The Iran-Contra Puzzle

The Iran-Contra Puzzle

Congressional Quarterly Inc.
1414 22nd Street N.W.
Washington, D.C. 20037

Congressional Quarterly Inc.

Congressional Quarterly Inc., an editorial research service and publishing company, serves clients in the fields of news, education, business, and government. It combines specific coverage of Congress, government, and politics by Congressional Quarterly with the more general subject range of an affiliated service, Editorial Research Reports.

Congressional Quarterly publishes the *Congressional Quarterly Weekly Report* and a variety of books, including college political science textbooks under the CQ Press imprint and public affairs paperbacks on developing issues and events. CQ also publishes information directories and reference books on the federal government, national elections, and politics, including the *Guide to Congress*, the *Guide to the U.S. Supreme Court*, the *Guide to U.S. Elections*, and *Politics in America*. The *CQ Almanac*, a compendium of legislation for one session of Congress, is published each year. *Congress and the Nation*, a record of government for a presidential term, is published every four years.

CQ publishes the *Congressional Monitor*, a daily report on current and future activities of congressional committees, and several newsletters including *Congressional Insight*, a weekly analysis of congressional action, and *Campaign Practices Reports*, a semimonthly update on campaign laws.

The online delivery of CQ's Washington Alert provides clients with immediate access to Congressional Quarterly's institutional information and expertise.

Copyright © 1987 Congressional Quarterly Inc.

Printed in the United States of America

Library of Congress Cataloging-in-Publication Data

The Iran-Contra puzzle.

    Bibliography: p.
    Includes index.
    1. Iran-Contra affair, 1985-   .   I. Congressional Quarterly, inc.
E876.I74 1987   973.927   87-24571
ISBN 0-87187-442-3

Editor: Patricia Ann O'Connor
Associate Editor: Colleen McGuiness
Major Contributors: John Felton, Steven Pressman
Contributing Editor: Margaret Thompson
Chronology: Stephen F. Stine, Michael V. Deaver
Contributors: Nadine Cohodas, Ann Davies, Carolyn McGovern, Robin D. Meszoly, Evamarie Socha, Elizabeth H. Summers, Pat Towell
Bibliography: Genevieve K. Clemens
Index: Jane Maddocks
Graphics: cover - Richard A. Pottern; pp. 5, 87 (Liman) - *Washington Post;* pp. 11, 22, 87 (Nields), 88, 91, 95, 96, 98, 99, 100 (Tambs), 102, 106, 107, 114, 117, 118, 119, 127, 135, 138, 140 - AP/Wide World Photos; pp. 19, 39, 169 - *New York Times*/Paul Hosefros; pp. 27, 101 - *Washington Post*/James K. W. Atherton; p. 31 - *Washington Post*/Frank Johnston; p. 45 - Rebecca Hammel; p. 49 - Murray H. Sill; p. 52 - U.S. Army/Arnold W. Kalmanson; pp. 67 (Durenberger), 150 (McCollum) - Paul Conklin; p. 73 - *Washington Post*/Jim Parcell; p. 79 - The White House/Bill Fitz-Patrick; pp. 85, 111, 116 (Sporkin) - *Washington Post*/Rich Lipski; p. 100 (Singlaub) - *New York Times*/José Lopez; pp. 103, 116 (Koch) - *Washington Post*/Fred Sweets; p. 115 - Bettmann Newsphotos; pp. 132, 150 (Fascell, Broomfield), 151 (Rudman, Boren, Heflin) - Teresa Zabala; pp. 150 (Hamilton, Brooks, Foley), 151 (Nunn) - Ken Heinen; pp. 150 (Cheney, Aspin, Boland, Courter, DeWine), 151 (Inouye, McClure) - Marty LeVor; pp. 150 (Jenkins), 151 (Cohen) - Sue Klemens; p. 150 (Rodino) - Art Stein; p. 151 (Hatch, Sarbanes) - Photo Response/Joseph McCary; p. 151 (Trible) - Karen Ruckman; p. 164 - *Washington Post*/Larry Morris

158227

Table of Contents

Part I

The Iran-Contra Affair: An Overview

Introduction

In the middle of his second term in office, an immensely popular Republican president is shaken by revelations that he secretly violated some of his most fundamental foreign policies and that his aides carried out possibly illegal covert operations.

Is the Iran-contra affair a political scandal, in the mold of Watergate nearly a decade and a half before, showing that deception and incompetence had reached the highest levels of government? Or is it a natural part of the political process, the latest evidence that the executive branch and Congress go through periods of not trusting each other?

Multiple investigations, private and public, appear to demonstrate that the Iran-contra affair is both. Frustrated with the standard procedures of government, zealous Reagan administration officials acted as if lofty goals—bringing democracy to Central America and winning freedom for Americans held hostage overseas—justified secrecy, skirting the law, and the misleading of Congress.

But because those goals were so admirable, each beholder judged for himself the seriousness of the scandal over the means used to achieve them. For some, the Iran-contra affair was more frightening than Watergate because it revealed that the entire U.S. national security apparatus had been distorted by flawed policies and actions. For others, the affair was overrated, a secondary matter blown out of proportion by "the media" and "liberals" who had never accepted the popularity of President Reagan.

With facts and revelations still tumbling out, it is impossible to tell which view ultimately will prevail. In the short term, however, the Iran-contra affair clearly curtailed the political effectiveness of the most popular president in a generation. The revelation that Ronald Reagan had been selling arms to Iran, the foreign government most hated by Americans, drove the president underground at a crucial point, just after the voters put the Democrats in charge of both houses of Congress. For all practical purposes, Reagan lost a full year of his presidency, as his administration and Congress were preoccupied with investigations and a bewildering array of charges and allegations.

Of all the revelations, perhaps the most important was that Reagan was not always the strong and effective leader that his aides had portrayed him to be. Nearly every report about the Iran-contra affair produced new evidence that

Reagan could be easily manipulated by White House aides, that he asked few questions, and that he did not always understand the full implications of the decisions he was asked to make. Friends and supporters said Reagan's managerial weakness was actually a strength: He never got lost in "detail," and his greatest asset was a genius for articulating the hopes and aspirations of average Americans. Even so, Reagan promised to improve his management style, and he appointed new aides who seemed likely to avoid the shortcuts that were one hallmark of the Iran-contra affair.

From the congressional viewpoint, Reagan's most important promise was to end the practice of carrying out policies in total secrecy just because they might prove unpopular. Just four days after the select House and Senate committees investigating the Iran-contra affair finished their twelve weeks of public hearings, Reagan sent Congress a letter promising to keep it informed about all covert operations. His August 7, 1987, pledge did little more than reaffirm existing law, but that was not the point. Critics said the president was acknowledging that he needed to cooperate more with Congress. Reagan's supporters said Congress, too, needed to be more receptive to the president's policies.

Mistrust between the two branches of government and the Reagan team's obsession for secrecy appeared to be the fundamental flaws that produced the Iran-contra affair. The administration used covert operations of dubious legality to implement policy in hopes of avoiding public debate and criticism. But when those operations were exposed, as they inevitably would be, the debate became more intense and more politically damaging than if the administration had openly confronted the underlying issues at the outset.

Lt. Col. Oliver L. North, a central figure in the Iran-contra affair, may have summed up the essence of the administration's troubles when he said he faced a choice between "lies and lives." To protect the lives of those with whom he was dealing in Iran and Central America, North said, he was forced to lie to Congress and to others in the administration whom he did not trust.

But Secretary of State George P. Shultz, one of those deceived by North, told the Iran-contra committees that government does not need to operate on that basis. "Nobody has to think they need to lie and cheat in order to be a public servant or to work in foreign policy," he said.

Roots of the Disaster

In many ways, the Iran-contra affair was a natural outgrowth of policies and procedures implemented early in the Reagan administration. National Security Council (NSC) staffers were confident, with some reason, that their actions simply carried out decisions that Reagan made throughout his presidency.

Once in the Oval Office in 1981, Reagan moved quickly to transform his broad philosophy of anticommunism into concrete foreign policy. Relying heavily on devices such as arms sales and military aid, the president bolstered friendly regimes that were fighting communist insurgencies. More controversial was his de facto introduction of the "Reagan doctrine": extending covert aid to a broad range of guerrilla groups that were attempting to overthrow Soviet-backed governments in the Third World.

Because of a convergence of events, the preeminent examples of both Reagan policies were to be found in Central America: in El Salvador, where Washington poured hundreds of millions of dollars to prop up weak civilian governments, and in Nicaragua, where he funded a rightist insurgency in hopes of toppling the revolutionary Sandinista regime, which had moved progressively to the left.

But Reagan confronted in Congress the still-powerful remnants of what some called the "post-Vietnam syndrome": a reluctance to make overseas commitments when U.S. interests were not clearly defined and when the means to be employed appeared to fall short of whatever goals were sought. Reacting to the Vietnam War, Congress in the mid-1970s had placed dozens of restrictions on many of the tools that presidents used to carry out their overseas policies, particularly foreign aid and the deployment of U.S. troops overseas. The Reagan administration chafed at those restrictions but never found a successful way to avoid them until the Iran-contra operations.

Almost from the opening days of the Reagan administration, El Salvador was the focus of a struggle in Washington over the extent to which the United States should rely on military means to deal with international problems. Reagan sought to use U.S. military assistance to bolster a series of Salvadoran governments beset by guerrillas on the left and "death squad" terrorists on the right. During three years of legislative disputes, Congress curtailed aid and put human rights conditions on it, effectively shifting U.S. policy toward a middle ground of moderating and stabilizing the civilian leadership in El Salvador.

The experience with El Salvador set the tone for the rest of Reagan's dealings with Congress on foreign policy—from his deployment of U.S. Marines to shore up the government of Lebanon to his continual campaign on behalf of the Nicaraguan contras. Congress at first went along with those policies but then withdrew support when it became clear that the original goals were not met.

The administration's battles were not only with Congress: Reagan never was able or willing to quell infighting and turf battles within and between the various agencies that dealt with foreign policy. Possibly more than any other recent president, Reagan was badgered constantly by "leaks" of secret information, including details of high-level policy deliberations. Although executive branch officials routinely blamed Congress for leaks, there was little doubt that the vast majority came from within the bureaucracy.

Some White House aides also concluded that the agencies of government that normally carry out foreign policy—particularly the State and Defense departments—were unwilling to take risks despite the potential for extraordinary gains. "The cost of failure is too high for them," said Adm. John M. Poindexter, Reagan's national security adviser in 1986.

Frustrated by leaks and the recalcitrance of Congress and the bureaucracy, the White House turned increasingly to covert action, both the "normal" kind conducted by the Central Intelligence Agency (CIA) through standard procedures required by laws enacted in the 1970s, and a new variety under which the National Security Council staff both formulated covert operations and implemented them.

From the White House point of view, the key virtue of both kinds of covert action was secrecy. By going covert, the White House could reduce the prospect of what Poindexter called "outside interference" with its policies.

In the first category of covert action, Reagan expanded to a massive scale an ongoing program of covert military aid to Moslem rebels in Afghanistan, and in late 1981 he ordered the CIA to fashion a serious fighting force out of the band of anti-Sandinista soldiers in Nicaragua. The administration also relied on covert action to accomplish political purposes: In 1984, the secret support by the CIA reportedly played a role in ensuring that moderate José Napoleón Duarte won the presidency in El Salvador. By 1987, Reagan had signed some three dozen "findings" authorizing CIA covert operations overseas, according to testimony to the Iran-contra investigating panels.

CIA-run operations had one major drawback, as far as the White House was concerned. By law, they had to be reported to Congress, where questions and objections likely would be raised. To get around that problem, the Reagan White House developed the concept of having the NSC staff conduct operations in secret, with involvement from the CIA and other agencies only as necessary and with no notice to Congress. North, an aggressive and tireless proponent of Reagan's policies, became a one-man covert action department, working out of his office in the Old Executive Office Building adjacent to the White House. By early 1986, North was managing a small network of private and public agents who were providing unofficial aid to the contras and helping sell U.S. weapons to Iran.

What Went Wrong

The Iran and contra operations carried the administration's fondness for covert action to the extreme, while demonstrating that secrecy and ideological zeal do not necessarily make for successful policy.

Testimony before the congressional committees showed that the Iran and contra operations ultimately failed, and were exposed, because of a series of fundamental flaws within the administration. Reagan's own investigatory commission, headed by former senator John Tower, R-Texas, said the basic fault was what it euphemistically called "management style"—the president's inability or unwillingness to grasp the details of his policies and to follow through to ensure that they were carried out properly.

Lt. Col. Oliver L. North, standing left, was sworn in July 7, 1987, to testify before the House and Senate select committees investigating the Iran-contra affair by Sen. Daniel K. Inouye, D-Hawaii, standing far right.

Reagan's 'Management Style'

As testimony before the Iran-contra panels demonstrated, the president's loose control over the White House meant that determined aides had free rein to carry out what they perceived as his ideological agenda. It was that management style that gave Poindexter, by his testimony, reason to assume that he had the right to make decisions on the president's behalf. Internal memos made clear the fact that Poindexter, North, and others all were certain they had wide latitude to implement Reagan's policies, with or without his knowledge. Poindexter, for example, insisted that the diversion of Iranian arms sales funds to the contras was merely a "detail" of the president's stated goal of aiding the Nicaraguan rebels, and so Poindexter felt free to approve it on his own.

The president's style of management had been a constant source of controversy throughout his presidency, and the Iran-contra investigations produced a confusing and somewhat conflicting picture of Reagan the boss.

In its report, the Tower Commission portrayed Reagan as a hands-off manager, one who asked few questions about what was being done in his name and who had little understanding of how his policies were being implemented. But key aides, starting with former national security adviser Robert C. McFarlane, testified to the select committees that Reagan was more than a rubber-stamp president, that he did understand substance and did have general knowl-

edge about his staff's activities. In particular, they pointed to the fact that Reagan occasionally overruled his own advisers, as when he decided to proceed with the Iranian arms deals over the objections of Shultz and Defense Secretary Caspar W. Weinberger.

The common ground in both versions was that the president set the overall direction and tone of his administration and knew that his aides were busy carrying out his policies but asked few questions about what they were doing.

Even after the main investigations were completed, it was not clear that Reagan fully understood what had happened. In his two formal speeches acknowledging mistakes—on March 4 and August 12, 1987—the president did not say what had gone wrong, and he attributed any failure to the implementation of policies, not to the policies themselves. In his August speech, Reagan said that at times he had been "mad as a hornet," but he did not say what he was mad at, the failures or the investigations and publicity about them.

Although Reagan said on several occasions that he accepted responsibility for what had gone wrong, he appeared to accept personal blame on only one count: allowing his emotional concern about the hostages to override his judgment that making concessions to Iran was wrong.

The president never acknowledged, as many Democrats had charged, that political considerations had been another driving factor behind the Iranian deals. Under that interpretation, the White House pursued the arms sales in hopes of getting the hostages released before the November 1986 congressional midterm elections. The primary evidence for this theory was North's frantic efforts a month before the election to make deals to free all the hostages. When Iran balked, the White House accepted a plan for the release of only one or two hostages, even though the plan contained elements violating U.S. policies.

Staff, Chief Advisers Faulted

As the Tower Commission noted, the White House staff failed to compensate for Reagan's weak grasp of details. McFarlane and Poindexter, in their daily briefings, apparently gave the president only the sketchiest information on which to make decisions. For example, Reagan apparently never read a lengthy memo justifying his January 17, 1986, decision to proceed with direct arms sales to Iran.

Standard procedures for making and implementing decisions were skirted: Key actors, such as Shultz and Weinberger, were excluded when they voiced objections, and there were no periodic reviews to determine whether the adopted policies were working.

Some critics, including the Tower board, charged that Shultz and Weinberger also failed in their duties. Shultz ceded jurisdiction over the Iran project to the NSC staff in mid-1985. Weinberger loyally carried out orders to supply missiles for Iran, and he reacted aggressively only when necessary to protect his own turf as secretary of defense, not to protest a policy with which he disagreed, critics said.

In the most recent manifestation of another long-term problem, White House aides and CIA director William J. Casey appeared to fashion intelligence assessments to suit their policies, instead of the other way around. Shultz and Weinberger were especially vocal in noting that the White House based decisions on Israeli-supplied intelligence projections that were at odds with official positions of the U.S. government. Casey's precise role remained one of the mysteries of the Iran-contra affair. At the very least, he appeared to overstep the traditional CIA role of providing objective information to the president and became an active exponent of particular policies.

On a more practical level, the administration's covert operations faltered because of lack of experience and sophistication on the part of those who ran them.

As the chief operative, North also was the chief fumbler, according to all available evidence. Although he fancied himself as a smooth diplomat and covert action specialist, North had little background in either field, and it showed. Rep. Ed Jenkins, D-Ga., noted perhaps the most important weakness in North's actions: his habit of making false promises to the Iranians. By misleading those with whom he was negotiating, Jenkins said, North was creating expectations that would later come back to haunt the United States.

To assist him, North recruited private agents who also were inexperienced in diplomacy and covert operations and whose prime interest was in making money. One of the most perplexing questions to arise from the Iranian dealings was why the White House relied so heavily on exiled Iranian businessman Manucher Ghorbanifar, a man known to top CIA officials as a "talented fabricator." Ghorbanifar may have been representing Iran or Israel or both. But his first concern, according to the evidence, was financial gain.

Aiding the Contras

U.S. involvement with the Nicaraguan contras began in late 1981, when Reagan authorized the CIA to help form a paramilitary force of about 500 fighters to harass the Sandinista government. In private briefings to Congress, the administration insisted that it was not trying to overthrow the regime in Managua but was merely hoping to use the rebels to block the flow of weapons from Nicaragua to the leftist guerrillas in nearby El Salvador. Led by rightist military officers, the guerrillas soon became known as contras, short for "counterrevolutionaries."

In spite of growing skepticism in Congress, the CIA continued to fund the contras through 1982 and 1983, providing a total of about $90 million. Amid news reports about the "secret war" in Nicaragua, the full House voted in July 1983 to cut off that funding. That move failed, but it led that October to the imposition of an absolute $24 million limit on CIA aid to the rebels in fiscal year 1984.

Congress Bans Aid

In April 1984, the *Wall Street Journal* revealed that the CIA had hired Latin American agents to mine the harbors of Nicaragua on behalf of the contras. That report created an uproar in Congress, largely because leaders of the Senate Intelligence Committee insisted they had never been told about the mining.

Political support for aid to the contras drained rapidly, and in October 1984 Congress voted into law the most restrictive of several versions of the "Boland amendment." Named after House Intelligence Committee chairman Edward P. Boland, D-Mass., it barred all aid to the contras by the CIA, Pentagon, or other agencies "involved in intelligence activities." The effect of the amendment was to cut off official U.S. support from mid-1984 until August 1985, when Congress voted "humanitarian" or nonmilitary aid to the contras.

As it became clear in 1984 that Congress would block further contra aid, North privately began recruiting agents to help the rebels, in place of the U.S. government. One of his first recruits was retired Air Force major general Richard V. Secord, who North said was recommended by Casey.

The administration also began seeking out alternative sources of financing for the contras. McFarlane approached Saudi Arabian King Fahd, who eventually agreed to provide $1 million a month. Fahd later upped his contribution and by 1985 had provided nearly $32 million. The administration also approached Taiwan, which gave $2 million to the contras, and gave serious consideration to asking South Africa to aid the contras. At the State Department's request, Brunei agreed to donate $10 million, but the money was sent mistakenly to the wrong Swiss bank account and never reached the contras.

North Fills Void

With the CIA phasing out of the contra-aid program, North quickly phased himself in. Working closely with Casey, North provided the contras with intelligence information and advice on military tactics. Through private agents such as Secord, North also arranged for the contras to buy several major covert shipments of arms from China, Poland, and other countries. The contras paid cash for those arms, using money supplied by the Saudis. Secord and his partner, Iranian-American businessman Albert Hakim, soon built up a network of secret Swiss bank accounts, filled with the profits from their arms sales to the contras. They later used those accounts to handle some $30 million generated by the Iranian arms sales.

North also began working closely with a group of conservative activists in Washington who were experts at raising money and spending it. Relying on North's ability to tell the contras' story compellingly, Washington fundraiser Carl R. "Spitz" Channell generated several million dollars in contributions from wealthy Americans, ostensibly for the contra cause. But much of the money went to support Channell's operations, along with a closely associated public relations firm headed by Richard R. Miller. Channell and Miller later pleaded guilty to tax fraud charges related to their contra-aid activities.

North testified that in January 1986 Ghorbanifar proposed aiding the contras with some of the profits from U.S. arms sales to Iran. North acknowledged that Ghorbanifar made the proposal as an incentive to encourage the Reagan administration to continue the sales. Poindexter quickly approved the idea but said he never told the president.

By the end of February 1986, the Secord and Hakim accounts were filled with millions of dollars generated by the various covert operations. Secord used some of the money to rent and buy airplanes and to hire pilots and support crews for a sophisticated operation that would deliver supplies to the contras inside Nicaragua. After many false starts, the air drops began in April and continued sporadically through the summer and into early fall. Secord testified that he spent about $3.5 million aiding the contras from the Iranian arms sale profits.

North's activities on behalf of the contras were an open secret in Washington and the subject of several newspaper stories in mid-1986. But when the House Intelligence Committee privately questioned him, North said he was complying with the Boland amendment. North later told the Iran-contra committees he justified that contention on the grounds that the Boland amendment barred involvement with the contras only by U.S. intelligence agencies, not by the NSC staff. Contra-aid supporters on the select committees embraced that justification, but Boland and other administration critics said North was violating at least the spirit of the law and probably was overstepping the letter of it. McFarlane said he assumed that the Boland law applied to the NSC staff, but Poindexter, his successor, said he had the opposite view.

On October 5, 1986, Nicaraguan troops shot down a supply plane; all on board were killed except loading specialist Eugene Hasenfus, a U.S. civilian hired by the Secord network. Captured by Nicaragua, Hasenfus later claimed that the contra-aid supply network was run by the CIA.

The downing of the Hasenfus plane, coupled with revelation a month later of the arms sales to Iran, ultimately led to exposure of the private contra-aid network. In testimony shortly after the Hasenfus plane went down, State Department and CIA officials insisted that the U.S. government had no involvement with it, either directly or indirectly. Those officials later acknowledged that their denials were misleading, at best.

Involvement with Iran

Like Nicaragua, Iran always had presented special problems for the Reagan administration. Reagan had been elected president in 1980 in part because the voters were disgusted with President Carter's inability to free the Americans who were held hostage at the U.S. Embassy in Tehran, and because Reagan projected the image of someone who knew what to do.

But once the embassy hostages were freed—through no active involvement by Reagan—Iran practically disappeared from the new administration's map. Aside from ritual denunciations of terrorism and calls for an end to the Persian Gulf war between Iran and Iraq, the administration appeared to be acting as if the radical Islamic regime in Tehran did not exist. That attitude persisted in spite of clear evidence that Iran played a major role in the October 1983 terrorist bombing that killed more than 240 U.S. Marines stationed in Beirut on a futile "peacekeeping" mission.

As pro-Iranian groups in Lebanon kidnapped one American after another, Reagan seemed to stand by helplessly, just as Carter had done. When asked about the hostages, Reagan and his aides said they were doing everything possible short of making deals with the hostage-takers. They also insisted that Reagan faced a more difficult situation than did Carter, since the hostages in Lebanon were held by shadowy groups that did not advertise their whereabouts, while the embassy hostages had been under the effective control of a government with which the United States could negotiate.

Israeli Arms Sales

In the meantime, some administration officials apparently viewed with sympathy Israel's attempts to use selective arms sales to curry favor with conservative military elements in Iran. Israel had had close ties to Iran before Shah Mohammed Reza Pahlavi was ousted in 1979. According to various reports, Israel as early as 1981 began supplying small quantities of spare parts and other military gear to the Iranian army in hopes of bolstering the factions opposed to the excesses of the radical Islamic regime of the Ayatollah Ruhollah Khomeini. There also was speculation that Israel wanted to prolong the Iran-Iraq War, with the particular goal of sapping the military strength of Iraq, an Arab country.

While U.S. intelligence officials knew that Israel was supplying military items to Iran, the Iran-contra hearings left unclear whether Washington in the early 1980s gave formal approval or merely signaled Israel to be cautious. Under U.S. arms sale laws, Israel was required to get official permission from Washington before shipping American-made weapons to another country, but Israel apparently never did so, relying instead on winks and nods from friendly U.S. officials. For the Israelis, anything short of adamant opposition may have been the same thing as a "green light" from Washington.

Whatever its extent, U.S. acquiescence in the Israeli sales was all the more ironic in that it occurred in spite of Reagan's embargo on direct arms sales to Iran and an aggressive campaign by the administration to halt arms exports by all countries to Iran. Under the rubric "Operation Staunch," the Reagan administration sent a series of special ambassadors to foreign capitals pleading for a halt to the arming of Iran. While it succeeded in blocking several planned shipments by West European countries, the effort had little overall impact on the flow of arms to Iran, which turned to China and Soviet-bloc countries for its military supplies.

Iran Policy Reappraised

As early as 1984, administration officials began raising questions about the underlying assumption of U.S. policy toward Iran: that little or nothing could be done to encourage moderation in Tehran until the aged Khomeini died. An NSC-initiated study examined that assumption in late 1984 and concluded that it was essentially correct.

The CIA in 1985 received new reports about potential instability in Iran, coupled with the possibility of renewed Soviet maneuvering to gain influence there. Based on those reports, the NSC produced a new study, on its own, which suggested a fundamental change in policy. The United States should encourage U.S. allies to help Iran meet its "import requirements," including those for weapons, in hopes of reducing Tehran's dependence on the Soviet Union. That proposal drew sharp rebukes from Shultz and Weinberger; the latter scribbled on his copy that encouraging arms sales to Iran was "absurd" and "roughly like inviting Quaddafi over for a cozy lunch."

The opposition by Shultz and Weinberger killed the NSC proposal for an official realignment of policy toward Iran; the study was never put in final form for submission to the president. But other events at the same time ensured that the essential thrust of the NSC draft became de facto U.S. policy. Throughout early and mid-1985, NSC consultant Michael Ledeen held a series of meetings with Israeli officials to discuss the need to gather more information about Iran. Those meetings apparently led Israel to conclude that Washington was ready for a broader review of its policy toward Iran. The White House also was impressed in June when a top Iranian official—Speaker of the Parliament Ali Akbar Hashemi Rafsanjani—played a role in freeing Americans taken hostage after the hijacking of a TWA jetliner to Lebanon.

The Iranian role in the TWA crisis, and the possibility that Iran might be willing to help gain the release of six other American hostages in Lebanon, proved irresistible to Reagan.

In spite of his tough talk about Iran and terrorism, Reagan by 1985 apparently was willing to take extraordinary steps to get the hostages released. Against the advice of many of his aides, the president had been meeting regularly with members of hostage families, many of whom made emotional pleas with him to be more aggressive in looking for ways to win freedom for the hostages. Several officials later said Reagan should not have met with the families because doing so put him under so much stress that he allowed his emotions to override his judgment—and Reagan seemed to embrace that view himself.

It was in that context that a pattern began to emerge: Israel approached the United States with proposals for weapons sales to Iran, and White House aides presented the idea to Reagan as a diplomatic move aimed at bolstering moderates there. But the aides got the president's attention by holding out the prospect of winning freedom for the hostages.

Events moved rapidly during the rest of 1985, with the administration accepting dramatic changes in policy toward Iran. First, according to McFarlane's testimony, Reagan in August approved Israeli shipments of TOW antitank missiles to Iran. Two shipments in August and September, totaling 508 missiles, resulted in the release of one American hostage from Lebanon, the Rev. Benjamin F. Weir. Because Iran paid more than triple the market price for the missiles, the shipments also produced huge profits for the Israeli arms dealers who handled them.

November 1985 Hawk Shipment

Three months later, in November, Israel proposed and the White House approved a major shipment of Hawk antiaircraft missiles to Iran. That shipment became so fouled up that only eighteen missiles ever arrived in Iran, and then only because the CIA, at North's request, provided one of its "proprietary" airlines to handle the job. No hostages were released in exchange for the shipment, although the White House had expected that all five Americans then held in Lebanon would be freed. Iran claimed the missiles were inadequate and demanded that the United States take them back, which it did in 1986.

The November shipment of Hawks later took on great legal and political significance, since Reagan had not given the legally required advance approval of CIA involvement and because Congress had not been told—as required by law—that Israel had transferred U.S.-made weapons to another country. To cover the CIA's tracks, Deputy Director John N. McMahon ordered the drafting of a presidential "finding" retroactively authorizing agency participation in the shipment. Poindexter testified that Reagan signed the finding on December 5, 1985. But Poindexter said he destroyed the document a year later because its stated focus on releasing hostages might prove "embarrassing" to the president if ever revealed.

The November Hawk shipment was important in another respect: It marked the first involvement in the Iranian deals by North and Secord, who North had recruited to aid the contras. At North's request, Secord spent a week in Lisbon trying unsuccessfully to route the shipment from Israel through Portugal to Iran.

On December 7, 1985, about ten days after the Hawk shipment was completed, Reagan and his top aides held their first serious discussion about the Iran initiative. Shultz and Weinberger argued strenuously against proceeding with additional arms deals that Israel was planning, and they left the White House meeting assuming that there would be none. McFarlane, who days before had handed in his resignation because of longstanding turf battles within the White House, then flew to London for meetings with Ghorbanifar, whom Israel had been pressing the United States to use in its dealings with Tehran. McFarlane said he was shocked by Ghorbanifar's lies and misrepresentations, and he returned to Washington convinced that the Iran initiative should be ended. Hearing of Ghorbanifar's involvement, top CIA officials also arranged to have him take a lie detector test, which he flunked.

But North argued for continuing the initiative, and Israel in January 1986 sent a representative to Washington who convinced Poindexter to carry on with the Iranian arms deals through Ghorbanifar. Israel's eagerness to get the United States involved was demonstrated by its willingness to risk sending another 500 of its TOW missiles to Iran in hopes of getting more U.S. hostages released. Poindexter later testified that he assumed Israel wanted the United States to give formal approval to the arms sales it had long been making to Iran. Shultz was more blunt, saying in a later White House meeting that Israel had "suckered" the United States into going along with its arms sales.

January 1986 'Finding'

After another inconclusive meeting among the president and his top aides, Reagan on January 17, 1986, signed a finding that authorized the CIA, working through third parties, to sell arms to Iran. The third parties turned out to be Ghorbanifar and Secord. One important and unusual provision of the finding was a directive that Congress not be told about it.

A key factor in Reagan's decision apparently was an informal intelligence assessment, provided by Poindexter and CIA director Casey, concluding that Iran was the weaker of the two parties in the Iran-Iraq War. That assessment matched the official Israeli view of the war, but it was directly opposite of the position embraced by all U.S. intelligence agencies. In later private meetings, Reagan cited the alleged Iranian military weakness as one justification for the arms sales.

Reagan's signature on the January 17 finding set off a series of U.S.-Iranian negotiations and arms deals. Early in 1986, North and Ghorbanifar were the principal actors, meeting secretly at various locations in Europe to arrange arms sales, supposedly to be accompanied by the release of hostages.

The first sale, of 1,000 TOW missiles in February, failed to produce a hostage release. Nevertheless, based on Ghorbanifar's assurances that Iran was ready for better relations, the White House moved ahead with plans for the next step up: a direct meeting in Tehran between high-level U.S. and Iranian officials. That meeting came in May, when McFarlane, North, and two other officials traveled to Tehran and spent three frustrating days negotiating with midlevel Iranian functionaries. McFarlane took with him a pallet of spare parts for Hawk missiles that Iran already owned. Negotiations about a larger shipment of parts collapsed because Iran was willing to release only two hostages and McFarlane insisted on the release of all five Americans then held in Lebanon.

The failure of the McFarlane mission dimmed White House enthusiasm for the Iran initiative, but only for a while. Casey, Poindexter, and others began talking about mounting a rescue mission to free the hostages, and North pursued another scheme of using Drug Enforcement Administration agents to locate the hostages and then bribe the Lebanese captors into releasing them.

In the meantime, some Iranian leaders appeared to be reconsidering the hardline stance that had led to collapse of the McFarlane mission. To get things moving again, Iran arranged in July 1986 for the release of another hostage, the Rev. Lawrence Jenco. In response, Reagan approved the shipment to Iran of another twelve pallets of Hawk spare parts.

Contact with 'Second Channel'

After months of searching for an alternative to Ghorbanifar as an intermediary with Iran, Secord and Hakim in August made contact with a so-called "second channel," who turned out to be a relative of Rafsanjani. He led an Iranian delegation to Washington for secret talks with North and others in mid-September, and those discussions led to one final arms sale in October: 500 more TOW missiles sent to Iran by Israel in exchange for release of hostage David P. Jacobsen.

As part of the October deal, the White House agreed to a nine-point plan, negotiated by Hakim, that included a promise to seek release of seventeen terrorists imprisoned in Kuwait for attacking Western embassies. Poindexter testified that he got Reagan's approval for that plan, even though it was contrary to the stated U.S. policy of demanding that Kuwait keep the seventeen terrorists in prison.

The White House denied that Reagan ever approved the plan, however, and Shultz said Reagan was astonished to hear about it.

The dumping of Ghorbanifar relieved the United States of the necessity of dealing with an untrustworthy intermediary, but it may have planted the seeds for the ultimate disclosure of the Iranian arms deals. On November 3, 1986, one day after Jacobsen was released, a pro-Syrian magazine in Lebanon revealed McFarlane's trip to Tehran. Rafsanjani immediately confirmed the report, insisting that Iran had rejected the U.S. overtures. The source of information for the Lebanese newspaper was not revealed, but many officials in Washington were convinced that Ghorbanifar had something to do with the disclosure—a charge he heatedly denied.

Aftermath of Disclosure

The administration's initial response to the disclosure was to deny that it had been dealing with Iran. Reagan told reporters there was "no foundation" to the reports. Poindexter also instructed White House spokesman Larry Speakes to say that the U.S. arms embargo against Iran remained in effect.

But as the days passed and as news reports produced a deluge of information—some accurate and some misleading—about U.S. dealings with Iran, administration officials became involved in a tug of war. Those who had opposed the initiative argued for prompt and full disclosure of the facts in hopes of reducing the ultimate political damage, while Poindexter insisted on trying to keep as much information secret as possible. Reagan, according to notes of White House meetings, apparently was caught in the middle. At one key session on November 10, he told his aides: "We must say something but not much." White House officials later said Reagan feared that publicity would kill any chance of winning the release of more hostages.

One of the administration's problems at the time was a lack of hard information about what had happened. Because officials made decisions almost casually and kept few formal records, there were conflicting recollections about what happened when. In an attempt to put the facts together, North and others began work in mid-November on a chronology. By November 20, the NSC staff had produced at least a dozen versions; some contained nearly all the essential facts and were labelled "maximum version," while others merely skimmed the surface.

McFarlane later said that he assumed one purpose of the exercise was to "protect" the president by minimizing his role. None of the chronologies mentioned Reagan's approval of the 1985 Israeli shipments, and none reported that money from the Iranian arms sales had been diverted to Secord's contra-aid network. In fact, the chronologies did not mention Secord at all.

Reagan made two attempts to explain the arms sales, first in a speech from the Oval Office on November 13 and then in a news conference on November 19. From a political standpoint, both efforts were disasters, raising more questions than they answered. The president's aides watched in disbelief as Reagan insisted during the press conference that the United States had not worked with Israel during the Iran arms deals. Minutes after the questioning ended, the White House issued a statement retracting that claim.

Congress in the meantime was demanding information, and the administration agreed that Casey and Poindexter would privately, and separately, brief the House and Senate Intelligence committees on November 21. The preparations for those briefings exposed, perhaps for the first time, the extent of uncertainty within the administration about the facts, especially about Israel's November 1985 shipment of Hawks to Iran.

At an important White House meeting on November 20, called to review Casey's proposed written testimony, North suggested a change stating that no one in the U.S. government knew until January 1986 that the November shipment included weapons. In effect, North was asking his colleagues to stand by a cover story developed in 1985 that Israel had shipped oil drilling equipment to Iran. Poindexter and Casey, the only others in the room who knew for certain that North's suggested statement was wrong, reportedly said nothing.

North told the Iran-contra committees that he and Casey later met privately and "fixed" the testimony. He never explained just how it was fixed, but the next day Casey did not tell the Intelligence committees that Israel had shipped the Hawk missiles to Iran.

North also testified to the Iran-contra committees that he and Casey previously had devised a "fall guy plan" to limit the political damage should word of the diversion ever be made public. Under that plan, North was to take full responsibility, he said. But North said Casey told him that Poindexter also would have to share blame because North was not senior enough to have made all the decisions.

Looking for Facts

As an attempt to cover up the 1985 Hawk shipment, the November 20 White House meeting failed, because State and Justice department officials raised the alarm. Hours after the meeting, Shultz went directly to Reagan and told him that parts of Casey's proposed testimony were untrue. Alerted by his aides, Attorney General Edwin Meese III gave Reagan the same message on November 21 and got approval to conduct a "fact-finding inquiry."

The true nature and extent of Meese's inquiry was a matter of sharp debate during the Iran-contra hearings and may continue to be so for years to come. Meese insisted that he was merely trying to straighten out conflicts in the recollections of various top officials and that he had no reason to look for criminal wrongdoing. Critics said Meese and his aides were too slow to recognize that a coverup was under way. Warren B. Rudman, R-N.H., vice chairman of the Senate Iran-contra committee, charged that Meese had "telegraphed" his moves to North and Poindexter, who then destroyed or altered incriminating documents. As Meese was proceeding, North shredded dozens, if not hundreds, of memos, telephone logs, and reports. He also instructed his secretary, Fawn Hall, to make substantial changes in other memos discussing his involvement with the contras. Poindexter testified that he, too, destroyed documents, including the December 1985 finding by which Reagan retroactively approved the Israeli Hawk shipment.

Diversion Memo Discovered

However haphazard it may have been, Meese's investigation did turn up the most damaging document of all: a memo North had written the previous April saying that $12 million from a proposed Iranian arms sale would be used to aid the contras. Confronted with the memo on November 23, North acknowledged that he had written it and that money had been diverted to the contras. He also pleaded with Meese to keep those facts secret, but Meese made no commitment.

Meese testified that he took the information to Reagan on November 24, who agreed with him that it would be necessary to make the diversion public. At a White House press conference the next day, Reagan announced that he had not been "fully informed" about one aspect of the Iranian arms deals and that, as a result, Poindexter had agreed to resign and North had been fired. The last part apparently came as news to North, who already had sent Poindexter a computer message resigning his post. Reagan refused to answer questions, but Meese, taking over the press conference, revealed the diversion and estimated it at $10 million-$30 million.

As White House officials knew it would, the connection between Iran and the contras created a sensation, transforming a controversy about flawed policy into a major political scandal. Hoping to stem at least some of the inevitable criticism, Reagan appointed a prestigious board to review the facts, headed by Tower; other members were former senator and secretary of state Edmund S. Muskie and former national security adviser and retired lieutenant general Brent Scowcroft. At first, Reagan gave the panel only sixty days to investigate and issue a report, but the members found the task too big and demanded, and got, until the following February.

Reagan also chose as his new national security adviser Frank C. Carlucci, a long-time foreign policy official who was widely respected in Washington.

Pressure from Capitol Hill

The appointment of the Tower board did not accomplish its primary purpose, that of quelling the demands on Capitol Hill for separate inquiries. Under political pressure, Reagan agreed to request appointment of an independent counsel, or special prosecutor, and a three-judge panel chose retired federal judge Lawrence E. Walsh, an Oklahoma Republican.

Congress began its own multiple investigations. The House and Senate Intelligence committees held closed-door hearings with key participants throughout late November and early December. The House Foreign Affairs Committee held two dramatic days of public hearings, during which North and Poindexter cited their Fifth Amendment privileges in refusing to testify.

Congressional leaders also agreed in December to appoint select committees to hold full hearings into the Iran-contra affair. Republicans wanted a limited inquiry that would answer questions quickly and curtail the political damage to their party. Democrats, who had just taken control of the Senate, slowed the process and made it clear that any inquiry would be thorough and run well into 1987.

Senate leaders named Daniel K. Inouye, D-Hawaii, and Rudman to head their eleven-member committee, and House leaders put Lee H. Hamilton, D-Ind., and Dick Cheney, R-Wyo., in charge of their fifteen-member committee.

Even before the select committees could get their investigations fully under way, the public got two hefty doses of facts that answered many of the outstanding questions.

First, after a partisan battle over the timing of a report, the Senate Intelligence Committee in late January 1987 made public a summary of its findings. Although crammed with details, the report contained no conclusions and thus was of limited help in advancing public understanding of what had happened and why.

Tower Commission Report

The Tower Commission report, released February 26, 1987, provided a much more complete picture of the Iran-contra affair—in large part because the commission's computer experts had unearthed dozens of internal White House memos that documented the activities of North, Poindexter, and others on an almost daily basis.

While cautiously worded, the Tower report served up a damning indictment of failures by Reagan and his aides throughout the events of the Iran-contra affair. Reagan, the Tower board said, had not paid close attention to what his aides were doing and had not asked the kinds of questions that would have revealed problems in time to correct them. Given the president's inattention to detail—which the board gingerly described as his "management style"—the White House staff failed to take compensating steps, such as taking troublesome issues to him for his review.

Introducing the Tower board at a press conference minutes after getting the report, Reagan clearly was stunned and confused; he stumbled in reading a prepared statement and rushed from the room to avoid questions from reporters. But Reagan quickly recovered the next day, effectively firing his chief of staff, Donald T. Regan, who the Tower panel had criticized for allowing "chaos" to descend upon the White House following disclosure of the Iranian arms sales. Reagan named former Senate majority leader Howard H. Baker, Jr., R-Tenn., to take Regan's place—an appointment that produced sighs of relief all over Capitol Hill, where Baker was highly popular.

A week later, on March 4, Reagan made yet another effort to explain the Iran initiative. In a prime-time speech, he said he accepted responsibility for any failures, but he did not apologize, as many supporters had encouraged him to do. Reagan also insisted that any flaws were in the "implementation" of his policies, not in the policies themselves.

The president acknowledged for the first time that the United States had traded arms for hostages. Recalling his denial the previous November of arms-for-hostages swaps, Reagan said: "My heart and my best intentions still tell me that is true, but the facts and the evidence tell me it is not."

Congressional Hearings

From the outset, it was clear that the congressional investigation into the Iran-contra affair would be plagued with several problems, chief among them partisanship and

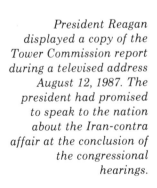

President Reagan displayed a copy of the Tower Commission report during a televised address August 12, 1987. The president had promised to speak to the nation about the Iran-contra affair at the conclusion of the congressional hearings.

the natural inclination of the public to compare it unfavorably with the Watergate probe of 1973-74.

Attempting to reduce partisan feuding, the congressional leaders agreed to limited agendas and tight time schedules for the investigations. The committees were to look into only the Iran arms sales and the administration's covert operations in support of the contras, and were to issue reports by late summer or early fall. They were not directed to examine the full range of administration foreign policies, nor where they to concentrate on other contra-related issues, such as alleged human rights violations by the contras or news media reports that certain contra leaders financed their operations with proceeds from drug smuggling.

Congressional leaders also made it clear that they did not expect the select committees to turn up evidence that might force the president from office—as the Senate Watergate committee had done more than a decade earlier.

The only issue that even raised the question of illegal action on the president's part was the diversion and whether he had approved it. Reagan insisted at every point that he knew nothing of the diversion until Meese told him about it on November 24, 1986, but opinion polls consistently showed that a majority of Americans did not believe him. Poindexter was considered the only person who could provide solid evidence refuting Reagan, but few members of the select committees expected him to do so.

Partly for that reason, congressional Democrats sought early in 1987 to play down the prospects of a direct confrontation between Congress and the president. House majority leader Thomas S. Foley, D-Wash., a member of the select committee, noted that memories of the trauma caused by Watergate would make it more difficult to consider impeachment. Besides that, Foley and others noted, Reagan was a popular and likable president, and Nixon had been neither.

The select committees spent the first four months of 1987 getting ready for hearings, reviewing documents, and privately interviewing hundreds of witnesses. Among them was Poindexter, who told a small group of committee lawyers and members on May 2 that he had never told Reagan about the diversion. Under an agreement with independent counsel Walsh, the committees sealed Poindexter's testimony and kept it secret. Walsh wanted more time to gather evidence against Poindexter, who would be testifying to the committees in public under a grant of limited immunity.

Perhaps the most important decision the committees made during the start-up period was to hold joint public hearings, thus avoiding the spectacle of two panels competing for witnesses and news coverage.

The committees began their public hearings May 5 with testimony by Secord. In twelve weeks of hearings that lasted until early August, the committees heard from thirty-two witnesses, several of whom received limited immunity against prosecution for their testimony.

The hearings filled in many of the details of the Iran-contra affair, painting a picture of twin covert operations run by the NSC staff and private agents with little supervision by either the president or his senior foreign policy advisers. Nearly every day produced important revelations, ranging from Secord's estimate that only about $3.5 million actually had been diverted to the contras, to Hall's dramatic description of how she altered important memos at North's request and helped him shred dozens of other documents.

The strong partisan inclination of some committee members also produced a pattern resembling two sets of hearings: The six House Republicans, joined by Sen. Orrin Hatch, R-Utah, staunchly defended Reagan at every turn and sought to play down the severity of administration mistakes, while most Democrats and some Republican members of the Senate panel sought to conduct a more aggressive investigation.

The most interesting split was among the Republicans. The House GOP members were accustomed to their minority status and to using the political version of guerrilla warfare to get attention. Doing what came naturally, they attempted to derail the hearings from an investigatory track by making lengthy speeches defending Reagan and condemning Congress for interfering in his foreign policy. But three Republican senators—Rudman, William S. Cohen of Maine, and Paul S. Trible, Jr., of Virginia—sought to distance their party from the failures of the Iran-contra affair. Rudman and Trible, in particular, targeted Secord and Hakim as likely villains and devoted much of their attention to the profits those two men may have made on the various arms deals.

Dramatic Testimony

For millions of Americans, however, the focal point of the hearings was North, who spent nearly six days at the witness table in July. Combative and articulate in his self-defense, North portrayed himself as a loyal soldier who had done only what was authorized and who had sought merely to serve his president. North's forceful presentation—aided by his appearance in a Marine Corps uniform adorned with medals—created a sensation. Opinion polls suddenly showed that many regarded him as a "hero," and popular magazines promoted "Olliemania." Hundreds of visitors, many wearing "Ollie North for President" T-shirts, waited in line for up to four hours to get into the hearings.

North's popularity put the committees on the defensive, especially the hard-driving lawyers who headed the investigation, Senate counsel Arthur L. Liman and House counsel John W. Nields, Jr. Republican defenders of Reagan were thrilled to find a witness who could articulate the president's foreign policy goals better than the president ever could. North received thousands of congratulatory telegrams, many condemning the committees.

North was followed to the witness table by Poindexter, who in a matter of minutes quelled the minuscule chance that Reagan would be impeached. Poindexter testified that he had never told Reagan about the diversion of funds to the contras. "On this whole issue, you know, the buck stops here with me," he said.

Poindexter testified that he viewed the diversion merely as an implementation "detail" of Reagan's overall policy of aiding the contras and so saw no need to tell the president about it. But Poindexter also said he realized that the diversion would be controversial if revealed; by not telling Reagan, Poindexter said he had hoped to protect him politically.

Committee Republicans, some of whom had heard Poindexter testify nearly three months before in private, greeted the statement as the ultimate vindication of Reagan's position. Several Democrats expressed skepticism, and a few insisted that he was not telling the truth, but all acknowledged that there was no way of proving that Poindexter was lying.

Committee members were unanimous, however, in condemning Poindexter for keeping such important information from the president. "It's my view that presidents ought to be allowed to create their own disasters," Rudman lectured Poindexter. "Nobody else ought to do it for them."

The remaining weeks of the hearings continued to produce dramatic testimony: Meese's defensive explanation of his inquiry the previous November; Shultz's gripping description of a "battle royal" in the administration over how much information to make public; Regan's claim that he knew little about the Iranian arms deals, in spite of a widespread assumption that he had run the White House with an iron fist; and Weinberger's devastating critique of the White House contention that the United States could bolster Iranian moderates by selling them weapons.

Drawing Conclusions

In closing statements summarizing the hearings, the four leaders of the committees stressed the dangers of bypassing standard procedures, allowing unelected aides to have too much power, and putting public policy in the hands of private agents. The leaders also acknowledged that Congress shared a measure of the blame and said the hearings demonstrated the need for cooperation between the legislative and executive branches of government.

Concentrating their fire on White House aides and private agents, the committee leaders virtually ignored Reagan's role in the Iran-contra affair. Inouye said the hearings had told "a chilling story, a story of deceit and duplicity and the arrogant disregard of the rule of law." But he did not mention Reagan's involvement in any of those things. Hamilton criticized the president only for failing to make "clean and crisp" decisions and for not knowing what his aides were doing.

In the weeks following the hearings, the committees turned their attention to the drafting of a report. Members said they assumed they could get relatively quick agreement on the basic facts of what had happened but would face a political struggle when it came to drawing conclu-

sions and making recommendations for corrective action.

There appeared to be broad agreement that the committees should not propose a wholesale rewriting of the laws dealing with the making and implementation of foreign policy. Instead, members said they were more likely to recommend limited steps such as tightening the requirements for presidents to tell Congress about covert operations, arms sales, and other foreign policy actions.

Reagan's August 7 letter to leaders of the Senate Intelligence Committee promising to tell Congress in advance about covert operations was one attempt to head off restrictive legislation. But the president said that under "extraordinary circumstances" he might have to delay notice to Congress for two working days. Senate Intelligence chairman David L. Boren, D-Okla., who had sought a firm notification promise from the president, said the commitment demonstrated "a good first step" toward a better relationship between the White House and Congress.

Five days later, on August 12, Reagan went on national television to review the lessons learned in the Iran-contra affair. While again taking responsibility for any mistakes made by his aides, the president appeared to minimize the seriousness of the Iran-contra affair and insisted he had already corrected any flaws in White House operations.

In response, Democratic leaders sought to remind the public that a Republican administration had made serious mistakes. But the Democrats also wanted to avoid appearing to be too eager to benefit from the president's troubles.

"Let there be no misunderstanding," Sen. George J. Mitchell, D-Maine, said in response to Reagan's speech. "The mistakes were not only in the execution of policies. The major mistakes were in the policies themselves. And the policies were the president's."

However, Mitchell immediately said that the Iran-contra affair "should be put behind us."

John Felton
September 1987

Revelations, Reactions, Investigations

The Iran issue exploded on the public scene shortly after the November 4, 1986, midterm elections with media reports that U.S.-made weapons and other military equipment had been shipped to Iran. The reported rationale for those sales was to gain freedom for American hostages held by pro-Iranian factions in Lebanon. The first account of the arms transactions appeared in a Syrian-backed magazine in Lebanon; U.S. officials publicly refused comment but provided details and speculation that kept the issue on the front pages.

Congressional leaders—none of whom had been informed about U.S. ties to Iran—demanded explanations, forcing the administration to abandon its official news blackout. President Ronald Reagan briefed key representatives and senators on November 12, and White House aides later consulted with several other top congressional leaders.

The next day, in a nationally televised White House speech, Reagan made the first official acknowledgment that the United States had directly shipped weapons and other military equipment to Iran's revolutionary government. However, he labeled as "wildly speculative and false" the reports that he had supplied the arms in direct exchange for Tehran's cooperation, beginning in September 1985, in the release of three American hostages.

"We did not—repeat—did not trade weapons or anything else for hostages—nor will we," he said. *(Text, p. D-1)*

The Iran arms sales became decidedly more controversial on November 25 when it was disclosed that some profits from the sales had been diverted to aid the guerrilla "contra" forces battling the leftist Sandinista government in Nicaragua. Two key figures in the affair were immediate staff casualties. Lt. Col. Oliver L. North, a National Security Council (NSC) aide was fired for his role in the arms dealings, and his immediate superior, Vice Adm. John M. Poindexter, resigned from his post as the president's national security adviser.

The two controversial policies—selling arms to Iran, apparently in exchange for American hostages, and arming the contras, possibly in violation of a legislative ban on such aid—triggered multiple investigations both within and outside Congress.

AFFAIR GOES PUBLIC: REVELATION, REACTION

While refusing to give more than sketchy details, Reagan and his aides insisted the arms transfers did not breach U.S. policy of refusing to negotiate with terrorists for the release of hostages. The shipments also did not violate a U.S. arms embargo in effect against Iran since 1979, White House officials said, because Reagan had authorized exemptions in a January 1986 covert "finding" made public almost one year later. *(Text, p. D-20)*

The issue was especially threatening to Reagan because of the stormy history of relations between the United States and Iran. Of all world leaders, perhaps none was more despised by the American public and politicians than the Ayatollah Ruhollah Khomeini, who assumed power after a 1979 coup. Khomeini characterized the United States as "the great Satan." When Iranian militants took over the U.S. Embassy in November 1979 and held Americans hostage there for more than a year, relations grew markedly bitter. *(U.S.-Iran relations, box, p. 16)*

On assuming the presidency, Reagan sought to keep alive Khomeini's negative image as a fomenter of terrorism. He also wanted to establish the United States as the foremost proponent of the principle of not making concessions to terrorists, saying he would not negotiate with or pay ransom to hostage-takers. In that context, the revelation that Reagan had authorized direct and indirect arms shipments to Iran—notorious for its support of terrorism—was especially shocking.

"We have been saying for years that we wouldn't deal with these people, and now it seems we're sending them weapons. What's going on here?" asked one frustrated Reagan supporter, William S. Broomfield, Mich., ranking Republican on the House Foreign Affairs Committee. Broomfield's comments were echoed by many others in Congress, with the harshest criticism coming from Democrats. "It's one of the dumbest things I've ever heard of," said Rep. Dave McCurdy, D-Okla., a member of the House

United States' Relations with Iran . . .

The disclosure in November 1986 of U.S. arms shipments to Iran brought sharply into focus what appeared to be a radical departure in America's policy toward that nation. Not only had the United States government and Iran's militant fundamentalist Islamic ruler, the Ayatollah Ruhollah Khomeini, been bitter enemies since Khomeini came to power in 1979, but President Ronald Reagan repeatedly had vowed that his administration would never engage in any concessions to terrorists in return for American hostages held by radical pro-Iran factions in Lebanon. However, as testimony during the Iran-contra investigations revealed, that policy apparently was overtaken by Reagan's keen interest in freeing the hostages and Iran's promises to assist if given U.S.-made arms.

The attempt to trade weapons for hostages, the manner in which it was conducted, and the impact of the sales on the bitter, longstanding Persian Gulf war between Iran and Iraq raised troubling questions about the administration's policy in the Middle East. One of the most pressing issues was the future of relations between the United States and Iran, which had slid dramatically from close ties to virulent animosity in less than ten years. U.S. allies in the region held contrasting views of Iran, further complicating the conduct of U.S. policy. The United States' closest ally in the region, Israel, considered Iraq to be its most bitter foe and, therefore, had played a major role in the shipment of U.S. arms to Iran. But the moderate Persian Gulf nations were fearful of an Iran victory in the Iran-Iraq War. The ambivalence became starkly apparent when, after selling to Iran arms that could be used in its war with Iraq, the Reagan administration proposed to outfit Kuwaiti tankers with American flags to assure the tankers safe passage in the Strait of Hormuz. The conservative Arab shiekdom of Kuwait supported Iraq in the war.

Road to Revolution

After months of civil disturbances, mass demonstrations, and crippling strikes, Shah Mohammed Reza Pahlavi left Iran January 16, 1979, for an "extended vacation," bringing to an end his thirty-seven-year reign. The shah, long championed by the United States as a guardian of stability in the turbulent Middle East, left behind a country in chaos—a populace steeped in Islamic tradition but swept away by the winds of modernization—a state without authority; an economy in shambles; rival factions battling for supremacy.

Within several weeks, the shah's monarchy had been replaced by an "Islamic republic" led by the seventy-seven-year-old doctrinaire Shiite Moslem,

the Ayatollah Khomeini. The ayatollah (or Moslem leader) had gone into exile in Iraq following Moslem-led anti-shah protests in 1963. In 1978, the Iraqi government, concerned with maintaining good relations with Iran, had expelled Khomeini, who went to France, where he orchestrated a campaign of opposition to the shah and became a symbol of the rebellion. Khomeini had made no secret of his desire to eradicate Western influence from Iran.

On February 1, 1979, Khomeini returned to Iran in triumph to lead the revolution. Greeted by an estimated million persons, he set out to achieve his goals. On February 11, armed revolutionaries and army sympathizers overthrew the caretaker government of Shahpur Bakhtiar (appointed by the shah as premier before the shah's departure) and sent him into exile in France. Three days later leftist guerrillas stormed the U.S. Embassy in Tehran and held some seventy employees hostage. The American personnel were freed later the same day by supporters of Khomeini.

On April 1, 1979, Khomeini proclaimed the formation of an Islamic republic, calling it "the first day of a government of God." Iranian voters had approved the new regime in a referendum March 30-31. The government acted through edicts issued by Khomeini from his headquarters at the holy city of Qum, about eighty miles south of the capital. Orders came down to reimpose Islamic customs on the Iranians who had been steadily assimilating Western ways. The government also moved quickly against those who had supported the shah; before the end of the year more than 600 officials of the deposed regime and common criminals had been shot. The former shah and his family were condemned to death in absentia. Khomeini also moved to break the strong ties that bound his predecessor so closely to the United States. Long before his fall, the shah had been labeled by dissidents as the "American shah."

The Hostage Crisis

Then, near the end of 1979, two events occurred that would plunge Iran and the United States into a 444-day confrontation. The exiled shah, having received permission from the U.S. government to enter the country for medical treatment, flew to New York on October 22 to undergo surgery. On November 1, Khomeini denounced the shah's admission to the United States and ordered Iranian students "to expend with all their might their attacks to force the U.S. to return the deposed and cruel shah." Three days later, on November 4, a mob stormed the U.S. Embassy in Tehran, taking as hostages sixty-six diplomatic personnel; subsequently, fourteen were released but the fifty-two others were held for more

... Troubled as U.S. Role in Gulf Grows

than fourteen months.

The militants immediately demanded the extradition of the shah in exchange for the hostages. Months of tense posturing followed, with President Jimmy Carter rejecting the demands that the shah be returned to stand trial for his "criminal" actions. Meanwhile, the shah was granted permanent asylum in Egypt in March 1980, where he died in July. Carter also ordered deportation proceedings against Iranian students who were in the United States illegally, halted imports of Iranian oil, and froze an estimated $12 billion in assets held by Iranians in U.S. banks. Attempts at negotiations—and international pressures by the United Nations and America's Western allies—failed. The administration then attempted a helicopter rescue mission, which ended tragically on April 25, 1980, when eight Americans were killed in an accident that occurred as the mission was attempting to leave the Iranian desert.

In part, Iran's willingness finally to discuss seriously the hostage situation was caused by its own internal problems, made more volatile by the eruption of a full-scale and costly war with Iraq on September 22, 1980. However, many analysts speculated that Reagan's landslide victory against Carter in November 1980 played a major role in the eventual release of the hostages, announced moments after the new president was sworn in January 20, 1981. Reagan's sharp campaign attacks on the militants as "barbarians" indicated that the Iranian government could not expect the new administration to approach the crisis in a conciliatory manner.

Persian Gulf War, U.S. Role

A small U.S. naval force had been stationed at Bahrain in the Persian Gulf since 1949. But in 1979, during the hostage crisis, the United States began maintaining a large fleet of ships in the Indian Ocean that sailed frequently into the Gulf of Oman at the entrance to the Persian Gulf. Then, in September 1980, Iraq attacked Iran, sparking a bloody war, which by 1982 had spread to the sea lanes on which each side depended to export its oil, vital to Western Europe and Japan. By 1987, more than 200 ships had been attacked by Iraqi and Iranian forces in the gulf. The U.S. force based at Bahrain had expanded to three destroyers and three frigates—all armed with antiaircraft missiles—and an unarmed flagship.

Kuwait approached the United States and Soviet Union in late 1986 in search of military protection for its fleet of tankers. Moscow quickly agreed to lease Kuwait three of its own tankers that would carry Kuwaiti oil under the Soviet flag. The prospect of a growing Soviet presence in the gulf greatly alarmed U.S. officials. Partly to prevent the Russians

from carving out a larger role in the area, the United States proposed early in 1987 to re-register Kuwaiti tankers as U.S. ships.

Then, on May 17, 1987, a French-built Mirage F-1 jet of the Iraqi air force, in an apparent accident, fired two Exocet missiles at the U.S. frigate *Stark*, which was steaming very slowly with its antimissile defenses not activated. The missiles hit—and one exploded—near a compartment where crewmen were sleeping. The blast and resulting fire killed 37 of the crew of 224. The attack on the ship drew widespread congressional attention to the administration's plan to escort Kuwaiti tankers in the gulf and put it in a highly charged context. Many members, including supporters of reflagging, concluded that the proposal entailed enough risk of conflict between U.S. and Iranian forces that the Reagan administration should consult more fully with Congress about the new policy. By the extraordinary majority of 91-5, the Senate May 21 voted to block reflagging of the Kuwaiti ships until the Pentagon sent Congress a report detailing the threats U.S. forces would face under the new program.

Ignoring widespread bipartisan opposition on Capitol Hill, Reagan in July allowed Kuwait to begin registering eleven of its ships under the U.S. flag, thereby entitling them to military protection. But two days after U.S. warships began convoying Kuwaiti oil tankers through the Persian Gulf, a mine explosion July 24 damaged one of the tankers and sparked renewed expressions of congressional concern over the U.S. role in the area. Nevertheless, the Reagan administration decided to expand the U.S. role in the region, sending mine-sweeping helicopters to help protect the Kuwaiti-owned, U.S.-flagged oil tankers, and asserting that the operation would go forward.

Congressional criticism continued, with some members demanding that the 1973 War Powers Act be brought into play. The act required the president to report to Congress any time U.S. forces were deployed into hostilities or into a situation in which hostilities were imminent. Thereafter, the forces must be withdrawn within ninety days unless Congress adopted a resolution approving their continued deployment.

The situation in the gulf grew more precarious in the fall of 1987. Although the United Nations Security Council had adopted a resolution calling for a cease-fire, the Iran-Iraq War, especially on the ground, showed little sign of abating. Other nations, including France and Japan (which depended on Persian Gulf oil), beefed up their own presence, as did the Soviet Union. But the situation remained extremely volatile, and the U.S. role remained a highly sensitive issue.

Armed Services and Intelligence committees. "If Jimmy Carter pulled that stunt, he would have been hung from the rafters."

Iran Arms Sales

In his November 13 speech, Reagan offered no apologies. Instead, he attacked the news media for revealing and speculating about the rationale behind the arms deals—that it was an arms-for-hostages trade.

The president sought to portray his policy in the context of seeking to foster better ties with "moderate" segments of a former ally that "encompasses some of the most critical geography in the world." The United States had three related goals, Reagan said: to seek an "honorable end" to the Iran-Iraq War, which had dragged on since September 1980; to eliminate state-sponsored terrorism and subversion; and to achieve the safe return of all hostages. By making "overtures" to Iran, Reagan said, the United States was not damaging any of its goals or policies. *(Iran-Iraq War, box, p. 16)*

The president said he had authorized the transfer to Iran of only "small amounts of defensive weapons and spare parts"—several shipments that, in total, would fit into one cargo plane and could not affect the outcome of the Iran-Iraq War.

A senior White House official told reporters that the amount of arms was greater than what could be carried by a Boeing 747 jumbo jet but less than the payload of a giant C-5 transport. The official defined "defensive" arms broadly to include such items as antiaircraft and antitank missiles. However, he excluded from the definition spare parts of U.S.-supplied F-4 warplanes—a major component of reported Israeli arms shipments to Iran made with U.S. concurrence. (It was later revealed that the shipments were considerably larger, totaling more than 2,000 TOW antitank missiles and some 200 spare parts for Hawk antiaircraft missiles.)

The purpose of the arms shipments, Reagan said, was not to buy freedom for hostages but to send Tehran "a signal that the United States was prepared to replace the animosity between us with a new relationship." According to a White House official, the weapons sales overture was intended to bolster "moderate elements" in Iran. "The people that we're dealing with have got to have some credibility within the country," he said.

The official acknowledged that arms shipments to Iran from Israel and the United States occurred about the same time as three U.S. hostages were freed by pro-Iranian factions in Lebanon. But he insisted that the shipments were not direct payments for the Americans' release. The three were: the Rev. Benjamin F. Weir, released in September 1985, about the same time as an Israeli arms shipment to Iran; the Rev. Lawrence Jenco, allowed to go in July 1986; and David P. Jacobsen, freed on November 2, 1986. The Jenco and Jacobsen releases occurred at about the same time the United States was directly involved in shipping arms to Iran.

Reagan gave only the barest details about one peculiar incident: the visit to Tehran in May 1986 by former national security adviser Robert C. McFarlane and four U.S. officials. Ali Akbar Hashemi Rafsanjani, Speaker of the Iranian Parliament, had said the Americans were carrying false Irish passports and bearing several gifts, including a key-shaped cake. *(McFarlane trip, What Happened chapter, p. 49)*

Many congressional leaders were upset that Reagan had refused for more than a year to tell them anything about his dealings with Iran. At the least, members saw that as a breach of trust between the two branches of government; at worst, some said, the administration might have violated or skirted the laws requiring notification to Congress of overseas arms shipments.

"The White House has been more willing to trust some of the factions in Iran than they were to trust the Republican and Democratic leadership of the House and the Senate," said Patrick J. Leahy, D-Vt., vice chairman of the Senate Intelligence Committee, in a comment indicative of the sentiments of many members. *(Legal questions, below, p. 23)*

In his speech, Reagan insisted that his actions were "in full compliance with federal law." An administration official said that statement was based, in part, on the fact that the president had secretly signed an executive "finding" January 17, 1986, authorizing the arms transfers to Iran. In effect, that order created exemptions to President Jimmy Carter's 1979 embargo on arms shipments to Iran.

Reagan skirted the issue of whether members of Congress had been notified about his previous actions in dealing with Iran. Instead, he put administration activities in the present and future tenses, saying "the relevant committees of Congress are being and will be fully informed."

A senior administration official said on November 13 that the House and Senate Intelligence committees had been notified about the operation before the affair was made public. But leaders and senior staffers of both panels disputed that statement and subsequent revelations seemed to substantiate their assertions.

Reagan vs. Democrats

As the Iran issue continued to dominate the front pages, Reagan defended his actions during a nationally televised news conference November 19. But he provoked as many questions as he answered. *(Text, p. D-3)*

The president rejected contentions that the secret arms shipments to Iran had been a policy misjudgment. "I don't think a mistake was made," he said. "It was a high-risk gamble, and it was a gamble that, as I've said, I believe the circumstances warranted. And I don't see that it has been a fiasco or a great failure of any kind."

Reagan insisted—as he had previously in his November 13 speech—that the arms shipments were intended to signal his good faith to moderates in Iran who might succeed the Khomeini regime. The shipments were not, he said, "ransom" payments for U.S. hostages held by pro-Iranian factions in Lebanon. Reagan played down the shipments as "minuscule" ones that did nothing to alter the military balance in the brutal Iran-Iraq War.

Although promising that he would not authorize any further arms shipments to Iran, the president rejected suggestions that he revoke his January 17 executive order authorizing previous shipments. He also repeatedly justified on secrecy grounds the decision not to tell Congress about the affair. Further, he said he had the right to "defer" legally required notifications to Congress on such matters.

Democrats went on the offensive, saying Reagan had damaged U.S. credibility by secretly buying freedom for American hostages while he was publicly espousing a tough policy of "no negotiating with terrorists." Their skepticism was expressed by Senate Democratic leader Robert C.

Byrd, W.Va., who said: "The point is, we were exchanging arms for hostages." Democrats also insisted that Reagan had to become more willing to compromise with Congress in order to reach a bipartisan consensus for his foreign policy. "Bipartisanship requires a two-way street," said David L. Boren, D-Okla., who assumed the chairmanship of the Senate Intelligence Committee when Democrats became a majority in the 100th Congress that convened in 1987.

Many congressional Republicans moved to shield the president from direct responsibility by placing the blame with key White House advisers, notably Poindexter and Chief of Staff Donald T. Regan. Still, some Republicans said Reagan could do much to make amends by agreeing that his arms dealings with Iran had been ill-construed. "The president ought to admit that a mistake was made and move on to something else," said Senate Republican leader Robert Dole, Kan.

Indicative of the mood on both aisles was that leaders of both parties suggested that Reagan should seek help from senior foreign policy advisers—including those who served in previous administrations—to revise the manner in which major foreign policy decisions were made.

Democrats argued that Reagan's explanations of the administration's dealings with Iran were incoherent and contradictory—signs that he had not clearly thought through the policy he intended his aides to follow. Incoming House Speaker Jim Wright, D-Texas, said the president's handling of questions was characteristic. Reagan, Wright commented, was "not careful with factual accuracy."

Perhaps an even more damaging critique came from Sam Nunn, D-Ga., the incoming chairman of the Senate Armed Services Committee, a respected expert on military affairs, and a major Democratic spokesman on foreign policy. Appearing before the press on November 20, Nunn

listed seven "contradictions," or misstatements, by Reagan on Iran. Nunn said other administration officials had given Congress evidence that called into question those statements. Among Reagan's comments were:

● That the United States provided only "defensive" arms to Iran. That description was "erroneous," Nunn said, given Iran's stated goal of settling its war with Iraq by toppling its government. "If you give them any weapons in that context, in my view, they are offensive weapons," he said. Nunn cited in particular TOW antitank missiles provided by the United States. Those missiles gave Iran a "very significant offensive capability," Nunn said, because Iraq depended on tanks to defend its territory.

● That arms shipments were "minuscule." Nunn said that description was "not in accord with all the information I have received" from other administration aides. Those officials, in private briefings, had acknowledged that the amount of arms was "very substantial," he said. Reagan and his aides said all U.S.-sponsored arms shipments could fit into one cargo plane; the aides described such a plane as being about the size of a giant C-5 cargo transport, which carries more than 100 tons.

(Wright said officials told him the United States had sold Iran 2,008 TOW missiles, which he valued at more than $12 million. Iran also received parts for 235 Hawk antiaircraft batteries, according to Wright.)

● That arms shipments did not shift the balance between Iran and Iraq. However, Nunn said, U.S. intervention could alter the "psychological balance" in Iran's favor, which Nunn said was a major factor in the stalemated war. Reagan also ignored the possibility that other nations would view the U.S. arms shipments as "the green light" to resume their own profit-making sales to Iran, Nunn said.

● That the United States did not swap arms for Iran's pressure on terrorist groups in Lebanon to release the three American hostages. That statement was "contrary to in-

On November 25, 1986, President Reagan disclosed that he had not been "fully informed" about the Iran arms deals. He then, with White House chief of staff Donald T. Regan, far left, and spokesman Larry Speakes looking on, turned over to Attorney General Edwin Meese III, at podium, the job of telling the press about the diversion of profits to the Nicaraguan contras.

History of U.S.-Nicaraguan Relations ...

The United States' relations with Nicaragua were a topic of heated debate well before the November 1986 disclosure that some proceeds from the U.S. arms sales to Iran were intended to be diverted for use by guerrilla forces in the Central American nation.

It became clear soon after Ronald Reagan entered office that he was deeply committed to the support of the "contras"—a diverse group of counter-revolutionaries—who were engaged in a paramilitary campaign against the country's Sandinista government, which Reagan considered to be Marxist and a willing tool of the Soviet Union and Cuba. But his policy encountered growing opposition from a skeptical faction in Congress, provoking numerous heated battles over the administration's requests for aid to the rebels.

Nicaragua under Somoza

Nicaragua is the largest (57,143 sq. mi.) and least densely populated (pop. 2.9 million) of the five Central American nations. A veritable backwater in Spanish colonial days, Nicaragua—together with Guatemala, El Salvador, Honduras, and Costa Rica—threw off Spanish rule in 1821 and for a brief period was part of the Mexican Empire. With the dissolution of the empire in 1823, Nicaragua became one of the five units of the United Provinces of Central America. The Central American union broke apart in 1838. From that point on, Nicaragua was nominally, if not always effectively, independent.

A revolt by Nicaragua's Liberal party against the Conservatives in 1893 brought José Santos Zelaya to the presidency, which he held for the next sixteen years. But the Nicaraguan leader antagonized the United States over a number of issues, forcing a confrontation that led to the dispatching of U.S. troops to Nicaragua and ultimately to Zelaya's resignation in 1909. Upheaval ensued, and U.S. Marines occupied Nicaragua for most of the period up to 1933, when Anastasio Somoza Garcia, an ambitious commander of the country's National Guard, came to power. He and his sons were to rule Nicaragua for more than four decades.

The long period of Somoza rule was based on absolute control of the National Guard and the Liberal party, and close ties to the United States. The Nicaraguan economy grew steadily under the Somozas, as did their own wealth. The instrument of destruction of the Somoza dynasty was the Frente Sandinista de Liberacion Nacional (FSLN), the Sandinist Front for the National Liberation. Founded in 1962, the front became a serious challenge to the government only in the 1970s, as discontent with the Somoza regime grew. By the mid-1970s,

the Sandinistas were waging open guerrilla warfare in several parts of Nicaragua, and the government responded by committing atrocities that only built further support for the guerrilla cause.

Sandinistas Take Over

In the waning days of the Somoza regime, the United States began distancing itself from the dictatorship. After Jimmy Carter became president in January 1977, Washington began pressuring Somoza to improve his human rights performance and to check the brutality of the National Guard. As the end drew closer, the United States reduced its embassy staff in Managua, the Nicaraguan capital, and recalled its military attachés to Washington. At the Organization of American States (OAS), the U.S. delegation pressed for the creation of an inter-American peacekeeping force to intervene in the Nicaraguan civil war. When that proposal was rejected, the Carter administration began direct talks with the FSLN and finally arranged for Somoza's departure to Miami.

Initially, relations between the United States and the Sandinista revolutionary government (a name taken from Augusto Sandino, a national hero who battled the U.S. Marine occupation of Nicaragua in the early 1930s) were good, although not particularly close. Recognizing that the revolution had shattered the Nicaraguan economy, the United States immediately dispatched a substantial amount of disaster relief. Congress appropriated $75 million in emergency assistance to Nicaragua, and international lending institutions (including the World Bank) provided approximately $200 million in funds for the new government.

Change in Policy

Even at that stage, however, there were divided opinions on whether to support the Sandinistas. There was, on the one hand, a view—more prevalent in Congress than elsewhere—that the Sandinistas were nationalists and social reformers who could be influenced to steer a moderate, albeit socialist, course and remain on good terms with the United States. On the other hand, the Central Intelligence Agency (CIA), the Defense Department, and the National Security Council felt that the Sandinista core was hard-line Marxist and that it would soon come under the sway of Cuba and the Soviet Union.

The latter view prevailed after Reagan became president. Washington quickly cut off Nicaraguan aid and initiated a covert insurgency program. U.S. representatives in multinational lending institutions began opposing loans to Nicaragua; U.S. exports were

... Is One of Controversy and Conflict

drastically reduced; and a trade embargo was declared in the spring of 1985.

The Sandinistas seized every opportunity to attack the United States in international forums, welcomed thousands of Cuban "advisers," established close political and economic relations with the Soviet Union, supplied arms to Marxist guerrillas in El Salvador and Guatemala, and rapidly converted their country into a tightly controlled socialist, if not communist, state. The rift between Managua and Washington by 1987 had become so great that most experts believed that there could be no reconciliation until there was a change of government in one, or both, of the capitals.

Disputes over Contra Aid

U.S. covert aid to the contras reportedly began in December 1981 with an executive order from the president authorizing actions by the CIA to disrupt arms shipments into Nicaragua. Administration officials argued they were not trying to overthrow the Sandinista government but were merely trying to stop the flow of Soviet- and Cuban-supplied arms to leftists in neighboring El Salvador. Democrats in the House of Representatives repeatedly tried to cut off the covert aid to the contras. In 1982 they succeeded in adding to a CIA authorization measure and to a defense appropriations bill an amendment prohibiting intelligence agency operations aimed specifically at overthrowing the Nicaraguan government. The provision was known as the Boland amendment for its sponsor, House Intelligence Committee chairman Edward P. Boland, D-Mass. (Boland amendment, box, p. 24)

In the spring of 1983, the Democratic majority in the House renewed attacks on aid to the rebels, contending that the administration was violating the Boland amendment. Four attempts were made that year and the next to end U.S. aid to the anti-Sandinista rebels. Though the House Democrats' efforts were initially blocked in the Republican Senate, a compromise eventually was reached on contra aid for fiscal 1984. The final measure provided that the administration could spend a maximum of $24 million for covert aid in fiscal 1984, but the president would have to return to Congress for more funds if he wanted to continue future aid.

In early 1984 the president asked Congress for an additional $21 million to support the contras. However, on April 6, a story appeared in the Wall Street Journal reporting direct CIA involvement in the mining of Nicaraguan harbors. The tone of the congressional debate grew more harsh, and many Republicans joined Democrats for the first time in opposing the aid. Congress refused the president's request. Immediately after that defeat, the administration sought $28 million to continue the covert aid in fiscal 1985. For the fourth time, the House banned the request, but a compromise was eventually reached that provided $14 million, with several stipulations, including congressional approval of the way the money was spent.

Elections were held in Nicaragua on November 4, 1984. Apart from the ruling Sandinista National Liberation Front, whose leader, Daniel Ortega, became president, only minor parties participated. Meanwhile, the so-called "Contadora" group of Colombia, Mexico, Panama, and Venezuela had begun work in 1983 to develop a negotiated solution to the conflicts in Central America. Among the group's principles were demilitarization of Central America, more economic aid from outside countries, and moves toward democracy.

Despite that impasse, the Reagan administration succeeded in 1986 in persuading Congress to renew support for the contras—$70 million in military aid and $30 million in nonmilitary aid. In 1986, Congress voted to approve $100 million in a military and nonmilitary aid program to the guerrillas, $40 million of which was left outstanding for approval in 1987. In March 1987 the House voted to temporarily halt aid, but the Senate sided with the president to go ahead with providing the $40 million.

Reagan had been planning to ask Congress in September 1987 for at least $105 million, and possibly as much as $150 million over eighteen months beginning in fiscal 1988, to continue arming and supplying the contras. The political future of any additional funding request was thrown into question August 7, 1987, with the signing of a peace plan by the presidents of five Central American countries, including Nicaragua. That action came just two days after the White House published its own peace plan that had been written with the cooperation of House Speaker Jim Wright, D-Texas. Contra-aid supporters urged Reagan to submit his request in September and demand congressional votes on it. But Wright said Reagan should wait for a few months to see if Nicaragua followed through with the August 7 plan, which would require it to restore freedom of the press and other rights and called for a reconciliation with the political opposition.

Meanwhile, the shape of U.S. policy in Central America remained uncertain. Not only were Congress and the administration disputing U.S. actions—and particularly the manner in which they were conducted—but the situation of other nations in the region gave rise to conflicting analyses. The extent of the threat the Sandinistas posed in exporting Marxism to Nicaragua's neighbors was one of the most central concerns.

formation I have received," Nunn said, citing Reagan's statements that the release of hostages was a sign of Iran's "good faith," reciprocated by U.S. arms sales.

● That the United States did not condone arms shipments to Iran by other countries, especially Israel. In his news conference, Reagan repeatedly denied that the United States was involved with or approved shipments to Iran by "third countries." Minutes after his November 19 news conference, the White House issued a statement correcting Reagan's comment, acknowledging that "there was a third country involved in our secret project with Iran." Top White House aides also said the United States gave official approval for at least one Israeli shipment to Iran in September 1985.

● That Congress did not have to be notified about the arms shipments to Iran. "The president seems to think that he can notify Congress any time he chooses to," Nunn said. "That is simply contrary to the letter and spirit of the law." Nunn noted that existing law called for prior notification to Congress of all but the most "extraordinary" covert operations. *(Arms sales controls, p. 24)*

● That the United States was providing arms to "moderates" in Iran, who were responsible for a "lessening" of terrorist activities by their country. "When we use the word 'lessening,' it means it is still there; it is simply less than it was," Nunn said. And Wright said Reagan erred in implying that none of the arms went to the Khomeini regime. "Whose army benefited from the arms?" he asked.

Bush Explains Policy

In a December 3 speech, Vice President George Bush offered the administration's most candid explanation up to that point of why the Iranian initiative was taken and its consequences. The speech was an effort to restore public confidence in Reagan and to minimize damage to Bush's own 1988 presidential aspirations. Bush previously had been conspicuously silent on the Iran-contra matter. *(Text of speech, p. D-16)*

Unlike Reagan, Bush admitted: "Clearly, mistakes were made." He was not specific, but he seemed to be referring to the funneling of Iranian arms profits to the contras—an activity in which Bush said he had not been involved. *(Subsequent testimony on Bush role, Select Investigating Committees chapter, p. 143)*

However, Bush defended the administration's underlying policy toward dealing with Iran—even though he acknowledged sharing the "hatred" of the American people toward the Khomeini regime. Although the method of the approach (selling arms) was "arguable," the goal of improving relations with Iran had merit, Bush contended, noting: "We may not like the current Iranian regime, and I've said we don't. But it would be irresponsible to ignore its geopolitical and strategic importance." Even so, Bush acknowledged, "the question remains of how the administration could violate its own policy of not selling arms to Iran. Simple human hope explains it perhaps better than anything else."

Bush continued: "The president hoped that we could open a channel that would serve the interests of the United States and of our allies in a variety of ways. Call it leadership. Given 20-20 hindsight, call it a mistaken tactic if you want to. It was risky but potentially of long-term value." With investigations under way, "Let the chips fall where they may. We want the truth," the vice president concluded.

In a speech December 2, 1986, Vice President George Bush admitted "mistakes were made," apparently referring to the diversion of arms profits to the contras.

Taking Aim at Regan

In the midst of Washington's furor, there seemed to be near-unanimous agreement on only one thing: The president's chief of staff, Regan, had to go. Republicans and Democrats alike argued that he had not served his boss well and should resign or be fired. But those who disagreed with that view were the most important players: Regan and Reagan.

The most important calls for firing Regan came from congressional leaders who said he had no defense on the question of whether he knew about the diversion of Iranian arms sales funds to the contras: If he did know, he should have stopped it; if he did not know what his subordinates were doing, he should have. *(Regan testimony, p. 135)*

House minority leader Robert H. Michel, R-Ill., considered one of the most cautious Republicans, on December 3 joined the call for Regan's departure, saying: "There have been enough inferences and enough statements made that when one does not pull his share of the load, I guess maybe he ought to think in terms of leaving."

Few leading members of Congress disagreed with that advice, and those who did offered ambiguous reasons in doing so. Alan K. Simpson, Wyo., the Senate Republican whip, noted that the president faced decisions on other pressing matters, including the budget. "You can't leave him alone to do that," he said.

Although some Republicans expressed hope that Regan's departure would go a long way toward calming the controversy, Michel quoted Reagan as saying that probably would not happen. "What good does it to fire, have a wholesale firing, if that does not solve the problem?" Michel asked in relating the president's views to reporters. "It doesn't kill the issue by firing this person or that person."

The demands for Regan's ouster came so quickly, and with such force, largely because the chief of staff had alienated many public officials in Washington with his boasts of personal power. "Always wrong, and with a loud voice," was the description of Regan by one prominent House Republican.

The pressure on Regan culminated with his resignation February 27, 1987. The president selected former senator Howard H. Baker, Jr. (R-Tenn., 1967-85), to be his new chief of staff. The choice was hailed on Capitol Hill; key lawmakers said Baker was ideally suited to repair battered White House relations with Congress.

Iran Sales: Legal Questions

Reagan's policy of supplying weapons and other military goods to Iran raised two kinds of legal questions, in addition to underlying policy issues: Did the president illegally or improperly fail to tell Congress about what he was doing, and did he violate or skirt laws limiting arms aid to terrorist countries?

The White House said that Attorney General Edwin Meese III certified all of Reagan's actions as legal and proper. Reagan himself, in his November 19 news conference, insisted that he had the right, in the interest of maintaining secrecy, to "defer" telling Congress about such matters.

But many members of Congress and their legal experts insisted that Reagan violated at least the spirit, and possibly the letter, of several U.S. laws. "It appears that laws have been broken," said Wright. He said Reagan withheld "vital information from the Congress for 18 months in contravention of the law." And Wright charged that Reagan skirted a ban on arms sales to terrorist countries.

Some of the president's supporters on Capitol Hill were slightly more charitable. After listening to Reagan's November 19 explanation, Richard G. Lugar, R-Ind., outgoing chairman of the Senate Foreign Relations Committee, said: "I suspect the president does not understand the law on informing Congress on these things."

Informing Congress

Responding to the Vietnam War and the revelations in the mid-1970s of various CIA misdeeds, Congress had enacted several laws requiring the administration to report on covert operations and other diplomatic and military actions overseas. The laws were based on the Washington axiom that information is power: The administration generated and possessed most information about policy, and it could shut members of Congress out of the policy-making process by keeping them in the dark.

Members of Congress also insisted that sharing information with Capitol Hill was beneficial: By consulting congressional leaders in advance, a president usually could gain their support and benefit from their experience.

The information-sharing laws most relevant to the Iran dealings concerned covert operations and arms sales.

Covert Operations. Legislation (PL 93-559) passed in 1974 required the president to tell Congress "in a timely fashion" about covert operations by the CIA and other intelligence agencies. It also required him to give personal approval to each covert operation by signing a "finding" stating its justification and general goals.

Complaining that it was having to report covert actions to seven congressional committees—with the resulting danger of leaks—the administration of Democrat Jimmy Carter in 1980 sought and won a revised law (PL 96-450) requiring that such notices be given only to the House and Senate Intelligence committees.

That law, inserted into the 1947 National Security Act as section 501, required the administration to tell the Intelligence panels in advance about most proposed intelligence operations, including covert actions; under undefined "extraordinary circumstances," that notice could be limited to the eight senior congressional leaders, four of whom were on the Intelligence panels.

If the administration did not notify the committees before an operation began, the president himself would have to do so afterward "in a timely fashion" and explain why the advance notice was not given.

The Senate Intelligence Committee, which drafted the 1980 law, said in a report (S Rept 96-730) that the legislation was "intended to mean that the committees shall be informed at the time of the presidential finding that authorizes" each covert operation. "Arrangements for notice are to be made forthwith, without delay." Wright told reporters on November 20, 1986, that the law was "not ambiguous" on the issue of timing. "It does not suggest you can do it and then tell the Congress 18 months later."

However, House Intelligence Committee member Henry J. Hyde, R-Ill., countered that the law was "deliberately vague" to give presidents flexibility. But he also said that Reagan had made a political mistake in failing to inform Congress at the outset.

The law contained one clause that both the Carter and Reagan administrations viewed as a possible loophole. The preamble stated that the requirements would be imposed "to the extent consistent with all applicable authorities and duties, including those conferred by the Constitution upon the executive and legislative branches of the government. . . ." Administration officials said that clause meant the president could cite his constitutional role as commander in chief as justification for withholding information from Congress.

Most members of Congress rejected the administration's explanations, noting that the Constitution said nothing about intelligence activities and that it did not excuse the president from obeying the law. "In that we are a government of laws and not a government of men, even the president of the United States is compelled to respect and obey the law," Wright said.

The Senate Intelligence Committee acknowledged in its 1980 report that there was a "gray area resulting from the overlap between the Constitutional authorities and duties of the [executive and legislative] branches."

In his news conference, Reagan put forward another reason for his decision to withhold notification. If he had told Congress about the arms sales dealings with Iran, he said, "I would not have been able to keep them as secret as they were." However, congressional sources noted the law specifically rejected such an argument by the president. Section 501(e) stated that the president could not use the possibility of "unauthorized disclosure" as a reason for withholding information from Congress.

Casey Agreement. In July 1984, after a blowup over the CIA's failure to tell Congress about its role in the mining of Nicaraguan harbors, CIA director William J. Casey agreed in writing to tell the Senate Intelligence Committee in advance about all "significant" covert actions. The agreement later was strengthened, committee sources said.

On November 21, 1986, Casey gave the House Intelligence panel a copy of Reagan's January 17 authorization for the Iran operation, which directed Casey not to tell Congress about it. There were reports that Reagan did so to

Boland Amendments on Aid to Contras ...

Congress's first legislation restricting U.S. support for the Nicaraguan contras in 1982 "sowed the seeds" of the Reagan administration's confusing policies in Central America, Robert C. McFarlane told the House and Senate select committees investigating the Iran-contra affair May 13, 1987. McFarlane, President Reagan's national security adviser from 1983 to 1985, said that Congress and the administration misled each other at the outset of the U.S. contra policy—launching fierce political battles. A central issue in the congressional Iran-contra investigations was whether the administration complied with aid restrictions.

The misleading started, McFarlane said, in December 1982, when Congress enacted the first "Boland amendment," named after Edward P. Boland, D-Mass., then chairman of the House Intelligence Committee and subsequently a member of the House Iran-contra panel. The amendment barred the United States from aiding any insurgent group "for the purpose of overthrowing" Nicaragua's leftist Sandinista government or provoking a war between Nicaragua and neighboring Honduras. The amendment did not prevent the administration from spending $24 million on the contras in 1983—on grounds that the purpose of the aid was to "interdict" Nicaraguan arms shipments to leftist guerrillas in neighboring El Salvador, not to oust the Sandinistas.

Repeatedly since the first Boland amendment, the administration shifted its stated rationale for helping the contras whenever Congress seemed ready to restrict it. Through most of 1983, the administration stuck to the contention that it was using the contras to stop the arms flow into El Salvador. At the end of 1983, Congress placed a $24 million limit on CIA aid to the contras during fiscal 1984 and then enacted a more stringent Boland amendment barring all aid. Reagan returned to Congress in 1985 and won approval for $27 million in "humanitarian," or nonmilitary, aid to the contras, as well as a classified amount to help them with communications and intelligence. During the 1984-85 political struggle, the administration said its contra policy was aimed at putting "pressure" on the Sandinistas to participate in regional peace efforts. In subsequent debates, the administration said its goal was to force the Managua regime to negotiate with the internal opposition, including the contras. That policy proved politically successful in 1986, when Congress voted $100 million in outright military and nonmilitary aid to the contras. Rather than shifting its policies to win votes in Congress, McFarlane told the select committees, the administration "should have stepped up to it" in the beginning and taken its case to the public. Following are brief descriptions of the various versions of the Boland amendments.

1982: Boland's Curbs

Administration officials first informed the House and Senate Intelligence committees in December 1981 of President Reagan's secret decision to channel money and arms through the CIA to the contras. In April 1982, the House Intelligence Committee rejected a move by some Democratic members to kill the covert aid. Instead, the committee voted to impose two restrictions. One required that the aid be used solely to interdict arms shipments from Nicaragua to leftist guerrillas in El Salvador. The second stipulated that funds were not to be used to overthrow the Nicaraguan government or to provoke a military exchange between Nicaragua and Honduras, where most of the Nicaraguan guerrillas were based. Language establishing those two restrictions was included in the classified portion of the fiscal 1983 authorization bill (PL 97-269) for the CIA and other intelligence agencies that was cleared by Congress in September 1982.

In December 1982, several Democrats attempted to amend the fiscal 1983 defense appropriations bill to bar U.S. aid to the Nicaraguan contras. Boland headed off that move by offering the language that had been incorporated into the intelligence authorization bill. The House approved the Boland amendment, 411-0, and the full Congress included it in the defense portion of the fiscal 1983 continuing appropriations resolution (PL 97-377).

That Boland amendment said: "None of the funds provided in this Act may be used by the Central Intelligence Agency or the Department of Defense to furnish military equipment, military training or advice, or other support for military activities, to any group or individual, not part of a country's armed forces, for the purpose of overthrowing the government of Nicaragua or provoking a military exchange between Nicaragua and Honduras."

The provision, subsequently extended by another law (PL 98-212), was in effect from December 21, 1982, to December 8, 1983.

1983: The Boland Cap

Early in 1983, publicity about the contra operation mushroomed, with the media carrying detailed reports on the war in Nicaragua.

Boland declared in April that the publicity showed that the amendment carrying his name was being violated because the Reagan administration appeared to be seeking to overthrow the government of Nicaragua. He later told the House that "one with any sense, any legal sense, would have to come to the conclusion that the operation is illegal, that the purpose and mission of the operation was to overthrow

... Spark Controversy over Interpretation

the government in Nicaragua."

With Boland and House Speaker Thomas P. O'Neill, Jr., D-Mass., leading the way, the House voted in July and again in October to force Reagan to stop giving financial or other support to the contras, but the Senate refused to follow suit. The issue was resolved by House-Senate conferees deliberating the fiscal 1984 defense appropriations bill (PL 98-212), which set a $24 million cap on funding for the contras in fiscal 1984. An identical provision was included in an intelligence authorization bill (PL 98-215) for fiscal 1984.

The second Boland amendment said: "During fiscal year 1984, not more than $24,000,000 of the funds available to the Central Intelligence Agency, the Department of Defense, or any other agency or entity of the United States involved in intelligence activities may be obligated or expended for the purpose or which would have the effect of supporting, directly or indirectly, military or paramilitary operations in Nicaragua by any nation, group, organization, movement or individual."

1984: The Boland Cutoff

In March 1984, Reagan asked Congress to approve $21 million for the contras, in addition to the $24 million limit then in the law.

As Congress was considering that request in early April, Reagan's Nicaraguan policy was shaken by the revelation that the CIA had provided the logistics and supervision for the mining of several Nicaraguan harbors. The mines had little explosive power, but they damaged several ships and caused a furor in Congress. Barry Goldwater, R-Ariz., chairman of the Senate Intelligence Committee, was particularly infuriated by the CIA's failure to give his committee advance notice of the mining. Both chambers adopted resolutions (which did not have the force of law) condemning the mining.

Nevertheless, the Senate twice approved the president's request; again the House refused to comply. When the dispute held up approval of a fiscal 1984 supplemental appropriations bill, the Senate backed down.

Reagan made no further effort to get the $21 million for fiscal 1984, but he did press Congress to approve $28 million in renewed aid to the contras for fiscal 1985.

The House rejected that request, too, and Congress resolved the issue in an omnibus continuing resolution (PL 98-473) that included fiscal 1985 funding for the Defense Department and CIA. Under enormous administration pressure, conferees in October adopted a complicated provision that rejected Reagan's request but gave him the opportunity to return to Congress for further funds in 1985.

Major elements of the third, and most comprehensive, Boland amendment:

● Said "During fiscal year 1985, no funds available to the Central Intelligence Agency, the Department of Defense, or any other agency or entity of the United States involved in intelligence activities may be obligated or expended for the purpose or which would have the effect of supporting, directly or indirectly, military or paramilitary operations in Nicaragua by any nation, group, organization, movement, or individual."

● Stated that the ban would cease to apply if, after February 28, 1985, the president submitted a report to Congress asking for aid for military or paramilitary operations in Nicaragua, and Congress approved it by passing a joint resolution. The president's report was to state that the Nicaraguan government was supporting guerrillas in El Salvador or other Central American countries and analyze the military significance of that support; justify the amount and type of aid sought for operations in Nicaragua; and explain the goals of U.S. policy for Central America and how the aid would further those goals.

● Expedited procedures for consideration of the joint resolution approving the president's request. The resolution was to be referred to the Appropriations committees in both chambers, which could report it no sooner than eight but no later than fifteen days after receiving it. Debate was limited to ten hours in each chamber, and motions to delay or amend the resolution were barred.

● Set a $14 million limit in fiscal 1985 on funds for military or paramilitary operations in Nicaragua, if approved by joint resolution.

The compromise also was included in the fiscal 1985 intelligence authorization bill (PL 98-618). It said: "No funds authorized to be appropriated by this Act or by the Intelligence Authorization Act for fiscal year 1984 (Public Law 98-215) may be obligated or expended for the purpose or which would have the effect of supporting, directly or indirectly, military or paramilitary operations in Nicaragua by any nation, group, organization, movement, or individual, except to the extent provided and under the terms and conditions specified by House Joint Resolution 648 [PL 98-473], making continuing appropriations for the fiscal year 1985, and for other purposes as enacted."

The last Boland amendment, fortified by a series of continuing resolutions, kept the complete cutoff of military aid to the contras in effect from October 1, 1984, to December 3, 1985, during which time it was revealed that U.S. officials had actively participated in soliciting private and third-country aid to the contras, and in contra resupply efforts.

protect the CIA director from congressional complaints if the operation became public. That tactic appeared to work: After listening to Casey, in subsequent hearings, Senate committee members said he had clearly violated the agreement, but they blamed the president for forcing him to do so.

Daniel Finn, minority counsel to the Senate committee, said the laws and the agreement with Casey "were not intended to deal with a case under which notification was not allowed" by the president.

Covert Arms Shipments. In 1985, Congress further amended the covert-action-notification law to require the Intelligence committees to be told whenever an intelligence agency provided weapons or defense services (such as training) to any entity outside the U.S. government. That provision, made permanent in the fiscal 1987 intelligence authorization law (PL 99-569), contained a major loophole: Notice was required only if each weapon or defense service was worth $1 million or more.

Congressional sources said it was possible that Reagan's shipments to Iran were exempt from the law because of the loophole. None of the items reportedly sold to Iran—including spare parts for antiaircraft missile batteries—cost more than $1 million apiece.

Regular Arms Sales. The Arms Export Control Act (PL 90-629), enacted in 1968 and amended frequently thereafter, required the administration to report to Congress all major arms sales to foreign countries made through "regular channels." Those included direct sales by the U.S. government to foreign governments and "commercial" sales overseas by private U.S. companies. The proviso also included so-called "third-party transfers": shipments of U.S.-originated arms from the country that first purchased them to another country.

The law required the president to report to Congress at the end of each quarter every "letter of offer" by the United States to sell any major military equipment valued at $1 million or more. The president also had to report to Congress thirty days in advance each proposed sale in which any item was valued at $14 million or more, or in which the total amount was $50 million or more.

The purpose of the advance notice was to give Congress the chance to block controversial arms sales. The legislature had come close to blocking several sales to Arab countries, but it stopped short each time. In early 1986, for example, Congress failed to override Reagan's veto of a resolution (S J Res 316) disapproving the sale of missiles to Saudi Arabia.

The president could waive all legal restrictions on his ability to make foreign arms sales by invoking "special authorities" included in section 614 of the permanent foreign aid laws. If he did this, however, he had to notify Congress that doing so was "vital" to the U.S. national security interests. Congressional sources said Reagan provided no arms sales notices about Iran to Capitol Hill and that it was uncertain whether that was required.

Several committees sent their legal experts scurrying to law books to resolve questions about Reagan's compliance with the law. But one senior Senate aide said the arms sale law, in particular, was "so byzantine that it could take months" for answers.

Antiterrorism Laws

The Export Administration Act of 1979 (PL 96-72) required the secretary of state to send Congress an annual report listing countries that had "repeatedly provided support for acts of international terrorism." Iran had been on that list each year since 1980.

The 1979 export law also required the secretaries of state and the Treasury to report to Congress thirty days before approving exports to those countries of goods or technology valued at $7 million or more. However, that notice was necessary only if the administration determined that an export would "make significant contributions to the military potential" of the country involved or would enhance its ability to support international terrorism.

Congressional sources said the Carter and Reagan administrations sent few reports to Congress in compliance with that requirement. In the Iran case, they said, the administration could have argued that reports were unnecessary on the grounds that the arms sales did not make "significant contributions" to Iran's military potential. Reagan administration officials had insisted that the United States shipped only small quantities of "defensive" arms that only marginally improved Iran's military capabilities.

Congress in 1986 toughened the restriction on arms sales to terrorist countries. A bill boosting funding for the security of U.S. embassies overseas included a flat ban on military exports to countries on the terrorism-supporting list. The president could waive the prohibition only by determining that such an export was "important to the national interests of the United States." If he did so, however, he had to report to Congress within ninety days justifying his decision.

Reagan signed that prohibition into law (PL 99-399) on August 27, 1986—months after at least two of the U.S. arms shipments to Iran occurred. The administration did not acknowledge making any shipments after that date, although later it was learned that additional arms were sent.

Reagan's approval of selling weapons to Iran clearly violated an embargo on all military exports to that nation imposed by President Carter in November 1979 after Americans were taken hostages at the U.S. Embassy there. Carter barred the exports in an executive order (No. 12170), which White House officials said remained in effect. However, White House spokesman Larry Speakes said Reagan created exceptions to the embargo on January 17, 1986, when he signed his secret executive order authorizing the Iran operation.

The Contra Bombshell

Reagan had made little progress in recovering from two solid weeks of controversy over his policy of secretly selling weapons to Iran when, on November 24, Attorney General Meese gave him evidence that apparently somewhere between $10 million and $30 million in profits from the Iranian arms deals had been diverted to the Nicaraguan contras. (Later, in testimony before the House and Senate Iran-contra committees, it was disclosed that the contras had actually received a much smaller amount.)

The next day, Reagan informed congressional leaders and announced that he had fired the NSC staffer who had helped manage the Iran operation, Lieutenant Colonel North. National security adviser Poindexter, who Meese said knew about the diversion of money to the contras, resigned and asked to be returned to the Navy.

At a hastily called November 25 news conference, a grim and shaken Reagan read a statement acknowledging that he had not been "fully informed" about the Iran arms deals. "This action raises serious questions of propriety," he said. However, he continued to insist that his Iran policy was "well founded." He conceded only that "in one aspect, implementation of that policy was seriously flawed." *(Text, p. D-7)*

Meese said at the news conference that no other top U.S. officials, including Reagan and cabinet members, knew about the transfer of Iranian money to the contras. Meese later amended his statement to say some persons with "tangential" ties to the government might have known about or been involved in the money transfers.

Asked why administration statements should be believed, Meese said Reagan had established credibility "by the full disclosure of the facts." He pledged that the Justice Department would continue to investigate the matter and that further information would be made public. Meese later ordered the FBI to launch a full-scale probe into possible criminal violations.

Many congressional leaders and others in Washington expressed skepticism that the diversion of arms profits to the contras had been carried out with the assent or knowledge of only two White House officials. "It defies credulity" that a middle-level official such as North could be making foreign policy, said Wright. If that was the case, he added, "if nobody knew of it, that in itself is a confession of a great void in the execution of our foreign policy." Dave Durenberger, R-Minn., Senate Intelligence Committee chairman in the 99th Congress, said: "Ollie North is not a Lone Ranger.... There are some undisclosed sources that gave him at least an amber light."

Within hours of Reagan's press conference, the most widely quoted statement on Capitol Hill was the famous question that then-senator Howard Baker had posed during the Watergate hearings of 1973: "What did the president know and when did he know it?"

Only sketchy details were available in 1986 about how the Iranian arms payments found their way to the contras. Meese said that Iran deposited money for the arms into one or more Swiss bank accounts and that some of those funds went to the contras.

Wright said congressional leaders were told that, in one transaction, Iran paid $19 million for antitank missiles and other items from Defense Department stockpiles. The CIA reimbursed $3 million to the Pentagon for the cost of the weapons, and about $12 million remained in a Swiss bank account, supposedly for use by the contras. That left about $4 million that might have gone to arms dealers as a commission or finder's fee, Wright said.

Congressional Response

The Iran-contra connection stunned members of Congress, many of whom were still flabbergasted by the underlying controversy over Reagan's arms sales to Tehran. Any official U.S. participation in diverting money to the contras between late 1984 and September 30, 1986, could have been illegal under several versions of the Boland amendment, barring direct or indirect U.S. military aid to the contras. *(Boland amendments, box, p. 24)*

Most Republicans rallied behind the president personally but criticized White House aides for misleading him and carrying out their own foreign policy. Some GOP leaders said critics should understand the president's dilemma, but at the same time insisted that Reagan remained firmly in control. "This nation is not rudderless," said Sen. John W. Warner, R-Va., a former secretary of the Navy. "The president is at the helm, and it's steady as she goes."

Members on both sides of the aisle called on Reagan to provide full information to Congress as quickly as possible.

Lt. Col. Oliver L. North, fired from his job as a National Security Council aide because of his involvement in the Iran-contra affair, was a star witness before the House and Senate select investigating committees.

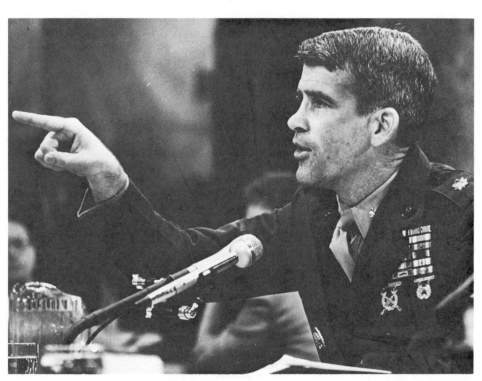

CIA's Covert Role in Iran-Contra Affair ...

Evidence that the Central Intelligence Agency (CIA) played a larger role than was previously thought in the effort to provide funds to the administration-supported guerrilla "contra" forces battling the leftist Sandinista government in Nicaragua gradually emerged during the House and Senate probes into the Iran-contra affair.

Testimony before the select committees indicated that CIA director William J. Casey, a close confidant of President Reagan, had approved active CIA support for the effort. Casey himself provided what some members of Congress later termed incomplete and misleading testimony in an appearance before the Senate Intelligence Committee on November 21, 1986. Shortly thereafter, Casey underwent surgery for a brain tumor, resigned his CIA post in February 1987, and died May 6.

Gates Nomination

The White House February 2 announced the selection of Robert M. Gates to succeed Casey. Initially, Congress hailed the appointment of Gates, a career intelligence and national security official who had been the CIA's deputy director since April 1986; and it was widely anticipated that his nomination would be quickly confirmed. Gates's appointment, however, surprised a number of observers, who had expected Reagan to choose either a well-known political figure or another high-level intelligence official with political connections. Nonetheless, the nomination of Gates—almost certainly made on the recommendation of Casey—was greeted enthusiastically in most quarters on Capitol Hill.

But the selection of Gates soon ran into tough going. After two intensive days of questioning by the Senate Intelligence Committee February 17-18, members expressed skepticism about the nominee's claims that the CIA did little wrong in the Iran-contra sales. On the one hand, Gates testified that high-level CIA officials were not aware of major aspects of the affair and knew almost nothing about it. But, on the other hand, Gates acknowledged several "shortcomings" in the CIA's manner of participating in the Iran arms sales, including violating "internal regulations" in arranging for a November 1985 shipment of Hawk missiles from Israel to Iran; failing to "communicate well enough internally about what was going on"; failing to protest "more vigorously" concerning its role in an operation "where there were significant elements unknown to us and where we mistrusted key figures"; tolerating "ground rules suggested by others that excluded some of our own experts"; accepting "a highly unusual funding mechanism" for the arms sale transfers; and failing to press Reagan to reverse his January 17, 1986, order not to tell Congress about the Iranian arms sales.

Gates testified that the CIA was conducting an internal investigation into specific aspects of the agency's involvement. Overall, he said, "the entire undertaking was a unique activity that we are all determined not to repeat." In addition to distancing the CIA from the Iran weapons sale operation, Gates said he would have done things differently had he been CIA director. Gates said that he had nothing to do with the initial decision making and that he was informed only sporadically about developments. Casey did not share all information with him, especially about the Iran project and U.S. involvement with the contras, Gates testified.

But some members of the panel faulted the nominee for his apparent lack of participation in decision making. Said Sen. William S. Cohen, R-Maine, in a view shared by others: "You did not know the details, moreover you didn't want to know the details. You basically didn't want to rock the boat...." Testimony released at the time of the confirmation hearing showed that Gates December 4, 1986, had told the panel that CIA officials "from the director on down, actively shunned information. We didn't want to know how the contras were being funded, in part, because we were concerned it would get us involved in crossing the line imposed by the law." Top officials, he added, "actively discouraged people from telling us things. We did not pursue lines of questioning. You know, we are not dumb. We knew the contras were getting a lot of money."

Given that situation, some committee members expressed concern that Gates had failed to act with any urgency on warnings that the arms sale revenue

Although the demands for an independent counsel came mainly from Democrats, Republican leaders joined in saying Congress should conduct its own investigations. Probes of the Iranian arms sales already were under way in both chambers, and leaders expanded the mandate of those inquiries to cover the connection with the contras.

While claiming they sought no partisan advantage, Democrats clearly were trying to exploit the political opportunity created by Reagan's sudden weakness. Some also appeared to be settling scores with a president who for years had mocked them as weak on national security issues: In the Iran affair Democrats were able to portray themselves as tougher than Reagan, saying they would not have armed Iran. Most Democrats, however, seemed to recognize the risks in appearing to attack an injured but still popular president. While rushing to the television studios to demand full investigations, Democratic leaders insisted they were not seeking to destroy yet another presidency. "We all

... Stirs Controversy as Directorship Changes

had been diverted. They also faulted him for his role in preparing Casey's November 21, 1986, testimony in which the director neglected to mention the diversion of funds to the contras, the CIA's distrust of key arms dealer Manucher Ghorbanifar, and the CIA's role in the November 1985 Israeli arms shipment to Iran, among other important points.

Gates Withdraws, Webster Appointed

Faced with growing Senate opposition to his appointment and the possibility of a protracted battle that could damage the CIA, Gates March 2 asked that his nomination be withdrawn. The next day, Reagan announced the nomination of William H. Webster to the CIA post. Gates's withdrawal and Webster's nomination were hailed on Capitol Hill. Senate leaders called Gates a victim of circumstances: an official who probably would have been confirmed had Congress and the administration not been consumed by investigations involving the agency. Before withdrawing his nomination, however, Gates sent the committee a "supplement" to written answers he had previously provided, denying charges that the CIA had more information about the diversion of funds than was made available to the attorney general in November 1986, that Casey's testimony had constituted a "cover-up," and that he had acquiesced in the Iran arms sale policy and had "turned a blind eye" to evidence that money from the sales was being diverted to the contras in Nicaragua. Gates said he took his concerns to Casey and others in October, but "I should have argued harder for notification [to Congress] and I should have been more aggressive. . . ."

The appointment of Webster, a sixty-three-year-old former federal judge who headed the FBI, won uniform praise from members of Congress, who lauded him for his integrity and intelligence, and—after his FBI appointment in 1978—for taking an agency tarnished by the Watergate scandal and restoring its sense of purpose and professionalism.

Before the Senate Intelligence Committee April 8-9, Webster assured members that he would keep Congress fully informed about CIA covert operations,

pledging that he would give Congress advance or immediate notice of such operations in almost all circumstances, and that he personally would avoid taking public positions on controversial policies.

The CIA director-nominee also fended off questions concerning the FBI's role in the Iran-contra arms sales. The questioning centered on three issues: the suspension in October-November 1986 of an FBI probe of Southern Air Transport, a Miami-based airline involved in shipping supplies to the contras (a Southern Air plane carrying contra supplies was downed in Nicaragua October 5, 1986); what Webster did or did not do in November when Attorney General Edwin Meese III was investigating White House actions in the Iran-contra affair; and Webster's response to an October 30, 1986, memo by an FBI agent warning that National Security Council aide Lt. Col. Oliver L. North might be prosecuted for his activities in Central America. Webster defended his decision to suspend for several weeks an inquiry into the operations of Southern Air, saying that North had called an FBI agent to warn that a continuing probe might disrupt U.S.-Iranian negotiations involving the exchange of arms for U.S. hostages in Lebanon. Webster also said that Meese's November inquiry did not indicate that there was criminal activity justifying the use of FBI agents. He acknowledged that he had probably read the October 30 memo regarding North. He initialed the memo but said he attached no importance to it because it contained only a "speculative comment" about North. Webster also said he disagreed with two procedures the administration used in the Iran affair in 1985-86: an "oral finding" by which Reagan authorized the first Israeli sale of U.S.-made weapons to Iran, and the president's retroactive approval of CIA assistance to Israel in shipping some of the arms to Iran. In conducting covert operations, Webster said, he would rely on an oral order from the president only in an emergency and would demand a written order as soon as practicable. He also said a retroactive authorization by the president would be improper.

The Senate Intelligence Committee unanimously approved Webster's nomination May 1; he was confirmed by the full Senate May 19 on a 94-1 vote.

want to see a strong president," Byrd said. "We don't want to see a fatally damaged presidency."

Nevertheless, many Democrats described the Iran case as merely the latest in a series of Reagan foreign policy fiascoes. They pointed to revelations in September 1986 that the administration had planned a "disinformation" campaign to mislead Libyan leader Muammar el-Qaddafi, Reagan's handling of the arrest in the Soviet Union of American journalist Nicholas Daniloff, and the president's

sudden lurch toward nuclear disarmament during his October 1986 summit meeting with Soviet leader Mikhail S. Gorbachev in Iceland.

North and the Contras

Contra officials denied receiving any of the money from the Iranian arms sales, although they said it was possible someone might have used the money to buy supplies for them without their knowledge. However, Wright quoted Meese as saying Adolfo Calero, one of three top contra leaders, drew $12 million in Iranian funds from a Swiss bank account. *(Calero testimony, p. 95)*

The new controversy had deep roots in the history of the contra assistance: After Congress cut off U.S. military support for the rebels in 1984, the administration turned to private anticommunist groups to keep weapons, uniforms, and other supplies flowing. North coordinated that private aid program, reportedly with the blessing of two consecutive national security advisers, both of whom also were involved in the Iran operation: McFarlane and Poindexter.

In 1985, when investigative reporters uncovered some of North's mysterious work on behalf of the contras, congressional critics demanded to know what the White House was doing. McFarlane told investigators that North was acting properly. Although reports of North's involvement in aiding the contras continued to surface in 1986, the administration brushed aside congressional efforts to investigate the matter. White House officials told Congress in the summer of 1986 that North was no longer involved with the contras and that private aid would not be necessary once the United States resumed official backing.

But congressional interest was renewed in October when a private plane carrying supplies to the contras was downed in Nicaragua and the sole surviving crewman, Eugene Hasenfus, claimed to be working for the CIA. In that context, word of North's involvement in skimming Iranian arms profits provoked special interest on the Hill and revived old issues the administration had hoped would die.

AFFAIR TRIGGERS MULTIPLE INVESTIGATIONS

To conduct "a comprehensive review" of the NSC's operations, Reagan on November 26, 1986, named a three-man committee headed by former senator John Tower, R-Texas. Other committee members were Edmund S. Muskie, former Democratic senator from Maine and a secretary of state during the Carter administration, and Brent Scowcroft, former president Gerald R. Ford's national security adviser.

Under heavy pressure from Capitol Hill, Reagan on December 2 supported a probe by an independent counsel, quelling some of the concern that his administration would cover up wrongdoing or be less than eager to ferret it out. "If illegal acts were undertaken, those who did so will be brought to justice," Reagan said in a nationally televised speech. *(Text, p. D-16)*

Reagan also named Frank C. Carlucci as national security adviser. That choice met with the approval of many critics who had worried about the quality of foreign policy advice the president was receiving. But Reagan stood by his refusal to fire Chief of Staff Regan or admit that he had made a mistake in selling arms to Iran.

Both houses of Congress moved to set up select committees to investigate the Iran-contra affair. Incoming House Speaker Wright on December 4 announced plans for a fifteen-member committee, to consolidate hearings and investigations planned by several committees. Senate lead-

ers agreed to establish an eleven-member select investigating panel the same day.

The agreement by leaders of both parties to appoint special committees killed the prospect, suggested by some, that a special session of Congress be convened for that purpose. Senate GOP leader Dole had campaigned for a special session so a panel selected by the Republican-controlled Senate could begin work as soon as possible. But key Democrats—the incoming majority—opposed the idea: Their Senate leader, Byrd, said it would heighten "an atmosphere of hysteria and crisis."

In the meantime, the Senate Intelligence Committee began closed hearings on December 1, and the House Foreign Affairs and Intelligence committees opened their own sessions the week of December 8. The Senate Intelligence panel was hampered by the refusal of two key witnesses to talk. Poindexter and North both declined to answer questions on Fifth Amendment grounds that doing so might incriminate them. Committee members informally discussed granting immunity to compel testimony, but the panel was reluctant to take such a step, largely because doing so might complicate the work of the independent counsel. *(Immunity issue, p. 57)*

Reagan's Steps, Walsh

By calling for an independent counsel, Reagan initially calmed some of the criticism that he had failed to realize the extent of the crisis and was unwilling to deal with it. "I certainly think the president went a long way, in getting back on track," said Sen. Nancy Landon Kassebaum, R-Kan. "Up to that time, he had appeared to be very uncertain, not clear about what was going on."

And administration officials insisted that Reagan was moving quickly to handle the situation. Defending the president whose administration he had been investigating, Attorney General Meese said ultimately "it will be shown that this president acted promptly, acted properly...."

But on Capitol Hill, some Democrats worried that the independent counsel's charter would not be broad enough. Sen. John Kerry, D-Mass., argued that the counsel should have authority to probe the White House-inspired network of private groups aiding the contras. If the counsel did not do so, he said, Congress would have to look into that matter. (Testimony from private donors later was provided to the House and Senate select Iran-contra investigation committees.)

Some Democrats also questioned Reagan's statement that he and his administration would "cooperate fully" with Congress. After North and Poindexter refused to answer questions before the Senate Intelligence panel on December 2-3, Vice Chairman Leahy said Reagan should "rewrite the script" in his speeches to indicate that there were major exceptions to the promised cooperation.

Reagan took steps to gain control over the NSC staff, which was responsible for the Iran-contra operations. The choice of Carlucci to succeed Poindexter had the most immediate impact. A former deputy director of the CIA and deputy secretary of defense, Carlucci was known as a hard-driving official who brooked no independent operations. He said that he would make sure he had more direct access to Reagan than did his predecessor. *(Carlucci appointment, box, p. 36)*

Reagan also said December 1 that he had directed the

Frank C. Carlucci was named December 2, 1986, to succeed John M. Poindexter as national security adviser.

NSC staff not to engage in covert operations.

Lawrence E. Walsh, a former federal district judge, diplomat, and deputy attorney general, was named December 19 to be the independent counsel. The special three-judge panel that named Walsh also instructed him to look into the "provision or coordination of support" for the contras since 1984. *(Walsh profile, box, p. 165)*

Permission to probe the contras followed requests from members of Congress, who wrote the three judges asking them to permit such an investigation. The jurisdiction set by the panel was broader than that requested by Attorney General Meese. Meese did not seek a probe generally into the "provision or coordination of support" for the contras. Furthermore, the panel appeared to have enlarged the time span that would be covered by the investigation. Meese's proposal referred to events "in or around January 1985," whereas Walsh's mandate covered events "in or about 1984" and following.

At a brief news conference December 19 after he was sworn in at the federal courthouse in Washington, D.C., Walsh said he wanted to coordinate with members of Congress investigating the Iran-contra affair. He added that he did not believe that the congressional investigations would infringe on the independent counsel's probe.

Intelligence, Foreign Affairs

The Senate and House Intelligence committees and the House Foreign Affairs Committee made progress in revealing some of the Iran-contra events during their December 1986 investigations.

Testifying before Foreign Affairs on December 8, Secretary of State George P. Shultz and former national security adviser McFarlane gave their views about how the administration conceived and conducted its policy toward Iran. Both painted a picture of an administration making important decisions on an ad hoc basis without the involvement of major policy makers. *(Text, p. C-2)*

Members of both parties said they were especially unhappy to hear senior officials describe how decisions on such a sensitive issue as arms sales to Iran could be made with little or no involvement by the secretary of state.

Shultz, McFarlane Testimony

Testimony produced the following major examples of departures from standard procedures. Further details emerged during the 1987 hearings by the House and Senate Iran-contra committees.

● The use of what McFarlane called an "oral finding" by Reagan in August 1985 to authorize secret talks with Iranians and to approve Israel's sale of U.S.-made weapons to Iran. McFarlane said Reagan's oral approval was equivalent to the standard, required written "finding"—the legal term for a presidential authorization for a covert operation by the CIA. Meese had determined, McFarlane said, that the authority "need not be a written finding" but merely had to involve approval by the president.

Congressional legal experts disputed the validity of an oral finding, saying that only a written authorization, reported to Congress, would have met the requirements of 1974 and 1980 laws (PL 93-559, PL 96-450) on covert action. Moreover, the August 1985 decision apparently had the effect of waiving the law (PL 90-629) that barred other countries from transferring U.S.-made arms to countries, such as Iran, that supported terrorism. Normally, the president had to report to Congress, in writing, whenever he gave permission for U.S.-made weapons to be transferred to third countries.

● Shultz's statement that he had not been told about Reagan's January 17, 1986, finding that authorized direct U.S. arms sales to Iran. The finding also was kept secret from other key officials, including those in antiterrorism units in the White House and at the State Department.

Asked about the finding, Shultz told the committee: "I was notified of it at about the same time you were notified of it"—in November 1986. Shultz said he had participated in a January 7, 1986, White House meeting on the issue and came away with the impression that Reagan was about to side with those advocating the arms sales to Iran.

After that meeting, Shultz said he had only "sporadic and fragmentary" knowledge of the arms sales and was unaware that Reagan had signed a finding. He also hinted that he did not even want to know about White House dealings with Iran. Because of the danger of leaks, he said he had decided that "I didn't need to know things that were not in my sphere to do something about."

Shultz also said he knew nothing about the diversion of Iranian arms sales money to the contras. Nevertheless, Shultz said he was aware of the U.S.-approved Israeli arms shipments in 1985.

● The use of private arms dealers and another country—Israel—to funnel weapons to Iran.

Normally, when the United States wanted to sell arms to another country, it would do so directly, with the State and Defense departments making all the arrangements. U.S. law (PL 90-629) also provided for "commercial" or private sales, but they were strictly regulated and had to be reported to Congress.

Iran-Contra Affair Revives Questions ...

The appointment of William H. Webster, who was serving as director of the FBI, to succeed William J. Casey as Central Intelligence Agency (CIA) director was likely to usher in a new era for the CIA in the wake of its alleged role in the administration's decision to sell arms to Iran and the diversion of some of the proceeds to aid the guerrillas ("contras") fighting the leftist Sandinista government in Nicaragua.

The CIA's role in the Iran-contra affair during 1985-86 led to considerable speculation. Casey's November 1986 testimony raised as many issues as it answered, but the CIA director soon thereafter was hospitalized for a brain tumor and died in May 1987, leaving numerous questions unanswered.

The purview of the CIA director is extremely wide: he not only heads the CIA, by far the most famous U.S. intelligence agency, but also manages a 120-member staff responsible for coordinating more than a dozen related agencies.

Casey left behind a CIA that was stronger than in many years but also more vulnerable than usual to political cross fire. By all accounts, he restored morale in the CIA and other intelligence agencies that had been damaged by a decade of post-Vietnam and post-Watergate disclosures and cutbacks. He did that mainly by pushing for, and getting, huge budget increases and by using every available forum to defend the work that intelligence employees did in secret. The spending increases fell victim to the federal government's overall budget cutbacks in 1985 and 1986, however. And Casey's other actions threw the CIA back into the same level of controversy raised by the mid-1970s congressional investigations into agency misdeeds.

Casey promoted CIA covert actions around the world, several of which caused political furors when revealed. He also made no secret of his mistrust of Congress, even of the members who had been most supportive of the intelligence agencies.

Casey's enthusiasm for the contras, and his dislike of Congress, apparently led him into one of the most damaging errors of his tenure: failing to clearly tell the Senate Intelligence Committee about a 1983 decision to use CIA contract personnel to mine Nicaraguan harbors. Early in 1984, when several ships were sunk and the CIA role was revealed, Senate committee members exploded. They said Casey had severely undermined whatever trust they had in him.

Disclosure Agreement

Casey later in 1984 signed an agreement with Senate committee members promising to notify Congress within forty-eight hours of starting or substantially changing covert operations that required presidential approval. The agreement, strengthened in 1985, had never been made public, as of mid-1987.

Casey's openness with the committees improved for about a year after he signed the agreement, congressional sources said. But when another major test of Casey's willingness to share information arose, the director resorted to his habit of keeping information from Capitol Hill.

That happened in late 1985 and early 1986, when CIA officials pressed Reagan to sign a "finding" legalizing the agency's participation in the Iran arms sales program. Casey submitted at least two proposed findings for Reagan's approval; both contained phrases ordering the CIA not to tell Congress about the arms sales, in spite of a 1980 law requiring "timely" notice of all covert actions. Reagan signed such a finding on December 5, 1985, and another one on January 17, 1986.

In addition to serving as a reminder of Casey's problems with Capitol Hill, the Iran-contra affair revived old questions about the proper roles of the CIA and its director. Some critics said that the agency was getting involved in, or being forced into, too many covert operations, and that the time and money spent on those operations distracted the CIA from its overriding responsibility to collect and analyze information on world events.

A related criticism, directed specifically at Casey, was that the CIA had become too central in making policy. Casey was a key adviser to the president, often battling with other officials such as Secre-

In the Iran case, however, the White House and the CIA arranged for weapons to be purchased from Pentagon stocks, shipped to Israel, and then transferred through private arms dealers to Iran—all without notification to Congress. Arms dealers then put the money that Iran paid for the weapons into secret Swiss bank accounts to reimburse private financiers who had provided advance money for the sales. The CIA reimbursed the Pentagon for its expenses.

Initial financing for at least some of the deals was handled by a syndicate led by Saudi arms merchant Adnan Khashoggi. One of the investors who expected to get substantial profits from the deals, based on inflated prices paid by Iran, was Roy M. Furmark, a New York businessman.

● Shultz's surprise revelation to the committee that the U.S. ambassador to Lebanon, John H. Kelly, from October 30 to November 4, 1986, had made secret "back-channel" communications with Poindexter, North, retired Air Force major general Richard V. Secord, and other officials in Washington without telling his boss—Shultz.

The secretary said he had been "shocked" to learn

...about Roles of CIA and Its Director

tary of State George P. Shultz. There also were charges, in some cases from disgruntled CIA employees, that Casey rejected intelligence assessments that did not support his own views. Casey rarely responded personally to such criticisms.

Notification of Congress

Angered by President Reagan's secret arms sales to Iran, some members of Congress began to fashion legislation to make certain they were informed about future "covert" operations. A bill (HR 1013) was introduced in the 100th Congress to stiffen requirements for notifying appropriate members about such activities. It was strongly endorsed by House Speaker Jim Wright, D-Texas, who said that Reagan could have avoided the "colossal misjudgments" of the Iran arms sale had he notified Congress of his intent.

The presidentially appointed commission to investigate the Iran-contra affair, chaired by former senator John Tower, R-Texas, however, reached a different conclusion, stating that the process itself was adequate, if those responsible would adhere to it. That opinion was shared by some key senators, who doubted that legislation was needed, thereby making unlikely enactment of new requirements.

Nonetheless, the debate over the House measure illustrated a deep sense of frustration of some members of Congress when it came to being kept informed about secret actions undertaken by the CIA and other executive branch agencies. The arguments over the legislation also pointed to the difficulties that Congress had in crafting laws to enable it to look over an administration's shoulder when covert actions were carried out. Part of the problem stemmed from the conflict between a president wishing to conduct secret foreign policy initiatives and members of Congress who opposed the use of covert methods to avert public discussion of controversial policies.

The potential of damaging leaks of sensitive information was often raised by those who did not want to force the administration to notify Capitol Hill about covert actions. But others claimed that members of Congress could be trusted with secrets, adding that many leaks came from executive branch officials. *(Leak issue, box, p. 65)*

Existing Law

The House and Senate Intelligence committees were kept apprised of ongoing covert operations through periodic briefings by the administration; they were also kept informed in conjunction with their jurisdiction over the CIA's budget, which included a contingency fund for covert actions. In addition to the annual budget review, the president under existing law was required to give prior notice of new covert actions to members of the two Intelligence committees.

But he could wait until after a covert action had been launched to tell members of Congress. In those cases, the president had to inform lawmakers in a "timely fashion," a phrase that was not defined when the law was enacted in 1980 as part of an intelligence authorization bill (PL 96-450).

Reagan's decision to sell weapons to Iran revived the debate over what Congress meant by "timely" notification. He did not tell legislators about his secret finding in January 1986 to authorize the sales until the operation was revealed in press accounts nearly ten months later.

The text of the finding was released in January 1987, nearly a year after it was signed. When he first approved the order, Reagan told Casey not to inform Congress about the operation "due to its extreme sensitivity and security risks."

A legal memorandum prepared by the Justice Department in December 1986 concluded that Reagan was "within his authority in maintaining the secrecy of this sensitive diplomatic initiative from Congress until such time as he believed that disclosure to Congress would not interfere with the success of the operation." The memo also said that the president had enough discretion under the 1980 notification requirement to choose a "reasonable moment" to inform Congress about a covert action.

---

about the communications, which dealt with the release during that time of American hostage Jacobsen. In response to a general request to all U.S. diplomats for information on the Iran-contra affair, Kelly on December 6 sent Shultz a cable describing his communications.

Shultz ordered Kelly back to Washington; the ambassador arrived on December 9 and was immediately interviewed by State Department officials. Shultz said Kelly's dealings with the White House had violated the normal chain of command, something that would be justified only by a "good reason."

● The mission to Tehran, late in May 1986, by McFarlane, North, another NSC staffer, Howard J. Teicher, and others aboard a plane carrying U.S.-made parts for Iranian antiaircraft missiles. The Americans met for four days with midlevel Iranians but reached no agreements, according to McFarlane. The unusual mission apparently was undertaken without the knowledge of State Department experts on Iran and the Middle East.

● The State Department's request that the sultan of Brunei make a donation to the contras.

Elliott Abrams, the assistant secretary of state for

inter-American affairs, reportedly asked the sultan of the oil-rich nation on the South China Sea to donate several million dollars to the contras, which he did, but the money was deposited in the wrong account and never reached the contras.

Shultz defended the action as legal, noting that the 1985 law (PL 99-83) authorizing U.S. nonmilitary aid to the contras had specifically said the State Department could seek similar aid from other countries.

● A request by North to Texas billionaire H. Ross Perot to make $2 million available as a ransom payment for American hostages in Lebanon. Perot confirmed that he shipped $2 million to a Swiss bank at North's request, but the money was never used.

Shultz told the committee he had been unaware of North's request to Perot and called it "outrageous."

Hostages Release as a Goal

The widely held impression that the administration was hypocritical in its denunciations of other countries for dealing with terrorists was a prominent issue in the congressional hearings. In all his 1986 public statements, Reagan had insisted that he did not swap the arms for hostages, and that the United States provided the small amounts of military hardware to Iran mainly as a way of boosting the standing of reformist elements there. However, the evidence compiled by the congressional committees appeared to indicate that securing release of U.S. hostages played a greater role in the Iranian arms sales than the president was admitting.

In testimony before Foreign Affairs, McFarlane said the United States approved the Israelis' arms shipments to Iran in August 1985, as a way of boosting the standing of moderates there who were opposed to terrorism and to the continuation of the Iran-Iraq War. The United States was not seeking to buy freedom for American hostages, he said.

But McFarlane said he became convinced by late November 1985 that the Iranians viewed their contacts with the United States as focusing on the hostage issue. All dealings "were being skewed toward the hostages alone," he said in a prepared statement to the committee. For that reason, McFarlane said, he recommended in December 1985 that the United States' approval for Israeli arms shipments to Iran be terminated. Reagan accepted that recommendation but a month later formally agreed to direct U.S. arms shipments to Iran.

While insisting that U.S. officials never saw the issue as a direct arms-for-hostages swap, McFarlane acknowledged that Reagan agreed to the sales in part because he was "terribly, terribly concerned" about the fate of the hostages. That concern, McFarlane said, was "a very leading underpinning of the whole initiative" toward Iran.

Shultz also acknowledged that freeing the hostages was one goal of the U.S. arms sales, and that "when you have something that has a variety of objectives to it, these things can get mixed up."

Who Was in Charge?

In a departure from previous custom that top personal aides to the president did not have to subject themselves to congressional scrutiny, White House chief of staff Regan testified under oath before both Intelligence committees December 16 and 18. Afterward, he told reporters that "I have done nothing wrong." Chiefs of staff had rarely ap-

peared before Congress, and Regan did so after the president waived the traditional claim of executive privilege.

The testimony of Regan and other high government officials seemed to confirm that key White House decisions were made on a surprisingly informal basis and that Reagan allowed wide latitude to even midlevel aides, such as North.

The committees focused many of their questions on how, and by whom, two important decisions were made: the approval in 1985 of Israeli shipments to Iran of U.S.-made weapons and military supplies, and the authorization for funds from the Iranian arms sales to be diverted to the contras. Senior aides to Reagan provided sharply conflicting testimony on the first matter, and they all denied knowing anything at all about the diversion.

Administration officials had given confusing and contradictory explanations of the U.S. decision to approve Israel's shipments of some 500 TOW antitank missiles to Iran in August and September 1985. Briefing reporters November 14 under the cloak of anonymity, Poindexter said the United States approved the Israeli shipments in advance—as part of an evolving White House policy of opening ties to "moderates" in Iran. But in later statements, Poindexter and other officials said the United States did not approve those Israeli shipments until after they were made—probably in November, when Israel was preparing to send Iran parts for U.S.-made Hawk antiaircraft missiles.

Regan and Meese both gave that version in their initial testimony on Capitol Hill. Regan told reporters December 18 that the president was informed of the proposed Israeli shipments in August 1985 but opposed them. After learning that the shipments had been made, Regan said, the United States decided to "put up with it. It had happened. It was water over the dam." However, McFarlane repeatedly insisted that the president approved of and did not oppose the Israeli shipments before they were made.

At the center of the disagreement was what happened at an August 6 White House meeting during which the issue was discussed. After listening to Regan, Meese, and McFarlane, Senate Intelligence members seemed to give credence to McFarlane's assertion that the president had approved the Israeli shipments. "I would characterize McFarlane's testimony as much more explicit, much more definitive" than that of other officials, Senate Intelligence chairman Durenberger said. "I think that with a little bit of reminding, the president would admit he gave some authorization" for the sale.

In addition to bearing on the truthfulness of key officials, the issue of U.S. authorization for the transactions was important because of the questionable legality of Israeli shipments unless the United States gave advance approval. Under PL 90-629, countries that bought U.S.-made weapons could not turn around and sell them to other countries without Washington's approval. Failure to get such approval could result in a cutoff of U.S. aid. Although Israel did not need to fear a suspension of aid, because of its longstanding ties with the United States, any public allegation that Israel violated U.S. law would embarrass both countries. Israeli officials insisted that they received prior U.S. approval for the 1985 sales.

The question of who authorized the diversion of Iranian arms sales profits to the contras proved equally troubling to the administration and congressional investigators. Regan told both Intelligence panels that the diversion was not an officially approved policy. "I can tell you that Col.

North or nobody else was ever authorized to divert funds from the proceeds of sales of arms to Iranians to the contras or anyone else," Regan said December 16. "I had no idea the funds were diverted," he said. Regan also said he believed the president was unaware that the contras had received funds from the Iranian arms sales. Meese December 19 said North had told him that only he, Poindexter, and McFarlane knew about the diversion.

But Reagan's denial of knowledge of the contra diversion was questioned by a number of members of Congress. In testimony before the House Foreign Affairs Committee in December, McFarlane helped promote speculation about the president's role in the affair. Noting that the national security adviser was not supposed to make decisions "on matters of policy change or initiative," McFarlane said of the fund diversion to the contras: "I find it hard to imagine that it was undertaken without higher authority."

Roadblocks to Probes

A major cause of important gaps in the Iran-contra chronology was the refusal of North and Poindexter to testify. Capitol Hill investigators said Poindexter and North seemed to be the only U.S. officials who knew most, or all, details about the Iran-contra affair. Both invoked their Fifth Amendment right to refuse to testify, on grounds that doing so might incriminate them, in closed sessions of the Intelligence committees and in an open Foreign Affairs Committee hearing December 9 that was broadcast live nationwide.

Referring to Reagan's description of North as a "national hero," Durenberger said: "Somebody is going to have to define for them what 'national hero' means. It doesn't mean you come in here and stiff the whole country." Senate Democratic leader Byrd was even more blunt, saying it was "a mockery for individuals to wear the uniform of our country and take the Fifth Amendment."

Research by the Library of Congress had produced no evidence of any other admiral in the nation's history refusing to testify before a committee by invoking his Fifth Amendment rights, said Lee H. Hamilton, D-Ind., who had been named to chair the House select Iran-contra committee and was outgoing chairman of the House Intelligence panel.

In addition to North and Poindexter, several private individuals involved in the affair came into public view. Three invoked the Fifth Amendment in refusing to testify in closed sessions of the Senate Intelligence Committee: retired Air Force major general Secord, who ran a Virginia company called Stanford Technology Trading Group International; his aide, retired colonel Robert C. Dutton; and Robert W. Owen, a former consultant to the State Department's nonmilitary aid program for the contras.

Two other NSC staff members appeared before Senate Intelligence December 12 but refused to testify: NSC staffer Teicher, who did not have an attorney and who was refused the services of the White House legal office; and Col. Robert L. Earl, an NSC staffer who pleaded inadequate time to prepare.

Turnover of Documents, Immunity Request

In his December 2 televised address from the Oval Office, Reagan had promised that his administration would "cooperate fully" with congressional inquiries. He cited as an example his "unprecedented step" of allowing McFar-

lane and Poindexter to testify before Congress on what they had done while serving as national security advisers. But within days, there were sharply conflicting reports from Capitol Hill about the extent of the administration's cooperation, particularly the refusal of Poindexter and North to testify.

Administration officials and their agencies were cooperating to various degrees, said congressional sources. In spite of CIA director Casey's legendary reluctance to hand over information to Capitol Hill, lower-level CIA officials were among the most cooperative, the sources said, while White House aides were the least forthcoming.

Representative Hamilton expressed frustration at the refusal of several agencies, especially the White House, to provide the House Intelligence Committee with documents. "I don't think we have any documentation," he said, noting that "there must be all kinds of" memorandums, legal opinions, and correspondence bearing on the affair.

Senate Intelligence was having better luck getting documents, although there were delays. Chairman Durenberger was among those saying that it was in the administration's best interest to get information to Congress. "I think it is one of the scandals that gets larger by our inability to get the facts," he told reporters.

Durenberger on December 5 asked the White House for a long list of documents. By December 8, he demanded the material within twenty-four hours—a deadline that was not met. Reagan spokesman Speakes said December 10 that the White House had given Senate Intelligence "all of the documents they have requested, which we could identify based on what they have asked for."

That statement was somewhat premature; about a half-dozen documents—less than half that the committee had requested—arrived on Capitol Hill on December 11. A Senate committee spokesman said they were helpful and that the White House was expected to provide further documents as soon as they could be found.

The White House refused to provide copies to the Foreign Affairs Committee, saying that panel did not have adequate facilities to store highly classified material.

Reagan December 16 asked the Senate Intelligence Committee to short-cut investigations by granting limited "use" immunity to Poindexter and North. But committee members refused. Speakes said Reagan was making that request because of "an urgent need for full disclosure of all facts," and that granting immunity to the two former aides was the fastest way of getting the information.

Meeting in closed session the following day, the committee rejected Reagan's request by "consensus," Durenberger said. Committee members, along with most other congressional leaders, called the request "premature."

Although the reaction against Reagan's request came from members of both parties, some Republicans charged that the uniformly negative response of Democrats demonstrated their partisan interest in keeping the Iran-contra issue alive. Byrd and other Democrats heatedly denied that charge and said they, too, wanted to settle the controversy as quickly as possible.

Even if it had approved Reagan's request, the existing Senate Intelligence Committee probably would not have had time to obtain the testimony from Poindexter and North before the Ninety-ninth Congress ended on January 3, 1987. At that point, the two special committees and the independent counsel were starting their work—and they would oppose any apparent interference by the Intelligence Committee.

Iran-Contra Crisis Raises Questions about . . .

Established in 1947 by the National Security Act (PL 80-253) as a cabinet-level agency in the president's Executive Office, the National Security Council (NSC) has had a major role in formulating controversial U.S. foreign policies and actions—a role that was questioned long before the Iran-contra affair became headlines in November 1986. The original mission of the NSC was to integrate domestic, foreign, and military policies of the executive branch. But critics charged that for many years the NSC process had been overly secretive and that senior agency officials vetoed or ignored recommendations of their own staff and frequently acted outside conventional channels.

Evolution of the NSC

The NSC has been the principal forum for foreign and defense policy deliberations; it consists of the president, the secretaries of state and defense, and a few other officials. In practice, the staff of the NSC became an adjunct to the president's advisers on personal and foreign policy.

During President Dwight D. Eisenhower's administration, the NSC assumed a major role in formulating the nation's foreign policy. The president, who firmly believed in methodical staff work, created a network of NSC staff committees to coordinate the flow to the president of advice and to oversee the administration's execution of foreign and defense policy decisions.

But by the time John F. Kennedy became president in 1961, there was growing criticism that the tightly structured NSC was stifling policy debate. Too many of the papers that made their way through the NSC to the president represented interdepartmental compromises that were masking important disagreements. As a result, Kennedy scrapped much of the existing NSC committee system and sought information from a widespread network of informal executive branch channels. At the same time, he urged upgrading the role of his national security adviser, McGeorge Bundy, a former Harvard University dean. Under Bundy, the NSC focused attention on day-to-day operations rather than the long-term planning that Eisenhower had mandated the NSC to perform.

The NSC staff was in eclipse through most of Lyndon B. Johnson's presidency. Having little experience in defense or foreign policy, Johnson instead relied heavily for advice on Secretary of State Dean Rusk and his defense secretaries, Robert McNamara and Clark Clifford.

A veteran of the Eisenhower system, President Richard Nixon vowed to restore to the NSC its systematic focus on long-range planning. He appointed to the post Henry A. Kissinger, who became the central conduit of all NSC information to the president. Kissinger dominated the foreign policy-making process, and eventually became secretary of state while retaining the NSC post.

In 1975, partially in response to criticism of Kissinger's pervasive control of foreign policy making, President Gerald R. Ford made him turn over the job of national security adviser to Lt. Gen. Brent Scowcroft, an Air Force officer who had served as a principal deputy on Kissinger's NSC staff. (Scowcroft was later to serve on the Tower Commission investigating the Iran-contra affair and the NSC's role in it.) *(Tower Commission, p. 71)*

President Jimmy Carter declared that he wanted the Departments of State and Defense to regain some of the power that had gravitated to the NSC under Kissinger. But he also selected as his national security adviser an activist geopolitical thinker in the Kissinger mold, Zbigniew Brzezinski.

President Ronald Reagan's initial national security adviser, Richard V. Allen, was an academic like his two predecessors, although he did not have their impressive credentials. Allen reported to the president through Edwin Meese III, then the White House counsel. During his NSC tenure, Allen had to face charges of alleged improprieties involving payments from a Japanese publishing firm and reportedly did not get along well with the secretaries of defense and state. He resigned in January 1982. His successor, William P. Clark, was a longtime Reagan ally but had no background in foreign affairs.

Clark brought Robert C. McFarlane with him to the NSC; Vice Adm. John M. Poindexter was already serving there as Allen's military assistant. Like Allen, Clark clashed with top cabinet officials, including Secretary of State George P. Shultz and Secretary of Defense Caspar W. Weinberger. When Clark resigned in 1983 to become secretary of the interior, McFarlane assumed the NSC post.

A former Marine officer with experience in the Pentagon and on the staff of the Senate Armed Services Committee, McFarlane proved effective in negotiating with centrist Reagan critics on Capitol Hill and in dealing with the press. But by December 1985 he had run afoul of White House chief of staff Donald T. Regan and resigned. Poindexter, McFarlane's deputy, picked up the baton in 1986. Despite a widely heralded Navy career, by all accounts, he lacked McFarlane's interest in (or skill at) dealing with the press and Congress.

NSC Expansion; Carlucci Appointment

From a staff of about forty professionals under Brzezinski, the NSC had grown during the Reagan

...the NSC and Its Role in Foreign Policy Making

administration to twenty-five senior interagency decision-making groups of high officials; fifty-five interagency groups; and more than 100 other task forces, working groups, and coordinating committees. But by 1986, their contribution to actual policy making had been considerably reduced, as Poindexter became increasingly concerned with security information leaks and relied on only a handful of close advisers.

With Poindexter's resignation November 25, 1986, in the wake of the Iran-contra revelations, Reagan nominated Frank C. Carlucci to be his fifth NSC adviser. Carlucci, then head of an international marketing division of Sears, Roebuck and Company, had served in a variety of government positions, including deputy secretary of defense in the Reagan administration, deputy chief of the Central Intelligence Agency (CIA) under President Carter, and several difficult and sometimes dangerous assignments in the Foreign Service. Carlucci's appointment (no Senate confirmation was needed) was generally hailed on Capitol Hill as bringing in a nonpartisan, tough manager who knew how to handle bureaucracies and get things done.

Debate on NSC Role

The NSC's involvement in covert operations was one of its many activities. At times, the agency had been the dominant institutional force in setting U.S. foreign policy, as it was under Kissinger. At other times, it was relegated to shuffling papers. Before the Iran-contra affair, there were no known cases of NSC operatives doing the kind of cloak-and-dagger work normally reserved for the CIA. In terms of secret missions abroad, however, a line could be traced at least to Kissinger's trip to China in 1971 to arrange a U.S. reconciliation with that country. Similarly, the NSC dispute with the State Department over the Iran-contra matter echoed past conflicts between the two agencies.

Like his predecessors, Reagan often resorted to the NSC because it was free from congressional and other outside controls. At issue in the Iran-contra affair, however, was whether the council's staff had gone beyond the limits set on NSC activities and was acting without control by Reagan or his chief of staff.

With Poindexter's resignation and the firing of his aide, Marine Corps lieutenant colonel Oliver L. North, the debate over the role of the NSC in formulating and carrying out U.S. foreign policy intensified. Although throughout most of its history, the council had been a pro forma group—largely because presidents chose for themselves which of their subordinates they wanted to use as counselors on any given issue—most of the 1987 controversy centered on the role of the NSC's professional staff in funneling policy options to the president and in monitoring agencies' execution of the president's decisions.

The NSC staff's involvement in the Iranian and contra policies raised a firestorm of objections on Capitol Hill. Critics contended that the Iran sale was only one of several Reagan White House initiatives that were shielded from review by professional diplomats in the State Department and from senior military officers, including the Joint Chiefs of Staff, who might have cautioned the White House against those policies. Because important and controversial areas of foreign policy were handled almost exclusively by the NSC staff, the policies were insulated from congressional oversight (the NSC staff members served as aides to the president, were not subject to Senate confirmation, and normally did not appear before congressional committees).

The Iran arms dealings revived calls for a change in the law to require Senate confirmation of the president's national security adviser, a proposal that had been talked about since the early 1970s, when President Nixon used NSC adviser Kissinger to make end-runs around the State Department.

In 1987, some members considered amending the 1947 National Security Act to specify that the NSC and its staff serve in a purely advisory role and should not carry out covert operations. (Existing law stated that the council, in addition to advising the president, could perform "such other functions as the president may direct.") But others on Capitol Hill warned against requiring constraints on the NSC, including Senate confirmation, arguing that the president should be entitled to confidential advice not directly accessible to Congress.

While opinion was not unanimous, most former national security advisers and foreign-policy scholars agreed that the NSC staff should not be a strong, independent force in decision making. According to that view, the NSC's role was that of a facilitator that presented the views of different departments to the president without prejudice and monitored the departments' actions to make sure presidential policies were being followed. In other words, the national security adviser would be a behind-the-scenes figure who would not contest the secretary of state's role as chief foreign-policy spokesperson for the administration. The adviser should, therefore, avoid a direct role in international negotiations and the management of covert operations.

Ultimately, however, the formal organization of the NSC would be less important than the way presidents decided to use it. They had always tailored the national security system to meet their own needs, and no structure could force them to employ it wisely.

Senate Intelligence Report Released

After working nearly full time for two weeks, the Senate Intelligence Committee wrapped up its Iran-contra probe on December 18. Its House counterpart held its final session December 23.

Leaders of the Intelligence panels said their investigations had uncovered substantial amounts of information but failed to answer some of the most important questions, especially those involving where the proceeds from the Iran arms sales went. Still unanswered were the following: Who authorized the reported diversion of funds to the contras; what happened to the money; and did Reagan give advance approval in 1985 to Israel's shipments of U.S. arms to Iran?

Because key figures, notably Poindexter and North, refused to testify, the committees had been stymied in their efforts to answer the first two questions. The hearings produced conflicting testimony from senior Reagan aides on the last question.

Nevertheless, Reagan pressed the Senate Intelligence Committee on December 23 to provide him with a report on its investigation so that he could present a declassified version to the public. The panel voted January 5, 1987, not to release the staff report, but much of the information in it subsequently was leaked to the news media. The report was rewritten under the auspices of the panel's new Democratic chairman, Senator Boren, and was made public January 29, 1987. Unlike the previously leaked staff report, the new document did not draw conclusions. Instead, it recited the history of U.S. dealings with Iran and aid to the contras, based on the testimony of more than thirty witnesses and thousands of pages of documents. Boren said the report generally showed "serious problems" in the administration's policy-making apparatus. In some cases, policy was made by "amateurs," he said, and the White House relied too heavily on private individuals, including foreign arms dealers, to carry it out. The committee listed in its report fourteen "unresolved issues" for the select House and Senate Iran-contra committees to investigate. Several of these centered on the role played by White House aides, other U.S. officials, and private individuals in the affair. The panel also implied that a broader inquiry into support for the contras by the government and private sources should be undertaken. *(Details on committee investigation and report, Senate Intelligence Committee chapter, p. 63; text of report, p. D-22)*

Tower Commission Report

The presidentially appointed three-member Tower Commission wrapped up its investigation of the Iran-contra affair and the NSC's role on February 26, 1987. The commission, in its report, cited Reagan's disengaged management style, which stressed delegation of authority, as one of several conditions that allowed for formation and implementation of the Iran-contra policy. The board also blamed White House staffers who were too willing to sidestep the institutional process for making and carrying out decisions. *(NSC box, p. 36)*

Although the commission said that the president's aides did not do enough to keep Reagan fully informed, in view of his style of delegating responsibility, it faulted the president for not asking what was being done and for not demanding that established procedures be followed. Reagan's deep concern for the hostages, the board said, led him

to pursue the Iran initiative that directly contradicted his publicly stated policy of refusing to deal with terrorists.

The Tower panel also came down hard on Chief of Staff Regan. Regan, the commission said, should have "insisted that an orderly process be observed" in carrying out policy, and he should have laid plans for handling the inevitable public disclosure of the arms sale. "He must bear primary responsibility for the chaos that descended upon the White House when such disclosure did occur," the panel's report said. Regan resigned the day after the report was issued.

Among the Tower Commission's major findings:

• The Iran-contra arms dealings represented a failure of people to use the foreign policy-making process properly, not a failure of the system itself.

• Although intended to improve political and diplomatic relations with Tehran, the Iran initiative almost from the beginning became an arms-for-hostages deal.

• Reagan did not seem to know that money from the Iran arms sales was secretly being diverted to the Nicaraguan contras.

• Chief of Staff Regan and former national security adviser Poindexter shared the blame for policy failures.

• Secretary of State Shultz and Secretary of Defense Caspar W. Weinberger, who opposed the Iran arms deals, should have done more than distance themselves from decisions.

• The Iran and contra operations were handled unprofessionally and never rigorously reviewed. Reagan knew little of his aides' actions and did almost nothing to find out.

The Tower Commission's key recommendations included:

• So the National Security Council would continue to have flexibility to provide each president with independent advice, Congress should not mandate changes in the NSC's structure and operation.

• In particular, the national security adviser should not be made subject to Senate confirmation.

• Every administration should carefully follow existing procedures for making, implementing, and reviewing foreign policy, especially for covert actions.

• Congress should consider merging the House and Senate Intelligence committees into a joint panel with a small staff. *(Details of Tower Commission and report, chapter, p. 71; text of report, p. D-52)*

Select Committees

As the Tower Commission released its report, the House and Senate select committees on the Iran-contra affair were gearing up for their own lengthy investigation. The Senate's eleven-member panel was chaired by Daniel K. Inouye, D-Hawaii; the House's fifteen-member committee was led by Lee H. Hamilton, D-Ind. Both chambers had formally voted to establish the panels in early January 1987, although the intention to do so had been announced in December 1986.

After receiving their respective charters from the House and Senate, the Iran-contra committees spent several weeks hiring staffs and laying the groundwork for an intensive investigation, expected to take at least three months. Staff investigators and attorneys talked with scores of potential witnesses (in all, there were more than

300 interviews) and examined stacks of documents. Several members of both panels participated actively in the behind-the-scenes work, but others—especially senior Democrats who chaired other committees—found little time to do so.

The launching of the committees in January was marred by partisan grumbling: Some Republicans charged that Democrats wanted a "witch hunt" to embarrass the Reagan administration, while a number of Democrats said the administration and its Capitol Hill backers favored a "cover-up."

Some of the sharpest differences prior to the start of the formal hearings on May 5 involved the committees and independent counsel Walsh, who repeatedly asked the panels to delay granting immunity to witnesses and to share with him material they gathered. At the same time, he said strict rules prevented him from turning over to the committees any information he compiled. *(Further details, p. 163)*

For the most part, the committees managed one task that had often seemed impossible on Capitol Hill: keeping secrets. Very little leaked out between the beginning of the investigations and the opening of the hearings, which consumed twelve weeks of testimony, ending August 6.

Although the House and Senate initially had established separate committees, leaders of both panels quickly had realized that merging their investigations and hearings was the only way to avoid excessive duplication. They announced March 18 that all hearings would be joint and that their staffs essentially would work as one unit. During the first week of hearings, and alternating weeks thereafter, the committees met Tuesday through Friday in the historic Caucus Room of the Senate Russell Office Building, which was oufitted with an expanded dais for the twenty-six members. (The Caucus Room was the site of the 1973 Watergate hearings.) The panels agreed to hold hearings in the intervening weeks on Monday through Thursday in committee rooms on the House side of Capitol Hill, starting with the hearing room of the Judiciary Committee, where articles of impeachment were voted against President Richard Nixon in 1974.

Among the central questions the committees sought answers to were: What happened to millions of dollars deposited in secret overseas bank accounts, supposedly for the benefit of the contras, and how much did President Reagan know about the possibly illegal activities of White House aides who ran the Iran and contra operations? Committee leaders hoped the hearings would answer dozens of questions about how the administration and private operatives ran U.S. policies toward Iran and Nicaragua. The broad outlines of the Iran-contra affair were well-known, because of press reports and investigations conducted by the Senate and House Intelligence committees and the Tower Commission. As the select committees hearings wore on, however, startling revelations were made about the nature of the operation, and the examination broadened to include consideration of recommendations about the constitutionality of the activities and changes in the way policy should be formulated and conducted in the future.

By their very nature, the joint hearings brought a summer of spectacle and drama to Washington, which had been consumed with the Iran-contra affair for months. Most of the hearings involving central figures were nationally televised, opening to full public view the questionable activities of dozens who apparently thought they were working to support Reagan's policies.

Former national security adviser John M. Poindexter testified before the House and Senate Iran-contra committees that President Reagan had not known about the diversion of funds from the Iranian arms sale to the contras.

The lead-off witness was retired Air Force major general Secord, who, among others, worked under instructions from Lieutenant Colonel North. Shortly thereafter, the panel received testimony from the president's former national security adviser, McFarlane. The final weeks were dramatic, as the panels heard testimony by the two key figures, North and Poindexter, followed by Secretary of State Shultz, Attorney General Meese, Defense Secretary Weinberger, and former White House chief of staff Regan.

The public hearings came to a close the first week of August, as members prepared to leave Washington for the summer recess. Committee staffers began working on the final report, scheduled for release in October.

If some committee Democrats were looking for ways to tarnish Reagan, some Republican members were likely to shift the focus away from the president and onto the shoulders of some of his aides. Rudman began to sound that theme in the closing days of the hearings when he repeatedly said that Reagan had been "ill-served" and "deceived" by senior aides.

A more benign view of the entire Iran-contra operation would probably be advanced by the six House Republicans with some of their Senate counterparts. Mistakes were made by Reagan, they might argue, but these were offset by mitigating factors. Among them: the need to keep the contras alive despite congressional "vacillation" and the long-term goal of improving relations with Iran while trying to free the hostages.

Leaders of both committees hoped to agree on a joint report. But the sharp differences among members could lead the panels to produce separate, competing documents—or at least differing sets of conclusions. Added to those would likely be a set of minority views.

Israel's Link in the Iran-Contra Affair ...

The Iran-contra affair brought under scrutiny once again the relationship between the United States and Israel—and the burdens both nations had placed on their longstanding friendship. The U.S.-Israel rapport had strong and emotional roots dating back to 1947 when Israel was created by a United Nations mandate; that relationship was somewhat shaken by the Iran-contra affair.

The two countries' close ties had been buffeted by ill winds in recent years. Relations had been tested by a number of events, including: Israel's vigorous lobbying on Capitol Hill to defeat American arms sales to Arab countries; Washington's unhappiness with the Israeli invasion of Lebanon in 1982; and the arrest and conviction of American Jonathan Jay Pollard, who was recruited by Israel to spy on the United States.

There was convincing evidence that Israeli officials helped initiate U.S. arms sales to Iran and urged Washington to continue the activity. Reports also surfaced that an Israeli official first suggested the idea of using money from Iranian arms sales for other unrelated activities. But the Israelis said it was Lt. Col. Oliver L. North who proposed the diversion to the contras. *(Israeli account, p. 141)*

The Iran-contra affair provided additional fuel to contentions that the United States and Israel did not always have identical interests in the Middle East. Israel sought a stalemate in the violent war between Iran and Iraq, whose leader, Saddam Hussein, was considered to be one of Israel's deadliest foes. The primary interest of the United States was to gain freedom for American hostages held in Lebanon by pro-Iranian fundamentalists. Both Israel and the United States saw the arms sales as a way to achieve their goals.

U.S. Commitment to Israel

After Israel declared its independence on May 14, 1948, the United States became the first country to formally recognize the Jewish state, carved out of Palestine by the British. The Soviet Union followed quickly. Thus the stage was set for decades of superpower competition in a region beset with bitter conflict between Jews and Arabs, the latter vehemently denying Israel's right to exist.

The establishment of the Israeli nation brought with it extensive American political, economic, and military involvement in the Middle East. That began with America's commitment to guarantee the independence and territorial integrity of Israel. Thereafter, five Arab-Israeli wars, various intra-Arab conflicts, and continuing uncertainty about the availability and cost of Arab oil had convinced successive U.S. administrations that peace in the Middle East was a most urgent concern.

The strong and longstanding U.S. support for Israel, however, evoked bitter anti-American feelings in many Arab countries, which turned to the Soviet Union for guidance and assistance. After the French decided in 1967 to cut off arms to Israel, U.S. policymakers felt they had no alternative but to step into an informal role of Israel's guarantor to counter Soviet assistance to Israel's enemies. No formal security pact was concluded, however. The signing of a defense treaty would have provided a rallying point for Arab hostility and would have jeopardized U.S. relations with its Arab friends. Moreover, Washington felt that an official defense pact might indirectly discourage Israel from negotiating on Arab lands it had acquired in the 1967 war. The U.S. commitment to Israel was reaffirmed by President Reagan in one of his first foreign policy pronouncements after taking office in 1981.

After Camp David, Relations Cool

The United States assumed a more active role in the Middle East in the late 1970s. President Jimmy Carter decided to abandon the previous administration's policy of step-by-step negotiations in favor of attempting to achieve a "comprehensive" settlement involving all nations in the region. Both the Arabs and Israelis rejected the overture, however. In the fall of 1978, Carter invited Egyptian president Anwar al-Sadat and Israeli prime minister Menachem Begin to meet with him at Camp David, Md., the presidential retreat. After thirteen days of arduous negotiations, the three agreed on two accords: a "Framework for Peace in the Middle East" and a "Framework for the Conclusion of a Peace Treaty between Egypt and

Independent Counsel

As Congress was gearing up to launch its own investigations, President Reagan agreed to appoint an independent counsel to conduct an inquiry into whether any criminal wrongdoing had been committed in the Iran-contra affair. Several members of Congress had written Attorney General Edwin Meese III to suggest the appointment.

Meese announced December 2, 1986, a week after his revelation of the Iran sales diversion to the contras, that he would recommend such an appointment to avoid any possible conflict of interest with the Justice Department's commitment to serve and be responsible to the executive branch. The president approved the suggestion. On December 19, a three-judge panel named former district court judge Walsh—who also had served as a diplomat and dep-

... Questions Raised but Ties Remain Strong

Israel."

But the euphoria and optimism resulting from the Camp David peace accords died in the early days of the Reagan presidency. The administration was accused by its critics of failing to push Egypt and Israel to make progress on granting West Bank Palestinians autonomy, as had been agreed to. In 1981, when the Israelis bombed a nuclear reactor in Iraq and the headquarters of the Palestine Liberation Organization (PLO) in Beirut, the United States responded by delaying the delivery to Israel of F-16 fighter jets. Relations between the two countries were further strained when the Israelis objected to proposed U.S. weapons sales to Saudi Arabia and when the Reagan administration became alarmed by various Israeli military moves against Iraq, Syria, and the PLO.

Friction between the United States and Israel intensified when Israel invaded Lebanon in 1982. Israel argued that it had to protect its northern border from hostile attack and would withdraw its forces only if Syria pulled out its troops at the same time. However, Israel began withdrawing from Lebanon early in 1985.

Policy Shift

Reagan's September 1, 1982, Middle East policy initiative—reaffirming U.S. support for Israel but calling for Palestinian self-government on the Israeli-occupied West Bank of the Jordan River "in association with" Jordan—created another strain in U.S.-Israeli relations. The president suggested further negotiations to determine the final legal status of the Israeli-held West Bank and Jerusalem (a city held dear by Arabs, Jews, and Christians). Reagan stated that Israel should halt further construction of settlements on the West Bank. Begin rejected the plan immediately, and Israel opposed any participation by PLO members.

U.S. Aid to Israel

The Reagan administration in 1982 actively opposed a move in Congress to increase aid to Israel beyond the president's request, which was another source of irritation between the two countries. Congress eventually compromised on the issue, giving Israel an increase in military aid that was substantial but fell far short of what Israel had wanted.

Although the bitterness that developed between the United States and Israel quickly evaporated after Begin resigned in September 1983, renewed cooperation between the two countries was limited by political turmoil in Israel itself. Begin was succeeded by his foreign minister, Yitzhak Shamir, but elections in 1984 gave a narrow edge to the opposition Labor Party under Shimon Peres. Negotiations resulted in the formation of a coalition government between the Labor and Likud parties, with Peres as prime minister and Shamir as deputy prime minister. They agreed to switch positions in two years (an agreement that subsequently was effected).

Peres made his first trip to Washington in October 1984, seeking a huge increase in U.S. aid to his country. Israel at the time was facing the most serious economic crisis in its thirty-six-year history. Its inflation approached 500 percent, and it had the heaviest foreign debt per capita in the world. But the Reagan administration equivocated, saying that any increases in economic aid would be delayed "pending the adoption of an effective Israeli economic stabilization program."

United States aid to Israel had been substantial, accounting for 12 percent of the Israeli government budget; in the 1980s the United States subsidized between one-fourth and one-third of Israel's defense spending.

As a Jewish state in the midst of hostile Arab neighbors, Israel needed to devote a disproportionate share of its resources to defense—up to one-third of the government budget. Israel maintained one of the world's most sophisticated defense establishments at an annual cost of about $5.5 billion. From 1973 to 1985, the United States had provided $18.5 billion for Israel's defense. Israel's $4.05 billion request for fiscal 1986 amounted to about a quarter of all American foreign aid.

Despite friction, Israel continued to need U.S. military, economic, and political support, and the United States needed to count on a reliable ally in the volatile region.

uty attorney general—to the post.

The creation of an independent counsel was challenged on grounds of its constitutionality; and Walsh ran into some conflicts with the House and Senate Iran-contra committees in his request that the panels hold off on receiving testimony from North, Poindexter, and others, on grounds that the committees' granting limited immunity (waiving the Fifth Amendment right to refuse to testify on the grounds that it might incriminate them, in return for guarantees that the testimony given could not be used in a court of law) would impede his criminal investigation.

Walsh and the committees reached a modus-vivendi shortly before North and Poindexter appeared before Congress in July. The counsel and the committees agreed to grant limited immunity for those witnesses, so that they could testify in public, on the stipulation that Walsh would not be hampered in his own investigations.

Throughout the hearings, however, a number of conflicts arose. Some questioned the appropriateness of appointing an independent counsel. Walsh contended that the committees' rather immediate calling of North and Poindexter to testify would impede his investigation. Some argued that Walsh was moving too slowly.

Nonetheless, an agreement was reached. North and Poindexter—the major targets of Walsh's probe—appeared before Congress, having been granted limited immunity. Their lawyers, well aware of the Walsh investigation, repeatedly cautioned their clients about making statements that might later be used against them in the possible criminal prosecution.

As the select committees' probe was winding up, the independent counsel continued to move ahead, having already handed down indictments for some of the persons who solicited private funds to aid the Nicaraguan contras. *(Immunity issue, p. 57; details on independent counsel, p. 163)*

What Happened

ARMS-FOR-HOSTAGES DEALINGS WITH IRAN

Between the November 1986 disclosure of the U.S. arms sales to Iran and diversion of some of the proceeds to the U.S.-supported contras fighting the leftist Sandinista government in Nicaragua and the fall of 1987, investigators poured over stacks of documents and interviewed hundreds of witnesses. The evidence produced in February 1987 by the three-person committee chaired by former senator John Tower, R-Texas, and later in the year by the House and Senate select committees investigating the Iran-contra affair was massive. It revealed a maze of intrigue, a startling lack of coordination and consultation both among key administration officials as well as between the White House and Congress, and a foreign policy carried out in large part by private individuals.

The investigations provided sometimes bewildering details about the affair; testimony by participants frequently was conflicting, and many questions were left unanswered. Nonetheless, by the fall of 1987, some pieces of the puzzle had dropped into place, and a general chronology had emerged.

Investigators traced the origin of U.S. arms sales to Iran to a White House effort late in 1984 to reassess overall policy toward Tehran. But intervention by Israel resulted in the policy developing faster than Washington had planned, and the initiative became inextricably linked with hostages rather than broader foreign policy objectives claimed by the administration: using arms sales as an "opening" to Iranian "moderates." The arms-for-hostages link came under widespread criticism. In its report, for example, the President's Special Review Board, or Tower Commission, said the United States "should never have been a party to the arms transfers. As arms-for-hostages trades, they could not help but create an incentive for

further hostage-taking."

Throughout the 1987 investigations, details of the development of U.S. arms sales to Iran emerged, beginning with the policy reviews in 1984 and continuing through the final shipment of missiles in late October 1986—just a few days before the secret dealings became public knowledge.

Roots of the Policy

The State Department in October 1984 produced an interagency study suggesting that there was little the United States could do to influence events in Iran. This study was requested by national security adviser Robert C. McFarlane, who was concerned that the United States had no plan for dealing with possible turmoil in Iran once the leader there, the Ayatollah Ruhollah Khomeini, died.

Concerns about Iran continued, however, and on May 20, 1985, the White House and CIA produced a special intelligence estimate raising the prospect of Soviet gains if Iran were to descend into chaos. On June 11, McFarlane's aides drafted a National Security Decision Directive outlining U.S. goals toward Iran. One was to encourage allies "to help Iran meet its import requirements," including "selected military equipment."

Secretary of State George P. Shultz and Defense Secretary Caspar W. Weinberger vigorously objected to the proposal; Weinberger called it "absurd." CIA director William J. Casey, however, was said to "strongly endorse" the thrust of the document, although he did not address the arms sale issue. Apparently because of the objections by Shultz and Weinberger, the proposal was scrapped and never submitted to Reagan.

While this debate was under way in Washington, two other sets of discussions were taking place.

Israeli officials and arms dealers were talking about using arms sales to Iran to obtain the release of American hostages in Lebanon and to open talks with Tehran, and Israeli and U.S. officials were conducting their own talks on Iran. Involved at that point were the men who later emerged as main characters in the arms sales saga: McFarlane, National Security Council (NSC) consultant Michael Ledeen, exiled Iranian businessman Manucher Ghorbanifar, Israeli arms dealers Adolph Schwimmer and Yaacov

Nimrodi, Saudi Arabian businessman Adnan Khashoggi, and Israeli officials David Kimche and Amiram Nir.

On May 4 or 5, 1985, Ledeen met in Jerusalem with Prime Minister Shimon Peres and asked if Israel would share with the United States its intelligence information on Iran. The Israeli response apparently came on July 3, when Kimche—director general of the Foreign Ministry—met with McFarlane in Washington. McFarlane testified that Kimche asked whether the United States was interested in talking to Iranians. To demonstrate their "bona fides," Kimche told McFarlane, the Iranians would try to win freedom for American hostages; the Iranians would need something in return, probably arms.

McFarlane said Reagan agreed to explore the proposal. The president's reaction, McFarlane told the Tower Commission February 21, 1987, was "quite enthusiastic and perhaps excessively enthusiastic, given the many uncertainties involved."

McFarlane noted that Reagan's approval came shortly after the conclusion of a Middle East hostage crisis. Two Lebanese men on June 14 had hijacked a TWA airliner, killed an American sailor on board, and held thirty-nine passengers hostage in Beirut. The hostages were released June 30—possibly after the intervention of Iranian officials. Reagan became emotionally involved in that hostage crisis, especially on July 2, when he welcomed the hostages back to the United States and placed flowers on the grave of Robert D. Stethem, the Navy diver who had been shot. (Numerous witnesses testified to the president's personal involvement in the fate of Americans held hostage in Lebanon, heightened by his meetings with their families.)

On July 13 Ledeen passed to McFarlane a message from Schwimmer, the Israeli arms dealer, saying the Iranians believed they could win freedom for the seven Americans then held hostage in Lebanon in return for 100 American-built TOW antitank missiles to be provided by Israel. McFarlane said he understood the deal was to be only part of a broader "private dialogue" with Iran.

Shultz, then traveling in Australia, agreed to opening talks with the Iranians but said in a cable to McFarlane that McFarlane should "handle this probe personally." Shultz also raised a caution about the Israeli proposal, noting that "Israel's interest and ours are not necessarily the same."

Reagan, recovering in Bethesda Naval Hospital from a cancer operation, approved the talks, according to testimony by McFarlane and White House chief of staff Donald T. Regan.

August 1985: The Disputed Decision

Exactly what happened in the next sequence of events was disputed by the participants. This sequence started with an August 2 White House meeting between McFarlane and Kimche, who asked for the U.S. position on arms sales to Iran. McFarlane said Washington would not sell arms directly to Tehran, but he promised an answer on whether the United States would approve of Israeli sales. How he got that answer was described by the Tower Commission as "murky."

Administration officials gave the following accounts of the events of early August 1985:

●McFarlane said he had numerous discussions with Reagan and other U.S. officials. Early in August, McFarlane said, Reagan told him in a telephone conversation that the United States should not sell its arms to Iran, but Israel could sell U.S.-made weapons, and could buy replacements from the United States, if the result did not upset the military balance in the region and if no major weapons systems were involved. McFarlane said he passed Reagan's approval on to Kimche and to top U.S. officials, including Shultz and Weinberger. McFarlane's version of events generally had been consistent in all of his public and private statements.

●Shultz and Weinberger both recalled meetings at which they expressed opposition to Israeli arms sales to Iran. Shultz cited a key White House meeting on August 6.

●Regan testified that the president expressed concern about swapping arms for hostages but supported developing contacts with Iran. Regan said the president was surprised and "upset" in September when McFarlane told him Israel had sold arms to Iran in hopes of freeing hostages. Regan told reporters December 18, 1986, that "to the best of my recollection the president was against the shipment."

●Reagan gave the Tower board three versions. On January 26, 1987, he supported McFarlane's story, saying that he had approved the Israeli shipment sometime in August but could not recall the exact date. Reagan gave the board a marked copy of McFarlane's January 16, 1986, testimony to the Senate Foreign Relations Committee, apparently indicating his agreement with what McFarlane had said.

Two weeks later, on February 11, Reagan told the board that, after discussing the matter repeatedly with Regan, he could not recall giving advance approval in August for an Israeli arms shipment.

Told by aides that his testimony was inconsistent, Reagan wrote a letter to the Tower panel February 20 saying that "I'm afraid that I let myself be influenced by others' recollections, not my own." Admitting he had no records, Reagan said: "The only honest answer is to state that try as I might, I cannot recall anything whatsoever about whether I approved an Israeli sale in advance or whether I approved replenishment of Israeli stocks around August of 1985. My answer therefore and the simple truth is, 'I don't remember—period.' "

In addition to bearing on the credibility of the individuals involved, the issue of whether Reagan gave advance approval for Israeli shipments of U.S. arms was important from a legal standpoint. Under U.S. law, any country buying American weapons could not transfer them to another nation without receiving Washington's approval in advance. Failure to do so could result in a loss of foreign aid.

Israel relied heavily on U.S. aid totaling $3 billion a year, and Israeli officials had said they would not have sold arms to Iran without approval.

The First Shipments

According to the Tower Commission, Israel's first supply of arms to Iran was in two parts: 100 TOW missiles on August 30, 1985, and 408 missiles on September 14. Iranian arms dealer Ghorbanifar testified the second shipment was supposed to contain 400 missiles, but eight extras were on the Israeli plane when it landed in Tabriz, Iran.

The number of missiles also may have startled the White House. McFarlane testified that he was "surprised by the move from 100 to at least 400" missiles.

Kimche called McFarlane early in September, saying that all U.S. hostages in Lebanon would be released, and McFarlane said he passed that word on to Reagan and other officials.

At about this time, Lt. Col. Oliver L. North, a National

At private fund-raisers, such as this 1986 one in Washington, National Security Council aide Oliver L. North told dramatic stories of the Nicaraguan contras' plight.

Security Council (NSC) aide, entered the Iran arms picture. Ledeen testified that North told him in September 1985 that he was handling "all the operational aspects" of the Iran sales.

The arms deal bore fruit September 15, but not to the extent that Israel and the United States had hoped. A pro-Iranian group released only one hostage, the Rev. Benjamin F. Weir.

The deals were financed in a peculiar manner that was to become the model for arms shipments to Iran.

To guarantee payment on the 100 TOWs, Ghorbanifar gave Saudi businessman Khashoggi a $1 million postdated check. Khashoggi deposited $1 million in a Swiss bank account controlled by Nimrodi (the Israeli arms dealer), Iran put $1.2 million into a Swiss account to pay for the shipment, Israel delivered the missiles, and Ghorbanifar gave Khashoggi the go-ahead to cash his check. Financing of the second shipment worked the same way. Khashoggi provided $4 million in up-front money for 400 missiles, and Iran paid $5 million once they were delivered, plus $250,000 for the extra eight missiles.

Sending Hawks to Iran

In spite of the disappointing results of the first shipments, Israel and the United States continued the contacts with Iran during the fall of 1985, and Israel launched plans for a more important shipment in November.

This planning occurred during a rush of world events in October and November, especially the hijacking of the *Achille Lauro* cruise ship and the first summit meeting in Geneva between Reagan and Soviet leader Mikhail S. Gorbachev. U.S. officials were preoccupied with those events, not Iran.

Apparently assuming that the United States had provided open-ended approval for arms shipments to Iran, Israel drafted plans to ship Hawk antiaircraft missiles in exchange for the release of four or five American hostages

in Lebanon. Early plans called for delivery of 80 or 120 missiles, according to documents, but in the end only 18 were delivered. Direct U.S. involvement in this shipment also was much greater than in the earlier shipments.

As before, the financing was circuitous. Ghorbanifar paid Israel $24 million in advance for 120 missiles, but Iran canceled the deal and demanded its money back. Nimrodi returned $19 million, deducting $5 million for the 18 missiles that were delivered. After Israel retrieved the missiles in February 1986, Iran apparently deducted about $4 million from a later payment to get its money back.

The November shipment was bungled at several points, resulting in a three-day delay. Iran ultimately returned seventeen of the missiles to Israel, saying they were out of date; the eighteenth missile was test-fired, possibly at an Iraqi target.

Most importantly, the shipment failed to meet its major goal: Not a single hostage was released.

Preparing for the shipment, North, at Casey's suggestion, in mid-November brought into the operation retired Air Force major general Richard V. Secord, asking him to help arrange for planes carrying the arms to pass through Portugal. The CIA also became involved in the operation, approving the use of its own airline (reportedly St. Lucia Airways) to fly cargo to Iran disguised as "oil drilling equipment."

Reagan gave the Tower board conflicting testimony about the November shipment, first saying that he had objected to it, leading to the return of the missiles to Israel. At his second appearance, Reagan told the board that neither he nor Regan could remember discussions about the shipment.

Discovering later that an agency-owned airline had been involved in an arms shipment to Iran, deputy CIA director John N. McMahon ordered preparation of a legal authorization—called a "finding"—to be signed by the president. Drafted by CIA general counsel Stanley Sporkin in November, the finding would have retroactively ap-

President's Contradictory Statements . . .

President Reagan's news conferences and nationwide addresses on the Iran-contra affair provided some indication of how much of a foreign policy debacle it was. The often contradictory statements showed the confusion surrounding it within his administration. Following are summaries of his major public statements.

November 13, 1986, Address

Seeking to defuse the revelation that the United States had sold arms to Iran, the president went on national television to refute speculation that the arms sales were made as a trade for release of American hostages. "We did not—repeat—did not trade weapons or anything else for hostages—nor will we," he said. The aim of the eighteen-month "secret diplomatic initiative" was "to renew a relationship with the nation of Iran, to bring an honorable end to the bloody six-year war between Iran and Iraq, to eliminate state-sponsored terrorism, and to effect the safe return of all hostages." Reagan also refuted as "unfounded" charges that the sales represented a tilt to Iran in the gulf war. *(Text, p. D-1)*

The president stated: "These modest [arms] deliveries, taken together, could easily fit into a single cargo plane." (It was subsequently revealed that the shipments were considerably larger.)

November 19, 1986, News Conference

Reagan's November 13 assurances failed to satisfy many Americans and members of Congress. Appearing before the press November 19, he defended his actions. During the half-hour of questions, he seemed unusually nervous and confused, provoking as many questions as he answered. "I don't think a mistake was made [in selling arms to Iran]," he said. "It was a high-risk gamble, and it was a gamble that, as I've said, I believe the circumstances warranted. And I don't see that it has been a fiasco or a great failure of any kind." *(Text, p. D-3)*

Reagan said he would not authorize any further arms shipments to Iran, but he rejected suggestions that he revoke a secret executive order (called a "finding") he had signed January 17, 1986, authorizing the previous shipments. He repeatedly justified on secrecy grounds his decision not to tell Congress about the dealings with Iran.

Inadequate briefing by his advisers led to one major stumble. In response to a question about Israel's role and reports of Israeli shipments of U.S.-made arms, Reagan replied that "we . . . have had nothing to do with other countries or their shipment of arms or doing what they're doing." Immediately after the news conference, the White House issued a retraction acknowledging that "There was a third country involved. . . ." But the statement continued to maintain that the amount of arms shipped was small.

November 25, 1986, Statement

Even as he was facing the press November 19, evidence was accumulating that the arms sales were intended primarily as a hostage trade-off. An even more damaging bombshell occurred November 25, when the administration revealed that profits from the shipments had been diverted to the U.S.-backed contra guerrilla forces in Nicaragua.

In his brief statement before reporters, the president said he had not been "fully informed" about the diversion. He also announced the resignation of national security adviser Vice Adm. John M. Poindexter and the firing of National Security Council (NSC) aide, Lt. Col. Oliver L. North (evidence increasingly implicated them in the Iran-contra affair), as well as his intention to appoint a special board to review the NSC's role and procedures. (On November 26, Reagan named former senator John Tower, R-Texas, to head the three-person review board.) *(Text, p. D-7)*

December 2, 1986, Address

In the wake of the startling events of November and mounting criticism, Reagan went on national television to assure Americans that "If illegal acts were undertaken [in the Iran-contra events] those who did so will be brought to justice." In a relatively short statement, the president said he had "done everything in my power to make all the facts . . . known to the American people. . . . I've pledged to get to the bottom of this matter." *(Text, p. D-16)*

The president announced the appointment of Frank C. Carlucci, a Washington insider, to succeed Poindexter as national security adviser. He also said that Attorney General Edwin Meese III had advised him "that his investigation has turned up reasonable grounds to believe that further investigation by an independent counsel would be appropriate." With the Tower Commission and independent counsel, "we will have in place a dual system for assuring a thorough review of all aspects of this matter."

March 4, 1987, Address

Reagan March 4 delivered what many observers called the most important speech of his presidency—a nationally televised admission that his policy of selling arms to Iran had gone wrong, coupled with promises to set his administration right. The president did not apologize, as many advisers and critics

... Show Confusion over Iran-Contra Policy

had suggested he should, but he repeated a previous acceptance of "full responsibility" for mistakes by others. Delivered with a firm voice and in a crisp manner, the speech helped calm fears that months of tumult had eroded the seventy-six-year-old president's energy and mental alertness. *(Text, p. D-81)*

The president was more explicit in acknowledging that the United States did swap arms for hostages. Reagan said of previous denials: "My heart and my best intentions still tell me that is true, but the facts and the evidence tell me it is not." The president admitted that he allowed his "personal concern for the hostages" to spill over into the broader goal of opening talks with Iran.

Reagan said he accepted "in total" the February recommendations of the Tower Commission on foreign policy procedures, and he noted changes he had already taken. *(Tower report text, p. D-52)*

March 19, 1987, News Conference

Answering questions in public about the Iran-contra affair for the first time in four months, Reagan March 19 defended his initial decision to sell arms to Iran—but said he "would not go down that same road again" because the sales deteriorated into an exchange of arms for hostages. On whether his initial decision to sell arms to Iran was a mistake, Reagan replied, "Well, if I hadn't thought it was right in the beginning, we never would have started that." *(Text, p. D-82)*

While decrying the arms-for-hostages angle, Reagan defended his underlying action in negotiating with Iranians who claimed to have influence over the hostage-takers in Lebanon. "So, I still believe that, if someone in my family was kidnapped and I went out and hired someone that I thought could get that person safely home, that would not be engaging in ransom of the victim," he said.

Reagan insisted that "there wasn't any thought of hostages" when the United States initiated the policy (the Tower board had concluded that freeing hostages was a goal of the arms sales "almost from the beginning"). He also repeatedly denied any knowledge that profits were diverted to the contras.

On other matter, Reagan said he had merely made a "misstatement" in his November 19, 1986, news conference when he denied that Israel was involved in the arms sales.

April 28, 1987, Session with Reporters

A week before the House and Senate select committees investigating the Iran-contra affair began public hearings, Reagan met with six reporters to discuss a wide range of issues, among them the Iran-

contra affair. He said he was "not worried" that Poindexter would implicate him in the diversion of profits to the contras because Poindexter "was an honorable man" and he, Reagan, was "not informed—as a matter of fact, . . . I did not know that there were any excess funds" until the affair was made public in November 1986. *(Text, p. D-86)*

August 12, 1987, Address

In his third nationally televised address on the subject, Reagan tried to close the book on the Iran-contra affair but found that contradictions and unanswered questions continued to dog his administration. *(Text, p. D-90)*

Reagan went further than before in acknowledging the mistakes of the Iran-contra affair and its political damage to his administration. But he also attempted to shift attention to other matters.

Referring to his previous address, the president commented, "As I said to you in March, I let my preoccupation with the hostages intrude into areas where it didn't belong. The image—the reality of Americans in chains, deprived of their freedom and families so far from home, burdened my thoughts. And this was a mistake." He said he offered no excuses for his actions. "I was stubborn in my pursuit of a policy that went astray."

Reagan took Poindexter's testimony that the national security adviser decided in February 1986 to approve the diversion on his own as vindicating the president's repeated assertions that he was unaware of that aspect of the affair. "Let me put this in capital letters. I did not know about the diversion of funds. Indeed, I didn't know there were excess funds."

At the same time, the president criticized Poindexter for taking the decision-making responsibility himself. Poindexter had told the Iran-contra committees that, on the diversion issue, "the buck stops here with me." But Reagan said in his address: "It stops with me. I am the one who is ultimately accountable to the American people. The admiral testified he wanted to protect me; yet, no president should ever be protected from the truth. No operation is so secret that it must be kept from the commander in chief. I had the right, the obligation, to make my own decision."

The president said he had acted to correct whatever mistakes were made. He cited several steps, including the hiring of new top aides, the banning of covert operations by the NSC staff, and a review of all ongoing covert operations by the CIA. Reagan noted that on August 7 he sent congressional leaders a letter promising to keep them better informed about covert actions.

proved CIA participation in the shipment and given blanket approval for future shipments designed to win release of hostages. The proposed finding also contained an unusual provision directing the CIA not to inform Congress about the operation. Adm. John M. Poindexter, who had replaced McFarlane as national security adviser in December, testified that he gave the document to the president December 5, and that the president signed it. But there was no evidence of his doing so. A year later, in the midst of the Iran-contra revelations, Poindexter shredded the finding, saying that its direct arms-for-hostage linkage might prove embarrassing to the administration.

Reagan Approves U.S. Role

The failure of the November arms-for-hostages swap resulted in a temporary suspension of U.S. dealings with Iran—but not before North proposed yet another trade.

On December 4—the day McFarlane announced his resignation and Reagan named Poindexter as his successor—North produced a plan for an even more ambitious arms deal. He proposed that Israel sell Iran 3,300 TOW missiles and fifty Hawk missiles in exchange for one French and five American hostages in Beirut. The arms were to be delivered in five stages over a twenty-four-hour period, coinciding with the release of hostages.

North's plan prompted one of the rare discussions on Iran involving all senior U.S. officials. At the White House on December 7, Shultz, Weinberger, and Regan argued against North's arms deals.

The next day—saying he was acting on Reagan's orders—McFarlane flew to London and told Ghorbanifar that the United States would engage in no more arms deals with Iran. At a White House meeting December 10, McFarlane reported on his trip. The Tower report cited conflicting evidence on whether anything was decided then. One odd memo by CIA director Casey said Reagan had "argued mildly" for allowing Israel to sell arms to Iran because of a concern that ending the deals would lead to retaliation against the hostages.

McFarlane officially left government service December 11, and later said he believed at that time that the arms-for-hostages dealing had ended.

During this time, Ghorbanifar traveled to Washington to meet with U.S. officials. During one trip, on January 11, 1986, the CIA gave him a lie detector test and Ghorbanifar was found to have lied on nearly every question. One top CIA official described Ghorbanifar as "a guy who lies with zest." The White House nonetheless continued to use Ghorbanifar as its contact with Iran.

North sent Poindexter another arms deal plan on December 9, 1985. North also continued meeting with Secord, Ghorbanifar, and Israeli officials.

On January 2, 1986, Nir gave Poindexter a proposal that appeared to revive the Iran initiative. Its greatest importance may have been its timing—Nir appeared in Washington "just when the initiative seemed to be dying," the Tower report said.

Under Nir's plan, Israel would exchange several pro-Iranian prisoners it held in Beirut, along with 3,000 TOW missiles, for the U.S. hostages. Reagan and his top aides discussed the plan January 7, 1986; as in previous meetings, Shultz and Weinberger were opposed and the others, especially Casey, were in favor.

The January 7 meeting may have been superfluous. A day earlier, Reagan had signed a draft version of a finding

authorizing arms sales to Iran. Regan testified that the president might have signed the document "in error." Reagan himself said he did not recall signing it.

Reagan signed a final version of the finding January 17 after Poindexter briefed him again on the arms plan Nir and North had produced. The plan outlined in Poindexter's memo had one major difference from what Nir had proposed: Rather than authorizing Israeli sales to Iran, Reagan for the first time approved direct sales by the United States. The plan called for shipping 1,000 TOW missiles to Iran; if the hostages were released, another 3,000 missiles would follow. Reagan's finding also directed that Congress not be told about it.

The president said he did not read the three-page memo from Poindexter describing the arms plan. Reagan also said he did not understand, or had not been told about, several aspects of the operation: the specifics of how it would be implemented, that Iran would be given intelligence information along with weapons, and that there were "downside risks" in having the NSC staff run the operation. Casey, Reagan said, never suggested that the CIA should run it.

Shultz said he was unaware of the finding until November 10, 1986, when Poindexter told him about it.

North put the operation into effect almost immediately, ordering the Pentagon to get ready to transfer 4,000 TOW missiles to the CIA, and ordering the CIA to prepare intelligence information to be turned over to Iran. The latter happened first; on June 25 or 26, CIA official Charles Allen met Ghorbanifar in London and gave him information about Iraqi military positions. In exchange, Ghorbanifar handed over information about Iranian terrorism.

North also drafted what he called a "notional timeline" for the Iran operation covering January 24 to February 25. It called for the delivery of 1,000 TOW missiles to Iran on February 8, to be followed the next day by the release of American hostages and pro-Iranian prisoners in Lebanon. Another 3,000 TOW missiles were then to be sent to Iran over the next two weeks, along with intelligence information. The plan called for Secord, rather than the CIA, to handle details of the arms shipments.

On February 11, according to North's timeline, "Khomeini steps down." That did not happen, and North gave no indication where he got the idea.

In any case, a U.S.-leased plane delivered 500 TOW missiles to Iran February 18 and returned to Israel the old Hawk missiles that Iran did not want.

North met in Frankfurt, West Germany, on February 24 with Ghorbanifar and an official from the Iranian prime minister's office—the first official contact in the arms deals between the two countries. The two sides agreed that U.S. hostages would be released, to be followed by a higher-level meeting between the United States and Iran. Poindexter around that time asked McFarlane if he would be willing to head a U.S. delegation, and McFarlane agreed. Three days after the Frankfurt meeting, another 500 TOWs were shipped to Iran.

Iran was charged $12 million for 1,000 missiles that the CIA had bought from the Pentagon for only $3.7 million, leaving about $6.7 million unaccounted for. As with previous deals, Khashoggi advanced money to finance the sale and Ghorbanifar offered postdated checks as a guarantee of payment by Iran. This transaction was complicated by Iran's apparent decision to deduct $4 million from its payment as a refund for the Hawk missiles it rejected.

Shultz testified that Poindexter said February 28 that

the American hostages would be released in a few days. They weren't.

McFarlane's Trip to Tehran

U.S. officials were disappointed that the shipments of missiles did not produce hostages. But despite that disappointment, they remained hopeful, and the effort was pursued.

In preparation for McFarlane's trip, North and other officials held several meetings with Ghorbanifar, including one in Washington early in April. After one false start, it was agreed that a delegation led by McFarlane would travel to Tehran in late May, coinciding with the release of all American hostages in Lebanon.

During this period—when top U.S. officials were at an economic summit meeting of industrialized nations in Tokyo—Shultz received evidence that U.S. arms dealings with Iran were continuing. He told the Tower board and the House and Senate select investigating committees that Poindexter and Casey both assured him the Iran operation had been ended.

Reagan on May 15 approved the McFarlane trip, along with a North-drafted statement of the "pillars" of U.S. foreign policy generally and the "principles" of U.S. policy toward Iran in particular. Among the principles, North stated: "We view the Iranian revolution as a fact. The U.S. is not trying to turn the clock back."

Reagan's approval triggered two major financial transactions: as an advance on the weapons delivery, Khashoggi deposited $15 million into a Swiss bank account controlled by North under the name "Lake Resources Inc.," and North shifted $6.5 million into a CIA Swiss account to cover the cost of the Hawk parts.

Although Iran had demanded 240 different parts for Hawk missiles, it was not clear whether Reagan knew in mid-May just what arms were to be shipped to Tehran. In any event, McFarlane's plane carried only one pallet of Hawk parts, and a second plane carrying other parts was never sent to Tehran once McFarlane realized that hostages would not be released.

The McFarlane delegation arrived in Tehran on May 25; its members included North, retired CIA officer George Cave, Nir, and a CIA official. The delegation stayed nearly four days, meeting with midlevel officials but none of the senior leaders promised by Ghorbanifar. In one cable to Poindexter in Washington on May 26, McFarlane said: "The incompetence of the Iranian government to do business requires a rethinking on our part of why there have been so many frustrating failures to deliver on their part."

Disappointed by the lack of substance, the delegation left Tehran on May 28, and the next day McFarlane reported to Reagan on the trip. McFarlane testified that he recommended ending the initiative to Iran.

The Tower board pinpointed one source of trouble that should have been apparent at this point: repeated misunderstandings between the Iranians and some Americans about what the dealings would produce. For example, the board said it compiled evidence that North and CIA officials knew that only one hostage would be released even if all the Hawk parts were delivered to Iran. McFarlane and Poindexter probably thought all hostages were to be released; as a result, McFarlane rejected any lesser deal with Iran.

On June 20, Reagan decided not to allow any further official meetings with the Iranians until the hostages were released. But North met again with Ghorbanifar in London on July 21, discussing the release of hostages in return for

Proceeds from the Iranian arms sales were used to fund the rebel forces, known as "contras," fighting the Sandinista-led government of Nicaragua.

the remaining Hawk parts. On July 26, a Lebanese group released one U.S. hostage, the Rev. Lawrence Jenco. North claimed in a memo that the release "undoubtedly" was a result of McFarlane's trip, and he later recommended that Reagan approve shipping the Hawk parts to Iran. Reagan did so July 30.

A New 'Channel'

The release of Jenco sparked new U.S. interest in the Iranian operation but did nothing to ease Washington's frustrations about the demonstrated unreliability of Ghorbanifar. A full year of dealings between the United States and Iran "had been marked by great confusion, broken promises and increasing frustration on the U.S. side," the Tower report said. North and others in Washington "apparently blamed these problems more on Mr. Ghorbanifar than on Iran."

In July 1986, an Iranian living in London suggested that the United States could deal with a second "channel" to Iran: the relative of someone the report called "a powerful Iranian official." News sources later identified that official as Ali Akbar Hashemi Rafsanjani, speaker of the Iranian parliament.

After introductory meetings in Europe, the new Iranian came to Washington September 19, 1986, and met with North, Cave, and a CIA official. Reagan was told about the new Iranian twice in September. From October 5-7, North, Cave, and Secord met with the Iranian in Frankfurt. North carried to that meeting a Bible signed by Reagan.

The Tower board reported that North, during the Frankfurt meetings, "misrepresented his access to the president and attributed to the president things the president never said." Among the latter, the board said, was a statement by North that the United States recognized that Saddam Hussein "must go"—a reference to the Iranian demand for the ouster of the Iraqi president. Reagan said that North's reported statements were an "absolute fiction."

During the meeting in early October, North agreed to sell Iran 500 TOW missiles in exchange for the release of two hostages. Plans for the exchange were completed at meetings October 26-28, at which the parties discussed a nine-point agenda—including arms sales—for future meetings.

It was subsequently disclosed that the plan included continued sale of arms to Iran in exchange for the release of U.S. hostages, as well as a U.S. promise to help win the release of seventeen terrorists jailed in Kuwait, the Da'Wa prisoners. Shultz later learned of the plan, and when he told the president of it on December 14, he said Reagan was "astonished" and angry.

Israel delivered 500 TOWS to Iran on October 29. Regan testified that the president gave his approval that same day. A week later, on November 7, the United States sent Israel replacements for the missiles. The CIA said Iran paid $4 million for these missiles, and North in a memo said Iran paid $7 million. The Pentagon charged the CIA slightly over $2 million, leaving $2 million to $5 million unaccounted for.

American hostage David P. Jacobsen was released in Lebanon on November 2, and the next day a Beirut magazine published an account of the McFarlane trip to Tehran in May. Rafsanjani on November 4 publicly confirmed the visit of McFarlane and his delegation.

DIVERSION OF FUNDS TO CONTRA AID NETWORK

The investigations painted a complex picture of the diversion of U.S. arms sales profits to the contras. North was the central figure in the contra supply network, a shadowy web of private individuals and secret bank accounts. With Poindexter's approval, he was aided by Secord and others. McFarlane also played a role, as, apparently did CIA director Casey. But, much to the relief of the White House, the Tower board and congressional committees could find no evidence that the president knew of the diversion.

Exactly how much the contras actually received was difficult to determine. Secord and his business partner, Albert Hakim, who managed the fund diversion, reaped substantial profits from the sales; and large sums from the Iranian arms deal remained in Swiss bank accounts at the time of the investigations. (Contra funds, box, p. 97; Secord-Hakim funds, box, p. 104)

The subject of using "residuals" from the arms sales for other unrelated activities first came up during a meeting in early January 1986 between North and Nir, the antiterrorism adviser to Israeli prime minister Peres. North testified that Nir did not specifically mention the contras. Israeli officials denied bringing up the diversion idea or having any role in the scheme. (Israeli version, box, p. 141)

At a meeting with Ghorbanifar later that month in London, North said the Iranian arms merchant suggested the use of profits to aid the contras. North said he thought it was "a neat idea." Ghorbanifar told the Tower board that North and Secord were worried about keeping aid flowing to the contras and that North asked him if the Iranians would pay $10,000 for each TOW missile instead of $6,500. "When told that Iran would pay that price, Mr. Ghorbanifar said Lt. Col. North was greatly relieved—'he was a changed man,'" said the report.

The following month, retired CIA officer Cave met with Ghorbanifar in Paris. Cave later wrote in a memorandum describing the March 7-8 meeting that Ghorbanifar "proposed that we use profits from these deals and others to fund support to the rebels in Afghanistan. We could do the same with Nicaragua." But Cave, testifying before the Tower panel, said that neither he nor Ghorbanifar ever mentioned the diversion during the Paris meeting.

Testifying before the Tower board, Attorney General Edwin Meese III said North told him in November 1986 that $3 million to $4 million was diverted to the contras after the February shipment of TOW missiles to Iran. According to Meese, North said that more money had been diverted after the May arms shipment; North did not remember how much.

Justice Department notes from Meese's interview with North indicated that North said Israeli officials handled the money and that he gave them the numbers of Swiss bank accounts opened by contra leader Adolfo Calero.

North Memo, Role of Others

One of the first pieces of evidence directly linking the Iran arms operation with the contra diversion was a White House memo prepared by North in early April 1986, entitled "Release of American Hostages in Beirut." The memo was written as a background to Reagan's approval of the secret mission to Tehran, headed, the following month, by McFarlane. The memo said that $12 million "will be used to purchase critically needed supplies for the Nicaraguan Democratic Resistance Forces." The money, North said, was needed to cover shortages in contra inventories "and to 'bridge' the period between now and when Congressionally-approved lethal assistance . . . can be delivered." *(Text of memo, p. D-79)*

At the time, Congress had prohibited U.S. military aid to the contras.

Investigators could find no evidence that North's memo, written for Poindexter, was seen by Reagan.

Another part of North's memo said that Iranian contacts had previously been told by U.S. officials that their aiding of Nicaragua's Sandinista regime "is unacceptable to us and they have agreed to discuss this matter in Tehran" during McFarlane's trip.

North's preoccupation with the contras surfaced in other discussions. A few weeks after his April memo was drafted, he sent a note to Donald Fortier, an NSC official at the time. In it, North warned about the future of U.S. support for the contras. The "picture is dismal unless a new source of 'bridge' funding can be identified. . . . We need to explore this problem urgently or there won't be a force to help when the Congress finally acts," said North.

Poindexter and North first discussed the diversion plan in February 1986. Although North kept Poindexter exhaustively informed about his Iran-related activities, the national security adviser asked for few details about North's contra activities. Poindexter said he did not advise the president of the diversion of Iranian arms sales profits to the contras because he believed that Reagan would have approved and because he wanted to "insulate" him from the decision. (Reagan had approved efforts to solicit contra aid from other countries—including Saudi Arabia, Brunei, China, and Taiwan—as well as private U.S. citizens.) In 1987 testimony, North said he assumed he had the full approval of his superiors—including the president.

CIA director Casey, who died May 6, 1987, after being hospitalized in December (and therefore could not testify), was intimately involved in the contra aid activities, North testified. North informed McFarlane of the diversion while standing on the tarmac at the Tel Aviv airport after the May 1986 mission to Iran. McFarlane was dejected after the failed four-day effort in Tehran to win release of the remaining U.S. hostages. According to McFarlane's testimony before the Tower Commission, "North said well, don't be too downhearted, that the one bright spot is that the government is availing itself of part of the money for application to Central America, as I recall, although I took it to be Nicaragua."

North apparently remained sanguine about the diversion nearly up to the day it was made public.

Assistant Secretary of Defense Richard L. Armitage testified that North told him sometime in November 1986, "It's going to be just fine . . . as soon as everyone knows that . . . the ayatollah is helping us with the contras."

Boland Amendments

The Tower report painted a picture of the Reagan administration wrapped up in a determined effort to keep the contras financed during a time when Congress had cut off military aid.

In December 1982, Congress passed its first version of the "Boland amendment," prohibiting the United States from trying to overthrow the Nicaraguan government. The next year Congress passed a second Boland amendment setting a $24 million cap on military aid to the contras. In October 1984 Congress went one step further by cutting off all funds to the contras and preventing the Pentagon, CIA, and any other agency "involved in intelligence activities" from supporting military operations in Nicaragua. *(Boland amendments, box, p. 24)*

Members of Congress argued that the Boland amendment proscriptions applied to the NSC staff on the grounds that the agency was involved in intelligence activities. That position was backed up in Reagan's Executive Order 12333, issued in December 1981, dealing with intelligence agencies and covert activities. It described the NSC as the "highest executive branch entity" that reviews and directs intelligence activities.

However, Reagan's Intelligence Oversight Board apparently provided the NSC with a legal justification for involvement in the contra supply network without violating the Boland amendment, according to the Tower report and testimony before the House and Senate Iran-contra committees.

A classified legal memo found in North's White House safe, apparently prepared by the intelligence board, said the NSC "is not covered by the prohibition" against aiding the contras for a variety of reasons, among them being that the NSC's role was to coordinate rather than implement covert action. "None of Lt. Col. North's activities during the past year constitutes a violation of the Boland amendment," said the memo.

But Poindexter worried about North's contra activities becoming public, as well as news of his own knowledge seeping out. "From now on, I don't want you to talk to anybody else, including [CIA Director] Casey, except me about any of your operational roles. In fact, you need to quietly generate a cover story that I have insisted that you stop," Poindexter told North in a message on May 15, 1986.

Three months later, when North was interviewed by the House Intelligence Committee, he denied any contra connections involving military operations or fund raising. Poindexter shortly afterward sent North a message: "Well done."

North's Secret Network

With congressionally approved money for the contras running out, North suggested to McFarlane in April 1985 that $15 million to $20 million be raised from private sources. Memos written by North at the time indicated that the funds were for arms and lethal aid.

"Evidence suggests that at least by November 1985, Lt. Col. North had assumed a direct operational role, co-ordinating logistical arrangements to ship privately purchased arms to the contras," said the Tower report.

Private contributions to the contras were funneled through a network of private individuals and secret bank accounts that North dubbed "Project Democracy." North told Poindexter in a July 1986 computer message that his Project Democracy assets were worth over $4.5 million and included six aircraft, warehouses, ships, leased houses, munitions, communications equipment, and a 6,520-foot runway in Costa Rica used as a secret airfield for contra supplies.

When Costa Rica decided to disclose the airfield's

existence and close it down, North and other U.S. officials discussed a plan to have North call Costa Rican president Oscar Arias and threaten to cancel $80 million in U.S. foreign aid along with Arias's upcoming meeting with Reagan. Assistant Secretary of State Elliott Abrams and Lewis Tambs, the U.S. ambassador to Costa Rica, confirmed the discussion with North but said that Tambs called Arias to persuade him to cancel the announcement. Tambs said he did not threaten the aid cutoff.

Later, Costa Rica announced the discovery and closure of the airstrip.

Under North's direction, retired Air Force general Secord began selling arms to the contras in late 1984. In 1985 he organized a private arms supply network at North's request, despite a total ban on U.S. arms aid to Nicaragua. By 1986 North had established a secret communications network, with fifteen encryption devices provided by the National Security Agency ostensibly to support his official counterterrorist activities as part of his NSC duties. One of the devices, which allowed for secure communications, was given to Secord and another to a CIA field officer posted in Costa Rica. "Through this mechanism, North coordinated the resupply of the contras with military equipment apparently purchased with funds provided by the network of private benefactors," said the Tower board.

Messages to North from Secord and the CIA officer asked him to spell out the logistics for arms deliveries to the contras, informed him of arms requirements, and kept him informed of how much money was involved, according to the report.

At least nine arms shipments were delivered to the contras through North's private network between March and June 1986.

North on at least two occasions contacted U.S. Customs Service officials to complain about their investigations into clandestine airline operations supplying the contras. North contacted assistant Customs commissioner William Rosenblatt after a C-123 cargo plane crashed October 5 in Nicaragua during a supply flight to the contras. The sole survivor, American Eugene Hasenfus, was captured and convicted on terrorism charges but later released. (Although administration officials initially denied any official U.S. connection, it was later revealed that the CIA and others in the U.S. government had been involved.)

Rosenblatt testified that North told him the Customs probe had focused on "good guys" who had not committed any crimes. Customs investigators then limited their inquiry into the individual aircraft that crashed rather than on the activities of Corporate Air Services Inc., an air freight company linked to the Hasenfus flight.

North earlier had complained to Customs commissioner William von Raab about an inquiry into another aircraft suspected of supporting the contras. But Rosenblatt and von Raab said North never asked them to close out their investigations.

In the Hasenfus case, North suggested to McFarlane that they find a "high-powered lawyer and benefactor" to provide a legal defense.

North also told McFarlane in the October 12, 1986, message that Reagan was briefed on the plan to assist Hasenfus before the president left for the U.S.-Soviet summit in Iceland. North said he was concerned that "when people begin to think of things other than meetings in cold places, he [Reagan] will remember this and nothing will have been done." (North's seemingly endless quest to aid the contras apparently led to personal strain; McFarlane noted the pressures on North in a June 1986 memo to Poindexter.)

As part of the Iran initiative, the United States sold TOW antitank missiles to Iran.

Effort to 'Blur' Reagan Role

Almost from the moment the Iranian arms sales became public, White House officials took steps to hide or obscure major facts, testimony revealed. Beginning in mid-November, efforts were undertaken to "blur" Reagan's role in the arms sales, apparently to protect the president politically.

McFarlane and North told of the frantic preparation at the White House on November 18 of a chronology of the Iranian arms deals. The main objective of those writing the chronology, McFarlane said, "was to describe a sequence of events that would distance the president from the initial approval of the Iran arms sale, distance him from it to blur his association with it." Drafted by North, the chronology said, among other things, that the U.S. officials believed the 1985 Israeli shipments to Iran consisted of oil drilling equipment, not missiles.

A more serious cover-up occurred with the destruction of important evidence related to the Iran-contra affair. North testified that he began shredding documents in October following the shooting down of the Hasenfus plane and after he learned from CIA director Casey that allega-tions were being made that proceeds were diverted from the Iran arms sales to the contras. After the arms sale disclosure was made public in early November, North said Casey advised him to destroy evidence related to the activity.

Further shredding took place later in the month, when Attorney General Meese was beginning his investigation into the Iranian arms sales that soon uncovered the contra diversion scheme. North's secretary at the time, Fawn Hall, said she altered several key documents and helped North destroy some documents and internal computer messages on November 21, shortly before Justice Department officials were scheduled to begin reviewing NSC files. Poindexter also said he shredded documents, including the December 1985 finding that laid out the arms-for-hostages policy.

Although the November 21-24 investigation by Attorney General Meese turned up the contra aid memo that North had neglected to shred, the Justice Department probe was faulted on several grounds, among them failure to immediately seal NSC files, to ask point-blank questions, and to take notes of meetings with key officials. But Meese defended the investigation, which led to North's firing and Poindexter's resignation.

Part II

The Investigations

Introduction

Almost immediately after the Iran-contra affair was disclosed in November 1986, numerous investigations were set in motion. During Attorney General Edwin Meese III's probe November 21-25, the Justice Department came upon the fact that some profits from the arms sales to Iran had gone to the Nicaraguan rebels, or contras. The diversion was discovered when Justice investigators found a memo by National Security Council (NSC) aide Lt. Col. Oliver L. North discussing the scheme. That memo was one of few that North had not disposed of after learning of the pending investigation. The Justice Department's inquiry subsequently was faulted for being insufficiently thorough. Some critics even suggested that it had been conducted with a view to putting the administration in a favorable light by appearing eager to "get to the bottom" of the affair, when many aspects were shielded from public view. Meese, however, later defended the scope of his probe, arguing that at the time, there was no substantial evidence of criminal conduct, which would warrant a different—more stringent—investigation.

To conduct "a comprehensive review" of the NSC's Iran-contra operations—carried out primarily by North, with the concurrence of his superior, President Reagan's national security adviser Vice Adm. John M. Poindexter—Reagan November 26 named a three-man commission, headed by former senator John Tower, R-Texas. The other two members were former senator and secretary of state Edmund S. Muskie, and former president Gerald R. Ford's national security adviser, Brent Scowcroft. In its report, issued February 26, 1987, the commission criticized the president for his ineffective management of the NSC, his advisers for failing to compensate for the Reagan's management style, and the White House staff for sacrificing institutional process in their pursuit of the Iran-contra policy. *(Tower Commission investigation, p. 71)*

The House and Senate Intelligence committees held hearings in November on the Iran arms sales. After the contra diversion had been revealed in December, the Intelligence panels, as well as the House Foreign Affairs Committee, held further hearings. The Senate Intelligence Committee, after news leaks and under administration pressure to make its findings public, released a report January 29, 1987. The report chronicled the administration's arms-for-hostages dealings but drew no conclusions concerning the propriety or legality of the affair. *(Senate Intelligence Committee investigation, p. 63)*

In the meantime, the Senate and House in December established special committees to investigate all aspects of the Iran-contra affair. Members of the panels were appointed December 16-17; they were constituted officially at the beginning of the 100th Congress in January 1987. During the first four months of the year, they developed a staff and interviewed hundreds of potential witnesses. Public hearings began in May and continued into early August, after which members heard closed testimony from CIA officials and the committees' staffs began drafting reports, scheduled to be released in October. *(Select committees investigation, p. 83)*

Also in December, a three-judge panel appointed Lawrence E. Walsh as independent counsel to investigate possible illegalities. Walsh was a former federal judge and president of the American Bar Association. His investigative charter was much broader than the Reagan administration had sought. *(Independent counsel investigation, p. 163)*

The multiple investigations raised two key procedural issues: whether the appointment of an independent counsel was constitutional, and whether, if it was, Walsh's investigation would be impeded by a congressional grant of limited (or "use") immunity to key witnesses. The principal argument against an independent counsel was that it represented a violation of the separation of powers doctrine, injecting the judiciary into matters belonging to the executive branch. North and his lawyers repeatedly raised that objection, and the case was continuing as of fall 1987. *(Independent counsel law, box, p. 58)*

The second issue pitted the congressional investigating committees against the independent counsel. Some members wanted to grant limited immunity quickly to essential witnesses—primarily North and Poindexter, who had invoked the Fifth Amendment in December, refusing to testify on the grounds that it might incriminate them—so that the facts could be uncovered in a more timely fashion and the hearings would not drag on. Walsh initially objected to such limited immunity grants because he said it would impede the independent counsel's criminal investigation. After prolonged negotiations among the select com-

Probe Continues a Rich Tradition ...

When twenty-six House and Senate members gathered in the Senate's historic Caucus Room May 5, 1987, to begin their Iran-contra hearings, they were continuing a rich tradition. Over the course of nearly two centuries, Congress had investigated scandals, wars, national security threats—real and imagined—and any number of other topics that captivated inquiring minds on Capitol Hill. Many of those investigations featured presidents and future presidents as investigators, witnesses, and targets.

"In my opinion, the power of investigation is one of the most important powers of the Congress," Harry S Truman declared in 1944, a few months before the feisty senator from Missouri was elected vice president. "The manner in which that power is exercised will largely determine the position and prestige of the Congress in the future."

Truman knew a thing or two about Hill inquiries. For more than three years he had chaired the Senate Special Committee to Investigate the National Defense Program, created in March 1941 to look into military and civilian preparedness for war. The panel existed for more than seven years, outlasting the U.S. combat role in World War II and the public's preoccupation with the war effort. But its work also paved the way for the establishment of the War Production Board and other methods of mobilizing people and industry.

As an assistant to the Navy secretary, future presidential candidate Adlai E. Stevenson served as a military liaison to the Truman Committee, as it was originally known. Later, the Navy's official contact person was a young captain named John F. Kennedy.

Second-Guessing in Wartime

A U.S. military defeat during the nation's infancy sparked Congress's first investigation. In 1792, the House instructed a select committee to examine why Gen. Arthur St. Clair and his troops had been routed by Indians in battles on the Ohio frontier. The committee exonerated St. Clair, blaming poor Army organization and the mismanagement of supplies that led to such things as "badness of gunpowder."

Seventy years later, Congress established its first joint investigating panel in response to another military action—one fought between the North and South. To Abraham Lincoln's consternation, the Joint Committee on the Conduct of the War routinely second-guessed the president's military moves and attempted to plot its own course during the Civil War. Controlled by critics who were convinced that Lincoln was not acting aggressively enough to secure a Union victory, the committee was welcomed by Gen. Robert E. Lee because of its divisive effect on Northern strategists.

Rooting Out Corruption

Other investigations dealt with money and favors. One looked into charges of widespread corruption surrounding the United States' purchase of Alaska from Russia in 1867.

Newspapers at the time reported that officials in Andrew Johnson's administration, along with private financiers, had used more than $2 million from the money to buy Alaska as bribes to members of Congress, lobbyists, and other government officials in exchange for their support of the sale. The House Committee on Public Expenditures ended its inquiry without bringing charges against any member of Congress. Instead, the panel lashed out at the "loose morality" of several Washington reporters who were accused of filling their stories with "nebulous gossip."

Congressional investigations hit something of a high-water mark during Ulysses S. Grant's two terms in the White House. Some thirty-five inquiries into a variety of subjects were launched on Capitol Hill between 1869 and 1877, according to a 1929 study of congressional investigating committees by a political scientist at the University of California at Los Angeles.

Probably the most famous scandal of the time was the Credit Mobilier affair in 1872-73, which triggered inquiries by a Senate committee and two House panels. The scandal involved an effort by Rep. Oakes Ames, R-Mass., to stave off legislative inquiries into corruption charges against the Union Pacific railroad and Credit Mobilier of America, a related company that had constructed the last portion of the transcontinental railroad in 1869. Ames, a shareholder in Credit Mobilier (his brother Oliver became president of the Union Pacific in 1866), arranged to sell some $33 million of stock in the company at artificially low prices to members of Congress and executive branch officials. Ames and another House member, New York Democrat James Brooks, were eventually censured by the House. Others, including Vice President Schuyler Colfax and Rep. James A. Garfield, R-Ohio, were implicated, but no action was taken against them. Garfield remained in the House until he was elected president in 1880, only to be assassinated seven months after entering office.

During the 1950s, two special Senate committees looked into corruption. One, headed at first by Estes Kefauver, D-Tenn., used the then-novel approach of televised hearings in 1950-51 to spotlight racketeering, drug trafficking, and other organized crime. The second panel, chaired by John L. McClellan, D-Ark., looked into shady labor union dealings. The inquiry was instrumental in the 1959 passage of the Landrum-Griffin Act aimed at stemming corruption in union affairs.

... Hill Investigations a Potent Tool

Looking for Subversives

After the United States emerged from World War I as a global power, members of Congress frequently pushed for inquiries into security threats posed by allegedly subversive elements loyal to other nations.

Beginning with the zeal of some members to look into pro-Nazi and fascist sympathizers, the drive to track down subversives later focused on the battle against communism. In 1938, the House established the Special Committee to Investigate Un-American Activities and Propaganda in the United States. Known popularly as the Dies Committee after its first chairman, Martin Dies, Jr., D-Texas, the panel embarked on a stormy path that weathered nearly four decades of controversy.

The original Dies Committee slipped out of existence in 1944, but the House, in a move that caught its Democratic leaders by surprise, voted to create a permanent House Un-American Activities Committee (HUAC) on January 3, 1945, the first day of the 79th Congress. By 1946—a year marked by the elections of Richard Nixon to the House and Joseph R. McCarthy to the Senate—the committee had turned its attention to hunting down communists in the United States.

The panel, with Nixon as a member, focused the following year on the movie industry. "From what I hear, I don't like [communism] because it isn't on the level," Gary Cooper assured the panel. Other Hollywood personalities—including Robert Montgomery; George Murphy, who served in the Senate as a Republican from California between 1965 and 1971; and an actor named Ronald Reagan—testified about the relatively mild and ineffective communist efforts to infiltrate the Screen Actors Guild.

It was the year of the "Hollywood Ten," mostly screenwriters such as Dalton Trumbo, who defiantly challenged the panel's conduct and later went to jail after being arrested for contempt of Congress. Nervous studio executives responded with the infamous blacklist, barring other suspected communists from Hollywood jobs, a practice that lingered into the 1950s.

The Un-American Activities Committee, with Nixon playing a key role, hit its stride in 1948 with a dramatic confrontation between Alger Hiss, a State Department official, and Whittaker Chambers, a senior editor with *Time* magazine and a former communist, who accused Hiss of having been a communist years earlier. While Hiss professed his innocence, Nixon doggedly pursued the matter. He eventually succeeded in refuting Hiss's claim that he did not know Chambers, paving the way for Hiss to be convicted and jailed for perjury.

Throughout the early 1950s, HUAC was overshadowed by McCarthy's more flamboyant hunt for communists. But McCarthy's investigation into alleged subversion in the U.S. Army—televised nationwide in 1954—ultimately convinced his Senate colleagues he had gone too far.

The Senate's vote to censure McCarthy in December 1954 for his tactics effectively ended his crusade, but HUAC continued its work. In the 1960s, the House panel pursued a new breed of suspected subversives—Vietnam War protesters and black militants. The committee also briefly examined the Ku Klux Klan, one of the few occasions when it looked into right-wing extremists.

The panel changed its name in 1969 to the Internal Security Committee, but its lifeblood was draining. The House abolished the panel in 1975.

Governmental Excesses

Even as that era was ending, however, another had begun in the annals of Hill inquiries. The Watergate scandal prompted a 1973-74 investigation by a Senate select panel that looked into widespread abuses of power by President Nixon and his top aides. The Watergate hearings led to the disclosure of tape recordings of Nixon's White House conversations and revelations that led to his downfall by showing his role in a cover-up of efforts to sabotage the Democrats in forthcoming elections.

In the summer of 1974, the House Judiciary Committee capped its own investigation by voting articles of impeachment against Nixon. Rather than face a House impeachment vote and probable conviction by the Senate, the president resigned on August 9, 1974.

Six months later, the Senate established a select panel to look into charges of another form of government abuse—activities by the CIA that exceeded its charter. President Gerald R. Ford named his own commission, headed by Vice President Nelson A. Rockefeller, to examine CIA operations. Among the members was California's outgoing governor, Ronald Reagan. The Senate panel, chaired by Frank Church, D-Idaho, conducted a fifteen-month inquiry that confirmed accounts of CIA spying on U.S. citizens, assassination plots against foreign leaders, and other abuses.

In the wake of the Senate's inquiry and a parallel probe conducted by a House special committee, both chambers created ongoing Intelligence committees with oversight jurisdiction over the CIA. Selected as the Senate committee's first chairman was Daniel K. Inouye, D-Hawaii, a veteran of the Watergate panel and subsequently chairman of the Senate select Iran-contra committee.

mittees, Walsh, and lawyers representing North and Poindexter, agreement was finally reached in June 1987 that granted the two witnesses limited immunity.

First Immunity Statutes

As a longstanding practice, Congress had authorized grants of immunity from prosecution to obtain testimony from individuals who would otherwise claim their Fifth Amendment constitutional right to remain silent in order to avoid possible self-incrimination.

When it approved the federal statute providing for punishment of recalcitrant witnesses before congressional committees, Congress in 1857 added a second section that contained an automatic and sweeping grant of immunity to those who were compelled by Congress to testify. As enacted, the law provided that "no person examined and testifying before either House of Congress or any committee of either House, shall be held to answer criminally in any court of justice, or subject to any penalty or forfeiture, for any fact or act touching which he shall be required to testify before either House of Congress, or any committee of either House, as to which he shall have testified, whether before or after this act; . . . . Provided, that nothing in this act shall be construed to exempt any witnesses from prosecution and punishment for perjury committed by him in testifying as aforesaid."

The disadvantages of this sort of immunity "bath" became evident in 1862 when it was revealed that embezzlers of millions in Indian trust bonds would escape prosecution because they had testified about their crime to a congressional committee and so, under the 1857 law, could not be prosecuted for it.

Congress repealed the 1857 law and replaced it in 1862 with a narrower immunity statute, stating that: "No testimony given by a witness before either House, or before any committee of either House . . . shall be used as evidence in any criminal proceedings against him in any court, except in a prosecution for perjury committed in giving such testimony." Thus, a witness's own testimony could not be used as evidence to convict him, but there was nothing to prevent its being used as a lead in discovering other evidence of crime.

An 1892 Supreme Court ruling raised questions about the adequacy of the 1862 immunity statute, but the law remained unchanged until 1954, when the Eisenhower administration proposed, and Congress adopted, the Immunity Act of 1954. The new law permitted either chamber of Congress by majority vote, or a congressional committee by two-thirds vote, to grant immunity to witnesses in national security investigations, provided an order was first obtained from a U.S. district court judge. The law further provided that the attorney general had to be notified in advance and given an opportunity to offer objections. The law also permitted the U.S. district courts to grant immunity to witnesses before the court or grand juries. The act granted immunity from prosecution for criminal activity revealed during compelled testimony. Under the 1954 law, witnesses who were compelled to relinquish their Fifth Amendment rights had to be granted "transactional" immunity, which shielded them completely from prosecution for any offense mentioned in or related to their testimony. In 1956 the Supreme Court upheld the 1954 immunity statute to those appearing before grand juries but made clear that it was proffering no opinion on provisions granting immunity to congressional witnesses.

1970 Revisions

In 1970 Congress passed an entirely new immunity law, part of the Organized Crime Control Act (PL 91-452), designed to compel testimony of recalcitrant witnesses. It set out the rules for granting immunity to persons appearing before congressional committees, courts, grand juries, and administrative agencies. Under the new law, witnesses who received immunity to waive their Fifth Amendment rights and testify were guaranteed that their testimony and the information it contained would not be used against them in any criminal prosecution, except for perjury, should they lie in their testimony. It did not, however, immunize them from all prosecutions for matters mentioned in their testimony, if the government had evidence of those crimes that was developed independently of their testimony.

By 5-2, the Supreme Court in 1972 upheld the constitutionality of the narrowed witness immunity provisions of the 1970 act. However, in its ruling in the case of *Kastigar* v. *United States,* the Court stressed that in any subsequent prosecution of a witness compelled to testify under a grant of immunity, the government must show that the evidence against the witness was derived from sources independent of the testimony.

Under the law, in place during the Iran-contra hearings, a congressional committee could immunize a witness only by a two-thirds vote of its members. The committee had to inform the attorney general—or an independent counsel, if one had been appointed—when it planned to grant a witness immunity. The attorney general or counsel then could attempt to dissuade the committee from acting but could not block it from doing so.

Watergate Witnesses

Congressional grants of immunity became an issue during the 1973 Senate Watergate Committee hearings, when more than two dozen witnesses were granted immunity from prosecution based on their testimony. In one of his first moves as Watergate special prosecutor, Archibald Cox June 4, 1973, urged the committee to delay its public hearings. One of his arguments for postponement was that a grant of immunity for certain witnesses before the committee might prevent them from being convicted later.

U.S. District Judge John J. Sirica denied Cox's request to delay the hearings. Sirica then approved grants of limited immunity—under the 1970 law—to White House counsel John W. Dean III and to Jeb Stuart Magruder, a former White House aide who was serving as deputy director of the Committee for the Re-Election of the President. Both were known to be under consideration for indictment in connection with the Watergate scandal and reportedly were prepared to offer evidence of the involvement of top White House officials, including the president. Both later served prison terms after pleading guilty to Watergate-related charges.

Samuel Dash, a professor at Georgetown University Law School who served as chief counsel of the Watergate Committee, recalled that his staff regularly notified Cox when the committee planned to immunize a witness. "Every time we notified them, they segregated all the evidence they had independent of us and submitted it to the court," Dash said. Early in the committee's investigation, Dean tried to obtain full immunity in exchange for his testimony, according to Dash. There was a certain irony to that attempt, he noted, recalling that Dean in 1969 had been part of a Justice Department team urging Congress to restrict the immunity that could be granted witnesses.

Iran-Contra Immunity Grants

The immunity issue in the Iran-contra matter came to a head in March 1987. Meeting with the House and Senate select committees, independent counsel Walsh asked members not to compel any testimony by Poindexter or North for ninety days in order to give him time to develop possible criminal cases against the two men. Most members were receptive to Walsh's plea, although pressure was growing in Congress to move ahead quickly with the hearings. However, they agreed to Walsh's request.

Meanwhile, the committees sought to obtain evidence from others involved in various aspects of the affair by granting them limited "use" immunity. At least a dozen witnesses had received immunity from the committees by the end of April. Committee members emphasized that persons given limited immunity would not necessarily escape prosecution.

"Nobody is really avoiding prosecution by what we're doing," said Warren B. Rudman, R-N.H., vice chairman of the Senate Iran-contra committee.

Senate Intelligence Committee

The story of U.S. arms sales to Iran was barely out when Congress moved in to begin investigations. The revelation, first published in a Lebanese magazine in early November 1986, sent congressional committees scrambling for further information.

Although more in-depth investigations would be held by a three-man commission (the Tower board) appointed by Reagan, by the House and Senate select committees on the Iran-contra affair, and by the independent counsel, the initial findings of the Senate Intelligence Committee paved the way for further probes into the way the Iran arms sales came about and the manner in which the profits from those sales were diverted—perhaps illegally—to assist the contras fighting the leftist Sandinista government in Nicaragua.

Three congressional committees immediately plunged into the Iran-contra embroglio—the House Foreign Affairs and House Intelligence committees, and, on the other side of Capitol Hill, the Senate Intelligence Committee. The Intelligence committees' hearings, conducted in November and December 1986, were behind closed doors, while most of Foreign Affairs' sessions were open to the public. Only one of the panels, the Senate Intelligence Committee, released a report of its findings. Controversy surrounded that report, but it was less about *what* was revealed than *how* it was revealed.

The staff of the Republican-led Intelligence Committee compiled the report in December after three weeks of closed hearings. The White House demanded that the report be made public—apparently because the committee found no direct evidence that President Reagan personally was aware of the scheme to divert Iranian arms sale profits to the contras.

Senate Democrats, however, said the report was incomplete and contained some inaccuracies. At their insistence, the committee voted January 5, 1987, not to release it. Nonetheless, White House and congressional sources leaked details of the report, and NBC News announced January 8 that it had obtained the entire document, a claim disputed by Dave Durenberger, R-Minn., committee chairman until January 6 (when party chairmanships changed hands from a Republican- to a Democratic-controlled Senate), and David L. Boren, D-Okla., the incoming chairman. *(Leak, box, p. 65)*

Although White House officials had pressed for release of the draft report, the thrust of it proved embarrassing. Principal findings included the conclusion that freeing American hostages held by pro-Iranian factions in Lebanon was a primary goal of the secret U.S. arms dealings with Tehran, despite the president's then-repeated assertions that the government would never trade arms for hostages. The report also demonstrated that Reagan exerted little control over his aides, and some senior officials kept others out of the decision-making process. Reagan approved the Iranian arms sales over the opposition of Secretary of State George P. Shultz and Defense Secretary Caspar W. Weinberger. The draft report said White House officials later withheld information about the sales from Shultz.

Under control of Democrats, the Senate panel voted 14-1 on January 29 to send a revised report to the Senate select committee investigating the Iran-contra affair. In a game of ping-pong, the select committee then voted unanimously to send the document back to the Intelligence panel with a recommendation that it be released.

Final Report

Officially titled "Preliminary Inquiry into the Sale of Arms to Iran and Possible Diversion of Funds to the Nicaraguan Resistance," the Senate panel's final report was a rewritten version of the 150-page document that the committee staff had prepared in December 1986. Unlike its staff report, the official Intelligence Committee document did not draw conclusions about culpability for the Iran-contra fiasco. Instead, it chronicled the history of U.S. relations with Iran and aid to the contras, based on the testimony of thirty-six witnesses and thousands of pages of documents. *(Text, p. D-22)*

The report listed fourteen "unresolved issues" in the Iran-contra affair that might be investigated by the House and Senate select committees. Among them were the roles played by White House aides as well as officials at the CIA, and the Defense and Justice departments. Examination of the activities of emissaries of foreign governments and private individuals working as consultants and intermediaries also was suggested. The role of private individuals in participating in—and perhaps formulating—the nation's foreign policy should be scrutinized, the report said. The panel also recommended a broader inquiry into support for the contras by federal and private sources; that investigation should include an examination of how funds were raised, administered, and distributed.

Release of the report came as the United States confronted a new wave of hostage-taking in Lebanon. Four persons—three Americans and an Indian national—were kidnapped in Lebanon January 24, and nationals of other countries were abducted in following days. In response, the State Department restricted private travel to Lebanon by Americans. Secretary of State Shultz said January 29 that Iran had "very strong ties" to the hostage-takers.

Notification of Congress

The first congressional hearings on the Iran arms sales (the diversion of profits to the contras had not yet been revealed) began on November 21, 1986, against a backdrop of growing criticism of the Reagan administration for failing in its obligation to inform the legislative branch about arms sales to Iran, particularly in light of laws strictly forbidding arms sales to allegedly terrorist nations, or countries supporting terrorism. The criticism on Capitol Hill was not alleviated by Reagan's November 13 and November 19 statements that arms were not "traded" for hostages and that the sales did not signify a change in the U.S. policy of not dealing with terrorists. In his November 19 news conference, the president repeatedly justified his decision not to inform Congress about the sales because, he said, the dealings were extremely sensitive.

The notification issue was extremely important to the Intelligence committees because it focused on longstanding constitutional disputes between the executive and legislative branches regarding their roles in approving and executing foreign policy. Some members of Congress said they needed to receive more information from the White House in order to perform their function of monitoring foreign policy decisions. An equally important argument was that congressional involvement beforehand could lead to better presidential decision making and sharing of responsibility. Some members challenged that the administration might have violated or skirted laws requiring notification to Congress of overseas arms shipments and covert operations. *(Box, p. 32)*

Those concerns were voiced by Senate Intelligence chairman Durenberger and ranking Democrat Patrick Leahy, Vt., who wrote Reagan that they were "deeply disturbed" by his refusal to inform Congress of the decision to sell arms to Iran. Durenberger said that failure to keep Congress abreast of developments would prove to be "incredibly deleterious to the course of American foreign policy."

INITIAL HEARINGS: STUNNING SILENCE

The Senate Intelligence panel, like the other initial congressional investigating committees, was hampered by the refusal of two key witnesses to talk. Rear Adm. John M. Poindexter, Reagan's former national security adviser, and Lt. Col. Oliver L. North, fired from his post on the National Security Council (NSC) staff, both cited the Fifth Amendment, declining to answer questions on grounds that doing so might incriminate them. Their refusal was somewhat unexpected because Intelligence Committee members had met privately with Poindexter at the White House to head off a confrontation over whether the former national security adviser would be called to testify.

Committee members informally discussed granting immunity to compel testimony. But the panel was reluctant to take such a step, largely because doing so might complicate the work of the independent counsel, who had not yet been appointed when the hearings began. President Reagan on December 16 asked the Intelligence Committee to grant "use" immunity, but the panel still felt immunity was premature because it might impede possible criminal investigations by the independent counsel. Testimony given by a witness before Congress could not be used against the witness, if granted limited or use immunity. Chairman Durenberger said he thought the committee could learn most of the facts "with or without" North and Poindexter; however, many gaps remained when the committee completed its inquiry. *(Immunity issue, p. 57)*

Reports of the destruction of NSC documents the weekend of November 22, 1986, by North and his secretary, Fawn Hall, prompted Durenberger to request that White House documents be saved. The Intelligence chairman, however, was unaware at the time that a more serious cover-up had been conducted, one aimed at concealing the diversion of some Iran arms sales proceeds to assist the contras—military aid that had been banned by legislation. Attorney General Edwin Meese III, who was instructed by Reagan to investigate the Iran arms sale affair, was soon criticized for not securing all documents immediately after his inquiry had turned up evidence of the diversion to the contras of arms sale proceeds, a discovery made public November 25. *(Meese testimony, p. 134)*

Director of the Central Intelligence Agency (CIA), William J. Casey, and State and Defense department officials gave closed-door testimony before the Senate Intelligence Committee November 21. Panel members said at the time the officials—including Richard H. Armacost, under secretary of state; Richard W. Murphy, assistant secretary of state for Near Eastern affairs; and Richard L. Armitage, assistant secretary of defense—had not been able to answer all questions, particularly about Israel's role in the initial shipments of U.S.-made arms to Iran in 1985. (Stories of the Israeli shipments had been circulating. When questioned about it at his November 19 press conference, Reagan denied that any "third country" was involved but immediately revoked that statement.)

After testifying December 10 and 11 before House Intelligence and Foreign Affairs committees, where he admitted to CIA errors of judgment, Casey was scheduled to return to Senate Intelligence on December 16. But a cerebral seizure hospitalized him December 15, and he was unable to testify further. Casey stepped down from the CIA post February 2, 1987, and died May 6. He was succeeded by FBI director William H. Webster. *(CIA, box, p. 28)*

Cabinet members testifying were Secretary of State Shultz, Secretary of Defense Weinberger, and Attorney General Meese. Shultz and Weinberger had participated in early discussions of the Iran plan, but both said they had disapproved of selling arms and negotiating with terrorists.

Intelligence Leak Spurs New Rules

The admission of Sen. Patrick J. Leahy, D-Vt., that he violated Senate Select Intelligence Committee rules by giving a reporter access to a draft report on the Iran-contra affair raised questions about congressional access to covert operations. Leahy had resigned from the panel in January 1987, soon after the leak.

The draft document contained no classified information, but the committee had voted not to release it.

Leahy's disclosure came on July 28, 1987, five days after leaders of the Intelligence panel used the occasion of Senate debate over a routine intelligence agencies authorization measure to publicize more stringent rules to govern the handling of secret information by committee members.

If the select committees investigating the Iran-contra affair were to recommend increased congressional access to information about covert operations in their final reports, both Leahy's rueful acknowledgment and the Senate committee's new, tougher rules likely would figure in the debate over tightening intelligence information.

Both events came in the wake of claims by two former White House aides, Lt. Col. Oliver L. North and Rear Adm. John M. Poindexter, that their earlier efforts to mislead congressional committees—including the Senate and House Intelligence panels—were justified by the risk that secret information would be leaked.

During a joint hearing of the Senate and House Iran-contra committees July 29, Rep. Dick Cheney, R-Wyo., cited Leahy's statement as proof that "there was legitimate cause for concern that Congress could not keep a secret, and a lot of evidence that ... various members of Congress had in fact been responsible for sensitive leaks."

In response, William S. Cohen, R-Maine, vice chairman of the Senate Intelligence Committee and a member of the Senate Iran-contra committee, declared that Leahy's resignation had been "a very strong signal" that the Intelligence Committee would not tolerate unauthorized disclosures and that the administration could have confidence that the Intelligence panels would keep secrets.

How NBC Got Its Scoop

The document, which an NBC television correspondent obtained from Leahy early in January 1987, was a draft preliminary report on the Iran-contra matter compiled the previous December by the Intelligence Committee staff. At that time, the Republican control of the Senate—and thus of the Intelligence panel—was in its final weeks.

Democrats on the committee complained that the report was incomplete and contained inaccuracies. On January 5, with Democrats newly ensconced as the majority, the panel voted not to release the document.

The White House then charged that the Democrats were suppressing the report because it found no direct evidence that President Reagan had been aware that Iran arms sales money had been diverted to contra guerrillas fighting Nicaragua's leftist government.

According to Leahy's July 28 statement, he allowed a reporter to look at part of the draft "to show that it was being held up because there were major gaps and other problems with it, and not because of a desire to embarrass the president."

Information from the committee report was revealed and a copy of the document displayed in an NBC newscast on January 11. Two days later Leahy resigned from the panel, months before he would have been required to under Senate rules limiting a senator to eight years' service on the committee.

Secrets in the Senate

In releasing its report February 26, 1987, the three-member Tower Commission said Congress should consider a joint Intelligence panel in hopes of cutting down on leaks of classified information. But supporters of the existing two-committee system—established in the mid-1970s—countered that it worked well and that the Iran-contra affair demonstrated that the CIA and other intelligence agencies needed more, not less, supervision by Congress.

Nonetheless, when David L. Boren, D-Okla., became chairman of the Intelligence Committee and Cohen its vice chairman in January 1987, new rules were adopted that sharply restricted members' ability to remove from the committee's offices any documents containing secret information:

● Secret documents, which previously could be taken by a member to his office for study, henceforth had to be read in the committee offices.

● Notes taken by a member during secret briefings would have to be filed in the committee offices where they could be reviewed only by their author.

In addition, Boren and Cohen emphasized repeatedly that they would seek the resignation from the committee of any member found to have leaked classified information.

"We have changed the way in which the Senate does business in that committee," Cohen said during debate on the intelligence bill in July. Boren seconded Cohen's argument, adding that the committee staff had been more tightly "compartmentalized," so that any staff member would have only information he needed to know for a specific purpose.

Subsequently, they said, both had been bypassed in the Iran arms deal, although Weinberger had approved the transfer of weapons from defense stocks to the CIA. Meese described what he had learned from his inquiry of late November. Further details of that inquiry were revealed in his testimony before the House and Senate select investigating committees. *(Box, p. 136)*

White House chief of staff Donald T. Regan testified in closed sessions of the Senate and House Intelligence committees, using White House records of the president's meetings to support his contention that Reagan lacked knowledge of and did not approve critical decisions.

From the NSC staff, Howard J. Teicher, and Lt. Col. Robert L. Earl refused to testify, though Teicher did answer questions the second time he was called. Earl, invoking the Sixth Amendment right to counsel, cited as his reason the delay in getting security clearance for private representation.

Robert C. McFarlane, Poindexter's predecessor as national security adviser, was the most forthcoming of the important witnesses. He testified before the Senate Intelligence Committee twice, December 1 and 18, and also appeared at House Intelligence and Foreign Affairs hearings. Before his December 1985 departure from the NSC post, McFarlane had been involved in the opening to Iran leading up to the first arms shipment in August 1985 and had traveled to Tehran in May 1986, a trip on which he first learned of the contra diversion from North. *(Testimony, p. 91)*

Private individuals who appeared before Senate Intelligence were consultants Robert W. Owen, North's liaison with the contras; retired Air Force major general Richard V. Secord, a central figure in both the private contra aid network and the Iranian arms sales; retired Air Force colonel Robert C. Dutton, an assistant to Secord in the contra aid network; and Michael Ledeen, an NSC consultant who played a major role in discussions with Israel on the Iran initiative. All but Ledeen, who had been an intermediary between the NSC and the Israelis, took the Fifth Amendment. Roy M. Furmark, a New York businessman and friend of Casey, testified in December 1986 before both Intelligence panels. Casey had said it was Furmark who tipped him off to the possible contra diversion.

Release of Report Debated

Partisan differences over the Iran scandal surfaced in early January 1987 on the question of whether to make public the draft report written by Intelligence Committee staffers. With the White House lobbying for release in the hope that it would vindicate the president's assertions that he had not been aware of the diversion scheme, Republicans on the committee urged publication. But they were outvoted 7-6 by the new Democratic majority, joined by Republican William S. Cohen of Maine, who became vice chairman of the committee and a member of the Senate Iran-contra panel.

Democrats also protested the opportunity given to the White House to review the original staff report. Sen. Lloyd Bentsen, D-Texas, pointed out that "the agencies being investigated had the right to edit the report and in fact did so." The White House had requested deletions of material on Israel's involvement for "diplomatic reasons."

Durenberger touched off a dispute after it was revealed in mid-January that he had briefed Reagan and his top aides in mid-December, while he was still chairman of the Intelligence panel, on the contents of the unreleased committee report. Durenberger said that White House officials requested the December 19 briefing at the same time that Reagan and his aides were pressing the panel to make public its conclusions. The committee decided a day earlier not to provide the White House with a written report, but Durenberger said there was a "consensus" in favor of a more informal discussion about it with Reagan. White House spokesman Larry Speakes gave a different account of the briefing: Durenberger had offered to come to the White House with ranking committee Democrat Leahy. Leahy, however, said he was not aware of Durenberger's briefing until he and other panel members were informed about it the week of January 19. Durenberger said he discussed the "general scope" of the report during his forty-five-minute session with Reagan and a longer meeting with Vice President George Bush on December 20.

The visits, on which Durenberger was accompanied by committee staff director Bernard McMahon, came a few days before Reagan December 23 requested a committee report so he could declassify information (an executive branch function) and make public the panel's findings.

A spokesman for the panel replied that the committee itself was considering releasing a report. Cohen and Daniel Patrick Moynihan, D-N.Y., said that the Senate Intelligence hearings for the most part could have been open because they had provided very little information that would impinge on national security.

"The President ordered this whole operation on Iran," commented Leahy. "He ordered his administration not to tell the Intelligence committees what he was doing. Now he wants the Intelligence Committee to tell him what his administration was doing during the time they were under orders not to tell the Intelligence Committee."

Portions of Report Leaked

A few days after the committee voted not to release the report, portions were leaked by White House and congressional sources to the news media. Several months later, on July 28, 1987, Leahy revealed that he was the source of the leak to NBC News. Leahy resigned his membership on the Senate Intelligence Committee soon after the leak. Durenberger said the report NBC obtained January 8 was a "rough, earlier draft." Chairman Boren said it was "not even a full summary" of the panel's work and that testimony of twelve of thirty-six witnesses had not been transcribed by that time.

The day after the NBC leak, the White House released two principal documents cited in the Senate staff report. The first was Reagan's January 17, 1986, "finding," an official document that authorized U.S. arms sales to Iran. The second was a companion background memo to Reagan prepared by North that linked future arms shipments to Iran with the release of all U.S. hostages held by pro-Iran terrorists in Lebanon. Although the memo justified the sales as helping to strengthen moderate elements in Iran, clearly freeing the hostages appeared to be the more compelling reason for the operation. (Although the memo suggested that future shipments would halt if hostages were not freed, arms deliveries continued through 1986 even though only two of the four hostages were released and three others were taken captive.) *(Texts, pp. D-20, D-21)*

The *New York Times* January 19 published another portion of the draft Senate report that presented conclusions condemning the administration's handling of the Iran arms sales. A Senate Intelligence Committee spokesman called the *Times'* action "irresponsible" and said some information in the account was incorrect.

As reported by the *Times,* the committee faulted Casey for his November 21, 1986, testimony, which "contained several misleading statements and omitted certain significant points." The report said Casey failed to tell the committee that Reagan's crucial January 17, 1986, finding authorizing Iranian arms sales was prepared in a "unique procedure" because key cabinet aides were excluded from deliberations. Casey also failed to tell the committee about the possible diversion of funds, although he had been aware for more than a month that his aides had "significant concern" about aspects of the arms sales program. The report also pointed out "significant inaccuracies" in Reagan's public statements of November 13 and 19 about the amount of arms sold and the role of Israel. *(Reagan statements, pp. D-1, D-3)*

The report noted that administration officials were particularly reluctant to heed CIA misgivings about the key intermediary—Iranian arms dealer Manucher Ghorbanifar—misgivings that subsequently were forcefully reiterated in testimony released by the House and Senate Iran-contra committees. *(CIA officials testimony, p. 139)*

The staff concluded that the administration, in carrying out the Iran arms sales, violated or skirted several laws and its own foreign policy guidelines.

REPORT PAVES WAY FOR SELECT COMMITTEES

Ten days after the *New York Times* publication, the committee, reorganized under Chairman Boren, released the rewritten final report. It was addressed to Chairman Daniel K. Inouye, D-Hawaii, of the Senate Iran-contra committee and was intended to provide lines of inquiry for the Senate-House select committees' investigation. The letter of transmittal noted, "It was never the goal nor the mandate of the Intelligence Committee during this initial phase to conduct a definitive investigation"; rather, its purpose was to "gather as much information as possible while recollections were fresh and to collect in one place as many documents as possible." In an indirect allusion to the leaked staff version of its report, the committee said its principal purpose was to summarize information gathered in the hearings and that it "could not appropriately reach conclusions or findings because of [the] preliminary nature" of the investigation.

Report's Major Findings

U.S. dealings with Iran resulted from a convergence of four developments in late 1984 and early 1985, according to the report. They included:

David L. Boren, D-Okla., left, succeeded Dave Durenberger, R-Minn., right, as chairman of the Senate Intelligence Committee when the Democrats resumed control of the Senate in January 1987.

● Suggestions by midlevel U.S. officials that it was time to review policy toward Iran, in part to thwart possible Soviet designs on that country.

● A campaign by private Middle Eastern arms dealers to promote weapons trade between the United States and Iran.

● Israel's interest in improving ties with Iran, which had been engaged for several years in a fierce war with Iraq, one of Israel's most feared enemies.

● Washington's desire to free American hostages held in Lebanon by terrorists considered sympathetic to and influenced by the Khomeini regime in Iran.

Testimony noted in the report indicated that President Reagan had a "deep personal concern" for the welfare of the hostages, and the possibility that they could be released "was brought up repeatedly in conjunction" with the arms sales. Although Reagan's initial public statements on the affair cited freedom for the hostages as only one of many reasons for dealing with Iran, the report indicated the hostages were an overriding concern at the White House. After the release of the Tower Commission findings in late February 1987, the White House acknowledged the policy ultimately became an arms-for-hostages plan.

The committee also confirmed reports that, three times in 1986, the United States gave Iran intelligence information on Iraqi military positions. Not addressed by the panel were allegations, denied by the CIA, that the CIA had deliberately supplied inaccurate intelligence. The sharing of intelligence was first mentioned in the committee's account of a London meeting between North and Ghorbanifar in January 1986. The CIA gathered the information at North's request and, after agency officials objected to providing the intelligence directly to Iran, furnished it instead to the NSC.

The report cited several cases in which the White House bypassed regular channels—especially the State Department—in dealing with Iran. Early in 1985, then-national security adviser McFarlane asked NSC consultant Ledeen to discuss the issue of weapons sales to Iran with Israeli prime minister Shimon Peres. When Secretary of State Shultz later learned of the initiative, he protested. Nonetheless, the White House continued to conduct its own dealings with Iran, and Shultz eventually wrote himself out of the operation.

Arms Transactions

The United States was involved in the following arms shipments to Iran, according to the report:

● 508 U.S.-made TOW antitank missiles were sent from Israel to Iran via a third country during August and September 1985. The panel cited conflicting testimony from White House officials about whether Reagan knew about and authorized the shipment in advance or months later. Based on McFarlane's account, the report said, "Israel did not feel bound to clear each specific transaction with the U.S.," but "proceeded on the basis of a general authority from the President based on a U.S. commitment to replace their stocks." The report quoted Shultz, who opposed the deal, as saying that four American hostages were supposed to be released in Lebanon in exchange for the arms. But on September 15, only one hostage was freed—the Rev. Benjamin F. Weir. McFarlane said Reagan was "elated." Washington later provided Israel with replacement missiles.

● Eighteen Hawk antiaircraft missiles, shipped by a CIA proprietary airline from Israel to Iran in late November 1985. Iran rejected the missiles, saying the ones they received were obsolete.

Two key actors were involved in making arrangements for this shipment: NSC staff member North and major general Secord, whom North had recruited to assist him.

North asked the CIA to supply an aircraft for a shipment of "oil drilling equipment" for a "humanitarian mission." When CIA deputy director John N. McMahon learned of the extent of the agency's role in the affair, he instructed that the CIA no longer support the NSC operation "without a Presidential Finding authorizing covert action." According to Poindexter's later testimony before the House and Senate Iran-contra committees, the president signed a retroactive finding in December authorizing CIA participation in the transfer. A finding authorizing continuation of the Iran initiative was signed by the president on January 17, 1986. Reagan ordered the CIA not to inform Congress about the operation.

● 1,000 TOW missiles, shipped by the CIA to Israel in February and then transferred in two deliveries to Iran. One plane picked up and returned to Israel Hawk missiles that Iran had rejected earlier. However, the transfer did not result in release of American hostages.

Meanwhile, North had begun to use an existing CIA Swiss bank account to finance the arms sales. He gave Secord authority to control the account and to arrange for CIA reimbursement of Defense Department costs for the weapons.

● A small quantity of spare parts for Hawk missiles, delivered to Tehran on a plane carrying a diplomatic delegation headed by McFarlane. The purpose of the May 25-28, 1986, mission was to establish high-level contacts between Iran and the United States, with the intention that they would result in the release of all American hostages held by pro-Iranian terrorists in Lebanon. McFarlane was able to meet with only midlevel officials, however, and no hostages were freed. Reagan had approved the trip and the arms delivery on May 15. (*McFarlane testimony, p. 91*)

● Additional Hawk spare parts, delivered to Iran on August 3, 1986. One hostage, the Rev. Lawrence Jenco, had been released in Lebanon on July 29—possibly as an Iranian signal of renewed interest in continuing the relationship with the United States.

In July and August the United States began developing a second channel of communication with Iran, through Albert Hakim, an Iranian-American in business with Secord. An advantage of developing this second channel was to reduce the role of Ghorbanifar. CIA analysts and others increasingly questioned his personal reliability and influence with highly placed Iranians.

● 500 TOW missiles, shipped from Israel to Iran in late October 1986. The United States reimbursed Israel for the missiles in early November. David P. Jacobsen, an American hostage, was released from Lebanon November 2. The next day a Lebanese magazine brought into the public arena the fact that the United States had been shipping weapons to Iran.

U.S. officials continued clandestine meetings with Iranians even after the arms dealings made headlines. In November 1986, a U.S. team led by North met with Iranian contacts and presented a Bible inscribed by Reagan. Representatives of the State Department and the CIA also met with Iranians in December; but the State Department official left the meeting when the Iranians demanded additional arms sales.

Contra Diversion

In its section dealing with the alleged diversion of Iran arms sale profits to the Nicaraguan contras, the Senate report did not include any direct evidence that Reagan was aware of the diversion plan. Reagan and his aides repeatedly had insisted that the president did not know of that activity.

When Attorney General Meese informed President Reagan and his chief of staff, Regan, on November 24, 1986, that the Justice Department had discovered the diversion scheme, "Meese said the president looked shocked and very surprised, as did Regan, who uttered an expletive," according to the report.

While it failed to resolve several outstanding questions about the contra funding, the Senate Intelligence Committee discussed in considerable detail its findings on the origins of the diversion, some of the key officials involved, and how it was carried out.

The committee traced a "direct connection" between the Iran weapons sales and contra funding to discussions in January 1986 between North and Amiram Nir, Israel's specialist in antiterrorism. According to the committee's report, notes from a November 1986 meeting between North and Meese indicated that Nir proposed using profits from the Iran arms sales to aid the contras. But Meese also testified that he was uncertain whether it was North or Nir who first suggested that proposal. (North subsequently told the House and Senate Iran-contra committees that Nir had suggested using the profits for other unrelated activities, but that it was Ghorbanifar who had suggested diverting funds to the contras.) The report said North told Meese that, soon after his meeting with Nir, he contacted a principal contra leader, Adolfo Calero. Shortly thereafter, three bank accounts were opened in Switzerland to facilitate the transaction of arms sale proceeds to the Nicaraguan rebels.

North gave the account numbers to the Israelis, who then deposited "residuals" from the arms sales, according to the Senate committee's account of Meese's interview with North. "North guessed the money got to the contras; they knew money came and were appreciative," said the report.

Israeli officials denied suggesting the contra diversion and insisted they only passed the money from the weapons sales into bank accounts at the request of their American contacts. At the same time, Israeli officials continued to press for arms sales whenever U.S. enthusiasm seemed to be waning. *(Israeli vs. North Account, box, p. 141)*

According to the report, Hakim, while acting as an interpreter between the Americans and Iranians at an early 1986 meeting on arms sales, proposed that the Iranians indirectly contribute to the contras by paying for overpriced merchandise. The account of Hakim's activities came from notes of a November meeting between Assistant Attorney General Charles J. Cooper and Thomas C. Green, a lawyer representing at that time both North and Secord. Green, according to Cooper's notes, said money from arms shipments in February and May 1986 was routed to the contras through Israel's and Hakim's financial networks. Green said Hakim and Secord "felt like they were doing the Lord's work. They believed they were not violating any laws."

The Diversion Memorandum

A White House memorandum drafted on or shortly after April 4, 1986, outlined the Iran arms program and its link to funding the contras. According to the report, a section of the memo said $12 million from the weapons sales would be used to buy for the contras "critically needed supplies." At the bottom of one page of the memo was a recommendation that presidential approval be obtained for portions of the plan dealing with Iran that did not include diverting money to the contras. The Intelligence panel's report noted that the memo was not signed "and it is not clear to the committee who, if anyone, saw it."

Meese confronted North with the memo, after Justice Department officials discovered it in NSC files in November 1986. Meese told the committee that North confirmed the memo's contents and was "surprised and visibly shaken." According to notes from Meese's inquiry, North said he had not discussed the matter with Reagan. North also told Meese that he would have had a record showing the president's approval if one had been given. (In later testimony, North said it was an oversight that he had not destroyed that memo, as he had countless others.)

The report said that North told Meese he had informed McFarlane about the contra diversion in April or May 1986. According to Meese, North said that the only three people who could have known about the scheme were himself, McFarlane, and Poindexter.

McFarlane told the Intelligence Committee that he learned about the contra diversion when he and North were returning from their unsuccessful mission to Tehran in May 1986.

When McFarlane asked North in November who had approved the contra program, the report said, "North responded that he would never do anything without it being approved by higher authority and that he could not account for who was involved beyond Poindexter." The report did not clarify exactly when North informed Poindexter of the contra program. Meese said Poindexter told him on November 24 that North had given his superior "enough hints" to let him know about the diversion, but that Poindexter "didn't inquire further" into the matter.

Additional Contra Connections

The Senate Intelligence Committee report included these other revelations about the diversion of funds to the contras:

● Evidence that a Swiss bank account suspected of being used by North, Hakim, and Secord to funnel Iranian funds to the contras was also used for U.S.-solicited contributions to the contras from other countries.

● Details about an offer in September 1986 by Israel to ship captured Soviet weapons to the contras. Poindexter briefed Reagan on the offer before the president met at the White House on September 15 with Israeli prime minister Peres. Regan said the president never told him what was discussed in private conversations with Peres and that the shipment of Soviet arms did not come up in an open White House meeting.

● Suspicions by CIA officials in September 1986 about the possible diversion of Iranian funds to the contras. There was evidence that the matter was brought to the attention of CIA director Casey in early October by CIA analysts.

The report also recounted an October 9 meeting involving Casey, North, and CIA deputy director Robert M. Gates at which North "made very cryptic references" to Swiss bank accounts and money for the contras, according to Gates's testimony before the committee. When Casey and Gates pressed North on CIA involvement in the diversion, North assured them that the agency was "completely clean," Gates said.

● Information (as of that time unconfirmed) showing Iranian funds intended for the contras were deposited into accounts in Crédit Fiducière Services, a Swiss bank. The bank then allegedly transferred money to its subsidiaries in Grand Cayman, which disbursed it to the contras.

Tower Commission

In the wake of a damaging report by a three-member special review commission appointed to investigate the Iran-contra affair, President Ronald Reagan pledged February 26, 1987, to do "whatever is necessary" to put his administration back on track. The commission said Reagan had lost control of his staff, which mismanaged a policy of arms sales to Iran and might have allowed funds from those sales to be diverted to the contra rebels in Nicaragua.

"I believe that the president was poorly advised and poorly served," said John Tower, chairman of the review board. "I think that he should have followed up more and monitored this operation more closely. I think he was not aware of a lot of the things that were going on and the way the operation was structured and who was involved in it. He very clearly didn't understand all that."

Although he had been warned to expect a harsh report, Reagan seemed taken aback by the depth of the criticism voiced by the three-member commission. Introducing the Tower panel at a crowded news conference minutes after its members had finished briefing him, Reagan appeared grim and shaken. The president read his brief remarks from a file card, referred reporters to the commission members, and departed.

Political advisers, summoned to the White House three days before the report was released, told the president that he had to act quickly and decisively to deal with the criticism of his administration and demonstrate that he was in charge.

When Reagan received the Tower report and introduced the commission to the press on Thursday, February 26, he promised to read the report that weekend and to respond further in an address to the nation the following week. The televised speech was given March 4. *(Reagan response, see below, p. 79; text of press conference, p. D-46)*

The president's chief spokesman, Marlin Fitzwater, said February 27 that Reagan was "rightfully angry at the mismanagement described in this report and he intends to make changes as soon as possible." Fitzwater said Reagan had not acted sooner—in spite of nearly four months of negative publicity about the arms deals—because he was waiting for the Tower panel to provide a "full accounting" of what went wrong.

As his first act in response to the Tower report, Reagan on February 27 replaced Chief of Staff Donald T. Regan, who had been sharply criticized by the Tower panel, and selected former Senate majority leader Howard H. Baker, Jr., to fill the post. Baker, a widely respected moderate and a popular choice, was expected to shore up Reagan's sagging relations with Capitol Hill.

Commission at Work

Reagan appointed the board November 26, 1986, the day after the administration announced that funds from the arms sales had been diverted. The purpose of the board was to conduct a "comprehensive review" of National Security Council (NSC) operations. Tower, a former senator, was joined on the commission by former senator and secretary of state Edmund S. Muskie and retired lieutenant general Brent Scowcroft, a former national security adviser. *(Commission Members, box, p. 72)*

The president's executive order 12575 of December 1, 1986, asked the board to investigate "the future role and procedures" of the NSC staff in "the development, coordination, oversight, and conduct of foreign and national security policy"; to review its "proper role" in operations; and to make recommendations on the NSC's implementation of policy. *(Text of executive order, p. D-15)*

Although executive departments and agencies were required to provide information to the commission, the investigation was somewhat hindered by limits to the commission's authority. Unable to subpoena documents or compel testimony, the commission had to depend on the departments to extract from their own files the documents they considered relevant. Several principal players in the Iran arms deal and in contra support operations declined to be interviewed. The independent counsel investigating the Iran-contra affair, Lawrence E. Walsh, and the FBI refused to contribute to the investigation. The Israeli government, which played a key role in the Iran initiative, first denied access to individuals, then, after agreeing to respond in writing, failed to do so.

However, the commission did interview eighty people, including the president on two occasions in 1987—January 26 and February 11. Notes from the president's diary, as well as from the NSC's files and computer system, were supplied. Others heard from were former presidents and vice presidents, secretaries of state, NSC advisers and members, and officials of the Central Intelligence Agency (CIA) and Joint Chiefs of Staff.

Given a sixty-day life span, the commission deter-

mined that the time constraint precluded a field investigation. The original deadline for issuing the report was January 29, 1987, but two extensions were requested—until February 19 and February 26—because the board acquired "new material," according to Herbert Hetu, spokesman for the review board.

Once written, the Tower report was declassified by experts from the Departments of State and Defense, CIA, National Security Agency, and NSC before it was released to the public.

Commission Findings

Taken as a whole, the Tower report described three foundations for the policy disaster known as the Iran-contra affair: Reagan's hands-off management style, the failure of his aides to compensate for the president's lack of attention to detail, and the willingness of White House staffers to sidestep the institutional process for making and carrying out decisions.

The panel squarely placed much of the blame on Reagan, saying he made little effort to find out what his staff was doing and allowed his compassion for the American hostages in Lebanon to override his stated policy of not dealing with terrorists. During most of the Iranian arms operation, the board said, Reagan knew few details and expressed little interest in actions taken in his name. "The president simply was not told the details of what was going on, and did not ask the kinds of forcing questions which would have brought many of these issues to the surface," Scowcroft said.

Reagan's principal failure, the board said, was that he did not demand that his staff—especially aides to the National Security Council—follow normal procedures. Reagan "should have ensured that the NSC system did not fail him," the report said. Instead, "he did not force his policy to undergo the most critical review of which the NSC participants and the process were capable. At no time did he insist upon accountability and performance review."

The Tower report contained a wealth of detail on how the Reagan administration made and implemented its Iran and contra policies. Drawing on interviews with most of the key participants and previously secret internal computer memos, the report provided virtually a day-by-day account of the arms sales and NSC aide Lt. Col. Oliver L. North's activities in support of the contras. *(See What Happened chapter, p. 43)*

The Initiative and the Diversion

Appointed to probe the operations of the NSC and its staff, the three members interpreted their mandate broadly, reviewing a wide range of actions by the administration. Among the most important, the panel looked at secret White House actions supporting the contras during a period when official U.S. aid to them was prohibited by law.

On the Iranian arms sales issue, the report found that a policy originally intended to improve relations with the radical government in Tehran quickly evolved into a series of arms swaps for hostages, largely because of Reagan's passionate concern about the hostages. Opening ties to Iran "may have been in the national interest," the panel said, but the United States "should never have become a party to the arms transfers" that were first suggested by Israel. The board did not blame Israel for inducing the United

---

Commission Members

On November 26, 1986, President Reagan named a distinguished three-member Special Review Board to study the role of the National Security Council (NSC) staff.

John Tower, chairman of the review board, served in the Senate (R-Texas) from 1961 to 1985. He first was elected to fill the vacancy created when Lyndon B. Johnson became vice president. While Tower was chairman of the Senate Armed Services Committee, committee staff included Robert C. McFarlane and Alton G. Keel, Jr., who later would become part of Reagan's NSC staff. Before becoming a U.S. senator, Tower taught at Midwestern State University in Texas. Smart and abrasive, he favored a hard-line policy toward the Soviet Union and supported Reagan's military buildup. He sharply criticized Congress for imposing excessive limitations on the president's freedom to conduct foreign policy. Until early 1986 Tower was a U.S. negotiator on long-range missiles at the Geneva arms talks.

Edmund S. Muskie became secretary of state in the Carter administration after Cyrus Vance resigned in April 1980 in protest against the abortive attempt to rescue Americans held hostage in Iran. Muskie served as a Democratic senator from Maine from 1959 to 1980. He was the first chairman of the Senate Budget Committee. Widely respected among Washington Democrats, he was the Democratic party's candidate for vice president in 1968 and a candidate for the party's presidential nomination in 1972.

Brent Scowcroft, a retired Air Force lieutenant general, succeeded Henry A. Kissinger as President Gerald R. Ford's national security adviser. Scowcroft had served as deputy to Kissinger during the Ford and Nixon administrations. A graduate of West Point, Scowcroft earned a Ph.D. in international relations from Columbia University. At the time of his appointment to the review board, Scowcroft was associated with Kissinger in an international consulting firm and had become a central figure in Washington's foreign policy establishment. He had been a key member of private and official study groups, including a 1983 presidential commission that recommended deployment of MX missiles and development of a complementary small missile.

The Tower Commission released its report on the Iran-contra affair February 26, 1987. Commission members, seated from left, were Edmund S. Muskie, Chairman John Tower, and Brent Scowcroft.

States into arms deals with Iran, but it did note that Israeli officials repeatedly provided rationales and encouragement.

The panel was unable to resolve fully one of the major mysteries in the entire Iran affair: When did Reagan first approve an Israeli shipment of U.S.-made arms to Iran? The president's aides disagreed about whether he gave the legally necessary approval before or after the first shipments in August and September 1985—or whether he had approved only replenishment of Israel's stocks of the weapons shipped to Iran. The testimony of Regan and former national security adviser Robert C. McFarlane differed on this point, and Reagan himself provided different versions in two interviews and one letter to the Tower Commission. In his letter, dated February 20, 1987, Reagan said he simply could not remember when he acted. Given those conflicts, the board chose to believe that Reagan probably approved the shipment in advance. *(Disputed August 1985 Decision, box, p. 75)*

The Tower report said there was "considerable evidence" that profits from the Iran arms sales were diverted to the Nicaraguan contras, although the commission did not obtain any hard proof. In addition, the report did not find any evidence that Reagan himself knew of the diversion—a point that White House aides had been emphasizing since the diversion was revealed in November 1986.

The report suggested that North, McFarlane, and national security adviser Vice Adm. John M. Poindexter might have lied to Congress about the private contra supply operation to mask possible violations of congressional proscriptions on aiding the rebels. Reagan apparently was not aware of the clandestine contra supply network, ac-

cording to the Tower board, although he met occasionally with individuals who were privately assisting the contras.

Key Recommendations

The Tower panel produced no major recommendations for legal or institutional changes, but its members said Reagan's administration and future ones should adhere to existing structures and procedures instead of creating ad hoc means of carrying out foreign policy.

The panel opposed several oft-recommended changes, such as requiring Senate confirmation of the national security adviser and barring the NSC staff from engaging in policy operations. Instead, it said the White House staff should be more responsive to congressional concerns, and the president should assign operational duties to his NSC staff only in highly unusual cases.

In using the existing system, the board said, the administration should carefully consider policies and their consequences before they are implemented, involve all the relevant agencies and experts in the government, review policies periodically to make sure they are working as intended, and limit the use of private individuals to carry out government policy.

One of the board's recommendations—that of merging the House and Senate Intelligence committees into a joint panel—in the past had encountered opposition on Capitol Hill. Supporters of the existing two-committee system countered that it worked well and that the Iran-contra affair demonstrated that the CIA and other intelligence agencies needed more—not less—supervision from Congress. *(Joint intelligence panel, box, p. 77)*

ESTABLISHED CHANNELS WERE 'LARGELY IGNORED'

In examining what went wrong in the Iran-contra affair, the Tower Commission discovered that essentially the bureaucracy was not given a chance to work.

The commission said in its report that White House aides who promoted the Iran arms dealings "largely ignored" established channels, handling the sales "almost casually and through informal channels." As a result, the panel said, President Reagan was cut off from advice from his appointees and from career specialists who could have highlighted the pitfalls that made swapping arms for hostages a foreordained disaster.

The review board's report contained a classic political science lesson: Presidents should subject their policy initiatives to systematic scrutiny, both by their politically appointed advisers and by career national security bureaucrats. That prescription conflicted with a conviction held by the New Right activists who made up Reagan's core constituency. In their view, the national security bureaucracies—the State Department, the intelligence agencies, and the senior military—were not tough enough in dealing with the Soviet Union and its allies.

The conservative activists pinned their hopes on dedicated and like-minded aides, who, free of routine bureaucratic constraints, could make bold global policy strokes. To many of these activists, North was the ideal agent of presidential initiatives.

But in their report, Tower and his fellow commission members firmly rejected such free-lancing. They emphasized instead the value of systematic consultation. "Using the process will not always produce brilliant ideas. But history suggests it can at least help prevent bad ideas from becoming presidential policy," they said.

There was plenty of responsibility to go around, the Tower group concluded. Some of the blame fell on Reagan, who did not involve himself in the details of policy and did not press his staff to evaluate the arms sales. But neither did his aides go out of their way to impress on Reagan the policy's risks. "The people in the system have a fundamental responsibility to keep the president aware and to keep under his sight the pitfalls of every policy that he wants to pursue," Scowcroft said February 26, 1987.

But by the same token, the review panel opposed any changes in the law governing the president's adviser for national security policy, the NSC, or its staff. "The problem at heart was one of people, not process," Scowcroft said. "It was not that the structure was faulty. It is that the structure was not used."

The Tower group's criticism of Reagan's Iran policy mirrored widespread criticism of two other key Reagan national security moves: his 1983 inauguration of the strategic defense initiative to develop a nationwide antimissile defense and his offer during the October 1986 Iceland meeting with Soviet leader Mikhail S. Gorbachev to dismantle all ballistic missiles. In those cases, too, critics on Capitol Hill and elsewhere charged that Reagan had plunged impulsively into radically new and risky policies without seeking the advice of senior political appointees or agency specialists.

Significant change had come to Reagan's NSC since the November 1986 revelations about the Iran-contra dealings. Vice Admiral Poindexter, who as Reagan's assistant for national security affairs had managed the NSC staff, resigned November 25. He was succeeded January 2, 1987, by Frank C. Carlucci, a veteran national security official with a reputation for straightening out bureaucratic foulups, a demonstrated nonpartisanship, and a strong command of management skills. Within days of taking over, Carlucci replaced several senior members of the NSC staff, banned conduct of covert operations by NSC staff members, and disbanded the staff's political-military section, through which North and other staffers had managed the Iranian arms deal.

Sen. David L. Boren, D-Okla., chairman of the Select Committee on Intelligence, commented February 26, 1987, that the Tower report "paints a picture of a system running out of control without adequate supervision by the president and the constitutional officers of our government." But he added that Carlucci's measures to bring the NSC "back within the limits of its original purposes, are welcome steps in the right direction."

Organizing to Advise

The basic problem in organizing a president's national security advisers, the Tower panel said, is balancing presidential innovation and bureaucratic caution. "The departments and agencies . . . tend to resist policy change," the report said. "Each has its own perspective based on long experience. The challenge for the president is to bring his perspective to bear on these bureaucracies, for they are his instruments . . . and he must work through them."

Echoing a generation of academic studies of how national security policy is made, the Tower Commission described the NSC as a marketplace of contending points of view. It should be the principal forum in which the president hears his advisers debate the merits of alternative policies, with an eye toward making up his own mind.

The council's members are the president, vice president, and secretaries of state and defense. The directors of central intelligence and of the Arms Control and Disarmament Agency are designated by law as "advisers" to the NSC, while most presidents routinely also have included the White House chief of staff and the chairman of the Joint Chiefs of Staff in NSC meetings.

Under the Tower panel's "marketplace" theory of NSC operations, a heavy burden falls on the president's assistant for national security affairs—the job held during the Iran arms affair by McFarlane and then Poindexter. The assistant should be "an honest broker," ensuring that the president's advisers fight for their respective points of view on a level playing field, the report said. "He assures that issues are clearly presented to the president; that all reasonable options, together with an analysis of their disadvantages and risks, are brought to his attention; and that the views of the president's other principal advisers are accurately conveyed."

But the assistant—aided by the NSC staff—also has other responsibilities, the Tower panel noted. He provides independent advice to the president, unhindered by the bureaucratic ties of the council members. He and the staff also monitor the way policies are carried out, ensuring that the president's intentions are fulfilled and that policies are reviewed so they do not become outdated. The assistant's role is particularly important in crises, when there is a premium on carrying out a president's wishes with speed,

Disputed August 1985 Decision

Exactly how the first shipment of arms from Israel to Iran was authorized, and by whom, was a matter of dispute, the Tower Commission found. On August 2, 1985, at a White House meeting with national security adviser Robert C. McFarlane, the director general of the Israeli foreign ministry, David Kimche, asked for the U.S. position on arms sales to Iran. McFarlane said Washington would not sell arms directly to Tehran, but he promised an answer on whether the United States would approve of Israeli sales. How he got that answer was "murky," the Tower report said.

The Tower board had testimony from McFarlane, Chief of Staff Donald T. Regan, Secretary of State George P. Shultz, and Secretary of Defense Caspar W. Weinberger on President Reagan's knowledge and reactions to the proposed arms transfers. Reagan himself gave the Tower board three versions. On January 26, 1987, he said he had approved the Israeli shipment sometime in August 1985 but could not recall the exact date. McFarlane had testified that Reagan had told him early in August that the United States should not sell arms to Iran, but that Israel could sell U.S.-made arms to Iran and could buy replacements from the United States.

On February 11, 1987, Reagan told the board that, after discussing the matter repeatedly with Regan, he could not recall giving advance approval in August for an Israeli arms shipment. Regan had testified to the Tower Commission that the president was surprised and "upset" in September 1985 when McFarlane told him Israel had sold arms to Iran in hopes of freeing the hostages. Regan also told the board that McFarlane had explained at the time that the Israelis had "simply taken it upon themselves to do this."

Told by aides that his testimony was inconsistent, Reagan wrote a letter to the Tower panel February 20, 1987, saying "In trying to recall events that happened eighteen months ago I'm afraid that I let myself be influenced by others' recollections, not my own.... I have no personal notes or records to help my recollection on this matter. The only honest answer is to state that try as I might, I cannot recall anything whatsoever about whether I approved an Israeli sale in advance or whether I approved replenishment of Israeli stocks around August of 1985. My answer therefore and the simple truth is, 'I don't remember—period.'"

Tower said, "Absent any evidence to the contrary, we have to conclude that the president's recollection of when the first shipment was approved was faulty." The board made a "plausible judgment," he added, that Reagan approved the shipment before it was made on August 30, 1985, as McFarlane had said.

---

precision, and secrecy.

Just as a president bears full responsibility for administration policies, he is free to decide how to organize and use the NSC, its staff, and the national security assistant in formulating policy, the review panel said. But it pointed out the dilemmas that any president faces in setting up his national security advisory system:

• The national security adviser has been immune to congressional interrogation and is not required to have Senate confirmation. The reasoning is that this aide should be beholden only to the president, so that the two can speak in confidence. But that arrangement could encounter opposition, the panel warned, if the president depends too heavily on his assistant to the exclusion of cabinet officers, who are subject to congressional oversight and who would be likely to reflect the institutional wisdom of the career bureaucracies they head.

• The assistant's role as manager of an administration's marketplace of policy ideas may be compromised if he becomes too vigorous an advocate for a particular point of view. "The president's access to the unedited views of the NSC principals may be impaired," the group warned.

• The more the assistant becomes the agent for carrying out presidential policy, the less able he will be to assess objectively how well the policy is being carried out and whether it is becoming outdated by events.

End-Running the System

The Tower Commission cited the Iran-contra arms dealings as a case study of the risks a president runs if he decides policy and carries it out through a small corps of advocates, without the systematic consultation of his principal national security advisers.

The president and his aides should have foreseen that the Iran arms transfer would arouse vehement public opposition. Moreover, funding for the Nicaraguan rebels had provoked years of intense political battles between Reagan and congressional opponents. Accordingly, the Tower panel said, "one would expect the decisions to undertake these activities would have been made only after intense and thorough consideration. In fact, a far different picture emerges." Neither policy was subjected to the administration's own routine procedures for interagency review or to the special procedures the president had set up in January 1985 for reviewing proposed covert operations.

According to the commission:

• The president was not given the benefit of hearing a thorough debate over the two policies. "At each significant step in the Iran initiative, deliberations among the NSC principals in the presence of the president should have been virtually automatic," the report said. "Two or three Cabinet-level reviews in a period of 17 months was not enough."

● Because of a concern for maintaining secrecy, the proposals were not thoroughly scrutinized by professionals in the relevant executive branch agencies. "This deprived those responsible for the [Iran] initiative of considerable expertise: on the situation in Iran; on the difficulties of dealing with terrorists; on the mechanics of conducting a diplomatic opening," the report said.

The Tower panel also complained that the president received no analysis by U.S. intelligence agencies of key aspects of the Iran dealings: Israel's initial proposal to transfer the arms, Israel's motivation in making the proposal, credibility questions about Iranian arms dealer Manucher Ghorbanifar or the other middlemen who purported to speak for the Tehran government, and the impact the proposed transfer would have on the military balance in the Middle East.

The only staff work on the proposed arms deal reviewed by the president was performed by NSC aides under the direction of the president's assistant, the review panel said. "These were, of course, the principal proponents of the initiative." The NSC staff work played down the risks involved in an arms transfer, ignored alternatives, and soft-pedaled the opposition of other members of the NSC.

● Decisions were made too informally for sound management. "Even when meetings among NSC principals did occur," the panel said, "often there was no prior notice of the agenda. No formal written minutes seem to have been kept. Decisions subsequently taken by the president were not formally recorded." As a result, the Tower Commission concluded, specific arms transfer proposals were considered "in a vacuum, without reference to the results of past proposals." If the administration had decided to carry out a top-to-bottom review of the policy afterward, the panel concluded, "it would have been extremely difficult to conduct."

Major Problems Ignored

Because of the shortcuts taken in considering the Iran and contra policies, the report contended, major problems were brushed aside:

● The Iran arms transfer was pursued regardless of severe internal contradictions between the goals of freeing U.S. hostages and opening long-term political ties with the Tehran government. For example, the Tower report said that to win the release of the hostages the United States would have had to exert influence with the pro-Iran group Hizballah, "which could involve the most radical elements of" the Tehran regime. The kind of strategic opening sought by the United States, however, involved what were regarded as more "moderate elements."

● Congress never was consulted on the arms sales, although consultation "could have been useful to the president, for it might have given him some sense of how the public would react to the initiative."

● Technical legal advice was not systematically sought on either policy, even though the laws governing each were highly complex. In the case of contra funding, the panel said, "the political cost to the president of illegal action by the NSC staff was particularly high, both because the NSC staff is the personal staff of the president and because of the history of serious conflict with the Congress over the issue of contra support." But the only legal advice obtained by the NSC staff on the contra issue came from the president's Intelligence Oversight Board, a three-member panel

intended to review intelligence failures. It was "an odd source," the Tower group said.

'Unprofessional' Approach

Because the Iran and contra policies were conducted by McFarlane, Poindexter, North, and other NSC staff members in isolation from the rest of the national security bureaucracy, the execution was "unprofessional," the Tower panel concluded. For example:

● In the Iran arms deal, North relied on "private intermediaries, businessmen and other financial brokers, and private operators and Iranians hostile to the United States. Some of these were individuals with questionable credentials and potentially large personal financial interests in the transactions." This invited kickbacks and payoffs and increased the risks that the news of the effort would leak, the review panel said.

● North used retired Air Force major general Richard V. Secord's network of associates in both the arms transfer and the contra funding efforts, risking the exposure of both if either one became public knowledge.

● Negotiations with Ghorbanifar and other Iranian middlemen "were handled in a way that revealed obvious inexperience," the review group said. "The discussions were too casual for dealing with intermediaries to a regime so hostile to U.S. interests. The U.S. hand was repeatedly tipped and unskillfully played."

● The arms transfer policy never was subjected to a searching review because of North's relative freedom of action. The president's assistant and the responsible officers on the NSC staff should have called for such a review, "but they were too involved with the initiative, both as advocates and as implementors," said the review panel.

Reagan's Management Style

The Tower Commission held Reagan responsible for the failure of his administration's policy-making process: "The NSC system will not work unless the president makes it work." All three members said that Reagan should have taken a more active role in managing his administration's national security policy. The panel concluded that the president "did not force his policy to undergo the most critical review of which the NSC participants and the process were capable.... The most powerful features of the NSC system—providing comprehensive analysis, alternatives and follow-up—were not utilized."

Given Reagan's management style of delegating to subordinates a great deal of responsibility for reviewing and carrying out policies, the panel said the White House staff had a special obligation to keep him informed.

"It was incumbent upon the other participants in the system to ensure that the president was absolutely clear about what was going on," Scowcroft said at the commission's press conference. "There should have been bells ringing, lights flashing and so on so that there was no question ... what the consequence of his pursuing this policy was." Instead, the commission painted a picture of administration aides obsessed with secrecy, running their own operations, and often hiding their doings from one another as well as from the president.

After the Tower report was released, Sen. Paul S. Trible, Jr., R-Va., a member of the select committee investigating the Iran-contra affair, told reporters he saw no need for Reagan to change his management style. "He has

Joint Intelligence Committee Proposal

Keeping secrets on Capitol Hill emerged as a fallout issue from the Iran-contra affair. With the backing of the Tower Commission, conservatives cited the Reagan administration's failures as justification for reviving a perennial idea that had not gained much ground before: merging the House and Senate Intelligence committees.

The Tower report recommended that Congress consider such a committee to reduce the number of leaks of classified information, thereby encouraging the executive branch to notify Congress of covert activities. A single committee with a smaller number of members and staffers "might tend to cure" presidents' obsession with leaks.

Critics of the idea countered that the administration was responsible for more leaks than Congress and that a joint committee would reduce congressional oversight of the intelligence agencies.

House and Senate Plans

Rep. Henry J. Hyde, R-Ill., the most persistent supporter of the single committee, introduced in 1987 a resolution calling for an eighteen-member committee. Each member would serve a maximum of six years. Of the nine members from each chamber, five would be appointed by the majority party and four by the minority party. The majority and minority leaders would serve as ex officio members.

A 1985 special Senate committee, chaired by Dan Quayle, R-Ind., suggested reforms in Senate rules, including a ten-member joint intelligence committee. Quayle, with cosponsors Minority Leader Robert Dole, R-Kan., and Bob Kasten, R-Wis., introduced legislation in the 100th Congress to set up such a panel. The plan would have five members from each chamber, three from the majority party and two from the minority. A House member would alternate in chairing the panel.

Authority and Jurisdiction Questions

The Tower Commission suggested that a joint panel be patterned after the old Joint Atomic Energy Committee, apparently the only joint committee of Congress ever to have permanent authority to report legislation. Under most proposals in 1987, a joint intelligence committee would handle legislation just as the Atomic Energy Committee did, by reporting identical bills simultaneously to the House and Senate. After each chamber had passed the legislation, Atomic Energy had acted as its own conference committee to resolve any differences. (The Joint Atomic Energy panel was abolished in 1977.)

One potential issue in the creation of a joint intelligence committee involved jurisdiction. The House Intelligence Committee had exclusive power over all intelligence programs, while the Senate committee shared jurisdiction with the Armed Services Committee. Hyde's proposal would have given a joint committee the exclusive jurisdiction of the House Intelligence Committee; Quayle's bill would have given the committee the more limited scope of the Senate Intelligence Committee.

Other Barriers to Change

There were other barriers to consolidating the intelligence committees. On the one hand, supporters of the existing two-committee system insisted the problem of Capitol Hill leaks was minor, pointing out that a study by the Senate Intelligence Committee in the first five months of 1986 found 147 newspaper articles divulging classified information; all but 12 cited administration rather than congressional sources. On the other hand, the Senate panel inaugurated new rules to prevent leaks after its January 1987 report on the Iran-contra affair was leaked.

Rep. Matthew F. McHugh, D-N.Y., argued that the existing system allowed members to learn how intelligence agencies really operated—a benefit for the agencies because it could "result in stronger support for the legitimate work of the intelligence community." The initial impact of a joint committee—reducing the number of members getting secret information—also presented the biggest political hurdle to its acceptance. In recent years, Senate and House members have stood in line to get on the intelligence committees. In 1986, for example, more than seventy members applied for seven slots.

Secrecy vs. Oversight

The proposal for a joint committee highlighted the tension between two principles with broad support in Congress and in the executive branch: protecting legitimate national security secrets and allowing Congress to review the budget and programs of intelligence agencies. Supporters of the existing system said it adequately balanced the conflict between secrecy and oversight, while critics insisted that oversight had interfered with keeping the secrets.

Events in the Iran-contra affair pointed out "that we did not have sufficient oversight," said Lee H. Hamilton, D-Ind., chairman of the House Iran-contra committee and former chairman of the House Intelligence Committee. The Tower Commission members, however, claimed that had the Reagan administration felt secure in disclosing the arms sale plan to Congress, congressional leaders might have been able to talk the administration out of it by pointing out political and policy flaws.

a sense of purpose, a core of deeply held values that animate all of his actions. He delegates substantial responsibility. That has worked well for six years," Trible said.

But Senate Armed Services Committee chairman Sam Nunn, D-Ga., contended that the Tower panel was too lenient on Reagan. If asked, Nunn said, he would have told Reagan: "'You've got to get involved enough to know what's going on in the broad sense. You've got to get involved enough to make sure you can at least referee the disputes between your own advisers.' . . . I'm not sure we can construct any group of people down there that can make up and compensate totally for that lack of presidential involvement in major matters."

Assigning Responsibility

The Tower panel faulted all Reagan's national security advisers for allowing the Iran arms transfer program to become settled policy as the result of such a casual review process: "None of the principals called for serious vetting [or review] of the initiative by even a restricted group of disinterested individuals. The intelligence questions do not appear to have been raised and the legal considerations, while raised, were not pressed. No one seems to have complained about the informality of the process. No one called for a thorough reexamination once the initiative did not meet expectations," the group concluded.

The panel criticized the following officials for particular derelictions of duty:

• Donald T. Regan, White House chief of staff, shared in the responsibility for the system's breakdown because he so vigorously asserted his personal control over the White House staff and attended "almost all the relevant meetings regarding the Iran initiative." He should have made contingency plans for the possibility that news of the arms transfer would leak. "He must bear primary responsibility for the chaos that descended upon the White House when such disclosure did occur."

• National security adviser John M. Poindexter was singled out for not exercising control over Lieutenant Colonel North in the Iran deal and the contra operations. Poindexter also "failed grievously" by either ignoring or not understanding the legal and political risks posed by the diversion of funds to the contras.

• CIA director William J. Casey also did not act on information about the contra diversion, which the board said he received a month before the activity became public. The panel also contended that Casey should have warned Reagan of the risk of letting North run the Iran arms operation, because the NSC staff was so close to the Oval Office. And it said Casey should have insisted on reviewing the assumptions embedded in the original Israeli arms transfer proposal and the credentials of Ghorbanifar and other Iranian intermediaries.

The panel also said that Casey should have kept pushing Reagan to consider notifying Congress about the arms transfer, since the CIA is the principal target of the law requiring that covert operations be reported.

• Defense Secretary Caspar W. Weinberger and Casey should have demanded a formal assessment of the effect on the Iran-Iraq military balance of providing arms and intelligence to Iran.

• Secretary of State George P. Shultz and Weinberger also were criticized for abdicating their responsibility to continue advising Reagan on the Iranian arms deal—which they opposed—and thereby remaining unsullied by the

policy. "They protected the record as to their own positions on this issue," the panel concluded. "They were not energetic in attempting to protect the president from the consequences of his personal commitment to freeing the hostages."

The Tower panel also produced evidence that White House officials attempted to cover up Reagan's role once the Iranian arms deals became public knowledge in November 1986. It cited testimony by McFarlane that he helped draft a chronology of events that tried to "blur" the president's approval of the arms sales.

Panel Recommendations

The Tower panel recommended that Reagan and future presidents accept the discipline of an orderly policy-making process that entails review of presidential initiatives by the government's career national security specialists. "It is through this process that the nation obtains both the best of the creativity of the president and the learning and expertise of the national security departments and agencies," the report said.

For the system to work, the commission said, the president's assistant for national security would have to ensure that issues and options were fully ventilated, including their legal implications and potential difficulties in implementing them. This would require him to keep NSC members informed of the president's thinking and to give them adequate notice of the agenda for NSC meetings.

Both the assistant and the other NSC principals should have direct access to the president, the panel recommended, but none of them should use private meetings with the president to circumvent the system of consultation. Moreover, it insisted, the assistant "should not use his proximity to the president to manipulate the process so as to produce his own position" as the chosen policy. Like the NSC staff, the assistant generally should not conduct policy, the panel recommended.

Members of the NSC staff should be drawn from across the agencies dealing with national security issues, with no one agency having a preponderant influence, the report said. As a rule, members should remain on the staff for no more than four years. The board also urged that the staff be organized hierarchically, with clear lines of control to thwart "energetic self-starters."

The review board recommended that the NSC staff be organized in a way that would foster institutional memory, either by creating a small permanent executive secretariat or by ensuring that staff members' tenures overlap. The panel also opposed three suggested changes in the NSC's charter:

• A ban on policy implementation by the NSC staff, partly because of the difficulty of defining "implementation."

• A cap on the size of the NSC staff, such as had been recommended by Senate Intelligence Committee chairman Boren. As with the ban on implementation, the review panel opposed legislation in this area that might be too rigid.

• A requirement that the Senate confirm the president's assistant for national security affairs.

The panel recommended that:

• The assistant to the president chair high-level interdepartmental committees to review issues within the NSC system.

• Presidents make rules "for restricted consideration of

covert action and that, once formulated, those procedures be strictly adhered to."

• Intelligence agencies and administration officials take care not to let officials' support for a policy bias intelligence estimates.

• The position of legal adviser to the NSC be upgraded. Carlucci said February 26, 1987, that he had named Paul S. Stevens as general counsel to the NSC with wide-ranging authority to attend any meetings and examine any issues.

• Congress consolidate the Senate and House Select Intelligence committees into a joint intelligence oversight committee. If administrations had to inform fewer members and staff aides of covert operations, they would have a harder time citing the risk of congressional leaks to justify refusal to inform Congress.

• Use of private individuals as diplomatic intermediaries be strictly limited and supervised. While opposing a flat ban on such "privatized" foreign policy initiatives, the review board warned that use of private and foreign sources gave those sources "powerful leverage in the form of demands for return favors or even blackmail."

HILL, WHITE HOUSE REACTION TO REPORT

For the most part, Capitol Hill reaction to the Tower report broke predictably along partisan lines. Most Republicans praised Reagan for having the "courage" to appoint

the Tower panel in the first place. "What we have here is a mistake, not a scandal," said Rep. Newt Gingrich, R-Ga. "If he [Reagan] has one mistake in six years, that's a pretty good track record."

Democrats used the report to bolster their longstanding claim that the president was dangerously "disengaged" from the making of policy. "This report shows that the president has been asleep at the switch," said Rep. Norman Y. Mineta, D-Calif. "He does not know what is going on at the highest levels of his own staff. He does not know who we are shipping arms to or why. He does not even remember what his own policies are."

The documented evidence in the Tower report led even some of Reagan's supporters to acknowledge that he, as well as his aides, had failed. "It does indicate that blunders were made of colossal proportions, and the president didn't adopt a hands-on approach toward the National Security Council," said Senate majority leader Robert Dole, R-Kan. William S. Cohen, R-Maine, vice chairman of the Senate Intelligence Committee, said the report "shows a situation [in] which the president conducted the office as if he were an absentee landlord, while the tenants were running around smashing the windows and breaking up the furniture."

Administration officials highlighted two findings that they said bolstered Reagan's previous statements. The board said it found no evidence that the president knew about or approved the alleged diversion of Iranian arms money to the contras or that he participated in any cover-up of wrongdoing.

Describing himself as a strong supporter of the president, Tower insisted to reporters that the Iran-contra affair was an "aberration" in an otherwise "pretty satisfactory" performance by the Reagan administration.

President Reagan confers with Howard H. Baker, Jr., who replaced Donald T. Regan as chief of staff.

Reagan critics, however, said the failures of the administration were more fundamental than a temporary mishap. They pointed to other blunders, among them the October 1986 summit meeting in Iceland during which Reagan suddenly agreed to a drastic proposal of nuclear disarmament, apparently with little consideration of the consequences and without consulting allies and key military aides. "I do not think it [the Iran-contra affair] was an aberration. I think it goes deeper than that," said Senator Nunn. "You can't have all these people running around town making foreign policy decisions on their own."

'Vigorous' Response Needed

There was wide agreement that Reagan could contain further damage to his presidency, and perhaps enhance prospects for his legislative agenda, by moving aggressively to deal with the management blunders pointed out by the Tower panel.

"One immediate step necessary is for the president to make it clear to everyone that his hand is firmly on the rudder, that he is in charge, that he is making the decisions and that there is a vigorous follow-up to ensure those decisions are being faithfully implemented," Dole said. Several members said that a politically astute staff at the White House would be especially needed while the independent counsel and special House and Senate committees pursued their investigations into the Iran-contra affair.

While the Tower report provided a wealth of new information about the Iran-contra affair, it did not affect plans by the House and Senate select Iran-contra committees to proceed with their inquiries. Several members of the Iran-contra panels applauded the Tower Commission's work but described the report as incomplete because it failed to resolve crucial questions stemming from the Iran initiative, particularly the mystery about what happened to money from the arms sales.

Dick Cheney of Wyoming, ranking Republican on the special House panel, said Reagan's response to the report would be "the test of how effective the last two years of his presidency will be."

The president had taken decisive action in December 1986, naming Carlucci as national security adviser and instructing him to revamp NSC procedures. The appointment of former FBI director William H. Webster to head the CIA had been another visible and positive step toward gaining firmer control of the national security apparatus.

New Chief of Staff

The departure of Chief of Staff Regan had been a major preoccupation in Washington. Republican leaders had begun calling for Regan's resignation early in December 1986, following the damaging revelation of the contra diversion. Both Reagan and his chief aide had resisted the demands, even when Nancy Reagan—reportedly the president's most influential adviser—joined the chorus. But the Tower report settled the issue. The report was harshly critical of Regan, whose "personal control over the White House staff" did not maintain "an orderly process" in carrying out policy. Regan resigned the day after the report was issued.

At a White House meeting that same day, four prominent Republicans urged Reagan to select a new staff chief who was familiar with Capitol Hill and could work with the Democratic leadership. Dole immediately said Baker would

fit that description. "Howard Baker has instant credibility," said Dole, Baker's successor as Senate Republican leader. Baker took over the top White House staff job March 2.

Reagan Speech

On March 4, 1987, Reagan delivered a major nationally televised address on the Iran-contra affair. At the heart of Reagan's twelve-minute speech were two statements, that he accepted "full responsibility" for his administration's actions, and that the United States did, in fact, trade arms to Iran for hostages. "As angry as I may be about activities undertaken without my knowledge, I am still accountable for those activities," the president said. *(Text of speech, p. D-81)*

In accepting responsibility, Reagan went no further than he already had in his January 27, 1987, State of the Union address. In that speech he said that he had taken "a risk" in dealing with Iran, that it had not worked, and "for that I assume full responsibility." In previous statements, Reagan had said "mistakes were made" but had never attributed any to himself. *(State of the Union address, p. D-22; December 6, 1986, radio address, p. D-18)*

The March 4 speech contained several indirect or passive references to mistakes but no clear-cut admissions of presidential error. As in the past, Reagan seemed to blame unnamed aides for most of the lapses in the Iran-contra affair. For example, he said inaccurate recordkeeping was at fault for his inability to remember just when he approved the first Israeli shipment of U.S.-made arms to Iran. And Reagan said he found the use of secret bank accounts "personally distasteful"—even though CIA and White House officials set up such accounts in Switzerland using the broad authority he granted them in writing on January 17, 1986.

The president acknowledged that the United States did swap arms for hostages. Recalling his earlier denials that weapons had been traded for hostages, Reagan said, "My heart and my best intentions still tell me that is true, but the facts and the evidence tell me it is not." The Tower report showed, he said, that "what began as a strategic opening to Iran deteriorated in its implementation into trading arms for hostages." Reagan said he had no excuses: "It was a mistake."

Paraphrasing a key finding of the Tower board, Reagan also admitted, "I asked so many questions about the hostages' welfare that I didn't ask enough about the specifics of the total Iran plan."

Reagan thus dropped his earlier justification for the arms sales that the Tower board rejected. The board quoted the president as basing his no-swap view on the fact that the United States was dealing with Iran and not directly with the groups that were holding Americans in captivity. After acknowledging the arms deals in his speech, Reagan dropped that issue and made no more references to Iran.

The president did not explain or justify numerous other statements by himself and other administration officials that proved inaccurate or misleading. For instance, investigators had found since Reagan's November 13, 1986, statement that the United States had sold a "limited" amount of weapons to Iran, that U.S. sales totaled more than 2,000 antitank missiles and some 200 parts for antiaircraft missiles. Reagan seemed to sweep aside his past accounts, saying he had been silent for three months because

"I felt it was improper to come to you with sketchy reports, or possibly even erroneous statements."

Reagan acknowledged the Tower board's criticism of his management style but defended his way of doing business, saying it had worked in the past: "When it came to managing the NSC staff, let's face it, my style didn't match its previous track record. I have already begun correcting this." In a meeting the previous day, March 3, the president had given general guidelines to the NSC staff, telling the staff that "there'll be no more freelancing by individuals when it comes to our national security."

Reagan also noted the Tower board's criticism of a general failure by the White House to keep track of decisions during the Iran arms sale program. "Well, rest assured," he said, "there's plenty of record-keeping now going on at 1600 Pennsylvania Avenue."

In addition to changing key personnel, Reagan said he had adopted "in total" the recommendations of the Tower board. He cited two specifics, a directive he issued in January 1987 barring the NSC staff from conducting covert operations and the creation of a new post of NSC legal adviser.

Reagan skirted, ignored, or said he had no answers to many remaining questions in the affair. Among these questions were what happened to the millions of dollars that seemed to have been diverted to the contras, why he and his aides had appeared to take a casual attitude toward legal requirements such as notifying Congress of covert operations and foreign arms sales, and how the Iran arms sales affected his stated antiterrorism policy.

Reactions to Speech

The March 4 speech was the highlight of a week-long public relations campaign to demonstrate that Reagan was on the job and in charge—not asleep at the switch, as the Tower Commission had seemed to portray him.

White House aides might have been spurred by Muskie's exceptionally harsh statements on CBS's "Face the Nation" program March 1. Muskie, the Tower board's sole Democrat, said that after interviewing Reagan twice, members "were all appalled by the absence of the kind of alertness and vigilance to his job and to these policies that one expects of a president." Asked if Reagan could function as president, Muskie had said, "We do not regard him as a

mental case. But we regard him as a president who didn't do his job."

The orchestrated White House response began March 2 with a press briefing by Baker to announce the withdrawal of the controversial nomination of Robert M. Gates to succeed William J. Casey as CIA director. Baker lavished praise on his new boss. "I do not see a hands-off president, or I do not see an AWOL president," he said. The next day, the White House staged two Reagan appearances with aides intended to show his grasp of foreign affairs. One was the private meeting with NSC staffers. Reagan also showed up in the White House press room—for the first time since late November 1986—to respond to Mikhail Gorbachev's February 28, 1987, offer to sign an agreement barring U.S. and Soviet medium-range nuclear missiles from Europe.

Against this backdrop of presidential activity, the substance of Reagan's March 4 speech seemed far less important than the manner of its delivery. Members of Congress on both sides of the aisle were relieved to see that Reagan was back to his normal upbeat self. "He did a lot to indicate that he's going to be an active president again," said Rep. William S. Broomfield, R-Mich. "That was important, after the worries and concerns people had."

But many Democrats—while reassured about Reagan's capacities—discounted the overall effort as another polished performance by a former actor. "If there was one thing the American people knew, it was that Ronald Reagan could deliver a good speech," said Sen. George J. Mitchell, D-Maine. "His ability to do that signifies nothing as to his ability to take control of the White House and the country."

After citing the Baker appointment, members reserved their highest praise for the president's confession that his earlier statement on not trading arms for hostages had been wrong. Several said such a retraction was a courageous move by a president who had hesitated to admit error.

Even his staunchest supporters acknowledged that, at best, Reagan could recover only some of the awesome political might he demonstrated before the Iran-contra affair. Citing the president's continuing vulnerability and the Democrats' control of Congress, Senate minority leader Dole predicted that Washington would be "in a holding pattern" until the next president took office in 1989.

Select Investigating Committees

During twelve weeks of nationally televised hearings that began May 5 and ended August 3, 1987, the twenty-six members of the House and Senate select committees investigating the Iran-contra affair heard testimony that revealed a startling mismanagement of U.S. foreign policy, involving possible illegal actions. However, the panels uncovered no evidence that President Reagan was aware of the diversion of Iran arms sale money to the contras fighting the leftist Sandinista government in Nicaragua, and many questions remained unanswered.

There never was much chance that the hearings would result in a grave constitutional crisis, as did the Watergate investigations of 1973-74. Because of Reagan's personal popularity, no one of any influence on Capitol Hill ever talked about trying to remove him from office. Even before the public hearings began, committee leaders privately had heard testimony that Reagan was not involved in the diversion—the one issue that had caused the president the most political trouble.

Under a pre-arranged agreement, the leaders kept that information secret for weeks. But because of it, they focused attention instead on the aides and private agents who carried out the president's policies, principally Reagan's national security adviser, Vice Adm. John M. Poindexter, and his aide, Lt. Col. Oliver L. North.

Also in contrast to Watergate and similar investigations of the past, the hearings were unlikely to result in sweeping legislative changes. Congress might tighten laws requiring the president to report on his foreign policy actions, but it almost certainly would not attempt to curtail his flexibility to any significant degree.

However, the committees' investigation served a purpose short of bringing down a president or leading to the enactment of major new laws. As noted by the four leaders of the two panels in their August 3 closing statements, the hearings offered a sobering reminder of the need for elected officials to take responsibility for the actions of government.

Summarizing what they had learned in forty days of public hearings, the committee leaders of both parties stressed the dangers of bypassing standard foreign policy-making procedures, allowing unelected aides to have too much power, and putting public policy in the hands of private agents.

Acknowledging that Congress shared a measure of blame, the leaders said the hearings demonstrated anew the importance of cooperation between the legislative and executive branches.

The hearings were still under way when Reagan's supporters began working to minimize any negative impact on the president. Administration officials and Republicans on Capitol Hill insisted that Reagan previously had corrected most of the mistakes evident in the Iran-contra affair by appointing new aides and instituting new White House procedures.

"If there ever was a crisis—which I doubt—it ended before these committees were established," said Dick Cheney, Wyo., ranking Republican on the House committee.

Reagan himself emphasized that theme in a speech August 12 outlining his agenda in the wake of the hearings. To demonstrate his willingness to take corrective action, Reagan August 7 sent a letter to the Senate Intelligence Committee promising new procedures for reporting covert operations to Congress.

Democrats faced a dilemma: While seeking to remind the public of the gravity of wrongdoing in a Republican administration, they clearly did not want to attack the president personally or to be seen as overly eager to profit politically from his problems.

In a strongly worded closing statement, Senate committee chairman Daniel K. Inouye, D-Hawaii, said the hearings had told "a chilling story, a story of deceit and duplicity and the arrogant disregard of the rule of law." But Inouye did not mention that the story involved Ronald Reagan. Inouye's House counterpart, Lee H. Hamilton, D-Ind., faulted the president only for failing to make "clean and crisp" decisions and for not knowing what his staff aides were doing.

As the hearings were concluding, Reagan demonstrated that lame-duck status had not sapped all of his ability to influence the political agenda.

In an unusual alliance with House Speaker Jim Wright, D-Texas, Reagan proposed a plan demanding a cease-fire and democratic reforms in Nicaragua. Both Wright and Reagan insisted the plan was meant to break years of deadlock in the Nicaraguan civil war. Instead, it might have helped break a deadlock in years-long peace talks among Central American leaders.

Two-Track Hearings

The hearings started out as a hard-hitting investigation into wrongdoing by White House officials and secret agents. Both committees hired experienced investigators and lawyers who privately interviewed hundreds of witnesses and reviewed thousands of documents.

The first phase of public hearings in May and June generally followed an investigative track. The committees produced substantial amounts of new information, both about the use of profits from the Iran arms sales and the secret White House campaign to aid the contras at a time when most U.S. aid was barred by law.

Perhaps the most significant news in that early phase was that two private agents recruited by North—retired Air Force major general Richard V. Secord and his associate, Iranian-American businessman Albert Hakim—spent only about $3.5 million from the diversion money to aid the contras, rather than the $10 million to $30 million estimated November 25, 1986, by Attorney General Edwin Meese III.

Secord and Hakim kept about $8 million from the Iran arms sales in secret Swiss bank accounts; at U.S. request, the money remained frozen and was likely to become the subject of protracted legal battles over who owned it.

As the hearings progressed, however, Reagan's avid Republican supporters on the committees hammered at a second theme: Congress's alleged interference in foreign policy. As committee lawyers and Democrats continued to ask detailed questions about who did what when, most Republicans made speeches defending Reagan and complaining about congressional "vacillation" on aid to the contras. The obvious goal of Republicans was to shift attention away from the mistakes of the Reagan administration and onto the failings of Congress. Starting with the appearance of North, the Republicans partly succeeded in that effort, putting the committee leadership on the defensive by reminding the public that Congress was no more perfect than the executive branch.

During his six days in the spotlight, former National Security Council (NSC) aide North wrested the initiative from the committees and made the Republicans' points better than they could. He came across on television—if not always in the hearing room—as an articulate and forceful advocate of presidential authority in foreign affairs. North's dramatic pitch for U.S. aid to the contras also produced an instant, if temporary, boost in public support of that cause.

In uniform and with a chestful of medals symbolizing a record of service in Vietnam, North created a media sensation. Pop magazines and even some committee Republicans called him a "hero," and visitors showed up wearing "Ollie North for President" T-shirts. Weeks after his testimony, public opinion polls showed North with a more favorable rating than Reagan or Congress. However, by summer's end "Olliemania" had died down considerably.

The investigatory momentum of the committees faltered again when Poindexter testified publicly that he never told Reagan about the diversion of Iran arms profits to the contras. Poindexter had told senior committee leaders the same thing privately on May 2, but that statement was kept secret until his public appearance.

Although several committee members said they simply could not believe Poindexter, his statement bolstered Reagan's longstanding claim of ignorance, and there was no documentary evidence to refute it. More important, that testimony killed any slim prospect of a dramatic confrontation between Congress and the president.

The panels devoted their final public sessions to testimony by current and former officials at the top of the Reagan administration. Those men, particularly Secretary of Defense Caspar W. Weinberger and Secretary of State George P. Shultz, denounced the actions of Poindexter and North and praised Reagan's leadership.

The Findings

The hearings showed that an intense disdain of standard governmental procedures helped motivate the Iran-contra affair. Military officers on the White House staff, still smarting from what they saw as political betrayal during the Vietnam War, took extraordinary precautions to keep their actions secret from Congress and their administration colleagues.

Rebuffed by Congress on aid to the contras and fearing congressional disapproval of arms sales to Iran, the administration used official and unofficial covert operations to implement significant foreign policies.

In one of the harshest comments summarizing the hearings, Senate committee vice chairman Warren B. Rudman, R-N.H., said Poindexter and North "showed total disrespect for the laws of the United States and our system of government, in effect adopting a position that the end justifies the means." Committee members were particularly incensed by assertions that Congress should play no role in formulating foreign policy. Inouye noted that Poindexter and North both said the need to confront a "dangerous world" justified secret executive action. "That is an excuse for autocracy, not for policy," Inouye said.

Remaining Questions

Even with their subpoena power, access to thousands of once secret documents, and testimony from numerous witnesses, the Iran-contra committees were unable to provide final answers to many important questions. On some issues, the panels were faced with flat-out contradictions: One witness said one thing, and another witness to the same event said something entirely different. Participants saw events from different perspectives or had different abilities to remember meetings and conversations one or two years earlier. And in all likelihood, some witnesses lied, even while testifying under oath. *(Contradictions, p. 145)*

On other issues, the committees simply did not have all the information they needed to make definitive judgments. Key documents that might have verified or refuted testimony were missing, thanks mostly to the shredding machine in North's office. And some of the most important participants were unavailable to the committees: former Central Intelligence Agency (CIA) director William J. Casey died as the hearings began; most foreigners involved were beyond the committees' reach; and the panels never even considered asking Reagan to testify, a request that probably would have been refused in any event.

Some panel members said the conflicts that emerged in the hearings did not prevent them from getting the Iran-contra story out before the American public. "The main thrust of the story is known. The participants are known," Senator Rudman told reporters. "The contradictions in testimony, in my view, quite frankly are not really important in terms of knowing the story."

Others, however, seemed more disturbed by the different Iran-contra accounts provided by key witnesses during the three months of public hearings. "Who do I believe?" asked Senator Inouye. "I'm in a dilemma like most Americans. Do I believe the admiral [Poindexter] or the colonel [North]? Or do I believe statements attributed to Mr. Casey? Do I believe the secretary of state? Do I believe the secretary of defense?"

The net result of the contradictions and unanswered questions, Inouye said, was that the picture of the Iran-contra affair that would be presented in the committee reports "obviously will have a few missing pieces."

COMMITTEES FORMED, GROUND RULES AGREED ON

Congress's dual-track approach toward investigating the Reagan administration's Iranian arms dealings got under way in December 1986 with the selection of special House and Senate committees.

Both chambers passed legislation (S Res 23, H Res 12) officially authorizing two Watergate-style panels immediately after the 100th Congress convened. The Senate on January 6, 1987, voted to establish its special eleven-member panel, formally named the Select Committee on Secret Military Assistance to Iran and the Nicaraguan Opposition. The next day, the House created, by a 416-2 vote, its fifteen-member Select Committee to Investigate Covert Arms Transactions with Iran.

In the Senate, incoming Majority Leader Robert C. Byrd, D-W.Va., had worked with outside legislative experts in mid-December 1986 to draft a committee charter.

"I think it's very evenhanded. It treats everyone fairly. It's a very broad charter that will get at the facts," said Rufus L. Edmisten, who helped in the drafting. Edmisten had been deputy chief counsel to the Senate Watergate committee and was later attorney general of North Carolina.

The Senate's select committee was chaired by Inouye, a former Intelligence Committee chairman and member of the Senate Watergate panel. The House chairman was Hamilton, the outgoing chairman of the Intelligence Committee.

The senior Republicans on the two panels were Senator Rudman and Representative Cheney. Cheney had served as White House chief of staff under President Ford.

Announcing the Senate membership on December 16, Byrd said he picked six Democrats "who will be fair, who will be tough, who will not be out to get anybody, and who will not be out to protect anybody." Besides Inouye, the Democrats were George J. Mitchell of Maine, Sam Nunn of Georgia, Paul S. Sarbanes of Maryland, Howell Heflin of Alabama, and David L. Boren of Oklahoma.

The GOP members named by Senate Republican leader Robert Dole, Kan., were Rudman, James A. McClure of Idaho, Orrin G. Hatch of Utah, William S. Cohen of Maine, and Paul S. Trible, Jr., of Virginia. Dole, who had been lobbied heavily by several GOP senators wanting to be on the panel, said he picked members who had been "fairly quiet" about the Iranian arms scandal, "not suggesting anybody be fired or prosecuted or anything else." *(Profiles, p. 149)*

House Committee Members

In the House, incoming Speaker Wright and Minority Leader Robert H. Michel, R-Ill., named their special com-

The Senate Iran-contra committee was chaired by Daniel K. Inouye, D-Hawaii, left. The chairman of the House panel was Lee H. Hamilton, D-Ind., right.

mittee members December 17. Wright said the nine Democratic members "represent our highest level of experience, knowledge, judgment and wisdom" and described chairman Hamilton as "impartial, judicious and fair."

Five of the Democrats were guaranteed a seat because they chaired committees with jurisdiction over various aspects of the Iran arms deal. These were: Dante B. Fascell of Florida, Foreign Affairs; Peter W. Rodino, Jr., of New Jersey, Judiciary; Jack Brooks of Texas, Government Operations; Les Aspin of Wisconsin, Armed Services; and Louis Stokes of Ohio, newly appointed chairman of Intelligence.

The remaining four positions went to Hamilton, Majority Leader Thomas S. Foley of Washington, Edward P. Boland of Massachusetts, and Ed Jenkins of Georgia.

In choosing his six members, Michel decided against naming all of the senior Republicans on the five committees. However, he appointed William S. Broomfield of Michigan, the senior Republican on Foreign Affairs, and Henry J. Hyde of Illinois, who was the ranking Republican on Intelligence.

Besides designating Cheney as the senior Republican on the panel, Michel dipped into the ranks of more junior House members for the remaining slots. They were filled by Michael DeWine of Ohio, Bill McCollum of Florida, and Jim Courter of New Jersey. Michel said he looked for Republicans with experience in foreign and intelligence matters, as well as those who had focused on legal issues on the Judiciary panel. Cheney, explaining the selection of some junior lawmakers, noted that members of Congress had no "necessary wisdom" simply because of their seniority. *(Profiles, p. 154)*

Ideological Splits, Watergate Threads

Ideologically, the House panel appeared more sharply divided than its Senate counterpart, with striking contrasts between ardent Democratic opponents and Republican supporters of Reagan's foreign policy, particularly on aid to the Nicaraguan contras.

Differences were a little softer on the Senate panel, where a more moderate to conservative tinge cut across party lines. For example, eight of the eleven Senate panel members—three Democrats and all five Republicans—voted to provide $100 million in military and other aid to the contras in a key March 1986 vote. In contrast, six of the nine Democrats on the House panel voted against contra aid in June, while three of them joined with all six Republicans in supporting Reagan's request.

Leaders of the two committees said they would try to cooperate with each other by exchanging information and trying to avoid competition. "Many of us are headline seekers, and we may find one committee trying to outdo the other one in scoops and headlines," said Inouye.

Although virtually everyone on Capitol Hill had been playing down comparisons between Iran and Watergate, the selection of the two special panels included several threads linking them to the Watergate period. Foremost was Inouye's selection, since he also served on the Watergate panel.

The Senate committee included two members—Cohen and Sarbanes—who were members of the House Judiciary Committee that voted articles of impeachment against Richard Nixon in 1974, shortly before he resigned the presidency. On the House committee, Rodino had been chairman of the Judiciary Committee that voted to impeach Nixon, and Brooks had served on the panel.

At his December 17 press conference, Inouye dropped several references to Watergate, at one point recalling that Nixon's status as a "wounded president" invited "mischief" by foreign adversaries such as the Soviet Union. "I'm not suggesting that our president [Reagan] is wounded badly, but there is no question that he has been injured," said Inouye.

Congressional leaders in both chambers, meanwhile, vowed that the panels would dig to the bottom of the administration's clandestine arms deals with Iran and the question of where the proceeds ended up.

Scope of Investigation

As approved the week of January 5, 1987, the charters set dates for both investigations. The Senate panel was scheduled to conclude its work by August 1, 1987, although its charter allowed the Senate to vote to continue the probe through October. The House panel had until October 30, 1987, to wrap up unless the House extended the deadline.

The charters also gave both panels broad mandates, allowing them to go far beyond the Iran-contra connection. For example, the charters were written broadly enough to cover inquiries into efforts to channel private funds to the contras in 1984-86, when Congress had prohibited the U.S. government from arming the rebels.

The House's charter contained virtually no limits. Besides the Iran sales and diversion to the contras, the resolution empowered the committee to look into the "operational activities and the conduct of foreign and national security policy" by NSC and other White House staff members. Another provision allowed the committee to look into "authorization and supervision or lack thereof" by the president and top officials over Iran-contra dealings and related matters.

The Senate resolution also authorized an inquiry into "the generation and use of any other money, item of value or service" to aid the contras.

Leaders of the House and Senate panels, however, said they would likely restrict their investigations, at least initially, to the Iran weapons sales and the diversion of profits. "It is not the intention of the committee to conduct an investigation into any private funding of the contras in which there is no direct or indirect government involvement," said Inouye.

Hamilton said the principal purpose of his investigation would be the Iran sales and money connection to the contras. But he added that the eventual scope of the committee's investigation would depend on "where the trail of evidence is going to lead."

In the House, several Republicans, including members of the Iran committee, criticized the breadth and duration of the investigation. Broomfield said, "This is not an investigation of the past six years of the Reagan administration. We should finish by April, not drag on until October." But Cheney reminded his GOP colleagues: "We are not here today because of a plot by anybody in the Congress to create problems for the administration or for our party.... We are here today because problems developed in the administration."

House and Senate Staff Members

After an organizational meeting January 8, Hamilton and Cheney announced top staffers on their panel: Chosen as chief counsel was John W. Nields, Jr. A Washington lawyer, Nields was chief counsel for the House ethics committee during its probe of the Korean bribery scandal in 1977-78.

Inouye and Rudman announced their top staff appointments on January 22. Arthur L. Liman was selected to be chief counsel. Known as a tough litigator, he was a member of Paul, Weiss, Rifkind, Wharton & Garrison, a blue-chip New York law firm. Liman specialized in complicated white-collar cases such as securities fraud, had been an assistant U.S. attorney in New York, and had been chief counsel to a special state commission set up in the early 1970s to investigate the uprising at the Attica, N.Y., state prison.

On March 18, 1987, the two panels voted to merge most of their activities, including public hearings. When the committees were formally constituted in January, leaders in both chambers were reluctant to establish a joint panel. But between that time and the start of public hearings in May, the two committees worked closely together. Staff members from both panels were present for all private interviews of witnesses, and the committees coordinated all major actions, such as seeking immunity for witnesses.

The vote to merge hearings and other operations was unanimous in both committees, and several members expressed enthusiasm.

"This is virtually an unprecedented agreement between the House and the Senate ... an excellent arrangement that'll let us get on with the business of resolving this matter as quickly as possible," said Representative Cheney. Senator Boren said the joint agreement "shows the American people that we're being responsible and trying to do this in a non-political non-sideshow fashion."

WEEK ONE:
SECORD TESTIMONY

The opening week of the Iran-contra hearings painted a graphic picture of important U.S. foreign policy matters managed by private agents, operating in secret, with little or no control exerted by responsible public officials.

Hou␣se and Senate select committees spent most of their May 5-8 hearings grilling retired Air Force major general Richard V. Secord, the key operative in secret U.S. arms sales to Iran and unofficial aid to the antigovernment contras in Nicaragua. Secord provided a wealth of details about the White House-inspired network that worked for nearly two years without any notice to Congress or the public. Secord had intimate knowledge of the details of the administration's privately conducted policies toward Iran and Nicaragua. At the instigation of NSC aide North, Secord began selling arms to the Nicaraguan rebels in late 1984, when official U.S. support was barred by law. A year later, he organized a private network to airlift military supplies to the contras and in 1986 made logistical arrangements for secret U.S. arms sales to Iran. *(Secord testimony text, p. C-8)*

Secord's testimony shed new light on the shadowy operations directed from the White House by North and his two bosses, first national security adviser Robert C. McFarlane, then Poindexter. In addition to aiding the

John W. Nields, Jr., left, served as chief counsel for the House select committee investigating the Iran-contra affair. Arthur L. Liman, right, was chief counsel for the Senate panel.

contras and arming Iran, North apparently was running three other covert activities, aimed at destabilizing Libyan leader Muammar el-Qaddafi and Cuban president Fidel Castro, and at buying freedom for U.S. hostages in Lebanon.

Often with the assistance of U.S. agencies, Secord's network of private companies used the standard devices of covert operations: Swiss bank accounts, coding machines, disguises, and clandestine meetings in the middle of the night. Appearing voluntarily before the committees, Secord described those activities with relish, admitting that he had once hoped to return to government heading the CIA's covert operations division.

With help from Secord and his business partner and money-manager, Albert Hakim, the committees made considerable progress in tracking the money generated by the private Iran-contra network. Secord himself provided at least a tentative answer to the question of how much was diverted to the contras from the Iran arms sales profits. He put the figure at $3.5 million, well below the $10 million to $30 million estimated in November 1986 by Attorney General Meese.

The fate of the money was at the forefront during the opening sessions, particularly some $8 million remaining in the control of Secord and Hakim. The money was what remained from $14 million in profits that their network made on the arms sale. The issue arose in large part because of what appeared as a fundamental flaw in the Iran-contra operation: Money generated privately by the sale of U.S. government property was kept under the control of private individuals answerable to no one in government. Some committee members and lawyers said the money belonged to the U.S. government; Secord insisted that the Pentagon was paid a fair price for its weapons and any profit was his to dispose of as he saw fit. *(Secord-Hakim funds, box, p. 104)*

Secord on May 7 agreed to a request by Senator Rudman for help in getting the money turned over to the U.S. Treasury. But the next day he said he hoped to channel the money to a private fund for the contras named after former CIA director Casey, who died just hours before the May 6 hearings got under way. Rudman said that use of the money for the contras, while "very laudable," was not satisfactory because it "belongs to the people of the United States."

Although the hearings were a unique experiment in bicameral investigation—and for the most part they demonstrated that Democrats and Republicans could work together to probe the actions of a Republican administration—partisanship, which had lurked beneath the surface of committee operations for nearly four months, made its inevitable appearance. The first signs came in the lengthy opening statements of panel members, with some Democrats attacking the administration and Republicans seeking to launch a philosophical defense of Reagan's activities. A more vivid demonstration came on May 7 and 8, when Republicans praised Secord's patriotism and sought to put his actions and those of the administration in the best possible light.

The White House carefully monitored the hearings, sending aides to take notes and subscribing to the official transcript. Frank C. Carlucci, Reagan's national security adviser, met privately with the Senate panel late May 7 for an undisclosed reason.

A Covert Operator in the Glare

Sitting ramrod straight a few feet from his interrogators, Secord came across as combative and self-assured. At times, he sought to emphasize his own importance, saying that only he made important decisions. At other times, challenged about the propriety of actions by his organization, Secord swore that he had merely responded patriotically to a request of his government. His main regret, he said, was that the secret operations became public.

During his first two days in the witness chair, Secord faced surprisingly gentle questioning from two lawyers from the House panel, chief counsel Nields and deputy minority counsel George Van Cleve. But on the third day, May 7, Senate committee counsel Liman ripped into Secord's assertion that he had not sought personal gain from the Iran and Nicaragua operations. In a withering cross-examination, Liman cast doubt on Secord's contention that he made no use of millions of dollars in profits generated by the arms sales. Later that day, Senator Boren raised embarrassing questions about Secord's past, especially his past

Richard V. Secord

friendship with former CIA agent Edwin P. Wilson. Wilson was convicted in 1983 on charges of illegally shipping munitions to Libya and plotting to murder an opponent of that nation's leader, Qaddafi. Secord left government in 1983— where he had served as a deputy assistant secretary of defense—under a cloud of suspicion about his ties to Wilson's shadowy network. (Wilson was in prison as of May 1987.)

On the first day of his testimony, Secord had said he hired for his Iran-contra organizations two other Wilson associates, former CIA employees Thomas G. Clines and Raphael Quintero. Secord said he trusted and respected both men. Boren recited the past legal troubles of Secord's associates, including Clines, who in 1983 pleaded guilty in a scheme to defraud the Pentagon on a shipping contract;

and Hakim, who reportedly admitted to bribing Iranian officials in the 1970s. Boren also revealed that the CIA in 1983 rejected a security clearance for Secord, and the Pentagon in 1986 removed him from a special consulting group for failure to submit required financial disclosure forms.

When Secord protested the innocence of his past associations and activities, Boren responded sarcastically: "It troubles me, because you obviously are a person that is proud of your reputation, why in the world, to paraphrase an old saying, would a sterling fellow like you get caught associating with people like Mr. Wilson, like Mr. Hakim, like Mr. Clines? What is a nice fellow like you doing in an operation like that?"

Another Senate committee member, Heflin, told Secord he made a favorable impression in his May 5-6 testimony but generated doubts in the minds of committee members with his later statements on financial matters. Heflin had told reporters May 7: "I don't think there's any question that his testimony to date will cause his indictment."

Apparently seeking to counter such statements, some Republicans professed admiration for Secord's military abilities. They pictured him as an experienced combat pilot, as a man who knew his way around the murky, complex worlds of arms sales, covert operations, and strategic planning. Representative Broomfield denounced Heflin's comments, saying that if Secord committed crimes, "I would hope that the committee would leave that to the special prosecutor. That's not our job."

Secord said he got support from Poindexter, who went to see him May 6 to shake his hand. "I was flattered," Secord said, adding that the two did not discuss serious matters.

Uncertainty about Reagan's Role

The first week of hearings shed little light on Reagan's participation in the Iranian and contra arms schemes. Reagan had said repeatedly that he did not know about the diversion of Iran arms profits to the contras or about potentially improper activities on behalf of the rebels. He acknowledged his involvement in the Iranian arms sales, however.

Secord told the committees that he assumed the president knew about and supported his activities. He said he based that assumption on comments by North and on the fact that three close Reagan aides were aware of most of what the Secord network did: McFarlane, Poindexter, and Casey. More important, Secord said in his opening statement May 5, he and his associates understood that their activities "were in furtherance of the president's policies. I also understood that this administration knew of my conduct and approved it."

Secord cited one instance in which North claimed to have told Reagan that it was "ironic" that Iran's leader, the Ayatollah Ruhollah Khomeini, was aiding the contras through the arms sales profits. Secord said he did not take the comment as a joke. North and Poindexter knew about the diversion, Secord said, adding that he was not sure about McFarlane or Casey. However, Secord acknowledged that he had no direct evidence that Reagan had any detailed knowledge of the specific activities of the Iran-contra network, including the diversion of Iranian arms sales profits.

Reagan said May 7 that Secord was "misinformed" in saying he might have known about the contra diversion.

However, Reagan said he had been aware that "Mr. Secord . . . was engaged with other private citizens in trying to get aid to the contras . . . and there's nothing against the law in that."

Control of the Money

In his questioning May 5-6, House counsel Nields sought to establish that North, acting as a government official, controlled the price of arms sold to Iran, and therefore the amount of profits generated by those sales. Secord said he consulted with North before establishing all prices—and never charged a price that North did not approve—but he insisted that the final pricing decisions were his, not North's.

In response to Nields's questions, Secord also acknowledged that he used proceeds from the arms sales for U.S. government purposes, as requested by North. Among those purposes were buying a Danish ship, the *Erria*, donating radios to a Caribbean country, aiding the contras, and making cash payments to agents of the Drug Enforcement Administration (DEA) who were working to find and rescue U.S. hostages in Lebanon. In each case, however, Secord again said he made the final decision. Referring to North's requests for aiding the contras, for example, Secord said: "We didn't always send as much money as he thought we should."

Secord acknowledged that he had no written authorization from U.S. officials to spend the money but argued that no one issued instructions to the contrary. "I didn't conceive of myself as a government person. I was a private person trying to help my government," he said.

Similarly, Secord rejected a contention by Senator Sarbanes that he was running a private CIA "completely outside" of government accountability procedures. "I was not trying to create my own CIA," he said. "My scope was much narrower than that."

A related issue was whether Secord and his associates wanted personal gain from the Iran-contra operations. Secord said he was paid a $6,000 per month salary by one of his companies, Stanford Technology Trading Group International, but insisted that there was no intention to profit personally from the Iran-contra operations of his companies. As an example, Secord said he renounced his share of profits from four private arms sales to the contras in 1985, insisting that he did not even know how much the profits were. Secord said he did so in hopes of returning to government service, and profiting from the sales might have created an "appearance" problem.

"There was no profit motivation in this Iranian initiative," he said, adding that prices for weapons were inflated solely to "create operational revenue" for the private network that transported the arms to Iran. One use of that revenue, he said, was to aid the contras. "The U.S. government did not provide one nickel for this operation," he said. "I was expected to raise the money to run the operation, all of it."

Almost to a man, committee members said they had trouble believing Secord's assertions. Rudman said Secord appeared to have "a rather casual interest in money." Even Hatch, Secord's most vocal supporter on the committees, said he had "difficulties" believing Secord's contention that he wanted no profits in four private arms sales to the contras in 1985. "In all honesty, I don't see any reason why you shouldn't have taken profits on it," Hatch said. "You had every right to."

The Profit Question

Both money issues—ownership and the profit motive—came to a head in Liman's grueling examination of Secord during the May 7 morning session. In a rapid-fire sequence of questions, Liman demanded to know what Secord had planned to do with the Iranian arms sales money and why he was building up enormous profits.

Under Liman's questioning, Secord insisted that he had no direct financial interest in the $8 million remaining in Swiss accounts because the money was controlled by Hakim. But he said that Hakim "responded" to his orders on how to use the money and that he had hired a lawyer and instituted legal action to block release to the U.S. government of the records from those accounts. Secord's assertion of a no-profit motive in the dealings later was challenged during Hakim's appearance before the committees June 3-5. *(See below, p. 103)*

In particular, Liman bore down on Secord's decision to retain $4 million worth of certificates of deposits that he had bought as insurance for planes that delivered arms to Iran. Liman noted that Secord kept the money long after the planes had returned safely from their missions, and that the money represented about half of the $8 million remaining unspent in the Secord organization's Swiss accounts.

Liman also cited private testimony by a Secord aide, retired Air Force colonel Robert C. Dutton, as evidence that Secord was planning to sell his organization's planes and other assets to the CIA once Congress allowed the agency to renew its involvement with the contras. Secord insisted he had no such plans and would have given the equipment—much of it bought with the Iranian arms profits—to the CIA.

Secord responded sharply to Liman, saying at one point: "I didn't come here voluntarily to be badgered by these questions that I have answered already repeatedly."

Liman and Boren also raised questions about whether some money from the Hakim-controlled Swiss accounts ended up in accounts that Secord himself controlled, including accounts for a company named "Korel," not previously disclosed in the Iran-contra investigations. Boren cited records, supplied by Hakim, showing that more than $1 million was distributed from 1984 to 1986 to accounts belonging to Korel and other companies. At least $200,000 went to accounts bearing Secord's names or initials, Boren said. Secord said he had no knowledge of those payments and had not seen the records to which Boren referred.

Secord's no-profit contentions appeared to break only once, when Boren cited Secord's comments to his colleagues that he hoped to profit from future arms sales to Iran if the United States normalized relations with that country. Secord acknowledged having made such comments.

Secord said he was inclined to sign a waiver, requested by the Senate committee, of his rights to secrecy over the Swiss accounts. But he said he wanted to consult further with his lawyer before signing the document, and he rejected a dramatic request by Boren during the hearing that he should sign the document "if you love your country." The Senate had filed suit against Secord seeking to compel him to sign the waiver, but a U.S. District Court judge rejected the Senate position as violating Secord's Fifth Amendment rights against self-incrimination.

(In mid-May, Secord filed a last-minute appeal of a Swiss order allowing U.S. access to secret bank records in which he might have an interest. Hakim already had appealed the order, meaning that it might be months before the bank records became available to independent counsel Lawrence E. Walsh, who was probing possible criminal violations. The Secord appeal caused some members of Congress to doubt his professed eagerness to cooperate with the inquiries.) *(Swiss bank records, p. 172)*

Contra Supply Network

Secord detailed the creation of the private contra aid network, which had expanded by early 1986 into an international web of secret arms deliveries. Throughout the period described by Secord, official U.S. military aid to the contras was prohibited by various versions of the "Boland amendment," named after Representative Boland. A member of the House select committee, Boland May 8 read Secord the law, saying its contra-aid ban was written in "very simple English words." Secord, however, contended the law "does not cover private funds." *(Boland amendments, box, p. 24)*

Secord said North asked him in mid-1984 to "contribute" his services to the contras, whose supplies were running low. After meeting with contra leader Adolfo Calero, and getting North's approval, Secord said he arranged four private arms sales to the contras. The sales were to have started in late 1984, but due to logistical foul-ups the first deliveries were not made until early 1985, he said.

Two of the sales, in February and April, were handled through a Canadian firm, Transworld Armaments. In his deposition, Hakim told the committee that Secord's organization had paid Transworld $1.5 million. The other sales, in March and May, were made by former CIA official Clines, and included ammunition, grenades, antitank rockets, and Soviet antiaircraft missiles. All four sales in 1985 were regular commercial transactions, Secord said, on which he and his associates made profits averaging 20 percent.

The private aid operation was developed later in 1985 in response to a request by North, Secord said. Eventually, the network owned five cargo planes and a landing strip in Costa Rica. It was managed from Washington, first by air delivery expert Richard B. Gadd, a retired Air Force colonel, and later by Dutton, who worked for Secord's firm, Stanford Technology Trading Group International. The air deliveries were made through Ilopango air base in El Salvador, with the cooperation of local officials, Secord told the panels.

Secord described several meetings on the contra aid program that he held with U.S. officials. A key meeting was an all-night session at a Miami airport hotel in mid-1985, during which Secord said he, North, and others agreed on the need to beef up the contras militarily. Secord said he also met three times with CIA director Casey, but that Casey never promised direct help for the contra aid network.

As described by Secord, North was the ever-present link at each step of the contra aid network. North recruited Secord to help the contras in mid-1984, arranged periodic meetings with high U.S. officials, and repeatedly sought to focus attention on the plight of the contras.

Under questioning by House Republican counsel Van Cleve, Secord said a half-dozen U.S. officials supported his private contra operation but lent no material assistance. The most concrete aid came from the CIA station chief in Costa Rica, who provided intelligence information. But Secord said no U.S. government money was spent to back his operation during the period when official U.S. aid to the contras was illegal.

Iranian Arms Sales

The hearings also filled in some details on the role of Secord's organization in U.S. arms sales to Iran.

One startling revelation was Secord's insistence that Iranian representatives did not promise in 1986 to release American hostages in Lebanon in exchange for U.S. arms sales. That sharply contradicted memos North wrote at the time to his boss, Poindexter, saying that Iran would release some or all of the hostages. In particular, Secord's assertion contradicted the understanding of members of a U.S. delegation to Tehran in May 1986. McFarlane, who led North and others in fruitless negotiations with Iranian officials, angrily left Tehran when the Iranians refused to agree to release of all the hostages.

Secord participated directly in several U.S.-Iran negotiating sessions, and he said he took the initiative in 1986 in recruiting a "second channel" (a relative of the speaker of Iran's parliament, Ali Akbar Hashemi Rafsanjani) to replace Iranian middleman Manucher Ghorbanifar. Secord said he never trusted Ghorbanifar, who came across as a salesman interested in profits more than in establishing ties between Iran and the United States.

North recruited Secord into the Iran arms sales operation in November 1985, at a time when Secord was planning his first private arms shipments to the contras. Secord traveled to Portugal, attempting unsuccessfully to persuade officials to allow an Israeli plane carrying Hawk antiaircraft missiles to land there on its circuitous route to Iran. The request was meant to disguise Israel's involvement in the arms transaction. When that effort failed, Secord arranged for a CIA-owned airline to fly the missiles on an unmarked plane to Iran from Israel. Secord denied suggestions by Boren that he or his contacts in Portugal had attempted to bribe local officials.

Secord's organization received $1 million from Israeli arms dealer Adolph "Al" Schwimmer for transportation expenses in the November shipment. But Secord said his actual costs totaled only $200,000. At North's request, he said, the remaining $800,000 later was used to help finance arms shipments to the contras.

In 1986, Secord hired planes and made other arrangements for three direct sales of U.S. arms to Iran: 1,000 TOW antitank missiles in February, Hawk missile spare parts in May and August, and more TOWs in October.

Secord Defends Actions

Secord at every point staunchly defended his actions and the underlying Reagan administration policies he said he was trying to support.

Secord said he believed so strongly in the Iran policy that he took the liberty of writing his own draft of a speech for Reagan to give in mid-November 1986, when the White House was trying to quiet the storm of controversy about the arms sales. In that draft, sent to the White House by a coded scrambling device, Secord said he suggested that Reagan should state his policy objectives, "to make no bones about it, that it was his operation, that he was responsible for it, had directed it, endorsed it, tried, we failed, and were going to try again." North later said the draft was rejected because "the line was thought to be too hard," Secord testified.

Secord said he tried twice to talk directly to Reagan, once by calling the White House and "demanding" to speak to the president. The second time was on November 25, after North was fired, when North and Secord met at a Virginia hotel. Reagan called North at the hotel, reportedly to express his regrets, and Secord said he reached for the telephone, unsuccessfully, just as North was hanging up. Vice President George Bush made a similar call, Secord said.

Asked what he would have said to the president, Secord gave his speech to the committees instead, saying the Iran policy was "worth a try" and that the American people "would understand the rationale" once they were given an explanation. In aiding the contras, he added, the private network had done "nothing wrong" because it "assiduously" stayed within U.S. laws.

WEEK TWO: MCFARLANE, OWEN, SIGUR

Ronald Reagan emerged from the second week of Congress's Iran-contra hearings May 11-14 as a far more actively involved participant than previously described in the arms scandal.

In his efforts both to channel aid to the Nicaraguan rebels and to win the release of American hostages held by pro-Iranian captors in Lebanon, Reagan was described in the hearings as a hands-on president who was personally involved in the Iran-contra dealings. This depiction contrasted sharply with earlier suggestions, such as that made by the Tower Commission, that Reagan was somewhat removed from decisions in the affair. *(Tower Commission, p. 71)*

McFarlane Testimony

Former national security adviser Robert C. McFarlane was the main witness in the four days of testimony, providing a detailed account of how and why the administration developed its covert policy of assisting the contras in Nicaragua. Unlike leadoff witness Secord, McFarlane already had testified on the Iran-contra affair before congressional committees and the Tower Commission. He said that secret plans to fund and arm the contras came largely in response to Congress's refusal to appropriate enough money to turn the rebels into an effective military force against the leftist Sandinista regime. *(McFarlane testimony text, p. C-23)*

McFarlane said Reagan made it clear to his staff that he wanted to keep the contras intact "body and soul" despite congressional restrictions on providing aid to them.

"I believe ... that President Reagan's motives and direction to his subordinates throughout this entire enterprise have always been in keeping with the law and national values," said McFarlane. "I don't think he is at fault here, and if anyone is, I am."

Nonetheless, some committee members dismissed McFarlane's zeal to accept blame. "I appreciate your willingness to shoulder great responsibilities. I admire you for

it, but I cannot accept that answer," said House select committee chairman Hamilton. "You spoke for the president, and the responsibility must rest with him as well as with you."

The former Marine officer for the most part maintained a calm composure during his testimony. On a few occasions, however, he displayed flashes of temper that caught committee members by surprise.

Reagan's Role

A central figure in Reagan's arms sales to Iran, McFarlane also spent much of his time at the witness table chronicling that ill-fated plan, which quickly degenerated into a weapons-for-hostages swap before it was revealed publicly in November 1986.

Although he said Reagan never acted unlawfully, McFarlane depicted the president as a willing participant in some of the Iran arms operations. He disclosed, for example, that Reagan personally approved a secret plan in early 1985 to pay up to $2 million in bribes and ransom for Americans held hostage by pro-Iran factions in Lebanon. The operation, which did not succeed, involved agents and informants connected to the Drug Enforcement Administration, and money for it came from the DEA, CIA, and from private sources.

Robert C. McFarlane

Some of the money to run the operation—linked to North—may have been diverted from contra bank accounts, an ironic twist given North's overarching scheme to funnel money from the sales of U.S. weapons to Iran.

White House officials denied that Reagan approved the ransom scheme. If he did, he may have violated the law by failing to issue a "finding" to authorize the covert operation and by not informing Congress. In a May 15 interview with regional editors, Reagan said he had "some trouble remembering" details of the rescue operation. "It's possible that what we're talking about was use of money to pay people and hire individuals who could effect a rescue of our people there. And I've never thought of that as 'ransom.' "

McFarlane also revealed that Reagan called the head of a Central American nation—thought to be Honduras—early in 1985 to persuade him to release a shipment of weapons from an unnamed source intended for the contras. A military official in that country seized the arms after Congress cut off military support to the contras, but Reagan's message succeeded in getting the weapons to the Nicaraguan resistance, said McFarlane. He later said he might have confused the incident with a similar event that occurred later in 1985.

During that period, McFarlane told the panels, Reagan had conveyed to his aides "the very strong wish that we not break faith with the contras," despite Congress's ban on arms aid. The goal, testified McFarlane, was to convince Congress and the American public that the rebels were "more than a ragtag military outfit," and that they deserved U.S. support.

Documents Show McFarlane Misled Congress . . .

In letters, private meetings, and sworn testimony during 1984-85, White House aides Robert C. McFarlane and Lt. Col. Oliver L. North misled Congress about the extent of White House involvement with the contras.

McFarlane, President Reagan's national security adviser during that period, repeatedly assured Congress that his aides, especially North, had stayed within the various versions of the Boland amendment, which barred U.S. military aid to the Nicaraguan rebels. McFarlane also told Congress that his aides had not solicited private or foreign donations.

But internal White House documents written at the time showed that North was deeply involved in aiding the contras while the Boland amendment was in effect. The House and Senate Iran-contra committees also heard testimony May 14, 1987, that North gave the contras military advice and secret intelligence information and served as a conduit for cash payments to contra leaders.

McFarlane acknowledged to the panels on May 11-13 that his 1985 denials were "too categorical."

The White House papers were among the more than seventy documents released during the first two weeks of the committees' hearings, which opened May 5. Beginning with a June 1985 report in the *Miami Herald,* news organizations disclosed North's role in arranging funds for the contras. Those reports prompted congressional committees to write McFarlane demanding to know what North was doing and whether his activities might have violated the law. Michael D. Barnes, D-Md., then chairman of the House Foreign Affairs Subcommittee on Western Hemisphere Affairs, wrote the first such letter on August 16, 1985, saying the reports "raise serious questions regarding the violation of the letter and spirit" of the Boland law.

McFarlane later said he turned those inquiries over to North, who composed letters denying any impropriety. McFarlane then signed the letters and sent them to Capitol Hill. The first North/McFarlane response was dated September 5, 1985; it was a letter to Lee H. Hamilton, D-Ind., then chairman of the House Intelligence Committee, and subsequently chairman of the House Iran-contra committee. In the letter written by North, McFarlane said he had "thoroughly examined" the charges about North's activities: "From that review I can state with deep personal conviction that at no time did I or any member of the National Security Council [NSC] staff violate the letter or spirit of the law."

In particular, the letter said that "at no time did we encourage military activity" by the contras. Further, it said that the NSC staff "did not solicit funds or other support for military or paramilitary activities either from Americans or third parties." McFarlane sent a similar letter to Barnes, dated September 12. The letter to Hamilton included a postscript saying that North had been harassed as a result of the press reports.

McFarlane: Assurances . . .

The committees followed up their inquiries with specific questions, and McFarlane met with the House Intelligence Committee on September 10, 1985. Responding to the additional questions, McFarlane on October 7, 1985, sent the Senate and House Intelligence committees an eight-page sheet of answers stamped "confidential." All answers denied press reports in June and August about North's involvement with the contras or gave an innocent interpretation of his activities.

Several of McFarlane's responses answered only part of the questions the committees had asked. For example, one question asked about a report in the *New York Times* that North knew in advance about contra attacks and had given the rebels "advice and assistance." The response, drafted for McFarlane by North, ignored the issue of whether North had ad-

McFarlane said he kept Reagan informed about the status of the contras, and that the president had a "far more liberal interpretation" about what U.S. officials could do lawfully to assist the rebels. A day later, however, the former national security adviser backed away from his May 13 statement, saying it was "probably a poor choice of words on my part." Instead, he said he meant to say that Reagan was deeply committed to helping the contras, but only in lawful ways.

McFarlane's Involvement

McFarlane's appearance before the two select committees featured a much tougher grilling than he previously had been subjected to by other committees in December 1986. Then, he was largely questioned on his role in the weapons sales to Iran, where McFarlane traveled on a secret mission in May 1986 in an unsuccessful attempt to free the hostages held by pro-Iranian terrorists in Lebanon.

McFarlane again was questioned closely about the Iran initiative. But he also faced a probing interrogation into his role in the administration's efforts to assist the contras in 1984-85, when the Boland amendment had cut off all U.S. arms aid. In the summer and fall of 1985, McFarlane on several occasions assured Congress that press accounts alleging improper activities by North in behalf of the contras were unfounded. His assurances persuaded Hamilton, then chairman of the House Intelligence Committee, to suspend

... on North Role in Contra Supply Network

vance knowledge of contra military actions. Instead, it said merely: "The allegation that Lt. Col. North offered the resistance tactical advice and direction is ... patently untrue."

More than a year later—in December 1986—McFarlane repeated his assurances to Congress that neither he nor his staff had violated the contra-aid bans. In closed testimony December 8, 1986, before the House Foreign Affairs Committee—a partial transcript of which was released May 11, 1987—McFarlane said he knew of no efforts by the White House staff to solicit funds for the contras. And McFarlane told House Intelligence on December 10 he had no reason to believe that North had violated the Boland law.

... and Second Thoughts

Confronted with North's memos explaining his work with the contras, McFarlane on May 11 told the Iran-contra panels that several "seemed to me to raise legitimate questions about compliance with the law." An "objective reading," McFarlane said, would take "passages in each of these memoranda to be either reflective of a past act that was not within the law or a recommendation that a future act be carried out that wouldn't be."

McFarlane acknowledged that his 1985 denials had expressed "too categorically" the opinion that the NSC staff had not violated the letter or spirit of the law. Looking back, McFarlane said, his suspicions "ought to have led me to be more probing and to get more concrete information one way or the other."

McFarlane also testified that North in the fall of 1985 had suggested altering a previous memo that had requested permission to ask "current donors" (presumably Saudi Arabia) to provide additional money to the contras. North suggested altering that memo to discuss the importance of persuading Congress to support the contras. McFarlane said he had

rejected North's suggestion and later destroyed the paper on which North had written his alterations.

What North's Memos Said

Buried in McFarlane's files at the White House was a one-page handwritten note headed "IV" and listing a series of six-digit numbers. McFarlane told the panels that those numbers represented the computer designations of super-secret memos written to him by North. McFarlane said those memos had later raised concerns in his mind about North's activities—but in spite of those concerns McFarlane assured Congress in 1985 that North was doing nothing improper.

The memos show that North kept close tabs on the military and financial activities of the contras throughout the period that the Boland amendments were in effect. Portions of the memos were quoted in the February 26, 1987, report of the Tower Commission, which reviewed White House involvement in the Iran-contra affair. The House and Senate select committees released the documents in full on May 11-12.

At least once a month—and occasionally twice a day—North generated ideas on behalf of the contras, ranging from helping them sink a Nicaraguan ship to having Reagan plead with the American people for donations to the "freedom fighters."

McFarlane rejected many of North's ideas, but he told the select panels he did not fault North because he was "energetic" and was supposed to "think up" ways to help the contras. The former national security adviser also acknowledged that North did not tell him about some of his activities, such as a July 1985, late-night meeting in Miami that led to the establishment of a private network that airlifted supplies to the contras. "I could imagine that Col. North kept that from me for my benefit, not his," McFarlane said.

an inquiry into charges that officials of the NSC had violated the Boland amendment. McFarlane repeated his denials in December 1986 testimony before the House Foreign Affairs Committee, which was conducting a preliminary inquiry into the affair. *(Boland amendments, box, p. 24)*

But under sharp questioning May 12 by House chief counsel Nields, McFarlane acknowledged that he had misled Congress into believing that North had done nothing wrong. He also disclosed that North himself had drafted the letters that McFarlane sent to Hamilton and other members of Congress steering them away from the charges against North.

"What did Congress have to do, what did they have to

ask you in order for you to tell them what you actually knew about North's conduct with the contras?" asked Nields.

"The responses that I gave in 1985 and the responses to the Congress in hearings in 1986 were clearly too categorical on my part," replied McFarlane. "Maybe if I had searched deeper, I could have found that out. But I didn't, and I am responsible for that."

He denied having deliberately deceived lawmakers. Instead, he said he relied on "tortured language" because he had misgivings about some of North's actions but was not fully convinced that his aide had acted unlawfully.

Committee lawyers and members also questioned McFarlane repeatedly on his involvement in other controversial aspects of the Iran-contra affair, donations to the contras by other countries, and the doctoring of White House memos and documents.

At the request of the administration, the committees had agreed not to identify by name certain countries that figured in U.S. fund-raising appeals for the contras. At least four of the countries, however, could be identified as Israel (1), Saudi Arabia (2), Taiwan (3), and China (4). McFarlane himself unintentionally mentioned King Fahd of Saudi Arabia during one discussion about "country two." And a document describing "country one" referred to "GOI"—the government of Israel.

"Country two" agreed in 1984 and 1985 to donate at least $24.5 million to the contras. Questioned about this during the hearings, McFarlane denied that he ever directly solicited money from the Saudis. He also turned aside suggestions that Saudi contributions to the contras were in any way linked to controversial U.S. arms sales to Saudi Arabia.

McFarlane said he discussed Reagan's commitment to the contras with Saudi officials beginning in mid-1984, which resulted in a Saudi agreement to contribute $1 million each month. McFarlane said Reagan reacted with "satisfaction and pleasure" when informed of the Saudi gift. The Saudis agreed early in 1985 to increase their contribution following a White House meeting in February between Reagan and King Fahd. But McFarlane and Reagan denied that a direct solicitation had been made. The Saudis eventually gave $16.5 million between February and April 1985, according to McFarlane.

"The president was not aware of any solicitations by members of the staff. He did not solicit any money," White House spokesman Marlin Fitzwater told reporters May 12. A day later, Reagan said that his diary indicated he never brought up the subject of Saudi aid to the contras when he met with Fahd. Instead, Reagan said his diary showed that "the king, before he left, told me that he was doing that, and that he was going to increase the aid."

"There's no question in my mind that there was a solicitation," Senate committee vice chairman Rudman told reporters May 14. "Now, it may have been a very diplomatically phrased solicitation, but I think it was a solicitation. The evidence says that."

Whether such a solicitation would have been unlawful, however, was not clear. Despite the Boland amendment, Rudman and others suggested that a president could not be prevented from asking other countries for assistance.

Doctored Chronology and Diversion

McFarlane was questioned very closely about his role in the preparation of a White House chronology of Iran-contra events in November 1986 that altered some of the facts to protect Reagan from culpability. In particular, McFarlane agreed to changes that masked Reagan's decision in August 1985 to approve Israel's selling of TOW antitank missiles to Iran and its ability to replace them from U.S. stocks. A doctored version of the chronology said that Reagan would not allow Israel to sell the missiles, and that he found out only afterward that Israel had shipped 508 TOWs in September 1985.

The chronology also was altered to indicate that U.S. officials did not learn until after the fact that Israel sent Hawk antiaircraft missiles to Tehran in November 1985. The document said that Reagan aides were under the impression that the Israelis were sending oil-drilling equipment to Iran, even though they knew at the time that the shipment contained the Hawks.

McFarlane said the changes were made by him and others to "minimize the president's role" in the original arms shipments to Iran. But under questioning by Nields May 12, McFarlane stopped short of saying that he deliberately falsified the chronology. "I am not trying to deny that it is not an accurate portrayal of the president's approval of these [Israeli] shipments which, indeed, occurred," said McFarlane.

"You are saying it is not an accurate portrayal?" asked Nields.

"It is not a complete portrayal," replied McFarlane.

Later, Senator Mitchell told McFarlane that there was "clear and convincing evidence" that he had participated in a "fix" of the White House chronology.

One question that remained elusive during McFarlane's testimony was whether Reagan knew about the diversion of funds to the contras from the profits earned in the Iran arms sales. McFarlane said he did not learn about the diversion until North told him at an airport in Tel Aviv in May 1986, when the two were returning to the United States after the Iran trip. The diversion scheme had been approved, North assured McFarlane, though McFarlane said he did not press his former aide about who had given that approval.

McFarlane said he assumed that authority would have had to come from either Reagan or Poindexter, McFarlane's successor. He said he did not discuss the matter with North again until the following November, only days before Attorney General Meese announced the diversion publicly.

At the time, McFarlane warned North, Poindexter, and others about a "problem" stemming from the diversion. "It just seemed to me that unless someone could stand up and say that this is on the basis of a finding, or it is chartered by specific decision by [Poindexter] or the president, that I could not imagine this kind of thinking being justified in law . . . ," said McFarlane.

McFarlane said North told him he was concerned about the fallout if news of the diversion got out. "I said, 'Well, that was approved, wasn't it?' " McFarlane testified. "Yes, you know it was. You know I wouldn't do anything without approval," McFarlane quoted North.

McFarlane also disclosed that North told him November 21, 1986, about a "shredding party" that was going to occur, presumably to destroy documents related to North's activities on the contras' behalf. McFarlane said he did not do anything to talk North out of destroying the documents. In one of his few displays of emotion during his testimony, McFarlane snapped at a question about the shredding from Representative Rodino, who asked whether McFarlane should have tried to tell North that destroying any documents might be illegal.

"That is right, and I deserve responsibility," barked McFarlane. "And I ought to be prosecuted to the full extent of the law and sent away." *(Further details, see Fawn Hall testimony, p. 110; North testimony, p. 119)*

North's Ties to Casey

McFarlane, in his testimony, speculated that North may have shielded his former boss from some of his actions in order to protect both McFarlane and Reagan.

At the same time, McFarlane said North apparently was taking orders from CIA director Casey, who shared

North's passionate support for the contras. The North-Casey tie bolstered the theory held by some that Casey was a linchpin in the secret war against the Sandinistas. He also emerged as a key figure in Reagan's decision to revive the flagging Iran weapons program in late 1985, after the president and other senior aides, including McFarlane, had decided to end the arms sales.

McFarlane said that Reagan reluctantly agreed to kill the program following a December 7, 1985, meeting at the White House, which Casey did not attend because he was out of town. McFarlane, who had just resigned as national security adviser, then went to London to inform Iranian and Israeli officials of Reagan's decision. But a December 9 memo by North said the London meeting had been "inconclusive" and then spelled out options for what to do next. Among these was a plan to draft a presidential "finding" to authorize direct U.S. arms sales and use Secord to arrange the transactions.

McFarlane said it was "conceivable" that Casey tried to resurrect the Iran operation after detecting reluctance on Reagan's part to end it.

Senator Sarbanes asked McFarlane if North's vigorous effort to continue the arms sales might also have been influenced by Secord's interest in generating profits that could be diverted to the contras. "It's possible, I suppose," said McFarlane.

Sigur, Owen Testimony

Further questions about third-country solicitations were directed May 14 at Gaston J. Sigur, Jr., a former NSC official who was at the time of the hearings assistant secretary of state for East Asian and Pacific affairs. Sigur was the first official still in the administration to testify before the select committees.

Acting at North's request, Sigur twice in 1985 asked an official from a foreign country—identified by sources as Taiwan—to donate to the contra cause, Sigur testified. In each case, Sigur said, the official and North later told him that the country donated $1 million.

Gaston J. Sigur, Jr.

Sigur said he discussed the approach to the country with McFarlane, who signaled approval. However, McFarlane vetoed the Taiwanese suggestion that any contribution be made directly to the United States. Instead, the money was deposited in the Lake Resources bank account in Geneva, controlled by North and Secord, according to Rudman.

While details about the diversion remained murky, a self-described "private foot soldier" for the contra cause told the committees about his delivery of military information and cash from North to contra leaders in late 1984 and early 1985.

Testifying under a grant of immunity, Robert W. Owen provided the panels May 14 with their first direct testimony about White House activities that might have violated the Boland amendment's cutoff of military aid. Owen continued his testimony on May 19. *(Owen testimony text, p. C-30)*

Code-named "T. C."—for "the courier"—the boyish-looking Owen described how he made cash payments to contra leaders, in Washington and Central America, using traveler's checks provided by North. In an explanation that raised more questions, Owen said he understood that the money originally came from Adolfo Calero, a major contra leader. Owen further stated that Johnathan Miller, a White House aide, assisted him in the money transfers. Miller promptly resigned his position after Owen implicated him during his testimony. *(See Calero testimony, below)*

Owen testified that he twice delivered maps from North to contra leaders in Central America. In both cases, sources said, the maps probably contained sensitive intelligence information about Sandinista military locations.

The first such delivery was in mid-November 1984. Owen said North gave him maps and photographs that were for use in a "potential" operation to destroy Sandinista military equipment. Owen quoted North as saying he got the information "across the river" or "up the river"—apparent references to the Pentagon or the CIA, both in Virginia across the Potomac River from downtown Washington. Owen said he delivered the material to Calero in Honduras, but the military operation was not conducted because the contras considered it "too risky."

The committees also released a letter from North to Calero, which Owen said he probably delivered early in 1985. The letter was addressed to "my friend" and signed "Steelhammer," one of North's code names, Owen said.

One paragraph told Calero that "next week, a sum in access [sic] of $20M will be deposited in the usual account." Sources said that probably was a reference to Saudi Arabian contributions totaling about $20 million at the time. North ended the letter with a warning to keep the information about the $20 million quiet. "The Congress must believe that there continues to be an urgent need for funding," the letter said.

WEEK THREE: OWEN, CALERO, SINGLAUB

The third week of hearings tightened the circle around evidence of Lieutenant Colonel North's involvement with the contras from 1984 to 1986. North was at the center of nearly all testimony before the committees May 19-21. Three witnesses described in detail North's role as general supervisor of the contras: contra leader Adolfo Calero; retired Army major general John K. Singlaub, a leader of anticommunist causes who provided private aid and weapons to the rebels; and Owen, who continued his testimony. *(Calero and Singlaub testimony text, p. C-34)*

The week's testimony added rich details to the unfolding story of how private operatives carried out the administration's policy of aiding the contras. Three wealthy Americans also told how North persuaded them to donate large sums to private groups, ostensibly to benefit the contras. The three were Colorado beer company executive Joseph Coors; Ellen Garwood, an heiress from Austin, Texas; and

William B. O'Boyle, a New York investor. *(Garwood and O'Boyle testimony text, p. C-37)*

North's Aid to Contras

Much of the week's hearings focused on North's activities. All six witnesses testified at length about their dealings with the NSC aide, and all six gave evidence raising questions about the legality or propriety of some of his activities. Of the six, Owen seemed to know North the best. Owen described himself as North's "eyes and ears" in Central America, and as a close friend. From 1984 to 1986, Owen saw North dozens of times and wrote him chatty letters filled with information and gossip about the contras.

Owen gave the panels several pieces of evidence about North's activities, particularly in 1985, when U.S. aid was absolutely banned. Owen said that North twice gave him maps and other intelligence information to take to Calero in Central America—but Owen insisted May 19 that doing so was not illegal because he understood the information had somehow been "declassified."

Calero saw North from another perspective; to him, North was the man in Washington to whom he could turn for money, advice, and consolation when Congress was cutting off funds. Calero said he told North "practically everything" he was doing. "I had no reservation. I had full confidence and trust in him," he said May 20.

Robert W. Owen

But North appeared wary of sharing information with Calero. The contra leader said North often left him in the dark, especially on the private air operation that aided the contras in 1986. Calero said North never told him that Secord was in charge of the operation, although he suspected as much. Asked if North shared many details about the delivery of supplies, Calero said: "No. I remember telling Col. North it was lousy."

North provided military advice, Calero said, citing in particular his suggestion that the contras needed to destroy Nicaragua's Soviet-supplied MI-24 Hind helicopter gunships. "It was best to take out helicopters on the ground," Calero quoted North as saying. "It was easier, cheaper."

Singlaub testified about North's help in planning a major arms purchase for the contras in 1985. Singlaub bought the weapons—including 10,000 rifles, grenade launchers, ammunition, and other items—from Poland and had them shipped to Central America. Singlaub said he got a list of the contras' weapons needs in March 1985 from military commander Enrique Bermudez. In April, Singlaub took the list to North, who approved it after making "insignificant changes." However, North and Calero deleted from the list about twenty Soviet-made surface-to-air missiles, Singlaub said, because Secord said he could provide trainers as well as missiles and Singlaub could not.

North also approved an appeal to Taiwan and South Korea for aid to the contras early in 1985, Singlaub said. After getting North's go-ahead, Singlaub asked high officials in both countries to provide such military aid. But he

said he never heard whether anything came of the request. (The committees had produced evidence that Taiwan gave $2 million for "humanitarian" contra aid later in 1985 after getting an appeal from North's associate, Sigur.)

All six witnesses during the week said they assumed that North was acting under orders, but none had direct knowledge of what those orders were or who gave them. None had any evidence of Reagan's involvement.

Owen said it never occurred to him that North might have been acting on his own. He described a brief telephone conversation he had with North November 25, 1986, the day North was fired. North said: "Well, you know, I would never do anything unless I had orders or other people knew what I was doing." Owen and Singlaub said North worked to keep his own involvement with the contras secret. Owen said North even asked him not to attend the funeral of a contra aid pilot, fearing that Owen's presence might attract attention that would expose North's role.

Washington and the Contras

The committees received conflicting testimony about the CIA's involvement with the contras during the period when direct aid by that agency was barred. Several witnesses had testified that specific CIA officials, especially those stationed in Central America, played active roles in helping the contras. But Calero complained bitterly about the lack of support, and Singlaub said former CIA director Casey—a longtime friend—refused to talk to him about Nicaragua.

Owen described frequent dealings with CIA officials, including agents in Costa Rica and Honduras. Agency officials helped plan various activities in support of the contras in 1985—even though CIA participation in such activities was expressly barred by the Boland amendment. Most deeply involved, Owen said, was the CIA station chief in Costa Rica, Joe Fernandez, who went by the name of Tomas Castillo. Castillo helped choose the site for an airstrip in Costa Rica to be used by the private contra aid supply network, and he helped develop a "cover story" that the farm on which the airstrip was located was actually an agricultural research station, Owen said. *(Castillo testimony, p. 100)*

Agency officials also gave North the maps and other intelligence information that Owen passed on to contra leaders in Central America, Owen said. Among those involved was the director of the CIA task force on Central America, who North called to straighten out a problem with one set of maps, Owen testified.

He also recounted an incident in March 1986, when North asked him to travel to Central America on a flight that was delivering U.S.-supplied medical goods to the contras. After the delivery, Owen said, North had arranged for the plane to transfer weapons from one contra faction to another. But the weapons were not where they were supposed to be, and Owen said CIA officials made several telephone calls trying to locate the materiel. Those efforts were unsuccessful, and the plane was forced to leave empty.

Calero insisted that the CIA gave the contras little help. "They got support from us," he said, acknowledging that he had called the CIA "more snoopers than helpers." Calero vigorously denied an implication by Senator Cohen that he was "controlled" by the CIA, saying his relationship with the agency was one of "mutual respect." But he acknowledged that the agency did all the purchasing and

The Contra Cash Flow

By the end of May 1987, the Senate and House Iran-contra committees had traced nearly $34 million worth of contributions to and expenditures by the contras between mid-1984 and January 1987. The information came from six bank accounts that contra leader Adolfo Calero said he maintained in Panama, the Cayman Islands, and Miami, Fla. *(Calero testimony, p. 98)*

Income

The contras took in $33.662 million in deposits and earned another $248,000 in interest. Nearly all the money—$32 million—came from a "foreign government," subsequently acknowledged by President Reagan to have been Saudi Arabia.

Between November 1985 and January 1987, the contras got another $1.045 million from Intel Cooperation Inc., one of several companies run by Washington public relations agent Richard R. Miller. Miller used that firm to funnel money that had been raised for the contras by his business associate, Carl R. "Spitz" Channell. Both Miller and Channell pleaded guilty to criminal charges in the Iran-contra affair. *(Details, p. 170)*

Lake Resources Inc., the shell company that handled the financial transactions of retired major general Richard V. Secord and his associate, Albert Hakim, contributed another $200,000 in October 1985. Some of that might have come indirectly from Taiwan, which put $2 million into Lake Resources' Swiss bank account earlier in 1985 at the request of the White House.

The committees identified another $417,000 as "miscellaneous deposits" into contra accounts. Calero said some of that money probably was used to establish a contra radio station.

Expenditures

The contras spent $33.814 million during the period covered by Calero's records.

The bulk—$19.178 million—went for arms purchases. Arms were bought from the following sources, according to the Iran-contra select committees: $11.35 million from Energy Resources Inc., controlled by Secord and Hakim; $5.3 million from retired major general John K. Singlaub and his associates; $2.095 million from two Miami arms dealers, Ronald J. Martin and James McCoy, operating as Gretch World and R & M Equipment Co.; and $432,000 from other sources.

The committees said the contras spent another $13.965 million on maintenance, equipment, and other items. About $4 million went to three agents in Honduras who changed dollars into local currency at favorable rates. Another $3.06 million was used to buy traveler's checks. Other money in this category went for various expenses, including $476,485 described as "FDN," the acronym for Calero's group, the Nicaraguan Democratic Force.

Calero's records also showed that the FDN donated $670,635 to other contra factions, including $600,635 listed as "Robelo," apparently meaning Alfonso Robelo, a contra leader who in the early 1980s was based in Costa Rica.

---

planning for the contras until Congress stopped that activity in 1984. The contra leader said that he developed a fondness for CIA director Casey, calling him "Uncle Bill."

Singlaub, on the other hand, seemed irritated by his old friend's refusal even to listen to his ideas about Nicaragua. The two men had known each other since World War II, when Singlaub parachuted into occupied France under Casey's supervision. But Singlaub said Casey "threatened to throw me out of the office" if he mentioned the contras.

Nevertheless, Singlaub said Casey agreed to meet in December 1985 with the president of a Washington arms concern, GeoMiliTech Consultants Co., to discuss a proposal for a complex three-way trade among the United States, Israel, and China. The end result of the trade was to be Soviet-style arms and ammunition that the United States could provide to "freedom fighters" in Nicaragua, Angola, Afghanistan, and elsewhere. Nothing came of the plan.

Singlaub also said the CIA in 1986 interfered with a plan of his to get famed Nicaraguan rebel Eden Pastora—known as "Commander Zero"—back into the war against the Sandinista government. Singlaub insisted he had tacit support for the plan from Elliott Abrams, the assistant secretary of state for inter-American affairs. But "someone in the CIA" later blocked a planned delivery of supplies to Pastora. *(See Abrams testimony, p. 103; Lewis A. Tambs testimony, p. 100)*

Singlaub said Abrams also approved his proposal to make follow-up trips to Taiwan and South Korea in 1986 seeking aid for the contras. But Abrams withdrew that approval after Singlaub arrived in Taiwan, saying the solicitation was going to be made instead by someone "at the highest level," which Singlaub "assumed to be someone in the White House."

Squeezing Out Calero

The week's testimony provided an intriguing explanation for North's apparent decision in 1985 to put Secord in charge of funneling private money to the contras—thus taking control of financial matters out of Calero's hands. The reason, Owen said, was that North became concerned about possible corruption in the contra forces and no longer trusted the leadership, especially Calero's brother who acted as a purchasing agent for the rebels in New Orleans.

In the summer of 1985, Owen testified, North and Secord decided that "it was potentially inappropriate that Adolfo Calero be using his brother, Mario Calero, to purchase goods" for the contras. There were rumors that "some money was going where it shouldn't go," he said, and North was concerned, even though there was no proof of improper behavior. North also was worried "that funds were being spent on things that probably were a waste of money," Owen said. As a result, he testified, North and Secord decided to use the latter's secret Swiss bank account to buy materiel for the contras, instead of providing money directly to them.

Calero acknowledged that his sources of direct funding suddenly dried up in 1985, after he received the last of a series of donations totaling $32 million from Saudi Arabia. But he vigorously denied the allegations of corruption, including any aimed at his brother. Calero insisted that neither he nor his brother profited from the contra-aid operations.

Calero also complained that Owen appeared to be a source of reports about corruption. Without naming names, Calero said that Owen "began to hang around with people in this country that had always badmouthed the FDN," the acronym for the main rebel army, the Nicaraguan Democratic Force.

Adolfo Calero

Owen apparently did become disenchanted with the Calero faction, filing reports to North on the FDN's refusal to cooperate with other contra groups. On March 17, 1986, Owen sent North a letter citing a long list of complaints about the Calero brothers, the State Department, and nearly everyone else involved in the contra effort. In a blast obviously aimed at Calero and his associates, Owen wrote to North: "This war has become a business to many of them. There is still a belief that the Marines are going to have to invade, so let's get set so we will automatically be the ones put into power."

Under questioning by Cohen, Calero debunked the Reagan administration's longstanding justifications for U.S. aid to the contras. The contras always have sought to topple the Sandinistas and to "restore democracy," Calero said. They never were fighting merely to interdict Nicaraguan arms supplies to leftist guerrillas in neighboring El Salvador or to "harass" the Managua regime—the two goals originally cited to Congress in 1982 and 1983. Calero said the contras also wanted more than negotiations between themselves and the Sandinistas—a goal sought by the administration in 1986.

When Cohen listed the administration's shifting goals, Calero said: "Well, we understood that you had to have a reason acceptable by this government in order for us to be supported. And since support means so much, we have to comply with conditions that we do not necessarily like or think are appropriate."

Using Traveler's Checks

The contra army runs on more than guns, boots, and beans. By Calero's testimony, one of its most important tools was the traveler's check—issued unsigned and free of charge by a friendly bank in the Cayman Islands. Calero gave the committees records showing that the FDN spent nearly $3.1 million in traveler's checks from 1984 to 1987. "Traveler's checks are a very handy way for people who are going to be traveling," he explained, prompting Cohen to say the contra leader might want to do a television commercial on their behalf.

Committee investigators spent the weekend of May 16-17 tracing the use of $90,000 of those checks, all of which Calero gave to North in 1985. Calero said North had asked for the money on several occasions, either saying or implying that it would be used to help free U.S. hostages in Lebanon, Calero said.

But Calero said he "sort of imagined," based on conversations with North, that some of the money also probably was used to make payments to other contra leaders who did not want to take money from the FDN. Owen had testified about paying some $30,000 to between six and ten contra leaders, using cash handed him by North.

With the help of the General Accounting Office and old-fashioned police work, the committees quickly traced about $30,000 of the checks. Of that, $25,300 worth were signed by three men identified by committee sources as agents or "associates" of the Drug Enforcement Administration, whom North was using to locate the hostages in Lebanon. North himself cashed another $2,440 in checks in 1985: $220 at local supermarkets, $340 at other retail stores in the Washington area, and $1,880 at hotels, airlines, and other outlets. Committee officials said the information seemed to indicate that North used some of the checks to pay his personal expenses, but cautioned that the evidence did not constitute conclusive proof. *(North testimony text, p. C-75)*

Calero said he gave the money to North because "I had trust that he would use that for the furthering of freedom's cause." However, he told Senator Rudman that he did not intend for the checks to be put to personal use.

Rudman drew Calero's attention to North's use of $100 in traveler's checks to buy snow tires on November 30, 1985. "When was the last time it snowed in Nicaragua?" Rudman asked. "Well sir, it does not snow in Nicaragua," Calero responded. "However, I am sure there is an explanation for that."

Running Cash

Hard cash also was handy for the contra-aid network, and Owen described three trips he took to New York in September and October 1985 to pick up money for North and Secord.

The first trip was on September 16, when North put Owen in touch with Secord, who instructed Owen to go to a Chinese market on the Lower West Side in New York. There, Owen met a man who, after the two identified themselves by their code names, went behind a counter, rolled up his pant leg, and pulled out a wad of $100 bills. Owen said he counted ninety-five bills. Returning to Washington, Owen met Secord at the Sheraton Carlton Hotel and handed over the cash, folded into a newspaper. Owen said he understood the unusual method of obtaining money was needed because September 16 was a bank holiday and Secord appeared to be short of cash.

Owen said he took two other trips to New York at the request of North and Secord. In both cases, Owen said he went to the sixth floor of a bank, asked for a person whose name he had been given, and received an envelope, which he took to North back in Washington. Owen at first told the panels that he did not know what was in the envelopes, but they appeared to contain cash. Later, he said he might have used some money from one of the envelopes to help pay his travel expenses. Committee investigators subsequently said they had tracked the money to accounts associated with the Secord-Hakim financial network.

Also in his courier role, Owen in 1985 delivered a bank account number to a Washington representative of Taiwan, which made two donations of $1 million each to the contras. Owen said North gave him the account number in an envelope, and he delivered the envelope to the office of the Taiwan representative.

The One-Two Punch

North and private fund-raiser Carl R. "Spitz" Channell acted as a team—Senator Rudman called them a "one-two punch"—in getting rich conservatives to donate money on behalf of the contras, according to testimony May 21. *(Channell indictment, p. 170)*

Two donors testified that North in 1985-86 gave them vivid descriptions of the contras' plight and that Channell followed with direct pleas for specific donations to his procontra, tax-exempt foundation, the National Endowment for the Preservation of Liberty.

The approach worked on both donors: Ellen Garwood said she gave $2.2 million to Channell's endowment, and William B. O'Boyle said he gave $160,000. Another donor, Colorado beer company executive Coors, said he sent $65,000 to Secord's Swiss bank account in 1985 at North's suggestion. Coors said he had approached CIA director Casey, a friend, offering to help the contras and was referred to North.

O'Boyle told of a private meeting with North during which the White House aide described a "very, very secret" plan for toppling the government of Nicaragua. O'Boyle related the plan reluctantly, and only after being ordered to do so. Under the plan, he said, the contras would seize a chunk of Nicaraguan territory and declare a provisional government, while the U.S. Navy would blockade Nicaraguan ports—leading to the swift ouster of the regime in Managua.

Panel members expressed fascination with the process by which North and Channell approached the contributors. Representative McCollum sought to emphasize that neither North nor any other administration official—including Reagan—directly asked for donations on behalf of the contras.

But Rudman scoffed at McCollum's assertions, saying it was "legal fiction" that North had not asked for the money. Noting that North's descriptions of the contras' plight invariably were followed by Channell's appeals for money, Rudman told Garwood: "Where we come from, we call that the old one-two punch."

Select committee members told the three donors that much of the money they contributed probably wound up supporting Channell's organizations rather than the contras.

Rivalry among Arms Dealers

Although the administration and many Americans viewed the contras as a charitable cause, arms dealers apparently saw them as a potential source of profits. Calero, Owen, and Singlaub each described cases in which arms dealers vied for the contras' business, but the competition drove prices up, not down. Calero said the contras got their money's worth only once, in 1985, when they bought a large shipment of rifles, ammunition, and other items through Singlaub. One of the world's most vocal anticommunists, Singlaub had bought the weapons from Poland at bargain-basement prices.

Singlaub said his deal encountered only one hitch. Mario Dellamico, a representative of a rival arms dealer, Ronald Martin of Miami, delayed the shipment when it

Joseph Coors, Ellen Garwood, and William B. O'Boyle, pictured standing from left, told how Lt. Col. Oliver L. North persuaded them to make large contributions to private groups, ostensibly to benefit the contras.

arrived in Guatemala and later went to Singlaub's Polish source demanding equivalent weapons prices.

Later in 1985, North insisted that the contras start buying weapons from Secord. Calero made four arms deals with Secord and told the committees he had been surprised to hear Secord's testimony that the weapons were sold at a markup averaging 20 to 30 percent. Secord implied, Calero said, that the weapons were being provided at cost. Calero expressed unhappiness with Secord's operation, saying one shipment of arms was so late that the contras called it

John K. Singlaub

"the slow boat from China"—where the arms originated.

WEEK FOUR: RODRIGUEZ, DUTTON, TAMBS, CASTILLO

The most direct testimony that the committees had thus far been given about involvement in contra activities by senior Reagan officials came May 28 from Lewis A. Tambs, who served as U.S. ambassador to Costa Rica, Nicaragua's southern neighbor, from July 1985 until December 1986. After he resigned his post, Tambs returned to Arizona State University to teach Latin American history. *(Tambs testimony text, p. C-43)*

Testimony by other key figures in the contra supply network depicted a clandestine project that was marred by infighting and unsafe conditions exacerbated by the lure of large profits. Conflicting accounts about running the operation were heard from retired Air Force colonel Robert C. Dutton, who handled day-to-day logistics, and former CIA agent Felix I. Rodriguez, who looked after a variety of chores for the operation in Central America. *(Dutton testimony text, p. C-39; Rodriguez, p. C-40)*

The Southern Front

Tambs said North told him at the time he assumed his diplomatic post that he should open a military front for the contras in southern Nicaragua. The former envoy said he understood that North's instruction came from a three-person Restricted Interagency Group (RIG): North, undersecretary of state Abrams, and a CIA representative. Tambs said he never asked Secretary of State Shultz about the contra military assignment because he assumed that North was acting in behalf of the RIG and under authority of his superiors. He said he never tried to find out who those superiors were.

At the time that Tambs received his order to assist the contras, a version of the Boland amendment then in effect prohibited U.S. government agencies from providing any direct or indirect military aid to the contras. But Tambs

said he never read that law, assuming instead that he had legal authority to help contra forces move from camps in Costa Rica into southern Nicaragua so that they could continue their fight to oust the leftist Sandinista government. "I'm not a lawyer. I probably wouldn't have understood it anyway," Tambs said, referring to the Boland amendment. Later he added, "I have difficulty reading a contract for a refrigerator."

Rather than deal directly with contra military leaders, Tambs entrusted that task to Tomas Castillo, a pseudonym for Joe Fernandez, the CIA station chief in Costa Rica at the time. Tambs said it would have been "unseemly" for him to meet with contra officials because of the sensitivity of his post. The Costa Rican government was worried that the Nicaraguans would invade the country to retaliate for the presence of contras along the border in northern Costa Rica, said Tambs.

Castillo testified before the select panels May 29; the session was behind closed doors so that his physical identity could be shielded. A transcript of Castillo's testimony was withheld temporarily, but committee members said he confirmed earlier accounts about his role in assisting the contras. *(Castillo testimony text, p. C-44)*

The Secret Airstrip

Shortly after he arrived in Costa Rica, Tambs testified, he received an order from North, conveyed through Castillo, to obtain permission from Costa Rican officials to

Lewis A. Tambs

build a secret airstrip to be used for private supply missions to contras in Nicaragua. Tambs said he discussed the airstrip privately with Abrams in September 1985 in Panama during a conference of U.S. diplomats in Central America. Tambs also said that Abrams was briefed on the progress of the airstrip during a visit to Costa Rica later that fall. Abrams "was abreast of all the developments [about the southern front] when I saw him on various occasions," former

ambassador Tambs told the select committees.

"Would you be surprised if you were told that Secretary Abrams has testified that he was not aware of the construction of the airstrip before it was started?" asked Inouye, apparently referring to a private deposition that Abrams gave to the committees. "I would be somewhat surprised, but ... well, he might have been distracted," replied Tambs, who said he was "convinced" that he discussed his southern front assignment with Abrams during the Panama meeting. "It was obvious to me he [Abrams] knew as much about it as I did," said Tambs. *(Abrams testimony, p. 107)*

Tambs said other high-level administration officials also were aware of the existence and purpose of the secret Costa Rican airstrip. He said he discussed the airfield with Poindexter in late December 1985 or January 1986, shortly after Poindexter became Reagan's national security adviser and visited Central America. Tambs also said he discussed the airfield the following July with CIA director Casey at the agency's headquarters in Virginia. Tambs said the two had a general discussion about the "Reagan doctrine" and its strategy of halting communism in Central America. Tambs said he assumed then that Casey was familiar with the airstrip project and the overall contra southern-front effort.

When Costa Rican officials decided to shut down the airfield in May or June 1986, Tambs said he complied with their wishes, instructing its U.S. operators to abandon the field. A few months later, in September, Tambs received a midnight phone call from North telling him that Costa Rican officials were planning to announce the existence of the then-secret airfield the next day at a press conference. Tambs, who was at a West Virginia resort, said North asked him to call Costa Rican President Oscar Arias and "dissuade" him from holding the press conference. Tambs testified that he made the call that night, persuading Arias to cancel the announcement.

In recounting the airfield incident, the Tower Commission said that North might have talked to Arias, threatening to cut off U.S. aid to Costa Rica unless the press conference was canceled. But Tambs told the Hill panels he did not think North ever called Arias.

'Commander Zero' Cables

Tambs also sparred with committee members over a series of cables between him and State Department officials in Washington concerning efforts to funnel supplies to contra military leader Eden Pastora, who was known as "Commander Zero." Tambs began the cable traffic on March 27, 1986, to report on an agreement between Pastora and Singlaub, who was working to raise funds for the contras and also was trying to persuade Pastora to resume an active part in the contras' war against the Sandinistas. In the agreement, Singlaub promised that the United States would provide weapons and other supplies. In exchange, Pastora agreed to cooperate with the other contra factions. *(Singlaub testimony, p. 95)*

In a sharply worded reply cable apparently drafted by Abrams's office but signed by Deputy Secretary of State John Whitehead, Tambs was told that Singlaub was in no position to commit U.S. support in return for his agreement with Pastora. "Your association with this initiative gives this document an unwarranted stamp of official approval," Tambs was told in the March 29 cable. In a subsequent cable, Shultz told Tambs that Pastora might try to "pressure or embarrass" the United States unless Tambs insisted more strongly that the government had no role in the Singlaub-Pastora accord.

Tambs testified that he never intended to suggest a direct U.S. role in Pastora's or Singlaub's activities. He said the reference to the United States in the agreement meant private individuals helping to supply the contras. Singlaub had told the committees May 20 that he had tacit support from Abrams for his effort to get Pastora back into the contra war, but that "someone in the CIA" blocked a planned weapons delivery to Pastora in 1986.

Logistics and Infighting

Dutton, who worked directly under Secord, told the panels May 27 that former CIA agent Rodriguez became a "detriment" to the contra operation after he tried to carve out a larger role for himself, including control over funds used to pay for fuel and other airlift expenses. Dutton also said that North and Secord became convinced that Rodriguez, who used the alias Max Gomez, posed a security risk to the operation after they suspected him of discussing it with others over open telephone lines instead of through secret-code devices.

But Dutton said it was impossible to remove Rodriguez from the operation because he was "well connected" to U.S. officials, whom he did not identify. Dutton also cited Rodriguez's ties to officials in El Salvador, where the supply effort was run from Ilopango air base, a large military installation.

Rodriguez provided a far different picture of the contra operation. Defending his role, he criticized Dutton and others for paying too little attention to faulty planes and equipment; these flaws, he said, resulted in dangerous conditions for the crews flying the Nicaraguan missions.

Robert C. Dutton

A Cuban native who worked for the CIA during the 1961 Bay of Pigs invasion, Rodriguez was recruited by North in September 1985 to assist in the contra supply operation. Rodriguez retired from the CIA in 1976; he later went to El Salvador to help its government battle leftist insurgents. He said he became disenchanted with the contra operation early in 1986, largely because he learned that Secord and others were involved. In particular, he was troubled by ties that some of them had with former CIA agent Edwin P. Wilson, who was serving a fifty-two-year prison term for selling explosives to Libyan leader Muammar el-Qaddafi.

Rodriguez said he first complained to North about the operation in February 1986 because of an incident involving a mechanic who was sent to work at Ilopango. Rodriguez said the man drank twenty-four beers during his first day on the job, and thirty-six beers the second day. "He was so old he looked like he was walking to a nursing home after that," said Rodriguez.

Secord came on the line after Rodriguez called North and gave permission to fire the mechanic. After that incident, Rodriguez said he grew more suspicious about the operation. "I don't know if I got a sixth feeling or something, but after I saw the people in there, I didn't feel comfortable with it," he told the committees. But he said North later persuaded him to stay after getting an unidentified U.S. ambassador in Central America to compliment Rodriguez on his work in the region. (According to a December 1986 chronology released by Vice President George Bush's office, Rodriguez May 1, 1986, met with Bush, North, and others to discuss counterinsurgency operations in El Salvador. At the meeting Rodriguez's performance in El Salvador received strong praise from U.S. ambassador to El Salvador Edwin G. Corr.)

Complaining to a Bush Aide

Rodriguez, however, said he continued to have reservations. In August, he complained about North's contra operation to Donald P. Gregg, national security adviser to Vice President Bush. Rodriguez and Gregg had become close friends while serving in Vietnam during the 1960s.

Rodriguez also met with Bush on a few occasions during his contra activities but said he never discussed anything "remotely connected" to the contras during his meetings with Bush. Instead, Rodriguez said the two talked about Rodriguez's efforts to help El Salvador battle leftist rebels.

During the August 8 meeting with Gregg at his White House office, Rodriguez pointed out North's involvement with Secord and others who had been associated with Wilson. He also told Gregg that arms dealers appeared to be making huge profits from the contras. Rodriguez said he heard about one incident where Thomas Clines, a Secord associate, charged nine dollars for hand grenades that cost him only three dollars.

Gregg's handwritten notes from the meeting mentioned that Rodriguez talked of North "using Ed Wilson group for supplies." The notes also said "a swap of weapons for $ [sic] was arranged to get aid for contras," an apparent reference to Secord's efforts to arm the Nicaraguan rebels. Rodriguez, however, testified that he did not discuss a weapons swap in his meeting with Gregg and did not know why Gregg put that in his notes. *(Gregg testimony, p. 143)*

Safety Concerns

During an earlier June 1986 meeting in Washington with North and Dutton, Rodriguez showed them a letter that bitterly complained about a "criminal disregard" for crew safety. The letter was written by pilot John Piowaty the day after he flew a mission in which the plane grazed a mountain. "I hope you have some answers for me and my fellow crew members. Better that than to have to face five widows. Better that than have to answer in a later court the souls of brave men dead because a professionally demanding mission was launched with a criminal disregard for the elements critical to its success." Hill staffers said they did not know specifically to whom the letter was written.

Felix I. Rodriguez

Rodriguez said Dutton at first asked if the letter was a joke when Rodriguez showed it to him in North's office. Rodriguez testified that Dutton later said he would take care of Piowaty's complaint by promoting him. A subsequent flow chart of the supply operation listed Piowaty as the maintenance director. Dutton was not asked about Piowaty's letter.

During the same June meeting with North, Rodriguez said he warned of the dangers of the contra operation being exposed, particularly in light of the ties that Secord and others had to Wilson. Rodriguez testified that he told North the situation would be "worse than Watergate, and this could destroy the president of the United States" if the operation became public. He also said that North adopted a defiant stance toward Congress at the same meeting. Drawing Rodriguez aside, North pointed to a television in his office showing part of a House debate in progress that

day on whether to resume aid to the contras. "Those people want me but they can't touch me because the old man loves my ass," Rodriguez quoted North. Rodriguez said he assumed the "old man" referred to Reagan.

A Series of Foul-Ups

In a related concern about the contra operation, Rodriguez told the panels he began to worry in the summer of 1986 that Secord and his associates might end the operation by taking the planes out of the area. Because contra leaders assumed that the planes belonged to them, Rodriguez put armed contra soldiers on the supply missions to ensure that the aircraft remained in Central America. He said that one of the guards was a seventeen-year-old soldier who later died in the cargo plane downed by the Sandinistas in October 1986.

Dutton, during his testimony, described North and Secord as "co-commanders" of the contra operation. He said North "indicated to me that we were working for the president of the United States" when the contra mission was first explained to him. Like Tambs, Dutton said he did not think there was anything illegal about the contra operation. "I had no need to question the legality of what we were doing. I just took it as an assumption that it was legal," he said.

Dutton, a twenty-six-year Air Force veteran, was involved in the unsuccessful effort to rescue American hostages in Tehran during Jimmy Carter's presidency. The day after he retired from the military in May 1986, he went to work for Secord. His job was to improve an operation that suffered from navigational foul-ups, lack of weather information, and other mishaps that prevented it on several occasions from fulfilling its mission of dropping supplies to the contras inside Nicaragua, primarily to the southern front. "We couldn't find the troops and they couldn't find us," he said. Asked if other U.S. officials helped, Dutton said there was "no way" the effort could have succeeded without the assistance of Castillo.

Castillo, for example, helped arrange permission for two supply flights to refuel at Costa Rica's international airport in mid-1986 after the secret airstrip had been closed down. In his own effort to assess some of the supply problems, Dutton flew on one of the flights into Nicaragua in September for a firsthand look. North later told him not to fly such missions because it was too risky.

Many of the bugs were worked out by September 1986, when as many as fifteen successful drops were made. Dutton said a total of about 185,000 pounds of weapons and other supplies were delivered to the contras that month. But the operation was exposed the next month after the Sandinistas shot down a contra supply cargo plane October 5. Two American crewmen died in the incident and a third, Eugene Hasenfus, was captured.

While the airlift was still under way, Dutton put together a photo album—displayed at the hearing—to give North a visual aid in explaining the operation. North told Dutton he planned to show it to the "top boss," whom Dutton understood to be Reagan.

One part of Dutton's testimony differed with a private deposition given to the committees by Shirley A. Napier, Secord's secretary. Dutton told the panels that Secord called Dutton to arrange for someone to pick up a "package" from Southern Air Transport in Miami and deliver it to North's White House office. Southern Air leased planes used in the contra operation.

According to Inouye, Napier told investigators that Dutton informed her she would be picking up $16,000 in cash. But Dutton testified that he did not know what the package contained until Napier arrived in Miami and signed for it. Dutton added that he did not know what North did with the money. *(Napier deposition, p. 151)*

Profit Questions

Dutton's testimony also clashed with Secord's on a crucial point pursued by several committee members—whether Secord was out to make a profit in the Iran-contra deals. Secord insisted during his May 5-8 testimony that he was not interested in profits. But Dutton told the committees that it was Secord who suggested that more than $4 million worth of supplies and other assets related to the contra operation be sold or leased to the CIA beginning in late 1986. Secord testified earlier that the suggestion to sell the assets to the CIA came from Dutton. "The idea was not mine," said Dutton. He said he wrote a document listing options for turning the operation over to the CIA, but that Secord had told him what to include.

Ranking Senate committee member Rudman also accused Secord of overcharging for profit. He said that an invoice for slightly more than $100,000 prepared in March 1986 contained as much as $40,000 to $50,000 in profits. The invoice, which Rudman said included inflated salaries for airlift crew, was paid by Lake Resources. That Panamanian shell company was controlled by Secord and Hakim and financed by profits earned from the sale of U.S. weapons to Iran and private donations to the contras. "I kind of get a little bit bewildered when people come up here and testify when they were just doing this for great patriotic reasons when the records are absolutely contrary," said Rudman.

Rodriguez said that North told him he wanted to buy better planes but that he could not because of a lack of funds. That prompted Republican senator Trible to ask Rodriguez how he felt now, knowing that Secord had "millions of dollars socked away in secret bank accounts."

"It infuriated a lot of people who believed strongly in the cause of democracy," said Rodriguez. Asked a few moments later if he considered Secord and others involved in the contra network as patriots, Rodriguez dryly replied: "I leave it to you and the American people to decide for yourself."

WEEK FIVE:
ABRAMS, HAKIM, LEWIS

As the hearings entered their fifth week, the Iran-contra committees began winding up the first phase of the probe, which focused on secret contra aid. Slowly, but determinedly, the panels were piecing together how the Reagan administration's zeal to rescue hostages and assist the Nicaraguan rebels mixed with the appetites of others for huge profits to cause a crisis in American diplomacy.

During the fifth week of testimony, the panels heard from two principal witnesses: Elliott Abrams, the assistant secretary of state for inter-American affairs (on June 2-3) and Albert Hakim, Secord's Iranian-born business partner who arranged the financial network behind the contra arms supplies and Iran arms sales (on June 3-5). The panels had granted immunity to Hakim, who was living in France at the time. Also appearing that week (on June 4) was David L. Lewis, who testified about accounts Hakim had set up to protect North's family's financial security. *(Abrams testimony text, p. C-47; Hakim, p. C-51; Lewis, p. C-59)*

Abrams explained a series of misleading statements he made to Congress in 1986 denying official U.S. involvement in contra-aid activities. He acknowledged that administration misconduct endangered one of Reagan's highest priorities: renewing official U.S. aid to the contras when the existing $100 million infusion expired.

Hakim provided a wealth of information about how he and Secord financed and carried out foreign policy. Using Swiss bank accounts, aging cargo planes, and dummy corporations, Secord and Hakim secretly sold arms to Iran and airlifted supplies to the contras at a time when official U.S. aid was sharply curtailed.

Hakim the Money Man

As the Iran-contra money manager, Hakim spent most of his time in the witness chair testifying about the bewildering network of overseas bank accounts and companies that he had established between 1984 and 1986. Hakim and Secord called this far-flung network "the enterprise."

But Hakim also shed new light on the negotiations between U.S. and Iranian officials in 1986 that led to arms sales in an effort to gain release of Americans held hostage by pro-Iran groups in Lebanon. A native of Iran who became a U.S. citizen, Hakim had no experience in foreign diplomacy, but he could speak Farsi—the official Iranian language—and so he acted as translator and negotiator when the CIA could not produce a Farsi-speaking agent. (It was later pointed out that if it had been fully advised of the transaction, the State Department could have provided one of a number of expert Farsi interpreters.)

Albert Hakim

In a startling revelation, Hakim said he and Secord in 1986 promised Iranian officials that the United States would "fight Russians" if they invaded. Senate panel chairman Inouye called it "just unbelievable" that private citizens would make such a pledge. When Senate committee counsel Liman asked Hakim if he was bothered by a citizen negotiating agreements with a foreign country, Hakim responded: "Mr. Liman, what bothered me was that we didn't have the competence within the government to do what I could do. That still bothers me."

Funds for North

Hakim further said he made several attempts in 1986 to provide financial security for North and his family—

Financial Maze of Iran-Contra Affair ...

When Attorney General Edwin Meese III disclosed the diversion of Iranian arms sales profits to the contras on November 25, 1986, one of the principal questions that was asked was: How much actually was diverted?

Meese estimated that between $10 million and $30 million had been diverted to the contras, apparently based on rough figures supplied by fired National Security Council aide Lt. Col. Oliver L. North. During their investigation, the House and Senate Iran-contra committees discovered that the diversion was far less than the bottom end of the range Meese gave.

New details about the money flow emerged May 6-7, 1987, when the Iran panels took testimony from retired major general Richard V. Secord, and the House committee released portions of private testimony given two weeks earlier by Secord's business partner, Albert Hakim.

Hakim had turned over to the panel the records of secret bank accounts used in financing the Iran arms sales and contra-aid operations. Most of the records involved Lake Resources Inc., a Panamanian shell corporation controlled by Hakim. However, Secord said he gave Hakim "oral direction" over use of the money.

Based on those records, Secord said it appeared that about $3.5 million in profits from the Iranian arms sales was used to support his private network that supplied weapons and other gear to the Nicaraguan rebels in 1986.

Secord's group in 1985 had sold the contras millions' worth of weapons but charged them prices that reflected an average profit of 20 percent, he said.

During its Iran-contra operations, from December 1984 through October 1986, the Secord-controlled organization took in $47.7 million and spent $40.2 million, according to Hakim's testimony. Of the income, about $30 million came from Iran arms sales and the rest was generated by Secord's private arms sales to the contras and private donations meant to benefit the contras. Nearly $8 million remained unspent in the Swiss accounts at the time of the select committees hearings; Secord said his organization had debts of about $500,000 that might need to be paid from the money.

Secord's Testimony

At the outset of his testimony May 5, Secord gave House committee counsel John W. Nields, Jr., the following breakdown of what happened to the $30 million in Iranian payments for U.S. arms delivered in 1986:

• $12.3 million was reimbursed to the Pentagon, through the Central Intelligence Agency (CIA), for the cost of the weapons, primarily TOW antitank missiles, and parts for Hawk antiaircraft missiles.

• $6.53 million was being held by a Swiss financial services firm, Compagnie de Services Fiduciaires, for Hakim's "benefit." Secord did not explain what he meant by that, except to say that Hakim could use the money as he wished. Secord swore he had no interest in the money, other than to pay off his organization's debts.

• $1.36 million remained in Lake Resources accounts.

• Some $3 million was spent to ship the arms to Iran.

• About $3.5 million was spent on the private network aiding the contras. That included the cost of weapons, salaries, and other expenses for air supply drops to the contras in Nicaragua and payments to contra leaders, including $10,000 a month to Alfonso Robelo and $5,000 a month to Arturo Cruz. Secord said leaders of the main contra group, the Nicaraguan Democratic Force (FDN), also got $200,000; some of that went in several deposits to accounts controlled by FDN leader Adolfo Calero, but Secord did not specify how much.

• About $2 million was unaccounted for, Secord said.

• About $1 million was used for other purposes related to neither Nicaragua nor Iran. That included, Secord said, $350,000 to buy a Danish-flag ship, the *Erria*, in April 1986; $100,000 to buy radio-telephone equipment for an unidentified Caribbean country, reportedly for a covert project against Cuban leader Fidel Castro; and unspecified "expense payments" in cash to Drug Enforcement Administration (DEA) agents in Europe who were working to locate and rescue U.S. hostages in Lebanon.

The *Erria* was purchased as a platform for broadcasting propaganda into Libya but later was used for at least one unsuccessful arms delivery to the contras.

The DEA refused comment on Secord's statement about what would appear to be an unusual use of its agents. Secord gave no details about what the agents were supposed to have done in return for the cash payments, which might have totaled several hundred thousand dollars, given the breakdown Secord provided.

Secord said his $3.5 million figure for the contras tracked with another way of calculating the net diversion of Iranian arms money. After February 1986, he said, his private aid network spent $5.5 million to $6 million on the contras. Of that, $1.65 million came from private donations and $470,000 already was in network-controlled bank accounts, the apparent result of Secord's commercial arms sales to the contras.

... Records of Secord-Hakim 'Enterprise'

Subtracting that $2 million-plus from the total amount spent by the private aid network produced a figure close to the $3.5 million netted from the Iran sales.

Although he refused to use the word "profit," Secord made it clear that his organization made money on all of its arms transactions—often at a high rate. *(Secord testimony, p. 87)*

Hakim's Records of 'The Enterprise'

A somewhat differing account of the cash flow was provided by Hakim.

Based on his records and information, the House and Senate Iran-contra committees were able to document the following overall receipts and expenditures from 1984 to 1986 of "the enterprise"—the companies and bank accounts involved in aiding the contras and selling arms to Iran on behalf of the U.S. government.

December 1984 - July 1985

Income: $11.4 million in payments from the Nicaraguan Democratic Force for weapons sold by Hakim and Secord.

Disbursements: $9.3 million total, including: $8.6 million to buy and transport arms for the contras; $600,000 in unidentified transactions; and $100,000 disbursed to Stanford Technology Trading Group International on behalf of Hakim and Secord, co-owners.

Remaining: $2.1 million total, including: $1.4 million in "capital accounts" for the benefit of Hakim, Secord, and others, and $700,000 in bank accounts.

August 1985 - December 1986

Income. $35.6 million total, including: $700,000 carried over from previous transactions; $1.8 million donated by private individuals on behalf of the contras (principally through the Washington public relations firm International Business Communications and its affiliates); $2 million from Taiwan; and $31.1 million generated by the sale of weapons to Iran.

Disbursements: $26 million total, including: $14.4 million to buy and transport U.S. arms to Iran; $7.9 million spent to aid the contras (apparently for arms shipments); $900,000 for three projects authorized by North (the purchase of the *Erria*, the purchase of radios for a Caribbean country, and the payment of cash to DEA agents); $600,000 paid to Secord and Hakim; a $900,000 bookkeeping loss on the sale of weapons to the CIA that had been intended for the contras; $700,000 in general expenses such as accounting and legal fees; and $600,000 un-

identified.

Remaining: $11 million, including: $1.4 million in bank accounts frozen by authorities in Switzerland and other countries; and $9.6 million in "capital accounts" for the benefit of Hakim, Secord, and others. The $11 million and $9.6 million figures include $1.4 million carried over from December 1984 to July 1985.

Capital Accounts

The panels provided two sets of figures for the "capital accounts" Hakim set up to benefit himself and others. This money represented part of the profits from the sales of arms to Iran and the Nicaraguan contras.

As of December 4, 1986, the accounts totaled $9.672 million; by May 27, 1987, they had shrunk to $6.667 million. Committee officials said that money had been invested with Merrill-Lynch in a London bank.

The capital accounts were:

Albert Hakim. Hakim established several accounts for his own benefit. They had $6.833 million in December 1986 and $4.679 million in May 1987. Hakim testified that $2.154 million was distributed from his accounts for "operational expenses and other purposes."

Korel Assets. Hakim testified that this account was for Secord's benefit; Secord testified that he knew nothing about it and had renounced his interest in the money. In December 1986 this account had $1.042 million, and in May 1987 it had $1.578 million. Hakim said he could not explain the large increase but attributed it to profitable investments and a "misallocation" by accountants. Hakim testified before the select committees June 5 that Secord withdrew slightly more than $82,000 from this account for his own use.

C. Tea. Hakim testified that this account was established for Thomas G. Clines, a former CIA official who was a major supplier of arms to the contras in 1985. The account stood at $990,000 in December 1986, but Hakim said Clines had subsequently withdrawn the money.

SciTech. Hakim testified that this account was established for Stanford Technology Trading Group International. The account had $605,984 in December 1986 and $193,717 in May 1987. Hakim did not explain the $412,267 in disbursements from that account.

B. Button. Hakim testified that he established this account in 1986 for North and his family. The account had $200,000 in December 1986 and $216,144 in May 1987.

There were no disbursements from it, according to committee records.

even though he knew it was illegal to make large gifts to U.S. government officials. Nothing came of the efforts, Hakim said, because lawyers could not find a way that was both "proper" and secret to get money to North.

In his first day of testimony, on June 3, Hakim sought to leave the impression that North had no way of knowing about the intended benefits. But under grilling the next day by Liman, he acknowledged that North might well have known about them (in subsequent testimony, North denied such knowledge). In any event, Hakim said, North never said anything to him about the matter.

Hakim said he was impressed by North at their first meeting in February 1986. "I really love this man," he said, praising North's willingness to die for his country.

About two months after meeting North, Hakim in May 1986 put $200,000 into an account for the benefit of North and his family. The money could be used either for death benefits if North were killed or to educate North's four children, Hakim said. Hakim named the account "B. Button"—short for "bellybutton," which he said was a private joke between himself and Secord. Hakim never explained the joke, however.

Liman focused on the timing, noting that Hakim sought to become North's benefactor weeks after meeting him. "So would it be a fair description, to use your term of 'love,' that it was love at first sight?" Liman asked. "You are correct on that, sir," Hakim replied, adding that North's own love of country and colleagues "immediately penetrated my system."

Also in May, Hakim signed a two-page set of instructions for the disposition of a $2 million reserve fund in the event that Hakim died. The money would pass first to Secord, and, if he died or became disabled, to North. Once obtaining control, Secord or North could have used the money as he wished, according to the instructions. Hakim said he wanted the $2 million to remain under control of the enterprise, which he said was headed by himself, Secord, and North.

In the fall of 1986, Hakim began working on a scheme to make one or more payments to the North family, either directly or through relatives. Hakim said he first considered funneling money through a relative, and he sent his Geneva-based attorney, Willard Zucker, to meet with North's wife, Betsy, to find out about the "family structure." Hakim said he understood that Zucker met with Mrs. North in Philadelphia, but that Zucker was unable to find a way to get money to the family. The panels released private testimony by a New Jersey lawyer, Harold G. Cohen, that tended to corroborate Hakim's assertions that Zucker and Mrs. North met on September 27, 1986.

With that idea dead, Hakim began working on a scheme to channel money to Mrs. North through a real estate agent, in the form of a commission for a real or phony property transaction. In his June 4 testimony, Washington attorney Lewis recounted a conversation in which Zucker explained how he planned the real estate deal. Lewis said he met in Geneva in October 1986 with Zucker, a longtime acquaintance, on unrelated business. At a lunch, Zucker described to Lewis a scheme under which a "wealthy client" of his would put money into the account of a Washington-area real estate agent, and the agent, in turn, would turn the same amount of money over to the wife of "someone in the White House." Lewis said he remembered—but was not certain—that the official's name was Oliver North. Lewis said he recalled that the amount involved was about $70,000.

In a related matter, the committees released one curious document that could be read as indicating that Hakim's organization in May 1986 paid $15,000 to Mrs. North, identified in the document as "Mrs. Bellybutton." However, Hakim said he did not recall such a payment, which would have been "irregular."

David L. Lewis

Secord knew of the $200,000 account in North's name and may well have told North about it, Hakim said. Hakim also said it was "my assumption" that Secord would tell North that he was named in the will making arrangements for the $2 million reserve. And Hakim also said North probably knew who Zucker was representing when he contacted Mrs. North.

Making Money

At the outset of his testimony, on June 3, Hakim stated repeatedly that he sought to make money on his Iran-contra dealings. His business, he said, was not "philanthropic." That statement stood in sharp contrast to Secord's assertions that he renounced his profits on 1985 arms sales to the contras and that he never intended to benefit from the Iranian deals. Several members said they had trouble believing Secord, and the panels produced evidence that Secord used some of the money for his own benefit.

Hakim acknowledged June 4 that some of the Iranians with whom he dealt also sought to make money on the sales. Hakim said he still had a "commitment" to pay some of those Iranians for helping to arrange contacts with high government officials in Tehran but did not know how much was owed.

Under questioning by Liman, Hakim said that U.S. officials—principally North—knew that Hakim, Secord, and some of the Iranians sought to make money on the arms sales. Hakim said he and Secord hoped for even greater profits on future arms sales to Iran. Asked by Liman if the two thought they could "make a bundle" over the years, Hakim said: "Yes, sir."

After listening to Hakim's convoluted explanation of the arms-for-hostages negotiations, Liman said he had the impression "that North is hustling you, that you are hustling North, that the Iranians are hustling you, that you are hustling the Iranians and that it really is, as you said here, a commercial type of environment." Hakim called that comment "unfair," but Liman later said he would "leave it to others" to judge its validity.

The committees also produced records that cast doubt on Secord's assertions in May that he did not want to profit from the enterprise's arms sales to the contras and Iran. One set of records showed that Secord in 1985-86 took more than $80,000 from an account that Hakim had set aside for Secord's benefit, using profits from the arms sales. According to those records and statements by Senator Trible, Secord bought a Piper Seneca airplane using a $52,500 check from the Swiss accounts, bought a Porsche car for some $30,000, and paid $2,300 to go with arms dealer Clines to what Trible called a "fat farm." The expenditures, while possibly legal, "raise a question about the credibility of Gen. Secord," Trible said.

Other committee documents indicated that Secord and Hakim earned huge profits on arms sold to the contras in 1985. In one deal, Secord and Hakim charged the contras $307,200 for arms that cost them $188,300, a 61 percent markup. Later, the rebels paid about $1.8 million for weapons that cost Secord and Hakim about $1.2 million, about a 50 percent markup. Hakim said Secord set the prices for the weapons they sold to the contras. *(Secord testimony, p. 87)*

Negotiating for the United States

Hakim proudly described for the committees his role in October 1986 in negotiating an agreement that led to the last shipment of U.S. weapons to Iran. But Liman cast Hakim's actions in a less positive light, noting that Hakim, a private businessman seeking a profit, was conducting foreign policy on behalf of the U.S. government.

The incident began with a meeting in Frankfurt, at which North presented a seven-point plan for the release of all American hostages held in Lebanon in return for the sale of 1,500 TOW antitank missiles by the United States. Iranian representatives rejected the plan, and North left for Washington. Hakim said he sought, at North's request, to reach an agreement with the Iranians and eventually drafted a new nine-point plan. It called for release of only one or two hostages, in return for the sale of 500 TOW missiles. It also included—contrary to U.S. policy—a promise that Hakim would produce a plan for the release of seventeen Moslem terrorists jailed in Kuwait.

Hakim said he sent the nine-point agreement to North in Washington and heard back that it had been approved by "the White House." That proposal, when finally brought to the president's attention, was dramatically denounced by him. *(See Shultz testimony, p. 132)*

Liman noted that Hakim, as a private citizen and businessman, was acting for the United States, "seeking not just to advance the United States' interests, but profit." But Hakim insisted that he was "serving a number of motivations," including advancing the interest of the United States.

One of the negotiating sessions that Hakim attended was a lengthy meeting in September at North's office adjacent to the White House. Late at night, after the session was concluded, North took a visiting Iranian official for a tour of the White House. The tour covered "every corner" of the White House, including the Oval Office and the super-secret Situation Room.

Influencing U.S. Elections

Hakim said on June 4 he had the "understanding" in the fall of 1986 that North—an active-duty military officer—wanted to gain the release of all U.S. hostages in Lebanon in hopes of improving the chances for Republicans in congressional elections. North never discussed the issue directly, Hakim said, but left the impression that he wanted to "remove this obstacle [the hostages] for the purpose of enhancing the president's [political] position."

In a prior deposition to the panels, Hakim put that statement in a broader context, saying that he had told North to stop focusing on the hostages. Hakim said North's

"prime objective at that time was to support the president in connection with the Republicans for the elections, and I found [emphasis on the hostages] to be counterproductive. And . . . this is not a good negotiating tactic." Hakim stood by that deposition June 4, adding that he felt under "political pressure" to help the hostages.

Abrams on the Line

One of the Reagan administration's most controversial figures acknowledged to the Iran-contra committees that he had misled Congress in the past—mostly because other officials had misled him.

Abrams, who had been appointed in July 1985 as the administration's senior official on Latin American affairs, including the contra program, retracted many of his past statements to Congress but staunchly defended his actions and insisted he intended to remain in office.

Abrams swore to the committees that he knew little about the activities of other U.S. government officials who were aiding the contras, including one ambassador who

Elliott Abrams

reported directly to him. He also claimed ignorance of major details about contra operations during 1984-85, including the fact that Saudi Arabia was the contras' main source of income. Near the end of his two grueling days of testimony June 2-3, several committee members said that Abrams might have to resign since he no longer had the trust of Congress. But Abrams found some defenders in powerful places. Secretary of State Shultz instructed State Department spokesman Charles Redman to say June 3 that Abrams was doing "a sensational job" and would be kept. At Shultz's request, White House spokesman Fitzwater the next day said that "we share the secretary's view." Shultz restated that position during his own testimony before the committees July 24-25. *(See p. 133)*

Always a combative witness at Hill hearings, Abrams did not shrink from challenging his questioners, and he displayed little of the contrite manner that some committee members appeared to be looking for. At the end of Abrams's first day on the stand, Senator Cohen told reporters: "You know when you deal with Elliott you are engaging in the crossing of verbal swords."

Misleading Congress

Committee members focused much of their attention on false or misleading statements that Abrams made to congressional panels in the fall of 1986 following disclosures about the private contra-aid supply network. Abrams later retracted or modified many of those statements. But in his appearance before the select committees, the assistant secretary defended his behavior, leading members to give little credence to his protestations that he fully accepted the need to keep Congress informed of administration actions. Abrams acknowledged that he previously had played games with words and deliberately gave misleading answers to questions. After hearing that, Senator Trible demonstrated the concern of committee members that Abrams might not yet be telling the truth. Questioning Abrams on a minor matter, Trible asked in frustration: "Am I asking the right question?" Abrams assured Trible that he was.

Others repeatedly complained that Abrams failed to ask other U.S. officials what was going on and, as a result, had misled Congress. Senator Rudman said Abrams appeared to have "an incomprehensible lack of curiosity" about elements of the contra-aid program. And Senator Cohen said Abrams was one of a "string of witnesses who suffer from either accommodating amnesia, bland indifference or deliberate ignorance." Cohen told Abrams he was "wrong at the top of your lungs."

House committee chairman Hamilton sternly lectured Abrams on his responsibilities to tell Congress the truth. "The object here is not to avoid a perjury indictment," Hamilton said. "The object is not to work to make your answer literally correct but nonetheless misleading. The object is to make the Constitution of the United States work."

Role in Contra Funding

The committees focused on Abrams's fall 1986 statements to Congress about two subjects: U.S. government involvement in the contra resupply network, and U.S. solicitation of foreign leaders to support the project.

As the administration's senior official on Central American affairs, Abrams had testified before several committees during October and November 1986. The testimony followed the October 5 downing in Nicaragua of a supply plane operated by the private contra-aid network, in which the sole survivor, Hasenfus, claimed to have been working for the CIA. Abrams acknowledged that he had given two House committees wrong and misleading information about the Hasenfus flight. On October 14, Abrams appeared before the House Foreign Affairs Subcommittee on Western Hemisphere Affairs and said no U.S. government official "was engaged in facilitating this flight or paying for it or directing it or anything like that. There is no U.S. government involvement, no government involvement, including anybody in the embassies overseas." (But the select committees during their investigation compiled testimony that several U.S. officials, including the ambassador to Costa Rica, the CIA station chief in Costa Rica, and the head of the U.S. military mission in El Salvador assisted the contra supply network.) Confronted on June 2 with the transcript of his Foreign Affairs testimony, Abrams said he had made similar statements to Shultz. "Every one of those statements, private and public, was completely honest and completely wrong," he said.

More generally, Abrams on June 3 acknowledged that he had given "categorical assurances" to Shultz, to Congress, and to the press that no one in the administration—including North—was violating the Boland amendment restrictions on contra aid. Abrams said he made those assurances without asking North directly whether he was violating the law "because I was confident that there was no such activity going on."

Abrams also said he did not tell the Senate Intelligence Committee about a $10 million Brunei gift intended for the contras because members asked about money from "Mid Eastern" countries, and Brunei is located in the South China Sea. Abrams insisted that Shultz had not "authorized" him to tell the panel about the Brunei donation. And he said he was "in a bind" because a November 25 hearing took place shortly after the bombshell White House announcement that profits from the Iran arms sales had gone to the contras.

Abrams stressed that he apologized to the Intelligence Committee on December 8. But Senator Boren, a member of both the Intelligence and select panels, said Abrams offered his apology only after a "heated exchange" with senators and after being told he should do so. Boren accused Abrams of trying to leave the impression with select committee members "that you came with a heavy heart" to the Intelligence Committee.

'Tin Cup' Diplomacy

Abrams gave the select panels new details on his solicitation of the government of Brunei. He joined the parade of witnesses who at one point adopted aliases: Abrams said he called himself "Mr. Kenilworth" during a trip to London in August 1986.

The solicitation of Brunei stemmed from a May 1986 decision by administration officials—apparently including Reagan—to ask foreign governments to provide "bridge" funds for the contras in the expectation that Congress later would approve renewing direct U.S. aid. In selecting countries to ask for money, Abrams said he used several criteria: They had to be rich, had to be friendly to the United States, and—at the insistence of Shultz—could not be a "right-wing dictatorship." Abrams said he narrowed his list to oil-producing countries but then excluded most Middle East nations because a State Department colleague said they had no interest in Central America. Abrams insisted that he was unaware until recently that Saudi Arabia had given some $32 million to the contras in 1984-85. Abrams also eliminated another oil-producing country, Venezuela, which had been critical of U.S. policy in Nicaragua. At that point, he said: "You are down to Brunei."

Abrams traveled to London in August 1986 and, by arrangement, walked in a park with a Brunei official. After giving a speech about the importance of Central America to the United States, Abrams directly asked for $10 million. He also handed over a card, provided by North, showing the Swiss Bank account of Lake Resources Inc.—the shell company controlled by Hakim and Secord.

Asked by Representative Broomfield about the propriety of soliciting money from a foreign country that might want something in return, Abrams said: "I have to tell you that I consider it is shameful for the United States to be going around rattling a tin cup. I did it because the contras were, as far as I knew, starved."

Congress had specifically authorized such solicitations, Abrams said, and "it would have been immoral in my view to have failed to use that authority, but it is a practice that I think is awful."

Working with North

Although acknowledging that he might have been "betrayed" by North, Abrams insisted that he trusted the NSC aide and disputed an assessment by Shultz that North was a "loose cannon." Abrams said Shultz asked him on September 4, 1985, to "monitor" North, particularly in light of persistent press reports about his activities on behalf of the contras. But Abrams admitted that he did little actual monitoring and asked North only cursory questions. "I wanted to know what my people were doing in detail," Abrams said. "With respect to people in other agencies, as long as I was sure they were not violating the law, that was what I needed to know, and I didn't need to know the details beyond that." Abrams said he did ask North whether he was abiding by the law, and North responded that he had cleared his actions with the White House counsel.

Abrams had told the Tower Commission that he was "careful not to ask North lots of questions." He did not need to ask questions, Abrams told the select committees, because former national security adviser McFarlane, North's boss through 1985, had assured Congress that North was abiding by the law. Under questioning, Abrams defended North for having suggested a plan under which the contras would capture parts of Nicaragua in hopes of provoking direct intervention in the war by the U.S. military. As described by Abrams, the plan bore some similarity to a "secret plan" that William B. O'Boyle, a private contributor to procontra causes, had said North described to him in 1986. Under that plan, the contras would seize Nicaraguan territory, and the U.S. Navy would block arms shipments to the government in Managua, causing its downfall. Although the plan "disappeared" and never was taken seriously, Abrams said North had the right to propose it and did so "through channels." *(O'Boyle testimony, p. 95)*

The Airstrip and Southern Front

By his testimony, Abrams in 1985-86 seemed to have remarkably little knowledge or curiosity about an airstrip built in Costa Rica by the contra supply network with the cooperation of U.S. officials. The airstrip was intended for emergency landings by supply planes after they had delivered weapons and other goods to contra camps deep inside Nicaragua.

Abrams said he learned of the existence of the strip in August or September 1985, shortly after becoming assistant secretary. But he said he asked few questions about it and assumed it was "obvious" that no U.S. officials were involved because that "would have been illegal."

In their previous testimony, former U.S. ambassador to Costa Rica Tambs and CIA station chief Castillo had described their roles in negotiating the airstrip. *(Testimony, p. 100)*

Abrams sought to play down the importance of the airstrip, saying it was only one of "hundreds" of such facilities in Central America. However, he stood by the hardball tactics that he and other U.S. officials used to keep the existence of the airstrip secret. Abrams gave his version—the third so far—of what the United States did in September 1986 to block disclosure of the facility.

The issue arose when a Costa Rican cabinet official planned a press conference at which he was going to expose the existence of the airstrip and its ties to the contras. North called Abrams late on a Friday night, asking if the State Department could put pressure on Costa Rican president Oscar Arias to cancel it. Abrams said he agreed and instructed Tambs by telephone to call Arias demanding that the press conference be canceled. Abrams said he told Tambs to imply that the United States might withdraw an invitation for Arias to visit unless he complied. Abrams testified that Tambs later called back to report that he had

spoken with Arias, who had agreed to call off the press conference.

In his testimony about the same incident Tambs had not mentioned the threat to cancel Arias's trip to Washington. The former ambassador testified only that he told Arias the press conference "would not be prudent" in light of a World Court case in which Nicaragua was accusing the United States of aggression.

North gave another version of the incident in a memo reproduced in the report of the Tower Commission. North told Poindexter, his boss at the time, that he had called Arias and threatened to cut off U.S. aid if the press conference were to be held.

Abrams insisted to the select panels that the U.S. pressure on Arias was an "absolutely legitimate diplomatic activity." But he did not directly answer a question from Senate committee attorney Mark A. Belnick about why high U.S. officials should have intervened with another government on behalf of an airstrip supposedly owned by private citizens—especially since Abrams professed not to know at the time about U.S. involvement in it.

Abrams flatly denied ever having instructed Tambs to open a "southern front" against Nicaragua. Tambs had testified that his main mission in Costa Rica was to help beef up a military operation against the Sandinistas in the southern part of Nicaragua. Tambs said he discussed that mission frequently with other U.S. officials, including Abrams, his direct supervisor. Tambs cited in particular a "hallway conversation" with Abrams during a September 1985 meeting of U.S. diplomats in Panama. Asked if such talks had occurred, Abrams told the committees: "At no time whatsoever." However, Abrams said he and Tambs discussed the need for unity among contra factions.

Singlaub and Pastora

Abrams also disputed two contentions before the select panels by Singlaub: that Abrams had given advance approval in 1986 for Singlaub to ask Taiwan and South Korea for donations to the contras, and that Abrams had approved a Singlaub plan to lure a famous contra leader back to fight the Sandinistas.

Singlaub had testified that Abrams early in 1986 approved Singlaub's plan to solicit aid to the contras from Taiwan and South Korea. Abrams agreed, Singlaub said, to send a "signal" at an appropriate time that Singlaub was acting on behalf of the U.S. government. But Singlaub testified that when he reached Taiwan, Abrams told him not to make the solicitations because high U.S. officials would be seeking the money. Abrams denied to the committees that he had given any such approval to Singlaub in advance and, in fact, said he told Singlaub to "knock it off" once Singlaub informed him of his plans. *(Singlaub testimony, p. 95)*

Abrams also disputed memos to him written at the time by a deputy, Richard Melton, that seemed to confirm Abrams's knowledge of the Singlaub solicitations. In one memo, dated May 15, 1986, Melton said he "had been instructed" to tell Singlaub that "the timing was not right." Abrams said the memo was wrong and cited Melton's private testimony to the select committees as supporting that contention. In any event, Abrams said he never approved the solicitation but merely was keeping Singlaub "strung along" because he generally approved of any efforts to aid the contras. "We didn't want to give him a definitive no," Abrams said. "But there was never any decision ... to give him the help he needed because that was something I felt I did not want to do."

Even so, Singlaub continued to pursue the matter, and for several weeks in the spring of 1986 Melton reported to Abrams that Singlaub was calling with questions about the status of his proposal.

Singlaub and Abrams gave conflicting testimony about an incident earlier in 1986: Singlaub's negotiation of an agreement to get contra leader Eden Pastora and his forces to reenter the fight against the Managua government in return for a promise of aid from the main contra army. Singlaub told the select panels he had discussed his plan in advance with Abrams, who did not object. He said he took Abrams's silence as approval. Abrams, however, insisted that he did not discuss the plan prior to Singlaub's action. Abrams said he relied on the "documentary evidence and my memory" in making that assertion.

Abrams testified that the first he knew about the matter was on March 27, 1986, when Tambs cabled the State Department that Singlaub and Pastora had signed an agreement under which Pastora would return to battle in exchange for a shipment of military supplies by "the United States." Abrams said he was angered by that cable because it implied that the U.S. government was giving official approval to the Singlaub plan. Abrams drafted, and Deputy Secretary of State John C. Whitehead sent, a heated cable denouncing Tambs for failing to dissociate the United States from Singlaub's activities. Abrams told the panels he found Tambs's cable "amazing." Abrams said he later discussed the matter with Singlaub and told the general that "there just wasn't anything we could do for Pastora in the military area."

The testimony about the Singlaub plan provided an insight into bickering among Reagan officials about Pastora, a former Sandinista hero. North and the CIA "hated Pastora with great passion," thinking him untrustworthy and "conceivably disloyal" to the contra cause, Abrams said. The undersecretary said he did not share that view, in part because of Singlaub's lobbying on Pastora's behalf. The infighting was of more than academic interest. Singlaub had told the committees that someone in the CIA sabotaged his agreement with Pastora by blocking the shipment of goods to Pastora's forces.

WEEK SIX:
HALL, SCIARONI

As they neared the end of the first phase of their inquiry—involving the contra supply operation—the committees were falling behind schedule. As a result, they agreed to cut down on the number of public witnesses during the second part of the hearings, which would focus on the Iran arms sales. Faced with a backlog of about twenty witnesses in the initial phase, the committees already had moved to speed up the hearings by enforcing procedures that strictly limited questioning by members and staff lawyers.

During the first six weeks of public hearings—which had featured eighteen witnesses and more than 100 hours of testimony—the committees had fleshed out the broad outlines and the intricate details of the administration's two secret foreign policy initiatives: funneling aid to the contras through a network of private operatives motivated by a commitment to the contra cause and a search for financial profits; and relying on many of those same private individuals to carry out a sensitive program to sell weapons to Iran in hopes of freeing American hostages held by pro-Iran factions in Lebanon. "What these committees have heard is a depressing story," said House select committee chairman Hamilton, as the first phase of the hearings drew to a close June 9. "It is a story of not telling the truth to the Congress and to the American people." (Text, p. C-64)

In week six of the public hearings, the committees heard from two witnesses who played supporting roles in the Iran-contra operation. Fawn Hall, former secretary to North, explained June 8-9 how and why she helped alter crucial White House documents relating to the contras. She also vigorously defended her former boss, who was fired from the NSC staff November 25, 1986, after Attorney General Meese announced that funds from the sale of weapons to Iran had been diverted to the contras. Hall was North's secretary from February 1983 until his firing. She then returned to her permanent post at the Pentagon. (Hall testimony text, p. C-61)

Preceding Hall at the witness table June 8 was Bretton G. Sciaroni, counsel to the president's Intelligence Oversight Board. Sciaroni wrote a legal memo for the board in September 1985 that said the Boland amendment barring aid to the contras did not apply to the NSC. Sciaroni's opinion, severely criticized by some committee members, also concluded that North's procontra activities did not violate the law. (Sciaroni testimony text, p. C-60)

A Secretary's Story

Hall's appearance had been eagerly awaited, largely because she brought a measure of glamour. More committee members than usual were on hand for the opening day of her testimony, and nearly every seat in the hearing room was taken. Senator Hatch observed to Hall: "You and the man you worked for motivated this country for quite a bit of time and you have captured the attention of the entire country."

Committee members were much kinder to Hall than they had been to other participants in the Iran-contra affair, especially those whose motives appeared questionable. But Hall responded firmly, with an edge to her voice, when members questioned the actions of North, whom she called "every secretary's dream of a boss."

Hall said that North never acted without his superiors' authorization. But, she added, North "was creative and never gave up" on his ideas. "He never sent information memorandums. It was always an action memorandum," she said, and those always were accepted, at least for review. "In the four years I worked for Col. North, in my recollection, I never saw a disapproved memorandum."

Hall confirmed a contention by the White House that North rarely dealt directly with Reagan. She said North never met alone with the president, to her knowledge, and the two men talked alone on the telephone only once—the day North was fired. Hall said North spoke almost daily with Secord and met with and talked on the telephone with CIA director Casey. Channell, a Washington fund-raiser for the contras, telephoned often, but North did not always return the calls, she said.

Although much of her story had leaked to the press, Hall's testimony was gripping. In a matter-of-fact tone, she described how she and North altered and shredded secret

Fawn Hall

White House documents the day before the Justice Department began its inquiry that led to disclosure of the Iran-contra connection. Four days later, on November 25, North was fired, and Hall smuggled copies of key documents out of the White House.

Hall testified that she believed strongly in the policies North was pursuing, presumably on behalf of the president. Asked by Senator Nunn how she got the information to support her beliefs, she said: "After working four years, twelve hours a day, five days a week, I wouldn't consider someone too bright if they didn't pick up something after all that." She was unable, however, to shed any light on Reagan's involvement in or knowledge of North's Iran-contra activities. Hall said, for example, that she had an "impression" that Reagan knew about North's work in raising money for the contras but offered no specific evidence.

Most of Hall's testimony, given under a grant of limited immunity, covered her actions in November 1986 as North's carefully crafted Iran-contra empire was crashing around him. Hall rejected the term "cover-up" as a description of her actions. "I would use the word 'protect,'" she told House panel member Stokes. "I believe that Col. North did what was right," Hall said. North had never done anything she saw as wrong, Hall said, "and therefore that is why I felt that I need not question someone I admired and respected."

Asked by Representative Foley if she realized that altering documents was wrong, Hall said she assumed that North must have had a "solid and very valid reason" for asking her to do it. "Sometimes you have to go above the written law," she said. Immediately retreating, Hall added: "I don't know, I felt, I believe in Col. North. Maybe that is not correct. It is not a fair thing to say, I felt uneasy to begin with and I agree with your assessment basically." Hall later retracted her original statement and acknowledged to Foley that her removal of documents was a "gross violation" of security standards.

Altering Documents

Late in the afternoon of November 21, 1986, Hall testified, North handed her four sensitive documents and asked her to make changes he had indicated in writing. All four were the original versions of "top secret" memos that had been in the NSC's central files since 1985. The four were among six memos that then-national security adviser McFarlane had noted in 1985 as raising questions about North's contra activities.

Hall said she did not know it at the time, but Friday, November 21, was the day that Reagan asked Meese to assemble information about the Iran matter. Meese's aides told NSC officials that they would be reviewing relevant documents the next morning. November 21 also was the day that CIA director Casey testified before the House and Senate Intelligence committees on the Iran arms deals.

Hall typed new versions of the four documents and destroyed the originals. But she said she did not have time to send the new versions to the NSC central files or to destroy copies of the originals in North's office. The altered memos carried a telltale sign: Hall used NSC stationery that had not existed in 1985, when the originals were produced.

The four memos altered by Hall were all written by North and sent to McFarlane. They were dated:

● February 6, 1985, reporting that a Nicaraguan cargo ship was about to pick up military supplies in Asia, apparently in China or North Korea. North suggested three options for dealing with the ship: seizing it and turning the weapons over to the contras; sinking it; or publicizing the shipment "as a means of preventing the delivery" of the arms to the Sandinistas. North recommended that contra leader Adolfo Calero be given information about the ship and "approached on the matter of seizing or sinking" it. Neither the "Approve" nor "Disapprove" box was checked on the memo. However, Poindexter, then McFarlane's deputy, wrote at the bottom of the memo: "We need to take action to make sure ship does not arrive in Nicaragua." Attached was a separate note from Poindexter to McFarlane recommending that the matter be discussed that day.

As altered, the memo did not mention seizing or sinking the ship. Instead, it recommended declassifying information about it "so we can have it placed in overseas news media."

● March 5, 1985, suggesting an increase in foreign aid for Guatemala because of the "extraordinary assistance" its military had provided for the contras. North attached to the memo copies of documents that a Guatemalan general had given the contras to help them buy weapons on the international market. North also gave McFarlane what he called a contra "wish list" of weapons. Six days later, McFarlane signed and sent to other top administration officials a North-drafted memo proposing the aid increase.

The altered version eliminated the reference to Guatemalan help to the contras and said, instead, that an aid increase was justified by domestic developments in Guatemala. However, Hall neglected to eliminate the attached documents and a reference to them at the bottom of the memo.

● March 16, 1985, suggesting a "fallback plan" for getting aid to the contras if Congress continued to ban assistance. North proposed an elaborate series of actions including a speech by Reagan asking for private contributions to the contras, to be followed by a public relations campaign and the creation of a nonprofit organization to accept those donations. North also suggested that the "current donors" be asked to provide an additional $25 million to $30 million to buy arms for the contras. That reference was to Saudi Arabia, which had given some $32 million to the Nicaraguan contras.

The altered version eliminated all of those proposals and suggested that Richard G. Lugar, R-Ind., then chairman of the Senate Foreign Relations Committee, and Dave Durenberger, R-Minn., then chairman of the Senate Intelligence Committee, be asked to suggest "fallback options."

● April 11, 1985, detailing military operations by the contras and warning that the rebels were running out of money. Scaling back his recommendations from the March 16 memo, North suggested that the "current donors [Saudi

The Secrets Game: Keeping the Lid on ...

Costa Rica, Honduras, Saudi Arabia, China, CIA agent Joe Fernandez, and former Israeli prime minister Shimon Peres.

Those were among the dozens of names that appeared almost daily in news reports about the Iran-contra hearings in Congress. But those names were rarely uttered in the hearings themselves, and nearly every reference to them was blacked out on the scores of documents introduced into evidence by the House and Senate select committees.

Largely for diplomatic reasons, the panels cooperated with the Reagan administration in an elaborate, and generally futile, effort to conceal a small portion of the Iran-contra details. Much of the information concerned countries and individuals involved in supporting the Nicaraguan rebels and selling U.S. arms to Iran. At the administration's insistence, the committees successfully kept secret substantial amounts of information only indirectly connected to the Iran-contra affair, such as the identities of intelligence agents and details about the military strengths of foreign countries.

The keeping of some secrets occurred in the context of nationally televised hearings that made public what one administration official called an "unprecedented deluge" of classified information. The committees and the administration worked closely in the time-consuming job of declassifying documents, officials said. The House panel took the position that it had the ultimate right to determine what information could be released and what could be censored. The Senate panel accepted the administration's position that the White House was the final arbiter.

"All of this information that the Hill has was given to them by us," said William B. Lytton III, deputy special counselor to the president.

Putting Secrets into View

Practically every day since the hearings opened May 5, 1987, the committees heard testimony about matters that under normal circumstances would be among Washington's most tightly held secrets: covert intelligence operations and sensitive dealings with foreign governments. The committees released stacks of documents, many of which previously were stamped "top secret." But key facts discussed in the testimony were obscured by code words, and many of the documents were heavily censored. The result was a crazy quilt of disclosure and classification that often seemed to make little sense.

A case in point involved Costa Rica and Honduras, the two countries adjacent to Nicaragua, whose government was under attack by the U.S.-backed contras. Except by accident, Costa Rica and Honduras were never mentioned in the hearings because their governments officially denied the fact that contras had launched operations from their territories. To avoid embarrassing those governments, the Reagan administration demanded that the committees not mention them, and the committees complied.

Some other countries were identified by code numbers—Israel was "country one" and China was "country four," for example. But Costa Rica and Honduras simply did not exist in public testimony and documents: Witnesses were requested not to utter their names, and censors smudged out all documentary references to them.

Committee and administration sources admitted that obscuring such details almost never had been successful, if only because the names of countries and individuals often were obvious in the context of the documents. "There is a finger-in-the-dam mentality," said one administration official. "Often we find ourselves trying to protect little bits of information that everybody already knows."

The futility of such efforts was demonstrated most vividly during the testimony in mid-May of former national security adviser Robert C. McFarlane. At the time, the panels were acceding to the administration's demand that Saudi Arabia ("country two") not be mentioned as the contributor of some $32 million to the contras. But McFarlane said in public session that the subject of contra aid came up during a visit to Washington by Saudi king Fahd. Reagan himself acknowledged that he had talked to Fahd about the contras.

Nevertheless, the administration insisted that protecting some kinds of information was valuable for foreign policy reasons. "If we don't mention country names, it may well be because those countries have asked us not to," Lytton said. "We have had diplomatic relations with them in the past and hope to in the future, after the congressmen are gone and the TV cameras are packed up."

One senior House committee member, who asked not to be identified, complained about the restraints. "There's a natural tendency by every ad-

Arabia] be approached" to provide $15 million to $20 million for the contras. North attached lists of weapons the contras had bought since July 1984—all through a network of dealers that he had organized.

The altered version deleted a reference to a then-pending arms shipment to the contras and dropped the recommended approach to Saudi Arabia. Instead, it suggested that McFarlane brief Reagan and urge him to take "concerted action" to get Congress to approve more money for the contras. Hall said she checked the "Approved" box

... When Everyone Already Seemed to Know

ministration to try to keep things secret, even if disclosure would do no harm," he said. "But this administration has gone overboard."

Even so, Hill sources said they could not point to material that had been withheld because its release would embarrass the administration. "There are embellishments that, if we had our druthers, we would have made public," the Senate aide said. "But the administration hasn't interfered with our getting the essential facts out."

'Redacting' Documents

At the start of most Iran-contra hearings, the select committees gave to reporters stacks of documents. About half of them at one time were classified "secret" or "top secret," indicating that their release to the public was a violation of law. Before reaching the hands of reporters, the documents had to go through a tedious review by lawyers from the White House, the State Department, and the CIA. The administration agreed to the select committees' request to declassify most of the thousands of documents—but often with substantial portions obscured by black ink. Two exceptions were CIA documents.

The committees received copies of the original, uncensored documents, which they used in their inquiry. All committee staff members obtained special security clearances. In reviewing documents for release, the lawyers worked from guidelines based, in part, on Reagan's 1982 executive order (No. 12356) governing secret information. Those rules required classification of "national security" information, such as descriptions of the sources and methods by which intelligence was obtained. However, the guidelines were general. They also were meant to apply to normal diplomatic and intelligence activity conducted by government agencies. But the hearings were based on the premise that the Iran-contra affair was far from normal, with government activities carried out by private individuals, none of whom had the usual security clearances.

The most striking example was the testimony of Albert Hakim, a businessman who managed the finances of the private network that sold arms to Iran and ferried weapons to the contras. Hakim told the committees he negotiated a nine-point agreement with Iran in October 1986.

At one point in the testimony, Senate committee chief counsel Arthur L. Liman referred to a deposition that Hakim had given privately. Hakim's lawyer protested that his client did not have a copy of the deposition. The reason: administration lawyers classified the deposition "top secret" because Hakim had disclosed secret information—and he lacked security clearances to read his own testimony.

Censoring Public Information

Scattered throughout the documents released by the committees were words, sentences, and entire pages that government lawyers deleted in hopes of preserving secrecy. Following are examples of deletions of information that had subsequently been entered on public record:

● At a top-secret hearing by the Senate Intelligence Committee December 8, 1986, Elliott Abrams, the assistant secretary of state for inter-American affairs, described his solicitation of $10 million from Brunei on behalf of the contras. Abrams told the committee that he made his request during a meeting in London. But a declassified committee transcript deleted the reference to London. The transcript was released June 5, three days after Abrams publicly described to the Iran-contra panels his walk in a London park with a Brunei official.

● Another transcript released by the committees, of McFarlane's private testimony in December 1986 to the House Foreign Affairs panel, heavily censored questioning by Mel Levine, D-Calif., about reports that the Saudis had helped finance the U.S. arms sales to Iran. Each of Levine's references to Saudi Arabia was deleted, even though he was quoting an Associated Press story.

● Among the most sensitive deletions were the names of U.S. intelligence officials, two of whom figured prominently in the contra supply network. In all documents, the CIA station chief in Costa Rica, Joe Fernandez, was referred to by his code name, "Tomas Castillo." His boss, Central American task force chief Alan Fiers, was unnamed. However, Fiers's predecessor, Duane "Dewey" Clarridge, was named in several documents.

● Censors followed an uncertain course when it came to Israel and top officials there. Israel was named in some documents as a participant in the Iran arms sales, but not in others. Nor was Israel named as a potential supporter of the contras.

---

on the memo.

Hall said she paid no attention to the specific changes she was making. But she recalled which documents she altered, telling deputy House minority counsel George Van Cleve she definitely had not changed one document—an

April 1985 memo in which North discussed the diversion of $12 million in Iranian arms sale profits to the contras. Justice Department lawyers found that memo in North's office in the Old Executive Office Building on November 22, when they went there to review documents.

Shredding and Removing Documents

Hall testified that her altering of the documents on November 21 was interrupted by "the shredding incident"—a session during which she and North destroyed a foot-and-a-half-high stack of memos and telephone logs.

Hall said North began destroying documents early in the evening, pulling files from cabinets and an office safe. She said she joined North and took over the shredding, dumping so many papers into the machine that it jammed. Hall said she called the NSC's Crisis Management Center, and an employee named "J. R." came to replace the machine's overfilled trash bag. Hall said she did not look at the documents she was shredding, and could not testify to exactly which ones were destroyed. However, Hall said she volunteered to shred computer-generated messages and logs of North's phone calls, because they contained "private" information and partly because they took up too much space.

After Reagan November 24 announced North's firing, White House security personnel arrived to advise that his office would be sealed. Hall said she called North and, talking softly to avoid being overheard, said she was concerned about the documents she had altered.

North told Hall to get clearance for his attorney, at the time, Thomas C. Green, to enter his office in the Old Executive Office Building. While waiting for North to return, Hall put in her boots copies of the memos she had altered. At her request, North's chief deputy, Lt. Col. Robert L. Earl, pulled from the files copies of internal NSC memos, and Hall said she put them in the back of her clothing.

Asked on June 9 whether she considered that her actions might have been illegal or improper, Hall said she was "emotionally distraught" and was trying to "protect what we were doing in the office." But Hall had trouble telling the panels from whom she was trying to keep the documents. In response to such questions, she talked about the importance of the Iran and contra "initiatives" and said she worried about leaks of classified information. "A lot of damage would be done if a lot of top-secret, sensitive, classified material was exposed in public, so that the Soviets and everyone else could read it," she told Senator Rudman, who responded: "It wasn't the KGB that was coming, Miss Hall. It was the FBI."

Diversion Memo

Hall provided some new information on one of the key documents in the Iran-contra affair: the April 1986 memo in which North described how $12 million in Iranian money was to be used to support the contras. Hall testified that one draft of the memo was sent to Poindexter, who ordered changes. She said she typed the changes and produced another draft. But Hall said she could not remember whether Poindexter ever got a final version, with his changes included, or whether anyone other than North and Poindexter had seen the drafts. Unlike North's other memos, the diversion memo was not dated and did not say who it was from and to whom it was written. The memo also did not include a standard cover sheet listing its classification and recipients.

The diversion memo might have been attached to another document, Hall said, but insisted she could not remember if that was the case. Meese said November 25 that Poindexter was the only top administration official, other than North, who knew about the diversion of Iranian money to the contras. (He later restated that point in July 29, 1987, testimony.)

Sciaroni Legal Opinion

The June 8 testimony by Sciaroni turned out to be a failed experiment for House panel Republicans.

As counsel for the three-member president's Intelligence Oversight Board, Sciaroni in 1985 briefly looked into North's contra activities. In a seven-page opinion dated September 12 and approved by the board, Sciaroni wrote that North's work did not violate the fiscal 1985 Boland amendment, which barred U.S. military involvement with the contras by intelligence agencies. In any event, the opinion said, the NSC staff was not covered by the Boland law because it was not an intelligence agency.

Sciaroni's contentions had been central to the arguments of conservative Republicans on the Iran-contra panels, and so House Republicans demanded that he be called.

Bretton G. Sciaroni

Representative Hyde used Sciaroni's presence to reiterate that the Boland law was "murky," and that Congress should have expressed itself more clearly.

But Sciaroni quickly faltered, admitting that his investigation of North's activities was cursory and that he had virtually no experience in examining such complex issues. Sciaroni said he began his August 1985 inquiry as a result of press reports that North was giving military advice and support to the contras. Congressional committees also were asking questions, adding to the urgency of the matter, he said.

Sciaroni's investigation was simple: He interviewed North, who worked on the same floor of the Old Executive Office Building, for about five minutes, and Cmdr. Paul Thompson, NSC counsel, for about half an hour. North denied any wrongdoing, and Thompson handed over an "inch-thick" stack of what he called the "relevant documents" on the matter, Sciaroni said. The documents provided little information about what North was doing, he added.

Sciaroni came under intense criticism for the fleeting nature of his investigation. Asked if he considered his work a "thorough investigation," Sciaroni said the allegations he was pursuing were "general." Sciaroni said he "had no reason to doubt" the North and Thompson denials. Sciaroni said he was not shown five memos in which North described his activities supporting the contras, including helping to procure weapons. Each of the documents would have been "relevant," Sciaroni said.

Sciaroni said his board was responsible for overseeing intelligence agencies but did not have subpoena power or the legal power to force compliance. In investigating the NSC staff, Sciaroni said he had to rely on voluntary cooperation.

Under questioning, Sciaroni stuck by his legal opinion that the Boland law did not prevent the NSC staff from helping the contras. The attorney produced statutes and executive orders to bolster his argument that the NSC staff was not one of the intelligence agencies barred from aiding the contras. If Congress wanted to limit actions by the NSC staff as well as by the CIA, he said, "it should have said so."

Several conservatives backed Sciaroni's argument, but other members of both parties ridiculed his reasoning. House panel counsel Nields directly challenged the core of Sciaroni's argument, noting that Boland, in an October 10, 1984, House floor statement, explained that his amendment barred all U.S. support for the contras, with "no exceptions." Sciaroni acknowledged to Nields that he based his opinion, in part, on the assumption that the NSC staff was not engaged in intelligence operations, such as aiding the contras. He said he had no way of knowing at the time that the NSC was running covert programs, because NSC staff members told him nothing about it.

Committee members also raised doubts about the competence of Sciaroni. The attorney said his memo on the Boland amendment was his first formal legal opinion since law school.

WEEK SEVEN: LEGAL ISSUES EXAMINED

As the hearings geared up for the "grand finale"— appearances by North, Poindexter, and cabinet and former top officials—the House and Senate select committees heard further testimony June 23-25 that the Reagan administration probably violated U.S. laws in helping Israel ship U.S.-made weapons to Iran in 1985. Possibly because they realized the illegality of the 1985 actions, senior administration officials had tried to conceal U.S. involvement in them as late as November 1986, when Congress and the Justice Department were beginning their investigations. Despite the belated concern about the propriety of the U.S. role in the sales, testimony indicated that the administration acted on the assumption that the president's discretion to conduct foreign policy was so broad that he could override certain laws, such as those requiring reports to Congress about all foreign arms sales.

The week's hearings also tarnished former NSC aide North's image. First, a private consultant testified that North had developed a scheme in November 1986 to disguise the fact that his associate, retired major general Secord, had paid for a $14,000 security system that had been installed at North's home in mid-1986. More dramatically, Charles J. Cooper, a Justice Department lawyer involved in the department's November 1986 inquiry, portrayed North as a polished liar. Because of North's false and misleading statements at that time, Cooper said he would not believe North even if he testified under oath.

The five witnesses during the seventh week were: Glenn A. Robinette (June 23), a private consultant and former CIA employee; Noel C. Koch (June 23), former deputy assistant secretary for international security affairs; Henry H. Gaffney, Jr. (June 23), director of plans for the Defense Security Assistance Agency; Stanley Sporkin (June 24), former CIA general counsel; and Cooper (June 25). *(Robinette testimony text, p. C-67; Koch and Gaffney,*

p. C-71; Sporkin, p. C-69; Cooper, p. C-73)

The panels also released June 25 depositions from State Department legal adviser Abraham D. Sofaer on proposed testimony by CIA director Casey on November 21, 1986; and by two U.S. officials in Portugal concerning U.S. attempts to help Israel ship arms to Iran via Portugal in November 1985. *(Sofaer testimony text, p. C-65)*

'Legal Gymnastics'

Although much of the June 23-25 testimony centered around arcane legal issues, the underlying theme was one of deception: Administration officials failed to follow standard procedures in approving Israel's 1985 arms shipments to Iran, then tried to disguise any impropriety, and finally found themselves caught in an expanding web of lies and misleading statements as they tried to cover up what they had done.

Henry H. Gaffney, Jr.

While much attention had been given to North's efforts to conceal his involvement with the contras, new testimony and documents indicated that other senior officials were more concerned at the time the story broke in November 1986 with covering up U.S. involvement in the Israeli shipments to Iran in 1985.

Israel transferred U.S.-made weapons to Iran twice in 1985: in August-September, when it shipped TOW anti-tank missiles, and in November, when it shipped eighteen Hawk antiaircraft missiles. The extent of U.S. involvement in the shipment of the TOW missiles was unclear. McFarlane, national security adviser at the time, had testified that Reagan approved the TOW shipments in advance— but Reagan said he did not remember giving the approval. The U.S. role in the November shipment was more direct; North arranged for a CIA-run airline to fly the missiles to Iran after Israel was foiled in its plan to ship them via Portugal.

The week's testimony made clear that the administration failed to satisfy several legal requirements for transfers to third countries of weapons sold by the United States. Pentagon officials testified June 23 that other countries could retransfer U.S.-origin weapons only with the advance written consent of the president. Such transfers also had to be reported to Congress.

Pentagon officials Gaffney and Koch said those procedures were not followed in Israel's shipments to Iran, meaning they probably were illegal. According to testimony, CIA officials quickly realized the impropriety of their agency's involvement in the November shipment, and they drafted a proposed covert action "finding," under which the president was to approve the action after the fact. Sporkin, CIA general counsel at that time, told the committees that the president could officially "ratify" prior deeds by the CIA by signing such a finding. (Sporkin subsequently was appointed a U.S. district court judge.)

Some on the committee, however, disputed Sporkin's contention that the president could waive legal requirements—such as notice to Congress of arms transfers—just by signing such a document. And Justice Department lawyer Cooper gave the panels evidence that Congress should have been told about the Israeli shipments in any event.

Noel C. Koch

Apparently concerned about the propriety of U.S. involvement with the Israeli shipments, administration officials decided to use an official CIA-run covert operation to sell weapons directly to Iran in 1986. But the administration continued to use what Senate committee member Nunn called "legal gymnastics" to avoid telling Congress. Under a 1980 law, the president must tell Congress about all covert operations—in advance, if possible, but in a "timely" manner if not. Reagan signed a new Iran arms sales finding on January 17, 1986, but Congress was not told about it until after the sales were public knowledge eleven months later.

Sporkin acknowledged that Congress was not given timely notice, but he insisted that the president was justified in delaying notice until after U.S. hostages in Lebanon were released. Although freeing the hostages was the actual goal of the arms sales, Reagan's January 17 finding was formally based on the much broader policy of improving relations with Iran. *(Legal requirements, p. 43)*

When the administration interprets laws to give itself the maximum flexibility, Nunn said, "it forces the Congress into the absurd position of legislating rigidities, and forces the president into no discretion and forces the agencies into a whole lot less flexibility." The net result, he added, "is to put us all into a rather unfortunate position in trying to conduct sensible foreign policy."

Writing a Finding

Sporkin led the committees through a description of how the administration drafted—and Reagan ultimately signed—the secret document authorizing U.S. arms sales to Iran in 1986. Covert action findings normally are among the most secret documents held by the U.S. government. The draft and final findings scrutinized by the Iran-contra committees were among the few ever made public. And Sporkin's testimony was the most extensive public description ever of how such a document was put together.

The process started with the CIA's effort to obtain presidential approval of its role in the 1985 Israeli sales. John N. McMahon, then the agency's deputy director, got events under way by asking Sporkin on November 25, 1985, to examine CIA actions in providing the airline that delivered the Israeli Hawk missiles to Iran. Sporkin said he determined, and McMahon agreed, that a finding was needed to ensure that the president knew about and approved what the agency had done. "We were engaged in a very high-profile kind of activity," Sporkin said. "I wanted to make sure this went to the top." The former CIA counsel said his demand for a finding was "stiff legal advice"—a contention later disputed by Senator Cohen, who said Sporkin merely was proposing that the agency "abide by the law."

Sporkin drafted a finding authorizing a wide range of U.S. actions to seek the release of U.S. hostages. It explicitly ratified "all prior actions taken by U.S. government officials in furtherance of this effort." The finding also directed the CIA not to tell Congress about the operation. The finding was undated, but Casey sent it to Poindexter on November 26, saying it "should go to the president for his signature." Poindexter testified in July that the finding was signed December 5.

Stanley Sporkin

Starting early in January 1986, CIA and White House officials drafted six more findings, aimed at approving future U.S. arms dealings with Iran. Sporkin said North insisted on deleting all references to the release of hostages because of opposition by the State Department. As described by Sporkin, North clearly was the driving force behind the findings. The NSC aide personally wrote a key draft, dated January 3, that was the basis for the final, official finding dated January 17. North also was responsible for inserting into the document language providing for "third parties" to be the conduit of arms between the United States and Iran. It was that language that enabled North to hire Secord to supervise shipment of the arms.

The November Probe

Cooper, the Justice Department lawyer, was an important witness for the committees because of his involvement in the department's investigation of the Iran-contra affair in November 1986. As the assistant attorney general heading the Office of Legal Counsel, Cooper was responsible for giving the department general legal advice. Cooper said Attorney General Meese first asked him to look into the legalities of the Iranian arms sales on November 7, a few days after a Lebanese magazine revealed the U.S. dealings with Iran. A week later, Cooper produced an opinion saying the U.S. sales were legal. However, Cooper said that opinion was based on incomplete and inaccurate information he received from administration officials.

As described by Cooper, the investigation appeared to have two distinct phases. In the first period, from early November through the morning of November 22, the aim was to pull together facts so the administration could have a coherent record of what happened. That phase culminated when Meese and others discovered serious discrepancies among the statements of key officials. The second phase ran from the middle of the day November 22, after Justice lawyers discovered a memo in North's files discussing the diversion of Iranian money to the contras, until November 25, when the diversion was announced. The aim of that inquiry was to find out what the memo meant and who knew about it.

One intriguing element emerging from Cooper's testimony was that the administration's motives in announcing the diversion might not have been as pure as Reagan had contended. Reagan insisted that he revealed the diversion solely because he felt obliged to get the information to the public as soon as possible. While not disputing that, Cooper testified that he and his colleagues were worried about the possibility of leaks because officials at the State Department and the CIA were discussing rumors that a diversion had occurred. Cooper said the investigators realized that the diversion would create both legal and political problems for the administration, with concern about the political fallout being the more important of the two. But he staunchly defended most aspects of the inquiry in the face of criticism by several panel members.

Select committee member Rodino, who also chaired the House Judiciary Committee, charged that Cooper and his colleagues were inexperienced in criminal matters and did not conduct the probe as "comprehensively" as it should have been. And Senator Rudman said Meese's decision to use lawyers from the civil side of the Justice Department to conduct the probe was "like having a group of the world's best cardiologists doing neurosurgery."

Cooper acknowledged only one major mistake by the Justice investigators: failing to move more quickly to protect White House documents. Meese ordered on November 25 that North's and Poindexter's offices be sealed. White House security officials took over North's office later that day but did not prevent his secretary, Fawn Hall, from smuggling out several documents. FBI agents did not establish full control over the offices until November 28, Cooper said.

Rudman said the Justice Department inadvertently warned North on November 21 that lawyers would be looking at his files the next day—enabling him to alter and shred documents before—and even after—the investigators arrived.

Preparing Casey Testimony

One of the most important events described throughout the hearings may have been a meeting in Poindexter's White House office on November 20, 1986, during which senior officials and lawyers reviewed a prepared statement that Casey was to give Capitol Hill the next day. Besides himself, Cooper said, those present at the meeting were Casey, Poindexter, Meese, and others, possibly including CIA deputy director Robert M. Gates.

In a dramatic narration June 25, Cooper described how those officials planned for Casey to give false testimony to the congressional Intelligence committees about the November 1985 Israeli arms shipment to Iran. The shipment was carried on a cargo plane provided by the CIA, at North's request. The CIA originally had drafted the testimony to say that agency officials did not know until January 1986 that the Israeli shipment contained missiles. Instead, the draft testimony said CIA officials thought the flight contained oil-drilling equipment.

Charles J. Cooper

Cooper said North had prepared a one-page insertion that went further, saying that "no one in the USG [U.S. government] found out" until January that the plane carried missiles. When North described his insertion at the November 20 meeting, Cooper said, no one objected to the language, including those in a position to know it was false: Casey and Poindexter. North corroborated this in his testimony before the select committees.

Cooper said he and Meese were not able to judge the accuracy of North's statement, and he testified that he was "under the impression" at the time that the Israeli shipment in fact had contained oil-drilling equipment. Three days before the November 20 meeting, however, Cooper had received a copy of a White House chronology clearly stating that Israel had shipped eighteen Hawk missiles to Iran. That chronology neglected to mention that the CIA provided the cargo plane that delivered the missiles.

Casey's proposed testimony worried another senior official who was not at the White House meeting: State Department legal adviser Sofaer. By that time, Sofaer had learned that Secretary of State Shultz had been told by McFarlane in November 1985 about the arms shipment, and Shultz's office had contemporaneous notes of the conversation.

As a result, Sofaer said he suspected that the story about oil-drilling parts was intended to shield the fact that arms had been delivered. "The whole thing smelled to me like the kind of thing you see in a trial . . . in a narcotics case, for example, when they refer to the drugs as 'shirts' or something like that," Sofaer said in a deposition released June 25. "I was scared that the president would be in trouble if the testimony was not changed, and if people were not forced to tell the truth about all this."

Sofaer called the White House shortly after the meeting in Poindexter's office broke up and voiced his concerns to counsel Peter Wallison. Repeating those concerns later to Cooper, Sofaer threatened to resign unless Casey's testimony was changed. He said that Cooper pledged to do the same. That evening, Shultz visited Reagan at his White House living quarters and warned that the proposed testimony was false.

Apparently as a result of Shultz's protest, Casey sidestepped the issue entirely when he testified to the House and Senate Intelligence committees on November 21. In reading his prepared statement, Casey deleted all references to missiles in the November shipment, leaving the impression that the plane carried oil-drilling equipment. The Iran-contra committees on June 26 released the full text of Casey's testimony to the House committee. In that session, Casey said the CIA had been asked to recommend an airline able to transport "bulky cargo" to an unspecified location in the Middle East. He said that the crew that flew the planes from Tel Aviv were informed that they were carrying "spare parts for the oil fields" in Iran. Casey said U.S. officials knew of only one arms shipment from Israel to Iran, which took place in September 1985. He said that transfer was done without U.S. knowledge and was not discovered until later. Those assertions subsequently were disputed by others in the administration. *(Text, p. C-1)*

A State Department official who accompanied Casey to the Intelligence Committee briefing hinted at U.S. awareness of the November shipment. Michael H. Armacost, under secretary for political affairs, said he had heard of shipments in September and November when asked about Israeli transfers of U.S. "military equipment" to Iran. Sources said that Armacost also told the Senate Intelligence Committee earlier in the day about the November shipment when Casey failed to do so.

Cooper's testimony seemed to shock even Republicans who had embraced most administration actions. By lying to

Meese, who was acting for Reagan, North and the others might have committed a crime, said Representative McCollum. "If it is not a crime, it is certainly one of the highest acts of insubordination and one of the most treacherous things that has ever occurred to a president, it seems to me, in our history," he said.

The CIA in Lisbon

The issue of what the CIA knew—and when—about the November 1985 shipment was clouded by other testimony revealed by the Iran-contra committees.

The panels on June 25 released unclassified versions of private depositions given by two U.S. officials in Portugal who said they knew early, during the November 1985 mission, that the Iran-bound plane contained Hawk missiles. Those officials were the CIA station chief in Portugal and the deputy chief of mission at the U.S. Embassy in Lisbon. The committees masked the identities of both officials, in part to avoid mentioning Portugal as the country through which the arms shipments were to have passed.

A third official, however, told the committees that he did not know at the time that the flight contained missiles. He was Duane "Dewey" Clarridge, then head of CIA covert operations in Europe. North had gone to Clarridge to get the CIA's help in clearing the Iran-bound shipment through Portugal.

The CIA station chief told the committees that he learned on November 23, 1985, that the plane was to carry missiles, to be exchanged for U.S. hostages in Lebanon. That information came from Secord, whom North had dispatched to Lisbon to make arrangements for the shipment. The CIA officer said he sent two cables to Clarridge on November 23, explaining his meetings with Secord, and the second cable specifically mentioned the missiles. The U.S. diplomat recalled seeing or hearing about the cables at the time. However, Clarridge told the committees that he never received the second cable, and the CIA could not locate it among Clarridge's files. *(Clarridge testimony, p. 140)*

The U.S. diplomat also revealed that the State Department and the White House were working at cross-purposes in trying to get Portugal to allow the flight to proceed to Iran from Lisbon.

The diplomat testified that the CIA station chief asked him to "pull out all the stops" in obtaining local approval for the Israeli flight. That order came in a telegram from Poindexter that was read to him by the CIA officer.

When the diplomat reached officials at the Portuguese foreign ministry on November 22, he learned that they already had turned down flight-clearance requests after being contacted by Secord. They were suspicious about the operation, believing that it ran contrary to the avowed U.S. policy of discouraging arms sales to Iran. But after the diplomat made his appeal, Portuguese officials agreed to provide clearance. They insisted, however, that the U.S. Embassy provide a written note stating the arms shipment was for humanitarian reasons and to help free American hostages. That put the diplomat in a bind, since writing such a note would contradict official policy toward Iran. Instead, he testified, Poindexter ordered him to deliver a "rather short and curt note" that basically said "thanks for not helping this humanitarian operation." State Department officials in Washington never saw the note, which irritated the Portuguese officials. The arms eventually were shipped by another route.

Home Security for North

Private security consultant Robinette testified June 23 that he had been hired and paid by Secord to provide North and his family with a security system worth nearly

Glenn A. Robinette

$14,000, and that North tried to cover up the fact that someone else had paid for the system. Secord paid Robinette $16,000, which included additional expenses, in two installments: $7,000 in cash and a $9,000 check drawn on a New York City bank that had been linked to Secord's Iran-contra network.

Robinette said Secord asked him early in 1986 to design a system to protect North's home in Great Falls, Va. North had complained about threatening phone calls and harassments such as punctured car tires and flashing lights at night.

Although he met with North and his wife, Betsy, to discuss the security system beginning in April 1986, Robinette said North never offered to pay for the work. He and North never had an explicit understanding about who would pay, Robinette testified. He was surprised, then, when North asked him in December 1986 to send a bill for the work completed the previous July. Robinette had already been paid by Secord but sent two invoices to North for $8,000. One was dated July 2, and the other—a copy of the first with a note attached—was dated September 22. Robinette said he originally had told North the system would cost somewhere between $8,000 and $8,500.

Robinette acknowledged that he sent the phony invoices in December to help North, who had just been fired from the NSC in the wake of the Iran-contra disclosures. North, meanwhile, responded to the fake invoices with two backdated letters. The first, dated May 18, was a formal letter apparently intended to appear as authorization for Robinette to proceed with the security system. North said in his letter he understood he had two options: paying the full amount over two years or having free use of the equipment until his retirement from the Marine Corps in 1988, after which he would make his home available for a "commercial endorsement" of Robinette's firm. Robinette told the panels that North had made up both options.

North's second phony letter, dated October 1, was informal and chatty, and expressed puzzlement about Robinette's invoice. "We just don't have the $8,000 without borrowing it," North wrote.

Robinette said he sent the fake invoices to help North. "I think you make a mistake if you lead with your heart instead of your head, which I did," he told the committees.

At the time he sent the phony bills, Robinette said, he was not aware that it was a federal crime for a government official to receive gifts or compensation other than his salary. During his testimony, North admitted that he had made a mistake in sending the letters.

Representative Hyde tried to defend North's acceptance of the security system, citing apparent threats to his family. But Senator Rudman said North could have gotten adequate protection from the government. "This government does not leave its employees out on a limb," he said.

WEEK EIGHT: NORTH TESTIMONY

Breaking seven months of self-imposed silence, Lieutenant Colonel North mounted a vigorous defense of his role in the Iran-contra operation, while insisting that several senior officials in the Reagan administration knew the full range of his activities.

In a week of dramatic testimony before the House and Senate Iran-contra committees July 7-10 (and concluding his testimony July 13-14), North clung to the belief that he never acted improperly or illegally while secretly aiding the Nicaraguan contras and arranging arms-for-hostages deals with Iran. *(July 13-14 testimony, p. 124; North testimony text, p. C-75)*

"I am not . . . at all ashamed of any of the things that I did," he said July 9. "I was given a mission and I tried to carry it out." But North said he always had been willing to be the "fall guy," accepting the blame if the operation were exposed and President Reagan threatened with political damage. That role, however, did not extend to his becoming the potential target of a criminal prosecution, he told the committees.

In carrying out his duties, North insisted that everything he did was on the authority of his superiors. He said he understood that to include Reagan but had no proof. His testimony also portrayed former CIA director Casey as a cornerstone figure in the Iran-contra operation, whom North consulted regularly on his activities. Casey frequently cited the need for an "off-the-shelf" covert operation that would not involve the CIA directly, according to North.

Since the November 1986 disclosure of the Iran-contra dealings, North's pivotal and often mysterious role had dominated the focus of the scandal. He had invoked his Fifth Amendment privilege against self-incrimination before congressional committees in December 1986, agreeing to testify at the Iran-contra select committees' hearings only after the special panels voted to obtain for him limited immunity from prosecution. Even with that immunity, North and his lawyer, Brendan V. Sullivan, Jr., sprinkled numerous references throughout the testimony to the seeming likelihood that North would face criminal charges sought by independent counsel Walsh. *(Walsh investigation, p. 163)*

'A Good Performer'

North's long-awaited appearance at the Capitol Hill hearings lived up to advance billing. Wearing a crisply pressed Marine uniform adorned with six rows of combat ribbons, North provided the kind of theater that had not been a regular feature of the hearings, which were entering their third month.

For the first time in weeks, television networks preempted their daytime soap operas and game shows to broadcast live from the Senate Caucus Room. The press tables were filled to capacity, and people waited in long lines for one of the few public seats.

As a witness, North seemed to alternate among the roles that others had carved out for him in past months. Occasionally, he sounded like the beleaguered hero that some considered him to be, a loyal military officer who fervently tried to serve his country the best way he knew how. At other times, a darker side emerged. For example, he admitted that he deliberately lied to Congress about his contra activities and destroyed stacks of documents in an all-night shredding frenzy in his White House office in November 1986.

Oliver L. North

"He's a good performer," said Democratic representative Brooks. "I guess the public likes a guy who says, 'Yeah, I lied and I'm glad I did it.'" Other members of Congress reported getting a flood of phone calls expressing support for North. And North said he had received thousands of letters and telegrams, virtually all of them positive. "Right now, North is an American hero," said Representative Broomfield. "He's doing a better job of explaining the [contra aid] policy than President Reagan ever did." But Broomfield warned that Reagan's supporters should not gloat. That was because North's testimony "shifts the focus of these hearings higher up the line" to the actions of officials such as Shultz, Meese, and Reagan himself.

Sympathy for North was accompanied by hints of open dissatisfaction with the conduct of the hearings among some panel members, particularly Reagan supporters. The specific target of the complaints was Senate counsel Liman, whose hard-hitting cross-examination of North July 9-10 was criticized by some House members.

In contrast to what others had said about him, North denied in his testimony that he was some sort of renegade NSC officer out to manage his own foreign policy. "I realize there's a lot of folks around that think there's a loose cannon on the gun deck of state at NSC," he told the committees July 7. "That wasn't what I heard while I worked there. I've only heard it since I left. People used to walk up to me and tell me what a great job I was doing."

If he sounded a bit betrayed by some of his former colleagues, North also reserved stinging criticism for Congress, as both an investigating body and as lawmakers involved in foreign policy. He told the committees that he had been caught "in the middle of a constitutional struggle" between the executive and legislative branches of government. In addition, he criticized members who, he charged, had concluded that he was guilty of illegal conduct before hearing his story. Like other witnesses, North also accused Congress of contributing to the Iran-contra affair by enacting inconsistent policies toward the Nicaraguan rebels.

More Questions Raised

While North addressed several key issues in the affair, under sharp questioning by Liman and House counsel Nields, some of his responses did not clear away the cloud of suspicion over Reagan and other White House officials. North only added to the speculation about Reagan's personal involvement in the Iran-contra affair with his testimony that he assumed the president was aware of virtually all of his activities.

The same held for other senior officials that North linked to crucial aspects of the operation, including North's potentially illegal campaign to help the contras fight a secret war against the Sandinistas. "I think he's given a number of people a reason for some sleepless nights," noted Senator Rudman.

Reagan officials took a low-key approach to North's testimony, telling reporters that few eyes were glued to television sets at the White House. "We think it's more important to carry on the business of government than to be watching TV," White House spokesman Fitzwater said July 7. He said short memos summarizing each day's testimony were prepared for Reagan to read at night.

Contradictory Statements

Reagan denied repeatedly that he knew about the diversion of Iran arms profits to the contras until the day before Meese announced it publicly in November 1986.

North testified that he never discussed the issue directly with Reagan, but that he had assumed at the time that the president knew of his plan to funnel some of the arms profits to the contras. North said Poindexter told him November 21, 1986, that Reagan did not know of the diversion, and that the president told North, "I just didn't know," during a November 25 telephone call. However, North also told the committees that he was surprised at Reagan's claim to the Tower Commission in January 1987 that he did not know North or other NSC officials were engaged in a covert operation to assist the contras.

During his testimony, North contradicted statements by other Reagan officials about their own roles, or professed lack of them, during the Iran-contra dealings. North, for example, said that Shultz and Assistant Secretary of State Abrams were aware of his covert efforts to assist the contras during the time that Congress prohibited U.S. military aid to the rebels. He told of an incident in September 1986 when Shultz, at a State Department reception for a retiring official, put his arm around North, telling him that he was doing a "remarkable job" for the contras.

Shultz denied that he knew about North's contra supply network; a State Department spokesman said that Shultz's comment to North referred only to his efforts to keep up the morale of the contras while U.S. aid was curtailed. (Shultz testimony, p. 132)

Abrams, in his testimony to the committees in June, said Shultz once referred to North as a "loose cannon" and instructed Abrams at the time to "monitor" the NSC aide's activities. Like Shultz, Abrams said he was not aware of the extent of North's contra activities. (Abrams testimony, p. 108)

North also discussed a mid-1986 meeting at the Pentagon at which he reviewed an item-by-item list of his covert contra actions with several other administration officials. Among those at the meeting, he said, were Abrams, Assistant Secretary of State Armitage, and CIA official Alan Fiers. "There was no doubt in their mind. These people knew what I was doing. They knew that it was a covert operation being conducted by this government to support the Nicaraguan resistance," said North.

Crucial parts of North's testimony also clashed with statements by McFarlane, who subsequently reappeared to rebut North's testimony. McFarlane told the committees in May that he instructed North during 1985 not to solicit contributions to the contras from foreign countries or private sources, when McFarlane considered such actions to be unlawful. (See p. 125; May testimony, p. 91)

North, asked about McFarlane's statement by Nields, testified that he never received such orders, and that McFarlane was aware of North's efforts to raise funds for the contras. "I never carried out a single act, not one, Mr. Nields, in which I did not have authority from my superiors ... I was authorized to do everything that I did." That included the effort that North began in the spring of 1984 to keep the contras together in "body and soul," a phrase that North attributed to Reagan. North said the contra assignment came from McFarlane.

North said he was the "only person left" in the U.S. government to work with the contras after Congress cut off military aid in October of that year under the Boland amendment. By the following summer, after newspaper accounts began questioning North's contra activities, the NSC aide began taking steps to shield himself from scrutiny, particularly on Capitol Hill.

Casey's Role

One of the most frequent names that cropped up during North's testimony was that of Casey, who died May 6, a day after the hearings started. Casey, according to North, was involved in virtually all of the NSC-directed Iran-contra activities. North said that Casey enthusiastically described the secret effort to aid the rebels as a "full-service covert operation." Both Casey and Poindexter were aware of North's scheme to divert Iran arms profits to the contras, a plan that Casey described as an "ultimate irony" because of the Ayatollah Ruhollah Khomeini's unknowing support for the Sandinista regime. "Director Casey was very enthusiastic about the whole program and advocated it," said North.

Liman pressed North on whether he thought Casey's proposal for a "CIA outside the CIA" was proper. "Are you not shocked that the director of the CIA was proposing an organization to do these kinds of things outside of his own organization?" asked Liman. "I don't see what would be wrong with that," North replied.

Casey was hospitalized in December 1986, a day before he was set to testify to the Senate Intelligence Committee about his role. He never recovered from his illness, preventing investigators from hearing his account of the scandal.

North said he did not tell Meese about Casey's knowledge of the diversion during a November 23 interview with the attorney general, who was then conducting a preliminary inquiry into the Iran arms sales. Justice Department officials, in the course of that investigation, had learned of the diversion a day earlier after discovering a memo that North had written in April 1986 mentioning the plan.

Asked by Liman why he hid Casey's knowledge, North said it was "always part of the plan" that the CIA head would not be linked to the covert effort to assist the contras. Casey from the outset wanted to preserve a "plausible deniability" to insulate the CIA from the operation, said North. Such insulation was needed because of the Boland amendment that barred the CIA and other intelligence agencies from helping the contras.

According to North, Casey suggested in 1984 that he consider using retired major general Secord to assist in a covert campaign to aid the contras. During his testimony in May, Secord said North asked him in mid-1984 to "contribute" his services to the effort. That led to Secord's assisting in arms sales to Iran and setting up a private supply operation to the contras managed by North in Washington. Secord and his business partner Hakim collected millions of dollars that flowed through shell companies and Swiss bank accounts that made up what they called the enterprise. Financial records analyzed by the select committees revealed that some $8 million in profits remained in various bank accounts connected to the Secord-Hakim venture when the operation came to a halt. North testified that he always thought Secord deserved "reasonable compensation" for his services but said he was surprised to learn that so much money remained unspent when only about $4 million ended up with the contras. North said July 10 the $8 million should be sent to the contras, which Secord had suggested in May. *(Secord testimony, p. 87)*

Diversion Scheme and Memos

It was North himself who first discussed the diversion scheme with Manucher Ghorbanifar, the Iranian arms merchant who served as the original intermediary between U.S. and Iranian officials. North said Ghorbanifar first suggested the idea in the bathroom of a London hotel during a meeting about Iran arms sales in January 1986. A few weeks earlier, Israeli official Amiram Nir had broached with North the idea of using "residuals" from the arms sales for other unrelated activities, North testified. He said Nir did not specifically mention the contras. At the London meeting, North said Ghorbanifar—whom North believed to be an Israeli intelligence agent—suggested the contra diversion as an "incentive" to sweeten the proposed sale of U.S. weapons to Iran. *(Israeli version, p. 141)*

North said he viewed Ghorbanifar as a "duplicitous sneak" who was reaping huge profits in the Iran deals. Nonetheless, North, always anxious to get money and arms to the contras, said he was immediately attracted to the diversion idea. "I thought using the ayatollah's money to support the Nicaraguan resistance was a right idea," he told the committees. "I didn't think it was wrong. I think it was a neat idea."

North outlined the diversion plan in five memos that he sent to Poindexter, each in connection with proposed arms sales to Iran during 1986. The purpose of the memos was to obtain Reagan's approval for the arms sales—and with them the diversion plan—but North testified that he never saw any of the memos come back with Reagan's signature. Still, North assumed that Reagan knew of the diversion plan until Poindexter told him in November that the president had never been aware of it.

Three of the arms sales that were the subjects of the memos took place—in February, May, and August. The other two fell through. All but one of the diversion messages—the April 1986 memo found by Justice Department aides—were destroyed by North, who said he had intended to shred all of them.

Liman grilled North on his extensive shredding of documents in October and November 1986. North claimed that he shredded papers on November 22, 1986, while Justice Department officials were in his office sifting through other documents. North said he figured at the time that the officials were looking for material related to arms shipments to Iran in 1985, while North was destroying contra-related documents. "They were working on their project. I was working on mine," he said. The documents he shredded "were beyond the pale of their inquiry." At the time, the Justice officials had not yet discovered North's

one remaining diversion memo. A Justice Department spokesman denied July 9 that North operated the shredder in his office while officials were examining documents there.

North said he began to get rid of documents in his office in October after learning from Casey that month that a former legal client, Roy Furmark, had heard of the diversion of Iran arms profits to the contras. North also said he was prodded by the October 5 capture in Nicaragua of American Eugene Hasenfus who was aboard a private contra supply plane shot down by the Sandinistas.

The Iran-contra operation continued to unravel in early November after a magazine in Lebanon reported McFarlane's highly secretive trip to Tehran the previous May. Within days of that disclosure, which Reagan dismissed as unfounded, Casey advised North to "clean things up" by getting rid of evidence relating to the operation. Casey at the time also advised North to hire a lawyer.

At Casey's suggestion, North said he destroyed a detailed ledger in early November that he had used to record financial transactions involving the contra supply operation. North said he used the ledger, supplied by Casey, to account for between $150,000 and $175,000 in cash and traveler's checks that North used to pay for expenses in the contra operation. Fawn Hall, North's former NSC secretary, told the committees in June about the ledger, but investigators did not know what had happened to it until North revealed that he destroyed it.

Tell Nothing to Congress

Several times during his testimony, North criticized Congress for failing to support the contras. "Plain and simple," he said July 9, "Congress is to blame because of the fickle, vacillating, unpredictable, on-again, off-again policy" toward the contras.

Saying that members of Congress could not be trusted to keep secrets about sensitive covert operations, North said he and other administration officials decided not to tell Congress anything of his efforts to assist the contras. "I didn't want to show Congress a single word of this whole thing," he said, reflecting the defiant attitude that the former NSC aide came to have toward Congress on contra matters.

North denied, however, that his attitude reflected a belief that he or anyone else in the administration had done anything illegal. Instead, North said his contra operation was designed as a way of "working around the problem" of the Boland amendment's ban on aid. "I think we found a legal way of complying with Boland," he said.

McFarlane testified in May that he and North misled members of Congress into believing that North's activities were not violating the letter or spirit of the anticontra law. McFarlane said he was convinced that Congress meant for the Boland amendment to apply to the NSC.

But North put a different spin on the Boland issue, citing opinions by Casey and others who did not think the law applied to NSC officials. Instead, North said he and McFarlane altered documents that sketched out North's activities in order to mislead Congress for other reasons. McFarlane "was cleaning up the historical record. He was trying to preserve the president from political damage, and I don't blame him for that." As for his own role, North was blunt about it when asked by Nields. "I will tell you right now, counsel, and all the members here gathered that I misled the Congress."

Bipartisan Comity Becomes a Casualty . . .

Twelve weeks of Iran-contra hearings, like the searing temperatures of a Washington summer, left some of the participants feeling increasingly hot under the collar.

As the hearings drew to a close, tempers flared more frequently, and tough rhetoric became more common. The confrontational edge reflected a central political reality surrounding the hearings—the fact that they largely represented a political struggle between Republican defenders of the Reagan administration and its Democratic critics.

At the outset, that struggle largely was masked by outward cordiality among the committees' members and witnesses. "When one considers the subject matter we're dealing with and the emotions that it has developed, the relationship among members is calm, cool and friendly," said Daniel K. Inouye, D-Hawaii, chairman of the Senate select Iran-contra committee.

But as the hearings drew to a close and the committees got ready to draft conclusions and recommendations, the signs of a bitter political confrontation became much more visible.

On one hand there were the president's most loyal supporters, who wanted to focus attention on the panels' approach and performance. On the other hand there were others, mostly Democrats, who wanted the focus on broader issues such as deceit by government officials, lying to Congress, and intense secrecy within the White House. Each side believed its preferred focus provided it with the political high ground.

The highly charged atmosphere that surrounded the appearances in July of two key Iran-contra figures exacerbated the political strains within the House and Senate committees.

The president's foremost supporters, all of them Republicans, quickly grabbed onto the perceived popularity of Lt. Col. Oliver L. North, the former National Security Council functionary, as an effective way of deflecting sharp criticism of Reagan's handling of the scandal.

And when Rear Adm. John M. Poindexter, Reagan's former national security adviser, repeatedly denied that he ever told the president about the diversion to the Nicaraguan rebels of funds from Iran weapons sales, these same members turned their sights on the performance of the committees themselves.

"Some people no doubt gleefully hope for another Watergate," said Sen. Orrin G. Hatch, R-Utah. "Those same people who were so taken by the original prospect of presidential involvement are now scurrying around, hoping that they can find a new line of fire."

Hatch, Reagan's staunchest supporter on the Senate panel, accused others on the committees July 20 of being "bound and determined to find something terribly wrong here, no matter what the facts turned out to be."

Members such as Hatch believed the testimony given by North and Poindexter helped to remove Reagan from the scandal's spotlight.

But many Democrats on the panels, joined by some Republicans, believed important and troubling questions remained about how the administration conducted foreign policy. "How was our government . . . reaching extraordinarily important judgments about what the United States ought to be doing?" Democratic senator Paul S. Sarbanes of Maryland wondered to reporters July 21. "It's very clear they cut the Congress out of it altogether. But I think it's equally clear they were cutting one another out of it to varying degrees."

The Lawyers: Fire and Fireworks

If the eleven days of testimony by North and Poindexter raised the volume level inside the hearings, they also increased friction among committee members over the conduct of Congress's Iran-contra investigation.

The most visible signs were the growing testiness by some members toward the roles of Senate chief counsel Arthur L. Liman and his House counterpart, John W. Nields, Jr. Both Liman and Nields emerged as tough questioners of the witnesses. The two lawyers drew mounting criticism from some members who felt they acted more like prosecutors than fact-finders.

An undercurrent of resentment surfaced in the wake of Liman's pointed questioning of North July 9. The next day, Rep. Bill McCollum, R-Fla., accused the Senate counsel of pursuing "a whole pattern of biased questions."

"He is acting like a prosecutor, not a prosecutor of Col. North so much, but as a prosecutor of the president," said McCollum. In an interview later, the Florida Republican said he thought Liman's approach reflected a conscious decision by Senate leaders to conduct hearings with a "predisposed bias" against the Reagan administration in the Iran-contra affair.

Adding to the harsh tone was the presence of feisty defense attorneys on the other side of the committee dais: Brendan V. Sullivan, Jr., and Richard W. Beckler. Representing North and Poindexter, respectively, they injected courtroom combat tactics into the already contentious political arena, challenging the nature and fairness of the congressional proceedings.

"Get off his back!" Sullivan snapped at one point

... in Political Battle over Reagan Policies

during Liman's grilling of North. Turning to North a few moments later, he told his client, "Don't answer the question." That led to some icy stares between Liman and Sullivan, who were separated by only a few feet in the Senate hearing room.

Inouye, for his part, dismissed Sullivan's objections, permitting the committee counsels to ask questions as they wished and directing North to answer them. He even suggested to Sullivan at one point that North himself ought to speak up if he objected to the questioning. "I'm not a potted plant," replied Sullivan. "I'm here as the lawyer. That's my job."

Committee members later said Sullivan was only doing his job in watching out for his client's interests. Still, his outburst clearly added to the increased intensity inside the Senate Caucus Room.

Beckler, Poindexter's aggressive lawyer, picked up where Sullivan left off in trying to depict his client as a victim of unjust treatment by the committees.

"I would hope that we can carry on the remainder of the testimony in a much more civil manner," Inouye said July 17, after Beckler angrily objected to one line of questioning during Poindexter's five-day stint on the House side of the Capitol.

"We don't have to yell at each other. And I must say that it gets a little tiring to be lectured at," Inouye said.

Squabbling among the Members

The long season of examining the Reagan administration's most embarrassing episode also took its toll on members. Frustrated by long hours of sitting around, awaiting their turn to ask questions and speak their mind, some of the members singled out others for criticism.

Several House Republicans were upset with Chairman Lee H. Hamilton, D-Ind., because of his sternly worded lectures to some of the major witnesses.

Hamilton's speeches often attracted widespread media coverage, further rankling the Republicans. He made headlines, for example, when he said July 21 that Poindexter had "locked the president" out of crucial Iran-contra decisions, while adding that Reagan had "created the environment" that allowed that to happen.

Accusing Hamilton of "pontificating," McCollum said the House select committee chairman "sounds almost like a judge passing judgment on a witness." Bothered by the impression that Hamilton was speaking for the entire committee, McCollum added, "I'm quite sure he's aware of what he's doing." McCollum said he and other House GOP members discussed Hamilton's actions among themselves but did not press their complaint with him privately or in public statements during the hearings.

One of the few signs of open hostility among committee members surfaced at the end of Poindexter's five days at the witness table. Senator Sarbanes triggered the incident when he charged Beckler with "coaching" Poindexter on some of his responses. Beckler jumped on Sarbanes immediately. "I have not coached my witness, and I'm not going to tolerate that kind of an accusation," shouted the lawyer.

A few moments later, Rep. Dick Cheney, R-Wyo., challenged Sarbanes's comments about Beckler with a caustic inference to other committee members, whom he did not name. "I'm certain that the senator would not want to leave the impression that somehow having a witness consult with counsel is inappropriate," said Cheney. "There are members of this committee who have their questions written for them by staff."

More Differences down the Road?

The differences among members likely would become even sharper as the panels prepared to write their reports that would close out Congress's Iran-contra investigation.

Members were expected to agree on some basic matters, such as faulting administration officials for keeping Congress in the dark about the Iran-contra dealings.

But other crucial questions were likely to be vigorously disputed, such as whether the Boland amendment, the law that prohibited U.S. military aid to the contras, applied to the president and his staff.

It was expected that all six House Republicans would unite in opposing conclusions that suggested highly improper or unlawful behavior by Reagan or other administration officials. At least two Senate Republicans—Hatch and James A. McClure, R-Idaho—would probably join them.

The key test would be the willingness of one or more of the remaining GOP senators to sign on to a strongly worded report pushed by committee Democrats. Those senators were Vice Chairman Warren B. Rudman of New Hampshire, William S. Cohen of Maine, and Paul S. Trible, Jr., of Virginia. Each of the three had been highly critical of various aspects of the administration's role in the Iran-contra affair. But it remained to be seen how far each was willing to go in signing a document casting blame on Reagan for the scandal.

As the hearings wound up, some committee members were anxious to put the short tempers and angry debates behind them. Said Inouye, "I want to be able to get up one morning and say, 'Aahh, it's over.'"

North's determination to keep Congress in the dark prompted a sharp retort from Nields. After North mentioned that news of his contra efforts had surfaced in the Soviet Union and Nicaragua, Nields shot back: "All of our enemies knew it and you wanted to conceal it from the United States Congress." North said he did so to avoid jeopardizing the administration's efforts to keep aid flowing to the contras. He also said the strategy permitted him to be the "deniable link" in the secret plan to assist the rebels. "I was supposed to be dropped like a hot rock when it all came down," he said. "And I was willing to serve in that capacity. I was not willing to become the victim of a criminal prosecution."

Role in Iran Arms Sales

Shifting back and forth between Iran and the contras, North also described in detail his role in a White House effort in November 1986 to falsify an account of Israeli-arranged arms deals with Iran in 1985.

The primary purpose of the chronology was to mask the potentially illegal CIA assistance in the sale of Hawk antiaircraft missiles in November of that year. North said he helped write a chronology on November 20, 1986, that said U.S. officials were assured by Israel at the time of the Hawk shipments that oil drilling parts were being sent, not weapons. The United States did not learn until the following January what had actually been delivered, according to the false chronology. North said several officials knew the chronology was "intentionally misleading" and that he had been asked to insert the false information by McFarlane, who was no longer in the government.

North conceded that disclosing the U.S. role in the 1985 shipment would have caused an "enormous international embarrassment" to Reagan because the deal in fact was structured as a straight arms-for-hostages swap.

On the same day that the false chronology was prepared, North and other officials met at the White House to review congressional testimony to be given the next day by Casey on the subject of Iran arms sales. During that meeting, and afterwards in Casey's office, North said he helped to "fix" the testimony by deleting references to any CIA knowledge of the 1985 Hawk shipment.

North also wanted to remove references in the testimony to the arms deal as an NSC operation, seeking instead to refer to it more generally as a U.S. government project. Asked by Nields who else knew of Casey's false account of the Hawk shipment, North offered a sweeping response: "There was a whole cabinet of people who met in November of 1985 and December of 1985, to include the secretaries of state and defense, the attorney general and others who participated in those activities."

His own role in the November 1985 shipment began after Israel was unable to obtain a landing clearance in Portugal for the flight carrying the Hawk missiles from Tel Aviv to Iran. North contacted CIA officials for assistance and also asked Secord—already helping him buy arms for the contras—to find a way to move the weapons from Israel to Iran. Secord, with help from the CIA, eventually chartered a CIA "proprietary" airline to deliver the weapons.

Legal Problems

But that action presented the administration with a troubling legal dilemma. The law required a presidential finding before the CIA could legally engage in a covert foreign policy operation. Such a finding was prepared in late November, after the Hawk missiles had been sent to Iran. Former CIA general counsel Sporkin had testified June 24 that he prepared a finding to authorize the CIA activity after the fact. *(Sporkin testimony, p. 115)*

But North added a critical wrinkle to the turn of events in November 1985. He told the committees that he saw a copy of the finding with Reagan's signature in Poindexter's office. If he did, the document would confirm Reagan's approval of an arms-for-hostages deal. If he did not, it appeared that the CIA illegally participated in the shipment. (It was not until Poindexter's testimony that the committees learned that Reagan signed the finding December 5.)

North said officials such as Shultz and Weinberger were not "enamored" of the Iran arms initiative. But he said he never heard either of them express strong resistance. "A lot of people were willing to let it go along, hoping it would succeed, and were willing to walk away when it failed or when it was exposed," said North.

WEEK NINE: NORTH, McFARLANE, POINDEXTER

Throughout his six days at the witness table that concluded July 14, North repeatedly said he never acted without the approval of Reagan's two national security advisers, McFarlane and Poindexter, who served during the Iran-contra affair. Minutes after North completed his testimony, McFarlane returned to the hearings to contradict some of North's statements, including a key element of North's account. McFarlane insisted that he did not give North explicit authorization for all of his contra-aid activities. McFarlane was followed July 15-17 by Poindexter, who completed his testimony the next week, July 20-21. Poindexter testified that he never told the president about the arms sale diversion. "On this whole issue, you know, the buck stops here with me," Poindexter told the committees on July 15. *(McFarlane July 14 testimony text, p. C-29; Poindexter, p. C-97)*

North Testimony

Aside from the pile of laudatory telegrams carried into the hearing room by North's wife, Betsy, his final two days of testimony July 13-14 did not provide many new revelations. Instead, committee members used much of their question time either to praise or admonish North for his actions. Many called him a patriot who served his country well.

Others chastised him for lying to Congress in the past and suggesting that the hearings had hurt foreign policy. "I wonder whether the damage has been caused by these hearings or by the acts which prompted these hearings," said House committee chairman Hamilton. "I wonder whether you would have the Congress do nothing after it has been lied to and misled and ignored." Both he and Senate chairman Inouye delivered impassioned speeches that, while singling out North for criticism, aimed broadly at the administration for its conduct. North sat virtually motionless, gazing up at the two chairmen as they lectured him. "Should we in the defense of democracy adopt and embrace one of the most important tenets of communism and Marxism, the ends justify the means?" said Inouye.

Earlier in the day, North enjoyed his own opportunity to speak about a subject dear to him—U.S. support for the contras. At the insistence of several contra supporters on the committees, North was permitted to describe a slide show he used to give to private groups to raise support for the rebels.

Knowing that McFarlane was getting ready to challenge some of North's account, the Marine officer repeated his assertion that he never did anything without the approval of his superiors. "I want to make it very clear again," said North. "Every single thing that I did that required a decision, I sought approval for. And if I didn't get approval, I didn't do it."

Bribes in the Bathroom

During his two final days of testimony, North provided further details about his efforts to assist the contras and manage the arms-for-hostages deals with the Iranians.

North had previously testified that the idea to divert profits from the weapons sales to the contras first came from Iranian arms merchant Ghorbanifar during a January 1986 meeting with North in London. North revealed July 14 that Ghorbanifar, whom North believed to be an Israeli intelligence agent, first offered him a $1 million bribe to proceed with a proposed arms sale the following month. North said he abruptly refused that offer but was immediately attracted to the diversion scheme. According to North, the discussion of the bribe and the diversion took place in a bathroom at the hotel where he was meeting with Ghorbanifar. The Iranian, in an ABC interview July 16, denied North's account. At a later meeting, North said, Iranian officials offered him a valuable Persian rug. He said he refused the gift, accepting instead a handful of pistachio nuts, a popular commodity in Iran.

His testimony also described a lack of diligence in accounting for the millions of dollars that flowed through the enterprise—the network of shell companies and secret bank accounts run by Secord and Hakim. North said the two men never provided him with details of their finances, and that he never asked for them. He called the Secord-Hakim venture an "imaginative solution to some short-term problems." Senator Trible asked North July 13 whether he knew that Secord and Hakim had earned "outlandish profits" as a result of the Iran-contra operation. North said he did not know about the profits, and that he never intended to make anyone rich. "The problem here is, they were getting rich," said Trible. Secord denied any interest in profits during his testimony to the committees in May. But his assertion had been placed in doubt by subsequent testimony and evidence.

Expedited Payments

In another area, documents released by the committees more tightly linked the NSC—and North in particular—with contra fund-raising groups. Throughout his testimony, North asserted that he never directly solicited contributions for the contras. But some of the documents showed a connection between the NSC and the State De-

partment's public diplomacy office for Latin America that awarded contracts to a conservative group involved in contra fund raising.

North said he might have made efforts to speed up payments to Richard R. Miller, an associate of fund-raiser Channell. Miller's firm, International Business Communications, had been awarded a State Department contract to promote public support—but not to raise money—for the contras. *(Miller tax fraud plea, p. 170)*

Miller worked closely with North in raising money from wealthy American conservatives that went to buy arms and military equipment for the contras. Miller acted under North's direction in setting up a Cayman Islands corporation to funnel money to the contras and to the Lake Resources account in Switzerland that paid for the contra supply operation.

One of the memos released by the committees said the public diplomacy office at the State Department was part of an interagency group that reported "directly to the NSC."

At another point, North testified that he pushed the idea of Vice President Bush meeting with high-level Iranian officials in 1986 to boost the prospects of improved ties between the United States and Iran. North said he thought Bush was a good choice because of a mediating role he had played in a tense meeting between opposing factions in El Salvador in 1983. Eventually, however, nothing came of North's plan to have Bush meet with the Iranians.

McFarlane Disputes North

Minutes after North completed his testimony, McFarlane returned to contradict some of North's statements. He originally testified in May, long before the committees had an opportunity to hear North's version of his Iran-contra role.

The clash between McFarlane and North stood in striking contrast to the close working and personal relationship the two had in the White House. Once describing North as "like a son of mine," McFarlane seemed almost pained in disputing some of North's testimony. The two men apparently did not see each other at the hearings; North quickly left the Senate Caucus Room after he completed his testimony and before McFarlane arrived.

McFarlane had asked the panels to let him testify a second time in order to challenge North's contention that he knew about and approved several Iran-contra actions during his tenure as national security adviser in 1984-85. McFarlane told the panels that North "went over the line from advice ... to an operational role" in helping the contras in military matters, "and that was not authorized." McFarlane said he was "generally aware" that the contras were obtaining weapons through a resupply program. But contrary to North's testimony, McFarlane said he never knew the extent of North's role. Instead, he instructed North in 1984 to undertake efforts to turn the contras into a more credible political force, an order that had come from Reagan, McFarlane testified.

After Congress passed the Boland amendment that fall, McFarlane said he told his staff that the law applied to NSC officials. "It is clear to me Mr. Boland did not want anyone in the United States government assisting the contras," McFarlane told the committees during his May testimony. But North testified that McFarlane never gave any explicit instructions to his staff that they were covered by the Boland amendment. North, citing legal judgments from Casey and private lawyers, told the committees he did not think the law applied to the NSC.

'Wanted to Get Rid of It'

That conclusion prompted a strong response during McFarlane's rebuttal testimony. "If you are a member of the staff ... and you hear the boss come to the meeting once a week and harangue and pound the table about how hard we've got to try to overturn the Boland amendment, what other conclusion is possible," he said. "I mean, I didn't like it. I wanted to get rid of it. We fought like crazy to get the votes. Now if it didn't apply to us, that was a lot of wasted effort."

In another dispute, McFarlane emphatically denied knowing anything about plans for the privately funded "full-service" covert organization envisioned by North and Casey to conduct a variety of missions in behalf of the U.S. government. McFarlane called it an "unthinkable" idea that "violates every tenet of my political beliefs." North had testified that McFarlane knew about the scheme for an "off-the-shelf" covert operation proposed by Casey.

In another matter involving the former CIA director, North testified that McFarlane approved of Casey's suggestion in the spring of 1984 that he recruit retired major general Secord into the clandestine effort to arm the contras. McFarlane, however, said he did not know of Secord's role in the contra supply operation until December 1985, when the two met in London in conjunction with the weapons-to-Iran program that Secord also had been working on. "No earlier offer or proposal, to my knowledge, either directly with Col. North or with the contras to engage [Secord] had ever come to my attention, as far as I recall," said McFarlane.

Other Disputes

McFarlane and North also clashed over an accounting of North's efforts to involve a U.S. ambassador in the contras' war against the Sandinistas.

North testified that McFarlane approved of his plan in mid-1985 to "encourage" Tambs, the U.S. envoy to Costa Rica, to help set up a military front for the contras in southern Nicaragua, flanking the Costa Rican border. McFarlane said he recalled discussing the opening of a military front with North, and that the idea of doing so made sense. But he said it would have taken a "long leap" for North to assume the authority to solicit Tambs's help from their general discussions about the southern front.

Tambs told the panels May 28 that his instructions came from North at the behest of a three-person Restricted Interagency Group consisting of North, Assistant Secretary of State Abrams, and a CIA official. (Tambs testimony, p. 100)

Yet another dispute between McFarlane and North took place over North's role in raising money for the contras. According to North's account, McFarlane knew of his aide's connection with a contra fund-raising group headed by Channell. McFarlane said he was aware of groups trying to raise money for television ads to promote Reagan's contra policy and his antimissile strategic defense initiative. But he said he did not know about North's efforts to help these groups "in the sense of raising money for direct linkage to the contras." According to McFarlane,

North denied to him at the time that he was trying to raise funds for the contras. During those discussions, McFarlane said he counted on North being truthful with him.

"Look Ollie," he said he told North at one point. "This is Bud. This is me. This is not some member of Congress. What's the story? Are you out raising money?" McFarlane said he believed his aide when North assured him he was doing nothing improper with Channell's group. Channell and Miller had pleaded guilty to charges that they defrauded the government by illegally seeking tax-deductible donations for the contras. Both men said they conspired with North in their fund raising.

Beyond North's specific role in the secret contra supply effort, McFarlane took exception to North's description of his role in efforts to cover up aspects of the Iran-contra episode in hopes of protecting the president. A major part of the cover-up took place in November 1986, when Reagan officials were preparing a chronology of events describing the sale of weapons to Iran in 1985-86. In doing so, the officials wanted to shield the CIA's role in helping to ship Hawk missiles from Israel to Iran in November 1985 in exchange for hostages. North testified that McFarlane directed him to write into the chronology that U.S. officials believed in 1985 that Israel was sending oil-drilling parts to Iran, and that the administration did not learn about the missiles until January 1986.

McFarlane denied telling North to do that. Instead, he said he first suggested saying in an earlier version of the chronology that a second shipment of "U.S. equipment" had gone from Israel to Iran after a sale of TOW antitank missiles in September 1985. McFarlane also said he did not participate in drafting the language of the later chronology that discussed oil-drilling parts.

In explaining his role, North had repeated several times his view that he would be the administration's designated "fall guy" when the Iran-contra operation unraveled. McFarlane disputed North's account. "No such plan existed, to my knowledge," he told the committees. "I know I wasn't party to any such planning before I left the government at the end of 1985." He said he never doubted, however, that North "would have offered to step forward to protect me or the commander-in-chief or both."

Poindexter Testimony

Poindexter's assertion that he never told the president about the arms sale diversion elicited a mixed reaction from the White House. Reagan on July 16 commented: "What's new about that? I've been saying it for seven months." Other White House officials said they were relieved, but not surprised, by Poindexter's statement. However, White House spokesman Fitzwater rebuked Poindexter for having done Reagan a "disservice" by not telling him. "We're saying that all of these decisions are presidential level, and the president has said that he should have known, and had he known, it wouldn't have happened," Fitzwater said.

Poindexter insisted that Reagan would have approved the diversion had he known, and he defended his decision not to tell the president. Asked July 17 about Fitzwater's "disservice" remark, he said: "I would have expected him to say that. That is the whole idea of deniability."

Although Poindexter backed Reagan on the issue that had dominated public discussion of the Iran-contra affair, his testimony undermined previous key White House assertions. Poindexter provided new ammunition for those who contended that swapping arms for hostages was the true basis for U.S. dealings with Iran. He revealed that Reagan in December 1985 signed a finding retroactively approving CIA participation in an Israeli arms shipment to Iran; the only goal mentioned in the document, which Poindexter destroyed a year later, was freeing hostages. Reagan had said he did not recall signing the document. After Poindexter's testimony, Fitzwater said Reagan "will not disagree" with his former aide on that matter.

John M. Poindexter

Poindexter also said Reagan knew about, and approved, some of North's procontra activities. Some committee members said those activities violated U.S. law.

But, in essence, Poindexter's testimony sharply reduced the prospects of a constitutional confrontation between Congress and the president, and it eliminated whatever tiny chance there had been that the Iran-contra inquiry could result in Reagan's impeachment or resignation. No committee members had suggested that Reagan might have committed an impeachable offense. But memories of Watergate—coupled with public skepticism that Reagan was telling the truth about the diversion—had been in the background.

Inability to Remember

Aside from his contention that Reagan never knew about the diversion of Iranian funds to the contras, perhaps the most striking feature of Poindexter's testimony was his inability to remember conversations and documents about which other witnesses gave vivid details.

When he served at the White House, the NSC aide often was described as a brilliant thinker able to absorb enormous amounts of detail. In his opening days of testimony, Poindexter showed his analytical ability but often seemed confused about the sequence of events and insisted that his memory on important points, such as his conversations with the president, was "fuzzy" or nonexistent. Poindexter's explanation was that he was busy at the time and that events that subsequently took on great importance did not register then. Except for his term as national security adviser, he said July 16, "I have never been hit with so many issues in such a short period of time."

Puffing on his pipe and pausing frequently as he gave slow, deliberate answers, Poindexter had the appearance of a college professor who accidentally stumbled onto a movie set. In style, he was a sharp contrast to North, who projected a dynamic and sympathetic image, especially on television. Heavily coached by his lawyers, North had aggressively confronted the panels with emotional speeches on his actions and views. Unlike North in his bemedaled Marine uniform, Poindexter chose to appear in civilian dress. He did so, he said, because the Iran-contra affair was "not a Navy issue." While at the White House, he said, he had tried to "make a very clear distinction" between his

role as a military officer and his subsequent role as a senior political appointee.

Like North, Poindexter was represented by a combative lawyer who sought to establish that the committees were taking advantage of his client. Richard W. Beckler, Poindexter's counsel, also claimed that the panels were colluding with independent counsel Walsh to prosecute his client. The panels had given North and Poindexter limited immunity against prosecution to make them testify.

The committees rejected those charges, and House panel chairman Hamilton heatedly denounced the latter one as "totally and absolutely false."

The Diversion Question

Although the question of when Reagan had learned of the diversion long had held a central place in the public's perception of the Iran-contra affair, many panel members had said for weeks that it was a side issue, key to judging the president's credibility but of little substantive importance.

Senate counsel Liman obviously intended to ask a series of questions leading up to the dramatic one of whether Reagan was ever told about the diversion scheme. But Poindexter spoiled that strategy, answering one of Liman's early warm-up questions with a long discourse putting the diversion issue into the "perspective" of Reagan's overall support for the contras.

By the time North suggested the diversion approach, Poindexter said, Reagan had approved efforts to get money to the contras from other countries and from private individuals. Using the Iranian money "fell in exactly the same category," he said. "In my view, it was a matter of implementation of the president's policy with regard to support of the contras," and so he gave North "general" approval.

Poindexter said he also viewed the diversion as only a short-term proposition to provide "bridge financing" of the contras until Congress approved Reagan's request of $100 million in official U.S. aid. Congress approved that money later in 1986.

Even while viewing the diversion as a continuation of Reagan's policy, Poindexter said he understood immediately that it would be a "politically volatile issue" if revealed. "So, although I was convinced that we could properly do it, and that the president would approve, if asked, I made a very deliberate decision not to ask the president so that I could insulate him from the decision and provide some future deniability for the president if it ever leaked out." By "future deniability," Poindexter said he meant that Reagan could be able to say truthfully that he did not know about the diversion.

Poindexter insisted that he "had the authority" to approve the diversion scheme on his own. In turn, Poindexter said he gave North "broad general authority" to carry out the plan.

Asked by Liman if he ever told Reagan about the diversion prior to Justice Department officials' November 22, 1986, discovery of information about it in North's office, Poindexter said: "I don't—I did not." Poindexter said his "best recollection" was that he discussed the matter with no one, other than North, until November 24, 1986, when Meese asked him about it.

Poindexter said he never told North that Reagan did not know about the diversion plan. North had testified that he asked Poindexter November 21 whether Reagan had approved the diversion and was told he had not. But Poindexter said he could not recall that conversation.

Not Asking for Details

Poindexter also testified that he asked North few questions about the diversion plan once he approved it. For example, he said he never asked North how much money was generated for the contras from the Iran arms sales because that was a "detail" and he did not want to get into "micromanagement of the project that Col. North was working on." North himself had testified that he never knew exactly how much money was spent on the contras out of the diversion fund.

Among the details about which Poindexter expressed general ignorance was North's use of the money for other covert operations, including several that were planned jointly with Israel. North testified that he and CIA director Casey developed a plan for an "off-the-shelf, stand-alone" private company, using Iran arms sale proceeds, that would conduct covert operations on behalf of the U.S. government. Poindexter said he recalled having "very preliminary discussions" with North about such covert actions, but insisted he knew no details and assumed nothing ever came of the ideas, although he found "attractive" features in privately run covert operations.

In one memo, dated September 15, 1986, North suggested that Poindexter brief Reagan on "initiatives" with Israel, presumably the covert plans. Although Poindexter wrote "done" next to North's recommendation, he told the panels "I seriously doubt" that he actually did so.

Poindexter said he could not recall seeing any of the five memos that North said he wrote mentioning the diversion plan in conjunction with Iran arms sales. Only one memo survived North's shredding of office documents: a famous April 1986 document, found by Justice Department investigators, which revealed the Iran-contra link.

On a related matter, Poindexter undermined the White House position that Reagan knew little about North's efforts in behalf of the contras. Poindexter said the president knew that North was helping the contras by doing such things as encouraging donations and supervising the construction of an airstrip in Costa Rica for the private network that ferried arms to the guerrillas. "He wanted to be sure that the contras were supported," Poindexter said of Reagan's instructions. But he said he did not give Reagan daily details because "the only thing that was important to him was that they [the contras] were staying alive." Reagan approved North's activities "in effect," Poindexter said, but never gave official approval to them by signing a covert-action finding. Poindexter could not explain Reagan's statement to the Tower Commission that he did not know about NSC actions on behalf of the rebels.

The 1985 Finding

Poindexter said he and Reagan paid scant attention to what was to become one of the most politically important documents of the Iran-contra affair: the 1985 finding approving the Israeli sale of U.S.-made weapons to Iran. Unlike all other administration documents on Iran arms sales, that finding was cast in straight arms-for-hostages terms and made no mention of broader "strategic" goals such as improving U.S. relations with Iran. It authorized the CIA to aid unspecified private parties "in their attempt to obtain the release of Americans held hostage in the Middle East."

Poindexter said the finding was "prepared by the CIA as a CYA effort," referring to the informal military term "cover your ass." According to previous testimony, the CIA wanted the protection of a presidential finding because of questions about the legality of the Israeli shipments.

Casey sent Poindexter the finding on November 26, 1985, asking for Reagan's signature. In spite of his doubts about the wisdom and legality of having the president ratify prior CIA actions, Poindexter said he gave the document to Reagan to sign nine days later, on December 5. Reagan read and signed it, he said. Poindexter said he then put the finding in a safe at the NSC offices and forgot about it.

A year later, on November 21, 1986, with the Iran arms sales public knowledge, Meese asked Poindexter to collect all documents about the sales, as part of a review of what the administration had done. Later that day, Cmdr. Paul Thompson, the NSC counsel, brought the documents to Poindexter's office and pulled the 1985 finding out of an envelope, saying: "They'll have a field day with this." Reading the finding, Poindexter said he realized that it would cause embarrassment "because the president was beaten about the head and shoulders" with charges that the Iranian arms sales amounted to swaps for hostages. "Well, this finding, unfortunately, gave that same impression," he added. "And so I decided to tear it up, and I tore it up, put it in the burn basket behind my desk."

Asked by Liman if he saw his role as shielding the president from political embarrassment, Poindexter said: "I think that it's always the responsibility of a staff to protect their leader, and certainly in this case, where the leader is the commander in chief. . . ."

Secrecy, Misleading Congress

More than any other witness—even including North—Poindexter demonstrated an obsession with protecting government secrets. His efforts to do so, he said, extended to keeping other top officials in the dark about the Iran-contra dealings. Leaking secret information, he said, "has become an art form in this city to help influence policy."

Poindexter said he never told anyone else in the administration about the diversion of Iran arms sale money to the contras, and he said he gave officials such as Shultz only limited information. Shultz, for his part, did not demand many details after opposing the entire idea of selling arms to Iran, Poindexter said.

Poindexter said he never discussed the diversion plan with Casey because he had to testify frequently before Congress "and I didn't want him to have to be evasive." And he said he did not reveal such matters to Chief of Staff Donald T. Regan because his position required frequent contact with the press.

North, McFarlane, and Poindexter all were involved in telling Congress in 1985 and 1986 that North was complying with legal curbs on aid to the contras. Of the three, Poindexter remained the only one still insisting that those statements were not false or misleading. Poindexter testified that he thought the administration was not violating the law. He said the Boland amendment did not apply to the NSC staff because it was not an intelligence agency. He acknowledged that he never sought advice from the Justice Department or White House lawyers on that question.

In asking North to withhold information from Congress, Poindexter said his main goal was to avoid the passage of "more restrictive" contra legislation.

The November Days

Liman and House committee chief counsel Nields led Poindexter through a description of the climactic days of the Iran-contra affair: November 17-25, 1986, when the secrets unraveled, leading to Poindexter's resignation and North's firing.

In the early days of that period, North and other officials wrote chronologies detailing the U.S. dealings with Iran. Poindexter acknowledged that some information in the chronologies was inaccurate—especially in sections dealing with the Israeli shipments to Iran in 1985—but he insisted he was "not sure what the right answers were" on those issues. "I was very fuzzy on 1985," when McFarlane handled most of the Iran dealings, he said.

A key development was a November 20 meeting in Poindexter's office, during which senior officials reviewed statements that Poindexter and Casey were to make the next day to the House and Senate Intelligence committees. One of those in attendance, Assistant Attorney General Cooper, told the Iran-contra panels that North proposed, and Casey and Poindexter accepted, inclusion of a false statement that no U.S. officials had known that a November 1985 Israeli shipment to Iran included weapons. Poindexter insisted that, a year after the shipment, he had forgotten that it included missiles. *(Cooper testimony, p. 117)*

Poindexter acknowledged that he participated in what later appeared to have been the wholesale destruction of White House documents in November—but he rejected any characterization of that as a "cover-up." The destruction of documents occurred shortly after the November 21 initiation of Meese's fact-finding inquiry. Meese told Poindexter that Justice Department lawyers would visit the NSC offices to review documents, and Poindexter passed the word on to North—a notice that might have prompted North to alter or shred key documents about his Iran-contra actions. Poindexter said he did not know then that North was altering and shredding papers.

On November 24, Poindexter said, Meese confronted him with North's April 1986 memo mentioning the Iran arms money diversion. Justice Department lawyers had discovered the memo in North's safe on November 22. Poindexter said he told Meese that he was "generally aware" of the diversion scheme and was ready to resign.

Early the next morning, Meese called Poindexter to his office and suggested that "the time had come" for him to quit. Poindexter said he then met Reagan at the Oval Office and the president accepted his resignation with "great regret."

Early Decisions on Iran

Standing by the administration's original statements of fall 1986, Poindexter said U.S. dealings with Iran were prompted by broad "strategic" concerns—such as ending the Iran-Iraq War and restoring ties with Iran—and were not solely based on a desire to win freedom for hostages. "The president never viewed this as an arms-for-hostages" deal, he said.

Poindexter also rejected North's contention that Shultz and Weinberger had raised only "muted" objections to the Iranian arms sales. At a key meeting on December 7, 1985, he said, both officials lodged "strong, vociferous objection and clearly laid out for the president" the reasons for not using arms sales as the means of opening relations with Iran. Casey spoke in favor of dealing with Iran, and

Reagan agreed, saying he was determined to get the hostages back.

Poindexter attributed to Meese the important decision that the United States would sell the weapons to Iran through private agents rather than allowing Israel to sell the weapons on Washington's behalf, as Israel wanted to do. Meese regarded direct U.S. sales as "a more straightforward way of doing it," Poindexter said. The decision was one of the most important in the Iran-contra affair because it enabled North to hire Secord as the agent who sold the arms to Iran and kept the profits. Because of a quirk in U.S. arms export control laws, the direct arms sales also made it easier for the administration to avoid—or at least postpone—telling Congress about the sales to Iran, Poindexter said.

In a disclosure that could have proved among the most embarrassing to Reagan, Poindexter said he got Reagan's approval in October 1986 for a "nine-point plan" that led to the release of hostage David P. Jacobsen and a final U.S. sale of 500 TOW antitank missiles to Iran. The plan was negotiated by Secord's associates, acting with North's authority. It included a provision that the United States would give Iran a plan that could lead to the release of seventeen terrorists imprisoned in Kuwait (the Da'Wa prisoners). This point was in opposition to official U.S. policy. Secretary of State Shultz, in his own testimony, vigorously disagreed that the president would have ever approved such a plan.

WEEK TEN: POINDEXTER, SHULTZ

The tenth week of hearings featured the final two days of testimony by former national security adviser Poindexter on July 20-21, followed by a two-day appearance July 23-24 by Secretary of State Shultz, the most senior administration official who was called by the committees. *(Shultz testimony text, p. C-112)*

Poindexter played a significant role in all phases of the Iran-contra affair; Shultz opposed the Iran dealings but had little involvement with them once President Reagan gave his approval. Shultz said he was unaware of the diversion scheme and of a secret White House-supervised operation to supply weapons to the contras through private agents.

In their separate appearances, the two men fleshed out a nearly complete picture of how the administration got itself into the Iran-contra affair. In its distrust of Congress and other agencies of government, the White House launched its own secret campaigns to aid the contras and negotiate arms-for-hostage deals with Iran, refusing to heed warning signs that its actions were illegal or unwise.

The two men rarely mentioned each other by name during their testimony, but they raised the question of how they ever got along with each other while serving as top aides to Reagan. Poindexter upbraided the State Department—and by implication, Shultz—for refusing to take risks and for failing to support the president once he decided to proceed with his policy toward Iran. Shultz harshly attacked the White House—principally Poindexter—for misleading the president and failing to give him sound advice on which to base his decisions. And he charged that Poindexter and other officials "deliberately deceived me." Shultz also faulted the CIA for skewing intelligence assessments to support White House policies.

Shultz commanded wide respect on Capitol Hill, and most committee members effusively heaped praise on him. Even Democratic representative Brooks, perhaps the most caustic administration critic on either committee, told Shultz: "You have injected a degree of honesty and integrity that has been sorely missing so far on the part of our witnesses."

Because of that respect, Shultz's testimony added to doubts about the credibility of his nemesis, Poindexter, who had been praised by committee members for his service to country but condemned by many for keeping information from the president. Noting that the two officials differed on both policy and the facts of what happened, Senate committee member Boren said: "In any conflict, I believe Mr. Shultz 100 percent. He has never misled me."

But Shultz's denunciations apparently did little to change minds of committee members about whether Poindexter could be believed on the central point of his testimony: that he never told Reagan about the diversion of Iranian money to the contras. Poindexter said he approved the diversion on his own and kept information about it from Reagan because of its "politically explosive" nature.

Some committee members said they never did believe Poindexter or were skeptical, and so the statements by Shultz merely reinforced their opinions. Senate committee chairman Inouye had been vocal in expressing skepticism about Poindexter's testimony, calling it "mind-boggling."

The skeptics pointed to three aspects of Poindexter's five-day testimony:

● His explanation that he was trying to protect Reagan from severe political damage. That explanation ran counter to his insistence that the diversion scheme was merely an implementation "detail" of the president's overall support of the contras.

● His general inability to recall key conversations and documents throughout the history of the Iran-contra affair, in spite of his reputation as a brilliant thinker with a keen memory.

● His account of his final days at the White House before he resigned November 25, 1986. Poindexter testified that Meese, Reagan, and others never asked him who approved the diversion scheme or any details about how it was implemented.

But other committee members said they continued to accept Poindexter's account, even after the testimony by Shultz. Boren noted that Shultz said he believed Reagan never knew about the diversion. "Shultz convinces me more [than Poindexter] that the president didn't know what was going on," Boren said.

Poindexter insisted throughout his testimony that the Iran-contra affair was of little consequence and had been "overblown" by news organizations and Congress. And he rejected criticisms of his actions even by some committee members who agreed with him on that score.

Poindexter Concludes

During the last three days of Poindexter's public testimony, committee members heard expressions of intense distrust of important institutions of American society, including Congress, other agencies of government, and the press. Because of the failings of those institutions, Poindexter said, the White House was justified in carrying out its policies in secret.

Poindexter's remarks—especially his harsh attacks on Congress—provoked strong reactions from members of the two committees, several of whom implied that he lacked a full understanding of the American constitutional system of government.

Poindexter said he was especially concerned about leaks of sensitive information by members of Congress, even while acknowledging that administration officials also leaked secrets in hopes of influencing policy. That fear of leaks, along with the desire to keep Congress from passing more restrictive legislation barring contra aid, justified the decision to withhold information in 1985 and 1986 about North's involvement with the contras, Poindexter told House committee chief counsel Nields on July 17.

"I felt that we were on strong legal ground with what we were doing and it was consistent with the president's policy, and I simply didn't want any outside interference," he said.

Poindexter was adamant in insisting that Congress give the president "an opportunity to carry out his foreign policy that he has undertaken."

Although he gave no specific examples, Poindexter said he often felt that "the press did not present a clear and complete picture to the American public about many of the issues that we were faced with," including the war in Nicaragua.

Poindexter also lashed out at the intelligence agencies and the State and Defense departments, all of which, he said, opposed arms dealings with Iran or failed to propose alternatives. "I think it is characteristic of all bureaucracies that they aren't willing to take any risks," he said. "As these hearings demonstrate, the cost of failure is too high for them."

Reagan and the Contras

Poindexter staunchly defended North's activities on behalf of the contras, insisting that they were legal and—while secret—were consistent with Reagan's publicly stated policy. If the White House did anything wrong, he said, it was in failing to confront Congress directly on the constitutionality of its legal restrictions on aid to the contras. In hindsight, he said, it was a "clear mistake" not to have challenged the various versions of the Boland amendment, which limited U.S. aid to the contras.

In his concluding testimony, Poindexter amplified on the discussions he had with Reagan about U.S. support for the contras during the 1984-86 Boland amendment period, when direct aid was sharply curtailed. While saying he generally avoided giving the president specifics, Poindexter recalled telling Reagan about the existence of an airstrip in Costa Rica that was used by the private contra-aid network. He said he informed Reagan not because the strip was financed by the Iran arms sale money, but because it was an example of cooperation by a "friendly government."

Poindexter said he did not tell Reagan about other contra-aid operations that had sparked controversy in the hearings. Among them was the fact that the U.S. ambassador to Costa Rica, Lewis Tambs, was working with contra leaders based there to expand a "southern front" against Nicaragua's Sandinista government. Asked by Representative Foley whether, in withholding such information from Reagan, he was trying to avoid burdening the president with details or was trying to protect him politically, Poindexter said: "My intention was to exclude [from Reagan's briefings] what I considered extraneous detail."

Another "detail" about which Reagan was not told, he said, was the fact that North was working with the private network that delivered supplies by air to contra base camps in Nicaragua. Poindexter also said he could not recall telling Reagan that Secord was involved in aiding the contras.

Questions on Decision Making

Although he stood by administration actions in the Iran-contra affair, Poindexter provided new ammunition for those who argued that the Reagan administration built its policies on a series of decisions that were made in haste and were not reviewed carefully in light of subsequent events.

In challenging administration actions, members of the House and Senate panels focused on two key matters: the signing and subsequent destruction of a 1985 finding retroactively approving CIA involvement in Israeli arms deals with Iran, and Poindexter's approval of the plan to divert Iran arms sale proceeds to the contras. *(Testimony on finding, p. 128)*

As astonished as they were by Poindexter's handling of the finding, committee members reserved their sharpest criticism for his self-reported decision not to tell Reagan about the diversion. Poindexter said that when North told him in February 1986 about the possibility of using Iranian arms sales profits to aid the contras, he thought about the matter for only a few minutes before approving it.

In a typical challenge to that decision, Representative DeWine told Poindexter: "In essence, you took the key player, the best player, out of the game. The premier politician of this generation, Ronald Reagan, did not have the opportunity to have the essential facts to make what in essence was a political judgment."

Once the plan was put into operation, Poindexter testified that he asked few questions about such details as how much money was being raised or how it was being spent. He said he had "complete confidence" in North and Secord.

Asked repeatedly if he knew about or approved of Secord and Hakim making substantial profits on the arms sales, Poindexter said he had not thought about that issue prior to the hearings. He said he assumed that the private operatives were entitled to "reasonable compensation" but never inquired into details or thought about what level of compensation would be reasonable.

While defending his decision to approve the diversion without involving Reagan, Poindexter did acknowledge a mistake in not discussing the matter with CIA director Casey. Poindexter said he decided not to tell Casey about the diversion because he did not want the CIA director to have to be "evasive" in discussing contra finances with members of Congress. But, unbeknown to Poindexter, North revealed the diversion scheme to Casey, who appeared to have been his chief mentor and confidant.

Relying on Israel

Near the end of Poindexter's testimony, on July 21, two Senate panel members raised questions about Washington's reliance on Israel during the early stages of the dealings with Iran.

Responding to questions by Nunn and McClure, Poindexter said Israel was the primary source for much of the information on which Reagan based his decisions in late 1985 and early 1986 to initiate contacts with Iran. The United States began selling arms to Iran in response to repeated requests by the Israeli government, he said. Israel had "selfish" reasons for pursuing the contacts and arms sales with Iran, Poindexter said, but "it turned out that we thought that was also in our interests, as well."

Under questioning by Nunn, Poindexter also testified that White House officials in 1985-86 accepted Israel's assessment of the military status of the Iran-Iraq War and rejected the official U.S. assessment offered by the CIA and other intelligence agencies. The two assessments differed on which country was in danger of losing the war: Israel said it was Iran, while the U.S. intelligence agencies were concerned about Iraq's position.

Acceptance of the Israeli assessment obviously was a key to the U.S. decision to proceed with the Iran arms sales. By selling arms to the country declared to be the underdog, Washington could stick to its position that it was not upsetting the Iran-Iraq military balance.

But accepting the Israeli intelligence assessment, and then selling arms to Iran, undermined the stated U.S. policy of trying to persuade all countries not to arm Iran, Nunn noted. A primary reason for targeting Iran was that it was unwilling to negotiate an end to the war, which Iraq had started; Iraq for several years had stated its willingness to negotiate. Selling Iran "a small amount of defensive arms," Poindexter said, "was important to get them to listen to us, and listen to our reasoning."

Shultz Tells of Deceit

In a vivid portrayal of a White House torn by secrecy and deceit, Secretary of State Shultz told the Iran-contra committees of deliberate efforts to mislead President Reagan about his Iran arms sale program. Shultz's extraordinary July 23-24 testimony provided a backstage view— from the vantage point of a sitting cabinet member—of a White House caught up in a widening scandal, with senior officials using the president as a shield to protect themselves.

Shultz also lashed out at the persistent efforts by CIA officials and NSC staffers to run foreign policy throughout the Iran-contra affair. Hitting hard at a theme that had run through Congress's investigation, Shultz insisted on the need for a rigid wall between intelligence gathering and policy decisions. His two days of testimony, riveting attention to vicious infighting among senior Reagan officials, represented an obvious—and seemingly successful—attempt to capture the high ground in the Iran-contra hearings.

Shultz's comments about the dangerous nature of covert actions run by the NSC were reassuring to several panel members concerned about government accountability. And he separated himself from other witnesses—notably Poindexter—who had defended the Iran-contra operation while criticizing the State Department for its objections to the Iran arms sales.

Senate chairman Inouye reminded Shultz July 23 that both had "lived through the agony and the nightmare of Watergate" and that Americans once again are "faced with this breakdown" of government-public trust. Shultz replied, "Nobody has to think they need to lie and cheat in order to be a public servant or to work in foreign policy."

Normally taciturn, Shultz dramatically described a "battle royal" inside the White House when the Iran arms scandal erupted in November 1986. He singled out Poindexter and Casey for having a "conflict of interest" because of a desire to protect their own roles as the chief advocates of the Iran-contra operation. Poindexter and Casey gave President Reagan incorrect information about the Iran initiative in the fall of 1986 and they relied on the president's communication skills to "bail them out," Shultz said.

George P. Shultz

Shultz said Reagan's heart and mind had been captured by officials who misled him. "I was in a battle to try to get what I saw as the facts to the president and see that he understood them," Shultz testified July 23. Under questioning by Mark A. Belnick, a Senate counsel, Shultz retraced the events in late 1986 when the White House was rocked by disclosures of arms sales to Iran in exchange for release of the hostages in Lebanon.

A day after Reagan's November 19 press conference assuring the public that he did not trade weapons for hostages, Shultz said he told the president in a "long, tough" talk at the White House that Reagan had made "wrong and misleading" statements about the arms deals. These included comments about the scope of and original U.S. role in the weapons purchases. The next day, Reagan directed Attorney General Meese to conduct the inquiry into the Iran arms sales that led to the discovery that profits were being diverted to the contras.

Casey's Involvement

Previous witnesses had portrayed Casey as a leading architect of the program to sell weapons to Iran and divert funds to the contras.

Shultz confirmed one incident in mid-1986 in which Casey apparently blocked a CIA report that linked Iran to continued terrorism. Representative Fascell said Casey might have "suppressed" the report and ordered it rewritten because it presented an "obstacle" to Reagan's arms program. Shultz said he was unsure of Casey's role but had heard that some of the original intelligence was not included in the report.

According to Shultz, Casey continued trying to keep the Iran arms initiative alive even after the American public was told about it November 25. Shultz described how Casey went behind his back to maintain the CIA's role after Shultz had persuaded Reagan to hand the Iran issue over to the State Department.

Unknown to Shultz, U.S. officials met with Iranians in December 1986 in Frankfurt to consider a nine-point plan originally worked out by North. The points included continued sale of arms to Iran in exchange for U.S. hostages and a promise to help win the release of the Da'Wa prisoners, seventeen terrorists jailed in Kuwait. Shultz later learned of the nine-point plan because a State Department

official, Charles Dunbar, attended the Frankfurt meeting, ostensibly to make sure the Iranians understood that no more arms deals would be arranged. But the Iranians kept the conversation focused on the nine-point plan.

After hearing about the meeting, Shultz said he told Reagan on December 14 about the negotiating plan. Saying the reference to freeing the terrorists in Kuwait made him "sick to my stomach," Shultz described Reagan as being "astonished" to learn of the U.S. negotiating position. "I have never seen him so mad," said Shultz. "His jaw set, and his eyes flashed, and both of us, I think, felt the same way about it. And I think in that meeting, I finally felt that the president deeply understands that something is radically wrong here."

Poindexter had told the committees that he had gotten Reagan's approval in October 1986 for the nine-point plan. But Shultz said he doubted that Poindexter gave Reagan a detailed description of the plan because it included such a "gross violation" of U.S. policy. *(Poindexter testimony, p. 129)*

Secretary in the Dark

Shultz, Reagan's chief foreign policy manager, described an environment in which he was kept in the dark about the Iran initiative and secret White House aid to the contras. Shultz's appearance also served as an opportunity to vindicate his own position within the administration. When the scandal broke, the secretary was branded by some critics as disloyal to Reagan because of his efforts to distance himself from the arms-for-hostages deals. Days after the arms deals became known, Shultz pointedly said that he was not speaking for the administration on the Iran arms deals.

Shultz testified that he had learned only on November 10 that Reagan had signed a secret intelligence finding the previous January 17 that authorized the direct sale of arms. Similarly, Shultz said Poindexter never told him about two earlier secret Iran arms-sales findings signed by Reagan in December 1985 and on January 6, 1986. But Senator Mitchell noted that Reagan, too, never told Shultz about the findings. "With all due respect, it wasn't just Adm. Poindexter who was keeping you in the dark, was it?" he asked. "I have a relationship with the president such that I don't think he is out to deceive me," replied Shultz, adding that Reagan probably assumed he knew about the findings.

For the most part, Shultz's testimony was warmly received by committee members, particularly because of his sharp denunciation of the Iran-contra operation. But some members raised doubts about his performance in the affair. The strongest criticism came from Representative DeWine, who accused Shultz July 24 of deliberately remaining uninformed about the details of the Iran arms program. "In my opinion, you purposely cut yourself out from the facts," said DeWine. "You permitted Adm. Poindexter to get between you and the president." DeWine's comments prompted a tart response from Shultz. "I'll just say that's one man's opinion, and I don't share it," he said.

Shultz rejected suggestions that he was not aggressive enough in battling the arms sales, saying that he argued "forcefully, fully" in front of Reagan. "I don't think there were any more arguments I could have thought up."

Representative Hyde told Shultz July 24 that he could have stopped the Iran arms initiative "dead in its tracks" if he had threatened to resign over it. But Shultz said he doubted that would have succeeded in changing Reagan's mind. "You can say I'll give up and leave, or I'll stay and fight," said Shultz, who acknowledged that Casey in November 1986 sent Reagan a note suggesting that the secretary of state be replaced.

Shultz vigorously defended his own role once the Iran deal was revealed. "Frankly, I felt I was the one loyal to the president, because I was the one who was trying to get him the facts so he could make a decision," he said.

Senator Rudman called Shultz a "hero," a term that had been used frequently to describe other participants in the affair, particularly North. But Rudman made it clear that Shultz's actions differed from others who had been given the laurels.

'A Piece of Junk'

Senator Sarbanes asked Shultz what he thought about a plan, endorsed by Poindexter, to use the proceeds from the Iran arms sales for a series of covert operations. "This is a piece of junk and it ought to be treated that way," Shultz said angrily.

On another key question, Shultz said he was not told that, beginning in 1984, Saudi Arabia and later Taiwan contributed millions of dollars to the contras at the behest of U.S. officials. Shultz said he originally argued against the soliciting of third-country support for the contras, doubting its legality and charging that it would jeopardize the chances of getting Congress to approve military aid. Shultz later approved a successful bid in 1986 to solicit $10 million for the contras from Brunei, an oil-rich Pacific nation. The secretary said he authorized that effort because Congress had specifically permitted the State Department to seek "humanitarian" contra aid from other countries. But Shultz said he did not know that the Lake Resources bank account in Geneva that was to receive Brunei's contribution was controlled by North, Secord, and Hakim. Instead, he said he thought the money would go directly into a bank account controlled by the contras.

The money never got to the contras because North inadvertently passed along an incorrect account number to Assistant Secretary of State Abrams. Abrams earlier testified that he had misled congressional committees by not telling them in 1986 what he knew about third-country contributions, including the Brunei gift. Asked about those statements, Shultz said Abrams was "full of remorse" for making a mistake. But Shultz gave Abrams a vote of confidence despite calls by dozens of members of Congress for his resignation. *(Abrams testimony, p. 107)*

Opposition to Arms Sales

As expected, Shultz's testimony focused on his opposition to the Iran arms sales. He said he had consistently rejected the use of arms as a means to free hostages and as a tool to improve relations with Iran. Despite his persistent objections to the idea, the arms sales proceeded without his knowledge, he testified. Shultz said he had known about the proposals to sell arms to Iran ever since Israeli officials first pressed the administration to undertake such an initiative beginning in mid-1985.

Shultz restated his opposition to the Israeli proposal to sell arms to Iran at an August 6, 1985, White House meeting attended by Reagan and McFarlane. According to McFarlane's testimony in May, Reagan approved the Israeli initiative sometime after the meeting, paving the way for Israel to ship 500 TOW antitank missiles to Iran in September. In exchange, the Rev. Benjamin F. Weir was released from captivity in Lebanon. But Shultz said he did not learn about the TOW shipment until the following December and was never told that Weir's release was linked to the weapons.

In November 1985, Shultz received hints of another arms transaction from McFarlane while attending the U.S.-Soviet summit in Geneva. According to Shultz, McFarlane telephoned him in Geneva and told him of what Shultz described to the panels as a "straight-out arms-for-hostages deal." Shultz said he told McFarlane he opposed the trade, but that it was too late to do anything about it.

Later, Shultz was told that the transaction did not take place, leading him to assume that Reagan had not abandoned his opposition to trading weapons for hostages. In fact, eighteen Hawk missiles had been sent to Iran, but no hostages were released. The missiles were rejected by Iran as obsolete and seventeen were subsequently returned to Israel.

In the wake of the November shipment, Poindexter never told Shultz that Reagan had signed an intelligence finding on December 5 that retroactively approved the CIA's role in the Hawk shipment. Poindexter testified that he destroyed the finding in November 1986 so that Reagan could deny his involvement.

The events in November 1985 later provided the basis for an incorrect version of the Iran arms deals told by Poindexter at a key November 10, 1986, White House meeting. At that meeting, attended by Reagan and several senior officials, Poindexter recounted what Shultz described in his testimony as a "cock and bull" story about the origin of the arms sales. According to Shultz, Poindexter described how North had first discovered that the Israelis had been shipping arms to Iran from a warehouse in Portugal, the same one from which North had been arranging secret weapons deliveries to the contras. That meeting did not address the White House's secret plan to aid the contras. Shultz was suspicious about Poindexter's story because he knew that the Israelis had first proposed a U.S. role in the Iranian arms sales much earlier in 1985.

Throughout the Iran initiative, Shultz said he and others at the State Department occasionally suspected that arms were being sold, but that he always received assurances that nothing of the sort was taking place. On January 17, 1986, for example, Shultz argued at a White House meeting on the subject that selling weapons would be "illegal and unwise." He said he did not learn until ten months later—at the November 10 meeting—that Reagan on that very same day had signed the finding that gave the legal authority to proceed with the sales.

On February 28, 1986, Poindexter briefed Shultz about a planned trip by McFarlane to establish contact with Iranian officials. A paper outlining the discussion points for the meeting raised the possibility of arms sales, but not until after the Iran-Iraq War ended and Iran renounced terrorism. Shultz said he interpreted the paper's proviso as a "reassurance" that Reagan had decided against going ahead with arms sales. What Poindexter did not tell Shultz, according to the secretary, was that the United States had shipped 500 TOWs to Iran the day before, along with 500 TOWs ten days earlier.

Hints in Tokyo

At the Tokyo economic summit in May 1986, Shultz learned that the U.S. Embassy in London had gotten wind of a possible arms deal. Shultz confronted Chief of Staff Regan and Poindexter, both of whom assured Shultz that nothing of the sort was planned. "We are not dealing with these people. This is not our deal," Shultz said Poindexter told him in Japan. The next day, according to White House documents, Poindexter sent a secret computer message to North, who was leaving for London to work on an arms deal. "Do not let anybody know you are in London or that you are going there. Do not have any contact with embassy," Poindexter advised.

Shultz said he did not learn about McFarlane's May 1986 mission to Tehran until after it took place. He said Poindexter, as well as Casey, told him that the trip had "fizzled" and that the Iran operation had been ordered to "stand down," which led him to believe that the program had been canceled.

A few weeks later, on July 2, Shultz received a memo from Under Secretary of State Armacost telling him to be aware of renewed hints about an arms-for-hostages deal. Armacost said the idea had some "merit to a point" but that it would create "confusion among our friends who will recall our frequent lectures on no deals for hostages and no arms for Iran."

Shultz during this period was the leading advocate of "Operation Staunch," Reagan's high-profile campaign to stop other countries from arming Iran, hoping a cutoff would help end the Iran-Iraq War.

Shultz said he did not recall asking questions in response to Armacost's memo, because he assumed from earlier talks with Reagan aides that no U.S. arms were going to Iran.

By early November, Shultz said it quickly became clear that a deliberate effort was under way to distort what the United States had done. Shultz, among other Reagan officials, was given a "press guidance" statement that said the U.S. arms embargo against Iran remained in effect, but only as long as Iran continued to advocate the use of terrorism. Shultz said the carefully crafted language "set my alarm bells ringing hard" because he realized that Reagan officials could justify the sales on grounds that Iran had abandoned terrorism. He said the press statement was "tricky and misleading." The secretary said he began to believe that others around Reagan were not telling him the truth about the arms shipments. "The only trouble is, as you look at the particular things that happened, when you get down into the dirt of the operational details, it always comes out arms for hostages," testified Shultz.

WEEK ELEVEN: MEESE, REGAN

In the final stages of their hearings, the committees heard from three high-level Reagan administration officials who corroborated much of the previous testimony given by Secretary of State Shultz. At the same time, the three— Attorney General Meese, former chief of staff Regan, and Defense Secretary Weinberger—testified that the administration was torn between disclosure and concealment of the basic facts about the Iran arms sale as details of the policy were unraveling in November 1986. Weinberger concluded

his testimony during the committees' twelfth week of public hearings. *(See p. 139)*

The three, as well as Shultz, said they favored making details of the arms sales public to avoid charges of a cover-up. But they also testified—and notes taken at meetings in mid-November verified—that the president and some of his aides, primarily Poindexter and Casey, initially feared that disclosure would endanger the lives of U.S. hostages and the Iranians with whom Washington was dealing.

As Shultz had, Meese, Regan, and Weinberger pointed to Poindexter as the official most insistent on withholding public information about the arms sale. The NSC aide, they said, argued that the president should say nothing about the Iran deals in hopes of keeping the initiative going and possibly winning the release of more hostages. *(Meese testimony text, p. C-120; Regan, p. C-126; Weinberger, p. C-130)*

Meese Testimony

The attorney general took the witness stand for two days on July 28-29, providing his account of investigations leading to the diversion of Iran arms sale proceeds to the contras. At the president's request, Meese had conducted an inquiry November 21-24, 1986, into the Iran arms sale, which unexpectedly uncovered (through a memo that North admitted he had "neglected" to shred) evidence that some of the profits were intended to support the Nicaraguan contras (an act widely interpreted as prohibited by Congress). Although sharply criticized for its lack of thoroughness, the informal investigation produced evidence of the diversion. *(Box, p. 136)*

The principal questions directed at Meese by the committees concerned the adequacy of his investigation, which the attorney general defended as successful. On the other hand, he acknowledged that during the initial fact-finding inquiry, he did not ask many pertinent questions of key officials, did not secure critical White House documents, and did not take notes on private meetings with those principally involved, including the late CIA director Casey, mentioned by some (including North) as playing a major role in the decision making. They also faulted his decision not to call on lawyers from the Criminal Division of the Justice Department, although, initially, there was no evidence of criminal activity.

Meese appeared after Assistant Attorney General Cooper had testified in June that the inquiry had been bungled. Republican senator Rudman had charged that Meese and his aides lacked the investigative instincts of a local police officer. And Democratic senator Mitchell, a former federal judge, termed the inquiry "inept, unprofessional." Some members privately expressed the conviction that the Meese probe had been launched more to plug leaks of embarrassing information than to disclose it.

With Meese sitting before them in the witness chair, those members who had been most critical softened their language but still asked questions demonstrating their skepticism. Most Republicans on the two committees defended Meese—at least against the unstated charge that he had participated in a cover-up. Throughout his two-day appearance, the attorney general staunchly defended his inquiry, saying it was a "fact-finding overview," not a criminal investigation, and that it produced the "essential facts" on which all subsequent probes rested.

Criticisms, Responses

Although members of the select committees sharply questioned specific aspects of Meese's weekend inquiry, many of them—including several former prosecutors—seemed most interested in the investigative techniques Meese and his aides used. Meese conducted formal interviews with only four persons: North, McFarlane, Shultz, and Sporkin. Aides took notes at each of those sessions, and the notes provided key evidence in all subsequent investigations. Meese had private one-on-one sessions with three other officials: Poindexter, Casey, and Bush. Those were brief "casual conversations," not interviews, he testified, so there was no need for him to take notes.

Several committee members expressed amazement at that contention, among them Senate committee chairman Inouye, who said he had been taught as a "junior prosecutor" always to take notes when gathering facts. "These were the important interviews, after you began to get suspicious that something was wrong," Inouye reminded the attorney general.

But Meese stood fast, saying: "I have a very good recollection" of those interviews even without notes.

Under repeated questioning, Meese acknowledged that in his one-on-one sessions he did not ask point-blank questions about the most important issues covered by his inquiry, especially the diversion.

Responding to Senator Nunn on July 29, for example, Meese said he did not directly ask Poindexter any of the following questions: who approved the diversion; whether Poindexter had told Reagan about the diversion or why he had not told the president; whether Poindexter thought he had authority on his own to al-

Edwin Meese III

low the diversion; and whether Poindexter had discussed the issue with Casey. Meese said some of those questions were unnecessary because Poindexter had told him that no one else in the White House knew about the diversion. Other questions simply did not occur to him, Meese said. Meese also said that he never asked Reagan if he had known about or approved the diversion, and that he did not ask North for details of the diversion scheme.

The issue of whether Meese should have called on the Justice Department's criminal division earlier in his inquiry dogged him throughout his testimony. Several Democrats hammered at it, drawing ammunition from Assistant Attorney General William Weld's July 16 deposition, in which he said he had wanted to be involved as early as November 21.

Meese compounded the questions, making conflicting statements about when he realized that criminal activity might have been involved. In the early stages of his testimony, he said he had "no hint" of wrongdoing even after his interview with North on November 23.

"I must say that it's always easy some eight months later to look back, and it certainly looks a lot different to us now than it did then, but at that time there was nothing that did give us that hint [of wrongdoing]," he told House committee counsel Nields on July 28. However, Meese later

testified that North's interview did raise the prospect of "criminal implications."

Meese also gave two dates for when he decided on the need for a criminal investigation: November 24 and November 25. In his deposition, Weld gave yet another account, saying he talked with Meese on November 25 and had the "impression" that Meese had put such an investigation on hold. Meese did not authorize one until the next day, Weld said.

On a related issue, Meese rejected repeated assertions that he and his aides should have moved more quickly during the inquiry to protect documents at NSC offices and that the failure to do so enabled North to destroy large quantities of official papers. Mitchell and Rudman had been particularly critical on that score.

Meese's Legal Advice

While emphasizing that he was not rendering formal advisories, Meese gave the panels opinions about several legal issues related to the Iran-contra affair. Among them were that:

● A "strong case" could be made that the Boland amendment, which barred military aid to the contras by U.S. intelligence agencies in fiscal years 1985-86, did not apply technically to the NSC staff. Meese said the NSC staff was not an intelligence agency, even though a Reagan executive order issued in 1981 defined the NSC as the top coordinator of actions by those agencies. But in a lengthy debate on July 29 with committee Democrats—including Representative Boland—Meese acknowledged that arguments could be made on both sides of the question about applicability to the NSC staff. In response to Senator Rudman, Meese also said the administration should not seek to evade such laws by use of technicalities. (The issue was important because North and Poindexter had argued that North's activities on behalf of the contras were legal because he was exempt from the Boland restrictions.) Meese said the Justice Department was never asked for a ruling on the matter.

● The president had a legal and constitutional right to delay notice to Congress of operations. Meese said he approved of the decision in January 1986 to delay notice to Congress of the Iran dealings, based on the fear that any leaks could endanger the hostages and the Iranians with whom the United States was dealing. But he said he agreed to the delay on the understanding that it was to be a "short-term" proposition of about thirty to sixty days. Instead, Congress was not told for more than ten months. As a general rule, Meese said Congress should be told in advance about covert operations, but in emergencies notice could be delayed for about forty-eight hours. (President Reagan subsequently informed Congress that he would implement the timely notice arrangement.)

Regan Testimony

Equipped with a quick and sometimes acerbic wit that injected humor into his testimony, Regan seemed to endear himself to many members of the Iran-contra committees July 30-31.

Like Shultz before him, Regan came across as a witness with nothing to hide and no hesitancy to cast aspersions on the activities of others who played pivotal Iran-

Attorney General's Iran-Contra Inquiry ...

Several weeks after the U.S. sale of arms to Iran was made public in November 1986, President Ronald Reagan instructed Attorney General Edwin Meese III to conduct an inquiry into the affair. Meese did so between November 21 and 24, but events on November 20 and November 25 also were essential. The Justice Department investigation uncovered evidence that funds from the Iran arms sales had been diverted to aid the contras in their battle against the Sandinista government in Nicaragua. Following is a review of the Meese inquiry, based on testimony before the House-Senate Iran-contra committees.

Thursday, November 20

On this day, it became clear to top administration officials—including Reagan—that there were major discrepancies and gaps in the accounts of what had happened early in the Iran initiative.

A key meeting was held in the afternoon. Those present included national security adviser Adm. John M. Poindexter, National Security Council (NSC) aide Lt. Col. Oliver L. North, CIA director William J. Casey, Meese, Assistant Attorney General Charles J. Cooper, NSC legal adviser Cmdr. Paul Thompson, and possibly others.

The meeting was called to review statements that Casey and Poindexter were to give the next day to the House and Senate Intelligence committees. One important issue was who in the U.S. government had known in November 1985 that Israel was shipping Hawk missiles to Iran.

North proposed an insert to Casey's testimony stating that no U.S. government officials knew until January 1986 that Hawks were in the shipment. Although that statement was untrue—because Reagan and his principal aides knew about the Hawks at the time—no one at the meeting objected to the insert. As approved at the meeting, the statement stuck to the cover story that U.S. officials thought the shipment contained oil-drilling parts, not weapons. Meese said he had no information on which to judge the accuracy of the insert.

North testified that he and Casey later met privately and "fixed" the testimony by deleting all references to the Hawks.

Later on November 20, State Department legal counsel Abraham D. Sofaer objected to Cooper about Casey's proposed testimony, saying that Secretary of State George P. Shultz had been aware of the Hawks shipment. Sofaer threatened to resign if the testimony was not corrected.

That night, Cooper called Meese, who was out of town, and urged him to return to help resolve the conflicts. Also that evening, Shultz visited Reagan at the White House and told him about the conflicting stories.

Friday, November 21

Meese arrived back in Washington and learned from Cooper that Casey's testimony to the Intelligence panels that morning had been altered. Meese then met with Reagan and suggested that someone should try to develop a "coherent overview of all the facts." Reagan agreed, assigning Meese to do it himself. White House chief of staff Donald T. Regan, who was present, suggested that Meese report back in time for a high-level meeting on Iran scheduled for November 24. Poindexter also was present at the meeting and, according to Meese, agreed with the need for a review of the facts.

Although the inquiry was to cover the entire Iran initiative, Meese said he decided to focus on the U.S. role in the 1985 Israeli shipments.

Meese then returned to the Justice Department and assembled a three-man team to help in the inquiry: Cooper; John N. Richardson, Jr., a key deputy; and William Bradford Reynolds, the assistant attorney general in charge of the Civil Rights Division. Meese and his three aides compiled a list of tasks and persons to be interviewed. Two persons not included on the list were Poindexter and Casey.

That afternoon, Meese called Poindexter and asked him to assemble all "relevant" documents about the Iran dealings so they could be reviewed the next morning by the team from Justice. At some point, Poindexter told North about the impending inquiry. Thereafter, North and his secretary altered and shredded relevant documents.

Meese and Cooper, meanwhile, conducted a two-hour interview with former national security adviser Robert C. McFarlane, who said he could not recollect the November 1985 shipment of Hawks. Although Cooper and Meese knew at that point that Shultz remembered talking to McFarlane in November 1985 about the Hawks, they did not ask McFarlane about the transaction.

Saturday, November 22

Meese and Cooper conducted an interview with Shultz, in his State Department office, during which Shultz raised the issue of the Hawk shipment, using notes by an aide to back up his contention that he had discussed the arms deal with McFarlane. Shultz also told Meese that Reagan recalled being aware of the Hawk shipment.

Later, Justice Department officials went to North's office to review documents. Among other things, they found an undated memo containing a

... Reveals Diversion, Raises Questions

one-paragraph mention of the diversion of Iran arms sale money to the contras.

Meese, meanwhile, interviewed former CIA general counsel Stanley Sporkin about his involvement in drafting the findings that authorized the Iran deals. Sporkin said CIA operatives had told him in November 1985 that Israel had shipped Hawks to Iran.

Later that afternoon, Meese was informed about the diversion memo. He then talked by telephone with North and scheduled an interview for the following afternoon.

Early that evening, Casey, who had asked Meese to stop by, told him that a friend, New York businessman Roy M. Furmark, had approached Casey in October with a story about how two Canadian businessmen were threatening to disclose the U.S.-Iranian arms deals because they had not been repaid $10 million they had lent to finance the deals. Casey said the Canadians were threatening to say that some of the Iran money had been used for "U.S. and Israeli projects," Meese testified.

In spite of Casey's disclosure, Meese said he did not ask Casey whether he knew about the Iran-contra diversion because "I felt that it was not appropriate to discuss this with anyone, even as good a friend as Mr. Casey, until after I found out what it was all about." Meese said he took no notes of his conversation with Casey.

Sunday, November 23

North went to Meese's office at the Justice Department for an interview that stretched over nearly four hours. Meese devoted the early part of the interview to the Iran arms deals but then showed North the diversion memo and asked if he had prepared it. Meese testified that North was "shocked" to see the reference to the diversion.

According to Meese's testimony, North said that Poindexter and McFarlane also knew about the diversion scheme, but he did not know whether Reagan was aware of it. But North misled Meese about several important aspects of the Iran deals. And North later apparently spent much of the night shredding documents at his office.

Monday, November 24

At Meese's request, McFarlane returned to the Justice Department in the morning for a follow-up interview. McFarlane said North had told him about the diversion the previous May.

Thereafter, Meese met with Reagan and Regan at the White House and told them what he had learned about the diversion scheme. Regan testified that his reaction was "horror" and Reagan's was "deep distress."

After lunch, Meese met with Vice President George Bush, who said he knew nothing about the diversion.

Regan, Poindexter, Shultz, Meese, and others then met for a review of the Iran situation but apparently did not discuss Meese's ongoing inquiry. According to Meese's notes, the officials discussed the 1985 Israeli shipments to Iran, and Poindexter said there was "no documentation" of them. Poindexter did not mention that he had destroyed a December 1985 "finding" giving Reagan's retroactive approval of the shipments.

After that meeting, Meese met with Poindexter for about ten minutes and told him about the diversion memo. Meese said Poindexter admitted knowing about the diversion but had not tried to stop it. Meese asked if anyone else in the White House knew about the diversion and was told "no." Meese said he asked no other questions and took no notes.

Reagan, Regan, and Meese then resumed their meeting that had been interrupted in the morning. Meese said he provided more details about his findings, including his conversation with Poindexter. Regan suggested that Poindexter should resign, but Reagan said he wanted to think about that matter overnight.

Tuesday, November 25

Meese testified that he was about to leave for work when Casey called and asked him to stop by his home, which was nearby. Casey told Meese that he had heard about the diversion issue from Regan and was surprised, Meese testified. But Meese said he did not ask Casey "point-blank" whether he had known anything about the diversion prior to Regan's revelation. Meese testified that he believed Casey did not know about the diversion—in spite of North's testimony that he and Casey discussed the issue several times.

While Meese was at Casey's home, Regan called and told Meese that he would be asking for Poindexter's resignation that morning. The president announced the resignation and North's firing at noon, and Meese revealed the diversion scheme and answered questions about it.

Meese met with the FBI director and other officials at the Justice Department that afternoon and reviewed steps for further investigation. The attorney general said he ordered the sealing of North's office, but that order was not passed to NSC security officers until late in the day. The Justice Department did not send formal letters to the White House on the sealing of offices and documents until November 28.

contra roles. Some of his barbs were directed at Poindexter and North, both of whom had admitted to getting rid of documents in an effort to hide Iran-contra activities. "It didn't occur to me that men of that caliber would be destroying documents," said Regan.

To Disclose or Not

As had Meese, Regan pointed to Poindexter as the official most insistent on containing the flow of information after the November 4, 1986, news report on the Iran arms sale. Regan said the president at first sided with Poindexter. Reagan was especially impressed by the arguments of hostage David P. Jacobsen, who visited the White House after his release in early November—a release prompted by the final Iran arms sale. Jacobsen pleaded with reporters not to pursue the arms-for-hostages story because doing so would jeopardize the safety of the remaining hostages. The president's initial decision was made despite the views of Shultz.

Donald T. Regan

According to notes made public by the committee, a crucial ninety-five-minute meeting with the president on November 10, 1986, at which the vice president and leading cabinet officials were present, made clear the dispute between administration officials. The notes from the meeting were kept by Shultz and deputy national security adviser Alton G. Keel, Jr. Poindexter led opposition to any kind of statement, saying the "news has peaked" and that no congressional hearings would be held until January, presumably because Congress had already adjourned for the year.

Regan quoted Reagan as saying: "We must say something but not much." Later in the meeting, according to the notes, Reagan expanded on that thought, saying: "We must say something because I'm being held out to dry." Keel quoted the president as telling his aides: "Don't talk specifics," such as the fact that the United States sold TOW antitank missiles to Iran. Meese, who was present, had testified that Reagan's position at the meeting was that "we should be very careful in statements to the press for a variety of reasons," primarily the concern for the safety of the hostages.

Two days later, on November 12, Reagan decided to make a public statement on the Iranian deals. In one meeting, Reagan and his aides apparently discussed an approach of denying false press reports while revealing as little true information as possible.

According to Keel's notes, for example, Reagan said: "Whenever we can, point to flat denial," citing as an example reports then circulating that former national security adviser McFarlane had visited Tehran the previous September. McFarlane did travel to Tehran—in May.

In his nationally televised address on November 13, Reagan emphasized several reports about secret U.S.-Iranian arms deals involving Danish ships and ports in Italy and Spain. "All these reports are quite exciting, but as far as we are concerned not one of them is true," he said.

Reagan gave no details about the deals that were made, except to deny that they were arms-for-hostages swaps.

Responding on July 27 to press reports about the November 10, 1986, meeting, White House spokesman Fitzwater said Reagan was concerned about the hostages but was not engaged in a cover-up.

Regan blamed Poindexter in particular for supplying faulty information that led the president to make several factual errors in his November 19, 1986, press conference on the issue. Reagan said, for example, that no other countries had been involved in sending arms to Iran, a remark—shortly retracted—that ignored Israel's role in the affair.

Regan noted that Poindexter had played a key role in rehearsing Reagan for the news conference. Apparently not wanting to disclose details to other White House aides who were present at the rehearsal, Poindexter made only "oblique" suggestions to the president for answers to anticipated questions. That "sort of confused the presidential mind," Regan said.

Regan confirmed reports that White House officials in December 1986 discussed protecting Poindexter and North from prosecution as a way of getting them to tell their stories. But he said Reagan quickly rejected any idea of a pardon because that would imply that a crime had been committed. "I'll be darned if I'm going to accuse them of a crime in advance," Regan quoted Reagan as saying.

Initial Opposition

Regan said he began to argue against continuing the Iran arms initiative after problems arose with the November 1985 shipment. He, Shultz, and Weinberger voiced objections at a key White House meeting on December 7. "It's an old Wall Street expression that I used—cut your losses," Regan testified.

After the president signed the January 17, 1986, finding that approved direct weapons sales to Iran, Regan said his concerns diminished because of the new procedures for sales directly to Iran, rather than through Israel, and because of Poindexter's assurances that the United States could win new contacts among the Iranians. However, Regan said that his views soured again in February when no hostages were released in Lebanon despite the shipment of 1,000 TOW missiles to Iran. He said he told Reagan that the United States had been "snookered again" and that the program should be ended. "How many times, you know, do we put up with this rug merchant kind of stuff," Regan said he told the president.

When Terry A. Smiljanich, a Senate committee lawyer, asked why the arms sales continued throughout 1986, Regan said the United States had become the victim of a "bait-and-switch" operation. But under later questioning by Senator Cohen, Regan also said the "bait" of the hostages helped to keep the arms program going. The president, he said, wanted to pursue a better relationship with Iran but also was strongly motivated by a desire to free the hostages. "The bait was still there," he said. "That was the bait to get arms."

White House in 'Chaos'?

During his testimony, Regan seemed eager to dispel a negative image in the February 1987 report by the Tower Commission, which said Regan bore "primary responsibility" as chief of staff for the "chaos" inside the White House. The day after the commission issued its report,

Reagan replaced Regan as chief of staff with Howard H. Baker, Jr. Obviously seeking to rebut the Tower report, Regan said he battled with other Reagan officials, notably Poindexter, to get to the bottom of the Iran-contra affair. *(Tower Commission, p. 71)*

"I'm not sure what could have been done about the chaos," he said. "I did try, in all honesty, to get this word out as quickly as I could—to make it public, to let the Congress know, to let the American public know."

Senator Heflin asked Regan if he had ended up as the "principal fall guy" in the Iran-contra affair. Pointedly referring to the widespread calls for his resignation at the time of the revelations, Regan replied: "I don't mind spears in the breast. It's knives in the back that concern me."

Regan's testimony brought the name of Nancy Reagan into the hearings for the first time. That happened on July 30, when Representative Courter asked about Regan getting a phone call from the first lady while he was driving to see Casey at the CIA on November 24, 1986. In her call, which Regan returned after his meeting with Casey, Nancy Reagan told him she thought there needed to be a "house cleaning" at the White House to get rid of aides who had "let Ronnie down" in the Iran-contra affair.

Regan and Nancy Reagan often did not agree, and she was considered a leading advocate of Regan stepping down as chief of staff after the Tower board issued its report. Regan said he had "the impression that mine was one of the heads that would have to roll."

Not in the Know

Despite his reputation for knowing every detail inside the White House, Regan testified he was not informed of several critical Iran-contra events during his two years as chief of staff. He said he was "aware in general" about the Iran initiative but was not kept abreast of important details. For example, he said he knew of the secret finding in January 1986 authorizing direct arms sales to Iran, but he did not learn until October that the president actually had signed it. Similarly, Regan said he never knew that Reagan had signed an earlier finding in December 1985 that provided retroactive approval for the CIA's assistance in shipping Hawk missiles from Israel to Iran. Poindexter testified that he gave the paper to the president, who signed it without question. Poindexter destroyed the document in November 1986. *(Poindexter testimony, p. 128)*

Most significantly, Regan said he never knew about the plan to divert profits from the Iran arms sales to the contras until Justice Department officials uncovered it in November 1986. No one ever told him, he said, that the Iran arms sales involved huge price markups to generate profits for the contras. Instead, he said he had assumed the weapons sales amounted to an "NPH deal," a Wall Street expression for "no profit here." Regan, however, told the committees that both he and the president knew at the time that the United States was sending Hawks to Iran, contrary to the attempt in 1986 to explain that oil-drilling parts had been sent instead. Regan said the oil-drilling account was part of a "cover story" concocted at the time of the Hawks shipment to conceal the fact that weapons had been sent, possibly illegally, to Iran.

In one revealing comment, Regan indicated that he, for one, realized in November 1986 that Meese's inquiry would not be enough to convince the public that the administration was forthcoming with the facts. Regan said he recommended creation of a review board—ultimately chaired by

Tower—because "nobody would believe it, if just Ed Meese looked into it."

WEEK TWELVE: WEINBERGER, CIA

After nearly twelve weeks of hearings by the House and Senate select committees investigating the Iran-contra affair, members wound up the public sessions by agreeing that there was no "smoking gun" evidence that President Reagan personally was involved in wrongdoing, such as engaging in a cover-up or approving the diversion of Iran arms sales money to the contras.

The final week of hearings included August 3 testimony by Defense Secretary Weinberger, who had appeared previously on July 31, and closed testimony by three CIA officials: Duane "Dewey" Clarridge, CIA counterterrorism chief (August 4); Alan Fiers, CIA Central America task force chief (August 4-5); and Clair George, CIA head of covert operations (August 5-6). The CIA officials' testimony was released later in August, as was that by two NSC aides. Testimony by aides to Vice President Bush and by NSC consultant Michael Ledeen was released in September. *(Fiers testimony text, p. C-139; George, p. C-141)*

Much of the last day of the public hearings was devoted to closing statements by committee leaders of both parties, who stressed the dangers of bypassing standard procedures, allowing unelected aides to have too much power, and putting public policy in the hands of private agents. Acknowledging that Congress shared a measure of blame, the leaders said the hearings demonstrated anew the importance of cooperation between the legislative and executive branches. *(Text of closing statements, p. C-134)*

Weinberger Testimony

On the opening day of his appearance, Weinberger corroborated Secretary of State Shultz's previous testimony that both had opposed the U.S.-Iran arms deals at crucial stages early in the process. Weinberger, in fact, said he argued in mid-1985 that going through with the Iran initiative would be like "asking [Libyan leader Muammar el-] Qaddafi to Washington for a cozy chat." He said he opposed the "whole policy," not just the arms sales, because it was based on the hope of establishing relations with Iranian moderates. "I didn't think there were any moderates still alive in Iran," he said.

Weinberger said that White House officials, apparently in the NSC, cut him off from intelligence reports prepared by his own agency in the fall of 1985 that dealt with aspects of the Iran arms sales. The defense secretary said he and Shultz also opposed the arms sales during key discussions in December 1985 and January 1986.

The Final Day

As the committees' concluding public witness, Weinberger spent more time August 3 listening to members' closing remarks than he did fielding questions from them. The reason was the panels' decision that only the four top committee members—Inouye, Rudman, Hamilton, and Cheney—would give closing statements. As a result, several other members used their ten-minute questioning time during Weinberger's appearance to give their own summaries of the hearings.

Weinberger also heard some of the committee members offer a defense against criticism leveled at him and Shultz in the Tower Commission report, which faulted the two for having "distanced themselves" from the Iran arms initiative instead of strenuously trying to move the White House away from the policy. *(Tower report, p. 71)*

Caspar W. Weinberger

Rudman disputed that conclusion, saying the commission did not receive as full an accounting of the Iran-contra affair as had the congressional committees. Both Weinberger and Shultz testified at the hearings that they vigorously opposed the idea of selling arms to Iran, but that Reagan decided to proceed despite their objections. "We did oppose it. We opposed it every step of the way," said Weinberger. He added that the Tower board's conclusion about himself and Shultz "can only be drawn by people who don't have any knowledge of the facts."

Weinberger also was questioned closely about intelligence reports coming into Washington during the Iran-contra affair about the status of the Iran-Iraq War. The intelligence issue played a prominent role in the hearings because Reagan apparently relied on information that Iran was losing the war as a justification for sending "defensive" weapons to that country.

According to notes taken by former White House chief of staff Regan at a key meeting November 10, 1986, Reagan said he had decided to send arms to Iran because that country was "weaker" in the war against Iraq. "Side with military superiority will win. We want to have things even," Regan's notes described the president as saying.

Both Shultz and Weinberger, however, testified that the intelligence reports they received at the time showed Iraq losing the war. Weinberger dismissed contrary intelligence claims August 3 as "absolute nonsense."

The defense secretary added that he did not remember Reagan mentioning Iraq's supposed advantage at the November 10 meeting. But he also said "minority intelligence views" might have been used by Poindexter and others to promote their proposal to sell weapons to Iran.

CIA, NSC Officials

After Weinberger's testimony, the committees closed their doors to receive testimony from three key CIA officials: Clarridge, Fiers, and George. All three provided further details on CIA involvement in the Iran-contra affair, North's role in it, and CIA misgivings about many aspects of the policy, as well as those who were conducting it. The committees released heavily censored transcripts of the hearings later in August, as well as testimony given earlier in closed sessions by NSC aides Lt. Col. Robert L. Earl (May 2, 15, 22, and 30) and Craig Coy (March 17 and June 1).

Clarridge: Casey's Role, Hawk Sale

Clarridge's testimony reinforced previous statements that CIA director Casey had played a hands-on role in many aspects of the Iran-contra affair. According to Clarridge, Casey wanted the agency to run the entire Iranian arms-for-hostages operation instead of turning it over to North and Poindexter at the NSC. Clarridge said no other senior CIA officials agreed with Casey because they mistrusted Manucher Ghorbanifar, the Iranian arms merchant who was serving as a middleman between U.S. and Iranian officials. "I cannot say that they didn't want to be involved at all," said Clarridge, referring to other CIA officials. "What I am saying is they did not want to run the operation, the Ghorbanifar piece of the operation."

In other parts of his testimony, Clarridge denied knowing that Hawk antiaircraft missiles were being shipped from Israel to Iran in November 1985, despite his active participation in the U.S.-assisted effort. Clarridge was the CIA's chief of the European division at the time of the Hawk shipment. On November 21, 1985, North asked him to sort out a problem that arose when Portugal refused to give landing clearances to an airplane carrying the missiles from Israel.

Clarridge, in turn, sent a cable to the CIA station chief in Lisbon, instructing him to "pull out all stops" in getting permission for the flight to land. But Clarridge testified that he thought the plane carried oil-drilling parts, not weapons. He said he did not remember when he realized that missiles were being shipped. He said he might have learned about the Hawks later in November, and that he did not find out officially until the following January.

Clarridge's testimony was at odds with the account given to the panels previously by the unidentified CIA station chief in Portugal. That official testified that he sent a cable to Clarridge November 23, telling him that the flight contained Hawk missiles. The station chief had learned that from Secord, who had been sent to Portugal by North to work out the missile shipment to Iran.

But Clarridge said he did not remember seeing the station chief's cable, and CIA officials did not find a copy in agency files. The station chief told the committees that he destroyed his copies of the cables to Clarridge as a routine precaution in December 1985.

Neil Eggleston, deputy counsel of the House panel, said there was "fairly convincing evidence" that the cable mentioning weapons was sent to Clarridge. In addition to the testimony from the CIA station chief in Portugal, the committees also obtained a deposition from a CIA dispatcher who remembered seeing a cable that mentioned Hawk missiles and Iran. A second crucial cable also was missing. That was one sent by Clarridge to the station chief in Portugal telling him the reason for helping Secord.

Eggleston reminded Clarridge that both North, who asked for Clarridge's help, and the CIA station chief, whom Clarridge ordered to assist in the operation, knew that weapons were aboard the flight. "The person who gave you the problem knew. The person you gave the problem to solve knew. . . . But you did not know?" asked Eggleston.

"That is the way it was," replied Clarridge.

Israeli vs. North Account

While the House and Senate Iran-contra committees wrestled over their final report on the scandal, information reported in September 1987 by the *Wall Street Journal*—and confirmed by the committees—raised fresh doubts about the testimony of one of the key players in the affair, former National Security Council (NSC) aide Lt. Col. Oliver L. North.

The information put North in conflict with members of the Israeli government who worked with him on the secret sale of weapons to Iran. And it fueled speculation by committee sources working on the report that the Reagan administration's intense efforts to funnel money and arms to the Nicaraguan contras might have been a driving force behind the sale of U.S. weapons to Iran and the diversion of profits to the rebels in Central America.

The new information suggested that North proposed a scheme to divert Iran arms sales profits to the contras in a meeting with an Israeli official in December 1985. In his public testimony in July, North said he had no recollection about such a discussion; instead, he said the diversion was suggested by Iranian arms merchant Manucher Ghorbanifar the following month. North testified that an Israeli official, Amiram Nir, originally suggested the use of "residuals" from the Iran arms sales for other unrelated activities. A few weeks later, Ghorbanifar raised the specific diversion scheme in the bathroom of a London hotel, where he and North met to discuss the Iran arms sales, according to North's testimony. *(North testimony, pp. 121, 125)*

But an account of the Iran-contra affair provided to congressional investigators by Israeli officials described North's meeting a month earlier in New York with an Israeli purchasing agent. The Israeli official kept notes of his meeting with North that indicated the NSC aide's interest in linking the Iran arms profits to the contras. Copies of the notes, written in Hebrew, were given to Warren B. Rudman, R-N.H., vice chairman of the Senate Iran-contra committee, during a private trip to Israel during the August 1987 congressional recess.

Arthur L. Liman, chief counsel for the Senate panel, knew about North's December meeting when he questioned North during the hearings in July. Liman, however, did not reveal the source of his information because of an agreement that the Israel-supplied account would be kept under wraps. "Do you recall whether the idea of using profit for the contras actually first came up in a meeting that you had with Israeli supply officials in the United States in or about December 1985?" Liman asked at the hearings.

"I don't recall that," replied North. "My recollection was that the first time it was specifically addressed was during a meeting [in January 1986] with Ghorbanifar. It may well have come up before, but I don't recall it."

A few moments later, Liman again asked North if he was the one who first raised the diversion scheme with Israeli officials in December 1985. "I have answered the question several times now," said North. He said he had "absolutely no recollection" of the diversion scheme being discussed before January.

Frantic efforts to route the Hawks through Portugal failed after Portuguese officials demanded a formal diplomatic note from the United States that would say arms were being shipped to Iran in exchange for U.S. hostages held in Lebanon. Eventually, the missiles were sent through another route after Clarridge asked CIA officers stationed elsewhere to assist in the delivery.

In response to several other questions from Eggleston, Clarridge said he could not recall various conversations with North ostensibly dealing with the Hawk shipment.

South Africa and Contra Aid

During his appearance, Clarridge was questioned closely about an apparent effort by the United States to obtain secret assistance for the contras from South Africa in 1984, although all references to South Africa were deleted in the heavily censored transcript of his testimony. The White House and CIA at the time were trying to locate alternative funding sources for the contras in the face of a funding cutoff voted by Congress.

In an earlier deposition given to the committees, Clarridge denied that he had any involvement in trying to arrange some kind of assistance from South Africa. He altered his position during his testimony, however, after reviewing a series of cables among CIA officials in early 1984 dealing with South Africa's potential offer. But Clarridge tried to play down the issue, saying there was a "misunderstanding" within the CIA about what the Pretoria government actually was offering. He said South African officials expected to be paid for their assistance to the contras and were also discussing another option, some kind of bilateral aid to an unidentified country in Central America.

Clarridge took a trip to South Africa in April 1984, but he said CIA director Casey had already decided not to accept any kind of offer. Even after Clarridge's trip, however, the CIA still seemed to be interested in pursuing the South African angle. But the talk died down after members of Congress reacted bitterly in the spring of 1984 to revelations that the CIA had mined Nicaraguan harbors.

"Current furor here over the Nicaraguan project urges that we postpone taking [South African officials] up on their offer of assistance," Clarridge said in a CIA cable written on May 11, 1984. Asked about the cable, Clarridge said that "assistance" meant the bilateral aid to a Central

American country contemplated by South Africa, not direct aid to the contras.

Fiers and George: Turf Battles

Both Fiers and George described in vivid detail a series of battles that beset the administration's policies toward Iran and Nicaragua.

On Iran, George complained that the White House shunted aside the experts at the CIA, refusing in particular to heed warnings about the reliability of Ghorbanifar. George also said the White House failed to accept a CIA assessment that the pro-Iranian Lebanese forces who were holding U.S. citizens hostage would never release all of them. NSC aide Earl had testified that the White House officials refused to involve the State Department in the Iranian initiative simply because they did not trust the diplomats there to keep it secret.

The testimony also provided new information about personality clashes. Fiers said that in 1984-85 the senior officials for Central America policy—Assistant Secretary of State Langhorne A. Motley and NSC aide Constantine Menges—"fought like cats and dogs" and would not speak to each other. George said he had to "referee" continual battles between Fiers and North, who served together on an exclusive committee handling policy toward Nicaragua.

Partly because of such clashes, the administration sidestepped normal procedures. North relied on a network of private agents—some of questionable reliability—to handle the daily details of arms sales to Iran and covert aid to the contras. Experts at the CIA and the State Department were excluded from these sensitive activities.

North and the CIA. Much of the testimony focused on North. In his July testimony, North portrayed himself as a hard-working covert operator who "got things done."

Fiers, George, Earl, and Coy all agreed with North's self-assessment, describing him as a dedicated officer who enjoyed an unusually close relationship with CIA director Casey. George said Casey was fond of "action people" such as North. Earl said the two men spoke to each other at least once a week.

However, both Fiers and George made it clear that they did not entirely trust North. They said he exaggerated his own importance, frequently told tall tales about his exploits and used his White House position to force the bureaucracy to cooperate with the plans he seemed to generate endlessly. And they acknowledged that they often found themselves in conflict with North, creating disputes that Casey usually had to step in to resolve.

Although Fiers and North were supposed to work closely together on Central America, the CIA official testified that he never knew exactly what North was doing. Shortly after taking over his post in 1984, Fiers said he became suspicious of North's activities and took his concerns to CIA higher-ups. Confronted directly, North told the CIA, according to Fiers: "No, I am not operating in Central America"—a statement that testimony showed to be untrue, since North was deeply involved in aiding the contras at the time.

"I never knew Col. North to be an absolute liar, but I never took anything he said at face value because I knew that he was bombastic and embellished the record, and threw curves, speed balls and spitballs to get what he wanted, and I knew it and I knew it well," Fiers said.

George also testified that North came up with "harebrained" schemes for covert operations in the Middle East and Central America. George said he was able to stop some of North's projects by appealing directly to Casey. But, he added, Casey's own fondness for direct action made him inclined to go along with North.

Ghorbanifar and Secord. Casey and White House officials overrode CIA objections to using two key operatives in the Iran-contra affair, George testified. He said he and others protested the involvement of Ghorbanifar and Secord.

The CIA had experience with Ghorbanifar dating to 1979 but found him to be "dishonest and untruthful," George said. In 1984, the CIA told its agents to avoid him. Late in 1985, Ghorbanifar turned up as the principal White House contact with Iran, causing CIA officials to protest and to demand that he be subjected to a polygraph test. Ghorbanifar flunked such a test on January 11, 1986. A CIA memo released by the committees said he "is clearly a fabricator and wheeler-dealer who has undertaken activities prejudicial to U.S. interests."

Nevertheless, the Reagan White House decided to use Ghorbanifar to develop a relationship with Iran, and it continued to use him throughout the first part of 1986 even though he never did deliver on promises to win the release of all U.S. hostages in Lebanon. Earl said it was "common knowledge" at the White House that Ghorbanifar was untrustworthy. But, he added, "as totally despicable and distrustworthy as he might have been, [Ghorbanifar] was at the time absolutely essential" as the U.S. contact with Iran.

After Ghorbanifar flunked the lie-detector test, George sent a new order to CIA agents telling them to stay away from Ghorbanifar. But a day or two later, on January 17, 1986, President Reagan signed the finding that authorized U.S. arms dealings with Iran. That directive, George said, "in its practical sense said: 'You'll be doing business with Mr. Ghorbanifar.'" George speculated that the White House agreed to use Ghorbanifar because of his ties to Israel. Although an Iranian, Ghorbanifar "is a recruited agent of the government of Israel," George said. North also had told the Iran-contra committees that Ghorbanifar worked for Israel.

George said he and other CIA officials also objected to Secord's involvement in the Iran program—and would have been even more opposed had they known that Secord also was helping North aid the contras. While admitting that he had no evidence that Secord was involved in illegal activities, George said he "worked the edges of the international arms market." George said he was concerned about Secord's past association with former CIA agent Edwin P. Wilson, who was serving a sentence in federal prison for illegal arms dealings with Libya.

Misleading Congress. Fiers and George were the latest in a string of administration figures admitting that they had misled Congress during its early inquiries into aspects of the Iran-contra affair.

The two men were present at a private House Intelligence Committee briefing October 14, 1986, nine days after Nicaragua shot down one of North's contra-supply planes. The downing of the plane put into motion the process of public exposure of North's contra-aid effort. George and Assistant Secretary of State Abrams, the two senior officials at the hearing, denied any U.S. government involvement in or knowledge of the downed plane—even though both knew of North's role in maintaining a network of air-supply operations to the contras. Fiers sat by silently as his colleagues uttered their denials.

Asked by committee members why he did not speak up, Fiers said he felt he was part of "the administration team." In retrospect, Fiers said, he should have been more forthcoming, "but I frankly was not going to be the first person to step up and do that." George said he, too, "didn't have the guts" to interrupt Abrams at the briefing. He acknowledged to Senator Cohen that he was "overly taken with trying to protect the Central Intelligence Agency."

But both men insisted they did not lie to Congress.

Aiding the Contras. Fiers and George both said they understood in 1984, when Congress was moving to cut off U.S. aid to the contras, that any CIA involvement in Central America would be controversial. But both insisted that they worked hard to stay within the law from 1984 to 1986, while pushing Congress to loosen the strings on what the CIA could do. Although they knew that North was working with the contras, both said that until late 1986 they did not realize the full extent of his involvement, or even of the participation by lower-level CIA employees who were helping him.

Remarkably, both CIA officials said their agency had little direct information during 1985 and early 1986 about where the contras were getting money to support their operations. Both said, for example, that they knew nothing about Saudi Arabian contributions to the contras totaling nearly $32 million. Fiers was CIA station chief in Saudi Arabia in 1984, when it made its first donations.

Fiers also said he could not recall—or he flatly denied—a number of incidents in which he or other CIA officials were alleged to have cooperated with North in aiding the contras during the period that CIA aid was restricted. In one case, Fiers said he could not recall North asking in February 1985 for secret maps showing the location of military bases in Nicaragua. North obtained the maps and sent them to the contras—an action Fiers said might have violated the legal restrictions on contra aid.

Fiers and George both insisted that they did not wittingly allow North to use the CIA to skirt the law. Fiers said he "let the reins out" early in 1986, allowing CIA officers to participate in some contra-aid activities that previously had been barred. That occurred during the period when Reagan was asking Congress to restore military aid to the contras. But Fiers said he later reimposed some of the restrictions.

Both CIA officials said they were troubled by the active assistance given North's contra-aid network by Tomas Castillo, the pseudonym for the CIA station chief in Costa Rica. They said Castillo skirted CIA policies against such assistance, but he may not have violated the law.

If Castillo breached CIA policy, George said, it may have been because he was placed in "an absolutely impossible situation." That happened, George said, when North gave Castillo instructions independent of the CIA and said they were coming from the White House.

Depositions from Bush Aides

The select committees September 8 disclosed documents related to earlier depositions given by two aides to Vice President Bush. Although the testimony provided no direct evidence that Bush knew about possibly illegal efforts to arm the Nicaraguan contras or to divert to them Iran arms sale profits, evidence revealed by the committees indicated that one of the stated purposes of a May 1986 meeting between Bush and a disaffected operative in the clandestine contra arms program was to discuss the supply effort. The evidence also suggested a warm relationship between Bush and North. In one case, Bush penned a note in November 1985 thanking North for his work in Central America and toward obtaining the release of American hostages in Lebanon.

Bush repeatedly maintained that he did not know about administration efforts to funnel weapons and cash to the contras until the scandal came to light in November 1986. In the wake of the aides' testimony, a spokesman for Bush reiterated that he was unaware of the supply effort.

Meetings with Rodriguez

One mystery remained the ties between Bush's office and Felix I. Rodriguez, a Bay of Pigs veteran and former CIA agent recruited by North in 1985 to aid in resupplying the contras. Rodriguez was a friend of Donald P. Gregg, Bush's national security adviser, who sponsored Rodriguez in a plan to help the government of El Salvador fend off leftist insurgents.

A briefing memo prepared for Bush before his May 1986 meeting with Rodriguez said one reason for the session was to discuss the "resupply of the contras" in addition to Rodriguez's activities in El Salvador.

But Gregg and his assistant, Army colonel Samuel J. Watson III, told congressional investigators that the contra supply program was not discussed in the meeting. The two aides said they did not know why the memo included the reference to the contras. In a separate deposition released by the committees, Phyllis Byrne, Gregg's secretary, testified that Watson had told her to include it in the memo. Watson did not recall telling Byrne to do so. *(Gregg testimony text, p. C-143; Watson, p. C-145)*

Gregg gave his deposition to committee investigators on May 18 while Watson and Byrne testified in separate closed sessions on June 16. Portions of their testimony were censored by the White House to remove sensitive references, such as identities of other countries and CIA agents.

Rodriguez, the main subject of the testimony by Bush's aides, appeared in open session May 27-28. He said he never discussed his contra activities in his meetings with Bush. *(Rodriguez testimony, p. 101)*

Bush, in a chronology released by his office December 15, 1986, had acknowledged meeting on three occasions with Rodriguez, but only to discuss efforts to help El Salvador fight rebels by using combat helicopters. Gregg and Watson said that was the subject that Rodriguez discussed with Bush at their May 1986 meeting at the White House. *(Chronology text, p. D-19)*

In their testimony, Gregg and Watson said it was three months later that they learned for the first time that North was coordinating an effort to resupply the contras. The two Bush aides said they met with Rodriguez on August 8, 1986. Rodriguez had sought the meeting to voice concerns about corruption inside the contra supply program. Although Rodriguez had such concerns months earlier, he said during his testimony that North had persuaded him to stick with the operation.

At the meeting, Rodriguez told Bush's aides that the supply operation included people he associated with Edwin P. Wilson, a former CIA agent imprisoned for smuggling explosives to Libya. According to Watson's testimony, Rodriguez said "a bunch of crooks" were involved in a "corrupt, shoddy, unsafe" operation to arm the contras. Among those he doubted were Thomas Clines, a former Wilson associate, and Secord.

Rodriguez also alerted Gregg and Watson to the possibility of the CIA taking over the supply effort, warning that the U.S. government should not be involved with those running the operation. Rodriguez "said this group of people was profiteering, that they were buying and selling arms, weapons, military supplies, to give to the contras . . . and that they were buying this stuff at low prices and charging the contras high prices," said Watson.

'Murky Business'

Gregg and Watson said Rodriguez did not tell them at the August meeting that he had been recruited by North. Nor did Gregg and Watson inform Bush about what Rodriguez told them, according to their testimony. "I frankly did not think it was vice presidential level," said Gregg.

Instead, he described what he had heard from Rodriguez as a "very murky business" involving a subject matter—the contras—that did not involve Bush directly. "We had never discussed the contras. We had no responsibility for it. We had no expertise in it. I wasn't at all certain what this amounted to," said Gregg.

Instead of telling Bush, his aides informed other administration officials about Rodriguez's concerns at a meeting on August 12, according to their testimony. This meeting included representatives from the NSC staff, State Department, CIA, and other agencies. Watson, in recounting the meeting, said most of the participants said very little and that it ended with vague assurances that Rodriguez's complaints would be looked into.

Neither Gregg nor Watson, however, specifically pressed North to explain his role in the contra supply effort as outlined by Rodriguez or to respond to Rodriguez's allegations about corrupt activities. Prior to the August meeting with Rodriguez, Gregg said he was generally aware that North was involved in efforts to help private individuals provide "humanitarian" contra aid.

Watson, describing an official trip to Central America in January 1986, said he learned there that a contra military officer was running a resupply operation for the rebels. He said that two CIA officers were advising contra leaders on "resupply techniques," but that he did not know anything about a private supply network involving U.S. officials. Watson, like Gregg, said he did not learn about the direct role of Americans in the supply program until Rodriguez told them in August 1986. Gregg said he notified Bush about Rodriguez's role in the contra supply program after Rodriguez told Gregg in December 1986 that North had recruited him for the supply effort. Asked for Bush's response, Gregg replied, "I do not remember that it evoked a large reaction."

According to Gregg, Rodriguez said North had asked him to keep his contra activities secret, and, in particular, not to tell Gregg. The Bush aide said North might have given those instructions to avoid "questions of possible illegality."

The testimony and documents released by the select committees included a "Dear Ollie" note in Bush's handwriting sent to North in November 1985. "One of the many things I have to be thankful for is the way in which you have performed, under fire, in tough situations," wrote Bush. "Your dedication and tireless work with the hostage thing and with Central America really gives me cause for great pride in you. . . ."

The "hostage thing" apparently referred to North's role in trying to secure the release of American hostages held by pro-Iran factions in Lebanon. The note, written on November 22, 1985, coincided with North's frantic efforts to move a shipment of U.S. arms from Israel to Iran in exchange for U.S. hostages. But it was not known whether Bush was referring to that specific operation.

A Penchant for Secrecy

The testimony from Bush's aides added to the portrait of administration officials intent upon secrecy. Watson, for example, described one episode in July 1986 when North, during a White House meeting, whispered to him an oblique complaint about Rodriguez's performance in the contra supply program. North quickly dropped the subject, however, when Watson pressed him for details. Watson recalled getting similar treatment from Earl, North's assistant on the NSC staff.

"I must tell you, these are bizarre conversations. People start talking to you and then when you ask them a question, they don't answer," Belnick, assistant Senate committee counsel, told Watson.

Watson previously had described North as a "very secretive type of person. He wanted people to think he was doing things very special, and I took it to be part of that." Watson also described how he was excluded from attending meetings of a Restricted Interagency Group (RIG), depicted as a key component in the administration's pro-contra efforts.

Despite his repeated requests to attend the sessions, Watson said he was kept out by Assistant Secretary of State Abrams, who chaired the RIG meetings.

Ledeen Testimony

The Reagan administration ignored an invitation in 1985 to establish ties with a senior Iranian official who said he was interested in improving relations with the United States, according to testimony from a key participant in the Iran arms sale dealings.

Testimony released September 27 from Michael Ledeen, a former consultant to the NSC, gave an account of his frustration in trying to convince administration officials to move away from selling arms to Iran in an exchange for hostages held by pro-Iran factions in Lebanon. The declassified transcripts of Ledeen's depositions were taken during four sessions in March, June, and September. *(Ledeen testimony text, p. C-146)*

According to Ledeen, the unidentified Iranian official who sought closer U.S. ties warned Ledeen that the White House's decision to sell weapons to Iran only served to reinforce the anti-American regime headed by the Ayatollah Ruhollah Khomeini. "It had strengthened the very people that it was necessary to remove if one were going to transform the Iranian government into something more reasonable," Ledeen told congressional investigators.

Testimony Leaves Doubts

Ledeen's account challenged administration claims that it was chiefly interested in bettering relations between Washington and Tehran when it decided to sell weapons to Iran.

Ledeen said he was introduced to the Iranian official in the fall of 1985 by Iranian arms merchant Ghorbanifar. The official told Ledeen that it was possible to change the nature of the Iranian regime through "peaceful, parliamentary methods," according to Ledeen's testimony. The official also asked the United States to supply him with pistols and other light weapons along with communications equipment to stay in touch with U.S. officials.

But Ledeen told congressional investigators that McFarlane, then Reagan's national security adviser, never responded to Ledeen's recommendation for further contacts with the official. He also said the U.S. government never followed up on other Iranian contacts arranged by Ghorbanifar.

Ledeen was ordered off the Iranian matter in late 1985 by Poindexter, after he replaced McFarlane as national security adviser. But Ledeen said he continued to discuss the Iranian contacts with other senior administration officials, including CIA director Casey and Defense Secretary Weinberger, in an effort to revive interest in the matter. According to Ledeen, Casey endorsed the idea of fostering improved relations with Iran. But he told Ledeen that the "politics of Washington" required that the hostage problem be solved before a broader Iran initiative could be pursued, Ledeen testified.

Ledeen's Role

Ledeen played a critical role in the early stages of the arms-for-hostages program because he was the first American to discuss Iran weapons deals directly with Israeli officials, who handled the initial sales in 1985. Ledeen said McFarlane asked him to meet with Israeli prime minister Shimon Peres in May 1985 in an effort to have the United States and Israel share intelligence information about Iran. At the meeting, Ledeen said Peres agreed to the information-sharing idea and also gave him a note asking U.S. approval for Israel to ship artillery pieces to Iran.

According to Ledeen, McFarlane told him to inform the Israelis that the artillery shipment "was okay, but just that one shipment and nothing else."

Ledeen said McFarlane told him in November 1986 to deny that McFarlane had directed him to meet with Peres in May 1985. McFarlane testified in May 1987 that Ledeen went to Israel on his own initiative. But Ledeen told congressional investigators he had "explicit approval" for the trip and related details of his conversations with Peres.

Within a couple of months of the Peres meeting, Ledeen had been introduced by Israeli officials to Ghorbanifar, who talked about the possibility of freeing American hostages in exchange for TOW antitank missiles. That led to a U.S.-approved Israeli delivery of 504 TOW missiles to Iran in August-September 1985, resulting in the mid-September release of the Rev. Benjamin F. Weir.

'Deceit and Illusion'

Despite Weir's release, Ledeen said he had turned against the arms-for-hostages program by October 1985. He testified that "so desperate was the Iranian need [for weapons] that they would resort to all manner of deceit and illusion to keep the weapons arriving." Ledeen also said Ghorbanifar shared his view at the time that the United States should no longer sell weapons in exchange for hostages. That statement was at odds with a portrait of Ghorbanifar drawn during the House and Senate select committees' public hearings. He was described by others as an untrustworthy businessman eager to make millions of dollars in weapons sales to Iran.

WRAP-UP: DISPUTES, REPORT

The TV lights were turned off, and the long lines of summer tourists dissipated. Most of the members of the House and Senate Iran-contra committees left Washington during the congressional August recess.

But the painstaking task of writing the final report loomed large, even though the document might be considered only an epilogue to the drama of the hearings. Contradictory testimony, open questions, and political battles awaited the drafters of the report.

The House and Senate panels were scheduled to release a final report on the scandal in late October. It was expected that the document would consist of an approximately 100-page section including an executive summary and conclusions and recommendations. In addition, the committees planned to release a much more lengthy narrative of the Iran-contra episode that would probably run some 1,000 pages and appear in two volumes. Representative Cheney said GOP members were likely to include a section on minority views in the final report.

Contradictions

The hearings produced dozens of contradictory statements, some of which might never be resolved. Some of the most important disputes included:

Poindexter vs. the White House. In his testimony, Poindexter insisted that Reagan would have approved the idea of diverting Iranian arms sales money to the contras. White House spokesman Fitzwater, saying he was speaking for Reagan, insisted that the president would not have approved the diversion. Asked about the White House refutation, Poindexter told the committees: "Clearly, there's a contradiction and I think that contradiction's going to have to stand."

North vs. McFarlane. North said July 7 that he "sought approval" from his superiors for "every one of my actions, and it is well documented." Later, he broadened that claim to say: "I was authorized to do everything that I did."

But North's former boss, McFarlane, who had testified in May, returned to the witness table July 14 and insisted that North did not tell him about many of his secret activities on behalf of the contras. The former national security adviser said he authorized North to lend "political" support to the contras but never gave approval for North to provide military and intelligence backing. For example, McFarlane testified that he ordered North and other NSC staff members not to solicit money for the contras; North said he never received such instructions.

North vs. Poindexter. In the same category, North said Poindexter was fully aware of his actions. Poindexter, while saying he gave North "general authority" to aid the contras, insisted that he did not know the details because he did not want to "micromanage" North's actions.

North and Poindexter also disagreed about the existence of the "diversion memos"—five memorandums North said he wrote in 1986 discussing arms sales to Iran and mentioning the diversion of profits to the contras. Poindexter said he did not recall any of the memos but conceded that he might have gotten one. As for the other four that North insisted he wrote, Poindexter said: "I frankly don't think they existed."

Finally, the two men had opposing recollections of whether North asked Poindexter on November 21, 1986, if Reagan knew about the diversion. North said that he did ask such a question and that Poindexter responded that Reagan was unaware of the diversion scheme. Poindexter said he recalled no such conversation.

Poindexter vs. McFarlane. Poindexter supported North in some of his testimony that ran contrary to McFarlane's. For example, Poindexter said he never heard McFarlane instruct the NSC staff not to solicit money for the contras. McFarlane and Poindexter also disagreed on the application of the Boland amendment to the NSC staff; McFarlane said he always assumed that the amendment did bar the NSC staff from providing military aid to the contras, but Poindexter insisted that the amendment did not apply to the NSC staff and swore that he never heard McFarlane say that it did.

North vs. Earl. In a deposition to the committees, Earl, North's former NSC deputy, related what North had told him after he and Reagan talked by telephone November 25, 1986. Reagan said, according to Earl's account, "It's important that I don't know" about the diversion. North himself testified that Reagan told him: "I just didn't know."

North vs. Justice Department. North testified that he shredded documents in his office on the morning of November 22, 1986, even while two Justice Department investigators were there reviewing files of the Iran arms sales. Meese and one of the investigators—Assistant Attorney General William Bradford Reynolds—heatedly denied that contention. Earl also said North did not shred documents in the presence of the Justice officials.

North vs. State Department. North said key State Department officials, including Shultz and Assistant Secretary of State Abrams, had to be aware of his actions in aiding the contras. North noted that Abrams served with him on a Restricted Interagency Group that directed U.S. policy toward Central America and so was aware of the "covert operation" in support of the contras. North also said Shultz congratulated him in 1986 on his backing of the contras. Abrams and Shultz insisted they did not know precisely what North was doing to aid the contras; in particular, both men said they never knew that North had given the contras intelligence information and had organized military resupply missions for them.

North vs. Meese. North implied repeatedly in his testimony that Meese was aware of Israeli arms shipments to Iran in 1985 that might have had explicit U.S. approval. On July 7, for example, he said he understood in November 1985 that Meese was aware of the delivery of Hawk missiles to Iran, and he said he was "led to believe" that CIA general counsel Sporkin got Meese's assent for a finding by which Reagan approved that shipment.

Meese testified that he knew nothing at the time about the 1985 shipments and learned about them only in the

course of his November 1986 inquiry into the matter.

North vs. Clarridge. North testified that he told CIA official Clarridge in November 1985 that the Israeli shipment to Iran contained Hawk missiles—not "oil drilling parts," as specified in a cover story widely used at the time. Clarridge told the committees in a private deposition that no one told him at the time about the missiles. Clarridge had helped arrange for a CIA-owned airline to make the shipment from Israel to Iran.

North vs. Congress. In his testimony, North complained about several activities of Congress, most notably its alleged leaking of classified information. But he made two specific charges that later were refuted. On April 15, 1986, North said, two senators tipped the press to the impending U.S. air raid on Libya, giving that country enough warning so that it was able to shoot down a U.S. aircraft. But Inouye noted earlier press accounts showing that the Reagan administration for weeks had been leaking information about possible U.S. military action, allowing Libya plenty of time to bolster its defenses.

North also charged that "a number of members of Congress" leaked information about the fact that the United States intercepted Libyan radio messages in 1985; those interceptions enabled the United States to capture the hijackers of the *Achille Lauro* cruise liner. But *Newsweek* magazine reported that the source of that information was "none other than North himself."

North vs. North. In an interview with Meese on November 23, 1986, North said that he and Poindexter were the only U.S. government officials who knew about the diversion scheme. But North told the committees that Casey knew about the diversion and was so pleased by it

---

Hearings, by the Numbers

In the aftermath of the Iran-contra hearings, which began May 5 and ended August 6, 1987, some statistics might help to tell the story of a congressional investigation.

For example, there were:
- Forty days of public hearings, plus four days of closed sessions.
- Twenty-five public sessions in the Senate Caucus Room, and fifteen in the House Foreign Affairs Committee room.
- Thirty-two witnesses, twenty-eight of them public.
- About 250 hours of public testimony.
- 311 subpoenas delivered by the select committees.
- 1,059 exhibits introduced into the record.
- 9,887 pages of transcripts of public testimony. A breakdown of those pages is lopsided. For instance, Lt. Col. Oliver L. North's six days at the witness table July 7-14 produced 1,388 transcript pages, while lawyer David L. Lewis's brief appearance June 4 yielded only 17 pages.

that he called it "the ultimate covert operation."

Meese testified that he believed North's statement to him, noting that North made it at a time when Casey was alive and able to refute or verify it. North said he did not tell Meese about Casey's knowledge because "it was always part of the plan" that Casey would never be linked to the NSC covert aid to the contras. Casey had warned that North and Poindexter would have to be the "fall guys" if the diversion ever was revealed, he testified.

Committee investigators floated another possible explanation of the contradiction: North testified to the committees without knowing what Poindexter would say and so might have wanted to invoke Casey's name as authority for the diversion in case Poindexter claimed not to have given his approval.

Poindexter vs. Poindexter. Former White House chief of staff Regan testified that when he confronted Poindexter about the diversion on November 25, Poindexter claimed to know practically nothing about it. But Poindexter testified that he had approved the diversion in advance and was fully aware of the implications of that decision, if not the daily details of how it was implemented.

Reagan vs. McFarlane. McFarlane said Reagan approved Israel's shipment of TOW missiles to Iran in August and September of 1985. But Reagan said repeatedly that he had no memory of having given such approval.

Reagan vs. Poindexter. Similarly, Poindexter said Reagan on December 5, 1985, signed a finding giving retroactive approval to CIA participation in Israel's shipment of Hawk missiles to Iran. Reagan said that he did not recall knowing about the Hawk shipment. And Fitzwater said Reagan did not remember signing the finding but would not dispute Poindexter's contention that he had.

Poindexter vs. Shultz. Poindexter testified that he recalled getting Reagan's approval in October 1986 for a nine-point plan that called for release of one or two U.S. hostages in return for a sale of 500 TOW missiles to Iran. One significant point called for the United States to develop a plan for the release of convicted terrorists held in Kuwait. But Shultz said Reagan was "totally surprised, astonished" in December 1986 when told about the reference to releasing the terrorists in Kuwait.

Writing the Final Report

Writing the closing chapter on the Iran-contra hearings was likely to touch off behind-the-scenes partisan wrangling as members debated the politically charged questions of why the scandal took place.

Reagan's Democratic detractors were likely to criticize his conduct, emphasizing wrongdoing and possibly illegal behavior at the highest level of the White House. His Republican supporters, however, could be expected to resist such an approach. Instead, they were likely to lobby for a report that said mistakes were made, despite Reagan's good intentions, largely because of overzealous aides.

General agreement among committee members could be expected on the basic facts surrounding Reagan's decision to sell arms to Iran and the diversion of profits to the Nicaraguan contras. Similarly, virtually all committee members agreed that Reagan wrongly kept Congress in the dark about his secret policy of selling weapons to Iran.

Committee lawyers and other aides began writing sections of the report while the members were on their August vacation. The schedule called for a draft to be submitted when members returned after Labor Day, with a final version expected in October.

An Incomplete Story

The report would serve as a blueprint for proposed changes in legislation and executive actions to prevent similar operations in the future. But like the hearings, the report would be incomplete because of gaps and conflicts that remained after three months of public hearings and hundreds of behind-the-scenes interviews with Iran-contra participants.

That meant it would be difficult, if not impossible, for the final report to live up to the promise that Senator Rudman gave on the opening day of the hearings May 5. "By the time these hearings are concluded," the vice chairman of the Senate panel said, "the American people will learn the answers to the five final questions: who, what, when, why and how."

While the answers to some of those questions were elusive, several committee members hinted at the themes they would like to see included in a report. Perhaps the most contentious issue was Reagan's personal role. He was likely to escape particularly harsh criticism because the committees did not uncover any direct evidence that he knew of the diversion of Iran arms sale profits to the contras. Nonetheless, some Democrats might try to weave into the report at least a milder judgment against Reagan that could face resistance from Republicans.

In his closing statement August 3, House committee chairman Hamilton suggested that Reagan's presidential style contributed to the behavior of officials in the Iran-contra affair. "The president's decisions [in the future] must be clean and crisp. Otherwise, as we have seen in these hearings, confusion follows and those who work for him cannot carry out his policies successfully." Similar themes were included in the February 26, 1987, Tower Commission report.

Beyond the crucial question of the diversion, some Democrats said Reagan should be held accountable for other aspects of the Iran-contra affair. Senator Mitchell cited issues such as the "incredibly stupid" decision to sell weapons to Iran and the secret White House effort to aid the contras. Mitchell acknowledged that definitive conclusions might be difficult to reach. But he said the testimony "seems clear" that Reagan was aware of the NSC's possibly unlawful efforts to funnel arms and cash to the contras during the period in 1984-86 when Congress had prohibited military aid.

Reagan told the Tower board that he was unaware of the NSC's activities but later backed away from that statement. "The one thing that comes through clearly here was that that law [prohibiting aid to the contras] was not observed," said Mitchell.

But Reagan's defenders were prepared to challenge vigorously efforts by other committee members to criticize Reagan. "How can they? The facts don't support that. Reagan has come out of this far better than anyone would have thought," said Senator Hatch. "I think the most significant thing really is that the hearings showed no venality, no corruption."

Profiles of Select Committees' Members

Congress wasted little time in deciding to establish select committees to investigate the Iran-contra affair in the wake of the November 1986 disclosures. On December 4, leaders of both chambers stated their intention to form special panels—fifteen members on the House side, and eleven on the Senate. Shortly thereafter, congressional leaders announced their appointments to the panels. The following provides political biographies of the twenty-six members. (Ages and committee memberships are given as of the beginning of the 100th Congress.)

Senate Democrats

Daniel K. Inouye, Hawaii, Chairman

Age 62. Elected in 1962. Committees: Appropriations; Commerce, Science and Transportation; Rules and Administration; Select Indian Affairs (chairman).

"This is a new experience for me," Inouye told a throng of reporters December 17, 1986, the day after his appointment as chairman. "You don't see me at press conferences. And I don't intend to be appearing before the mike . . . this often."

Despite his stated aversion to publicity, Inouye was hardly a stranger to national prominence. As a member of the Senate Watergate Committee in 1973, Inouye captured the attention of millions of television viewers when he unwittingly exclaimed "What a liar!" into a live microphone after listening to testimony by White House aide John Ehrlichman. Ehrlichman's lawyer, John Wilson, later added to Inouye's burgeoning popularity by referring to him as "that little Jap," which resulted in an outpouring of public support for the senator.

Besides the uproar caused by that incident, Inouye's service on the Watergate panel also earned him a reputation as a tough interrogator of witnesses.

Several years after Watergate, Inouye figured in another dramatic Senate episode—that chamber's 1981 debate over the fate of Sen. Harrison A. Williams, Jr., D-N.J., who faced expulsion because of his involvement in the Abscam bribery scandal. Inouye acted as Williams's defense lawyer on the floor, where he denounced the government's "sting" tactics in setting up the Abscam operation. In doing so, he described the government's case against Williams as an attack upon the institution itself. "The integrity of the Senate is challenged by this investigation, and the Constitution compels us to reject its advance," he said. Williams resigned before the Senate could vote on his expulsion.

Inouye also served as the first chairman of the Senate Intelligence Committee when that panel was established in 1976.

Through the years, he positioned himself to place a stamp on foreign aid. With the Democrats' retaking Senate control in January 1987, Inouye assumed the chairmanship of the Appropriations Subcommittee on Foreign Operations, a post he held before the GOP captured the Senate in 1980.

Inouye voted against President Reagan's request for $100 million in military and other aid to Nicaraguan contras when the Senate approved the money in March 1986. He once unsuccessfully pushed an amendment to provide $6 million to the contras to allow them to leave for another country. He also charged at one point that CIA support for the contras was "slowly but surely eroding whatever credibility is left" to that agency.

In another foreign policy controversy, Inouye in 1985 cautioned other members of Congress to be patient in dealing with then-Philippine president Ferdinand E. Marcos. Three months before the authoritarian Marcos was ousted from his position, Inouye in late 1985 was trying to convince others that the Philippine leader would not necessarily renege on a pledge to hold free elections. "You are bound to have, in a nation like that, incidents of illegal activity. You can find the same thing in any state in the union here," Inouye said at the time. Inouye said he had always felt a "special closeness" to the Philippines, in part because it shared with Hawaii the status of an island long dominated by the U.S. mainland.

A member of Hawaii's Territorial Legislature before statehood, Inouye served two terms in the U.S. House after Hawaii entered the union in 1959. He easily won election to the Senate in 1962 when the incumbent, Oren E. Long, retired and endorsed Inouye to succeed him.

Since then, Inouye coasted to reelection victories against nominal opposition, winning 74 percent in his 1986 campaign.

Born in Honolulu on September 7, 1924, Inouye originally wanted to be a surgeon. But that ambition changed after he lost his right arm during World War II, when Inouye fought in Italy and France with an all-Japanese regiment. Instead, he became a lawyer and then went into politics.

David L. Boren, Okla.

Age 45. Elected in 1978. Committees: Select Intelligence (chairman); Agriculture, Nutrition and Forestry; Finance; Small Business.

The incoming chairman of the Senate Intelligence Committee in the 100th Congress, Boren had not played much of a role in foreign policy matters. Instead, he focused on the economy, agriculture, and legislation to limit the influence of political action committees.

He voted for military aid to Nicaraguan contras, and supported the administration on other foreign and defense policies.

Boren figured decisively in the Senate's razor-thin approval in August 1986 of funds requested by Reagan for funding of the "Bigeye" chemical bomb. Boren voted for an

House, Senate Iran-Contra Investigators ...

Lee H. Hamilton, D-Ind.
House Chairman

Dante B. Fascell, D-Fla.
Vice Chairman

Dick Cheney, Wyo.
Ranking Republican

House Committee Members

Les Aspin
D-Wis.

Edward P. Boland
D-Mass.

Jack Brooks
D-Texas

William S. Broomfield
R-Mich.

Jim Courter
R-N.J.

Michael DeWine
R-Ohio

Thomas S. Foley
D-Wash.

Henry J. Hyde
R-Ill.

Ed Jenkins
D-Ga.

Bill McCollum
R-Fla.

Peter W. Rodino, Jr.
D-N.J.

Louis Stokes
D-Ohio

amendment to delete funds for the production of the chemical bomb, but he switched his position after supporters told him the amendment could delay production longer than he wanted.

A former governor, Boren was one of two Rhodes scholars to sit on the select panel.

Howell Heflin, Ala.

Age 65. Elected 1978. Committees: Judiciary; Agriculture, Nutrition and Forestry; Select Ethics (chairman).

For Heflin, a seat on the select committee had a familar feel to it. Unlike some of the other business of legislating, investigating the Iran arms deal was like prac-

... A Roundup of the Membership Roster

Daniel K. Inouye, D-Hawaii
Senate Chairman

Warren B. Rudman
R-N.H., Vice Chairman

Senate
Committee
Members

David L. Boren
D-Okla.

William S. Cohen
R-Maine

Orrin G. Hatch
R-Utah

Howell Heflin
D-Ala.

James A. McClure
R-Idaho

George J. Mitchell
D-Maine

Sam Nunn
D-Ga.

Paul S. Sarbanes
D-Md.

Paul S. Trible, Jr.
R-Va.

ticing law, and Heflin, a former chief justice of the Alabama Supreme Court, never really left that profession.

Colleagues still called him "Judge," and despite eight years in Washington, he did not seem comfortable with life in the Senate. Heflin liked to ruminate over issues and did not like having to become an instant expert.

A former trial lawyer, Heflin was one of the chamber's best storytellers—a gift known mostly to colleagues who listened to him in private, though he occasionally spun out a yarn to make a point in committee or on the floor.

On the generally polarized Judiciary panel, Heflin and fellow conservative Democrat Dennis DeConcini, Ariz., often held the swing votes. Heflin cast a decisive and politically difficult vote in June 1986, opposing the nomination of Alabama U.S. attorney Jefferson B. Sessions III for a federal judgeship. He cited allegations that Sessions was insensitive on racial issues.

George J. Mitchell, Maine

Age 53. Appointed 1980; elected 1982. Committees: Governmental Affairs, Environment and Public Works, Finance, Veterans' Affairs.

A former federal judge, Mitchell earned a reputation as a thoughtful moderate who weighed the facts before making a decision. His soft-spoken, judicious image appeared strong enough to have overshadowed any partisan taint he received as chairman of the Democratic Senatorial Campaign Committee during 1985-86.

Nevertheless, Mitchell was politically savvy enough to have risen quickly in the Democratic ranks. As chairman of the campaign committee in 1986, Mitchell oversaw the return of Senate control to the Democrats. To show their appreciation, they elected him in November as deputy president pro tempore, a job held only by Hubert H. Humphrey, D-Minn. (1949-64, 1971-78).

Mitchell was named a U.S. attorney in 1977 and became a judge two years later. He was appointed to the Senate in 1980 to succeed Edmund S. Muskie, who became secretary of state.

Sam Nunn, Ga.

Age 48. Elected 1972. Committees: Armed Services (chairman), Select Intelligence, Governmental Affairs, Small Business.

Nunn long had been known as Capitol Hill's most prestigious voice on defense, with a reputation for mastering complex issues. He sharply criticized President Jimmy Carter's defense budget as too stingy. But Nunn was equally critical of Reagan's program, arguing that Reagan was undermining defense over the long run by seeking more rapid spending increases than the traffic would bear.

On the Governmental Affairs Permanent Subcommittee on Investigations, he also probed organized crime, labor racketeering, and government control of secret information.

A voracious reader who recruited highly qualified aides, Nunn also was known as a formidably effective interrogator in committee hearings. On most politically charged security issues, he was a moderate hawk. He supported aid to the Nicaraguan contras. After the covert arms sales to Iran became public in November 1986, he warned that U.S. interests could suffer if presidential leadership were crippled by the controversy.

Some critics said Nunn was too painstaking in reaching his positions. And some liberals found him too conservative. But after the 1984 election, Nunn assumed a higher national profile, helping to form the Democratic Leadership Council with the aim of pulling the party toward the political center.

Nunn's name had been mentioned in the 1988 presidential sweepstakes, but he announced in 1987 that he would not be a candidate.

Paul S. Sarbanes, Md.

Age 53. Elected 1976. Committees: Foreign Relations;

Banking, Housing and Urban Affairs; Joint Economic (chairman).

Throughout six years in the House and ten in the Senate, Sarbanes often utilized his skills as a lawyer to play key roles in legally oriented matters.

As a member of the House Judiciary Committee that debated impeachment charges against President Nixon, Sarbanes had the task of arguing for an obstruction-of-justice article, perhaps the most important raised against Nixon. The panel approved the article, 27-11.

During President Carter's administration, Sarbanes was the Senate floor manager for ratification of the controversial Panama Canal treaties.

And in September 1986, Sarbanes was the vice chairman of a special twelve-member Senate panel that heard testimony and then reported to the Senate on the recommended impeachment of federal Judge Harry E. Claiborne of Nevada, who had been imprisoned after his conviction on charges of filing false income tax returns.

The Rhodes scholar son of Greek immigrant parents, Sarbanes was known for his deliberative style. On Foreign Relations, he sharply criticized Reagan's foreign policy and opposed military aid to the contras.

Senate Republicans

Warren B. Rudman, N.H., Vice Chairman

Age 56. Elected 1980. Committees: Appropriations, Budget, Governmental Affairs, Small Business, Select Ethics.

Rudman brought to the committee six years of experience as attorney general of New Hampshire, from 1970 to 1976. He reorganized that appointive office, which had been relatively inactive, and created a consumer protection division.

He quickly won a reputation as one of the most talented legislators of the Senate class of 1980—a group that included many unimpressive members—and a very effective senator by any measure.

The most frequently heard complaint about Rudman on Capitol Hill was that, even by the Senate's standards, he conveyed a well-developed sense of his own importance. But it was widely conceded that he had a striking list of legislative achievements.

One of his priorities was defense of the Legal Services Corporation (LSC), a perennial target of Reagan administration budget cuts. The Appropriations Subcommittee on Commerce, Justice, State and the Judiciary, which funds the agency, was chaired by Paul Laxalt, R-Nev., from 1983 to 1985, but Laxalt left much of the work of running the panel to Rudman. In 1986, Rudman took the chairman's title as well. He protected LSC against conservatives' complaints that agency officials were improperly engaged in political activity.

Rudman also was an unofficial leader of the Appropriations Subcommittee on Defense between 1981 and 1984. Chairman Ted Stevens, R-Alaska, who was majority whip and who had a long commute to visit his constituents, relied heavily on Rudman to develop issues in hearings and to carry the defense panel's flag on the floor.

Positioned solidly in the GOP mainstream on most issues, Rudman was generally supportive of Reagan's defense buildup, but he became known for his willingness to judge issues independently and his tenacity in following through.

His first major battle came in 1983, when he blocked production of the Viper—an antitank rocket in a throwaway launcher designed as a last-ditch defense for Army troops. Rudman persuaded his colleagues to stop production of the rocket, on the strength of tests showing that its warhead was too puny to stop Soviet tanks and data showing that it cost far more than comparable foreign weapons.

The Army countered with the kind of delaying tactics that frequently bamboozled congressional critics. But Rudman hung tough and the Viper was canceled, one of the few major weapons in recent decades to be killed off so late in its production cycle.

Early in 1985, he proposed a reduction of 10 percent (nearly 180,000 people) in Pentagon support personnel, which he claimed would save nearly $13 billion over three years with no adverse impact on U.S. combat power. He lost that fight, though Congress approved only a fraction of the increase Reagan requested for personnel costs in the fiscal 1986 budget.

By the end of 1985, Rudman was pursuing an even more sweeping attack on the deficit: the deficit-reduction act, which he cosponsored with Phil Gramm, R-Texas, and Ernest F. Hollings, D-S.C., establishing declining deficit targets over a five-year period enforced by a novel procedure for automatic, across-the-board reductions in federal spending.

The Gramm-Rudman act made the New Hampshire legislator's name a household word, and Rudman played a pivotal role in developing and refining the measure. When constitutional doubts were raised during debates about the requirement for automatic reductions, Rudman took the lead in forging a compromise that added the General Accounting Office (GAO) to the scheme and provided a fallback procedure for instituting the cuts if the automatic device were struck down by courts.

The Supreme Court in July 1986 found the automatic scheme unconstitutional because the GAO's power of review exceeded constitutional limits. Rudman, Gramm, and Hollings twice persuaded the Senate to pass a new version of the automatic procedure, but House leaders balked at the enhanced role envisioned for the Office of Management and Budget, and the Gramm-Rudman fix went no further. Nevertheless, Gramm-Rudman was not without impact. Its deficit targets narrowed debate, establishing for the first time a clear measure of success or failure on the deficit. It also provided important procedural checks that came into play on spending bills.

William S. Cohen, Maine

Age 46. Elected 1978. Committees: Armed Services, Select Intelligence, Governmental Affairs, Special Aging.

Telegenic and laid-back, Cohen projected an introspection and bemused detachment from the political rough-and-tumble that belied his willingness to go to the mat with his opponents.

He gained national prominence in 1974 as a freshman on the House Judiciary Committee during impeachment proceedings against President Nixon. Cohen's careful questioning of witnesses won him attention even before he became one of six committee Republicans who voted for impeachment.

Among Senate Republicans, his position typically was somewhat left of center, though he backed contra aid.

As chairman of the Governmental Affairs Subcommittee on Oversight of Government Management, he successfully challenged Reagan's plan for a wholesale purge of the Social Security disability rolls. In 1984, Congress cleared Cohen's bill to make it more difficult for the government to take away disability benefits.

In the national security area, he was a leading critic of two of Reagan's most cherished programs, the MX missile and the strategic defense initiative (SDI). In 1983, Cohen, Nunn, and other centrists threatened to kill MX production unless Reagan shifted his nuclear weapons planning and his arms control proposals to the Soviets. The changes were needed, the group said, to make the nuclear balance more stable.

Cohen successfully urged Reagan to propose to the Russians a "build-down" of nuclear missiles: a formula under which both countries could modernize their arsenals while cutting them back. Cohen's critics claimed he was using build-down to hide his opposition to a nuclear weapons freeze, a proposal popular in Maine.

In 1986, Cohen joined Armed Services Democrats in dismissing Reagan's vision of SDI as a nationwide shield against nuclear missiles.

Orrin G. Hatch, Utah

Age 52. Elected 1976. Committees: Judiciary, Select Intelligence, Labor and Human Resources.

Hatch was considered one of the Senate's most articulate conservatives and one of its staunchest supporters of Reagan.

Under GOP leadership, he chaired the Labor Committee and the Judiciary Subcommittee on the Constitution. In the latter post, he made an impact because of his strong interest in constitutional and civil rights law.

A former trial lawyer, Hatch enjoyed legal debates. He served on the special committee considering the impeachment of U.S. District Judge Harry E. Claiborne and was one of three senators who voted against conviction on any grounds. Hatch cited allegations of government abuse in assembling the case against Claiborne.

When Hatch was first elected, he was seen as an archconservative. But his image changed—in part because of the arrival of more conservative colleagues and in part because Hatch demonstrated a preference for working through compromise and consensus.

James A. McClure, Idaho

Age 62. Elected 1972. Committees: Appropriations, Energy and Natural Resources, Rules and Administration.

One of the most conservative members of the Senate, McClure was another consistent supporter of Reagan on defense and foreign policy.

He was the first of five candidates defeated for majority leader when Senate Republicans picked their leaders at the outset of the Ninety-ninth Congress. At the time, some said they feared his intense loyalty to Reagan could create problems for more independent-minded senators in the 1986 elections.

McClure focused much of his legislative attention on energy and the environment. He had chaired the Energy Committee and the Appropriations subcommittee with jurisdiction over the Interior Department.

McClure began his political career as a county prosecuting attorney, later serving as a city attorney and in the Idaho Senate. He served in the U.S. House from 1967 to 1973.

Paul S. Trible, Jr., Va.

Age 40. Elected 1982. Committees: Foreign Relations; Commerce, Science and Transportation; Governmental Affairs.

The most junior member of the Senate select panel, Trible was a loyal Reagan supporter.

He co-chaired Reagan's 1980 campaign in Virginia, and used a seat on Foreign Relations to back Reagan's foreign policy initiatives.

In one break with the White House, however, Trible voted in May 1986 against the sale of arms to Saudi Arabia and stood fast a few weeks later when the Senate sustained Reagan's veto of a resolution blocking the sale.

Like several others on the Senate select panel, Trible had experience as a prosecutor. His post as prosecuting lawyer in Essex County led to election to the House in 1976. His contacts from the Reagan presidential campaign helped him win his Senate seat.

In a committee that included members with Watergate probe experience, Trible had one link of his own: He worked at the Justice Department on litigation involving the secret Nixon tapes.

House Democrats

Lee H. Hamilton, Ind., Chairman

Age 55. Elected 1964. Committees: Foreign Affairs; Science, Space and Technology; Joint Economic.

In spite of his many official and unofficial leadership roles over the years, Hamilton avoided the spotlight, especially when television cameras were around. During his first two decades in Congress, Hamilton appeared rarely on nationally televised news shows and generally avoided reporters.

Early in December 1986, when the rumor mill produced his name as the logical choice to head the House select committee, some Democrats complained that Hamilton would yield center stage to the more glamorous and publicity-conscious Senate committee. Apparently heeding that criticism, Hamilton suddenly began accepting invitations for network news and talk shows, and he stepped up his criticism of the White House for refusing to cooperate with congressional investigations.

There never was much doubt that Hamilton would head the House committee, because his qualifications for the post were almost unique.

He had chaired the Foreign Affairs Subcommittee on Europe and the Middle East for a decade, developing a reputation for fairness and competence in handling some of the most sensitive foreign policy issues facing Congress. In 1985 and 1986, he also headed the Intelligence Committee, again winning praise from Republicans and Democrats alike in spite of his strong opposition to President Reagan on some key issues.

Hamilton took center stage in the House once before: in late 1983 and early 1984, when political pressure was

building in Congress to force Reagan to remove 1,200 U.S. Marines from their hazardous "peacekeeping" duties in Lebanon. At the request of Speaker Thomas P. O'Neill, Jr., D-Mass., Hamilton led House Democrats in drafting a resolution calling for the "prompt and orderly withdrawal" of the Marines. Just as some Democrats were having second thoughts, however, Reagan preempted congressional action by ordering the Marines out of Lebanon.

As chairman of the Middle East subcommittee, Hamilton occupied uncomfortable ground on the sensitive question of U.S. relations with Israel. Like nearly all other American politicians, Hamilton was pro-Israel. But unlike most other members of the committee, he occasionally questioned the closeness of the relationship between the United States and Israel and voiced support for the idea of "balance" in U.S. policy toward Israel and its Arab neighbors.

Among his colleagues in Congress, Hamilton was respected primarily for his thoughtful, no-nonsense approach to issues. Hamilton rarely raised his voice, but other members listened when he did.

Hamilton was particularly outspoken in opposing aid to the Nicaraguan contras, saying that the administration had not developed a rational strategy for ousting the regime in Managua.

He also attempted unsuccessfully in 1986 to reverse a new Reagan policy of aiding the UNITA guerrillas in Angola. His opposition to the Angola involvement was sparked as much by procedural as by policy issues; along with other Democrats on the Intelligence Committee, Hamilton was angered that Reagan decided to provide the aid over their opposition.

Although acknowledging that some covert CIA operations were necessary, Hamilton said that it was "virtually impossible" for the United States to keep secret its involvement in large-scale paramilitary actions overseas.

Hamilton was an untiring advocate of congressional involvement in foreign-policy making, saying that one lesson of the Vietnam War was that presidents must get public and legislative support before embarking on foreign adventures. He was among the first to call any president to account for failing to consult with Congress before making major foreign policy decisions, and he was an aggressive seeker of details about what administration officials were doing.

To the chagrin of reporters, Hamilton also was one of the most determined protectors of official secrets on Capitol Hill. In all of his leadership positions—and especially as Intelligence chairman—he made a point of refusing to divulge classified information, even when other members appeared willing to do so.

Dante B. Fascell, Fla., Vice Chairman

Age 69. Elected 1954. Committees: Foreign Affairs (chairman), Select Narcotics Abuse and Control.

Fascell wanted very much to be chairman of the select committee, if only to assert the primacy of his own panel on foreign policy. Even after incoming Speaker Jim Wright, D-Texas, announced plans for the special panel on December 4, Fascell proceeded with previously scheduled Foreign Affairs hearings. Televised live by the networks, the hearings thrust Fascell into the limelight and provided the public's first direct look at the two central characters in the Iran-contra affair: Vice Adm. John M. Poindexter and Lt. Col. Oliver L. North.

Fascell's failure to get the special committee chairmanship marked a rare setback; blunt and tenacious, he was widely regarded as one of the most accomplished legislators and skilled politicians in the House. Other members said he had few equals in his ability to negotiate deals and collect votes to get legislation passed. That ability was especially important in 1985, when Fascell was responsible for easing a foreign aid authorization bill through the House, which had not passed one in four years.

Some liberals complained about Fascell's support of the Reagan administration on Central America; in the early 1980s, he backed Reagan's requests for military aid to El Salvador, and he was one of the few top Democrats in the House to support U.S. aid to the Nicaraguan rebels. In at least one case—during House action on El Salvador aid in 1985—liberals accused Fascell of double-crossing them by lobbying actively on behalf of the White House.

Fascell acknowledged that his position on Central America reflected the leanings of his district, which was heavily populated by conservative Cuban exiles.

Edward P. Boland, Mass.

Age 75. Elected 1952. Committee: Appropriations.

As chairman of the House Intelligence Committee from 1977 to 1984, Boland was best-known for his efforts to curb aid to the Nicaraguan rebels. But he did so only when it became clear that U.S. involvement in the war was growing despite congressional reservations.

The Boland amendment of 1982 forbade the CIA from arming the contras. Boland offered the ban to head off an effort by some Democrats to cut off all U.S. aid. After it became apparent in 1983 that the administration was still bent on helping overthrow the Nicaraguan government, Boland joined those trying to stop funding of the contras. But after negotiations with the Senate, a $24 million cap was set instead. In 1984, however, after news of the CIA's role in the mining of Nicaragua's harbors, all aid officially was cut off.

Boland seemed uncomfortable in his high-profile role as Reagan critic. Not only did he shun publicity, but debate over the volatile issue disrupted the nonpartisan tone he tried to set for the panel. Nevertheless, Boland commanded respect from Democrats and Republicans. As one of the few congressmen to receive daily intelligence reports for six years, he was one of the best-informed on the select panel.

Les Aspin, Wis.

Age 48. Elected 1970. Committee: Armed Services (chairman).

Like a handful of other members who concentrated on national security, Aspin was a defense intellectual. But he also was an aficionado of congressional politics, who plainly relished the broker's role. In the 1970s, he acquired the reputation of "liberal Pentagon critic" with his barrage of imaginative press releases attacking Pentagon foibles.

But by the time Reagan took office, Aspin differed with most liberals over many issues, notably the MX missile and aid to the contras, both of which Aspin supported. In part, these were disagreements over the merits. But they also reflected Aspin's belief that the Democratic Party had to shed a destructive image of reflexive opposition to all controversial weapons and to all uses of force.

Aspin clashed with liberals in 1983 when he organized key House Democrats in backing MX in return for changes in Reagan's nuclear arms plans and negotiating stance with the Soviets. Over the next two years, Democratic leaders adopted opposition to MX as a party position. But Aspin continued to support the missile.

In 1985, House Democrats elected Aspin to replace Melvin Price, Ill., as Armed Services chairman. Some liberals who backed him later said he had promised to oppose MX, a claim Aspin denied. In the summer of 1986, after Aspin voted to arm the contras, liberals vowed to oust him. Nonetheless, Aspin retained the chairmanship.

Jack Brooks, Texas

Age 64. Elected 1952. Committees: Government Operations (chairman), Judiciary.

Crusty and cantankerous were two words commonly used to describe Brooks. On Government Operations, he dueled with the Reagan administration. He challenged the Office of Management and Budget as overzealous in regulatory affairs and took on the administration over its efforts to boost polygraph tests of federal workers. He was also among the House members who played a role in mounting a legal challenge before the Supreme Court to the Gramm-Rudman-Hollings budget-balancing law.

Brooks, a lawyer, was a member of the Judiciary Committee during its impeachment proceedings against President Nixon. "He didn't even need to hear the evidence. He was ready to impeach," a Brooks aide said later.

Brooks opposed contra aid and many other Reagan initiatives.

Thomas S. Foley, Wash.

Age 57. Elected 1964. House majority leader. Committee: Budget.

Considered the epitome of the "nonpartisan" politician, Hill leaders sought Foley for the select panels in the hope of avoiding witch-hunt charges.

He was widely respected for his intelligence, ability to argue both sides of an issue, and skills as a negotiator. A former assistant state attorney general, he said he grew up wanting to be a judge. Although he never achieved that goal, he often took a judicial stance in House politics. He played a key role in recrafting the Gramm-Rudman-Hollings budget bill to make it more acceptable to House Democrats, although he was never an enthusiast for the legislation.

Foley also was active in the debate over aiding the contras. In 1984, he sponsored a floor amendment forbidding the use of U.S. troops in El Salvador or Nicaragua without Hill approval or unless U.S. national security was threatened. While others were voicing dismay, Foley's initial reaction to revelations about the Iran-contra arms link was to express concern the scandal might cripple another presidency.

Foley served as majority whip from 1981 to 1987.

Ed Jenkins, Ga.

Age 54. Elected 1976. Committees: Budget, Ways and Means.

Jenkins, with neither Foreign Affairs nor Intelligence committee experience, was a surprise choice for the select panel. But as a Southern moderate-conservative who supported contra aid, he was expected to give panel Democrats some regional and philosophical balance.

During 1986, he made his mark in leading an almost successful House attempt to override Reagan's veto of a bill sharply restricting textile imports.

More importantly, Jenkins cultivated respect as an articulate spokesman for Southern conservatives. He won the esteem of Ways and Means chairman Dan Rostenkowski, D-Ill., in 1981 when he tried to convince other Southerners to oppose President Reagan's tax cuts and helped to fashion a Democratic alternative. In 1984, he was named to the "Speaker's Cabinet" set up to improve relations between House leaders and Democratic members.

A former federal prosecutor, Jenkins was inclined to do his House politicking behind the scenes.

Peter W. Rodino, Jr., N.J.

Age 77. Elected 1948. Committees: Judiciary (chairman), Select Narcotics Abuse and Control.

The appointment of Rodino to the Iran-contra committee marked the third time he had been involved in a sensitive intergovernmental dispute.

His first—and the one that put him in the history books—was his stewardship of the Judiciary panel in 1974 when it was considering articles of impeachment against President Nixon. Rodino's sober, deliberate style proved to be the right touch for handling the wrenching national crisis.

In 1986, Rodino presided over another impeachment proceeding—one which led to the removal from office of imprisoned federal Judge Harry E. Claiborne of Las Vegas.

Rodino's job at Judiciary changed considerably after Reagan was elected. Where the chairman had used the panel to push liberal ideas, he turned it into a graveyard for New Right initiatives like constitutional amendments to ban abortion, allow public school prayer, and require a balanced federal budget.

But Rodino's inaction backfired at times when he misread his opponents' strength. Balanced budget advocates forced a floor vote in 1982, and the proposed amendment was defeated only after deft maneuvering by House leaders. In 1984, Republicans pushed a crime bill through, and in 1986, proponents of a bill to ease gun laws muscled their way past Rodino.

Louis Stokes, Ohio

Age 61. Elected 1968. Committees: Appropriations, Select Intelligence (chairman).

Stokes was no stranger to sensitive congressional inquiries. As chairman of the ethics committee during the Ninety-seventh and Ninety-eighth Congresses, he presided over the investigations of several House members, among them Gerry E. Studds, D-Mass.; Dan Crane, R-Ill.; and George V. Hansen, R-Idaho.

His committee also looked into charges that former representative Geraldine A. Ferraro, D-N.Y., a 1984 vice presidential candidate, had violated campaign disclosure laws by omitting some of her husband's financial dealings.

He was a consistent opponent of Reagan's foreign policies in Central America and elsewhere. In domestic areas, he became a chief critic of the administration's spending priorities, often seeking to add spending in areas targeted for cuts.

A lawyer, Stokes held no political office prior to his election.

House Republicans

Dick Cheney, Wyo., Ranking Republican

Age 45. Elected 1978. Committees: Interior and Insular Affairs, Select Intelligence. Chairman, GOP Policy Committee.

Although he brought no legal background to the select committee, Cheney had considerable administrative experience and insight into the workings of the White House.

The Wyomingite was White House chief of staff under President Ford and said when the Iran-contra arms dealings came to light, that in a well-run office, such a transaction would not have been carried out without the knowledge of those in charge. However, he expressed confidence early on that when all the facts were known, the president would come out clean.

While generally a Reagan loyalist, Cheney had been critical of White House operations under Chief of Staff Donald T. Regan.

Cheney was a leader of the 1985 revolt by House Republicans against Reagan's tax-overhaul initiative, presumably because of its adverse impact on business. But the rebellion also was a thinly veiled protest against administration failure to consult and cajole House Republicans on important bills. At the time, Cheney charged that the administration had "cut out Republicans in the House and on the Ways and Means Committee and tried to jam [the bill] through and it didn't work." Only after President Reagan came to Capitol Hill to lobby Republican members personally to vote for the legislation was the package approved. Cheney led the tax fight as head of the Republican Policy Committee, a post he assumed in 1981.

While Cheney amassed a solid right-wing, conservative voting record, he gave a more moderate impression to those who talked with him.

He was thoughtful and willing to listen to both sides of an argument. In addition, Cheney had a perspective on congressional politics that was broader than most.

As a political science graduate student, he came to Washington in the late 1960s as a congressional fellow to work in the office of Rep. William A. Steiger, R-Wis. (1967-78).

He then worked for Donald H. Rumsfeld at the Office of Economic Opportunity during the Nixon administration and later went with Rumsfeld to the White House. When Rumsfeld became secretary of defense in 1975, Cheney took over the job of chief of staff.

A student of Washington politics, Cheney also became an experienced user of the news media to get his message across.

William S. Broomfield, Mich.

Age 64. Elected 1956. Committees: Foreign Affairs, Small Business.

Although a staunch supporter of President Reagan, Broomfield was more at home with traditional Midwest Republicanism than more strident ideological conservatism. Along with a dwindling number of senior Republicans, Broomfield was identified first as a House member, second as a Republican, and third as a conservative.

The Iran-contra affair caused Broomfield great anguish. At first, he expressed feelings of anger and betrayal: anger that the administration had sidestepped Congress and betrayal that Reagan had carried out a secret foreign policy directly contradicting his public one on Iran. He also said that CIA director William J. Casey's December 10, 1986, closed-door testimony before the Foreign Affairs Committee provided evidence of "serious errors of judgment by senior CIA officials."

As ranking Republican on Foreign Affairs, Broomfield carried Reagan's water on issues ranging from arms control to Central America. In many cases, Broomfield's efforts failed in the liberal-dominated committee but succeeded on the floor, where Republicans and conservative Democrats produced a majority. In 1984, for example, Reagan's request for major increases in aid to El Salvador was rejected in the committee but narrowly approved by the full House.

Jim Courter, N.J.

Age 45. Elected 1978. Committees: Armed Services, Select Aging.

A handsome and articulate member of the GOP mainstream, Courter emerged as one of the most active Republicans on House Armed Services. However, he blended a hard line on defense and foreign policy with a highly critical stance toward the way the Pentagon did business.

He was a Reagan loyalist on most controversial issues, supporting contra military aid, for example. But he also was an active member—and for a period a co-chairman—of the Military Reform Caucus, a bipartisan group of senators and House members who suspected that the Pentagon often subordinated military effectiveness to bureaucratic interests.

Many of the caucus members were liberals who would attack the Pentagon in any case. But Courter's critiques were driven partly by fear that public perception of Pentagon mismanagement was undermining support for Reagan's military buildup.

To counter instances of waste and mismanagement, Courter pushed various measures intended to subject new weapons to more realistic tests and to increase the amount of competition in contracting.

Though he was more conservative than many leading New Jersey Republicans, Courter had good relations with party leaders, notably Gov. Thomas H. Kean. He was regarded as a possible candidate in 1988 for the Senate seat held by Frank R. Lautenberg, D-N.J.

Michael DeWine, Ohio

Age 40. Elected 1982. Committees: Judiciary, Foreign Affairs.

DeWine brought four years of prosecutorial experience to the House select committee. Prior to coming to Congress in 1983 and before serving a term in the Ohio Senate, he was the prosecuting attorney in Greene County, Ohio.

In Congress, Dewine was a member of the Judiciary Committee and was active on criminal law issues. He was a vigorous supporter of capital punishment.

In 1986, DeWine was one of nine House "managers,"

or prosecutors, who helped win a conviction at the impeachment trial of U.S. District Judge Claiborne of Las Vegas.

DeWine gained increasing visibility on the Foreign Affairs panel. After closed hearings on the Iran arms deal, DeWine castigated Stephen J. Solarz, D-N.Y., for asserting that he believed President Reagan knew that funds from the sales were diverted to Nicaraguan contras. DeWine's blast brought him coverage on all three networks.

Henry J. Hyde, Ill.

Age 62. Elected 1974. Committees: Foreign Affairs, Select Intelligence, Judiciary.

In the first few years of his House career, Hyde was known as one of the principal opponents of legalized abortion. Beginning in 1981, however, Hyde's association with the antiabortion movement became much more tenuous. He continued to oppose abortion but turned his attention to foreign affairs.

In this area, Hyde became one of the administration's chief defenders. His favorite admonition to colleagues was that "you can't have 535 secretaries of state."

That was quintessential Hyde, who was considered to have one of the quickest wits in the House and to be one of its best off-the-cuff debaters.

Despite his interest in Foreign Affairs, Hyde remained an important player at Judiciary, and in 1982, he had a critical role in developing legislation to renew and revise the landmark 1965 Voting Rights Act. Hyde originally believed the law had achieved its purpose of opening the ballot box to minorities. But during subcommittee hearings in 1981, he became convinced that more needed to be done, and that was a turning point. From then on, the debate was not whether the voting rights law needed to be renewed, but rather what the new legislation would look like.

Bill McCollum, Fla.

Age 42. Elected 1980. Committees: Judiciary; Banking, Finance and Urban Affairs.

Sober and hard-working, McCollum devoted much of his first term in the Senate to Judiciary Committee matters. He was a lawyer by training, and on a panel of other lawyers he could easily hold his own. McCollum served on the Subcommittee on Immigration, Refugees and International Law, and he was an important participant in the six-year fight to revise the immigration laws.

McCollum approached the issue from a conservative perspective and was a leading opponent of a provision to grant legal status to millions of illegal aliens who could prove they had been in the United States for a period of time. He said the provision rewarded lawbreakers and was a slap in the face to people who had waited for years to enter the United States legally.

In a related immigration matter, McCollum successfully sponsored a 1986 bill to crack down on the practice of sham marriages to gain entry into the United States.

Committee Members' Role in Probe

After three months of public hearings into the Iran-contra affair, many of the twenty-six members of the House and Senate select committees had become more widely known because of constant television exposure and other forms of media attention.

The eleven senators and fifteen House members also carved out a myriad of roles for themselves during the course of their investigation.

A glimpse at each member's role in the investigations could provide an indication of what to expect in the final report.

Senate Committee

Daniel K. Inouye, D-Hawaii, chairman. A veteran of the Senate Watergate Committee investigation in 1973-74, Inouye sprinkled numerous references to the Nixon-era scandal throughout the Iran-contra hearings while stopping short of directly comparing the two episodes. He used words like "chilling" and "mind-boggling" to describe some of the Iran-contra testimony. But Inouye was frustrated that the whole Iran-contra story might never come out because of conflicts among key witnesses that apparently could not be resolved.

For the most part, Inouye was credited by his colleagues on the Senate committee with leading an effective and fair investigation. In particular, he enjoyed a close working relationship with Warren B. Rudman, the Republican vice chairman. Almost without exception, the two appeared together when making comments to the media and rarely disagreed publicly.

Normally even-tempered, Inouye found himself in a glaring contest with Brendan V. Sullivan, Jr., the aggressive attorney representing Lt. Col. Oliver L. North. Sullivan ripped into the chairman when Inouye, speaking at the end of North's testimony about the military's honor code, made a reference to the Nuremberg war-crimes trials. But Inouye said outside the hearing room that Sullivan was only carrying out his responsibilities as a good defense lawyer.

Warren B. Rudman, R-N.H., vice chairman. The acid-tongued Rudman was scored in some home-state editorials for his seeming attacks on the administration's actions in the Iran-contra affair. But his rhetoric was probably harsher than his instincts, and he was not likely to endorse any kind of strong committee denunciation of President Reagan himself.

He hammered away at North's efforts to raise money for the Nicaraguan contras among rich U.S. conservatives, describing a "one-two punch" that combined pitches by North and fund-raiser Carl R. "Spitz" Channell.

With pro-North telegrams pouring in as the colonel was ending his dramatic testimony, Rudman jumped to defend Inouye against those who found fault with the chairman's conduct. Rudman angrily denounced letter-writers who used ethnic slurs in criticizing Inouye, a decorated veteran who lost an arm in World War II.

Democrats

David L. Boren, of Oklahoma. The chairman of the Senate Intelligence Committee, Boren concentrated on the CIA's role in the Iran-contra affair. A centrist, he made numerous speeches about the need to put aside partisan differences in order to agree on an "American foreign policy." At one point, Boren took a jab at the committee counsels, saying members could ask better questions. But Boren himself relied more on speechmaking than questioning during his time to interrogate witnesses. Boren indicated he planned to conduct more extensive oversight hearings into CIA activities.

Howell Heflin, of Alabama. Some observers expected the former chief justice of the Alabama Supreme Court to emerge as the Iran-contra hearings' equivalent of Watergate's Sam Ervin. Instead, Heflin remained a backbencher, often asking vague and clumsily worded questions. Speaking in a heavy drawl, he once quipped that an interpreter was needed to help him communicate with witness Adolfo Calero, a contra leader who spoke English with a thick Spanish accent. Heflin sometimes asked detailed questions about various matters, such as the U.S. effort to solicit $10 million for the contras from the oil-rich nation of Brunei.

George J. Mitchell, of Maine. He used his skills as a former prosecutor and federal judge in becoming one of the Senate committee's most effective questioners. When most committee members heaped praise on North during his six days of testimony in July, Mitchell also lauded North's "deep devotion" to the nation. But he added that others who disagreed with North were no less patriotic and could still love "God and . . . country."

Sam Nunn, of Georgia. The one committee member talked about as a 1988 presidential candidate, Nunn spent much of his time analyzing the origins of Reagan's Iran arms policy. A highly respected expert on defense with a reputation for careful study of issues and attention to detail, Nunn was skeptical of the reliance by national security adviser John M. Poindexter on arguably inaccurate and self-serving intelligence information to justify the Iran initiative. In questioning Poindexter, he also underscored a series of contradictions among key players in the affair.

Paul S. Sarbanes, of Maryland. A methodical and detailed questioner, the Maryland liberal focused much of his attention on a proposal to generate funds for covert activities through a complex scheme involving the transfer of high-technology items and weapons among the United States, Israel, and China. The plan never got anywhere, and Secretary of State George P. Shultz dismissed the idea as "nutty." Sarbanes touched off a hot exchange when he accused Richard W. Beckler, lawyer for Poindexter, of coaching his client at the witness table.

Republicans

William S. Cohen, of Maine. At the outset of the hearings, he figured to be Reagan's sharpest critic among Republicans on the Senate panel. Cohen used his literary and poetic skills in delivering a number of eloquent speeches illustrating his view of what went wrong in the Iran-contra affair. But he backed away from direct blasts at the president, saying the public did not want Reagan "pilloried or politically paralyzed for being human."

Orrin G. Hatch, of Utah. Reagan's most vocal defender on the Senate committee, he spent much of his time criticizing the scope and duration of the congressional investigation. In a challenge to independent counsel Lawrence E. Walsh, he said there would be "one lot of hell raised" if North were prosecuted for his role in the Iran-contra affair. During his questioning time, Hatch often answered his own rapid-fire queries before the witness had time to jump in.

James A. McClure, of Idaho. Virtually alone among committee members, he repeatedly tried to cast Israel as the guiding force behind the ill-fated policy of selling U.S. weapons to Iran in exchange for American hostages. By pointing out Israel's different objectives in promoting U.S.-Iranian relations, he tried to take the heat off White House officials, who, McClure suggested, were merely responding favorably to Israeli overtures. Other members shied away from the politically sensitive issue.

Paul S. Trible, Jr., of Virginia. A cautious conservative who in 1987 announced his retirement from the Senate the next year, Trible represented a state where support for Reagan was deep. Trible skirted direct criticism of the president and his aides. Instead, the Virginian focused on the private business operation run by retired major general Richard V. Secord and his partner Albert Hakim. Trible lashed out at "profiteering" by the Secord-Hakim "enterprise" and was likely to try to pound away at that theme in the committees' final report.

House Committee

Lee H. Hamilton, D-Ind., chairman. Although a sharp critic of many Reagan policies, Hamilton tried to use his chairmanship primarily to promote unity and bipartisanship. GOP members of his panel gave him high marks for fairness on procedural points. But Republicans complained about the harsh tone of some of the statements he made about the Iran-contra affair, saying he was trying to make it appear he spoke for the committee. While asking few questions of witnesses, he delivered lengthy summaries following testimony by some of the key Iran-contra players: former national security adviser Robert C. McFarlane, Assistant Secretary of State Elliott Abrams, North, and Poindexter. These statements stressed that the administration had misled Congress and abused the normal foreign policy processes. He told North: "Democracy has its frustrations. You've experienced some of them. But we, you and I, know of no better system of government; and when that democratic process is subverted, we risk all that we cherish."

His most difficult moments came during the five days of testimony by Poindexter, when he overruled repeated objections by Poindexter's attorney, Beckler. Hamilton succeeded in doing so without inflaming an already tense atmosphere.

Dante B. Fascell, D-Fla., vice chairman. As chairman of the House Foreign Affairs Committee, Fascell wanted to head the select committee but was passed over by Speaker Jim Wright, D-Texas. In spite of his disappointment, Fascell was an active member of the committee, focusing on side issues, such as the activities of Channell and Richard R. Miller, the Washington consultants who raised money for the contras and funneled it to Swiss bank accounts controlled by North's private contra-aid network. Fascell headed the committee's investigation into some $400,000 worth of secret, nonbid contracts that Miller's public relations firm got from the State Department to promote the contras in the United States. In response to North's testimony, Fascell asked rhetorically: "Why don't I feel good?"

Dick Cheney, R-Wyo., ranking minority member. A respected House GOP leader, Cheney worked closely with Hamilton to keep the sharply divided panel functioning as smoothly as possible. But he joined his fellow party members in justifying administration actions when possible and playing down possible illegalities or policy misjudgments. He said he was not troubled by North's shredding of documents because all White House officials destroyed sensitive documents. Cheney served as White House chief of staff under President Gerald R. Ford. While insisting that Congress intervened too much in foreign affairs, Cheney said it was "stupid" for officials to lie to Congress because that damaged their credibility and that of the president.

Democrats

Les Aspin, of Wisconsin. Chairman of the Armed Services Committee, Aspin was the missing member of the Iran-contra panel. Saying he was busy with other matters (primarily the defense authorization bill and the Persian Gulf situation), Aspin did not attend any hearings during the first several weeks, and showed up sporadically thereafter. He asked his first questions (of Poindexter) on July 20, focusing on how much money actually was diverted to the contras from the profits of Iran arms sales.

Edward P. Boland, of Massachusetts. As could be expected, he focused on administration efforts to skirt various versions of the Boland amendment, which limited U.S. aid to the contras in fiscal 1983-86. When Secord claimed the law was vague, Boland responded that it was "simple English" and should have been understood by the administration. Otherwise, he made few speeches justifying the law or condemning the White House for skirting it, devoting his question time during hearings to specific factual inquiries. For the most part, he relied on prepared questions but did follow up when he got unexpected answers.

Jack Brooks, of Texas. The most partisan and outspoken Democrat on either committee, Brooks had harsh criticism of several witnesses, telling reporters that Abrams and Poindexter each was a "lying son of a bitch." Brooks also chaired the Government Operations Committee and took a special interest in issues under that panel's jurisdiction; for example, he told Poindexter that he had violated the Presidential Records Act by shredding a "finding" by which Reagan retroactively approved Israeli shipments of U.S.-made arms to Iran in 1985. Brooks voted against granting limited immunity to North for his testimony. A perpetual cigar-smoker, Brooks violated the committees' no-smoking rule, sitting several seats away from his colleagues.

Thomas S. Foley, of Washington. The House majority leader, Foley was unable to attend several of the hearings, but he spent more time on committee business than many of his colleagues thought possible. He proved to be one of the best members of either panel in pursuing extended lines of questioning on complicated matters. Foley effectively demolished the credibility of one witness sponsored by the House Republicans: Bretton Sciaroni, counsel of the Intelligence Oversight Board, who wrote a legal opinion saying that restrictions on U.S. aid to the contras did not apply to the staff of the National Security Council. Foley demonstrated that Sciaroni had virtually no experience in such matters and had failed bar examinations prior to getting hired at the White House.

Ed Jenkins, of Georgia. His cool Southern demeanor provided a calming counterpoint to some hot situations in the hearings. For example, he was the first member to quiz North after three days of tense probing by committee lawyers, and his matter-of-fact questioning was effective in pointing out the pitfalls of North's activities, especially his dealings with Iran. At several points he chastised the administration for soliciting contra aid from Taiwan during a period when Congress was acting on a textile import bill that would have affected that country.

Peter W. Rodino, Jr., of New Jersey. Chairman of the Judiciary Committee, he concentrated on legal issues, such as the Justice Department's "fact-finding" inquiry in November 1986 into the Iran arms sales and the suspension of investigations into the contra-supply activities of Southern Air Transport and into allegations of drug smuggling and gunrunning by contra groups. But Rodino, who thirteen years earlier had led the Judiciary panel's impeachment proceedings against President Richard Nixon, did not ask the consistently sharp questions that would make a mark on the Iran-contra inquiry.

Louis Stokes, of Ohio. One of the few members of either committee willing to do so, Stokes said publicly that he did not believe Poindexter's testimony that he never told Reagan about the diversion of Iran arms-sales profits to the contras. Chairman of the House Intelligence Committee, Stokes asked detailed questions about the administration's control, or lack of it, over covert operations. Stokes joined Senator Mitchell in lecturing North on democracy, saying he had served in a segregated Army unit in World War II but was as willing to fight for his country as North had been.

Republicans

William S. Broomfield, of Michigan. The ranking GOP member on the Foreign Affairs Committee, Broomfield generally limited himself to reading staff-prepared questions and statements defending Reagan. Like his fellow House Republicans, he supported all White House aid to the contras—calling North a "hero" for carrying it out—but condemned the arms sales to Iran. Broomfield headed efforts to curtail the hearings, calling for the immediate granting of limited immunity to North before most others were ready to act.

Jim Courter, of New Jersey. Along with Bill McCollum, Courter was the House Republican most open in attacking the committee leadership, primarily by challenging the questioning of the chief counsels. He pushed for permission for North to give a slide show describing the Soviet threat in Central America.

Michael DeWine, of Ohio. Then forty, DeWine was one of the committee's youngest members. He appeared to have trouble staying awake during hearings, nodding off almost daily. He actively looked into the case of Sam Hall (the brother of Rep. Tony P. Hall, D-Ohio), who claimed to be working for a mysterious group aiding the Nicaraguan rebels. And he accused Secretary of State George P. Shultz of protecting himself instead of supporting the president.

Henry J. Hyde, of Illinois. Aside from Senator Hatch, Hyde was one of the most persistent Reagan defenders on the panels. He said the administration should not have lied to Congress but implied that Congress brought that on itself by failing to keep secrets. Along with Hatch, he led the effort to point to the "positive" side of U.S. dealings with Iran—the attempt to improve diplomatic relations with a strategically important country. Hyde rarely asked questions, preferring to give long speeches consisting of one-liners and quotations. At one point he started to ask Poindexter a question, but said, "I'd rather answer it myself," and proceeded to do so.

Bill McCollum, of Florida. A staunch administration defender and critic of the hearings, McCollum attacked Nields and Liman for asking "biased" questions of witnesses. He made news in June when he said the testimony of Charles J. Cooper, a Justice Department lawyer, about a November 20, 1986, meeting at the White House showed that Casey, Poindexter, and North were engaged in "criminal" behavior and had committed "one of the most treacherous" acts ever against a president. But he did not raise the subject when North and Poindexter testified.

Independent Counsel

Shortly after the disclosure in November 1986 of U.S. arms sales to Iran and diversion of the proceeds to the contras fighting the leftist Sandinista government in Nicaragua, steps were set in motion by Attorney General Edwin Meese III and members of Congress to appoint an independent counsel to investigate the affair.

At the beginning, there was uncertainty about such action; legislation enacted in 1978 and extended in 1982 required that either the attorney general or a majority of either political party on the Senate Judiciary Committee or House Judiciary Committee had to cite evidence of criminal misconduct to trigger appointment of an independent investigator. *(Background, p. 166)*

After Meese publicly discussed results of his inquiry on November 25, members of Congress began to call for the establishment of an independent counsel. On behalf of eleven of twenty-one Democrats on the House Judiciary Committee, Rep. John Conyers, Jr., D-Mich., chairman of the Judiciary Subcommittee on Criminal Justice, wrote the attorney general to request such an appointment. Previously, on October 17, the members had asked Meese to name an independent counsel to probe charges that Reagan administration officials were illegally involved in private efforts to supply the Nicaraguan contras.

Following the November 25 revelation, Conyers said the need for an independent counsel was "even more compelling" in light of the diversion of Iran arms sale proceeds to the contras.

Thereafter, House Judiciary chairman Peter W. Rodino, Jr., D-N.J., and Dan Glickman, D-Kan., chairman of the Administrative Law and Governmental Relations Subcommittee, also wrote a letter to the attorney general suggesting an independent investigation of the entire affair. They did not ask specifically for appointment of an independent counsel, but they told Meese a Justice Department probe alone would "not serve the national interest, the president's interest or the interest of those who may be the subjects of the investigation."

Meese Petitions for Counsel

Responding to mounting public and congressional pressure, Meese announced at a December 2, 1986, news conference that his preliminary investigation of the arms deals had produced evidence of possible criminal violations and that he would seek appointment of an independent counsel. Meese also said he was taking that action to avoid any conflict of interest that could result from a Justice Department investigation of the executive branch.

Once the independent counsel was officially appointed, the Justice Department's role in the matter moved off center stage. Nonetheless, Meese's role continued to be scrutinized; some members of Congress criticized his handling of the early stages of the investigation. They questioned whether the FBI should have been called in sooner to protect documents and whether it was even appropriate for Meese to conduct an investigation, given that he had advised the president that the Iranian arms sales were legal. Meese aggressively defended his actions at the December 2 news conference and again before the House-Senate select committees investigating the Iran-contra affair July 28-29, 1987. *(Meese press conference, p. D-7; testimony, p. C-120)*

On December 4, the attorney general filed a petition for an independent counsel, with a three-judge panel appointed to review the request, determine the scope of the inquiry, and select the counsel. The panel included Appeals Court judges Lewis Morgan from the Eleventh Circuit, Walter Mansfield from the Second Circuit, and George MacKinnon from the D.C. Circuit. All three senior, or semiretired, judges had been appointed to the panel by former chief justice Warren E. Burger.

What to Investigate

Although only the three-judge panel could officially determine the scope of the independent counsel's investigation, there was considerable speculation about what criminal laws might have been violated. And discussions among lawyers reflected the cloudy legal nature of the Iran-contra affair. While many people thought there might have been a criminal violation, they were unable to put their finger on exactly what law or laws had been violated.

For example, allegations (later substantiated) that Lt. Col. Oliver L. North, a National Security Council (NSC) aide, had shredded documents related to the affair could be construed as an obstruction of justice. But criminal law specialists said it was not clear that shredding documents

On December 19, 1986, Lawrence E. Walsh was named independent counsel to investigate the Iran-contra affair.

would be sufficient evidence to justify prosecution on grounds of violating Section 1505 of Title 18 of the U.S. Code, which referred to "obstruction of proceedings before departments, agencies, and committees." The second paragraph of the statute made it a crime to "corruptly" influence, obstruct, or impede or endeavor to influence, obstruct, or impede "the due and proper administration of the law under which any pending proceedings is being had before any department or agency of the United States" or before Congress. Criminal law specialists said it was not clear that documents were shredded during any "proceeding."

Other statutes that could be involved, according to lawyers' initial evaluations included:

●U.S. Code Section 641, which covered anyone who embezzles, steals, purloins, or "knowingly converts to his use or the use of another, or without authority, sells, conveys, or disposes of any record, voucher, money or thing of value of the United States or any department or agency thereof...."

●U.S. Code Section 1001, the basic criminal fraud statute, which made it a crime for anyone who "in any matter within the jurisdiction of the United States knowingly and willfully falsifies, conceals or covers up by any trick, scheme or device a material fact" or "makes any false oral or written statements."

●U.S. Code Section 371, the general federal conspiracy law, which made it illegal for two or more persons to conspire either to commit any offense against the United States or to defraud the United States or any agency. For this statute to be applicable, there had to be evidence of an "offense against the United States," or some fraud against the country.

Independent Counsel's Mandate

In filing his petition before the three-judge panel, Meese said the independent counsel "should have jurisdiction sufficiently broad to investigate and prosecute any and all violations of U.S. federal criminal law" that were "in connection with the sale or shipment of military arms to Iran and the transfer or diversion of funds realized in connection with such sale or shipment." Meese specified that the transactions that should be covered occurred between January 1985 and the end of 1986. When Meese's petition was made public, however, some members of Congress objected that it was too narrow. All eight Democrats on the Senate Judiciary Committee sent a private letter to the panel, arguing for a broader investigation. Conyers, one of the signatories, said the independent counsel also should investigate possible illegal funding of the contra effort, in addition to the Iran arms sales. Meese said December 9 that the Justice Department would continue to investigate contra funding on its own, but Conyers and Don Edwards, D-Calif., another Judiciary member, responded that it was inappropriate for the department to conduct such a sensitive investigation of the executive branch.

The three-judge panel December 19 named Lawrence E. Walsh, a former federal district judge, diplomat, and deputy attorney general, to the position of independent counsel. At the same time, the court broadened the scope and time span of the inquiry, instructing Walsh to look into the "provision or coordination of support" for the contras beginning in 1984. *(Walsh background, box, p. 165)*

At a brief news conference December 19 after he was sworn in at the federal courthouse in Washington, D.C., Walsh said he planned to meet with Meese and the chairmen of the House and Senate Iran-contra committees, Rep. Lee H. Hamilton, D-Ind., and Sen. Daniel K. Inouye, D-Hawaii. Walsh said he wanted to coordinate his activities with the congressional investigation. In response to a question, Walsh said he did not believe that the two would be in conflict. He said a grand jury was being impaneled for the investigation (the jury was selected January 28, 1987). Walsh declined at that time to comment on the immunity issue despite several questions on the subject. President Reagan December 16 had asked Congress to grant immunity to North and his boss, Reagan's former national security adviser Rear Adm. John M. Poindexter. Both had invoked their Fifth Amendment right to refuse to testify before congressional committees. Investigating committees at the time refused to grant the request. Some members and legal experts had said that such a move could hamper the independent counsel's investigation because the two could not be prosecuted for any criminal law violations that came to light as a direct result of their testimony.

COURT CHALLENGES TO COUNSEL STATUTE

Walsh faced several challenges as he got his investigation under way, not the least of which was one to the very existence of his office.

The legality of the independent counsel was first

raised in another case. Washington, D.C., federal district judge Thomas Penfield Jackson February 25 blocked one counsel from seeking an indictment against former White House aide Michael K. Deaver, who had been under investigation for allegedly lying to a House subcommittee and to a grand jury about his lobbying activities after he resigned as deputy White House chief of staff in May 1985. Deaver's attorneys challenged the independent counsel statute, passed as Title VI of the 1978 Ethics in Government Act (PL 95-521), amended in 1982, as a violation of the separation of powers doctrine and thereby unconstitutional. They argued that it gave the judiciary too much sway over the executive branch. On February 24, North's lawyers had filed a similar lawsuit, seeking an injunction against Walsh's inquiry.

Following the Deaver ruling, Walsh said his investigation would continue "without interruption." "We believe the independent counsel statute is constitutional," he said. "The lawsuit against our office should be dismissed." He filed such a motion on March 2.

On March 5, Attorney General Meese attempted to circumvent the legal issue by appointing Walsh to head a new independent counsel office within the Justice Department. Meese said the appointment was "parallel" to Walsh's selection by the three-judge panel the previous December. Meese also filed a motion to dismiss North's lawsuit and characterized his own appointment of Walsh as an "insurance policy" so that the investigation could "go forward unimpeded." As long as there was a legal challenge to Walsh's court appointment, there was "a question mark over Walsh's activities," Meese argued. With the Justice Department appointment, "we remove that question mark."

In a statement after Meese's action, Walsh said, "We welcome the attorney general's willingness to eliminate any doubt which may have arisen as to the continuity of [the counsel's] investigation." He also restated his belief that the independent counsel statute was constitutional.

Arguments in North's Lawsuit

Although the Justice Department moved to dismiss North's suit, it chose to do so on grounds that were narrower than Walsh's argument.

Walsh's motion contended that the counsel statute was constitutional. Further, Walsh said that his probe could be hampered without prompt resolution of the lawsuit. "As long as [North's] action remains pending, it invites potential witnesses to withhold cooperation, or to challenge the validity of grand jury process served upon them," Walsh said. "Thus the mere pendency of this action may irreparably injure the ongoing criminal investigation."

In arguing that the law was constitutional, Walsh noted that the Watergate special prosecutor, whose appointment was similar to Walsh's, was upheld by the Supreme Court in a 1974 case involving access to President Richard Nixon's tapes of his White House conversations. Walsh also cited Article II of the Constitution, which allowed the courts to appoint "inferior officers" of the United States. Such court authority was confirmed by the Supreme Court in an 1880 case, Walsh said.

"Reduced to its essentials," Walsh said, North's "argument is that he can only be investigated by a prosecutor subject to the domination of the president and attorney general, even though both the president and attorney general have determined that, in order to avoid the potential

---

Walsh Profile

The selection December 19, 1986, of Lawrence E. Walsh to be independent counsel for the Iran-contra investigation came after a two-week search by a three-judge panel. His name, however, had surfaced days before the official announcement, and it was not a surprise when word finally came.

Walsh had had a multifaceted career, holding important jobs in the public and private sectors. A lifelong Republican, he served several administrations. President Dwight D. Eisenhower appointed him to the federal bench in New York in 1954, and three and one-half years later made him deputy attorney general. In 1969, President Richard Nixon tapped him to become an ambassador with the U.S. delegation to the Vietnam peace conference in Paris.

Rep. Dan Glickman, D-Kan., whose Judiciary subcommittee had jurisdiction over the special prosecutor law (PL 97-409), said he was not disturbed by Walsh's Republican affiliation. "I think it's probably even better," Glickman said. "He probably will do his best to be independent."

Walsh was born in Port Maitland, Nova Scotia, in 1912. He earned a bachelor's degree and law degree at Columbia University, the latter in 1935. He was admitted to the New York bar in 1936.

For the next two years he served as a special assistant attorney general in New York. From 1938-41 he worked as a deputy assistant district attorney under Thomas E. Dewey. After Dewey was elected governor, Walsh served as the governor's counsel. He also served as counsel to the New York Public Service Commission and as general counsel and executive director of the Waterfront Commission of New York.

In 1961, Walsh became a partner in the New York law firm of Davis, Polk and Wardwell, where he worked until 1981. During that time he served a year—1975-76—as president of the American Bar Association.

In 1981, Walsh went to Oklahoma, where he became a member of its bar and was with the firm of Crowe and Dunlevy.

---

for conflict of interest, this investigation should be conducted by a prosecutor independent of their control."

"Neither the words of the Constitution nor the decision of the courts mandate the illogical result [North] seeks," Walsh concluded.

A friend-of-court brief making similar points was filed March 5 by six constitutional law specialists on behalf of Common Cause, a public interest research and lobbying group headquartered in Washington, D.C. Citing Article II language, the Common Cause brief argued that North's

Controversy Surrounds Effort to Renew ...

One of the prominent themes running throughout the Iran-contra investigations was the legality and position of the independent counsel (previously called the special prosecutor). Legislation authorizing the independent counsel was due to expire at the end of 1987, so Congress—in the midst of the Iran-contra imbroglio—was obliged to take another look at it.

Establishment of Special Prosecutor

The special prosecutor law traced its origins to the Watergate crisis. The idea of an independent investigator emerged April 30, 1973, when the Senate Judiciary Committee refused to confirm Elliot L. Richardson as attorney general until he had appointed a special prosecutor for the Watergate investigation. *(Box, p. 170)*

But it was not until five years later, in 1978, that the special prosecutor law was enacted as Title VI of the Ethics in Government Act (PL 95-521). The legislation was an amalgam of several proposals with a common theme: that an independent investigator was needed to handle politically sensitive cases. The objective was to eliminate a potential conflict of interest in having the attorney general, a political appointee, investigate the president who appointed him or other top executive branch officials.

Overhaul of 1978 Law

Legislation to revamp the law was introduced in February 1982 by Sen. William S. Cohen, R-Maine, then chairman of the Oversight of Government Management Subcommittee of the Governmental Affairs Committee (and later a member of the Senate Iran-contra committee), and Carl Levin, D-Mich., the ranking subcommittee Democrat. Their action followed hearings in May 1981 and an extensive subcommittee report in October that concluded the attorney general needed more flexibility in administering the law.

Despite the infrequent application of the act, Cohen had little trouble finding witnesses anxious to testify about its operation. The law was never popular with attorneys general, who believed that its very existence implied that they were incapable of conducting impartial investigations of high government officials.

"The special prosecutor statute is predicated on the assumption that the attorney general will lack impartiality, or at least will be perceived to do so, in any investigation and prosecution of senior administration members. I do not believe this conclusion to be warranted in the ordinary case," former attorney general Richardson wrote in a February letter to Cohen.

However, Richardson, like most of the witnesses who testified in 1981, agreed that some type of special prosecutor provision remained necessary to assure the public that high officials suspected of wrongdoings would not get special treatment from the Justice Department.

The Reagan administration took a different view. In his testimony, Rudolph Giuliani, associate attorney general, called for repeal of the act. He contended the law was unconstitutional because it

"quarrel is not with the ethics act but with the Constitution itself."

The brief added that the 1978 ethics act was carefully tailored to respond to specific conflict-of-interest problems that arose when top executive branch aides were accused of wrongdoing. "Congress has limited the president's power to control an officer charged with investigating his closest aides; it has not injected itself into the functions of the executive branch," the brief said.

Although Walsh presented a constitutional and a procedural defense, the Justice Department sought dismissal of North's suit on procedural grounds alone. In a memorandum supporting its motion, the department said North filed his lawsuit prematurely. The memo said that North "has failed to demonstrate that the investigation undertaken by the Independent Counsel has caused him any cognizable injury.... No formal charges have been made against [North], and, indeed, none may ever be made."

The Justice Department's lawyers also said that "in short, [North] seeks adjudication of fundamental constitutional issues in advance of the strict necessity to do so."

Many members of Congress had asked the Justice Department to defend the law on constitutional, as well as procedural, grounds. But at a Senate Judiciary Committee hearing March 4, Meese expressed his own doubts about the constitutionality of the law. "There are serious concerns in the department and among legal scholars generally as to the constitutionality of the independent counsel statute," he said. (The Justice Department subsequently filed a brief challenging the law.) Several committee members disagreed and insisted the legislation had been carefully drafted to conform to constitutional separation of powers.

"In view of the situation that exists today," warned Howard M. Metzenbaum, D-Ohio, "if the attorney general isn't in court defending the constitutionality of the law, the perception of the American people is going to be devastating to this administration."

Legal Issues Persist

Over the next few months, the legal confrontation between North and the independent counsel continued.

... Law Authorizing Independent Counsel

involved the judiciary—through the appointment of a special prosecutor—in the enforcement of laws, an executive branch function. Attorney General William French Smith voiced similar concerns. Cohen, disturbed by the Justice Department's statements, wrote in his panel's report that "the subcommittee is gravely concerned that Attorney General Smith's announcement doubting the constitutionality of the present law will undermine the operation of the provisions in the next case that arises under the act."

1982 Revisions

In its report recommending changes in the law, Cohen's subcommittee said the standards for triggering the appointment of a special prosecutor should be tightened. (Existing legislation required the attorney general to seek a special prosecutor unless he could conclude that the matter was so unsubstantiated that no further investigation or prosecution was warranted.)

The report highlighted a number of other problem areas. Chief among them were provisions spelling out which officials could be subject to a special prosecutor inquiry. The panel concluded that existing law embraced both too few individuals and too many—too few because it did not cover a president's family, and too many because it applied to many executive branch officials whose prosecution by the Justice Department would not raise conflict-of-interest problems.

The subcommittee also determined that the act allowed prosecutions of government officials for too long a time after alleged criminal activities had occurred. The report pointed out that some persons could be covered for sixteen years—eight years during the terms of the president who appointed them and another eight years if a new president of the same party were elected and served two terms.

The final legislation (PL 97-409) approved by Congress in December 1982 extended the law for five years. Generally, the bill followed the subcommittees' recommended revisions, tightening the standards that would call for creation of special prosecutor (renamed the independent counsel), circumscribing the list of officials covered by the law (to those officials who occupied top-level executive positions close to either the president or the attorney general), and reducing coverage to two years after an official left office.

1987 Extension

With the independent counsel law about to expire, House and Senate committees by fall 1987 approved similar bills that would extend and revise independent counsel legislation. But the effort to renew the law promised to be one of the more bitter fights between the Reagan administration and the 100th Congress. The Justice Department in August said the law was unconstitutional because it violated the separation of powers doctrine by allowing a three-judge panel to appoint the counsel—a situation, it was argued, that permitted the judiciary to intrude on the executive branch's responsibility for prosecutions.

U.S. District Court Judge Barrington D. Parker March 12 dismissed North's suit, stating that there were "good reasons to believe" that the independent counsel legislation would be upheld. Parker also dismissed North's challenge to the attorney general's appointment of Walsh within the Justice Department. He said North could not show irreparable harm from the independent counsel probe and that it was not appropriate to interfere with an ongoing criminal investigation. "The nation demands an expeditious and complete disclosure of our government's involvement in the Iran-contra affair," Parker said.

At a March 9 hearing on North's challenge, Guy M. Struve, a member of Walsh's staff, contended that the attorney general had the authority to delegate prosecutorial authority. He also noted that Article II of the Constitution allowed Congress to let the president or the courts appoint "inferior officers." Struve argued that the independent counsel was such an officer. In a spirited rebuttal, Barry Simon, one of North's lawyers, charged that Walsh and his investigation team were "essentially a group of vigilantes—private citizens who cannot enforce the law."

Simon contended that only a prosecutor appointed by the president could conduct a probe, appear in a grand jury room, issue subpoenas, and question witnesses. Simon also challenged the notion that the independent counsel was an inferior officer. "He's not inferior to anybody," North's lawyer asserted.

In his twenty-one page opinion, Parker said he agreed with Walsh's office that North had not shown any injury. Parker also said there was a "strong policy against intervening in criminal investigations" that persuaded him not to consider North's challenge. Again, in May, U.S. District Court Judge Aubrey E. Robinson, Jr., ruled that Meese's back-up appointment of Walsh within the Justice Department was legal.

Nonetheless, North and his attorneys continued their legal challenges. On June 8, a three-judge panel of the U.S. District Court of Appeals for the District of Columbia declined to rule on North's claim that the independent counsel had no authority to investigate him. A principal reason for North's challenge was to block Walsh's subpoena for a sample of the former NSC aide's handwriting.

North renewed his battle against the Walsh inquiry in August, with his lawyers restating previous assertions that Walsh in fact remained outside the Justice Department and that the independent counsel position was unconstitutional. Again, however, the U.S. District Court of Appeals for the District of Columbia August 20 dismissed North's arguments, upholding Robinson's ruling, rejecting the contention that Walsh's investigation was unconstitutional and stating that North had to comply with the grand jury subpoena for a sample of his handwriting or face contempt charges and possible imprisonment. The court did not rule on the constitutionality of the 1978 act establishing the independent counsel, but in its thirty-one page opinion, it did say, "We hold that Walsh and the associate counsel derive the necessary legal authority from the attorney general's regulation of March 5, 1987, regardless of whether they also have the authority pursuant to their appointment under the [1978 Ethics in Government] act."

Justice Department Challenges Law

In late summer 1987, the Justice Department challenged the constitutionality of the independent counsel law in another case under investigation. The issue was raised in the case of Theodore B. Olson, a former assistant attorney general accused of giving false testimony to Congress in 1983. Olson and two others subpoenaed in the case filed suit claiming the law was unconstitutional.

U.S. District Court Judge Robinson in July 1987 ruled in the case that the independent counsel was constitutional. When the decision was appealed, the Justice Department on August 31 filed a brief with the federal appeals court in Washington, D.C., arguing that the provision establishing the counsel in the 1978 Ethics in Government Act should be overturned because it violated constitutional separation of powers. At the same time, the Justice Department said that it had offered backup appointments to the counsels so as not to interfere with existing investigations.

Walsh said he intended to submit a brief supporting the constitutionality of the act.

COUNSEL, CONGRESS NEGOTIATE IMMUNITY

At the time of Walsh's appointment, House and Senate committees were already at work investigating the Iran-contra affair, and two select committees were soon to be named. These congressional probes would pose two principal problems for Walsh's investigation, according to criminal law specialists. One was the committees' willingness to grant immunity from prosecution to witnesses in exchange for their testimony—an issue that was to recur throughout the first half of 1987. The other was the widespread publicity that usually resulted from congressional hearings and the difficulty that could arise in finding an unbiased jury to hear evidence in any future trial.

The immunity issue was "a real problem," said Philip Heymann, a Harvard law professor who worked with the first Watergate prosecutor, Archibald Cox, and who was a former head of the Justice Department's criminal division.

"The Congress always wants to move ahead and wants to get the information," he said. "And prosecutions go much slower than hearings." The publicity problem, he added, resulted from the sometimes conflicting goals of a prosecutor, who had to make his case before a judge and a jury, and of Congress, which was interested in gathering information and making policy decisions. "The very purpose of a congressional investigation is to get information to the public as well as the Congress," Heymann said. "And prosecutors always worry about that infecting juries."

Calls for Immunity

As full-scale investigations into the Iran-contra affair were launched in January 1987, the immunity issue began to heat up. Some Republican members of the investigating committees had embraced the White House argument that the entire investigation could be concluded quickly by using grants of immunity to force key witnesses to testify. Under a 1970 law (PL 91-452), congressional committees could, on a two-thirds vote of members, grant limited, or "use," immunity to witnesses; doing so would compel them to testify or face jail for contempt. They could not, however, be criminally prosecuted based on the information they provided while under congressional immunity. (Background, p. 57)

On the two select committees, the most vocal advocates of early grants of immunity were Sen. Orrin G. Hatch, R-Utah, and Rep. William S. Broomfield, R-Mich. Broomfield acknowledged that granting immunity to North could jeopardize any criminal prosecution of him. But the "greater interest" was resolving the Iran-contra affair quickly, he said. "I really sincerely believe, regardless of who is in the White House, this isn't in the best interests of our country to have this prolonged investigation."

But the Democratic and Republican members of both committees opposed as "premature" the early granting of immunity. "You're going to have to have a little better idea of what you're going to get from a grant of immunity before you start giving it," said Sen. Howell Heflin, D-Ala., a former chief justice of the Alabama supreme court.

Walsh Arguments

In a January 13 letter and thirteen-page legal memorandum, Walsh asked the two panels not to grant immunity to any witnesses before he had completed his inquiry. Walsh said such action on the part of Congress would:

● Create "serious—and perhaps insurmountable—barriers to the prosecution of the immunized witnesses." Walsh noted that once a congressional committee had granted immunity to a witness, the independent counsel could prosecute that person only if he could prove that the evidence came from sources other than the immunized testimony. Offering such proof to a court would be "very difficult," Walsh said.

● Result in intensive publicity, allowing potential defendants to claim that "an unbiased jury cannot be assembled" for any subsequent trials. Walsh cited cases from the Watergate investigations to bolster his point that prosecuting individuals was difficult once they have testified in nationally televised congressional hearings.

● Reduce the ability of the independent counsel to obtain "complete and truthful" testimony. Normally, Walsh said, prosecutors offered immunity only after considering "the relative culpability of all the targets of investigation"

Carl R. "Spitz" Channell pleaded guilty to conspiring to defraud the government by soliciting money for military aid to the contras while claiming the contribution was for a tax-exempt organization.

and after they knew what kind of testimony the prospective witnesses would give. Immunized witnesses generally gave truthful testimony because they feared being prosecuted for perjury; but those witnesses might also restrict their remarks to evidence that could be confirmed independently, thus limiting their value to prosecutors, Walsh said.

"We certainly will hear him out and respect his view," Hamilton said. "But in the final analysis, our committee has the legal authority to grant immunity, and we will do what we think is in the best interest of our investigation."

Congress and the independent counsel had "different responsibilities" that might conflict, Hamilton acknowledged. Walsh's task was to prosecute persons who might have violated laws, while the committees were trying to find out what went wrong in the administration's foreign policy apparatus, he said. Another potential conflict between Walsh and the Hill committees involved the sharing of information. In a memo on the relationship between his office and the committees, Walsh said the two sides "should cooperate with one another as fully as possible"—especially in the sharing of information. Walsh called on the committees to give him all testimony and documents they had obtained, and he said he would try to reciprocate.

But Walsh said he probably would not be able to share with Congress any evidence presented to the grand jury investigating the Iran-contra affair—especially if the committees intended to make the information public during their hearings. To divulge grand jury information, Walsh said, would require permission from the federal district court in Washington that supervised his work.

Congress vs. Walsh

But the pace of Walsh's investigation and the immunity issue continued to concern members of the House and Senate Iran-contra committees. Even before the panels began their public inquiry, members expressed frustration over the possibility of a lengthy investigation by the independent counsel that would restrict their own probe. In fact, the opening of the committees' public hearings was postponed to May 1987 as a result of negotiations with Walsh over whether and when to grant immunity to North and Poindexter.

The conflicts between Congress and the independent counsel emerged in March, when some members of the committees began pushing for immunity for Poindexter and North. One, Sen. Paul S. Trible, Jr., R-Va., wrote in the March 11 *Washington Post* that the public benefit of obtaining testimony from the two "far outweighs the risks to Walsh's potential prosecution of them."

To head off early grants of immunity, Walsh met with the House committee March 10 and the Senate panel March 11. He told reporters that he asked each committee not to compel public or private testimony by Poindexter or North for ninety days. The main reason for the request, he said, was to "protect against any unnecessary frustration of the prosecution [of those men] by a premature granting of immunity."

House committee leaders said a solid majority supported Walsh's request. "We want to work out an arrangement that will be acceptable to the Senate and also to the independent counsel," said House chairman Hamilton. However, some panel members expressed displeasure about the possibility of postponing the hearings. Several Senate members argued that the committee should move ahead with an application for immunity for Poindexter, who, as the president's national security adviser, could be expected to describe how much Reagan was told about the Iran-contra affair. The committees did vote to apply for limited (or "use") immunity from prosecution for other witnesses.

By the end of April, the committees had conferred immunity on at least eleven witnesses, according to an "interim report" issued April 28 by independent counsel Walsh. Those eleven were: Joan Corbin and Shirley A. Napier, secretaries to retired major general Richard V. Secord; John C. Cupp, Edward de Garay, Cynthia F. Dondlinger, Robert C. Dutton, Richard B. Gadd, and Robert W. Owen, all of whom were reported to be either directly involved with the contra supply network or with companies said to have some connection with it; Lt. Col. Robert L. Earl, an ex-NSC aide who had worked for North; Fawn Hall, North's former secretary at the NSC; and Albert Hakim, Secord's business partner who established the complex arrangement for handling the Iran-contra financial transactions.

In addition to those listed by Walsh, Tomas Castillo, the pseudonym for the CIA station chief in Costa Rica who helped coordinate logistics for the contra aid, also was reported to have been granted immunity by the committees. Walsh said he had asked for a delay of up to twenty days in grants of immunity for at least four witnesses: Earl, Gadd, Hakim, and Owen.

Walsh Rebuttal

Walsh responded to the congressional criticism of his request for delaying North's and Poindexter's immunity in his seventeen-page interim report in which he said there was "ample basis" for continuing his broad criminal investigation. "Most lines of inquiry are proving fruitful. None

Demands for Independent Investigators . . .

While independent counsels, known until 1982 as "special prosecutors," reached prominence during the Watergate crisis that led to the resignation of President Richard Nixon in 1974, demands for independent investigators of high-level wrongdoing date back much further.

The first special prosecutor was named more than a century ago to investigate whether President Ulysses S. Grant's personal secretary was involved in a ring of tax-evading whiskey distillers. A special prosecutor also was appointed to probe the "Teapot Dome" scandal of the Harding administration and alleged tax fixing during the Truman years.

Watergate and Its Aftermath

In early 1973, members of Congress demanded a special prosecutor to look into the June 17, 1972, burglary of Democratic National Committee headquarters by men tied to President Nixon's reelection campaign.

Nixon had nominated Elliot L. Richardson as attorney general, but the Senate Judiciary Committee blocked his confirmation until Richardson promised to appoint a special prosecutor to investigate the Watergate affair. Richardson subsequently selected Harvard law professor Archibald Cox and promised him complete independence.

Within a few months, Cox was demanding secret tape recordings Nixon had made of his White House conversations. Cox refused to accept transcript summaries Nixon was offering, and the president ordered Richardson to fire Cox. Richardson balked and re-

signed. His deputy, William D. Ruckelshaus, was fired after refusing to carry out Nixon's order. Solicitor General Robert H. Bork finally fired Cox, setting off a public outcry and the House impeachment probe that eventually led to Nixon's August 9, 1974, resignation.

Five years after the firings, Congress passed the Ethics in Government Act of 1978 (PL 95-521), which included provisions designed to guard against conflict of interest among government officials. The new law set up a mechanism for court appointment of a temporary special prosecutor to probe allegations against high government or campaign officials.

The Reagan administration opposed reauthorization of the law in 1981-82, contending it unconstitutionally involved the judiciary—through the appointment of a special prosecutor—in the enforcement of laws, an executive branch function. However, Congress in late 1982 cleared a five-year reauthorization of the law.

Recent Experience, Pending Suits

From 1978 through mid-1987, independent counsels had been appointed in nine public cases. According to congressional staffers, there were other cases that were not made public.

In addition to the Walsh investigation into the Iran-contra affair, the public cases included:

● **Hamilton Jordan,** President Jimmy Carter's chief of staff, accused in 1979 of using cocaine. The special prosecutor, former U.S. attorney Arthur H. Christy, announced May 28, 1980, that there was

---

has yet been abandoned," Walsh wrote in his report. He also repeated previous warnings that additional grants of immunity by the congressional panels could harm his ability to prosecute Iran-contra participants. *(Walsh interim report, p. D-87)*

Among those committee members defending Walsh's position was Sen. David L. Boren, D-Okla., who said, "You can't hurry up the timetable of the legal process. You've got to gather your evidence. You have to go through the process." Walsh, said Boren, "has a job to do that is not exactly consistent with our job." Each side, he added, had been "very reasonable in striking a balance and compromise."

Limited Immunity Granted

After a protracted skirmish among the committees, Walsh, and lawyers for North and Poindexter, agreement was reached to give the two former NSC aides limited immunity to testify before the congressional committees. The ground rules for the testimony were circumscribed and

caused considerable political and logistic problems for the congressional probes. But the grants of limited immunity also were troublesome for Walsh's investigation, although the extent could not be foreseen until the committees had concluded their inquiry and Walsh had finished his investigation.

FIRST CONVICTIONS IN IRAN-CONTRA AFFAIR

The first conviction obtained by Walsh in the Iran-contra investigation came on April 29, 1987, when conservative fund-raiser Carl R. "Spitz" Channell pleaded guilty to conspiring to defraud the government by soliciting money for military aid to the contras while claiming the

... Have Been Heard over the Past Century

insufficient evidence to prosecute Jordan.

• **Tim Kraft,** Carter's national campaign manager, also accused of using cocaine. This 1980 investigation, stemming from the Jordan case, was conducted by Gerald J. Gallinghouse, a former U.S. attorney. It ended in March 1981 with no indictment.

• **Raymond J. Donovan,** alleged to have violated federal law before becoming President Reagan's labor secretary. Leon Silverman, a former assistant U.S. deputy attorney general, was appointed in 1981 as special prosecutor. The probe ended in September 1982 with insufficient evidence of Donovan's ties to organized crime.

• **Edwin Meese III,** Reagan's attorney general, subject of allegations of misconduct involving his personal financial dealings. Independent counsel Jacob Stein, a Washington trial lawyer, looked into the allegations in 1984 but found no basis for criminal charges.

• **Theodore B. Olson,** a former assistant attorney general, accused of giving false testimony to Congress in 1983 about the administration's withholding of Environmental Protection Agency documents concerning the Superfund toxic waste program. James C. McKay, a Washington attorney, was appointed independent counsel on April 24, 1986, but withdrew a month later to avoid possible conflict of interest with his law firm. He was replaced by Alexia Morrison, a former assistant U.S. attorney for the District of Columbia.

• **Michael K. Deaver,** former White House aide, accused of illegally using his official and personal ties with President Reagan on behalf of his lobbying clients. The court in May 1986 named former U.S. attorney Whitney North Seymour, Jr., to head the investigation. Deaver was indicted March 18, 1987, for perjury, becoming the first person to face criminal charges sought by an independent counsel under the Ethics in Government Act.

• **Lyn Nofziger,** former White House aide, accused of violating federal laws in lobbying for several clients including Wedtech Corp., a defense contractor based in Bronx, N.Y. Washington attorney McKay was appointed independent counsel in February 1987. Nofziger was indicted July 17 on charges that his lobbying for Wedtech and two other clients violated the Ethics in Government Act.

• **Meese,** under pressure from members of Congress and the press, asked independent counsel McKay to investigate also his involvement with Wedtech. Upon formal application by the Justice Department, Meese was included in McKay's investigation in May 1987.

Some cases have never reached the stage of appointing an independent counsel. Circumstances where preliminary investigation uncovered insufficient evidence to warrant naming a special prosecutor have included charges that President Carter and Vice President Walter F. Mondale illegally solicited political contributions at a White House luncheon; that President Reagan's first national security adviser, Richard V. Allen, had taken bribes from foreigners; and that CIA director William J. Casey had violated the foreign agents registration law when he represented Indonesia in a case before the federal government.

money was for a tax-exempt organization, the National Endowment for the Preservation of Liberty (NEPL). The next day, the Internal Revenue Service revoked NEPL's tax-exempt status.

In a short hearing April 29 before a federal district court in Washington, D.C., Channell said he conspired with North and others to supply funds to the contras. As part of the plea agreement, Channell agreed to cooperate with prosecutors. He could receive a maximum five-year prison term and a fine of up to $25,000. But he would not be sentenced until the Walsh investigation was completed. *(Hearings on private funds solicitations, p. 95)*

In papers filed April 29, shortly before Channell's guilty plea, prosecutors said more than $2 million was illegally collected by NEPL in 1986 from three contributors. NEPL showed up in an organizational chart prepared by North and found among his White House papers during the Tower Commission's investigation of the Iran-contra affair. North had listed NEPL under "resources development." *(Tower Commission, p. 71)*

NEPL, which collected funds for the contras from 1984 to 1986, was reported to have funneled about $5.8 million to another organization, International Business Communications (IBC), a public relations firm headed by Richard R. Miller, later indicted by the grand jury.

IBC was a source of controversy; between 1984 and 1986, the State Department awarded the company six noncompetitive contracts to publicize the contras' cause in the United States. During the court proceeding April 29, Channell named Miller as one of his co-conspirators. "I categorically deny that I conspired with Mr. Channell or anyone else for that purpose or any illegal purpose. I am confident that ... my conduct will be vindicated," Miller stated.

According to press accounts, another Channell associate was David C. Fischer, a former special assistant to President Reagan. Fischer reportedly helped arrange meetings with Reagan for Channell contributors. Fischer was described as Reagan's "right-hand man, his door opener" while he worked for Reagan from 1977 to April 1985.

At a news conference March 19, Reagan confirmed meeting with Channell's supporters, but said he believed the purpose was to thank them for funding television commercials in support of the contras. "I thought that was worth a thanks," he said.

A week after Channell pleaded guilty, Miller became the second person to do so in Walsh's investigation, even after categorically denying the charges. In a brief court proceeding May 6, he admitted to conspiracy to defraud the government in an illegal fund-raising scheme to buy military equipment for the Nicaraguan contras. Both Channell and Miller said they also conspired with North.

During the guilty plea proceeding, Miller said that in the fall of 1985 he asked North to determine the price of a piece of military equipment and that subsequently, at a meeting in a Washington, D.C., hotel, he asked a contributor to buy the item for the contras. The type of military equipment and the price were not disclosed. Miller said he knew it was likely the contributor would take an improper tax deduction for the equipment by calling it a charitable contribution. The formal charge against Miller cited four unidentified donors who provided more than $3.1 million for the contras between the fall of 1985 and 1986.

Swiss Bank Records

In August, the independent counsel's office received news that Switzerland's supreme court ruled that the records of bank accounts used by participants in the Iran-contra affair could be handed over to the U.S. investigators.

Walsh said August 20 that he was pleased that the Swiss court had "reaffirmed our right ... to receive the evidence located in Switzerland." The Swiss court action made it possible for the independent counsel to review detailed records of the accounts into which the Iran arms sales proceeds and private contributions to the contras, perhaps illegally obtained, were utilized. That subject had consumed several days of the House-Senate select committees' inquiries. (*Hakim testimony, p. C-51; Secord-Hakim funds, box, p. 104*)

Walsh's battles over the constitutionality of the independent counsel position continued into the fall of 1987. Meanwhile, the office persevered in its probe, with the likelihood that further indictments would be handed down. There was also a possibility that Walsh might interview Reagan. When he was appointed to the position in December 1986, the independent counsel had said he would "talk to anyone necessary" in the executive branch who could provide relevant information. Administration officials in early September 1987 said they anticipated that the president would agree to be interviewed, if requested, citing his many pledges of full cooperation with the Iran-contra investigations.

Appendix

Chronology

1979

January 16. *Shah Leaves Iran.* Shah Mohammed Reza Pahlavi leaves Iran for a "vacation" abroad, thus ending his thirty-seven-year rule.

February 1. *Khomeini Returns.* Ayatollah Ruhollah Khomeini returns to Iran after fifteen years in exile.

February 11. *Khomeini Government.* A provisional government formed by Khomeini takes power.

July 17. *Nicaraguan Revolution.* The forty-two-year dictatorship of Anastasio Somoza in Nicaragua ends when Somoza resigns and leaves Nicaragua. Somoza had been ousted by a broadly based revolution headed by a guerrilla group known as the Sandinista National Liberation Front. A new government is formed several days later by the Sandinistas and other groups. The junta proclaims its alliance with Cuba and other "anti-imperialists," but it also seeks U.S. aid. Shortly after the revolution, the United States supplies $61 million in aid. More aid is provided in 1980.

November 4. *U.S. Hostages in Iran.* Demanding the return of the shah, who is in New York for medical treatment, militants storm the U.S. Embassy in Tehran and seize sixty-six American hostages. Thirteen (five women and eight blacks) are freed November 19-20 and another in July 1980, but the remaining fifty-two are held fourteen months.

November 9. *No Military Deliveries to Iran.* President Carter blocks delivery of $300 million in military equipment and spare parts to Iran.

November 9. *Aid to Nicaragua.* President Carter submits to Congress an aid package that includes $75 million in economic aid for Nicaragua.

November 14. *Iranian Assets Frozen.* President Carter freezes Iranian assets in the United States.

December 24-27. *Soviets Invade Afghanistan.* The Soviet Union begins airlifting troops and supplies into Afghanistan in a move to put down a rebellion by Moslem tribesmen who oppose Marxist rule. On December 27, about 20,000 Soviet troops cross the border and invade the country.

1980

March. *Sandinistas Visit USSR.* The first major Sandinista delegation arrives in Moscow and signs economic, technical, scientific, and cultural agreements. The delegation also signs a party-to-party agreement between the Sandinista National Liberation Front and the Soviet Communist party.

April 7. *Ties with Iran Severed.* President Carter severs diplomatic relations with Iran and imposes an embargo on American exports, except food and medicine, to Iran.

April 17. *Iranian Imports Banned.* President Carter bans all imports from Iran and prohibits travel there by U.S. citizens. U.S. military equipment previously purchased by Iran and impounded after the U.S. Embassy takeover is made available for sale to other nations.

April 25. *Failed Rescue Mission.* A U.S. mission to rescue American hostages is aborted in the Iranian desert because of equipment failures.

May 31. *Aid to Nicaragua.* Nearly seven months after requesting rapid congressional action, President Carter signs into law legislation authorizing $75 million in emergency economic aid for Nicaragua (PL 96-257). Carter said the money was needed to strengthen moderate elements in the country. The Senate routinely passed the measure, but conservatives in the House succeeded in delaying passage and adding a number of restrictions to the bill. Further delays were encountered before the money was actually released September 12.

September 22. *Iran-Iraq War.* The Iran-Iraq dispute escalates into full-scale war. Iraq attacks Iran.

1981

January 19. *U.S.-Iran Relations.* Direct, formal communications between Washington and Tehran resume with the establishment, pursuant to the Algiers Accord, of the Iran-United States Claims Tribunal at the Hague. Economic sanctions are partially lifted, but the arms embargo is reinforced, according to the report issued in February 1987 by the President's Special Review Board (Tower Commission).

January 20. *Reagan Inauguration.* Ronald Reagan is inaugurated president.

January 20. *Hostages Freed.* American hostages in Iran are released.

February. *Nicaraguan Aid Suspended.* The Reagan administration suspends the final $15 million payment of the $75 million Nicaraguan aid package enacted in 1980.

June 7. *Iraqi Reactor Attack.* Israeli planes bomb an Iraqi nuclear reactor.

August. *North Joins NSC.* Lt. Col. Oliver L. North joins the staff of the National Security Council (NSC).

December. *Contra Aid.* President Reagan signs a National Intelligence Finding establishing U.S. support for the Nicaraguan resistance forces, or contras.

1982

March. *Contra Aid.* Reports surface that the Reagan administration has begun efforts to support the Nicaraguan contras.

June 8. *'Project Democracy.'* President Reagan proposes "Project Democracy"—a new program to promote democracy overseas—during a speech before the British Parliament. Rather than placing the program totally under government auspices as Reagan had proposed, Congress in 1983 authorized funds for the National Endowment for Democracy (NED), the new agency that was to funnel the money to private organizations, such as unions and businesses, to carry out the program. Lt. Col. Oliver L. North later referred to his covert operations as "Project Democracy." A February 15, 1987, *New York Times* article reported that National Security Council (NSC) aide North's dealings with Iran and the contras had begun as "the secret side" of the public Project Democracy program and that the "covert side was intended to carry out foreign policy tasks that other Government agencies were unable or unwilling to pursue." But the President's Special Review Board (Tower Commission) found no link between North's Project Democracy and NED.

July. *Iranian Support for Terrorism.* The United States becomes aware of Iranian support for international terrorism and groups engaged in hostage-taking, according to the Tower Commission.

July 19. *University President Kidnapped.* David Dodge, the president of the American University of Beirut, is kidnapped. He is freed July 20, 1983.

December 21. *First Boland Amendment.* The first Boland amendment, named for House Intelligence Committee chairman Edward P. Boland, D-Mass., is signed into law. It bars the CIA and the Defense Department from spending funds toward overthrowing the Sandinista regime in Nicaragua or provoking a military conflict between Nicaragua and Honduras. The amendment, contained in an omnibus appropriations bill for fiscal 1973 (PL 97-377), was in effect from December 21, 1982, to December 8, 1983.

1983

Spring. *'Operation Staunch.'* The State Department begins "Operation Staunch," a program aimed at discouraging other countries from selling arms to Iran, according to the December 10, 1986, *Washington Post.* The *Post* said the program was begun after Secretary of State George P. Shultz became increasingly concerned about the Iran-Iraq War and its effect on Persian Gulf oil supplies.

April 27. *Reagan on Central America.* In an address to a joint session of Congress, President Reagan defends his Central America policy. He devotes much of his speech to a harsh attack on the leftist government of Nicaragua, saying it "has treated us as an enemy." In his only direct reference to U.S. activities against Nicaragua, he says the United States is not seeking the overthrow of the Nicaraguan government but is merely trying to prevent the flow of Soviet- and Cuban-supplied arms through Nicaragua to the guerrillas in El Salvador.

May 4. *Reagan Supports Contras.* President Reagan, in an interview, calls the Nicaraguan contras "freedom fighters" and acknowledges that the United States is aiding them. He criticizes the attempts of Democratic leaders to cut off military aid to the contras.

May 25. *State Department Role.* In a memo released by the House and Senate committees investigating the Iran-contra affair, Shultz asks to be the administration's "sole delegate" in carrying out Central American policy. But, according to the September 19, 1987, *Washington Post,* Shultz, who is concerned with the National Security Council's role, is told: "No one agency can do it alone."

July 20. *Hostage Released.* The president of the American University of Beirut, David Dodge, who was kidnapped on July 19, 1982, is released.

September. *Presidential Finding on Contras.* President Reagan signs a second presidential finding authorizing "material support and guidance" to the contras, according to the February 1987 report of the President's Special Review Board (Tower Commission). The objective is to induce the Sandinista government to negotiate with its neighbors and to pressure the Sandinistas and their allies into halting aid to leftist guerrillas in El Salvador.

October 17. *McFarlane Appointment.* President Reagan announces the appointment of Robert C. McFarlane as national security adviser.

October 23. *Beirut Attack.* In Beirut, 241 U.S. servicemen are killed in a truck-bomb attack by a suicidal driver linked to a pro-Iranian Lebanese Shia group.

November 3. *Rodriguez-Gregg Meeting.* Former CIA operative Felix I. Rodriguez, returning from a trip to Central America, meets with Donald Gregg, an aide to Vice President George Bush, to discuss the general situation in the region, according to a chronology released by the vice president's office on December 15, 1986.

November 18. *Project Democracy Approved.* Congress approves funding for the National Endowment for Democracy, the new agency that is to funnel money to Project Democracy programs. Approval comes after CIA director William J. Casey publicly pledges that the CIA will not take part in the organization's affairs.

December 8. *Second Boland Amendment.* The second Boland amendment, named for House Intelligence Committee chairman Edward P. Boland, D-Mass., is signed into law. It sets a $24 million cap on military funds to the contras supplied by the Pentagon, CIA, "or any other agency or entity of the United States involved in intelligence activities." This version, contained in a fiscal 1984 defense appropriations bill (PL 98-212), was in effect from December 8, 1983, to September 30, 1984.

December 12. *Bombings in Kuwait.* A wave of car bombings strikes the U.S. and French embassies and other targets in Kuwait. The imprisonment of seventeen terrorists convicted of the bombings—the Da'Wa prisoners—will become an issue in U.S.-Iran negotiations.

1984

January 13. *Iran Policy Review.* In a memo to national security adviser Robert C. McFarlane, National Security Council (NSC) official Geoffrey Kemp recommends the administration reevaluate its attitude toward Iran. Kemp, the NSC's senior director for Near East and South Asian affairs, views the Khomeini government as a menace to U.S. interests and suggests a revival of covert operations against it.

January 20. *'Operation Staunch'.* Secretary of State George P. Shultz designates Iran as a sponsor of international terrorism. The administration, under a program called "Operation Staunch," actively pressures U.S. allies to not sell arms to Iran because of Iran's sponsorship of international terrorism and its continuation of the war with Iraq.

January 23. *Exports to Iran.* Evidence of Iranian complicity in terrorist activities prompts the United States to impose additional controls on exports to Iran, according to the February 1987 report of the President's Special Review Board (Tower Commission).

February 10. *University Professor Kidnapped.* Frank Reiger, head of the electrical engineering department at the American University of Beirut, is kidnapped. He is freed April 15.

March 7. *Newsman Kidnapped.* Jeremy Levin, Beirut bureau chief for the U.S. Cable News Network, is kidnapped in Beirut.

March 16. *CIA Station Chief Kidnapped.* William Buckley, the CIA station chief in Beirut, is kidnapped.

March 27. *Israeli Contra Aid Solicited.* CIA director William J. Casey sends a memo to McFarlane expressing his concern that Congress would not approve supplemental funds "to carry out the Nicaraguan covert action project." According to McFarlane's May 11, 1987, testimony before the House and Senate Iran-contra committees, Casey then declares his "full agreement" that McFarlane "explore funding alternatives with ... the others." "The others," according to McFarlane, referred to "Country One," identified by news sources as Israel. McFarlane testified that Country One refused. In the same memo, Casey suggests establishing a "foundation" run by a private citizen who would organize, raise, and disburse nongovernmental funds to the contras.

April. *Saudi Contra Aid Solicited.* The CIA solicits Saudi Arabia to make contributions to the Nicaraguan contras, according to the November 28, 1986, *Washington Post.* The solicitation was first reported by the *Post* in May 1984. The CIA is reportedly down to its last $1 million in

funds authorized by Congress when CIA director Casey dispatches a senior official in the operations directorate to seek additional funds. When the Saudi government declines initially, Casey turns to Israel, according to the *Post* report.

April 6. *CIA Role in Harbor Mining.* The *Wall Street Journal* reports that the CIA provided logistics and supervision for the mining of Nicaraguan harbors. Although the mines' existence had been public knowledge since early January, this is the first firm report of CIA participation. It creates an uproar in Congress, where President Reagan is seeking additional aid for the contras.

Early May. *Reagan-Saudi Meeting.* President Reagan meets at the White House with the Saudi ambassador to the United States, Prince Bandar bin Sultan.

May 8. *Cleric Kidnapped.* American Presbyterian minister Benjamin F. Weir is kidnapped in Beirut. He is freed September 15, 1985.

May 24. *Saudi Arms Sale Proposal.* As the Iran-Iraq War produces attacks on Persian Gulf shipping, the Reagan administration announces its intention to resubmit to Congress a proposal to sell Saudi Arabia 1,200 Stinger antiaircraft missiles. The proposal had been withdrawn March 21 in the face of overwhelming opposition in Congress.

May 28. *Arms Sent to Saudis.* The United States delivers to Saudi Arabia a controversial cargo of 400 Stinger missiles and 200 missile launchers, valued at $40 million. Invoking presidential powers as provided for in the Arms Export Control Act, Reagan sends Congress formal notice of the sale on May 30 and effectively bypasses the thirty-day notification period.

May/June. *Saudi Contra Aid.* National security adviser McFarlane meets with Saudi ambassador Bandar bin Sultan who, according to McFarlane, offers to contribute $5 million to the contras, the *Washington Post* reported March 19, 1987. Contra bank records showed a total of $8 million deposited from July 6, 1984, to February 7, 1985. Bandar denied any Saudi contributions to the contras. McFarlane told the House and Senate Iran-contra committees May 11, 1987, that he had discussed Reagan's commitment to the contras with Saudi officials beginning in mid-1984 and that the Saudis agreed to contribute $1 million a month to the contras.

June 25. *Contra Aid Rejected.* Breaking a month-long deadlock over a Reagan request for an additional $21 million for the contras, the Republican-controlled Senate bows to House opposition and agrees to remove the funds from a fiscal 1984 supplemental appropriations measure.

Summer. *'Arms for Hostages' Idea.* International arms dealers, including Saudi Arabian Adnan Khashoggi and Iranian exile Manucher Ghorbanifar, are interested in bringing the United States into an arms relationship with Iran, and discuss this at a series of meetings, according to documents and testimony received by the Senate Intelligence Committee during its investigation into the Iran-contra affair. The discussions, which continue into early 1985, reportedly include the idea of an "arms for hostages" deal, in part as a means of establishing each country's bona fides.

Summer. *Iran Seeks TOW Missiles.* Iranian purchasing agents approach international arms merchants with requests for TOW (tube-launched, optically-tracked, wire-guided) antitank missiles, according to the Tower Commission report.

July. *Private Contra Aid Network.* Retired Air Force

major general Richard V. Secord and Marine lieutenant colonel Oliver L. North first discuss private assistance to the contras during a meeting in North's NSC office, according to Secord's May 5, 1987, testimony before the House and Senate Iran-contra committees. After meeting with contra leader Adolfo Calero and getting NSC aide North's approval, Secord arranges four arms sales to the contras. The first two deals, in February and April 1985, are made with a Canadian firm, Transworld Armaments. But complications ensue and Secord calls on ex-CIA operative Thomas G. Clines for assistance with the two other sales in March and May 1985.

July 6. *First $1 Million from Saudis.* The first $1 million in contra aid from the Saudis is deposited in a Cayman Islands bank account belonging to the contras, according to the March 19, 1987, *Washington Post.*

August. *Ghorbanifar Called 'Fabricator.'* The CIA issues a notice to other government agencies that Iranian arms dealer Ghorbanifar is a "fabricator," according to the Senate Intelligence Committee's report on the Iran-contra affair. Ghorbanifar later becomes a central figure in arranging for the sale of U.S. weapons to Iran.

August 7. *Shultz Not Told of Saudi Funds.* According to Secretary of State Shultz's July 23, 1987, testimony before the House and Senate Iran-contra committees, McFarlane misleads Under Secretary of State Michael H. Armacost about the source of contra funding. McFarlane claims to be ignorant of the source of the $1 million a month subsidy that he had arranged personally with the Saudi ambassador to Washington.

August 31. *U.S.-Iran Relations Study.* McFarlane requests an interagency study of U.S. relations with Iran after Khomeini. McFarlane receives the study October 19.

September 2. *Contra Air Attack.* In a memo to national security adviser McFarlane, NSC aide North tells of a contra air attack in Nicaraguan territory that he and a CIA official had urged contra leader Adolfo Calero to postpone. Nevertheless, the attack took place, resulting in the loss of the contras' only operating helicopter on the northern front. In the memo, according to the Tower report, North requests permission to solicit funds from a private donor for the purchase of a replacement "civilian" helicopter. McFarlane disapproves the request and writes at the bottom of the memo, "Let's wait a week or two." After apparently reconsidering, McFarlane scratched out his previous notation and wrote, "I don't think this is legal."

September 15. *CIA Plane Shipment Reported.* The *Washington Post* reports that the CIA sent to the contras three Cessna 02A observation planes equipped with rocket pods. The *Post* reports that the Air Force had declared the planes "surplus" and had transferred them to a secret Joint Chiefs of Staff operation code-named "Elephant Herd." From there the planes were transferred to the CIA and then ultimately to the contras. Congressional critics charged that the transfer of excess equipment at no charge to the recipient could be part of an administration attempt to circumvent spending limits on aid to the contras, according to the *Post.*

September 27. *Restrictions on Exports to Iran.* The State Department announces new restrictions on exports to Iran.

October. *North Fills Void.* After October 1984, the NSC staff—particularly North—moves to fill the void left by congressional restrictions on aid to the contras, according to the Tower Commission report. Between 1984 and 1986, North performs activities the CIA is unable to under-

take, including the facilitation of outside fund-raising efforts and oversight of a private network to supply lethal equipment to the contras.

October 12. *Third Boland Amendment.* The third, and most comprehensive, Boland amendment, named for House Intelligence Committee chairman Edward P. Boland, D-Mass., is signed into law. It bars the Pentagon, CIA, "or any other agency or entity of the United States involved in intelligence activities" from either directly or indirectly providing military aid to the contras. This version, contained in an omnibus spending bill for fiscal 1985 (PL 98-473), was in effect from October 1, 1984, to December 3, 1985.

October 14. *Controversial Contra Manual.* The Associated Press reports that the CIA in 1983 had approved a manual that appeared to advocate the kidnapping and killing of Nicaraguan government officials by the contras. Although the administration found low-level agency employees responsible for the manual, the findings and reports on the matter by the House and Senate Intelligence committees seemed to add to congressional doubts about continuing aid to the contras. The CIA in mid-November punishes six officials for their part in the manual.

October 19. *U.S.-Iran Relations Study.* McFarlane receives from the State Department a response to his request for an interagency study on U.S. relations with Iran. The report, entitled, "Iran: The Post-Khomeini Era," incorporates a Special National Intelligence Estimate (SNIE), which concludes that the United States has "no influential contacts" within the Iranian government or among Iranian political groups. The report conveys an impression of relative American powerlessness to affect events in Iran. It concludes that the possibility of resuming arms shipments to Iran depends on Iran's willingness to restore formal relations, which itself turns on Iran's perception of the importance of such shipments and the American perception of the impact of such shipments on the regional balance of power. A revised SNIE circulates in May 1985.

November 7. *Intelligence Support for Contras.* McFarlane receives a memo from North seeking permission to continue providing contra leader Adolfo Calero with intelligence information. North assures McFarlane that, contrary to concerns expressed by CIA director Casey, he had not discussed details of contra military operations and finances with a CIA official. The CIA official had declined to participate in a meeting with Calero because of new statutory prohibitions, according to the Tower report.

November 8. *Contra Aid Ban.* The fiscal 1985 intelligence authorization act (PL 98-618) is signed into law, barring aid to the contras. Partly because the wording of the provision banning aid was narrower than the Boland amendment enacted October 12, the President's Intelligence Oversight Board, according to the Tower report, decided in September 1985 the ban did not cover the NSC and, presumably, its staff.

November 19-21. *Hostage Ransom Proposed.* Theodore G. Shackley, a former CIA official, is introduced to Iranian arms dealer Manucher Ghorbanifar in Hamburg, West Germany, by the former head of SAVAK's counterespionage department, Gen. Manucher Hashemi. Ghorbanifar suggests to Shackley that the United States pay a cash ransom for the return of U.S. hostages held in Beirut, with Ghorbanifar working as the middleman, according to the Tower report. He also suggests that Iran would be willing to exchange captured Soviet weapons for U.S.-made TOW missiles. The State Department replies in December, according to Shackley, that it would work the problem out through other channels.

December. *Contra Arms Purchase.* According to the February 15, 1987, *New York Times,* the first known shipment of weapons for the contras arranged by North's Project Democracy network leaves Portugal for Honduras.

December 3. *University Librarian Kidnapped.* Peter Kilburn, librarian at the American University of Beirut, fails to report to work. The extremist group Islamic Jihad says he has been kidnapped.

December 4-12. *Kuwaiti Airline Hijacking.* Four Arabs hijack a Kuwaiti passenger plane and divert it to Tehran. The hijackers demand the release of seventeen Arabs (the Da'Wa prisoners) imprisoned for terrorist attacks in December 1983 that included the bombing of the American and French embassies in Kuwait. Two American hostages aboard the plane are killed December 4 and 6. Iranian police storm the plane and free the hostages December 9. The U.S. government later accuses Iran of backing the operation and demands the extradition of the hijackers on December 11. The Iranian government refuses the extradition request December 12.

December 11. *CIA Influence in Iran.* In a letter to the deputy national security adviser, Vice Adm. John M. Poindexter, the CIA professes only a limited capability to influence events in Iran over the near term, according to the Tower Commission report. The CIA's deputy director of operations tells Poindexter that he considers Marxist Mujaheddin E Khalq to be well organized, influenced by the Soviets, and likely to succeed Khomeini. The State Department distills these views in a draft National Security Decision Directive (NSDD) sent to McFarlane December 14. NSC staff member Howard J. Teicher told the Tower Commission that the interagency study failed to identify any new ideas for significantly expanding U.S. influence in Iran.

December 21. *Contra Arms Purchase.* Defex, a Portuguese arms trading company, sends to the Portuguese Arms Directorate three "end-user" certificates, requesting arms shipments to Guatemala, according to the January 17, 1987, *Washington Post.* The *Post* reported that Guatemalan officials denied any connection with the shipments and that the arms apparently were being purchased for the contras. U.S. and Portuguese officials were reported to believe that nearly 800 tons of Portuguese arms and ammunition were purchased in 1985 and 1986. The "end-user" certificates were said to have been given to Defex by Energy Resources International, a company controlled by Richard Secord and Albert Hakim. Requests for clearance to ship the arms by air were filed in January 1985.

December 21. *Gregg-Rodriguez Meeting.* Former CIA operative Felix I. Rodriguez meets with Donald Gregg, Vice President George Bush's national security adviser, and expresses an interest in working with the El Salvador Air Force as an adviser on counterinsurgency, according to a chronology released by Bush's office December 15, 1986. Gregg subsequently called U.S. ambassador to El Salvador Thomas R. Pickering, Assistant Secretary of State Langhorne Motley, and Deputy Assistant Secretary of Defense Nestor D. Sanchez to recommend that they meet with Rodriguez. Rodriguez met with these officials and later with Gen. Paul F. Gorman, who was in charge of the U.S. Army's Southern Command that oversees U.S. military operations in Central America.

Late 1984. *Iran Policy Reappraisal.* Donald Fortier, the NSC's top global strategist, identifies Iran as one of three world flash points where existing U.S. policy needs review. A formal reappraisal of U.S. policy toward Iran begins when the NSC issues a National Security Study Directive for the CIA, State Department, and Department of Defense to look into ways of improving U.S.-Iran relations.

1985

January. *Israelis-Ghorbanifar Discussions.* In a series of meetings beginning in January, Iran and the American hostages in Lebanon are discussed by Yaacov Nimrodi and Adolph "Al" Schwimmer, Israeli arms merchants; Amiram Nir, antiterrorism adviser to Israeli prime minister Shimon Peres; and Manucher Ghorbanifar, an exiled Iranian arms merchant. According to the report issued in February 1987 by the President's Special Review Board (Tower Commission), they conclude that a plan to gain the release of American hostages and "open up a dialogue with Iran" was realistic with U.S support. The Tower Commission found "rather cryptic evidence" of a March meeting in Cologne, West Germany, that involved Iranians, including probably Dr. Shahabadi, chief of the Iranian buying office and a friend of Saudi arms merchant Adnan Khashoggi. New York businessman Roy M. Furmark, who participated in at least one of the meetings, told CIA national intelligence officer Charles Allen that "profit was certainly a motive" of the Israelis and Ghorbanifar, but that the group did see their efforts as promoting stability in the region and the release of the hostages.

January 8. *Priest Kidnapped.* Rev. Lawrence Jenco, director of Catholic Relief Services, is kidnapped in Lebanon.

January 10. *Contra Arms Purchase.* Defex, a Portuguese arms trading company, sends a letter to the Lisbon government requesting permission to arrange transit through Portugal to Guatemala of one-half million rounds of 7.62mm ammunition from Romania, according to the January 17, 1987, *Washington Post.* Defex was reported to be acting on behalf of Energy Resources International, a company controlled by Richard V. Secord, a retired Air Force major general, and his Iranian-American partner, Albert Hakim. The arms were destined for the contras, according to the *Post.*

January 18. *Covert Action Findings.* A National Security Decision Directive (NSDD) is signed by President Ronald Reagan requiring additional interagency evaluations of all covert activities, notification of Congress in accordance with statutes, and presidential approval in writing of all covert action findings made pursuant to section 501 of the National Security Act.

January 22. *Rodriguez-Bush Meeting.* Former CIA operative Felix I. Rodriguez meets with Vice President George Bush and Donald P. Gregg, Bush's national security adviser. Bush is told of Rodriguez's interest in working with the El Salvador Air Force on counterinsurgency, according to a chronology of contacts with Rodriguez released by Bush's office December 15, 1986.

February-May. *Contra Arms Purchases.* The first of four private arms sales arranged by Secord for the contras occurs. According to Secord's May 1987 testimony before the House and Senate select committees investigating the Iran-contra affair, Secord arranged four private arms sales to the contras that were to begin in late 1984 but due to logistical foul-ups were not made until early 1985. Two of the sales, in February and April, were handled through a Canadian firm, Transworld Armaments, and the other sales, in March and May, were made by former CIA official Thomas Clines. These were regular commercial transactions; the private aid network was developed later in 1985.

According to the March 6, 1987, *Washington Post*, Calero said that, during the period of the congressional ban on contra aid, the contras obtained arms through three intermediaries: Secord, retired major general John K. Singlaub, and retired lieutenant colonel James McCoy, who worked with Ronald J. Martin of R. M. Equipment Co.

February. *Contra Aid Deposit.* National Security Council (NSC) aide Lt. Col. Oliver L. North sends a letter to Calero urging the contras to use some of their funds for "my British friend and his services"—an apparent reference to retired British commando David Walker, according to the May 16, 1987, *Washington Post.* In May 14, 1987, testimony before the House and Senate Iran-contra committees, Robert W. Owen, North's liaison with the contras, said that North had suggested that Walker and others had been involved in some sabotage work in Managua.

February 6. *North Proposes Ship Interception.* The Tower Commission found that in 1985 North became increasingly involved in operational activities in support of the contras. In a memo to national security adviser Robert C. McFarlane, North discusses a Nicaraguan vessel, called the MONIMBO, which was suspected of carrying arms via North Korea to Nicaragua. North recommends providing contra leader Calero with information on the MONIMBO so that the vessel might be seized or sunk. North suggests using the special operations unit of "a friendly nation" to assist in the operation. Vice Adm. John M. Poindexter, the deputy national security adviser, attaches a note to the memo indicating his agreement. The project apparently was abandoned when the friendly government rejected involvement, according to the Tower report.

February 6. *Singlaub Activities.* North briefs McFarlane on Singlaub's efforts to raise funds in Asia for the contras and requests permission to coordinate Singlaub's contacts with two Asian countries that had offered to make a contribution. The Tower Commission found no evidence that McFarlane approved North's request, but both Asian countries eventually made contributions.

February 8. *Gorman Voices Concern over Rodriguez.* Gen. Paul F. Gorman, commander of the U.S. Army's Southern Command, sends a cable to the State Department stating that NSC aide North has assured him that Rodriguez is to focus "on forces operating elsewhere in Centam" and will play only a consulting role in El Salvador, according to the August 20, 1987, *Washington Post* account of documents released by the House and Senate Iran-contra committees.

February 11-12. *King Fahd Visit.* Saudi Arabian king Fahd pays a state visit to the White House. The king has breakfast with President Reagan. According to the May 11, 1987, testimony of former national security adviser McFarlane before the House and Senate Iran-contra committees, McFarlane is informed within a day or two of the visit that Fahd has offered to pay up to $2 million a month for the contras. The Saudis were reported to have given $1 million a month to the contras from July 1984 to February 1985. McFarlane testified that the Saudis eventually gave

$16.5 million between February and April 1985. Both Reagan and McFarlane denied that a direct solicitation had been made.

February 13. *American Hostage Escapes.* Hostage Jeremy Levin escapes from his captors in Lebanon and is turned over to U.S. authorities by Syria.

February 14. *Contra Arms Purchase.* The Portuguese company Defex files another five Guatemalan end-user certificates, according to the January 17, 1987, *Washington Post.* Energy Resources International, Secord and Hakim's company, is the new Guatemalan agent listed. The certificates request 10,000 rifles (3,787 were ultimately provided); 10,000 pounds of TNT (6,700 pounds were provided); 1,500 detonators; 150 M79 grenade launchers with 10,000 grenades (not made in Portugal, so were not provided); 150 60mm mortars; 3,000 60mm grenades; 100 81mm mortars; 2,000 81mm grenades; 150 machine guns; and 30 57mm recoilless rifles. The first installment of these weapons is cleared for shipment by air on March 19.

February 14. *Rodriguez's Contra Role.* After meeting with Rodriguez, General Gorman states in a cable to U.S. ambassador to El Salvador Thomas R. Pickering and Col. James Steele, commander of the U.S. military forces in El Salvador, that the primary role of Rodriguez is to assist the Nicaraguan Democratic Force (FDN), the main military arm of the contras, according to the August 20, 1987, *Washington Post* account of documents released by the House and Senate Iran-contra committees.

February 19. *Rodriguez's Contra Role.* North notes that General Gorman wants to get Rodriguez out of the counterinsurgency effort in El Salvador. North writes: "FR told his priority should be FDN," according to the August 20, 1987, *Washington Post* account of documents released by the House and Senate Iran-contra committees.

February 19. *Rodriguez-Gregg Meeting.* Rodriguez meets with Bush adviser Gregg to report on his progress in El Salvador, according to the chronology released December 15, 1986, by Bush's office. Rodriguez moves to El Salvador in March 1985.

February 28. *Contra Arms Purchase.* A plane, contracted by R. M. Equipment Co. and carrying 9,450 rifle magazines, 20 mortar tripods, and other military supplies, reportedly departs from Miami and arrives in Tegucigalpa, Honduras. According to the May 2, 1987, *Miami Herald*, the weapons are intended for the contras, but when the contra leadership refuses to pay for the cargo, valued at $43,150, the supplies are placed in a Honduran warehouse. The *Herald* reported that R. M. Equipment had served as the broker for as much as $15 million worth of military supplies for the contras.

March 5. *Singlaub Activities.* North requests from the ambassador of an unnamed Central American country "a multiple entry visa" for Singlaub. On March 14, after returning from his trip, Singlaub tells North that he promised contra leaders that he would recruit and send "a few American trainers," described as "civilian (former military or CIA personnel) who will do training only and not participate in combat operations."

March 5. *Contra Arms Purchases.* North sends McFarlane a memo describing a plan to ship weapons to the contras via an unnamed country (identified by news sources as Guatemala), with shipments to start on or about March 10. North, according to the Tower Commission report, attaches copies of "end-user" certificates for nearly $8 million in munitions for the contras. North calls for increased U.S. aid to Guatemala.

March 11. *American Journalist Kidnapped.* Terry A. Anderson, chief Middle East correspondent for the Associated Press, is kidnapped in Beirut.

March 16. *North Plan for Private Aid to Contras.* NSC aide North sends a memo to McFarlane, outlining a fall-back plan if Congress does not vote to resume aid to the contras. He recommends that President Reagan make a public request for private funds "to support liberty and democracy in the Americas." McFarlane writes "not yet" in the margin of the memo. North also suggests that White House counsel Fred Fielding be asked to "conduct a very private evaluation of the president's role." The Tower Commission report indicates that McFarlane agreed to some of North's recommendations, including the establishment of the Nicaraguan Freedom Fund Inc., a 501(c)3 tax-exempt corporation.

April. *Israeli Contact Suggested.* National Security Council consultant Michael Ledeen, during a trip to Europe, meets with a European intelligence official who has just returned from Iran. The official tells Ledeen, according to Ledeen's testimony before the Senate Intelligence Committee and the Tower Commission, that the political situation is more "fluid" than previously thought and suggests that the United States contact the Israelis to learn about Iran's internal affairs.

April. *IOB Opinion.* Bretton G. Sciaroni, general counsel of the Intelligence Oversight Board (IOB), sends North a copy of his legal opinion on the "legal basis for covert action" in Central America, according to Sciaroni's testimony June 8, 1987, before the House and Senate Iran-contra committees.

April 4. *Reagan Cease-fire Proposal.* President Reagan proposes a sixty-day cease-fire between the contras and Sandinista troops, along with church-mediated negotiations. Reagan proposes the cease-fire as a means of encouraging Congress to release $14 million in unspent fiscal 1985 funds, which the president claims would be used only for nonmilitary aid, if the Sandanistas accept the cease-fire by June 1. If no agreement is reached within sixty days after the talks start, Reagan would resume arms aid unless both sides are opposed.

April 9. *Ledeen Role Questioned.* In a memo to McFarlane, the NSC director for political-military affairs, Donald Fortier, disapproves of suggestions to use Ledeen as "the primary channel for working the Iran issue" with foreign governments. But Ledeen, on his own initiative, sets up a meeting with Israeli prime minister Shimon Peres. McFarlane suggests to Fortier that they hold off on sending Ledeen to Israel until after McFarlane has a chance to speak with Secretary of State George P. Shultz on the matter.

April 10. *Contra Arms Purchase.* The Portuguese company Defex files more end-user certificates for military equipment allegedly ordered by the Guatemalan government but actually slated for the contras. Energy Resources International is listed as the arms purchaser, according to the January 17, 1987, *Washington Post.*

April 11. *North on Contra Funds.* North tells McFarlane in a memorandum that he is worried about funds for the contras running out and suggests that $15-$20 million be acquired from "current donors [Saudi Arabia]," in order to allow the contra force to grow to 30,000-35,000. According to the Tower report, North also writes that between July 1984 and February 1985, the Nicaraguan Democratic force (FDN) received $1 million a month for a total of $8 million, and from February 22 to April 9, 1985, $16.5 mil-

lion more had been received for a grand total of $24.5 million. North indicates that $17,145,594 already had been spent for "arms, munitions, combat operations, and support activities." He attaches a list of contra arms purchases during this period.

April 18. *North Diagram.* North sketches a diagram linking him with Robert W. Owen, head of the Institute for Democracy Education and Assistance Inc. (IDEA); Andrew Messing, Jr., the executive director of the National Defense Council, a procontra group; and Linda Guell, director of Western Goals Foundation, one of conservative fund-raiser Carl R. "Spitz" Channell's organizations. North writes "weapons" under Owen's name, "funds" under Messing's name, and "money" under Guell's name. The sketch is included in the Tower Commission report.

April 23. *House Rejects Contra Aid Resumption.* The House overwhelmingly votes to reject a resolution to release $14 million in aid to the contras. An hour earlier the Senate narrowly had approved the resolution.

May. *Contra Arms Purchase.* Contra leader Adolfo Calero places a $5.3 million order for small arms and ammunition with Singlaub, according to the March 6, 1987, *New York Times.* Calero, in his May 20, 1987, testimony before the House and Senate Iran-contra committees, said that Singlaub offered AK47 rifles at $135 a piece, compared with Secord's price of $250 each.

May 4 or 5. *Ledeen-Peres Meeting.* NSC consultant Ledeen, according to his testimony before the Senate Intelligence Committee and the Tower Commission, meets with Israeli prime minister Peres to ask for his help in obtaining intelligence information on Iran. Peres sets up a group of people outside the government, headed by former chief of Israel's military intelligence Shlomo Gazit, to study the Iran question and Iranian terrorist issue. Ledeen testified that he had discussed with McFarlane the possibility of opening ties with Iran through Israeli intermediaries. Ledeen told the Tower Commission that during his meeting with Peres, the Israeli prime minister asked him to ask McFarlane if the United States might approve an Israeli arms shipment to Iran. Ledeen recalled that it was "either ammunition for artillery pieces or some quantity of artillery pieces, but it had to do with artillery." Ledeen said that McFarlane authorized him to tell Peres "it's okay, but just that and nothing else."

May 13. *Ledeen Report.* Ledeen returns to the United States from Israel and calls Fortier to tell him that his meeting with Peres developed some "very positive feedback," according to a memo from Fortier to Poindexter.

May 17. *CIA Memo on Iran Policy.* Graham Fuller, the CIA national intelligence officer for Near East and South Asia, submits a five-page memo to CIA director Casey, entitled, "Toward a Policy on Iran." Fuller states that a succession struggle in Iran was in the making and that "the US has almost no cards to play; the USSR has many." He writes: "Our urgent need is to develop a broad spectrum of policy moves designed to give us some leverage in the race for influence in Tehran." After analyzing a number of alternative courses, Fuller concludes that the "best course ... was to have friendly states sell arms that would not affect the strategic balance as a means of showing Tehran that it had alternatives to the Soviet Union."

May 20. *Intelligence Assessment of Iran.* The intelligence community circulates a revision of its October 1984 "Special National Intelligence Estimate" (SNIE) on Iran. The study suggests that the degree to which European and other friendly states "can fill a military gap for Iran will be a critical measure of the West's ability to blunt Soviet influence."

May 28. *Hospital Director Kidnapped.* David P. Jacobsen, director of the American University of Beirut Hospital, is kidnapped.

May 28. *Israeli Help Proposed.* While working on a draft of a new National Security Decision Directive (NSDD) on Iran, Fortier writes McFarlane: "I think the Israeli option is one we have to pursue even though we may have to pay a certain price for the help."

May 30. *Shultz Not Told of Ledeen Mission.* U.S. ambassador to Israel Samuel Lewis reports to Secretary of State Shultz that Ledeen is in Israel on a "secret mission for the White House." According to Shultz's December 16, 1986, testimony before the Senate Intelligence Committee, he had been unaware of Ledeen's efforts in Israel.

June. *Coors's Contribution.* Colorado businessman Joseph Coors tells CIA director Casey that he wants to make a contribution to assist the contras. According to Coors's May 21, 1987, testimony before the House and Senate Iran-contra committees, Casey says he cannot do anything but arranges for Coors to meet with North. North suggests Coors contribute $65,000 for the purchase of a Maule cargo aircraft, which Coors thought would be used by the contras but which in fact became part of the assets of Secord's contra supply operation. North, according to Coors, turns over the Swiss bank account number of Lake Resources and the money was deposited in August 1985.

June 3. *CIA Station Chief Dies.* William Buckley, the CIA station chief in Beirut who was kidnapped March 16, 1984, probably dies of "pneumonia-like symptoms" while still being held hostage in Lebanon, according to NSC chronologies cited in the Tower report.

June 4. *Iran Memo Sent to Shultz.* CIA director Casey forwards a copy of Graham Fuller's May 17 memo on Iran policy to Secretary of State Shultz.

June 5. *Gregg-Rodriguez Meeting.* Rodriguez meets with Bush aide Gregg and Col. James Steele, commander of U.S. military forces in El Salvador, to discuss the situation in El Salvador, according to a chronology released December 15, 1986, by Bush's office.

June 5. *Shultz Complains about Ledeen.* After learning of Ledeen's contacts with Israeli officials about Iran, Shultz complains in a memo to McFarlane that the State Department had been bypassed. According to his testimony before the Senate Intelligence Committee, Shultz tells McFarlane that Israel's agenda "is not the same as ours" and that an intelligence relationship with Israel concerning Iran "could seriously skew our own perception and analysis of the Iranian scene."

June 7. *McFarlane Responds to Shultz.* McFarlane, responding to Shultz's message of June 5, says the Ledeen-Israeli contacts had been an Israeli initiative and that Ledeen had been acting "on his own hook." McFarlane writes, "I am turning it [the initiative] off entirely," but added "I am not convinced that that is wise."

June 7. *Shackley Report on Hostages.* Former CIA official Theodore G. Shackley prepares a second report on "American Hostages in Lebanon." (He made his first report in November 1984.) Shackley gives the June report to Ledeen, who passes it on to North. Shackley reports that Tehran is interested in two things: (1) a dialogue with a responsible American who can identify what he represents; (2) a discussion of a quid pro quo that involves items other than money.

June 7. *Reagan and Ransom.* North requests and receives McFarlane's approval for efforts to secure the release of hostages in Lebanon. One plan, to be implemented by NSC and Drug Enforcement Administration (DEA) personnel, involves the private ransoming of two U.S. hostages for $2 million. The Tower Commission says that evidence suggested that the private source of these funds was Texas businessman H. Ross Perot.

According to McFarlane's May 11, 1987, testimony before the House and Senate Iran-contra committees, President Reagan approves and Attorney General Edwin Meese III authorizes a June 1985 plan to pay up to $2 million in bribes and ransom for two American hostages. The operation, which did not succeed, was to be financed by DEA, CIA, and private sources. An NSC document, released the day of McFarlane's testimony, indicated that $500,000 was to be used as "bribes" and the remaining $1.5 million was to be paid upon release of the hostages. White House officials denied that Reagan had approved the paying of "ransom" for the hostages' release.

June 9. *University Official Kidnapped.* Thomas Sutherland, acting dean of agriculture at the American University of Beirut, is kidnapped.

June 11. *Draft NSC Proposals on Iran.* NSC aides Donald Fortier and Howard J. Teicher submit to McFarlane a draft National Security Decision Directive (NSDD) based on a May 20 intelligence report on Iran. The draft defines immediate U.S. interests and longer-term goals and recommends steps to meet those goals. First on the list is the suggestion that U.S. allies should be encouraged to "help Iran meet its import requirements. . . . This includes provision of selected military equipment as determined on a case-by-case basis."

June 12. *House Votes Contra Aid.* The House reverses its April 23 decision and votes 248-184 to provide the contras with $27 million in nonmilitary aid. Nicaraguan president Daniel Ortega's visit to the Soviet Union in late April to request both economic and military aid was seen as a major reason for the congressional turnaround on contra aid.

June 14. *TWA Hijacking.* TWA flight 847 is hijacked and diverted to Beirut with 135 U.S. citizens aboard. According to testimony by White House chief of staff Donald T. Regan before the Senate Intelligence Committee, McFarlane during the crisis mentions the possibility of using the Israeli channel to Iran. Regan said that he had been unaware of any such contacts with Iran prior to this time.

June 17. *Draft NSC Proposals on Iran.* McFarlane sends the recently drafted NSDD on Iran to Shultz, Defense Secretary Caspar W. Weinberger, and Casey.

June 17. *Hostage Swap Discussed.* According to the Tower report, Casey learns from a wartime friend, John Shaheen, that Iranian arms dealer Cyrus Hashemi claimed that he had discussed with the Iranian foreign ministry an exchange of U.S. hostages for the release of seventeen terrorists imprisoned in Kuwait (Da'Wa prisoners) and TOW (tube-launched, optically tracked, wire-guided) anti-tank missiles. Hashemi, under indictment for attempting to sell arms to Iran, wanted the charges dropped. Hashemi was indicted in April 1986 on similar charges.

June 19. *Iran and TWA Hijacking.* Iran sends the United States a message to the effect that Tehran wants to do as much as it can to end the TWA hijacking crisis, according to the Tower report.

June 21. *U.S. Response to Iran.* The United States responds to the Iranian offer of assistance: "[i]t is the view of the United States that the government of Iran cannot escape its responsibilities . . . to help secure the release of the hostages. . . ," according to the Tower report.

June 29. *Shultz Responds to Draft NSDD.* Shultz responds to the June 11 draft NSDD in a written memo to McFarlane. Shultz calls the proposal to permit or encourage a flow of Western arms to Iran "perverse" and "contrary to our interest."

June 30. *TWA Hostages Released.* Hostages on TWA flight 847 are released after the alleged secret intervention of the leader of the Iranian parliament, Ali Akbar Hashemi Rafsanjani. The development produces what one U.S. source calls "a great stirring of interest" within the administration in the prospect of improving relations with Iran. In a speech following the hostages' release, President Reagan restates U.S. policy, insisting that the United States gives "no reward" to terrorists. "We make no concessions, we make no deals," he says. One American was killed during the hijacking ordeal.

June or July. *Taiwan Contributes to Contras.* Taiwan, solicited by Assistant Secretary of State Gaston J. Sigur, Jr., contributes $1 million for the contras, according to Sigur's May 14, 1987, testimony before the House and Senate Iran-contra committees.

July. *'Southern Front,' Costa Rican Airstrip.* Prior to assuming his post as U.S. ambassador to Costa Rica, Lewis A. Tambs is told by North that he is to open a military front for the contras in southern Nicaragua, according to Tambs's testimony before the House and Senate Iran-contra committees May 28, 1987.

He also testified that shortly after he arrived in Costa Rica North told him to obtain permission from Costa Rican officials to build a secret airstrip to be used for contra supply missions. The runway is constructed in the summer of 1985. It is used for direct contra supply efforts from July 1985 to February 1986 and then for emergency use of damaged aircraft until its closing in September 1986.

July. *Private Contra Aid Airlift.* Secord meets in early July with North and Calero in an all-night session in an airport hotel in Miami. According to Secord's May 5, 1987, testimony before the House and Senate Iran-contra committees, North confronts Calero that evening about private contra funds being "wasted, squandered, and even worse, some people might be lining their pockets." At the meeting, the three decide to launch an airlift operation in Central America to supply the contras. Secord testified that he was advised by former CIA employees Clines and Rafael Quintero not to get involved with the operation, but pleas from North persuaded Secord to lend a hand.

July. *North Contacts FBI.* North asks an FBI official to postpone an interview with Mousalreza Ebrahim Zadeh, who was the target of an FBI bank fraud investigation. North was concerned that Zadeh, an Iranian who had been posing as a Saudi Arabian prince, would change his mind about pursuing a scheme to sell Saudi oil to raise money for the contras. According to then-FBI director William H. Webster's testimony before the Senate Intelligence Committee in April 1987, the FBI had not planned to question Zadeh at that time.

July 1. *Khashoggi-Ghorbanifar Report.* Khashoggi sends to McFarlane an analysis, prepared by or with the assistance of Ghorbanifar, of prospects for improved U.S.-Iranian relations. The report, dated February 5, 1985, includes a narrative by Ghorbanifar, which says that "if it proves necessary to bribe some Iranian it can be done under the cover of a gift," according to the March 5, 1987, *New York Times.* McFarlane testified that he did not recall

seeing the analysis, according to the Senate Intelligence Committee's report issued January 29, 1987.

July 2. *Reagan Meets with Hijacking Victims.* President Reagan attends a ceremony upon the return of the hijacking victims aboard TWA flight 847. One American, U.S. Navy diver Robert Dean Stethem, was killed in Beirut during the June 1985 hijacking. During the ceremony, the plane's pilot, John L. Testrake, states the hope that the administration's efforts to free the American hostages held in Lebanon will soon succeed. McFarlane told the Tower Commission that the Reagans stayed an extra half hour to greet each of the families there and that "it was a very moving moment and it had an impact on him."

July 3. *Kimche-McFarlane Meeting.* David Kimche, director general of the Israeli foreign ministry, tells McFarlane in a meeting at the White House that Israel has succeeded in opening a dialogue with Iranian officials. Kimche says that Iran is willing to renew relations with the United States and as a sign of good faith would seek the release of U.S. hostages held in Lebanon. Kimche tells McFarlane the Iranians at some point may request arms. McFarlane told the Tower Commission that he reported this conversation to the president before Reagan entered the hospital July 13 for a cancer operation. He said he also informed Shultz, Weinberger, and Casey.

July 8. *Reagan Criticizes Iran.* Reagan, in a speech to the American Bar Association, says countries such as Iran, Libya, North Korea, Cuba, and Nicaragua were united "by one simple criminal phenomenon—their fanatical hatred of the United States, our people, our way of life, our international stature." He also says Iran is part of a "new international version of Murder Incorporated."

July 9. *Channell's Contra Effort.* Conservative fundraiser Carl R. "Spitz" Channell meets with North; Richard R. Miller, president of International Business Communications; and several others at the Hay-Adams Hotel in Washington, D.C., to discuss efforts to raise money and secretly supply the contras with military aid, according to Channell's April 29, 1987, testimony in the U.S. District Court in Washington, D.C.

July 10. *Contra Traveler's Checks.* North cashes two $500 traveler's checks to purchase tickets from Pan American Airways. The blank checks were given to North by contra leader Calero and were drawn on a Cayman Islands bank account.

July 11. *Ledeen-Israeli Contacts.* Upon the suggestion of Kimche, Leeden meets with Israeli arms dealer Adolph "Al" Schwimmer. Leeden, testifying before the Senate Intelligence Committee and the Tower panel, said that Schwimmer recommends that he meet with Ghorbanifar. Leeden testified that he discussed with McFarlane the possibility of meeting with Ghorbanifar during the summer and McFarlane agreed.

July 11. *Hostage-Arms Swap Proposed.* According to the Tower report, Israeli arms dealer Schwimmer relays through Ledeen a message from Prime Minister Peres to McFarlane that the Iranians were interested in opening ties to the West and that the Iranians had suggested that seven U.S. hostages might be released in exchange for 100 TOW missiles.

July 13. *Reagan Surgery.* President Reagan undergoes cancer surgery. The prognosis is excellent.

July 14. *McFarlane-Shultz Communications on Iran.* McFarlane sends a cable to Shultz telling him of the possible opening to Iran and the proposed arms-for-hostages arrangement. McFarlane tells Shultz that he had instructed Ledeen to say that the United States did not "favor such a process." However, the issue had been raised again in McFarlane's July 3 meeting with Kimche and in a special message from Peres. McFarlane says he has reviewed the proposal: "On balance I tend to favor going ahead." Shultz responds that the United States should show some interest, but proceed with caution for the time being. Shultz points out "the fraud that seems to accompany so many deals involving arms and Iran, and the complications arising from our 'blessing' an Israel-Iran relationship where Israel's interests and ours are not necessarily the same."

Mid-July. *McFarlane Briefs Reagan on Iran.* Several days after the president's surgery, McFarlane visits Reagan in the hospital. According to his testimony before the Senate Intelligence Committee, McFarlane requests permission to use an Israeli contact with an Iranian to reach Iranian officials. White House chief of staff Regan, who testified that he attended the meeting, said that they met for twenty to twenty-five minutes during which time the president asked many questions and then gave McFarlane the go-ahead. Chief of Staff Regan also said that McFarlane referred specifically to Ghorbanifar as the Iranian contact. McFarlane denied that he made any mention of Ghorbanifar and told Intelligence Committee members that he had not become aware of Ghorbanifar until December 1985. The Senate report says, "It should be noted, however, that McFarlane made reference to Ghorbanifar in his July 14 cable to Shultz describing the proposal."

July 16. *Weinberger Responds to Draft NSDD.* Weinberger, in his initial reaction to the June 11 draft NSDD that recommended the United States encourage a flow of Western arms to Iran, writes in the margin, "This is almost too absurd to comment on." In his formal comments, Weinberger strongly opposes the arms sales proposal.

July 16. *Ghorbanifar Called 'Fabricator.'* Secretary of State Shultz sees an intelligence report that refers to Ghorbanifar as "a talented fabricator."

July 18. *Casey Responds to Draft NSDD.* CIA director Casey writes McFarlane that he "strongly endorse[s]" the "thrust" of the June 11 draft NSDD and supports the idea of improving U.S. leverage in the region. Casey does not address the issue of limited arms sales to Iran, according to the Tower report.

July 29. *Contra Arms Purchase.* The Lisbon government receives an end-user certificate from Portuguese weapons trading company Defex for the purchase of arms supposedly going to Guatemala but actually purchased for the contras. Energy Resources International, a company controlled by Secord and Hakim, is once again listed as the agent. According to the January 17, 1987, *Washington Post,* additional arms shipment clearances are granted by the Lisbon government on: May 7, 1985 (by ship); December 15, 1985 (by air); March 2, 1986 (by air); April 12, 1986 (by air); May 24, 1986 (by air); August 22, 1986 (by ship).

Late July. *Ledeen-Ghorbanifar Meeting.* Ledeen meets with Ghorbanifar in Israel. The meeting also is attended by Kimche, Schwimmer, and Nimrodi. Ghorbanifar says that both the United States and Iran would have to send clear signals showing a desire to renew ties. Ghorbanifar suggests that the Iranians might secure the release of U.S. hostages in Lebanon in exchange for U.S. shipments of arms.

Late July. *Khashoggi to Finance Sales.* Furmark, Ghorbanifar, Nimrodi, Nir, and Schwimmer meet to discuss the opening of relations between Iran and the United States. Furmark told the Tower Commission that, when it became apparent that the Israelis would not ship arms without payment and the Iranians would not pay until they inspected the shipment, Khashoggi offered to put up $1 million for advanced payment to Israel, to be repaid through Ghorbanifar after the Iranians inspected the shipment.

August. *IOB Examines North's Contra Activities.* Because of press reports that NSC aide North has been giving military advice and support to the contras, Bretton G. Sciaroni, counsel to the president's Intelligence Oversight Board, begins an inquiry into North's activities. He issues an opinion September 12.

August. *Coors Contributes to Contras.* Joseph Coors deposits $65,000 in the Lake Resources' Swiss bank account, according to his May 21, 1987, testimony before the House and Senate Iran-contra committees.

August 2. *McFarlane-Kimche Meeting.* McFarlane meets with Kimche and tells him that Iranian "moderates" wish to establish a dialogue with the Reagan administration and are willing to obtain the release of U.S. hostages in Lebanon in return for shipments of arms to Iran. According to the Tower Commission report, Kimche says that the shipment of 100 TOW missiles to Iran could result in the release of all American hostages in Beirut. McFarlane tells him that the United States probably would not agree to selling arms to Iran but says that he will discuss the possibility of Israel delivering the arms. McFarlane told the Tower Commission that he reported to the president within two or three days of his meeting with Kimche.

Early August. *Approval of Israeli Sale to Iran.* In and around the first two weeks of August, most NSC principals have an opportunity to discuss Israel's request to transfer arms to Iran, according to the Tower Commission. But the commission points out that what transpired was "quite murky" and there apparently was no written record of the decision-making process.

McFarlane said that he discussed the proposal with President Reagan "several times" and on at least one occasion with the full NSC. McFarlane said Reagan called him within days after the meeting and gave his approval for Israel to transfer arms to Iran and buy replacements from the United States.

A conflicting version of events was provided by Chief of Staff Regan, who told the Tower Commission the president had not given prior approval to Israel's sale of arms to Iran. President Reagan at first told the Tower Commission that he had approved the arms shipments, then later said he had not approved the transfer in advance, and finally said that he could not remember whether he had approved it in advance or not. The Tower Commission concluded: "We are persuaded that he [Reagan] most likely provided this approval prior to the first shipment by Israel."

August 6. *Shultz Opposes Arms Sale.* Shultz meets with Reagan and McFarlane to discuss the transfer of 100 TOW missiles from Israel to Iran in return for the release of four or more hostages, according to Shultz's testimony before the Tower Commission. Shultz voices his opposition to the deal. He told the Tower Commission that he did "not recall the president having decided at that meeting to approve the Iranian offer."

August 8. *Meeting on Arms Sale.* A National Security Planning Group meeting is held in the White House residence, according to the Senate Intelligence Committee report. McFarlane, Poindexter, Vice President Bush,

Shultz, Weinberger, Regan, and Casey are all present. At this time, McFarlane and Poindexter brief Reagan and the others on the Kimche proposal to supply Iran with TOWs from Israel in exchange for the release of U.S. hostages. There was conflicting testimony on who supported the proposal, but Shultz and Weinberger clearly opposed the deal. There was also conflicting testimony on whether or not arms shipments were approved by the president at this time.

August 15. *Contra Aid Resumed.* Legislation (PL 99-88) appropriating $27 million in "humanitarian" aid to the contras is signed into law. Most of the money is set aside for uniforms and other logistical support for the contras. The money was authorized in foreign aid legislation (PL 99-83), which became law August 8. Both measures barred the CIA or the Defense Department from administering the aid.

Mid-August. *Draft NSDD Shelved.* After negative reactions from Shultz and Weinberger to a June 11 draft NSDD that recommended encouraging friendly nations to sell arms to Iran, NSC aide Teicher, one of its authors, is advised to do nothing and "basically to stand down," Teicher told the Tower Commission.

Mid-August. *Ledeen-McFarlane Meeting.* Ledeen returns from his trip to Israel and, according to Ledeen's testimony before the Senate Intelligence Committee, is informed by McFarlane that "the program of contact with Iran would go forward and that a test of the kind Ghorbanifar had proposed would occur." Ledeen said McFarlane told him to work out the arrangements with Kimche for receipt of the hostages.

August 17-30. *Financing of Arms Deal.* According to the Tower Commission report, Ghorbanifar August 17 gives Saudi arms merchant Adnan Khashoggi a post-dated check for $1 million as a guarantee of payment by Iran. Khashoggi then deposits $1 million in an Israeli bank account in Switzerland. Israeli arms dealer Yaacov Nimrodi notifies Israeli officials the money has been received for 100 TOW missiles. Iran transfers $1,217,410 to Ghorbanifar August 27. After the 100 TOWs are delivered to Iran August 30, Ghorbanifar notifies Khashoggi that the post-dated check is covered.

August 20. *McFarlane Denies NSC Contra Role.* Responding to congressional concern about North's involvement in contra fund-raising and supply activities, McFarlane writes Lee Hamilton, D-Ind., chairman of the House Intelligence Committee: "I can state with deep personal conviction that at no time did I or any member of the National Security Council staff violate the letter or spirit of the law [barring military aid to the contras.]" In their testimony before the House and Senate Iran-contra committees in 1987, both McFarlane and North admitted they had misled Congress on North's contra activities.

August 21. *Ledeen-Kimche Meeting.* Ledeen meets with Kimche, who, according to the Tower report, gives Ledeen documents obtained from Ghorbanifar. Kimche tells Ledeen not to expect Iran to meet every promise, but that "he thought that even something significantly less than what they had promised would still be significant ...," according to Ledeen's testimony before the Tower Commission.

August 29 or 30. *Passport for North.* The NSC arranges with the State Department to have a passport created in the name of "William P. Goode." The NSC staff explains to State Department officials that the passport was for North in preparation for "a sensitive operation to

Europe in connection with our hostages in Lebanon."

August 30. *Israel Sends TOW Missiles to Iran.* According to the Tower report, Israel ships 100 U.S.-made TOW antitank missiles to Iran, the first installment of a two-part sale to Iran. A second shipment of 408 missiles is sent on September 14. (The Senate Intelligence Committee report said documents the committee received indicated 508 TOWs left Israel August 30, transited a third country, and arrived in Iran September 13.)

Late August-Early September. *North Plans for Hostage Release.* North is directed to prepare contingency plans for extracting hostages from Lebanon.

September. *Abrams Told to Monitor North.* Shultz becomes concerned about North's activities on the NSC and requests Assistant Secretary of State Elliott Abrams to "monitor Ollie," according to Abrams June 2, 1987, testimony before the House and Senate Iran-contra committees.

September. *Tambs's 'Southern Front' Assignment.* Lewis A. Tambs, the U.S. ambassador to Costa Rica, meets with Assistant Secretary of State Abrams, during a meeting in Panama of U.S. ambassadors in Central America. According to Tambs's May 28, 1987, testimony before the House and Senate Iran-contra committees, Tambs holds a hallway conversation with Abrams in which they discuss the ambassador's assignment to open a "southern front" for the contras. Abrams also participates in a discussion of a secret airstrip being built in Costa Rica for private supply missions to the Nicaraguan contras, according to Tambs. During his June 2, 1987, testimony before the committees, Abrams denied ever having the discussion with Tambs of his "southern front" assignment. Abrams said he learned of the airstrip in August or September 1985.

September 4. *Ghorbanifar Prediction to Ledeen.* Ledeen meets with Kimche, Ghorbanifar, Schwimmer, and Nimrodi in Paris. According to Ledeen's testimony before the Senate Intelligence Committee and Tower Commission, Ghorbanifar tells Ledeen to look for a change in tone on the part of Iranian officials. Two weeks later, on the anniversary of the Iranian revolution, the president and prime minister of Iran make sharp attacks against the Soviet Union, but not against the United States.

September 4. *North's Hostage Release Role.* According to the Tower Commission report, the American ambassador to Lebanon, Reginald Bartholomew, reports that North is handling an operation that would lead to the release of all seven American hostages held in Lebanon and that a U.S. team had been deployed to Beirut.

Early September. *Ghorbanifar Called a 'Talented Fabricator.'* Leeden hands over intelligence information to the CIA on Ghorbanifar and on Iran's involvement in terrorism. According to a senior CIA analyst's testimony before the Senate Intelligence Committee, this was the first time Leeden had identified Ghorbanifar by name to the CIA. Ledeen testified that the question of Ghorbanifar's bona fides first came up in September 1985. But Shultz testified that he had seen an intelligence report on July 16, 1985, which called Ghorbanifar a "talented fabricator."

September 9 or 12. *North Says Hostage Release Possible.* North calls an unnamed CIA analyst on September 9 and requests increased intelligence collection on Lebanon and Iran, according to the CIA analyst's testimony before the Senate Intelligence Committee. North tells him American hostages in Lebanon may be released. The Tower report said North on September 12 asks Charles Allen, national intelligence officer for counterterrorism, for increased intelligence efforts and tells Allen that captured CIA operative Buckley may be released within the next few hours to days.

September 10-12. *Israeli Says Hostage to Be Freed.* Kimche tells McFarlane that the United States could expect one hostage to be released within a few days and asks him to select one. McFarlane chooses Buckley, according to McFarlane's May 11, 1987, testimony before the House and Senate Iran-contra committees. Buckley, it is discovered, had died and Rev. Benjamin F. Weir is released on September 15.

September 12. *McFarlane Denies NSC Role.* McFarlane writes Rep. Michael D. Barnes, D-Md., assuring him that there have not been and would not be any expenditures of NSC funds "which would have the effect of supporting directly or indirectly military or paramilitary operations in Nicaragua by any nation, group, organization, movement or individual. . . ."

September 12. *IOB Opinion on North's Activities.* Sciaroni, counsel for the three-member president's Intelligence Oversight Board, writes a legal opinion saying that North's activities had not violated the fiscal 1985 Boland amendment, named for House Intelligence Committee chairman Edward P. Boland, D-Mass., which barred military aid to the contras by the Pentagon, CIA, or any agency or entity involved in intelligence activities. Sciaroni concludes that, in any event, the National Security Council was not covered by the Boland amendment because it was not an intelligence agency.

September 14-18. *Financing of Arms Deal.* According to the Tower Commission report, Ghorbanifar gives Khashoggi a post-dated check for $4 million as a guarantee of payment by Iran. Khashoggi September 14 deposits $4 million in an Israeli bank account in Switzerland. Nimrodi notifies Israeli officials that the money has been received for the TOW missiles. After 408 TOWs are delivered to Iran September 14, Iran transfers $5 million to Ghorbanifar September 18 and he notifies Khashoggi that the post-dated check is covered. Ghorbanifar pays Nimrodi $250,000 for eight additional TOWs.

September 14. *Israel Sends More TOWs to Iran.* Israel delivers 408 TOW missiles to Iran. The Tower Commission report said there was some evidence that all or part of the TOW shipment was returned to Israel because it contained defective or otherwise unacceptable missiles, and that Israel replaced and reshipped the missiles.

September 15. *Hostage Released.* The Rev. Benjamin F. Weir is released after sixteen months of captivity in Lebanon. The announcement of his release is delayed until September 18 in the hope that other hostages will be freed. The *Washington Post* reported on August 9, 1987, that a joint U.S.-Israeli rescue mission was planned to locate and rescue any U.S. hostages in Lebanon not freed as a result of the arms shipments. The team was unable to locate the other hostages, so the rescue never took place.

September 16. *Running Cash for North and Secord.* Robert W. Owen travels to New York City on the first of three trips to pick up money to be delivered to either North or Secord upon his return to Washington, D.C. According to Owen's May 19, 1987, testimony before the House and Senate Iran-contra committees, on this trip he is sent to a Chinese market in the lower West Side of Manhattan, where an unidentified man walks behind the counter, rolls up his pants leg, and hands over a wad of money totalling $9,500. Owen testified that upon his return he met Secord at a hotel and handed over the cash, folded in a newspaper.

September 17. *Rescue Mission Discussed.* According to the August 9, 1987, *Washington Post,* notes taken at a luncheon indicate that McFarlane discussed with Shultz, Weinberger, and Casey "possible military activities," said to be a reference to the proposed U.S.-Israeli rescue mission to free the hostages held in Lebanon.

September 20, 1985-April 11, 1986. *Funds Transferred to Lake Resources.* In seven transfers between these dates, Channell's National Endowment for the Preservation of Liberty (NEPL) funnels a total of $1.74 million to the Lake Resources account at Credit Suisse Bank in Geneva, according to the March 7, 1987, *Washington Post.* Of this, $1.31 million was funneled through a Cayman Islands corporation called I. C. Inc. (later renamed Intel Co-operation Inc.) and the $430,000 difference was transferred directly to Lake Resources, a Panama-registered company controlled by North, Secord, and Hakim that may have been the most important conduit through which Iranian arms sales and contra aid money passed.

September 20. *North Letter to Rodriguez.* North writes Rodriguez in El Salvador to tell him that within the next fifteen days two new planes will be sent to Honduras to conduct night air drops of military supplies to the contras "deep inside" Nicaragua. North asks him to help with the servicing of the new aircraft. The letter, according to the April 26, 1987, *Washington Post,* instructs Rodriguez not to inform the CIA station chief in El Salvador or others of his activities for the contras. Rodriguez also is told to destroy the letter.

September 26. *North Meetings.* According to North's calendar, North has meetings with Ledeen and then with Schwimmer.

October. *Taiwan Contributes to Contras.* Encouraged by NSC aide North, Assistant Secretary of State Sigur asks Taiwan for a second contribution to the contras. Taiwan had contributed $1 million in June or July 1985. Taiwan agrees to contribute another $1 million, according to Sigur's May 14, 1987, testimony before the House and Senate Iran-contra committees.

October 1. *IBC Contract.* The State Department awards a $276,000 secret contract to Richard R. Miller's International Business Communications Inc. (IBC) to promote support for military aid to the Nicaraguan contras, according to an Associated Press story in the February 7, 1987, *Washington Post.* The contract is not signed until September 1986.

October 4. *False Report of Buckley's Death.* William Buckley, the CIA station chief in Beirut who was abducted March 16, 1984, is reported to have been tortured and killed. Members of the Islamic Jihad announce the execution in retaliation for an October 1 Israeli air raid on the Palestine Liberation Organization (PLO) headquarters in Tunis. The report is said to have led to a series of meetings in Europe among U.S. (CIA and NSC), Israeli, and Iranian intermediaries. According to chronologies produced by the NSC, this announcement was false and Buckley probably died on June 3, 1985.

October 7. *McFarlane Denies NSC Contra Role.* Responding to an inquiry from Rep. Lee H. Hamilton, D-Ind., chairman of the House Intelligence Committee, as to the nature of the NSC staff's involvement in fund raising for the contras, McFarlane writes: "There is no official or unofficial relationship with any member of the NSC staff regarding fund raising for the Nicaraguan democratic opposition."

October 7. *Cruise Ship Hijacking.* An Italian cruise

ship, the *Achille Lauro,* is seized by four Palestinian hijackers. The hijackers later kill American Leon Klinghoffer and push his body off the ship.

October 8. *North Meets with Intermediaries.* North's calendar indicates that he met with Ledeen, Schwimmer, Nimrodi, and Ghorbanifar in the Old Executive Office Building, according to the Tower report.

October 10. *Reagan Thanks Channell.* The March 7, 1987, *Washington Post* reported that President Reagan writes Channell to thank him and his organization, the National Endowment for the Preservation of Liberty (NEPL), for their "remarkable contribution to the course of democracy in Central America. Keep up the good work."

October 17. *Reagan Meets with Channell.* President Reagan and White House officials meet with Channell and selected donors to Channell's NEPL.

October 21. *McFarlane Denies NSC Role in Contra Fund Raising.* McFarlane receives an inquiry from Rep. Richard J. Durbin, D-Ill., as to whether there were any efforts underway in the administration to facilitate the sending of private donations to the contras. McFarlane replies: "No."

Early November. *Israeli Inquires about Arms Replacements.* Yitzhak Rabin, Israel's defense minister, asks McFarlane whether U.S. policy would still permit Israel to buy replacements for arms transferred to Iran. McFarlane confirms that it would, although he indicates U.S. reservations about any trade of arms for hostages, according to testimony before the Tower Commission.

Early November. *Reagan Told of Israeli Arms Plan.* McFarlane tells President Reagan, on the margins of his briefings for the Geneva summit, to expect a shipment of missiles from Israel, through a third country, to Iran, and that hostages would come out, according to Chief of Staff Regan's testimony before the Tower Commission. In his January 16, 1987, meeting with the Tower Commission, the president said he did not remember how the November shipment came about. He said he objected to the shipment and that, as a result, the shipment was returned to Israel. In his second meeting with the commission, Reagan said that neither he nor his chief of staff remembered any meeting or conversation in general about the shipment and that he did not remember anything about a call-back of the shipment.

November 7. *North-Miller-Channell Meeting.* Lt. Col. North, IBC president Miller, and Channell meet at the Hay-Adams Hotel in Washington, D.C., to discuss raising private funds for the Nicaraguan contras. Shortly thereafter, Barbara Newington of Greenwich, Conn., donates $1 million to Channell's NEPL.

November 9. *Kimche-McFarlane-North Meeting.* Kimche meets with McFarlane and North. McFarlane tells Casey and CIA deputy director John N. McMahon November 14 that Kimche had indicated that the Israelis planned to provide some arms to moderates in Iran who would oppose Khomeini, according to McMahon's testimony before the Tower Commission.

November 14. *Waite Report on Hostages.* Terry Waite, special envoy of the archbishop of Canterbury, travels to Beirut. Waite says that the kidnappers remain under intense pressure and it is possible the hostages may be killed in the near future, according to a December 5, 1985, memo written by North. Waite also reports that CIA station chief William Buckley is dead.

November 14. *Casey on Intelligence Leaks.* In response to criticism of the CIA voiced by Senate Intelligence Committee chairman Dave Durenberger, R-Minn., CIA director Casey wrote to Durenberger: "When congressional oversight of the intelligence community is conducted off-the-cuff through the news media and involves the repeated compromise of sensitive intelligence sources and methods, not to mention unsubstantiated appraisals of performance, it is time to acknowledge that the process has gone seriously awry." The CIA made Casey's letter public.

November 17 or 18. *Rabin Asks for Help on Arms Transfer.* While in Geneva for the U.S.-Soviet summit, McFarlane receives a call from Israeli defense minister Rabin. Rabin indicates some difficulties in transferring arms from Israel to Iran, through a European country—identified in news reports as Portugal. McFarlane then calls Poindexter and North and asks them to find out what the problem is.

November 18. *Shultz Informed of Arms Sale.* According to the Tower report, McFarlane tells Shultz of an imminent Israeli shipment of 100 Hawk antiaircraft missiles to Iran in exchange for the release of four American hostages. Shultz says that if he had known about it sooner, he would have stopped it. Shultz tells an associate November 22 that "Bud [McFarlane] says he's cleared with the president" on the plan.

November 19. *North Seeks Secord's Assistance.* North, acting on behalf of McFarlane, sends a letter to Secord requesting his assistance in arranging the transfer of arms from Israel to Iran through a third country (Portugal). Secord that day makes arrangements for transshipment of the Israeli Hawk missiles.

November 19-21. *Reagan Briefed in Geneva.* While attending the U.S.-Soviet summit, President Reagan is told by McFarlane that the Israelis are considering shipping arms to Iran and, if successful, hostages might be freed, according to Chief of Staff Regan's testimony before the Senate Intelligence Committee.

November 20. *North Informs Poindexter.* North sends a message to Poindexter outlining a planned shipment of arms to Iran via a third country (identified in news accounts as Portugal). According to the Senate Intelligence Committee and Tower reports, the message tells of the scheduled November 22 delivery of eighty Hawk missiles. The missiles are to be loaded on three chartered aircraft, which would take off at two-hour intervals for Tabriz. In return, the message says, five U.S. hostages would be released. North indicates that no planes are to land in Tabriz until the hostages are released. A sum of $18 million already had been deposited by Iranian middlemen for the purchase of the missiles. North says that in accordance with Poindexter's instructions "I have told their [Israel's] agent that we will sell them 120 items [Hawks] at a price that they can meet."

November 21. *CIA Aid Requested.* North calls Duane "Dewey" Clarridge, chief of the European division of the CIA's directorate of operations, to ask for help in obtaining an overflight clearance of an Israeli plane. According to the Tower report, the next day Clarridge used CIA communications channels to help obtain the clearance. When Portugal denies the aircraft landing rights, North asks Clarridge to find a reliable commercial substitute for the Israeli plane. Clarridge puts Secord in contact with a carrier that is a CIA proprietary. The February 24, 1987, *Washington Post* identified the carrier as St. Lucia Airways.

November 22. *Bush Note to North.* Bush sends a handwritten "Dear Ollie" note to North in which he says:

"Your dedication and tireless work with the hostage thing and with Central America really gives me cause for great pride in you. . . ." The note was released in September 1987 by the House and Senate Iran-contra committees. Following its release, Bush reiterated that he had been unaware of the contra supply effort until it became public in late 1986.

November 22. *Aircraft for Hawk Shipment.* North tells Poindexter that Secord will charter two aircraft "in the name of LAKE Resources (our Swiss Co.)" from a CIA proprietary. The planes are to pick up the cargo in Israel and deliver it to Portugal, where it will be transferred to three Israeli-chartered planes for the flight to Iran. Later that day North informs Poindexter that Israel has allowed the lease on the three chartered planes to expire, but that Secord has suggested using "one of our LAKE Resources A/C [aircraft]" that had been set to take "a load of ammo" (from Portugal, according to the January 14, 1987, *Washington Post*) to the contras. North says he will tell contra leader Calero that the shipment will be several days late. North writes: "Too bad, this was to be our first direct flight to the resistance field . . . inside Nicaragua. The ammo was already palletized w/parachutes attached." (According to the Senate Intelligence Committee report, another plane ultimately was used for the Iran arms transfer. And testimony given to the House and Senate Iran-contra committees indicated the shipment was not routed through Portugal.) The *Post* quoted one member of Congress as saying this was "the first overlap" between the Iran and contra operations.

November 22-25. *Financing of Arms Deal.* According to the Tower Commission report, Ghorbanifar deposits $24 million in an Israeli bank account in Switzerland. Nimrodi notifies Israeli officials that the money has been received for 120 Hawk missiles. Iran transfers $24.72 million to Ghorbanifar November 22. A CIA proprietary aircraft flies eighteen Hawks to Iran November 25. Iran rejects the missiles and cancels the deal. (The missiles are returned to Israel in February 1986.) Nimrodi returns Ghorbanifar's money, less $5 million for the Hawks delivered.

November 25. *Hawks Delivered to Iran.* A cargo of eighteen Hawk missiles is flown to Iran by a CIA proprietary airline. The cargo is listed as oil-drilling equipment. No hostages are released. The Iranians are disappointed with the shipment and seventeen Hawks eventually are returned to Israel (the other Hawk had been test-fired).

November 25. *CIA Calls for Presidential 'Finding.'* When CIA deputy director McMahon learns that a CIA proprietary has flown arms to Iran and that the CIA asked foreign governments to grant overflight clearances, he asks for a presidential "finding" authorizing the covert action.

November 26. *Draft Finding Sent to White House.* A draft finding, prepared by CIA general counsel Stanley Sporkin, is sent to Poindexter after Casey gives his approval. The finding retroactively sanctions CIA participation in the Hawk shipment and directs Casey not to brief Congress, unless the president tells him otherwise. Poindexter testified before the House and Senate Iran-contra committees, July 15, 1987, that Reagan signed the finding on or around December 5, 1985. Poindexter also testified that he destroyed the finding November 21, 1986, because he thought that its arms-for-hostage terms could be embarrassing for the president.

November 30. *North Cashes Contra Traveler's Check.* North cashes a $100 traveler's check at National Tire Wholesalers in Virginia and purchases two snow tires.

Contra leader Calero had given North traveler's checks drawn on a Cayman Islands bank account in which the Saudis reportedly had deposited $32 million for the contras.

December. *Iran Funds Diverted to Contras.* North asks Secord to divert funds from an Iran arms sale to the contras, according to Secord's May 1987 testimony before the House and Senate Iran-contra committees. Secord's organization had received $1 million from Israeli arms dealer Schwimmer for transportation expenses in the November 1985 Hawk shipment, but Secord said his actual costs totaled only $200,000. At North's request, the remaining $800,000 later is used to help finance arms shipments to the contras.

December 4. *Poindexter Named to Succeed McFarlane.* Poindexer is named by Reagan to replace McFarlane who is resigning as national security adviser.

December 4. *Operation Code for Iran, Contra Activities.* North tells Poindexter he is using an "operation code" for the Iranian affair "similar to the one used to oversee deliveries" to the contras, according to a PROF (Professional Office, or computer mail system) note included in the Tower report.

December 4. *Congress Permits Intelligence Aid to Contras.* Legislation (PL 99-169) allowing U.S. intelligence agencies to supply the contras with limited intelligence information and some communications equipment becomes law. The bill bars the CIA from using its contingency fund to resume covert military aid to the contras.

December 5. *Reagan Signs Intelligence Finding.* On or about this date, President Reagan signs an intelligence finding providing retroactive authorization for the November 1985 arms-for-hostage deal with Iran, according to Poindexter's July 15, 1987, testimony before the House and Senate Iran-contra committees. Poindexter said he destroyed the document November 21, 1986, to protect the president from "significant political embarrassment." A White House spokesman July 16, 1987, said the president does not recall signing the finding but "he doesn't disagree with the contention that he did . . . ."

December 5. *North Outlines New Arms-for-Hostages Plan.* Poindexter receives from North a message briefing him on developments in Iran, U.S. arms shipments, and the hostage situation. In the message, which was included in the Tower report, North outlines a new plan that calls for 3,300 TOW missiles and fifty Improved Hawk missiles to be transferred to Iran in exchange for the release of all U.S. hostages and one French hostage in Lebanon. The deliveries are to take place in five installments over a twenty-four-hour period on or about December 12, 1985. If during any of the transactions, no hostages are released, the deliveries are to stop. North says that he is to meet in London with Secord, Kimche, and Schwimmer to discuss whether or not to proceed.

December 5. *Poindexter-Shultz Conversation.* Poindexter telephones Secretary of State Shultz to brief him on the Iran initiative. Shultz, in his July 23, 1987, testimony before the House and Senate Iran-contra committees, said that he was told more than he had been before about developments in the last half of 1985. But Poindexter does not mention the fact that President Reagan had signed an intelligence finding that day.

December 7. *Reagan, Top Advisers Discuss New Proposal.* President Reagan meets with Shultz, Weinberger, Regan, McMahon, McFarlane, and Poindexter to discuss the Iran initiative. Most of the testimony received by the Senate Intelligence Committee and the Tower Commission indicated that at this meeting there was a consensus to dispatch McFarlane to London to inform the Iranians that the United States wanted the U.S. hostages released and was interested in better relations with Iran but was making no offer of arms. Shultz told the House and Senate Iran-contra committees July 23, 1987, that at this meeting Weinberger warned the president that there were legal problems, to which the president responded: "[T]he American people will never forgive me if I fail to get these hostages out over this legal question."

December 7. *Poindexter-Shultz on Initiative.* Poindexter tells Shultz privately that the Iran project had fallen apart during Thanksgiving week. According to Shultz's testimony before the Tower Commission, Poindexter says that he recommended to the president that "we disengage," but that Reagan did not want to.

December 8. *McFarlane-Kimche Meeting.* McFarlane joins North in London. He meets privately with Kimche and tells him that his mission is "to close down" the operation, according to the Senate Intelligence Committee report. McFarlane told the Tower Commission that Kimche was upset and said he thought the United States was missing a big opportunity.

December 8. *McFarlane Meets with Ghorbanifar, Israelis.* In a three-hour meeting with North, Kimche, Nimrodi, and Ghorbanifar, McFarlane tells Ghorbanifar to relay to the Iranians that the United States was interested in improving relations with Iran, but that there would be no sale of U.S. weapons nor would the United States approve sales by others. According to McFarlane's testimony, Ghorbanifar argued for continued U.S. arms transfers. McFarlane claims he came away from the meeting convinced that they should no longer do business with Ghorbanifar.

December 9. *North Memo on London Meeting, Options.* North writes a memo to McFarlane and Poindexter summarizing the London meeting and setting forth a new plan of action. He outlines five options available, including the possibility of direct U.S. arms deliveries to Iran with Secord's help. According to the memo, disclosed in the Tower report, Ghorbanifar had refused to relay McFarlane's message that there would be no more arms deliveries until all the hostages were released. The Iranian said it would lead to the execution of one or more hostages.

December 10. *McFarlane Reports on London Meeting.* After returning from London, McFarlane reports back to President Reagan in a meeting at the White House that includes Weinberger, Casey, Regan, and Poindexter. (Shultz was in Europe.) McFarlane reports that an impasse in the talks developed when he refused to discuss the transfer of arms to Iran. McFarlane describes Ghorbanifar as "devious" and suggests that they no longer use him as an intermediary. McFarlane told the Tower board that he left government December 11 thinking the initiative had been discontinued. According to the Tower panel, CIA director Casey December 10 prepares a memo on the White House meeting. Casey says that the president "argued mildly" for the continuation of Israeli arms deliveries to Iran without any U.S. commitment other than replenishment. Reagan testified before the Tower panel January 26, 1987, that he agreed at the December 10 meeting to reject the latest arms-for-hostages plan. The Tower Commission report states that North, Ghorbanifar, Ledeen, Secord, and Nir met variously among themselves during the rest of December.

December 19. *Ledeen-Casey Meeting.* According to

the Tower report, Ledeen meets with Casey. Ledeen testified before the Senate Intelligence Committee that, upon his return to the United States in late December, he suggested to Casey and other CIA officials that the United States should continue working with Ghorbanifar. Ledeen had met with Ghorbanifar in Europe earlier in December at Ghorbanifar's request. Casey subsequently requests that Ghorbanifar submit to a polygraph test.

December 20. *Rodriguez in Washington.* Felix Rodriguez attends a Christmas party in Washington, D.C., and is introduced to the staff of Donald P. Gregg, Vice President Bush's national security adviser, according to a chronology released by Bush's office December 15, 1986.

December 22-23. *Ghorbanifar Meeting.* Ghorbanifar and Ledeen meet with the chief of the CIA's Iran desk. According to the CIA official's report of the meeting, only Ledeen was present and he told of his relationship with Ghorbanifar. The CIA report, which was provided to the Tower panel, recalled Ledeen's confidence in Ghorbanifar as a "wonderful man ... almost too good to be true." Ledeen says that the Iranians had been overcharged and that $200,000 had been turned over to Ghorbanifar to promote his contacts within Iran. The CIA official is also told that Ghorbanifar is holding $40 million that the Iranians wanted returned.

December 23. *Casey Tells Reagan of Ghorbanifar Visit.* Casey sends a memo to President Reagan that includes a paragraph on Ghorbanifar's visit to Washington and tells him of Ghorbanifar's upcoming polygraph. Casey states: "It is necessary to be careful in talking with Ghorbanifar."

December 23. *North-Nir Meeting.* North briefs Amiram Nir on the Iran initiative in light of McFarlane's meetings in London earlier in December, according to the Tower report.

December 23. *North Meets with Ledeen, Secord.* North meets with Ledeen at the Madison Hotel at 2:30 p.m., according to North's calendar, which was provided to the Tower Commission. He then meets with Secord at the Hay-Adams Hotel at 3:45 p.m.

December 24. *North Meets with Israeli Intelligence Officers.* North meets with Gen. Uri Simhoni and Col. Moshe Zur, according to notations made on North's calendar. North's secretary, Fawn Hall, describes the visitors as "Israeli intelligence," according to the Tower report.

Late December. *NSC Warned about Ghorbanifar.* Allen gives the NSC staff a copy of an August 1984 CIA "burn notice" on Ghorbanifar to the effect that he was a fabricator whose information should not be trusted.

1986

January 2. *Poindexter, North Meet with Nir.* Vice Adm. John M. Poindexter, President Ronald Reagan's national security adviser, and Lt. Col. Oliver L. North, a National Security Council (NSC) aide, meet with Amiram Nir, who is an antiterrorism adviser to Israeli prime minister Shimon Peres. Nir proposes that Israel sell 4,000 TOW (tube-launched, optically-tracked, wire-guided) antitank missiles to Iran and buy replacements from the United States. According to his plan, the United States can back out of the deal if all U.S hostages in Lebanon are not released after the first 500 missiles are delivered to Iran.

According to notes taken by Attorney General Edwin Meese III in his November 23, 1986, interview with North that were later turned over to the Senate Intelligence Committee, North and Nir discuss at an early January meeting the diversion of funds from Iranian arms sale proceeds to the contras. But North in July 1987 told the House and Senate select committees investigating the Iran-contra affair that Nir mentioned using "residuals" from the arms sales for other unrelated activities but that Nir did not specifically mention the contras. A different version was provided by Israeli officials. According to news reports in September 1987, the Israelis said the diversion of Iran arms profits to the contras was suggested by North in a December 1985 meeting in New York with an Israeli purchasing agent. In his July testimony, North said he did not remember such a discussion.

January 3. *Presidential 'Finding' Drafted.* NSC aide North and CIA general counsel Stanley Sporkin work on a draft of a presidential "finding" authorizing an Iran initiative. North, according to a Central Intelligence Agency (CIA) chronology cited in the report of the President's Special Review Board (Tower Commission), does not want to mention the hostage rescue in the draft but Sporkin insists that hostages should be mentioned.

January 4. *Draft Finding Submitted to Poindexter.* North submits to Poindexter the draft finding and memorandum on plans to sell TOW missiles to Iran in exchange for improved relations and the release of U.S. hostages. North indicates that the finding was based on discussions with Nir and Sporkin and that he had had a phone conversation with CIA director William J. Casey about the finding and the overall approach.

January 5. *Shultz Informed of Israeli Proposal.* Poindexter tells Secretary of State George P. Shultz that the Israelis had taken action to "revive" the Iran initiative. Poindexter says that Nir has proposed exchanging certain Hizballah prisoners and 3,000 missiles for the release of American hostages in Beirut.

January 6. *Draft Finding Given to Reagan.* Poindexter briefs President Reagan on the proposed revival of the Iran initiative and gives him a draft finding authorizing it. Also present at the meeting are Vice President George Bush, White House chief of staff Donald T. Regan, and NSC aide Donald Fortier. The president signs the finding. Regan told the Tower Commission the draft may have been "signed in error." The president told the panel that he did not recall signing the draft.

January 7. *Reagan, Top Advisers Discuss Iran Initiative.* The Israeli arms sales proposal advanced by Nir January 2 is discussed at a White House meeting attended by Reagan, Bush, Regan, Shultz, Secretary of Defense Caspar W. Weinberger, Casey, Meese, and Poindexter. Weinberger and Shultz continue to express opposition to the plan. Although Reagan apparently does not make a decision at this meeting, according to the Tower report, several of the participants later said they thought the president supported the proposal.

January 9. *Finding Authorizes Intelligence Aid to Contras.* President Reagan signs a finding authorizing the CIA to provide intelligence advice, training, and communications equipment to the contras, the January 14, 1987, *Washington Post* reported. The estimated cost of the aid in 1986 was $13 million. Limited intelligence and communications aid was permitted under legislation (PL 99-169) signed into law December 4, 1985.

January 11. *Ghorbanifar Takes Polygraph Test.* Iranian arms merchant Manucher Ghorbanifar takes a polygraph test at the request of CIA director Casey. Ghorbanifar, the middleman in U.S. arms deals with Iran, shows deception on virtually all relevant questions. During a break in the polygraph test, Ghorbanifar says that the Israelis had "doubled" the cost of the November 1985 Hawk missile shipment apparently because Americans were involved. He also comments that the Israelis are retaining the full $24 million they received for the shipment and the Iranians wanted it returned.

January 13. *CIA Interviews Ghorbanifar.* At Casey's request, Charles Allen, CIA national intelligence officer, spends five hours interviewing Ghorbanifar to obtain a general overview of the information he possesses. Allen produces a nine-page report January 29. North meets with Ghorbanifar the evening of January 13.

January 14. *North Meets with Casey.* North meets with Casey to discuss Weinberger's resistance to the proposed Iran initiative.

January 15. *Nir Voices Israeli Concerns.* North informs Poindexter that Nir has said that Israel is about to withdraw from the Iran initiative so that it cannot be blamed for the deaths of American hostages. Nir also said that Israel is upset because the United States has not replenished TOWs sold by Israel to Iran in September 1985 and that it cannot deliver 1,000 additional TOWs without a U.S. promise to replenish.

January 16. *Final Draft of Finding Discussed.* Poindexter, Casey, Meese, Sporkin, and Weinberger meet to review the final draft of the Iran initiative finding. The question of notifying Congress is discussed. Meese gives his opinion that withholding notification is legal.

January 16 or 17. *CIA Warning on Ghorbanifar.* The CIA issues a third "burn notice" saying it is going to do no further business with Ghorbanifar, according to the testimony of Clair George, CIA deputy director for covert operations, before the House and Senate Iran-contra committees August 4-5, 1987.

January 16. *North Questions Ledeen's Reliability.* North sends a memo to Poindexter questioning the reliability of Michael Ledeen, an NSC consultant, as a go-between for the United States and Ghorbanifar. North also suggests the possibility of a secret business arrangement among Ghorbanifar, Israeli arms dealer Adolph "Al" Schwimmer, and Ledeen. In a January 24 message to Poindexter, North says Casey shares their concerns about Ledeen and tells Poindexter there is further evidence of a business arrangement among Schwimmer, Israeli arms dealer Yaacov Nimrodi, Ghorbanifar, and Ledeen. "Perhaps because of these doubts," according to the Tower report, "Ledeen ceased to be an official American contact with Ghorbanifar."

January 17. *Finding Authorizes Arms Sales to Iran.* Reagan signs a secret finding authorizing the sale of weapons to Iran for the purpose of establishing a more moderate government in Iran, obtaining intelligence on Iran, facilitating the release of American hostages in Beirut, and preventing additional terrorist acts. The finding is almost identical to the January 6 draft, but with the addition of the words "and third parties" to the first sentence's listing of those entities to receive U.S. assistance in their contacts with Iranians, according to the Tower report. The order instructs Casey to refrain from reporting the finding to Congress, until otherwise directed.

A cover memorandum to the January 17 finding signals a major change in the Iran initiatve. Rather than accepting Nir's proposal that Israel sell 3,000 TOW missiles to Iran, the memorandum proposes instead that the CIA purchase 4,000 TOWs from the Defense Department and ship them directly to Iran. President Reagan told the Tower panel that he was briefed on the contents of the memo but did not read it. He said that he understood that the plan was for the United States to become a direct supplier of arms to Iran. President Reagan writes in his diary, "I agreed to sell TOWs to Iran." Present at the meeting are: Bush, Poindexter, Regan, and Fortier. Neither Shultz, Weinberger, nor Casey attends the meeting.

January 17. *Shultz Opposes Iran Arms Sales.* Shultz argues at a White House meeting that selling weapons to Iran would be "illegal and unwise." He learned ten months later that Reagan that same day signed a finding authorizing the sales, according to Shultz's July 23, 1987, testimony before the House and Senate Iran-contra committees.

January 17. *Defense Department Makes Missile Arrangements.* Secretary of Defense Weinberger receives a phone call from Poindexter informing him of the president's action. According to the Senate Intelligence Committee report, Weinberger directs his military aide, Maj. Gen. Colin Powell, to arrange for the transfer of 3,504 TOW missiles to the CIA under the Economy Act. (The Tower Commission report listed the number of missiles needed as 4,508—4,000 to be sold to Iran and 508 to go to Israel to replace the TOWs sold in August-September 1985.)

January 18. *CIA Formally Joins Iran Initiative Efforts.* Poindexter, North, retired Air Force major general Richard V. Secord, Sporkin, George, and the CIA chief of the Near East division meet to discuss the logistics and financing of arms sales to Iran. The meeting marks the formal entrance of the CIA into the operation.

January 19-21. *Rodriguez-Watson Meeting in El Salvador.* Col. Samuel Watson, Vice President Bush's deputy national security adviser, meets in El Salvador to discuss counterinsurgency operations with Felix I. Rodriguez, a former CIA operative who helped coordinate the contra supply network; Col. James Steele, commander of U.S. military forces in El Salvador; and others, according to a chronology of contacts with Rodriguez that was released by Bush's office December 15, 1986. Watson also visits two contra military camps in Honduras.

January 21. *North Requests Swiss Bank Account.* North requests the CIA to open a Swiss bank account to receive payment to the CIA for the actual cost of the missiles sold to Iran and transportation. CIA officials told the Senate Intelligence Committee that they decided to use an existing account for several months until a new account was opened.

Late January. *Ghorbanifar Suggests Diversion to Contras.* Sometime between January 17, when the presidential finding was signed, and Jaunary 24, North meets with Ghorbanifar in London to brief him on what the United States is prepared to do. Nir is also present. In his July 8, 1987, testimony before the House and Senate Iran-contra committees, North said that Ghorbanifar took him into the bathroom and suggested that "residuals" from the arms sale could be used to support the contras. Ghorbanifar later reportedly denied suggesting the diversion. Poindexter told the Iran-contra committees July 15, 1987, that North first mentioned the possibility of diversion to him sometime in February 1986 following a meeting in London.

The diversion idea has been attributed to several others. During a November 23, 1986, interview with Attorney General Meese, North said he had discussed the diversion possibility with Nir in early January 1986. North later told the Iran-contra committees that diversion to the contras had not been specifically mentioned. During a November 24, 1986, meeting with Assistant Attorney General Charles J. Cooper, Thomas C. Green, Secord's attorney, attributed the idea to Secord's business partner, Albert Hakim, who supposedly suggested it in early 1986. And news reports in September 1987 indicated the Israelis attribute the diversion scheme to North who was said to have suggested it at a December 1985 meeting with an Israeli official. North told the Iran-contra committees he had no recollection of such a discussion.

January 24. *North Outlines Plan for Hostages' Release.* North, after returning from a meeting with Ghorbanifar in London, completes a plan called "Operation Recovery" and submits it to Poindexter. The memorandum, presented in the form of a "notional timeline," outlines the operation beginning January 24 and ending February 25. The plan calls for a sample of U.S. intelligence on Iraq to be given to Ghorbanifar, who would send it on to Iran. Funds for the purchase of 1,000 TOW missiles would be transferred through several Swiss bank accounts and ultimately $6 million would be transferred to a CIA account. The CIA would wire the $6 million to the Defense Department, which would release the TOWs to the CIA. Upon delivery of the missiles to Iran, all U.S. hostages and 50 Hizballah prisoners held in southern Lebanon would be released. After that, 3,000 more TOWs would be sold and delivered to Iran, and 508 missiles would go to Israel to replace those sold to Iran in August-September 1985. The Hawk missiles sold to Iran in November 1985 and later rejected by Iran are to be returned to Israel. North's plan anticipates that Iranian leader Ayatollah Ruhollah Khomeini would step down, February 11, 1986. Regarding the suggestion that Khomeini would depart, the Tower Commission said that it "found no evidence that would give any credence to this assumption."

January 25. *CIA Objects to Intelligence Release.* North and CIA officials meet to discuss intelligence information that is to be passed to Iran. According to testimony given to the Senate Intelligence Committee, then CIA deputy director for intelligence Robert M. Gates objected to the release of certain intelligence, but he is overruled by the NSC.

January 26. *Limited Intelligence Passed to Iranians.* CIA deputy director John N. McMahon convinces North to provide the Iranians with only limited intelligence information on the Iraqi front. McMahon had argued that the intelligence posed a greater threat to upsetting the balance of the Iran-Iraq War than providing the Iranians with TOW missiles. The intelligence information is transmitted to Ghorbanifar in London by CIA official Allen. In exchange, Ghorbanifar provides Allen with information on Iranian terrorism, according to the Tower Commission report.

January 28. *CIA Assistance to Contras Defined.* A CIA analysis concludes that an intelligence authorization measure (PL 99-169) enacted in December 1985, which had allowed the CIA to provide the contras with intelligence and communications assistance, did not authorize the CIA to provide the contras with "specialized logistics training," according to the Tower Commission report.

January 30. *Reagan Meets with Channell and Do-*

nors. President Reagan meets with Carl R. "Spitz" Channell and major donors to Channell's National Endowment for the Preservation of Liberty. Linda Chavez, deputy assistant to the president for public liaison, and Elliott Abrams, assistant secretary of state for inter-American affairs, attend the meeting, according to the March 7, 1987, *Washington Post.*

January-March. *Encryption Devices.* North receives fifteen KL43 encryption devices from the National Security Agency for use in transmitting classified messages between members of the contra support network.

February. *Poindexter Approves Diversion to Contras.* Poindexter approves North's proposal to use proceeds from the Iranian arms sales to support the contras, according to Poindexter's July 15, 1987, testimony before the House and Senate Iran-contra committees. North raises the issue sometime in February just after returning from a meeting in London, Poindexter testified. North had a meeting in London in late January, at which he said Ghorbanifar suggested diversion of funds to the contras. North also met with Ghorbanifar in London in early February.

February 5. *North Travels to London.* North travels to London to meet with Ghorbanifar, Nir, and Ghorbanifar's Tehran contact. According to Ghorbanifar's testimony before the Tower panel, the meeting was in Frankfurt and North, Secord, a CIA officer, Nir, and several Iranian officials attended.

February 8 or 9. *Arms Sale Timetable Reviewed.* Following his February 7 return from London, North discusses the arms transfer timetable with CIA official Allen; another CIA official; retired Air Force major general Richard V. Secord, a key figure in North's Iranian and contra operations; and Noel Koch, deputy assistant secretary of defense for international security affairs.

February 10-April 11. *Financing of Arms Deal.* According to the Tower Commission report, Ghorbanifar gives Saudi Arabian arms merchant Adnan Khashoggi post-dated checks amounting to $12 million as a guarantee of payment by Iran. Khashoggi February 10 deposits $10 million in the Lake Resources account. Lake Resources transfers $3.7 million to a CIA account February 10-11. After the CIA certifies the availability of funds to the Defense Department, 1,000 TOWs are signed over to the CIA February 13. Southern Air Transport flies the TOWs to Israel February 14. After the TOWs are delivered to Iran February 17 and 27, Iran's March 3 payment of $7.85 million passes through several accounts. Then Khashoggi is told the post-dated checks are covered and is repaid $12 million from the Lake Resources account by April 11. (The Tower Commission concluded that the difference between the $7.85 million Iran transferred and the $12 million repaid Khashoggi was covered by the $5 million Israel withheld pending return of the November 1985 Hawk shipment that was rejected by Iran. Seventeen Hawks were returned to Israel February 18.)

February 13. *'Operation Rescue.'* North reports to Poindexter that "Operation Rescue" is under way.

February 17. *TOWs Delivered to Iran.* A shipment of 500 TOW missiles is flown from Israel to Iran. The Hawk missiles delivered to Iran in November 1985 and later deemed obsolete by Iranian officials are picked up by the same plane and returned to Israel.

February 18. *North Requests False Passports.* A memo from North to Poindexter describes Albert Hakim as vice president of one of the European companies set up to "handle aid to resistance movement." Hakim is Secord's Iranian-American business partner. North requests false passports and documents for a delegation scheduled to travel to West Germany to meet with Ghorbanifar. North also suggests that Hakim be provided with a one-time false identification as a Defense Intelligence Agency official.

February 20. *Iranian Fails to Show Up for Meeting.* North, Nir, Secord, and the CIA chief of the Near East division, meet Ghorbanifar in Frankfurt, West Germany, and await the arrival of Ghorbanifar's contact, a representative from the Iranian prime minister's office, but he fails to show. The meeting is rescheduled for February 24. Documents and testimony received by the Senate Intelligence Committee indicated North, Secord, and Hakim met with Ghorbanifar in Europe and turned over a second set of intelligence materials. However, the committee could not ascertain the exact meeting date.

February 24-26. *Frankfurt Meeting with Iranian Official.* North, the CIA chief of Near East division, Secord, Nir, and Hakim meet in Frankfurt with Ghorbanifar and an official from the Iranian prime minister's office. In a February 27 memo to McFarlane, North says that this was the first contact between the U.S and Iranian governments in more than five years. He reports that Iran "is terrified of a new Soviet threat" and that U.S hostages in Lebanon will be released during the next meeting. The CIA official at the meeting said in his report that, during two meetings February 25-26, agreement was reached that the United States would ship 1,000 TOWs to Iran and one or two hostages would be released.

February 25. *Reagan Requests Contra Aid.* Reagan asks Congress for $100 million in aid for the contras, including $70 million in military assistance.

February 27. *TOWs Delivered to Iran.* The second shipment of 500 TOW missiles is delivered to Bandar Abbas, Iran. No hostages are released. After meeting with Ghorbanifar, Hakim, and the Iranian official, Secord reports to North that the Iranian emphasized the need for a quick meeting and that the official said "he would possibly, *repeat,* possibly surprise us by getting some hostages released before meeting."

February 27. *McFarlane to Meet with Iranians.* In a memo to North, McFarlane mentions that Poindexter has asked him whether he could meet with Iranian officials sometime during the next week. Poindexter tells McFarlane, according to the Tower Commission report, that "the president is on board." McFarlane congratulates North and says that, if the world knew of his efforts, "they would make you Secretary of State. But they can't know and would complain if they did—such is the state of democracy in the late 20th century."

February 27. *North Describes Support for Effort.* In a second February 27 memo to McFarlane, North says that he has met with Casey, Poindexter, and George, and that "all have now agreed to press on. Believe we are indeed headed in the right direction." He says that Secord has indicated that McFarlane is to meet with Ali Akbar Hashemi Rafsanjani, the speaker of the Iranian parliament.

February 27. *Poindexter Meets with CIA Officials.* Poindexter meets with CIA director Casey, George, and the CIA chief of the Near East division.

February 27. *Owen Cites CIA Contra Role.* In a memo made public May 19, 1987, during his testimony before the House and Senate Iran-contra committees, Robert W. Owen reports to North that the CIA is giving orders concerning the handling of "lethal supplies" to the contras.

Owen served as North's liaison with the contras.

February 27. *Secord Purchases Munitions for Contras.* Secord withdraws $222,000 from a Lake Resources account to purchase munitions for the contras. The May 10, 1987, *Washington Post* reports that after the February 1986 arms sale to Iran, much larger sums of money began flowing into the Lake Resources accounts. North alludes to Secord's trip to Europe and his arranging an "arms delivery for the Nic resistance" in a February 27 memo to McFarlane.

February 28. *Poindexter Briefs Shultz.* Shultz is informed by Poindexter that the hostages would be released the following week and is briefed on McFarlane's upcoming meeting with an Iranian official. Shultz told the Tower panel that at this time Poindexter said nothing about providing arms to Iran in exchange for hostages. Shultz also said that he was told the Iranians were interested in obtaining intelligence information on Soviet activities on the Iranian border and in Afghanistan.

Late February. *Peres Letter to Reagan.* Israeli prime minister Shimon Peres writes to Reagan urging him to continue his efforts to gain a strategic opening in Iran and pledges Israeli assistance.

March. *Lawsuit against Secord.* Secord hires retired CIA technical services specialist Glenn A. Robinette to dig up "derogatory" information on two American journalists, Martha Honey and Tony Avirgan, who had filed a lawsuit against Secord and two dozen other defendants charging them with complicity in a 1984 attempt to assassinate former Nicaraguan contra leader Eden Pastora. Robinette testified June 23, 1987, before the House and Senate Iran-contra committees, that Secord paid him $4,000 a month for his efforts and said that during a November 1986 trip to Costa Rica he passed out approximately $7,000 to informers.

March-June 1986. *North, Secord Coordinate 'Drops' to Contras.* According to the Tower Commission report, messages sent to North from Secord and others indicate the contra supply effort carried out at least nine "drops" of weapons to the contras during this period. Some of the classified messages sent to North on his private communications network: "(a) asked him to direct where and when to make contra munitions drops; (b) informed him of arms requirements; and (c) apprised him of payments, balances, and deficits," the commission reported.

March 5. *Congressional Notification.* Maj. Gen. Vincent Russo sends a message to Maj. Gen. Powell, Weinberger's military aide, stating his belief that the CIA has the responsibility of notifying Congress of the Defense Department's transfer of TOW missiles to the CIA. The Army's office of the general counsel February 13 had determined the responsibility of congressional notification lay with the CIA rather than the Army, according to the Senate Intelligence Committee report.

March 5. *U.S.-Iranian Meeting Discussed.* Poindexter, Casey, another CIA official, and George Cave, a retired CIA officer and Iranian affairs expert who was serving as a fulltime consultant to the CIA, discuss the planned meeting between U.S. and Iranian officials. Cave, who joined the team as an interpreter, told the Tower Commission he was "a little bit horrified when I found out that [Ghorbanifar] was involved in this."

March 8. *North, Cave, and CIA Official Meet with Ghorbanifar.* North, Cave, and the CIA chief of the Near East division meet in Paris with Ghorbanifar. North tells Ghorbanifar that the United States is interested in meeting with senior Iranian officials as long as the hostages are released before or during the meeting, according to North's March 10 report to McFarlane. North also indicates U.S. willingness to assist Iran in opposing the Soviets, if the hostages are released quickly. Ghorbanifar presents a list of 240 spare parts needed by Iran for its Hawk missiles. Earlier in March Ghorbanifar had said that the Iranians also wanted Phoenix and Harpoon missiles but at the Paris meetings the Americans argue that the Iranian launchers were in such disrepair they would be unable to use these missiles. Cave wrote in his report on the meeting that Ghorbanifar "proposed that we use profits from these deals and others to fund support for the rebels in Afghanistan. We could do the same with Nicaragua." However, in his testimony before the Tower Commission, Cave said neither he nor Ghorbanifar mentioned a diversion.

March 11. *McFarlane Meeting in Frankfurt Canceled.* Poindexter tells Secretary of State Shultz that a planned trip by McFarlane to meet with Iranian contacts in Frankfurt had fallen through because McFarlane objected to the idea.

March 13-17. *Ghorbanifar Meets with Iranian Officials.* Ghorbanifar travels to Tehran and has what he subsequently described as difficult meetings with several high officials. Nir, according to the Senate Intelligence Committee report, worries that Ghorbanifar might be losing his influence with Tehran and urges U.S. officials to work more closely with Ghorbanifar.

March 17. *Owen Criticizes Contra Leaders.* After returning from a trip to Central America, Owen sends a report to North, referring to him by his code name, "B.G." or "Blood and Guts." In the report, Owen voices his concern for the contra fighting forces and expresses his contempt for many of the contra political leaders who treat the Sandinista-contra war like a "business." Owen also refers to the $100 million contra aid package pending before Congress, saying that should the funds be approved, it would be like "pouring money down a sinkhole."

March 26. *Iranian Proposes High-Level Meeting.* North, in a memo to McFarlane, says that Hakim spoke twice the previous day with the Iranian representative from the prime minister's office. According to North's memo, the Iranian official proposed a meeting the next week between the U.S. delegation and an Iranian delegation led by Rafsanjani. The Iranian official also proposed that during the meeting the remaining U.S. hostages would be released and the United States would start delivering immediately the 3,000 TOW missiles. The Iranian called for U.S. agreement at the meeting to the delivery of spare parts.

March 26. *North Efforts to Acquire Missiles for Contras.* Three months after McFarlane's resignation as national security adviser, North notifies him of his efforts, with Secord's assistance, to obtain Blowpipe launchers and missiles for the contras.

March 31. *Contra Aid Expires.* The $27 million authorization and appropriation for nonmilitary aid to the contras, which became law in August 1985, expire.

Spring. *Soviet Threat to Iran Downplayed.* Casey gives the White House a new Special National Intelligence Estimate (SNIE), which concludes that the Soviets are less likely to attack Iran or have influence in post-Khomeini Iran than was presumed in 1985, according to the January 13, 1987, *Washington Post.* A May 17, 1985, memo by Graham Fuller, the CIA national intelligence officer for Near East and South Asia, had warned of the leverage the Soviet Union was developing in Iran. His warning was a factor in the reevaluation of U.S. policy toward Iran.

April. *Secord Meets with U.S. Ambassador in El Salvador.* Secord, during a brief visit to El Salvador, discusses the contra supply effort with Edwin G. Corr, the U.S. ambassador to El Salvador. Secord testifies May 6, 1987, before the House and Senate Iran-contra committees that Corr "was sympathetic with our operation, and I know that he kept track of it." Secord said that Corr's support was "moral," not active.

April. *Wealthy Contributor to Contras.* North meets with millionaire William B. O'Boyle and shows him photos of a new Nicaraguan airport that he says will be used for Soviet bombers and reconnaissance planes, according to O'Boyle's May 21, 1987, testimony before the House and Senate Iran-contra committees. North later tells O'Boyle that the contras need Blowpipe surface-to-air missiles, which cost $20,000 apiece, and describes a "very, very secret plan" for the contras to oust the Sandinista government. O'Boyle also met with conservative fund-raiser Channell and eventually contributed $160,000.

April. *CIA Provides Information to Contra Network.* "Tomas Castillo," the pseudonym used by the CIA station chief in Costa Rica, requests "flight vector information" from CIA headquarters for a cargo plane dropping "lethal material" to the contras within Nicaraguan territory. According to Castillo's May 29, 1987, testimony before the House and Senate Iran-contra committees, the CIA provided information on Nicaraguan radar and surface-to-air missile sites as well as weather conditions.

April. *North Contacts FBI.* North asks Oliver B. "Buck" Revell, FBI executive assistant director, to delay a grand jury appearance of public relations consultant Richard R. Miller. Miller was to testify in a bank fraud investigation of Mousalreza Ebrahim Zadeh, an Iranian who was posing as a Saudi prince. Miller had been asked by North to serve as an intermediary with Zadeh on a possible contribution to the contras. Revell at first said he had asked for a delay but later told then-FBI director William H. Webster and the Senate Intelligence Committee that he had not.

April 3. *NEPL Funds Transfer to Lake Resources.* North scribbles a note to himself that says, "call Copp [Secord alias], 650k to LAKE," according to the Tower Commission report. The report cited an April 16 message from Secord that says "650k received today as reported by the banker." The March 7, 1987, *Washington Post* reported a chain of money transfers from Channell's NEPL to Miller's public relations firm, International Business Communications, and then on to a Cayman Islands firm (I. C. Inc., later renamed Intel Co-operation Inc.) and finally ending in the transfer of $650,000 into the Lake Resources account in Switzerland April 11. The April 18, 1987, *Washington Post* reported that the money may have been used to construct an airstrip in Costa Rica.

April 3-4. *North, CIA Officials Meet with Ghorbanifar.* Ghorbanifar meets in Washington with North, Allen, and the CIA chief of the Near East division. Ghorbanifar tells them that Iran wants Hawk radars and mobile I-Hawk missile batteries in addition to the TOW missiles. U.S. officials, according to the Senate Intelligence Committee report, say that the 240 Hawks would be supplied only after the release of hostages.

April 4-7. *North Memo Mentions Diversion to Contras.* North writes a memorandum for Poindexter to transmit to the president reviewing negotiations with Iran and seeking approval for a trip by McFarlane and others to

Tehran. Within hours of the arrival of the U.S. delegation, which is to be met by Rafsanjani, U.S. hostages are to be released, and then Hawk missile parts are to be delivered to Iran, according to the plan North outlines. The memo specifies how profits from the sale of the weapons to Iran are to be spent. North writes: "$12 million will be used to purchase critically needed supplies for the Nicaraguan Democratic Resistance Forces." North's memo, entitled "Release of American Hostages in Beirut," was found November 22, 1986, in North's desk during a Justice Department inquiry into the Iran arms sales. The contra diversion was disclosed to the public November 25. Poindexter testified May 15, 1987, before the House and Senate Iran-contra committees that he did not tell the president about the diversion of funds.

April 8. *IOB Says Contra Training Permitted.* The Intelligence Oversight Board (IOB), according to the Tower Commission report, provides Poindexter with an interagency memorandum concluding that, under the "communications" and "advice" provision of the fiscal 1986 Intelligence Authorization Act, any U.S. agency may lawfully provide basic military training to the contras, "so long as such training does not amount to the participation in the planning or execution of military or paramilitary operations in Nicaragua."

April 11. *Drop by Private Supply Network.* An L-100 cargo plane parachutes ammunition at a contra "drop zone" along the Costa Rican border, the so-called southern front, according to the Tower report.

April 12. *Castillo Confirms 'Drop' to Contras.* North receives a secure message from CIA field officer Castillo, who confirms the successful drop of weapons to contras on the southern front. The CIA official also outlines plans for follow-up air drops over the course of the next two-three weeks and says, "My objective is creation of 2,500 man force which can strike northwest and link up with Quiche [the Quiche Indians of Nicaragua] to form solid southern force."

April 14. *U.S. Hostage Killed.* The United States bombs targets in Libya and applies heavy pressure on allies to isolate and punish states involved in terrorism, in whose number it counts Iran. Senate Intelligence Committee findings show that the attack may have resulted in the execution of hostage Peter Kilburn at the behest of Libyan leader Muammar el-Qaddafi. Two British hostages in Beirut, Leigh Douglas and Philip Padfield, also are killed. (The men were found dead April 17.)

April 15. *Wealthy Contributor to Contras.* Texas millionaire Ellen St. John Garwood reportedly transfers money and stock totalling $2 million to Channell's National Endowment for the Preservation of Liberty after meeting on several occasions with NSC aide North, according to the May 22, 1987, *Washington Post.*

Mid-April. *CIA Requests Hawk Parts.* The CIA formally requests from the Army 234 spare parts for Hawk missiles. By the end of April, according to the Senate Intelligence Committee report, the cost of the spare parts was fixed at $4.4 million.

April 16. *Poindexter: Hostages First, Then Arms.* North writes Poindexter seeking approval for a meeting with Ghorbanifar in Frankfurt on April 18, according to the Tower report. Poindexter approves the request but insists that no arms are to be turned over to the Iranians without first gaining the release of hostages. He authorizes North to tell Ghorbanifar: "The President is getting very annoyed at their continual stalling." The North-Ghorbanifar meeting is delayed until May 6 in London.

April 21. *Iranian Seeks Additional Concessions.* North reports to McFarlane that the Iranian contact is trying to gain additional concessions before securing the release of U.S. hostages. According to North, George Cave believes that the delays and attempts to force new concessions are a consequence of internal disputes over what Iran should do in the wake of the U.S. bombing of Libya and the murder of hostage Peter Kilburn. In a cover note, Poindexter reaffirms his position that the Hawk parts should be turned over to Iran only after the release of the hostages. Poindexter tells McFarlane: "The President is getting quite discouraged by this effort. This will be our last attempt to make a deal with the Iranians."

April 22. *North on Contra Needs.* North sends a memo to Fortier expressing his concern for the rapid depletion of funds authorized by Congress for the contras. North, according to the Tower panel, writes, "[T]he picture is dismal unless a new source of 'bridge' funding can be identified. . . . We need to explore this problem urgently or there won't be a force to help when the Congress finally acts."

April 22. *Indictments for Arms Sales to Iran.* The U.S. Customs Service announces arrests in a major "sting" operation involving the sale of arms to Iran. With the cooperation of Iranian arms dealer Cyrus Hashemi, a total of eighteen individuals are indicted in New York for conspiring to sell arms to the Khomeini regime. Ghorbanifar is arrested in Switzerland and jailed for a day because he was an investor in the failed scheme.

April 23. *White House Meetings on Central America.* Two meetings on Central American affairs are held at the White House, according to the Senate Intelligence Committee. One focuses on Elliott Abrams's trip to the region and is attended by Reagan, Bush, Deputy Secretary of State John C. Whitehead, Abrams, Regan, Poindexter, Fortier, and North. The second meeting is attended by Reagan, North, Regan, Poindexter, a Costa Rican security official and his wife, and Castillo. The Tower Commission described a three-minute photo session with this group in 1986.

April 24. *Iran Operation Analysis.* Major Julius Christensen, a member of the Director of Central Intelligence/Hostage Location Task Force, sends to North an analysis of options for gaining the release of hostages. Christensen says that the longer the operation is dragged out, the greater the risk of exposure.

April 28. *Danish Freighter Purchased.* Hakim travels to Copenhagen to negotiate for the purchase of the Danish ship *Erria*, according to the February 2, 1987, *New York Times.* The Tower report said that the ship was used to carry out a series of weapons deliveries to the contras through two Central American countries. The ship, which cost $350,000, was used for purposes not related to Iran or Nicaragua, according to Secord's May 5, 1987, testimony before the House and Senate Iran-contra committees. It was purchased primarily for the purpose of transmitting propaganda messages into Libya.

April 29. *North Suggests Tehran Meeting.* North sends a memo to Poindexter emphasizing the need to move quickly on the Iran project. North suggests that he, Cave, and Nir should schedule a trip to Tehran May 2 to meet with their Iranian contact.

April 30. *Rodriguez-Watson Meeting.* Rodriguez meets with Watson, Bush's deputy national security adviser, to discuss insurgency in El Salvador and the need for

helicopter parts, according to a chronology released by Bush's office December 15, 1986.

May. *Perot Ransom Attempt Fails.* Texas billionaire H. Ross Perot is asked by North to deposit $2 million in a Swiss bank account and then to fly $1 million in cash to Cyprus for use as ransom for U.S. hostages in Lebanon. Perot agrees, but the deal falls through. Details of the operation were revealed during Secord's May 1987 testimony before the House and Senate Iran-contra committees.

May. *Hakim Establishes Account for North.* Hakim places $200,000 into a Swiss bank account prior to North's secret mission to Tehran. According to his June 3, 1987, testimony before the House and Senate Iran-contra committees, the money in the account, code-named "B. Button" (short for "bellybutton"), could be used either for death benefits if North were killed or to educate North's four children. Also in May, Hakim signs a paper providing for the disposition of a $2 million reserve fund to North should both Hakim and Secord die or become disabled.

May 1. *Rodriguez-Bush Meeting.* Rodriguez meets with the vice president for approximately ten minutes, according to a chronology released by Bush's office December 15, 1986. The meeting is attended by Donald P. Gregg, Bush's national security adviser, and Watson, along with former senator Nicholas F. Brady, R-N.J. (1982). During the meeting, Rodriguez shows pictures taken during counterinsurgency operations in El Salvador. At the end of the session, U.S. ambassador to El Salvador Corr and North join the group in Bush's office, at which time Corr praises Rodriguez's work in El Salvador.

Bush later repeatedly denies that he discussed contra supply operations with Rodriguez, although a briefing memo prepared for Bush for this May meeting and released in September 1987 by the House and Senate Iran-contra committees lists "resupply of the contras" as a topic to be discussed. The vice president does not recall reading the mention of the contras, according to the September 9, 1987, *Washington Post.* Gregg and Watson also told the committees the topic was not discussed at the meeting.

May 2. *North on Contra Offensive.* North informs Poindexter that he believes the contras were preparing to launch a major offensive to capture a "principal coastal population center" in Nicaragua and proclaim independence. According to the Tower report, North suggests that the United States should be prepared to assist the contras.

May 3. *Shultz Protests Iran Deal.* Secretary of State Shultz is informed that the U.S. Embassy in Great Britain has learned that Ghorbanifar, Nir, and Khashoggi had approached British entrepreneur Roland "Tiny" Rowland in hopes of securing a line of credit to help finance the shipment of arms to Iran. Shultz again voices his opposition. Shultz told the Tower Commission that both Poindexter and Casey soon informed him that the operation had ended and the people involved had been told to "stand down."

May 5. *North to Avoid Embassy in London.* After the early May flap over the discovery by the U.S. Embassy in London of the Iran arms deal, North stresses to Poindexter the urgent need to conclude the current operation. Poindexter directs North to travel to London and instructs him to keep quiet about the trip and avoid all contact with embassy personnel.

May 6. *North-Ghorbanifar Meeting.* North and Cave meet with Ghorbanifar, who assures them that a U.S. delegation would meet with senior Iranian officials. Ghorbanifar also adds that the Iranians wanted all Hawk missiles to be delivered with the delegation, but an agreement is reached, according to the Tower report, which calls for one quarter (one pallet) of the Hawk spare parts to accompany the delegation. The Defense Department is to be paid $6.5 million, but Iran is to be charged $15 million.

May 8. *North on Hostage Release.* North informs Poindexter that the week of May 19 has been set for the release of the hostages.

May 8. *Israelis Offer to Aid Contras.* North informs Poindexter of an Israeli offer to assist in Central America. The Tower report said that former U.S. ambassador to Costa Rica Lewis A. Tambs and a CIA official in Central America knew of no Israeli arms shipment to the contras.

May 12. *Reagan Briefed on McFarlane Trip.* During a national security briefing, Poindexter discusses with President Reagan McFarlane's upcoming trip to Iran to secure the release of hostages, according to notes taken by NSC executive secretary Rodney McDaniel. The Tower Commission report said the notes indicated that Reagan directed the press not be told about the trip.

May 14–August. *Financing of Arms Deal.* According to the Tower Commission report, Ghorbanifar gives Khashoggi post-dated checks amounting to $18 million as a guarantee of payment by Iran. Khashoggi May 14 deposits $15 million in the Lake Resources account. Lake Resources transfers $6.5 million to a CIA account May 15. After the CIA May 16 certifies the availability of funds to the Defense Department, Hawk spare parts and 508 TOWs are signed over to the CIA May 16 and 19. Southern Air Transport flies the arms to Israel May 23–24. The Hawk spare parts are delivered to Iran May 25 and August 3. Iran makes payments in July and August totaling $8 million, which pass through several accounts. Then Khashoggi is told July 24 that he can expose $3 million against Ghorbanifar's checks and another $5 million in August. By August, Khashoggi has been repaid $8 million out of the Lake Resources account.

May 15. *McFarlane Trip Approved.* President Reagan approves McFarlane's trip to Tehran, according to NSC executive secretary McDaniel's notes.

May 15. *Reagan's Contra Options.* In a memo to Reagan, Poindexter refers to contra funds stalled in Congress and suggests options: reprogramming; presidential appeals for private donations; and presidential overture to certain heads of state, according to the Senate Intelligence Committee report.

May 15. *Lower Profile for North.* Poindexter tells North in a memorandum that he is afraid North is letting his operational activities become too public. "From now on," he writes, "I don't want you to talk to anybody else, including Casey, except me about any of your operational roles. In fact, you need to quietly generate a cover story that I have insisted that you stop."

May 15. *Ghorbanifar Contact with Libyan.* According to the Tower report, North tells Poindexter that Ghorbanifar had been reminded the United States wanted an Iranian commitment against terrorism. North also reports that Ghorbanifar had transmitted a secure message concerning Howaldi Al Homadi (or Hamadi) who, according to Ghorbanifar, is the head of Libya's internal security force and the "defacto number 2 man in the country." Ghorbanifar said in his message that Homadi was willing to meet in Europe with North or other U.S. officials to improve U.S.–Libyan relations. Ghorbanifar said that Homadi would promise to end attacks against the United States; to work

out a schedule to get terrorists out of Libya; and to transfer business contacts from the Eastern bloc to the West.

May 15. *DEA Rescue Operation.* Secord's financial records show a cash payment of $30,000 to the Drug Enforcement Administration (DEA). According to Secord's May 6, 1987, testimony before the House and Senate Iran-contra committees, North was using DEA agents working out of Cyprus for another hostage-rescue operation.

May 16. *Contra Funds.* President Reagan, according to Senate Intelligence Committee findings, holds a National Security Planning Group (NSPG) meeting at which it is decided that two options to obtain funds for the contras should be explored: (1) seek to get reprogramming through Congress; (2) solicit third-country assistance for the contras. Shultz is asked to provide a list of countries that might be approached.

May 16. *Reagan's Contra Role.* Following the NSPG meeting, North sends a memo to Poindexter about the contra operation. He reports that the contras have more than $6 million available for immediate disbursement, but he stresses the need for "going forward with the reprogramming proposal and getting the requisite authority for CIA involvement," according to the Tower Commission report. North says that the more money there is for the contras, the more visible the program becomes and the more inquisitive members of Congress will become. "While I care not a whit what they say about me, it could well become a political embarrassment for the president and you," North wrote. He suggests much of the risk could be avoided by providing $15 million under an authorized CIA program. He goes on to say, "I have no idea what Don Regan does or does not know re my private U.S. operation but the President obviously knows why he has been meeting with several select people to thank them for their 'support for Democracy' in CentAM [*sic*]." Later that day Poindexter tells North that "Don Regan knows very little of your operation and that is just as well."

May 18. *Ghorbanifar Assurances on McFarlane Trip.* A CIA official is assured by Ghorbanifar that American hostages will be turned over upon the arrival of McFarlane in Tehran and that the U.S. delegation will be able to meet with high-ranking Iranian officials.

May 19. *Poindexter Excludes Shultz, Weinberger.* North "strongly urged" Poindexter to include Shultz and Weinberger along with Casey in a "quiet" meeting with President Reagan to review McFarlane's planned trip to Tehran. The Tower report shows that Poindexter responded in a memo "I don't want a meeting with RR [Ronald Reagan], Shultz and Weinberger."

May 20. *Bush Speaks with Rodriguez.* Vice President Bush speaks briefly with Rodriguez and El Salvador air force commander Juan Rafael Bustillo at a large reception in Miami on Cuban Independence Day, according to a chronology released by Bush's office December 15, 1986.

May 21. *Poindexter, Reagan Discuss McFarlane Trip.* Poindexter discusses with President Reagan the "Terms of Reference" for McFarlane's secret mission to Iran.

May 22. *Final Plan for Tehran Trip.* North submits to Poindexter the final plan for the U.S. delegation to travel to Iran, U.S. hostages to be released, and Hawk spare parts to be delivered.

May 23–25. *Trip Under Way.* McFarlane and his delegation travel from the United States to Iran via Europe and Israel.

May 25. *Delegation Arrives in Tehran.* McFarlane,

North, Cave, NSC staff member Howard J. Teicher, Nir, and a CIA communicator arrive in Tehran on a plane that also carries a pallet of Hawk spare parts, which was loaded in Israel. The delegation also brings a chocolate cake from a kosher bakery in Tel Aviv—"more a joke than anything else between North and Ghorbanifar," Teicher told the Tower Commission. The delegation is not met by any senior Iranian officials. They later meet with Ghorbanifar, officials in the Iranian prime minister's office, and another functionary.

May 27. *Report to Reagan.* President Reagan receives a written brief on the McFarlane trip to Tehran.

May 27-28. *Fruitless Mission.* McFarlane demands May 27 that the hostages be released by 6:30 a.m. the next day. On May 28, McFarlane is told the Iranians think they can get two hostages out now and the remaining two after delivery of the Hawk missle spare parts. McFarlane rejects the offer and the delegation leaves Tehran, but not before the Hawk spare parts are taken from the aircraft by the Iranians.

Ghorbanifar, in testimony before the Tower panel, claims that the U.S. delegation was entirely to blame for the failure of the mission. He said the failure to hold a preparatory meeting may have resulted in misunderstandings on both sides. Ghorbanifar also said that the U.S. delegation was not met by Iranian officials because the plane arrived in Tehran several hours ahead of schedule. The Tower panel reported that North, Cave, Allen, and another CIA official knew as early as mid-April that, if the U.S. delegation was not accompanied by all the Hawk spare parts, only one hostage would be released. The Tower panel suggested that McFarlane may not have been aware of this.

May 28. *McFarlane Told of Contra Diversion.* McFarlane told the Tower Commission that, while at the Tel Aviv airport after his return from Tehran, North told him that the mission was not a complete failure and that "the government is availing itself of part of the money (from the Iran initiative) for application to Central America."

May 29. *McFarlane Reports to Reagan.* McFarlane reports directly to President Reagan on his trip to Tehran and suggests that the arms-for-hostages initiative be discontinued, according to notes taken by McDaniel. The meeting was attended by Poindexter, Bush, Regan, Teicher, and North.

June 3. *Secord's Druze Force.* North tells Poindexter that Secord, with Nir's assistance, has three people in Beirut and a forty-man Druze (a Moslem sect) force "working 'for' us," according to the Tower report.

June 6. *Military Rescue Planning.* At his regular national security briefing, President Reagan approves military planning to rescue the hostages in Beirut.

June 6. *Ghorbanifar Pushes Initiative.* Ghorbanifar, according to the Tower report, does not give up on the arms-for-hostages initiative and presses his Iranian contact for another meeting with the United States. Ghorbanifar also pressures Cave to contact the Iranian. Cave does so June 13 and suggests a meeting in Europe to plan a second secret trip of U.S. delegates to Iran, during which U.S. hostages would be freed and then the Hawk spare parts and radars would be delivered. The next day the Iranian tells Ghorbanifar that Iranian officials would meet a U.S. delegation in Europe if the remaining Hawk spare parts and radars are delivered first. If everything is delivered, all hostages would be freed; if half the equipment is delivered, half the hostages would be freed.

June 10. *Rafsanjani Speech.* Iran's speaker of parlia-

ment, Rafsanjani, gives a speech in which he guardedly encourages better Iranian-U.S. relations, according to an NSC chronology of events compiled in November 1986.

June 10. *Third Country Aid to Contras.* North sends a memo to Poindexter on third country assistance to the contras in which he wonders how much Shultz knows about earlier contributions. He mentions the need to go back to the head of an unnamed allied country to acquire British-made antiaircraft Blowpipe missiles, according to the Tower report. In the memo, North says he would love to carry a letter from Reagan regarding the Blowpipes.

June 10. *McFarlane Concerns about North.* McFarlane voices concern about political opponents uncovering North's contra activities and about pressures being put on North. He suggests to Poindexter that North be either transferred or sent to Bethesda Naval Hospital for a disability review board, according to the Tower report. McFarlane mentions that the Marine Corps "has already tried to survey him once." Poindexter tells McFarlane that he would think about McFarlane's concerns.

June 11. *Third Country Aid to Contras.* In a memo to North, Poindexter says that he thinks Shultz knows nothing about earlier contributions to the contras. Poindexter says that Abrams has recommended Shultz solicit a contribution from Brunei, according to the Tower report.

June 20. *Opposite Directions for Reagan, Ghorbanifar.* President Reagan directs that no further meetings would be held with Iranian officials until U.S. hostages are released. On the same day, Ghorbanifar supplies his Iranian contact with a detailed analysis of the price and availability of the remaining Hawk spare parts. Ghorbanifar, according to the Tower report, also says the United States would throw in as a gift ten diesel generators used to operate the Hawks. Ghorbanifar and his Tehran contact continue discussions for the rest of June.

June 24. *Cave-Iranian Contacts.* In late June, Cave has several phone conversations with the Iranian official in Tehran to discuss the possibility of an arms-for-hostages deal. On June 24, North tells Poindexter that the Iranian is trying to reach Cave to arrange for the release of one hostage, according to the Tower report.

June 24. *Resolution on NSC Contra Aid.* Legislation (H Res 485) is introduced directing President Reagan to turn over to the House of Representatives information on the activities of Lt. Col. North or any other NSC staff member in support of the contras.

June 25. *Rodriguez-Watson Meeting.* Watson meets with Rodriguez in the Old Executive Office Building to discuss counterinsurgency in El Salvador. Rodriguez reportedly is accompanied to the office by retired Air Force colonel Robert C. Dutton, who does not attend the meeting. The meeting, originally omitted from the chronology released by Bush's office December 15, 1986, was made public May 14, 1987.

June 25. *Hostage Location 'Breakthrough.'* North, in a memo to Poindexter, says that the CIA believes it has made a "major breakthrough" in discovering the location of at least two of the four U.S. hostages in Lebanon. He also tells Poindexter that negotiations between Cave and the Iranian seem to be at a standstill. The conversations, however, continue, as the two sides make proposals and counterproposals and haggle over the prices of weapons.

June 26. *Reagan 'Contra' Victory.* The House, for the first time in three years, approves by a 221-209 vote a Reagan request for military aid to the contras. Contra aid legislation (PL 99-500) was signed into law October 18.

June 27. *North-Iranian Meeting.* According to North's calendar, he meets with an Iranian named "Tabatabaie [*sic*]" and possibly with Sen. Jesse Helms, R-N.C.

July. *The Second Channel.* Hakim is contacted sometime in July by an Iranian living in London who proposes a new Iranian contact to replace Ghorbanifar. The contact later is identified by news sources as a relative of Rafsanjani.

Early July. *North Cuts Off Nir.* North is told by Nir that a hostage will be released shortly. A hostage briefing team is sent to Germany but no release occurs. North contacts CIA official Charles Allen to request that he take over day-to-day contact with Nir. Allen told the Tower panel that Nir was "alarmed" about losing direct contact with North and began working closely with Ghorbanifar and others to obtain the release of a U.S. hostage. In a message to Poindexter about this time, North says that he has "lost face" because of his failure to secure the release of an American hostage.

July 2. *Shultz Told Iran Initiative Proceeding.* Under Secretary of State Michael H. Armacost sends a memo to Secretary of State Shultz informing him of a renewed "conjecture" about an NSC-sponsored arms-for-hostages deal. He reports "The story is that one hostage may be released tomorrow in Lebanon."

July 8 or 9. *Ghorbanifar Letter.* Ghorbanifar writes a letter to his Iranian contact outlining possible solutions to the stalemate in U.S.-Iranian negotiations.

July 10. *A Contact with Tehran.* North informs Poindexter that two senior foreign government officials had visited Tehran and reported a feeler by Rafsanjani to the effect that the Americans knew what had to be done to improve relations. North proposes sending a message to the Iranians through this channel expressing U.S. willingness to open talks with the Iranian government. Poindexter approves, according to the Tower report.

July 11. *Israeli Help Sought.* North tells Poindexter the United States has asked Israel to help in a hostage rescue plan.

July 12. *CIA Concern over Private Network Ties.* Castillo, the CIA station chief in Costa Rica, is ordered in a cable to back away from his plan to use contras to transmit flight information to pilots for the contra supply network. Castillo had been supplying this information with a secret coding machine provided by North. The cable, sent by Central American task force chief Alan Fiers, says the CIA has kept its distance from the private network and told Congress it has no relationship with the network. Castillo told the House and Senate Iran-contra committees May 29, 1987, that he did not interpret the cable as an order for him to stop his own contacts with the network.

July 15. *Poindexter Expresses Confidence in North.* North writes a memo to Poindexter expressing his deep disappointment that the national security adviser has lost confidence in his ability to manage contra policy matters. Poindexter responds to North in a memo saying, "Now you are getting emotional again. . . . I just wanted to lower your visibility so you wouldn't be such a good target for the Libs [*sic*]." Poindexter reassures North that he plans to retain him.

July 15. *'Project Democracy' Assets.* North describes in a note to Poindexter the assets owned by "Project Democracy," a term North uses to describe the dummy corporations established to act as owners of the equipment and money used in the private contra aid network. The

assets include six aircraft, warehouses, supplies, maintenance facilities, ships, boats, leased houses, vehicles, ordnance, munitions, communications equipment, and a 6,520-foot runway in Costa Rica, according to the Tower report. Total value is placed at more than $4.5 million. Project Democracy wants to sell the equipment to the CIA for about $2.25 million, once Congress renews aid to the contras but North says the CIA is not interested. Poindexter subsequently replies to North that he had told CIA deputy director Gates that he thought "the private effort should be phased out" and asks North to talk to Casey about this.

Mid-July. *Contra Debt.* The contras have a debt of more than $2.5 million, according to testimony before the Tower panel by the head of the CIA's Central American task force.

July 17. *Another Contact with Tehran.* North reports to Poindexter a second opportunity for direct contact with the Iranian government through an official of a foreign country. (A message had been sent to Iran earlier in July through another foreign country.) This second contact had informed Secretary of State Shultz of Iran's interest in easing relations with the United States. North prepares a response, although according to the Tower report, it is unknown whether Poindexter approved sending it.

July 18. *Reagan Informed of Iranian Contacts.* Poindexter informs President Reagan of recent contacts with Iranian officials.

July 21. *Report of Possible Hostage Release.* North, Cave, and Nir meet with Ghorbanifar in London to discuss the release of the hostages in exchange for the Hawk missile spare parts that remained undelivered from McFarlane's trip to Tehran in May. Nir reports to North that the Iranians claimed to have taken action that morning to release one American hostage in Beirut. North reports to Poindexter that in the meantime Cave would proceed to Frankfurt to meet with an Iranian named Tabatabai, who allegedly had good connections with Rafsanjani and other Iranian "pragmatists," to determine whether he should be used as a contact.

July 23. *'Deal Was Off.'* When no hostage is released, Ghorbanifar is instructed to tell his Iranian contact that "the deal was off," according to a July 26 memo from Casey to Poindexter.

July 24. *Iranian Transfer of Funds.* The Iranians transfer $4 million to a Swiss bank account as partial payment for Hawk missile spare parts removed from the McFarlane delegation's plane in May.

July 25. *Second Channel.* North tells Poindexter that Cave is in Frankfurt to meet with the second channel to evaluate him as a potential intermediary with Iran.

July 26. *Jenco Released.* Rev. Lawrence Jenco, who was kidnapped January 8, 1985, is released in Lebanon.

July 26. *Next Step Pondered.* Poindexter briefs President Reagan on Jenco's release. In a message to McFarlane, Poindexter attributes Jenco's release to McFarlane's trip to Tehran and Ghorbanifar's proddings of his Iranian contact. Poindexter says Ghorbanifar "has cooked up a story" that, if a hostage is released, the United States would deliver the remaining Hawk spare parts. Both Poindexter and McFarlane agree that the United States must reaffirm its position that all the hostages must be released first.

Casey sends Poindexter a memo the same day in which he concludes that the Ghorbanifar-Iranian connection has worked for a second time. The CIA director says that, if there is no U.S. government contact as a result of Jenco's release, it is possible that one or more hostages may be murdered. He suggests continuation of the Ghorbanifar-Iranian contact to see what would lead to the release of the remaining hostages.

July 27. *Frankfurt Meeting.* North, Cave, Nir, and Ghorbanifar meet in Frankfurt and talk by phone with the Iranian contact. In his report to Poindexter on the discussions, North says that, despite their protestations that the United States wanted all hostages freed before any weapons would be delivered, "this is clearly not the way they want to proceed." He says the United States will have to do something in order to prevent the death of one of the hostages.

July 29. *Delivery of Hawk Parts Approved.* North sends a memo to Poindexter requesting that he obtain President Reagan's approval for the delivery of remaining Hawk missile spare parts to Iran, to be followed by a meeting with the Iranians in Europe. According to the Tower report, a notation by Poindexter indicates Reagan gave his approval July 30.

July 29. *Bush-Nir Meeting.* At the King David Hotel in Jerusalem, Vice President Bush meets with Nir at North's request. Nir briefs Bush on negotiations with Iran. According to a three-page memo prepared August 6 by Bush's chief of staff, Craig L. Fuller, which was reproduced in the Tower report, Nir told Bush that "we are dealing with the most radical elements."

Early August. *Rodriguez Complaint.* Dutton, an assistant to Secord, meets with North and Rodriguez, who was helping to coordinate the contra supply network from an air base in El Salvador. Rodriguez, according to May 5, 1987, testimony by Secord before the House and Senate Iran-contra committees, complains about the shoddy equipment being used in the operation.

Early August. *Brunei Solicitation.* In light of the contra's debt problem, the United States decides to solicit funds from a third country. Assistant Secretary of State Abrams confers with Shultz's executive assistant, Charlie Hill, on where contra funds from third-country solicitations should be deposited: a Bahamian bank account opened by the CIA to receive the funds or a Swiss bank account suggested by North. They decide on the latter.

On August 8, Abrams, using the pseudonym "Mr. Kenilworth," travels to London, solicits a $10 million contribution from a Brunei official during a walk in a park, and passes him the account number supplied by North, which turns out to be incorrect.

August 3. *Hawk Spare Parts Delivered.* The remaining 240 Hawk spare parts (twelve pallets) are delivered to Iran, according to the Senate Intelligence Committee and Tower reports.

August 5. *Webster Questions Arms Sales.* FBI director Webster, who has just learned about the Iranian arms sales, is assured by Attorney General Meese that the sales were authorized, according to the June 28, 1987, *Washington Post.*

August 6. *Intelligence Committee Interviews North.* North is interviewed by members of the House Intelligence Committee. According to the Tower Commission report, an NSC account of the meeting said that North told committee members that he gave no military advice to the contras and knew of no specific military operations. He also said that he had not been in touch with retired Army major general John K. Singlaub for twenty months and that he had never provided guidance to Robert Owen, who was

North's liaison with the contras. Poindexter sent North a copy of the NSC account with the message "Well Done."

August 8. *Contra Aid Discussed with Bush Aides.* Rodriguez meets with Bush aides Gregg and Watson to voice concern about corruption inside the contra supply program. A chronology released by Bush's office December 15, 1986, said this was the first time Rodriguez had discussed the private contra aid network in any of his meetings with the vice president's staff. However, a briefing memo prepared for Bush before a May 1986 meeting with Rodriguez indicated that one reason for the meeting was to discuss "resupply of the Contras." In testimony released by the House and Senate Iran-contra committees September 8, 1987, both Gregg and Watson said the contra supply program was not discussed at the May meeting.

August 12. *Rodriguez's Concerns Relayed.* Gregg and Watson meet with U.S. ambassador to El Salvador Corr, Deputy Assistant Secretary of State William G. Walker, NSC staffers Raymond F. Burghardt and Robert L. Earl, and a CIA officer to relay Rodriguez's concerns about the private aid network.

August 25. *Second Channel.* Hakim and Secord meet with the proposed second channel and other Iranians in Brussels, according to the Tower report.

August 27. *Antiterrorism Law Signed.* Reagan signs into law antiterrorism legislation (PL 99-399) that includes a flat ban on military exports to countries designated as supporters of terrorism. Iran was on the list at that time. The president could waive the prohibition if he determined the exports were in the national interest, but he was required to send a report to Congress within ninety days justifying his decision.

August 27. *Iran Seeking TOWs.* During discussions in Brussels between Secord and the second Iranian channel, the Iranian says that his government is trying to purchase TOW missiles in Madrid for $13,000 apiece. The United States was not involved in the effort, according to a memo written by Secord to North.

September 2. *North on Contacts with Iran.* North sends Poindexter a memo entitled "Next Steps with Iran" in which he discusses various activities under way to free the hostages and improve relations with Iran, including contacts with Iran through two "friendly" countries, through Ghorbanifar and the official in the Iranian prime minister's office, and possibly through the second channel. (Another activity was deleted from the Tower report.) North says the Ghorbanifar connection is the only proven means by which a hostage has been released. He tells Poindexter that the CIA favors proceeding with Ghorbanifar's efforts, which involve a sequential arms-for-hostages plan, and pursuing the other activities as subsidiary efforts.

September 2. *IBC Contract.* The State Department signs a secret $276,000 contract with Richard R. Miller's public relations firm, International Business Communications (IBC), eleven months after its effective date of October 1, 1985. According to an Associated Press article in the February 7, 1987, *Washington Post*, IBC hosted meetings to plan a procontra ad campaign and paid for contra leaders to visit the United States to seek congressional and public support.

September 7 or 8. *Address by Shah's Son.* The son of the deceased shah of Iran pirates Iran's national network broadcast frequency and makes an eleven-minute speech on Iranian television. The broadcast, according to a September 8 memo from North to Poindexter, reportedly sparks protest in Tehran and elsewhere from supporters of the shah's family. Ghorbanifar's Iranian contact asks Cave how the United States could profess to accept the Iranian revolution and still sponsor such an event, according to the Tower report.

September 8. *North Supports Ghorbanifar Connection.* North updates his September 2 memo to Poindexter and says, pursuant to "guidance," he had sought the simultaneous release of all three American hostages but that the proposal had been rejected by the Iranian official. He reiterates CIA support for the sequential plan proposed by the official. North states: "[O]ur window of opportunity may be better than it will ever be again, if we are able to consummate the release of the hostages before the Iranian offensive begins [against Iraq, thought to be planned on or about September 22]."

September 9. *School Director Kidnapped.* Frank Herbert Reed, the American director of the Lebanese International School in West Beirut, is kidnapped.

September 9. *New Orders after Reagan Briefing.* The president is briefed on the proposed second channel, prospects for hostages' release, and the possibility of a rescue operation. Later that day Poindexter tells North to pursue the second channel and to stop using Ghorbanifar as an intermediary in arms shipments, unless in the future there is no other channel, according to a September 10 memo written by Allen to Casey. Allen says that North will have to raise about $4 million to cut Ghorbanifar out.

September 9. *Contra Airfield in Costa Rica.* North informs Poindexter that the Costa Rican government had decided to hold a press conference announcing the existence of a secret airstrip in that country that had been used for direct supply of the contras from July 1985 to February 1986, and thereafter as the primary abort base for damaged aircraft. According to the Tower report, North told Poindexter that he had a conference call with U.S. ambassador to Costa Rica Tambs and Assistant Secretary of State Abrams. North says that he was selected to call Costa Rican President Oscar Arias to tell him that, if he held the press conference, the United States would cancel $80 million in promised U.S. foreign aid and Arias's upcoming visit with Reagan. Poindexter responds: "You did the right thing, but let's try to keep it quiet."

Abrams, in his June 2, 1987, testimony before the House and Senate Iran-contra committees, gave another version of what happened. He said that he directed Tambs to call the Costa Rican president and imply that his visit to the United States might be cancelled if the press conference were not called off. Tambs had told the committees May 28, 1987, that he called Arias and persuaded him the press conference "would not be prudent" in light of the World Court case in which Nicaragua was accusing the United States of aggression. He said he did not threaten to cancel Arias's trip to Washington.

September 10. *Nir Visit.* Nir meets with North and Poindexter in Washington.

September 12. *University Official Kidnapped.* Joseph J. Cicippio, acting comptroller at the American University of Beirut, is kidnapped in Lebanon.

September 12. *Israel Offers Soviet Weapons.* Israeli defense minister Yitzhak Rabin, North, Nir, and Gen. Hagai Regev meet in Washington. Rabin, according to the Tower Commission report, offers "a significant quantity" of captured Soviet bloc weapons to the United States for use by the contras. Rabin refuses to give them directly to the contras. The arms are to be picked up by a foreign flag

ship that week and delivered to the contras.

September 15. *U.S.-Israeli 'Initiatives.'* North suggests in a memo on the president's upcoming meeting with Israeli prime minister Peres that Poindexter brief Reagan on "initiatives" with Israel, presumably covert plans. Although Poindexter initialed the memo and wrote "done," he told the House and Senate Iran-contra committees during his July 1987 testimony that he "seriously" doubted that he actually briefed Reagan on this matter.

September 15. *Weapons Shipment Recalled to Israel.* North reports to Poindexter that orders were passed to a ship to proceed to Haifa to pick up the arms offered by Rabin September 12. Poindexter tells North that "Absolutely nobody else should know about this." Rabin reported to the State Department that the ship had left Israel but had been recalled when it appeared the Iran arms story would become public.

September 15. *Peres Visit.* Israeli prime minister Peres meets with President Reagan in Washington.

September 19-20. *Meeting with Second Channel.* North, Cave, and Secord meet with the second Iranian channel and two other Iranians in Washington, according to the Tower report. (Hakim indicated in his June 4, 1987, testimony before the House and Senate Iran-contra committees that he also participated in the meetings.) The two sides concentrate on the hostage issue and Iran's urgent need for weapons and intelligence information to be used in offensive operations against Iraq. North agrees "in principle" to provide weapons requested by the Iranians. The parties discuss establishing a secret eight-man U.S.-Iran commission to work on future relations. North tells the second channel that "there is no official message from the United States," unless it comes from North, Secord, or Cave. Charles Allen told the Tower panel that at one point the Iranian channel said that Khomeini's son had briefed his father in detail on contacts with the United States.

September 23. *Reagan Briefed.* President Reagan is briefed on discussions held with the second Iranian channel.

September 26. *VOA Editorial.* The Voice of America broadcasts an editorial in Farsi, in which Iran, among others, is thanked for its assistance in the successful resolution of the September 5 hijacking of Pan American flight #73 in Pakistan. The editorial, agreed upon during the September 19-20 meetings with the second channel, was to be a signal from the U.S. government that the two sides were moving in the right direction.

Late September. *Khashoggi's Financial Problems.* Saudi arms merchant Khashoggi asks Roy M. Furmark to seek Casey's assistance in either refunding the $10 million Khashoggi was owed for financing Iranian arms deals or completing the weapons shipment, according to Furmark's testimony before the Senate Intelligence Committee. Furmark, a New York businessman and a lawyer for Khashoggi, was a friend and former legal client of Casey.

September 26-November 7. *Financing of Arms Deal.* According to the Tower Commission report, Iran deposits $7 million into the Lake Resources account. Lake Resources transfers $2.037 million to a CIA account that has been closed. Because the funds are not immediately available to the Defense Department, North asks Israel to ship 500 TOW missiles from its own inventory. Israel delivers the TOWs October 30-31. On November 3, 500 TOWs are released to the CIA. The replacements are delivered to Israel November 7.

September 30. *Contra Airfield in Costa Rica.* In a

memo to Poindexter, North says that the Udall Corporation, a "Project Democracy" proprietary that built a secret airstrip in northern Costa Rica in summer 1985, had been closed and its assets disposed of because of press reports on the airstrip in early September.

October. *Soviet Tank Deal.* A ship leased by "Project Democracy," North's network of dummy corporations, is sent to the Middle East to pick up an Iranian-captured Soviet tank in exchange for U.S.-made weapons. The arrangement falls through, according to the February 15, 1987, *New York Times* and later testimony.

October 1. *Diversion Suspected.* CIA national intelligence officer Allen reports to CIA deputy director Gates his suspicion that funds from Iranian arms sales were being diverted to the contras. Gates is said to be deeply disturbed by this and asks Allen to brief Casey, which he does on October 7, according to the Tower report.

October 2. *Next Steps.* North sends Poindexter a memo entitled "Next Steps for Iran," in which he requests approval of plans for an October 6 meeting with the second Iranian channel. North recommends giving the contact a mix of factual and bogus intelligence and presenting him with a Bible inscribed by Reagan. He also suggests that Secord brief Nir on the new channel—and on Nir's new supporting, rather than primary, role—in such a way that Nir and other Israelis still perceive this as a "joint venture." North suggests they keep the Ghorbanifar connection on hold until they see what the new channel produces. Poindexter gives his approval and meets that evening with Casey and Gates to discuss the intelligence proposal.

October 3. *McFarlane Gets Update.* Both Poindexter and North report to McFarlane on the new channel. Poindexter says he may ask McFarlane to undertake negotiations after the hostages are released.

October 3. *Poindexter-Kuwaiti Meeting.* Poindexter meets with the Kuwaiti foreign minister, the *Washington Post* reported July 25, 1987. According to a December 1986 State Department document released by the House and Senate Iran-contra committees, Poindexter may have requested that Kuwait "do something" about the Lebanese terrorists imprisoned in Kuwait (the Da'Wa prisoners).

October 4. *McFarlane Offers Help.* McFarlane offers to take a few months off to work on the Iranian hostage problem.

October 5. *Contra Supply Aircraft Downed.* A Southern Air Transport C-123 cargo plane carrying weapons and other supplies to the contras is shot down in Nicaragua. Three crew members, including two Americans, are killed. Eugene Hasenfus, an American, parachutes to safety and is captured.

October 5-6. *Rodriguez Alerts Bush's Office.* Rodriguez calls Watson twice to say that he has received information that one of the contra supply aircraft is missing, possibly in Nicaragua. According to the chronology prepared by Bush's office detailing contacts between the office and Rodriguez, Watson passes this information on to the White House Situation Room and the NSC staff.

October 6. *Southern Air Investigation.* The FBI begins an investigation in Miami of Southern Air Transport after the downing of one of its planes in Nicaragua. According to testimony by FBI director Webster in April 1987 before the Senate Intelligence Committee, North contacted FBI official Oliver B. "Buck" Revell shortly after the inquiry began to express his concern that the probe could disrupt U.S.-Iranian negotiations involving the swap of arms for U.S. hostages in Lebanon.

October 5-7. *Meeting with Second Channel.* North, Cave, Hakim, and Secord meet in Frankfurt, West Germany, with the second Iranian channel and an Iranian Revolutionary Guard intelligence official. The Americans present a Bible to the Iranians inscribed by President Reagan October 3 with a passage from Galatians 3:8 ("And the Scripture, forseeing that God would justify the Gentiles by faith, preached the gospel beforehand to Abraham, saying, 'All the nations shall be blessed in you.' "). According to the Tower report, North during the meeting misrepresents his access to the president and attributes to the president things Reagan never said.

North presents the Iranians with a seven-point proposal for the provision of weapons and other items in exchange for, among other things, the release of the remaining hostages. The Iranians counter with a six-point proposal that promises, in part, the release of one hostage. They make clear that they cannot secure the release of all the hostages. North then leaves for Washington.

According to Hakim's testimony June 4, 1987, before the House and Senate Iran-contra committees, Hakim eventually drafts a nine-point plan that calls for the release of only one or two hostages in return for the sale of 500 TOW missiles. It also states—contrary to U.S. policy—that Hakim will produce a plan for the release of seventeen terrorists jailed in Kuwait (the Da'Wa prisoners). Hakim testified that he sent the plan to North and later heard that it had been approved "by the White House." Hakim also told the committees that he had the "understanding" in the fall of 1986 that North hoped the release of the hostages would improve the chances of Republicans in the upcoming congressional elections.

October 7. *Casey Told of Canadians' Threat, Diversion Suspicion.* According to testimony before the Senate Intelligence Committee and Tower Commission, Furmark tells Casey that two Canadian middlemen in the Iran arms sales, Donald Fraser and Ernest Miller of Toronto, were threatening to sue and blow the lid of secrecy off the deals because they had not been repaid the $10 million they had loaned Khashoggi for the deals. They had been promised repayment within thirty days at a 20 percent interest rate. Casey that same day tells Poindexter of his conversation with Furmark. Casey meets later that day with Allen, who tells the CIA director of his suspicion that funds were being diverted to the contras.

October 8. *Soviet Weapons Shipment.* The Danish freighter *Iceland Saga* arrives at a U.S. Army munitions depot near Wilmington, N.C., with a cargo of Soviet bloc and Portuguese weapons and ammunition. The shipment had originated in the Polish port of Szczecin three months earlier, when it reportedly had been loaded onto the *Erria,* the ship purchased by Hakim. According to the February 21, 1987, *Los Angeles Times,* Secord and Hakim had purchased the weapons for $2.2 million and planned to sell them to the contras. But when that deal fell through, the CIA purchased the weapons from the two for $1.2 million, the *Times* reported.

October 9. *North Questioned on CIA Involvement.* North visits CIA headquarters to brief Casey and Gates on the Frankfurt meeting with the new Iranian contact. According to testimony by Gates before the Senate Intelligence Committee, he asks North at this briefing whether the CIA has been involved in North's efforts on behalf of private funding for the contras. North responds that the CIA is "completely clean" of involvement in the private contra funding and makes a "cryptic" reference to the link between the Iran arms sales and efforts to assist the contras but neither Casey nor Gates pursue the Iran connection. They later discuss the fact that they did not understand North's comments, according to Gates's testimony.

October 10. *Scheme to Channel Money to North.* Hakim's Geneva-based lawyer, Willard I. Zucker, discusses with Washington, D.C., attorney David L. Lewis a scheme to channel $70,000 to the wife of "someone in the White House" through a real estate agent, in the form of a commission for a real or phony property transaction. Lewis told the House and Senate Iran-contra committees June 4, 1987, that he remembered—but was not certain—that the official's name was Oliver North.

October 12. *Hasenfus Defense Fund.* North asks McFarlane's help in finding a high-powered lawyer and benefactor to raise funds for the legal defense of Hasenfus, who was captured in Nicaragua following the October 5 crash of a contra supply plane. North say he has located approximately $100,000.

October 14. *CIA Contra Role.* In testimony before the House Intelligence Committee, Assistant Secretary of State Abrams and CIA deputy director of operations Clair George deny any U.S. government involvement in or knowledge of the contra supply plane downed in Nicaragua October 5. That same day Abrams tells a House Foreign Affairs subcommittee that there was "no U.S. government involvement" in the flight.

October 15. *CIA Officials Meet with Poindexter.* Casey and Gates meet with Poindexter to discuss a memo prepared by Allen stating that money from the Iranian arms sales is being "distributed to other projects of the U.S. and Israel" and warning of the potential for exposure of the Iran initiative. Casey and Gates suggest, according to Gates's testimony to the Senate Intelligence Committee, that Poindexter consider having the president reveal the Iran initiative to the public rather than having it "leak in dribs and drabs." Casey advises Poindexter to get a White House counsel involved right away. Gates orders a review of CIA involvement. The CIA general counsel Dave Doherty, according to documents received by the Senate Intelligence Committee, reports that there is "nothing amiss from the CIA standpoint."

October 16. *Allen-Furmark Meeting.* Under Casey's direction, Allen meets with Furmark to discuss his clients' financial claims stemming from the Iran arms sales. Allen told the Tower Commission that in an October 17 memo "I laid out how deeply troubled I was because I could see this thing blowing up and we were going to have an incredible mess on our hands." Furmark recommends another arms shipment to Iran so investors can be repaid partially and the process can be kept going to free the hostages.

October 17. *Call for Independent Probe.* Members of the House Judiciary Committee ask Attorney General Meese to name an independent counsel to probe charges that Reagan officials were illegally involved in private efforts to supply the contras.

October 18. *Contra Aid Approved.* President Reagan signs into law an omnibus spending bill (PL 99-500) that includes $100 million in contra aid. This version of the bill is flawed (several pages are missing) and is replaced by a new version (PL 99-591) signed October 30.

October 21. *American Author Kidnapped.* American author and book salesman Edward Austin Tracy is kidnapped in Beirut.

October 22. *Ghorbanifar Alleges Diversion.* Allen

and Cave meet with Furmark in New York. Furmark tells them that Ghorbanifar believes that the bulk of the $15 million that had been raised by the Canadian investors and an Arab investor for the May 1986 Hawk missile spare parts deal had gone to the contras.

October 23. *Memo on Diversion Allegation.* Allen and Cave report to Casey on their October 22 meeting with Furmark. A memo containing Ghorbanifar's allegation that funds were diverted from the Iran arms sales to the contras is drafted for Casey to send to Poindexter, but Casey later discovers that he had failed to sign, date, and deliver the memo to Poindexter. The memo also shows that Furmark believes Nir had received $2 million of the $8 million paid by the Iranians to Ghorbanifar.

October 24. *Casey Conversation with Poindexter.* Casey talks to Poindexter about the Iran operation, according to Allen's testimony before the Tower Commission.

October 26-28. *Nine-Point Plan Discussed.* North and his team hold a second meeting in Frankfurt with the new Iranian channel and other Iranian officials at which the payment and delivery schedule for 500 TOW missiles is finalized. The parties discuss a nine-point U.S. agenda with Iran that includes the transfer of the TOWs and an unspecified number of Hawk spare parts, development of a plan for the release of seventeen Da'Wa terrorists held in Kuwait, the delivery of additional arms including 1,000 more TOWs, and military intelligence. The Iranians agree to the release of one and perhaps two hostages, and to work to create the conditions for the release of other hostages. North tells the Iranian channel, according to the Tower report, that in exchange for his efforts to gain the release of a third hostage, the United States would provide a technician to help with the Phoenix missiles Iran already has.

The Iranians inform the Americans that the story of McFarlane's mission to Tehran has been published in a small Hizballah newspaper in Lebanon.

October 29. *Release of Two Hostages Expected.* North sends a message to Poindexter stating that Iranian officials have assured them that two of the three hostages held by Hizballah would be released in the next few days. North tells Poindexter: "This is the damndest operation I have ever seen. Pls let me go on to other things."

October 30-31. *TOW Missiles Delivered to Iran.* Israel ships 500 TOW missiles to Iran at the request of the United States. (Israel receives 500 replacement TOWs November 7.)

October 30. *Southern Air Inquiry Suspended.* Stephen Trott, head of the Justice Department's criminal division, asks FBI director Webster for a ten-day suspension of "non-urgent" aspects of the FBI's inquiry into Southern Air Transport. The FBI had begun investigating Southern Air shortly after the October 5 downing in Nicaragua of a contra supply plane. Webster told the Senate Intelligence Committee April 8-9, 1987, that Trott requested the delay because the company was involved in a "sensitive" operation to secure release of U.S. hostages in Lebanon. Poindexter had pursuaded Attorney General Meese to request the delay, the Justice Department revealed December 18, 1986.

October 30. *FBI Memo on North.* An FBI agent warns in a memo that North might be prosecuted for his activities in Central America. Webster told the Senate Intelligence Committee in April 1987 that, although he had initialed the memo, he did not remember it and attached no importance to it.

October 30. *Contra Aid Approved.* President Reagan

American Hostages in Lebanon

Name	Position	Date Kidnapped	Status as of September 1987
David Dodge	President, American University of Beirut	July 19, 1982	Released July 20, 1983
Frank Reiger	Department head, American University of Beirut	February 10, 1984	Released April 15, 1984
Jeremy Levin	Bureau chief, Cable News Network	March 7, 1984	Released February 14, 1985
William Buckley	Station chief, Central Intelligence Agency	March 16, 1984	Died June 3, 1985 [1]
Benjamin F. Weir	Presbyterian minister	May 8, 1984	Released September 15, 1985
Peter Kilburn	Librarian, American University of Beirut	December 3, 1984	Killed April 14, 1986 [2]
Lawrence M. Jenco	Director, Catholic Relief Services	January 8, 1985	Released July 26, 1986
Terry A. Anderson	Chief Middle East correspondent, Associated Press	May 16, 1985	Still held
David P. Jacobsen	Director, American University of Beirut hospital	May 28, 1985	Released November 2, 1986
Thomas Sutherland	Acting dean of agriculture, American University of Beirut	June 9, 1985	Still held
Frank H. Reed	Director, Lebanese International School	September 9, 1986	Still held
Joseph J. Cicippio	Acting comptroller, American University of Beirut	September 12, 1986	Still held
Edward A. Tracy	Writer	October 21, 1986	Still held
Alann Steen	Professor, Beirut University College	January 24, 1987	Still held
Jesse J. Turner	Assistant professor, Beirut University College	January 24, 1987	Still held
Robert Polhill	Professor, Beirut University College	January 24, 1987	Still held
Charles Glass	Journalist	June 17, 1987	Escaped August 18, 1987 [3]

[1] Died in captivity probably on this date.
[2] Executed possibly in retaliation for U.S. attack on Libya.
[3] There was some speculation that Glass was allowed to escape.

signs into law a bill (PL 99-591) appropriating $70 million in military aid and $30 million in nonmilitary aid for the contras. (A flawed version of the omnibus spending bill (PL 99-500) had been signed on October 18, but PL 99-591 replaces that law.) The bill lifts most of the restrictions Congress imposed in 1984-85 on direct U.S. involvement with the contras and allows the CIA to resume management of the contra aid program. However, the separate fiscal 1987 intelligence authorization bill (PL 99-569), signed into law October 27, 1986, bars the CIA from using its multimillion-dollar contingency fund to aid the contras. (Previous contra assistance—$27 million in nonmilitary aid—had run out March 31, 1986.)

Early November. *Soviet Tank Swap Fails.* Soviet-made AK-47 rifles are loaded onto the freighter *Erria* in Israel, in the first phase of a plan to trade the rifles to Iran for one or more Soviet T-72 tanks that Iran had captured from Iraq. According to news reports, the *Erria* waits in the Gulf of Oman for about a month before abandoning the venture, which had been arranged by Hakim.

November 2. *Jacobsen Released.* Hostage David P. Jacobsen, who was kidnapped May 28, 1985, is released in Beirut.

November 3. *Magazine Reports McFarlane Visit.* A pro-Syrian Beirut weekly magazine *Ash-Shiraa* discloses McFarlane's secret trip to Tehran in May. Hassan Sabra, the publisher and editor of the magazine, says that the information was leaked through the office of Ayatollah Hussein Ali Montazeri, the designated heir to Iranian leader Khomeini. In a December 6 interview with an Associated Press reporter, Sabra says the leak is part of Iran's ongoing power struggle. Iranian speaker of parliament Rafsanjani November 4 confirms the visit of McFarlane.

November 3. *Shultz Advice.* When the Iran story breaks, Shultz urges Poindexter to go public to make it "clear that this was a special one time operation based on humanitarian grounds and decided by the president within his Constitutional responsibility to act in the service of the national interest," according to documents and testimony received by the Senate Intelligence Committee. Shultz said that he did not know at this time about the January 17, 1986, presidential finding. Poindexter rejects Shultz's advice.

November 5-20. *Chronology Compiled.* Under presidential orders, North, Poindexter, McFarlane, Lt. Col. Robert L. Earl, and Craig P. Coy begin compiling a chronology of the Iran initiative. From November 5-20, they produce a series of chronologies, ranging from merely a list of events to "Maximum Versions," which mix events with rationale. The final version, completed November 20, is entitled "Historical Chronology." The Tower report described the chronologies that were produced as "often conflicting and occasionally far from what we believe transpired." The report went on: "At best, these chronologies suggest a sense of confusion about both the facts and what to say about them. At worst, they suggest an attempt to limit the information that got to the President, the Cabinet, and the American public." This later was confirmed.

November 6. *Reagan Denies McFarlane Trip.* During a bill-signing ceremony, President Reagan tells reporters that stories about McFarlane traveling to Tehran have "no foundation."

November 6. *Casey, Gates Meeting with Poindexter.* According to the Senate Intelligence Committee report, Casey and Gates meet with Poindexter at the White House. Casey recommends that Poindexter bring in the White House counsel, but Poindexter says he does not trust the counsel and would talk to NSC legal adviser Cmdr. Paul Thompson instead. Gates testified that he learned at this meeting that Casey previously had recommended that North obtain legal counsel.

November 6. *Rodriguez-Watson Meeting.* Rodriguez speaks at the National War College on "low intensity conflict" in El Salvador. He later has dinner with Colonel Watson.

November 6. *Canadians Threaten Lawsuit.* Furmark tells CIA officer Allen that the Canadian middlemen who had helped Khashoggi finance an Iran arms deal are planning to sue the Saudi arms merchant and the private firm into which they had paid $11 million (reported earlier as $10 million), according to the Senate Intelligence Committee report. Documents received by the committee indicated Furmark said he persuaded the Canadians to delay their lawsuit.

November 7. *Israel Reimbursed.* According to the Tower report, Israel receives from the United States 500 TOW missiles to replace those shipped to Iran in October 1986.

November 7. *Reagan Decides Not to Comment.* According to notes taken by the NSC executive secretary and released to the Tower Commission, Reagan decides not to respond to questions on the Iran initiative for fear of jeopardizing the remaining hostages. White House spokesman Larry Speakes tells reporters to ease off on the inquiry. "Lives are at stake," he says, "and American interest is at stake."

November 7. *Administration Acknowledges Iran Contacts.* Administration officials admit that Reagan, eighteen months earlier, approved contacts with Iran to improve relations with that country, end Iran's support for terrorism, and help gain the release of hostages, according to the December 4, 1986, *New York Times*. The plan made no mention of arms sales, but, according to the officials, the United States accepted an Israeli offer to ship older U.S.-made spare parts and weapons to Iran. The *Times* said it was unclear if the president approved arms shipments.

November 7. *Rodriguez-Bush Aides Meeting.* In a meeting with Bush aides Gregg and Watson, Rodriguez describes his role in El Salvador "as primarily directed toward the insurgency in that country," according to a chronology of contacts with Rodriguez released by Bush's office December 15, 1986. The chronology goes on to say that Rodriguez indicates that "he, himself, had been able to assist the Contra resupply effort."

November 8-10. *U.S.-Iran Meetings.* Another round of meetings is held in Geneva between U.S. officials and Iranian representatives to discuss the release of hostages, the Da'Wa prisoners in Kuwait, the Israeli role in the arms transfers, and Iranian intelligence requirements. The new Iranian channel admits, according to the Senate Intelligence Committee report, that Iran still owes Ghorbanifar $10 million but also says that Ghorbanifar owes Iran 1,000 TOW missiles. According to the July 30, 1987, *Washington Post*, U.S. and Iranian representatives agree to delay planned shipments of medicine and weapons "until the situation cooled down."

November 10. *White House Meeting.* President Reagan meets with Vice President Bush, Shultz, Weinberger, Meese, Casey, Regan, Poindexter, and Alton G. Keel, Jr., at a ninety-five minute White House session. Shultz claims that it was during this meeting that he first learned about the January 17 presidential finding approving arms sales to Iran. Poindexter tells the meeting that North has just returned from Geneva with news that the United States "might get two more hostages by weekend," according to the July 30, 1987, *Washington Post*. Both Shultz and Regan told the House and Senate Iran-contra committees that Poindexter made misleading statements about the Iran initiative during the meeting.

Notes taken by Regan indicate the president says: "We must say something because I'm being held out to dry." According to notes taken by Keel, Reagan directs that "we don't talk TOWs, we don't talk specifics." (In a press statement July 27, 1987, White House spokesman Marlin Fitzwater said the president was concerned for the safety of the hostages and was not trying to cover up the Iran arms deals.) The president also requests those present to affirm that there had been no ransoming or bargaining with terrorists.

November 11-12. *Rodriguez-Bush Aides Meeting.* Rodriguez and El Salvador Air Force commander Bustillo have dinner with Watson November 11 and meet with Gregg the next day. Bustillo tells Gregg that he would welcome Rodriguez's return to El Salvador to continue his assistance in the counterinsurgency operation, according to the chronology released by Bush's office December 15, 1986.

November 12. *Southern Air Inquiry.* FBI director Webster calls Associate Attorney General Trott to see if the FBI's investigation of Southern Air Transport could be resumed. The investigation had been suspended October 30. Trott does not respond with a go-ahead until November 20, and then there are further delays.

November 12. *Reagan on Arms Sales.* In a meeting with congressional leaders, President Reagan says he approved the delivery of arms to Iran to foster renewed dialogue with "moderate" elements in Iran.

November 12. *Buchanan Urges Disclosure.* White House communications director Patrick J. Buchanan, citing adverse public opinion, urges Chief of Staff Regan to make "earliest and fullest disclosure" of details concerning the Iran arms sales. Buchanan warns that "the story will not die," according to the July 31, 1987, *Washington Post.*

November 12. *Public Statement Preparations.* Reagan decides to make a public statement on the Iranian arms deals. In one meeting, Reagan and his aides apparently discuss an approach of denying false press reports while revealing as little true information as possible. According to notes taken during the meeting, which were made public by the House and Senate Iran-contra committees, Reagan says: "Whenever we can, point to flat denial," citing as an example the then-current reports that McFarlane had visited Tehran the previous September. McFarlane went to Tehran in May.

November 13. *Reagan's Speech.* In a nationally televised speech from the White House, President Reagan announces that arms shipments to Iran were not ransom payments for American hostages but good faith gestures intended to open a "dialogue" with moderates there. The president's speech represents the first official acknowledgment that the United States directly shipped weapons and other military equipment to Iran. Reagan says that U.S. shipments, in total, would fit in one cargo plane.

November 14. *Shultz Meets with Reagan.* In a meeting with President Reagan, Shultz urges the president to announce that there would be "no more arms sales" to Iran, according to Shultz's testimony before the House and Senate Iran-contra committees July 23, 1987. On Novem-

ber 15, Shultz submits to Chief of Staff Regan a draft paper again calling for an end to the sales. Shultz is told the White House is not then in a position to adopt the proposal.

November 15. *Hasenfus Sentenced.* Hasenfus, the sole survivor of a contra supply plane downed October 5, 1986, is sentenced by a Nicaraguan people's revolutionary tribunal to thirty years imprisonment.

November 16. *Shultz Opposes Arms Sales.* Secretary of State Shultz, appearing on the CBS television show "Face the Nation," says that he is opposed to any more arms sales to Iran under the current conditions. When questioned, Shultz says he does not speak for the administration on this issue.

November 16. *Joint Chiefs Not Informed.* Poindexter says that the Joint Chiefs of Staff were not informed in advance about the arms shipments, according to the December 4, 1986, *New York Times.*

November 17. *Reagan Says No More Sales.* Reagan says that he has "absolutely no plans" to send more arms to Iran, according to the December 4, 1986, *New York Times.*

November 18. *McFarlane Role in Compiling Chronology.* During November, McFarlane reviews various versions of the NSC staff's chronology. According to the Tower report, McFarlane described in his testimony a process that obscured essential facts and left ambiguous the president's role. In a November 18 memo, McFarlane attempts to "gild the President's motives." His version, which McFarlane testified was "misleading, at least, and wrong, at worst," is incorporated into the chronology.

November 19. *Shultz Cautions Reagan.* According to his testimony on July 23, 1987, before the House and Senate Iran-contra committees, Shultz tells the president prior to his news conference that they both had been lied to and deceived and that the president should be careful about saying there had been no arms for hostages.

November 19. *Reagan Press Conference.* President Reagan, in a scheduled news conference, tells reporters he has ruled out future arms deliveries to Iran. He insists that the covert operation was not a mistake. Reagan denies that Israel was involved in the Iran initiative, but after the press conference the White House issues a statement acknowledging that a third country was involved. Reagan reiterates that all the shipments of weapons he has authorized or condoned would fit into a single cargo aircraft.

November 19. *Casey Briefed.* Casey is briefed in preparation for his November 21 appearance before the Senate Intelligence Committee. Casey may have been told that there might be a problem in the area of diversion of Iran arms sale funds to the contras, according to the Senate Intelligence Committee report.

November 19. *Shultz Confronts Reagan.* Shultz calls Reagan immediately after the president's news conference to tell him he had made wrong and misleading statements and to ask for a meeting the next day, according to Shultz's testimony before the House and Senate Iran-contra committees on July 23, 1987.

November 20. *Meeting on Casey Testimony.* North, Poindexter, Casey, Meese, Assistant Attorney General Charles J. Cooper, NSC legal adviser Thompson, and others, possibly including CIA deputy director Gates, meet in Poindexter's office to review a prepared statement Casey is to give to the congressional Intelligence committees the next day.

According to Cooper's June 25, 1987, testimony before the House and Senate Iran-contra committees, the CIA's original draft said CIA officials did not know until January 1986 that a November 1985 Israeli shipment to Iran contained Hawk missiles rather than oil-drilling equipment. At the meeting a statement from North is inserted saying that no one in the U.S. government knew until January 1986. Cooper said no one objected to the substitute language, including those who knew it was false.

According to CIA deputy director for operations Clair George's testimony before the Iran-contra committees on August 4 and 5, 1987, someone at the meeting mentions that funds may have been used from the Iran arms sales for other purposes, to which Casey responds that he knows "absolutely nothing about that."

November 20. *Reagan Warned of Casey's Testimony.* Shultz has a "long, tough discussion" with the president, in which he points out incorrect information being given to Reagan, according to Shultz's July 23, 1987, testimony before the House and Senate Iran-contra committees. Shultz tells Reagan that CIA director Casey is planning to present false testimony on the arms sales during his appearance on Capitol Hill the next day. State Department legal adviser Abraham D. Sofaer, according to his deposition to the Iran-contra committees, threatens to resign unless Casey's testimony is changed.

November 20. *House Leader on Shipments.* Contradicting earlier reports released by the White House, House majority leader Jim Wright, D-Texas, issues a public statement saying that officials had told him 2,008 TOW anti-tank missiles and parts for 235 Hawk antiaircraft missiles were shipped to Iran via Israel. Previous statements by Reagan and White House officials had indicated significantly fewer weapons had been shipped.

November 20. *'Historical Chronology.'* The NSC staff prepares its final chronology, a seventeen-page document entitled "Historical Chronology."

November 20. *Southern Air Inquiry.* FBI director Webster is told by Associate Attorney General Trott to proceed with the investigation of Southern Air Transport (SAT). According to Webster's April 8, 1987, testimony before the Senate Intelligence Committee, there are further delays and the inquiry is not resumed for another four to five days.

November 21. *Congressional Investigations.* The first congressional investigations into the Iran arms sales begin when the House and Senate Intelligence committees hear testimony from CIA director Casey and top State and Defense Department aides. Poindexter testifies before the Senate Intelligence Committee.

November 21. *Casey Testimony.* Apparently as a result of Shultz's protest to Reagan the night before, Casey avoids all references to Hawk missiles in the November 1985 shipment to Iran, leaving the impression that the plane carried oil-drilling equipment. Casey also testifies that U.S. officials knew of only one arms shipment from Israel to Iran, which occurred in September 1985, but Under Secretary of State Armacost tells the committee he had heard of Israeli shipments in September and November.

November 21. *Reagan Authorizes Inquiry.* Attorney General Meese tells Reagan that there is "a lot of confusion" about the facts of the Iran dealings and suggests that someone should try to develop a "coherent overview of all the facts." The president agrees and assigns Meese to do it.

November 21. *Meese-Webster Conversation.* Meese speaks briefly with Webster about Meese's inquiry into the Iran arms sales and both agree that it would not be appropriate to bring the FBI into the matter.

November 21. *Poindexter Destroys Finding.* Meese tells Poindexter to assemble all "relevant" documents on the Iran dealings so they could be reviewed by a Justice Department team the next day. According to Poindexter's July 15, 1987, testimony before the House and Senate Iran-contra committees, the national security adviser tears up the only signed copy of the December 5, 1985, finding that gave retroactive approval to the CIA's participation in the November 1985 Israeli shipment of Hawk missiles to Iran. Poindexter said he wanted to protect the president from political embarrassment.

November 21. *McFarlane Interview, Memo.* In an interview with Meese and Cooper, McFarlane says he cannot recollect the November 1985 Hawk missile shipment to Iran, although Shultz remembered talking to McFarlane about it at the time of the shipment. After the interview, McFarlane sends a memo to Poindexter in which he states that, during a meeting he had with the president in July 1985 while Reagan was in the hospital recovering from cancer surgery, the president "was all for letting the Israelis do anything they wanted." The memo was turned over to the Tower Commission.

November 21. *North Shreds Documents.* Poindexter tells North about the impending inquiry. North shreds memos, telephone logs, and other documents, and has his secretary, Fawn Hall, alter documents about his activities involving the contras.

November 21. *Earlier Israeli Shipments Reported.* A State Department memo reportedly refers to Israeli arms deals with Iran before 1985, according to the August 6, 1987, *Washington Post.* Sen. James A. McClure, R-Idaho, requested that the memo be declassified but the White House refused, the *Post* reported.

November 22. *Diversion Memo Discovered.* Justice Department officials discover in North's office an undated memo containing a one-paragraph mention of the diversion of Iran-arms-sale money to the contras.

November 22. *Meese Inquiry.* Meese interviews Shultz and former CIA general counsel Stanley Sporkin. In a meeting at Casey's home, Casey tells Meese of Furmark's story that two Canadian investors in the Iran arms sales, who were owed $10 million, were threatening to disclose the deals and to say that some of the money had been used for "U.S. and Israeli projects." Meese does not ask Casey whether he knew about the diversion of funds to the contras, according to Meese's July 28, 1987, testimony before the House and Senate Iran-contra committees.

November 22. *Poindexter Meets with North, Casey.* Poindexter has a two-hour lunch with North and Casey. Poindexter said during his July 20, 1987, testimony before the House and Senate Iran-contra committees that he could not recall any details of the discussion that day, except that Casey had told him about his November 21 appearances before the Intelligence committees. Poindexter said the diversion to the contras was not discussed.

November 23. *Meese Confronts North.* During a nearly four-hour interview, Meese shows North the diversion memo that was discovered in North's office November 22, and asks if he prepared it. North is shocked to see the reference to diversion, according to Meese's testimony before the Senate Intelligence Committee December 17, 1986, and the House and Senate Iran-contra committees July 28, 1987. North tells Meese that Poindexter and McFarlane knew about the diversion scheme but that he does not know whether Reagan knew, Meese later testified.

November 23-24. *North Shreds Documents.* North

returns to his office in the White House at 11:00 p.m. and shreds documents for five hours.

November 23. *Casey Seeks Shultz Resignation.* CIA director Casey suggests to the president in a letter disclosed July 24, 1987, during the Iran-contra hearings, that the State Department "needed a new pitcher."

November 24. *Meese Tells Reagan of Diversion.* After another interview with McFarlane, Meese at 11:00 a.m. meets with the president and Regan and tells them about the diversion scheme.

November 24. *Meese Inquiry.* After informing the president of the diversion discovery, Meese tells Vice President Bush, who says he had not known about it. Meese, Regan, Poindexter, Shultz, and others meet to review the Iran situation but apparently do not discuss Meese's inquiry. Meese meets with Poindexter for about ten minutes and tells him about the diversion memo. Poindexter admits knowing about the diversion, but says no one else at the White House knew. Meese meets again with the president and Regan. The chief of staff suggests Poindexter should resign. Regan later tells Casey about the diversion issue.

November 24. *Whitehead on NSC Role.* Deputy Secretary of State Whitehead appears before an open session of the House Foreign Affairs Committee and challenges the wisdom of having NSC aides carry out policy. He calls for "a review of the functioning" of the NSC.

November 24. *Attorney Meets with Cooper.* Washington attorney Thomas C. Green, who at that time represents North and Hakim, meets with Assistant Attorney General Cooper. According to the Senate Intelligence Committee, Green reportedly tells Cooper that, during a meeting in Europe in early 1986, Hakim told the Iranians they should make a contribution over the arms purchase price for use of the contras or "of us." Green tells Cooper that this was the basis upon which the February 1986 shipment of TOWs was priced and that the same thing happened in May 1986.

November 24. *Casey-Furmark Meeting.* In a meeting with Furmark, Casey says that there had been $30,000 in the Lake Resources account and that he does not know where the money is, according to the Senate Intelligence Committee report.

November 24. *Nancy Reagan on 'Housecleaning.'* According to Regan's testimony before the House and Senate Iran-contra committees July 30, 1987, first lady Nancy Reagan calls him and states that "there would have to be a housecleaning of people who had let Ronnie down." Regan responds that he will recommend that Poindexter be relieved of his position.

November 25. *Meese Inquiry.* Casey tells Meese that he was surprised to hear of the diversion, but Meese does not ask him "point blank" if he had known about the diversion before Regan told him. Later in the day Meese meets with FBI director Webster and other officials to review steps for further investigation.

November 25. *Poindexter Resigns, North Fired.* President Reagan accepts national security adviser Poindexter's resignation and fires NSC aide North for their role in the diversion of funds to the contras.

November 25. *Diversion Disclosed.* Reagan briefs the National Security Council and congressional leaders. In a hastily called news conference, Reagan says that he had not been "fully informed" about the Iran arms deals. Meese reveals that an estimated $10 million-$30 million may have been diverted from the Iran arms sales to the contras. Meese says that no other top U.S. officials, includ-ing Reagan and cabinet members, knew about the diversion. The attorney general later amends his statement to say some members with "tangential" ties to the government may have known about or been involved in the money transfers.

November 25. *North Documents Smuggled Out.* Meese orders the sealing of North's office. The order is passed to NSC security officers late in the day. After security personnel have arrived, Fawn Hall, North's secretary, smuggles out of the White House copies of memos she had altered for North and file copies of internal NSC memos, according to Hall's June 8, 1987, testimony before the House and Senate Iran-contra committees.

November 25. *Abrams 'Perhaps Misleading' Testimony.* When asked about third-country solicitations for the contras during a Senate Intelligence Committee hearing, Assistant Secretary of State Abrams fails to reveal his August 1986 solicitation of $10 million from the government of Brunei. Abrams describes his response as "literally correct and perhaps misleading," during his June 2, 1987, testimony before the House and Senate Iran-contra committees.

November 26. *Reagan Appoints Investigative Panel.* President Reagan announces the formation of a three-man special commission to conduct "a comprehensive review" of the operations of the president's eighty-member National Security Council (NSC) staff. Appointed to head the investigative panel is former Texas senator and chairman of the Senate Armed Services Committee John Tower. Other members are: former Maine senator and secretary of state Edmund S. Muskie and President Gerald Ford's national security adviser Brent Scowcroft. The President's Special Review Board, which came to be known as the Tower Commission, is formally established December 1, 1986, by Executive Order 12575.

November 26. *Israeli Role.* Israeli foreign minister Peres says that Israel had "no part in the contra issue," the *New York Times* reported November 27, 1986.

November 26. *Criminal Investigation.* Meese authorizes a criminal investigation into the transfer of funds from Iranian arms sales to the contras, according to Assistant Attorney General William Weld's deposition to the House and Senate Iran-contra committees.

November 26. *Contra Denial.* Contra leaders deny receiving the alleged $10 million to $30 million in diverted funds.

November 28. *Congressional Call for Independent Probe.* In a letter to Attorney General Meese, Rep. John Conyers, Jr., D-Mich., acting on behalf of eleven of the twenty-one Democrats on the House Judiciary Committee, calls for appointment of an independent counsel to investigate the Iran-contra affair. Conyers chairs that panel's Subcommittee on Criminal Justice.

December 1. *Tower Commission Established.* President Reagan signs an executive order establishing a special three-man commission to review the operations of the NSC staff and to recommend reforms.

December 1. *North Cites Fifth; McFarlane, McMahon Testify.* North appears before the Senate Intelligence Committee in a closed session and invokes his Fifth Amendment right to refuse to testify on grounds that doing so may incriminate himself. Former national security adviser McFarlane and John N. McMahon, former deputy director of the CIA, testify before the committee in closed session.

December 2. *Independent Counsel; NSC Director.*

President Reagan, in a four-minute nationally televised speech, calls for the appointment of an independent counsel to investigate arms sales to Iran and diversion of arms sale profits to the contras. Reagan also announces his selection of Frank C. Carlucci to replace Vice Adm. John M. Poindexter as national security adviser.

December 2. *Independent Counsel.* Attorney General Meese says his preliminary investigation produced evidence of possible criminal law violations and that he will seek the appointment of an independent counsel. During a forty-minute news conference, Meese defends his handling of the affair. A petition for a court-appointed independent counsel is filed December 4.

December 3. *Poindexter Cites Fifth.* Former national security adviser Poindexter appears before the Senate Intelligence Committee in closed session and invokes his Fifth Amendment right to refuse to testify.

December 4. *Gates, Dash Testify.* CIA deputy director Gates testifies in a closed session of the Senate Intelligence Committee. Samuel Dash, the former chief counsel and staff director of the Senate Watergate Committee, testifies before the committee on the possible use of legal immunity during congressional investigations.

December 4. *Congressional Investigating Committees.* The House announces plans to appoint a fifteen-member select committee to investigate the Iran-contra affair. Senate leaders agree on an eleven-member panel.

December 5. *GAO on Contra Aid Handling.* The General Accounting Office (GAO) issues a report that the $27 million appropriated for "humanitarian" aid to the contras in fiscal 1986 "could not be fully tracked or verified." The GAO found some funds were diverted to buy military items and noted discrepancies in record-keeping. A State Department official defends its monitoring procedures and says there was "no significant diversion" of the money.

December 6. *Reagan Says 'Mistakes' Made.* In his weekly radio address, President Reagan says "mistakes were made" in the secret shipment of arms to Iran. Reagan says that the U.S. effort to establish ties with "responsible moderates" in Iran came to light and was "broken off."

December 8. *Shultz Testifies.* Secretary of State Shultz testifies before the House Foreign Affairs Committee in open session. He states that, after participating in a January 7, 1986, meeting on the Iran arms sales, he had only "sporadic and fragmentary" knowledge of the arms sales and was unaware Reagan had signed the January 17, 1986, finding authorizing direct U.S. arms shipment to Iran. He reveals that, without his knowledge, U.S. ambassador to Lebanon John H. Kelly had "back-channel" communications from October 30 to November 4, 1986, with Poindexter, North, Secord, and other officials in Washington regarding the release of a hostage. The secretary defends as legal the solicitation of a contra donation from Brunei.

December 8. *McFarlane Testifies.* Former national security adviser McFarlane testifies before the House Foreign Affairs Committee in open session that an "oral finding" by the president in August 1985 authorized Israel's sale of U.S.-made weapons to Iran. He tells the panel that by November 1985 the dealings with Iran "were being skewed toward the hostages alone" and he recommended in December 1985 that U.S. approval for Israeli arms shipments to Iran be ended. Reagan accepted that recommendation but a month later approved direct U.S. sales to Iran, according to McFarlane.

December 8. *Owen Cites Fifth; Abrams Testifies.* Owen, North's liaison with the contras, appears before the Senate Intelligence Committee in closed session and invokes his Fifth Amendment right to refuse to testify. Assistant Secretary of State Abrams appears before the committee and apologizes for withholding information from the committee on November 25 on State Department solicitation of a $10 million gift to the contras from the sultan of Brunei.

December 9. *Poindexter, North Cite Fifth.* Poindexter and North appear before the House Foreign Affairs Committee in open session and invoke their Fifth Amendment right to refuse to testify.

December 9. *North Cites Fifth.* North appears before the House Intelligence Committee in closed session and invokes his Fifth Amendment right to refuse to testify.

December 9. *Secord Cites Fifth; Ledeen Testifies.* Secord appears before the Senate Intelligence Committee in closed session and invokes his Fifth Amendment right to refuse to testify. Michael Ledeen, a former NSC consultant, testifies before the committee in closed session.

December 10. *Poindexter Cites Fifth; Gates, Mc-Farlane Testify.* Poindexter appears for ten minutes before the House Intelligence Committee in closed session and invokes his Fifth Amendment right to refuse to testify. Gates and McFarlane testify before the committee in closed session.

December 10. *Casey Testifies.* CIA director Casey testifies before the House Foreign Affairs Committee in closed session.

December 10. *Dutton Cites Fifth.* Dutton, assistant to Secord at Stanford Technology Trading Group, appears before the Senate Intelligence Committee in closed session and invokes his Fifth Amendment right to refuse to testify.

December 11. *Casey Testifies.* CIA director Casey testifies before the House Intelligence Committee in closed session.

December 11. *Furmark Testifies.* Furmark testifies before the Senate Intelligence Committee in closed session.

December 12. *Another Meeting with Iranians.* State Department and CIA officials meet with Iranian representatives. Shultz told the House and Senate Iran-contra committees July 23, 1987, that the plan was for the State Department to take over Iran policy but that Casey had gone behind his back to persuade the White House to maintain the CIA's policy role.

At the meeting State Department official Charles Dunbar tells the Iranians there would be no more arms sales, but the Iranians focus on the nine-point plan negotiated in October 1986 that includes the continued sale of arms to Iran in exchange for the release of hostages and a promise to develop a plan to win the release of seventeen terrorists jailed in Kuwait (the Da'Wa prisoners). According to the Senate Intelligence Committee report, after this unsuccessful session, the CIA officer (identified elsewhere as George Cave) met privately with an Iranian representative without the State Department's knowledge or approval.

December 12. *American Arrested in Nicaragua.* U.S. citizen Sam N. Hall is arrested on spy charges in Nicaragua. Hall is the brother of Rep. Tony P. Hall, D-Ohio.

December 12. *Teicher, Earl Refuse to Testify.* NSC aide Teicher refuses to testify before the Senate Intelligence Committee in closed session because he does not have an attorney and has been refused the services of the

White House legal office. Lt. Col. Robert L. Earl, another NSC staff member, also refuses to testify before the committee in closed session on the grounds he has had inadequate time to prepare.

December 14. *Shultz Reports on U.S.-Iran Meeting.* Shultz tells President Reagan about the December 12 meeting with the Iranians and about the nine-point plan. Shultz says, during his July 23, 1987, testimony before the House and Senate Iran-contra committees, that Reagan was "astonished" to learn of the U.S. negotiating position and that he had never seen the president so mad. Poindexter had told the committees July 15, 1987, that he had gotten Reagan's approval in October 1986 of the nine-point plan but Shultz said he doubted Poindexter gave Reagan a detailed description of the plan.

December 14. *Political Use of Diverted Funds Alleged.* The *Sunday Sun* of Lowell, Massachusetts, publishes an article alleging that profits from the Iran arms sales were used to finance a private, procontra lobbying effort and possibly election-related activities.

December 15. *Casey Hospitalized.* CIA director Casey is hospitalized after suffering a seizure in his office.

December 15. *Bush Chronology.* Vice President Bush's office releases a chronology of contacts Bush and his staff had with Felix I. Rodriguez, a former CIA operative who helped coordinate the contra supply network while working on counterinsurgency efforts in El Salvador. Bush denies any knowledge of Rodriguez's contra supply efforts. According to the chronology, Rodriguez first talked with Bush's top national security aides about the contra supply network on August 8, 1986. Following the downing in Nicaragua of a contra supply plane October 5, 1986, Rodriguez contacted a Bush staff member who passed the information on to the White House and NSC staff.

December 15. *Swiss Accounts Frozen.* Responding to a petition from the U.S. Justice Department, the Swiss government orders the Credit Suisse bank to freeze accounts linked to North, Secord, and Hakim, according to the December 18, 1986, *Washington Post.*

December 15. *Intelligence Data Reported Given to Iraq.* The *Washington Post* reports that the United States had been supplying Iraq with intelligence on Iran since 1984.

December 16. *Reagan Asks Immunity for Ex-Aides.* President Reagan asks the Senate Intelligence Committee to consider granting limited "use" immunity to former White House aides Poindexter and North, in order to compel their testimony. Committee members December 17 reject the plea as "premature."

December 16. *Senate Investigating Committee.* Senate leaders appoint an eleven-member panel—six Democrats and five Republicans—to investigate the Iran-contra affair. Daniel K. Inouye, D-Hawaii, will chair the committee, and Warren B. Rudman, R-N.H., will be vice chairman.

December 16. *Regan Testifies.* White House chief of staff Regan testifies before the Senate Intelligence Committee in closed session. Regan's appearance before the panel is highly unusual. Chiefs of staff rarely testify before Congress, and Regan did so after the president waived the traditional claim of executive privilege.

December 16. *Shultz, Teicher Testify.* Secretary of State Shultz and NSC staffer Teicher testify before the Senate Intelligence Committee in closed session.

December 17. *House Investigating Committee.* House leaders appoint a fifteen-member panel—nine Dem-

ocrats and six Republicans—to investigate the Iran-contra affair. Lee H. Hamilton, D-Ind., will chair the committee; Dante B. Fascell, D-Fla., will be vice chairman; and Dick Cheney, R-Wyo., will be ranking Republican.

December 17. *Weinberger, Meese Testify.* Secretary of Defense Weinberger and Attorney General Meese testify before the Senate Intelligence Committee in closed session.

December 17. *Weapons Pricing Issue.* Sen. William Cohen, R-Maine, says the Senate Intelligence Committee had received evidence that the Pentagon had provided weapons at "at least wholesale" prices and then, in some cases, the arms were sold to Iran at a mark-up of 400 percent.

December 17. *NSC Staff Changes.* The *Washington Post* reports the resignations of NSC staffers Teicher, senior director of political-military affairs; Alton G. Keel, Jr., acting director; and Rodney B. McDaniel, executive secretary.

December 17. *Hasenfus Released.* Under the direct order of Nicaraguan leader Daniel Ortega, Hasenfus is pardoned and released from custody as a "Christmas goodwill gesture." Hasenfus was captured after his airplane crashed October 5 in Nicaragua while transporting supplies to the contras.

December 17. *Swiss Accounts Frozen.* Responding to a supplemental request from the U.S. Justice Department, the Swiss government orders the Credit Suisse bank to freeze the accounts of six individuals and three companies, according to the December 18, 1986, *Washington Post.* The individuals are thought to include Khashoggi, Ghorbanifar, and probably two Canadian investors in the Iran arms deals, Donald Fraser and Ernest Miller. The three companies are identified as Hyde Park Holding and Investment, a Lake Resources Inc. affiliate, and Stanford Technology Trading Group affiliate.

December 18. *Casey Surgery.* CIA director Casey undergoes surgery to remove a cancerous tumor from his brain.

December 18. *Weinberger, Regan, Furmark Testify.* Secretary of Defense Weinberger, Regan, and Furmark testify before the House Intelligence Committee in closed session.

December 18. *McFarlane Testifies.* Former national security adviser McFarlane testifies before a closed session of the Senate Intelligence Committee.

December 18. *Push for Regan Resignation Reported.* The *Washington Post* reports that White House political director Mitchell E. Daniels, Jr., has suggested that White House chief of staff Regan resign. According to the report, Daniels told Regan there was a widespread consensus among Republicans that he should resign. Daniels declined to comment on the *Post* report.

December 18. *Shultz Reassures Kuwait.* According to his testimony before the House and Senate Iran-contra committees July 24, 1987, Secretary of State Shultz, after hearing that Poindexter may have asked Kuwait to "do something" about the terrorists jailed in Kuwait (the Da'Wa prisoners), cables the Kuwaiti foreign minister to affirm that there has been no change in the U.S. policy against terrorism.

December 18. *Shultz Warns Ambassadors.* The *Washington Post* reports that John H. Kelly, the U.S. ambassador to Lebanon, has been "admonished" by Secretary of State Shultz for engaging in back-channel communications with the NSC staff to make arrangements concerning the release of hostage David Jacobsen. Shultz sent a cable warning all U.S. ambassadors against using back-channel communications unless directed to do so by the president.

December 18. *Pentagon Probe.* A Pentagon spokesman announces that the Army inspector general's office will investigate whether the Pentagon received adequate compensation for weapons sold to Iran. The CIA reportedly reimbursed the Pentagon about $12 million for 2,008 TOW antitank missiles, spare parts for Hawk antiaircraft missiles, and other military supplies.

December 19. *Independent Counsel Selected.* A three-judge panel names Lawrence E. Walsh, a former prosecutor, federal judge, and president of the American Bar Association, as independent counsel to investigate the Iran-contra affair. Walsh is given broad authority to investigate not only the actual sale of arms to Iran and the diversion of funds to the contras, but also the "provision or coordination of support" for the contras since 1984.

December 19. *Durenberger Meets with President.* Senate Intelligence Committee chairman Dave Durenberger, R-Minn., and committee staff director Bernard McMahon brief President Reagan, White House counsel Peter J. Wallison, Regan, and Keel on the contents of the committee's unreleased report. The committee had decided at a December 18 business meeting not to provide the White House with a written report. The committee is not notified about the briefing until January 20, 1987.

December 19. *Meese Testifies.* Attorney General Meese testifies before the House Intelligence Committee in closed session.

December 19. *White House Taping System.* The *Washington Post* reports that a sophisticated White House communications system, capable of recording some phone calls and meetings, and preserving messages and documents written on NSC computer terminals, may contain information on the Iran arms affair. The taping system is in the White House Situation Room and has been used to record some of President Reagan's key foreign policy meetings, according to the *Post.* White House spokesman Larry Speakes says on December 21 that no tapes were made of discussions relating to the Iran arms sales.

December 20. *Durenberger Meets with Bush.* Senate Intelligence Committee chairman Durenberger and committee staff director Bernard McMahon brief Vice President Bush, Craig Fuller, and another Bush staff member on the contents of the committee's unreleased report. The committee is not informed of this meeting until January 20, 1987.

December 21. *Waite to Return to Lebanon.* Terry Waite, Anglican church envoy, announces his plan to return to Lebanon before Christmas in an attempt to win the release of the remaining U.S. hostages held there.

December 21. *Wright Urges Pardon.* In a television interview, Representative Wright, the incoming speaker of the House, urges Reagan to pardon North and Poindexter to give them the "ultimate immunity" in exchange for their testimony. White House spokesman Speakes December 22 says Reagan had ruled out a pardon for the two.

December 22. *Request for Documents Refused.* The *Washington Post* reports that Assistant Attorney General John Bolton refused to release documents requested December 11 by House Judiciary Committee chairman Peter W. Rodino, Jr., D-N.J. Bolton said that some documents requested by Rodino included "highly classified" information and that no Judiciary Committee staff member had the proper clearance to review them. Rodino raises the

document issue when Attorney General Meese appeared before the House and Senate Iran-contra committees July 28, 1987.

December 23. *Secord Cites Fifth.* Secord appears before the Senate Intelligence Committee in closed session and invokes his Fifth Amendment right to refuse to testify.

December 24. *North Hospitalization Reported.* The *Washington Post* and *New York Times* report tht North was hospitalized for emotional distress in December 1974, following his return from an overseas assignment. The story was first disclosed by the *Miami Herald* December 23. The *Times* reports that former national security adviser Richard V. Allen was unaware of this when he hired North in 1981. The White House and North refuse comment on the story.

December 26. *Abshire Appointment.* Former U.S. ambassador to NATO David Abshire is appointed by President Reagan to coordinate White House responses to all probes into the Iran-contra affair. He will have cabinet rank and will serve as a special counselor to the president.

1987

January 2. *Rodriguez Statement.* Felix I. Rodriguez, a former CIA operative who helped coordinate the contra supply network while working on counterinsurgency in El Salvador, denies reports that he had discussed rebel supply operations with Vice President George Bush. Rodriguez, also known as Max Gomez, says his meetings with Bush dealt only with El Salvador. In a written statement released in Miami, Rodriguez says that he became "marginally involved" with the contra supply effort in late 1985, but fails to provide details on his role in the operation.

January 3. *Israel Denies Knowledge of Diversion.* Israeli prime minister Yitzhak Shamir says during Israel's English-language broadcast that Israel could prove it had no previous knowlege of arms sales proceeds being diverted to the contras. David Kimche, former director general of the Israeli Foreign Ministry, also denies allegations that Israel knew of the diversion of funds. Kimche says he met twice with North in 1985, with other people present, and that the subject of the contras was not raised.

January 4. *Iran Pushes Assets Return.* Iran's prime minister Mir Hussein Moussavi says that if the United States does not return more than $500 million in frozen Iranian assets within "a definite period of time," Tehran will take the case to the World Court. The assets were seized shortly after U.S. Embassy personnel in Tehran were taken hostage in November 1979.

January 5. *Senate Intelligence Report.* The Senate Select Intelligence Committee votes 7-6 not to make public a 150-page report of the committee's findings during its November-December 1986 inquiry into the Iran-contra affair.

January 5. *Iranian Arms Sale Case.* A thirty-four-page memorandum, filed by lawyers for one of eighteen arms dealers accused of conspiring since November 1985 to sell $2 billion worth of arms to Iran, alleges that the key informant in the case had played a role in the U.S. government's arms shipments to Iran. An April 1986 "sting" operation had exposed the private arms deal with the help of Iranian arms dealer Cyrus Hashemi. Attorneys for Samuel Evans, former lawyer for Saudi Arabian arms merchant Adnan Khashoggi, contend that the accused arms dealers thought they were negotiating arms transactions that eventually would have received U.S. government approval.

January 6. *Senate Investigative Committee.* The Senate votes 88-4 to establish the Select Committee on Secret Military Assistance to Iran and the Nicaraguan Opposition. The eleven-member panel, six Democrats and five Republicans, is chaired by Daniel K. Inouye, D-Hawaii.

January 6. *North's Document Shredding.* White House spokesman Larry Speakes tells reporters that news reports "grossly misrepresented" possible document-shredding by former National Security Council (NSC) aide Lt. Col. Oliver L. North. "If there was shredding, it was very limited," he states.

January 7. *House Investigative Committee.* The House votes 416-2 to establish the Select Committee on Secret Military Assistance to Iran and the Nicaraguan Opposition. The fifteen-member panel, nine Democrats and six Republicans, is chaired by Lee H. Hamilton, D-Ind.

January 7. *Senate Intelligence Report.* The new chairman of the Senate Intelligence Committee, David L. Boren, D-Okla., reacting to White House participation in the editing of the Senate committee's report, states that it was "very inappropriate" for members of the White House to join in editing the committee's unpublished report. White House spokesman Speakes denies that massive revisions were made but says some changes were necessary to protect intelligence sources and methods.

January 7. *FBI Probe of Break-ins.* The Justice Department orders an FBI investigation of break-ins at the offices of organizations opposing the Reagan administration's support of the Nicaraguan contras, the Associated Press reports.

January 8. *Senate Intelligence Report Leaked.* NBC News reports that it has obtained a copy of the Senate Intelligence Committee report, which committee members voted not to release, and broadcasts some details. Committee members say it is a rough draft and incomplete. Sen. Patrick J. Leahy, D-Vt., discloses July 28, 1987, that he was the one who leaked the document. Leahy resigns from the committee January 13.

NBC reports that North resisted the advice of Secretary of State George P. Shultz and Secretary of Defense Caspar W. Weinberger to end the arms shipments and reportedly wrote in a memo that "if the program is terminated, then the hostages will die."

January 9. *Background Paper Leaked.* The *Washington Post* reports on leaked portions of a background paper that was prepared by the NSC to accompany the January 17, 1986, finding authorizing the Iran initiative. The paper outlined U.S. policy and reasserted U.S. opposition to negotiating with terrorist states, but said that arms sales to Iran "may well be our *only* way to achieve the release of the Americans held in Beirut."

January 9. *'Finding,' Background Paper Released.* The White House releases President Reagan's January 17, 1986, "finding" officially authorizing the Iran initiative and the companion background memo justifying U.S. arms sales as helping strengthen "moderate" elements in Iran.

January 10. *Israeli Diversion Role Alleged.* The *Washington Post* reports that sources with access to the unpublished Senate Intelligence Committee report said that during a January 1986 meeting with White House aides, Amiran Nir, antiterrorism adviser to then-Israeli

prime minister Shimon Peres, made the first suggestion that proceeds from Iranian arms sales be diverted to the contras. North, however, told the House and Senate Iran-contra commitees in July 1987, that Nir had suggested using the proceeds for other projects but had not mentioned the contras.

January 11. *Israel Not a Scapegoat.* U.S. Ambassador to Israel Thomas Pickering tells Israeli prime minister Yitzhak Shamir that the United States does not hold Israel responsible for events surrounding U.S.-backed arms shipments to Iran.

January 11. *Israeli Inquiry Proposed.* Amnon Rubinstein, leader of Israel's Shinui Party and a member of Israel's coalition government, calls for an investigation into Israel's role in the Iran-contra affair.

January 12. *New NSC Guidelines.* Frank C. Carlucci, who succeeded Vice Adm. John M. Poindexter as Reagan's national security adviser, issues new guidelines barring the NSC staff from undertaking covert activities.

January 12. *Waite Returns to Lebanon.* Terry Waite, Anglican Church emissary for the Archbishop of Canterbury, returns to Lebanon to negotiate the release of the remaining foreign hostages.

January 12. *Iraq Condemns United States.* Iraq's first deputy prime minister, Taha Yassin Ramadan, accuses the United States of having supplied Iraq with faulty intelligence information, that resulted in the deaths of thousands of Iraqi soldiers. Ramadan's condemnation, reported in the January 13, 1987, *Wall Street Journal*, comes amidst allegations that the United States had passed false information to both Iran and Iraq, although the CIA denied the reports. In his harshest statement since news of U.S. arms sales to Iran surfaced, Ramadan says, "The arms scandal is expressive of a bigger U.S. program in the region aimed at conspiring with Iran against Iraq."

January 13. *Walsh Urges Delaying Immunity.* In a letter to the House and Senate Iran-contra committees, independent counsel Lawrence E. Walsh asks the two panels not to grant immunity to any witnesses before he has completed his inquiry. He says a premature grant of immunity would create "serious—and perhaps insurmountable—barriers to the prosecution of the immunized witnesses."

January 13. *Intelligence Committee Restrictions.* The Senate Intelligence Committee places new restrictions on senators and staff members to prevent leaks of committee reports and hearings. Senator Leahy, who, it later was revealed, leaked the committee's draft report on the Iran-contra affair, resigns from the committee.

January 13. *Rescue Mission Explored.* NBC News reports that Israel, at the request of President Reagan, conducted intelligence missions throughout 1986 to locate hostages held in Lebanon's Bekaa Valley, but was not successful in finding them.

January 14. *Vance Testifies.* The Senate Foreign Relations Committee begins hearings to review details of the Iran-contra affair. Cyrus R. Vance, secretary of state during the Carter administration, sharply criticizes Reagan's agreement to sell arms to Iran.

January 16. *McFarlane Testifies.* Robert C. McFarlane, Reagan's former national security adviser, testifies before the Senate Foreign Relations Committee in open session. He repeats his earlier assertions that Reagan gave prior approval to Israel's 1985 arms shipments to Iran. He testifies that in the summer of 1985 he informed Secretary of State Shultz and Secretary of Defense Weinberger that President Reagan had approved Israeli arms shipments to

Iran, which both Shultz and Weinberger deny.

January 17. *CIA Station Chief Recalled.* The *Washington Post* reports that the CIA the previous week recalled its station chief in Costa Rica because of "unauthorized contacts" with the private contra aid network during a period when Congress had barred U.S. military assistance to the contras. The station chief, later identified as going by the pseudonym of Tomas Castillo, subsequently was suspended, according to an Associated Press (AP) article in the January 25, 1987, *Washington Post.* An AP article in the February 2, 1987, *Washington Post* said Castillo was being forced to take early retirement in the spring of 1987.

January 17. *Contra Arms Purchases.* The *Washington Post* reports that nearly 800 tons of Portuguese arms and ammunition were purchased—with apparently false documents—for the Nicaraguan contras. Arms shipments totaling an estimated $5.6 million reportedly were sent from Lisbon to the contras over an eighteen-month period ending in August 1986. The shipments officially were purchased for Guatemala but actually were destined for the contras. According to the *Post,* certificates were filed with the Portuguese government by Energy Resources International, a company that, it was later learned, was controlled by retired Air Force major general Richard V. Secord and his Iranian-American business partner, Albert Hakim. Guatemalan officials denied any connection with the arms purchases.

January 19. *Intelligence Panel Conclusions Published.* The *New York Times* publishes a twenty-three-page section of the Senate Intelligence Committee's draft report on the Iran-contra affair. The Senate panel January 5 had dropped the section, which contained the staff's conclusions, prior to its vote not to release the full report. A committee spokesman branded the *Times* action as "irresponsible" and said some information in the report was incorrect. The staff conclusions condemned the administration's handling of the Iran policy and said that top officials ignored or did not receive repeated warnings in 1986 that the U.S. initiative toward Iran had "gone wrong." The CIA role was criticized and CIA director William J. Casey's testimony November 21, 1986, was termed "misleading" and "incomplete." The staff concluded that the administration had violated or skirted several laws and its own foreign policy guidelines.

January 20. *McFarlane on May 1986 Trip.* Former national security adviser McFarlane says on ABC's "Nightline" that, prior to his trip to Iran in May 1986, he was told the release of four U.S. hostages already had been arranged by U.S. intelligence officials and the White House directed him not to negotiate with Iranian officials during the trip.

January 20. *Waite Disappears.* Anglican Church emissary Terry Waite meets in Beirut with representatives of the Shiite faction reportedly holding Western hostages. Waite, on his fifth mission to Lebanon to negotiate the release of hostages, agrees to drop from the public eye to meet with kidnappers. When Waite fails to reappear weeks later, authorities assume he has been taken captive.

Moslem militia officials on January 30 confirm reports that he has been taken hostage.

January 21. *Meetings with Iranians Continued.* In a closed session of the House Foreign Affairs Committee, Secretary of State Shultz tells committee members that U.S. officials had continued to meet with the Iranians to discuss arms and hostages in December 1986, weeks after the Iran-contra affair first became public. Shultz testifies, according to subsequent news reports, that State Department and CIA officials attended a December 13, 1986, meeting in Europe at which the Iranians put forward a nine-point agenda negotiated in October that included shipment of more U.S weapons and spare parts and a promise to work for the release of seventeen terrorists held in Kuwait (the Da'Wa prisoners), in return for the release of American hostages in Lebanon.

January 21. *Tower Commission Deadline Extended.* White House spokesman Speakes announces that the President's Special Review Board (Tower Commission), after gaining White House approval to interview President Reagan on January 26 and receiving additional documents from U.S. intelligence agencies, had had its report deadline extended to February 19.

January 22. *Shultz Target of Criticism.* Following Secretary of State Shultz's testimony before the House Foreign Affairs Committee January 21, White House officials accused Shultz of not being "a team player," the *New York Times* reports.

January 22. *Singapore Solicitated for Contra Aid.* Administration officials acknowledge that the United States had asked Singapore to supply the Nicaraguan contras with long-range communications equipment, but that Singapore had not provided the aid. Secretary of State Shultz told investigators of the request.

January 23. *Third Country Aid to Contras.* The *Washington Post* reports that the Reagan administration had solicited funds for the Nicaraguan contras from at least six countries, including Israel, Saudi Arabia, Brunei, Singapore, South Korea, and Taiwan. According to the *Post,* information provided to congressional committees also showed that Israel had transferred arms to the contras as early as 1984 in response to U.S. requests. Israel denied aiding the contras.

January 23. *Pentagon Undercharges CIA.* Pentagon spokesman Robert B. Sims releases an unclassified audit summary indicating that the Pentagon undercharged the CIA by almost $2.6 million for antitank missiles sold to Iran in 1986. Pentagon investigators called it "an honest mistake" resulting primarily from the sale of two versions of the TOW antitank missile. The Army had sold the CIA both old and new models but had charged the agency at the lower rate of the older model. Sims said the missiles were turned over to the CIA in 1986 in three installments: 1,000 in February, 508 in May, and 500 in November.

January 23. *Iranian Scorns U.S. Overtures.* Iran's president, Hojatolislam Ali Khamenei, scorns U.S. efforts to maintain contacts with Iranian officials even after the November 1986 disclosure of U.S. arms sales to Iran.

January 24. *Four Kidnapped in Lebanon.* In the largest single kidnapping of American citizens in the city of Beirut, terrorists, disguised as Lebanese police, abduct three Americans and one Indian from the Beirut University College campus. The three Americans are Alann Steen, professor of journalism; Jesse Jonathan Turner, assistant professor of computer science and math; and Robert Polhill, professor of business studies and accounting. Mithileshwar Singh, chairman of the business school, is said to be an Indian citizen who is a permanent resident of the United States.

January 26. *Reagan Meets with Tower Commission.* In a seventy-six-minute interview, President Reagan tells the Tower Commission that he approved the shipment of arms by Israel to Iran sometime in August 1985. He also says that he approved the replenishment of any arms transferred by Israel to Iran. Reagan later tells the commission that he had not approved the August shipment in advance, and finally tells them that he cannot remember whether he did or did not give prior approval. Reagan also tells the panel that he did not know that the NSC staff was engaged in aiding the contras.

January 27. *State of the Union Address.* During his State of the Union address to Congress, President Reagan says that his "one major regret" was that efforts to establish contacts with Iran and to win the release of American hostages were unsuccessful. He concedes that "serious mistakes were made."

January 28. *Walsh Impanels Grand Jury.* Independent counsel Walsh impanels a grand jury to hear evidence of any illegalities that might have been committed by administration officials and private individuals who were working on behalf of the United States.

January 28. *Contra Ability Questioned.* The Associated Press reports that a former U.S. commander of military forces in Central America, retired Army general Paul Gorman, told the Senate Armed Services Committee that the contras would be unable to topple the Sandinista government by conventional means. Gorman said that, instead of assisting the contras militarily, the U.S. government should be providing economic aid to those democratic countries bordering Nicaragua, particularly Honduras and Costa Rica.

January 28. *Rafsanjani Displays Bible.* The speaker of Iran's parliament, Ali Akbar Hashemi Rafsanjani, displays a Bible that he says was given to him by former national security adviser McFarlane during his trip to Tehran in May 1986. The Bible, inscribed with a verse from Galatians 3:8 and signed "Ronald Reagan Oct. 3, 1986," actually was presented to the second Iranian channel by North and his team at an October 1986 meeting in Frankfurt. Rafsanjani also passes out photocopies of an Irish passport issued in the name of Sean Devlin but with McFarlane's picture.

January 28. *U.S. Ban on Travel to Lebanon.* In the aftermath of recent American kidnappings in Lebanon, the administration bars most Americans from traveling to Lebanon. The order gives Americans living in Lebanon thirty days to leave. Violators would be subject to up to five years imprisonment and a $2,000 fine. Families of hostages, journalists, and certain humanitarian workers are exempt from the order.

January 28. *American Freed in Nicaragua.* Sam Hall, brother of Rep. Tony P. Hall, D-Ohio, is released from custody after Nicaraguan medical officials found him to be mentally unbalanced. Sam Hall was arrested December 12, 1986, and confessed December 22 that he had been spying on behalf of three men, code-named Tinker, Evers, and Chance, but that as far as he knew he was not working for the U.S. government.

January 29. *Senate Intelligence Report Released.* The Senate Intelligence Committee votes 14-1 to send its report detailing events surrounding the Iran-contra affair to the Senate Iran-contra committee. That committee votes to send the report back to the Intelligence panel with a recommendation that it be released. Based on the testimony of thirty-six witnesses and thousands of pages of documents, the report presents the most complete chronology of the affair up to that time. The report lists fourteen "unresolved issues" that the Senate select panel might want to review.

January 29. *Hasenfus Testifies.* Eugene Hasenfus, the sole survivor of the contra supply plane downed in Nicaragua October 5, 1986, testifies before the House Iran-contra committee.

January 31. *Arms for Hostages.* U.S. News & World Report releases an interview with Secretary of State Shultz in which Shultz speculates that arms sales to Iran may have escalated kidnappings of U.S. citizens in Lebanon. "The structure of the arms deliveries and the connection with the hostages may have gotten pretty tightly connected, in which case the perception of the Iranians—whatever the perception in this country was—would be that hostages are a thing of value. Once you get that established in somebody's mind, then you have problems," he said.

January 31. *U.S. Reporter Detained.* A *Wall Street Journal* reporter, Gerald F. Seib, is detained by Iranian police. Seib was among more than fifty Western journalists invited to Iran to observe Iran's war efforts against Iraq.

February 2. *Casey Resigns.* CIA director Casey resigns and President Reagan nominates CIA deputy director Robert M. Gates as Casey's successor.

February 2. *Reagan's Notes.* The White House announces that President Reagan would be willing to turn over "relevant excerpts" of his personal notes about the decision to sell arms to Iran, if requested by the House and Senate Iran-contra committees.

February 2. *Private Arms Sales to Iran.* The *New York Times* reports that high-ranking Pentagon officials learned more than a year ago of efforts by private arms dealers to ship U.S. jet fighters and other weapons to Iran, but allowed the efforts to continue in hopes of receiving intelligence information and access to Soviet tanks captured from Iraq by Iran. The *Times* says it obtained more than 4,000 pages of confidential documents and interviewed 150 government officials, arms dealers, and intelligence sources over an eight-week period. A key source for the report on the $1 billion private transaction—called "Demavand" after Iran's highest mountain—was Oregon businessman Richard J. Brenneke, a former CIA employee who said he had extensive intelligence connections. According to the *Times*, the Pentagon confirmed it was told of Demavand as early as December 1985, but various arms dealers said some high government officials knew of the project by early 1984.

February 3. *Iran Holds U.S. Reporter.* In a radio broadcast, Iran acknowledges holding *Wall Street Journal* reporter Seib, calling him "a spy for the Zionist regime." Seib is released February 6.

February 4. *Poindexter, North Testimony Requested.* In a letter to President Reagan, John Tower, chairman of the Tower Commission, requests that the president order former NSC aides Poindexter and North to appear and cooperate with the panel. Reagan refuses the request February 6.

February 5. *Israeli Role.* The *Los Angeles Times* reports that Israeli prime minister Shamir has refused to allow Israeli officials to testify before the House and Senate Iran-contra committees. Shamir said that he would consider responding to written questions on a government-to-government basis.

February 6. *Reagan Refuses to Order Testimony.* In a letter to the Tower Commission, White House counsel Peter J. Wallison informs the panel that President Reagan will not use his presidential powers to force North and Poindexter to appear and cooperate with the panel, as requested February 4, because it would violate their rights under the Constitution and the Uniform Code of Military Justice.

February 6. *White House Documents Released.* President Reagan meets with David M. Abshire, his special counselor on the Iran-contra affair, to review congressional requests for documents. An estimated 3,000 NSC documents are released to the Senate Iran-contra committee.

February 7. *State Department Contract with IBC.* An Associated Press story in the *Washington Post* reports that the State Department awarded a $276,186 contract in 1986 to International Business Communications (IBC), a public relations firm headed by Richard R. Miller, to generate support for contra aid. The contract was effective as of October 1, 1985, but was not signed until September 2, 1986.

February 7. *Casey Support for Contra Aid.* The *Miami Herald* quotes an unidentified intelligence officer as saying that CIA director Casey played an important role in helping North provide aid to the contras. "Without Casey's help at every stage," the source said, "Ollie North would not have been able to do any of what he did for the contras."

February 9. *McFarlane Drug Overdose.* McFarlane is admitted to the Bethesda Naval Hospital after an apparent suicide attempt. McFarlane, according to police reports, took an overdose of twenty to thirty tablets of the tranquilizer Valium. McFarlane had been scheduled to testify before the Tower Commission that morning.

February 10. *Reagan Notes.* The Tower Commission receives President Reagan's personal notes on the Iran arms sales. Panel members read them while a White House courier stands by. They are not allowed to keep or copy the notes, according to the February 12 *New York Times.*

February 11. *Reagan Meets with Tower Commission.* President Reagan meets with the three-member Tower Commission and extends its reporting deadline from February 19 to February 26. In a seventy-minute interview, Reagan tells the panel that after going over the matter with White House chief of staff Donald T. Regan, he does not recall authorizing, in advance, the August 1985 Israeli shipment of arms to Iran. The president thus reverses his January 26 testimony before the panel.

February 11. *Hostage Swap under Discussion.* The *Washington Post* reports that secret negotiations are under way on the proposal to exchange four professors abducted from the Beirut University College campus January 24, 1987, for 400 Arab prisoners held in Israeli prisons. According to reports, Islamic Jihad for the Liberation of Palestine, the group held responsible for the kidnappings, has provided a list of 310 Lebanese and 90 Palestinians.

February 12. *Walsh Expands Inquiry.* The *New York Times* reports that independent counsel Walsh has assumed responsibility for at least three Justice Department inquiries into private American arms supplies to the contras. Two of the inquiries, according to the *Times,* are being handled by investigators in Miami and involve the October 5, 1986, downing of a U.S. cargo plane over Nicaragua. The third inquiry is being conducted in Macon, Ga., and involves the provision of supplies to the contras.

February 15. *'Project Democracy.'* The *New York Times* reports that NSC aide North's Iran-contra operations began as the covert side of "Project Democracy," a well-publicized program established in 1983 to promote democratic institutions abroad. The Tower Commission, however, could find no connection between the real Project Democracy run by the National Endowment for Democ-

racy and North's covert operations network that he labeled "Project Democracy."

February 17-18. *Gates Confirmation Hearings.* Gates undergoes tough questioning from Senate Intelligence Committee members during hearings on his nomination to be the next director of the CIA.

February 18. *Israeli Role.* Israeli prime minister Shamir tells U.S. congressional leaders that he will provide written accounts of Israeli involvement in the transfer of arms to Iran if U.S. officials drop their attempts to seek the testimony of Israeli citizens and government officials.

February 18. *Hussein Interview.* In an interview with the *Financial Times* of London, Jordanian king Ibn Talal Hussein says that U.S. arms sales to Iran were "diametrically opposed to every assurance I received." Hussein said that the United States had promised to prevent the supply of arms to Iran.

February 19. *McFarlane Interview.* Former national security adviser McFarlane is interviewed by the Tower Commission in his room at the Bethesda Naval Hospital. McFarlane reportedly reiterates during three hours of questioning that Reagan gave oral approval of the Israeli shipment of arms to Iran in 1985. McFarlane, according to the *Los Angeles Times,* says he helped draft an inaccurate chronology of the Iran arms affair to protect Reagan from political damage.

February 19. *Break-in Victims Testify.* Witnesses working for organizations that oppose President Reagan's policies in Central America testify before the House Judiciary Subcommittee on Civil and Constitutional Rights on break-ins at their offices. Witnesses claim they were victims of political burglaries. While office equipment and other valuables were left untouched, files were rifled. The February 20 *Washington Post* reported that, according to the Center for Constitutional Rights, there had been fifty-eight break-ins in the last two years at churches, offices, and houses of people sympathetic to the Sandinista government in Nicaragua and leftist rebels in El Salvador.

February 20. *Reagan's Letter to Tower Commission.* After giving the Tower Commission contradictory testimony on January 26 and February 11 as to when he approved Israeli arms shipments to Iran, Reagan sends the commission a letter saying, "I cannot recall anything whatsoever about whether I approved an Israeli sale in advance or whether I approved replenishment of Israeli stocks around August of 1985. My answer therefore, and the simple truth is, 'I don't remember—period.' "

February 20. *Cover-up Plan.* The *New York Times* and *Los Angeles Times* report that McFarlane told the Tower Commission February 19 that he and other administration officials took part in an effort to conceal President Reagan's role in initiating the sale of weapons to Iran. A November 18, 1986, document written by McFarlane at the request of Poindexter outlines a plan by which Reagan could "plausibly" deny approving the August 1985 arms sale to Iran. White House spokesman Marlin Fitzwater says that President Reagan was unaware of any cover-up attempt.

February 20. *Contra Leader Salary.* Arturo Cruz, Sr., one of three top contra officials, tells the *Los Angeles Times* that ex-NSC aide North arranged a salary for him amounting to $7,000 a month from January to November 1986. According to Cruz, North said the funds came from a "private foreign source."

February 20. *Break-in Investigations.* The Associated Press reports that Oliver B. "Buck" Revell, the FBI's executive assistant director, testified that the FBI was "not involved in any capacity" in break-ins against organizations opposed to President Reagan's policy in Central America.

February 20. *Records of Swiss Accounts Sought.* The *Washington Post* reports that the U.S. Justice Department, in hopes of tracking diverted funds from Iranian arms sales to the contras, has sent a request to Swiss authorities for the release of the records of twenty Swiss bank accounts controlled by corporations and individuals associated with the Iran-contra affair.

February 21. *McFarlane Interview.* The Tower Commission interviews McFarlane for the third time. During the three-hour session, McFarlane reportedly repeats his assertion that Reagan gave his oral aproval in August 1985 for Israel to ship arms to Iran.

February 24. *Channell's Activities.* The *Los Angeles Times* reports that political fund-raiser Carl R. "Spitz" Channell used tax-exempt contributions from his organization, the National Endowment for the Preservation of Liberty (NEPL), to help finance military aid for the contras. According to the *Times,* Jane McLaughlin, a former employee of NEPL, told investigators that Channell had set up an account code named "Toys," and had raised $2.2 million, which she claimed helped purchase weapons for the contras.

February 24. *CIA Proprietary Allegations.* The *Washington Post* reports that since 1985 the Caribbean-based St. Lucia Airways has flown secret missions to strategically important regions around the world, including flights from the United States to Tehran November 25, 1985, and to Tel Aviv May 23, 1986. The Senate Intelligence Committee and Tower Commission reports said the November 25, 1985, Hawk missile shipment to Iran was delivered by a CIA proprietary airline. St. Lucia Airways officials denied any links to the CIA or any other U.S. government branches.

February 26. *Tower Report Released.* At an 11:00 a.m. press conference President Reagan presents the three-member Tower Commission, which, after three months of research and interviews, has completed its report. The panel blames the Iran-contra debacle on key White House staffers and on the president himself, saying Reagan failed to understand or control what his appointees were doing.

February 26. *First Grants of Immunity.* The House and Senate Iran-contra committees vote to grant limited immunity to three witnesses: Fawn Hall, former secretary to North; retired colonel Robert C. Dutton, an assistant to Secord; and Edward de Garay, owner of an air freight company allegedly involved in the contra aid network.

February 26. *Private Contra Funding.* The *Washington Post* reports that three groups supplied the contras with millions of dollars in weapons after the October 1984 congressional ban on U.S. government aid to the Nicaraguan rebels. The *Post* identifies the leaders of the three groups as retired Army major general John K. Singlaub, Secord, and Ronald J. Martin, the head of a Miami-based company, R. M. Equipment Co.

February 27. *Regan Resigns.* White House chief of staff Regan offers a terse resignation letter to the president on the day after the Tower Commission report blamed him for the "chaos" in the White House after the Iran initiative became public. The president accepts Regan's resignation with regrets and announces that former Senate majority leader Howard H. Baker, Jr., would be the new chief of staff in the White House.

March 2. *Gates Nomination Withdrawn.* Responding to a written request by CIA deputy director Gates, President Reagan withdraws his nomination of Gates to succeed Casey as the director of the CIA. Gates states in a letter to the president that the Senate's intention to delay his confirmation until after the Senate Iran-contra committee has completed its investigation would "be harmful to the Central Intelligence Agency, the intelligence community and potentially to our national security." Just hours before he asked that his nomination be withdrawn, Gates had sent a four-page letter to the Senate Intelligence Committee denying seven of what he called "the most egregious allegations against me" concerning his role in the Iran-contra affair.

March 2. *Hostage Rescue Plan.* The *New York Times* reports that there had been an elaborate plan to rescue hostage Peter Kilburn, who was killed possibly in retaliation for the U.S. attack on Libya April 14, 1986.

March 2. *North Court Challenge.* Independent counsel Walsh requests that the U.S. District Court in Washington, D.C., dismiss a lawsuit filed by former NSC aide North, challenging the constitutionality of Walsh's appointment as independent counsel. In a forty-five-page legal memorandum, Walsh says that North's efforts are clearly "a considered attempt to disrupt the ongoing criminal investigation."

March 3. *Webster Nomination.* President Reagan nominates FBI director William H. Webster to succeed Casey as the director of the CIA.

March 4. *Reagan Response to Tower Report.* In a brief nationally televised speech, President Reagan responds to the findings of the Tower Commission and pledges to implement those recommendations made in the report. Reagan admits that "mistakes" were made and that "what began as a strategic opening to Iran deteriorated in its implementation into trading arms for hostages."

March 5. *Khashoggi Disputes Tower Report.* The *New York Times* reports that arms dealer Adnan Khashoggi denied that, after putting up $10 million for the February 1986 arms sale to Iran, he was reimbursed twice for his efforts. The Tower Commission report indicates that Khashoggi was paid $12 million by Manucher Ghorbanifar and $12 million by Lake Resources, the account controlled by North, Secord, and Hakim. Khashoggi told the *Times* that he never received a payment from Lake Resources.

March 5. *Calero Receives Saudi Funds.* In a meeting with reporters in Washington, D.C., contra leader Adolfo Calero says that during the congressional ban on aid to the contras, the Nicaraguan Democratic Force (FDN), the rebels' main military faction, received about $32 million from non-American sources from July 1984 to March 1985, $18 million of which was used to buy weapons. Sources say most of the money came from Saudi Arabia.

March 5. *Walsh Given 'Parallel' Appointment.* Attorney General Edwin Meese III appoints Walsh to head a new independent counsel office within the Justice Department in an effort to circumvent North's lawsuit challenging the constitutionality of the independent counsel statute. The "parallel" appointment, according to Meese, is "to remove any doubts concerning the legitimacy of his activities that might arise now or in the future." Meese also files a request that North's suit be dismissed on procedural grounds, but he does not address the constitutional issue.

March 5. *Contra Aid.* President Reagan certifies to Congress that the remaining $40 million from the $100 million in contra aid approved by Congress in 1986 should be released. The money could be released by Reagan only after he certified that no peace pact had been reached in Central America and that Nicaragua's government had not made a serious effort to negotiate with its opponents.

March 5. *Weinberger Disputes Tower Report.* Secretary of Defense Weinberger tells reporters at a Boston news conference that the Tower panel's criticisms of him were "naked conclusions" unsupported by the evidence. On a March 6 appearance on NBC's "Today" show, he says that he and Shultz had repeatedly voiced their opposition to the sale of arms to Iran.

March 6. *North Court Challenge.* North's lawyers file a challenge to Walsh's March 5 "parallel" appointment to a position within the Justice Department.

March 6. *Contra Funds from Swiss Account.* Calero says that the contras received $200,000 from the Swiss bank account of Lake Resources Inc., which was controlled by North, Secord, and Hakim. According to the March 7, 1987, *Washington Post,* this is the first confirmation that the contras received money from a Swiss account that may also have contained money diverted from the Iran arms sales.

March 6. *Reagan's Conflicting Testimony.* The *Washington Post* reports that the White House requested that the Tower Commission not report Reagan's conflicting testimony as to when he first approved the August 1985 Israeli arms shipments to Iran.

March 7. *Private Contra Funds.* The *Washington Post* reports that more than $1.7 million was funneled in 1985 and 1986 by Carl R. "Spitz" Channell from his tax-exempt National Endowment for the Preservation of Liberty (NEPL) to a Swiss bank account used by North for aiding the contras and financing arms sales to Iran. The *Post*'s story is based on an eighty-seven-page report, written by Miller's public relations firm International Business Communications (IBC), in which IBC attempts to reconstruct what happened to the $4.93 million it received from NEPL from May 1985 to December 1986.

March 10-11. *Walsh Asks for Immunity Delay.* Independent counsel Walsh asks the House and Senate Iran-contra committees to delay granting immunity to North and Poindexter for at least ninety days. Both committees March 11 vote limited or "use" immunity for Hakim.

March 10. *Reagan Expresses Confidence in Aides.* White House spokesman Fitzwater says that President Reagan, though he failed to defend Secretaries Weinberger and Shultz from criticisms in the Tower Commission report during his March 4 televised address, expresses his full support for the two. Fitzwater says that Reagan in his March 14 weekly radio address will confirm that both secretaries staunchly opposed U.S. arms sales to Iran.

March 11. *House Vote on Contra Aid.* The House votes 230-196 to freeze $40 million in contra aid, the second installment of $100 million in aid approved by Congress in October 1986.

March 12. *Walsh Seeks to Interview Israelis.* The *Washington Post* reports that, despite earlier Israeli government refusals, independent counsel Walsh is seeking permission to interview Israeli citizens who may have played a part in the Iran-contra affair. The Israeli government has offered to respond to written questions by U.S. investigators. The offer was accepted by leaders of the congressional investigative committees, but Walsh maintains that he was "not a party to that agreement," according to the *Post.*

March 12. *North Court Challenge Dismissed.* U.S. District Court Judge Barrington D. Parker dismisses on procedural grounds North's lawsuit challenging the constitutionality of the independent counsel law.

March 14. *Reagan Defends Cabinet Members.* In his weekly radio broadcast, President Reagan defends Secretary of Defense Weinberger and Secretary of State Shultz. In reference to the Iran arms sale, Reagan said that Weinberger and Shultz "were right and I was wrong."

March 15. *Bush Defends Aide.* Vice President George Bush defends his national security adviser Donald P. Gregg in a taped interview with CBS's "60 Minutes." Gregg had told reporters, shortly after the October 5, 1986, downing of a cargo plane over Nicaragua, that he had never discussed the contras with Rodriguez, but a chronology issued by Bush's office December 15 indicated Gregg met with Rodriguez in August 1986 to discuss problems with the contra supply effort. In response to a reporter's questions, Bush insists that Gregg forgot about the meeting.

March 17. *Poindexter Cites Fifth.* Former national security adviser Poindexter is called before the House Government Operations Subcommittee on National Security to answer questions on the administration's computer security policy. Poindexter cites his Fifth Amendment right to refuse to testify on the grounds he may incriminate himself.

March 18. *Joint Hearings and Immunity Decisions.* The House and Senate Iran-contra committees agree to hold joint hearings beginning May 5, 1987. The committees also approve an agreement worked out with Walsh on the timing of testimony by North and Poindexter. Limited immunity was voted for six witnesses: retired lieutenant colonel Richard B. Gadd, John C. Cupp, and Cynthia F. Dondlinger, all three of whom were employees of a Secord-controlled firm called American National Mangement Corp.; Col. Robert L. Earl, an ex-NSC aid to North; Robert W. Owen, North's liaison with the contras; and Tomas Castillo, the pseudonym for the former CIA station chief in Costa Rica.

March 19. *Reagan Press Conference.* For the first time in four months, President Reagan holds a press conference, during which he defends his Iran policy and denies ever being told about the diversion to the contras.

March 19. *Saudi Contra Aid.* The *Washington Post* reports that McFarlane, in a two-page letter written to his attorney Leonard Garment just before McFarlane's February 9 suicide attempt, disclosed information about Saudi Arabian contributions to the contras. McFarlane, in letters to the chairmen of the Senate Intelligence Committee and the House Iran-contra committee, said that he had not fully disclosed what he knew of foreign contributions to the contras.

March 25. *Effort to Block Contra Aid Fails.* After three unsuccessful attempts to end a filibuster blocking consideration of a House-passed moratorium on aid to the contras, Senate Democrats abandon their efforts to prevent release of $40 million in aid to the contras.

April 8. *Reagan Diaries.* The White House agrees to release to the House and Senate Iran-contra committees pertinent entries in President Reagan's diaries between January 1, 1984, and December 19, 1986. Under the agreement, White House counsel Arthur B. Culvahouse, Jr., will single out Iran-contra-related entries, but Reagan will have to authorize their release.

April 8-9. *Webster Testifies.* FBI director Webster, nominated to be CIA director, is questioned about his role and that of the FBI in the Iran-contra affair, during confirmation hearings before the Senate Intelligence Committee.

April 8. *Meese Testimony Released.* The Senate Intelligence Committee releases Attorney General Meese's testimony before the committee in December 1986 in closed session. According to Meese's testimony, he was asked by then-national security adviser Poindexter to delay investigations by the U.S. Customs Service and FBI into Southern Air Transport so that persons who might be interviewed could carry out plans to deliver arms to Iran in exchange for U.S. hostages.

April 15. *Walsh Grants Immunity to Two.* Cupp and Dondlinger, employees of Secord's American National Management Corp. of Vienna, Va., are granted immunity by independent counsel Walsh, according to their lawyers.

April 15. *Swiss Bank Records.* The Swiss government rejects efforts by two companies and five individuals to block the release of their bank records to U.S. investigators. The decision can be appealed to Switzerland's Federal Court.

April 16. *Judge Rejects Senate Request.* Chief U.S. District Court Judge Aubrey E. Robinson, Jr., denies a request by the Senate Iran-contra committee that he order Secord to authorize an inspection of his foreign bank records. Accounts in Switzerland and the Cayman Islands are thought to have been used to handle the diversion of funds from Iranian arms sales to the contras. Robinson said that to order Secord to sign a "consent directive" would violate Secord's Fifth Amendment rights.

April 20. *Rafsanjani's Press Conference.* Speaking before twenty foreign journalists, Iranian speaker of parliament Rafsanjani says that "We do not expect our relations [with the United States] to be severed until doomsday." Rafsanjani expresses dismay that Iran had been overcharged for arms deliveries. He tells reporters that if the United States had maintained ties, more U.S. hostages might have been released.

April 20. *Hakim's Bank Records.* Congressional investigators interview Hakim in Paris, and he turns over copies of financial records of secret bank accounts in Switzerland and elsewhere.

April 23. *Diversion Documented.* Senators Inouye and Warren B. Rudman, R-N.H., say that Hakim's Swiss bank records show that money was diverted from the Iran arms deal to the contras, according to the April 24 *Washington Post.*

April 28. *Walsh Report.* In a seventeen-page interim report to Congress, independent counsel Walsh responds to congressional criticism of his inquiry and says there is "ample basis" for continuing a broad criminal investigation. He rejects calls from congressional critics to narrow the scope of the investigation. He repeats earlier warnings that additional grants of immunity could harm his ability to prosecute Iran-contra participants.

April 28. *Reagan Defends His Role in the Affair.* During a half-hour interview with reporters on a variety of subjects, President Reagan reasserts that he knew nothing of the diversion of funds to the contras until notified by Attorney General Meese on November 24, 1986. Reagan tells reporters that he is not worried about the possibility of Poindexter implicating him when his former national security adviser testifies before congressional investigative committees.

April 29. *Channell Pleads Guilty.* In a hearing before the U.S. District Court in Washington, D.C., political fundraiser Channell pleads guilty to conspiring to defraud the government by soliciting money for military aid to the contras while claiming the money was for his tax-exempt National Endowment for the Preservation of Liberty. Channell named North and IBC's Miller as co-conspirators in the case. Miller issues a statement following the hearing "categorically" denying that he had conspired with Channell to secretly raise funds for the contras.

April 30. *Webster Testifies.* FBI director Webster is called back before the Senate Intelligence Committee to answer new questions about the FBI's role in the Iran-contra affair. Webster is questioned about two occasions on which North asked FBI officials for delays in its investigation of Mousalreza Ebrahim Zadeh, an Iranian posing as a Saudi prince who had offered to contribute to the contras.

May 1. *Fischer Hired by Channell.* The *Washington Post* reports that during 1985, Channell hired former Reagan aide David C. Fischer on a $20,000-a-month retainer to arrange meetings between President Reagan and Channell's major contributors. (Originally Fischer was to be paid $50,000 per meeting.) According to the *Post*, Fischer left the White House staff on April 7, 1985, but failed to turn in his White House pass until November 24, 1986, the day before Attorney General Meese announced the diversion of funds from Iranian arms sales to the contras.

May 1. *Senate Committee Approves Webster Nomination.* The Senate Intelligence Committee votes 15-0 in favor of confirming FBI director Webster as director of the CIA.

May 1. *Saudi Ambassador Refuses to Answer Questions.* Saudi ambassador to the United States Bandar bin Sultan writes a letter to Secretary of State Shultz stating his unwillingness to answer any written questions on the Iran-contra affair submitted to him by independent counsel Walsh or the congressional Iran-contra committees. The ambassador said that to do so could jeopardize longterm relationships between Saudi Arabia and the United States.

May 3. *Tambs Interview.* The *New York Times* reports that former U.S. Ambassador to Costa Rica, Lewis A. Tambs, in his first interview since resigning as ambassador in January 1987, insisted that he was acting on instructions from a Restricted Interagency Group (RIG), when he helped establish a contra "southern front" and urged Costa Rican officials to permit contra supply planes to use a secret airstrip in Costa Rica. Tambs identified the three key RIG officials as North of the NSC; Alan Fiers, head of the CIA's Central American Task Force; and Elliot Abrams, assistant secretary of state for inter-American affairs.

May 3. *Reagan Urges Support for Contra Aid.* Speaking before a gathering on Ellis Island of the American Newspaper Publishers Association, Reagan renews his appeal for contra aid. The president's speech stresses the restoration of democracy in Nicaragua rather than military conflict, in what was described by White House officials as a deliberate change in tone aimed at winning congressional support for contra aid, according to the May 4 *Washington Post.*

May 5. *Secord Testifies.* The Senate Select Committee on Secret Military Assistance to Iran and the Nicaraguan Opposition and the House Select Committee to Investigate Covert Arms Transactions with Iran begin joint public hearings.

After nearly two hours of opening remarks by the members of the committees, retired Air Force major general Richard V. Secord voluntarily testifies before the panel without legal immunity. Secord reveals that about $3.5 million of the $14 million in profits from the 1986 sale of U.S. arms to Iran was used to support the private network that supplied weapons and other gear to the Nicaraguan contras. A total of $8 million from the arms profits remains in Swiss bank accounts controlled by his business partner, Hakim. Secord says that he received logistical assistance from CIA director Casey, who in the last of three meetings with Secord said that he thought Shultz could solicit the $10 million Secord needed for his contra aid operation from a country that later was identified as Brunei.

Secord says that he received advice, cooperation, and contacts from then-U.S. ambassador to Costa Rica Louis Tambs, as well as the U.S. ambassador in El Salvador, CIA field officers in Costa Rica and Honduras, and Col. James Steele, the chief of the U.S. military forces in El Salvador. Secord also testifies that U.S. Drug Enforcement Administration (DEA) operatives received an undisclosed amount of money from Swiss bank accounts to finance their efforts to track down and rescue hostages held in Lebanon.

May 5. *Frozen Iranian Assets.* The Iran-United States Claims Tribunal orders the United States to release $451.4 million in frozen Iranian assets.

May 6. *Casey Dies.* Former CIA director Casey dies of pneumonia and cancer at the age of seventy-four.

May 6. *Miller Pleads Guilty.* International Business Communications (IBC) president Miller pleads guilty to conspiring to defraud the U.S. government. Miller was part of an illegal fund-raising scheme to buy military equipment for the Nicaraguan contras under the cover of a tax-exempt organization.

May 6. *Contra Factions Agree to Merge.* The U.S.-backed United Nicaraguan Opposition and the Costa Rican-based Southern Opposition Bloc agree to merge under the name of the Nicaraguan Resistance. Under the agreement, a new fifty-four-member assembly will be formed. A six-member directorate subsequently is elected.

May 6. *Secord Testifies.* In his second day of testimony before the House and Senate Iran-contra committees, Secord tells investigators he assumed the president knew of his activities. He says that former NSC aide North had remarked that he had mentioned to the president that "it was very ironic that some of the Ayatollah's money was being used to support the contras." Secord says North may have been joking, but he had not taken it as a joke. He also points out that three close Reagan aides were aware of most of what the Secord network did: Casey, McFarlane, and Poindexter. During his testimony, Secord states that he had shredded some documents on the contra operation.

May 7. *Secord Testifies.* In Secord's third day of testimony before the House and Senate Iran-contra committees, Senate committee counsel Arthur L. Liman grills Secord on money issues—ownership and the profit motive. Secord insists that he had no direct financial interest in the $8 million that remains unspent in Swiss bank accounts. At the urging of Senate committee vice chairman Rudman, Secord agrees to help recover the $8 million from Swiss accounts. Liman questions Secord on various proposals to sell or lease to the CIA planes, ships, communication equipment, and buildings used by the contra aid network. Secord denies that he ever had planned to profit from the venture and says he would have given the equipment to the CIA.

May 8. *Secord Testifies.* In his fourth day of testimony before the House and Senate Iran-contra committees, Secord states that since the opening of a Justice Department investigation in November 1986, he has met with North on at least four occasions. Secord also tells the panels that he would recommend to Hakim that unspent profits held in Swiss bank accounts be donated to the William J. Casey Fund for the Nicaraguan Freedom Fighters. Senate committee vice chairman Rudman replies, "I must tell you that in my view you or no one else has a right to send that money anywhere. That money belongs to the people of the United States. . . ."

May 8. *Calero Aids Hostage Rescue Attempt.* Contra leader Calero says that, during the summer of 1985, he turned over $50,000 in traveler's checks to NSC aide North for the purpose of aiding a Drug Enforcement Administration operation to gain the release of U.S. hostages in Lebanon. The money, according to Calero, was taken from Nicaraguan Democratic Force funds and turned over to North voluntarily for what Calero thought to be a "humanitarian and worthy effort."

May 11. *McFarlane Testifies.* In his first day of testimony before the House and Senate Iran-contra committees, former national security adviser Robert C. McFarlane tells of early efforts by the Reagan administration to gain the release of U.S. hostages in Lebanon. McFarlane said that in 1985 the president personally approved and the attorney general authorized a plan to pay $2 million to kidnappers for the release of two hostages held in Lebanon. The first $500,000 was to be used as "bribes" and the remaining $1.5 million was to be made available to the kidnappers following the release of the hostages. McFarlane tells the committees of Reagan's knowledge of efforts to solicit contra aid from third countries. He also says that Reagan contacted the head of a Central American country to ask that a contra arms shipment seized by a local military official be released. McFarlane testifies that shortly after Attorney General Meese began a probe into the diversion of funds from Iranian arms sales to the contras on November 21, 1986, North told McFarlane that he planned a "shredding party" to destroy secret NSC documents.

May 12. *McFarlane Testifies.* In his second day of testimony before the House and Senate Iran-contra committees, McFarlane admits that during his December 1986 testimony before congressional investigative panels, he withheld information relating to Saudi Arabia's contra aid donations and his role in soliciting the funds. McFarlane is also questioned about his part in the November 1986 preparation of a White House chronology that obscured Reagan's role in the original arms shipments to Iran.

May 12. *Misplaced Brunei Contribution.* Senator Inouye announces that a $10 million contribution made by the sultan of Brunei was deposited in the wrong Swiss bank account because North gave an incorrect account number to Assistant Secretary of State Abrams, who then relayed the number to the sultan. As a result the $10 million ended up in the account of a wealthy Swiss import-export executive, where it earned $253,000 in interest. The money eventually was returned to the sultan.

May 13. *McFarlane Testifies.* In his third day of testimony before the House and Senate Iran-contra committees, McFarlane says that he discovered in the fall of 1985 that North was in close contact with CIA director Casey and may have been taking instructions directly from him concerning contra support strategy. On the question of whether the Boland amendment's ban on providing aid to the contras applied to NSC officials, McFarlane states: "It was clear to me Mr. Boland didn't want anybody in the U.S. government assisting the contras."

May 14. *Saudi Contra Aid.* The *Washington Post* reports that, according to a diplomatic source, McFarlane on two occasions solicited funds from Saudi Arabia to aid the contras. The source made his claim after President Reagan acknowledged discussing contra aid with Saudi king Fahd ibn Abdul Aziz during his February 11, 1985, visit to the United States, but denied that there had been a solicitation.

May 14. *McFarlane Testifies.* In his fourth day of testimony before the House and Senate Iran-contra committees, McFarlane insists that President Reagan personally approved the authorization of $2 million to be used by Drug Enforcement Administration agents in Lebanon to seek the release of U.S. hostages held there. McFarlane's testimony conflicts with assertions by Reagan that he knew nothing about the operation. McFarlane again denies that he solicited contra aid from Saudi Arabia.

May 14. *Sigur Testifies.* Assistant Secretary of State Gaston J. Sigur, Jr., tells the House and Senate Iran-contra committees about his role in twice soliciting contributions for the contras from Taiwan in 1985. Each request led to a $1 million contribution.

May 14. *Owen Testifies.* In his first day of testimony before the House and Senate Iran-contra committees, Owen says that beginning in November 1984 he worked as a courier, shuttling money, maps, and intelligence information from North to the contras in Central America.

May 14. *White House Aide Resigns.* Johnathan Miller, the manager of White House administrative affairs, resigns just one hour after Owen tells the House and Senate Iran-contra committees that Miller, who was assigned temporarily to the NSC staff in March 1985, helped convert into cash $6,000 to $7,000 in traveler's checks, which had come from contra leader Calero. The cash was then delivered to contra leader Arturo Cruz.

May 14. *Bush Chronology Revision.* The office of Vice President Bush revises a chronology issued December 15, 1986, on contacts between members of his staff and Rodriguez, to include a June 25, 1986, meeting between Bush's deputy national security adviser Col. Samuel J. Watson III and Rodriguez in the Old Executive Office Building. According to Watson's records, the two discussed counterinsurgency methods in El Salvador.

May 14. *Reagan Interview.* In an interview with reporters from several weekly news magazines, the president states that in November 1986 when he called former NSC aide North a national hero, he was referring to North's military service record from action in Vietnam. When questioned about whether the Boland amendment's ban on intelligence agencies providing support to the contras applied to the NSC, Reagan is quoted in the May 23, 1987, *National Journal* as saying that the "NSC is not an intelligence operation, it's simply advisory to me." While maintaining that he did not personally solicit aid for the contras, the president says there was nothing in the law that would have prevented him from doing it.

May 15. *Reagan Meets with Reporters.* During a twenty-two-minute meeting with reporters from southeast television stations and newspapers, President Reagan says that he was "having some trouble remembering" details of a June 1985 plan to rescue hostages in Lebanon using $2 million in ransom money put up by Texas billionaire H. Ross Perot. McFarlane told the House and Senate Iran-contra committees that the president had approved it. While reasserting that he had not solicited contra donations from third countries, Reagan said that the Boland amendment did not specifically restrict him or his national security adviser from doing so.

May 17. *Iraq Strikes U.S. Ship.* The USS *Stark* is fired upon by an Iraqi missile, seriously damaging the vessel, killing thirty-seven crew members, and wounding twenty-one others. The ship is struck eighty-five miles from its final destination of Bahrain in the Persian Gulf. The Iraqi government calls the attack a tragic error.

May 17. *Baker Says Not Ransom.* White House chief of staff Howard H. Baker, Jr., appearing on NBC's "Meet the Press," says that President Reagan "did not pay ransom" in approving a 1985 plan to have Drug Enforcement Administration (DEA) agents pay for the release of hostages in Lebanon. Baker insists that the money was intended to "bribe" guards and informants as DEA agents made their way through a series of checkpoints.

May 19. *Owen Testifies.* In his second day of testimony before the House and Senate Iran-contra committees, Owen, who describes himself as North's "eyes and ears" in Central America, testifies about aid North and CIA officials gave the contras, at a time when the Boland amendment's ban on military aid was in effect. Owen also gives details of his cash-running assignments and tells of his concerns that funds were being misused by the contras. Owen ends his testimony with a poem written by American privateer John Hull, praising North and the contra effort. Its closing lines are: "In our lifetime, you have given us a legend. For the future, you are giving our children a chance to live as free individuals and for these things, we say thank you, Ollie North."

May 19. *Webster Confirmed.* FBI director Webster is approved by the Senate 94-1 to be director of the CIA.

May 20. *Calero Testifies.* In testimony before the House and Senate Iran-contra committees, contra leader Adolfo Calero testifies that North supplied the contras with military advice. He provides a financial rundown of contra operations, detailing weapons purchases and the use of more than $3 million in traveler's checks for a variety of expenses. He says that he gave North $90,000 in traveler's checks between March and July 1985 to assist in a hostage-rescue operation. Investigators determine that $25,300 of the total amount was used by DEA agents in their attempt to locate and rescue hostages in Lebanon. Approximately $2,440 of the funds, according to investigators, was used by North at grocery stores, gas stations, and other consumer outlets. North testified that he sometimes used his own money for contra-related expenses and later reimbursed himself with traveler's checks.

May 20. *Singlaub Testifies.* In testimony before the House and Senate Iran-contra committees, retired Army major general Singlaub describes his role in trying to raise money for the contras and arranging for weapons sales to the rebels. Singlaub says the contras in 1985 provided him with a list of needed weapons, which he then took to North for approval. Singlaub describes trips to Taiwan and South Korea in 1986 to seek contra aid.

May 20. *Walsh Subpoenas Israeli.* In an effort to gain testimony before the grand jury investigating the Iran-contra affair, the office of independent counsel Walsh issues a subpoena to the former director general of the Israeli Foreign Ministry, David Kimche, who is on a business trip to New York. The Israeli Embassy says that the subpoena breaches an agreement between Israel and the United States that no Israeli citizen involved in the Iran-contra affair would be compelled to testify personally.

May 21. *Wealthy Contributors Testify.* Three

wealthy Americans—New York investor William B. O'Boyle, Texas heiress Ellen Garwood, and Colorado beer company executive Joseph Coors—tell how North persuaded them to donate large sums of money to private groups. The money was ostensibly for the contras, but committee members told the three much of their money probably ended up paying for overhead in Channell's organizations.

May 22. *North Court Challenge.* North revives his court challenge to the independent counsel law, when he asks the U.S. Court of Appeals to declare the law unconstitutional. North's attorneys file a seventy-seven-page brief. A lower court had dismissed North's lawsuit March 12.

May 27. *Dutton Testifies.* In testimony before the House and Senate Iran-contra committees, retired Air Force colonel Robert C. Dutton, who supervised day-to-day logistics for the contra supply network, provides details about the supply effort. He says there was no way the operation could have succeeded without the help of Castillo. A photo album Dutton compiled for North to use as a visual aid in explaining the contra supply effort is displayed at the hearing.

May 27. *Rodriguez Testifies.* In his first day of testimony before the House and Senate Iran-contra committees, Felix I. Rodriguez explains how he became disillusioned with the contra supply network because of its faulty equipment and the ties that several participants had to Edwin Wilson, an ex-CIA agent imprisoned for selling explosives to Libya. He testifies that he voiced his concerns to both North and Bush aide Gregg. He says he did not discuss his contra work with Bush.

May 28. *Rodriguez Testifies.* In his second day of testimony before the House and Senate Iran-contra committees, Rodriguez answers further question on his discussion of the contra aid network with Gregg.

May 28. *Tambs Testifies.* In testimony before the House and Senate Iran-contra committees, former U.S. ambassador to Costa Rica Lewis A. Tambs says that in mid-1985 North asked him to assist in opening a "southern front" for the contras, an order he understood came from a Restricted Interagency Group consisting of North, Abrams, and a CIA representative. He also testifies that North told him to get permission to build a secret airstrip in Costa Rica to be used by the contra supply planes. He says he discussed the airstrip with Abrams. Tambs entrusted the contra mission to the CIA station chief in Costa Rica, according to Tambs's testimony.

May 29. *Castillo Testifies.* In closed session testimony before the House and Senate Iran-contra committees, the former CIA station chief in Costa Rica, who uses the pseudonym Tomas Castillo, recounts his role in the contra supply operation and implicates some of his superiors at the CIA in potentially unlawful activities to assist the contras. In Castillo's declassified testimony, made available to the public on June 1, he says that he kept his superiors informed of his activities and that, while they expressed concern about his connection with the supply network, they never gave him a direct order to stop.

June 2. *Abrams Testifies.* In his first day of testimony before the House and Senate Iran-contra committees, Assistant Secretary of State Elliott Abrams is questioned about his knowledge of the opening of a southern front in Nicaragua and the construction of an airstrip in Costa Rica. He admits to misleading Congress about aid to the contras, but he claims that often that was because

others in the administration did not tell him about their contra activities. Abrams also details his role in soliciting $10 million in contra aid from the country of Brunei.

June 3. *Abrams Testifies.* In his second day of testimony before the House and Senate Iran-contra committees, Abrams comes under intense questioning and criticism about his previous misleading statements on Capitol Hill. Secretary of State Shultz reaffirms his support for Abrams and says he has done a "sensational job."

June 3. *Hakim Testifies.* In his first day of testimony before the House and Senate Iran-contra committees, Albert Hakim tells of his efforts to provide financially for North and his family, including a secret $200,000 bank account and a plan to pay North's wife, Betsy, for a fictitious job. Hakim states repeatedly that he had been interested in making money on his Iran-contra dealings.

June 3. *Walsh Urges Delay in North Immunity.* Independent counsel Walsh meets with members of the House and Senate Iran-contra committees to urge that they either deny or delay granting immunity to North.

June 4. *Limited Immunity for North.* Despite efforts by Walsh to persuade members of the House and Senate Iran-contra committees to refuse or delay granting North limited immunity, the committees vote to start the process of granting immunity to North to force him to testify.

June 4. *Hakim Testifies.* In his second day of testimony before the House and Senate Iran-contra committees, Hakim describes his role in discussions with the second Iranian channel, including his negotiation of a controversial nine-point plan that included a promise to help win the release of seventeen terrorists jailed in Kuwait (the Da'Wa prisoners). Hakim is again questioned about his attempts to provide financial security for North and his family. Hakim also says that during October 1986 talks with Iranians in Frankfurt, he had the understanding that North wanted to gain the release of hostages to improve the political chances for the Republicans in the November congressional elections.

June 4. *Lewis Testifies.* In testimony before the House and Senate Iran-contra committees, Washington attorney David M. Lewis testifies briefly to recount what Hakim's Geneva-based lawyer, Willard Zucker, had told him about Hakim's plan to give money to Betsy North.

June 5. *Hakim Testifies.* In his third day of testimony before the House and Senate Iran-contra committees, Hakim testifies that Secord told the Iranians that the United States would "fight Russians in Iran" if the Soviet Union invaded Iran. Secord also suggested that the United States would work with Iran to depose Iraqi president Saddam Hussein. Hakim again is questioned about profits made by "the enterprise"—the companies and bank accounts involved in the Iran-contra affair.

June 6. *Walsh Subpoenas Three Israelis.* The *Washington Post* reports that independent counsel Walsh, claiming that he was not party to an agreement between Israel and congressional committees investigating the Iran-contra affair, issues subpoenas for three Israelis: Israeli arms dealers Adolf "Al" Schwimmer and Yaacov Nimrodi, and Amiram Nir, an antiterrorism adviser to Israeli prime ministers Peres and later Shamir.

June 8. *Sciaroni Testifies.* In testimony before the House and Senate Iran-contra committees, Bretton G. Sciaroni, counsel to the President's Intelligence Oversight Board, tells of his September 12, 1985, legal opinion that the Boland amendment did not apply to the National Security Council and that North's activities did not violate the law. But he admits that his investigation was cursory and that he had no experience in examining such complex issues.

June 8. *North Court Challenge.* A three-judge panel of the U.S. Court of Appeals for the District of Columbia declines to rule on North's claim that the independent counsel law is unconstitutional. The case is sent back to U.S. District Court Judge Aubrey Robinson with instructions to take testimony, if necessary, to determine whether Walsh has the legal authority to continue his inquiry.

June 8. *Hall Testifies.* In her first day of testimony before the House and Senate Iran-contra committees, Fawn Hall, former secretary to NSC aide North, says that, in an effort to protect North, she aided him in shredding a stack of NSC documents, altered other documents at his request, and smuggled some out of the White House.

June 9. *Hall Testifies.* In her second day of testimony before the House and Senate Iran-contra committees, Hall again is questioned about her role in shredding and altering documents and in smuggling others out of the White House. When asked if she realized that altering documents was wrong, Hall responds that "sometimes you have to go above the written law." She later retracts her statement.

June 9. *First Phase of Hearings Ends.* The House and Senate Iran-contra committees conclude six weeks of hearings into the Iran-contra affair. During this first phase of public hearings, which lasted from May 5 to June 9, committee members heard more than 100 hours of testimony from eighteen witnesses.

June 12. *Letter Demands Abrams Resignation.* One-hundred-twenty-nine House Democrats send a letter to Secretary of State Shultz demanding the resignation or "immediate replacement" of Abrams. They say that because Abrams "knowingly and deliberately misled Congress" in his testimony on secret aid to the contras, he can no longer "function effectively" as assistant secretary for inter-American affairs.

June 15. *North Ordered to Testify.* U.S. District Court Judge Louis Oberdorfer signs an order granting North limited or "use" immunity from prosecution for his testimony before the House and Senate Iran-contra committees.

June 16. *Napier Deposition.* The House and Senate Iran-contra committees release a deposition from Shirley A. Napier, one of Secord's secretaries. In her April 10 deposition, she said that she and others destroyed documents on the contra supply operation in early December 1986. Secord, however, testified that no documents were shredded after November 25. On May 11, a few days after Secord testified, Napier filed an affidavit stating that the shredding took place in November.

June 17. *North Refuses to Testify in Private.* In an unexpected move, North's attorney, Brendan V. Sullivan, Jr., informs lawyers for the Iran-contra committees that his client would not give a private deposition before his public testimony in July. The committees decide—at least for now—not to pursue time-consuming contempt of court charges against North. A new agreement between Sullivan and the committees is reached June 23.

June 17. *Journalist Kidnapped.* Charles Glass, an American TV journalist and writer, is kidnapped in Lebanon.

June 18. *Gadd Deposition.* The House and Senate Iran-contra committees release a deposition from retired Air Force colonel Richard B. Gadd in which he describes his role in helping organize the contra supply operation.

June 23. *Robinette Testifies.* In testimony before the House and Senate Iran-contra committees, former CIA technical services specialist Glenn A. Robinette says that North requested phony invoices for the installation of an electric security fence around North's Great Falls, Va., home, in a scheme to cover up the fact that Secord paid for the nearly $14,000 security system. Robinette also testifies that in March 1986 Secord hired him to dig up "derogatory" information on two free-lance journalists who were preparing a lawsuit against Secord and others.

June 23. *Koch Testifies.* In testimony before the House and Senate Iran-contra committees, Noel C. Koch, a former deputy assistant secretary of defense, describes his role in the pricing of TOW missiles for sale to Iran. Koch says that in the fall of 1985 North told him that the continued detention of American hostages was "really eating" Reagan and that the president wanted the hostages "out by Christmas." Koch tells the committee he resigned as trustee of the Richard Secord Legal Defense Fund upon discovering suspicious deposits totaling $500,000 from a Swiss bank account used by Hakim.

June 23. *Gaffney Testifies.* In testimony before the House and Senate Iran-contra committees, Henry H. Gaffney, Jr., director of plans for the Defense Security Assistance Agency, states that Israel's transfer of U.S.-made weapons to Iran in 1985 probably violated U.S. law.

June 23. *Agreement Reached on North Testimony.* The House and Senate Iran-contra committees announce that an agreement has been reached with North's attorney that will allow North to begin his public testimony July 7. North is to be questioned July 1 about Reagan's knowledge and role in the diversion of Iran arms sales money to the contras.

June 24. *Sporkin Testifies.* In testimony before the House and Senate Iran-contra committees, former CIA general counsel Stanley Sporkin tells of the drafting of two covert action findings, one giving retroactive approval to CIA involvement in the November 1985 Hawk missile shipment to Iran and the other authorizing the Iran initiative.

June 25. *CIA Depositions.* The House and Senate Iran-contra committees release declassified depositions from three CIA officials. Two say they knew that Hawk missiles were being shipped to Iran in November 1985. But the third official, Duane "Dewey" Clarridge, then head of CIA covert operations in Europe, testifies that he was unaware at the time that the flight carried missiles.

June 25. *Cooper Testifies.* In testimony before the House and Senate Iran-contra committees, Assistant Attorney General Charles J. Cooper describes a November 20, 1986, White House meeting at which administration officials planned for CIA director Casey to give false testimony to the congressional Intelligence committees about the November 1985 Israeli arms shipment to Iran. Cooper testifies about the Justice Department's November 1986 inquiry into the Iran-contra affair.

June 30. *North Documents.* North turns over to the House and Senate Iran-contra committees seven binders of documents and personal memorandums relating to the Iran-contra affair. Sections of North's notebooks were deleted, which, according to North's lawyer, contained private or nonrelevant material. Committee officials, however, reserve the right to allow their chief counsels to inspect the original notebooks.

July 1. *North Questioned.* After agreeing the previous week to limit their questioning to President Reagan's involvement in the diversion of funds from Iranian arms sales to the contras, House and Senate Iran-contra committee investigators interrogate North in a nearly two-hour closed session meeting.

July 7. *North Testifies.* In his first day of testimony before the House and Senate Iran-contra committees, former NSC aide Lt. Col. Oliver L. North insists that all his activities had been authorized. North claims that he had sent five memorandums to Poindexter seeking the president's approval of proposed arms sales to Iran in 1986. The memos, according to North, also mentioned the diversion of profits from the arms sales to the contras. North testifies that none of the memos were ever returned to him with the president's signature, but he had assumed Reagan knew of the diversion plan until Poindexter told him November 21, 1986, that the president had not been aware of the plan. North says that he had seen in Poindexter's office a finding signed by the president authorizing CIA assistance in the November 1985 transfer of arms from Israel to Iran. The former NSC aide tells the committees that he began shredding documents as early as October 1986 after the October 5 downing of a contra supply plane in Nicaragua and after learning from CIA director Casey that businessman Roy Furmark had heard that funds may have been diverted to the contras from the sale of U.S. weapons to Iran.

July 8. *North Testifies.* In his second day of testimony before the House and Senate Iran-contra committees, North admits that he purposely misled Congress about his involvement in aiding the contras during a time when the Boland amendment's ban on U.S. government aid was in effect. Suggestions by North that Congress could not be trusted with information relating to covert activities draws a sharp response from Senate committee chairman Inouye, who insists that most leaks came from the administration rather than Congress. North tells the committees that the diversion idea was first suggested by Iranian arms dealer Manucher Ghorbanifar, a key intermediary in U.S.-Iranian negotiations. North says he thought it was a neat idea—and still does. North tells the committee that Poindexter, McFarlane, and Casey knew of the diversion. According to North, Casey enthusiastically supported the diversion scheme and called it a "full-service covert operation." North discusses his use of traveler's checks from contra leader Calero and vehemently denies profiting from any of the Iran-contra operations, but does admit that his December 1986 effort to conceal that someone else had paid for a security fence for his home was the "greatest misjudgment" of his life.

July 9. *North Testifies.* In his third day of testimony before the House and Senate Iran-contra committees, under cross-examination by Senate chief counsel Arthur L. Liman, North explains how he and CIA director Casey agreed in November 1986 that North would take the "fall" should the Iran-contra operation be uncovered but that Casey thought someone higher up would have to go because North was not senior enough. North testifies that he had had no reservations about taking the blame for the operation until the November 25, 1986, press conference in which Attorney General Meese indicated that the Iran-contra affair might become a criminal matter.

July 9. *North Shredding.* The Justice Department issues a statement disputing North's July 9 claim that he continued to shred documents November 22-23, 1986, while Justice Department investigators reviewed his files in the next room. North said that the officials were aware of his actions, but never questioned him or tried to intervene.

July 10. *North Testifies.* In his fourth day of testi-

mony before the House and Senate Iran-contra committees, North says that CIA director Casey was interested in establishing an "off-the-shelf, sustaining, stand-alone" organization outside of the CIA to run covert operations.

July 10. *North Court Challenge.* U.S. District Court Judge Robinson issues a ruling holding that independent counsel Walsh's March 5, 1987, backup appointment by the Justice Department was valid and Walsh may proceed with a secret grand jury request. The details are under seal, but Walsh is believed to be seeking a handwriting sample from North.

July 10. *December 1985 Finding.* An administration official says that President Reagan has "no recollection" of signing a secret arms-for-hostages finding in early December 1985. North testified that he saw a signed copy in Poindexter's office.

July 11. *North Defense Fund.* The *Washington Post* reports that North's defense fund has grown to approximately $130,000.

July 13. *North Testifies.* In his fifth day of testimony before the House and Senate Iran-contra committees, North is questioned by committee members who use much of their time to either praise or admonish North for his actions.

July 14. *North Testifies.* In his sixth and final day of testimony before the House and Senate Iran-contra committees, North again is questioned by committee members. In response to one question, North reveals that, during a conversation in the bathroom of a London hotel, Ghorbanifar offered him a $1 million bribe to ensure that the February 1986 arms shipment to Iran was carried out. The offer was made at the same meeting in which Ghorbanifar allegedly suggested diverting proceeds from the arms sale to the contras. In their closing statements, chairmen Inouye and Hamilton express concern for North's role in the conduct of foreign policy and reprimand him for lying to Congress, U.S. government officials, and the Iranians to achieve his ends.

July 14. *McFarlane Testifies.* Former national security adviser McFarlane returns briefly to testify before the House and Senate Iran-contra committees. He disputes North's repeated assertions that he received explicit authorization for all of his contra-aid activities.

July 15. *Poindexter Testifies.* In his first day of testimony before the House and Senate Iran-contra committees, former national security adviser Rear Adm. John M. Poindexter ends months of speculation with his statement that he never told the president about the diversion of funds from the Iranian arms sales to the contras. Poindexter insists that Reagan would have approved the diversion had he been briefed on the operation, but says that he decided to withhold the details of the operation in order to insulate the president and provide "some future deniability," if it was ever disclosed. Poindexter testifies that Reagan signed a secret finding in early December 1985 giving retroactive approval to CIA participation in a November Israeli shipment of arms to Iran. Poindexter says he destroyed the finding a year later, on November 21, 1986, to protect the president from political embarrassment because the finding gave the impression it was a straight arms-for-hostages swap. He asserts that the NSC staff was exempt from the restrictions of the Boland amendment.

July 15. *White House Reaction.* The White House, in response to Poindexter's first day of testimony before the House and Senate Iran-contra committees, says that the former national security adviser "vindicated" the president by maintaining that he had not told Reagan that profits from the sale of arms to Iran had been used to support the contras.

July 16. *Poindexter Testifies.* In his second day of testimony before the House and Senate Iran-contra committees, Poindexter tells investigators that he destroyed documents in late November 1986 relating to the Iran-contra affair and that he made no effort to prevent North from destroying a notebook that contained information about the November 1985 Hawk shipment to Iran. When asked about events surrounding his November 25, 1986, resignation, Poindexter says that in his final meeting with President Reagan, Meese, and White House chief of staff Regan, he was not asked what he knew about the diversion of funds to the contras.

July 16. *White House Disputes Poindexter Statement.* White House spokesman Fitzwater disputes Poindexter's July 15 assertion before the House and Senate Iran-contra committees that Reagan would have approved a plan to divert proceeds from the sale of arms to Iran to assist the contras. Fitzwater says that contrary to Poindexter's belief, the diversion "wouldn't have happened," and that any official who fails to seek presidential approval for sensitive policy decisions does the president a "disservice."

July 16. *North Court Challenge.* Attorneys for North appeal a ruling by U.S. District Court Judge Robinson that North must comply with a grand jury subpoena issued by independent counsel Walsh.

July 17. *Poindexter Testifies.* In his third day of testimony before the House and Senate Iran-contra committees, Poindexter calls the White House assertion that Reagan would not have approved the diversion of funds to the contras an "expected" response. "I understand that he [Fitzwater] said that, and I would have expected him to say that. That's the whole idea of deniability." He still insists the president would have approved the diversion plan. Poindexter tells the committees he withheld information on NSC contra activities from Congress to avoid publicity and more restrictive legislation.

July 20. *Poindexter Testifies.* In his fourth day of testimony before the House and Senate Iran-contra committees, Poindexter is questioned by committee members. He reiterates his belief that he was carrying out policies that served the long-term interests of the United States and he says that he is not going to be apologetic about it.

July 20. *White House Dismisses Talk of Pardons.* White House spokesman Fitzwater says that a preemptive presidential pardon for Poindexter or North is not being considered.

July 21. *Funds Returned to Brunei.* The Malaysian national news agency reports that the sultan of Brunei's $10 million contribution to the contras has been returned. The funds had never reached the contras because North had given the wrong Swiss bank account number to Assistant Secretary of State Abrams, who then passed the information on to the sultan. A Brunei spokesman said the contribution was intended to aid Central America's poor and not to supply arms to the contras.

July 21. *Panel Disputes Contra-Drug Connection.* The House Select Committee on Narcotics Abuse and Control reports that it has found no evidence to substantiate charges that the contras were involved in drug smuggling. Rep. James A. Traficant, Jr., D-Ohio, taking issue with the finding, claims that planes that had taken supplies to the contras had come back with drugs. He says he does not know how this could have occurred without someone in the United States knowing about it. The investigation is to be continued by another panel.

July 21. *Poindexter Testifies.* In his fifth and last day of testimony before the House and Senate Iran-contra committees, Poindexter is criticized for his secrecy and exclusion of the president in crucial decision making. House chairman Hamilton lectures Poindexter: "[Y]ou locked the president himself out of the process," while serving him as national security adviser. But Hamilton goes on to say that Reagan "created the environment" in which Poindexter and North operated. Reagan loyalist Rep. Bill McCollum, R-Fla., criticizes Poindexter for the secrecy of NSC decision making on the contra issue that "got us where we are today." After Hamilton's closing remarks, Poindexter says that he disagrees with the chairman's interpretation of many events and that he is leaving "with my head held high."

July 21. *Reflagging of Kuwaiti Tankers.* The U.S. flag is raised on the first two Kuwaiti tankers to receive American protection while transitting the Persian Gulf.

July 23. *Shultz Testifies.* In his first day of testimony before the House and Senate Iran-contra committees, Secretary of State George P. Shultz describes an environment in which he was kept in the dark about the Iran-contra operations. He says that he had to fight a "battle royal" to get all the facts out once the Iran arms scandal erupted in November 1986. He tells of his discussion with Reagan after the November 1986 news conference in which he pointed out to the president those statements he thought were "wrong or misleading." Shultz also claims that White House aide Johnathan S. Miller was "trying to lock me out of trips" abroad by blocking his travel requests.

Sen. Sam Nunn, D-Ga., remarks that Shultz's testimony revealing such infighting contains "elements of an internal coup." Shultz's denunciation of deception and lying, and his stated efforts to keep the president informed impresses many on the investigating committees. Senator Rudman praises the secretary of state as a "real" hero.

July 24. *Shultz Testifies.* In his second day of testimony before the House and Senate Iran-contra committees, Shultz claims that the president was a hero for instructing that nothing be covered up and says that he does not believe the president wished to deceive him about the Iran arms sales. While acknowledging that Abrams had made a mistake when he misled Congress about solicitations of aid from Brunei for the contras and stating that no one needed his permission to tell the truth, Shultz defends him as a "first class" person with a "real instinct for public service." Some Republicans criticize Shultz for not being aggressive enough in his opposition to the Iran policy. When Rep. Henry J. Hyde, R-Ill., suggests that Shultz could have threatened to resign in protest, Shultz responds: "That's not the way to play the game at all."

July 24. *State Department Contracts Investigated.* The State Department's inspector general reports that he has found no evidence that International Business Communications (IBC) illegally used State Department funds to lobby Congress to support the administration's Central America policy. His report states that the State Department's Office of Public Diplomacy for Latin America and the Caribbean, however, did award more than $400,000 in contracts to the company without seeking competitive bids and that one contract was classified secret in order to hide the fact that there had been no competitive bidding.

Rep. Dante B. Fascell, D-Fla., who chairs the Foreign Affairs Committee, which has been investigating the IBC contracts, states that the evidence suggests that North secretly directed the public diplomacy office and used the office to help IBC when it was a vital link in the contra supply effort, according to the July 25 *Washington Post.* IBC president Miller pleaded guilty May 6, 1987, to conspiracy to defraud the government by using tax-deductible contributions for military aid to the contras.

July 24. *Kuwaiti Tanker Damaged.* The first U.S.-flagged Kuwaiti tanker to pass through the Persian Gulf hits an underwater mine en route to Kuwait.

July 26. *Flap over* Post *Article.* The *Washington Post* publishes a report, based on notes taken by deputy national security adviser Alton G. Keel, Jr., during a White House meeting on November 10, 1986, that alleges the president actively led the initial effort to cover up details of the arms-for-hostages deals. The next day, White House spokesman Fitzwater, referring to the *Post* article, declares that "some members of the press are so hungry to try to destroy the president that they've lost all perspective." Fitzwater defends the president's decision on the grounds that the lives of the hostages were at stake.

July 28. *Owen Immunity.* The *Washington Post* reports that independent counsel Walsh earlier in the month granted limited immunity to Owen.

July 28. *Leahy Leaked Report.* Sen. Patrick J. Leahy, D-Vt., announces that he resigned from the Senate Intelligence Committee in January 1987 after he violated committee rules by giving an NBC reporter access to a draft report on the Iran-contra affair.

July 28. *Meese Testifies.* In his first day of testimony before the House and Senate Iran-contra committees, Attorney General Edwin Meese III describes and defends his four-day inquiry in November 1986 into the Iran-contra affair.

July 28. *Contra Abuses Reported.* The Nicaraguan Association for Human Rights issues its first report, which describes abuses committed by the contra forces, including execution of prisoners, forcible recruitment of Menonites as soldiers, and abductions and executions of civilians. The organization, which is mandated by Congress to monitor contra activities as a condition of U.S. aid, reports that some contra leaders viewed the investigation as "little more than a public-relations effort," an allegation denied by contra spokesmen.

July 29. *Meese Testifies.* In his second day of testimony before the House and Senate Iran-contra committees, Meese admits that he took no new precautions, such as the securing of documents, after discovering the diversion of funds to the contras and its possible "criminal implications." Meese's testimony also reveals that, during meetings with Reagan, Bush, McFarlane, Casey, Regan, and Poindexter after the diversion discovery, no notes were taken, although notes had been taken during earlier interviews with North, McFarlane, and Shultz. Meese characterizes the unrecorded meetings as "casual conversations . . . simply to confirm information we already had" and, therefore, did not require note taking. In a lengthy debate with Rep. Edward P. Boland, D-Mass., author of the Boland amendments, Meese acknowledges that arguments can be made on both sides of the question of the amendment's applicability to the NSC staff.

July 29. *North Contempt Citation.* In response to petitions filed by the *Washington Post, Wall Street Journal,* and the interest group Public Citizen challenging the

secrecy that has surrounded the contempt charges against North, U.S. District Court Judge Robinson directs North's lawyer and independent counsel Walsh to submit edited versions of their pleadings that do not reveal matters before the grand jury and, therefore, can be made public. Each side will have an opportunity to contest the proposed disclosures of the other.

July 30. *Regan Testifies.* In testimony before the House and Senate Iran-contra committees, former White House chief of staff Donald T. Regan offers an image of himself as "aware in general" about the Iran initiative but not kept abreast of the important details. Regan testifies that both he and the president did know that the November 1985 Israeli shipment to Iran contained Hawk missiles. He also states that he advised the president that the United States was being "snookered" by "rug merchants," and that the Iran initiative ought to be halted. He says that he was not aware of the contra diversion and describes President Reagan's shock upon learning of it.

July 31. *Reagan on Law Breaking.* During a picture taking session in the White House, President Reagan says that he has not heard "a single word" during testimony before the House and Senate Iran-contra committees indicating that laws had been violated. White House spokesman Fitzwater clarifies this statement August 3 by saying that Reagan meant his statement to apply only to the limited portions of the hearings he had watched on television.

July 31. *Regan Testifies.* In his second day of testimony before the House and Senate Iran-contra committees, Regan states that when the topic was broached with him in December 1986, the president immediately rejected pardoning Poindexter or North because he did not know what crime had been committed. When questioned about the president's erroneous assertion during the November 10, 1986, White House meeting that Iran was the weaker side in the Iran-Iraq War, Regan does not recall anyone correcting the president.

July 31. *Weinberger Testifies.* In his first day of testimony before the House and Senate Iran-contra committees, Secretary of Defense Caspar W. Weinberger relates that he forcefully opposed arms sales to Iran. Weinberger states that Reagan's decision to supply Iran with arms was partially a result of claims by Poindexter that he had intelligence that Iran was losing the war with Iraq; the secretary characterizes those reports as "absolute nonsense." And he scoffs at the notion of establishing relations with Iranian moderates: "I didn't think there were any moderates still alive in Iran."

August 1. *Pentagon Role.* The *Washington Post* reports that a House Armed Services Committee report concluded that there was no evidence that the Defense Department purposely undervalued the weapons it sold to the CIA for shipment to Iran in order to create profits to aid the contras. Secretary of Defense Weinberger told the House and Senate Iran-contra committees July 31 that the undercharging resulted from "a series of unfortunate but totally innocent errors."

August 1. *Gadd Immunity.* According to the *New York Times,* Lt. Col. Richard B. Gadd has been granted full immunity from prosecution by independent counsel Walsh. Gadd helped establish the contra aid network in late 1985.

August 3. *Weinberger Testifies, Public Hearings Conclude.* In his second day of testimony before the House and Senate Iran-contra committees, Weinberger spent more time listening to members' closing statements than answering questions. Some committee members defend Weinberger against the Tower Commission's criticism that he and Shultz distanced themselves from the Iran initiative. Weinberger insists that they vigorously opposed the arms sales to Iran. He is questioned closely about the erroneous intelligence—showing that Iran was losing the war—that was used to justify sales to Iran.

During this second phase of public hearings, which lasted from June 23 to August 3, committee members heard from twelve witnesses.

August 4. *Clarridge Testifies.* Duane "Dewey" Clarridge, head of the CIA's counterterrorism section, testifies before a closed session of the House and Senate Iran-contra committees. A declassified transcript of his testimony is released August 19. Clarridge tells the committees that CIA director Casey had wanted to run the entire Iran arms-for-hostages operation rather than turn it over to the NSC, but no other senior CIA officials agreed with Casey. Clarridge denies that he knew a November 1985 shipment to Iran contained Hawk missiles, despite his active role in facilitating the shipment.

August 4. *Wright Cites Law Violations.* House Speaker Jim Wright, D-Texas, reacting to the president's July 31, 1987, statement that he had heard no testimony indicating laws had been broken, contends that laws were violated in seven instances. Declaring that the law was "flouted," Wright cites failures to notify Congress despite legal requirements and violation of the Boland amendment ban on U.S. aid to the contras. Reagan's statement had been clarified August 3 to indicate that he was talking about only those parts of the hearings he had seen on television.

August 4-5. *George Testifies.* CIA deputy director for covert operations Clair George testifies in closed session before the House and Senate Iran-contra committees. A declassified transcript of his testimony is released the week of August 24. George states that the White House and CIA director Casey ignored the advice of CIA experts, including their objections to using Iranian arms dealer Ghorbanifar and retired lieutenant general Secord in the Iran operation. George expresses his admiration of Casey, whom he claims would not have approved the autonomous spy agency idea that North attributed to him. He calls the plan for Drug Enforcement Administration agents to ransom the hostages a "fake" and a "scam" pulled on the United States by unscrupulous people in the Middle East. George apologizes for his congressional testimony on October 14, 1986, in which he denied U.S. government involvement in supplying aid to the contras.

August 5. *Bush Defends His Role.* Vice President Bush blames the House and Senate Iran-contra committees for the public perception that "I was lying" when he said he had had no knowlege of the diversion of funds to the contras. He states in an interview that the "distorted view" arose because the members of the committees were claiming that "everything was evil." According to the August 6 *Washington Post*, Bush explains his failure to warn the president against arms sales to Iran by claiming that he had been closed out of the decision-making process and denied information. He also claims that he had not heard any strong objections and thus was unaware of any conflict of opinions within the administration over the arms sales. Bush says he was at the Army-Navy football game on December 7, 1985, when the Iran initiative was discussed at a White House meeting. A spokesman later says that Bush

does not recall "a showdown session" at a January 7, 1986, meeting on the arms sales and perhaps was not there for all of it. North and Poindexter receive praise from Bush, who states that talking about presidential pardons for the two was "premature." Bush also states his view that the Boland amendment did not apply to the NSC staff.

August 5. *Fiers Testifies.* Alan Fiers, head of the CIA's Central American Task Force, testifies before a closed session of the House and Senate Iran-contra committees. A declassified transcript of his testimony is released the week of August 24. Fiers tells the committees that he knew North was working with the contras but did not know until late 1986 the full extent of his involvement. He says he was troubled by the active assistance given North by CIA station chief Castillo. He admits that he misled Congress both in his testimony on the CIA role in the contra aid network and in his silence while other officials denied U.S. involvement in the effort. Fiers repeats allegations that associates of one-time contra leader Eden Pastora were involved in running cocaine to the United States to raise revenue and states that it was a major reason for the 1984 cut-off of all funding for Pastora's army. Fiers also states that he never took what North told him at "face value" because North tended to "embellish the record."

August 5. *U.S. Peace Plan.* President Reagan unveils a peace plan for Central America, which was largely drafted by House Speaker Wright. The plan calls for a cease-fire between the leftist Sandinista government and the contras, to be accompanied by political freedoms. Simultaneously, U.S. military aid to the contras would be halted and Nicaragua would stop accepting arms aid from the Soviet Union or its allies.

August 5. *North Court Challenge.* North's attorneys appear before the U.S. Circuit Court of Appeals for the District of Columbia to argue against the July 10, 1987, ruling that found the independent counsel's backup appointment by the Department of Justice to be valid.

August 6. *Further Hearings.* House chairman Hamilton states that witnesses are being recalled by the House and Senate Iran-contra committees during closed door sessions in order to follow up on some leads.

August 7. *Israeli Testimony Controversy.* The *Washington Post* reports that out-of-court negotiations between the government of Israel and independent counsel Walsh on the testimony of Israelis involved in the Iran arms sales have broken down. U.S. District Court Judge Robinson has decided to rule on whether the Israelis will be required to answer questions that Walsh is to submit to him. Walsh has pressed for their testimony despite the decision of the House and Senate Iran-contra committees not to call Israeli witnesses and the agreement of the State Department with the Israeli view that questions should be directed to the government of Israel.

August 7. *New Covert Operation Procedures.* President Reagan and leaders of the Senate Intelligence Committee announce agreement on new covert operation standards and on procedures for telling Congress about them. Reagan agrees to notify Congress within two days after ordering covert actions in emergencies.

August 7. *Central American Peace Plan.* The presidents of Costa Rica, El Salvador, Guatemala, Honduras, and Nicaragua sign a peace pact in Guatemala City. The agreement proposes that governments confronting insurgencies offer amnesty to their opponents, and begin "democratization measures." The accord calls for a cease-fire simultaneously with agreement that no country would assist an insurgency against another. The plan differs from the U.S. initiative put forward August 5 in that it does not require Nicaragua to forswear Soviet-bloc military aid. The agreement is to take effect in ninety days.

August 8. *U.S.-Iran Trade.* The *Washington Post* reports that the United States imported more than $612 million worth of oil ($505.8 million) and luxury goods ($107 million) from Iran in 1986, while the Iranians purchased only $34 million in U.S. goods. (The figures do not include secret weapons sales to Iran.)

August 8. *Webster Announces Investigation.* CIA director Webster tells the American Bar Association convention that he will have an outside counsel investigate the role that the CIA played in the Iran-contra affair to determine whether CIA rules or statutes were violated.

August 9. *Walsh on Immunity.* Independent counsel Walsh tells reporters that the House and Senate Iran-contra committees' decision to grant "central figures" limited immunity in exchange for their testimony has been "the most serious external threat" to his investigation.

August 12. *Reagan Address.* Reagan acknowledges the mistakes in the Iran-contra affair in a nationally televised speech and states that he will not make excuses. Reagan directly criticizes Poindexter for attempting to shield him from the diversion policy, asserting that the buck "stops with me." The president admits that he was "stubborn" to pursue the selling of arms to Iran after receiving the advice of Weinberger and Shultz against the exchange of arms for hostages. Speaking of his future agenda, Reagan stresses bipartisanship and cites the administration's peace initiative in Central America as an example. Reagan says that he welcomes the Central American peace pact signed August 7, but affirms that his administration would not "abandon those who are fighting for democracy and freedom."

August 16. *Israeli Sales to Iran.* The *Washington Post* reports that Israeli officials sought the Reagan administration's approval of its arms dealings with Iran as early as 1981. The *Post* reports that signals the Israelis received from the United States were mixed: sometimes, vigorous objection; other times, implicit approval.

August 18. *Hostage Escapes.* Charles Glass escapes from his captors in Beirut amid speculation that he was allowed to escape due to Syrian efforts to secure his release. He was kidnapped June 17.

August 20. *Walsh's Authority Upheld.* The U.S. Circuit Court of Appeals in the District of Columbia upholds U.S. District Court Judge Robinson's July 10, 1987, ruling that independent counsel Walsh's backup appointment by Attorney General Meese is legal. It also rules that North must comply with a grand jury subpoena for a sample of his handwriting or face contempt of court charges.

August 20. *Swiss Bank Records.* Switzerland's Federal Court, its highest tribunal, rules that records of secret bank accounts of Iran-contra participants, including Secord, Hakim, and Ghorbanifar, may be released to the independent counsel.

August 21. *Contras Accept Peace Pact.* Leaders of the contras meet with El Salvadoran president José Napoleón Duarte for five hours. The contras reportedly accept the Central American peace plan signed in Guatamala, but say they will not lay down their arms.

August 24-25. *Reagan's Radio Message.* In a three-minute message broadcast by Radio Liberacion, a U.S.-sponsored clandestine radio station that beams into Nicaragua, President Reagan pledges continued support for the contras until the Sandinistas establish democracy.

August 27. *Reagan Speaks to Contra Leaders.* President Reagan reassures contra leaders that they will receive adequate funding until the cease-fire and democratization called for in the Central American peace pact are implemented. The contras propose a plan that would provide "humanitarian" aid after U.S. assistance expires on September 30 and would place military aid in an escrow account while negotiations progress. The White House calls the proposal "constructive" but says the administration will have to study it.

August 27. *Earl and Coy Testimony.* The House and Senate Iran-contra committees released the May 1987 testimony of Marine Lt. Col. Robert L. Earl and the March and June testimony of Craig P. Coy. Most of the testimony of the two former aides to North has been superseded by North's July appearance before the committees. However, their information was important in helping the committees prepare for his testimony.

August 31. *Justice Challenges Independent Counsel.* For the first time, the Justice Department argues, in a brief filed in a federal appeals court in another case under investigation, that the 1978 Ethics in Government Act should be overturned because it violates constitutional separation of powers. The Justice Department claims that it is committed to protecting investigations already under way by issuing "backup appointments." Walsh already has such an appointment.

September 3. *Contempt Files to Be Opened.* An appellate court grants motions by the *Washington Post, Wall Street Journal,* and the interest group Public Citizen to open records of contempt action against North. The records will be opened after twenty-eight days, during which time North's lawyers and Walsh may censor documents.

September 8. *Bush Aides' Testimony.* The House and Senate Iran-contra committees release the closed door testimony of Donald P. Gregg, the vice president's national security adviser, and Col. Samuel J. Watson III, Bush's deputy national security adviser. They reiterate that Rodriguez did not discuss the contra aid network with them until August 1986, although a briefing memo prepared for Bush lists contra aid as a topic of discussion at a May 1986 meeting. Both say they do not know why the memo included the reference to the contras and that the topic was not discussed.

September 10. *Poindexter's Closed Door Testimony.* The House and Senate Iran-contra committees release some 500 pages of documents and depositions given by Poindexter in four different closed sessions that preceded his July 1987 public testimony. Poindexter said June 17 that he never made a distinction between raising outside money for lethal aid to the contras and for procontra ad campaigns. His comments seem to suggest that the president knew the purpose of private and foreign funds earmarked for the contras. He said Reagan would talk in "generic terms about how he thought it was appropriate for private individuals to support the contras. . . . I don't recall a distinction being made between lethal and non-lethal aid." Reagan has claimed that the purpose of donations from private Americans was to pay for advertising aimed at promoting the contra cause in Congress.

In other matters, Poindexter said that CIA director Casey had talked of buying a plane for the contras "with his own private money." His testimony did not indicate what, if anything, ever came of the airplane idea. Poindexter also testified that he did not send North on an advance trip to Tehran for fear that North would be taken hostage. He believed that the Iranians would not dare take McFarlane captive during his May 1986 trip.

September 19. *Latin American Diplomacy Office.* The *Washington Post*, quoting White House and State Department documents released by the House and Senate Iran-contra committees, reports that then-national security adviser William P. Clark and his assistant Walter Raymond, Jr., succeeded in their efforts in 1983 to have the State Department's Office of Public Diplomacy for Latin America and the Caribbean report directly to the NSC and to win the appointment of Otto Reich as the office's director. In a memo to the president in May 1983, Shultz requested that he be made the "sole delegate" in carrying out Central American policy and that he be given the "dominant voice" in State Department personnel selection. Shultz received an unsigned White House memo in response that stated:"No single agency can do it alone."

September 21. *Israeli Account of Diversion Idea.* The *Wall Street Journal* reports that the House and Senate Iran-contra committees have notes from an early December 1985 meeting between North and an Israeli official that indicate North proposed diverting funds from the Iranian arms sales to the contras. North stated in his July 1987 testimony before the committees that Iranian arms merchant Ghorbanifar proposed the diversion scheme in January 1986.

September 21. *Persian Gulf Conflict.* U.S. helicopters attack an Iranian ship reportedly laying mines in international waters used by U.S. warships and tankers they escort through the Persian Gulf.

September 22. *Arias Addresses Congress.* The principal author of the Central American peace pact that was signed in Guatemala August 7, Costa Rican president Oscar Arias, addresses an unofficial meeting of the House and Senate. He urges that the United States "give peace a chance." Arias met with Reagan before going to Capitol Hill.

September 25. *Poindexter Retirement.* The Navy announces that Navy Secretary James H. Webb has approved Poindexter's request to retire, effective October 1, but will defer a decision on Poindexter's request to retire with the rank of vice admiral until the conclusion of the independent counsel's investigation.

September 26. *Woodward Book on Covert Activities.* The *Washington Post* reports that Bob Woodward, in his new book *VEIL: The Secret Wars of the CIA, 1981-1987*, said that former CIA director Casey nodded affirmatively when Woodward asked him if he had known about the diversion of Iranian arms sales profits to the contras. When asked why, Casey reportedly said, "I believed." The conversation, according to Woodward, took place in Casey's hospital room several days after he had undergone surgery for a brain tumor. Sophia Casey, his widow, claimed that Woodward, an assistant managing editor of the *Post*, never got in to Casey's hospital room and called the story "a lie," the *Post* reported September 28. The story was reaffirmed by Woodward after Sophia Casey made her comments.

September 28. *Casey's Knowledge.* Hamilton, chairman of the House Iran-contra committee, states that he believes Casey not only knew about the diversion of funds to the contras but was a "primary actor" in arranging for it, the *Washington Post* reported September 29. Inouye, his

counterpart on the Senate committee, states that he would not be surprised if Casey knew.

September 28. *Ledeen Testimony.* The House and Senate Iran-contra committees release the declassified testimony of former NSC consultant Michael Ledeen. Behind closed doors, Leeden testified that Reagan administration officials ignored his recommendation that they meet with a senior Iranian official who was interested in improving relations with the United States. He said the Iranian warned that U.S. arms sales to Iran only reinforced the Khomeini regime. Ledeen claims that he opposed the arms-for-hostages deals but was told by CIA director Casey in December 1985 that releasing the hostages must take priority over changing the Iranian government. Ledeen also said McFarlane had approved his trip to Israel to meet with Israeli prime minister Peres in May 1985, despite McFarlane's May testimony to the contrary.

October 4. *'White Propaganda.'* The General Accounting Office (GAO) issues a report claiming that the State Department's Office of Public Diplomacy for Latin America and the Caribbean violated a law banning the use of department funds "for publicity or propaganda purposes not authorized by Congress," according to the October 5 *Washington Post*. The report cites a March 13, 1985, memo in which Johnathan S. Miller, then an employee of the Public Diplomacy Office, tells White House communications director Patrick J. Buchanan about the Public Diplomacy Office's "white propaganda" operations. The memo states that "consultants" wrote articles to appear on the op-ed pages of the *New York Times* and *Washington Post* under the names of contra leaders Alfonso Robelo, Calero, and Cruz. (Miller was on loan to the National Security Council when it was revealed in May 1987 that he had helped Owen cash traveler's checks to give to the contras. He resigned immediately after being implicated.)

October 6. *Ortega Issues Warning.* Nicaraguan president Daniel Ortega warns that if the United States continues to aid the contras after the Central American peace pact takes effect on November 7, the pact will have been violated and Nicaragua will no longer be obliged to observe it. He says, however, that no matter what action Congress takes on Reagan's contra aid request, his country is committed to continuing efforts to implement the pact.

October 7. *Reagan on Peace Plan.* In a speech before the Organization of American States, Reagan describes the Central American peace pact signed August 7 as "a step in the right direction," but claims that the plan does not consider U.S. security interests since it does not address the presence of Soviet-bloc and Cuban forces in the region. He says that only the August 5 peace plan that he and House Speaker Wright sponsored would eliminate "communist colonialism on the American mainland." Reagan states that he will proceed with his request for $270 million in aid to the contras over an eighteen-month period, but says that military aid could be converted into humanitarian assistance should the Sandinistas make satisfactory progress toward democracy.

October 8. *Ortega Speech.* In a speech before the United Nations, Nicaraguan president Ortega is harshly critical of President Reagan and his policies. Ortega, however, suggests a U.S.-Nicaraguan meeting to work out an agreement guaranteeing mutual security.

October 8. *Persian Gulf Conflict.* U.S. helicopters sink one Iranian boat and disable two others, which reportedly had fired on a U.S. helicopter flying over international waters in the Persian Gulf.

Profiles

Elliott Abrams, assistant secretary of state for inter-American affairs. As the senior official on Latin American affairs since July 1985, Abrams worked closely with Lt. Col. Oliver L. North on issues involving the Nicaraguan contras. Abrams participated in the U.S. effort to elicit financial support from foreign governments for the contras; his efforts resulted in a $10 million donation from the sultan of Brunei (an oil-rich island in the Pacific).

Testifying before the House and Senate select committees investigating the Iran-contra affair in June 1987, Abrams acknowledged that he had misled Congress in the past about U.S. contra aid and U.S. solicitation of foreign leaders to support the contras. Abrams retracted many of his earlier statements, but he defended his actions and, backed by Secretary of State George P. Shultz, stated his intent to remain in office despite congressional calls for his resignation.

David M. Abshire, special counselor to the president with cabinet rank. In December 1986, Reagan appointed Abshire, who was serving as NATO ambassador, to coordinate White House strategy on the Iran-contra affair.

Charles Allen, senior CIA intelligence officer. Allen in October 1986 raised concerns with CIA officials, including director William J. Casey, about the Iran arms deals. Allen warned that profits from the arms sales might have been diverted to other purposes, including contra aid.

Oscar Arias, president of Costa Rica and chief architect of the August 7, 1987, peace plan signed by the presidents of five Central American countries.

Howard H. Baker, Jr., White House chief of staff, replacing Donald T. Regan, who resigned abruptly in February 1987. Baker, a widely respected moderate, retired from the Senate in 1985, in part to plan a run for the presidency in 1988. In moving to the chief of staff post, he said he was giving up his presidential bid. As a Republican senator from Tennessee (1967-85), Baker gained national attention as vice chairman of the Senate Watergate Committee in 1973-74.

George Bush, vice president of the United States. Bush said he supported the Iran arms deals as a way of improving relations with Tehran. He participated in the discussion of the January 17, 1986, presidential finding that authorized the Iran initiative, including U.S. arms sales to Iran. In July 1986, Bush met in Jerusalem with Israeli official Amiram Nir, who briefed him on the arms deals and hostage situation. At that meeting, according to a memo by a Bush aide, Nir made clear that the United States was dealing with radicals, not moderates, within Iran.

Several top Bush aides were in contact with Felix I. Rodriguez, a major figure in the contra supply effort who worked out of El Salvador. Bush stated that he was not himself involved in the contra arms supply operation and denied knowledge of any diversion of funds to the contras from the Iran arms sales.

Previous positions held by Bush included serving as director of Central Intelligence in 1976-77.

Adolfo Calero, member of the Nicaraguan Resistance group and political head of the largest contra faction, the Nicaraguan Democratic Force, which controlled nearly all of the 10,000-plus contras battling the Sandinista government. Until February 16, 1987, Calero was one of the three members of the United Nicaraguan Opposition (UNO), the contra directorate formed in 1985 at the behest of the Reagan administration. Contra leaders reorganized and replaced the UNO with the Nicaraguan Resistance group in May 1987.

Calero provided the House and Senate Iran-contra committees with financial records that showed nearly $34 million worth of contributions to and expenditures by the contras between mid-1984 and January 1987.

Frank C. Carlucci, national security adviser. Appointed by President Ronald Reagan in December 1986 to replace then-Vice Adm. John M. Poindexter. Carlucci, a former deputy director of the CIA and deputy secretary of defense, had a reputation for straightening out bureaucratic foul-ups and brooking no independent operations. Soon after taking over as national security adviser, he removed the National Security Council (NSC) staff from an operational role in covert activities and disbanded the NSC political-military section through which Lt. Col. Oliver L. North and others had operated the Iran arms deal.

William J. Casey, director of the CIA from 1981 to 1987. A longtime friend and supporter of President Ronald Reagan, Casey was deeply involved in administration policy making. He was a key figure in Reagan's decision to revive the Iran arms sales in 1986, and, like the president, was an enthusiastic supporter of the contra cause.

As the CIA's combative and controversial director, he restored agency morale, increased its budget, and promoted covert operations. Casey resigned February 2, 1987, because of ill health; he died of cancer three months later on May 6, just as the Iran-contra hearings were getting under way.

Through the testimony of other participants in the Iran-contra affair, most notably that of Lt. Col. Oliver L. North, Casey emerged as a cornerstone figure in both the Iran arms deals and secret contra supply operations. North testified that he had consulted with Casey frequently on both operations and that Casey had supported the diversion of profits scheme. Casey had claimed not to have known about the diversion until shortly before it was revealed in late November 1986. Duane "Dewey" Clarridge, head of the CIA's counterterrorism section, testified that Casey had wanted the CIA to run the entire Iran operation instead of the National Security Council, but that no other senior CIA officials had agreed with him.

North also testified that Casey had envisioned a privately funded covert organization outside the CIA that would conduct a variety of missions for the government.

Tomas Castillo (alias of Joe Fernandez), CIA station chief in Costa Rica from mid-1984 until December 1986. Castillo assisted in coordinating the contra aid network. He helped select the site for an airstrip to be constructed for the contra supply network and supplied flight/drop information. During closed testimony before the House and Senate Iran-contra committees in May 1987, Castillo described CIA involvement in activities to aid the contras while the congressional ban on such aid was in effect.

George Cave, retired CIA official recruited by the administration to serve as translator and note-taker for many of the talks between U.S. and Iranian intermediaries in 1986. Cave had served in Iran and was fluent in Farsi. He reportedly had warned U.S. officials in early 1986 about the unreliability of Manucher Ghorbanifar, a key middleman in the U.S.-Iran arms deals. CIA deputy director Clair George told the Tower Commission that Cave had begun his involvement in the Iran initiative as an interpreter but had "become a player." This assessment was borne out by Cave's July 1986 trip to Europe to discuss the possibility of opening a second Iranian channel.

Pedro Joaquín Chamorro, Jr., contra leader and member of the Nicaraguan Resistance group, a political directorate of exiled rebels opposed to the Sandinista government. Chamorro, former editor of the Nicaraguan opposition newspaper *La Prensa,* replaced Adolfo Calero in February 1987 as one of the three members of the United Nicaraguan Opposition (UNO), the original contra umbrella group formed in 1985 to receive U.S. aid. The contras in May 1987 replaced UNO with the Nicaraguan Resistance.

Chamorro's father, editor of *La Prensa* and a staunch opponent of the Somoza government, had been assassinated in early 1978. Although Somoza denied involvement, the murder consolidated opposition to the regime, which was ousted by the Sandinistas the following year.

Carl R. "Spitz" Channell, fund-raiser who ran several organizations that provided the contras with financial and political support from 1984 to 1986. Much of the money raised by Channell's efforts was funneled to Swiss bank accounts controlled by Lt. Col. Oliver L. North and others. On April 29, 1987, Channell pleaded guilty to con-

spiracy to defraud the government by soliciting funds to provide military aid for the contras while claiming the money was for a tax-exempt organization, the National Endowment for the Preservation of Liberty. Channell said he had conspired with North and others.

Duane "Dewey" Clarridge, head of the CIA's counterterrorism section. Clarridge was the CIA Central American Task Force chief who managed U.S. support of the Nicaraguan contras from 1981 to 1984. Clarridge later became head of CIA covert operations in Europe. Lt. Col. Oliver L. North approached Clarridge to get CIA help in clearing a November 1985 Iran-bound shipment through Portugal. Clarridge testified that he did not know the shipment contained Hawk antiaircraft missiles, although a cable stating that it was missiles supposedly was sent to him. Clarridge said he did not remember seeing the cable, and it could not be found in agency files.

Thomas Clines, ex-CIA official hired by Richard V. Secord to help supply arms to the contras. Clines was an associate of Edwin P. Wilson, a former CIA agent convicted in 1983 on charges of illegally selling explosives to Libya. Clines pleaded guilty in 1984 to charges in the case of a company that allegedly defrauded the Pentagon on a contract for transporting military goods to Egypt.

Charles J. Cooper, assistant attorney general who was asked by Attorney General Edwin Meese III in early November 1986 to look into the Iran arms sales. Cooper produced an opinion saying the U.S. sales were legal. But he later said the opinion was based on incomplete, inaccurate information given him at the time. Testifying before the House and Senate Iran-contra committees in June 1987, Cooper told how Justice Department investigators had discovered a memo in Lt. Col. Oliver L. North's office on November 22, 1986, discussing the contra diversion. He said the Justice Department had erred by not moving more quickly to protect documents that were shredded by North and his secretary, Fawn Hall.

Cooper also described how, during a November 20 White House meeting, Reagan officials planned for CIA director William J. Casey to give false testimony to the congressional Intelligence committees about the November 1985 Israeli arms shipment to Iran.

Joseph Coors, Colorado brewery executive who was one of the three private donors to testify before the House and Senate Iran-contra committees in May 1987 about their efforts to aid the contras. Coors said that in 1985, at Lt. Col. Oliver L. North's suggestion, he had sent $65,000 to retired major general Richard V. Secord's Swiss bank account. Coors said he had approached CIA director William J. Casey first with an offer to help the contras and that Casey then referred him to North.

Craig P. Coy, former aide to Lt. Col. Oliver L. North at the National Security Council. Coy told the House and Senate Iran-contra committees that he had known little about the contra-aid network but that North had assured him that all North's activities had been authorized. Coy helped prepare the chronology of the Iran arms initiative along with other members of the NSC staff.

Arturo Cruz, Sr., contra leader widely respected on Capitol Hill. Cruz resigned from the political directorate of contra factions, the United Nicaraguan Opposition (UNO), in March 1987 amid internal wrangling over contra reforms. When the contras reorganized their directorate in May, Cruz was the only one of the three original UNO leaders not to return.

During the Iran-contra investigations, Cruz admitted

that Lt. Col. Oliver L. North had arranged for him to receive monthly payments of $7,000 from January to November 1986.

John C. Cupp, former Army Green Beret sergeant who worked as security chief for American National Management Corp., a Virginia firm involved in the private contra aid network. Cupp reportedly helped retired lieutenant colonel Richard B. Gadd recruit pilots, mechanics, and others for contra supply missions.

Edward de Garay, chairman of Corporate Air Services, a Pennsylvania company that acted as paymaster for the private contra aid network. His firm was the employer of record of the crew of the cargo plane carrying supplies for the contras that was downed by the Nicaraguan military in October 1986.

Cynthia F. Dondlinger, accountant and contract officer for American National Management Corp., a Virginia firm involved in the private contra aid network.

Col. Robert C. Dutton, retired Air Force officer who supervised day-to-day logistics for the contra supply effort. Dutton compiled a photo album with pictures of the contra aid operation. He worked under retired major general Richard V. Secord and described Secord and Lt. Col. Oliver L. North as "co-commanders" of the operation. Testifying before the Iran-contra committees in May 1987, Dutton indicated that Secord might have been interested in profiting from the contra operation.

Lt. Col. Robert L. Earl, deputy to Lt. Col. Oliver L. North on the counterterrorism unit at the National Security Council until late 1986. Earl helped shred documents in November 1986 with North's secretary, Fawn Hall.

Earl told the House and Senate Iran-contra committees that he had had little direct information about North's contra-aid network but that North had assured him that North's activities had been authorized. Earl testified that North had told him in 1986 that he had informed Casey about the diversion of funds to the contras. Earl participated in the NSC's chronology writing in November 1986.

Joe Fernandez. *See* Tomas Castillo.

Alan Fiers, chief of the CIA Central American Task Force since October 1984, succeeding Duane "Dewey" Clarridge. Fiers had been CIA station chief in Saudi Arabia in 1984 when that country made its first donations to the contras.

Fiers had served with Lt. Col. Oliver North and Assistant Secretary of State Elliott Abrams as members of the Restricted Interagency Group (RIG), a key component in the administration's procontra efforts. But Fiers told the House and Senate Iran-contra committees that he never knew exactly what North was doing. During his testimony, Fiers either denied or said he could not recall incidents in which he or other CIA officials allegedly cooperated with North in aiding the contras during the period that CIA aid was restricted. He testified that in early 1986 he allowed CIA officers to participate in some contra aid activities that had previously been barred, but he later reimposed some of the restrictions.

David Fischer, former special assistant to President Ronald Reagan and an associate of Carl R. "Spitz" Channell. Fischer allegedly helped arrange meetings with Reagan for Channell contributors.

Donald Fortier, former deputy national security adviser for political-military affairs. Fortier worked for national security adviser Robert C. McFarlane and his successor, then-Vice Adm. John M. Poindexter. With NSC aide Howard J. Teicher, Fortier coauthored in June 1985 a

Iran-Contra Code Names

Public hearings and reports on the Iran-contra affair gave followers a rare glimpse of clandestine operators, complete with phony passports, false identities, aliases, and code names.

Pseudonyms in covert operations were customary, retired major general Richard V. Secord told the House and Senate select committees investigating the Iran-contra affair. But few seemed to relish their use as much as National Security Council aide Lt. Col. Oliver L. North, who chose such colorful code names as "Blood and Guts" and "Steelhammer."

Following are some of the pseudonyms and code names used by, or given to (as in the case of Betsy North), participants in the Iran-contra affair. The list was compiled from testimony, documents, and news reports.

Name	Pseudonyms/Code Names
Elliott Abrams	Mr. Kenilworth
Adolfo Calero	"The Sparkplug"
George Cave	Sam O'Neil
Joe Fernandez	Tomas Castillo
Manucher Ghorbanifar	Nicholas Kralis "The Merchant"
Robert C. McFarlane	Sean Devlin
Amiram Nir	Mr. Miller
Oliver L. North	Mr. Goode or William P. Goode Mr. Green "Blood and Guts" or "B.G." Steelhammer
Betsy North	Mrs. Bellybutton
Robert W. Owen	"The Courier" or "T.C."
Luis Posada Carriles	Ramon Medina
Felix I. Rodriguez	Max Gomez
Richard V. Secord	Major General Adams Dick Copp or Mr. Copp

National Security Decision Directive (NSDD) that outlined a strategy for improving U.S. relations with Iran. The directive included a proposal for allowing arms sales to Iran.

Fortier died of cancer in August 1986.

Graham Fuller, CIA national intelligence officer for the Near East and South Asia. In a May 1985 memorandum submitted to CIA director William J. Casey, Fuller warned that the Soviet Union was developing significant leverage in Iran at a time when the regime of the Ayatollah Ruhollah Khomeini was faltering. He said the United States should develop new policies to gain influence in Iran. He suggested encouraging "friendly states" to sell arms to Iran to show there were alternatives to the Soviet Union.

Roy M. Furmark, a New York businessman involved in deals in the Middle East and a former law client and longtime friend of CIA chief William J. Casey. Furmark was part of the private network of individuals, including Adnan Khashoggi and Manucher Ghorbanifar, involved in the Iran arms sales. In early October 1986, Furmark told Casey that two Canadian financiers who had not been paid for their role in arms shipments to Iran were threatening to reveal the secret arms operation. Later in October Furmark told CIA officials of Ghorbanifar's belief that money from the Iran arms sales had been diverted to the contras.

Richard B. Gadd, retired Air Force lieutenant colonel who was involved in the contra supply effort. Gadd established three companies in 1983 that handled classified military operations, specializing in the charter of commercial aircraft for Pentagon and CIA covert operations. Airmach, one of Gadd's companies, received a State Department contract in 1986 to deliver nonmilitary aid to the contras. Gadd handled the covert program to ship arms to the contras from January to April 1986; he hired pilots and cargo handlers and located planes to be used to deliver military goods to contra camps inside Nicaragua.

Henry H. Gaffney, Jr., a senior Pentagon official, who testified before the House and Senate Iran-contra committees in June 1987 that Israel's transfer of U.S.-made weapons to Iran in 1985 had probably violated U.S. law. The panel quizzed him on a memo he had written in late 1985 or early 1986 that predicted negative consequences—such as angering Arab countries—if arms were sold to Iran.

Ellen Garwood, a Texas heiress who said that she had contributed $2.2 million to the contras through Carl R. "Spitz" Channell's organization, the National Endowment for the Preservation of Liberty. Garwood testified before the House and Senate Iran-contra committees on May 21, 1987, along with Joseph Coors and William B. O'Boyle.

Robert M. Gates, a career intelligence and national security official who became the CIA's deputy director in April 1986. Reagan nominated Gates in February 1987 to succeed the ailing William J. Casey as director of the CIA. During confirmation hearings, however, Senate members became increasingly concerned about Gates's role in the Iran operation, suggesting that he had ignored evidence of wrongdoing. Gates withdrew from consideration in March rather than face a prolonged political battle.

Clair George, deputy director for covert operations at the CIA since July 1984. George became actively involved in the Iran arms shipments following President Reagan's signing of the January 17, 1986, finding authorizing the initiative. He told the House and Senate Iran-contra committees that the White House shunted aside the experts at the CIA, in particular their warnings about the reliability of Manucher Ghorbanifar and their assessment that pro-Iranian Lebanese forces holding the American hostages would never release all of them. George ordered CIA agents to stay clear of Ghorbanifar after he failed a lie-detector test.

George also told the committees that, while he had known of North's work with the contras, he had not realized the full extent of his involvement or of the lower-level CIA employees who were helping him. George apologized for his October 14, 1986, testimony before the House Intelligence Committee, in which he denied any U.S. government involvement in or knowledge of the contra supply plane downed in Nicaragua October 5.

Manucher Ghorbanifar, exiled Iranian arms merchant who played a key role in initiating and arranging financial support for arms shipments to Iran. Ghorbanifar acted as an intermediary for U.S., Israeli, and Iranian officials in 1985 and 1986. Despite CIA warnings that Ghorbanifar was unreliable, National Security Council and Israeli officials continued to do business with him until September 1986. In July 1987, Lt. Col. Oliver L. North told the House and Senate Iran-contra committees that he considered Ghorbanifar an Israeli agent and that CIA director William J. Casey had told him Ghorbanifar worked for Israeli intelligence. CIA official Clair George said the same thing in his August testimony before the committees.

Francis Gomez, former official of the United States Information Agency. Gomez was associated with three companies that were active in the contra aid network, including Richard R. Miller's International Business Communications.

Max Gomez. *See* Felix I. Rodriguez.

Thomas C. Green, attorney for Richard V. Secord and, until November 26, 1986, for Lt. Col. Oliver L. North. Green was present when North's former secretary, Fawn Hall, handed over to North documents that she had smuggled from North's office after North was fired November 25. Hall told the House and Senate Iran-contra committees that Green never advised her that removing the documents was improper. She also stated that Green asked what she would say if questioned about shredding documents. When she replied that shredding occurred every day, his response was something to the effect of "good."

Donald P. Gregg, Vice President George Bush's national security adviser. Gregg had numerous contacts with former CIA operative Felix I. Rodriguez, a longtime friend who helped coordinate the contra supply effort.

According to a chronology released by the vice president's office December 15, 1986, Rodrgiguez first mentioned the contra supply network in August 1986. Gregg's prior meetings reportedly had concerned Rodriguez's counterinsurgency work in El Salvador. Gregg reiterated this in his testimony before the House and Senate Iran-contra committees.

Albert Hakim, Iranian-born businessman who, with his partner, retired major general Richard V. Secord, arranged the financial network behind the Iran arms sales and contra arms supply efforts in 1985 and 1986. Testifying before the House and Senate Iran-contra committees in June 1987, Hakim described a labyrinth of shell companies and foreign bank accounts. He told of his role as interpreter and negotiator in the arms-for-hostages dealings with Iranians in 1986. His efforts included negotiating a nine-point plan that in some respects contradicted U.S. policy. Hakim also told of his attempts to provide financially for Lt. Col. Oliver L. North and his family.

Fawn Hall, secretary to Lt. Col. Oliver L. North from February 1983 to November 1986. Testifying before the House and Senate Iran-contra committees in June 1987, Hall strongly defended North's conduct in the Iran-contra affair. She described how she had shredded some documents and altered others in November 1986 in an effort to protect her boss from Iran-contra disclosures. She also told of smuggling documents from the White House after North was fired from his NSC position on November 25, 1986. After North was fired, Hall returned to her permanent post at the Pentagon.

Lee H. Hamilton, D-Ind., chairman of the fifteen-member House Select Committee to Investigate Covert Arms Transactions with Iran. A member of the House since 1965, Hamilton had served as chairman of the House Intelligence Committee and the Foreign Affairs Subcommittee on Europe and the Middle East. He had been an outspoken critic of U.S. aid to the contras and an aggressive advocate of congressional involvement in foreign policy making. *(Profiles of House Iran-contra committee members, p. 154)*

Eugene Hasenfus, the sole surviving crewman of a C-123 cargo plane shot down over southern Nicaragua on October 5, 1986. The plane was carrying supplies to the contras, and the episode exposed the U.S. air supply operation. Hasenfus was captured, convicted on terrorism charges, and sentenced to thirty years in prison for his role. At his Nicaraguan trial Hasenfus confessed that he had been smuggling weapons to the contras. Nicaraguan president Daniel Ortega pardoned and released him on December 17, 1986.

Daniel K. Inouye, D-Hawaii, chairman of the eleven-member Senate Select Committee on Secret Military Assistance to Iran and the Nicaraguan Opposition. A twenty-four-year veteran of the Senate, Inouye was a member of the Senate Watergate Committee in 1973-74. His service on that panel earned him a reputation as a tough interrogator of witnesses. A former Intelligence Committee chairman, Inouye headed the Appropriations Subcommittee on Foreign Operations from 1976 to 1980 and again in 1987. *(Profiles of Senate Iran-contra committee members, p. 149)*

Alton G. Keel, Jr., National Security Council deputy director. Notes taken by Keel during the November 10, 1986, meeting, in which President Ronald Reagan and top advisers discussed how the administration would handle the exposure of U.S. dealings with Iran, indicated that the administration would give no specifics and would state the position of not dealing with terrorists.

John H. Kelly, U.S. ambassador to Lebanon. Bypassing the State Department, Kelly in late October and early November 1986 made secret "back channel" communications with National Security Council staff members and with retired major general Richard V. Secord regarding hostage negotiations with Iran.

Adnan Khashoggi, wealthy Saudi Arabian businessman and leading financier for shipments of U.S. arms to Iran. Khashoggi brought arms merchant Manucher Ghorbanifar and Israeli officials together to arrange the arms transfers to Iran. He also brought in other private investors to help finance the arms sales.

Ayatollah Ruhollah Khomeini, Shiite Moslem leader of Iran who returned from a fifteen-year exile in February 1979 to establish an Islamic republic.

David Kimche, former director general of the Israeli Foreign Ministry. While serving with the foreign ministry, Kimche discussed arms sales to Iran with Reagan officials. In July 1985, he proposed that the United States establish contacts with Iran and attempt to win freedom for the American hostages held in Lebanon in exchange for weapons.

Noel C. Koch, former deputy assistant secretary of defense and close friend of retired major general Richard V. Secord. At the Pentagon, he helped negotiate the price of TOW missiles sold to Iran and protested that the United States was swapping arms for hostages in contradiction to its stated policy. In June 1987, he testified before the House and Senate Iran-contra committees that Lt. Col. Oliver L. North had told him President Reagan was determined to get the American hostages back.

Koch told the committees that he resigned from the Richard Secord Legal Defense Fund when he discovered suspicious deposits totaling $500,000 from a Swiss bank account used by Secord's associate, Albert Hakim.

William G. Langton, president of Southern Air Transport, a Miami company that delivered some U.S. arms to Iran in early 1986 and leased planes to the private contra aid network.

Michael Ledeen, National Security Council consultant on terrorism with close ties to Israel. In 1985, Ledeen met with top U.S. and Israeli officials and with the private network of arms dealers. He played a major role in establishing the U.S.-Israeli connection in the arms sales to Iran. The Tower Commission report speculated that Ledeen eventually was dropped as an official American contact with Iranian arms dealer Manucher Ghorbanifar, a close friend of Ledeen, because of concerns that Ledeen had some financial arrangement with Ghorbanifar and Israeli arms dealers.

David L. Lewis, Washington attorney and acquaintance of Albert Hakim's Geneva-based lawyer, Willard I. Zucker. Lewis testified in early June 1987 before the House and Senate Iran-contra hearings. He recounted what Zucker had told him about Hakim's plan to give money to Betsy North, wife of Lt. Col. Oliver L. North. According to Lewis, Zucker had said a "wealthy client" wanted to get the money to the wife of "someone in the White House." Lewis said he was not certain that Zucker had mentioned North's name.

Robert H. Lilac, Lt. Col. Oliver L. North's supervisor at the National Security Council in 1981 and associate of retired major general Richard V. Secord. In 1984, Lilac was vice president of a Secord company, American Marketing and Consulting Inc., which bought a cargo plane for the contras. Lilac denied any involvement in the contra aid network.

Arthur L. Liman, chief counsel of the Senate Select Committee on Secret Military Assistance to Iran and the Nicaraguan Opposition. As a partner with a New York law firm, Liman had specialized in complicated white-collar criminal cases. He previously had served as an assistant U.S. attorney in New York.

Ronald J. Martin, Miami arms broker, head of R. M. Equipment Co., which reportedly bought weapons in Portugal and elsewhere on behalf of the private contra aid network.

Lt. Col. James McCoy, retired Army officer and Miami arms broker who was a major source of weapons for the contras.

Robert C. McFarlane, national security adviser from October 1983 to December 1985. McFarlane supervised early National Security Council (NSC) efforts to aid the contras and played a central role in ongoing secret contacts with Iran, even after leaving his NSC post. He made a secret trip to Tehran in May 1986 in hopes of winning freedom for U.S. hostages held by pro-Iranian terrorists in Lebanon. McFarlane took an overdose of Valium in February 1987 and was hospitalized briefly.

Testifying before the House and Senate Iran-contra committees in May 1987, McFarlane admitted that he had misled Congress in the past regarding the contra activities of his aide, Lt. Col. Oliver L. North. He also admitted that he had helped alter a chronology of the Iran arms deals prepared by the White House in November 1986, in an attempt to protect the president. McFarlane made a return appearance before the committees in July 1987 to refute some of North's testimony.

John N. McMahon, CIA deputy director from 1982 to 1986 who balked at agency participation in the Iran arms deals without presidential authorization. When McMahon discovered in November 1985 that a CIA proprietary airline had delivered weapons to Iran at the request of Lt. Col. Oliver L. North, he refused further agency participation without a finding, or authorization, signed by the president. According to then-national security adviser Vice Adm. John M. Poindexter, the president signed a finding on December 5, 1985, giving retroactive approval to CIA participation in the November Hawk missile delivery to Israel.

At meetings of top administration officials in December 1985 and January 1986, McMahon argued against providing Iran with arms or intelligence information. He resigned in March 1986.

Ramon Medina. *See* Luis Posada Carriles.

Edwin Meese III, attorney general of the United States. Meese knew of the U.S. plan to sell arms to Iran and in January 1986 provided the administration with legal advice on the Iran initiative. He stated, however, that he was not kept informed of the Iran deals after January.

In November 1986, Meese began a Justice Department fact-finding inquiry to pull together a coherent record of what had happened in the Iran arms sales. During this investigation, Justice Department lawyers discovered a memo in Lt. Col. Oliver L. North's files that mentioned the diversion of funds from the Iran arms sales to the Nicaraguan contras. Meese made a public statement November 25, announcing the diversion of funds. On December 2, Meese announced that he would seek appointment of an independent counsel to investigate possible criminal activities.

Members of the House and Senate Iran-contra committees questioned Meese's failures to ask point-blank questions and to make notes of some interviews during his November inquiry. They also criticized him for not taking adequate steps to preserve crucial White House documents and for being slow to bring the Justice Department's Criminal Division into the inquiry. During his testimony, Meese defended his initial probe of the Iran arms deals as adequate and successful, saying that his basic discoveries of the Iran-contra story were valid and had held up.

Johnathan Miller, former deputy assistant to the president for administration and management. As a State Department official on loan to the National Security Council, Miller helped Robert W. Owen, Lt. Col. Oliver L. North's liaison with the contras, convert traveler's checks into cash to give to the contra leaders while the congressional ban on U.S. aid was in effect. Implicated by Owen's testimony before the House and Senate Iran-contra com-

mittees, Miller resigned May 14, 1987. He was the first Reagan official to resign as a result of the congressional hearings on the Iran-contra affair.

Richard R. Miller, president of International Business Communications Inc., a Washington public relations firm that had secret contracts with the State Department to publicize the contras' cause in the United States. His firm also helped funnel donations from U.S. tax-exempt groups headed by Carl R. "Spitz" Channell to secret Swiss bank accounts controlled by Lt. Col. Oliver L. North and others. Miller pleaded guilty May 6, 1987, to conspiracy to defraud the government because of his part in an illegal fund-raising scheme to buy military equipment for the contras. Miller named Channell and North as part of the conspiracy.

Edmund S. Muskie, member of the President's Special Review Board (Tower Commission) appointed by Reagan in November 1986 to study the National Security Council staff's role in the Iran-contra affair. Muskie, a former Democratic senator from Maine (1959-80), served as secretary of state during Jimmy Carter's last year as president (1980-81).

John W. Nields, Jr., chief counsel of the House Select Committee to Investigate Covert Arms Transactions with Iran. Nields is an attorney with a Washington law firm. He served as chief counsel to the House Committee on Standards and Official Conduct, which investigated the Korean lobbying scandal in 1977-78.

Yaacov Nimrodi, arms merchant and former Israeli military attaché in Iran. Nimrodi was a member of the network of middlemen, including Amiram Nir, Adolph "Al" Schwimmer, Manucher Ghorbanifar, and Adnan Khashoggi, who facilitated some of the U.S. arms shipments to Iran.

Amiram Nir, Israel's chief antiterrorism official and adviser to Israeli prime minister Shimon Peres. Nir in January 1986 became the main Israeli contact with the United States regarding arms sales to Iran. He met with top U.S. officials throughout 1986 in support of the arms deals, and he accompanied former national security adviser Robert C. McFarlane on his trip to Iran in May 1986.

Lt. Col. Oliver L. North, former deputy director of political-military affairs at the National Security Council (NSC). North helped supervise arms shipments to Iran in 1985 and 1986 and coordinated assistance to the contras beginning in 1984. North assembled and took charge of a network of private operatives who raised money and provided the Iran-contra operations with banking, arms purchasing, and other services. He was fired from his NSC post on November 25, 1986, the day Attorney General Edwin Meese III announced that profits from sales of arms to Iran had been diverted to the contras.

North invoked his Fifth Amendment right to refuse to testify during preliminary congressional investigations into the Iran-contra affair in December 1986.

Seven months later in July 1987, he testified before the House and Senate Iran-contra committees with limited immunity. North defended himself, stating that he had done nothing without the authority of his superiors. He said that he had consulted regularly with national security adviser John M. Poindexter and CIA director William J. Casey regarding his Iran-contra activities. North said that he had been willing to be the administration's "fall guy," but not if that meant a criminal prosecution, a possible outcome of the investigation of independent counsel Lawrence E. Walsh.

During his appearances before the Iran-contra committees, the articulate North won the sympathy and support of many Americans and was hailed by some as an American hero. His emotionally charged testimony at that time also sparked public support for the contra cause.

William B. O'Boyle, a New York investor who contributed $160,000 to Carl R. "Spitz" Channell's fund-raising efforts on behalf of the contras. Testifying before the House and Senate Iran-contra committees in May 1987, O'Boyle said that, as part of the solicitation, Lt. Col. Oliver L. North had privately told him of a secret plan to topple the Nicaraguan government.

Daniel Ortega, Nicaraguan president whose Sandinista government came to power in 1979. Ortega was the popular leader of rebels fighting the American-backed Somoza regime that had ruled Nicaragua for forty years. The rebels, who took their name from the assassinated nationalist hero Augusto César Sandino, forced President Anastasio Somoza to resign in July 1979, and Ortega established his "Government of Reconstruction."

President Jimmy Carter had met with Ortega in September 1979 and promised American aid for the beleaguered country. However, U.S. relations with Ortega's government shifted with Ronald Reagan's arrival in the White House in 1981. As the Sandinista's military buildup took place, ties with the Soviet Union and Cuba increased, and government repression of internal opposition grew, the United States began to back the contras in their fight against Ortega's leftist government.

Robert W. Owen, former aide to Lt. Col. Oliver L. North. Owen, serving as North's courier and personal representative, delivered intelligence information and money to contra leaders in Washington and Central America in late 1984 and 1985. His testimony before the House and Senate Iran-contra committees linked North directly with about $90,000 worth of traveler's checks. Owen also said that White House aide Johnathan Miller had assisted him in money transfers to the contras. Miller resigned immediately after Owen's discussion of his role.

Shimon Peres, foreign minister of Israel since 1986. Peres was prime minister from 1984 to 1986, during the time the United States, with Israel's encouragement and assistance, began the Iran initiative. National Security Council consultant Michael Ledeen met with Peres in May 1985 to ask for Israel's help in acquiring intelligence information on Iran. At this meeting, Peres asked if the United States would approve an Israeli arms shipment to Iran. Representatives of Peres subsequently suggested that arms could be traded for the release of American hostages in Lebanon.

H. Ross Perot, Texas billionaire who, responding to a request by Lt. Col. Oliver L. North, transferred $2 million to a Swiss bank in May 1986 to serve as ransom payment for American hostages in Lebanon. The money was never used, however.

Rear Adm. John M. Poindexter, national security adviser from December 1985 to November 1986. President Ronald Reagan appointed Poindexter, formerly Robert C. McFarlane's deputy, to replace McFarlane in December 1985. National Security Council (NSC) aide Lt. Col. Oliver L. North kept Poindexter informed about the Iran arms deals and the contra supply operations. Poindexter, in turn, briefed Reagan almost daily on foreign policy during the height of the Iran-contra dealings. Poindexter resigned November 25, 1986, the day Attorney General Edwin Meese III revealed the diversion of funds from the Iran

arms sales to the Nicaraguan contras. Poindexter, who held the rank of vice admiral while serving as national security adviser, reverted to his previous rank of rear admiral upon leaving the White House. His request to retire from the Navy as of October 1, 1987, was approved but a decision as to whether he could retire as a vice admiral was deferred pending resolution of the independent counsel's investigation, the Navy announced in September.

Poindexter's style was marked by an obsession for secrecy. He was the least visible national security adviser in decades. In August 1985, he had set up a secret computer code, called "Private Blank Check," through which he and North could communicate without the knowledge of other NSC staffers. In his testimony before the House and Senate Iran-contra committees in July 1987, Poindexter made clear his mistrust of Congress. He admitted withholding information from Congress and destroying information, including a December 1985 presidential finding that gave retroactive approval for CIA assistance to Israel in shipping missiles to Iran in November 1985. Most significantly, Poindexter took responsibility for approving the diversion of Iranian profits to the contras and said that he had not told Reagan about the plan because of its "politically explosive" nature. Committee members and top Reagan officials who testified came down hard on Poindexter, holding him responsible for many of the administration's Iran-contra troubles.

Luis Posada Carriles (alias Ramon Medina), Cuban exile who worked with Felix I. Rodriguez in El Salvador managing contra aid flights into Nicaragua.

Rafael Quintero, Cuban-American who helped coordinate the contra arms supply effort out of El Salvador under the direction of ex-CIA official Thomas Clines. Quintero fought at the 1961 Bay of Pigs attempted invasion of Cuba and was a veteran of many CIA covert operations.

Ali Akbar Hashemi Rafsanjani, speaker of the Iranian parliament and a prominent figure in U.S. contacts with Iran. Rafsanjani in June 1985 persuaded Lebanese Shiite terrorists to release some of the hostages held on a hijacked TWA flight. U.S. officials hoped that he could help obtain the release of American hostages held in Lebanon as well. In 1986, a relative of Rafsanjani became the so-called second channel, replacing Manucher Ghorbanifar as the middleman in the Iran initiative.

Ronald Reagan, president of the United States. The Iran-contra scandal, which broke upon the public scene in November 1986, became the most serious problem of Reagan's two terms in office. In December 1985 and January 1986, Reagan had signed a series of presidential findings that authorized arms sales to Iran. According to former national security adviser Robert C. McFarlane, he also had given prior approval to Israeli shipments of U.S. arms to Iran in 1985. The arms deals contradicted the administration's embargo on arms sales to the Iranian regime. Reagan in November 1986 characterized the deals as attempts to improve relations between the United States and Iran, to strengthen the position of Iranian "moderates," and to encourage release of the Americans held hostage by pro-Iranian terrorists in Lebanon. In March 1987, however, the president admitted that the strategy had deteriorated into a straight arms-for-hostages trade, a "mistake." Reagan accepted full responsibility for the Iran initiative but stated that he had not known about the diversion of profits from the arms sales to the Nicaraguan contras.

Reagan was a strong supporter of the Nicaraguan

rebels. In his testimony before the House and Senate Iran-contra committees, McFarlane stated that Reagan had wanted the National Security Council to do all it could to help keep the contras intact "body and soul" while the congressional restrictions on U.S. aid were in effect.

The Tower Commission faulted Reagan's management style, saying he had allowed his aides too much latitude, that they had neglected to report critical details to him, and that White House record keeping had been lax. The board concluded, however, that Reagan had been candid and had had no intent to mislead the public. Testimony before the Iran-contra committees bore out many of the Tower Commission's assessments. At the end of the public hearings, Reagan appeared to have been cleared of wrongdoing.

Donald T. Regan, White House chief of staff from 1985 to 1987. Regan apparently knew generally of the Iran initiative but was not informed of important details. He maintained that he did not know of the diversion of profits from the Iran arms sales to the contras until Attorney General Edwin Meese III's public announcement in November 1986.

The Tower Commission concluded that Regan, as a chief of staff who asserted his personal control over White House staffers and who attended almost every relevant meeting on the Iran initiative, should bear primary responsibility for the chaos that fell upon the White House with disclosure of the Iran arms deals. Regan resigned February 27, 1987, the day after the Tower board issued its report; he was replaced immediately by former senator Howard H. Baker, Jr.

Testifying before the House and Senate Iran-contra committees in July 1987, Regan described how events had gone beyond his control. He said he had battled to get the facts of the Iran-contra affair and to disclose them to Congress and to the public.

Oliver B. "Buck" Revell, executive assistant director of the FBI who was contacted several times by Lt. Col. Oliver L. North about FBI activities related to the Iran-contra affair. North asked Revell in April 1986 to delay a grand jury appearance by Richard R. Miller, a public relations consultant who was to testify in an investigation involving a potential contributor to the contras. Revell at first said he had asked for the delay but later said that he had not.

North also called Revell shortly after the start of an FBI inquiry into Southern Air Transport in October 1986 to voice concern that the probe could disrupt U.S.-Iranian negotiations.

Alfonso Robelo, contra leader of the Democratic Nicaraguan Movement and one of the directors of the Nicaraguan Resistance group. Robelo, with Adolfo Calero and Arturo Cruz, was a director of the United Nicaraguan Opposition (UNO), the political coalition group established in 1985 at the behest of the U.S. government. When UNO broke down under internal pressures, the contras replaced it with the Nicaraguan Resistance group.

During the Iran-contra hearings, retired major general Richard V. Secord testified that Robelo was given monthly payments of $10,000 from funds diverted from the Iran arms sales to the private network aiding the contras.

Glenn A. Robinette, security consultant, formerly employed by the CIA. Testifying before the House and Senate Iran-contra committees in June 1987, Robinette said that in 1986, under instructions from retired major general Richard V. Secord, he had installed a $14,000 security system at Lt. Col. Oliver L. North's home in Great Falls, Va., after North had complained of death threats.

Although Secord had paid for the system, Robinette said that North asked for receipts for the work in July 1986. Robinette sent two phony invoices in December. North then sent two predated letters to appear as authorization for the project.

Felix I. Rodriguez (alias Max Gomez), a veteran of the 1961 Bay of Pigs attempt to invade Cuba and former CIA operative recruited by Lt. Col. Oliver L. North to help coordinate the contra supply network working out of El Salvador. Rodriguez served as a liaison with private American crews involved in the contra effort while he worked for the Salvadoran air force on counterinsurgency efforts. He discussed the contra operation with aides to Vice President George Bush. Bush, who discussed insurgency in El Salvador with Rodriguez, said he was "not informed" of the contra discussions Rodriguez had with his staff.

Adolph "Al" Schwimmer, Israeli arms dealer and an adviser to Israeli prime minister Shimon Peres. Schwimmer, with others, including Amiram Nir, Yaacov Nimrodi, and Manucher Ghorbanifar, participated in early discussions of the Iran initiative and in the subsequent arms sales negotiations.

Bretton G. Sciaroni, counsel for President Ronald Reagan's Intelligence Oversight Board. Appearing before the House and Senate Iran-contra committees in June 1987, Sciaroni testified about a legal memo he had written in September 1985 that said the Boland amendment restrictions on U.S. aid to the contras did not apply to the National Security Council (NSC) and that Lt. Col. Oliver L. North's activities did not violate the law. His conclusion was based on conversations with North and with NSC counsel Cmdr. Paul Thompson. Sciaroni said Thompson had given him a stack of documents regarding North's activities but had omitted key memos. Some panel members criticized Sciaroni's legal expertise and background.

Brent Scowcroft, a member of the President's Special Review Board (Tower Commission), the panel established by Reagan to investigate the National Security Council staff's role in the Iran-contra affair. A retired Air Force lieutenant general, Scowcroft became President Gerald R. Ford's national security adviser after serving as deputy to Henry A. Kissinger during Kissinger's service as adviser to Ford and President Richard Nixon. A member of Kissinger's international consulting firm, Scowcroft was an important figure in Washington's foreign policy establishment.

Richard V. Secord, retired Air Force major general and a key operative in the Iran-contra affair. Secord ran a network of private companies involved in selling arms to Iran and funneling profits and other contributions to the contras. With his partner, Albert Hakim, Secord worked closely with Lt. Col. Oliver L. North. Secord began selling arms to the contras in late 1984 at North's instigation. In 1985, he organized a private network to airlift military supplies to the Nicaraguan rebels, and he made logistical arrangements in 1985-86 for secret U.S. arms sales to Iran.

As the first witness to testify before the House and Senate Iran-contra committees, Secord detailed how the network of private individuals, companies, and bank accounts—which he called "the enterprise"—worked in selling arms to Iran and in aiding the contras. He denied repeatedly that he had any interest in profiting from the Iran-contra operation. Secord said he had hoped that, if he performed a real service in aiding the contras, he would have a good chance of going back into the government.

Secord had left government in 1983—he was a deputy assistant secretary of defense—under a cloud of suspicion about his ties to Edwin P. Wilson's shadowy network. Wilson, a former CIA agent, was convicted in 1983 on charges of illegally shipping munitions to Libya and plotting to kill an opponent of Libyan leader Muammar el-Qaddafi.

Theodore G. Shackley, former top CIA official and business associate of Edwin P. Wilson, the ex-CIA agent imprisoned for selling explosives to Libya. Shackley met with Iranian middleman Manucher Ghorbanifar in late 1984 to discuss possible arms sales to Iran and release of American hostages in Lebanon. He later drafted a memo to the State Department but said he played no further role in the Iran-contra affair. Shackley ran a Virginia consulting firm, TGS International Inc., and reportedly did consulting work for Albert Hakim.

George P. Shultz, secretary of state. Shultz was one of the administration's strongest opponents of arms sales to Iran. Shultz maintained that he was only partially informed about details of the Iran arms deals and that he knew nothing about the diversion of funds to the contras. The National Security Council staff and CIA cut Shultz and the State Department out of crucial decisions regarding the Iran arms deals and the contra supply operations. Shultz, for example, was not told about a series of presidential findings, written in December 1985 and January 1986, that authorized U.S. arms sales to Iran. When Shultz attempted to investigate Lt. Col. Oliver L. North's activities in behalf of the contras, North assured him that he had done nothing improper.

The Tower Commission criticized Shultz for not being more forceful in opposing the Iran arms deals and for protecting his own position. When he testified before the House and Senate Iran-contra committees in late July 1987, however, Shultz said that he had spoken out forcefully and fully against the sale of arms to Iran. He described a "battle royal" in the White House after disclosure of the Iran-contra affair in November 1986 and told of his attempts to get the facts to the president.

Gaston J. Sigur, Jr., assistant secretary of state for East Asian and Pacific affairs. Sigur twice solicited contributions for the contras from Taiwan in 1985. Each request led to a $1 million contribution sent to a Swiss bank account.

John K. Singlaub, retired Army major general and chairman of the World Anticommunist League, who worked to raise money worldwide for the contras. Singlaub was one of the major conduits of arms to the contras while the congressional ban on aid was in effect.

Stanley Sporkin, former CIA general counsel who helped draft presidential findings in December 1985 and January 1986 that authorized U.S. arms sales to Iran. Sporkin left the CIA post to become a U.S. district court judge in February 1986.

Col. James Steele, U.S. Army officer and former commander of U.S. military forces in El Salvador. Steele reportedly helped supervise contra aid flights out of El Salvador's Ilopango air base. He denied doing anything improper.

Lewis A. Tambs, U.S. ambassador to Costa Rica from July 1985 to December 1986. Tambs testified that Lt. Col. Oliver L. North instructed him to help open up a southern front for the Nicaraguan contras. Tambs obtained permission from Costa Rican officials to build a secret airstrip to be used for contra supply missions.

Tambs retired from his Costa Rican post in December 1986 to return to Arizona State University to teach Latin American history.

Howard J. Teicher, former senior director of the National Security Council's office of political-military affairs and Lt. Col. Oliver L. North's nominal superior. Teicher and Donald Fortier coauthored in June 1985 a National Security Decision Directive (NSDD) that set out a strategy for improving U.S. relations with Iran. One provision in the NSDD would have allowed the sale of arms to Iran. Teicher accompanied former national security adviser Robert C. McFarlane on his May 1986 trip to Iran. Teicher resigned from the NSC staff in December 1986.

John Tower, chairman of the President's Special Review Board (Tower Commission), established by Reagan in November 1986 to investigate the National Security Council staff's role in the Iran-contra affair. A Republican senator from Texas during 1961 to 1985, Tower chaired the Armed Services Committee. His conservative credentials and hard-line approach helped protect the panel's work from right-wing criticism.

Lawrence E. Walsh, independent counsel appointed in December 1986 by a special three-judge panel to investigate and, if warranted, to prosecute alleged violations of federal criminal laws by Lt. Col. Oliver L. North and other Iran-contra participants. An attorney with an Oklahoma law firm, Walsh had been appointed to several positions during the Eisenhower and Nixon administrations, including federal district judge, diplomat, and deputy attorney general.

Col. Samuel J. Watson, deputy national security adviser to Vice President George Bush. Watson, with Bush aide Donald P. Gregg, had numerous contacts with Felix I. Rodriguez, who helped coordinate the contra supply effort.

William H. Webster, director of the CIA, replacing William J. Casey who resigned in February 1987. Reagan nominated Webster in March 1987 to serve as CIA chief after Robert M. Gates's nomination for the post ran into trouble on Capitol Hill. A former federal judge and head of the FBI since 1978, Webster had earned a reputation for integrity and intelligence. The Senate overwhelmingly confirmed his nomination in May 1987.

Caspar W. Weinberger, secretary of defense. Weinberger steadfastly opposed U.S. arms sales to Iran throughout 1985 and 1986, believing that there was no "moderate" element in Iran with which to deal. He maintained that he was uninformed about the Iran arms deals and knew nothing about the diversion of profits from those sales to the Nicaraguan contras. The Tower Commission criticized Weinberger for not being more forceful in his opposition to the arms deals and for protecting his own position.

Ben B. Wickham, Jr., CIA station chief in Nicaragua from 1982 to 1984. Wickham reportedly resigned in 1985 to work for the contra aid network.

Willard I. Zucker, American lawyer living in Geneva who ran Compagnie de Services Fiduciaires SA, the financial services company that acted as banker and lawyer for the operations of retired major general Richard V. Secord and Albert Hakim.

Testimony

Following are excerpts from testimony of witnesses who appeared before congressional committees investigating the sale of arms to Iran and the diversion of funds to the Nicaraguan contras. Preliminary examinations into the Iran-contra affair were begun in 1986 by the House and Senate Intelligence committees and the House Foreign Affairs Committee. Soon after the 100th Congress convened in January 1987, the Senate officially created its special panel, the Select Committee on Secret Military Assistance to Iran and the Nicaraguan Opposition, and the House established its Select Committee to Investigate Covert Arms Transactions with Iran. *(Senate Intelligence Committee report, p. D-22)*

HOUSE INTELLIGENCE COMMITTEE

The House Intelligence Committee opened the first formal inquiry into arms sales to Iran November 21, 1986, when Director of Central Intelligence William J. Casey and other CIA, State, and Defense Department officials testified in a closed hearing, parts of which were later made public. In his testimony, Casey sidestepped the issue of whether the United States knew Israel was shipping Hawk missiles to Iran in November 1985. Following are excerpts from the declassified version of the testimony released June 26, 1987, by the House and Senate select Iran-contra committees:

CASEY: The CIA's involvement began in late November of 1985 when the agency was there asked to recommend a reliable airline that could transport bulky cargo to an unspecified location in the Middle East. This requirement specified that the carrier had to be reliable and able to move rapidly, quickly.

A proprietary of ours which regularly took on commercial ventures was designated. When the plane got to Tel Aviv the crew was informed that the cargo was spare parts for the oil fields and that it was to go to Tabriz.

Our [... classified ...] back in Washington decided that in order to protect the plane, our [... classified ...] should be asked to get flight clearances into Iran, and this was done.

On 25 Nov., 1985, the plane dropped the cargo in Tehran. To the best of our knowledge, neither the Israelis nor the Iranians knew that they were dealing with a CIA proprietary, and believed it to be just another commercial charter airliner. The airliner was paid the normal commercial rate which amounted to approximately $127,000.

This little activity was authorized by our associate deputy director for operations. I was out of the country at the time and then Deputy Director John McMahon was in charge. He approved the flight as an urgent mission in keeping with proprietary normal business, but he directed that we would not provide any future flights into Iran in the absence of a finding. This flight was done without a finding.

* * *

[Rep. Anthony C.] BEILENSON [D-Calif.]: Thank you, Mr. Chairman.

Most of the things I wanted to ask about have been asked, but let me ask a couple other things if I may.

First, I was out of the room for a couple minutes and I may have missed this, but with respect to weaponry provided to the Iranians, so far as we are directly involved and concerned it was something like 2,008 TOWs [antitank missiles].

CASEY: Yes.

BEILENSON: And spare parts for Hawk missiles?

CASEY: That is right.

BEILENSON: Has there been beyond that through Israel, for example, any major transfers of arms to Iran?

CASEY: Well, we suspect there have been and we do know that the Israelis provided some weapons to them before we got involved, but that is in a very complicated way, some of that has been aborted, some of that has been adjusted, so that we take responsibility for the 2,008 TOWs plus the Hawk missile parts.

BEILENSON: Have the Israelis made any shipments that require notification or require permission from the U.S. before transferring to Iran, do you know?

CASEY: There was one shipment that was made in the summer of 1985 which we heard about later, that for a time in order to keep this going we waived, or didn't take action on the failure of the Israelis to get the necessary permission and we have since I believe straightened that out.

BEILENSON: Have we replenished the Israelis?

CASEY: We have replenished the Israelis, yes, one shipment they made was replenished.

BEILENSON: Just that one?

CASEY: Yes.

* * *

[Rep. Lee H.] HAMILTON [D-Ind.]: The president did not approve any arms shipments by Israel directly into Iran?

[Charles] ALLEN [national intelligence officer for counterterrorism and narcotics]: We don't know.

[Clair] GEORGE [CIA deputy director for operations]: We don't know.

ALLEN: We don't know that and—

GEORGE: What do you mean we don't know it?

ALLEN: We don't know.

HAMILTON: You mean the president hasn't told you?

ALLEN: We have no knowledge of that as part of this project whatsoever.

GEORGE: We received the missiles, we transported them to Israel and away they go. We don't know whether or what transpires. We bring them to Kelly Air Force Base I should say.

CASEY: I don't have the details on this at my command, Mr. Chairman, but there was a shipment, the Israelis made a shipment in violation, a shipment which violated our law and I think for a time we didn't do anything about it and later on we required that the Israelis correct that. Just how that was done I don't have that at my fingertips.

HAMILTON: Have we asked the Israelis how much they have shipped to Iran?

CASEY: I don't think so. Do you know, Mike?

[Michael H.] ARMACOST [under secretary of state for political affairs]: In our contacts, Mr. Chairman, we have normally been approaching them as we have approached many countries on Operation Staunch, requesting that no arms be shipped and the general answer we have in our diplomatic engagement has been that as a government they are not shipping any arms, although there is occasionally a caveat they are not entirely sure that some private activity might not be taking place.

[Rep. Robert A.] ROE [D-N.J.]: Will the chairman yield?

HAMILTON: I yield.

ROE: I am curious on the point, how do we monitor, how does the United States monitor exactly what the chairman is saying, the transshipment, when we made an agreement with a country that they cannot go to a third country? How do we monitor that, or do we monitor that, and not only in Israel. And how do we monitor the third country shipment?

[Richard L.] ARMITAGE [assistant secretary of defense for international security affairs]: Usually with the security people, and they don't, they don't go out and do a hands-on inspection. Generally when equipment is used in an offensive way or transferred to third countries, we find out about it from the country to which it is transferred or from whoever is on the receiving end of offensive use of the weapon. That is what triggers our consultations with the Congress.

ARMACOST: In the case of the Operation Staunch directed against Iran, [. . . classified . . .] when we find a shipment is going in we have made representations to the country concerned.

HAMILTON: Are you aware of any shipments by Israel to Iran of American military equipment?

ARMACOST: I think I—

HAMILTON: Other than the ones stated here?

ARMACOST: I have heard about two recently, and I was otherwise unaware, the September and November shipments. Other than that, it has been our supposition there is quite a lot going on but I am not aware of any specific shipments and we have not been able to pin that down.

HOUSE FOREIGN AFFAIRS COMMITTEE

Following are excerpts from the New York Times *text of the December 8, 1986, testimony of Secretary of State George P. Shultz and from the* Washington Post *text of*

the December 8, 1986, testimony of former national security adviser Robert C. McFarlane before the House Foreign Affairs Committee:

George P. Shultz

. . . You asked in one way or another about my role in the diversion of funds for aid to the Nicaraguan resistance. My role in that was zero. I knew nothing about it, until it came out. So I don't have anything that I can contribute to your deliberations on exactly how that came about. . . .

The hearings you are holding . . . come at a crucial point for the nation. The president has recognized that serious problems have been created on our conduct of foreign affairs by the manner in which some individuals implemented our effort to establish better contacts with Iran, and by the diversion of funds from arms sales to the Nicaraguan democratic resistance.

He has taken the lead in rectifying any problems that may exist. . . .

I want to put to rest now any doubt as to my readiness to respond to questions about my prior knowledge and activity. I have already made all the information at my disposal available to the FBI. I have been interviewed by the Department of Justice. I am ready in this open session to bring forward all the materials I properly can, and at whatever appropriate time you choose I am prepared to make a statement and to answer questions in closed session, giving classified details of my knowledge and activities. . . .

Reagan's Foreign Policy Leadership

Where do we stand after six years of President Reagan's leadership in foreign affairs? Working with Congress and with the broad support of the American people, President Reagan's policies have brought us to a threshold of a new and remarkably different world, a world in which America's interests, America's pride and America's ideals are flourishing. . . .

Only a few years ago, the democracies of the world were believed to be an embattled, shrinking handful of nations. Today, people struggling under oppressive regimes of the right and the left can see democracy as a vital force for the future. Vital but nonviolent movements toward more open societies have succeeded. The failure of closed, command economies is more evident every day. A new wind of change is blowing. People who are ready to stand up for freedom and have no choice but to fight for their rights now know that communism's march is not inevitable.

President Reagan is a freedom fighter and the world knows it. And I stand with Ronald Reagan. Strong defenses, sound alliances and support for the free economic and political development of peoples everywhere, that's what President Reagan stands for. His policies are not the policies of a party, they are the policies of all the American people. They are inevitable policies if our country is to remain the best and greatest on Earth, and the hope of humanity everywhere. . . .

Shultz's Opposition

Q: Now, it has been alleged that you were opposed to this Iranian initiative. . . . If you were, did you convey your concern to the president and, if you did, when did you do it?

A: I conveyed my concerns on many occasions, in two full meetings, on another occasion, according to my records, and I don't think anyone involved in this is under any illusion whatever about my views. . . .

I supported and continue to support, as my statement indicates, the idea of trying to see if we can't rearrange the furniture a little bit insofar as Iran is concerned. And there are various ways to try to do that which I support, and which is the president's basic intent. So I support his policy. However, when it comes to the use of arms, I have a different view. But I do believe that it's a legitimate subject for debate as a policy matter. The president listened to views, pro and con, and he has said publicly that in the end he decided that he should send a signal—I think that was his word—to Iran to show our serious intent. And so he authorized some arms shipments to Iran for that purpose. . . .

Soliciting Foreign Contributions

Q: Over the weekend, we read about the Sultan of Brunei contributing large sums of money into a secret Swiss bank account to support the contras. I wonder how many other Third World countries have done the same thing, who has control of this fund and who handles it, basically? What knowledge do you have on that particular fund that circumvents what I believe the spirit of the law in support of the contra effort in Nicaragua?

A: First of all, it would not be proper for me to talk about any particular third country and so I will not do that. I did see a report in the press that during a visit to Brunei last summer, I raised this issue, or sold the Sultan on transferring funds. That is not correct. I did visit Brunei, it was the only ASEAN [Association of Southeast Asian Nations] country that I had not visited and I wanted to visit each of them, just as I try to stop in the Pacific island states . . . on that same trip. But there were no conversations with any Bruneian during that visit by me of this matter.

'Perfectly Proper Activity'

Having said that, let me go on and say—first reminding you that in August 1985, Congress approved $27 million in humanitarian aid for the Nicaraguan democratic resistance. The funds were appropriated in December for obligation through March 31, 1986. At the time the Congress expressly confirmed that, in addition to expending this $27 million the law did not preclude—I'm quoting from the law that you passed—"activities of the Department of State to solicit such humanitarian assistance for the Nicaraguan democratic resistance." So it was a perfectly proper activity for the Department of State, for me, to do that. There's nothing illegal about it, there's nothing improper about it. . . .

We went about it very carefully and considered it last summer because, with the delays, you remember, in enacting the final appropriations—even though both houses had voted—the resistance was having great trouble. They were incurring debts, they didn't have funds. And so, in discussions with Assistant Secretary [Elliott] Abrams, we tried to think through where we might properly solicit some funds. We wanted to be very careful that we lived completely by the spirit, let alone the letter, of the law and didn't get involved with a country where it might be thought that we had tremendous leverage, say, because of our aid program or something of that kind. So we were very, very careful about that.

And we did successfully persuade one government to make a contribution. So that is what we did. The discussions with the government were conducted by Assistant Secretary Abrams, but with my authority explicitly. . . .

Error of Shipping Arms

Q: I have two things I'd like you to comment on. Mr. [Robert C.] McFarlane has said publicly, "I talked to the secretary of state repeatedly and often of every item in the relationship with Iran."

And secondly, I'd like you to clarify for me what the administration believes the mistakes to have been. . . . Was the mistake in supplying arms to Iran? Was the mistake in diverting funds to the contras? Was the mistake in not informing the Congress. . . ?

A: Well, very clearly it was a mistake to get involved in the illegal arms transfer—or funds transfer.

Q: To the contras?

A: To the extent—I don't know the ins and outs of that, I don't want to act like a judge passing judgment on what happened. I don't have the facts. But from what I have seen and what the attorney general said, some things took place that were illegal. And so that's clearly a mistake. I might say it's not only a mistake because it's illegal but it has—it has confused the situation insofar as our support for the Nicaraguan resistance is concerned. And unfairly to them, because they have no part in that. And so it's a mistake from that standpoint as well.

Shultz's Knowledge of Shipments

I do not know in detail—in fact, I don't know much at all—about the arms transfers that apparently took place in the calendar year 1986. I know more about what took place during 1985, and I'm prepared in a closed session, based on documents that I have, cable traffic and notes that were taken at the time—and I don't claim that my notes encompass everything that I knew, but I've tried to stick in what I've prepared for a closed session to things that I could be pretty confident of. Recognizing that in these things, when you go into them and you are questioned and people remind you of this or that, it jogs your memory.

But at any rate, I knew that arms transfers to Iran were periodically considered after June 1985 as part of an effort to improve relations with Iran and secure the release of our hostages. There was a lot—there was considerable discussion between Mr. McFarlane and I about that, and at least on one occasion that I distinctly recall, with the president.

I learned not as a result of being involved in the development of the plan but, so to speak, as a plan was about to be implemented. I learned in various ways of two proposed transfers during 1985, but I was never informed and had the impression that they were not consummated. I later learned—heard—that one shipment had misfired, that is, it had been delivered but due to Iranian rejection of the arms involved, was not—not consummated.

I knew that in December 1985, following a full-scale discussion of this matter with the president, that we instructed a mission that talked with the Iranians that were being—that were the interlocutors, or representing themselves as the interlocutors—they were told on instructions that we would engage the Iranians in a dialogue if they release our hostages but that we would not sell them arms. That was an explicit part of the instruction that the president had authorized.

So there was, you might say, a period of time from more or less the middle of 1985 until this period following the December meeting in which there was a fair amount of discussion of the subject—and I expressed my views during that period—in which some things were apparently structured. I can't tell you exactly how, but which, so far as I could see, never came off. And at the end of this process, after a full discussion, wanting to see the dialogue with Iran continue but not—but having become convinced that there shouldn't be an arms transfer connected with it, the instructions that I referred to were the instructions of the mission. . . .

The subject was reviewed again by the president in a full-scale meeting in January of 1986. This was not a meeting in which an explicit decision was stated. People made arguments, I made my arguments.

However, I could fairly conclude from the meeting that the point of view that I thought had prevailed in December was not—didn't seem to be prevailing. But it wasn't as though there was some sharp decision.

I learned in November that a finding was made authorizing among other things arms sales, but I was not informed of that finding at the time so I can't tell you anything about the thinking that went into the finding as such. That came as a—

Q: The finding was in January, Mr. Secretary.

A: The finding was in January, and I was notified of it at about the same time you were notified of it. I did not learn about any transfers of arms during 1986 in a direct way. But, as is always the case, you have bits and pieces of evidence float in and so I weighed in on the basis of that, restating my views. What I heard was conflicting: at times that there was some sort of deal or signal in the works, and at other times that the operation was closed down. And, in fact, the word used at one time with me was that the people involved had been told to stand down.

So, again, there was this ambiguity from my standpoint. I would say to you that I did take the position in part because of all the problems that we have with leaks, and recognizing that if the president's initiative had any chance of success it would have to be a secret initiative for all the reasons that have been developed—perfectly good reasons. That whenever I would be called upon to do something to carry out those policies, I needed to know, but I didn't need to know things that were not in my sphere to do something about.

'Back Channel' Messages

Now this past weekend, our ambassador in Beirut, Mr. John Kelly, responded to an all-posts directive that we put out. We put out a directive from the State Department—I don't have the date of it but shortly after this investigation started—telling our posts to discover anything that they had about this, to secure it and to make it available here in Washington. So I got a response from Mr. John Kelly and I will read his response.

"I met in Washington in July or August 1986 with Robert McFarlane, who briefed me on the hostage negotiations involving arms to Iran as an inducement. Between the dates of Oct. 30 and Nov. 4, 1986, I had numerous conversations with Lt. Col. Oliver North and Richard V. Secord, relating to the hostage negotiations with Iran. During that period, I received and sent numerous 'back channel' messages to and from the White House, Admiral Poindexter, concerning the hostage negotiations. Those messages were transmitted and received in what is referred to as the 'privacy channel,' using CIA communications facilities.

"In accordance with our standard practice at Embassy Beirut"—which they have to do, given the situation there—"all of that message traffic was destroyed thereafter, at my direction." That is a standing order in a post like Beirut; nothing wrong with that. "I would assume that copies may be available at CIA headquarters or at the White House situation room. With regard to my conversations with McFarlane, North and Secord, I stand ready to discuss them with appropriate officials upon the Department's direction."

I have instructed Ambassador Kelly to return to Washington immediately, bringing with him all records of such activities, to be available to the FBI and other appropriate investigative bodies. I am, to put it mildly, shocked to learn this, after the event, from an ambassador, but at any rate, I'm just reading you this report.

Agreed with Reagan's Objective

Throughout the entire period, I opposed the transfer of arms to Iran until Iran stopped the war in the Gulf, ended its support for terrorism and obtained the release of the hostages. Throughout the entire period, I fully agreed with the president's objective of finding a way to modify Iran's behavior in a manner consistent with our strategic interests, and those of our friends in the region and around the world.

The president has confirmed publicly that he believed in principle, in the light of all the circumstances, that we should use a limited amount of arms to send a signal. There are legitimate arguments to be made in favor of this decision and the president has made them. And I fully accept their legitimacy, and the legitimacy and propriety of the president's decision, and right to make that decision, and support that.

It's difficult for me to talk about particular incidents without violating security requirements, to give you a full accounting—which, as I've said, I'm perfectly prepared to do. But it must be done in a way that is proper. But I believe a review of the classified record, if you go through it with me, will support the statements that I have made. And it will also show that my knowledge of what took place was sporadic and fragmentary, and materially incomplete. So I'm not the witness to tell you all of the things that took place because I'm not informed.

Insofar as any question—I'm repeating, but I want to repeat—any question of diversion of funds to support the Nicaraguan democratic resistance, my knowledge was not fragmentary, it was non-existent....

State Department's Involvement

Q: Did the Inter-American Affairs Bureau at State have any knowledge of, or was it involved in the coordination of, funds for the contras from the Iran arms sales?

A: No.

Q: Was the bureau aware of any—

A: Let me say, not to their knowledge. If there were some funds put somewhere, that were useful, then they were trying to provide, properly, humanitarian aid when that was authorized.

And, since the $100 million authorized, they've been involved in that. And there is an explicit congressional mandate for the State Department to play a strong role in that, and we're trying to do that. But nobody in our bureau, that I know of—and I'm certain Elliott Abrams and his group had no knowledge of this Iranian funds transfer question at all. Zero.

Q: Well, was the bureau aware of the method by which the contras were receiving lethal aid during the period in which the Boland amendment was in effect?

A: We are—we don't presume to know everything that a person may do somewhere in the government. It was clear that—from private sources, presumably—some aid was flowing to the people fighting for freedom and independence in Nicaragua. And personally, I applaud that. There's a lot of aid flowing from America to the Nicaraguan communists, quite a few Americans down there. That's their right to be. And it shouldn't be surprising that there are Americans who want to help the people fighting for freedom.

Q: To what extent do intelligence operatives from other agencies apprise the bureau of their activities with respect to coordinating funding for contra operations, and does the assistant secretary for inter-American affairs receive such reports?

A: He does, and he chairs the inter-agency group that includes people from all of the agencies involved whose task it is to evaluate what is going on and to make recommendations, if needed, for new legislation or what our policy should be, and to oversee the tactics involved.

Q: . . . Are you apprised on a regular basis of the department's involvement in contra operations by Assistant Secretary Abrams, and do these reports include summaries of the intelligence community's operations?

A: Well, I see reports from time to time. I see Elliott Abrams frequently. And so I try to keep abreast of what is going on, as best I can. . . .

Q: Can you tell us whether you were under any constraint, or whether the department was under any constraint, not to reveal any of the information with regard to the Iranian arms sales?

A: No. We were, of course, bound by the decisions that would be made about something that was to be held in confidence. But as far as our measuring up to our responsibilities were concerned, we were engaged, you might say, in an argument about what should be done. And there were these incidents that came along that I have pointed up for you, without being in a position to—for various reasons; partly lack of knowledge, partly because of the nature of the open hearing here—to give you full information about them.

Necessity to Consult Congress

Q: But once the project was under way, didn't you feel that the department had a necessity of consulting with the Congress with regard to these initiatives?

A: Well, I don't feel that we should sort of bring all our internal debates to the Congress, particularly on something like this. Of course, policy toward Iran, policy toward terrorism, all of these basic things that have been laid out, we have discussed here in the committee many times.

Q: . . . Once that was under way and some of that was brought to the department's attention, wasn't there then a responsibility to the department to consult with Congress?

A: Well, perhaps so. I don't—I'm not here to claim that my actions in all of this were all that they should be. You'll have to judge that for yourself. And I can tell you what I knew and what I didn't.

Chain of Command

Q: You mention Ambassador Kelly's report to the CIA but a failure to report to your office. Is that an unusual or a unique situation, or something that's in violation of any of the State Department's regulations?

A: I hope it's unique. Ambassadors—there is supposed to be, I say supposed to be—a chain of command that goes from the president, to me—not to the NSC, to me—and through the assistant secretary, by and large, to the ambassador. That's the chain of command.

Q: And was that a violation, sir?

A: And if something comes up that causes an ambassador to go outside the chain of command, there needs to be a good reason. Now it may be very well that Ambassador Kelly will say that he was told on the authority of the president that he was supposed to do this and that. And I would think that he would have checked with me to see if that were so.

Q: Who would enable such an ambassador to waive that responsibility?

A: At this point, all I can tell you is the cable that I got. I don't consider it a satisfactory situation.

I do have to—I think we should recognize, however, what life is like in Washington. Now, come on, here we are. And who was it? The Canadian ambassador coined the phrase, "It's never over." Nothing ever gets settled in this town. It's not like running a company, or even a university. It's—it's a seething debating society in which the debate never stops, in which people never give up, including me. And so that's the atmosphere in which you administer. And what I try to do is stay as close to the president as I can, and I feel very close to him. And I admire and respect him tremendously. I think he has transformed the situation, done a marvelous job. And I try to stay very close to him and I support his policies.

I don't win every argument, by a long shot, but I am in the argument. And when the president decides something, then I do my best to make it work....

Damage to U.S. Credibility

Q: For six years the administration has said it would never yield to the demands of terrorists, pay ransom for hostages, or sell arms to states that sponsor and support terrorism. It now turns out that we've done all three. How could this have happened? How much damage has it done to our credibility, and what assurance can you give us that it won't happen again?

A: Well, the president decided to give a signal. I'm just quoting the president here, and he's made a public statement of what he authorized and why. And he has acknowledged that in doing so he recognized that there were risks as well as potential benefits, and he had to weigh that. And right now, because of the way this has blown up, the emphasis is all on the risks. I dare say that if somehow we had our hostages all returned, and we saw a different kind of situation in one way or another emerging in Iran, and this came out, people would say, well, the president showed guts....

Perot Ransom Payment

Q: Were you consulted or informed about the request of Lt. Col. North to Ross Perot to pay $2 million in ransom money for the release of our hostages? And is it conceivable to you that Lt. Col. North would have made such a request without the approval of the president or some higher authority?

A: I was not informed. And, so far as I know, the president wasn't informed. But I have no knowledge about Lt. Col. North's activities in this regard. I think the offer of Mr. Perot, if that is what took place—I don't know, I just read about it—I think it's outrageous.

A Constitutional Confrontation?

Q: ... In the past when those of us have differed with you, the issues have entirely been those of judgment and policy. It appears today we have a political crisis that's become a constitutional confrontation.

A: I don't believe it's a constitutional confrontation at all. What the president has done is—is move out people who seem to be involved, he has put in a new and outstanding National Security Council director, he has appointed—or asked for the appointment of a special prosecutor. He has said that he will make available to the Congress, and instructed me to come here and talk to you. Where is the constitutional crisis? There is no constitutional crisis....

Foreign Policy Duplicity

Q: ... Now as the Cabinet officer who is responsible for the conduct of this nation's foreign policy, if you are telling us this morning—and I believe all of us feel you're stating the truth—that your role was zero, or non-existent, then how is it—

A: My role was non-existent insofar as the apparent reported use of funds generated by sales of arms to Iran and the diversion of those funds to help the Nicaraguan resistance. I knew nothing about that. I did not say that I knew nothing about any of the other things. On the contrary, I tried to tell you what I knew about it.

Q: I appreciate that clarification. But nonetheless, many of these activities were directly contrary to stated policies of our government. My question is, how is it possible for this duplicitous activity to go on? In other words, how is it possible that another agency, aside from the State Department, is engaged in activity, or operations, that are contrary to the official policy of the United States? Shouldn't the State Department assert its natural, constitutional, proper role over the conduct of the foreign policy so we don't end up with contradictory policies that possibly confuse not only our allies but people here in America?

A: First of all, the president made a public statement explaining his reasoning for sending a signal. A signal involving arms transfers that you have characterized in various ways and which have been widely characterized as such.

There is a whole other side to that argument which the president presented, explaining to the American people and to you why he decided to send that signal. Knowing full well the risks involved but seeking an objective that, if it could be achieved I'm sure everybody would applaud. So that's the decision that the president made, legitimately.

Now insofar as the State Department is concerned, I believe it is correct to say that we do not have a foreign policy in the State Department. The president has a foreign policy. I work for the president and we are engaged in a process—and I am by directive and by common understanding and, I hope, by my association with the president—principal foreign policy adviser to him. But it is the president's policy....

Robert C. McFarlane

It wasn't until the summer of last year that [moderate political] elements surfaced [in Iran] and we became aware that elements that were both in the government and close to it as advisers wanted to know whether the United States had any interest in such a discourse.

The elements making the proposal from within Iran, high officials, made clear that for them to be able to sustain that dialogue and over time exert any influence to change policy within Iran, they would need to strengthen themselves. And in their terms this would require them to reach out to elements within the military, the revolutionary guards, or both and that the currency of that undertaking was arms....

The president acknowledged, faced with this opportunity, that any elements within Iran who truly were committed to change and reform were certainly going to be very vulnerable.

And he acknowledged that the transfer, indirectly, of weapons to support these individuals and allow them to build a constituency would indeed not be a violation of policy but to the extent that it dealt with people who opposed Iranian policy, opposed terrorism, that modest levels which could not affect the balance in the war with Iraq nor could be applied to terrorist undertakings would be sensible....

Q: Did you ever receive any instructions ... not to inform the House or Senate select committees on intelligence of the Iranian initiative or related activities?

A: Never in my recollection did I have any explicit proscription of that.... But I understand after I left that there were other decisions taken....

Q: [McFarlane was asked for comment on a news article stating that President Reagan gave general authorization to proceed with sale or resale of arms as early as fall 1985.]

A: ... In sum, to say that the president authorized the indirect delivery of small levels of arms to Iran for the purpose of strengthening elements that were against terrorism and that that was communicated ultimately to the Iranian authorities and that in the conduct of that, that certain transfers occurred, which were reviewed again in December of last year.

Q: When did that authorization occur?

A: In August of 1985....

Q: Was it your understanding at the time that these weapons, be they offensive or defensive, would be utilized to allow Iran to continue its war with Iraq?

A: No.

Q: What was your understanding...?

A: Well, sir, the value, the utility of these systems, which could not have had a significant effect on the war, was it engendered the political figures involved to be able to consolidate more of a power base within Iran.

Q: In any of your conversations with the president or any other White House representatives, did you ever discuss the issue of diversion of payments from Iran to the Nicaraguan contras?

A: No.

Q: Did you ever discuss with the president the component that hostage negotiations played in this policy?

A: Yes.... It seemed to me that after two or three months, roughly in November ... there was a skewing of the emphasis toward the hostages and, as important as they are, the more fundamental issue was the political stability of [the] U.S.-Iranian relationship. I recommended that we reorient it as originally planned and start dealing directly with the Iranians and make clear that we could not be party to the transfer of U.S. weapons. The president agreed....

Q: I'm very curious as to how it's possible ... for a lieutenant colonel on the NSC staff to have the authority by himself to divert millions of dollars in arms sales to aid to the contras....

A: The events ... occurred after I left the government, and I can't really account for how a diversion such as has been alleged could have occurred.

Q: Is it possible?

A: Of course, it's theoretically possible. As to whether it is plausible ... I can only comment on the basis of my knowledge of the individuals concerned.... Lt. Col. [Oliver L.] North is a person of integrity ... and thus would not have acted contrary to U.S. law, nor would he have taken initiatives without higher authority. Similarly, Adm. [John M.] Poindexter is a man of integrity ... and it seems to me very, very unlikely he would have acted in any way contrary to law....

Q: When did you first learn of this diversion of funds?

A: ... From the Iranian relationship to Central American accounts in May of this year in connection with a mission I was asked to undertake to Iran. Either en route or returning, I was advised in a very summary fashion that the U.S. government had applied certain Iranian funds to Central American programs.... I took it to have been a matter of established approved policy sanctioned by higher authority than the officer who conveyed it, who was Lt. Col. North....

Q: On that flight back from Tehran, when you learned first of the diversion of funds ... did you ask Lt. Col. North whether he was acting on the authority of the president or a person of higher rank....

A: No....

Q: Did you say, "Ollie, you're breaking the law"...?

A: When you are told in a very brief space of time a finding has been approved which allows the transfer of arms, that some have been transferred, further that no hostages have come out and yet an arrangement is now in place for all of them to come, and the government is applying some of these monies to Central America—the several elements here were all elements with which I had no knowledge prior to the time but were presented as elements

within an integral whole which ... did not seem to me to be at the time a matter where the authority did not exist.

Q: Who ... could have directed Adm. Poindexter to allow Lt. Col. North to take such action?

A: I firmly believe that the president did not know of and did not approve of such actions. I also ... find it hard to imagine that Adm. Poindexter did....

Q: I'm a little puzzled about how these weapons got to the military in Iran without the leaders knowing about it.

A: That is a central question to be answered ... best ... in a closed session.... I think you can be very confident that very high-level officials within the Iranian government were both aware of and supportive of this entire initiative. We certainly would not have undertaken it with people of lesser standing....

Q: When you had discussions with those moderate elements, did you raise [the] issue of their bringing forward hostages ... to prove their good faith?

A: Yes.

Q: What then did you ask them to do other than that? Did you think that by opening the channels and asking them to get out the hostages we were then dealing with moderate elements which would justify a policy exception which would leave in shambles every single policy which we had in place? ...

A: I didn't have any of those thoughts in mind.... I believe it is not in United States' interests to have the eternal enmity of ... Iran. It's plausible to believe that some in Iran ... might also agree....

Q: Isn't it true that you actually resigned your NSC directorship in order to perpetuate this policy as a private citizen?

A: That is absolutely false and an outrageous statement....

Q: The *Miami Herald* has been carrying a story ... that there had been knowledge prior to the condoning of the transshipment of American arms through Israel to Iran.... Was [there] any discussion of the appropriateness of the transshipment with [knowledge] that Iran had in fact paid for the blowing up of the Marine barracks?

A: At the time of the attack on the barracks in October of '83, the reports that elements within Lebanon that had links to Iran might well have been responsible....

Q: On the trip to or from Iran, did Lt. Col. North also tell you he had asked Ross Perot to make a $2 million ransom payment?

A: ... In the return, when we made an intervening stop in the Middle East ... I was advised on whether or not Lt. Col. North planned to travel to another location at the time. In context, the issue ... was to see whether a separate and entirely distinct effort ... was maturing or working out or not. I was advised at the time that it involved Mr. Perot. The nitty-gritty of it I wasn't advised of.

Q: Were you told that it involved the payment of ransom?

A: No, in the way it was portrayed to me, it wasn't a ransom. My impression was that it involved sources and source payments ... but it wasn't a matter of dealing directly with the captors.

Q: ... Would it be fair to say that it was your view at the time that this decision to divert funds from Iran to the contras must have been approved by the president himself?

A: No ... I have described a model of decision-making that existed when I was in the government, but I don't know how decisions were reached since....

Q: Would it have been conceivable to you that the policy could have been approved without the approval of the president?

A: It is conceivable....

Q: The finding ... in August of last year by the president—you said it was an oral finding. And as I understand it, that was a finding which allowed, which constituted the formal approval in your judgment by this government at the proper level of authority and in the proper manner, to approve the shipment of arms from Israel to Iran in August of 1985. Is that correct?

A: I'd be glad to deal with the countries involved in a closed session.... The thrust of your point is correct, that the president in August provided the decision basis for events that followed.

Q: Am I correct in my recollection that you said it was an oral finding by the president...?

A: That's correct.

Q: Can you tell us in whose presence. . . ?

A: The decision followed consultation and advice by the president with his Cabinet officers—the secretary of state, defense, the chief of staff, the director of central intelligence, myself.

Q: To whom did the president orally convey this finding?

A: To me and . . . his Cabinet officers in separate but related talks . . . one-on-one or in groups.

Q: Can we assume that . . . every statutory member at least of the National Security Council was made aware at that time. . . ?

A: I believe you can. . . .

Q: This had the effect of authorizing the transfer of U.S.-supplied weapons from a third country to Iran. Is that correct?

A: That is correct. . . .

Q: Was there a legal opinion rendered at the time with respect to that authorization?

A: The legal considerations were discussed, but in terms of something formally in writing, no, sir. . . .

Q: Was the chief of staff, Mr. [Donald T.] Regan . . . [informed] at the same time as you. . . ?

A: . . . There isn't any doubt but that each member of the NSC was involved and conscious of the course of the arguments pro and con, Mr. Regan and all others. . . .

HOUSE, SENATE SELECT COMMITTEES

Hearings before the House and Senate select Iran-contra committees began May 5, 1987, and ended August 6, 1987. Thirty-two witnesses appeared before the committees; twenty-eight testified publicly. Following are excerpts from the hearings transcripts provided by the House Office of the Clerk:

Opening Statements

Following are excerpts of the May 5, 1987, opening statements of Daniel K. Inouye, D-Hawaii, chairman of the Senate select committee, and Lee H. Hamilton, D-Ind., chairman of the House select committee:

INOUYE: . . . Ladies and gentlemen, 200 years ago, the framers of our Constitution provided for more perfect union by establishing a strong national government built on a system of checks and balances.

The Founding Fathers did not believe that effective government and checks and balances were inconsistent. On the contrary, it was their premise that no branch had such a monopoly on truth that it should be free to act with total independence.

The unique genius of the American system was that by dividing power, it promoted sound policy based on reasoned and open discourse and mutual trust between the branches. These hearings this morning and for the days to follow will examine what happened when the trust which is the lubricant of our system is breached by high officials of our government.

The story is not a pretty one. As it unfolds in these proceedings, the American people will have every right to ask how could this have happened here. And as we answer that question, the American people will have every right to demand that it will never happen again.

Indeed, it should never have happened at all.

The constitutionally mandated relationship between the Executive and Legislative Branches of this Nation has stood the test of time. It has survived the shock of civil war, outlasted the mightiest monarchies and dictatorships, and seen us successfully through the turbulence of world wars.

There is no reason this same carefully calibrated system could not have guided us through the difficult choices we faced in Central America and Iran.

The formulation of American foreign policy has always been a matter of discourse between the President and Congress. Without detracting from their own primary responsibility, Presidents have understood that Congress has an indispensable role in foreign policy.

We must ratify the treaties, confirm the major foreign policy officials, authorize and appropriate the funds and exercise the oversight. Bipartisanship in the execution of foreign policy requires prior consultation in the development of foreign policy.

In short, it is a working relationship. The President may be the senior partner in foreign policy, but he is not the sole proprietor.

Indeed, this fact was seemingly recognized by this Administration. In 1984, the Administration pledged its complete cooperation with Congress. It entered into an unambiguous agreement with the Senate Intelligence Committee promising advance notification of anticipated covert activities.

As recently as the summer of 1986, the Director of Central Intelligence reaffirmed this agreement and lauded the successful partnership that had developed between the Executive and the Intelligence Committee.

But at the very moment, these promises of cooperation, notification, and partnership were being made and reaffirmed, the secret chain of events which would explode in the Iran/contra affair was well in motion.

The story is one not of covert activity alone, but of covert foreign policy. Not secret diplomacy, which Congress has always accepted, but secret policy making, which the Constitution has always rejected.

It is a tale of working outside the system, and of utilizing irregular channels and private parties accountable to no one on matters of national security while ignoring the Congress and even the traditional agencies of executive foreign policy making.

The story is both sad and sordid; it is filled with inconsistencies and often unexplainable conduct. None of the participants emerges unblemished. People of great character and ability holding positions of trust and authority in our government were drawn into a web of deception and despair.

Congress, too, is not immune from scrutiny in these hearings. We cannot avoid asking whether appropriations bills which changed from year to year and sometimes within the same year were an effective way of controlling foreign policy.

Nor can we avoid asking whether we were vigilant enough in carrying out our oversight functions.

Let it be clear, however, that our concern in this inquiry is not with the merits of any particular policy, but with flawed policy-making processes.

Purpose of Hearings

Our hearings are neither pro-contra nor anti-contra, neither pro-Administration nor anti-Administration. We are not prosecutors; and this is not an adversarial proceeding. We meet here as American citizens, united in a common effort to find the facts lest we repeat the mistakes.

Our purpose is self-examination, not recrimination. To this end, we will deal with questions of the greatest sensitivity to our national security, questions we address precisely because we in Congress do recognize the paramount importance of foreign policy. And so we will consider in these hearings the following questions:

First, were the statutory restrictions on the United States aid to the contras violated?

Second, was Congress misled?

Third, were the Executive Branch's own internal checks and balances bypassed in policy decisions in Nicaragua and Iran?

Fourth, was there a public foreign policy and simultaneously was there a very different covert foreign policy?

Fifth, was American foreign policy privatized;

And, finally, were decisions on the most significant matters of national security driven or influenced by private profit motives?

We do not deal here with civil disagreements over the direction of U.S. foreign policy, or with the creative tensions between the branches of government.

Those are normal and healthy, and they do not end in shredding of documents. Only a contempt for law leads to altered documents and perjured statements.

By eliciting and examining the entire story, we believe our Nation will emerge stronger. We also believe that sunlight is the best disinfectant. Our country is not divided or disspirited. These hearings do not represent our democracy's weakness, but its strength. . . .

* * *

HAMILTON: . . . Let me address several questions.

First, what went wrong? Our answer to that question today must be tentative, not final. But after four months of investigation, the examination of over 100,000 documents, and the interview of hundreds of witnesses by the committees, we can begin to address that question.

These hearings will show, I believe, that many things went wrong. Significant foreign policy decisions on Iran, terrorism, Nicaragua were made in secret. For months, some individuals, in and out of government, went to great lengths to conceal activities from the Congress, from appropriate officials in the Executive Branch, and from the American people.

This excessive secrecy led policy astray. A small number of officials made policy outside the democratic process.

Secret policies, different from stated policies, cast doubt on our political process and our credibility in the eyes of Americans and friends and allies around the world.

Some officials apparently did not understand how our democracy works. Their conduct demonstrated a fundamental distrust and disrespect for democratic principles and the orderly processes of constitutional government.

Apparently, we had one policy in public and another policy in private. We said one thing to our friends and allies, and we did another.

Where the law required notice to the Congress, efforts were made to circumvent the law. When Congress inquired, it was not always told the truth.

Where Congress prohibited the involvement of government agencies, private individuals and enterprises were recruited and directed by government officials to perform prohibited activities.

Where complex decisions should have involved the expertise of many in government, a few officials relied on outsiders and even foreigners to formulate and execute American policy.

High officials did not ask the questions they should have asked. Activities were undertaken without authority. Checks and balances were ignored. Important meetings occurred without adequate preparation. Established procedures were circumvented. Accurate records were not kept, and legal questions were not addressed.

Three Phases

Secondly, what should you look for in these hearings?

These hearings will have three phases. In phase one, we will examine the policy of support for the contras. Reasonable people may differ about the wisdom of this policy, and our hearings will not address the merits of the issue.

Our concern here begins in 1984 when Congress and the President enacted the Boland Amendment. This law prohibited any agency engaged in intelligence activities from spending money in direct or indirect support of the contras.

These hearings will be devoted to finding out what was done during the period that the Boland Amendment was in effect to supply the contras.

By whom was it done and at whose direction? What funds were raised? Who raised them? Where did they come from, and how were they spent? What was the involvement of high officials, and what did they know about the contra supply operation?

In phase two, we will examine the series of secret arms sales to Iran. We will try to find out how this policy began, why it contin-

ued, how it became a change of arms for hostages, and what happened to the proceeds from the sales. We will want to know who was involved, what they did, at whose direction they acted, and whom they kept informed.

In phase three, we will try to assess responsibility. Who was responsible for devising these policies and supervising their execution? Did high officials abdicate responsibilities? Were high officials misinformed and misled? What was the extent of the President's knowledge and involvement?

The final question is what do we hope to achieve in these hearings? We are here to investigate and to inform, not to prosecute. We will follow the facts where they lead.

We do not seek radical change. We seek to restore the established and constitutional ways of doing the nation's business. We seek to show that these misdeeds are not the way we do business in this country.

These joint hearings are a part and only a part of the process of discovering truth about these events. Others have investigated, and we build upon their work.

As we have better understood these events, changes have already been made in the way we conduct our nation's business. More changes will be made. Our constitutional process is working, and the purpose of these hearings is to contribute to the self-cleansing process of our democracy.

We have no desire to prolong these hearings. We, too, want to get back to the work on other important matters on the congressional agenda, but we do have a constitutional responsibility to fulfill. We want to carry out that responsibility carefully, fairly, and faithfully.

Our system of government is effective only if it enjoys respect and trust, and this inquiry will achieve its purpose if we can contribute to rebuilding that respect and trust. . . .

Richard V. Secord

Following are excerpts from the May 5, 1987, testimony of retired Air Force major general Richard V. Secord. A key player in the Iran-contra affair, Secord helped to arrange the shipment from Israel to Iran of Hawk antiaircraft missiles in November 1985. He also ran a private contra-aid network.

SECORD: . . . In the summer of 1984, and again in November of 1985, the current Administration asked me for assistance. On each occasion, first with respect to the contras and later in connection with the Iran initiative, I responded to the request for help. I made no secret then and make no secret now of my view that containment of the Sandinista regime and our relations with Iran should be subjects of vital and strategic interest to the United States.

In these undertakings, I coordinated my efforts with various government officials, and I asked other men to assist me in their private capacity.

All of them worked long and difficult hours. Many worked in the face of constant danger, some died. There was indeed compensation paid to the private parties, but no one undertook these missions for compensation alone.

We believed very much in the significance of what we were doing and that our conduct was in furtherance of the President's policies.

I also understood that this Administration knew of my conduct and approved it. I feel exactly the same about the men in government with whom I was in contact.

It should come as no surprise that I have a great deal of respect and admiration for [Rear] Adm. [John M.] Poindexter and for Lt. Col. [Oliver L.] North.

They are both dedicated and honest men who in my view tried diligently and conscientiously to carry out the policies of the President in an appropriate manner.

All of us have had to suffer and endure a painful assault upon our motives and integrity inspired by incredible misinformation and speculation mainly in the media.

Principally, for this reason, and out of respect for the men whom I invited to join with me, as well as the request of this committee to come forward, I have decided to set the record straight to the best of my ability and to testify voluntarily without any immunity whatsoever.

It is my hope that the members of this committee and my fellow Americans will suspend judgment, not only about us, but also about the objectives and the policies we were pursuing, until after all the facts are placed upon the record.

As you will shortly see, we did have some success. We also had our share of failure. But in all these endeavors, at least we tried. And I for one am not ashamed of having tried.

If we were unconventional in some of our methods, it was only because conventional wisdom had been exhausted. If we had been successful in every respect, we would not be here today.

In agreeing to testify, I have returned to the position I embraced at the time the Attorney General of the United States prematurely went public with his grossly inaccurate disclosures about our operations.

The decision of Mr. [Edwin] Meese [III] and possibly others to succumb to anxiety and ignorance is particularly unforgivable, in my judgment, in light of the fact that had he been receptive, he could have been advised of the facts surrounding these events before his announcement.

This reasonable option was rejected and we were instead betrayed, abandoned and left to defend ourselves.

In the face of that abandonment, my instincts were equally self-protective and I have refused until now to testify.

With the passage of time, I have reconsidered and I am now prepared to explain to all of you and to the American public precisely what I did.

I am ready to answer your questions, Mr. Chairman.

[Sen. Daniel K.] INOUYE [D-Hawaii]: Thank you very much, Mr. Secord.

Mr. Nields, please proceed.

[John W.] NIELDS [Jr., House committee chief counsel]: Thank you, Mr. Chairman.

Mr. Secord, I take it there came a time in November of 1985 when you became involved in the sale of military, U.S. military equipment to Iran.

SECORD: That is correct.

NIELDS: Was that something you were asked to do or something that you volunteered for?

SECORD: I was asked by Lt. Col. North to assist.

NIELDS: Did that request come orally or in writing, or both?

SECORD: Both.

* * *

NIELDS: Mr. Secord, the letter [from Robert C. McFarlane, former national security adviser, to Secord] begins, "Your discreet assistance is again required in support of our national interests." Had your assistance been required earlier, in support of our national interests?

SECORD: One year earlier, in 1984, I had been asked if I would be interested in trying to assist the contras.

NIELDS: And who asked you if you were interested in that?

SECORD: Col. North.

NIELDS: And were you, in fact, involved in assisting the contras in November of 1985, at the time you received this letter?

SECORD: Yes.

NIELDS: What was the nature of the project that you were then engaged in having to do with the contras?

SECORD: In November of 1985, I was at the very beginning of a complex project we referred to as the "airlift project," a project which was designed to ultimately make airdrops, parachute airdrops to various contra forces.

NIELDS: In Nicaragua?

SECORD: In Nicaragua.

Tracing the Money Trail

NIELDS: Now Mr. Secord, such an operation, I take it, requires finances.

SECORD: Yes, it requires millions of dollars.

NIELDS: Where was the money supposed to come from to support this air supply operation?

SECORD: The money was coming from donated funds and these funds were coming, as I understand it, from private individuals and from some friendly countries.

NIELDS: And where were these monies being put?

SECORD: In November of 1985 they were being deposited in a Swiss bank account in favor of a company, a Panamanian company, Lake Resources Inc.

NIELDS: And who controlled the Lake Resources Inc. account?

SECORD: Mr. Albert Hakim was the person who was in control of this account and others that were created for various support purposes—but there was, at my request, and really under my oral direction.

NIELDS: And was Mr. Hakim then a business associate of yours?

SECORD: Yes, he was.

NIELDS: How did the donors know where to put the money, to your knowledge.

SECORD: I gave the account's name and number to Col. North and he, in turn gave it to whoever was interested.

NIELDS: I take it then, Mr. Secord, that at the time you received this letter requesting your assistance on the Iranian initiative, there was then in existence in Switzerland a bank account containing money for the benefit of the contras.

And that bank account was Lake Resources.

SECORD: Yes.

NIELDS: At a later point in time, February of 1986, and forward, were the proceeds of arms sales to Iran also put into the same Lake Resources bank account?

SECORD: Yes, they were.

NIELDS: What was the total amount of money representing the purchase price of arms sold to Iran that was put into the Lake Resources or related Swiss bank accounts?

SECORD: Something over $30 million.

NIELDS: I take it by your answer that means something just a very little bit over $30 million?

SECORD: Yes.

NIELDS: So if you were speaking in round numbers, it would be $30 million?

SECORD: Yes, sir.

NIELDS: How much money was paid, to your knowledge, either directly or indirectly to the United States Treasury out of that money?

SECORD: I believe it was about $12.3 million.

NIELDS: So in round numbers, $12 million?

SECORD: $12 million.

NIELDS: I want to ask you some questions about, I think you'll agree there is a difference there of approximately $18 million. I want to ask you some questions about where that money went.

Before I do, let me ask you this. Up until a few days ago, did you have access to the records necessary to determine where that money went?

SECORD: No.

NIELDS: Who did?

SECORD: The committee, the House and Senate Select Committee had these records which they received recently from Mr. Albert Hakim.

NIELDS: So that prior to that time Mr. Hakim had the records?

SECORD: Correct.

NIELDS: Mr. Hakim identified in testimony given to this committee some eight Swiss bank accounts relating to the flow of this money that you just have been testifying about. Those records were then subpoenaed from him by the committees, both and they are now undergoing a preliminary by accountants working for the two committees.

The records reflect that there is now in the bank accounts approximately $1,360,000. In addition, Mr. Hakim has testified to the committees that $6,527,000 of this money is presently being held in an account for his benefit by a Swiss fiduciary. Those two numbers total approximately $8 million, and if you subtract that from the $18 million difference that you testified about a moment ago, that leaves $10 million presently unaccounted for.

I want to ask you what happened to that $10 million, how it was spent and again before I do, I am going to ask you whether you have been given access to printouts of the disbursements from these various bank accounts by the committee during these past few days?

SECORD: Yes, I have.

NIELDS: And have you reviewed those together with the members of the committee?

SECORD: Yes, I have.

NIELDS: Based on that review, can you give us now an approximate amount of money from the process of the sales of arms to Iran which went to the benefit of the contras?

SECORD: Based upon my review of Mr. Hakim's records, in which I identified all disbursements that I could locate, which were identified with the various contra projects, it appears that approximately $3.5 million of these funds were expended in support of the airlift project, the various contra projects.

NIELDS: How did you arrive at that number?

SECORD: By going through Mr. Hakim's records in detail and identifying the disbursements that were made for these projects.

NIELDS: And what was the total amount of disbursements that you identified from February 1986.

SECORD: Between $5 and $6 million.

NIELDS: And did you then try to determine what other sources of funds those disbursements might have come from?

SECORD: Yes. And we located donations that came in during the time frame for the contra projects of $1.649 million. In addition to that, there were in the accounts in February of 1986 some $470,000. So if you total those two numbers, you have about $2 million.

NIELDS: And you have assumed that all of that $2 million was spent on contra projects?

SECORD: It was.

NIELDS: And then the remaining amount of money that was spent on contra projects, I take it, had to come out of the proceeds of the arms sales to Iran.

SECORD: That is the method we used, that is correct.

Contra Funding

NIELDS: Can you give us a little bit more detail on the subject of just what kinds of expenditures for the benefit of the contras were made out of these bank accounts?

SECORD: The airlift project had three components to it. The procurement and the operations of the aircraft, of course. That meant two C-123K transport aircraft, two Caribou aircraft, and one light utility airplane, a Maule. So there were five aircraft to support it.

We also were required to construct an emergency landing field in one of the Central American countries. That was the second component, and the third component was the procurement of limited quantities of munitions for the purpose of troops, air drops, to the southern contras, the contras located in the southern part of Nicaragua.

NIELDS: Did you have to spend money on salaries in addition?

SECORD: Yes, of course. To support the airlift operation we spent money on salaries, fuels, spare parts, on maintenance, on support for the air crews.

NIELDS: Was there any money paid to contra leaders?

SECORD: Yes.

NIELDS: Who and how much?

SECORD: There was a monthly disbursement of $10,000 a month to one contra leader and $5,000 a month to another. That is [contra leaders, Alfonso] Robelo and [Arturo] Cruz, and on several occasions we made disbursement to Mr. Adolfo Calero's account with the FDN, the main body of the contras.

NIELDS: During this period of time were there any payments directly to Mr. Calero, past February 1986?

SECORD: I believe there were some. I would have to look at the records to refresh my memory on that point, but I think there was $200,000 disbursed during that period for the FDN contras.

NIELDS: In any event, your memory is there was $200,000 at some point in time, and you would be willing to refresh your memory on that question by further consultation with the records?

SECORD: Yes, sir.

NIELDS: Now by my calculation, after approximately $3 [and a half] or so million was spent on the contras, there is still something over $6 million which we have not yet accounted for.

How was that money spent?

SECORD: Well, there were in the vicinity—and we added these expenses up, too, by looking at Mr. Hakim's records—there were in the vicinity of $3 million spent in support of the Iran project, basically on the transportation of materials from the United States to Iran.

NIELDS: And that still leaves a little over $3 million unaccounted for.

What was that money spent on?

Let me rephrase that question.

Were there other projects on which money was spent that were neither Iran nor Nicaragua related?

SECORD: Yes. There was a requirement to procure a small ship in April of 1986, and then to operate that ship from then until the end of the year, ultimately, and that was a substantial expense.

The procurement cost was about $350,000, and there were monthly operational costs. We have not yet audited those accounts.

NIELDS: And when you said there was a requirement, was the ship bought for private purposes or was this ship bought for governmental purposes?

SECORD: This ship was bought for, initially, to be used on another government project which is not related to Iran.

NIELDS: Was it related to Nicaragua?

SECORD: No.

NIELDS: And at whose request was the ship purchased?

SECORD: I received the request from Col. North.

NIELDS: Were there any other projects or purposes for which money was spent?

SECORD: Yes. There was a $100,000 expenditure to buy radio-telephone equipment for a Caribbean country. This was a request that we received from Col. North.

And then there were expense payments made. And we have yet to determine the exact amount of these payments—made to U.S. Drug Enforcement Agency [DEA] agents who were working on a separate project to try and locate and rescue some American hostages in Lebanon.

NIELDS: How were those expense payments made?

SECORD: They were made in cash.

NIELDS: How?

SECORD: In some cases the cash was given to Col. North. He would give the money to the agents for the expense bills that they submitted, and in some cases the money was picked up by the DEA people in Europe.

NIELDS: Was any explanation ever given to you as to why the DEA agents' expenses were being paid for in cash out of Lake Resources' bank account?

SECORD: Yes. I was told that the director of the Drug Enforcement Agency had agreed to detail some agents to this project from time to time, but the expenses of these agents would have to be borne by outside financing. So, we financed it.

Unaccounted Funds

NIELDS: . . . Are there some additional expenditures that at this point in time you have not yet been able to identify the purpose of?

SECORD: That is correct.

This unquantified balance that we're talking about right now, the $2 million to $3 million, probably something on the order of $2 million, we have not yet been able to identify the other elements of overhead and expense that had to be paid out of this, and I'm sure we will get to this before too long.

NIELDS: And once again, I think I should emphasize that your answers today are approximate ones; is that correct?

SECORD: Yes, these are just approximate, based on our first audit of the accounts.

NIELDS: ... Just to review, I understand you've testified that $30 million came into these accounts, representing the purchase price of arms sold to Iran, that the cost of those goods to Lake Resources was $12 million. Am I correct so far?

SECORD: Correct.

NIELDS: Leaving a difference of $18 million.

Eight million dollars remains either in a bank or custody of a fiduciary company in Switzerland, leaving a remainder of $10 million. Of that, something over $3 [and a half] million dollars was spent for the benefit of the contras. Am I correct so far?

SECORD: Correct.

NIELDS: Leaving a difference of $6.5 million or so. And of that, approximately $3 million was spent on expenses in transporting arms to Iran, leaving a difference of approximately $3.5 million. Of that, something over $1 million was devoted to purposes that you've identified in your testimony today that are neither Iran-related nor Nicaragua-related, leaving a difference of approximately $2 million, and that figure you have not yet been able to give the committee the precise purpose of?

SECORD: That is correct.

* * *

Meeting with Casey

NIELDS: You've made several references to the Director of Central Intelligence [William J. Casey], did you actually meet with him in connection with Nicaragua?

SECORD: Yes.

NIELDS: On how many occasions?

SECORD: Three occasions.

NIELDS: When was the first occasion?

SECORD: A few days before Christmas 1985, was my first meeting. I went to his office at Langley, met with him.

NIELDS: How was the meeting arranged?

SECORD: He called me in my office and asked if I could be over there in a few minutes. I wheeled right over there, I got in a little late, because it was bad weather that day. But he saw me anyway.

NIELDS: Do you know why he called you?

SECORD: Later I determined he called me because North had suggested to him it might be a good idea for him to call me, but he, himself, did call me.

NIELDS: Will you describe your meeting?

SECORD: Yes. The meeting probably lasted 45 minutes, I would guess. As I said, just the two of us were there. It was a little bit humorous because at the start of the meeting he was doing most of the talking and I was making a few comments but we were talking about two different countries. I didn't realize it for about five minutes.

He was talking about Iran, and I was talking about the Nicaraguan scene, so we were hemispheres apart for awhile.

The director was not the easiest guy I have ever communicated with, but I have great respect for the man, I want to make that very clear to the committee. He had a lot of strategic vision.

After we got the talking past each other problem straightened out, and we got around quickly to the subject of Central America, which was the purpose of the meeting, he was talking about Iran only because he knew I had something to do with the Iran matter which was not yet discussed and I won't get into that right now. We talked about the situation in Latin America.

I told him that I was not an expert on that area, that I felt inadequate about that area because I really did [not] have any first hand knowledge of the geography, the people or anything else. But he was well aware that we were cranking up this airlift operation, knew of its importance.

He asked me for my estimate of the situation, by that he meant the overall military-political situation, and I gave him a

brief explanation, and I told him that among other things that I felt that the contra had no chance of prevailing, none whatsoever, if we didn't get this airlift operation into the field, and even with it, even if we were very successful I had grave reservations about their ability to achieve any military victories, of course—any significant military victories.

I didn't see any real moves to create a viable southern front and it never was done successfully thereafter.

Although I knew they had many thousands more men that they could successfully arm and train, I didn't see the logistics capability, I didn't see the intelligence capability and I did not see the leadership which is going to be required for a decisive military victory there.

Of course, it's possible that sufficient pressure could be generated by keeping them in the field to bring the Sandinistas to the table. I believe he shared my view of that situation, at least at that time.

He told me that they were very appreciative of what I was doing, and he said I had his admiration and asked what he could do, and I explained to him that I needed intelligence information, as I've just discussed with you gentlemen. He took some notes on that; he was noncommittal, he didn't promise me anything.

But he said he would look into it. Just as I was leaving that particular discussion, I said to him, Mr. Director, if and when you get your hunting license back—this was kind of a crude way of referring to hoped for congressional action—whatever assets we are creating right now—by that I had in mind the airfield which was just being scratched out and our airlift operation, and the material that went with it is yours, just walk in and it is yours. That I assure you. He said, thanks very much, and I left.

NIELDS: You were referring to the assets you were developing in connection with this air resupply operation?

SECORD: That is correct. As I said earlier, it was not a profit-making picture for us. We were just trying to hold the line until we could get out of there.

NIELDS: When was your next meeting with Director Casey?

SECORD: The next meeting was at my request and it was a very brief meeting that took place in—I believe it took place in early February 1986. I don't have any notes on it, but I remember it fairly well.

NIELDS: How was that set up?.

SECORD: I called North and asked him to set it up, and he did.

NIELDS: This one was at your request?

SECORD: My request. I went to see him because I was unhappy, and I told him, Mr. Director, you and I are both too old to waste time beating around the bush. I have come here to complain.

Complain about what?

I said, complain about your organization.

What organization?

The Central—the task force, I said.

He said, What task force?

I said, the Central American task force.

Oh, that one. What's the problem?

I said, the problem is I'm not getting any support. I wanted intelligence information, guidance; whatever support you can give us, I want. We want every bit of support that we can get from you. Instead what we are getting is a lot of questions about the nature of [retired colonel Richard B.] Gadd's [contra-aid supplier] organization, how is it organized, who owns it, who has the share, what Secord is doing. It was like an investigation of our organization. They were not supporting it.

I didn't need to be investigated, I needed to be supported, and that was the nature of my complaint, and I stated it firmly. Again he said he would look into it. The meeting was a brief meeting.

The last time I saw the director was quite a bit later, and I'm sorry but I cannot tell you what month it was in. I think it was before the May journey of Mr. McFarlane to Tehran in '86, but it might have been after, I'm not sure. But it was about that time frame.

This meeting concerned itself also with contra matters. I happened to be in North's office discussing something when the director called Col. North, and North said that was the director, he wants to see me, would you like to go with me?

I thought we were leaving the building, but we weren't. We were just going around the corner to another office where he happened to be, the director happened to be. I went in and he said, good to see you again, General.

North and I sat down with him and the subject was raised—and I believe this was a continuing discussion Col. North was having with the director, because it went right into the middle of a problem, and that was the growing shortage of funds to support the contras.

North said that this was becoming a really critical problem, that donations to the cause were tailing off, they hadn't been materializing as they should, there were shortages in virtually everything, even food by this time.

The director stated that he wasn't at all confident that they would be able to get a new bill out of Congress in too short a period of time. He said that some people over here, meaning the executive offices, seemed to think they were going to be able to get a new bill rather rapidly off the Hill. But he didn't share that view.

North turned to me and asked me to give my estimate of the situation, so I had to give my estimate of the situation again. So I ran through quickly what I thought I knew about the situation at the time. I told him that this airlift operation, which was my area of concern, was also short of funds, we needed a lot of things, we needed a lot of new equipment.

I wanted in particular to buy some navigation systems for the new airplanes but they were very expensive. We didn't have good weather radars either, and so on.

Casey asked me how much money is needed, and I said, well, it depends on what period of time you are talking about. Unless the Government, the U.S. Government, gets back into the support of the contras, you know, we're not going to make it.

That was the message I wanted to impart. It had to be done fairly soon, because these private efforts, while they can bring a little bit, they cannot supplant the kind of effort that can be put forth by a nation. No private organization ever has enough resources to do that kind of a job.

I have already mentioned intelligence and there are other areas. He said, well, a few months, the end of the summer, something like that, I guessed. I said it would take about $10 million, I thought.

And, he said $10 million, $10 million, and then he mentioned the country which he thought might be willing to donate this kind of money. But then he said, but I can't approach them.

Why, I don't know. Why he couldn't approach them, I don't know and he didn't say. But he said that two or three times. And then he said, he looked at me and said, but you can.

And I said, Mr. Director, I'm not an official of the U.S. government. I don't think these people are particularly interested in solicitation from private citizens. I think that would be very foolish.

And then he mused about it again and North said somebody better damn well start looking into this thing right away because it is a rather desperate situation.

The director stated that he believed that George [P. Shultz], meaning the Secretary of State, could make such an approach, though, and that was the bottom line. He said that he would speak to the Secretary of State about this matter.

That was the last time I ever met with the director, although again he thanked me for the efforts that I had been involved with.

* * *

Secord resumed his testimony May 6, 1987. One of the topics touched upon was Secord's dealings with Manucher Ghorbanifar, a middleman in the Iran arms deal.

NIELDS: ... You went to Paris and you had a meeting [in December 1985]?

SECORD: Yes.

NIELDS: Who did you meet with?

SECORD: With Mr. Ghorbanifar and he was accompanied by Yaakov Nimrodi, an Israeli citizen.

NIELDS: What was Mr. Nimrodi's role?

SECORD: He was a business associate of Al Schwimmer.

NIELDS: Did you talk about what had happened, or did you talk about what was going to happen?

SECORD: We talked about what had happened, and Ghorbanifar engaged me in quite a bit of conversation about how he thought the game should continue in the future. He had a number of proposals in mind which were interesting. I took notes on these and later, of course, reported the essence of my discussions with Ghorbanifar to North.

I was in no position to negotiate any kind of deal with Ghorbanifar or with anyone else, so I was basically in a receiving mode.

NIELDS: What were Mr. Ghorbanifar's proposals?

SECORD: His proposals all were various sets of arms for hostage proposals. He was very in what I would characterize as U.S. high-technology weapon systems, specifically missile systems, for their F-14s. Harpoon missiles, other air intercept missions were mentioned a few times and TOW [antitank] missiles, and even though the I-Hawk missiles were sitting on the ground in Iran and he knew that they were not wanted. He still talked from time to time about shipping I-Hawk missiles.

He came up with different formulas—so many Phoenix's for so many Boxes, as he called them, which was his code word for hostages. It was blatantly a set of proposals of arms for hostages.

He had a boilerplate kind of salesmanship pattern, which he put out very glibly, which talked about the strategic setting and things that he knew Americans would like to hear. The Russian threat, the Iranians were being held hostage by the hostages themselves, and they needed to move on. But it was my impression that Ghorbanifar was more interested in business than he was in foreign policy.

* * *

Details of the Meeting

NIELDS: Would you describe the discussions?

SECORD: Briefly, yes. The meeting went on for quite a long while, several hours, and there was—it was badly seated, I may say, because they had Mr. McFarlane seated at a table smaller than this, directly across from Mr. Ghorbanifar. They were practically nose to nose throughout this entire session. And then the rest of us were seated around the room, essentially listening.

McFarlane said that he was there to listen to what had happened and to listen to any proposals that they might have. Ghorbanifar ran through again the whole litany of things that I have mentioned to you here today. He started with his overview, his strategy setting. As I said, it was very good. I have heard him make that address several times. He almost has like a tape.

Very quickly that meeting degenerated. It degenerated into propositions of U.S. arms for U.S. hostages in Lebanon. Ghorbanifar pursued that line with Mr. McFarlane for a long time, far too long. I was glad when the meeting was over, and McFarlane was very, very unhappy with this session. He told me—

NIELDS: Are you now referring to something that happened after the meeting?

SECORD: Yes. He told me after the meeting that he was very unhappy. But it was apparent in the meeting itself. I mean, no U.S. official could agree to such a proposition.

NIELDS: What did he say at the meeting?

SECORD: He said he would report this information back to the president. He committed to nothing. He didn't say he would do anything or wouldn't do anything. He just left.

NIELDS: How long did the meeting last?

SECORD: It lasted several hours, maybe three or four hours. I don't remember. It was too long. It just went on and on, and Ghorbanifar was making his best salesman pitch.

NIELDS: What did you do after the meeting?

SECORD: Taxied back to the hotel, picked up the bags and went straight to the London Airport, whereupon we departed for Washington, Andrews Air Force Base in the plane. The three of us came back that night together, so I had an opportunity to toss this around with Mr. McFarlane and with Col. North on the way home, and we conferred quite a bit.

NIELDS: What did you say and what did they say?

SECORD: McFarlane said, this was one of the most despicable characters I have ever met. I found that interesting because he was far from the most despicable character I have ever met.

NIELDS: Who are we talking about?

SECORD: Mr. Ghorbanifar.

NIELDS: Was Mr. Ghorbanifar, if not the most despicable character you have ever met, nonetheless despicable?

SECORD: The argument he was advancing was repulsive to all of us, but he's smooth. He was on the wrong line but he was making a hard pitch and he had a lot of tenacity and he just wouldn't stop.

Ghorbanifar wanted—as I have said twice before—the game to continue. That was his objective. He may have posed as an agent of Iran but he was really his own agent. He was a businessman, interested in making money, and that was it. So I didn't argue with Mr. McFarlane on that point.

I did, however, sense in my discussions with him that the Iranian initiative was dead. This seemed to me to be the case. I have made a counter-argument with him and wrote a short, handwritten point paper for him on the airplane. It was my position then, and it had been for a long time, that we had essentially a blank in our strategy planning for that area. Since the revolution in Iran, we had nothing in Iran, we had no idea of what was going on in Iran, we had no relations with Iran, yet it was a vitally strategic piece of territory which is unique in the world.

It seemed to me that if we didn't try to do something to regain a measure of influence or at least relations with Iran, then the Soviets surely would, over time, achieve a powerful sphere of influence there, and where that would lead no one can tell. . . .

* * *

Getting Weapons to Iran

SECORD: . . . We started moving the TOWs out of Texas on the 19th of February, 1986.

NIELDS: Did you move them all at the same time?

SECORD: Yes. We moved all 1,000 TOWs on two Southern Air Transport 707 aircraft to Israel, and then beginning I think about the 22nd or so of February, we transferred the first 500 TOWs to Tehran.

NIELDS: How was that done?

SECORD: That was done in a secret way by an Israeli 707 aircraft which had been sterilized, that is all markings removed from it, and it was chartered by me. I agreed to pay the Israeli government a price for the use of the airplane, and I had to furnish the crew.

NIELDS: Where did the crew come from?

SECORD: The crew came from Southern Air Transport. We actually had two crews that were used. They were specially selected from their pilots and they were screened by me, and if there are any heroes in this story, it has to be them. They were tremendous, they were fantastic, they were professional, and they pulled it off beautifully.

NIELDS: How did they actually go?

SECORD: They went by a route I had devised so as to keep them out of any other country's air space. It turned out, with the loads we carried, we could barely fly a long route down the Red Sea in international air space, around the southern end of the Saudi Arabian peninsula and up the Sea of Oman and coast into Iran east of Bandar Abbas. We computed with good weather we could make it safely, pretty safely, to Bandar Abbas.

Of course, planning a route like this on paper and actually flying it are sometimes two different things. Your fuel flow specifics have to be proved. But we were fairly confident that we could do it safely, and we also devised a covert command control and communications system whereby I could control these missions from my command post in Israel.

NIELDS: Is that where you were during these flights?

SECORD: Yes. There have been a lot of reports, even this morning, in the news that I flew to Tehran. I never went to Tehran.

NIELDS: Did this first shipment of 500 TOWs down the Red Sea and into Iran go smoothly?

SECORD: Yes, it went very smoothly. The weather was not bad, and they landed at the airfield in Bandar Abbas on the southern coast of Iran and discharged the 500 TOWs, offloaded them there, and then flew empty to Tehran, where they onloaded—they were supposed to onload the 18 Hawks that had been sitting there all this time. There were only 17 Hawks provided to them. They claimed that they had torn down the 18th one looking for something special.

Of course, there was nothing special. And, therefore, they were only returning 17 Hawks. It took almost 12 hours to load those 17 Hawks into the aircraft, and I was in quite a sweat because I was out of contact with them a lot longer than I thought should have been the case.

But finally they came up on the air as they departed Iranian air space and flew uneventfully back to Tel Aviv, and it lifted quite a load from my shoulders. . . .

* * *

Arms Sale Profit

NIELDS: After this transaction, did you have any discussions with Oliver North about how to use this $2.6 million surplus?

SECORD: Yes.

NIELDS: Would you describe that?

SECORD: Col. North's position was consistent throughout in February and later that he wanted me to use all available surpluses to support the contra project.

NIELDS: Did you have a number of conversations with him?

SECORD: I was comfortable with that. I had a number of conversations with him about this matter over a period of time. There was always a certain amount of tension on this subject because North wasn't running this operation, I was, along with Hakim, and of course, he wasn't sitting around worrying about having enough money to execute it, because we couldn't be in a position of being forced to go back to Ghorbanifar for the money if we had an overrun.

That would have been ridiculous, we could never get away with that. We had to keep sufficient revenues in these accounts to stay fluid so that we could go on to the next operation.

And remember, not one dime of U.S. money went into this operation. So we had to be very, very careful on this. So, I was perfectly willing to send funds to the contra project from these surpluses, and as the bank records which you got from Mr. Hakim show, we did.

But never was I able to send as much as Ollie North thought we should.

* * *

Personal Profit?

NIELDS: Mr. Secord, did you receive any money personally out of the Iran initiative?

SECORD: The only money that I received personally was my salary from Stanford Technology.

NIELDS: And how much was that?

SECORD: $6,000 a month.

NIELDS: Did you receive any other money at all out of the Iranian initiative?

SECORD: No, I did not. I told you that I foreswore my share of the earlier profits, and there were no profits given to me.

NIELDS: Earlier profits refers to—

SECORD: The arms brokering that took place in 1985.

NIELDS: Did that have anything to do with the Iranian initiative to begin with?

SECORD: No.

NIELDS: Was it ever—

SECORD: Your question was Iranian initiative?

NIELDS: Right.

SECORD: The answer is no.

NIELDS: Was it ever contemplated that you would obtain profits or any other kind of remuneration in connection with the Iranian initiative?

SECORD: No, and there was no profit motivation in this Iranian initiative. We did not price these weapons to generate personal profits. We didn't have in mind a personal profit residue of any kind in this operation. We priced them to create operational revenue. We needed money to operate this thing. The U.S. government did not provide one nickel for this operation. I was expected to raise the money to run the operation—all of it. This is what the government expected me to do.

We cut the price on our last transaction down to a very low price for these TOWs because we felt at that time we had a sufficient pool of money for continued operations. This operation was aborted and the residue, the seed there, the $8 million still on deposit is on deposit because we didn't take any of the money.

NIELDS: Was any of the money from the Iranian initiative set aside for you?

SECORD: No.

NIELDS: Was any of it set aside on the books of Mr. Hakim for you?

SECORD: Not as far as I know.

NIELDS: Was any of it set aside on the books being handled on Mr. Hakim's behalf for you?

SECORD: No, and when we looked through Mr. Hakim's records we could not identify any such accounts.

NIELDS: Mr. Secord, the Senate committee is in litigation with you, attempting to compel a waiver of foreign bank secrecy requirements. So far, you have prevailed in that litigation. But since then, you have made a decision to come forward and testify without immunity. Will you at any time subsequent to that decision to testify, voluntarily, will you voluntarily execute the waivers that you have previously been asked to?

SECORD: I am inclined to sign such a waiver, Mr. Nields. I probably will, but I reserve the right to consult on this complex matter with my counsel, and will be in touch with you.

NIELDS: Now, are you willing to provide the committees with all of your tax returns and related financial information?

SECORD: Yes, I have already provided you with the tax returns and any other financial statement information you wish, I will be happy to give to you.

Whose Money Was It?

NIELDS: Mr. Secord, I think you have testified that the three transactions with Iran threw off a surplus when you take the price received and deduct the aggregate cost of goods plus expenses. You have testified that it threw off an aggregate surplus of $14 million.

My question to you, sir, is whose money was that?

SECORD: Well, that is an interesting question, Mr. Nields, and it is—... The number $14 million is not the relevant number. The number that is relevant to your question I believe is the $8 million that is in these accounts right now.

NIELDS: Let me make it perfectly clear, Mr. Secord, I am not asking you—you may answer this later—but my question now is at the time the surplus was created, whose money was it?

SECORD: It is the enterprise's money and it was there for continuing operations.

NIELDS: Who decided, who was entitled to decide how it would be spent?

SECORD: These decisions were being made by me and they were being relayed to Mr. Hakim, who implemented the decisions.

NIELDS: Are you asserting, Mr. Secord, that you were entitled to decide to use that money for any purpose that you wanted?

SECORD: Yes.

NIELDS: Now, some of the money was used to buy a boat. Is that correct?

SECORD: Correct.

NIELDS: That was done at Mr. North's request?

SECORD: Yes.

NIELDS: For a U.S. requirement. And that was for a governmental purpose?

SECORD: Yes.

NIELDS: Some money was spent to buy Motorola radios?

SECORD: Yes.

NIELDS: That was at Mr. North's direction?

SECORD: At his request.

NIELDS: And that was for a governmental purpose?

SECORD: I think it was for—it was in the form of a donation.

NIELDS: To a foreign government.

SECORD: Yes.

NIELDS: Was this something that Mr. North wanted to do to satisfy himself personally, or was there some official purpose to giving a donation to a foreign government?

SECORD: I think he had had some request for assistance from the U.S. representative in this country.

NIELDS: Did you understand he was acting in his official capacity or his personal capacity when he asked you to give money to this Caribbean country?

SECORD: I always understood him to be in his official capacity.

NIELDS: So you understood this to be a governmental request?

SECORD: That is a hard question. I didn't think of it in that way. I suppose the answer is basically yes.

NIELDS: And Mr. North asked you to give him some cash that he could give to some DEA agents?

SECORD: Yes. We gave cash to him for that purpose, and also we gave it directly to the DEA agents.

NIELDS: And that was a governmental purpose?

SECORD: Yes.

NIELDS: And a lot of the money was spent on Iranian expenses?

SECORD: Correct.

NIELDS: And that was a governmental purpose?

SECORD: Yes, sir.

NIELDS: And money was spent on the contras?

SECORD: Yes.

NIELDS: That was also at Mr. North's request?

SECORD: His suggestion.

NIELDS: Well, I think you indicated he did more than suggest. He urged you continually, as I understand.

SECORD: Yes, he did, he urged me to do it, but it was my decision, and as I testified earlier, we didn't always send as much money as he thought we should.

NIELDS: Now, you have asserted a moment ago that in spite of the fact that you were using the money for governmental purposes at Mr. North's request, that you were entitled to take all of the money, $14 million, and spend it for any personal purpose that you wished.

SECORD: I didn't say personal purpose. You asked if I could spend it for any purpose I wished, and my answer technically is yes.

NIELDS: Including your personal purpose?

SECORD: We—never contemplated such a thing. Never.

NIELDS: Were you entitled to use it for a personal purpose?

SECORD: In my opinion, yes.

NIELDS: So you could have gone off and bought an island in the Mediterranean with the $14 million?

SECORD: Yes, Mr. Nields, but I did not go to Bimini. I guess I am trying to make the point, the money is still there, Mr. Nields. It is still there. It is intact.

NIELDS: Was this expressed in writing anywhere?

SECORD: No, sir, this was a covert operation, and it was being run under my direction. Mr. Hakim followed my guidance.

NIELDS: Was this a covert operation of the U.S. government?

SECORD: It was in support of a U.S. government covert operation, and I tried to use covert tactics in order to support that operation.

NIELDS: In any event, there was nothing in writing that expressed your entitlement to use this money for any purpose you wished?

SECORD: No, and there was nothing in writing which prohibited it either.

NIELDS: Did you have any discussions with Col. North or anyone else in the U.S. government in which they agreed to such an arrangement?

SECORD: There were a lot of lawyers in the room, in the situation room, when we were discussing the financing in January of 1986, and my role was laid out as that of the commercial cutout. None of these lawyers told me that I was anything other than the commercial operator. None of these lawyers told me I was a government agent. I wasn't paid a government salary. I didn't get a nickel of government money. I didn't conceive of myself as a government person. I was a private person trying to help my government.

NIELDS: Well, in the letter which I think has been marked Exhibit 1, signed by Oliver North, it states that "Your discrete [sic] assistance is again required in support of our national interests."

SECORD: Right.

NIELDS: Did you understand that you were performing functions in the national interest or in your personal interest?

SECORD: I was performing functions privately in the national interest.

NIELDS: And you assert that you were entitled to use the money generated from the sale of U.S. military equipment for your own personal purposes?

SECORD: I didn't say that. I said that technically that that could have been done. That is a hypothetical question because nothing like that was done.

Pricing the Weapons

NIELDS: Now, I take it that the money that came into these Swiss accounts was the purchase price for military equipment in U.S. stocks. Is that correct?

SECORD: That was correct.

NIELDS: In fact—

SECORD: That is partly correct. The money that came into the Swiss account was intended to procure the equipment and to transport the equipment to Iran.

NIELDS: Well, it was the purchase price that Ghorbanifar was paying for the arms, wasn't it?

SECORD: Yes.

NIELDS: And he was paying for arms that were in U.S. government stocks.

SECORD: The government could have charged anything they wanted to for these weapons. The government charged what they thought they were supposed to charge.

NIELDS: My only question was, were these arms in U.S. government stocks?

SECORD: Yes.

NIELDS: And, indeed, the price was paid before those arms left U.S. government stocks?

SECORD: That is right.

NIELDS: That was a requirement?

SECORD: That is correct.

NIELDS: And Col. North was the government official who decided how much money was to be charged to Ghorbanifar; isn't that also true?

SECORD: Col. North decided how much?

NIELDS: That is my question.

SECORD: No. I decided how much I would charge.

NIELDS: Did you do that in conjunction with Col. North?

SECORD: I had to because he was getting basic prices for me.

NIELDS: Also Col. North knew what the price was going to be before he decided whether the government would sell those arms; isn't that right?

SECORD: He didn't decide what the government would sell those arms for. The Pentagon did. He relayed that information to me after it was relayed to him by CIA logisticians.

NIELDS: Mr. Secord, this was an important government project that you were working on, was it not?

SECORD: Yes.

NIELDS: And the price that was being charged to the Iranians was an important fact in that project, wasn't it?

SECORD: It was a very important fact to me. If I didn't have

sufficient funds to operate the enterprise with, it couldn't be done.

NIELDS: Well, it was important in another way, wasn't it? If you charged too much, you could jeopardize the whole program.

SECORD: Yes. But that was never a factor.

NIELDS: Well, it was a factor, was it not, in the fact that the program eventually fell apart?

SECORD: I don't believe that the program fell apart because of the dispute over the microfiche list. When we discussed this matter with the second channel, they said that it was not an issue, not an important issue.

NIELDS: Well, Mr. Ghorbanifar was quite unhappy about the price that was being charged?

SECORD: Because Mr. Ghorbanifar was being deceptive with us and was dealing with financiers. He had told me he was dealing with Iranian money, and he was not, so he got himself painted into a corner.

NIELDS: Well, eventually, I think, according to your prior testimony, he claimed that he had never been fully paid for the arms and consequently had not been able to reimburse Mr. [Adnan] Khashoggi [Saudi Arabian arms merchant], and Mr. Khashoggi threatened to expose the entire operation.

SECORD: That is correct.

NIELDS: And Mr. Ghorbanifar was eventually extremely unhappy and there was a leak and the operation was exposed.

SECORD: That is also correct.

NIELDS: Wouldn't you agree that the price charged, if too high a price had been charged, that was a fact which could jeopardize the entire operation?

SECORD: If too high a price were charged, it could jeopardize the operation. But too high a price was not charged.

NIELDS: What I am asking is, wasn't it a question that the U.S. government had an interest in?

SECORD: Well, looking back at it, I suppose you could say that. But I don't recall any discussions about that factor at that time.

NIELDS: Was there ever a price charged that Col. North was not aware of in advance?

SECORD: No, because I informed him completely on everything that we did.

NIELDS: Was there ever a price charged that he didn't agree with?

SECORD: No.

NIELDS: But you are asserting that you had the power to decide what price to charge and to keep the difference between whatever price you charged and the price paid to the U.S. government, plus expenses?

SECORD: That is correct.

NIELDS: In your opening statement you made a reference to Mr. Attorney General Meese's statement on the 25th of November—

SECORD: Yes, sir.

NIELDS: —1986.

SECORD: Right.

NIELDS: And I think you had some uncomplimentary things to say about the statement.

What was it that you objected to in it?

SECORD: When I learned that the—that an internal inquiry was going on, I was fearful that there would be a rush to judgment, and I asked my attorney, Mr. [Tom] Green, to go and lay out the outlines of this operation to the Justice Department, to the No. 2 man in that investigation, [William] Bradford Reynolds.

Mr. Green was not aware of any of the details of the Iranian operation. He was not aware there was such a thing until about this time—just shortly before this time—and I had to hurriedly give him a briefing myself.

But he did go and talk on two days, for two days, Monday and Tuesday. That would have been the 24th and 25th of November. And on the 25th of November, Mr. Reynolds informed him—Mr. Green—that he agreed with Mr. Green's thrust, which was that we should slow down, take this thing a step at a time, we will lay it out for you, give you all the details that we can.

We should not rush into the public with this story until you at least have the facts. You couldn't possibly have ascertained the facts in a weekend investigation.

Mr. Reynolds agreed. Minutes later, obviously unbeknownst to Mr. Reynolds, Mr. Meese went before the American people and made his pronouncements and betrayed all of us and it is unforgivable.

NIELDS: What else did you do or what did you do, if anything, after he made the announcement?

SECORD: Well, I was stunned. You mean just before he made the announcement or just after?

NIELDS: Well, I think it was just after. Did there come a time when you made a call to Adm. Poindexter?

SECORD: Yes, sir, but it was just before the announcement that morning. I had heard because I had received a call from North's office, in fact, I received two calls from there, that the national security adviser Poindexter was resigning and that North was also resigning.

That is what they said. I called Poindexter, it was difficult for me to get through, but I insisted and I was rude in getting through. I asked John what in the world is going on.

He said that it was too late—that it was my intention to urge him not to quit, but to stand in there and fight and let's get this thing straightened out.

But he said it was too late, the resignation had already gone forward and I said, I want to talk to the President personally myself. I insist on it. And I told his aide that I demanded to talk to the President.

He said it was too late, they had already built a wall around the President.

I was very, very frustrated. But time was rushing forward and shortly after my brief conversation with John Poindexter, Mr. Meese made his announcement.

NIELDS: Did you on another occasion later in the same day after the announcement make a request to speak to the President?

Let me rephrase the question.

Were you and Oliver North together later on in the day in a hotel?

SECORD: Oh, yes, yes.

By this time my office was just untenable, the press were besieging it. So I went to a nearby hotel for a few hours to consult with my attorney and Oliver North came to the hotel.

. . . I presume that what you are getting at is the telephone conversation that was received—the telephone call that was received.

NIELDS: I take it there was a telephone call received while you were there?

SECORD: Yes.

NIELDS: For whom?

SECORD: The call came in for—there were two phone calls that came in for Col. North. One call was from the President. I didn't realize it was the President for a few seconds until I saw him stand up at attention. He is a good Marine, you know.

And he said, "Yes, Mr. President. Yes, Mr. President. Thank you very much, Mr. President."

And then he said that I am just sorry it had to end this way; I was trying to serve you the best way I knew how, Mr. President.

I said, "Let me have the phone," but it was too late. He hung up.

I wasn't fast enough.

NIELDS: What was it you wanted to tell the President?

SECORD: I wanted to tell the President that I would like to see him and try to bring some rationality back into this matter. There is no reason to back away from these operations. I mean, maybe there were mistaken judgments taken in the policy, maybe not. I happen to think that it was a good policy.

It was worth the try. But in any case, once you have made a decision like this to back away from it is a terrible mistake in my judgment. They are defensible. The American people would understand the rationale that underlies such a policy. We have done nothing wrong, moreover, in trying to privately support the contras.

We have not broken any law, especially we have not—we were assiduous in making sure that we didn't violate any law pertaining to the contras, and I have in mind the Boland Amendment when I

am speaking of this.

The Iranian initiative was completely legal. Lawyers worked on that as hard as they could. We made some progress in both areas. Some credit could be taken, it seemed to me.

So my advice would have been let's stake out our position; don't cut and run.

But I didn't get a chance to make that kind of a speech. I have made it now.

NIELDS: Mr. Meese had emphasized in his press conference of that day, the so-called diversion, the use of Iranian arms sales proceeds for the contras. What was your understanding of the President's knowledge of that issue and what was your basis for it?

SECORD: Well, I have no direct first-hand knowledge about what the president knew or didn't know as I think everyone knows, I never spoke with the President on this. I was told on a number of occasions and I even recorded it once in a December 1984 memo to myself that the President was informed of my participation in the contra and later in the Iranian operations. I had talked with the director of the CIA, who was a close confidant of the president.

I assumed that he was passing information to him. I talked with two different national security advisers in the two years in question. I was told by Adm. Poindexter in January of 1986 that not only was he pleased with the work that I had been doing, but the president was, as well.

On a few occasions I heard Oliver North offhand and I think in a humorous vein remark that in some conversations with the President he had mentioned that it was very ironic that some of the Ayatollah's money was being used to support the contras. Whether he actually said this to the President or whether he was joking with me, I am not sure. It was not said to me in a way that I took it as a joke.

NIELDS: Earlier you said that, when you were in the room in which they were working on the finding, you said that the Israelis' role in this transaction was to provide a cover, and if there was an exposure to take the hit. What did you mean?

SECORD: Well, the Israelis played an important role in this. They were, as I said, joint venture partners. One role which was fairly clear to me was that in this covert operation at least the first level of deniability, normally you have different levels of cover involved in a covert operation and if a certain amount of exposure resulted the first level of deniability or protection for the U.S., if you will, could be that the Israelis would take the blame for the shipments.

NIELDS: In other words, that the Israelis would say it was the Israelis who were shipping the arms to Iran?

SECORD: This was an option that was available.

NIELDS: That would have meant that it would have been the American people and the Congress who would not have found out that arms were shipped to Iran by this country?

SECORD: If that option were exercised, that is true. That option was never exercised. . . .

* * *

On May 7, 1987, Secord was interrogated by Arthur L. Liman, chief counsel for the Senate select Iran-contra committee. In sometimes pointed exchanges, Liman questioned Secord about his arms dealings and what happened to the profits.

LIMAN: Is it a fact that Mr. North, Col. North, dealt directly with the Iranian official?

SECORD: After we were able to arrange it, yes.

LIMAN: Is it a fact that Mr. McFarlane dealt directly with the Iranian official in Tehran?

SECORD: Yes. Secretly.

LIMAN: Was Mr. McFarlane posing as a representative from Timbuktu or as a representative of the United States?

SECORD: Obviously from the United States.

LIMAN: Did you carry over a Bible to the Iranians inscribed by the President of the United States?

SECORD: They did, yes.

LIMAN: And you were aware of it?

SECORD: Yes.

LIMAN: And the President of the United States didn't disguise who he was, did he?

SECORD: No.

LIMAN: So it is still your testimony that the purpose of putting you in as an intermediary was to conceal the fact that the United States was dealing with Iran from the Iranians?

SECORD: Sure. And it makes sense. The Iranians had to be able to say they were not dealing with the Great Satan directly, they were dealing with a company, they were dealing through Europe.

LIMAN: Did Lake [Resources Inc., a conduit for the arms money] ever send a single invoice to the Iranians?

SECORD: No.

LIMAN: Did it ever issue a single piece of paper to the Iranians saying you are buying these from Lake?

SECORD: Mr. Nields—excuse me—Mr. Liman, there's no question the covert operation was designed to be concealed from Congress. There is no question of that. I mean, they didn't—they chose not to notify the Congress. But that wasn't my decision. It wasn't my decision at all. I wasn't involved in that decision.

* * *

Profiteering?

LIMAN: Is your position, Mr. Secord, that Oliver North was prepared to let you generate whatever profits you could to use as you saw fit?

SECORD: It's my position that he knew that I was generating money to keep the enterprise going. He well knew, at least in a macro sense, what the numbers were, and he had a trust in me and my men and he felt that we were doing the right thing.

LIMAN: I don't think you answered the question. Is it your position that Oliver North was prepared to let you spend whatever the profit was as you saw fit?

SECORD: Yes.

LIMAN: And that you never told him before you were brought into this transaction as a "commercial outcut," end of quote, that the money would be dedicated for the contras?

SECORD: No, definitely not. He had an expectation, I think he had a legitimate expectation that we would support the contras to the extent that we could. After all, this airlift project was mine. I conceived of it, others were operating it but I conceived of it, wanted it to function correctly. It had to have money. It was always short of money. You have documents that prove that.

We sent the money that we thought that we could spare from the Iranian initiative.

* * *

LIMAN: Did you ask Col. North to assist you in selling these assets [airplanes] to the CIA?

SECORD: No. But we talked—North and I did talk about whether the costs for these things should be reimbursed by CIA or not, and concluded—my recollection—that the best possible option was to simply transfer it, simply let them take over and walk away. By this time frame, I wanted out of this operation in the worst possible way. It had dragged on for too long.

It was becoming very dangerous. We couldn't get support. We were short of money. I wanted out of it. That is the important point I would like the committee to understand. That is what was in my mind at that time.

LIMAN: If you wanted out of it, why didn't you just stop and turn over all the money to the government?

SECORD: Believe me, I thought about it.

LIMAN: You did think about it?

SECORD: More than once about it.

LIMAN: Did you talk to anyone about it?

SECORD: I talked to North about it, yes.

LIMAN: Did you talk to [Albert] Hakim [Secord's business partner] about it?

SECORD: Many times.

LIMAN: Did Hakim ever indicate to you any willingness to let go of this money?

SECORD: You are going to talk to him soon. Ask him that question. I am not going to presume to put words in his mouth.

LIMAN: I was only asking him what he said to you, only asking you what he said to you.

SECORD: No.

I am reminded of another point that might be of importance. The U.S. Government never asked me for the money.

LIMAN: And as long as—who in the U.S. Government knew you had this kind of money?

SECORD: Well, Col. North knew. His boss, Adm. Poindexter knew. I know. I don't think the CIA had an accurate figure on it, but they knew there was money there.

LIMAN: By the CIA, who do you mean knew were generating these profits?

SECORD: The CIA knew prices were being charged in excess of the cost. They knew that we had to operate our enterprise. They knew that they weren't funding it. They knew I had to fund it.

LIMAN: Did they know that the money was being funneled to your Central American operation?

SECORD: I don't think they did.

LIMAN: Did they know that the money was being used to buy a ship for another covert activity?

SECORD: I don't believe they did.

LIMAN: Did they know that the money was being used for some kind of operation that was employing the DEA agents?

SECORD: I don't know on that point. They may have known.

* * *

Panel members questioned Secord during the afternoon of May 7, 1987.

[Rep. Louis] STOKES [D-Ohio]: Mr. Secord, you told us as a private citizen you were in charge of the commercial cutout used in the Iran operation. The government sold you the missiles, or the spare parts, and then you sold them to Iran. Once they were sold to you, they were no longer the property of the United States government; is that correct?

SECORD: That is correct.

STOKES: Are you also saying to us that at that point the U.S. Government no longer had the ability to be able to order you to conduct this covert operation in any way they wanted to conduct it?

SECORD: Well, I think they had great faith that I would follow the directions that were given, and I did, of course.

STOKES: Well, if we accept this version, aren't we, in effect, accepting the fact that the United States Government contracted out its foreign policy to you, subject to you carrying out their best wishes?

SECORD: I don't think they viewed it that way, sir. I think that they viewed me as a logistics and commercial—logistics operator and commercial go-between, and certainly didn't view me as being a foreign policy negotiator or anything like that.

STOKES: A few moments ago you were asked by Mr. Liman about your operation, which to a large degree parallels the CIA operation, that is, their reserve for contingencies. You operated your own fund, you bought ships, airplanes, things of that sort.

That obviously was for the purpose of circumventing the Boland amendment; is that correct?

SECORD: I didn't see it that way.

STOKES: Well, under the Boland amendment all agencies, all individuals in our Government were prohibited from utilizing any appropriated funds for use of the contras. You understood that?

SECORD: Yes, sir.

STOKES: Under your operation private funds, non-appropriated funds, could be used for any purpose you saw fit and that included for the use of the contras?

SECORD: Well, I felt a responsibility. I knew why the funds were donated. I felt a responsibility to make sure they got to the contra project, and they did.

STOKES: Doesn't it look to you like we have two governments? There is one Government run by the United States which Mr. Reagan is head of, where you cannot utilize appropriated funds for the purposes we have already enunciated, and this other government run by you, that you can utilize these funds for whatever purposes you deem necessary, though they be contrary to the use for which appropriated funds can be put?

SECORD: I am not sure what answer you are looking for.

STOKES: Well, I guess—

SECORD: I understand what you are saying, but I am—I didn't see it that way. I didn't see it that way. The President has certain rights in the foreign policy area. I never saw myself as being a foreign policy operative. I believe that the funds that we had were private funds and could be sent to the contra project, which project we believed deeply in, and we did that.

STOKES: Is it your view having been a general, having performed in government as you have, that this fits within the constitutional framework of our government?

SECORD: I did, sir.

STOKES: You saw nothing wrong with those operations?

SECORD: I did not see anything wrong with it then.

STOKES: Did Colonel North's salary come from appropriated funds?

SECORD: I am sure it did. . . . All U.S. Government appropriated funds.

STOKES: How about the airplane pilots who flew Mr. North around the world to the various meetings he had with you and others?

SECORD: To the extent they were government pilots, of course they were paid the same way.

STOKES: Then how do you square this fact away with the fact that you say no appropriated funds were used in any manner in conjunction with your operation?

SECORD: It never ever occurred to me that someone would construe normal governmental salaries as being attached by Boland.

STOKES: Well, when the Boland amendment passed on the floor of the House, the author of the amendment, Mr. Boland, stated on the floor that it would include salaries. Were you aware of that?

SECORD: No. I didn't have the legislative history, sir. I can tell you, sir, that I was aware that Boland was a legislative compromise. I can tell you that I have heard from a distinguished counsel, the chief counsel for the Senate Committee, that Boland is a piece of Swiss cheese; that Boland is an act which, if you had the I.Q. of a genius, you could not trace its meandering.

I think there was considerable confusion and misunderstanding about the intentions of Boland.

* * *

[Sen. David L.] BOREN [D-Okla.]: Do you think it is strange for a private citizen to be taking an action of such importance for the foreign policy of the United States as purporting to represent this country in the opening of communications with an element in the government of a foreign power?

SECORD: It is very strange, sir. I looked for, as hard as I could, a better channel [than arms middleman Manucher Ghorbanifar]. The one we had was corrupt, and when I found what I thought was the right channel, I turned this over to the government and they vetted it and eventually agreed with us. . . .

BOREN: . . . So you see nothing strange at all in terms of the way we make foreign policy in this country for a person who is purely a private citizen with no official government capacity to be making the kinds of decisions and deciding about the identity of people within the government, some of whom have relationships to very high government officials in the government of Iran. . . .

SECORD: I think it is very strange, very unusual.

BOREN: Do you think it is appropriate? We are in the bicentennial year of the Constitution. Do you think it is appropriate that important foreign policy decisions of this country should be made by Mr. Richard Secord, private citizen, instead of by the Congress of the United States, the Secretary of State, and the President of the United States?

SECORD: Looking back at it, I think that you could make that criticism very easily, but I must tell you, sir, that I was doing the best I could under the circumstances, and I thought I was

carrying out the President's policy, and I was not trying to usurp anybody's authority. And I did not. . . .

BOREN: Mr. Secord, again I go back to this being the bicentennial year of the Constitution. Does it not disturb you as an American, setting aside your own great confidence in yourself, which has been clearly expressed to us—you obviously have more confidence than you have in the CIA in terms of you said you could not run their covert operations better than they, you have more confidence in your legal judgment than in the judgment of the Attorney General whom you have roundly condemned for making public the diversion of funds—you seem to have more confidence in yourself than you do in even the President's own staff because you drafted a speech to give to Colonel North for the President of the United States to read to explain this. . . .

Now, is it right for you, as a private individual, to use American taxpayers' money to make these kinds of decisions, even when the National Security Council, albeit a shockingly low level at the National Security Council, is telling you not to continue?

SECORD: I find it difficult to respond to that string of assertions.

BOREN: I can understand why you would find it difficult to respond, because concerning—have you read the Constitution of the United States, Mr. Secord?

SECORD: Yes, Senator Boren.

BOREN: Do you believe in it?

SECORD: Of course. I have sworn to uphold it and I have fought for it quite a few times.

BOREN: I understand you have fought for it. No one takes anything away from that.

But does it not trouble you? Did you not wake up some mornings and think, how did I, as a private individual, start exercising all this responsibility to make foreign policy of the United States of America in lieu of the Congress, the Secretary of State, the President of the United States, members of the National Security Council? Did you not have even a moment of humility about your judgment in substituting yourself for the constitutional process of this country?

SECORD: I don't agree with what you are saying about what I did. I thought I was doing the right things at the time, but I can tell you I was troubled all along the way, troubled all along the way. . . .

BOREN: Now, let me ask you about profit motive. You have said that in all of this you had no profit motive and that you renounced any profits that you might make.

Isn't it true, though, in terms of your conversation with our staff when you were being questioned that you commented that while you and Mr. Hakim did not expect to—or at least you did not expect to make or desire to make a profit out of the current operation—that you felt that if you could open the door to improve relationships between the United States and Iran, given the fact you had previously represented this government in Iran when you were an official of this government and you had particularly dealt with the Shah and his government in the arms field—Mr. Hakim was involved in the armaments field during that same period.

Is it not true that you told our staff during questioning by them that you and Mr. Hakim had talked about the fact that once the channels were open, you really saw a great opportunity to make a good deal of money in terms of taking advantage of that new openness between Iran and the United States?

SECORD: Yes, sir

BOREN: So, it is not really quite correct to say that that evil thought of making a little profit down the road didn't just lurk somewhere in the back of your mind through all this?

SECORD: I am like Mr. Liman—I am not the philanthropist, either. I have to make a living.

* * *

[Sen. Orrin G.] HATCH [R-Utah]: General, let me talk a little about some personal things in your life.

We have heard a great deal about your distinguished career. You graduated from West Point and served as a command pilot, you had 4,500 flying hours. You have been extensively decorated with the Distinguished Service Medal, the Legion of Merit, the Distinguished Service Cross; you served in Laos, Thailand, Iran and you were Deputy Assistant Secretary of Defense with responsibilities in the Mideast.

I understand you are married and have three children; is that correct?

SECORD: Yes, sir.

HATCH: And you live in McLean, Virginia; is that correct?

SECORD: Yes, sir.

HATCH: Are your children in high school, do they go to public or private schools?

SECORD: Public schools. I have one child who is a senior in high school and I have a daughter who is in college in D.C. and I have a daughter who is older and married. . . .

HATCH: Did your net worth or personal lifestyle improve as a result of your involvement in the contra/Iranian operations?

SECORD: It has not improved. It's deteriorated. My personal financial situation has gotten much worse recently. Of course, legal bills—as was pointed out earlier—are climbing.

HATCH: And they are ongoing and you haven't been paying them, I take it, at this point?

SECORD: My lawyer must be a philanthropist. . . .

HATCH: . . . There are going to be some who feel that the $8 million in that account can be used for your benefit and there may be some question about the other $2.5 million, where that went. So I think it pays to clear these things up as much as you can.

But as far as you are concerned, what is going to happen with the $8 million?

SECORD: I don't know yet. There are bills, quite a few bills, to be paid. . . .

HATCH: . . . To be honest with you, it looks to me like with all of the running around the world you have done, and being away from your family and putting these things together, it has been a pretty doggone thankless task, and frankly, you didn't get rich from it, although it remains to be seen what you will do with the $8 million and what happened to the other $2.5.

But nevertheless, I don't think anybody can make the claim here that you have gotten rich off of this. And frankly, I will be honest with you. One of the difficulties with your story is that—your unwillingness to take profits on the arms transfer.

In all honesty, I don't see any reason why you shouldn't have taken profits on it. You had every right to. To me, I will accept your story at face value that you wanted to come back into the government, you would have liked to have worked in security, and intelligence, and I will just say this:

If we assume everything you say here is true, sir, and we assume that you have testified candidly, I would have to say you make one heck of a good intelligence person, because there is no question about your intelligence, and there is no question about your ability to understand an awful lot of what intelligence is all about. . . .

* * *

[Sen. Warren B.] RUDMAN, [R-N.H.]: You testified both in deposition and here today that there were bills to be paid, and my understanding is that those bills, including the debt benefit, which I am aware of, are less than $500,000 according to your own testimony, although it is possible that Hakim may have some other bills that you are unaware of.

I understand that. But at least we are talking somewhere in the vicinity of $6 to $7 million that will be left when that is done. Do you agree with that?

SECORD: It is entirely possible. I don't know what the nature of Hakim's bills might be, and I don't know about this litigation of the ship.

Aside from those two uncertainties, your arithmetic seems accurate. . . .

RUDMAN: . . . The operations over, you have testified repeatedly that you direct Hakim—the money is frozen. We all understand that.

I consider I am probably a United States official. I would like to ask you a question. I believe this committee can make arrangements within 48 hours, have the United States assert claims in

those accounts that we are aware of.

Will you direct Mr. Hakim to do the same and return all of those funds to the Treasury of the United States? Will you cooperate with this committee to that end?

[Thomas C.] GREEN [Secord's lawyer]: Indulge us one minute.

RUDMAN: After you have paid your lawyer, Mr. Secord.

GREEN: If you make that a first priority, it might facilitate this decision.

SECORD: Of course, as you might imagine, we have talked about this question. We expected to get a question of this nature.

RUDMAN: I am surprised it wasn't asked before now, but we would sure like an answer. I am going to stick with you until we get some idea of what your answer is in a definitive way.

SECORD: It is a fair question.

RUDMAN: I would say so.

SECORD: It is a difficult situation I find myself in. I told you I am in a precarious financial situation. I don't want to prejudice any claim Mr. Hakim is going to make. He is going to be here, I am told, in a few days.

RUDMAN: We will see about that. We certainly hope so, but he is, of course, not within our reach.

SECORD: But he will be very shortly. I am informed that he will be.

RUDMAN: Good.

SECORD: And I want to confer with him as soon as he gets here with counsels, and continue with the auditing of these accounts, find out what is there, find out what claims he might wish to assert, and then we will come back to you with the firm position.

I don't want to stake out a position right now, but I will tell you one of my options is to stake out no position, and beyond that I can't go right now.

RUDMAN: Well, if Mr. Hakim does appear here he will be asked a question.

We have a list of the bills that we believe are presently legitimate. Mr. Hakim might even claim additional bills. He might even claim he is entitled to a profit, which well may be.

That is, I believe, in the free enterprise system. He may claim he is due some money, but I don't think, General, that this government, whose goods were sold and who this money rightfully belongs to, ought to be deprived of the major share of those funds when those claims are paid. Do you agree with that?

SECORD: I personally agree with you, Senator.

RUDMAN: And then you will assist us once we get Mr. Hakim before us, to that end?

SECORD: Yes, sir.

Secord resumed his testimony May 8, 1987:

[Rep. Dick] CHENEY [R-Wyo.]: One of the problems I have with the [contra] operation, General, is that it seems to me we have this dilemma. Many of us on this committee are very strong supporters of the contra cause and while you were running your operation in Central America we were doing battle in the Congress to try to build support for the policy that was ultimately adopted last year when Congress approved the $100 million in military and humanitarian assistance for the contras.

But I am concerned in a sense that in winning the short term victory of keeping the contras alive through the operation that you ran, we may have done damage to our capacity to build public and congressional support for a long term program of support for the contras.

And I wonder if that subject was ever discussed, was ever the subject of talks between yourself, Col. North, or the others involved in the operation?

SECORD: I don't recall any specific discussions of that nature, but I agree with your analysis. I, too, am afraid that the revelation is going to badly damage the cause.

CHENEY: We will do our best to renew that program later this year, but that is a subject for debate in other committees. Was there ever any discussion of what would happen if the operation had its cover blown?

SECORD: Yes. Yes, we discussed that. We simply expected

that we would be no longer able to function and would have to pull out.

CHENEY: . . . Gen. Secord, you have stated that you believed your activities did not violate the Boland Amendment because you were a private citizen. You have also stated that you received legal advice to the effect that your operation did not violate the Neutrality Act or that you carried it out in such a way that it was consistent with the Neutrality Act.

It has been suggested that because Col. North encouraged support and sometimes assisted your effort that you engaged in effect in circumventing the Boland Amendment. But if your activities were permitted, how would it have been possible for you to have circumvented the Boland Amendment?

SECORD: We do not have the view that we were circumventing the Boland Amendment. We simply read the Boland Amendment and believed it did not apply because we were private.

* * *

[Sen. Sam] NUNN [D-Ga.]: . . . Have you had any conversation with either Adm. Poindexter or Col. North subsequent to November of 1986 regarding what they told the President of the United States about diversion of contra funds?

SECORD: I don't believe so. No, sir.

NUNN: Have you ever had a conversation with them about that subject other than the one you alluded to with Col. North earlier?

SECORD: Never, sir.

NUNN: That is the only time it has come up?

SECORD: Yes, sir.

NUNN: Have you ever had a conversation with any other governmental official about whether the President of the United States was told about the diversion of funds to the contras?

SECORD: I don't believe so. I haven't spoken to very many government officials since the revelation.

NUNN: This is a pretty important point. Is it one that you would have a vague recollection on if you had? You say you don't believe so. Are you certain?

SECORD: You are talking about Administration officials, not counsels for the committee or things like that?

NUNN: I am talking about Administration officials now.

SECORD: I don't believe so, sir.

NUNN: Would you remember it if you had? It is a pretty key point here.

SECORD: I have had conversations with a lot of people, Sen. Nunn, but I don't remember talking to any government official about that point.

NUNN: How about anyone else other than the counsel for this committee? Have you had any conversations with anyone, whether governmental official or not, regarding whether President Reagan was told about the diversion of funds to the contras?

SECORD: It has been discussed in brief terms with Mr. [Lawrence E.] Walsh's [the independent counsel] staff.

NUNN: That is the independent counsel?

SECORD: Yes, sir.

NUNN: Beyond that, beyond the investigations ongoing and the investigators, have you had that discussion with anyone else?

SECORD: About—

NUNN: About whether the President of the United States knew that there were funds being diverted to the contras from the Iranian arms sale?

SECORD: Well, I have speculated with some of my friends that there was a good chance, but I had no evidence of it, as I testified.

NUNN: You told some of your friends that there was a good chance of what?

SECORD: That the President would know. I felt that the President had a pretty good flow of information coming into him so there was a good chance he would know. But I don't know. And I don't know today.

NUNN: You stated in answer to a question from Sen. [James A.] McClure [R-Idaho] a few minutes ago that, rather unequivocally, I thought that you were not an agent in any way of the United States Government. Is that your position?

SECORD: Yes, sir. I never thought of myself as an agent of the U.S. Government.

NUNN: Have you had a chance to examine the January 17 finding—actually it is the January 17 memorandum for the President from John Poindexter, subject, covert action finding regarding Iran. Have you had a chance to look at that?

It is Exhibit 9 in the book.

SECORD: I have not looked at it. I have looked at the finding, but not at that memo.

NUNN: Would you take a look at page 2 of that memo in Exhibit 9, paragraph 1?

Do you follow up at the top where it says Gen. William French Smith determined that under an appropriate finding you could authorize the CIA to sell arms outside the provisions of the laws and reporting requirements for foreign military sales? Do you follow me?

SECORD: Yes, sir.

NUNN: The next line is the one I really wanted to call your attention to, quoting, "the objectives of the Israelis' plan could be met if the CIA using an authorized agent as necessary purchased arms from the Department of Defense under the Economy Act and then transferred them to Iran directly after receiving an appropriate payment from Iran."

You see that?

SECORD: Yes, sir. And I was never informed of that. I have never seen the memo until it was placed in this book here.

NUNN: If you had known that, would that have changed your view about your legal circumstances?

SECORD: If—I believe that I would have been wise enough to try to find out what they meant by the word 'agent' in that language.

NUNN: So your testimony here today is you never knew about that?

SECORD: I did not know about it.

NUNN: Did you know about it before today?

SECORD: No. I knew there was a memo. I have read about it in the press, but I have never seen that until today.

NUNN: Now, I call your attention, Gen. Secord, to Exhibit 8, if you would flip the page back. This is a memorandum from Ollie North dated August 31, 1985, and I refer you down to the last paragraph. Do you see that?

SECORD: The most recent proposal?

NUNN: Yes. Could you just read that first sentence for us?

SECORD: The most recent proposal (Copp as agent for the CIA in sales to the Israelis, who will then deliver weapons to the Iranians), can only work if we can get the Israelis to come up on their price.

NUNN: Who was Copp?

SECORD: That was a pseudonym for me.

NUNN: Had you seen this memorandum before?

SECORD: Never before. Never.

NUNN: Had Ollie North ever told you that he looked on you as an agent of the CIA?

SECORD: No, and I think that he will not say that I was.

NUNN: This memorandum says it though, does it not?

SECORD: It appears to.

NUNN: You stated that you viewed Ollie North as a man that is honest, a man of integrity, is that right?

SECORD: Yes sir.

NUNN: But you also said that you believed he was rather flamboyant and when you—when he talks to you about whether the President knew and the question about the Ayatollah, using the Ayatollah's funds to fund the Contras, that you didn't know whether that was a joke or serious. What is your testimony on that? I am a little bit confused.

SECORD: You described it correctly.

NUNN: One day you said you didn't take it as a joke. The next day you said that he was flamboyant and—

SECORD: What I said, sir—I believe what I said is, he did not say it in a way that I took it to be a joke, but I also said that I was skeptical of this, of the accuracy of this.

NUNN: Well, does this mean that you do have doubts about Col. Oliver North's honesty and integrity?

SECORD: No sir, I don't have any doubts about honesty and integrity, but people sometimes say things that are a little bit exaggerated.

NUNN: How do you view this memorandum where he says you are an agent of the CIA.

SECORD: I don't think that he knew what the technical meaning of the word agent is and I certainly was not an agent of the CIA.

NUNN: And he never told you this?

SECORD: Never.

NUNN: I am a little bit puzzled here, Gen. Secord, about how you concluded, and if you concluded that what you were doing in terms of the Contra diversion was authorized. What gave you certainty that that diversion of funds to the Contras was indeed authorized, and who did you believe authorized it?

SECORD: It was my belief, and the belief of Albert Hakim that those funds were the funds of the enterprise and could be spent on projects as the enterprise so desired.

* * *

NUNN: ... October '86 you had 500 TOW missiles that you charged the Iranians $3,600,000, you paid the CIA $2,037,000, is that approximately correct?

SECORD: Of course, that is correct, but we also had a lot of expenses, as I testified earlier

NUNN: I understand. In terms of markup, this is two cases—in one case, you tripled the price, in another you doubled the price, and in another case it was about a 76 percent markup. They average out about 130, 140 percent markup.

SECORD: I don't think you are including the expenses, and the Defense Department does include expenses.

NUNN: How much then would you deduct for expenses? Would it get it down to 100 percent markup?

SECORD: Perhaps. I haven't made that calculation.

NUNN: Is that the way to make friends, to make people happy?

SECORD: I testified to the circumstances we were operating in, Senator. The Iranians were perfectly willing to pay this price. I had to have the necessary operating revenues in order to make this project go.

NUNN: Is that the way you believe the U.S. should go about if we chose to establish a strategic relationship with a country that has been hostile?

SECORD: No, sir. I prefer the foreign military sales form, but in this case it was not a foreign military sale; it was a covert action through commercial companies.

NUNN: Did it bother you that the strategic relationship may have been in jeopardy if the Iranians found out about the price?

SECORD: No, because we were able to explain it.

NUNN: You got the money in advance from the Iranians before the arms were delivered?

SECORD: We had to have it in advance, yes, sir.

NUNN: You got the money before hostages were released, did you not, at least the sales that are relevant thereto?

SECORD: I believe that is correct.

NUNN: Did you worry that the Iranians might find out about the markup and retaliate against the hostages?

SECORD: No. It was not a worry of mine at the time, and when we discussed these prices after the microfiche incident, when we discussed these prices with the second channel representatives of the Iranian Government, there was no problem....

NUNN: It seems there are three or four theories floating around about the Iranian arms sale. One is trying to establish a strategic relationship, the second relating to the hostages, a third theory would be that it was primarily a contra fund-raising exercise, and a fourth theory is that it was primarily a profit-making venture for those involved. Of those four theories, which would you subscribe to?

SECORD: One and two.

NUNN: It seems to me the pricing was more compatible with three and four.

SECORD: I don't agree with that.

NUNN: I think we will leave that for others to judge.

* * *

[Rep. William S.] BROOMFIELD [R-Mich.]: ... I have been involved with foreign policy for more than 25 years as a Member of the House Foreign Affairs Committee, and from that perspective, I think a great deal of blame for this foreign policy foul-up rests right at the doorstep of Congress. Over those years, as everyone knows, there has been a great change in the Constitutional role of Congress in making foreign policy. Since Vietnam, Congress likes to boast that it has been an equal partner with the President in shaping foreign policy. I think Congress ought to shoulder the blame for an on-again/off-again foreign policy.

President Reagan, who still carries the burden of making foreign policy, must deal almost daily with the 535 Secretaries of State in the House and Senate who seldom can form a simple majority around a single issue.

I guess what I am trying to say, General, is that the problems you are confronting in trying to assist your country were the direct results of Congress' inability to maintain a consistent policy line regarding Nicaragua. If Congress had been able to get its act together, there would have been no need for the covert efforts to bridge the gap in our policy.

I have several questions I would like to ask you. As a former senior U.S. official with experience in covert operations, what do you think are the proper roles of the President and Congress with respect to such operations?

SECORD: I believe that the proper roles are well spelled out in Hughes/Ryan. When I went into this, I wasn't very familiar with those acts. When I dealt with the CIA in my earlier years, there were no such acts. Given the political circumstances that exist in our country today, I understand the necessity for the President to notify the Congress on such serious matters as covert operations.

In this particular set of circumstances we have been talking about with respect to Iran, hindsight was wonderful, but it seems to me that there was a big political error on the part of the President not to at least notify the eight men, which he could have opted to do. I think that would have been—made the Congress, like it or not, a partner in the venture, and I think it would have been much wiser for him to do that, especially since we were dealing with foreigners. I don't think we should have had to worry so much about security of eight men. I don't have a problem with how it is spelled out now in my mind.

What I have a problem with is the continual assumption in this country that covert operations are wrong. This is a dangerous world we live in today, and sometimes the President, who has security responsibility for this nation, in my opinion, has to have this tool available. He uses it seldom, but sometimes you have to use it.

BROOMFIELD: General, what effect do you believe that these highly publicized proceedings will have on the willingness of foreign countries and individuals to cooperate with the United States on proper covert operations in the future?

SECORD: In my opinion, the whole world is laughing at us. We have been hearing a lot of talk about the cleansing effect of these kinds of hearings. I don't believe that. I don't think it does that. I think it opens up our guts to the rest of the world, they not only don't trust us like they used to, they also laugh at us.

* * *

[Sen. William S.] COHEN [R-Maine]: ... Did Oliver North ever tell you that President Reagan would be most grateful if this individual that you contacted on his behalf, on this country's behalf, to raise funds, would be very grateful if his country would contribute?

Let me rephrase that. You approached a certain individual from a country we will call country X, which is not geographically proximate to the United States, right?

SECORD: Right.

COHEN: And you approached that particular individual at Oliver North's behest—

SECORD: Yes, sir.

COHEN: And did he tell you at that time to tell this individual that the President would be most grateful for a contribution from that country?

SECORD: No. He asked me to refer to a conversation that Mr. McFarlane apparently had had with the individual.

COHEN: In your conversation with that individual, you said that "The President of the United States would be most grateful for your assistance in this matter?"

SECORD: He asked my opinion, and I said it was my opinion that since this was a high priority matter with the President of the United States, that he would be happy with it. Yes, that is my opinion. No one said to me the President said to do this.

COHEN: You had two contacts with this individual?

SECORD: I had two contacts with him with respect to solicitation for a donation.

COHEN: And you had additional contacts with him for other purposes?

SECORD: Not until very recently, and that was around the 20th of November, I think. 1986.

COHEN: Of 1986?

SECORD: Yes.

COHEN: I will come back to that in a moment. What did you mean when you said the President would be most grateful or happy to have this contribution. What did that imply, in your judgment?

SECORD: In my judgment, I was saying what I believed to be true, that the President would welcome donations to the contras.

COHEN: Do you think that is an appropriate policy to pursue, to have foreign governments contributing to programs or policies of the United States that have been at least circumscribed by the Congress, if not rejected by the Congress?

SECORD: I don't think it is particularly inappropriate. It is not my preference. I believe it was made legal in some legislation.

COHEN: That was long after you had approached him, though, wasn't it?

SECORD: It wasn't illegal then. It is not my preference to be frank with you. It is unseemly, I think, but in this case, there was a pretty desperate situation.

COHEN: Why would a country want to contribute to a program of the United States?

SECORD: Because they have great trust in the United States, because they expect the United States as the leader of the free world and the defender of the free world. They want to protect the United States to the extent they can.

COHEN: Do they expect some sort of reciprocity in the future?

SECORD: I don't see how in this case. They might be thinking that it might improve relations to a small degree.

COHEN: It is a fair assumption that if one country contributes to a program, or several do, that they would expect something in return in the way of evenhanded treatment in the future, or perhaps beneficial treatment with a controversial program in the future. That might enhance their opportunity to have a President who has been grateful for a contribution?

SECORD: I agree with you, sir.

COHEN: That is part of the unseemly aspect of it, when you have other countries who are making contributions and creating at least an implied sort of obligation without the knowledge or consent of Congress or the American people?

SECORD: I agree with an earlier statement by a Senator, who said, I think—where there is a quid there is a quo.

* * *

[Sen. Howell] HEFLIN [D-Ala.]: The most troublesome testimony to me was why was this surplus of six to ten million dollars not spent to help the contras, when you state that the contras so desperately needed help, and Col. North was urging you to help them more.

Also I have considerable uncertainty in my mind as to whether you did or did not mislead Col. North into believing that $12 million from the arms sale had been spent on the contras, when only around $3 million had.

In fairness to you, I would like for you to address these issues and to give you ample time to address them and particularly the

question of why a surplus instead of contra assistance.

SECORD: Sir, I have tried my best to testify as to the requirement for the surplus for operating revenues in those accounts. We had to go forward in an ad hoc basis. We were walking into darkness all the time. We didn't know what was going to happen next.

I had to have monies, I couldn't go back for more money. I had to err on the conservative side, if you will, if there were to be errors. There were overruns, unexpected contingencies. We were dealing with the second channel. I had the question of whether to buy an airplane or not. All these things were floating around.

With respect to the $12 million you referred to, I believe that number appears in the famous memo which was supposedly written in the spring of 1986. I don't know where Ollie North got that number from. It is a completely alien number and he knew it was. It was far, far more money than any of us ever anticipated generating at that time or at any other time in the operation.

So I think you are just going to have to ask Col. North. I think he will testify to it honestly, but I believe that the story as I have spun it out here, sir, will be corroborated by the people that follow me.

* * *

[Rep. Thomas S.] FOLEY [D-Wash.]: Mr. Secord, when you met with firms prior to sale of arms from Iran, you indicated at that time you were not an agent for the CIA or for the U.S. Government or agent thereof?

SECORD: That was my belief.

FOLEY: That you were a commercial cutout and had, as Sen. McClure indicated, an arms-length relationship with the agency?

SECORD: That is correct.

FOLEY: You could have sold those arms to any country in the world and been within your legal rights?

SECORD: In theory.

FOLEY: But as a practical matter, you were not designated as a commercial cutout except under the understanding that you could carry out the wishes of the CIA in making the sales to Iran?

SECORD: There was no such explicit discussion with those lawyers, but it was clear that is where they were to go, and they trusted me.

FOLEY: So you had a moral obligation to follow the direction of the CIA in that regard?

SECORD: No question.

FOLEY: And you undertook that responsibility without any thought of varying in any way from their wishes in that respect?

SECORD: You are correct.

FOLEY: But you still did not consider yourself an agent?

SECORD: No.

FOLEY: What is the distinction?

SECORD: I don't see how I am an agent of the Government, Mr. Foley. I wasn't paid a nickel by the Government. I had no contract, there are no terms of references, no instructions, no nothing. I was in a room full of lawyers at one time. They didn't try to make me an agent.

FOLEY: But you were an instrument of the policy or you saw yourself as an agent?

SECORD: Indeed.

FOLEY: You made a decision apparently with Mr. Hakim not to share personally in the benefits of any of these sales?

SECORD: That is right.

* * *

[Sen. Paul S.] TRIBLE [Jr., R-Va.]: . . . You are living in a world very different than any of us. You are dealing in a world of foreign bank accounts, investments, changing parts and big dollars, big dollars which you can't really explain where they came from, who provided them, or really the purpose to which they would be directed.

SECORD: I don't agree with that.

TRIBLE: I understand that and the record will speak for itself, and that was the point of raising the question. To raise the question and give you an opportunity to respond.

SECORD: Thank you, sir.

TRIBLE: . . . What you have done is you have wrapped yourself and these activities in the American flag, in an attempt to justify what you have done. I am convinced that you are a man who loves this country and I am convinced that you are a man who has sought to advance the interests of this country as you saw them.

But there are some deeply troubling aspects to your testimony and I guess that is the point of the hard questions that have been posed.

Money, secret bank accounts, dealing with very, very dark figures. Millions and millions of dollars. Many people on this committee find it hard to believe that a man who prides himself so much on being in command—"this is my enterprise," "this is my idea," "these are my dollars"—could know so little, care no more, would forswear so much as you have done. Suffice it to say that your testimony about the dollars and the bank accounts and the characters that you have been working with is deeply troubling. . . .

Today your actions and your testimony are being judged by 200 million Americans. Regardless of the size of the jury, be it 200 million or smaller, some people are going to believe you are a patriot, and others will believe you are a privateer. I think you are both. I think you are a man who pursued national interests as he saw it because he loved his country, but also a man who pursued at the same time enormous profits. . . .

* * *

[Rep. Edward P.] BOLAND [D-Mass.]: Now I would like to direct your attention to the period October 3, 1984, through December 19, 1985, just the matter of a little amendment. It has been variously described. It was described, I think, by you as like Swiss cheese, full of holes.

SECORD: No, sir, I didn't say that.

BOLAND: And I think perhaps even the counsel for the Senate indicated that he—that yesterday I think he mentioned the same, that characterization that you applied to it.

Can you indicate what your activity on behalf of the contras at that time during that period, October 3, 1984, through December 19, 1985—I have a list of them here, but you were pretty well involved in the contra activities during that period, were you not?

SECORD: Yes, sir.

BOLAND: What was the role of Oliver North in those activities?

SECORD: Oliver North introduced me to the contra leaders. Oliver North collected the information from me. He kept track of what was going on during these operations. He urged me ahead when the time came to try and create the air operation which I described earlier.

He urged me strongly to move forward in that area and I did.

BOLAND: Now, were other members of the United States Government providing assistance to these activities?

SECORD: Yes, sir, I have testified to this previously.

BOLAND: You responded to a question from Stokes that while you didn't know the legislative history of the amendment, you were aware of various legal opinions that apparently led you to conclude that its meaning was less than clear, and that was the reference made here today, too—not by you.

Let me read the Boland amendment that was in effect between October 3, 1984, and December 19, 1985.

"During fiscal year 1985, no funds available to the Central Intelligence Agency, the Department of Defense or any other agency or entity of the United States Government involved in intelligence activity may be obligated or expended for the purpose of or which would have the effect of supporting, directly or indirectly, military or paramilitary operations in Nicaragua by any nation, group or organization, movement or individual."

General, they are very simple English words. If you have demonstrated anything here in the last four days, it is your magnificent knowledge of the English language, literally.

Now, what would be your literal interpretation or your literal opinion, unadorned opinion of that particular amendment?

SECORD: . . . I am not a lawyer, obviously, but I believe that it is an anti-appropriations act, pure and simple, and does not cover private funds.

BOLAND: General, you understand words. I just read the amendment.

SECORD: Yes, sir.

BOLAND: The words are simple. They are unadorned. They are literate.

SECORD: It means to me—

BOLAND: They are clear.

* * *

INOUYE: The folks outside the Beltway are asking, why don't they take the deposit in Perpetual or Riggs or Maryland National, why in Geneva or Zurich?

Is it true that when you make a deposit in Switzerland, you have to pay a fee?

SECORD: I am not aware of that, Mr. Chairman. It is possible they charge a fee. I know they charge a lot of fees.

INOUYE: The banks around here if you make a deposit even if for a checking account would pay you interest, isn't that correct?

SECORD: Yes, sir.

INOUYE: Do these Swiss banks pay interest?

SECORD: I don't think that the checking accounts do. They have other accounts that are interest-bearing.

INOUYE: Does your account receive any interest?

SECORD: Hakim managed the funds in such a way as to try to draw interest when he could. That is reflected in the record.

INOUYE: Did Mr. Hakim have to pay a fee?

SECORD: Yes. He paid a lot of fees. I think they are required.

INOUYE: Why open a Swiss account? You don't make any money on it?

SECORD: In order to maintain secrecy under Swiss law.

INOUYE: Oh, you don't want others to know that you have an account?

SECORD: That is right.

INOUYE: What sort of people make those deposits?

SECORD: Well, I think a lot of different kinds of people do it for different reasons. We were doing it, sir, to try to maintain secrecy.

Robert C. McFarlane

Following are excerpts from the May 11, 1987, opening statement and testimony of former national security adviser Robert C. McFarlane:

MCFARLANE: . . . There was a powerful—and to many, persuasive—case that to lose in Nicaragua would invite the Soviets to step up their investment in aggression significantly in other developing nations of the world.

We had to win this one. And this is where the Administration made its first mistake. For, if we had such a large strategic vehicle, it was clearly unwise to rely on covert activity as the core of our policy.

There are two basic reasons for this. The first is, that you can never achieve a sufficient level of resources through a covert policy to cope with a determined effort backed by the Soviet Union.

The Congress views covert actions—properly, in my judgment—as an instrument to be used with great selectivity as an adjunct of policy, not as its foundation, and surely not as a vehicle for waging war with a Soviet proxy.

The other reason for not making covert action the core of policy is that you cannot get public and Congressional support for such a policy. If you decide to engage in conflict with a Soviet client in whom the Russians are prepared to make a substantial investment, you must have the American people and the U.S. Congress solidly behind you. Yet, it is virtually impossible, almost as a matter of definition, to rally public support behind a policy that you can't even talk about. . . .

People turned to covert actions because they thought they could not get Congressional support for more overt activities. . . .

In the meantime, the President repeatedly made clear in public and in private that he did not intend to break faith with the contras. He directed that we continue—make continued efforts to bring the movement into the good graces of Congress and the American people and that we assure the contras of continuing Administration support—to help them hold body and soul together—until the time when Congress would again agree to support them.

Congressional restrictions made it impractical for either the Defense Department or the Central Intelligence Agency to function even as a liaison with the contras. The State Department has always been disinclined to be associated with a covert action. But the President had made clear that he wanted a job done. The net result was that the job fell to the National Security Council [NSC] staff. . . .

I did make a special point of stressing to my staff that we were to operate at all times within the law, and that in particular we were not to solicit, encourage, coerce or otherwise broker financial contributions to the contras. . . .

[Arthur L.] LIMAN [Senate committee chief counsel]: Did you come up with a plan for a third country to take over the assistance and management of the contra effort?

MCFARLANE: There was never any concrete plan, either written or discussed orally in these meetings.

LIMAN: Was it a concept of yours, sir?

MCFARLANE: The possibility of third-country contributions I had thought of, that is correct. Others of the Administration had also, and we had talked about it.

LIMAN: And what was the concept that you talked about?

MCFARLANE: At times, since existing law did not prohibit that, there was a hope that perhaps a short bridging of finance by another country, or more than one, would sustain the movement until the administration could make a better case and be more persuasive with the public and the Congress.

LIMAN: Did you have any discussion about the possibility of in effect farming out the whole contra support operation to another country, which would not only provide the funding, but give it some direction?

MCFARLANE: There was some consideration of that.

LIMAN: And whose idea was that?

MCFARLANE: I believe it was probably mine.

LIMAN: Now, did you report this contribution to the President of the United States?

MCFARLANE: Yes, I did.

LIMAN: How often would you meet with the President of the United States as national security adviser?

MCFARLANE: Normally at least once a day, and usually more often, but the date at 9:30 each morning always called for a national security brief that normally tended on towards a half hour.

LIMAN: And when did you tell the President about this, and what did you tell him?

MCFARLANE: I suspect it was within a day, not more than a couple of days, unless we were traveling, and in that meeting with the President, I provided to him in writing a note card which made clear that country two had chosen to volunteer from $1 million per month through the end of the year for contras subsistence, and after that meeting was over, I was called to come back and pick up the note card which, as I recall, it expressed the President's satisfaction and pleasure that this had occurred.

LIMAN: Now it says that you were to assure the contras of continuing administration support to help them hold body and soul together until the time when Congress would again agree to support them. Tell us exactly what kind of support you were to assure the contras of during this period when you were prohibited from spending any money to support them?

MCFARLANE: Well, basically it was smoke and mirrors. It was a matter of trying to demonstrate simply by the presence of a White House person, someone close enough to the President to achieve simply by dint of that proximity, credibility with the contra leaders and to make clear that you are going to have to make do money-wise on someone else. But the President, whose political influence is not insignificant, is going to make your cause

a very high priority cause for himself, second or third on his foreign policy agenda.

But I also made very clear that this has to be done within the law. . . .

LIMAN: And as I understand the line that you were drawing, you couldn't come right out and say, "I want a contribution." Am I correct? That would be a solicitation.

MCFARLANE: That is correct.

LIMAN: But you could express the concerns about the fact that the contras were running out of funds?

MCFARLANE: That is correct.

LIMAN: And if in response to those concerns the foreign leader offered the money, you could tell him where to deposit it?

MCFARLANE: Well, of course, when it was legal the previous summer, he would have known that.

LIMAN: But you could tell him thank you when he offered it in February?

MCFARLANE: Yes.

LIMAN: And it was that kind of line that you found you had to walk in order to keep the contras going?

MCFARLANE: That is correct.

LIMAN: Mr. McFarlane, you understand that [Lt. Col.] Oliver [L.] North had a deep commitment to the contra cause; am I correct?

MCFARLANE: Yes, I did.

LIMAN: This was something that was not just an assignment for him, it was something in which he had a conviction?

MCFARLANE: That is correct.

LIMAN: And he had a conviction that was a conviction shared by the President, by you, and by the administration?

MCFARLANE: That is correct.

LIMAN: And he was also a person who brought enormous energy to what he was doing?

MCFARLANE: Yes, he did.

LIMAN: And is it fair to say he was also a person who was difficult to control when he was in pursuit of an objective?

MCFARLANE: Well, I think Col. North always responded to firm guidance when it was given.

LIMAN: Was he a person who ran with the ball?

MCFARLANE: Yes, he was. He was a very solid, determined, energetic, devoted officer.

LIMAN: Is there question, Mr. McFarlane, as to whether in giving him this task you gave it to a person who would run with the ball very, very far?

MCFARLANE: Well, I thought surely that Ollie was probably the mission-oriented, can-do professional on the staff, and I believe that the interpretation of guidance I had given to him would probably be certainly carried out but that probably he would on occasion go beyond, and I could foresee that.

LIMAN: Well, here you are being told by the director [of Central Intelligence] that if you rely on third countries for lethal support for the contras, and it gets out, Congress could penalize those countries as well as the contras; right?

MCFARLANE: Yes.

LIMAN: And you acknowledged that that was a serious issue? And that you would leave it to the President to decide?

MCFARLANE: Yes.

LIMAN: Did you bring it to the President? Do you have any recollection of that, sir?

MCFARLANE: I know that I did not.

LIMAN: Then why did you tell the CIA that you were going to leave it to the President and not to do it?

MCFARLANE: Well, first, you assume that this is an accurate record there. The first time I have seen this document, but the—two things here.

First of all, when the director would come to the meeting, he would carry a notebook about like this, with inserts such as this one, with the CIA overlay imprinted on it. Occasionally, when there was something he wanted me to follow up on after the meeting, he would give me a clean memorandum, without the CIA lettering on it; and he didn't on this subject.

But concerning this one, over time I found that from the spring of 1984 through the summer, through 1985, in fact, as a consistent matter, I normally disagreed with the director on how a given matter ought to be taken on and promoted with the Congress.

And I also found—and it didn't do very much good to argue about it, and the easy way to resolve a given conflict was just to acknowledge that the only way you are going to solve this is to elevate it to the boss. . . .

LIMAN: Did there come a time when you received a call from an Israeli representative telling you that as a result, an American hostage would be allowed to go free?

MCFARLANE: Yes . . . it was the report from Mr. [David] Kimche [a senior Israeli official] in Israel that, as a practical matter, they had run into difficulties with the Iranian intermediaries, that nonetheless, he believed that while his expectations that all hostages would be released had not been fulfilled, or would not be fulfilled, that we ought to continue the dialogue with them anyway, and that the United States could expect one hostage to be released within a couple of days.

His call must have been on or about the 10th to 12th of September.

LIMAN: Were you asked to play God and choose one hostage?

MCFARLANE: Yes. And I asked for Mr. [William] Buckley.

LIMAN: And that was the subject of some anguish to be put in the position of having to choose?

MCFARLANE: Yes.

LIMAN: And it brought home to you, I take it, what it really meant to be negotiating for hostages?

MCFARLANE: Well, it was very clear that this was not a— the kind of exchange that was proper.

LIMAN: And did you report to the President that as a result of the Israeli shipment, a hostage would be released?

MCFARLANE: Yes, I did.

LIMAN: And you told him ultimately that it was Mr. [Benjamin] Weir?

MCFARLANE: Yes, I did. I believe it was on a Sunday when we got word of that: I called Reverend Weir's family and arranged—and Col. North arranged, I believe, for the rendezvous of the family with him in Norfolk [Va.].

* * *

LIMAN: . . . We were in this Catch-22, that to sell arms would violate our policy, and to take a tough position might result in the hostages being killed?

MCFARLANE: Yes. I had to say I did not think personally that that was likely.

LIMAN: But did you not report that to the President, that that was a possibility when you returned?

MCFARLANE: Others report that I did; and I can accept that I did. I believe, frankly, Ollie reported that. He was in the meeting.

LIMAN: But it was reported to the President—

MCFARLANE: Yes.

* * *

McFarlane's Trip to Tehran

MCFARLANE: We left Tehran in the morning, Tehran time . . . and went back to Israel and upon arrival in the afternoon, by which time people in Washington would have been at work, I asked the communicator to set up the secure radio right there at Ben-Gurion, the airstrip. And while waiting for him to do that, the others in my party were unloading the baggage and personal effects from the aircraft and I suppose I was obviously dispirited by the events in Tehran, and Col. North, I think, in an effort to be supportive, mentioned to me offhandedly that I shouldn't count it a total loss, that we are applying some of the funds from the Iranian connection to Central America, or words to that effect. And I was a little startled.

I went ahead at the time to get on the radio by this time connected to [Rear] Adm. [John M.] Poindexter and reported the completion of the mission and asked for instructions recommending that I simply proceed back to Washington and he acknowl-

edged that and said, fine, go ahead, he would advise the President, and that he would look forward to getting my debrief when I got back.

As I recall, I got off the radio and by this time there was someone from the Shin Bet that picked me up and took me around the airfield to the other side of it where an aircraft was waiting to take us ultimately back to the United States.

Col. North had gone on, I was told, to see about whether or not a separate effort to secure the release of hostages that involved perhaps the DEA [Drug Enforcement Administration] connection that was being played out in Cyprus had been fruitful or not and ultimately I went back to Washington.

LIMAN: Let's make the record absolutely clear. When you said that you communicated with Washington through this secure link, and that you got the approval from the President to return, you did not communicate to Washington what Col. North had just told you about the application of the proceeds of the sale?

MCFARLANE: No, I didn't.

LIMAN: Did you ask Col. North whether he had obtained any approval from Adm. Poindexter or anyone else for the application of the proceeds?

MCFARLANE: No, I didn't.

LIMAN: Did you give any thought as to how the proceeds could be applied to Central America?

MCFARLANE: No, I didn't. I was operating, Mr. Liman, under the context of a request to return and carry out a mission in government as someone who was not in the government, who had no authority to know nor need to know matters beyond what it required to carry out my mission.

LIMAN: Were you uncomfortable with what he told you?

MCFARLANE: Yes. It was of a piece with a half dozen items that I had learned which seemed to me either unorthodox or very risky, but I was not in the government and I took it to be part and parcel of a number of things that I learned, however.

* * *

MCFARLANE: [On November 25, 1986] I heard on the BBC that the attorney general had had a press conference in Washington and had announced the channeling of money to Central America, and the staff changes, and that as part of his briefing, that I had been identified as someone who was witting of that channeling.

. . . I wrote out a statement that I believe was an accurate expression of my knowledge of this matter. It said, basically, that I had learned of it in connection with the trip to Tehran in May, that at the time I was advised I took it to be a matter of approved policy, and that during my own service in government, it had not been raised nor discussed, but that then I called back to the White House and asked for Col. North to read it to him and see if it was an accurate statement of fact.

And I got him on the phone and I said, here is what I have heard and I am sorry. I have a statement that I intend to release if it is accurate. I read it to him. He said, "Yes, that is accurate."

And I asked again, "Ollie, it was approved, wasn't it?"

And he said, "Yes, but it was approved. You know I wasn't doing anything that wasn't approved."

And I said, "Then don't worry, you did the right thing. Just tell it like it was."

Then I think we had a few words that I tried to be consoling, and he talked about the difference between how the matter was to be treated and his first meeting that day before the attorney general's conference and the rather brutal fashion in which he learned of his discharge. . . .

LIMAN: Did you ask Col. North how they discovered this?

MCFARLANE: I believe that he said that—I asked what happened, I think, and he said, they must have found the memo, or words to that effect.

LIMAN: Did he say, "I missed one"?

MCFARLANE: Something like that.

* * *

On May 12, 1987, McFarlane was questioned by John

W. Nields, Jr., and Richard Leon, two counsels for the House committee.

NIELDS: I take it what Mr. North is trying to do here [in a memo sent to McFarlane March 5, 1985] is to reward a certain Central American country for assistance that it had provided to the contras in obtaining arms?

MCFARLANE: Well, I think that any objective person would see it that way. I don't intend to what the Navy calls see a lawyer about it, but the fact that a country on its merits deserves foreign aid is a condition which Ollie could very well wrap into a more romantic portrayal of why they ought to be getting it. Now, it isn't worth arguing about.

Yes, for me, to ask Cabinet officers and the Chairman of the Joint Chiefs whether they thought Guatemala was deserving of foreign aid is a reasonable thing to do. On its merits it was worth endorsing. In March when it came across, I don't recall having gotten—paying attention to it at all. When it came up in August, I do recall saying that this is just one more kind of example of hyperbole where innocent propositions are given a rather lurid kind of cast that was just not true.

NIELDS: But North's purpose in this memo is to reward this Central American country for helping the contras get arms?

MCFARLANE: That I think is correct, yes.

NIELDS: And he says so here, and these are his words, I understand, not yours, "the real purpose of your memo is to find a way by which we can compensate the Central American country for the extraordinary assistance they have provided the Nicaraguan Freedom Fighters."

MCFARLANE: Yes.

NIELDS: Then he goes on to say, at tab 2, "Are end user certificate, which is the Central American country provided for the purchase of nearly $800 million worth of munitions to be delivered to the FDN [the main contra political faction]."

MCFARLANE: Yes.

NIELDS: An end user certificate, I take it, is a certificate that states the actual final user of munitions?

MCFARLANE: That is correct.

NIELDS: And in this case, this Central American country was not the final user of the munitions?

MCFARLANE: Yes.

NIELDS: So the end user certificates were false?

MCFARLANE: That is right, in the normal course of CIA security of a movement the requirement is to identify a country and by working through intelligence sources, and sister services, to gain the cooperation of another country's intelligence service to provide end user certificates. And it isn't beyond imagination—in fact I assume that when the agency was authorized and took part in training the contras that that was part of the training, how you do that.

NIELDS: And I take it that North's purpose here is to reward the Central American country for having these false end user certificates?

MCFARLANE: I think that is true. It may be interesting to note that the U.S. was providing military assistance to other Central American countries, to Salvador, to Honduras, and to Panama in much lesser sums, but Guatemala was the exception and it was because the Congress had understandable complaints about their human rights record and the killing of peasants and others by militia forces of internal security forces but that had begun to change for about a year's time and there had been a new government and for me raising the question—

NIELDS: Without getting into what Central American country we are talking about, and you have listed a number, I take it it is fair to say that Mr. North was in touch with people from that Central American country?

MCFARLANE: Yes.

NIELDS: And, indeed, he had obtained what he refers to as a wish list from that country?

MCFARLANE: Yes.

NIELDS: And he has been in touch with them, would you not infer, in connection with their having provided these end user certificates?

MCFARLANE: I suppose....

NIELDS: The wish list ... is a list of various kinds of military equipment that this country wants.

MCFARLANE: Yes.

NIELDS: And North had obtained that wish list?

MCFARLANE: Yes.

* * *

NIELDS: And what he is writing [in a memo]—he is asking you if you will make a recommendation to the Secretaries of Defense and State that this Central American country be rewarded?

MCFARLANE: I don't think it was quite accurate. He is asking that I ask them for their views on whether this country merits the aid, I believe.

NIELDS: Well, he is asking you to send a memorandum which recommends that they be given some aid?

MCFARLANE: Yes, and I felt that way. I didn't feel that way because they were giving support to the contras alone, although, gosh, that certainly wouldn't disqualify them for me.

NIELDS: And you did eventually send that memorandum?

MCFARLANE: Yes.

NIELDS: And he says in his memo to you at the top of page two, your memo does not refer to the arrangements which have been made for supporting the resistance, referring to the Nicaraguan resistance, I take it.

MCFARLANE: Yes.

NIELDS: And in fact, your memorandum did not make any such reference?

MCFARLANE: No.

* * *

LEON: As I recall your testimony, when you first learned of that country's [Saudi Arabia's] decision to give more money and double its contribution from the prior year, when you first learned of that, my understanding of your testimony is you were the first to learn that; is that correct?

MCFARLANE: That is likely, I think, yes.

LEON: Before accepting it from that country, in light of the risks that [the] Boland [amendment] might present, did you decide to find out from anybody in the Administration as to whether or not it should be accepted before first assessing the legal consequences of accepting it?

MCFARLANE: No. At the time to me it did seem to be a clear case of a voluntary chipping in, of a donation by this party.

LEON: So you didn't see—you didn't perceive any legal problem with respect to accepting the gift at that time?

MCFARLANE: No, I didn't.

LEON: Even in light of your understanding of Boland—

MCFARLANE: That is right.

LEON: Involvement potentially in this money being generated?

MCFARLANE: That is right.

LEON: And you informed the President with regard to that second gift again in writing in the note to this book?

MCFARLANE: Yes, I believe so.

LEON: Now, on that occasion, was there a reason you informed him in that manner in any way because you were concerned about the legality of your conduct vis-à-vis that contribution?

MCFARLANE: Not at all. I informed him because I had no way of knowing whether he knew about it or not. I had no reason for knowing whether it came up in the conversation that he had had, and apparently, there may have been some ambiguity in what I said yesterday on that score.

I didn't intend to imply that in that meeting the President raised this issue with the Head of State of the other government. I know for a fact he did not.

LEON: OK. How is it that you know for a fact he did not?

MCFARLANE: Because I had occasion to check on this when I was asked about it six weeks ago during these investigative proceedings, and all I knew or my basis for knowing was the debrief I got at the end of the meeting from the President, in which he made no mention of this subject having come up, and so, based on that, my own opinion was he did not.

But I didn't know whether there might have been something else in his diary, and I was informed that there was by a senior White House official, but that it had not been raised by the President.

* * *

McFarlane on North

MCFARLANE: . . . I am afraid that in the past two days that Ollie is really getting a bum rap which appears to be endorsed from me, and I don't intend that.

I think Col. North is a man of immense devotion to the preservation of human life. That sounds like a platitude, but it isn't at all. He is a person of very deep and profound conviction, belief in God, who relies on his conscience, as all of us do, but one that is formed in scholarly pursuit of scriptures and passionate in its extreme energy.

He is quite cynical about government. Ollie is a man that is a veteran of an experience in Vietnam, of which I was very conscious, and I think not uncommon to the experience of many people—that is a situation that anyone who exposes himself to the loss of life, his own, has to deal, and that is, is it worth it?

And for him it was an easy determination that, yes, it was, because there were enough daily shows of evidence by Vietnamese people, young and old, children, others, of their satisfaction that he was there. And yet, that personal justification was in very sharp tension with the reality that we were losing.

Now, in the wake of his service there, having to cope with the vivid reminders of how worth it it was and how tragic a loss of life of Vietnamese—tens of thousands occurred from it—I believe that he committed himself to assuring that he would never be party to such a thing again if he could prevent it.

And I think for him, when it became a matter of association with the contra movement, that it was again a circumstance where we had made a commitment to people, that he could see we were just about to break, and that the bottom-line consequence of that would be the death of a lot of people, contras, and that he couldn't be party to that. . .

I think Mr. North acted not out of a motive of self-gain but out of a very human commitment to the preservation of life. . . .

* * *

[Sen. Paul S.] SARBANES [D-Md.]: In all of this, who or what are you trying to shield or protect?

MCFARLANE: Very likely myself, my reputation, my own record of performance.

SARBANES: And only that?

MCFARLANE: Well, I believe, Sen. Sarbanes, that President Reagan's motives and direction to his subordinates throughout this entire enterprise has always been in keeping with the law and national values. I don't think he is at fault here and if anybody is, I am.

* * *

McFarlane resumed his testimony, May 13, 1987:

[Rep. Jim] COURTER [R-N.J.]: It seems to me looking at the even most restrictive amendments that were passed by Congress relative to Central America, that they referred—and we have a copy of them on the wall over here—they referred to the fact that no funds available to certain organizations. I know that Mr. [Edward P.] Boland [D-Mass.], who asked questions just a few moments ago, said the operable words are "no funds."

I want to ask you whether you think—and I would hold—that the operable words there are "available to" and then you read on.

The question is that if the Congress was true, if the Congress was clear, they would have prohibited money from the United States going to Central America rather than money designated to individual agencies going to Central America; is that correct?

MCFARLANE: I think it is legally correct, Mr. Courter;

but—and I think that—in that same context—are ways that I as a person not paid by the NSC could condone doing, not being covered by the law. But I didn't because neither you nor I should engage in this kind of interpretation for convenience, self-serving interpretations.

I mean, it was clear to me Mr. Boland didn't want anybody in the U.S. Government assisting the contras. We lost. Okay. Don't do it. That's the right thing to do.

But there were people after the vote here saying, well, the CIA can't do it, and the Defense Department can't do it, who were the only people good at doing it, but all the rest of you can do it. Now, that's just not reasonable.

* * *

INOUYE: Did you feel that it was your duty and responsibility to report to the President on the first contribution [from Saudi Arabia to the contras]?

MCFARLANE: Yes, sir.

INOUYE: On the second contribution?

MCFARLANE: Yes, sir.

INOUYE: Did you also feel that he, the President, should be notified because of his deep concern for the body and soul of the contras?

MCFARLANE: Yes, sir.

INOUYE: That he would be interested in any sort of assistance?

MCFARLANE: Yes, sir.

INOUYE: If that is the case, why wasn't he notified about the diversion?

MCFARLANE: Again, Mr. Chairman, I don't know. I wasn't in the Administration at the time. I operated under the assumption that he had been or at least that the decision to do it was approved as part of the normal process, and I was wrong, but I didn't know that.

INOUYE: If you were in charge at that time, would you have notified the President of the diversion?

MCFARLANE: I would not have allowed the diversion to occur.

INOUYE: Assuming that it did?

MCFARLANE: Yes, sir, I would.

INOUYE: Did you during your term as director advise the President of some of the extraordinary activities of Col. North?

MCFARLANE: Well, I think I did make clear to the President that Col. North was a very—a very tireless, hard-working, devoted officer. That is true.

* * *

[Sen. Warren B.] RUDMAN [R-N.H.]: My question is based on your general testimony here that you did have concerns about whether Col. North was crossing the line that you had set for your people, did you ever inform the President of North's activities to the extent that there were some activities that you were concerned might be crossing the line?

MCFARLANE: I remember that I was periodically concerned about the almost certain temptation to raise money that would come up whenever Ollie would go out and talk to groups throughout the country.

It would have been silly not to expect that that would happen and so I would mention occasionally that Ollie was doing quite a lot of speaking around the country and it was clear there was a lot of sentiment in support of the contras, but that was proscribed and we had to be very careful not to do that. I was telling the staff not to.

RUDMAN: I guess my question is did you ever give the President any cause for alarm in his mind as the President that people who worked for him might be doing things proscribed by the Congress?

MCFARLANE: No, sir. The President, in fact, would often provide his own views on that subject generically, and there is no doubt in my mind that he had a far more liberal interpretation of that than I did, I think. But that I was making sure that things as far as I knew or could tell didn't go beyond the law.

* * *

RUDMAN: You are familiar with Exhibit 38-A involving the DEA caper?

MCFARLANE: Yes, sir.

RUDMAN: That describes a plan to bribe some people to free two hostages for a million dollars apiece?

MCFARLANE: Yes, sir.

RUDMAN: You approved it?

MCFARLANE: The Attorney General approved it.

RUDMAN: And the Attorney General approved it. You both approved it.

MCFARLANE: Yes, sir.

RUDMAN: Did it involve the use of a couple of agents and ransom money to be supplied by [H.] Ross Perot [businessman], if he was willing to provide it?

Was that an intelligence activity? And if it wasn't, what kind of an activity was it?

MCFARLANE: Well, it wasn't intelligence in the context of gathering intelligence. It was within the scope of the 1947 Act concerning the CIA.

RUDMAN: It was within that scope, was it not?

MCFARLANE: I think it was.

RUDMAN: In fact, Oliver North tried to carry this out, which was a policy that had been approved by you. In fact, there was $200,000 used to try to start the process?

MCFARLANE: That's correct.

RUDMAN: On the face of that memoranda, there is an acknowledgement that the Attorney General of the United States, Mr. [Edwin] Meese [III], whom you probably discussed it with since DEA was under his jurisdiction, approved it?

MCFARLANE: Yes, sir.

RUDMAN: To your knowledge, was a finding ever signed for this activity?

MCFARLANE: No, sir.

RUDMAN: Were congressional committees, House or Senate Intelligence Committees ever notified of this activity?

MCFARLANE: No, sir.

RUDMAN: Should they have been?

MCFARLANE: No, sir.

* * *

McFarlane resumed his testimony May 14, 1987:

[Rep. Jack] BROOKS [D-Texas]: Now, Mr. McFarlane, you testified on two occasions that you asked Col. North if he had approval for diverting funds from the Iranian arms sales to the contras, and he said, yes, that he would never do anything without approval. What do you think he meant by approval? By whom?

MCFARLANE: I had the impression that that had to mean at least by Adm. Poindexter, and that I have no basis for judging beyond that. He made no other comment on it.

BROOKS: Well, based on your knowledge of the structure in the White House and the National Security Council, do you believe that only Poindexter would have made a major decision like that to divert funds to the contras, or would that decision have necessitated the approval of the Chief Executive of the country?

MCFARLANE: Mr. Chairman, I think my own knowledge on it extends only to what I have said. Something of that magnitude, assuming it were brought to the Admiral's attention, I am sure he would not undertake on his own authority, but because I cannot say conclusively that it was indeed brought to his attention and not to anybody else's, I am speculating here.

BROOKS: When you were head of the National Security Council and a decision like that would have been made, would you have made a unilateral decision to extend money to the contras in violation of the Congressional law?

MCFARLANE: No, sir.

BROOKS: Not without checking with the President; is that right?

MCFARLANE: That is right, sir. . . .

BROOKS: . . . Now, Mr. McFarlane, are you aware of any U.S. funds other than those from the Iranian arms sales that found their way into the contra effort or were intended to go to the contras directly or indirectly such as AID [Agency for Interna-

tional Development] funds, State Department funds, currency exchange activities or any other device for transferring money?

MCFARLANE: No, sir.

BROOKS: Now, yesterday you testified that you discussed activities of Col. North and the Boland amendment with President Reagan, and you indicated that you were concerned that Col. North might try to raise money during his speaking engagements on behalf of the contras, but that the President had a far more liberal interpretation of the Boland amendment than you did— and what did you mean by a "more liberal interpretation?"

Could you describe the conversations that led to . . . your conclusions?

MCFARLANE: Yes, sir. I think it is probably a poor choice of words on my part. What I intended was to reflect that in our conversations the President often noted his belief that the tradition in the United States of helping freedom fighters, as he referred to them, was very clear and he thought entirely legal.

He would refer occasionally to the volunteers that fought in the Spanish Civil War in the 1930s, referred to others that have gone overseas to fight before we were formally at war, joined other countries' armed forces, and said that he believed that this tradition that goes all the way back to our own Revolution and the assistance we got from the French is one that we should be— should identify with and support, but that is not to say that he urged or in any way authorized me or anyone else to take any illegal activity.

And on your first point, sir, if I implied that I was telling him about possible violations of law by Col. North, I didn't intend that.

* * *

[Rep. Lee H.] HAMILTON [D-Ind.]: Now what concerns me is the disparity between your opening remarks and the remainder of your testimony. The approach to making—to the making of foreign policy set forth in your opening statement is in my view quite at odds with the foreign policy process you have described in your subsequent testimony.

To my mind, at least, they are hard, if not impossible to reconcile. I will not go into a lot of detail here, but let me quote some of your words. When questioned about various aspects of your involvement in providing assistance to the contras, you have told us that you "used some tortured language"; that you did not provide "a full account"; that you were "too categorical"; and that you gave the Congress in response to congressional inquiries "incomplete statements."

In testimony under oath before the Foreign Affairs Committee last year when you were asked about the contributions, you responded, "I have no idea of the extent of that or anything else."

And you said, "I have seen the reports and heard that Country Two [Saudi Arabia] contributed. The concrete character of that is beyond my ken."

Now, I have been impressed as I have sat here for these hours again and again with the clear discrepancies [in] what you and others in the administration told the Congress that the administration was or was not doing and what, in fact, was done. And so I ask myself how can the Congress find out what has happened?

If the National Security Adviser of the President of the United States and other high officials do not provide complete and accurate answers to the Congress, what can we do? How must we frame our questions to get the facts?

Must we put every Executive Branch official under oath who comes before us? Must we regard every claim of executive privilege and every statement of explanation with great skepticism? When can we be assured that we are hearing the whole truth?

How can we get a total account of what is happening so that we can be a responsible partner rather than an adversary in the process?

How can our system of government work if the Administration is not candid in its answers to the Congress?

The Congress only knows one way to get information, and that is through the process that we are engaged in here. Sen. Sarbanes asked you who or what you were trying to shield or protect and you said in short that you were trying to protect yourself and repeatedly during these hearings you have volunteered to take the blame, the whole blame on yourself.

I appreciate your willingness to shoulder great responsibilities, I admire you for it, but I cannot accept that answer. As the National Security Adviser you are the spokesman for the President of the United States and when we write to you we do not write to Mr. McFarlane, we write to you as the representative of the President, and when you spoke to the Congress and when you wrote to the Congress we accepted your words and your assurances as those of the President.

You spoke for the President. And the responsibility must rest with him as well as with you. You cannot, it seems to me, accept responsibility for mistakes as admirable as that may be and thereby absolve the President of responsibility.

* * *

At the conclusion of North's testimony July 14, 1987, McFarlane again took the witness stand. He refuted claims that he had authorized many of North's covert activities. (North testimony, p. C-75)

[Sen. Sam] NUNN [D-Ga.]: . . . Let me ask you something you have already testified to but since it came up in this recent testimony—did you authorize or did you know that Col. North was asking Ambassador [to Costa Rica Lewis A.] Tambs to open a Southern Front [in Nicaragua]?

MCFARLANE: When I heard that testimony I did recall that Col. North discussed with me whether or not it would be worthwhile for a Southern Front to be opened by the contras. That was manifestly in the interest of the contras, if they could do it and bring it off to do that, so there wasn't a serious matter of argument on that score.

With regard to having Ambassador Tambs involved with it, I am not sure what that would be. Surely Ambassador Tambs was not to be the man in the field that somehow organized the effort and supported it. My recollection is that the limit of the exchange was on whether or not the contras opening a Southern Front was a good idea, and I said if they can do it that's fine.

NUNN: Well, that could have implied, could it not, to Col. North, that he had the authority in that case? It seems to me that based on what you have said he would be entitled to assume that he had authority when you said that what he had proposed was a good idea.

MCFARLANE: Well, to say that it is useful for a Southern Front to be opened seems to me a long lead, but I think certainly I am not perfect and I can be misunderstood. I am only saying that with regard to directing Ambassador Tambs to become involved in anything, I just don't believe that occurred.

NUNN: One other question that you previously testified to that came up this morning, the Channell group [run by Carl R. "Spitz" Channell]. Did you know again that Col. North was associated with the Channell group in the overall contra effort—I won't call it solicitation, because we have been through that one in length, but whatever it was, did you know that he was involved with the Channell group?

MCFARLANE: No, sir, I didn't. The existence of the Channell group came to my attention when I suppose everyone else's here, a few months ago. I had heard earlier that some group was promoting ads on television for SDI [the strategic defense initiative] and for the contra movement, but in the sense of raising money for direct linkage to the contras, no, I was never aware of that.

* * *

[Rep. William S.] BROOMFIELD [R-Mich.]: . . . I would like to know, in retrospect, do you think your differences of recollection on several key factors with Col. North is a matter of intentional misstatements on the part of Col. North or an honest difference of opinion?

MCFARLANE: I don't think Col. North would ever make a deliberate misstatement or a lie. I don't believe that. That leaves only the possibilities of differing interpretations between us, and I think that must account for these disagreements. They are cer-tainly not ones that are malicious, I am sure, on his part and don't derogate from what were his motives that were entirely patriotic.

BROOMFIELD: If there were misunderstandings about Col. North's orders, do you consider that your fault as a supervisor, or did Lt. Col. North intentionally mislead you?

MCFARLANE: I believe that he is a thoroughly honest man of integrity and would not deliberately mislead me ever.

I believe in earlier testimony I said that if he failed to inform me of something he was doing, which he thought might be questionable, he probably did it to protect me. So I would not hold him to account even if there were voids of information.

* * *

'Body and Soul'

[Rep. Thomas S.] FOLEY [D-Wash.]: Mr. McFarlane, did you give Col. North a direct instruction from the President that he should keep the contras together, body and soul, as a viable fighting force?

MCFARLANE: I did, and I explained what I believed that meant, that it was to spend his time trying to turn them into a credible political organization by incorporating acknowledged leaders within Nicaragua into the military leadership and also working with him to come up with a platform so that they would be seen by Congressmen as a political movement of real substance interested in negotiation; and he did that. And I think if anything is missing from the past six days, it is to acknowledge that enormous diplomacy of Col. North in being able to pull off what was an extremely solid platform and peace proposals.

FOLEY: Was the instruction also to assist the contras in a military way to keep them as a viable military fighting force in the field?

MCFARLANE: No, sir.

FOLEY: Did you receive these instructions from the President personally?

MCFARLANE: Clearly the President wanted the contras to survive and stated so to me many times, and I translated that expressed wish of the President to Col. North and others on my staff. He also, the President, expressed this to the Secretary of State and Defense, Director Casey. It was no secret.

FOLEY: So he, the President, told you that he wanted to see this result occur, and you translated that into a direction directed to Col. North, is that correct?

MCFARLANE: That is correct.

FOLEY: The President didn't say, "Tell Col. North that I want him to do this"?

MCFARLANE: No, sir.

* * *

Raising Funds for the Contras?

[Sen. Paul S.] SARBANES [D-Md.]: . . . Col. North said here that in the early days of 1984, when it was seen that money was running out, there were discussions within the Administration as to the alternatives and that Director Casey suggested Gen. Secord [retired major general Richard V. Secord] to him as a person who could act outside of the Government of the United States, provide assistance in this contra support effort. And he then said, "The person who suggested Gen. Secord to me, and I then took the name to Mr. McFarlane, was Director Casey."

Now, I take it it is your testimony that you didn't know about Gen. Secord's role in any of this until the Honduran meeting in December of 1985; is that correct?

MCFARLANE: That is correct, Sen. Sarbanes, and I think that the statement is also reinforced by the facts that are on the public record.

Specifically, in 1984 to my knowledge, there was no meeting or deliberate plan developed to plan for the contingency of a congressional cutoff.

The reason why you wouldn't need to do that was because as we have learned separately a country, a second, third country had volunteered to support and continue to sustain the needs of the contras.

That same country continued that into 1985, so as a practical matter at least from my point of view, there wasn't any need for there to be some new creation, because the funding level was carried on.

SARBANES: Did the account number in which these countries that were being solicited would deposit their money come to you from Col. North?

MCFARLANE: Yes, sir, I testified to that.

SARBANES: And did Col. North solicit third countries for money with your authorization?

MCFARLANE: Did he solicit from third countries—

SARBANES: With your authorization?

MCFARLANE: No, sir.

SARBANES: Well, now, Col. North said he was asked, Mr. McFarlane has testified that he gave you instructions not to solicit money from foreign countries or private sources. Did he give you those instructions? And then Col. North said this litany, I never carried out a single act, not one that did not have authority from my superiors, and it was then pointed out that that wasn't the question. The question was did McFarlane give you such instructions. He said no, I never heard those instructions, instructions from you not to solicit money from foreign countries or private sources.

As I recall your testimony when you were here before us it was your opinion that you had given such instructions repeatedly and explicitly to all members of the National Security Council staff, is that correct?

MCFARLANE: It is and I can identify with certainty an occasion where Col. North and I talked about the several speeches, which I encouraged, and exactly what happened at each one of them and he explained to me that he at no time was party to taking of money or even facilitating getting it from a potential giver to a bank account and so forth. And quite honestly trying to put myself in his position I could imagine where that would have been very hard to do. And I said look Ollie, with some fairly candid Marine Corps expletives, this is Bud, this is me, this is not some Member of Congress—what is the story? Are you out raising money? And he said I have never in any fashion breached the law concerning any activities, nor have I ever raised money.

He was very emphatic. I believed him.

* * *

COURTER: You indicated from my recollection, it feels like a number of months ago when you testified, a lot has gone over the bridge, you indicated that it was your opinion that the Boland Amendment covered the National Security Council, it that correct?

MCFARLANE: Yes, sir. It was not a legal judgment, but one that I thought the only politically sensible course.

COURTER: You also indicated that you had not read nor was it brought to your attention the fact that the Intelligence Oversight Board wrote an opinion that indicated that the National Security Council was not covered by Boland, you were unaware of that opinion?

MCFARLANE: I was unaware of it.

COURTER: Did you in writing ever indicate to those people in your office while you were the head of the National Security Council of your opinion that the Boland amendment covered the National Security Council?

MCFARLANE: No, sir, I never did. But I would like to add that if you are a member of the staff and you are sitting there and you hear the boss come to the meeting once a week and had a rage and pound the table about how hard we have got to try to overturn the Boland Amendment, what other conclusion is possible? I didn't like it. I wanted to get rid of it. We fought like crazy to get the votes. If it didn't apply to us that was a lot of wasted effort.

* * *

[Sen. William S.] COHEN [R-Maine]: ... You indicated there was discussion between yourself and Col. North, I believe it was on the 21st, about going out to his house, having a conversation, having to leave, and there was a discussion in the car on the way back into town about a shredding party.

Would you restate that for us, please, because Col. North has indicated that no such statement was made.

MCFARLANE: It was at [former NSC counsel Michael] Ledeen's house on the morning of the 21st, a Friday. I got a call from Mr. Ledeen shortly before 11:00, I think, asking if I would come by to see him. I don't recall his saying that Col. North would be there, because he wanted to summarize for me how he believed he had participated, and I went there at about 11:00.

We got down to sitting in the den at about 15 or 20 minutes later. He took 15 or 20 minutes to go through a summary, which was basically that he had been not a designated agent, but a person who did report information that he learned. And I said that I understood that to be essentially correct.

And about that time, Col. North arrived in a taxi, and when he came in, he said to Mr. Ledeen that he was going to have to turn around and go back because something had come up at the office and that he would like to arrange to come back and see Mr. Ledeen later in the day, and he asked me if I would give him a ride back downtown. And I said that I was—that I would. And as we—I waited for him about another five minutes outside, and he came back out—and I don't have any absolutely rock-solid certainty of all the things we talked about, but I believe with confidence that he mentioned that he thought or he was worried about the fact that Mr. Ledeen had—might have gotten some profit out of the Iranian business, which he has since said that he does not believe, and I agree.

We went on downtown, and I think we talked abut our families. I think Col. North made a reference to his confidence that things would go all right and that he had put his trust in the Lord in a spiritual reference and that he was concerned that it not involve the President and the President be protected; and, as I recall it, either then or perhaps in my office on Sunday, but on one of those two occasions, he said that there was going to have to be a shredding party.

I told him that, "To the extent you are worried about whatever involves me, Ollie, don't worry about it. Testify on the truth. You always did what I told you, I believe, and I will back you up." I dropped him off, and that is all I remember about it.

COHEN: What did you think he meant by protecting the President?

MCFARLANE: Well, I really believe, sir, that it was a kind of an instinctive statement by a subordinate about what he believed his duty to be. I don't think it was any more conspiratorial than that, that here he was, a Lieutenant Colonel, talking to someone, me, that he saw as his superior, and he wanted to acknowledge to me both that he believed he had an obligation to protect me and the President, and he did say that it is important that the President not be hurt by this.

And yet, I took it as really something that is instinctive among subordinates to the Commander in Chief, and not a conspiratorial reference.

COHEN: In fact, that was the instinct that led the group to try to reconstruct the chronology to be presented to the Congressional committees thereafter, wasn't it?

MCFARLANE: I think that is overdrawn, but I think we all had an instinct that the President should not be harmed.

Robert W. Owen

Following are excerpts from the May 14, 1987, testimony of Robert W. Owen, who delivered payments from Lt. Col. Oliver L. North to the contras:

[Neil] EGGLESTON [House deputy general counsel]: When you say that Col. North asked you to do some work for him, what is it that he asked you to do?

OWEN: He asked me to go change traveler's checks into dollars.

EGGLESTON: What did he want you to do with the dollars?

OWEN: Once I completed the transaction, I set up an appointment with the contra leader and paid him with the cash.

EGGLESTON: When you first had the conversation with

Col. North about you cashing the checks, where were you?

OWEN: In the Old Executive Office Building in his office.

EGGLESTON: Did he hand you the traveler's checks in his office?

OWEN: Yes, he did.

EGGLESTON: Did you see where he got the traveler's checks from?

OWEN: Yes, I did.

EGGLESTON: Where did he get the traveler's checks from?

OWEN: Out of a safe in his office. Unfortunately, it must have been an unlucky safe. It was the safe where the thousand dollars for Richard [V.] Allen [Reagan's first national security adviser] was found.

EGGLESTON: I take it you know that because Col. North told you that?

OWEN: Yes.

EGGLESTON: Indeed did Col. North make a joke about that?

OWEN: He did.

EGGLESTON: Did he on several occasions joke about the fact that the safe where he was keeping these traveler's checks was the same safe Mr. Allen had used?

OWEN: He made some comments to that effect.

EGGLESTON: I take it you don't know whether that was the same safe Mr. Allen uses?

OWEN: It makes a nice story.

EGGLESTON: This is based on what Mr. North said to you?

OWEN: Yes.

EGGLESTON: Did you, in fact, cash these traveler's checks?

OWEN: I did.

EGGLESTON: Cash them in your own name?

OWEN: Yes.

EGGLESTON: Did you, in fact, give them to a contra leader?

OWEN: Yes, I did.

EGGLESTON: Where did you give it to the contra leader?

OWEN: In my apartment.

EGGLESTON: Was anyone else present at that time you provided the funds to the contra leader?

OWEN: No.

EGGLESTON: What was the amount of the funds that you provided?

OWEN: I am not sure whether it was six or seven thousand dollars.

EGGLESTON: Was there anyone else present at the time that you received the traveler's checks from Col. North?

OWEN: Yes.

EGGLESTON: Who was that?

OWEN: An individual named Johnathan Miller.

EGGLESTON: What was Johnathan Miller's position at that time?

OWEN: At that time he was either on loan to the NSC [National Security Council] or working out of the State Department from the Office of Public Diplomacy for Latin America.

EGGLESTON: Did Mr. Miller also cash checks?

OWEN: It was felt that there were probably too many checks for me to cash in the amount of time that I had, so he did cash some traveler's checks.

EGGLESTON: Do you have a recollection of the dollar amount that you cashed as opposed to the dollar amount Mr. Miller cashed?

OWEN: I think he may have done $3,000 and I did $4,000 or both did $3,500 or $3,000 and $3,000.

EGGLESTON: Did you go together to cash the checks?

OWEN: No. We went our separate ways.

EGGLESTON: And you then met back someplace where you received the cash from him?

OWEN: Yes.

EGGLESTON: Where did you meet back?

OWEN: I believe we met at Col. North's office.

EGGLESTON: Was Col. North there?

OWEN: I don't remember.

EGGLESTON: But Mr. Miller gave you the cash and you

then made the appointment to pay the money to the contra leader.

OWEN: Yes.

EGGLESTON: Did you make any other payments to this contra leader?

OWEN: No, not directly to him.

EGGLESTON: Did you know whether Col. North made any arrangements to make further payments to this contra leader?

OWEN: There was a discussion that the contra leader wanted to find a way that he could both be paid to continue with the Nicaraguan resistance and do some work for the pay that he was receiving. I believe Col. North may have talked to some various foundations to see if there was some work available for him.

EGGLESTON: Did you have any conversation with Col. North about the reason that the U.S. Government could no longer pay this contra leader?

OWEN: It was a concern of Members on the Hill that if this person was receiving funds from a U.S. agency that it would be illegal for him to be up on the Hill. . . .

EGGLESTON: Do you know where Col. North obtained the traveler's checks that were located in his safe?

OWEN: I believe they were traveler's checks provided to him by [contra leader] Adolfo Calero. . . .

* * *

Owen resumed his testimony May 19, 1987:

EGGLESTON: Mr. Owen, in the fall, September and October of 1985, did you have occasion to take trips up to New York at the instructions of Col. North?

OWEN: The first time I went, it was not at the instruction of Col. North, but yes, I took three trips to New York.

EGGLESTON: And the first time, did there come a time when you went up on a bank holiday?

OWEN: Yes, on Sept. 16th, I believe it was Rosh Hashanah, and the banks were closed, I was asked to go up there.

EGGLESTON: And you were asked to go by Col. North?

OWEN: No, Col. North gave me a phone number to call, and a person to ask for, and that person was Mr. Copp, who obviously was [retired major general Richard V.] Secord.

EGGLESTON: Did you know at that time he was Mr. Secord?

OWEN: I had a very good idea, yes.

EGGLESTON: You, I take it, then, had a conversation with Secord?

OWEN: Yes, sir, I did. He gave me instructions, the address, and in essence a code to use when I went and approached the person.

EGGLESTON: Where did you go?

OWEN: I flew up to New York and I took a cab down to the Lower West Side, and I was instructed to go to a corner Chinese market.

EGGLESTON: And you went to the market?

OWEN: Yes, sir.

EGGLESTON: Did you give a code name?

OWEN: I asked for the person, I don't remember his name, and then I said that—I used the code name, saying this person sent me—and I am afraid I don't remember—I think it was something like "Mooey," or something along those lines.

EGGLESTON: Did that person then give you anything?

OWEN: Yes, he did. He walked behind the counter. I believe he rolled up his pant leg and pulled out a wad of $100 bills. Not I believe, I know he pulled out a wad of $100 bills.

EGGLESTON: Did he give a part of this wad to you?

OWEN: He gave the whole wad to me. He asked me if I wanted to count it. I did not know how much I was supposed to be getting, but I decided I had better count it anyways.

EGGLESTON: And how many $100 bills did he give you?

OWEN: There were 95; it was $9,500.

EGGLESTON: After getting the bills from him, the $9,500 in cash, did you return to D.C.?

OWEN: Yes, I did.

EGGLESTON: And did you meet with Gen. Secord?

OWEN: Yes, I did. I was told that he would be waiting for me at the Sheraton Carlton. I went in the lobby. I saw him sitting in the bar. I went downstairs, used the house phone, and called the bar and asked to speak with him. And then I met him in the lobby.

EGGLESTON: Did you give him the cash?

OWEN: Yes, sir, I did. I had folded it in a newspaper and handed him the newspaper.

EGGLESTON: Did you know the reason that you took this trip?

OWEN: I just knew that obviously they were short of cash and they must have needed it, it was a bank holiday, and this was the easiest way for them to get it.

EGGLESTON: But you do not know, you were not told the reason that they needed this $9,500 in cash?

OWEN: No, sir, I was not.

EGGLESTON: Did you have any conversation with Gen. Secord about the reason that the amount was only $9,500?

OWEN: Yes, sir, I suggested to Mr. Secord that perhaps the money-changer had taken his 5 percent, and he said, no, he assured me that that was to stay within the legal law, so that no more than $10,000 was transmitted in one transaction; so they kept it under the $10,000 so it would not have to be reported.

EGGLESTON: You understood that there was some reporting requirements when people deal in amounts of cash in excess of $10,000?

OWEN: Yes, sir, and every time I would travel to Central America, there were always large signs posted, saying that if you have $10,000 or more that you are taking in or bringing out, you have to declare it.

Trips to New York

EGGLESTON: Did you take any other trips to New York in order to obtain cash?

OWEN: Yes, I took two more.

EGGLESTON: And on whose instructions did you take those trips?

OWEN: Again, Gen. Secord's.

EGGLESTON: And did you have conversations with Col. North before taking those trips?

OWEN: Yes, I did.

EGGLESTON: Is it actually Col. North who asked you to take the trips?

OWEN: I guess that is questionable, I mean, it was both for Col. North and Gen. Secord.

EGGLESTON: How did you get the money on those occasions?

OWEN: I went to a bank, which was I think in the mid-40s in Manhattan, and I went up to the sixth floor, and unfortunately I don't remember the name of the bank, asked for a person whose name I had been given, and told them that I was expected to pick up an envelope, and they provided me with an envelope each time.

EGGLESTON: Do you remember the name of the person who you were to speak to?

OWEN: No, sir.

EGGLESTON: And did you see inside the envelope?

OWEN: No, sir, I did not.

EGGLESTON: It was sealed at the time you got it?

OWEN: Yes, it was.

EGGLESTON: And did you have to sign any receipt for it?

OWEN: No.

EGGLESTON: You were simply handed the envelope filled with cash or whatever was in it?

OWEN: Yes, I can't necessarily testify that it was cash, because I didn't know, but it certainly felt the same shape and size.

EGGLESTON: And on those two occasions, after getting the envelopes from the bank, the person at the bank, what did you do with the envelopes?

OWEN: I returned to Washington, and on these two occasions I believe I took the envelopes to Col. North, in his office.

*   *   *

EGGLESTON: Do you recall that there actually came a time when Col. North met with Members of Congress?

OWEN: I believe he met with them in August of 1986.

EGGLESTON: Did you have any conversations with him prior to the time that he had that meeting about the way he was going to respond to those questions?

OWEN: I don't think so. I did talk with him after he had those conversations.

EGGLESTON: You did have a conversation with him afterwards, after the meeting?

OWEN: Yes, sir.

EGGLESTON: And did he say anything to you about what he had said to the Members of Congress about his association with you?

OWEN: Yes, he did. Col. North at that time, obviously, was very busy. I never wanted to take up much of his time when I did get in to talk with him.

I asked him if he had had the meeting. He said he had. He said that my name was brought up. And his comment to that question was, yes, I know Rob Owen. I have met him several times. But I think that that was the extent of his remarks.

EGGLESTON: Did the Resolution of Inquiry [an action taken by Congress in August 1986 to look into North's activities] also call for the production of various documents? Do you recall that?

OWEN: Yes.

EGGLESTON: Do you know whether Col. North provided to the Members of Congress the various TC memos [memos Owen had written to North] that you had provided to him?

OWEN: I would doubt that he did. I think that that would be an exposure on his part.

EGGLESTON: I take it similarly you don't believe that he advised them that you had carried maps down to the contras on at least three occasions in late 1984 and early 1985?

OWEN: I don't believe he did.

Meetings with North

EGGLESTON: And if Col. North said he had met with you several times, I take it that he had met with you quite a number of times by August of 1986; is that correct?

OWEN: I would say so. I have no idea of the number though.

EGGLESTON: Indeed, if you were to add up in his calendar for 1985, it appeared that you had about 20 or so meetings with him reflected in his calendar and up until August of 1986, about 20 or so additional meetings, would that sound consistent with what you think probably happened?

OWEN: Easily. We wouldn't always meet in his office. We would meet in a variety of different places.

EGGLESTON: Is there a reason that you would sometimes meet outside of his office?

OWEN: I was concerned that my showing up on his calendar too many times would be potentially detrimental and might be used at some point against him. And I think he had the same concern.

EGGLESTON: Because the people who are visiting the Old Executive Office Building are reflected on a computer for admission purposes; is that the problem?

OWEN: Yes, and each time you have to sign in, and the computer keeps track.

EGGLESTON: And as a result you met in other places, not just in the Old Executive Office Building?

OWEN: Yes, sir.

EGGLESTON: There had been a previous investigation of Col. North in the summer of 1985. Were you aware of that?

OWEN: Sir, I can't remember that one specifically, but I know there are a number of investigations that constantly involved Col. North. We had some conversations about them.

There were different times when he thought that he was probably going to be moved and he said I will just let the chips fall where they may. Often times when information came out, he and I would talk, and he would—he said on several occasions that he would always be the fall guy if this story ever broke.

EGGLESTON: Let me ask you about that. Did Col. North indicate to you whether or not his superiors at the NSC knew what it was that he was doing in Central America?

OWEN: It was my understanding that he did. I was never given any clear indication. I once asked him what he did with my memos, and he said I take them across the street. I just assumed that that would probably go to the National Security Adviser, either Robert [C.] McFarlane or [Adm.] John [M.] Poindexter.

EGGLESTON: Did he ever indicate to you whether or not the President knew what he and you were doing in Central America?

OWEN: I don't think the President has time to know who Robert Owen is. But I imagine that he had an idea that Col. North was doing things to help the Nicaraguan democratic resistance.

EGGLESTON: But you have no specific information about just what it was that the President may have known about Col. North's activities?

OWEN: No, I don't have specific information, but I was always under the assumption that he knew what he was doing, or at least had a general idea. He may not have gotten into the specifics.

* * *

Breaking the Law?

EGGLESTON: Mr. Owen, throughout the—particularly the spring of 1985, but throughout the time that you were involved in these various projects with Col. North, at the time that you were standing on the street corners making cash payments through open windows of cars, did there come times when you would talk or joke with Col. North about whether or not you were all going to go to jail for your activities?

OWEN: There were a couple of occasions that we would laugh about it and joke, yes.

EGGLESTON: You and Col. North would joke about it?

OWEN: Yes, and I hate to bring this poor person's name up again, I think he has already been through too much, but Johnathan Miller would also joke about it as well.

EGGLESTON: And was part of the reason that you would joke or talk about whether or not you were going to jail for your activities, was part of the reason the generally furtive and secretive nature of what it was that you were doing?

OWEN: Sir, I am not trained as a secret agent, and I haven't been through any of this before. When you are involved in something that is new and different from changing traveler's checks to traveling with documents to providing funds to different people, I think that there is always a sense of nervousness about it.

We were in a politically charged atmosphere. Obviously the Congress was deeply divided. The feeling was that should our efforts be found out, there would be people who would want to try and find something illegal and try and throw us in jail.

But quite frankly, in my personal view, I wasn't that concerned. If I was, I probably would have gone and talked to a lawyer about it, but I felt that I was working with a member of the National Security Council, someone who had access to the President of the United States, and believed it was the right thing to do.

A Private Citizen

EGGLESTON: It is true, was it not, you were not a government official?

OWEN: That's right. I was not.

EGGLESTON: And you did not have a security clearance.

OWEN: No, sir, I did not.

EGGLESTON: And you were essentially acting at that time as a private individual under the direction or under the guidance of a marine lieutenant colonel, who was the deputy director of the office of political military affairs at the NSC.

OWEN: Well, in a way it would be also, obviously, since I was being paid by Adolfo Calero, I was working with him, but I guess you could say that I probably did more for Col. North than I did for Adolfo Calero.

EGGLESTON: Well, at the time you were making the payments to the contra leaders, you were acting, really, at the request of Col. North; is that fair?

OWEN: But there were contra funds that were not Col. North's funds.

EGGLESTON: Nevertheless, it is not Adolfo Calero who asked you to make those payments. It was Col. North.

OWEN: Yes, sir.

EGGLESTON: And at the time that you took the maps down [to the contra leaders], it was because Col. North provided them to you, not because Adolfo Calero had asked you for them.

OWEN: Yes, sir.

EGGLESTON: And similarly, when you went out to New York and obtained the cash, it was because Col. North and Gen. Secord wanted you to do it, not because Adolfo Calero had specifically asked you to do it.

OWEN: That's right.

EGGLESTON: Did you regard yourself as a private individual who was acting in furtherance of a covert operation in Central America?

OWEN: I guess you could say that. I was a private citizen who believed in what I was doing. I thought I was doing it, certainly, under the auspices of the United States Government, but I was still a private citizen.

* * *

North—His Own Boss?

[Richard] LEON [House committee counsel]: Let's get back to the point you were making about Ollie saying he was a member of the National Security Council on the staff of the President. You testified you never met Robert McFarlane; is that correct?

OWEN: That's right, I have not.

LEON: You have never met Adm. Poindexter?

OWEN: I have not.

LEON: And you did testify, I believe, that Ollie on at least one occasion said to you that he was sending his memos across the street, which you implied to mean to the NSC directorate?

OWEN: Yes, sir.

LEON: Do you recall who was the director at the time he made that statement?

OWEN: I think it was Bud McFarlane.

LEON: Did you ever receive any indication that McFarlane had in fact reviewed those memoranda?

OWEN: No, sir, I don't. I did not.

LEON: And did you ever demand any insurance from Ollie North that such approval had been sought and obtained from his superiors?

OWEN: No, I did not. When I walked into the Old Executive Office Building, which is right next door to the White House, and I talked to a man who is associated with it, and is a U.S. Government representative, who works, [I] know, very closely with the national security advisers. I believe that was good enough for me.

I wasn't about to go and try to track down a legal opinion.

LEON: So did you take the notion that he was acting under the authority of the supervisors, so to speak, on blind faith?

OWEN: Yes, I did. I also was in his office on a number of occasions when he would have conversations over the phone with different people, and that gave me cause to think that obviously they had some idea what he was doing, too.

LEON: Did it ever cross your mind, Mr. Owen, that perhaps Col. North was acting out on his own on a limb?

OWEN: It never did.

* * *

[Sen. William S.] COHEN [R-Maine]: You indicated earlier Oliver North called you.

OWEN: No, sir, I called him.

COHEN: At that point you had a conversation, and he said, "I will never do anything without authority from others"?

OWEN: Yes, sir. I believe that is what he said.

COHEN: You believed him?

OWEN: Yes, sir.

COHEN: During the course of your relationship with him you never had cause to doubt that he would do anything but under orders from his superiors, right?

OWEN: Yes, sir.

'Shredding Party'

COHEN: Now, you have been watching these hearings rather closely since you, quote, from various members, including myself, and you have heard some testimony that Oliver North engaged in a "shredding party."

OWEN: Yes, sir.

COHEN: Do you believe he shredded documents based upon authority or orders from others?

OWEN: Sir, I believe if he shredded documents, he would have done it to protect the President, because he felt obligated to do that.

COHEN: In other words, he would have acted on his own?

OWEN: Yes, sir.

COHEN: So, it is possible, then, that Col. North acted during the course of your relationship with him on orders other than his superior's?

OWEN: It is possible, sir. Many people point or say Col. North is a cowboy. I don't believe that. I believe that he was acting either under the wing of certain people in the Administration.

My personal view—I don't know whether you want that or not—would be Director [of Central Intelligence William J.] Casey probably knew everything that Col. North was doing and was fully aware of it. There may have been others, as well.

* * *

[Sen. Daniel K.] INOUYE [D-Hawaii]: . . . Throughout these hours you have referred to patriots and patriotism and heroes. Somehow I guess the suggestion that if you are against the President's policy in Central America you are less than patriotic; is that the correct assumption to make?

OWEN: No, sir. I haven't meant to convey that assumption whatsoever. I believe that there is always in a democracy a need for difference of opinion.

It is my belief that the people who are willing to put their lives on the line, we are patriotic. That does not mean to say those who are against the President's policy are any less patriotic.

INOUYE: So those of us who may argue for and vote for measures that you may disagree with may still be patriots?

OWEN: Sir, you are a great American. And I fully believe that.

INOUYE: I just wanted the record to be clear, because somehow I felt like something less than a patriot all day long.

OWEN: I would never even begin to suggest that. You have given a tremendous amount to this country and I would never take that away from you.

Calero and Singlaub

Following are excerpts from the May 20, 1987, testimony of contra leader Adolfo Calero and retired Army major general John K. Singlaub, a contra supporter:

[Paul] BARBADORO [Senate deputy chief counsel]: Let's go back to the summer of 1984. You received your first substantial deposit [from Saudi Arabia into a contra account] in July of 1984, correct?

CALERO: Yes, $1 million.

BARBADORO: Before you received that $1 million, did [Lt.] Col. [Oliver L.] North or anyone else tell you that it was going to be arriving?

CALERO: No, I was never told when or how much would be arriving.

BARBADORO: Did you tell Col. North that you had received the million dollars?

CALERO: Yes, I did.

BARBADORO: Did he tell you where the million had come from?

CALERO: No, he didn't.

BARBADORO: Did you ask him?

CALERO: No. I didn't care where it had come from.

BARBADORO: You were happy to get the money and you didn't care where it had come from, is that right?

CALERO: Yes, I had other, much more important worries than to find out where it had come from.

BARBADORO: Did Col. North tell you that you could be expecting more money deposited in the future?

CALERO: Well, I remember that every time we got money, I mean, we were very happily surprised or some sort. I don't think that anybody told me that there will be something coming. As a matter of fact, I could not plan for arms purchases because we didn't know, we made our first arms purchases after we had received an amount and it wasn't until the third receipt that we figured, well, this might be something that will be followed up.

BARBADORO: You mentioned additional deposits. After July you continued to receive deposits of $1 million a month, did you not?

CALERO: Yes, sir.

BARBADORO: And did you continue to keep Col. North informed when you had received deposits?

CALERO: Yes, yes.

BARBADORO: You continued to receive those deposits until February of 1985, correct?

CALERO: Yes.

BARBADORO: What happened in February of 1985?

CALERO: Then we received two substantial deposits, I believe, of $7.5 million or five million, and in March we got $7.5 million. The thing is we got eight million and between February and March we got $24 [million].

BARBADORO: Mr. Calero, could you look at Exhibit AC-2, which is a listing of deposits to your account by source, and by date, that was drawn from bank account records that you provided us?

Does that refresh your memory about what deposits you received in February and March?

CALERO: Yes.

BARBADORO: Could you please tell us what those deposits were?

CALERO: One million between July 1984 and February 1984. In February 1984—

BARBADORO: 1985, isn't that?

CALERO: 1985, excuse me. We received five million and four million. And in March of 1985, we received two deposits of $7.5 million each.

BARBADORO: So between July of 1984 and March of 1985, how much did you receive in total from this source?

CALERO: $32 million.

BARBADORO: After March did you get any additional money from this source?

CALERO: No, we did not.

* * *

Buying Arms

BARBADORO: How did you determine what arms to buy and how much to pay for them?

CALERO: Well, I knew what was being used and we had prepared before with the CIA budget, which listed all the materials that we were going to buy with the new funding, which never came, but—so I knew what we had to get and I consulted with our military men.

BARBADORO: Did you also consult with Col. North?

CALERO: Oh, I told him, I used to tell Col. North practically everything. I had no reservation. I had full confidence and trust in him.

BARBADORO: So you discussed your purchases with Col. North in advance, is that right?

CALERO: I discussed our needs and probably told him that I was going to purchase, yes.

BARBADORO: Did you also tell him after you made a purchase what you had purchased and how much you had paid and who you had bought it from?

CALERO: Yes. Yes.

* * *

The Contra Cause

COHEN: When you joined the FDN [the main contra political faction], I assume you did so out of a commitment to remove the Sandinistas [the Nicaraguan government] from power. You saw them as a cancer on the country, did you not?

CALERO: Yes, sir.

COHEN: And there has never been any doubt in your mind, or those of your followers, that your intent and goal was to declare them out of Nicaraguan society?

CALERO: Yes, sir.

COHEN: You didn't join the FDN simply to interdict arms going into El Salvador?

CALERO: No, sir. But I felt that there was no contradiction there.

COHEN: Right. But that was not your purpose.

CALERO: That was not.

COHEN: Your men were not going out there to fight and lay down their lives to simply stop the flow of weapons going to a neighboring country?

CALERO: No, sir, definitely not.

COHEN: And you were not jeopardizing your lives simply to harass the Sandinistas on the periphery to keep them preoccupied?

CALERO: No, sir.

COHEN: Your goal from the beginning has been to remove the Sandinistas militarily?

CALERO: Well, we have always thought—we had the recent experience of Somoza [the dictatorship of Anastasio Somoza overthrown by the Sandinistas in 1979]—that to change the situation in Nicaragua, we had to have a strong military offensive, plus a political offensive.

COHEN: But you—

CALERO: And diplomatic offensive.

COHEN: You never believed the Sandinistas were going to negotiate away their power?

CALERO: Not without military pressure.

COHEN: Even with military pressure, from your own studies of history, have you ever known a communist government to negotiate away its power?

CALERO: Never.

COHEN: So it has never been your intent really to try to negotiate with the Sandinistas unless it was surrender on their part?

CALERO: Well, or unless it was a life-saving situation on their part.

COHEN: Well, if you were on the outskirts of Managua [capital of Nicaragua] and the Sandinistas said, "Can't we talk at this point," are you going to lay down your weapons?

CALERO: I don't believe in surrendering and then negotiating.

COHEN: The reason I raise these questions is because there were a number of representations made to the United States Congress. You commented very eloquently in your opening statement about the on-and-off-again policies, the contradictions, the internal divisions, not only within Nicaragua but within the United States Congress and the United States itself, and part of the difficulty has come about by virtue of the fact that the Administration over a period of time has represented different things to the United States Congress and therefore the American people, namely, that we are only using you for the purpose of interdicting the flow of arms.

This would be the purpose of providing you with a limited amount of weapons and materiel, not to help remove the Sandinistas but to stop the flow of weapons going elsewhere. That lasted for a short period of time and then we had another rationale, which was to simply harass the Sandinistas to keep them from consolidating their power.

But that is not the reason that you are out there fighting, and

that representation, if that were represented to you that that is what we were doing, that would not be—let me rephrase it.

Would it be somewhat of a deceit to you to suggest we were only there to use you to help us prevent the flow of arms going elsewhere?

CALERO: Well, we understood that you had to have a reason acceptable by this government in order for us to be supported.

And since support to us means so much, we have to comply with conditions that we do not necessarily like or think are appropriate.

COHEN: You didn't like the particular conditions that were laid down to you?

CALERO: No, no, no, but we had very little choice.

COHEN: You had no choice under the circumstances?

CALERO: Right.

* * *

[Rep. Dick] CHENEY [R-Wyo.]: You also were asked earlier and I'd like to focus again on this effort on the extent to which the CIA provided assistance to the FDN during that period of time the Boland Amendment was in effect [1984-85]. Obviously, we are aware that CIA was heavily involved prior to enactment of the Boland legislation in 1984. I believe in the deposition when you were interviewed by committee staff earlier you talked about the subject that was mentioned by Sen. [William S.] Cohen [R-Maine], I believe, that you referred to them [CIA officials] during that period of time as "snoopers" rather than "helpers." Can you elaborate on that at all? Did they provide any guidance or assistance in terms of your military activities during the time the Boland Amendment was in effect?

CALERO: Well, I complained about that and said we were receiving absolutely no assistance, no help, that there could be ways for them to make some indications to us that would be only logical and within the boundaries of their activity, but no, they were always after information from us.

* * *

Use of Contra Funds

[Sen. Warren B.] RUDMAN [R-N.H.]: You gave Col. North $90,000 in traveler's checks [in early 1985]?

CALERO: Yes, sir.

RUDMAN: There were blanks at both ends, which is unusual, which made them fully negotiable, is that correct?

CALERO: The bank did us that favor.

RUDMAN: That is a friendly bank. At any rate, some of those checks were used for DEA [Drug Enforcement Administration] agents, which we have advised you about, and some were used for other purposes, such as helping other contra leaders.

We don't know what a lot of it was used for. As a matter of fact, those charts don't really prove anything other than those checks that appear to be cashed at retail establishments by a signatory that says Oliver North.

We don't know whether that is Oliver North's signature, we believe it is.

CALERO: Yes, sir.

RUDMAN: But certainly, there was never any intention on your part that any of your hard-earned funds would be used for anybody's personal use, other than for the cause, is that not correct?

CALERO: Yes, sir.

RUDMAN: And looking at the last item of the first column on the right-hand sheet, the National Tire Wholesalers, for two snow tires purchased with that, when was the last time it snowed in Nicaragua?

CALERO: Well, sir, it does not snow in Nicaragua.

RUDMAN: I didn't think so.

CALERO: However, I am sure there is an explanation for that.

RUDMAN: I hope there is, Mr. Calero, because this draws no inferences to guilt or innocence, all we know is that we went to a lot of trouble to trace $90,000 worth of checks, and we were as surprised as you are to see those.

Col. North will get here, and I hope he can explain himself. This is not a trial. We are not trying to establish guilt or innocence. We are trying to find out what happened. You would agree that you never intended your hard-worked-for money to be used for anyone's use, including your own?

CALERO: Yes, sir.

RUDMAN: I thank you, and I think it is important that the American people have a chance to hear what you have to say.

* * *

Singlaub's Role

[Ken] BALLEN [House deputy counsel]: In April '85 did you meet with Col. Oliver North?

SINGLAUB: Yes.

BALLEN: Did you have with you the list [of weapons for the contras] developed with Enrique Bermudez [a contra military commander]?

SINGLAUB: Yes, I did. I wanted to get his concurrence and make sure that we weren't doing something that was in conflict with what others were doing, so I took the list to him. To the best of my recollection, he made some additions and subtractions to the list, or changed the mix a little bit, still keeping within the constraints of the total amount [of money] that Calero had said was available for this purchase.

BALLEN: When you say "he," you are referring to Col. North made these changes to the list?

SINGLAUB: That's right, yes. They were insignificant, but we accepted his suggestions.

I had also consulted with other experts, making sure that we were getting the right—the best kind of weapons mix.

BALLEN: After Col. North made these suggestions to the list of arms, did you come to any agreement with Col. North as to a final list during this meeting?

SINGLAUB: Yes, we definitely did. I said I wanted to have a list that was not going to change at the whim of someone, and we did reach a clear-cut statement of what we were going to buy.

It did not include, by the way—the ultimate list—any surface-to-air missiles.

BALLEN: General, prior to traveling to the FDN basecamp in March, had you ever had discussions with Col. North about the legality of arms purchases for the Nicaraguan resistance?

SINGLAUB: Yes, I did. I don't remember whether that took place in '84 or early '85, but I did ask for his advice, what are the parameters within which I must operate if I am going to do this.

He said he had discussed this with lawyers and at the time I believe that he had discussed it with someone in the Justice Department. He gave me the rules.

BALLEN: What did he tell you?

SINGLAUB: First of all, that the funds could not be solicited in the United States and banked in the United States; they would have to be deposited outside of this country; secondly, that we could not use any U.S. carrier, either air or surface, to move them; could not use any bank—U.S. bank to do it, and that it, of course, would not be purchased in the United States. It had to be—all of the transaction—done outside of the country.

BALLEN: These were the rules, if I understand your testimony, that Col. North gave you in order for you to be capable of buying weapons for the Nicaraguan resistance, keeping within United States laws?

SINGLAUB: That's correct.

BALLEN: And you had this conversation with him prior to traveling to Central America in March of '85?

SINGLAUB: To the best of my belief, it was prior to the trip down there, yes.

BALLEN: Let me direct your attention, sir, back again to April of '85. You testified that Col. North gave his approval to the list.

SINGLAUB: Right.

BALLEN: After Col. North gave the approval on the proposed arms purchase that you were to conduct, did you then take any steps to procure the arms?

SINGLAUB: Yes. I met with an arms dealer who had been certified to me by a friend, who had been in a position to purchase this type of weapon system from the East Bloc [reportedly from Poland]. He gave me the name of and assisted in and introduced me to an arms dealer from—who was in that business and was considered reliable.

BALLEN: Did you subsequently meet with the arms dealer referred to?

SINGLAUB: Yes, I did.

BALLEN: Do you recall where that meeting took place?

SINGLAUB: Yes. It took place in the Sheraton-Carlton Hotel on 16th and K Sts. in this city [Washington, D.C.].

BALLEN: What month would that be, sir?

SINGLAUB: That was in April of 1985, toward the end of it.

BALLEN: And what, if anything, did you say to the arms dealer concerning your discussion, prior discussion with Col. North on this proposed transaction?

SINGLAUB: Well, I am not certain of the exact words. I believe that I assured him that this list had the blessing of my contacts in the National Security Council. I don't remember at the time whether I actually used Col. North's name or simply stated that it had been blessed in the National Security Council by the contacts that I have been using to keep the Government informed.

BALLEN: Did the arms dealer that you met with say whether or not he was able to procure these items on the list?

SINGLAUB: Yes, he assured me, assured us—Adolfo Calero was with me at this meeting—that he could procure these weapons and ship them as directed.

* * *

BALLEN: Gen. Singlaub, let me ask you this question. Did you come to any agreement with Col. North about your activities, your profile and visibility with the news media?

SINGLAUB: Yes. He indicated that he understood and agreed that I would have to maintain a high profile in order to do this, getting these other benefits to include one that I discussed with him and that is that if I had high visibility, I might be the lightening rod and take the attention away from himself and others who were involved in the covert side of support.

BALLEN: You discussed that with Col. North?

SINGLAUB: Yes. We discussed it and reached agreement that there was little that I could do except to accept this high profile.

BALLEN: And did he agree that one of the benefits of this would be that, as you testified, it would divert attention away from his activities and covert operations?

SINGLAUB: Yes. Since this was one of his concerns, that was brought up as one of the advantages of my high visibility.

BALLEN: And after this meeting with Col. North, did you continue to give interviews with the press and continue to take a high profile, high visibility role?

SINGLAUB: Yes, I did.

* * *

A Lighthouse

[Rep. William S.] BROOMFIELD [R-Mich.]: Mr. Calero, the United States is often referred to as—indeed, we like to think of it as a lighthouse beaming a bright light, symbolizing freedom and hope to the oppressed world. In short, a beacon of liberty.

If that was so, would you say that to the people of Nicaragua yearning for freedom the United States is now viewed more like a lighthouse whose beam is growing dimmer currently or a lighthouse temporarily encased in a fog bank of itself by indulgent self-examination?

If it is the latter, what can we do short of voting more aid to ensure that the beacon light shines brightly again for you and your oppressed brethren?

CALERO: You use the image of the lighthouse. I would say the lighthouse that goes on and off really represents a tremendous danger for ships because you cannot—you cannot count on it, and it is best not to count on something that is being shut on and off, and being put on and off.

I certainly think that we will bring about conscience in this country to keep up the support of our effort, which is not only for us but for all of us.

BROOMFIELD: Mr. Calero, I wasn't here. You probably answered this question, but I think a key question in this investigation is, did you receive any aid from the so-called diversion of funds from the arms sales in Iran?

CALERO: It is becoming more apparent every day that we didn't, which is something that we have held right from the beginning, and nonetheless we are in need of money. We have a debt of $1.9 million in Central American region, which cannot be paid out of the $100 million [voted by Congress in 1986] because there was a prohibition set on paying back debts, but we have to incur that debt in order to keep alive between the time of the end of the Nicaraguan Humanitarian Assistance Office, the humanitarian aid, and the beginning of the $100 million.

* * *

Singlaub resumed his testimony May 21, 1987:

[Sen. Warren B.] RUDMAN [R-N.H.]: ... Since this whole story has broken, you have found out that Gen. Secord was in a very unique position. Gen. Secord was the recipient either in trust or otherwise of a huge amount of money that represented a mark-up on U.S. goods; is that correct?

SINGLAUB: That is right, yes, sir.

RUDMAN: And he was also in the position of controlling those monies to buy what the contras might want from him?

SINGLAUB: I have learned that, yes.

RUDMAN: You have learned that. And during that period that that money was being held, the contras needed a lot of things, did they not, Gen. Singlaub?

SINGLAUB: I must say that that is a source of great irritation to me; that I was working very hard during that time to get a few hundred thousand dollars. If I had any knowledge that that money had been in a bank and was available, I would have been even more furious.

RUDMAN: And, in fact, there were millions of dollars in accounts and we have had testimony under oath to this committee that that money was being held for the enterprise; that is Gen. Secord's testimony. Certainly you could have done a lot with that $8 million to help the contra cause, could you have not?

SINGLAUB: That is correct. The contras could have used it.

RUDMAN: General, do you have a Swiss bank account?

SINGLAUB: No.

RUDMAN: You have never had a Swiss bank account?

SINGLAUB: Never.

RUDMAN: I will ask you a question which you may not wish to answer, and I will not press you on it, but I will simply ask it.

You don't seem to be one who is hesitant to express a view. So if you feel like expressing one, I will give you that opportunity.

Do you think that in the light of what you heard in terms of the Maule airplanes and who claims they own them, and all of the other aircraft, and who own those aircraft, and money in Swiss bank accounts and doubling the price of arms, do you think Gen. Secord and his associates triggered the—treated the contras as someone they really wanted to help or someone they wished to profit by?

SINGLAUB: You are right. I would prefer not to answer that.

O'Boyle and Garwood

On May 21, 1987, private contributors William B. O'Boyle, Ellen Garwood, and Joseph Coors testified about the money they had donated to the contra cause and what they thought they were buying with their money. Following are excerpts from O'Boyle and Garwood's testimony:

[Thomas] FRYMAN [House staff counsel]: What did [fund-raiser Carl R. "Spitz"] Channell say after [Lt.] Col. [Oliver L.] North arrived [at a breakfast in Washington, D.C., in early 1986]?

O'BOYLE: Well, he introduced me as someone who was willing to provide money for weapons. I don't recall his exact words, but that was, in effect, what he said.

FRYMAN: What did Col. North say in response to this?

Missiles, Planes for the Contras

O'BOYLE: Well, Col. North made the point that he could not ask for money himself as a government employee, but that he could provide information and he did that. He began to explain the type of weapons which were needed.

FRYMAN: Did he have any sort of paper with him as he was describing these types of weapons?

O'BOYLE: As I recall, he had a small notebook which he referred to.

FRYMAN: What types of weapons did he indicate were needed?

O'BOYLE: Well, he talked about blowpipe missiles, which were $20,000 apiece, but which had to be purchased in packs of 10. These were necessary to counteract the Hind helicopter gunships which the Russians had been supplying to the Sandinistas and were wreaking havoc upon the contras.

We also talked about Stinger missiles. He described the ammunition needs, referred to a type of NATO [North Atlantic Treaty Organization] ammunition. He referred to a type of Eastern Bloc ammunition that was being used by the contras that they needed.

He gave the prices for those. He also described a certain kind of aircraft that was needed.

FRYMAN: What type of aircraft was that?

O'BOYLE: It was a Maule aircraft.

FRYMAN: Is that a brand of aircraft?

O'BOYLE: Yes. Maule is a manufacturer of the aircraft.

FRYMAN: That is spelled M-a-u-l-e?

O'BOYLE: Yes.

FRYMAN: What did he indicate was the need for the Maule aircraft?

O'BOYLE: Well, apparently these Maule aircraft were used to supply—for two reasons. One was to fly supply missions which would deliver supplies to the contras. These are light aircraft, easily repaired, relatively easy to fly.

They can carry a heavy load so they can—and short takeoff and landing so they can dump supplies out to the contras; and also, they had apparently some kind of very sophisticated surveillance and communications on board and as they flew up and down the borders or wherever they flew, they could report back to Washington what was going on.

FRYMAN: And he identified the Maule aircraft as one of the types of weapons that were needed by the contras; is that correct?

O'BOYLE: Well, I don't want to quibble with you about the word "weapons," but it was on the list. It was on that list.

FRYMAN: It was one of the items that was given to you in response to Mr. Channell's comment that you wanted to make a contribution for weapons.

O'BOYLE: That is right.

FRYMAN: Was there a price identified for these planes?

O'BOYLE: Yes, they were quoted at $65,000 each. Apparently, that was a reduced price.

FRYMAN: Now you say while Col. North was there, he stated that he could not himself ask for a contribution.

O'BOYLE: That is right.

FRYMAN: What happened after he left?

O'BOYLE: Well, Mr. Channell and I talked a bit more, pretty much about what we had been talking about all along. I indicated that I would be willing to think this over and I would get back to Mr. Channell if I decided I wanted to contribute.

FRYMAN: In the breakfast meeting with Col. North, was there any further discussion about a meeting with President Reagan with contributors?

OWEN: Not as far as I recall, no.

FRYMAN: What decision did you make about making a contribution?

O'BOYLE: I decided that I would make a contribution.

FRYMAN: And what amount did you decide to contribute?

O'BOYLE: I decided to contribute $130,000.

FRYMAN: What was this to be for?

O'BOYLE: Two of the Maule aircraft.

FRYMAN: How did you make this contribution?

O'BOYLE: I hand delivered the check to Mr. Channell in Washington a few days later.

* * *

A 'One-Two Punch'

[Sen. Warren B.] RUDMAN [R-N.H.]: We all appreciate your testimony this morning, and obviously you are here to give us information. All of you exercised your rights as individual Americans to do what you wished to do and we all understand that.

I want to ask Ms. Garwood a question because we kind of got a—I guess what I can best describe it as a theory of legal fiction, not by Mrs. Garwood, but generally floating around that somehow, because you were never asked directly by certain people to give money, that they didn't ask you.

I want to just go through a meeting that hasn't been covered but is covered in your deposition. It was a meeting in Dallas in September, 1985, if I'm correct, of the U.S. Council of World Freedom, and Mr. Channell went to that meeting and told you he wanted to take you to meet Col. North at the airport following the meeting because Col. North was going to be coming through Dallas, was going to stop to meet; is that correct?

GARWOOD: Yes, sir.

RUDMAN: Mr. Calero was also at that meeting of the U.S. Council, I believe?

GARWOOD: Yes, he was.

RUDMAN: And Mr. Channell—Mr. North met with you at the airport that day.

GARWOOD: Yes.

RUDMAN: And Mr. North told you of it, according to your deposition, that there was a need for all sorts of things down in Nicaragua, particularly, I believe, possibly trucks and other supplies.

GARWOOD: Yes. He told me the terrible news that supplies had arrived but there was no way to transport them. Much of the supplies arrived to feed the starving people of Ethiopia [was] left on the docks and rotted.

RUDMAN: And they didn't have trucks to move them with.

GARWOOD: That's right.

RUDMAN: And then Col. North left and Mr. Channell took you back to your hotel in a cab; is that correct.

GARWOOD: Yes.

RUDMAN: And then essentially within a short time frame after Col. North telling you, Mrs. Garwood, that trucks were needed, Mr. Channell said to you, Ms. Garwood, you can help.

GARWOOD: Yes.

RUDMAN: And in fact you did.

GARWOOD: Yes, I did.

RUDMAN: Then there, you issued a check or shortly thereafter issued a check for $22,000?

GARWOOD: Yes, sir.

RUDMAN: From where we come from we call that the old one-two punch, is what we call that.

GARWOOD: What do you mean by that?

RUDMAN: Well, I don't speak Texas, but let me see if I can explain it. Col. North was telling you of a terrible need, knowing that you were a person of some means, but obviously was precluded or thought he was precluded from asking directly for money, but he set forth this dire situation and moments later his friend, who took you to the airport to meet him, could incidentally, ask you for money.

GARWOOD: Yes, sir. I think what Col. North and Mr. Channell both knew mostly about me was not that I had a lot of funds so much as I was deeply interested in protecting the independence of the United States, and that the target of the Soviets is not really Nicaragua, it's our country, and anything that I could do to help those freedom-seeking people prevent another Cuba down there and Soviet stronghold was really to defend our country.

RUDMAN: Oh, I agree with you, Mrs. Garwood, sure.

GARWOOD: I would easily want to give what I could.

RUDMAN: Obviously Col. North was telling you of the sad plight of these people and moments later Mr. Channell would ask you for money and that is what I called the one-two punch.

GARWOOD: They didn't have to do a one-two punch with me. They knew I already was so interested and so eager to help defend our country that all they had to do was ask me and if I had it, I would give it.

RUDMAN: OK. I think I've made the point and that is a very good example.

That didn't take place here in Washington; Col. North made a special stop in Dallas to talk with Mrs. Garwood to tell Mrs. Garwood about the sad plight which we all understand and many of us understand and have supported to help those people in Central America, but then shortly after you were solicited by Mr. Channell, and that to me it's a fiction for anyone to assume that somehow that's not a solicitation. The whole event was a solicitation done by two different people.

Would you disagree with that?

GARWOOD: It was clarifying for me beliefs that I already had and showing me how desperate things were. I don't—they practically knew they didn't have to solicit anything from me, that if I could help simply as Mr. Coors has said he wanted to help and Mr. O'Boyle, I didn't actually have to say it, they knew too much of my history to believe anything else. And so they didn't have to solicit.

I was more than eager to give.

RUDMAN: I appreciate that.

* * *

The Nicaragua Plan

[Rep. Louis] STOKES [D-Ohio]: Mr. O'Boyle, you had made the inquiry yourself of Mr. North as to what was the plan for Nicaragua; is that correct?

O'BOYLE: That is correct.

STOKES: And then in response to that, he then said to you something to the effect that he would share it with you, but it was really a secret, is that correct?

O'BOYLE: Yes.

STOKES: After that, what did he than say?

O'BOYLE: Are you requiring me to answer that?

STOKES: Yes, sir.

O'BOYLE: He said that there were two—or there was one plan that had two different—there were two plans in one, so to speak.

One would be implemented if Congress approved the money last year for the contras. One would be implemented if Congress did not approve the money.

They involved the Nicaraguan contras seizing a part of Nicaragua, establishing a provisional capital, a provisional government, and the U.S. Navy coming down, blockading the country, preventing the suppliers coming in from Cuba to support the Sandinistas, and at that point, supposedly, the Sandinistas would fall and the contra government would come into power and then Nicaragua would be restored to democracy.

And if the Congress did approve the money, this would happen on a slower time schedule, giving the contras more time to consolidate their position. If they did not approve the money, it would happen on a shorter time scale which would be something of a desperation move, but kind of a last ditch effort, you might say, on the part of the contras. That was the plan.

STOKES: Did he say anything in terms of the plan of any involvement by the United States or its forces?

O'BOYLE: Yes. He indicated that part of the plan would involve having our Navy go down and blockade the country.

STOKES: Is this your best recollection of the entire plan?

O'BOYLE: Yes, it is.

STOKES: And after he told you about the plan, did you say anything further to him?

O'BOYLE: We discussed one or two other matters that I have already reviewed here with you, but nothing else about that particular plan.

STOKES: So in essence that was it?

O'BOYLE: Yes.

STOKES: Thank you very much, Mr. O'Boyle. Thank you, Mr. Chairman.

[Sen. Daniel K.] INOUYE [D-Hawaii]: I think it should be noted that this is what Col. North told Mr. O'Boyle, that no documents with the classified indicators placed thereupon were used for this briefing, isn't that correct?

O'BOYLE: Only a map was used.

INOUYE: You don't—

O'BOYLE: I don't recall that it was classified.

INOUYE: Therefore, you are not certain whether the map itself was classified?

O'BOYLE: I don't think it was.

Robert C. Dutton

Following are excerpts from the May 27, 1987, testimony of retired colonel Robert C. Dutton who, starting in May 1986, ran a private airlift to aid the Nicaraguan contras:

[Ken] BALLEN [House deputy counsel]: Did you ever arrange for cash to be delivered to [Lt. Col.] Oliver [L.] North at the White House?

DUTTON: On one occasion.

BALLEN: Do you recall when that was?

DUTTON: I don't recall the date of it.

BALLEN: How much cash was involved?

DUTTON: I found out after the fact that it was, I believe, $16,000.

BALLEN: What were the circumstances? How did this come about?

DUTTON: Gen. Secord [retired major general Richard V. Secord] called the office [Stanford Technology Trading Group International (STTGI)] and spoke to me and said that he wanted to get Bill Olmsted [code name for one of the operatives in the contra-aid network] an airline ticket to fly down to Miami, pick up a package and bring it up to Col. North and asked that I have Shirley Napier, our administrative assistant, get that taken care of.

He called later in the day and said he was unable to locate Mr. Olmsted and, therefore, Shirley should cancel the ticket. Shirley was standing there and commented that she could fly to Miami as easily as anyone else and would be willing to do that.

I mentioned that to Gen. Secord and he said, all right, let her fly down and pick up the package at Southern Air [Transport, a Miami-based air carrier company that rented airplanes and services to the airlift operation]. She went down and I don't recall if she told me the next morning or that evening that she had signed a handwritten receipt for $16,000 cash and she had delivered it, I believe, to Fawn Hall, Col. North's secretary.

BALLEN: Did you have discussions with Gen. Secord or Col. North afterwards as to the purpose of this cash being delivered to Col. North?

DUTTON: I can't remember the specific conversation but I seem to remember that Col. North wasn't pleased that we had used Shirley, but Gen. Secord said to do it and so we did it.

BALLEN: But you never discussed the purpose of the cash with anyone?

DUTTON: No.

BALLEN: So you don't know why Col. North was receiving it?

DUTTON: No, I do not.

* * *

Keeping Record

In the course of Dutton's testimony, it was revealed that he had kept a photograph album of the Central American operation:

BALLEN: Was someone taking photographs of the drop zones [where Dutton's operation attempted to drop off supplies for the contras]?

DUTTON: Yes, the air crew.

BALLEN: Why were they taking photographs?

DUTTON: To document what they were doing. There had been people that had said, you know, if they continue to be unsuccessful, we will wait for the day they take the loads out and throw them in the ocean someplace and say we delivered them, they just can't find them.

That wasn't the way the operation was going to operate, and they were going to prove that they were doing the job they were sent there to do. The drop zone was identifiable, and they took the picture before the load was on it and after the load was on it.

BALLEN: Did you ask them to take pictures?

DUTTON: I believe I did during that lengthy stay when I was there in September [1986].

BALLEN: When did you return from Central America in September?

DUTTON: I believe it was the 20th of September.

BALLEN: Did you take any of those photographs with you?

DUTTON: Yes. Just before I left, they had gotten them back, and they were sitting on the coffee table. I went through and sorted out the ones that I thought gave the best evidence of the operation, what it was, what we were doing and how we were doing it.

BALLEN: What did you do with the photographs once you returned?

DUTTON: I went into an office and sorted them into order and asked Shirley Napier to get me a photo album, which she did, and I made annotations on them, I had annotations from crew members that described the drop zone, and I put together sort of a photographic document that said here is the operation, here are the assets, here are the people, here is the kind of weather they are having to fly in, here are the loads actually on the drop zone, and then I had a session with the problems we ran into, pictures of the aircraft stuck in the mud and that sort of thing.

BALLEN: Why did you prepare this photograph album?

DUTTON: I thought it was direct evidence of what was there. I thought it might be beneficial if Col. North wanted to show it to people he was working with to say, here is a set, and what it looks like, not just written messages.

BALLEN: What did you do with the photograph album after you prepared it?

DUTTON: I finished it on a Friday or Saturday morning. Col. North and Gen. Secord were at our offices in Virginia. Gen. Secord looked through it. He liked it. Col. North came out of a meeting they were having and this was the first time I had seen him since I had gotten back from that operation. He was very pleased with what had happened. I showed him the album and he liked it and said he would like to take it and show it to his top boss.

BALLEN: Who did you understand Col. North to be referring to when he said he would like to take the photograph album to show it to his top boss?

DUTTON: I understood that to be the President.

BALLEN: Why did you understand that?

DUTTON: I never heard him use the term talking about anybody else he was working with as a top boss. He didn't refer to [Rear] Adm. [John M.] Poindexter that way. It was my impression.

BALLEN: Did he refer to Director [of Central Intelligence William J.] Casey as the top boss?

DUTTON: No.

BALLEN: How did he refer to Director Casey to you?

DUTTON: If he didn't refer to Mr. Casey, he called him Bill.

* * *

Shredding Documents

[Arthur L.] LIMAN [Senate committee chief counsel]: Was there a shredding party at your organization in November and December [1986]?

DUTTON: Excuse me, sir, we don't have shredding parties. There was some business done in the office. We had a great concern about the security of the office because we were being inundated by people that were very interested in what had happened in Central America. They found out that STTGI was involved. It was Gen. Secord's desire that we don't have any superfluous material laying around the office. I had duplicate messages of KL-43 traffic [coded messages] that I shredded. I didn't consider that a shredding party.

LIMAN: Did you ask Ms. Napier to shred?

DUTTON: No.

LIMAN: Was she asked to shred papers?

DUTTON: I understand she was, yes.

LIMAN: Do you know what she was shredding?

DUTTON: Telephone logs.

LIMAN: Did you see her shred other records?

DUTTON: No, I did not.

LIMAN: Is it your testimony that the only records that were shredded were duplicate records?

DUTTON: My testimony is of my records the only thing shredded were duplicate records.

LIMAN: Would it have been everyone else's in that organization?

DUTTON: The only other thing that I can testify to is the telephone log and that I assisted her in shredding because she was having trouble with it.

LIMAN: How did you protect operational security if you shred a duplicate but keep an original?

DUTTON: This wasn't trying to protect operational security necessarily. There wasn't a need for me to carry a huge bundle of excess messages around, two or three copies of the same message, so I got rid of the ones I didn't need. I kept the originals and you have those.

LIMAN: Were you carrying them around?

DUTTON: They were locked in my desk. But I don't consider that secure enough. When we got to this point I shredded the ones that were duplicates, packaged the rest of them, stapled them and put them in my office.

LIMAN: Who made the decision to have the shredding take place at the offices?

DUTTON: For the telephone log I understand it was Gen. Secord, for mine it was my decision.

LIMAN: And was it all done at or about the same time?

DUTTON: I don't believe so. My records—I would say maybe within a month of each other, or a couple of weeks of each other, but it wasn't all done at the same time.

LIMAN: Did you see them do the shredding?

DUTTON: No, I did not.

*   *   *

[Rep. Louis] STOKES [D-Ohio]: Would it be a fair statement to say that . . . in the 26 years you have been in the military service of the United States that you had never seen a lieutenant colonel with the power and authority of Lt. Col. North?

DUTTON: Not with that much power, but I have observed what I would consider junior ranking officers that could make the Pentagon sit up and talk, and they are just that dynamic. And Col. North was one of those. I made the comment, I think, to Gen. Secord that I have seen Col. Norths before, and they are something to behold.

STOKES: Well, would you say that he surpassed any that you had ever seen before?

DUTTON: On an order of magnitude.

*   *   *

[Rep. Henry J.] HYDE [R-Ill.]: Now, we hear much about the power of a lieutenant colonel, a lowly lieutenant colonel in the marines, and how he had this enormous power. It just seems to me, and I wonder if you don't agree, that Col. North wasn't acting in his capacity as a colonel in the Marine Corps but he was acting as an official of the National Security Council when he called people, when he sent memos, when he issued directives or whatever it was he did.

It wasn't in the rank of colonel in the Marine Corps, but as a relatively high official with the approval of, perhaps of his immediate superiors in the National Security Council.

It just seems to me, I mean, some members of this prosecutoral exercise probably made it to the Boy Scouts, but not much beyond. I haven't checked on everybody. A few I have. They still wield enormous power as Senators, as members of Congress. So it just seems to me kind of a false issue to be talking about his rank while he was assigned to the National Security Council.

I don't suppose you have any comment on that and I don't solicit one, but I want to make the point.

DUTTON: The only point I would make, sir, is I would never refer to a lieutenant colonel as "lowly." That is a good way to lose support.

HYDE: I suppose if you are a lieutenant or a lesser rank, you are right.

Now, one last question. In your work, because of its covert nature, I know you used code names. Some of them are very interesting: steel hammer, blood and butts, and you had encryption devices to communicate with each other to keep things from the public gaze, and you talked in obscure murky terms to conceal the reality. I understand that.

I have read some of these messages, and I figured out a lot of the obscure language. DZ, I guess, is drop zone—is that it? And some of the language is obscure to me, and I wonder if you could tell me what it is. I will read you the code, and you tell me what you really meant.

For instance, your Exhibit 9, RCD 9. "Send Fawn. Can't continue on milk and cookies. Regards, Bob." What was the reality behind that code message?

DUTTON: Sir, that is highly classified.

HYDE: Oh, I wouldn't want that disclosed in public.

DUTTON: Sir, at that point in time we had finally been successful, and it was time to put just a slight bit of levity into what was going on. We had been dead serious for a long time, and the idea of sending Fawn just struck me at a weak moment.

HYDE: No one can say you exercise poor judgment all the time, Colonel.

DUTTON: Thank you.

Felix I. Rodriguez

Following are excerpts from the May 27, 1987, testimony of Felix I. Rodriguez, who went by the alias Max Gomez. Rodriguez worked for the contra-aid network in El Salvador. On June 25, 1986, he met in Washington, D.C., with Lt. Col. Oliver L. North and retired colonel Robert C. Dutton.

[Paul] BARBADORO [Senate deputy chief counsel]: Mr. Rodriguez, did you also complain to Col. North about the condition of the aircraft that were being used in the resupply operation?

RODRIGUEZ: Yes, sir, I did.

BARBADORO: What did you tell him?

RODRIGUEZ: We explained to him the poor condition of the aircraft. I brought up with me a concern that was written by one of the pilots and it was right after one of their aircraft almost crashed, it had such poor equipment that it was about ten miles off south where it was flying at nighttime and it hit the top of a mountain, destroyed the left jet engine and we took pieces of wood about this size from inside the engine and this crew wrote a letter of complaint to them the following day. I got hold of a copy.

I brought it up with me. I gave it to the Colonel and the Colonel started reading this letter and he looked at Mr. Dutton look at me, and say this is a joke? I say, I don't believe it is a joke.

The people who wrote it almost got killed the day before they wrote it. He looked at Dutton, and said do you know about this letter and Dutton say, yes, but he didn't think it was important to bring it to your attention.

So the Colonel said, you know, a letter like this if it goes to the press would do a lot of harm. He say, well, Mr. Dutton answered, don't worry about it. He is now our chief maintenance officer for the whole program we have increased his salary tremendously starting next month.

BARBADORO: Mr. Rodriguez, take a look at Exhibit FIR-4. Is that the letter that you showed to Col. North?

RODRIGUEZ: Yes, sir, that is the letter.

BARBADORO: Who wrote that letter?

RODRIGUEZ: Mr. Piowaty.

BARBADORO: Who is he?

RODRIGUEZ: He is one of the pilots that was in the operation. A retired colonel, if I recall, lieutenant colonel.

BARBADORO: What was wrong with these aircraft?

RODRIGUEZ: They were very old, the communication equipment were very old. The radars were very old and—well, you have all it in the letter explaining all the anomalies and problems that they had. You can read some of them if you wish [to know] what his complaint was.

BARBADORO: Well, did the planes have inadequate radar?

RODRIGUEZ: According to all that he wrote here it didn't have anything adequate.

BARBADORO: To your knowledge, did the planes have any equipment to detect radar?

RODRIGUEZ: Well I—when I came back, I brought back—this was a small radar detector, I would imagine it was to detect the radar system inside Nicaragua. It couldn't have been that expensive because it was a Fox-XX made by Radio Shack.

BARBADORO: It was a radar detector used for cars; is that right?

RODRIGUEZ: In this case it was being used by airplanes.

BARBADORO: And they were using a radar detector for cars to detect radar in the airplanes?

RODRIGUEZ: Yes, sir.

BARBADORO: Were there other problems with the aircraft?

RODRIGUEZ: Ask me if anything was right and I might be able to answer.

BARBADORO: Well, is it fair to say that the aircraft were frequently broken down?

RODRIGUEZ: They were frequently flying not too much. Most of the time they were broken down, sir.

BARBADORO: They were broken down more often than they were working, isn't that right?

RODRIGUEZ: Yes, sir. They were very old and they were hard to maintain.

BARBADORO: And in your opinion did these aircraft because of their poor condition pose a safety risk for the people flying them?

RODRIGUEZ: Absolutely, sir.

BARBADORO: And, in fact, one of the aircraft hit the top of a mountain and that is what prompted this letter to be written, isn't that right?

RODRIGUEZ: Yes, sir.

BARBADORO: What was Col. North's reaction when you showed him this letter?

RODRIGUEZ: Well, I just explained to you the reaction that he took, he looked at Dutton.

BARBADORO: Could you repeat it, please?

RODRIGUEZ: He looked at Mr. Dutton and say—well, first of all, he look at me and say is this a joke? I say, no, I don't think it is a joke, the people who wrote it almost got killed the day before. He looked to Mr. Dutton and said do you know about this?

And Dutton said, yes, but I didn't think it was important to bring to your attention. So he said the situation like this if the press got a hold of it, it would bring a lot of problems; so Mr. Dutton answered, you don't have to worry about it, he is now our chief maintenance pilot and his salary has been increased starting next month.

BARBADORO: So Mr. Dutton's reaction was to promote the person complaining rather than to improve the aircraft?

RODRIGUEZ: Well, apparently he had taken that decision before this is the way it sounded to me.

BARBADORO: After discussing the condition of the aircraft with Mr. Dutton present, did you ask to speak to Col. North alone?

RODRIGUEZ: Yes, sir, I did.

BARBADORO: What did you say to Col. North when you spoke to him alone?

RODRIGUEZ: I was very concerned with the whole thing and I asked if I could talk to him briefly alone, and I looked straight at him and said, Colonel—it is pretty hard for me to go over this here—

BARBADORO: I would like you to repeat what you told him, please.

RODRIGUEZ: I said, Colonel, I have learned that people are stealing here, you have to understand that there are hand grenades bought at nine dollars apiece—bought at three dollars apiece and sold at nine dollars apiece, and if this is known and the people which are involved, connected to the Wilson case before [in which Edwin P. Wilson, a renegade CIA agent, was convicted in 1983 of illegally selling arms to Libya] is going to be worse than Watergate, and this could destroy the President of the United States.

He told me that that was not the case, that Mr. [Thomas] Clines [a member of the contra-aid network and former CIA official and associate of Wilson] was a patriot, that Mr. Clines was not buying any equipment from anybody, that he was just helping him in the transportation of equipment. [In 1984, Cline pleaded guilty to charges of allegedly defrauding the Pentagon on a contract for transporting military goods to Egypt.]

So, at that point I told him I was going to leave to go down to pick up some pictures and I left the room.

BARBADORO: Was that your last meeting with Col. North?

RODRIGUEZ: Yes, sir.

BARBADORO: At some point before the end of the meeting, Col. North also made a reference to Congress, did he not?

RODRIGUEZ: Yes, sir. That was the day, if I recall, when you all had the voting on the aid to the contras. I learned from listening to all the testimony here, he's the kind who goes to the dramatic side. So he was looking at the TV where the hearings were taking place—or the voting was taking place—

BARBADORO: A Congressional debate was going on and it was being shown on TV; right?

RODRIGUEZ: He looked at the TV and said, those people want me but they cannot touch me because the old man love my ass. I'm sorry but you told me to say it that way.

* * *

In the fall of 1986, Rodriguez met with Donald Gregg, Vice President George Bush's national security adviser, to discuss problems in the airlift operation.

BARBADORO: And that meeting with Mr. Gregg occurred in Washington on August 8th, didn't it?

RODRIGUEZ: That's correct, sir.

BARBADORO: Who else was at that meeting?

RODRIGUEZ: At that meeting I believe, if he didn't arrive, he was not there but arrived a little later, Mr. Watson, Col. [Samuel] Watson [III, aide to Vice President Bush].

BARBADORO: And in that meeting, you told Don Gregg that Ollie North was connected with the—what you referred to as the Wilson group in running this resupply operation, didn't you?

RODRIGUEZ: Yes, sir. At that meeting, I think I started by telling Don, Don, I am sorry, I thought I never had to come to you with this, but I think it is about time that I put it up to you what is going on right now, and I went on to explain to him my concern about the situation, and my concern of what might happen if they continued with the operation.

BARBADORO: Exactly what did you tell him?

RODRIGUEZ: That I was very disturbed with the situation that had arose down there. I explained that there has been a operation to support a Nicaraguan freedom fighter from where I was. I don't recall in detail whether I gave him what I was involved or not. I am sure that I knew about it and explained to him that I had a report from somebody that Tom Clines had been involved in purchasing equipment for them and explained the incident of the hand grenade that I was told and also another incident that I learned that for example, Mr. Gadd [retired colonel Richard B. Gadd, contra-aid supplier], was using a couple of people in the wrong way in the country south—I don't know how—what number you refer to—and that their salary was a hundred dollars a day for one and $150 for the other one.

I was told that Mr. Dutton had found out that he was actually charging $400 a day for one and $450 a day for the other one. He was making $600 a day on those people in a period of six months that would amount to a hundred thousand dollars. You can do quite good with a hundred thousand dollars in support of these people.

BARBADORO: Did you tell him that [retired major general] Richard [V.] Secord was involved in the operation?

RODRIGUEZ: Yes, sir.

BARBADORO: Did you tell him Tom Clines was involved in the operation?

RODRIGUEZ: Yes, sir. I was concerned that even if they had done nothing wrong in this, the reputation they had, the Peter Maas book [*Manhunt*, about Wilson and his exploits], it would be a disaster if it was known by everybody, and the press.

BARBADORO: It would be a disaster because Ollie North was involved with this group; isn't that right?

RODRIGUEZ: Ollie North represented the Administration and these people were involved in this sort of deal before.

BARBADORO: What was Don Gregg's reaction when you told him that this group of people was involved with Ollie North in this resupply operation?

RODRIGUEZ: He was pretty surprised. He was pretty mad, if I recall, and—even though I told him I didn't want to make a big wave on it. He merely got on the telephone and called upstairs to Col. North's office and he was not there, so he spoke to [Lt. Col. Robert L.] Earl [North's deputy on the National Security Council staff] and asked him—told him that he had heard an outrageous report from my friend Felix—the way he put it—and he wanted him to come down to listen for himself and if he had known that people like Tom Clines were being used, it was outrageous. He knew who he was. He had something like a thief about him. Not very nice.

* * *

Rodriguez resumed his testimony May 28, 1987:

[Sen. George J.] MITCHELL [D-Maine]: Let me see if I understand this now. You were meeting with Mr. Gregg in his office. You were telling him about your concerns with the Nicaraguan resupply operation.

RODRIGUEZ: Right.

MITCHELL: He was taking notes.

RODRIGUEZ: Right.

MITCHELL: These three pages of notes are his notes of that conversation and it is your testimony that every other sentence in these notes reflects what you said to him except for this one sentence that is in the middle?

RODRIGUEZ: That is correct. You can say that.

MITCHELL: So all of the sentences that he wrote before that one sentence correctly reflect what you said and all of the sentences that he wrote after that one sentence accurately reflect what you said, but that one sentence regarding a swap of weapons for dollars arranged to get aid for the contras you did not say?

RODRIGUEZ: No, sir.

MITCHELL: Do you have any explanation for how that could have appeared in his notes under these circumstances?

RODRIGUEZ: No, sir.

MITCHELL: Apart from what you said to Mr. Gregg, were you aware at that time of any swap of weapons for dollars to get aid to the contras?

RODRIGUEZ: No, sir. We didn't know exactly where it was coming from, had no idea. As a matter of fact, we thought we were very short in funds the way it was arriving down there.

MITCHELL: When did you first learn about a swap of weapons for dollars to get aid to the contras?

RODRIGUEZ: Through the press, sir.

MITCHELL: Through the press? You had no knowledge of it?

RODRIGUEZ: No, sir. None whatsoever.

MITCHELL: Would you agree, Mr. Rodriguez, that it is somewhat puzzling that a sequence of handwritten notes taken by someone with whom you were meeting and which in every other detail accurately reflects what you said should have in the middle of it one sentence which you now say you did not say at that time?

RODRIGUEZ: I don't know exactly what he wrote, what he meant. He could answer that. He would have no reason to puzzle me at all. I have a lot of respect for Mr. Gregg.

* * *

MITCHELL: . . . Would it be fair to say, Mr. Rodriguez, that this [contra-supply] operation was controlled by the United States Government?

RODRIGUEZ: I would not say so, sir.

MITCHELL: No. What would you say?

RODRIGUEZ: I didn't consider that. I considered that Col. North had the interest of helping the Nicaraguan Freedom Fighters. I respect him for it. I helped him and I will continue to help anybody under the circumstances because I believe very strongly in the situation that they were having, as I testified to you before, and perhaps a lot of this was done in the spirit that I did.

But if you have a problem, you would feel the same way. When you lose your country and feel abandoned, if anybody comes to your help under those circumstances, it would be immoral for me not to go to him for help in any way or form.

MITCHELL: We respect and admire you for that, Mr. Rodriguez.

Of course, you would agree the nature of your particular beliefs has nothing to do with the question of whether or not this was controlled by the Government.

RODRIGUEZ: In my opinion, it was controlled by Col. North to a great extent. I personally didn't believe the Government itself was involved.

MITCHELL: Did you think Col. North was acting as a private citizen in this matter?

RODRIGUEZ: Sir, it is not for me to determine that.

MITCHELL: I'm not asking you to determine that. I'm asking you what you thought.

Did you believe Col. North was acting as a private citizen outside of his capacity?

RODRIGUEZ: I'm sure he had guidelines, sir. But I believe he felt so strongly about it, he would do a lot of things on his own that at the time to me he was even kind of a very powerful lieutenant colonel.

MITCHELL: Did you think Col. [James] Steele [former commander of U.S. military forces in El Salvador] was acting as a private citizen in this matter?

RODRIGUEZ: No. Col. Steele was not involved in this type of operation.

MITCHELL: Did you think CIA officials involved were acting as private citizens in this matter?

RODRIGUEZ: I had not much knowledge of that at that time.

MITCHELL: To the extent they were involved, did you believe they were acting as private citizens?

RODRIGUEZ: No, sir.

MITCHELL: When you came to see Mr. Gregg to express your complaints, did you express them to him as a private citizen?

RODRIGUEZ: No, sir. At that time I considered, first of all, that the Congress had approved the aid to the Nicaragua Freedom Fighters. So at that point I didn't consider it illegal to talk to him. I felt that at that point in time it was preparation for the U.S. Government officially to take over the program and he should have the benefit of my ideas at that time, that he didn't know what was being done there, so that the State would not be making—using the wrong people for this operation.

MITCHELL: That is true, but—and I understand that. That has nothing to do with the question of whether or not Mr. Gregg was a Government official.

RODRIGUEZ: No. He was. No question about that. I am not denying that, sir.

MITCHELL: Notwithstanding all of that, it is your contention that this was not a Government operation?

RODRIGUEZ: It was not, as far as I knew.

Lewis A. Tambs

Following are excerpts from the May 28, 1987, testimony of Lewis A. Tambs, former U.S. ambassador to Costa Rica (July 1985-December 1986). Tambs was questioned on the role the administration may have played in the contra-aid operation.

[Mark A.] BELNICK [Senate committee lawyer]: Now, sir, in early July 1985, before you left to take up your new post as Ambassador to Costa Rica, did you have a conversation with [Lt.] Col. [Oliver L.] North in which he asked you to undertake a certain assignment in your new ambassadorial position?

TAMBS: That is correct.

BELNICK: Could you tell the committee what Col. North asked you to do.

TAMBS: Col. North asked me to go down and open up the southern front.

BELNICK: Was anybody else present in this conversation but you and Col. North?

TAMBS: Not that I recall.

BELNICK: Where did the conversation take place?

TAMBS: It was in his office.

BELNICK: And what did you say to him?

TAMBS: What did I say to him?

BELNICK: Yes, sir.

TAMBS: Well, I don't recall my exact words, but I said, if that is what they want, that is what we will try and do, in effect.

BELNICK: I am sorry.

TAMBS: I say in fact that is what I believe I said.

BELNICK: All right. Did he say anything more?

TAMBS: No.

BELNICK: What did you understand Col. North to mean when he said we want you to go down there and open the southern front?

TAMBS: Well, my understanding was—we are not talking about a front, Mr. Belnick, in the sense you had in France in World War I. We are talking about some isolated resistance groups which would distract the Sandinista Army from the area on the upper Honduran border, and—

BELNICK: And what was your instruction to be? What were you supposed to do, as you understood it from Col. North, to help open that southern front?

TAMBS: Well, as I understood it, Mr. Belnick, first of all, we would encourage the freedom fighters who were basically in Costa Rica, to fight. And the war was in Nicaragua. The war was not in Costa Rica, and so that is what I understood my instructions were.

BELNICK: So you understood this to mean you were to encourage them to in effect open a military front inside Nicaragua?

TAMBS: Yes, sir.

* * *

The Administration's War?

BELNICK: So that you understood as of July 1985, based on your conversation with Col. North, that it was the Administration's policy that United States officials—you, in particular—ought to push and work for the opening of a southern military front against the Sandinistas in Nicaragua, right?

TAMBS: Yes.

BELNICK: Didn't you consider that this position was in some conflict with the Boland Amendment then in force?

TAMBS: They have a saying in the Foreign Service, [it] is "When you take the king's shilling, you do the king's bidding."

To my knowledge, the Boland Amendment was very limited. It had been passed when I was ambassador in Colombia, and I have never read it. I hadn't read it then, obviously, and the assumption is on my part—was that if these were instructions that had been cleared, obviously with legal counsel or White House staff, you can't really expect people in the field to be constitutional lawyers, because I think you can see what the implications would be—that if any officer in the field, be he in the Foreign Service or CIA or whatever, if he, in effect, is obliged to check with his own personal lawyer before he carries out an order given to him by a legitimate superior, the entire government is going to come to immobilization and paralysis.

The people in the field who are trying to do a job are going, I think—in every case or in most cases—are going to assume that orders from Washington are legal and legitimate, and I certainly do not want to see the United States Government brought to paralysis while people are getting private legal counsel [before] they carry out orders from their legitimate superiors.

* * *

Personal Feelings

[Sen. Warren B.] RUDMAN [R-N.H.]: . . . Ambassador Tambs, it is good to see you again. You have been a very candid witness, very refreshing. You are a private citizen, came into government service in what, 1982?

TAMBS: Yes, sir.

RUDMAN: And in for about four or five years and out again. Back to your former pursuits. You have taken full accountability for what you did. You let it stand out there. You don't run and hide. And you have been very candid. . . .

I was kind of interested in your interview with *The New York Times* on the 3rd of May [1987], because it is quite a contrast, not to your testimony here today, but to what I guess you stand for.

Let me just recount a few bits of that to you verbatim. . . . There were three quotes I thought stood out.

The first one, this is you speaking, " 'Now the people who gave us the orders are trying to paint us as running amuck,' said Tambs, a professor of history at Arizona State University in his first interview on the subject since leaving office. 'It is insane.' "

The next quote was, " 'I am terribly afraid they may now have forgotten giving their approval,' Mr. Tambs said. 'These guys are trying to save their jobs.' " You were asked who you were referring to and I am not sure of the other quotes on this. You said the RIG [Restricted Interagency Group, an executive branch policy coordinating group]. "I believe they are talking about Mr. [Elliott] Abrams [assistant secretary of state], the fellow in the CIA and North." . . .

And then you finally said, "It is absolutely outrageous to fry low level officers here carrying out their orders." Those are all accurate statements?

TAMBS: That is correct, yes, indeed.

RUDMAN: I am just very interested, knowing you to be the measured kind of a fellow you are, that something had to happen over a several-month period to cause you to give that interview and make what I believe to be very accurate statements, but still difficult things to say.

Tell us why that finally came about and what your personal feelings were as to what was happening to you. Did you feel you were kind of being hung out to dry?

TAMBS: No, the fact is as Ambassador I am responsible and was responsible. What I find to be disconcerting, to put it mildly, is to see officers who were carrying out what they believed to be orders from their legitimate superiors now in effect seeing their careers sacrificed. And I am referring specifically to the senior CIA person in Costa Rica, and you have a situation which I think is one which will essentially paralyze the government in the foreign service, and that is if an officer receives an order, first of all, he is going to wonder whether it is legal and consult his lawyer.

But secondly, if he feels—if he carries out an order and his senior officer is going to cut and run if there is an investigation, and investigations, of course, are right and proper, and as I suggested to you today when the question was asked about the aircraft landing at the international airport, those orders to service it were given it by me, and those officers were in effect carrying out orders from their legitimate superior.

RUDMAN: But everything you did in relation to the southern front and all of the things involved thereto, things involved even with [retired Army major general John K.] Singlaub [a contra supporter] other than the agreement which we have already discussed today, all those things were essentially a result of directions that you got from relatively high-ranking officials in the White House, the [Central Intelligence] agency and the State Department.

TAMBS: That is correct, sir.

RUDMAN: And you assumed that they had authority to give them.

TAMBS: Yes.

RUDMAN: And you carried out their orders to the best of your ability.

TAMBS: Yes, sir.

RUDMAN: And now that you did, and you are no longer a part of the establishment, you know you are off in Arizona teaching so you are not part of the establishment. People are kind of suggesting in their testimony that old Tambs did it all by himself. Does that outrage you?

TAMBS: Well, it is very complimentary in a way, isn't it? At the same time, when we discussed the RIG, I thought they were doing a splendid job, and I was delighted to be working with them because they wanted to win.

RUDMAN: And they ought to stand up and tell us what a splendid job they were trying to do, shouldn't they?

TAMBS: I can't speak for them, but—

RUDMAN: But you would advise that?

TAMBS: Yes.

RUDMAN: I won't get into depositions here, but I am not going to get into some of them because some of them would not be seemly, to use your word, to get into here, but I will tell you, Ambassador Tambs, that when the depositions of certain people you have referred to become public as to what they specifically said was their knowledge and what they did and who they told, I think that you all will probably burn up. That is what I think.

Tomas Castillo

At the end of week four of the Iran-contra hearings, the special panel investigating the affair went behind closed doors to hear the testimony of Tomas Castillo (alias for Joe Fernandez), former CIA station chief in Costa Rica. Following are excerpts from Castillo's testimony, which was unavailable until June 1, 1987, after it had been declassified:

CASTILLO: I hope I will be able to convey to each of you a clear understanding that I and the other men and women of the CIA's clandestine service, both those under my command at the station in [. . . classified . . .] and those at CIA headquarters who supported our efforts, performed our duties in the best tradition of the service. To the best of my recollection neither they nor I ever intentionally violated any law of the United States in spirit or otherwise.

To the contrary, the deliberate, persistent and resourceful efforts over a two-year period of my superiors, as well as those officers who served under me, in particular given the constraints and changing national policies under which we were required to operate are a testimonial to the high standard of conduct which this country expects of its intelligence officers.

If there were any lapses they resulted from decisions made under the pressures of fast moving events, from the characteristic can-do attitude of the clandestine service, of clandestine service operations officers or simply from emotional concerns for patriotic Nicaraguans whom the United States has supported, albeit intermittently, in their efforts to pursue the ideals of peace and freedom, which we in this country not only enjoy, but often take for granted.

I believe that it would be grievously harmful to the morale of the CIA officers who were [. . . classified . . .] working with the southern front of the Nicaraguan resistance to suppose, without any basis in fact, that they ever engaged in a conspiracy to violate the laws of the United States.

These honorable men and women were placed in an extremely difficult situation, which was not of their own making.

Specifically, they were required as an integral part of their duties as intelligence officers, to gather intelligence, and to carry out political action operations in order to hold together the many diverse, even opposing factions within the resistance.

The very fact that the resistance [. . . classified . . .] is more focused and politically and militarily viable than it has ever been is a remarkable accomplishment [. . . classified . . .].

You may question whether my officers—and I understood the legal constraints of the Boland Amendment [in effect 1982-85, it restricted U.S. aid to the Nicaraguan contras]. Of course, we did— or we thought we did—notwithstanding the fact that there were no lawyers assigned to my station and the cable guidance from lawyers on these matters was understandably terse and narrow and did not pretend to address every eventuality.

The application of the Boland Amendment in humanitarian legal terms in the field operational environment led us to feel that we were in the middle of a mine field with each step becoming a critical decision. My officers and I tried diligently to adhere to the constraints of the Boland Amendment as we understood them, and I believe we were—and I believe we generally were successful.

In addition, we in the field were impacted greatly by the political considerations, which attended the various incarnations of the Boland Amendment, considerations arising out of political sensitivities here in Washington, which were difficult for us to appreciate.

While we were doing our best to keep faith with the legal constraints of the amendments and at the same time carry out our duties with respect to the Nicaraguan resistance, we were faced with political dimensions of a broad issue of support for the Nicaraguan resistance.

Those dimensions adversely affected our operations on several occasions. It was—it often seemed to us that the next upcoming vote in Congress on support for the resistance was the most important consideration governing the perceptions of what activities were permissible.

Regard also the urgency or necessity of a beneficial operational action—I can recall CIA lawyers disapproving certain operational activities which were acceptable under the terms of the Boland Amendments themselves because of a possible negative political impact at home.

You can imagine my difficulty in trying to reconcile such decisions with the duties of my office. Regardless, as Chief of Station, I was directly and specifically involved in all of the operational activities concerning the Nicaraguan resistance, and the officers under my command followed my guidance.

Therefore, I am fully and unequivocally responsible for all of their actions.

* * *

The Southern Front

[Paul] BARBADORO [Senate deputy chief counsel]: Both you and your superiors at CIA Headquarters [in Washington, D.C.] thought at that time it would be a good idea to build up the Southern Front military forces, didn't you?

CASTILLO: Well, in the long-range view—

BARBADORO: This was a good idea to have a strengthened Southern force?

CASTILLO: It would have been natural for the Southern Front to exist, applying military pressure on the Sandinista Army, to relieve pressure from the—against the FDN [the main contra political faction].

BARBADORO: So it was a good idea to build up the Southern Front?

CASTILLO: Yes, sir.

BARBADORO: It was also a good idea, you thought, to unite the Southern Front with the FDN, isn't that right?

CASTILLO: Yes, sir.

BARBADORO: But is it fair to say that in the—once the Boland Amendment came into effect, you had a problem and that problem was you weren't allowed to supply these Southern Front forces that were fighting in Southern Nicaragua?

CASTILLO: Well, sir, the Boland Amendment that these people had to exist, make it on their own until, if it came about, there would be a reinstitution of their funding. That didn't make the plan that they had of unification of the military effort or any of the other political activities—that didn't change.

What changed was the way we had to deal with them. We no longer had any leverage. We could no longer apply the influence as a result of being able to give them that support, or at least the support that came through us and apply that leverage in political areas.

In other words, my primary responsibility was the development of a Democratic pluralistic political program with them to advise and guide them on gaining—telling their story to the world, that these were Democrats, that they were trying to rescue their revolution. Obviously, there are many individual parochial interests that these Nicaraguan politicians have.

Our difficulty was with Boland, we were no longer able to influence that direction, especially in terms of unification.

BARBADORO: I don't mean to cut you off, but isn't it true that you were trying to get the Southern Front troops inside Nicaragua fighting, and one of the problems you faced was how were these troops going to be supplied once they got inside Nicaragua?

CASTILLO: No question.

BARBADORO: And you couldn't supply them because of the Boland Amendment?

CASTILLO: That is correct.

BARBADORO: And because they were independent from the FDN, you had problems getting the FDN to share their more abundant supplies with these forces?

CASTILLO: Correct.

*   *   *

State Department Connections

BARBADORO: Do you recall a conversation with Assistant Secretary of State [Elliott] Abrams about the construction of the airstrip [in Costa Rica to be used by the private contra aid supply network]?

CASTILLO: Yes, sir.

BARBADORO: When was that conversation?

CASTILLO: I think he had just assumed that position when he made a visit [. . . classified . . .] but I cannot recall the date. It is sometime between—between September and October, 1985. But it is a guess.

BARBADORO: Who was present during that conversation?

CASTILLO: Two station officers.

BARBADORO: And what happened in the conversation?

CASTILLO: At the end of the briefing that we gave Assistant Secretary Abrams he turned to me and asked me about Point West [the site where the airstrip was located]—"tell me about Point West."

I was, frankly, quite surprised that he would ask about Point West because I did not know how he would have known that I knew about Point West, since it was a—I thought it was a compartmented [restricted by classification] subject.

BARBADORO: And what did you say to him when he mentioned Point West?

CASTILLO: Well, I explained that [. . . classified . . .] what happened so far; that I don't think at that time there had been—I don't believe that the negotiation for the place had even been completed. I don't think by that time construction had begun.

BARBADORO: Did he say how he learned of Point West?

CASTILLO: I asked him how he had learned about it and he said that [Lt.] Col. [Oliver L.] North told him about it. I then asked him if the Chief of the Central American Forces knew about—also knew, and he said he did.

*   *   *

Getting Supplies

BARBADORO: Did there come a time when Col. North suggested to you that he might be able to help in the resupply of the Southern Front troops?

CASTILLO: Yes.

BARBADORO: When was that?

CASTILLO: Early '86.

BARBADORO: Was that in a telephone conversation or a face-to-face visit?

CASTILLO: I don't remember.

BARBADORO: What did he say that he thought he could do?

CASTILLO: I don't remember the precise wording of the exchange, and so what I am giving you is my impression, and it is my impression that he said that supplies could be delivered to the Southern Force.

BARBADORO: Did he say how that was going to be done?

CASTILLO: By air.

BARBADORO: Who was going to do it?

CASTILLO: Private benefactors.

BARBADORO: Did he specify who?

CASTILLO: No. At no time did he ever specify who.

BARBADORO: Did he suggest to you what your role could be in assisting with this effort?

CASTILLO: Passing information about drop zones and time which we would obtain from the commanders inside Nicaragua.

*   *   *

The Airstrip

[Neil] EGGLESTON [House deputy general counsel]: You had indicated that you thought I think that the establishment of an airfield down in Costa Rica would be significant in order to be able to supply whatever contras may enter into Nicaragua and fight inside Nicaragua, is that correct?

CASTILLO: Yes, sir.

EGGLESTON: Let me just ask you, if you could, to explain, you were asked by Mr. Barbadoro the reason that you didn't report [the airstrip], and what I think you told Mr. Barbadoro is that you had essentially a passive role and were merely observing.

What I am confused about is it seems to me the role of any station is a passive role. We have reports that you make about airdrops inside Nicaragua. Much of your reporting must certainly be about various activities that take place inside of a country and are in the nature of a passive role.

Is there a reason, other than that, that you did not report on the development of this airstrip which was taking place in a corner of Costa Rica?

CASTILLO: Let me try and put it in perspective. There were very precarious times. I did not want to ever give the appearance that I was trying to circumvent or that I might be circumventing, that my actions might be misunderstood.

At the same time, we have had longstanding prohibition against reporting on any activities of American citizens abroad. You weigh one against the other and you say well, what are their activities? They are clearing a piece of land. Whatever their intentions might have been, it is simply that. It wasn't an illegal activity, it was an activity that I had certain tangential interests in [. . . classified . . .].

I have to look out for his [apparently a reference to former ambassador to Costa Rica Lewis A. Tambs] interests in terms of these people might be a gang of cowboys that come there and start to create problems or get involved in some sort of illegal activity. I felt that I had at least a responsibility to passively monitor and be generally assured that these people weren't irresponsible.

By the same token, reporting to headquarters on something that essentially did not involve at that time an intelligence activity, it is a judgment call, and I chose not to. At the same time it was evident from the conversation even before construction began, the conversation with Assistant Secretary Abrams, that they knew about it.

So that either Mr. [Raphael] Quintero [an associate of retired major general Richard V. Secord who was stationed in El Salvador to run the contra resupply network] or whoever he was reporting to, was informing Col. North and that Col. North was informing Assistant Secretary Abrams and [. . . classified . . .].

EGGLESTON: So you are telling me that—if I could parse that out for a second. You have indicated that there are a couple of reasons you didn't report. You said they were clearing a plot of land and there is nothing illegal about that. They weren't clearing a plot of land to establish an apple orchard, you knew they were going to establish an airfield there apparently under the direction or control of Col. North, to resupply contras in the southern part of Nicaragua.

That is correct, is it not?

CASTILLO: Well, yes, it was correct that they were going to construct an airfield. How much Col. North was involved in the decision-making process, I don't know. He was connected to it. That it was an airfield to be used eventually for the contras, yes, that is true, but in and of itself, it wasn't necessarily an illegal or an intelligence activity, by my interpretation.

EGGLESTON: And—

CASTILLO: Anybody can fault me on the judgment call on it, but that is what I decided. I decided not to make it a matter of official record.

* * *

[Sen. Sam] NUNN [D-Ga.]: So it is a crazy telegram [from the Central American Task Force July 12, 1986, on the CIA's relationship with private benefactors of the contra-aid effort], isn't it.

CASTILLO: Yes, sir.

NUNN: It is not only strange it is almost crazy?

CASTILLO: Well, [. . . classified . . .] the following month when I went up to see him, also heard my views concerning this because I was obviously still irked that the problem [having the contras take over the communications duties on the supply drops, a task which had been done by the CIA] had not been solved.

NUNN: Well, I agree with you. I am agreeing with you. I am agreeing with your interpretation of it.

The second point that strikes me is we have repeatedly briefed Congress that we do not have any relationship with the PBS [private benefactors]. They are telling you they have been briefing Congress that there was no relationship right after you had had a meeting with them discussing in [. . . classified . . .] that the relationship was unorthodox and in your view, too close?

CASTILLO: Yes, sir.

NUNN: They are basically telling you here that what you are doing is not what they are telling Congress, isn't that right?

CASTILLO: Well, it is for them to answer first of all, what they were thinking when they sent this cable. My reading from my personal standpoint, was I wasn't going to get subjective about the degree of what they had told or what the relationship was, all I know is I had that problem. I wanted the problem resolved. This cable said—

NUNN: Said you didn't have—

CASTILLO: We are nowhere.

NUNN: It also said to you that they are basically misleading Congress, it seems to me.

CASTILLO: Well, I wouldn't have taken it that way because the relationship was not improper. The relationship was proper.

It was passing of information during the time that the Boland Amendment permitted it.

NUNN: But it was something that you felt was unorthodox, and you wanted to be moved out, you wanted the CIA to get out of it by extension, so there was something in your mind causing you concern or you wouldn't have raised these points. Something was causing you serious concern, and you shared that with your superiors, as you should have, and they basically came back with zero.

CASTILLO: Yes, sir.

NUNN: Let me move on to one other point. Let's just summarize this. You have been in the business a long time. Isn't this cable in effect a CYA ["cover-your-ass"] cable?

CASTILLO: Yes, sir.

NUNN: They were covering their rear end back in Washing-

ton, weren't they?

CASTILLO: Yes, sir.

NUNN: And they were putting it all on your head?

CASTILLO: Well, they just weren't resolving my problem.

NUNN: Leaving it all on your head?

CASTILLO: They were satisfying their situation, but not mine.

NUNN: They were leaving you hanging out there wherever you were before you raised the problem, you were still hanging out there by yourself, weren't you?

CASTILLO: Well, that is perhaps one way of looking at it.

* * *

[Sen. William S.] COHEN [R-Maine]: Let me refer you quickly to the incident involving the potential killing of two Senators [senators Cohen and Gary Hart, D-Colo. (1975-87) who took a trip to Managua, Nicaragua, in September 1983 to visit Sandinista and contra officials]. You mentioned that [Eden] Pastora [a.k.a. "Commander Zero," a contra military leader] was the one who orchestrated the attack upon the airport in Nicaragua.

CASTILLO: Yes, sir.

COHEN: Who approved that particular raid?

CASTILLO: I don't think it was ever—Pastora didn't submit his plans for approval.

COHEN: Would it surprise you if I told you that [. . . classified (a CIA official). . .] informed both Sen. Hart and myself that that had been approved?

CASTILLO: It would be a surprise to me. Well, I wasn't in the approval area, but it would have been my impression that he didn't submit his plans for approval to CIA.

* * *

An Active Role?

[Rep. Peter W.] RODINO [Jr., D-N.J.]: You started off in your statement this morning, and in answer to one of the questions, too, you stated, "My view was to develop political organizations," and you talked about your role as passing passive information, and it seems to me that you alluded to this line because it seems this is the way you felt you would be within the Boland amendment. Is that correct?

CASTILLO: That is correct, sir.

RODINO: Now, let me ask you, on Exhibit 6, there is a message sent by [. . . classified . . .] 4-12-86, and it is apparently sent by you, and I read from it this. Do you know the third sentence from the bottom? It says, "My objective is creation of 2,500-man force which can strike northwest and link up with Quiche [the Quiche Indians of Nicaragua] to form solid southern force. Likewise, envisage formidable opposition on Atlantic Coast resupplied at or by sea. Realize this may be overly ambitious planning but with your help believe we can pull it off."

Does that seem to be passive information?

CASTILLO: Sir, that portion of that cable has caused me a great deal of concern.

RODINO: It causes me a great deal of concern.

CASTILLO: And it should. And I would like to explain it within the context in which it was written.

RODINO: But it was written?

CASTILLO: Oh, yes, I wrote that.

RODINO: OK.

CASTILLO: It was done—first of all, let me explain that the communication between North and I—and this is one of many either telephone or on the K.L. 43 [encryption machine] dealing with political matters. It is an informal communication.

In other words, I wrote this late at night, to a friend, not to headquarters, not formal, wasn't going to be read by hundreds of people as our other staff cables are.

It was written in an off-handed style. This certainly should—there certainly should have been more appropriate wording. Let me say that essentially what it was, it was representing or I was advocating the views and taking the words as my own or making the words my own, but I was actually advocating the views of the southern front commanders.

I am not a military officer. I have no military experience. I have no military background. This was their expectations, and I assumed them in terms of this particular message as my views in that informal method of communication that I used with Col. North.

Essentially, where it said, "your help," essentially what it was, it was a pulling together of all the U.S. Government elements for the purpose of what this was. But it is brainstorming. It was nothing more than that.

Elliott Abrams

Following are excerpts from the June 2, 1987, testimony of Assistant Secretary of State Elliott Abrams:

[Mark A.] BELNICK [Senate committee lawyer]: Did you have any conversations with Ambassador [Lewis A.] Tambs before he took up his post as Ambassador to Costa Rica in the summer of 1985?

ABRAMS: Yes, sir. It is customary, when an ambassador is going out to his post, for his—to meet with his assistant secretary. And at some point in the stream I had such a meeting with him. It took place in my office, as Assistant Secretary of State for Human Rights.

BELNICK: What did you discuss on that occasion?

ABRAMS: We discussed Costa Rica. We discussed mostly Costa Rica in the context of the regional security problem—that is, in the context of Nicaragua—and we talked about regional policy, I think, more than we did—I didn't know really enough to talk about, and I'm sure he did—Costa Rica and politics and economics and so forth.

So we talked more about the regional issues.

The Southern Front

BELNICK: Did you ever tell Ambassador Tambs, either on that occasion or any time subsequently, that one of his missions as Ambassador to Costa Rica was to assist the opening of a Southern Military Front in Nicaragua against the Sandinista regime?

ABRAMS: At no time whatsoever.

BELNICK: Did Ambassador Tambs ever tell you that any such instruction had been given to him by Col. North or anyone else?

ABRAMS: He did not. However, the circumstances of Ambassador Tambs' departure [were] somewhat bizarre. In the fall of 1986, President [Oscar] Arias [of Costa Rica] came to the U.S. for an official visit. The morning of, or perhaps the day before—I don't recall exactly—the visit, and without any notice to the Department of State, none whatsoever, Ambassador Tambs announced to his staff in San Jose at the embassy, "I quit. My mission was to found a Southern Front. I was sent here to set up a Southern Front. I have completed that mission and therefore it is time for me to go."

We found out about it because a member of the staff telephoned the Department and said, hey, do you know that Ambassador Tambs just resigned, and we said, no. In fact, we don't have an ambassador in Costa Rica today, in part because of having no lead time, we haven't been able to get somebody in place and confirmed and so forth. We are still working on that.

I knew at that point, that is, the day of the visit, he told President Arias on the airplane, again before he told the Department. So I found out at that point that he believed that this was his mission in Costa Rica.

BELNICK: Have you ever discussed that belief with him, personally, directly?

ABRAMS: I don't believe I have talked to him. We saw each other during the visit.

The answer to your question is no.

BELNICK: All right, sir.

ABRAMS: I should say, by the way, it is not my practice—with one exception—it is not my practice to meet with people alone. Being part of a hierarchy, it is important to spread information both up and down and sideways, and it is a lot easier to do if there is someone who is a note-taker.

The meeting with Ambassador Tambs to which I referred, in the spring of '85, had present the desk officer for Costa Rica.

BELNICK: Did [Lt.] Col. [Oliver L.] North ever tell you that he had discussed opening a Southern Military Front with Ambassador Tambs?

ABRAMS: No, sir.

BELNICK: Did you ever hear anything like that from the [CIA's Central American] Task Force Chief [Alan Fiers]?

ABRAMS: No.

BELNICK: All right.

ABRAMS: It is part of the duties of all our our ambassadors to Central America to support the resistance. We are now talking about the summer of 1985. I read in my opening statement from the policy of the United States, as enacted by Congress, and Congress had just approved $27 million for us to support a fighting force.

So it was the duty of every ambassador to support United States policy, to try to get the government of the country to which he was assigned, this wasn't true only in Central America, but most importantly in Central America, to support that policy.

Ambassador Tambs certainly had that responsibility and the responsibility of working with the resistance in Costa Rica. He did not have the responsibility to, quote, "set up a southern front."

* * *

Airstrip in Costa Rica

BELNICK: Did there come a time you learned one of the things he [Ambassador Tambs] was doing was talking to the Costa Rican government about the construction of an airstrip at a site known as Point West to be used in contra supply?

ABRAMS: Yes.

BELNICK: When did you first learn of that proposed airstrip project?

ABRAMS: I learned of the project rather earlier than I learned of his involvement with the Costa Rican government. Of that, I learned when he testified here. I learned of that in—I learned of the existence of the airstrip probably in August, being that I was sworn in late in July. Probably in August of 1985, maybe September of 1985. But that's the time period.

BELNICK: How did you learn of the project at that time?

ABRAMS: I don't recall any conversation in particular in which I was told of it. The—as you know, the former [CIA] station chief has testified that I told him that it was Col. North. That's perfectly logical and plausible to me.

BELNICK: You don't recall whether you learned about the airstrip from Col. North or from someone in the [Central Intelligence] Agency?

ABRAMS: That's correct. I don't recall.

BELNICK: What do you recall learning?

ABRAMS: That there was an airstrip being built by the private benefactors, as we used to call them, in Costa Rica, that this was a project which was either under way or about to be under way, period.

BELNICK: Did you learn whether the United States Government or any U.S. Government officials were involved in that project?

ABRAMS: Well, it was pretty clear from the way it was told to me that no U.S. Government officials were involved in the project. That would have been illegal.

BELNICK: Did someone tell you specifically no U.S. Government officials were involved?

ABRAMS: I doubt it was said in so many words. It was obvious no U.S. Government officials could be involved.

BELNICK: How was it obvious?

ABRAMS: It would have been illegal.

BELNICK: Therefore you assumed no one was involved?

ABRAMS: Yes.

BELNICK: Did you ask Col. North whether he was involved

with the airstrip project or the private benefactors constructing it?

ABRAMS: No.

* * *

BELNICK: Sir, you knew that the senior CIA representative in Costa Rica [CIA station chief Tomas Castillo] was involved in some way with the airstrip?

ABRAMS: I did not.

BELNICK: You knew he was knowledgeable about it?

ABRAMS: I did not.

BELNICK: Didn't there come a time in the fall of 1985 when you were in Costa Rica meeting with the senior CIA representative and two of his assistants, correct?

ABRAMS: That is correct.

BELNICK: And you asked him, what about the airstrip, because you were surprised he hadn't mentioned it to you; is that correct?

ABRAMS: That's correct.

BELNICK: And because you were surprised—excuse me, weren't you surprised because you believed that he knew about the airstrip?

ABRAMS: I was surprised because I had spent at least, I would say by memory, at least an hour with the station chief and two of his staff members. And they gave me what was purported by them and believed by me to be a totally complete briefing on everything going on in Costa Rica. There wasn't supposed to be a lawn getting mowed in Costa Rica without them knowing about it.

I have since sort of—I was new in the job. I had kind of exaggerated the degree to which we can know the degree to what is going on in another country. But that was my view.

They gave me a full, complete, total briefing. I knew something they didn't seem to know. I had been told there was an airstrip being built. Come on, how is it possible they did not know this?

I said to the station chief when the briefing was theoretically over, "Isn't there an airstrip being built someplace?"

I believe he has testified correctly that he nearly had a cardiac. I thought he was going to fall off his chair. He looked at me and he looked at the two guys, and he looked at me and looked at the two guys. It became apparent that his real concern was them. He said something to the effect that they don't know about that or they didn't know about that. They knew about it then.

It just seemed to me obvious that if somebody is building a—I mean, he was supposed to be reporting on things like this. It was very odd to me he didn't know about it.

Of course, he did know about it. He said to me, "Yes, these two guys didn't know about that. Yes." And he showed me—my memory is he actually had a map or we had a map or there was a map in the room. He showed me where it was, and he said something to the effect that "It isn't open yet" or "It isn't stated yet."

In other words, this is an airstrip which is not in use, was what stayed in my mind. That was the end of that.

BELNICK: Did you ask the station chief why it was such a secret from others who were working with him?

ABRAMS: No. I had no reason to question who in his station he was telling what.

BELNICK: Did you ask the station chief whether anybody from our government was involved in the construction of the airstrip?

ABRAMS: No. It had been presented to me, I think, as a private benefactor effort. I did not assume and do not assume people are violating the law.

BELNICK: Did I hear you correctly say a few moments ago that the first time you knew that Ambassador Tambs had spoken to the Costa Rican government or negotiated with the government about the airstrip was when he testified here last week?

ABRAMS: That is correct. He never reported that to the Department of State.

BELNICK: Did you ever ask him once you found out about the airstrip whether he had had any contact with the Costa Rican government about that matter?

ABRAMS: No. It would never have occurred to me that an ambassador would do something like that without checking with the Department.

BELNICK: Did you ask him to check with the Costa Rican government as to their knowledge or approval of the airstrip?

ABRAMS: No.

BELNICK: That was something you wanted to stay away from?

ABRAMS: No. It was—I mean, if the private—if some group of private benefactors had gotten permission to do this, you know, here you get into it again. That was exactly the kind of thing where you start getting—put yourself in the middle of that, what may have been a negotiation between the benefactors, what seemed to be, and the Costa Rican government.

That is exactly where you are going to get accused of facilitating.

* * *

BELNICK: Now, sir, do you recall—jumping ahead in time to September 1986—receiving a telephone call from Col.—

ABRAMS: To?

BELNICK: September 1986? That you received a telephone call from Col. North telling you that there was going to be a press conference held by an official of Costa Rica to discuss the airstrip?

ABRAMS: Well, I don't remember the exact date, but yes. I remember the call.

BELNICK: Tell me what you remember about that call and what happened?

ABRAMS: As I recall, it was Friday night. It was late. It was about eleven o'clock. And he called and said do you remember that there was an airstrip and that this airstrip would at that point not have been in use because there was no contra military activity under way in Costa Rica really after May 8, after the inauguration of President Arias?

Yes, I remember that.

Well, the Minister of Public Security, he said, was going to give a press conference and he was going to talk about the airstrip and he was going to reveal all sorts of things about the airstrip, including apparently what role, if any—I shouldn't say "if any"—what role, he was apparently going to say the previous government of Costa Rica had had approving it or so forth. This was a very bad thing he said, and it would do no one any good and raise all sorts of awkward questions about the previous government and we ought to try to stop it.

And I said I agree with that. And he said, well, what we need to do is, let me get Tambs on the line and would you instruct Tambs to call President Arias and tell him not to have this press conference?

I said, I will. Sounds right to me. So he called back, I don't know, you know, half an hour later, something like that, with Ambassador Tambs on the line. Ambassador Tambs, I remembered, was in the U.S. I believe he testified he was in West Virginia, which, I think, is my memory.

And we explained this to Tambs, that is, that there was going to be this press conference, it had nothing to do with the use of the airstrip. The airstrip, as far as I knew, was long since, since you are talking about September, so it is May to September, out of use.

But there was no good going to come out of that press conference for the United States or for Costa Rica. Would you please call President Arias, I said, call him up and ask him not to allow that—cancel the press conference? Tell your Minister of Public Security not to hold that press conference with an implied threat.

This was—well, this was before his official visit to the U.S. I don't recall whether at that moment we knew when he was coming, but the issue of his official visit was in the air. And I instructed Ambassador Tambs to advert to the visit in a way which made it clear to President Arias that his visit was at risk. That is to say, something like this is a needless, a gratuitous complication of U.S. /Costa Rican relations, it is an exceedingly odd thing to do, gratuitously, in the period when we are all contemplating an official visit.

It was supposed to be diplomatic, but the message was supposed to be clear.

BELNICK: Almost a contradiction in terms here?

ABRAMS: No, no, no. Be a good diplomat. Get the message through clearly. So he said, I will do that. And he—there was another conversation then an hour or two later, midnight, one o'clock, something like that, in which Ambassador Tambs reported he had done so and the press conference was cancelled. That was the end of that night's activities.

BELNICK: You are aware that Col. North has written a PROF message [a White House internal computer message] in which he says that he spoke to the head of State in Costa Rica, had a conversation with him and conveyed the threat or at least the notion that the aid might be cut off if this press conference took place.

Do you have any knowledge as to whether Col. North had such a conversation with the Chief of State of Costa Rica?

ABRAMS: Not—well, to my personal knowledge, no. I do know President Arias has flatly denied it and that Col. North did not tell me that he had had such a conversation.

* * *

Proposed Military Action

BELNICK: Was that a time when Col. North proposed at a RIG meeting [Restricted Interagency Group, an executive branch policy coordinating group] the seizure of certain territory in Nicaragua?

ABRAMS: He proposed it. I can't tell you what the context was. There certainly was such a proposal. Maybe it was in a RIG meeting, I don't recall.

BELNICK: Do you recall the specifics of that proposal?

ABRAMS: Let me see what I can—how much I can recall. The idea was that the resistance would take a location on the Atlantic Coast of Nicaragua. What comes to mind is Peria Blanca. But it would take a town or city and his idea was that would be the—was that that would be Khe Sanh [the location of a siege of 6,000 U.S. Marines in South Vietnam in 1967-68] I think was the analogy he used, and that one of two things would be bound to happen.

Either seeing these freedom fighters killed day by day, we would rescue them or seeing them fighting to the last man in Alamo-style fight, the public perception of their bravery would change. That was the basic idea, though he hoped, of course, that we would intervene.

BELNICK: What was your response to that proposal?

ABRAMS: Interesting proposal. I did not have any idea whether it was militarily feasible. I generally got my ideas about what was militarily feasible from Col. North and from the CIA and from DOD [the Department of Defense], of course.

As I recall, maybe it was a RIG meeting because I think we did get from DOD and CIA, have been sort of said that it is the craziest idea we ever heard, they couldn't do that, it is not going to happen and it disappeared relatively fast.

BELNICK: Did you ever make a report, that idea?

ABRAMS: No. It disappeared.

* * *

BELNICK: You testified to the House Foreign Affairs Committee on October 15, 1986, and you said, "I will say that no American intelligence or Defense or any other kind of Government official was engaged in facilitating this flight [of Eugene Hasenfus in October 1986. Hasenfus' plane was shot down over Nicaragua, two crewman were killed and Hasenfus was captured by the Sandinistas] or paying for it or directing it or anything like that, there is no U.S. Government involvement, no Government involvement, including anybody in the embassies overseas."

You made those statements.

ABRAMS: I made those statements and I made a similar statement on October 14 to Secretary [of State George P.] Shultz and every one of those statements, private and public, was completely honest and completely wrong.

* * *

BELNICK: Isn't it true, sir, that the only reason you didn't ask Col. North point blank or in so many words whether he was

involved or whether there was any U.S. official involved in the Hasenfus flight is because you were afraid that you'd get the wrong answer?

ABRAMS: No. It is not.

BELNICK: Well, sir, can you give us any other plausible reason for not asking the man who you believed knew more even than the CIA who was responsible for that flight?

ABRAMS: Mr. Belnick, I have told you really all day today that it was very clear indeed that Col. North was not violating the law, that, as Mr. [Robert C.] McFarlane [former national security adviser] had previously assured Congress, there was no facilitating, there was no directing, there was no coordinating going on by Col. North or anybody else under his direction in the U.S. Government.

I worked with him, as others did, in the RIG over the course of that year in question, that is to say, from roughly, let us say, September 1985 to September 1986; and in that year, had occasion to watch Col. North at work and had occasion to watch him use proper channels in his work with me repeatedly, and I had no reason whatsoever to believe that he was violating the law.

BELNICK: And you were willing to give categorical assurances to the Secretary of State, under oath to Congress, to the public, and the press without ever asking the question point blank of the man you knew knew the most in the Government; isn't that right?

ABRAMS: That is correct. Not only was I willing, Mr. Belnick, I did it because I was confident that there was no such activity going on.

BELNICK: And you turned out to be wrong?

ABRAMS: That is correct.

* * *

Abrams resumed his testimony June 3, 1987:

[Sen. Warren B.] RUDMAN [R-N.H.]: . . . I would rather ask you some questions about process which I find difficult to really comprehend. You said yesterday, and I think I am quoting you accurately, "There are things I didn't want to know as long as they were legal."

Do you recall saying that?

ABRAMS: Something to that effect, yes.

RUDMAN: You know I find that a difficult statement to comprehend. How could you possibly know if they were legal if you didn't know what they were? I don't understand that. It just doesn't make any sense to me at all, knowing your background.

ABRAMS: Well, the answer has two parts. First of all, you just can't function at all unless you put trust in your colleagues and I did that in all my colleagues. You just—you cannot function if you ask somebody a direct question and the answer you get is pretty direct, you have to really rely on that.

But in addition I tried to explain yesterday that we were in a position, I think, in which we were damned if we did and damned if we didn't because whether I would be accused of facilitating Gen. Singlaub's [retired Army major general John K. Singlaub] work if I met with him. I met with him. I am accused of it. I bet if I had said to Col. North, "Do you know the names, the actual names of benefactors?" And, assuming the answer was, yes, "Tell me the names. I just want to know the names." And he would have told me and not that he had not had anything to do with them, but just that he knew the names—that I would sit here today, and I would be accused again of facilitating that. So we were caught.

RUDMAN: It seems to me you were operating on the general theory, for better or for worse—I happen to think for worse—it was the old adage, curiosity killed the cat, and in this case, the cat would have been Elliott Abrams. I think that is what you are saying.

ABRAMS: What I am really trying to say is we were in a legislative and political situation where almost anything you did and anything you didn't do, it was just so controversial you couldn't make a move without somebody going to lower the boom.

RUDMAN: I accept your answer. I think you made it clear, but let me get down to a specific. I find it incomprehensible your lack of curiosity on the Hasenfus affair, particularly since the

Secretary of State was relying on your judgment, your personal reputation as well as the reputation of the government was at stake. . . .

I mean, Mr. Abrams, when the Hasenfus affair occurred, you are, if you are anything, savvy, you are tough, you are bright. You showed a remarkable lack of curiosity with North as to asking him not just, "Ollie, do you know," but close the door and figuratively put up against the wall and say, "North, I have to know what the truth is here," and push him and push him and push him.

If you had done that, and he continued to not disclose to you, you could feel more comfortable here. You relied on a cursory examination of this man knowing by your own statement that he, more than anyone else in the government, knew what was going on in the private network.

How do you explain that? I have difficulty with that.

ABRAMS: I think, Senator, first of all, the day this happened, we did contact the NSC [National Security Council], CIA, and I am not sure about DOD, I suspect we did, and I know the NSC staff did contact the DOD.

But with respect—I think you are playing the movie backwards from the end. You know the end, and I know the end, now we know what happened, now we know what I should have done.

But I didn't know then what I should have done, and I didn't know any of this and now it has all come out and it is really rather incredible and it keeps getting more incredible as the days roll by, and—

RUDMAN: It is going to get more incredible by the end of this week, I can assure you.

ABRAMS: But I was not at the end of the movie. I was in the middle of the movie, and I didn't know the ending.

* * *

An Issue of Trust

[Sen. David L.] **BOREN** [D-Okla.]: You talked about trust. I know my time is up. You talked about trust and Chairman [of the House Foreign Affairs Committee Dante B.] Fascell [D-Fla.] said we must rebuild our Central American policies.

It is essential that we have a policy. Otherwise we are going to allow the communists a beachhead in a very critical part of the world to our own security.

We have to rebuild trust and [some] sort of partnership between the Congress and the Executive Branch if we are to have a consistent policy. As you know I have voted for support to the contras.

Do you think that you can rebuild that kind of trust—given your own record, do you think you are in a position to take a leadership role to rebuild the kind of trust between the Congress, when it has been clear before the Foreign Relations Committee, before the Intelligence Committee, before the American people on national television, that the wrong impression has been created by you, and that even the apology which was wrung out of you before the Intelligence Committee was not one that you felt so strongly about, there was so much on your heart the minute you stepped through the door you had to render an apology before the meeting got started, do you think that you can play a constructive role in the future to rebuild a relationship of trust given what has gone on in the past?

ABRAMS: I do, Senator, and I think perhaps more importantly the Secretary does.

I cannot promise you I will never be misled or wrong. I will be wrong, but the answer to your question is yes.

BOREN: I have to say to you, and I am sorry to say this, that as one who feels very strongly that we must begin from this point forward to rebuild a bipartisan foreign policy, particularly in Central America, rebuild trust so that the Congress and the Executive Branch can work to go to put our Central American policy back together, that I am afraid there is too much in the record at this point for you to be able to effectively able to play that role.

I am sorry to say that, but I feel strongly about that, and I hope you will ponder it?

ABRAMS: I am sorry you feel that way, and I hope that the briefings that I have given on about 10 occasions since then to the Intelligence Committee and its staff have revealed the fact that we are working together and are continuing and I hope to continue to work together with Congress.

* * *

The Administration's Fall Guy?

[Sen. George J.] **MITCHELL** [D-Maine]: You are obviously an extremely intelligent, very articulate man, and I think you have worked hard on behalf of the policy in which you believe. I tend to agree that you have been treated very shabbily, particularly if—and I believe you when you say you didn't know that the statements you were making were untrue, no one corrected you. I have the impression that baseball has a designated hitter. This committee has designated questioners. It looks to me like you are one of the administration's designated fall guys.

I think that is unfortunate, and it concerns me that your anger or outrage doesn't appear at all directed at those who place you in the position of repeatedly making public statements that you believe to be true, but which others knew to be untrue, and which has therefore resulted in your integrity being called into question as opposed to theirs, and really you are in a position where all public officials were constantly making public statements.

They were written down and in the last analysis you don't have much beyond your own reputation for integrity, and your own word.

ABRAMS: Senator, I have feelings about this, and my wife has more, which I think it is—you know, I just don't think it is fair to express all of those at this point here, but I would disagree with one thing that you said.

Last night after this hearing was over, I went back and saw the Secretary. We watched some of the hearings—who made some public comments at noon yesterday, and others last night, and it is not his view nor is it my view that I am a fall guy. I am and plan to be Assistant Secretary of State for Inter-American Affairs.

MITCHELL: I hope for your sake you are not, but I think what is going to happen is truly inexorable, Mr. Abrams.

* * *

A Formula for Disaster

[Sen. Sam] **NUNN** [D-Ga.]: Wrapping it all up because the yellow light is on [the light indicates how much time a Congressman has left for questioning the witness], how do we operate in the executive branch? Forget about Congress. Forget about the Intelligence Committee. How does the executive branch operate when so many people are misleading so many other people and particularly with you in a key position, and you were being misled over and over and over again according to your testimony.

ABRAMS: You can't operate that way and I think that we, in the executive branch and you, in the Congress, know the way in which that was operating in the executive branch was a disaster, and the thing just fell apart.

It was being operated by the NSC keeping the Department of State in the dark, and that is a formula for disaster.

* * *

Making Foreign Policy

[Rep. Lee H.] **HAMILTON** [D-Ind.]: I want to thank you for your testimony. I know you to be a dedicated and able public servant, and your appearance is very much appreciated by me and all members of the committee.

The point I want to make is that I think the tactics that were employed by the Administration in carrying out its policy in Central America impeded if they did not defeat the policy objectives that you sought.

It means [what] the Executive pursued undermined the ends you desire. I think you recognized that early, and I appreciated that. Let me try to be specific about the meetings, and I don't mean to beat a dead horse here, because you have had long sessions, and you have testified well.

First, you misled the Congress because you gave Congress

information that was not true in some instances. You acknowledged that you made statements that were not true, and that at least in some instances, your testimony taken as a whole is misleading.

It is not my intention to go through all of that, because we have talked about it for a long time. But we have here not a single inadvertent statement, but a pattern of statements upon which the Congress and its committees rely, and over a period of time, whether intentionally or not, you and your colleagues kept from the Congress critically important facts about policy.

By no stretch of the imagination can the approach of the Administration in presenting and defending its policy be considered candid or forthcoming or cooperative, and those characteristics, I believe, lie at the heart of successful foreign policy making in this country.

Second, you, the Administration, relied on secrecy as the chief means to carry out key aspects of your foreign policy goals. The Executive tried to implement its policy in secret, and you said, I think earlier today, that ultimately you can't do it that way, and you and I agreed on that point.

Now, let me just make one comment about secrecy, almost parenthetically, if I may. The Administration kept from the Congress information about soliciting funds from Brunei [$10 million solicited in August 1986 by Abrams], and if I understand your testimony correctly, you said that you wanted to maintain the Sultan's request for confidentiality.

I really do not see why we in the U.S. should let a foreign Sultan dictate the requirements of our foreign policy. These are matters that ought to be determined by our processes, not theirs. We simply cannot let a Sultan or a King undermine the established constitutional procedures of our government.

Third, I think you diminish the role of Congress in the foreign policy process. You told us in the opening statement, and we all agreed with it, that Congress must be a powerful participant in the making of foreign policy, but your actions as you acknowledge were not compatible with your rhetoric.

You said that unless Members of Congress ask exactly the right questions, they won't get the right answer, with regard to one hearing at least, and that is precisely the wrong tactic.

The object here is not to avoid a perjury indictment. The object is not to work to make your answer literally correct but nonetheless misleading. The object is to make the Constitution of the United States work. Congress is a partner, not an adversary.

Congress is an adviser, not an obstacle, and the Executive and the Congress are meant to work together, and those of us who have responsibility for carrying out that task must make the system work.

Fourth, you, as others have pointed out, kept yourself ignorant about an important part of policy for which you had responsibility. I was impressed with your testimony about your emphasis on the compartmentalization of policy-making. You did your thing, Col. North did his thing, you said you did not need to know what Col. North was doing, and for you, it was enough to know that the State Department was not in violation of the law.

That may satisfy you, but it cannot satisfy the Congress. For whatever reasons, and I don't want to judge those reasons, you did not ask the questions that you should have asked about the private network. You looked the other way. You chose not to be informed about a key element of policy directly under your jurisdiction.

Let me try to conclude. We cannot advance U.S. interests if public officials who testify before the Congress resort to legalisms and word games, claim ignorance about things they either know about or should know about, and at critical points tell the Congress things that are not true.

I am aware, and I don't need to be reminded that the performance of the Congress in all of this is not flawless. I happened to agree with your observation the other day that this humanitarian aid program that we asked you to administer was simply unworkable, and that neither you nor anybody else could administer it well.

But I hope you recognize that the Congress cannot play its constitutional role if it cannot trust the testimony of representatives of the President as truthful and fully informed. The Presi-

dent cannot sustain his policy if he tries to carry that policy out secretly, and his representatives mislead the Congress and the American people.

Now, whether or not the policy of aiding the contras is wise, it means you chose to achieve that policy, hiding facts from the Congress. I don't say you did that intentionally. Relying on secret means to carry out elements of that policy, circumventing the foreign policy process, choosing to remain ignorant of key facts, I think undermined your policy and made it much more difficult for you to carry the day.

Under the Constitution, the President and the Congress play a key role in making foreign policy. Members of this committee of both parties have a deeply-felt desire to show that our government system of shared powers works, and I do not see how that can be done unless those of us who are charged with that responsibility speak to one another the truth.

You may respond.

ABRAMS: Well, I guess I would say I agree with the general points you have made. I would say with respect to myself, that I described some testimony yesterday, the testimony immediately after the Hasenfus shootdown as honest and wrong, and I would repeat that statement today, and I cannot promise that I won't be wrong again.

We try our best, we will try our best to inform ourselves of all the facts before we come up here. With regard to the Senate Intelligence Committee hearing [November 25, 1986, on the Iranian arms deal], you mentioned diminishing the role of Congress with regard to one hearing at least, I would say with regard to one hearing, under extraordinary circumstances, the day of the Meese announcement [November 25, 1986, on the diversion of arms deal funds to the contras] and corrected by me at my initiative about a week later, after discussing this with the Secretary's office, the legal advisor, the FBI [Federal Bureau of Investigation], and coming back to the Congress.

That said, again—I will agree with you that the manner in which this policy was conducted over the past, what, three years, I guess, has in fact undermined support for the policy in the public and in Congress.

It isn't a speculative proposition. I think that your points can be demonstrated that you can't run a government that way, and you can't sustain support for a policy that way.

Albert Hakim

Following are excerpts of the June 3, 1987, testimony of Albert Hakim, a business partner of retired major general Richard V. Secord. Hakim set up a $200,000 Swiss bank account, called the "Button account," with money from the Iran arms deal. The money was to be used to support Lt. Col. Oliver L. North's wife and children in the eventuality that North died during the Iran-contra operation.

[John W.] NIELDS [Jr., House committee chief counsel]: Now the last account [being reviewed by the panel] is the Button account, and it has $200,000 in it, and your records reflect that that was put into the Button account May 20, 1986. Is Button short for something?

HAKIM: In this case, no. The name, Button, actually came as the result of a joke between Mr. [Willard] Zucker [Hakim's financial adviser and lawyer in Switzerland] and myself at a time that we were having a discussion. Actually, the complete name is Bellybutton, and this was a name that I decided to use at the time because we laughed about the joke, and I simply took the name and used it for this set aside.

NIELDS: Does it refer to a person?

HAKIM: Yes, it does.

NIELDS: Who?

HAKIM: Lt. Col. North.

NIELDS: Can you explain the circumstances surrounding the setting up of an account for Lt. Col. North?

HAKIM: I must start by saying that when I established this account, Lt. Col. North had absolutely no idea about this. This occurred during the time that the so-called [Robert C.] McFarlane Tehran trip [to negotiate for the release of the hostages] was about to take place.

NIELDS: That took place approximately the 24th, 25th of May, 1986, and this account was set up on May 20th?

HAKIM: I am talking about the time when the concept and idea came to my mind. We knew that such a trip was going to take place, and by this time I had become extremely fond of Lt. Col. North. To me, he is an amazing person. I know it is something in this man that—he has got two loves. One is his country, and to a point that he is, in my mind, the biggest satisfaction that can be given to him is if he would enter into an environment that he could get killed for his country. I sensed that so many times.

The other love that he has is his family, and he especially during the time of the second channel [Iranian officials who became the contacts in the Iranian arms deal after the first contacts did not work out], I witnessed him being torn apart between these two loves.

But coming back to how this thing came about, I came up with the idea that Ollie had to be assured, and it started out with putting this money aside as a death benefit for him, and I had also learned through scattered discussions—it was not that there was one discussion that this issue was analyzed—I had heard through various remarks that Ollie was not spending time at home, and he was not attending to his family, to his kids' education and so forth, and I had become emotionally very attached to Ollie, still am, and I really love this man.

I talked to Richard, Gen. Secord, I said that I thought it would be wise to set aside $500,000 to cover the—as a death benefit for Ollie. . . .

NIELDS: Richard what?

HAKIM: Opposed.

NIELDS: Was against it?

HAKIM: Against it, yes. As a matter of fact, he made a remark that the point of reference that I use is my own lifestyle and I have no understanding of what a soldier's life is, and that there are benefits that the government provides, and I came up with the figure of $200,000. Gen. Secord made no opposition to this. He did not disagree, and yet he did not come right out and say that, fine, go ahead and do it. And I did not pursue this.

That is how this was developed and the reason I came up with this figure in addition to the fact that Gen. Secord had been opposed to my original idea, I figured that the interest on $200,000 could cover a good part of a child's university education.

NIELDS: Did you tell Col. North that you had set this money aside?

HAKIM: I cannot recall having told Col. North that I have set money aside for his family's benefit, but I do recall my reaction to the times that we were discussing his family problem, basically for not being able to attend to his family, and also his concern about the education of his kids and his concern what would happen if he should get killed and so on.

The way I remarked to him was, "Ollie, you are part of the family for as long as one of us is alive, you need not worry about your family." That is what I remember having told him. I do not recall sitting him down and saying that I have set aside $200,000 for your family's benefit.

NIELDS: You have referred to this at times as a death benefit. I take it this was shortly before the trip to Tehran in May of 1986?

HAKIM: You are correct.

NIELDS: You have also said some things about his children's education. Did you ever take any steps to get some part of this money or any other money into his possession for his children's education?

HAKIM: The answer is yes. I consulted Mr. Zucker and he—I gave him an Iranian proverb. I told him that I want to do this, but the proverb is that if you want to fix the eyebrow, we don't want to blind the eye, meaning that I want to find a proper way of getting this money to his kid without compromising Ollie's position or his family, and consequently, we came to the conclusion that Mr.

Zucker, during his forthcoming trip to the U.S. to contact Mrs. [Betsy] North, without mentioning my name, to tell her that there is a certain person who admires her husband and wishes to help out with the university and the education expenses of the children.

And I provided him with the telephone number, home telephone number of Mrs. North, and I was told later that Mr. Zucker did call Mrs. North and as a result of that, a meeting took place, I believe in Mr. Zucker's attorney's offices in Philadelphia.

NIELDS: Did Mr. Zucker tell you anything about what happened during that meeting?

HAKIM: What I can recall the purpose of his meeting was, was to learn more about the family structure of Mr. and Mrs. North, to see who is who, what the family structure is, who are the relatives.

I have never met Mrs. North or any of the children, and I do not have any personal knowledge to this date about Col. North's family structure. Bill Zucker basically wanted to learn about the family, and when I asked him, he said that he has an idea about the family structure, and I believe what he had in mind was to see if he could find a proper way of getting the money in some sort of fashion, which was never determined, through the relatives to North's family, and the bottom line of that investigation was that he could not find a proper way to do that.

NIELDS: Did you and Mr. Zucker ever talk about another way to do that?

HAKIM: Yes. I was persistent and I had additional discussion with Mr. Zucker. The idea that we came up with was maybe we could arrange for a part-time job for Mrs. North, and since we did not know what the qualifications of Mrs. North were, we decided that maybe if Mr. Zucker could find someone that could offer that position to her, and even if she did not qualify, we could make use of the Button set aside to cover her salary, and Mr. Zucker told me that he knew of a land real estate developer that he was going to contact and see if he could find a way, approaching the problem that way.

And that was the last time we discussed about this issue, and to the best of my knowledge, no money was sent to North's family and no solution, no proper solution was found.

NIELDS: Just so we understand, the idea of this real estate development company was to have that company pay Mrs. North some kind of a salary and to have the Button account pay the real estate company?

HAKIM: That is correct.

NIELDS: You have indicated that you told Mr. Zucker not to tell Mrs. North what the source of this money was.

HAKIM: That is correct.

NIELDS: But I take it Mr. North knew who Mr. Zucker was.

HAKIM: Yes, he did. Although they had not met.

NIELDS: And did you mention to anyone else the fact that you had given Mr. Zucker the Norths' telephone number?

HAKIM: I believe I told this to Gen. Secord, that this is what I was doing.

NIELDS: Mr. Hakim, I have to ask you this question. Since you have testified that you told Mr. Zucker not to mention your name, were you attempting to compromise Mr. North without his knowledge or did you act in the belief that this wouldn't happen unless—that a meeting would never take place in Philadelphia unless Mr. North knew of it and approved of it?

HAKIM: I did not absolutely have the intention of compromising Oliver North in any way or form. Basically what I did, I put a wheel into motion and then if North's family wanted to open the door to my motion, they could. If they wanted to close the door to it, they also could do that.

I just simply went ahead and put this action into motion and left the rest up to them.

*　*　*

On March 5, 1986, Hakim deposited $2 million in funds earned from the Iran arms deal into a Swiss bank account. Hakim made provisions for control of the money, which was to be used for the contra-aid network, should he, Secord, or North die during the Iran-contra operation.

House counsel Nields is referring to the first of two legal documents drawn up by Hakim.

NIELDS: I take it your idea here was that if anything should happen to you, Gen. Secord would control the account, and if anything happened to him, Oliver North would control the account?

HAKIM: We went up the ladder, yes.

NIELDS: With North at the top of the ladder, Secord in the middle and you at the bottom?

HAKIM: That is correct, sir.

NIELDS: And I take it the idea was you wanted to keep the higher the person was on the ladder, the farther you wanted to keep him away from the money in these accounts, or having his name associated with them?

HAKIM: That is correct.

NIELDS: But you still had to have it associated in some document, otherwise you might lose control of the $2 million.

HAKIM: Lose control of the $2 million for the enterprise [the contra-supply operation].

NIELDS: And this was an enterprise ultimately in which North was at the top?

HAKIM: That is correct. That was my judgment.

* * *

NIELDS: Now, Exhibit 20 is similar to the other document that was executed in the event of your death, except that it does not mention Lt. Col. North; is that correct?

HAKIM: That is correct.

NIELDS: And what was the reason for not having North's name on this document?

HAKIM: We had created certain obligations in connection with opening the second channel that would not have been appropriate for a government official to get involved in handling those commitments.

NIELDS: These were commitments to officials or people you believed to be officials of the Iranian Government?

HAKIM: As well as businessmen.

NIELDS: Both?

HAKIM: Yes.

NIELDS: And when you say commitments, you mean that you had an obligation to pay them some money?

HAKIM: That is putting it very bluntly, yes.

NIELDS: But accurately?

HAKIM: Yes.

NIELDS: And I take it from what you are saying that one of the purposes of this second $2 million sub-account was that it could be used for that purpose.

HAKIM: But it was company expense, so those commitments, I regarded them as company expense.

* * *

In February 1986 Hakim joined a special U.S. delegation headed by North in Frankfurt, West Germany. The delegation met with Iranian officials to discuss the weapons deal; Hakim posed as "a special interpreter for the President of the United States, to impress the Iranians."

HAKIM: Well, Col. North was heading the U.S. delegation and his emphasis was to establish, to take steps that would take us to establishing a relationship with Iran, normalizing the relationship. It was a long-term objective and at the same time he was referring to removal of obstacles and the obstacles, he meant the hostages. But he approached—the approach of Col. North was long-term where the approach of the Iranian official was highly only focused on purchase of weapons.

And I would bring them around and get them across to talk about the same thing. They would continue for a short while to discuss about the long-term relationship, but before I knew it they were back, each one, to what I call back to their own frequencies, and I didn't see the meeting going well. I didn't have a good feeling about it because I was convinced that the gentleman who came

from Iran had definite requirements, and he did not want to divert his attention from the requirements that he had and later on my assessment proved to be correct.

NIELDS: Now, after this meeting, did you return home to the United States? I don't mean immediately, Mr. Hakim. I mean eventually.

HAKIM: Oh, yes, eventually I did come back to the United States, yes.

NIELDS: And did you for a time have direct telephone conversations with the Iranian official?

HAKIM: Yes, but prior to that.... [Before returning to the United States, Hakim met with an Iranian official in the Frankfurt Sheraton Hotel lobby.] He had a personal message for me to carry to the President of the United States. He approached me and Gen. Secord was also present and we had a very short discussion in the lobby, and the cultural difference became so evident during this short and brief discussion that I gave even less of a chance for success with the approach that we were taking.

The message was if I could whisper into the ears of President Reagan to go ahead for whatever money is needed, to supply the arms—this may not be meaningful to the committee but—

NIELDS: What do you mean by for whatever money?

HAKIM: Basically, he was trying to bypass all the people and make the deal with the President, and if the—

NIELDS: For money?

HAKIM: Yes. You know, tell him that money is no problem and if he could get the weapons given to them and make a deal.

* * *

Hakim resumed his testimony in the afternoon of June 4, 1987. He described a meeting that took place in North's office with Iranian representatives including "the second channel." After the meeting, Hakim and North took the second channel on a tour of the White House.

HAKIM: . . . Towards the end of the day, after we broke and arranged to have the meeting the next day at our offices, Col. North and I took our guest for a tour of the White House, and we took him to every corner of the White House, and by then—

NIELDS: Did that include the Oval Office?

NIELDS: Yes. We went—also we did not actually walk into the Oval Office, the doors were open. There was a little barrier, rope barrier in front there, but we showed him the rooms and Col. North, by this time, was also impressed by this gentleman, and he was feeling, after many months of frustration, he was feeling upbeat. It is interesting to note while we were passing by one of the corridors, stepping down the stairs, we came across a picture that was hanging on the wall. It portrayed the table and like a conference table and there were dogs sitting around the table and I remember one of the dogs I think was taking a little nap, and Ollie was feeling very upbeat and he asked me to translate for our guest that this represented our Cabinet, and that was [Director of Central Intelligence William J.] Casey taking a nap. That broke the ice.

* * *

The testimony subsequently returned to the topic of Hakim setting up the Button account for North's family.

[Arthur L.] LIMAN [Senate committee chief counsel]: The point that I obviously am pressing you on, Mr. Hakim, is that this story that Col. North was not going to know who was offering to provide money to the family is pretty preposterous, isn't it?

HAKIM: Well, I wouldn't go that far, Mr. Liman.

We have not in the examination that you are conducting focused on a very important element, and the discussion of myself with Gen. Secord, the direction that your questioning is taking is eliminating the double direction of my strategy, which one direction was to Gen. Secord and another direction was towards Mr. Zucker.

LIMAN: The reason I didn't mention it was because you didn't mention that other part of your strategy yesterday. So why don't you tell us about that. . . .

HAKIM: I definitely brought that subject up. There was no focus on it.

LIMAN: You brought the subject up with Gen. Secord?

HAKIM: Yes, sir. . . .

LIMAN: What did you tell him?

HAKIM: I told him that I intended to help with the education of Col. North's child. I told him that I am going to have Mr. Zucker examine this. I told him I will be giving the telephone number of Mrs. North to Zucker and I am going to leave it up to him to come up, if possible, with a method that we can achieve our objective.

LIMAN: And when you testified yesterday at page 101 that it is very possible, those were your words, that Col. North would not have known who was behind this arrangement in contacting his wife and so forth, that was really an overstatement, wasn't it?

HAKIM: If everybody would have been done as I was hoping to be done, that would not have been an overstatement.

LIMAN: But is it a fact that you regarded it as inconceivable that Col. North would not have known?

HAKIM: I probably depended too much on the genius of Mr. Zucker.

LIMAN: Did you testify at your deposition in the last session at page 70 that it was inconceivable? . . .

Look on line 7, page 70. "Is there any doubt in your mind that if Zucker contacted Mrs. North, that Oliver North would know who was sending Zucker?

"Answer. I would have found it, maybe it would have taken time, but eventually I would have found it impossible for him not to know."

It goes on.

HAKIM: That is my testimony.

LIMAN: That still is your testimony?

HAKIM: Yes sir.

LIMAN: Is it a fact that the reason—the reason that you could make this approach to Mrs. North was because Gen. Secord led you to believe that North would not object to it?

HAKIM: The way I look at this structure, Mr. Liman, is that I believe I already used those words. I put the wheel into motion. It would have been—assuming that we would have found a way—it would have been up to Mrs. North and Col. North to accept or to refuse this assistance.

LIMAN: Now, when you say you put the wheel into motion, were you ever told by Col. North that he objected to the fact that his wife met with Zucker in Philadelphia?

HAKIM: I don't recall any discussion with Col. North in that area.

LIMAN: You in fact received a report from Zucker that he had the meeting?

HAKIM: Yes.

LIMAN: You received a report from him that he had gone over the family structure?

HAKIM: Yes sir.

LIMAN: You received a report from him that he could not find a way of transferring money through relatives?

HAKIM: That is correct.

LIMAN: You continued after that to deal with North and the [second] channel, is that so?

HAKIM: We were—these were two independent—

LIMAN: Were you seeing North?

HAKIM: Yes.

LIMAN: Talking to him?

HAKIM: Yes. Generally speaking.

LIMAN: Did he ever in any of the conversations after the Philadelphia trip say to you, "I object to this attempt to transfer money to my family?"

HAKIM: No such discussions took place.

LIMAN: Did he, in fact, encourage you to continue on the second channel?

HAKIM: There was no relevance between the two.

LIMAN: Well, you understood that if Col. North took your overture as being something that was unwelcome, he could cut you out, right.

HAKIM: I could cut him out, sir. He needed me.

LIMAN: Did you need him too?

HAKIM: The currency needed me. I was helping out. I made my resources available, all of my resources available to the country.

LIMAN: Are you saying, Mr. Hakim, that among your resources were TOW [antitank] missiles [a reference to the weapons that were sold to Iran as part of the arms deal]?

HAKIM: I was making my resources available to the United States, not Iran. TOW missiles were made available by the United States to Iran.

LIMAN: Didn't you testify that as you saw the structure, you would deal principally with Secord and Secord would deal with North?

HAKIM: You are correct, sir.

LIMAN: And that North was, therefore, on the top of that particular structure with respect to the negotiations with Iran?

HAKIM: As far as I was concerned.

LIMAN: And he may have—he did have superiors, but your contact in the government was principally North and [George] Cave [a retired CIA official who acted as translator and note-taker for many of the 1986 talks between the U.S. and Iranian officials], correct?

HAKIM: That is correct.

LIMAN: And at no time after you attempted to pass money to the North family through this arrangement between North and—Mrs. North and Zucker—did Mr. North ever protest to you?

HAKIM: That subject was never discussed.

LIMAN: That means he never said anything to you that that approach was unwelcome, correct?

HAKIM: I don't know if he knew.

LIMAN: Well, if what you were trying to do was proper and lawful, why didn't you just simply say to North, "Col. North, I want to help with the education of the children."?

HAKIM: I did not have the knowledge I—I sought the advice of my attorney to look into this to see if we could find a proper way of doing it because—unlike Iran, if I know very well making—if you—you refer to it as kickback. Kickbacks available to American officials [are] illegal.

LIMAN: Mr. Hakim, isn't it a fact that you knew that the passing of money to the North family, even if it was for the education of the children, was not proper?

HAKIM: That is why I consulted a lawyer.

LIMAN: And isn't it a fact that the instructions to the lawyer were to transfer the money in a way which would be secret?

HAKIM: In a way that it would be proper.

LIMAN: Secret also?

HAKIM: Secret also.

*   *   *

LIMAN: . . . Just see what it is you admit and what it is you don't.

HAKIM: I will admit to the truth.

LIMAN: Good.

You admit you set up an account of $200,000 for the benefit of the North family, correct?

HAKIM: Yes, Mr. Liman.

LIMAN: You admit that that account was kept secret, correct?

HAKIM: Up to a certain point.

LIMAN: Until you revealed it to us?

HAKIM: Yes, sir.

LIMAN: You admit that you tried to pass money to the North family through Zucker?

HAKIM: I testified to that.

LIMAN: You say that you were looking for a proper way to pass it, correct?

HAKIM: I asked Mr. Zucker, my attorney, to look for a proper way.

LIMAN: You admit that you told Secord of this and he never objected?

HAKIM: That is correct.

LIMAN: You admit that Zucker told you that he met with Mrs. North?

HAKIM: Yes, sir.

LIMAN: And you admit that at no time after that meeting did Col. North ever object?

HAKIM: I testified that.

LIMAN: Now, you said—and I will—you repeated it just earlier, "Basically, what I did was I put a wheel in motion, and then if the North family wanted to open the door to my notion, they could. If they wanted to close the door to it, they could also do that."

HAKIM: Assuming that the cycle of the wheel will be completed and they—a way will have been found.

LIMAN: The question is, did they ever close the door to it or did you just simply stop trying?

HAKIM: The cycle never finished, sir. The wheel started, never got off the ground.

LIMAN: And it didn't get off the ground because Zucker couldn't find a way of transferring it?

HAKIM: A proper way of transferring it.

* * *

LIMAN: Why didn't you tell Col. North that you were making provisions for him in the will with respect to $2 million [in a Swiss bank account set aside for the enterprise] which could be used for personal purposes?

HAKIM: I told Gen. Secord. That was the pattern of our operation.

LIMAN: And when you told Gen. Secord, did you contemplate that Gen. Secord would tell Col. North?

HAKIM: Gen. Secord knows what he has to do. I don't know what he would have done. But my assumption would have been that he would tell Col. North, but I don't have firsthand information, sir.

* * *

Dealing with Iran

LIMAN: If I understand your testimony, your conclusion was that the way to open the door to Iran was, at least in part, through commercial channels.

HAKIM: I believe that is the only way to open the door to Iran, then and now.

LIMAN: And you saw that the—if business could be done with Iran, it would provide opportunities for both you and Gen. Secord for profit; is that fair to say?

HAKIM: Yes.

LIMAN: And it would also be beneficial to the United States.

HAKIM: Of course.

LIMAN: And that's what you meant in your opening statement when you said that this was a unique opportunity; it could be personally profitable to you and Gen. Secord, it could be good for the United States, it could be good for Iran, it could be good for the whole region there; is that fair to say?

HAKIM: Correct. That is fair.

LIMAN: And one of the factors that you recognized and that you discussed with Gen. Secord was that the Iranian market was about $15 billion a year if it could be opened; is that correct?

HAKIM: I discussed that with Gen. Secord, among other people. I still do.

LIMAN: Did you discuss that with Lt. Col. North?

HAKIM: No sir. I'm saying with other businessmen.

LIMAN: And if you could be instrumental in opening up this channel, you would have at least an inside track on doing some good business there.

HAKIM: Yes, sir.

LIMAN: Indeed, you thought you and Gen. Secord could make a bundle if this succeeded?

HAKIM: Yes, sir.

LIMAN: And you made no secret of that, you reported that to the American officials you were dealing with?

HAKIM: That's correct.

LIMAN: So that there was no mistake on their part that both

you and Gen. Secord had a dual motive?

HAKIM: I spoke for myself. I left Mr. Secord to make his position clear himself.

* * *

A Political Motive

LIMAN: But even at this late date, which is October [1986], after you had been working on this second channel since July, Col. North still was contemplating that all of the hostages would be released; correct?

HAKIM: Col. North not only had the desire of re-establishing the relationship with Iran, it did not for a moment leave his mind the American hostages being kept in Lebanon. That was in his mind at all times.

LIMAN: Did he tell you that he was under political pressure to get them released?

HAKIM: He did not have such a discussion with me, but that was my definite impression and understanding, that that was the case.

LIMAN: Well, what gave you that impression?

HAKIM: When we got closer to the time for the elections, my understanding was that Col. North wanted to remove this obstacle for the purpose of enhancing the President's position.

LIMAN: Well, did you reach the conclusion and so testify to it that you believed that his—North's prime objective was to get the hostages released in time for the elections?

HAKIM: I would say this would be unfair to say that it was his prime objective. But definitely he was trying to achieve that goal.

LIMAN: If you look at page 202 of May 31, would you tell me whether you testified that that was your impression of Col. North, namely that it was his prime objective to get the hostages released in time for the election?

HAKIM: . . . I've read that, sir.

LIMAN: Was it true what you testified?

HAKIM: What I testified is correct, sir, but my understanding of your question is different than the context that is in my deposition.

Here I am advising Col. North that his strategy for negotiation is wrong. Col. North wanted to achieve—as I earlier testified a few moments ago—he wanted to achieve both. And I told him, as I testified here, that this is a wrong approach to put his emphasis and show as his prime objective the release of hostages.

I told him, as I testified, he should low-key that and he should put his attention more on the long-term relationship.

LIMAN: Mr. Hakim—

HAKIM: There is no question Col. North wanted to get the hostages out as quickly as possible.

LIMAN: Mr. Hakim?

HAKIM: Yes, sir.

LIMAN: If you misspoke at your deposition, you can so state. . . . Would you look at that passage and tell me whether or not that statement is still something that you stand by? If it is, I will read it. If it is not, I won't.

HAKIM: You should read the whole thing, sir. If you want to, go back. You are taking part, only a small part of my whole testimony in connection with this subject. Let's go further.

LIMAN: "Question: Let me ask you to focus on this particular period of time. What was your perception of how the hostage problem should be resolved?"

Is that the question? You see the question there?

HAKIM: Yes, sir.

LIMAN: And your answer was, "Answer: I did not approve of Col. North's focusing on hostages. My suggestion was that, 'You should low key that. You should not show any interest or hunger in getting the hostages back,' because his prime objective at that time was to support the President in connection with the Republicans for the elections, and I found that to be counterproductive. And, like I said, this is not a good negotiating tactic. 'You should low-key that. And then, to the contrary, tell them you are not interested in that.' " Is that what you testified?

HAKIM: The testimony is correct, sir.

LIMAN: Is that true?

HAKIM: That is true, but—

LIMAN: That is what he said to you to what your impression was?

HAKIM: That is correct.

LIMAN: And did you also testify that you felt under political pressure?

HAKIM: I felt under political pressure or he—

LIMAN: That you were put under political pressure?

HAKIM: Yes.

LIMAN: And now that was just what you observed from the way in which Col. North was acting? Those were your conclusions, or did he say that to you?

HAKIM: The subject—the subject of the elections was definitely discussed during our attempt in trying to re-establish the relationship with Iran, sir.

LIMAN: And what was said?

HAKIM: As I testified earlier, that he wanted to gain the release of the hostages to enhance the position of the President.

I just testified to that a few minutes ago.

* * *

LIMAN: . . . You can get an impression here that North is hustling you, that you are hustling North, that the Iranians are hustling you, that you are hustling the Iranians and that it really is, as you said before, a commercial type of environment, is that an unfair impression that I have?

HAKIM: Yes. That is [unfair].

LIMAN: When you were told that this agreement [that Hakim negotiated with the Iranians, October 1986] that you had negotiated had been approved by the President of the United States, you must have felt very proud?

HAKIM: : I felt proud throughout, sir. I felt proud being part of the time.

LIMAN: Did you feel like you had been the Secretary of State for a day?

HAKIM: I would not accept that position for any money in the world, sir.

LIMAN: Well, you had it better than the Secretary of State in some sense. You didn't have to get confirmed; correct?

HAKIM: I still believe that I have it better than the Secretary.

LIMAN: And—

HAKIM: I can achieve more, too.

LIMAN: And if this initiative had succeeded, did you ever make any calculation as to how much you and Gen. Secord would make?

HAKIM: In what period of time, sir?

LIMAN: People tend to think in terms of three-to-five-year plans.

HAKIM: Many millions.

LIMAN: Did it bother you at all that here you—and I say it respectfully—a private citizen was left with this kind of task of negotiating an agreement in which if it succeeded, you stood to benefit very substantially?

HAKIM: Mr. Liman, what bothered me was that we didn't have the competence within the government to do what I could do. That still bothers me.

* * *

Hakim resumed his testimony June 5, 1987. He described a background document, written by Secord, for an October 1986 meeting between U.S. and Iranian officials in Frankfurt, West Germany.

HAKIM: This refers to the meeting that finally led to my having the discussion with the Iranians regarding the development of the nine points [of the U.S. proposal to the Iranians to negotiate the release of the hostages through an arms deal].

LIMAN: So this was the meeting in Germany?

HAKIM: Yes, sir.

LIMAN: Now, if you look at it, it says on one of the points, "As I said in Brussels, we will fight Russians in Iran in case of invasion with or without the Government of Iran's assistance." Who is the "I"; is that Secord?

HAKIM: It says U.S.

LIMAN: That is U.S.—

HAKIM: U.S. will.

LIMAN: The United States will fight the Russians, not—

HAKIM: That is my understanding, yes.

LIMAN: And the "I" who is saying this to the Iranians is Gen. Secord?

HAKIM: Yes, sir.

LIMAN: And were you present when he was committing to the Iranians that we would go to war with the Russians if they invaded Iran?

HAKIM: The way I recall this, Mr. Liman, it was a bargaining method that Gen. Secord used to get the attention of the Iranians.

LIMAN: But you told us earlier that one of the problems with the first channel [the first Iranian contacts in the arms deal, including Manucher Ghorbanifar] was that Mr. Ghorbanifar was always promising more than he could deliver; is that correct?

HAKIM: That is correct.

LIMAN: And you had warned Gen. Secord and [Lt.] Col. [Oliver L.] North that it was important to deal straight with the Iranians; is that so?

HAKIM: That was when I got to know the people of the second channel [the Iranian officials who became the contacts in the arms deal after the first contact did not work out], yes.

LIMAN: And you were there when Gen. Secord was making these kinds of statements and giving these kinds of assurances to representatives of the Iranian Government?

HAKIM: This was the first meeting.

LIMAN: And if you go down to the next sentence, that is also in Secord's handwriting, am I correct?

HAKIM: Yes, sir.

LIMAN: And am I also correct that Secord wrote—have said to the Iranians, we will cooperate to depose the leader, the President of Iraq, is that what he was saying?

HAKIM: As I mentioned, he left these with me to use as ideas for patching up things.

LIMAN: Well, I mean was it you who was saying that we will cooperate to depose—

HAKIM: No, Gen. Secord wrote this.

LIMAN: And it was Gen. Secord who also said it, wasn't it? Did he say it to the Iranians or did he not?

HAKIM: I think it [was] more than Gen. Secord. If I recall correctly, it was the attitude of the total delegation.

LIMAN: By that you mean Col. North—

HAKIM: As well as Mr. [George] Cave [a retired CIA official who acted as a translator and note-taker for many of the 1986 talks between U.S. and Iranian officials] and Gen. Secord.

LIMAN: Now is the "we"—we will cooperate—is that the enterprise or is that again the United States of America?

HAKIM: My understanding is the United States.

LIMAN: Did you find it surprising that Gen. Secord, a private citizen, and a Lieutenant Colonel, an annuitant, as we will call them, of the CIA, could, without any congressional approval, or anything more that you knew of make these kinds of representations to the leader of the Iranian delegation?

HAKIM: My impression, Mr. Liman, was from the very beginning that the President of the United States was supporting this mission. It was cleared with him. And in my mind I can't go further than the President's authorities, and I can't judge the policy of the President.

LIMAN: But in fairness, you got that impression because Col. North dropped the name of the President and because he had the kind of access in the White House that he had, and because he could deliver the TOWs and the Hawks and the other things that were promised, right?

HAKIM: Yes.

LIMAN: It wasn't because Gen. Secord told you that he met with the President, because he has made it clear that he didn't.

HAKIM: That is correct, sir.

* * *

A Business Proposition

LIMAN: Finally, there is now presently, as I understand it in Merrill Lynch in London some $6.67 million.

HAKIM: This is the result of our investigation of yesterday, yes.

LIMAN: And is that money blocked?

HAKIM: Yes, sir.

LIMAN: And there is another $1,400,000 in bank accounts that was not distributed as profit of the enterprise in Switzerland; is that roughly correct?

HAKIM: That is also frozen, yes.

LIMAN: And that is frozen?

HAKIM: Yes.

LIMAN: Now, you testified that when you started on the Iran initiative, none of the surplus was supposed to be for your personal financial benefit.

HAKIM: You are referring to the first channel?

LIMAN: The first channel.

HAKIM: Yes, sir.

LIMAN: Did you have a different understanding on this profit with respect to the second channel?

HAKIM: Yes, and I believe I testified to that.

LIMAN: And with whom did you have that understanding?

HAKIM: I testified that everyone involved on both sides, the American and the Iranian sides, they both were aware of that.

LIMAN: Are you prepared to deed over this money to the United States Government?

HAKIM: Mr. Liman, I have so many questions about this money and the enterprise in my mind that you cannot imagine. I— So not being able to clarify those questions in mind, I don't think I am in a position to do so.

LIMAN: There is one acid test of whether you considered the money yours, your partner's, or whether you consider it money that belongs to the United States, and that is whether you are prepared to deed it over. I take it the answer is you are not.

HAKIM: You are right....

It is not a question of acid test. There are commitments, it is a business, you have to look at it to see who are the people involved. Definitely the U.S. Government is one of the elements. I am saying it is not a question of doing a heroic thing and passing an acid test, it is a business situation and should be treated as such.

LIMAN: One of the commitments that you are referring to, or liabilities, is the commitment to this group of intermediaries who introduced you to the second channel?

HAKIM: Also [they] are unpaid.

LIMAN: Let's talk about that one. I know you have some other bills as well?

HAKIM: Also myself. There are a lot of issues that are not [clarified].

LIMAN: Mr. Hakim, the question is whether you expect that the U.S. Government should be paid out of proceeds of U.S. arms sales money that was necessary for you to offer to various intermediaries in order to open up a second channel....

You should recognize [the] obligations that you made?

HAKIM: I would like to address it differently. Definitely is an obligation of the enterprise.

If we ever decided what the enterprise is, I believe then we can answer your question.

LIMAN: Well, I think that is a good answer. At this moment, the enterprise as you see it is still there?

HAKIM: Effectively, yes, there is a monster sitting there with a few heads.

LIMAN: And how long do you contemplate that the enterprise will continue?

HAKIM: It all depends on how cooperative we all can be.

LIMAN: And one of the things that you define as cooperation is satisfying obligations to the third parties; is that fair to say?

HAKIM: No. That is not what I tried to communicate. I was trying to communicate that there are legal matters involved with this.

There are different countries involved with this. And it takes cooperation on the part of all people to try to resolve this.

LIMAN: Do you not have, subject to blocking the order, power to dispose of that money?

HAKIM: I have to examine that, sir. I don't think I have—

LIMAN: I am sorry, go ahead.

HAKIM: I have not addressed this thing for a long time. I need to see if I can do that.

LIMAN: You expect some of that money out of these enterprise accounts for your own benefit?

HAKIM: Yes, sir.

LIMAN: Have you defined in your own mind, however?

HAKIM: I have bigger problems to deal with and haven't sat down to do that yet.

* * *

The Enterprise

[Sen. Paul S.] SARBANES [D-Md.]: What were the purposes of the enterprise?

HAKIM: This is one of my questions, sir, that I have outstanding on mine, because this enterprise—my understanding was from Gen. Secord—was created to be a private corporation, if you will, and as a conventional businessman I expected the business would be conducted more or less in a conventional manner except the fact that it had to be operated covertly, and I applied all the rules and understandings and accepted practices that are applied to conventional business structures.

But as the—as we got deeper into our activities, I saw signs and symptoms that made me to wonder whether this enterprise was a private structure or it was not, because I saw a definite sign of inconsistency. I saw that on one hand we were acting as a private organization. At one point I saw the influence of Col. North, who was not a private individual, in what we were doing. I saw times—

SARBANES: Col. North, actually you perceived that Col. North could, in effect, call on the enterprise for money for whatever purpose he might have, did you not?

HAKIM: Yes, and then I also said that sometimes Gen. Secord would totally accept, sometimes partially accept, sometimes not accept his requirements. That is why I am saying I started to wonder.

SARBANES: But in your deposition on May 24th, at page 44, you said, "Richard said that you never know what Ollie would need next.

"Question: I take it at one point Ollie needed a ship, and you used the money to buy a ship.

"Answer: Yes.

"And at one point Ollie needed Motorola radios and you used the money to buy Motorola radios.

"Answer: Yes.

"And I take it at one point he wanted some money for DEA [Drug Enforcement Administration] agents in cash, and you used it for that purpose.

"Answer: Well, I don't know whether he initiated that. Richard told me that such and such people will come to you and give you so much.

"Question: But it wouldn't come as a surprise to you to learn that that also was originated by Ollie?

"Answer: I would be surprised if it didn't."

You then went on, in effect to say—is it fair to say that it was your understanding that during that period of time that this differential surplus, profit, whatever we call it, was being used and was to be used in North's direction?

"Answer: This was what I tried to explain earlier. Everything that you mention are examples of these contradictions. Yes.

"Is the answer yes?

"Answer: Yes."

Is that a correct statement of your perception of North's ability to call on the enterprise?

HAKIM: Yes, sir.

* * *

A Motive for Profit?

[Rep. Michael] DeWINE [R-Ohio]: I just, you know, I understand your statement that you do, in fact, like Ollie North, any witness who has testified says he likes Ollie North, so I understand that. But wasn't there really, Mr. Hakim, another overriding motive? Isn't this really the way you have alway done business? In fact, you don't see anything unusual about this, do you? This is just part of the cost of doing business? This is just part of the price that it takes to make these millions of dollars that you obviously have made so far?

HAKIM: Senator, I would like to make—sir, Congressman, I would like to make the following statement.

DeWINE: Sure.

HAKIM: I do not disagree with your line of logic, but it has one very big gap in it. You take out of all this that I am a human being, I have all the emotions of a human being, I am not a machine, I do get attached to people, I can provide you with tangible facts that my attachment to people is great, I can go back to the very beginning of my business career and provide you with witnesses.

By you eliminating that important fact and also undercutting my understanding that in Rome, I do as the Romans do, you are leaving a bad taint on me. I understand how business is conducted in the United States. I understand the ethics here. I also understand the way business is conducted elsewhere, and also there is—please do not eliminate the human element of my structure.

DeWINE: Well, I appreciate those comments, and, as I said, as I prefaced my comments to you and my question to you—

HAKIM: But definitely, definitely, I assure you that in no way I wanted to compromise Ollie. That would have been the last thing that I could have done, and looking at it cold-bloodedly, one—we got to a point that they needed me to open the second channel. I did not need to do any favors to Ollie. I testified to that yesterday. These things happened at a time that emotional issues were involved, and when I opened the second channel, I really, from the business point of view, I was in control. They needed me. I had the entree to Iran. If they wanted to—if they were unhappy with the first channel and so on.

I am trying to also add to this business rationale. Really it was the human end of this and not the business motivation for the set-asides, sir. . . .

DeWINE: Mr. Hakim, would it be a fair summary then that what you are testifying today is that when Secord told you that, when Gen. Secord told you that you still considered this as his money, he could come back and get the money if he wanted after that, is that my understanding?

HAKIM: Your understanding is correct and you should add to that that Gen. Secord would never make a good businessman. He was born a general and will die a general.

With all due respect to him really, he is a great soldier and I have a lot of respect for him.

* * *

[Rep. Jack] BROOKS [D-Texas]: Well, I want to thank you for your candid education of Americans in the way of doing business that you have prospered in doing, and I think it was an interesting description of how you do business, and I enjoyed it.

HAKIM: Thank you, sir.

BROOKS: I think they would shoot me in East Texas if I did it, but it works good in lots of places. It has been a pleasure to do business with you.

* * *

Paying Taxes

[Sen. David L.] BOREN [D-Okla.]: What about taxes? You say you have given some indication in your answers, and I have been listening to your answers, that you have some doubt, you apparently don't accept my hypothesis that this money [the profit made in the Iranian arms deal] belongs to the taxpayers, so I presume that the $15 million either belongs to the taxpayers or it became yours and Gen. Secord's to do with as you please.

If any other American taxpayer were to get $15 million to do with as they please, they would have to pay taxes on that money. I don't believe you can have it both ways. How can you explain that you either won't give it back, either it belongs to the taxpayers and

you should give it back, or you should pay taxes on it, should you not?

HAKIM: If you are on behalf of the U.S. Government giving me $15 million today, I will pay taxes on it.

BOREN: You kept $15 million that belongs to the taxpayers.

HAKIM: That is not what the records show.

* * *

[Rep. Jim] COURTER [R-N.J.]: I would like the United States taxpayers to receive a windfall when they can and if we can get some of this money fine but it is my understanding that the United States Government received all the money that it contracted for with regard to the sale of the weapons, is that correct?

HAKIM: You are correct.

COURTER: We sold weapons that totaled $12 million, the contract was that we receive $12 million, we asked for $12 million and we got $12 million before in fact we got rid of the weapons.

HAKIM: You are correct, sir.

* * *

Ethics versus Profits

[Rep. Louis] STOKES [D-Ohio]: . . . Mr. Hakim, you mentioned ethics this morning, and I was rather struck yesterday when you talked about acting as Secretary of State due to the incompetence of the officials of the United States. Did it strike you that while you were working in behalf of the business enterprise owned by yourself and Gen. Secord that there was a conflict of interest between your profit motive and your being able to represent the best interests of the United States?

HAKIM: First, I would like to very much clarify this issue of the acting as the Secretary of State.

STOKES: I am just referring to your statement yesterday.

HAKIM: Yes, but I also said that I would not accept the job for any money in the world. My total focus of yesterday's discussion, Mr. Stokes, was for that one particular day where I testified that I was remaining behind to patch things up, to patch things up doesn't require the skill of the Secretary of State, it requires the skill of an Iranian who speaks the language and understands the culture, and this is what I was referring to.

And then to patch up the relationship so the two parties can get back together would not compromise the interests of the United States.

STOKES: Mr. Chairman, indulge me, if you would, I have just one further question.

In response to a question posed to you, I think, by Sen. [George J.] Mitchell [D-Maine] earlier today when you referred to having been dropped and stabbed in late 1986 and he pursued that with you, let me just ask you this: What did you feel at that time the obligation of the United States was to you?

HAKIM: I felt that the body that asked me to come forward and help with this, could come out at least to listen to us, even tell us that "You are on your own, there is nothing we can do"; you know, we were not called upon. Our request to meet, you know, we thought that we were doing this on the behest of the President.

My only contact was Gen. Secord. I requested him to contact the President. He said he had already tried and failed.

I earlier testified that to this date I really don't know what the layer or element or part of the U.S. Government was who retained us, but in my mind there is no doubt that I could not have gotten to the White House, participated in various meetings, gone to the Situation Room, given the phony passport without some authority within the U.S. Government structure having retained us. I expected them to come out and say, "Hey, fellows, you are on your own. For these reasons we cannot help you," or, "We will help you."

There was total silence, as if we didn't exist.

STOKES: You really felt the President of the United States should have come and said something to you in your behalf, is that it?

HAKIM: I believed that if he could not do that, he should have arranged for us to be heard.

* * *

The President's Authority?

[Sen. Sam] NUNN [D-Ga.]: As an American citizen, did it bother you that a retired general and a lieutenant colonel on the NSC [National Security Council] staff and a businessman were holding out to the Iranian delegation that America would get involved in a war against the Soviet Union in Iran even without the cooperation of the Iranian government, and that we would also cooperate with them to depose the President of Iraq?

Did that bother you as an American citizen?

HAKIM: If I believed at the time that Col. North and Gen. Secord did not have the approval of the higher-ups to attend these meetings, it would definitely have bothered me, but I was continuously under the impression that they had their authority to participate in those meetings.

NUNN: So you thought they were really speaking for the President when they held out these propositions?

HAKIM: That was my impression.

* * *

[Sen. Paul S.] TRIBLE [Jr., R-Va.]: I would like to say a couple of words about what we have heard thus far and how this kind of fits together in my mind.

Mr. Chairman, I must say this smacks of a soap opera. It is a saga of greed and a flair for the dramatic. It is part James Bond and part Jimmy Durante and it would be very laughable but for the destructive consequences for people and policy.

What we have established, I think, through this testimony is the sheer folly of operating outside official channels. Without oversight and accountability, consultation, checks and balances, people and policy get into big trouble.

Your testimony and the records that you have furnished this committee have been very helpful, Mr. Hakim. It tells us a lot, not only about yourself, but other witnesses.

For example, it calls into serious question the truthfulness of the testimony of your partner, Gen. Secord. Gen. Secord said he was only advancing national interests and yet the evidence shows that he was actively promoting his own self-interest.

He said that he has forsworn all profits from this enterprise. I would label that a contingent disclaimer of profits, contingent on his getting Federal employment.

You obviously didn't believe him because you continued to put more and more of the profits into his account, but the evidence shows that over $300,000 was transferred to his benefit for his investments and for his personal use.

Gen. Secord also said that the arms markup was 20 or 30 percent. We have learned from your records that the markup was huge, 50 or 60 percent or more that your enterprise was gouging the contras, the very people that Gen. Secord said he was so fervently hopeful in helping.

Mr. Chairman, I think it may well be necessary in view of the testimony of Mr. Hakim to call Gen. Secord again to give him a chance to respond out of fairness to Gen. Secord and Mr. Hakim and also for the further information of this committee.

* * *

[Sen. Daniel K.] INOUYE [D-Hawaii]: During the past two days, panel members and citizens in the audience have chuckled over some of your responses. They have found your testimony fascinating and exotic. But I must confess to you that I found it rather sad.

To be told that here we had an American citizen, not just one, but two, not cleared to handle certain classified material sharing the secrets of this Nation, secrets that even we here have been denied—I would be tempted to show you one of the documents that this committee received from one of our agencies, and it says, "Reviewed and cleared," and all it has is a blank piece of paper.

You were given the KL-43 [encryption machine], a most secret device, something that the KGB would love to grab hold of, and now we are told that it is lying in an attorney's safe or closet.

We have been told that phony passports were issued by this Government.

We are told that persons not cleared have had access to the Situation Room, and I doubt if three of us on this panel have ever seen the Situation Room, it is considered so secret, and then to find that Iranians who have been sneaked in in the dark of the night have been given a special tour of the White House—to say that it is stranger than fiction is an understatement.

But then we find an American general, who should know better, an American lieutenant colonel, who everyone suggests is second only to the President of the United States, committing this country, its power and majesty, to defend Iran without even consultation with the Congress of the United States, is just unbelievable.

And then to come out that we will participate in deposing a chief of state of a country, and we are supposed to be neutral in that area.

Did these things bother you? I realize you are not a diplomat or politician, but I think of all the people in this room, you are the most knowledgeable of things in the Middle East.

Did it not concern you that something was drastically wrong?

HAKIM: When I look back, Mr. Chairman, I share your opinion. At the time it didn't occur to me.

David L. Lewis

Following are excerpts from the June 4, 1987, testimony of David L. Lewis, a Washington, D.C., lawyer. He described a lunch in Geneva, Switzerland, where he met with Willard Zucker, Albert Hakim's lawyer and financial adviser.

[John W.] NIELDS [Jr., House committee chief counsel]: And did you have a conversation with Mr. Zucker while the others were absent?

LEWIS: Yes, I did.

NIELDS: And would you describe that conversation?

LEWIS: We got into a discussion of the real estate transaction [the business transaction that would be used to transfer money to North's family by giving Mrs. North real estate commissions]. I guess I was asking some questions about the nature of the property or what was involved, and Mr. Zucker then indicated to me that there wasn't a specific property involved.

NIELDS: Did you say was not a specific—

LEWIS: Was not a specific property involved, that—I guess I got the impression—I don't recall the exact words—he had a wealthy client who wanted to, in a sense, get money to or award someone here in the U.S. and was looking for a business transaction to do it in. And we discussed ways that might be done and—but then as we went on, he began to indicate to me that, in fact, it was not necessary that there even be a real estate deal.

He essentially was looking for a cover for someone to merely pay money to a certain person here in the U.S. I then asked him who the person was, and he said the person was the wife of someone in the White House, that they were not paying the money—the money was earned by the person in the White House in some unrelated matter, but they did not want to pay the money to the person in the White House because of his sensitive position.

I then asked him who the person in the White House was and, to the best of my recollection, he said it was Lt. Col. Oliver North.

NIELDS: Did he say anything more about how this transaction might be structured?

LEWIS: Yes. He explained it to me in what I call—I don't think he used this wording—mirror transaction. What he was suggesting is that someone here in the U.S. would pay money to Col. North's wife, or the woman, whatever, and—

NIELDS: Was that someone the real estate—

LEWIS: The real estate broker, whoever was going to do this, would pay money to the designated person here, and at the same time a similar sum of money would be deposited in the payer's bank account in Switzerland or anywhere else in the world the payer wanted.

NIELDS: When you say the payer, you are referring again to the real estate broker?

LEWIS: That's right.

NIELDS: So the real estate broker would have a Swiss bank account and Mr. Zucker's client would put money into that bank account, simultaneously the broker in the U.S. would pay money to this person in the U.S.?

LEWIS: That's correct.

NIELDS: Did Mr. Zucker mention an amount of money?

LEWIS: Well, I believe he did. I don't have a specific recollection of that amount.

NIELDS: Do you recall telling Spencer Oliver [general counsel of the House Foreign Affairs Committee and a part-time staffer of the House committee investigating the Iran-contra affair] that it was $70,000?

LEWIS: I don't specifically recall that, but that amount in that range, I think, seems—does ring a bell, but I can't tell you now I recall a specific amount.

NIELDS: I take it whatever you told Spencer Oliver would have been the best of your recollection at that time?

LEWIS: That's correct.

NIELDS: Can you say $70,000 is approximately that amount of money?

LEWIS: I think I can.

NIELDS: Did anything come of this conversation?

LEWIS: No, not that I know of.

NIELDS: Did you take any steps to pursue it?

LEWIS: None.

Bretton G. Sciaroni

Following are excerpts from the June 8, 1987, testimony of Bretton G. Sciaroni, counsel on the president's Intelligence Oversight Board (IOB). In September 1985 Sciaroni looked into allegations, raised by press reports of Lt. Col. Oliver L. North's assistance to the contras, that the National Security Council (NSC) staff was violating the Boland amendment.

[John W.] NIELDS [Jr., House committee chief counsel]: I take it the Intelligence Oversight Board is not truly set up to conduct large-scale investigations.

SCIARONI: Right. We have an investigatory authority but we do not have things such as subpoena power, ability to put people under oath.

NIELDS: So you need to rely, to a considerable degree, on the cooperation of people in the Intelligence [community]?

SCIARONI: That's absolutely true.

NIELDS: And in order to get that cooperation, it is important to remain on good working terms with them?

SCIARONI: Well, if they are members of the intelligence community, they are required by law to provide help in the course of our duties.

The NSC is not part of the intelligence community, as has been pointed out. So in that particular case, I am dependent upon the good will of the officials, unless I have reason to believe something has been hidden from me.

NIELDS: In any event, it would have been difficult for you to have said, Ollie, I'm now going to have to review all of the files in your office?

SCIARONI: That's true.

NIELDS: And did you not do that?

SCIARONI: No.

NIELDS: And as a result, you ended up your investigation believing that the NSC had not raised funds or given military support or helped give military support to the contras?

SCIARONI: I had no reason to believe that.

NIELDS: You wrote that down in your report as a conclusion, did you not?

SCIARONI: That is true.

NIELDS: It now appears that that was incorrect?

SCIARONI: That is true.

NIELDS: So that at least part of the report that you wrote ended up as a result of concealment of facts from you to be based on misinformation?

SCIARONI: Well, I wouldn't choose to characterize it until you could hear from the other participants about why those things weren't shown to me.

NIELDS: Well, I am simply asking you, sir, isn't it true that the conclusion was based on failure to communicate information to you?

SCIARONI: True.

NIELDS: You didn't have the facts?

SCIARONI: That is true.

NIELDS: And it was the incorrect facts in part upon which your opinion was based?

SCIARONI: That is absolutely correct.

NIELDS: Indeed, one of the reasons, and I emphasize at the moment only one of them, but one of the bases for your legal conclusion was that the NSC was not an operational organization.

SCIARONI: It is not typically an operational organization, that is true.

NIELDS: And you were not told at that time that it was, in fact, involved in intelligence operations?

SCIARONI: No, I was not told that.

* * *

A History of the Boland Amendment

[Rep. Henry J.] HYDE [R-Ill.]: Now, you are aware, are you not, that the Tower Commission [appointed by the president to investigate the Iran-contra affair] viewed the Boland Amendment [which restricted U.S. aid to the Nicaraguan contras] as very murky, and I quote from page Roman Numeral 321, "The result was an intense political struggle between the President and Congress over how to define U.S. policy towards Nicaragua. Congress sought to restrict the President's ability to implement his policy. What emerged was a highly ambiguous legal environment."

That is the opinion, and I assume they are talking about the Boland Amendment because they mention it. They say on December 21 [1982] Congress passed [the] first Boland prohibiting the Department of Defense [DOD] and CIA from spending funds to overthrow Nicaragua or provoke conflict between Nicaragua and Honduras. The following year $24 million was authorized for the contras. On October 3, '84, Congress cut off all funding for the contras and prohibited DOD, CIA and any other agency or entity involved in intelligence activities from directly or indirectly supporting military operations in Nicaragua. Then the Tower Commission goes on and says the 1984 prohibition was subject to conflicting interpretation.

On the one hand, several of its congressional supporters believed the legislation covered the activities of the NSC staff. On the other hand, it appears that Col. North and [Rear] Adm. [John M.] Poindexter [former national security adviser] received legal advice from the President's IOB, the restrictions on lethal assistance did not cover the NSC staff. Confusion only increased.

In December 1985, Congress approved classified amounts of funds to the contras. That was a short time after [Rep. Edward P.] Boland [D-Mass.] had said that the U.S. Government was out of the business of supporting the contras, no money at all, for communications and advice.

The authorization was subject to a classified annex negotiated by the Senate and House Intelligence committees; an exchange of letters initiated the day the law passed evidencing the extreme difficulty even the Chairmen of the two committees had in deciding what the annex permitted or proscribed, and we have excerpts up there of the Chairman of the Senate committee saying one thing, the Chairman of the House committee saying another.

So it is interesting that members of Congress and the NSC have to adhere to a law that is murky at best.

SCIARONI: Let me just make a comment about that. I work a great deal with attorneys from the Central Intelligence Agency, and over the last two years they have had to go into a scramble, it seems, several times a year to try to figure out what the law is, what the intent of the Congress is, and try to make sense of that operationally for them.

I have a great appreciation for the kind of headaches this has caused for them out there, because the Congress has changed its course numerous times as you have elaborated.

* * *

Applying the Boland Amendment

[Sen. George J.] MITCHELL [D-Maine]: Mr. Sciaroni, as I understand your opinion, the National Security Council staff is not covered by the Boland Amendment because the National Security Council is not specifically identified either in the Boland Amendment itself or in section 101 of the Intelligence Authorization Act of 1985; is that correct?

SCIARONI: That is correct.

MITCHELL: So, if an agency is listed, it is covered, and if an agency isn't listed, it is not covered. That is your opinion?

SCIARONI: That is correct.

MITCHELL: And in your opinion, it didn't make any difference what the employees of any agency were actually doing. If the agency is listed, they are covered by Boland; if the agency isn't listed, they are not covered by Boland. That is your opinion?

SCIARONI: It would stress credulity to think anyone would do those kinds of things the Boland Amendment tried to prohibit.

MITCHELL: Supposing they did just that, supposing employees of the Department of Agriculture, which are not listed in those pieces of legislation, engaged directly in the prohibited type of activity—that is, intelligence activity—would they be covered by the Boland Amendment?

SCIARONI: They wouldn't, but it is an unlikely situation operationally—

MITCHELL: Have you not been following these hearings, Mr. Sciaroni?

SCIARONI: Yes, I have.

MITCHELL: There is very little you could say that would qualify it as highly unlikely. . . .

* * *

Sciaroni's Investigation

[Rep. Thomas S.] FOLEY [D-Wash.]: . . . You considered this question that had arisen about U.S. activities in support of the contras as being a serious and important matter for the board to investigate?

SCIARONI: The articles were quite prominent in August of 1985.

FOLEY: It was a major issue, was it not?

SCIARONI: It was.

FOLEY: And you considered it was important for the board to involve itself in this matter?

SCIARONI: I thought so.

FOLEY: That is why you undertook this investigation?

SCIARONI: Right.

FOLEY: Which you considered to be one that required serious and thorough examination; would that be fair?

SCIARONI: That's fair.

FOLEY: Did you think you gave serious and thorough examination to the question?

SCIARONI: I believe I did.

FOLEY: As a result of having spoken to two people, one for no more than half an hour and another for five minutes, you consider that was a thorough investigation?

SCIARONI: The charges that had been leveled were general in nature, and once I had asked the questions about what Col. North's activities were and been given the answers, I had no reason to doubt them.

FOLEY: You asked the counsel of the NSC, Cmdr. Paul B. Thompson, to give you information regarding those allegations, and it is your testimony now that he gave you inadequate and incomplete information?

SCIARONI: That would appear to be the case.

FOLEY: You believe he misled you?

SCIARONI: You should ask Cmdr. Thompson.

FOLEY: What do you believe? I'm asking you if you wish to

state your opinion now. Do you believe now that he knew that that information was incomplete and gave it to mislead you, gave you inadequate information to mislead you?

SCIARONI: Sir, I wouldn't care to characterize. You ought to put the question to him, why those memoranda weren't shown to me.

FOLEY: In other words, you at this time, knowing that you were given inadequate information by Cmdr. Thompson, are unwilling to characterize as to whether he gave such inadequate information to you deliberately?

SCIARONI: I have my personal view on that, sir.

FOLEY: That is what I was asking for, your personal view. You don't care to give it?

SCIARONI: I really wouldn't.

FOLEY: With respect to Col. North, the person you asked about his illegal activities, in this five-minute investigation in his office—do you believe he told you the full truth?

SCIARONI: It would appear not.

FOLEY: You believe he deliberately misled you?

SCIARONI: These are questions we should hear from Col. North about, why he denied that he was doing these activities.

FOLEY: I assume you know that he knew what his activities were and he told you at the time that he was not involved in any illegal activity?

SCIARONI: Right.

FOLEY: And you took his word for it and went back and wrote a report based on that?

SCIARONI: You don't consider that another official is not going to tell you, you know—answer your questions.

FOLEY: Why do you investigate another official, if the investigation consists of asking him if he did anything wrong and taking his word when he said he didn't?

SCIARONI: Both Cmdr. Thompson and Col. North knew what the mandate of the board was. I have to believe they understood the seriousness of my coming to ask them questions about activities, alleged activities out of the NSC.

* * *

[Sen. Warren B.] RUDMAN [R-N.H.]: Did you ever read Dickens, Mr. Sciaroni?

SCIARONI: On occasion.

RUDMAN: Did you ever read "Oliver Twist"?

SCIARONI: It has been quite a while.

RUDMAN: Remember Mr. Bumble?

SCIARONI: Well—

RUDMAN: I want to just tell you this because it's good for everyone to understand, the American people watching this about our laws and how we make them. He said if the law supposes that, Mr. Bumble, the law is an ass, an idiot. This Congress assumes, Mr. Sciaroni, that when it passes a law, that an outrageous, blatant attempt to subvert the law will be recognized by the courts for what it is, because courts always recognize attempts to subvert the law. This is not a contract between adversaries; this is the intent of the United States Congress.

I want to just tell you, Mr. Sciaroni, I think your opinion on that issue is just dead wrong.

Fawn Hall

Following are excerpts from the June 8, 1987, testimony of Fawn Hall, who worked as Lt. Col. Oliver L. North's secretary. Hall was quizzed about four secret National Security Council (NSC) documents she altered at North's request on November 21, 1986.

[Mark A.] BELNICK [Senate committee lawyer]: Did you pay attention to any of those changes when Col. North handed you the documents and said, "Here, make these changes"?

HALL: No, I didn't.

BELNICK: Did you ask Col. North why he wanted you to make those changes?

HALL: No, I didn't.

BELNICK: Did you read the changes that he made?

HALL: No, I didn't.

BELNICK: Did you appreciate the significance of the changes that Col. North was asking you to make to those original System 4 [secret] documents?

HALL: No, I didn't.

BELNICK: Weren't you curious?

HALL: It was a policy of mine not to ask questions and just to follow instructions. I believed in Col. North and what he was doing. I had no right to question him.

BELNICK: And so you took the original documents and made the changes that Col. North told you to make?

HALL: Yes, I did.

* * *

BELNICK: You weren't totally comfortable with what you were doing, were you, Ms. Hall?

HALL: I would say that I wasn't totally comfortable, yes. But as I've said before, I believe Col. North had a good reason for doing what he was doing. I'm not going to question that.

BELNICK: He didn't tell you what that reason was?

HALL: No, he didn't.

* * *

Changing Documents

BELNICK: Let's turn, then, to Exhibit 5.

Exhibit 5 bears the System 4 number 402007, which you recognize as another of the numbers on [former national security adviser Robert C.] McFarlane's list [of secret documents], correct?

HALL: Yes, sir.

BELNICK: That document [was] prepared on April 11, 1985, and contained a discussion of FDN [the main contra political faction] military operations which had been made possible by funding that had been provided through the donors after the cutoff of American aid by Congress.

On page 2, Col. North concludes that the money on hand will be insufficient to enable the resistance to grow to a larger force than it achieved unless efforts were made to seek additional funds of $15 to $20 million from the current donors.

By the way, Ms. Hall, did Col. North ever identify to you or describe to you who he meant by the "present donors" or the "current donors" in [this] memorandum?

HALL: No, he didn't.

BELNICK: In any event, Col. North recommends that those donors be approached for more aid and on page 3 of the memo, that recommendation is stated succinctly.

He attaches to the memo a list of expenditures and outlays by the resistance. Let's compare that document, Exhibit 5, with Exhibit FH-5-A. And as we look at those pages, in general information that seems to have been acquired actively by Col. North has been deleted and instead there are phrases such as according to information, they, the resistance, have given us, there is a more passive tense used when describing the type of knowledge that Col. North had, but the most dramatic change on the document comes at the end. All references to the present donors or funding by the present donors have been deleted from the document and instead of making a recommendation that the current donors be approached for increased aid, the recommendation is that Congress be approached for increased aid.

The specific recommendation then at the very end of the memo on page 3 is "that you brief the President on the current situation and urge concerted action on immediate Congressional approval of a $14 million CIA supplemental and a $75- to $100 million for the next fiscal year."

Again, you have checked the approved box on page 3 of that memo?

HALL: Yes, sir.

* * *

Hall resumed her testimony June 9, 1987:

[Sen. Warren B.] **RUDMAN [R-N.H.]:** Mr. Chairman, before I ask Ms. Hall a few questions, I just want to get the record straight on something. I think my colleague from Utah, [Republican] Sen. [Orrin G.] Hatch, makes a very good point, and all of us in this committee have tried assiduously to avoid casting any aspersions of guilt or innocence on anyone. That is not our job and certainly before people of America.

But so that anyone watching might not misunderstand, we have wanted Col. North here since last January. Col. North's not being here to answer these charges is his choice, not ours. And I would say it is his legal choice, and I am not critical of that. He has every right, as an American citizen, to invoke his constitutional privileges. That is what this country is all about.

But let the record show that the reason Col. North is still a mystery man is because he hasn't been before this committee for a whole lot of reasons, some having to do with his wishing to take immunity, others having to do with the Independent Counsel [Lawrence E. Walsh] wanting more time, but I think it is important that the American people don't misunderstand that we are not kind of holding Col. North out in the corridor and letting people make statements about him before we hear from him ourselves. I wish we had heard Col. North, Mr. Chairman, last February, and [Rear] Adm. [John M.] Poindexter. I had made it clear that when it came to balancing the interests of this country on prosecution versus getting the cloud out from over the President, we should have had them here months ago. I stand by that position. Some people disagree, but I believe it. But that is why he is not here.

Smuggling Documents

RUDMAN: Ms. Hall, thank you very much for being so candid in your testimony. I don't have any real factual problems with your testimony. I want to just clear up some things that I don't understand. I want to get to Mr. [Thomas C.] Green [North's lawyer at the time] for just a moment. Let me describe the situation as the transcript and your deposition indicates it, so we understand fully Mr. Green's participation.

As I understand it, you left the office with some documents in your boots and in your back, behind your back, as you described it. You walked out of the building, you wanted to maybe remove the documents at this point. Mr. Green, I believe, told you, "No, don't pass them to me here or to Col. North here," is that correct?

HALL: I don't believe he used those words, sir.

RUDMAN: Well, what did he say?

HALL: When I was on the elevator, he said, "Why don't you just wait for a few minutes," or "Let's see, let me—"

RUDMAN: That is good, that is fine.

HALL: I am just trying to remember what I remembered him saying. We walked outside, and Tom said, "Why don't you wait until we get in the car?"

RUDMAN: That is Mr. Green you are speaking of?

HALL: Mr. Green, yes, I am sorry.

RUDMAN: So at that point, Mr. Green knew that you had documents on you, on your person?

HALL: We would have to assume so, I don't know....

RUDMAN: ...Mr. Green knew when you got into his car that you had documents on your person, is that true?

HALL: I would say that he knew, yes.

RUDMAN: And then you proceeded to remove documents from your boots and from other parts of your clothing, is that correct?

HALL: That is correct, sir.

RUDMAN: And you handed those documents to Col. North or Mr. Green?

HALL: I handed them to Col. North.

RUDMAN: And Mr. Green was aware of that transfer of those documents?

HALL: Yes, he was.

RUDMAN: And I guess we can say, in fairness to everyone, that it is not normal to take documents out of the White House in one's boots and clothing, so Mr. Green certainly realized that there was something that was concealed that was being taken out of the White House?

HALL: Yes, sir. . . .

RUDMAN: And Congressman [Louis] Stokes [D-Ohio], when he described it, he called it a cover-up. You corrected him and said, "I did not look at it as a cover-up. I looked at it as protecting."

HALL: That's correct.

RUDMAN: Who are you protecting it from?

HALL: I was protecting the initiative.

RUDMAN: From whom?

HALL: From everyone, because I felt that—I knew we were trying to get back the hostages and I knew we were dealing with Iranian moderates and if this is exposed, there would be people whose lives would be lost.

And I also felt that it divulged—if this breaks out, we are sitting up here talking about all kinds of things, we are revealing sources and revealing everything. In my opinion, I don't think this is proper.

RUDMAN: I would observe, Ms. Hall, that—

HALL: A lot of damage would be done if a lot of top secret, sensitive, classified material was exposed in public, so that the Soviets and everyone else could read it. That is how I felt.

RUDMAN: Ms. Hall, did you know that it was White House personnel that were standing in the office barring people from leaving? You did know that.

HALL: I knew it was an NSC official, yes.

RUDMAN: It wasn't the KGB that was coming, Ms. Hall, it was the FBI [Federal Bureau of Investigation].

HALL: That's true, sir, but we do in this country have a tendency to have classified documents get on the front page of *The New York Times*—excuse me, I didn't mean to say that—but other newspapers in general.

Sorry about that. I didn't mean it.

* * *

North's Style of Operation

[Rep. Dick] CHENEY [R-Wyo.]: Let me come back to a point Mr. DeWine raised. He asked about Col. North's relationship with Adm. Poindexter and Mr. McFarlane.

I would like to explore his working relationship in terms of his style of operation.

We all know that there are people who, when given direction by a superior, will follow explicit through step by step to undertake a certain task.

There are others who demonstrate initiative. If assigned a problem, they will go out on their own and find creative ways of addressing the problem, and a third category, those who don't wait to receive an assignment, but identify a problem and decide on a course of action and try to persuade their superiors to follow that course of action.

Which model would Col. North fit most closely with?

HALL: Probably the latter. He was creative and never gave up. There was always a means to achieve a goal. I don't believe that he would do anything without authorization.

CHENEY: Do you perceive a conflict there at all in terms of showing and demonstrating initiative on the one hand, and on the other hand, waiting for authorization to undertake an activity?

HALL: I don't see a conflict, no. I think they can work hand in hand.

CHENEY: Did you ever have the sense that he was developing policy options and then taking those to his superiors, to Mr. McFarlane and Adm. Poindexter trying to persuade them to pursue that course of action?

HALL: He had ideas to overcome barriers and to find the means. I would say that he was creative in his work and I would say that many of his policies were accepted and authorized many times.

CHENEY: Are you aware of any policy options he developed that were turned down?

HALL: I don't remember ever receiving a disapproved memorandum. He never sent information memorandums. It was always an action memorandum.

CHENEY: And every action memorandum was approved?

HALL: I don't remember one being disapproved. There might have been one back from Adm. Poindexter with a notation of some kind. In the four years I worked for Col. North, in my recollection, I never saw a disapproved memorandum.

* * *

[Rep. Thomas S.] FOLEY [D-Wash.]: Without any reference to possible obstruction of justice, which is not the purpose of this committee to determine, did you not know that alteration of existing documents in a major, fundamental way was a violation of the responsibility of those who possess those documents?

HALL: I agree with you, sir, and at the time, as I stated before, I felt uneasy but sometimes, like I said before, I believed in Col. North and there was a very solid and very valid reason he must have been doing this for and sometimes you have to go above the written law, I believe.

I don't know, I felt—I believed in Col. North. Maybe that is not correct. It is not a fair thing to say. I felt uneasy to begin with and I agree with your assessment basically.

FOLEY: That unauthorized destruction of documents is a gross violation of security.

HALL: I don't know that destruction—OK, you are talking about the altered documents.

FOLEY: The shredding.

HALL: The shredding. I don't know that it was unauthorized.

FOLEY: You are not sure whether Col. North had—

HALL: I don't believe—

FOLEY: You are not sure whether Col. North did not have superiors' approval to destroy those documents?

HALL: I have no idea, sir.

FOLEY: But normally speaking, you would not be engaged in that kind of shredding as a routine daily or routine weekly or monthly activity of your office?

HALL: Sir, we never shredded to the volume we did. In my eyes, those documents could have been shredded, the PROFs [White House computerized messages] in my office could have been shredded every single day. If I completed a phone log, I could have shredded it that minute. There is no reason why it couldn't have been shredded earlier.

FOLEY: Do you have any doubt that it was an unusual shredding?

HALL: It was unusual. I have said that.

FOLEY: Finally, under any circumstances, the removal of classified documents from the offices to which they were assigned, removal from those offices and from the building was a gross violation of the security of those documents which for any other purpose, any purpose at all, would justify the severest discipline, isn't that true?

HALL: I agree that it was a gross violation and I honestly, sir, did not know the severity of what I was doing at the time. I wish I could re-do it.

FOLEY: I am not asking particularly the state of mind, but your judgment now and your judgment in any situation in which you were calmly analyzing the circumstances would be that such a removal could not be justified for any purpose when it was secretive and designed to take the documents outside the confined area without authority; isn't that correct?

HALL: Sir, I don't agree that it can't be justified by any means. I believe that it was definitely wrong and there would have to be extraneous reasons for doing that. I mean, we could make up scenarios, the KGB was coming in the door, and you would take them out then. It can be justified in circumstances. It was not in this case.

FOLEY: You are satisfied it was not in this case?

HALL: Yes.

FOLEY: Thank you.

* * *

[Sen. Paul S.] TRIBLE [Jr., R-Va.]: Ms. Hall, in your dialogue with Congressman Foley, you seemed to suggest there were times when one could go above the law. Did you really mean to say that?

HALL: No, and I said, I believe I retracted that. I tried to—

TRIBLE: Let me give you an opportunity to do that.

HALL: We all say things out of emotion that we don't necessarily mean.

TRIBLE: I just wanted to give you an opportunity to set the record straight.

HALL: I don't feel that.

TRIBLE: You were not suggesting that you were serving some higher good that permitted you to undertake these activities?

HALL: No.

* * *

[Rep. Bill] McCOLLUM [R-Fla.]: . . . Has there ever been any indication to you that anyone higher than Col. North ordered the shredding of documents on November 21st or knew anything about it?

HALL: I don't know, sir. I didn't ask Col. North and he didn't offer information as to why he was shredding.

McCOLLUM: There is nobody else you know of at all, any other source?

HALL: No, sir. Honestly, I don't know.

McCOLLUM: At any time did you overhear Col. North or anyone else say that they had personally discussed with President Reagan fund raising for the contras?

HALL: I don't remember someone discussing it. I am aware that the President met with many of the contributors that contributed to the contra effort, and I believe he might have met with some individually. I don't know.

McCOLLUM: But you don't ever recall overhearing anyone discuss their conversation with the President about the subject?

HALL: No, sir. It was my impression that he probably knew, but I don't remember.

McCOLLUM: At any time did you ever overhear Col. North or anyone else say that they had personally discussed with President Reagan the diversion of moneys from the arms transactions for the benefit of the contras?

HALL: No, sir. . . .

McCOLLUM: At any time, did you overhear Col. North or anyone else say that they had personally discussed with President Reagan any matter whatsoever concerning the Iranian arms deal or the hostage rescue efforts?

HALL: There were several meetings, I believe, with the President on those issues.

McCOLLUM: That Col. North had?

HALL: Yes, or that he attended.

McCOLLUM: And he mentioned to you the fact that he had discussed those things with the President personally?

HALL: No, he didn't, sir. Col. North attended the meetings at which the President was present that those matters were discussed.

McCOLLUM: But other than those occasions, you do not recall any discussions that someone described to you with the President about the Iranian arms matters or about the hostage rescue efforts?

HALL: No, sir.

Close of First Phase of Hearings

On June 9, 1987, at the end of the first phase of the Iran-contra hearings, Lee H. Hamilton, D-Ind., chairman of the House select committee, reviewed the information that had been revealed over the previous six weeks of testimony:

HAMILTON: I would like to make some statements about Phase I, which we are concluding, of our hearings. . . .

For the past six weeks these committees have been meeting to try to find out what went wrong in the processes of the American Government and why. We have heard about 110 hours or more of testimony from about 18 witnesses. Surely it seems to me these committees have heard some of the most extraordinary testimony ever given to the United States Congress. Let me mention a few things that stand out in my mind.

An elaborate private network was set up to carry out the foreign policy of the United States.

Private citizens, many with divided loyalties and profit motives, sold arms and negotiated for the release of American hostages.

Private citizens were given top secret codes and encryption devices and had access to Swiss bank accounts used for United States covert actions and operations.

The President was involved in private and third country fund raising for the contras.

Wealthy private contributors were courted at the White House, solicited in coordination with government officials, and given what they told was secret information.

American policy became dependent on the contributions of private individuals and third countries.

The President approved the payment of fines, or funds rather, to terrorists to secure the release of hostages.

Senior officials did not know and chose not to know important facts about policy.

A National Security Adviser and an Assistant Secretary of State withheld information and did not tell the Congress the truth concerning U.S. involvement in the contra supply operation and the solicitation of funds from third countries.

When official involvement with the contras was prohibited, officials of the National Security Council raised money, helped procure arms, and set up a private network to ship arms to the contras.

A United States Ambassador negotiated an agreement with Costa Rica for a secret airstrip.

The CIA agent facilitated supply flights.

An official designated by the Secretary of State as a loose cannon, carried out highly sensitive negotiations to obtain the release of American hostages. He gave the approval of the White House to a plan to depose Saddam Hussein [president of Iraq] and to go to war with the Soviet Union in defense of Iran.

This same official participated with others in an effort to rewrite chronologies, altered critical documents, and organized a shredding party to destroy these documents.

This money from the sale of U.S. arms to Iran was diverted to the contras and for the use of several private individuals.

Money raised for the contras was used to finance a DEA [Drug Enforcement Administration] operation to seek release of hostages.

Contra funds were also provided to [Lt.] Col. [Oliver L.] North, perhaps even—although this is not proven—for personal use.

What these committees have heard is a depressing story. It is a story of not telling the truth to the Congress and to the American people.

It is a story about remarkable confusion in the processes of government. Those involved, whether public officials or private citizens, had no doubt they were acting on the authority of the President of the United States.

At the outset, Chairman [Daniel K.] Inouye [D-Hawaii] appropriately asked how could this have happened here? The question now is how can we prevent if from happening again?

For me, these events raise several questions and concerns.

First, our Government cannot function cloaked in secrecy. It cannot function unless officials tell the truth.

The Constitution only works when the two branches of Government trust one another and cooperate.

Policy failed here because the process of government failed.

As Mr. [Robert C.] McFarlane told these committees, when the President and the Congress cannot agree to charge ahead is to invite disaster.

Second, privatization of foreign policy is a prescription for confusion and failure.

The advancement of American national interests depends on the full use of the many resources of the United States Government.

We are ill-served when it is otherwise.

The use of private parties to carry out the high purposes of government make us the subject of puzzlement and ridicule.

Third, accountability, including personal responsibility, has been absent.

My concern is not simply the accountability of funds, but accountability for policy.

Who supervised Col. North?

Who was responsible for U.S. funds earned from the sale of U.S. arms?

Who asked whether actions taken were lawful?

Accountability requires supervision, and acceptance of responsibility up the chain of command.

High officials cannot look the other way or distance themselves from key aspects of policy or the actions of those they supervise.

Accountability requires rigorous oversight by the Congress and a full exercise of the process of checks and balances under the Constitution.

It requires, above all, the operation of the normal processes of government.

These committees have heard a great deal during these past six weeks and we have got much to reflect upon.

When these hearings resume later in June, probably June 22nd, with other witnesses which we will announce later, my guess is that the committees will return to these themes making the shared powers of the Constitution work, the privatization of American foreign policy, and the accountability and responsibility of public officials.

Abraham D. Sofaer

Following are excerpts from the June 18, 1987, private testimony of State Department legal adviser Abraham D. Sofaer. Sofaer told the committees about his opposition to CIA director William J. Casey's November 21, 1986, planned testimony before the House Intelligence Committee and to the administration's efforts to cover up the Iran-contra affair. (Casey testimony, p. C-1)

[Mark A.] BELNICK [Senate committee lawyer]: What was your first official involvement in matters pertaining to the Iran initiative subsequent to Nov. 1, 1986? And if you want to use your notes to refresh your recollection, that's fine.

SOFAER: It was on Nov. 18th, 1986, when a conference was called by the White House counsel related to the Iran arms issue.

BELNICK: Who was at that conference, do you recall?

SOFAER: [Peter] Wallison was there, who was White House counsel; [Assistant Attorney General Charles J.] Cooper; Thompson, [then counsel to the national security adviser] Paul Thompson of the NSC [National Security Council]; Dave Doherty, CIA general counsel; and a couple of other people may have been there. But those people were definitely all there.

BELNICK: And this meeting was at the White House?

SOFAER: Yes.

BELNICK: And by whom had the meeting been called?

SOFAER: I seem to recall that it was Wallison.

BELNICK: Tell us what you recall having transpired at the meeting. And you're free to refer to your notes if that helps.

SOFAER: Thank you. Wallison said that we needed the facts relating to the arms sales to Iran. By that time it was clear that such sales had occurred. Initially, denials were published in the press and even I was doubtful that it was true. But by then it was quite clear that it had occurred. There was going to be a press conference with the president. And Wallison, as his lawyer, no doubt wanted to know more about it. One of the major lessons I learned at the meeting was that he knew as little as I did.

At that meeting I found that Cooper—

BELNICK: Now that's Chuck Cooper from the Justice Department?

SOFAER: Yes, Chuck Cooper, who is assistant attorney general in the Department of Justice. And Paul Thompson of the NSC, and to an extent, Doherty, although he didn't say as much, they knew a lot more than Wallison did.

Cooper's knowledge, however, seemed to be related to the legal issues. He explained that there was a finding adopted on Jan. 17 or so of—

BELNICK: This is Cooper now?

SOFAER: Cooper. And that from January '86 on all activities were pursuant to that finding and all arms shipped were pursuant to the Economy Act. At least this is my understanding. It may have been Thompson who said this, but I think Cooper already was aware of a finding. I'm not sure.

BELNICK: Did Mr. Cooper say for how long he had been aware?

SOFAER: No, he didn't.

BELNICK: Did you understand—did he give you the impression that he had known about it all along?

SOFAER: No.

BELNICK: Or that this was something he had just found out in the course of—

SOFAER: He gave me the impression that he had been assigned the job of figuring out the legal issues involved. And he had looked at a 1981 opinion that was written by the legal adviser. Actually it was written by Jim Michel [James H. Michel, then State Department deputy legal adviser], signed off by the legal adviser, and sent over to Attorney General [William French] Smith who had approved it, relating to the transfer of certain arms. [. . . classified . . .]

BELNICK: Judge, you've said and your notes indicate that Peter Wallison, then the president's counsel, said at the meeting that he needed facts and that he couldn't give advice without the facts, correct?

SOFAER: Yes.

BELNICK: Who was he asking for the facts?

SOFAER: He was asking Thompson essentially, and to an extent, Cooper.

BELNICK: And what was Thompson's response?

SOFAER: Thompson said that on that day the White House was going to brief Intelligence Committee staff on the Hill. We pressed him for at least as much information as he was going to give to the congressional staffers and he refused.

BELNICK: Did he tell you why?

SOFAER: He said that [Rear Adm. John M.] Poindexter had instructed him not to give out any information to anyone who didn't need to know it. Our position was that, in order to advise our clients on the legal issues involved, we did need to know it. And at a minimum, we should be told what was going to be told to staffers.

BELNICK: And he continued to refuse?

SOFAER: Flatly refused, with considerable embarrassment.

BELNICK: But on instructions, as he put it, from Adm. Poindexter, who was then the president's national security adviser?

SOFAER: Yes. He also said that—

BELNICK: Just so I get this straight, being a civilian. Paul Thompson was then counsel to the National Security Council?

SOFAER: He was counsel to the national security adviser. I don't think he had the same rank or title that Paul Stevens [Paul S. Stevens, NSC special assistant to the president and legal adviser] has now.

BELNICK: Let me ask you. Do counsel to different departments, such as the National Security Council or the legal adviser himself, your position, do they have each as their ultimate client the president of the United States?

SOFAER: Absolutely.

BELNICK: And Peter Wallison—

SOFAER: Particularly someone like myself who's nominated by the president.

BELNICK: So that in addition to being the legal adviser to the secretary of state, you're also one of the president's lawyers?

SOFAER: Yes.

BELNICK: And the same would be true of Thompson for that matter?

SOFAER: I would say so.

BELNICK: And certainly Peter Wallison directly was counsel to the president, correct?

SOFAER: Correct.

BELNICK: And you're telling us that at this meeting counsel to the president was asking another counsel to the president [... classified ...] for facts so that he could give the president advice and Thompson said, no, on orders from Adm. Poindexter?

SOFAER: Yes.

BELNICK: Didn't you find that unusual?

SOFAER: Absolutely.

BELNICK: And disturbing?

SOFAER: Very disturbing. He gave as his reason that the lawyers who needed to work on the issue—and I gathered by that he meant Doherty in the CIA and Cooper from the Department of Justice—had been briefed adequately to work on the issue. And that [... classified ...] those were the people in charge of legality as he put it.

BELNICK: According to Thompson?

SOFAER: Right. And he said that from the political point of view that things seemed calm and the committees seemed to be accepting the position of the White House and there was really no need to get the issue more broadly briefed.

* * *

BELNICK: Now during your briefing with [Charles] Hill [executive assistant to Secretary of State George P. Shultz] did someone from the CIA arrive with a draft of Director Casey's proposed testimony for Nov. 21?

SOFAER: Yes, right in the middle of that briefing. We took a break and [Michael H.] Armacost and I went down to his office where we met with David Gries [director of the CIA Office of Congressional Affairs].

BELNICK: He was with the CIA?

SOFAER: Yes. And he had brought over a draft of Casey's testimony.

BELNICK: You reviewed the draft?

SOFAER: Yes.

BELNICK: And what did you find noteworthy in your review of it?

SOFAER: (Pause.)

BELNICK: Let me ask specifically. Was there any discussion of the November 1985 transfer in Director Casey's draft testimony?

SOFAER: Yes, there was a discussion of a transfer, but not of Hawk missiles. It was of oil drilling bits.

BELNICK: Did it say anything about Hawk missiles?

SOFAER: Nothing.

BELNICK: By the way, do you know who had prepared Director Casey's draft testimony?

SOFAER: No.

BELNICK: Gries didn't tell you?

SOFAER: No.

BELNICK: Did you say anything to Gries when you saw the reference to oil drilling equipment in the draft testimony?

SOFAER: I expressed skepticism as to the oil drilling bits.

BELNICK: What did you say, as best you remember?

SOFAER: I said, was he sure that this was a correct story. And particularly, was he sure that the CIA and the NSC did not know that these were weapons rather than oil drilling bits.

BELNICK: What did Gries respond?

SOFAER: He didn't know anything really. I don't think he had any personal knowledge of this matter.

BELNICK: Did you find anything else in the draft testimony that caused you concern or that you took particular note of?

SOFAER: Yes. First of all, I saw the prices, the money for the missiles, and it seemed low to me. It was either by then or later that day I started collecting information on the prices of TOW [antitank] missiles. That was one.

Another thing that I saw that made me skeptical was the assertion that the CIA said they would help out, but only this one time. The CIA said they would assist Israel in shipping these oil drilling bits from [... classified ...] by finding an airline for them or giving them the name of an airline, but this is the only time they would do that without a finding.

This made me skeptical because I didn't see any reason why they would be reluctant to help Israel get the name of an airline if all they were doing was shipping oil drilling bits. So that story did not hang together.

And then I saw the name of Southern Air Transport [a Miami-based air carrier company, formerly controlled by the CIA, which rented airplanes and services to the contra-resupply airlift] in the testimony. That made me concerned.

BELNICK: Why?

SOFAER: I associated that name with [Eugene] Hasenfus [who was shot down over Nicaragua in October 1986 as a part of the contra-resupply effort] or the whole Central American thing. I don't know whether Hasenfus had gone down yet.

BELNICK: He had.

SOFAER: I associated the name with that. And to me it was a red flag indicating a possible connection to Central America.

* * *

BELNICK: Tell us what the conversation was with Wallison at 6:25 p.m. on Nov. 20.

SOFAER: He said that, according to North, all North did was to give the Israelis the name of a proprietary airline. They, then, made the arrangements to use the airline. That he, North, denies that he knew it was Hawk missiles or arms. He says he understood it was drill bits.

Then Wallison said to me the president keeps getting deeper into this because people are operating in his name.

BELNICK: Who did you understand Wallison to be referring to when he said people are operating in his name?

SOFAER: People were operating in his name. I understood it to be Poindexter, North and others were taking actions, had taken actions without the president's approval.

BELNICK: Taken actions during the period of the—

SOFAER: Yes, September and November, right.

BELNICK: Tell us, then, about the evening conversation or conversations that you had with Cooper on Nov. 20?

SOFAER: Cooper said that Ollie North said that there had been no call and that he had no knowledge of any of this.

BELNICK: Any of the—

SOFAER: The arms. And he denied the call to the CIA, as well, at that point.

BELNICK: What call to the CIA?

SOFAER: The urgent call for an airline, to have an airline arranged. All he did was provide the name of a proprietary from the CIA. That is, he apparently did get, from the CIA at some point, the name of an airline which he passed on to the Israelis.

I said that that was nonsense, that it couldn't be correct, that we had a contemporaneous note of [former national security adviser Robert C.] McFarlane's call. I guess my note said that [... classified ...] Ollie North said there was no call, I gather would be the November '85 call. [... classified ...]

BELNICK: You said that there were contemporaneous notes at the State Department?

SOFAER: Yes, I told Cooper that we had a contemporaneous note of the call in Nov. '85.

BELNICK: Do you remember Cooper's succinct response?

SOFAER: He expressed shock in a way that would not be polite to mention in a public record.

BELNICK: Shock at hearing about the note?

SOFAER: Yes.

BELNICK: Did you tell Cooper you had a concern about the course that events were on?

SOFAER: Yes, I told him that both Armacost and I were extremely concerned that people were not telling the full truth and we were scared—I was scared that the president would be in trouble if the testimony was not changed and if people were not forced to tell the truth about all this.

BELNICK: Did you indicate to Cooper that you might have to resign or would have to resign if the testimony were not changed to reflect what you believed to be the truth?

SOFAER: Yes, I did. The reason for that was I believed in the secretary of state and if he had a note indicating that he believed that something had happened, I assumed that that would be the truth and that would force me to have to indicate that in some forceful way.

BELNICK: To put it bluntly, Judge, you told Cooper that if Director Casey gave testimony that said no one in the United States government knew that the November transfer was Hawks, you were going to resign from the government?

SOFAER: Yes.

BELNICK: Did Cooper respond?

SOFAER: Yes, he said that he would leave with me.

* * *

BELNICK: Did you hear again from Cooper late in the evening on Nov. 20, that he had reached the attorney general?

SOFAER: Yes. Let me say that I was more concerned about cover-up than I was about anything else. I believed that Cooper and I and a number of other people had a duty to insure that no cover-up occurred. On the other hand, we also could have, if we had the true facts, we could deal with it. We could then see whether there was any proper legal basis for what had occurred.

I was not assuming that anything that had been done was illegal. What I knew was that a cover-up was illegal and that whatever you might be able to say about the legality of something you did, there is no way you could claim that a cover-up was legal.

BELNICK: It was your position you could deal with the facts, but not with the alteration of facts?

SOFAER: Absolutely. You might be able to deal with the facts, and you have to face the facts, whatever they were, yes.

Cooper told me, at 11:28 p.m. that night, Nov. 20, according to my notes, that he had told the attorney general about this. Apparently he had called him out of town and he, the attorney general, fully shared the concerns we shared and he canceled a trip.

There were many questions about Charlie Hill's notes that Cooper and the attorney general had. When were they taken? What was written down in them? The attorney general was very interested in those notes.

That he had called Paul Thompson and he was told earlier that [Lt. Col. Oliver L.] Ollie North had adhered to his prior story, that Paul Thompson then called Poindexter, who tried to reach McFarlane and he couldn't reach him.

Then he told me that references in Casey's testimony had been changed.

BELNICK: The references to the oil drill story?

SOFAER: Right, that it had been adjusted correctly to avoid the issue. I wrote my notes that way because—

BELNICK: Wrote your notes that way?

SOFAER: Yes, because what he told me was not an indication that the matter had been dealt with fully, in a satisfactory way, but at least the misleading of Congress was avoided.

I congratulated him and we agreed that the president should not be placed at risk until the truth is known. That is, we were satisfied with that fix because at least there wasn't a lie out there and the president wasn't at risk. We could then go further, investigate further, et cetera.

At this point, no formal investigation had been authorized by the president and I gather it was the next day or so that Cooper called me and said the president had authorized the attorney general to investigate.

* * *

BELNICK: On Nov. 21, did you also receive a telephone call from Bud McFarlane?

SOFAER: Yes, I did.

BELNICK: Please tell us about that call.

SOFAER: Mr. McFarlane asked me if—

BELNICK: He called you?

SOFAER: Yes. He asked me if there were—he said that he had heard that there were notes, contemporaneous notes kept by the secretary [of state] of conversations between him and the secretary and others relating to the Iran arms matter.

BELNICK: Did he specifically mention the November '85 shipment, or just generally the Iran matter?

SOFAER: I don't recall, but he said he had heard that there were notes. And I assumed that he had heard that from the attorney general and that it related to the note that I had told the attorney general about.

BELNICK: What else did Mr. McFarlane say?

SOFAER: He asked if I had the notes and if he could have access to them.

BELNICK: What did you say?

SOFAER: I said I didn't have the notes and that I would pass on his request.

BELNICK: Did he ask you whether the notes would be given to the Justice Department?

SOFAER: Yes, he did.

BELNICK: And you told him they would be?

SOFAER: Yes, I said I was sure they would be.

BELNICK: Did you hear from the secretary of state's office subsequent to McFarlane's call?

SOFAER: Yes.

BELNICK: What did you hear and from whom?

SOFAER: I heard from Charlie Hill and/or Nick Platt [then executive secretary of the State Department and special assistant to the secretary of state]—might have been both, might have been one—that McFarlane had called the secretary and had asked to see him about the possibility of some notes that he, the secretary, had kept.

BELNICK: Were you asked for your advice about that meeting?

SOFAER: Yes.

BELNICK: What advice did you give?

SOFAER: I advised the secretary not to see Mr. McFarlane.

BELNICK: Why or why not?

SOFAER: The reasons are spelled out in a memorandum I wrote to the secretary, "Not for the System." It's entitled "Not for the System" because it was not to be distributed to other people.

BELNICK: And is that memorandum the one that we've just marked Sofaer Exhibit 6?

SOFAER: Yes.

BELNICK: And this is a memo you did send to the secretary?

SOFAER: Yes, definitely, on that day.

BELNICK: Do you know if the secretary followed your advice?

SOFAER: Yes.

BELNICK: And he did not see Mr. McFarlane, as far as you know?

SOFAER: Yes, as far as I know. He may have spoken to him on the phone to tell him that he couldn't see him, but I believe that he didn't see him.

Glenn A. Robinette

Following are excerpts from the June 23, 1987, testimony of Glenn A. Robinette, a private security consultant who worked for the CIA for more than twenty years. Robinette testified that retired Air Force major general Richard V. Secord paid for installation of a security system at the home of Lt. Col. Oliver L. North in 1986, and that North participated in an apparent effort to cover up that fact.

[Paul] BARBADORO [Senate deputy chief counsel]: Did you meet with Col. North again five days later on the 10th of May?

ROBINETTE: Yes, I did, sir.

BARBADORO: And what was the purpose of that meeting?

ROBINETTE: I had reached a point then where I had formulated more specific ideas as to what would be useful and fit into their lifestyles.

BARBADORO: Where did you meet with Col. North this time?

ROBINETTE: I met with Col. North at Gen. Secord's office in the Tysons Corner area of Virginia, that is Stanford Technology.

BARBADORO: Was Gen. Secord at this meeting as well?

ROBINETTE: Yes, he was.

BARBADORO: Was there any discussion at this second meeting about how much you thought this system might cost?

ROBINETTE: Yes, there was.

BARBADORO: What did you say about it?

ROBINETTE: At this time, I described in more specific detail as to what I thought would be a useful system to protect the family and the children from any threats.

I believe at this time was the first time, or in more specific detail when Col. North mentioned his concern of terrorists, terrorism.

I summarized by telling him—after describing the system, summarized then by telling him the estimated cost in my opinion of the system.

BARBADORO: And what was that estimated cost?

ROBINETTE: Somewhere around $8,000 and $8,500.

BARBADORO: What was his reaction when you told him about the cost of the system?

ROBINETTE: He concurred and said, "Please try to keep it along those lines. Remember, I am a poor lieutenant colonel."

BARBADORO: Other than that reference, was there any discussion at the meeting about who was going to pay for the system?

ROBINETTE: No, sir.

* * *

BARBADORO: Mr. Robinette, I just want to summarize your testimony with you to date.

ROBINETTE: Yes, sir.

BARBADORO: You said so far you paid [two Laurel, Md., security systems companies] approximately $13,900 to install the security system, correct?

ROBINETTE: Yes, sir.

BARBADORO: And you, in turn, received a total of $16,000 in reimbursement from Richard Secord, is that right?

ROBINETTE: Yes, sir.

BARBADORO: A $7,000 payment in May, and a $9,000 payment in August, is that right?

ROBINETTE: Yes, sir.

BARBADORO: And is it fair to say that during this entire period of time you never went to Col. North to seek reimbursement for this system, and Col. North never offered to pay you for this system, is that right?

ROBINETTE: That is correct, sir.

BARBADORO: The only person you went to was Gen. Secord, and he paid you for the system, is that right?

ROBINETTE: Yes, sir.

* * *

BARBADORO: But let's be clear about something, Mr. Robinette, when you sent these bills to Col. North, you never expected him to pay you for this system, did you?

ROBINETTE: I had been paid.

No, I didn't expect him to pay.

BARBADORO: Gen. Secord had paid you in full for the system, right?

ROBINETTE: Yes, sir; I just commented, I had been paid for it.

BARBADORO: The real reason that you sent those bills to Col. North was to protect him; wasn't it?

ROBINETTE: I believe so, yes, sir, and—

BARBADORO: You were trying to provide him with a cover story, weren't you?

ROBINETTE: Yes, sir; I was trying to help Col. North.

I think my action was one in which the action was one of heart rather than head. And I think you make a mistake if you lead with your heart instead of your head, which I did.

BARBADORO: What you were doing, though, was to provide him with a cover story that made it look like Col. North was supposed to pay for the system, not Gen. Secord; is that right?

ROBINETTE: Yes; he was in the middle of major problems.

He had been fired, and I had some affectionate feelings for the family, and I was trying to assist him for what it was worth.

BARBADORO: Did Col. North ask you in a telephone conversation to send him backdated bills, and a second notice, and a first notice?

ROBINETTE: No, sir, he did not.

BARBADORO: Did you do that on your own?

ROBINETTE: Entirely on my own.

* * *

BARBADORO: Within a few days after sending the bills to Col. North, you got something back from him; did you?

ROBINETTE: Yes, sir, I would say within a week.

BARBADORO: And what you got back were two letters that appeared to correspond to the two bills you had sent; correct?

ROBINETTE: That is correct, sir.

BARBADORO: And so what you had done is you had sent phony bills, and he had sent back phony letters?

ROBINETTE: Yes, sir.

BARBADORO: Did the letters come from Col. North in one envelope or did they come separately?

ROBINETTE: I believe both of the letters came in one envelope.

BARBADORO: And here again did you receive originals or copies?

ROBINETTE: I think I got copies, sir.

BARBADORO: Mr. Robinette, take a look at Exhibit 9-A, which is a letter from Col. North to you, dated 18 May, 1986, which the committee has had enlarged and reproduced, and it will be displayed to my right. Is that one of the letters you received from Col. North?

ROBINETTE: Yes, it is, sir.

BARBADORO: Let me first ask you about the address on the letter. It is 703 Kentland Drive, Great Falls. That is where Col. North lives, isn't it?

ROBINETTE: Yes, sir.

BARBADORO: And you knew that because you had been out to the house several times.

ROBINETTE: A number of times to meet the family.

BARBADORO: Is it fair to say, Mr. Robinette, that this letter suggests that you and Col. North discussed two options as to how Col. North might pay for this security system?

ROBINETTE: I think it is fair to say that, sir.

BARBADORO: And the letter is dated 18 May, so what he is trying to do is to suggest that back in May you and Col. North had discussed your two payment options; correct?

ROBINETTE: Yes.

BARBADORO: The first option that the letter discussed is that you will loan Col. North the security equipment until he retires from the Marine Corps, and that in exchange, Col. North will make his home available for commercial endorsement of the security system; did you ever discuss this payment option with Col. North?

ROBINETTE: Not to my recollection, sir.

BARBADORO: The second payment option discussed is that you would allow Col. North to pay off the system in 24 equal monthly increments. Did you ever discuss this payment option with Col. North?

ROBINETTE: Not to my recollection, sir.

BARBADORO: In fact, you and Col. North never discussed any payment options, did you?

ROBINETTE: Not to my recollection, sir.

BARBADORO: You were looking to Gen. Secord to pay for this system?

ROBINETTE: Yes, sir.

BARBADORO: Let me turn to the second letter Exhibit 9-B.

That letter is also from Col. North to you, and it is dated 1 Oct., 1986. Is that the letter you received from Col. North for the first time in December?

ROBINETTE: Yes, sir.

BARBADORO: And this letter appears the way it is drafted to respond to your phony second notice dated Sept. 22, 1986; correct?

ROBINETTE: Yes, sir.

BARBADORO: The address on this letter is different from the first letter. It says 703 Kentland Drive, Falls Church, Virginia. Do you know why it says Falls Church rather than Great Falls?

ROBINETTE: No, sir.

BARBADORO: Do you know that Col. North once lived in Falls Church?

ROBINETTE: No, sir, I know nothing about Col. North's earlier residences.

BARBADORO: Mr. Robinette, is it fair to characterize this letter as suggesting, attempting to suggest that you and Col. North had agreed on what I had earlier described as the first option for payment, that is that you and Col. North had agreed that Col. North could endorse the security system when he retired from the Marine Corps instead of paying you? Is that what this letter suggests?

ROBINETTE: I believe so, sir.

BARBADORO: Did you and Col. North ever agree on such a payment plan?

ROBINETTE: No, sir.

BARBADORO: This whole proposal, these two options, and the suggestion that there was an agreement is made up, isn't it?

ROBINETTE: It is not to my knowledge—I have never heard of it, sir.

BARBADORO: You were one of the parties to this supposed agreement; correct?

ROBINETTE: Yes, sir.

BARBADORO: And there was never any agreement between you and Col. North as to either of these options; correct?

ROBINETTE: Yes, sir.

[Mark] TOUHEY [Robinette's lawyer]: Excuse me, Counsel.

(Witness confers with his attorney.)

BARBADORO: Mr. Robinette, these two letters—the first one is dated May 18, 1986, and the second is dated Oct. 1, 1986—both those dates are false; right?

ROBINETTE: Yes, sir.

BARBADORO: The first time you received these letters was in December 1986; right?

ROBINETTE: That is correct, sir.

BARBADORO: And isn't it true that what these letters are are simply cooked up responses to the phony bills you sent Col. North in December?

ROBINETTE: I would presume so, sir.

Stanley Sporkin

Following are excerpts from the June 24, 1987, testimony of U.S. District Court Judge Stanley Sporkin, the former CIA general counsel. Sporkin described how the administration drafted the secret intelligence "finding" authorizing U.S. arms sales to Iran and told of his role in including a reference to the release of U.S. hostages in the document.

[Tim] WOODCOCK [Senate committee counsel]: Now, Judge Sporkin, if I may, let me direct your attention to what has been marked as SS No. 4. That is the finding which was drafted into formal form by your assistant on Nov. 25; is that correct?

SPORKIN: That is correct.

WOODCOCK: Let me go over some of the provisions of this document with you. This document contains a provision for not notifying Congress; is that correct?

SPORKIN: That is correct.

WOODCOCK: And do you recall how it is that that provision came into being?

SPORKIN: Yes. If I may, let me explain to you what happened here.

I told you, as a lawyer, when you are sizing up a problem, I saw

there were three major areas I had to deal with. One was to make sure that this project was fully authorized from the top, from the highest authority in the land. The second problem I had to deal with was how to maintain the security of the project so that if it was viable, it would be able to be accomplished. And the third area, which we will get into, is how do we deal with that very small window of 48 hours or so in which the agency [the CIA] had been involved in activity. And I had to deal with those three.

I dealt with the number one by saying we do it through a finding, because that goes to the president of the United States. I dealt with the secrecy and the security end of it by utilizing a provision that I don't recall; it might have been used one other time in my tenure, but one that is very rarely used and only in extreme circumstances, and that was in the non-notification to the Congress. And the third area, to take care of that 48-hour window, was to make sure that this activity had been authorized and that the president was willing to ratify it so that my people or the people of the agency knew that they were operating under presidential authority.

So those are the three issues and that's the way I dealt with it.

* * *

WOODCOCK: Let me direct your attention, if I may, to Dec. 9, 1985. On that day you had a meeting with Lt. Col. Oliver [L.] North, is that right?

SPORKIN: That's what the records indicate.

WOODCOCK: Now, when you went to that meeting you were not the only one that was scheduled to arrive, is that correct?

SPORKIN: My recollection is that the deputy director [former CIA deputy director John McMahon] told me, asked me to join him at a meeting with Mr. North.

WOODCOCK: And that again is Mr. McMahon asking you to join him in a meeting with Mr. North?

SPORKIN: That is correct.

WOODCOCK: You went to the meeting but Mr. McMahon didn't arrive, is that correct?

SPORKIN: That is correct. Well, I think he might have told me he wasn't coming. I mean at some point, he may have said I can't make it, you go ahead and run it, not run it, attend it.

WOODCOCK: As a matter of fact, he did not arrive, is that correct?

SPORKIN: That is correct.

WOODCOCK: Nevertheless you and Lt. Col. North did have a meeting on that day, is that right?

SPORKIN: That is correct.

WOODCOCK: The subject of the meeting was the Iran initiative?

SPORKIN: I'm sure it was.

WOODCOCK: Now, do you recall at this point what Mr. McMahon's frame of mind was with respect to the initiative?

SPORKIN: What I can recall is I think, I gathered that the deputy director would have preferred that the agency's role be extremely limited if at all.

WOODCOCK: Was this position of Mr. McMahon understood by Lt. Col. North?

SPORKIN: Yes. As a matter of fact, I might even have learned it from Mr. North.

WOODCOCK: Do you recall whether Lt. Col. North had any reaction to it himself?

SPORKIN: He would have been just as happy to have the CIA out of it as would the deputy director. I just don't think that Col. North wanted to do any more business I think with Mr. McMahon as Mr. McMahon wanted to do business with Mr. North. So I think it was agreed that, or at least discussed that if there is some way to find a way to have the CIA take a very minor role or take no role at all.

WOODCOCK: Let me paraphrase your answer if I may. Your answer suggests perhaps two things are going on here. One is that Mr. North and Mr. McMahon did not together form a mutual admiration society, is that right?

SPORKIN: I can't really say that. I've told you what—

WOODCOCK: There was some difference there, is that right?

SPORKIN: Yes, I think—well, I think that McMahon, that the deputy director—if this were going to be a CIA covert operation then the CIA ought to handle it and I don't think he wanted—and again I'm doing things that I would tell people not to do, I'm trying to bring things together for you, and I think that that was his view, that he did not want to have the agency involved unless we were going to run the whole operation and I think North, I don't think wanted to become overly involved with Mr. McMahon. They are two very strong people, and I don't think both of them together can be running the same operation.

* * *

WOODCOCK: Now in reading this document, that is the memorandum that you saw on Jan. 5th, did it become crystal clear to you that one of the objectives of the finding was to obtain the release of American hostages?

SPORKIN: Yes.

WOODCOCK: Now, what was your reaction to that since the finding up to that point did not include any reference to the release of American hostages?

SPORKIN: Well, again, either because of that or because of what I said happened on Friday night, I was concerned about that being omitted from the finding.

WOODCOCK: So what did you do?

SPORKIN: Well, I thought about it, and I didn't raise it at that time as I recall, but it was sort of gnawing on me a little bit, and we got up to leave, we went out to a little hall and I—it happened very quickly, I saw Lt. Col. North, and I said tell me again or tell me why we're not putting hostages in this document.

WOODCOCK: And it is just you and North at this point, is that right?

SPORKIN: That is correct. And he said that, mentioned that either the secretary of state or the Department of State did not want it in. And I said, well, you know, it doesn't sound right to me, and I said let's go back and see the director [William J. Casey]. And we went back to the director.

WOODCOCK: What was your concern about the omission of the reference to hostages?

SPORKIN: Well, it bothered me that, I guess there were a number of concerns but certainly an important concern was that this was an element in the proposed course of action and it wasn't in there, and the one thing about findings that I believe were analogous to the business, the securities laws business is it's almost like an offering statement that you make a document that contains everything because it's sort of an insurance policy kind of thing, that therefore people that carry that out know that they are protected if they carry out in the terms that are set forth in the document.

And so I went back to the director and I raised it with him.

WOODCOCK: What was his response?

SPORKIN: Well, he hurried us out. You know, he listened to Lt. Col. North, who was not himself, it was clear that he was presenting a position that he didn't necessarily believe in. He was presenting what I believe he thought was the Department of State's position, they didn't want it in. I think he gave all the arguments it looks like a hostage-for-arms shipment, it didn't look right and I think he gave all the arguments. My argument was but that's the fact, we are going with a very, this is going to be a very sensitive finding, this is a very important element of that finding.

There is a proposal not to notify Congress and nobody wants to put in what in my view is a very important element of that and I said I thought it ought to be in there. And the director agreed with me.

WOODCOCK: Turning just for a moment to Lt. Col. North's statement of a position of what you felt was either the secretary of state or the State Department, did you have an understanding as to whether the opposition emanating from the State Department was to simply include the reference to hostages or were they more fundamentally opposed to the issue altogether?

SPORKIN: I didn't get the latter, and, again, that is not fair to them. That was not what—I did not get from them that was their point, but, again, that could have very well been their point but it is my perception, my perception is they didn't want it

included in the finding.

WOODCOCK: It wasn't clear, at least from the way Col. North was describing it, that the State Department had an opposition fundamentally to the program as policy; is that correct?

SPORKIN: I don't know whether—whether—again, I am going to discuss this with you, but it is going to be difficult for me to back up what I am saying, but I don't know whether the point was being made that if that was in that it would be considered an arms-for-hostage and they would be out.

However, a program that involved these kinds of things did not upset them and, therefore, they could buy into it. But I would think it would have to be an honest program. It was not a—we weren't just, this is not window dressing.

So I think, I mean, again to be fair, that may well have been my thinking of what was going on at the time. In other words, it had to be an honest program where it would be for these items and not for the hostages?

WOODCOCK: In other words, you were not going to have a situation in which you had a covert finding that was so covert there were terms that were even secret from the text of the finding itself; is that right?

SPORKIN: No, I don't think that is what I just said. You know—I will leave what I said.

WOODCOCK: You didn't check with anybody in the State Department to determine precisely what their position was; is that right?

SPORKIN: No, sir. I did not.

WOODCOCK: And that wouldn't have been your job anyway; is that right?

SPORKIN: Well, I was, I thought I could operate right within the agency. But we went back to the director, had a discussion, and the director agreed that the hostages was part of the program and ought to be in there.

* * *

WOODCOCK: Now, on Jan. 20, you attended yet another meeting—you attended a meeting; is that corect?

SPORKIN: That is correct.

WOODCOCK: Where was that held?

SPORKIN: That was in the situation room.

WOODCOCK: At the White House; is that correct?

SPORKIN: That is correct.

WOODCOCK: And Clair George was present and he was the deputy director of CIA operations; is that correct?

SPORKIN: That is correct.

WOODCOCK: You, yourself, were there?

SPORKIN: That is correct.

WOODCOCK: Gen. Secord [retired major general Richard V. Secord] was there?

SPORKIN: That is correct.

WOODCOCK: The deputy chief of Near East affairs from the CIA [whose identity was not disclosed] was there?

SPORKIN: Right.

WOODCOCK: And Lt. Col. North?

SPORKIN: That is correct.

WOODCOCK: I gather from what we discussed earlier, you were not eager to go to this meeting; is that correct?

SPORKIN: Well, yes. I was not eager at all to go. I was winding my way down at the agency at this time and the meeting, as I recall, occurred on Martin Luther King's birthday, which I think was the 20th of January.

I was called at home by Mr. George and asked me if I would accompany him in a meeting.

As you can see now, from the time I came there, until now, how things have turned full cycle. I say, well, I don't see any reason why I ought to be at that meeting. You know, I am trying to wind my way down. Why do you need me?

He said, no, we need you.

WOODCOCK: So you went?

SPORKIN: Well, I reluctantly went. Only because he said that he wanted his lawyer there. So I went. Now, I was—my recollection is I was told it was going to be [then national security adviser Vice] Adm. [John M.] Poindexter, North, Mr. George, his deputy, and me. But when I got there, I found it was Mr. Secord.

I don't believe I would have attended that meeting if I had known that Mr. Secord would have been there. Not because it was Mr. Secord. It is just that I didn't think I wanted to be involved in a matter involving agents and operations not affiliated with the agency.

WOODCOCK: Now, when you got there, you saw Mr. Secord?

SPORKIN: Right.

WOODCOCK: Are you saying from your testimony that your background knowledge of Mr. Secord did not cause you any concern?

SPORKIN: I didn't—did I—what I said was it wasn't—I didn't know he was going to be there. My not wanting to go to the meeting had nothing to do with him since I didn't know about him.

My not wanting to go to the meeting was because I didn't think I wanted to be involved.

WOODCOCK: When you got there and saw him, did that cause you concern?

SPORKIN: Yes, it did.

WOODCOCK: And you did not take an active participation in the meeting; is that correct?

SPORKIN: Well, what happened is I had two choices. One is I would get up and leave and leave a bad taste in people's mouths when I was a week or so away from leaving the whole agency. Or, two, I could sit by and say very little. And what I did is I sat by and said very little.

WOODCOCK: You did not see a copy of the presidential finding of Jan. 17 at this meeting; is that correct?

SPORKIN: I didn't see that. I didn't see anybody editing anything. I can tell you exactly what I said, as I can recall.

Number one, they were talking about a meeting that was going to be held in London, and I said, look, folks, at this meeting you have to assure yourself of two things. We are going to get the hostages and we are going to get paid for the product we are giving up.

I told them, I said, look, you have to realize you don't bring lawsuits on these matters if they don't fulfill their end of the bargain. So you have got to take steps to make sure that we are going to get what we are bargaining for.

That, I think, is essentially what I had to say at that meeting.

WOODCOCK: You referred to an upcoming meeting in London. Did you have an understanding that that event might be the event that would lead to the release—the immediate release of the hostages?

SPORKIN: I thought that was going to be a very important event, yes.

WOODCOCK: And you connected that with the release of the hostages; is that right?

SPORKIN: I think I did.

WOODCOCK: You went to no further meetings on this subject after Jan. 20?

SPORKIN: No. I was asked the next day to go to another meeting. At that point I said, folks, that is it. The ball game is over.

Gaffney and Koch

Following are excerpts from the June 23, 1987, testimony of Henry H. Gaffney, Jr., and Noel C. Koch. Gaffney, a senior Pentagon official, and Koch, a former senior Pentagon official and close friend of retired Air Force major general Richard V. Secord, told the panel about the Reagan administration's secret arms-for-hostages deals with Iran.

[Joe] **SABA** [House staff counsel]: Dr. Gaffney, I just want to summarize, for clarity, for Hawk missiles sold by the United States to Israel and in Israel's stocks in 1985, Israel's agreement with the United States was that Israel would not transfer those Hawks without obtaining the advance written consent of the United States government.

GAFFNEY: That is correct.

SABA: And the advance written consent of the United States government is by our law given by the president who has delegated that to the secretary of state?

GAFFNEY: That is my understanding.

SABA: And neither the president nor his designee, the secretary of state, can give that consent unless certain conditions are satisfied in advance of that consent and the transfer?

GAFFNEY: That is correct.

SABA: And that these conditions are, first, the United States could legally sell to the third country?

GAFFNEY: Yes.

SABA: In which case it must be demonstrated that the United States in the fall of 1985 could make a direct sale to Iran?

GAFFNEY: Yes.

SABA: And that it was your opinion at that time that we could not?

GAFFNEY: That is correct.

SABA: And, second, even if a direct sale could be made and if that sale exceeded in value $14 million, prior to giving his consent, the Congress must be notified of the sale?

GAFFNEY: That is correct. That is what the law requires.

SABA: And that, third, if those first two conditions are satisfied, notwithstanding their satisfaction, the United States must obtain from the transferee country—which in this case would be Iran—written assurance that it would accept the conditions of transfer, including obtaining consent of the president of the United States to further transfer?

GAFFNEY: Yes, sir.

SABA: Dr. Gaffney, I will tell you that Gen. Secord has testified here that on Nov. 18—sorry, on Nov. 25, 1985, 18 Hawk missiles went from Israel to Iran. Dr. Gaffney, do you know of any change or reversal of American policy on the 25th of November, 1985, or of any change in the United States' position of neutrality at that time?

GAFFNEY: None, to my knowledge. None that had come to our agency.

SABA: Mr. Koch?

KOCH: I am aware of none.

SABA: Dr. Gaffney and Mr. Koch, do either of you know of any congressional notification sent by the president or any of his authorized designees to the Congress stating that the president would permit Israel to transfer Hawks to Iran that year?

GAFFNEY: Not to my knowledge, nothing recorded in our agency.

KOCH: No.

SABA: Dr. Gaffney and Mr. Koch, do either of you know of any written consent granted by the president or the secretary of state or any authorized designee to Israel permitting the transfer of those weapons?

GAFFNEY: No.

KOCH: No.

SABA: And do either of you know, has the Ayatollah Khomeini or any of his authorized designees provided to us in advance of that transfer a writing stating that the Ayatollah will consent to inform the president of the United States in advance upon further transfer or use of those weapons?

GAFFNEY: I have seen no such document.

KOCH: I think you would have to ask the Ayatollah.

SABA: So, Dr. Gaffney, in the absence of those conditions being met, and assuming a transfer, I take it that transfer was first a breach of the LOA [letter of offer and acceptance, signed by Israel]?

GAFFNEY: Yes, I would assume so.

SABA: And I take it for those who may have participated in it, it constituted a violation of the Arms Export Control Act?

GAFFNEY: As far as I can see.

* * *

[John] **SAXON** [Senate committee counsel]: Mr. Koch, Mr. Saba asked you earlier, from the outset when you first heard of this initiative and thought that we were giving arms to Iran and not selling them through Israel, that you stated objections to the policy. As the top terrorism policy maker at the Pentagon during this period, what would you say your objections were to the arms-to-Iran initiative?

KOCH: There is a question of not making concessions to terrorists. It was about the last shred of a fig leaf that we had that constituted any kind of a pretense in having a policy toward dealing with terrorism at all. And so to have shed that one, it seemed to me, left us in a very difficult position, in addition to which there would be second order consequences to our having done this.

So I was concerned that we looked very bad with our allies and again, never mind the question of Operation Staunch [the U.S. effort to stop countries from sending arms to Iran] or anything else, I am looking purely through the prism of someone having to deal with their counter-terrorism officials.

And so we had tried with varying degrees of success to get the cooperation of our friends in Europe and elsewhere. It had taken us a long time to do that. I had been involved in most of it and in front of most of it and it had taken a lot of time and now it seemed to me that this was unwinding.

My response to Mr. Saba was predicated on the assumption at the time that this was a straight-out ransom, not that there was a question of sales involved, but rather that we were going to give them X number of Hawk missiles in exchange for hostages, which I thought was ridiculous. I don't think we should ransom hostages.

As it evolved, either as an effort to rationalize the effort or the question of pursuing a sensible policy toward the gulf that was emerging, that we were evolving a policy toward the gulf in which we were going to try to restore our relationships with Iran.

If that was the object, then it seemed to me that was support-able, and if that was the object, then clearly logic took you to a point at which you had to have those hostages back because the American people wouldn't stand for restoration of relations with Iran in circumstances in which they thought they were holding our hostages—which, incidentally, they are not. That is a misperception.

SAXON: So if I understand your testimony here this afternoon, Mr. Koch, and in your previous sworn statements in depositions to the committee, is it fair to say that you believed that the arms initiative was contrary to our stated policy of not shipping arms to Iran?

KOCH: That is correct.

SAXON: It was contrary to our policy of pressuring our allies not to ship arms to Iran?

KOCH: That is correct.

SAXON: It was contrary to our policy of not dealing with or making concessions to terrorists?

KOCH: That is correct.

SAXON: And in your opinion, did you believe that the ship-ping of arms to Iran would lead to the increased shipment of arms to Iran by our allies?

KOCH: Yes, but that wasn't a consideration of mine alone.

SAXON: And did you believe it would, perhaps, lead to the taking of additional hostages?

KOCH: I thought that was a definite possibility.

SAXON: Did you ever hear Secretary [of Defense Caspar W.] Weinberger verbalize these objections?

KOCH: In summary form, sure, they were not elaborated, but those were his concerns.

SAXON: And it would be your understanding then that he shared these concerns?

KOCH: That would be my understanding.

* * *

[Rep. Jim] COURTER [R-N.J.]: One of the things that bothers me is we are trying to draw some lessons from these events, and one of those lessons that we, I think, may be drawing is the fact that people inside the White House did not use the normal structure, did not use the normal process—the structure being the various departments and agencies and the process means coordi-nating and going through those—but yet your testimony, in es-sence, is that State Department, being perhaps the most superior of equals, was running into problems in operations because the

other agencies and departments were not working with it properly and smoothly and that we, therefore, turned to, once again, [Lt. Col.] Oliver [L.] North to in kind of a Herculean way solve the problems that were best suited for the various structures and departments and agencies that were placed there.

KOCH: I would like to correct the notion that there was a widespread perception of Oliver North as Herculean within the administration. I don't know where this has grown from, but those that worked with him know he worked very hard, he was very intelligent, but there heroic dimensions never revealed themselves before this thing became public, and so we didn't say, "Oh, my God, all else is lost. Let's call in Ollie."

COURTER: I know, but it almost sounds that way to me. It seems rather absurd that you would do that, but when there was a problem with hostages, Oliver North was dragged into that. If there was a terrorism problem, he was dragged into that. If there was to be an attempt to free hostages on the *Achille Lauro* [the Italian cruise liner hijacked by Palestinian terrorists in October 1985], he had to do that. When it came to opening up an effort to either swap weapons for hostages or initiating an effort to create liaison and communication with the second generation Iranians, he was chosen to do that. We want to keep the effort of the resistance in Central America alive, he was given that task as well.

It seems to me that all roads began and ended with Oliver North.

KOCH: Yes, sir, but you may be turning the logic upside down. The question that is always raised is how could a lieutenant colonel—I don't know why they say lowly lieutenant colonel, but they do—have amassed such power? And maybe a more useful way of looking at it is to conclude that all these things that got dumped on him—not that he got dragged into them, but rather they got dumped on him—is because people in the administration didn't take them very seriously. They were not neat and clean. There was not a lot of money in them. There wasn't any glory in them. The possibility of a failure was substantial, and so everybody else wanted to be out giving speeches and trying to beat the woods for a vice presidency somewhere when they got out and got a job. The difficult work got shoveled off on people like Ollie.

COURTER: That is precisely my point. He shouldn't have been tasked with so much, and apparently he was. Risks were involved. The things that required certain risks seemed to be placed on his desk rather than others.

KOCH: Right. I mean, it was—there were, to put it bluntly, failures in leadership here when you had to try to get these departments to function together, when the heads of at least two of those departments could never get along together, it was con-stant bickering, and it permeated their relationships between our respective departments; and nobody would inflict any discipline on that process and say, "That is fine, but let's do it on behalf of the administration." When you had that kind of situation, what evolved out of that as a result of that was an inability to make sensible policy in a sensible way. What came out of that was that you went off on this privatization route.

* * *

[Sen. William S.] COHEN [R-Maine]: Sen. [Warren B.] Rudman [R-N.H.] said to you that had the administration listened to the two of you, we wouldn't be in this mess today and be having these hearings. If they had listened to Secretary Weinberger, we wouldn't be here today; right?

KOCH: That is right.

COHEN: If we had listened to Secretary [of State George P.] Shultz, we wouldn't be here today?

KOCH: If we could have listened to both, and they spoke with one voice, we might not be here today either.

COHEN: And if we listened to [former national security adviser Robert C.] Bud McFarlane, who after his trip to London came back to the White House and said, "We are making a mistake," we wouldn't be here today. There you have three of the top national security advisers, as such, on the foreign policy and defense policy, all three saying, "Don't do it"?

KOCH: Yes, sir.

COHEN: And yet the program went on, to continue a theme

by Sen. [Paul S.] Sarbanes [D-Md.]?

KOCH: Yes, sir.

COHEN: You could only conclude that that had to be because somebody in the White House wanted it to continue, that somebody being the president of the United States?

KOCH: Logic takes you there.

COHEN: There is no other conclusion that one could come to, is there?

KOCH: I understand that.

Charles J. Cooper

Following are excerpts from the June 25, 1987, testimony of Assistant Attorney General Charles J. Cooper, the Justice Department lawyer involved in the November 1986 inquiry into the Iran-contra affair. Cooper related his account of a November 20, 1986, meeting at the White House during which senior administration officials and lawyers discussed prepared testimony CIA director William J. Casey was to give on Capitol Hill the next day. (Casey testimony, p. C-1)

[Pam] NAUGHTON [House staff counsel]: Now, going down to the sixth paragraph on the insertion, which is CJC [Charles J. Cooper] Exhibit 6, I would read that into the record. It states, "To the best of our knowledge," and then there are some handwritten delineations, "neither the Israelis nor the Iranians knew that they"—and it says "was dealing with a CIA proprietary; nor did airline personnel know what they were carrying. No one"—first of all, the original language read, "We in CIA did not find out that our airline had hauled Hawk missiles into Iran until mid-January, when we were told by the Iranians."

The first part of that sentence is crossed out, and handwritten instead is wherein "no one in the USG"—assuming U.S. government—"found out that our airline had hauled Hawk missiles into Iran until mid-January, when we were told by the Iranians."

Now, Mr. Cooper, who proposed the change in that language from no one in the CIA knew it was Hawks to no one in the U.S. government knew it was Hawks until January?

COOPER: Lt. Col. [Oliver L.] North, and it is my distinct recollection that he was the author of all of the interlineations that you see on this page.

NAUGHTON: And when Col. North made the assertion that no one in the United States government knew that they were Hawk missiles until January of 1986 in this proposed testimony to Congress, did anyone in the room dispute that fact?

COOPER: No.

NAUGHTON: Did Mr. Poindexter [Rear Adm. John M. Poindexter] dispute it?

COOPER: No.

NAUGHTON: Did Mr. Casey dispute that?

COOPER: No.

NAUGHTON: Did they remain silent?

COOPER: They reacted the same way I did, at least that was my impression, that—OK, if that is the way it was, fine. I mean, they did not appear to me to have any personal knowledge of this matter.

NAUGHTON: And they accepted that change; is that correct?

COOPER: Yes.

NAUGHTON: What was your impression of the deference that Mr. Poindexter and Mr. Casey gave to Oliver North in your observation in this meeting?

COOPER: Well, I did not—no impression was retained on my memory, in particular of any deference that they gave him. They gave him the deference that one gives to a person who has superior knowledge of the facts or has the only basis for having any knowledge of the facts, whether that is because they have been reported to him or because he personally knows.

But he stated this with authority, that no one in the USG found out. In fact, I can recall crisply that he wanted to eliminate

the inference that someone in the United States government knew about this, even if the CIA didn't.

NAUGHTON: So, Mr. North's position was that if the document read no one in the CIA knew of it, that would infer that someone in the government did?

COOPER: Yes.

NAUGHTON: And he wanted to erase that inference; is that correct?

COOPER: Yes. And I thought if that was correct, that we certainly ought to do that.

NAUGHTON: Now, in your deposition, do you recall telling us that Mr. Poindexter and Mr. Casey gave absolute deference to Col. North during that meeting?

COOPER: Well, I would be surprised if that is my formulation, but the record will speak for itself. I do not—with respect to factual matters, everybody in the room was deferring to North, yes. If that is the sense of which I used the term, but it was not like these men, these Cabinet officials were somehow in awe or in deference, or taking some kind of a particularly deferential or respectful position vis-à-vis North, although they quite obviously knew him very well, and he was comfortable around them, and they were comfortable around him.

I had never met—I don't think I had ever met anyone there except—well, I certainly hadn't met North before, and I don't believe I had met Mr. Casey before that time. I was deferential to them, I can recall that.

* * *

On November 23, 1987, Cooper joined Attorney General Edwin Meese III, John N. Richardson, Jr., assistant to the attorney general and chief of staff, and William Bradford Reynolds, assistant attorney general, civil rights division, in interviewing Oliver North. The meeting, which took place in Meese's office, stemmed from Justice Department lawyers' discovery of a memo in North's files discussing the diversion of Iranian money to the contras. The aim of the meeting was to find out what the memo meant, and who knew about it.

NAUGHTON: Was Col. North eventually questioned about the contra diversion memo?

COOPER: Yes, he was.

NAUGHTON: And who presented the memo to him?

COOPER: The attorney general. The attorney general was the dominant interviewer by far during the time that he was there.

NAUGHTON: Can you tell us how he was presented the memo?

COOPER: I can only tell you what my recollection of it is and it is hazy, but it is my recollection that the attorney general handed him the memorandum and began asking him some questions that had nothing to do with the diversion, questions that do not now stick in my mind. And that—and I do not recall having seen any—during this period I don't recall having seen any register on Mr. North's face that this memo had particular significance, but certainly it did when the attorney general asked him about the contra diversion.

NAUGHTON: Can you recall as specifically as you can what the attorney general asked him?

COOPER: I think the attorney general was asking about finances, finances that were involved in this whole Iran initiative, and he asked him about the monies that went to the Nicaraguan resistance.

NAUGHTON: What was Oliver North's reaction when the attorney general asked him if any of these funds went to the Nicaraguan resistance?

COOPER: He appeared to be visibly surprised and not expecting to hear that question.

NAUGHTON: Can you describe to us what his reaction was?

COOPER: Well, I think he—my best recollection is that he paused for a moment, silent, before he responded, and then he responded that—in a way that was responsive, and certainly did not—he acknowledged the transfer to the contras. But it was just obvious surprise on his face.

NAUGHTON: Did he ask if there was a cover memo?

COOPER: Yes, he did. I have a general recollection to that effect. Whether it was immediately, I don't recall, but he did ask that question.

NAUGHTON: Did the attorney general ask Oliver North should we have found one?

COOPER: The attorney general asked something to the effect—first of all, I think Mr. Reynolds said, no, there was no cover memo and somebody—and I suspect it was the attorney general—I think that it was—said essentially, "Why did you ask that question? Is there a cover memo with this? Should we have found one?"

North's response, again to the best of my recollection, was, "No, I just wondered," or something to that effect.

NAUGHTON: Did anyone in the room ask him if there indeed was or had been a cover memo?

COOPER: I don't recall. It is entirely possible and there was some conversation about a cover memo, but, you know, at some point we became or at least I became satisfied that it was North's view that there was no cover memo. And I also have a vague recollection that he—and I do recall that this is confirmed by the notes—that he offered to re-examine his files and the documents in a search for such a cover memo if there was one.

NAUGHTON: Did you ask him to do that?

COOPER: I don't think we asked him to do it, but I don't think we told him not to do it or anything like that. It just—he made the suggestion. I don't recall the reaction to it.

* * *

NAUGHTON: To whom did Mr. North say the memo was addressed?

COOPER: I don't think he—I don't recall his discussing who it was addressed to specifically, although I do recall him saying it was for Poindexter or that it had been given to Poindexter or something to that effect, that he did not think it had gone any further.

NAUGHTON: Did Col. North say that he believed anyone else had seen it?

COOPER: No. In fact, my recollection is to the contrary of that.

NAUGHTON: Did he say whether or not the president had seen it, to his knowledge?

COOPER: Yes. He did not think that the memo had gone to the president.

NAUGHTON: Did you ask him who in the government knew of the diversion?

COOPER: Yes, we did.

NAUGHTON: And who did he say knew of the diversion?

COOPER: He identified Mr. Poindexter, Mr. [Robert C.] McFarlane and himself in the government.

* * *

[Rep. Bill] McCOLLUM [R-Fla.]: So when Col. North told Attorney General Meese on Nov. 20, in that meeting regarding the Casey testimony, that there was no one in the United States government in November 1985 aware that there was a Hawk missile shipment going into Iran, and they didn't find out about that until January after that, he was lying, wasn't he? Isn't that a fact?

Isn't it also a fact that when Adm. Poindexter and Mr. McFarlane and Director Casey—well, at least I think it was so with Casey, but certainly when Adm. Poindexter and Mr. McFarlane were silent and they didn't refute that fact in the attorney general's presence on Nov. 20, and let this testimony apparently be put that way with regard to the Hawk missiles and the lack of awareness, they, too, were lying, weren't they?

COOPER: I believe so.

McCOLLUM: And after the attorney general was formally charged with the investigation the next morning and he spoke with Mr. McFarlane, had a meeting with him and Mr. McFarlane told the attorney general he didn't know there were missile parts in the missile shipment until he came back into the picture in May 1986,

he was lying then, too, wasn't he?

COOPER: It appears that he was.

McCOLLUM: And when Col. North told the attorney general on Sunday the 23rd of November that he had first thought that the shipment of the 1985 things over to Iran on that plane load were oil drilling equipment and he didn't learn until later from Gen. Secord [retired major general Richard V. Secord] that there were missile parts, he was lying even on Sunday when he said that, wasn't he?

COOPER: Yes, I believe he was.

McCOLLUM: So the point of it all is that we had a group of people, at least three and possibly four—Col. North, Adm. Poindexter, Mr. McFarlane and probably Director Casey—who were deliberately deceiving and lying to the attorney general of the United States about the involvement of the United States on the shipment of these missiles in November 1985; isn't that a fact?

COOPER: I think it is.

McCOLLUM: So if we want to call it a cover-up or whatever it is, we can still say for sure that we had one attorney general who got pretty darn mad when he began to realize this fact as you were revealing certain portions of this to him, didn't he?

COOPER: Oh, yes, he was.

* * *

McCOLLUM: So we have a whole series running from November 1985 through November 1986 where at least three or four specific instances the attorney general of the United States, our top legal officer, would be of the closest men to the president of the United States who was being misled and was not being fully informed, and yet was being called upon to make judgments and decisions.

I think that that in itself may well be a crime. If it is not a crime, it is certainly one of the highest acts of insubordination and one of the most treacherous things that has ever occurred to a president, it seems to me, in our history.

* * *

[Sen. William S.] COHEN [R-Maine]: One other point I would like to raise is an exhibit I would like to offer into evidence. Mr. Cooper, you drafted on Dec. 17, 1986, a memorandum for the attorney general, and it deals with the timely notification requirement of Section 501(b) of the National Security Act. I would like to summarize what I believe your conclusions are. If I am incorrect you may correct me.

I think you indicated that in essence, since the statute acknowledges the president's right not to give prior notice, it necessarily follows that the president has sole and absolute discretion to determine what constitutes timely notice after the action is under way. And that timely notice could be a matter of days, it could be a matter of weeks, it could be a matter of months, or in this case, even a year and a half before the so-called "gang of eight" were notified because you give the total discretion to him until the action is actually terminated or completed.

I would concede one point. You indicated that Section 501(b) is clumsily drafted, and I would concede that 501(b) might be clumsily drafted, but the fact is that even if we were to employ the considerable talents of someone like yourself, and to draft it in a very concrete fashion, that under your interpretation Congress could not constitutionally require the president to report a covert action within any specified time period. So even if we didn't draft it clumsily, we still couldn't draft it in a way to specify a time frame.

Sen. [Sam] Nunn [D-Ga.] made, I think, an important point yesterday. He indicated that Congress necessarily has to recognize the need for flexibility in giving the president as much as possible in covert actions, and I agree with that. But unfortunately flexibility is too often taken as license, and then after the fact it is rationalized as a constitutional power that cannot be diluted or diminished by congressional action.

That leaves Congress with two essential options. One is to treat the presidency as a monarchy with absolute powers in foreign policy, what I would lightheartedly call the Hyde view [after House committee member Henry J. Hyde, R-Ill.]. The second option would be for Congress to refuse to propose any funds for covert actions in the future, which I believe would be a mistake, and a serious one, and I will call that the hidebound rule.

I think that comity is important, but it has to run in two directions on Pennsylvania Avenue, and if it doesn't run in two directions, I think that we are going to find ourselves in a very debilitating confrontational paralysis, unless that comity flows in both directions. Unfortunately I find under your interpretation of the notification requirement, we really don't have much in the way of options other than those two, and you may be correct. I hope that is not the situation.

* * *

[Rep. Jim] COURTER [R-N.J.]: Referring your attention again to the first part of my question, with respect to the lack of candor, at least on the part of Mr. North and Mr. Poindexter, if not Mr. Casey, on the Hawk shipment, can you posit to me a credible reason why they would be less than candid?

I can think of three reasons why they would, and two perhaps why they wouldn't. One reason, obviously is the fact that if they were less than candid, it would be a lie. The second, they were talking to Ed Meese, who, since it was his department that drafted the finding, surely knew of the arrangement about weapon sales to Iran.

And third, they were knowledgeable of the fact that Ed Meese was specifically appointed by the president to bring all the relevant information to the president. It would be like lying to the president.

Now, there are three good reasons why they should have been candid to you. Can you think of any reason why they were not? What were they trying to accomplish by that?

COOPER: To keep—to prevent or at least to delay the truth of the matter from surfacing. I mean, that was apparently their purpose. I really don't—I don't have a good sense for what was the immediate motivation, the personal goals, the purposes they sought to accomplish.

COURTER: That was the result of their not being candid or lying, but I just don't see that that is a motive at this particular juncture when the whole world is falling in, when the president of the United States is on the line, when he appoints Ed Meese to gather all the facts.

The only two reasons I think of is number one, protecting Israel at the expense of the government of the United States, which doesn't seem logical, and the other reason—I would like your opinion on this—that perhaps they felt the presidential finding [the secret intelligence "finding," signed by President Reagan January 17, 1986, authorizing the Iran arms sales] had no retroactive effect, and therefore, did not cover the first shipment?

COOPER: That may well be what they concluded, and this was some kind of an effort to keep from disclosure the failure to get a finding for the November matter. That is entirely possible.

* * *

[Rep. Louis] STOKES [D-Ohio]: Lastly, when you and the attorney general interviewed Col. North, he was not under oath at that time, was he?

COOPER: No, sir, he was not.

STOKES: Based upon your testimony here today, would you agree that, or evaluate the testimony that he gave you at that time as being false?

COOPER: I believe it was false in some respects, yes, sir.

STOKES: Based upon everything you know about Col. North as a result of your contact with him and your interview of him, let me ask you this: Would you believe him under oath?

COOPER: Congressman, I would not, but I personally don't believe an oath in any way enhances the obligation of truthfulness.

STOKES: And in effect, you are saying you would not believe him whether he was under oath or not?

COOPER: That is—well, I have to regretfully say that, yes, sir, I have to say that.

* * *

[Senate committee Chairman Daniel K.] INOUYE [D-Hawaii]: I am just curious, why did it take so long to secure this [North's] office, because on the 7th of November you were going to have doubts; the 17th of November, you [were] quite clear that something was wrong; on the 20th, you felt compelled to call in the admiral and the colonel; on the 21st, the admiral was told that the office would be searched; on the 23rd, you confronted the colonel with the memo; on the 25th, you call the press conference. In the interim we have shredding parties.

Why did it take so long?

COOPER: Again, Mr. Chairman, not until the 25th was the decision made that we, indeed, could and should go forward with a criminal investigation. During this period of time, obviously, evidence was lost, and that is regrettable, and in hindsight, obviously, one wishes that extraordinary measures of some kind had been taken and people had perceived the need to take extraordinary measures. But not until the 25th did we definitely have an understanding of the implications of the diversion that satisfied us that there was a potential criminal predicate and, therefore, go forward with the investigation at that moment.

INOUYE: On the 25th of November?

COOPER: That is my recollection, yes.

INOUYE: But yet it was about five days beyond that when this office was sealed.

COOPER: Yes, sir, and—well, by the FBI. And I don't really have a good understanding for why that is true.

Oliver L. North

Following are excerpts from the July 7, 1987, testimony of Lt. Col. Oliver L. North. Throughout his testimony, North, a star witness in the Iran-contra hearings, repeated that he was only following orders but that, while assuming presidential approval, he had never received direct orders from President Reagan.

[John W.] NIELDS [Jr., House committee chief counsel]: It was not true the United States Government had no connection with Mr. Hasenfus' airplane that went down in Nicaragua? [Piloted by Eugene Hasenfus, the plane was shot down over Nicaragua, in October 1986, while transporting weapons to the contras.]

NORTH: No, it was not true. I had an indirect connection at flight, and many others I would point out.

NIELDS: In certain communist countries, the government's activities are kept secret from the people, but that is not the way we do things in America, is it?

NORTH: Counsel, I would like to go back to what I said just a few minutes ago.

I think it is very important for the American people to understand that this is a dangerous world, we live at risk and that this Nation is at risk in a dangerous world, and that they ought not be led to believe as a consequence of these hearings that this Nation cannot or should not conduct covert operations.

By their very nature, covert operations or special activities are a lie. There is great deceit, deception practiced in the conduct of covert operations.

They are at essence a lie.

We make every effort to deceive the enemy as to our intent, our conduct, and to deny the association of the United States with those activities.

The intelligence committees hold hearings on all kinds of these activities conducted by our intelligence services. The American people ought not to be led to believe by the way you are asking that question that we intentionally deceived the American people or had that intent to begin with.

The effort to conduct these covert operations was made in such a way that our adversaries would not have knowledge of them or that we could deny American association with them or the association of this Government with those activities.

And that is not wrong.

NIELDS: The American people were told by this Government that our Government had nothing to do with the Hasenfus airplane, and that was false, and it is a principal purpose of these hearings to replace secrecy and deception with disclosure and truth, and that is one of the reasons we have called you here, sir.

And one question the American people would like to know the answer to is what did the President know about the diversion of the proceeds of Iranian arms sales to the contras.

Can you tell us what you knew about that, sir?

NORTH: You just took a long leap from Mr. Hasenfus' airplane.

As I told this committee several days, and if you will indulge me, Counsel, in a brief summary of what I said, I never personally discussed the use of the residuals or profits from the sale of United States weapons to Iran for the purpose of supporting the Nicaraguan resistance with the President.

I never raised it with him and he never raised it with me during my tenure at the National Security Council [NSC] staff. Throughout the conduct of my entire tenure at the National Security Council, I assumed that the President was aware of what I was doing and had, through my superiors, approved it.

I sought approval of my superiors for every one of my actions, and it is well documented.

I assumed when I had approval to proceed from either Judge [William P.] Clark, [Robert C.] Bud McFarlane, or [Rear] Adm. [John M.] Poindexter [each has served as national security adviser], that they had, indeed, solicited and obtained the approval of the President.

To my recollection, Adm. Poindexter never told me that he met with the President on the issue of using residuals from the Iranian sales to support the Nicaraguan resistance or that he discussed the residuals or profits for use by the contras with the President, or that he got the President's specific approval, nor did he tell me that the President had approved such a transaction.

But again, I wish to reiterate that throughout, I believe that the President had indeed authorized such activity. No other person with whom I was in contact with during my tenure at the White House told me that he or she ever discussed the issue of the residuals or profits with the President.

In late November, two other things occurred which relate to this issue.

On or about Friday, November 21, I asked Adm. Poindexter directly, "Does the President know?" He told me he did not.

And on November 25, the day I was reassigned back to the United States Marine Corps for service, the President of the United States called me. In the course of that call, the President said to me, words to the effect that, "I just didn't know."

Those are the facts as I know them, Mr. Nields. I was glad that when you introduced this, you said that you wanted to hear the truth. I came to tell you the truth, the good, the bad, and the ugly.

I am here to tell it all—pleasant and unpleasant—and I am here to accept responsibility for that which I did.

I will not accept responsibility for that which I did not do.

* * *

The Memoranda

NIELDS: . . . You had a specific reason for believing that the President had approved, you wrote memoranda, did you not, seeking the President's approval for the diversion?

NORTH: I did.

NIELDS: And indeed, you wrote more than one of them?

NORTH: I did.

NIELDS: How many did you write?

NORTH: Again, I will estimate there may have been as many as five. Again, I am trying to recall without access to those particular documents. You may have six, and I am not trying to disassemble at all with you.

NIELDS: And these five were written, I take it, on each occasion where there was a proposed sale of arms to the Iranians that you felt had reached sufficiently final form to seek the Presi-

dent's approval?

NORTH: Yes.

NIELDS: And the first one was in February or January of 1986; is that correct?

NORTH: As I recall, it was. . . .

NIELDS: This is a draft, but I think you just testified that on five different occasions, you put one of those drafts in final form.

NORTH: It is my recollection that each time we prepared to conduct one of those transactions, and not all of them went through to fruition, there were only three that actually transpired during the time that I was supervising this activity, but it is my recollection that there were probably five times total, that we actually got to a point where we thought, one, that the sale would take place; and, number two, that we would have the hostages released and a dialogue with the Iranians as a consequence.

NIELDS: And you sent those memoranda up the line?

NORTH: It is my recollection I sent each one of those up the line, and that on the three where I had approval to proceed, I thought that I had received authority from the President. I want to make it very clear that no memorandum ever came back to me with the President's initials on it, or the President's name on it or a note from the President on it. None of these memoranda.

I do have, as you know, in the files that you have of mine, many, many of my memoranda do have the President's initials on them, but none of these had the President's initials on them. . . .

NIELDS: Frequently, you would send memoranda to the National Security Adviser seeking his approval for something. Is that correct?

NORTH: Judging by the pile of paper you just sent me, I obviously sent too many. . . . But, yes, I did send memoranda to my boss.

NIELDS: Seeking his approval?

NORTH: Yes, sir.

NIELDS: What line under the heading "Recommendations," in which you sought his approval?

NORTH: Yes.

NIELDS: And sometimes you sent memoranda up the line with a recommendation that he brief the President on something.

NORTH: As I recall, yes.

NIELDS: And occasionally, you sent up a memorandum recommending that he obtain the President's approval?

NORTH: That is correct.

NIELDS: And that is what you did in this case?

NORTH: Apparently so. Those are the words that I had typed on a piece of paper.

NIELDS: Because you specifically wanted, before proceeding on a matter of this degree of importance, to have the President's approval.

NORTH: Yes.

NIELDS: Now, at any time did Adm. Poindexter tell you, "Don't send any more memos like this."?

NORTH: I don't recall such an instruction, and had I been given it, I would have followed it. There were times when we, in both the case of Adm. Poindexter and Mr. McFarlane, decided no more memoranda on certain subjects, and they would be handled with verbal briefings.

NIELDS: But that was not the case with respect to these memoranda seeking approval of the diversions?

NORTH: You insist on referring to it as diversions. My use of Webster['s dictionary] leads me to believe those were residuals. The only thing we did was divert money out of Mr. [Manucher] Ghorbanifar's [a middleman in the Iranian arms deal] pocket and put it to a better use.

NIELDS: I am not asking you about words now, Colonel. I am asking you whether you didn't continue to send memoranda seeking approval of diversions or residuals, whatever the word, for the benefit of the contras, up to the President for approval?

NORTH: I did not send them to the President, Mr. Nields. This memorandum went to the National Security Adviser, seeking that he obtain the President's approval. There is a big difference. This is not a memorandum to the President.

* * *

Shredding Documents

NIELDS: That is the whole reason for shredding documents, isn't it, Col. North, so that you can later say you don't remember whether you had them, you don't remember what is in them?

NORTH: No, Mr. Nields. The reason for shredding documents and the reason the Government of the United States gave me a shredder—I mean, I didn't buy it myself—was to destroy documents that were no longer relevant, that did not apply or should not be divulged.

Again I want to go back to the whole intent of a covert operation. Part of a covert operation is to offer plausible deniability of the association of the Government of the United States with the activity, part of it is to deceive our adversaries, part of it is to insure those people who are at great peril carrying out those activities are not further endangered. All those are good and sufficient reasons to destroy documents, and that is why the Government buys shredders by the tens and dozens and gives them to people running covert operations; not so they can have convenient memories.

I came here to tell you the truth, to tell you and this committee and the American people the truth, and I am trying to do that, Mr. Nields, and I don't like the insinuation I'm up here having a convenient memory lapse like perhaps others have had.

NIELDS: You shredded these documents on Friday, the 21st of November 1986?

NORTH: I started shredding documents as early as my return from Europe in October. I have absolutely no recollection when those documents were shredded, none whatsoever.

NIELDS: There has been testimony before the committee you engaged in shredding of documents on November 21, 1986. You deny that?

NORTH: I do not deny I engaged in shredding on November 21. I will also tell this committee I engaged in shredding almost every day I had a shredder and put things in burn bags when I didn't.

Every single day I was on National Security Council staff, some documents were destroyed, and I don't want you to have the impression that these documents that I referred to seeking approval disappeared on the 21st. Because I can't say that. In fact, I am quite sure, by virtue of the conversations I remember about the 21st, that those documents were already gone.

They were gone by virtue of the fact that we saw these operations unraveling as early as the mid part of October. We lost the Hasenfus airplane, and the discussion the Director of Central Intelligence [William J. Casey] had had with a private citizen about what he knew of a contra diversion, as you put it, and at that point I began to, one, recognize I would be leaving the NSC, because that was a purpose for my departure, to offer the scapegoat, if you will, and, second of all, recognizing what was coming down, I didn't want some new person walking in there opening files that would possibly expose people at risk.

So I do not want you to leave with the idea that those documents were shredded just on the 21st. They might have been shredded on the 19th or the 11th of November when I came back from a series of trips to Europe.

* * *

Political Damage?

NIELDS: I am asking you whether, in your judgment, the President was suffering domestic political damage as a result of the publicity surrounding the Iranian arms initiative?

NORTH: Yes.

NIELDS: And you were concerned about that?

NORTH: Always.

NIELDS: And can you think of any document, the disclosure of which would have caused him more domestic political damage than a document reflecting his approval of the diversion?

NORTH: The answer to your question is yes. I can think of a lot of documents that would cause domestic political damage.

NIELDS: In your files?

NORTH: Not necessarily in my files.

NIELDS: Well, let's talk about the ones that were in your files that you were concerned about shredding.

My question to you is can you think of any document in your files that you were thinking about shredding which would have caused him more domestic political damage than one of these diversion memos reflecting his approval?

NORTH: Can I give you more than a one-word answer?

NIELDS: Why don't you try one word and then explain.

NORTH: All right, Mr. Nields.

Yes. The answer is yes, I can think of many documents that could be damaging to the President.

NIELDS: That wasn't the question.

[Brendan V.] SULLIVAN [Jr., North's lawyer]: It was the question.

NIELDS: No, it was not.

The question was can you think of any documents which would have been more damaging?

NORTH: I suppose so. And I suppose those had already been destroyed. And I want to go back once again to what I tried to say at the very beginning.

I happen to believe that this Nation needs to be able to conduct deniable covert operations. I believe that this President, like all Presidents, needs to have an ability to disassociate himself from those activities and that the U.S. role should remain hidden or deniable and not be revealed.

That is, after all, the essence of those operations.

The reason I destroyed documents—

NIELDS: That was not the question, sir.

NORTH: I want to answer that.

NIELDS: That was not the question.

NORTH: That is important.

NIELDS: The question on the table is different.

Are there any documents or were there in your files that you were thinking about shredding on November 21st that would have been any more damaging politically than one of these diversion memos reflecting presidential approval?

That is the question.

NORTH: The way you have asked the question, I can tell you absolutely not because I don't think the documents existed on November 21st.

NIELDS: Well, that is my next question.

Are you here telling the committee that you don't remember whether on November 21st there was a document in your files reflecting presidential approval of the diversion?

NORTH: As a matter of fact, I will tell you specifically that I thought they were all gone because by the time I was told at some point early on November 21st that there would be an inquiry conducted by [Attorney General Edwin] Meese [III], I assured Adm. Poindexter, incorrectly, it seems, that all of those documents no longer existed. And so that is early on November 21st because I believe the decision to make an inquiry, to have the Attorney General or Mr. Meese, in his role as a friend of the President, conduct a fact-finding excursion on what happened in September and November in 1985, I assured the Admiral, "Don't worry. It is all taken care of."

. . . I started shredding documents in earnest after a discussion with Director Casey in early October, when he told me that Mr. [Roy M.] Furmark [a New York businessman and friend of Casey who had, in October 1986, asked Casey to look into complaints by Canadian financiers that they had not been paid for their role in the Iranian arms deal] had come to him and talked to him about the use of Iran arms sales money to support the resistance.

That followed shortly—was preceded shortly by the crash or shootdown of the aircraft Mr. Hasenfus was on. And Director Casey and I had a lengthy discussion about the fact that this whole thing was coming unraveled and that things ought to be "cleaned up," and I started cleaning things up.

NIELDS: And when you cleaned them up, did you or did you not shred documents that reflected the President's approval of the diversion?

SULLIVAN: Objection. How many times do we have to have the question asked, Mr. Chairman? The witness has done it—answered that question I think about 10 times this morning. I request respectfully that he move on to a new subject.

[Sen. Daniel K.] INOUYE [D-Hawaii]: I must overrule this. I have some difficulty in trying to get a clear answer myself. I am certain counsel is having that difficulty. Please proceed.

SULLIVAN: What is your question, counsel?

NIELDS: Have you forgotten the question?

SULLIVAN: I have, and I have to make objections. You ask it again.

NIELDS: You did, and it was overruled and the question stands. I would like the witness to answer it, if he remembers it.

SULLIVAN: He obviously doesn't remember it. He just asked you to repeat it.

NIELDS: You did. He did not, sir. Do you remember the question?

NORTH: My memory has been shredded. If you would be so kind as to repeat the question?

NIELDS: You have testified that you shredded documents shortly after you heard from Director Casey that Furmark had said monies had been used from the Iranian arms sales for the benefit of the contras.

NORTH: That is correct.

NIELDS: My question to you is, did you or did you not shred documents that reflected Presidential approval of the diversion?

NORTH: I have absolutely no recollection of destroying any document which gave me an indication that the President had seen the document or that the President had specifically approved. I assumed that the three transactions which I supervised or managed or coordinated, whatever word you are comfortable with—and I can accept all three—were approved by the President.

I never recalled seeing a single document which gave me a clear indication that the President had specifically approved that action.

* * *

False Documents

NIELDS: Was the Attorney General aware in November of 1985 that 18 Hawk missiles had been shipped to Iran?

NORTH: I did not specifically address it to the Attorney General in November of 1985. I do remember discussions that included the Attorney General subsequent to this event.

I believe there was one that Mr. McFarlane referred me to in December that I believe may well have addressed this issue because, when he joined me in London, we talked about how to fix the problems that had been created by the September and November shipments.

One of the issues that had already come up by then was a draft finding prepared in concert with Mr. [Stanley] Sporkin, who was at the time the general counsel of the Central Intelligence Agency. I was led to believe, or at least came to believe, in 1985 that Mr. Sporkin had gotten the acquiescence or support—either he or Director Casey—of the Attorney General in that November finding.

The November finding specifically referred to prior actions.

NIELDS: Ratified them?

NORTH: Ratified prior actions.

NIELDS: Was that finding ever signed?

NORTH: It is my understanding that the finding was signed.

NIELDS: What is the basis for your understanding?

NORTH: I believe, although I do not recall specifically, but I believe I saw a signed copy of that finding.

NIELDS: Where?

NORTH: Adm. Poindexter's office.

NIELDS: Did you have a copy of it in your office?

NORTH: I did not. I had a draft copy.

NIELDS: When did you see the signed finding?

NORTH: I think I may have seen a signed copy of it in early December.

NIELDS: Of what year?

NORTH: 1986—sorry—'5.

NIELDS: That finding referred only to arms and hostages; isn't that true? It didn't refer to any broader purposes?

NORTH: Exactly. That, as I indicated a few moments ago, I perceived to be a serious deficiency in that finding.

NIELDS: And a serious problem therefore with exposure of the Hawk shipment?

NORTH: Exactly. The exposure of the Hawk shipment—again, my priorities, safety of the hostages, safety of the second channel, the international repercussions of a—what clearly in that initial finding sent to the National Security Adviser by Director Casey was nothing more than an arms for hostages swap....

NIELDS: Did you discuss the wisdom of putting out a false version of the facts with Adm. Poindexter?

NORTH: I may have. I don't recall a specific discussion. Again, it was—he and I knew what had transpired back in November of '85. He and I knew that this version of the document was wrong, intentionally misleading, showing a separation between the United States and Israel on the activity....

NIELDS: By putting out this false version of the facts, you were committing, were you not, the entire administration to telling a false story?

NORTH: Well, I am not trying to pass the buck here. October? I did a lot of things, and I want to stand up and say that I'm proud of them. I don't want you to think, Counsel, that I went about this all on my own. I realize there's a lot of folks around that think there's a loose cannon on the gun deck of State at NSC. That wasn't what I heard while I worked there. I've only heard it since I left. People used to walk up to me and tell me what a great job I was doing.

The fact is there were many, many people, to include the former Assistant to the President for National Security Affairs, the current National Security Adviser, the Attorney General of the United States of America, the Director of Central Intelligence, all of whom knew that to be wrong.

NIELDS: We understand that, Colonel. I take it one of your functions was to give people above you in the hierarchy advice?

NORTH: That is correct.

NIELDS: And by putting out this story, you were committing, among other people, the President of the United States to telling a version of the facts which wasn't true?

NORTH: Counsel, I think I have answered the question as best I can. I am not too sure who you want to blame for committing who. If you want to blame me for committing others, that is fine....

NIELDS: Can there ever be good and sufficient reasons to put out a false story about the President's activities without asking him?

NORTH: Counsel, I don't know that the President ever used this version. I know that other people did. But I don't know that the President of the United States was ever given this version. I don't know that the President ever was—had this put before him and said "use this." And I don't know that he's ever said that.

NIELDS: Well, once other people put this version out, and you have indicated that others did—I take it Director Casey among them?

NORTH: Director Casey certainly put out a part of that. And, as I said, not all of that middle paragraph you have just shown me is incorrect.

NIELDS: But some of it is, and Director Casey used it in his testimony, did he not?

NORTH: I have not seen Director Casey's testimony. I would have to see it to tell you whether he did or didn't.

NIELDS: It has been provided to you.

NORTH: So was a mountain of paper, Counsel, bigger than I am.

NIELDS: You were present, I take it, at a meeting on the 20th of November in Adm. Poindexter's office?

NORTH: ... Yes, I was.

NIELDS: And the purpose of that meeting—I take it present at the meeting were, among other people, Director Casey, Adm. Poindexter, you, Mr. [Charles J.] Cooper from the Attorney General's Office, the Attorney General, Paul Thompson [an NSC lawyer]?

NORTH: I recall—quite honestly, I didn't recall Mr. Cooper being present, but I do recall that the others were present. I also believe that Director Casey had one of his staff present with him....

NIELDS: And I take it that the subject of the November Hawk shipment and what he [Casey] would testify about it was discussed?

NORTH: As I recall, that was the subject of discussion, and—I had worked, as I recall, on various issues with CIA officers.

Director Casey had been away, and as I recall, had been brought back early from a trip; and I had been working with a number of his staff on various testimony preparations; and at the meeting on the 20th, I recall it a lot differently than perhaps some other people have.

My principal objective in that session was to create some closure between a CIA version, which showed this to be an "NSC operation," and make it more visible as a U.S. Government operation.

The CIA version of their chronology had said this is the NSC this this, the NSC that that, the NSC et cetera. My effort was to try and make closure between their version and one that would say this was the U.S. Government that did A, B and C. Nonetheless, the portion that dealt with the November Hawk shipments was in part in error.

Now, I understand there is a lot of heroes walking around that have claimed credit for exposing the fraud, et cetera. Let me just make note as to what I recall and what I recorded at the time.

I have my notes. After we left that meeting, I do not recall, incidentally, a great debate over whether the U.S. Government knew or whether the CIA knew what was aboard the airplane.

I very clearly knew what was on that airplane. So did Director Casey know that I knew what was on that airplane. The issue, as far as I was concerned, was what did the CIA know? I had told the CIA after my discussions—this is going back to 1985—after my discussions with the Israelis, which occurred the night Mr. McFarlane called, I believe I flew up to New York, and we can go through that whole 1986 chronology if you wish.

There were subsequent discussions of the Israelis. Gen. Secord [retired major general Richard V. Secord] went over. We eventually got a CIA proprietary to fly Hawks from Israel to Iran.

I knew it, and by then the CIA knew that they were flying something for me. I never told—I don't believe—the CIA what was really on those airplanes. I don't believe. I knew. And so, in working the chronology, it was important that the CIA be able to say that they did not know what was on the airplanes at the time, and I don't believe they did. They certainly found out shortly thereafter because of the same sensitive intelligence I referred to earlier.

There was no doubt that shortly thereafter, everybody who had access to that very sensitive intelligence knew what was going on. There was a discussion, as I recall, relatively brief, in Adm. Poindexter's office which included Adm. Poindexter, Director Casey, myself, Mr. Thompson, I believe Mr. [George] Cave [a retired CIA official who acted as a translator and note-taker for many of the 1986 talks between U.S. and Iranian officials], and the Attorney General, and if he says he was there, Mr. Cooper.

I just don't remember him. May have been the first time I ever met the man. I then went back to Director Casey's office over in the Old Executive Office Building, the one that was just down the hall from my basement.

And in that room, Director Casey and I fixed that testimony and removed the offensive portions. Now, we fixed it by omission. We left out—it wasn't made accurate, it wasn't made fulsome, it was fixed by omission.

*   *   *

NIELDS: I would like to go back to the reason for putting out a false version of facts in the NSC chronologies concerning the Hawk shipment.

Was the reason the fact that the pre-finding shipments by the Israelis were in violation of law?

NORTH: Well, let me just preamble that by virtue of saying I don't believe that anything I did while I was at the NSC was a violation of law, nor do I believe that anything we did while I was at the NSC was a violation of law. I didn't believe it then; I don't believe it now.

If I believed it then, I wouldn't have done it.

*   *   *

Aid to the Contras

NIELDS: . . . Following October of 1984, was the U.S. Government support for the war in Nicaragua managed by you?

That was the only question.

NORTH: The U.S. contact with the Nicaraguan resistance was me, and I turned to others to help carry out that activity.

NIELDS: Did you manage it?

NORTH: I tried. In terms of coalescing the activities that went on, yes.

NIELDS: Now, you said you were given the job. Who gave it to you?

NORTH: I guess it fell to me by default. Mr. McFarlane was the one who originally tasked me to go make contact with the resistance, assure them of our unflagging support. I made a trip in the spring of 1984 to that effect and basically it just persisted thereafter.

NIELDS: Maybe it would be most useful to get into specifics of the areas of your support.

I take it one area of your support was to endeavor to raise money from sources other than the U.S. Treasury.

NORTH: That's correct. Boland proscriptions did not allow us to do so and so we sought a means of complying with those Boland proscriptions by going elsewhere for those monies. [The Boland amendments restricted U.S. aid to the Nicaraguan contras.]

NIELDS: And you went to foreign countries?

NORTH: I did not physically go to those foreign countries.

NIELDS: Representatives of—

NORTH: Representatives of foreign countries and I had discussions about those matters, yes. . . .

NIELDS: And you asked them for money for the contras?

NORTH: Well, I want to be a little bit more specific about that. I don't recall going hat in hand to anybody asking for money.

I do recall sitting and talking about how grateful this country would be if the issue that they had discussed with others were indeed brought to fruition.

For example, a representative of Country Three [Taiwan] and I met and we talked about an issue that had been raised with him beforehand by others outside of the Government. And I told him I thought that was a dandy idea and I told him where he could send the money and he did so.

NIELDS: Before we get into the specifics and I am going to ask you more about Country Three in a minute, Mr. McFarlane has testified that he gave you instructions not to solicit money from foreign countries or private sources.

Did he give you those instructions?

NORTH: I never carried out a single act, not one, Mr. Nields, in which I did not have authority from my superiors. I haven't in the 23 years that I have been in the uniformed services of the United States of America ever violated an order, not one.

NIELDS: But that wasn't the question.

NORTH: That is the answer to your question.

NIELDS: No. The question was, did Mr. McFarlane give you such instructions?

NORTH: No. I never heard those instructions.

NIELDS: And I take it that it was your understanding from what you have just said that quite to the contrary, you were authorized to seek money from foreign countries?

NORTH: I was authorized to do everything that I did.

NIELDS: Well, again, that isn't the question.

NORTH: I was authorized to have a meeting—in this particular case, in specific, by Mr. McFarlane—for the purpose of talking to the man about a suggestion that had been made to him by others and to encourage that process along, and I did so.

I had already provided to Mr. McFarlane a card with the address of an account, an offshore account which would support the Nicaraguan resistance and, thank God, somebody put money into that account and the Nicaraguan resistance didn't die, as perhaps others intended.

Certainly the Sandinistas and Moscow and Cuba intended that and they didn't die. They grew in strength and numbers and effectiveness as a consequence, and I think that is a good thing.

And Mr. McFarlane was the person who asked me for the card on the account and with the account and I gave it to him and I don't know who he gave it to. But whoever he gave it to gave a lot of money.

I don't know if Mr. McFarlane asked that person for the money or not. I did not go to the representative of Country Three and ask him for money. He suggested that he put money there and I told him where to send it and, thank God, that he did so, too.

NIELDS: I take it you are saying not only did Mr. McFarlane not instruct you not to seek money from foreign countries, but that he was aware of each and every one of your actions to obtain money from foreign countries and approved of it?

NORTH: I believe so, yes.

* * *

Who Was in Charge?

NIELDS: Who was in charge [of the covert operation to aid the contras]? You were a government official. He [Gen. Secord] was not. He's a major general. You are a lieutenant colonel. Are you telling this committee that because he had a higher rank when he was with the government that he was the boss?

NORTH: Well, he was the boss of what? He was the boss of the organizations and the commercial enterprises that he set up to assist the Nicaraguan resistance, and that I eventually asked him to expand out into other covert operations, and he did those things.

NIELDS: He did those at your request, did he not?

NORTH: That's correct. But you said "direction." I think he would probably take umbrage with that.

NIELDS: I am not asking you whether he would take umbrage; I am asking you whether the United States Government retained control over this covert operation.

NORTH: I tried to, Counsel. Tried to.

NIELDS: And indeed all of the money that went into that bank account in Switzerland resulted from your efforts?

NORTH: I don't know that, no because you say "that bank account." I'm not sure to this day exactly how much money went into that bank account or which bank account.

NIELDS: Well, I can tell you that the committees' records reflect that the monies that went into those bank accounts came from the proceeds of sales of arms to Iran, from Country Three, directly or indirectly from [fund-raiser Carl R.] Spitz Channell's organizations, a little bit from the Government of Israel and one deposit from Joseph Coors.

And my question to you is: Isn't it true that you were responsible for directing all of that money into those accounts?

NORTH: My sense is that the ones you have just identified—except that I don't know that it is the Government of Israel; I believe it was an Israeli private citizen—I would agree that I am the person that caused that money to go into those accounts.

* * *

Who Knew?

NIELDS: . . . Were your activities in that respect [soliciting money from foreign countries for contra aid] known to others in the White House other than the National Security Advisers?

NORTH: Well, I want to go back to something I said at the very beginning of all this, Mr. Nields. I assumed that those matters which required the attention and decision of the President of the United States did indeed get them. I assumed that.

I never asked that. I never walked up to the President and said, "Oh, by the way, Mr. President, yesterday, I met with so-and-so from Country Four." Nor did he ever say, "I am glad you had a meeting with Country Four and it went well."

NIELDS: Do you know whether or not the President was aware of your activities seeking funds and operational support for the contras from third countries?

NORTH: I do not know. I assume that he did.

NIELDS: What was the basis of your assumption?

NORTH: Just that there was a lot going on, and it was very obvious that the Nicaraguan resistance survived. I sent forward innumerable documents, some of which you have just shown us as Exhibits that demonstrated I was keeping my superiors fully informed as to what was going on.

* * *

NIELDS: Was the President aware of your U.S. operation to raise funds for the contras from private contributors?

NORTH: Well, I think that the PROFs note [White House internal computer messages] right there indicates that I believed he was. But I didn't ever walk in and by the way say to him, "Mr. President, this is what I—" I know I have been accused of those kinds of things, but I didn't do that.

The fact is that I assumed, and I think that is a fairly clear indication I am sending my boss what I thought was going to be a very private not is [*sic*] that would never see the light of day anywhere else, and I said to him what I felt. And I was asking him for guidance.

NIELDS: And he certainly didn't tell you to stop?

NORTH: Why would he? We were conducting a covert operation to support the Nicaraguan resistance, to carry out the President of the United States' stated, publicly articulated foreign policy.

Why should he tell me to stop? We weren't breaking any laws. We were simply trying to keep an operation covert.

* * *

On July 8, 1987, House counsel Nields questioned North on the $17 million profit garnered by the sale of arms to Iran. In particular, Nields focused on the question: Whose idea was it to divert money from the arms sale to the Nicaraguan contras?

NIELDS: My question to you is: Who in the United States Government chose to structure the transaction so that there would be $17 million left in Mr. Secord's bank accounts?

NORTH: Well, I don't know that it was structured to leave $17 million in the account to start with. It was structured so—so by the time we got to the February transaction, it was structured in such a way that Gen. Secord would become the person who actually conducted the transactions. But the Government of the United States would be paid exactly what it asked for whatever was shipped, and that was what we did with the 1,000 TOWs [antitank missiles] in February and that is what we did with the Hawk parts—excuse me—the Hawk parts and TOWs later in the autumn.

In each case the decision was made to allow Gen. Secord to be the broker, if you will, for that transaction, that it would be his accounts that would then transfer monies to the Israeli—to the various people who needed to be paid, to include the Government of the United States.

I initially thought that the money was coming from the Israelis in the person of Mr. Ghorbanifar—who was widely regarded in our Government, at least in the CIA people I talked to, as an Israeli agent—to Mr. Secord's account, to the CIA, and then to the Pentagon to pay for the weapons or the materiel, whatever it was that was being shipped.

That was done for a number of purposes: one, to accrue sufficient funds to pay for Israeli replenishments for what had been shipped in '85; second of all, to generate revenues to support the Nicaraguan resistance; and, third, to cover the costs of these transactions and ultimately further the cause of the approach we made with the second channel [Iranian contacts in the arms deal].

NIELDS: Who made the decision to structure the transaction in such a way that there was $17 million left for these purposes that you have described?

NORTH: You keep coming back to $17 million. I have just told you that I got approval to structure the transaction in such a way that there would be residuals remaining from the transaction for the purposes I just told you.

NIELDS: Whose idea was it?

NORTH: If I may—I am going to ask you for the latitude to make a longer discourse than 10 words. . . .

Mr. [Amiram] Nir [an Israeli agent] was the first person to suggest that there be a residual and that the residual be applied to the purpose of purchasing replenishments and supporting other activities.

At that point in time, in early January, he did not raise with me the specifics of supporting the Nicaraguan resistance. That proposal came out of a meeting in—as I recall, later in January, where I met with Mr. Nir and Mr. Ghorbanifar—I am going to say London [England] or it may have been Frankfurt [West Germany] or it may have been elsewhere—and in that meeting I expressed our grave reservations as to how the structure—which at that point in time focused on several thousand TOWs—would result in what we wanted. . . .

I expressed our reservations that the arrangements that were being made by Mr. Ghorbanifar—and by then acting on our behalf as well as the Israelis'—were not going to lead to what we wanted.

What we wanted as a part of that overall program was to establish a higher level meeting well above my pay grade. In fact, I suggested a number of people—and I'm sure you have seen it in my messages to my superiors—a number of people who could meet with senior Iranian officials and various ways in which that could happen.

In that January meeting I told him that I was not confident that we were headed in the right direction, and I tape recorded that meeting. Mr. Ghorbanifar by then was aware of my role in support for the Nicaraguan resistance. He had seen my name in the newspapers. He is a very well read individual. I had been told by the Central Intelligence Agency, by Director Casey himself and by others in the CIA, that they believed Mr. Ghorbanifar to be an Israeli intelligence agent.

Mr. Ghorbanifar took me into the bathroom and Mr. Ghorbanifar suggested several incentives to make that February transaction work, and the attractive incentive for me was the one he made that residuals could flow to support the Nicaraguan resistance.

He made it point blank and he made it by my understanding with the full knowledge and acquiescence and support, if not the original idea of the Israeli intelligence services, if not the Israeli Government. . . . And I saw that idea of using the [Iranian leader] Ayatollah Khomeini's money to support the Nicaraguan freedom fighters as a good one.

I still do. I don't think it is wrong. I think it was a neat idea and I came back and I advocated that and we did it. We did it on three occasions.

These three occasions were February, May and October, and in each one of those occasions, as a consequence of that whole process, we got three Americans back and there was no terrorism while we were engaged in it against Americans.

For almost 18 months, there was no action against Americans until it started to come unraveled. . . .

* * *

NIELDS: Who decided how that $10 million [from the Iranian arms sale] was going to be used—you, Mr. Secord, or someone else?

NORTH: I described for Gen. Secord the purposes to which I thought that money ought to be applied, and throughout my long experience with Gen. Secord, who after all, had been referred to me by Director Casey, who was the one that suggested him back in 1984 as the person to assist us outside the government to comply with the Boland proscriptions, I relied on Gen. Secord to carry that transaction out.

There were points in time when we discussed these activities. I had to tell him what the government was going to charge for various commodities, but ultimately the decision was his.

And yet, I wish to point out he always, to my knowledge, did what I asked.

NIELDS: Are you testifying that the transaction was set up, structured in such a way that it was up to Gen. Secord to decide how the residuals were going to be used?

NORTH: Well, I won't put it all on his back. There was always a concert of opinion that the purpose of the residuals were as follows: To sustain the Iranian operation, to support the Nicaraguan resistance, to continue other activities which the Israelis very clearly wanted, and so did we, and to pay for a replacemnt for the original Israeli TOWs shipped in 1985.

And we, I think, used that money for that purpose.

NIELDS: And whose decision was it how those monies were to be used?

NORTH: Well, I got North—I believed my boss, I talked to Adm. Poindexter about it, I talked to Director Casey about it, and I communicated it back to Gen. Secord and said, here is what we have to do, you figure out how you are going to allocate those monies to accomplish those purposes, and to my knowledge, he did so. . . .

NIELDS: I don't want to belabor the point, but let me see if I can ask the question simply once and see if you can answer this one way or the other.

Whose decision was it whether the moneys would be used for the contras or not? Somebody in the U.S. Government, or Gen. Secord?

NORTH: The decision was made that residuals from those transactions would be applied to support the Nicaragua resistance with the authority that I got from my superiors, Adm. Poindexter, with the concurrence of William J. Casey and I thought at the time the President of the United States.

I later learned that the President was unaware of that aspect of these transactions. . . .

NIELDS: . . . If those higher-ups in the United States Government from whom you sought approval decided that the $10 million should not, any part of it, be sent to the contras but should all come back to the United States Treasury, that is what would have happened, isn't it?

NORTH: Yes.

NIELDS: So it was our money that was going to the contras, wasn't it?

NORTH: I disagree with your conclusion, Counsel.

INOUYE: Is this a good time for a recess?

NORTH: I am sorry, Mr. Chairman.

INOUYE: Please proceed.

NORTH: I disagree with your conclusion. If my boss told me, "Ollie, every penny that comes from this thing goes right back into the Treasury of the United States of America," that is exactly what I would have asked Gen. Secord to do. And I am confident that is exactly what he would have done. Okay?

I was never asked to do that. I got approval to do what I did and I didn't do anything without approval.

* * *

The Money Trail

NIELDS: Was it your understanding as of November of 1986 that there was $8 million either in Swiss bank accounts or in investment accounts at CSF [Compaignie de Services Fiduciaires, a financial services company in Switzerland that handled all financial matters for Secord and Albert Hakim, Secord's business associate]?

NORTH: No.

NIELDS: Was it your understanding that most of that money had already been spent for the contras?

NORTH: It was my understanding throughout that money was being spent for the purposes I defined earlier. . . .

NIELDS: How much money, according to your understanding, remained in these Swiss bank accounts under his [Secord's] control as of November 1986?

NORTH: I did not know. In fact, at the very end of this whole thing, and to this day, I still do not know how much money was under his control and where it was.

I simply relied on the fact that I had a relationship of trust between myself and Gen. Secord, between Gen. Secord and Director Casey, obviously, that those activities were being carried out. . . .

NIELDS: . . . Our testimony that the committee has taken has shown that some approximately $4 million from all of the sales were used for the contras.

My question is this: would it have surprised you in November of 1986 to learn that Gen. Secord had used $4 million of the proceeds of the Iranian arms sales for the contras and had $8 million remaining in the pot?

NORTH: I was surprised. And I want to note I still don't understand that, and I am not willing at this point to accuse anybody, but I was surprised.

* * *

NIELDS: Col. North, did you have any personal interest in any of the monies that flowed from the arms sales to Iran or that were kept in Swiss accounts under Gen. Secord's control?

NORTH: Not one penny.

NIELDS: There has been testimony, as I am sure you are aware, that a death benefit account was set up by Mr. Hakim with the name Button, for the benefit of your family in the event of your death.

[Were you] aware of any such account?

NORTH: No. I was totally unaware of it. The first I heard of it was through these hearings.

I had never heard of it before, and it was a shock, an absolute shock.

NIELDS: There is a testamentary document which has been introduced in evidence relating to a particular $2 million sub-account set up, also by Mr. Hakim, which provides that on his death, Gen. Secord can control the use of the funds, and in the event of his death, you can control the use of the funds, and it also contains a provision that if everybody dies, it will be distributed to their estates.

Were you aware of such a document?

NORTH: No. I never heard of it until these hearings. I was shocked, and I have absolutely no idea where that all came from whatsoever, never heard of it before.

NIELDS: And you never heard of the idea, either, I take it?

NORTH: No, never. I did at one point express concern after I would guess in February, March, April, somewhere after I had met Mr. Hakim, became aware what his role was in the financial network that had been established, I did at some point express concern to Gen. Secord, "Suppose both of you guys go down on the same airplane flight back and forth to Europe; what happens then?"

I was told, "Don't worry, arrangements will be made so these operations can continue," but nobody ever told me that a single penny was set aside for my purposes, for my benefit whatsoever, ever, and I never heard of Buttons or Belly Buttons until this hearing began.

* * *

North's Home Security System

NIELDS: There had been testimony that several thousand dollars was spent on a fence, a security system, that was put in at your residence and that the moneys to pay for it came from Gen. Secord, and my question to you is, were you—I take it there was a security system put in at your residence?

NORTH: There is a security system in at my residence. It has since this April been sufficiently supplemented that it is now extraordinary.

NIELDS: And I take it—Were you aware that that security system was paid for by Gen. Secord?

NORTH: I am going to waffle an answer. I am going to say yes and no, and if you would indulge me, I will give you another one of my very straightforward, but rather lengthy, answers.

The issue of the security system was first broached immediately after a threat on my life by Abu Nidal. Abu Nidal is, as I am sure you on the Intelligence Committees know, the principal, foremost assassin in the world today. He is a brutal murderer. When I was first alerted to that threat by the Federal Bureau of Investigations [FBI] in late April, I was simply told that there was a threat that had been promulgated by Abu Bakar, who is the press spokesman for Fatah Revolutionary Council, which is the

name of the Abu Nidal group. He targeted me for assassination. . . .

The FBI was then contacted again and asked what protection can be offered. The FBI correctly said "We don't offer protection." I then sought other types of protection. I went to my superiors and said, "What can be done?" Contrary to what was said some days ago, this Lieutenant Colonel was not offered at that time any protection by the government of the United States, Sen. [Warren B.] Rudman [R-N.H.]. I asked for, and I was told that the only thing that I could do is to immediately PCS, permanent change of station—you and I, as Marines, know well what that means—and jerked out of our home and sent to Camp Lejune [North Carolina] in that I was preparing at the time to go to Tehran and we didn't want to tell the whole world that that was deemed not to be the appropriate thing to do.

The next thing we tried to do was to find a secure telephone to put in my home to justify the installation of a U.S. Government security system. That too was impossible or not feasible or couldn't be done. . . .

At some point along in there, either Gen. Secord raised with me or I raised with him this threat, and I told him I couldn't get U.S. Government protection; I couldn't find a contractor to come out and do it myself; and he said, "Don't worry about that, I have got a friend, or an associate"—I don't remember the words—"who is an expert. This guy has a company that does these things."

And he, shortly thereafter, I believe it was around the 5th of May, introduced me to Mr. Glenn Robinette. He was introduced to me as a man who, one, had been a former CIA, or perhaps I understood at the time FBI, I don't remember, technical expert; a man who owned a security company and a man who could immediately go out and do a survey and an estimate.

He did. Over the course of the next few days, he went out to my home, I called my wife or told my wife, whatever, that he would be out and went through the situation. He came up with an estimate of $8500 max, as I recall it was $8,000 to $8,500, and he could furthermore immediately install the system.

Now, I want you to know that I would be more than willing—and if anybody else is watching overseas, and I am sure they are—I will be glad to meet Abu Nidal on equal terms anywhere in the world. Okay? There is an even deal for him.

But I am not willing to have my wife and four children meet Abu Nidal or his organization on his terms. I want you to know what was going through my mind. I was about to leave for Tehran. I had already been told by Director Casey that I should be prepared to take my own life.

I had already been told that the Government of the United States on an earlier proposal for a trip, might even disavow that I had gone on the trip, on an earlier proposal, and we can come back to that at some time, if you like.

So, having been—having asked for some type of U.S. Government protection for my wife and children, and having been denied that, and perhaps for fully legitimate reasons and if there is a law that prevents the protection of American Government employees and their families from people like Abu Nidal, then gentlemen, please fix it, because this kid won't be around much longer, as I am sure you know. . . .

Now, let me go to your next question, because I know it is coming, and it deserves an answer. I never got a bill, . . .

Now, I then went on the trip to Tehran. I came back. I never got a bill. I didn't ask for a bill, and I never received one. I never asked, where is the bill, until well after it was too late, and I will cover that.

When I didn't get a bill, I basically understood what had happened, and I don't know exactly how it worked out, but I believe that an accommodation was worked between Mr. Robinette and Gen. Secord to make a gift out of that security system, that I did not pay for.

When I came to the end of my tenure at the NSC, it was, to say the least, a busy time. There were other things to be done besides shredding documents when I left. There was a lot of work to be done, and one of the things I did was to sit and contemplate the previous five and a half years of my work, and I am proud of that work.

I believed that we accomplished a lot. But there was one thing that just didn't look right, and that was that for the first time in my life, I had accepted something that I had not paid for, and even though I honestly believe that the Government of the United States should have paid for it, should have put it in, I then picked up the phone and asked for a bill.

I got a bill. In fact, I got two of them. I didn't ask that they be back-dated, but after all, Mr. Robinette is an old hand in the CIA. Right? The bills came with the old original dates, and I think there was another bill with later date on it.

Then, as I told you yesterday, I was going to tell you the truth, the good, the bad and the ugly, this is the truth, I did probably the grossest misjudgment that I have made in my life. I then tried to paper over that whole thing by sending two phony documents back to Mr. Robinette. It was not an exercise in good judgment.

I don't believe I have any particular monopoly on bad judgment. I think it was a gross error in judgment for this committee to put my home address up on the screen for the whole world to see, when I have got twenty security agents guarding my wife, my children and me right now.

* * *

The Traveler's Checks

NIELDS: There has been testimony about use of traveler's checks. I would like to give you an opportunity to answer or explain that testimony.

I take it you have it in mind?

NORTH: I do have it in mind, counsel. I appreciate the opportunity.

Again you will have to indulge me a bit.

When I began the covert operation in 1986—excuse me—1984 in support of the resistance, we had enormous problems trying to solve near time, real time, what I call operational problems. The end result of that was that I talked to Director Casey about the difficulties.

He had suggested establishing an operational account and I did so. There were two sources of monies for that operational account. One was traveler's checks from [contra leader] Adolfo Calero and the other one was cash eventually from Gen. Secord.

My recollection is that the very first traveler's checks came either very late '84 or certainly early 1985 and that the sum total of traveler's checks was probably in excess of $100,000 or thereabouts.

I also had cash which I estimated to be somewhere in the neighborhood of 50 to 75 thousand dollars in cash, so we are talking about an operational account that went from somewhere around 150 to 175 thousand dollars. At various points in time there would be considerable sums in it and at various points in time there would be none in it.

My recollection is that I got the traveler's checks in packages of less than $10,000. I understand that others have remembered elsewise, but that is how I remember it.

Those funds were used to support the operations that we were conducting. They were used to support the covert operation in Nicaragua, and then eventually were used to support other activities as well.

The fact that I had those funds available was known to Mr. McFarlane, to Adm. Poindexter, to Director Casey, and eventually to Adm. Art [Arthur] Moreau [former assistant to the chairman of the Joint Chiefs of Staff] over at the Pentagon....

What is important that you realize is that meticulous records were kept on all of this. I kept a detailed account of every single penny that came into that account and that left that account. All of the transactions were recorded on a ledger that Director Casey gave me for that purpose. Every time I got a group of traveler's checks in, I would report them, and I would report them when they went out, even going so far as to record the traveler's check numbers themselves.

The ledger for this operational account was given to me by Director Casey, and when he told me to do so, I destroyed it because it had within it the details of every single person who had been supported by this fund, the addresses, their names, and placed them at extraordinary risk.

Every transaction that you showed on that chart that you had up on the wall or the screen, or wherever it was—hard to tell when you see it on video tape—but when you had it up there, you showed a group of traveler's checks with my name on it. Every single one of those traveler's checks which bore my name were used by me to defray an actual operational expense as it happened. I would cash a check, for example, at Miami Airport and hand the money to a resistance person I met with there, or I flew, myself, off to some place because we were trying to avoid the use of appropriated funds, we used this account to live within Boland and to hide the fact that NSC travel was being conducted.

Unlike the CIA, the NSC travel voucher system doesn't have a covert cover. We had one dickens of a time trying to protect my travel, and, as you undoubtedly know, gentlemen, I made an enormous amount of travel. The schedule was brutal, much of it was paid for out of that operational account.

There were times when that account was down to zero. No money in it, I didn't have any traveler's checks, and I had handed out all the cash—not to myself, but to others. Under those circumstances, I would use my own money. Lt. Col. Oliver North's paycheck money, his own money that he had earned, and I would use it for an operational expense. I would, therefore, make a notation in the ledger, "Spent $250 on going to Atlanta to meet with somebody," and the next time I got cash or traveler's checks, I would use those checks to reimburse myself every single penny, and the checks that you saw that came to me was used to pay an operational expense on the scene or to reimburse myself. I never took a penny that didn't belong to me.

Every single one of those checks—and I would also point out to you, Counsel, that you don't have them all, because by my own recognition and memory there were checks used in 1986, and the ones that you depicted earlier were only 1985. I used those traveler's checks right up until shortly before I was fired, but only for the purpose that you saw.

I realize that this hearing is a difficult thing. Believe me, gentlemen, it is not as difficult for you as it is for a guy that has got to come up here and tell the truth, and that is what I am trying to do. I want to make it very clear that when you put up things like Parklane Hosiery—and you all snicker at it—and you know that I have got a beautiful secretary and the good Lord gave her the gift of beauty, and that people snicker that Ollie North might have been doing a little hanky-panky with his secretary, Ollie North has been loyal to his wife since the day he married her, and the fact is I went to my best friend, and I asked her, "Did I ever go to Parklane Hosiery?" And you know what she told me? "Of course, you did, you old buffoon, you went there to buy leotards for our two little girls." And the reason I wrote the check, Parklane Hosiery, just like the checks at Giant, is because I was owed my money for what I had spent in pursuing that covert operation.

You gentlemen may not agree that we should have been pursuing covert operations at the NSC, but we were. We had an operational account, and we used the money for legitimate purposes within that cover operation. Does that answer your question, sir?

NIELDS: Yes.

NORTH: Thank you.

* * *

Who Was Involved?

NIELDS: Col. North, you testified yesterday concerning approval that you received for the plan to use the proceeds of arms sales to Iran for the contras and you testified about Adm. Poindexter and the President.

Who else, if anyone, and I don't mean to imply anything in the question, but leaving those two people aside, who else in the Government was aware of either the plan or the fact of using proceeds of arms sales to Iran for the contras?

NORTH: Well, if I may clarify, what I testified to yesterday is my assumption that the President knew and then I subsequently testified that I was told he did not know.

I know that Adm. Poindexter knew, I know that Mr. McFarlane knew at a point in time when he was no longer in the

Government, and Director Casey knew.

Aside from that, I can't speak with certainty as to who else inside the Government knew for sure, although there were certainly a number of people who by the time November of 1986 came along certainly had great suspicions or belief that it was happening.

But the only ones that I know for sure whom I confirmed it with were those three.

* * *

NIELDS: . . . Among other things you directed those who were operating the resupply operation down in Central America with respect to when they [the contras] should make drops, how they should make them, where they should make them and so on?

NORTH: I don't think that "directed" is the right term. I am not trying to back away from any of the things that I did, but it is hard to direct a war from a desk in Washington, and I was not trying to direct a war from a desk in Washington.

I provided as much support for those activities as I was physically able. I went down frequently to coordinate with people in the region and I would receive and try to coordinate those activities based on information that I received from a multiple of sources. And so "directing" I don't think is quite the right phrase to use.

NIELDS: But you did from time to time give instructions about where items should be dropped—

NORTH: Yes.

NIELDS: —when they should be dropped, how they should be dropped?

NORTH: Well, again, I mean they are going to be dropped by parachute, number one. But I would have communications in—that would indicate we needed a unit in a certain place, needed a certain number of items, and I would pick up the phone and—the KL-43 [an encryphon machine]—and ask those guys to see if they could do that. Sometimes they could, sometimes they couldn't.

* * *

NIELDS: Was the President of the United States aware of your—the fact that you were running a resupply operation in Nicaragua?

NORTH: Again, I have absolutely no idea of what the President's knowledge specifically was about what I was doing. I made every effort to keep my superiors fully apprised as to what I was doing and the effect that it was having in the region. And you have tons of documents taken from me, some of which I personally surrendered to you, and you alone and—others that were taken from my files that make that abundantly clear.

I don't know to this day what the President knew I personally was doing. I hope to God that people were keeping him apprised as to the effect of it, because if we had not done it, there wouldn't have been a Nicaraguan resistance around when the Congress got around to putting up a hundred million dollars for it, sir.

* * *

Misleading Congress

NIELDS: . . . I take it you did considerably more which you did not tell the committee about? [North previously acknowledged that he had made false and misleading statements to congressional committees about his involvement with the contras.]

NORTH: . . . I will tell you right now, Counsel, and all the members here gathered, that I misled the Congress. I misled—

NIELDS: At that meeting [at the White House in August 1986 with members of the House Intelligence Committee]?

NORTH: At that meeting.

NIELDS: Face to face?

NORTH: Face to face.

NIELDS: You made false statements to them about your activities in support of the contras?

NORTH: I did.

Furthermore, I did so with a purpose, and I did so with a purpose of hopefully avoiding the very kind of thing that we have before us now, and avoiding a shut-off of help for the Nicaraguan

resistance, and avoiding an elimination of the resistance facilities in three Central American countries wherein we had promised those heads of state on my specific orders, on specific orders to me—I had gone down there and assured them of our absolute and total discretion.

NIELDS: Would you—

NORTH: And I am admitting to you that I participated in preparation of documents for the Congress that were erroneous, misleading, evasive and wrong, and I did it again here when I appeared before that committee convened in the White House Situation Room, and I make no excuses for what I did.

I will tell you now that I am under oath and I was not then.

NIELDS: We do live in a democracy, don't we?

NORTH: We do, sir, thank God.

NIELDS: In which it is the people, not one Marine lieutenant colonel, that get to decide the important policy decisions for the nation?

NORTH: Yes.

NIELDS: And part of that—

NORTH: I want to point out part of that answer is that this Marine lieutenant colonel was not making all of those decisions on his own. As I indicated yesterday in my testimony, Mr. Nields, I sought approval for everything that I did.

NIELDS: But you denied Congress the facts.

NORTH: I did.

NIELDS: You denied the elected representatives of our people the facts upon which they needed to make a very important decision for this nation?

NORTH: I did because of what I have just described to you as our concerns. And I did it because we have had incredible leaks from discussions with closed committees of the Congress. . . .

NIELDS: Were you instructed to do it?

NORTH: I was not specifically instructed, no.

NIELDS: Were you generally instructed?

NORTH: Yes.

NIELDS: By whom?

NORTH: By my superiors. I—

NIELDS: Who?

NORTH: I prepared draft answers that they signed and sent.

* * *

NIELDS: As a result of the fact that the operations you have been testifying about were conducted in the covert manner that you have been testifying about, as I understand your testimony, you and others put out a false version of facts relating to the 1985 Hawk shipment.

You altered documents in official NSC files. You shredded documents shortly after you heard that representatives of the Attorney General of the United States were coming into your office to review them.

You wrote false and misleading letters to the Congress of the United States.

The Government lied to the American people about the connection to the Hasenfus plane.

You received a personal financial benefit from operating funds of the covert organization without knowing where it came from—

NORTH: Sir—

NIELDS: I am referring to the security fence.

Eight million dollars of operation funds was handled in a manner that you didn't know what had happened to it or whether it existed.

My question to you is whether this is an inevitable—these things are inevitable consequences of conducting covert operations or whether these are things that happened because of this—these two particular covert actions? If you have an answer.

NORTH: I have tried over the course of the last two days, Counsel, to answer every one of your questions accurately.

I have tried to give you answers and explanations where needed for why I did what I did and the facts as they were known to me about what others did.

I am not here to impugn the testimony of others or to make excuses for anything that I did.

I have accepted the responsibility for those things that I did and some of that has not come easily.

I would also expect, as you keep raising the American people, that the tens of thousands of American people who have written to me and communicated with me since I was relieved of my duties at the NSC and in particular over the course of the last two days, some of them seem to believe and with very, very few exceptions, perhaps 50 out of 40,000 or 50,000, perhaps 50, the remaining 50,000 or so who have communicated seem to believe that they think it is right that somebody would do something under those circumstances and I tried to do it to the very best of my abilities.

If they are found lacking, it is not for not having tried enough.

I sincerely believe that I did everything within the law. I made serious judgment errors and I have admitted those, but I tried and I don't regret having done it.

NIELDS: I have no further questions, Mr. Chairman.

INOUYE: Thank you very much.

Col. North, for the past two days, together with my colleagues on this panel, I have sat here very patiently listening to statements suggesting that Members of Congress cannot be trusted with the secrets of this land.

Although I have not discussed this in public before, but I did serve on the Intelligence Committee for eight years, serving as chairman for the first two years.

In fact, it was my assignment to organize the Intelligence Committee.

During that period, according to the Federal Bureau of Investigation, the Central Intelligence Agency and the National Security Agency, there wasn't a single leak from that Senate Select Committee on Intelligence.

I am certain you are well aware that most of the leaks in this city come from the other side of Pennsylvania [Ave.].

Secondly, I am a recipient of the Distinguished Service Medal of Intelligence, the highest non-military decoration that can be given to a non-military person. And last year just before Mr. Casey went to the hospital, he presented me with a Central Intelligence Agency medal.

Thirdly, a few days ago, Gen. [William E.] Odom, Director of the National Security Agency, communicated with me to advise me that since the creation of these two select committees, they have not seen any leaks emanating from these two committees.

I don't know who you are talking about, but I can assure you that these committees, the House and the Senate Select Committees, can be trusted.

The sessions of this day and yesterday have clearly demonstrated that if we had gone through the regular process that we have followed with all other witnesses, and that is going into Executive Session, taking depositions, we would not have had to have delays that we have experienced today over classified information.

Like you, I do not wish to see secrets of this land inadvertently and decently made public.

* * *

On July 9, 1987, North was permitted to read his opening statement. He had not been able to do so previously because committee rules require that copies of such statements be available to the committee forty-eight hours in advance. North failed to comply with the rules by holding on to his statement until his first day of testimony.

NORTH: As you all know by now, my name is Oliver North, Lieutenant Colonel, United States Marine Corps.

My best friend is my wife, Betsy, to whom I have been married for 19 years and with whom I have four wonderful children, ages 18, 16, 11, and 6.

I came to the National Security Council six years ago to work in the Administration of a great President. As a staff member, I came to understand his goals and his desires.

I admired his policies, his strength and his ability to bring our country together.

I observed the President to be a leader who cared deeply about people and believed that the interests of our country were advanced by recognizing that ours is a Nation at risk in a dangerous world—and acting accordingly.

He tried, and in my opinion succeeded, in advancing the cause of world peace by strengthening our country, by acting to restore and sustain democracy throughout the world, and by having the courage to take decisive action when needed.

I also believe that we must guard against a rather perverse side of American life and that is the tendency to launch vicious attacks and criticisms against our elected officials.

President Reagan has made enormous contributions and he deserves our respect and our admiration.

The National Security Council is in essence the President's staff. It helps to formulate and coordinate national security policy.

Some, perhaps on this committee, believe the NSC was devoid of experienced leadership. I believe that is wrong.

While at the NSC, I worked most closely with three people: Mr. Robert McFarlane, Adm. John Poindexter, and CIA Director Bill Casey.

Bud McFarlane is a man who devoted 30 years of his life to public service in a number of responsible positions.

At the NSC, he worked long hours, made great contributions, and I admire him for those efforts.

Adm. Poindexter is a distinguished Naval officer who served in a number of important positions of responsibility. He, too, was a tireless worker with a similar record of public service, and I, too, admire him greatly.

William Casey was a renowned lawyer, war veteran of heroic proportions, and a former Chairman of the SEC [Securities and Exchange Commission].

I understood that he was also a close personal friend and adviser to President Reagan.

There is nearly a century of combined public service by these three men.

As a member of the NSC staff, I knew that I held a position of responsibility, but I knew full well what my position was. I did not engage in fantasy that I was the President or Vice President or Cabinet member or even Director of the National Security Council.

I was simply a staff member with a demonstrated ability to get the job done. Over time, I was made responsible for managing a number of complex and sensitive covert operations that we have discussed here to date.

I reported directly to Mr. McFarlane and to Adm. Poindexter.

I coordinated directly with others, including Director Casey.

My authority to act always flowed, I believe, from my superiors. My military training inculcated in me a strong belief in the chain of command.

Insofar as I recall, I always acted on major matters with specific approval after informing my superiors of the facts as I knew them, the risks and the potential benefits.

I readily admit that I was action oriented, that I took pride in the fact I was counted upon as a man who got the job, and I don't mean this by way of criticism, but there were occasions when my superiors confronted with accomplishing goals or difficult tasks would simply say, "Fix it, Ollie, or take care of it."

Since graduating from the Naval Academy in 1968, I have strived to be the best Marine officer that one can be. In combat my goal was always to understand the objective, follow orders, and accomplish the mission and to keep alive the men who served under me.

One of the few good things that has come from the last seven months of worldwide notoriety has been the renewed contact that I have had with some of the finest people in the world, those with whom I served in Vietnam. Among the 50,000 or so messages of support that have arrived since I left the NSC are those who recount the horrors we lived through and who now relate stories of their families and careers.

After Vietnam I worked with my fellow officers to train good Marines to be ready in case we were called upon elsewhere in the world, but at the same time to hope that we never were. I honestly believe that any soldier who has ever been to a war truly hopes he will never see one again.

My Marine Corps career was untracked in 1981 when I was detailed to the National Security Council. I was uneasy at the beginning, but I came to believe that it was important work, and as years passed and responsibilities grew, I got further from that which I loved—the Marine Corps and Marines.

During 1984, '85 and '86, there were periods of time we worked two days in every one. My guess is that the average workday lasted at least 14 hours. To respond to various crises, the need for such was frequent and we would often go without a night's sleep hoping to recoup the next night or thereafter.

If I had to estimate the number of meetings and discussions and phone calls over that five years, it would surely be in the tens of thousands. My only real regret is that I virtually abandoned my family for work during these years, and that work consisted of my first few years on the staff as a project officer for a highly classified and compartmented national security project which is not a part of this inquiry.

I worked hard on the political-military strategy for restoring and sustaining democracy in Central America, and particularly El Salvador. We sought to achieve the democratic outcome in Nicaragua this administration still supports, which involved keeping the contras together in both body and soul. We made efforts to open a new relationship with Iran and recover our hostages. We worked on the development of a concerted policy regarding terrorists and terrorism, and a capability for dealing in a concerted manner with that threat. We worked on various crises such as TWA-847, the capture of the *Achille Lauro*, the rescue of American students in Grenada and restoration of democracy on that small island, and the U.S. raid on Libya in response to their terrorist attacks. And as some may be willing to admit, there were efforts made to work with the Congress on legislative programs.

There were many problems. I believe that we worked as hard as we could to solve them, and sometimes we succeeded and sometimes we failed. But at least we tried, and I want to tell you that I, for one, will never regret having tried.

I believe that this is a strange process that you are putting me and others through. Apparently the President has chosen not to assert his prerogatives, and you have been permitted to make the rules. You called before you the officials of the Executive Branch. You put them under oath for what must be collectively thousands of hours of testimony. You dissect that testimony to find inconsistencies and declare some to be truthful and others to be liars. You make the rulings as to what is proper and what is not proper. You put the testimony which you think is helpful to your goals up before the people and leave others out. It is sort of like a baseball game in which you are both the player and the umpire. It is a game in which you call the balls and strikes and where you determine who is out and who is safe. And in the end you determine the score and declare yourselves the winner.

From where I sit, it is not the fairest process. One thing is, I think, for certain, that you will not investigate yourselves in this matter. There is not much chance that you will conclude at the end of these hearings that the Boland Amendments and the frequent policy changes therefore were unwise, or that your restrictions should not have been imposed on the Executive Branch. You are not likely to conclude that the administration acted properly by trying to sustain the freedom fighters in Nicaragua, when they were abandoned, and you are not likely to conclude by commending the President of the United States, who tried valiantly to recover our citizens and achieve an opening for strategically vital Iran.

I would not be frank with you if I did not admit that the last several months have been very difficult for me and my family. It has been difficult to be in the front pages of every newspaper in the land day after day, to be the lead story on national television day after day, to be photographed thousands of times by bands of travelers who chase us around since November just because my name arose at the hearings.

It is difficult to be caught in the middle of the constitutional struggle between the Executive and Legislative Branches over who will formulate and direct the foreign policy of this nation.

It is difficult to be vilified by people in and out of this body, some of who have proclaimed I am guilty of criminal conduct even before they heard me. Others have said that I would not tell the truth when I came here to testify, and one member asked a person testifying before this body whether he would believe me under oath. I asked when I got here, if you don't believe me, why call me at all?

It has been difficult to see questions raised about my character and morality, my honesty, because only partial evidence was provided. And as I indicated yesterday, I think it was insensitive of this committee to place before the cameras my home address at a time when my family and I are under 24-hour armed guard by over a dozen Government agents of the Naval Investigative Service because of fear that terrorists will seek revenge for my official acts and carry out their announced intentions to kill me.

It is also difficult to comprehend that my work at the NSC, all of which was approved and carried out in the best interests of our country, has led to two massive parallel investigations staffed by over 200 people. It is mind-boggling to me that one of those investigations is criminal and that some here have attempted to criminalize policy differences between co-equal branches of Government and the Executive's conduct of foreign affairs.

I believe it is inevitable that the Congress will in the end blame the Executive Branch, but I suggest to you that it is the Congress which must accept at least some of the blame in the Nicaraguan Freedom Fighters matter.

Plain and simple, the Congress is to blame because of the fickle, vacillating, unpredictable, "on again/off again" policy toward the Nicaraguan Democratic Resistance, the so-called contras.

I do not believe that the support of the Nicaraguan Freedom Fighters can be treated as the passage of a budget. I suppose if the budget doesn't get passed on time again this year, it will be inevitably another extension of a month or two. But the contras, the Nicaraguan Freedom Fighters, are people living, breathing—young men and women who have had to suffer a desperate struggle for liberty with sporadic and confusing support from the United States of America.

Armies need food and consistent help, they need a flow of money, of arms, clothing and medical supplies. The Congress of the United States allowed the Executive to encourage them, to do battle and then abandon them. The Congress of the United States left soldiers in the field unsupported and vulnerable to their communist enemies.

When the Executive Branch did everything possible within the law to prevent them from being wiped out by Moscow's surrogates in Havana and Managua, you then had this investigation to blame the problem on the Executive Branch.

It does not make sense to me. In my opinion, these hearings have caused serious damage to our national interests. Our adversaries laugh at us and our friends recoil in horror.

I suppose it would be one thing if the Intelligence Committees wanted to hear all of this in private and thereafter pass laws which in the view of Congress make for better policies or better functioning of Government, but to hold them publicly for the whole world to see strikes me as very harmful. Not only does it embarrass our friends and allies with whom we have worked, many of whom have helped us in various programs, but it must also make them very wary of helping us again.

I believe that these hearings, perhaps unintentionally so, have revealed matters of great secrecy in the operation of our Government, and sources and methods of intelligence activities have clearly been revealed, to the detriment of our security.

As a result of rumor and speculation and innuendo, I have been accused of almost every crime imaginable, while rumors have abounded. Some media reports have suggested I was guilty of espionage for the way I handled U.S. intelligence, some have said I was guilty of treason and suggested in front of my 11-year-old daughter that I should be given the death penalty. Some said I stole $10 million, some said I was second only in power to the President of the United States, and others that I condoned drug trafficking to generate funds for the contras, or that I personally ordered assassinations, or that I was conducting my own foreign policy. It has even been suggested I was the personal confidant of the President of the United States.

These and many other stories are patently untrue. I don't

mind telling you that I am angry at what some have attempted to do to me and my family.

I believe that these committee hearings will show that you have struck some blows, but I am going to walk from here with head high and my shoulders straight because I am proud of what we accomplished. I am proud of the efforts that we made, and I am proud of the fight that we fought. I am proud of serving in the administration of a great President. I am not ashamed of anything in my professional or personal conduct.

As we go through this process, I ask that you continue to please keep an open mind. Please be open-minded and able to admit that perhaps your preliminary conclusions about me were wrong, and please also do not mistake my attitude for lack of respect. I am in awe of this great institution, just as I am in awe of the Presidency. Both are equal branches of government with separate areas of responsibility under the Constitution that I have taken an oath to support and defend, and I have done so, as many of you have.

Although I do not agree with what you are doing or the way it is being done, I do understand your interest in obtaining the facts, and I have taken an oath to tell the truth in helping you to do so.

In closing, Mr. Chairman, and I thank you for this opportunity, I would just simply like to thank the tens of thousands of Americans who have communicated their support, encouragement and prayers for me and my family in this difficult time.

Thank you, sir.

INOUYE: Thank you very much, Col. North. I wish the record to show that the panel did not amend, delete or strike out any word or words or phrases from this opening statement. Furthermore, we did not put on testimony words which we thought were helpful to our goals and leave the rest out. I am certain you will agree with me, Colonel, that every word you wanted to present to the people of the United States was presented. Isn't that correct, sir?

NORTH: Yes, Mr. Chairman, it was, and I was not referring to my testimony, but that which preceded me, sir, about me.

INOUYE: Secondly, you have suggested that these hearings have disclosed matters of great secrecy in the operation of our government and sources and methods of intelligence activities have clearly been revealed to the detriment of our national security. May I once again advise you that according to the Director of the National Security Agency, Gen. Odom, not a single bit of classified material has been leaked by activities of this joint panel.

*   *   *

[George] VAN CLEVE [House minority counsel]: What I want to do is I want to find out as best I can, and again at about the same period of time, say early to mid-1985, exactly what it was you thought that you personally as a member of the NSC staff were prohibited from doing by the Boland Amendment.

As I have reviewed your testimony yesterday, and it is not entirely clear to me, so you knew that there were restrictions being imposed on the Government by the Boland Amendment, but what was your understanding of the restrictions that applied to your activity as a member of the NSC?

NORTH: My understanding was that, first of all, we were to work to comply with Boland and that we were to work to keep alive the Nicaraguan resistance.

Second, I did not view, nor did my superiors view that the National Security Council staff was covered by Boland.

There were people who were concerned about that, and we sought and obtained legal advice to the effect that it was not; not the least of those was Director Casey.

*   *   *

False Statements

VAN CLEVE: Col. North, I don't want to ask you to repeat your testimony of yesterday afternoon, but I believe that you did admit that correspondence with Congress you drafted together with Robert McFarlane in 1985 and 1986 was misleading.

NORTH: It was indeed.

VAN CLEVE: You have also admitted you altered some of the documents in which you most clearly described your role and Mr. McFarlane's role in assisting the contras; is that correct?

NORTH: I did.

VAN CLEVE: I take it you intended to mislead the Congress?

NORTH: I did.

VAN CLEVE: If you weren't violating the Boland Amendment, why was it necessary?

NORTH: I want to, first of all, say that I am not justifying that either. I happen to have very high regard for Chairman [of the House Select Committee investigating the Iran-contra affair, Lee H.] Hamilton [D-Ind.], and any of the things that I have said about leaks from the Congress, I did not mean to impugn Congressman Hamilton or Sen. Inouye.

What I was concerned about—and I think my superiors were concerned about—is the fact that we had lives at risk, we had a program at great risk. I do not believe that there ought to be circumstances in which people like myself have to make judgments over lives or lies.

And, as I advocated back in June a year ago, I think that we need to have some kind of process by which the Executive can, in and of itself, discreetly prepare to talk to discreet members of Congress about what should be done.

We, after all, have to go to the Congress to get appropriated funds. If we are to conduct covert operations as they are currently specified in the National Security Act and Hughes-Ryan [Law] and by Executive Order 12333, we have to come to the Congress to get those monies.

What I am suggesting, gentlemen, is that the process has not worked. It has been indiscreet at both ends, at both ends of Pennsylvania Avenue, and I am not justifying what I did except to say to you if I had divulged what I was doing, if Mr. McFarlane had divulged what I was doing, many, many lives were at stake.

*   *   *

Hostage Release

VAN CLEVE: Did the Iranians, to your knowledge, ever agree that all of the hostages would be released prior to or on Mr. McFarlane's arrival in Tehran?

NORTH: It turns out that the Iranians did not. Manucher Ghorbanifar told us that they had agreed to that. And what had happened was we had gone too far down the line with Ghorbanifar. What was his—his process, if you will, was to tell the Iranians one thing and tell us another. Then let the two sides sit down and duke it out.

Well, as I said, we knew Ghorbanifar for what he was. We did not know of the letters that he had sent to Tehran committing us to certain things until after we got there.

When we exchanged letters face to face with the Iranians in Tehran, it was very obvious that he had lied to both sides and we knew that he did this, but we didn't know that the lie was quite so blatant.

We had expectations from him, communicated to us directly and through the Israelis, that that would be the outcome if things went well in Tehran.

We did not know all of the expectations of the Iranians as to what it would take to make things go well. . . .

*   *   *

A Question of Lying

VAN CLEVE: Can you assure this committee you are not here now lying to protect your Commander in Chief?

NORTH: I am not lying to protect anybody, Counsel. I came here to tell the truth.

I told you that I was going to tell it to you, the good, the bad, and the ugly. Some of it has been ugly to me. I don't know how many other witnesses have gone through the ordeal that I have before arriving here and seeing their names smeared all over the newspapers and by some members of this committee. But I committed when I raised my right hand and took an oath as a midshipman that I would tell the truth, and I took an oath when I arrived here before this committee to tell the truth, and I have done so, painful though it may be for me and for others. I have told you the truth, Counsel, as best I am able.

Under questioning from Senate chief counsel Arthur L. Liman, North told the select committees July 9 that he was meant to be the fall guy for the administration if the Iran-contra affair were ever made public. North said he willingly accepted that role until he found out that he was also the subject of a criminal investigation.

LIMAN: Now, after you were dismissed [from the National Security Council], did Adm. Poindexter call you and say to you that he would confirm that he had given the authority [to conduct the arms deal and diversion of funds to the contras]?

NORTH: I honestly don't recall a conversation with Adm. Poindexter after I was dismissed. He may have called, I don't remember it.

LIMAN: Do you recall any conversation with him in which he said, "Col. North, don't worry, even if you destroy all the documents, I will stand up and say I approved it"?

NORTH: No. I recall no such conversation.

LIMAN: So that you were—once the documents were destroyed, you were out there without any kind of assurance that anyone would stand behind you; is that fair to say?

NORTH: That was the plan, and it was planned that I would be out there. Everything had gone right according to plan, right up until about 12:05 in the afternoon the next day [after November 21], or several days thereafter.

LIMAN: And when the plan changed was when you had the IC [independent counsel Lawrence E. Walsh, appointed by a panel of federal judges December 19, 1986], or the criminal investigation announced?

NORTH: Well, I don't know where—in who else's mind the plan changed, Counsel. I know that when I heard the words "criminal investigation" or criminal behavior or whatever the words were that were used in the press conference, or shortly thereafter—I don't—it was certainly profound at that point that my mind changed considerably.

LIMAN: Now, you had—

NORTH: I think if you will indulge me for a second, over the five and a half years that I had served on the NSC staff, I had, as I hope I have testified here today, sought every possible means to do what needed to be done within the law.

We had done in extremis to find a way to live within the constraints and proscriptions of Boland and I had sought a means in 1985 in working with various lawyers, various counsel, to find a way to implement a policy that started without my acquiescence or support or direction or anything else, and work very, very hard to find legal ways to carry out the policy of the President; and there was probably not another person on the planet Earth as shocked as I was to hear that someone thought it was criminal, and I can tell you that that shock was compounded when I heard later that there was to be an Independent Counsel, and further compounded when I was the only name in the appointment order for that Independent Counsel, the only person on the planet Earth named in that appointment order, Counsel.

* * *

Casey's Role

LIMAN: Col. North, as late as November 23, were you still prepared to conceal from the Attorney General facts relating to Director Casey?

NORTH: I was prepared at that point to continue not to reveal the diversion, as you put it, had even occurred. You recall, I removed those files. His people had been going through them that day. I thought I had gotten them all.

LIMAN: Well, who were you protecting?

NORTH: What do you mean, who was I protecting? I was

protecting the lives and safety of the people engaged in the operation.

LIMAN: Explain to us how telling the Attorney General of the United States that Director Casey approved a diversion would jeopardize lives, other than perhaps put him in jeopardy of the kind of investigation that you have been through?

NORTH: Well, I don't know, other than the fact that this investigation could indeed result in lives being put in jeopardy. I don't think that a specific—you know—thought went through my mind on that issue.

LIMAN: Was it just instinctive that you don't mention the name of the Director when you are talking to the Attorney General about knowledge of support for the contras?

NORTH: It was instinctive, Counsel, from my earliest days of contact with the Director, that his relationship and mine not be something that was publicly bandied about. And until these hearings, I don't believe that most people in Washington knew that the Director and I communed as often as we did.

* * *

Taking the Fall

LIMAN: Colonel, in November of 1986, after the Iranian venture had been publicized initially in Lebanon and in papers all over the world, did you discuss the diversion with Director Casey?

NORTH: Oh, sure.

LIMAN: Now tell us about that, whatever you can recall.

NORTH: Well, I don't recall the—I mean, we had several discussions about it.

LIMAN: I will take all several.

NORTH: My recollection is that Director Casey agreed with my assessment, that the time had come for someone to stand up and take the hit or the fall. He, quite frankly, did not think that I was senior enough to do that and suggested that—I am trying to recall—suggested that it was probably going to go up the line, or something like that.

LIMAN: Did he suggest who else could take the hit?

NORTH: He suggested it might be Adm. Poindexter....

LIMAN: Did he discuss anyone else who might have to take the hit?

NORTH: No. But he was concerned that the President not be damaged by it, and I shared that belief....

LIMAN: So that at the time you were having your conversation with Casey, you were still laboring under the assumption that the President of the United States knew, correct?

NORTH: Yes.

LIMAN: And did Director Casey tell you, "The President doesn't know"?

NORTH: No.

LIMAN: And when you and Director Casey were talking about the fact that someone had to take the hit, why did you understand that it was necessary for someone to take the hit?

NORTH: I think he and I certainly could see they were going to have a major international, and perhaps—and we obviously do—a domestic political drama on this thing, and that it would be helpful if someone were, as we had originally planned, when it comes time for this thing to go down the tubes, here is the guy who gets fingered for it.

And, again, none of us, at least certainly not me, and no one I ever talked to, ever imagined that we had done anything criminally wrong.

* * *

LIMAN: ... Can you explain to me, someone who has never been in a position such as yours, as to why you would be concerned about the security of documents locked in an NSC office, subject to all sorts of security regulations and access restrictions, but not concerned about keeping them at home? [After he was fired from the NSC, North took steno pads filled with personal notes about the Iran-contra affair home with him.]

NORTH: Well, again, as I said, I may have had a few of them at home, I don't really recall how many, if indeed there were. I removed the rest of them on the 25th [of November], along with several hundred pages of other documents for one purpose, and that was to protect myself.

Because after the press conference, my perspective changed, and it became one of protecting myself, and that was the reason to remove those notebooks from the NSC and take those documents from the White House with me.

Shredding Documents

LIMAN: Now, when did you do your shredding before the 25th? Which was the last preceding day in which you did shredding that was out of the ordinary?

NORTH: It is entirely likely that I was shredding documents as late as the morning of the 25th....

LIMAN: Do you remember shredding documents during the lunch hour on the 22nd when the representatives of the Attorney General's office had left for their lunch?

NORTH: I remember shredding documents while they were in there reading documents.

LIMAN: Do you remember—shredding them in their presence?

NORTH: I mean, they were sitting in my office and the shredder was right outside and I walked out and shredded documents.

LIMAN: More than a few pieces of paper, right?

NORTH: Pardon?

LIMAN: It would be more than a few pieces of paper?

NORTH: That is a pretty high-speed shredder. It eats them pretty quick.

I'm not trying to be light about it. They were sitting in my office reading and I would finish reading a document and say, "We don't need that anymore." I would walk up and I'd go out and shred it. They could hear it. The shredder was right outside the door....

LIMAN: Did anyone say to you, "Colonel, what are you doing"?

NORTH: No, and I didn't think anything of it either. What you've got to understand, Counsel, is that I didn't think I had done anything wrong.

LIMAN: Well, I understand that you—

NORTH: And I don't think that they necessarily thought I had done anything wrong....

LIMAN: Do you deny, Colonel, that one of the reasons that you were shredding documents that Saturday was to avoid the political embarrassment of having these documents be seen by the Attorney General's staff?

NORTH: I do not deny that.

* * *

LIMAN: ... You then testified that you were given a task of keeping the body and soul of the contras together, correct?

NORTH: That's correct.

LIMAN: Whose words are "the body and soul"?

NORTH: As they were relayed to me, they were the words of the President.

LIMAN: And did you understand those words to mean to keep them together in the field as a fighting force until Congress turned money back on?

NORTH: And more. To keep them together as a viable political opposition, to keep them alive in the field, to bridge the time between the time when we would have no money and the time when the Congress would vote again, to keep the effort alive, because the President committed publicly to go back, in his words, again and again and again to support the Nicaraguan resistance.

And I not only do that, but I went down and talked, as you now know from my notebooks, with the heads of states of Central America and other countries, with the political leadership of those other countries, in an effort to do just exactly that.

LIMAN: Now, did the job—

NORTH: And I also believe, sir, that that action, direction to me as a member of the President's staff, was just as legal as that proscription taking away funding.

LIMAN: And did you understand that that direction was

emanating from the President of the United States himself?

NORTH: I did....

LIMAN: Your counsel has asked to read what the Tower Board Report says, and it is in the last paragraph on the page. "The President told the Board on January 26, 1987, that he did not know that the NSC staff was engaged in helping the contras." Take that sentence. [Issued February 26, 1987, the report marked the culmination of an investigation into the Iran-contra affair by the President's Special Review Board, chaired by former senator John Tower, R-Texas]

NORTH: I read it.

LIMAN: Does that come as a surprise to you?

NORTH: Yes.

LIMAN: Now, who was it who conveyed the instructions of the President that you should keep the body and the soul of the contras together?

NORTH: Mr. Robert C. McFarlane.

LIMAN: Over the course of the period that you were at the NSC, you reported, as you have testified, regularly to Mr. McFarlane and Mr. Poindexter, Adm. Poindexter, on what you were doing to carry out this mission, correct?

NORTH: You have far more than my testimony to confirm that.

* * *

Presidential Authority

LIMAN: So, it comes down to the fact that because of your belief that the President is the sole authority on foreign policy, he could do whatever he wanted to? In that field?

NORTH: Would you repeat that question, please?

LIMAN: Does it come down to the fact that from your point of view as the action officer, the staff officer, the person who had to run this covert operation, that if the President wanted it, that was enough?

NORTH: And was within the limits of the law, that is correct.

LIMAN: As you saw it?

NORTH: Yes.

LIMAN: And when the former National Security Officer, National Security Adviser says, "I didn't know anything about this and we were complying with Boland," and when the President of the United States says, "I knew nothing about the NSC staff assisting the contras," you looked upon that as just another exercise in deniability; is that the fact?

NORTH: You will have to take that up with them, Counsel.

* * *

North resumed his testimony July 10, 1987:

LIMAN: Did you, when you returned from London with Mr. McFarlane [in December 1985], brief the President of the United States?

NORTH: I was in that briefing as I recall, yes.

LIMAN: And—

NORTH: And I probably made some contributions to it, but my recollection is that Mr. McFarlane and I went to the regular morning briefing with the President. I may be incorrect in that. It was a long time ago.

LIMAN: Did you also prepare a report on the meeting?

NORTH: I probably did. I prepared papers on almost everything.

LIMAN: Did you—do you recall telling the President of the United States that if the Iranian venture was discontinued at that time, that the lives of the hostages might be taken?

NORTH: I recall certainly very clearly putting that kind of message forward. I don't necessarily recall saying it point blank to the President that morning, but I very clearly saw that as a possibility. Certainly the Israelis did, and I think, to at least a certain extent, that was shared by the people with whom I worked at the CIA.

Our concern was that having started the route, wisely or unwisely, but having started that in August and September and having a disaster on our hands in November as a consequence of what the Iranians clearly saw as a double-cross, that we had indeed increased the jeopardy to the hostages rather than reduced it. That kind of—

LIMAN: If you look at Exhibit 51, it is a memorandum of December 9 from you to Mr. McFarlane and Adm. Poindexter. It is a December 9 memo headed "Next Steps." At page 3, in describing the options, it says, "Do nothing: very dangerous, since United States has in fact pursued earlier Presidential decision to play along with Ghorbanifar's plan. U.S. reversal now in midstream could ignite Iran fire—hostages would be our minimum losses."

Remember that, Colonel?

NORTH: Yes, I wrote this document. But I think it is important, Counsel, to point out that I was presenting forward, as I try to do in most cases, options that we had if we wished to pursue any initiative in getting our Americans back.

LIMAN: Part of your role was to point out to the President or his National Security Adviser the opportunities and the risks, correct?

NORTH: That is correct.

LIMAN: And you were pointing out the risks of abandoning further arms sales to Iran in terms of saying that they might take out reprisals on the hostages; isn't that so?

NORTH: That's correct. At the least.

LIMAN: Yes. And when you say "at the least," did Ghorbanifar make those threats or was that an opinion that you and some of your colleagues and the Israelis formed?

NORTH: I don't recall Ghorbanifar making that kind of a threat. Ghorbanifar was obviously in a very difficult situation. He had made commitments on behalf of the Israelis perhaps or others that what they were delivering in December would be responsive to what they had asked for, and he had a big problem on his hands.

At the same time, the Israelis saw their original initiative foundering. I know that Mr. [David] Kimche [former director general of Israel's foreign ministry], with whom I conversed on this both in London and before and after, expressed this kind of a view.

LIMAN: Now, at the briefing that you had with the President of the United States, did he ask Mr. McFarlane's opinion as to whether you should go forward?

NORTH: I don't recall that part of the discussion.

LIMAN: Did you express a view as to whether you should go forward?

NORTH: If I did—and again, I do not recall that specifically—but if I did, it was to advocate that we do something, that this whole thing not lead to the kind of outcome that is forecast right there.

LIMAN: You mean the loss of the hostages?

NORTH: Exactly.

LIMAN: And—

NORTH: And the potential for further reprisals. I think that is important.

LIMAN: Was there any discussion about the fact that having started down the road of dealing with Iran on arms, we were now becoming hostage to that very process?

NORTH: I always felt that way, and I think that is articulated in this memorandum.

LIMAN: And was there any discussion of the fact that if we started selling them arms, that once we stopped we were going to run the risk that more hostages would be taken?

NORTH: Yes, and there was frequently discussion of that aspect of this whole initiative. But again, and I want to make it very clear, we believed, I believed then and I still believe today, that had we been able to get to a point where we would have had a meeting with, for example, the Vice President [George Bush] and [Ali Akbar Hashemi] Rafsanjani [speaker of the Iranian parliament], which was the proposal that I had advocated at some point along in here, by virtue of intermediate-level or low-level staff contact like I was going to do, that we could get beyond that risk, and that once you had established the dialogue that we were seeking to establish, that we could in effect start working an outcome to the Iran-Iraq War which would then lead to a reduced need for this kind of thing to begin with....

LIMAN: Colonel—Colonel, there is a saying that "failure is an orphan." The committee has heard testimony and will hear

testimony that Secretary [of State George P.] Shultz was opposed to this venture, the Secretary of Defense [Caspar W. Weinberger] was opposed to it. At the meeting on December 7, the Chief of Staff [Donald T. Regan] was opposed to it. Mr. McFarlane said that when he returned from London, he was opposed to it, and testified under oath.

Had you become the principal advocate of having this program go forward?

NORTH: I don't believe I was the principal advocate. Certainly Director Casey was always a supporter of it, because he saw several objectives that could be achieved by it.

And I would simply observe that, like some of my other activities, the opposition that I heard was far more muted while we were doing it than it ever was after it failed or after it was exposed. And I kind of get the feeling, Counsel, that there were a lot of people who were kind of willing to let it go along, hoping against hope that it would succeed, and willing to walk away when it failed.

I am not necessarily advocating that that is the way things ought to be, but this was a high-risk venture. We had an established person to take the spear, and we had hoped we had established plausible deniability of a direct connection with the U.S. Government. And I am not necessarily saying that is a bad thing, high-risk operations like this or activities like this. It is understandable that people don't complain too loudly while they are happening as long as they can be assured of protection if it goes wrong.

LIMAN: Colonel, when you said there was an established person to take the spear, again you are referring to yourself? I think that can be answered yes or no.

NORTH: Yes.

* * *

LIMAN: ...Mr. Hakim testified under oath here that you told him that the President was exerting pressure on you to get the hostages back by—in time for the elections in November of 1986.

NORTH: The President of the United States never told me that, nor did any other person. I may have said that to Mr. Hakim to entice him to greater effort. But I certainly didn't hear that from the President.

LIMAN: That was your idea?

NORTH: Yes.

LIMAN: And no one in the Administration gave you that idea?

NORTH: No one ever. I can assure you, Counsel, that the President's concerns for the hostages outweighed his political ambitions or political concerns. They were truly humanitarian, and I don't think it would be right to leave any doubt about that.

In fact, the President was willing to take great political risk in pursuing this initiative.

LIMAN: Did you, when you told Hakim this, think it was right to attribute that to the President?

NORTH: Well, as you have in the tape recordings I made with every meeting I had with the Iranians, I said a lot of things that weren't true. Again, I would have told them they could have free tickets to Disney World or a trip on the Space Shuttle if it would have gotten Americans home.

LIMAN: Whose side did you think Hakim was on, the Iranians or ours?

NORTH: Oh, he is on our side.

LIMAN: Did you think that he needed inducement in order to get the deal done?

NORTH: I think exhausted men who are working very, very hard sometimes need all kinds of inducements.

* * *

Freeing the Hostages

LIMAN: Do you remember that it was, in fact, the stated policy of the President that he would try to get the hostages back by an initial shipment of TOWs, but if they didn't deliver them all it [the shipments] would stop?

NORTH: That was clearly the intent when this [the president's January 17 finding] was prepared in January [1986], that's correct. . . .

LIMAN: Did you receive instructions from Adm. Poindexter before the Tehran trip [May 1986] that there would be no delivery of arms unless all the hostages were released?

NORTH: I recall that being the specific objective, and I think that was our specific objective in each of these transactions, that we would seek to limit any further transfers unless we got them all home immediately.

But I think it is important to recognize that those of us who were engaged in the endeavor, particularly myself, Gen. Secord, Cave, recognized that there was probably going to have to be some give and take, and I think that we made every effort to achieve the primary objective, all the hostages home, and then proceed with the initiative in its broader sense as we had originally defined it, but that the Iranians were unwilling throughout—not necessarily just because of Mr. Ghorbanifar, but to proceed apace so that they did not lose all of what they considered to be their leverage.

I do not believe at any point that we had solid evidence, nor do we today—did we at the point in time when I left, anyway—that the Iranians exercised the kind of total control over the Hizballah [a pro-Iranian group that held U.S. hostages] in Lebanon that many people imagined. In other words, they, the Iranians, were unable—not just unwilling, but unable—to snap their fingers and cause all of the hostages to be released at any given moment.

LIMAN: Who was calling the shots on these negotiations for the United States?

NORTH: On the trip that I went with Mr. McFarlane, clearly he was the chief negotiator.

LIMAN: And on the instructions that preceded the trip, the authorization as to how far you could go, who called the shots on that?

NORTH: Well, certainly Adm. Poindexter gave the guidance.

* * *

LIMAN: Gen. Secord, who was over in Israel, indicated that he thought we should have grabbed the deal for the two hostages [proposed by Iran]. Did you advocate that when you were in Tehran?

NORTH: I don't know what that has to do with this.

LIMAN: Did you?

NORTH: I did.

LIMAN: And you were overruled?

NORTH: I was.

LIMAN: And you were overruled by higher authority?

NORTH: Mr. McFarlane was in charge of the trip.

LIMAN: And Mr. McFarlane was in communication with Washington?

NORTH: And so was I.

LIMAN: And were you told by Adm. Poindexter that the deal is clear, all the hostages have to be released or no more arms?

NORTH: I don't believe I communicated that directly to Adm. Poindexter. I certainly articulated my opinion to Mr. McFarlane. Mr. McFarlane made a decision and I saluted smartly and carried it out.

LIMAN: Didn't Mr. McFarlane have instructions from the President of the United States on what he could give and what he couldn't?

NORTH: Apparently so. . . .

LIMAN: Was the American foreign policy being driven to a great extent by concern about the welfare for these hostages?

NORTH: Undoubtedly it was, but I viewed, and I think certainly Adm. Poindexter viewed, and in all of my discussions with the Iranians and Israelis and others, I viewed the hostages as an obstacle. The obstacle had to be overcome like a hurdle you could proceed down the track, to use a little allegory.

What I am saying to you is that if we could have gotten beyond the hostage issue, it would have been palatable, publicly, internationally and every other way, to have meetings with high-level Iranian officials, first privately and ultimately publicly, and I viewed it all as a step-by-step process.

* * *

LIMAN: Now, you also discussed the use of the residuals of profit for the contras with Adm. Poindexter, correct?

NORTH: Correct.

LIMAN: And that was before you put it in any memoranda?

NORTH: Yes, I—and I don't recall specifically on this case—but my normal modus operandi on making a proposal such as that would be to go over and sit down with the Admiral and talk to him.

Normally the Admiral would like to think about it. I mean, the Admiral was not a hip-shooter, as I am accused of being.

LIMAN: A cautious man?

NORTH: I think so.

LIMAN: A man who is prudent, man who plays by the book?

NORTH: My sense is that he is exactly that. . . .

LIMAN: Did he discuss the risks of using the funds for the contras with you?

NORTH: Yes.

LIMAN: What did he say?

NORTH: "This had better never come out." And I took steps to ensure that it didn't, and they failed.

LIMAN: And did he discuss that with you when you first raised it, "This had better not come out"?

NORTH: I don't recall that specific discussion then. We certainly had it later.

* * *

A Secret CIA

LIMAN: Now, Director Casey was in charge of the CIA and had at his disposal an Operations Directorate, correct?

NORTH: Certainly.

LIMAN: And, as I understand your testimony, Director Casey was proposing to you that a CIA outside of the CIA be created. Fair?

NORTH: No.

LIMAN: Well, wasn't this an organization that would be able to do covert policy to advance U.S. foreign policy interests?

NORTH: Well, not necessarily all covert. The Director was interested in the ability to go to an existing, as he put it, off-the-shelf, sustaining, stand-alone entity that could perform certain activities on behalf of the United States. And as I tried to describe to the committee last night in the executive session, several of those activities were discussed with both Director Casey and with Adm. Poindexter.

Some of those were to be conducted jointly by other friendly intelligence services, but they needed money.

LIMAN: Colonel—

NORTH: Yes, Counsel.

LIMAN: You understood that the CIA is funded by the United States Government, correct?

NORTH: That is correct.

LIMAN: You understood that the United States Government put certain limitations on what the CIA could do, correct?

NORTH: That is correct.

LIMAN: And I ask you today, after all you have gone through, are you not shocked that the Director of Central Intelligence is proposing to you the creation of an organization to do these kinds of things outside of his own organization?

NORTH: Counsel, I can tell you I am not shocked. I don't see that it was necessarily inconsistent with the laws, regulations, statutes and all that obtain. I don't see that it would necessarily be unconstitutional. I don't see that it would necessarily be in any way a violation of anything that I know of. And if indeed the Director had chosen to use one of these entities out there to support an operation in the Middle East or South America or Africa, and an appropriate finding were done and the appropriate activities were authorized by the Commander in Chief, the head of state in his capacity to do so, maybe I am overly naive, but I don't see what would be wrong with that.

LIMAN: Maybe you are.

But did the Director ever tell you that he contemplated that this private organization would operate pursuant to Presidential findings?

NORTH: We never got that far.

LIMAN: Did the Director ever tell you that this private organization would be subject to oversight pursuant to the laws of the United States by Congress?

NORTH: Again, the discussion didn't get that far.

* * *

On July 13, 1987, committee members questioned North and lectured him on democracy and patriotism.

[Sen. George J.] MITCHELL [D-Maine]: The questions last week were mostly about the facts. They are important. But it is also important to consider some of the broader policy and legal issues. One of the purposes of the committee is to consider the relevant laws to see how they worked or didn't work in this case, and recommend changes in those laws, if appropriate.

In other words, to try to find out how and why these important policy decisions were made and whether we ought to change the manner in which decisions are made.

I would like to try to do that, at least to some extent, this morning; and so, perhaps, out of all of this we could all learn something.

Now, you said last week that you have obeyed the law. You haven't claimed, and I understand you don't now claim that you are in any way above or exempt from the requirements of the law; is that correct?

NORTH: That is correct, sir.

MITCHELL: And you agree, don't you, that every American, whatever his or her position, must obey the law?

NORTH: I do.

MITCHELL: That is true, even if a person doesn't agree with the particular law?

NORTH: Yes, sir.

MITCHELL: Now, if the law is properly enacted and is constitutional, but that law is in conflict with the President's policy, domestic or foreign, which is controlling, the law or the President's policy?

NORTH: Well, certainly, as I have indicated in my earlier testimony, the law is the law, and as you have also indicated in my testimony, I do not believe that any of us are above the law and certainly in this case, while I am not a lawyer, and do not profess to be able to play the various issues pro and con, I continue to believe that the President's policy was within the law, that what we did was constitutional in its essence, that the President's decisions to continue to support the Nicaraguan democratic opposition in the way that they were carried out from 1984 through my departure in 1986 fully fit within the strictures of the particular statutory constraints that were contained in Boland.

So I don't see, Senator, that there is a distance at all between what was passed and what we did. Certainly, there are folks who can argue the constitutionality of Boland as to whether or not the Congress has the authority to tell a President that he can or cannot ask a Head of State or send his agents, in this case myself, out to talk to foreign leaders.

It is my understanding of the Constitution and the laws that there is no separation between what we did and the Boland constraints. In my going out to talk with foreign Heads of State or foreign leaders or to arrange for non-U.S. Government monies to be used, that met the rigorous constraints imposed by Boland.

* * *

MITCHELL: . . . Now, of course, the concern which you expressed about leaks is a real one. There have been leaks by Members of Congress and I believe every member of this committee joins me in dismay when a Member of Congress leaks sensitive information. But let's be clear. The fact that a few Members of Congress leak doesn't mean that all Members of Congress leak. Just as the fact that some members of the Administration leak cannot be fairly said to mean that all members of the Administration leak.

Now obviously just in these matters, generally every time you tell one person a secret you increase the odds that the secret won't be kept. So there has to be a judgment. How much benefit does the President get from the advice of independently elected congressional leaders against how much the risk of leak increases by their knowledge.

Let's apply that to the facts of this case. Many people in the Executive Branch of our Government knew. Private American citizens, some without security clearances, knew. Some Israelis knew, some of them government officials, some private citizens. Some Iranian officials knew. Some Canadians knew. At least one Saudi Arabian knew. And Mr. Ghorbanifar, an Iranian citizen, who you said is an Israeli agent and who you and others have described as a liar and a cheat, he knew.

In those circumstances, how much would the risk of disclosure have been increased by telling eight of the highest elected officials in the United States Congress, and against that, how much did the President lose when he was deprived of the independent advice of those eight officials?

* * *

Covert Operations

MITCHELL: You made a strong statement in favor of covert action. Gen. Secord made a similar statement when he was here. Let me assure you there's no dispute on the need for some covert action. I know of no member of this committee who favors prohibiting all covert action. We all recognize that there are going to be circumstances in which the United States simply must conduct covert actions in the national interest; but the problem is that covert actions by their very nature conflict in some respects with democratic values.

You've said that covert actions require secrecy and deception. Our democratic process places a high value on the very opposite characteristics of openness and truth. So the real question and the much more difficult question is how to conduct covert operations in an open, democratic society in a lawful manner, in which public officials are accountable for their acts.

So my first question to you is, do you believe that the President has unrestricted power to conduct covert action?

NORTH: Within the limits of the constitutional authority to prosecute the foreign policy of the United States, the President has a very wide mandate to carry out activities, secretly or publicly, as he chooses.

Well, I do not believe that the things we did in pursuing the two principal covert actions we have discussed and some of the subsidiary activities that were pursued as a consequence of the revenues generated were in any way prohibited; and the fact is that the President, since the founding of the Republic, has always held that he could send his agents, he could discuss things and negotiate with foreign leaders, and to do so within the framework of the constitutional authority as the head of state and the Commander in Chief has widely been held to be within his Presidential purview.

* * *

MITCHELL: . . . You have talked here often eloquently about the need for a democratic outcome in Nicaragua. There's no disagreement on that. There's disagreement as how best to achieve that objective. Many Americans agree with the President's policy; many do not. Many patriotic Americans, strongly anti-communist, believe there's a better way to contain the Sandinistas, to bring about a democratic outcome in Nicaragua and to bring peace to Central America.

Many patriotic Americans are concerned in the pursuit of democracy abroad we not compromise it in any way here at home. You and others have urged consistency in our policies, you have said repeatedly that if we are not consistent our allies and other nations will question our reliability. That is a real concern. But if it's bad to change policies, it's worse to have two different policies at the same time; one public policy and an opposite policy in private. It's difficult to conceive of a greater inconsistency than that. It's hard to imagine anything that would give our allies more cause to consider us unreliable than that we say one thing in public and secretly do the opposite. And that's exactly what was done when arms were sold to Iran and arms were swapped for hostages.

Now, you have talked a lot about patriotism and the love of our country. Most nations derive from a single tribe, a single race; they practice a single religion. Common racial, ethnic, religious heritages are the glue of nationhood for many. The United States is different; we have all races, all religions, we have a limited common heritage. The glue of nationhood for us is the American ideal of individual liberty and equal justice. The rule of law is critical in our society. It's the great equalizer, because in America everybody is equal before the law. We must never allow the end to justify the means where the law is concerned. However important and noble an objective, and surely democracy abroad is important and is noble. It cannot be achieved at the expense of the rule of law in our country. . . .

Now, you have addressed several pleas to this committee, very eloquently. None more eloquent than last Friday when in response to a question by Rep. [Dick] Cheney [R-Wyo.] you asked that Congress not cut off aid to the contras for the love of God and for the love of country. I now address a plea to you. Of all the qualities which the American people find compelling about you, none is more impressive than your obvious deep devotion to this country. Please remember that others share that devotion and recognize that it is possible for an American to disagree with you on aid to the contras and still love God and still love this country just as much as you do.

Although he's regularly asked to do so, God does not take sides in American politics. And in America, disagreement with the policies of the Government is not evidence of lack of patriotism.

I want to repeat that: In America, disagreement with the policies of the Government is not evidence of lack of patriotism.

Indeed, it is the very fact that Americans can criticize their Government openly and without fear of reprisal that is the essence of our freedom, and that will keep us free.

I have one final plea. Debate this issue forcefully and vigorously as you have and as you surely will, but, please, do it in a way that respects the patriotism and the motives of those who disagree with you, as you would have them respect yours.

* * *

[Sen. Orrin G.] HATCH [R-Utah]: Now, I'll just be honest with you. Based upon what I have heard thus far, with your admission of mistakes, with your admission of some of the things you did you feel were wrong in retrospect—and it's always easier to do these things in retrospect—I don't want you prosecuted. I don't. I don't think many people in America do. And I think there's going to be one lot of hell raised if you are. That doesn't mean they won't. It doesn't mean that sticklers in the law won't pursue the last pound of flesh, but I'll tell you, I don't want you prosecuted.

Now, there may be something in the remaining part of this testimony or these hearings that might change my attitude, but as of right now, I don't want that to happen. And I don't think many people who've watched this, whether they believe in what you did or didn't, want that to happen.

* * *

[Sen. Paul S.] SARBANES [D-Md.]: . . . Once we start going down the path of people saying, "Well, we are not going to respect that decision that has been made through the constituted channels, we are going to go outside of it, shroud it in secrecy," then I think we are facing very deep difficulties. And that is why I simply close by making the point that the depth of one's conviction and the well-meaning aspect to it is not enough in and of itself. That view has to prevail.

Now, you have been very persuasive, you have been persuasive in the past as you have dealt with the Congress and with others. But the essence of our constitutional system, the thing that makes it respected throughout the world, it commands the allegiance and the support of the American people is that it gives us a process by which we can resolve these sharply held differences among ourselves, and we have to maintain that process. The substantive goal does not justify compromising the means we have put into place.

* * *

[Sen. William S.] COHEN [R-Maine]: . . . Long after the sheer force of your personality has faded from this room, and that may be a very long time indeed, and long after these cameras that are here today are clicked off, I think the American people are going to be left to deal with the policy implications of what has occurred and what has been said in this room.

Number one, and this is somewhat disturbing to me, but we will have to resolve this as a committee or committees in the Congress or country. We will have to determine whether any Administration can avoid complying with an established law by going black, as it has been said, or taking it covert.

And then, once having decided to take a program covert, whether notice can be withheld by a President in his sole discretion until such time as he decides or she decides if the action is completed, which could be days, it could be weeks, it could be months, or in this case, even possibly years.

Number two, we are going to have to decide whether even in covert actions, deception should be practiced upon Congress by deletion or official documents reduced to confetti while false statements are given to public officials. I think the answer is quite clear on that.

Number three, whether those in the Executive Branch may authorize the covert sale of U.S. assets, inflate the prices to be paid, and then fund programs that were either not known or authorized by Congress, and in fact, maybe even rejected by Congress.

Number four, whether it is appropriate to use private entrepreneurs to carry out covert objectives without specific and very rigid guidelines to make sure that profit motives don't contradict or corrode the public purpose.

Number five, whether it is a tolerable practice to authorize a covert solicitation of foreign countries to pay for programs either not authorized by Congress or rejected by Congress. . . .

The final point would be whether Congress should adopt policies that deal as severely with Members of Congress who reveal our Nation's secrets as they would with those who would lie about them. And that I think we call—calls for a resounding yes by members of this committee and this Congress. We must deal as severely with ourselves as we would with those who would lie to cover up any covert activity.

Finally, I want to just recall the words of Gen. [John K.] Singlaub [a contra supporter]. I know he is somebody that you admire. He has appeared before this committee. I think we are all satisfied of his dedication and patriotism. He retired from the Army because he was upset. He was upset because President [Jimmy] Carter had declared a unilateral withdrawal of troops from South Korea. . . .

After his retirement, he said the following. He said, "This Administration doesn't want to hear anything that is contrary to the decisions they have already made. That is a bad thing. It is the first symptom of a totalitarian regime when you start rejecting any legitimate criticism, any advice from the loyal opposition."

Well, if Gen. Singlaub is right, and we have to ask what it means to reject not the voice of the loyal opposition, but the voice of the majority in Congress and the country. Because I think that has been clear by—on the part of a number of us. Democracy demands not only that the rights of the minority be protected, but that the rules of the majority be respected. That is true even if you and I believe the majority is wrong.

We have to respect the rule of law until we can change the law itself, because otherwise the rule of law will be reduced to the law of rule. I think that is one of the central lessons of this hearing.

* * *

[Rep. Peter W.] RODINO [Jr., D-N.J.]: Col. North, when Adm. Poindexter told you that the President did not know [of the diversion], that was a result of your having asked him whether or not the President knew?

NORTH: Yes, sir. My recall on that is that on the 21st [of November] the Attorney General had told him, I mean this is the way it was conveyed to me, that he was going to conduct a fact-finding inquiry into the activities that had occurred in 1985. Specifically the August, September and November transfers of Israeli equipment to Iran. And as a consequence of that inquiry in which the Admiral told me to lay out everything, I told him that I had destroyed the references to the use of residuals to support the Nicaraguan Resistance, and I specifically asked him, as I remember it, "By the way, does the President know about this?" Since it's my recollection he had said that the President had asked the Attorney General to look into this. And he at that point said, no, the President does not know about it.

RODINO: Did Adm. Poindexter tell you that he had talked with the President and learned that he didn't know?

NORTH: No. As I remember, it was a very brief conversation, and I think basically just the way I described it to you as I remember.

RODINO: Did you ask him whether or not the five memos which you had sent forward requesting that the President be advised had been sent forward for the President's knowledge?

NORTH: No, because I had—what precipitated this conversation was my assurance to him that those memoranda no longer existed.

RODINO: Was this a surprise to you?

NORTH: I think so, yes. But by that point in time I was one, exhausted, and, number two, I suppose nothing much surprises you after that point.

RODINO: Did this, Col. North, at this point then send a flash through your mind that now you were the fall guy, that this was what was being said to you?

NORTH: No, not at all. Because in that same conversation I told the Admiral again that I thought I ought to go right away, that I ought to live now in an effort to diffuse this thing. Director Casey had by that point suggested to me it was probably going to take someone above my pay grade as he put it or above my level at the NSC or within the Administration to take this on the nose as it were. And I thought that we at least ought to make an effort to diffuse it at the lowest level possible before it worked its way up.

* * *

Taking the Fifth

[Rep. Jack] BROOKS [D-Texas]: Col. North, I want to thank you for your testimony before these committees. As you know, I didn't vote to grant you immunity from prosecution because of the general principle, I think, government officials should be fully accountable for their actions.

You have stated numerous times during the past few days that you didn't think you had broken any laws. You may not have. In any case, you felt so strongly, if you felt so strongly that you hadn't, I had a little difficulty understanding your reluctance to testify without immunity.

NORTH: It is very simple.

BROOKS: Nevertheless, you—

SULLIVAN: Excuse me.

BROOKS: Counsel, did you have an answer to a question?

SULLIVAN: I was so shocked at your statement with regard to the Fifth Amendment that I interrupted before you were through. I want to apologize. You may—

BROOKS: That is a new first for you.

SULLIVAN: Well, I interrupt when I find things so appalling, Congressman.

BROOKS: Yes.

SULLIVAN: Do you know anything about the Fifth Amendment and its purpose?

BROOKS: I said, and I would say again, I had a little difficulty understanding why the Colonel, if he thought he had broken no laws whatsoever, was reluctant, it seemed in discussions with the counsel for the committee and with you about immunity. I didn't vote for it. And if you don't like that, I am sorry.

SULLIVAN: I don't care if you voted for immunity. We prefer not to be up here at all.

BROOKS: Thank you.

SULLIVAN: But don't ask any questions about the Fifth Amendment.

BROOKS: Mr. Chairman, I have had quite enough listening to Mr. Sullivan. He is a distinguished criminal lawyer, but you know we didn't hire him as our lawyer, and I don't need him to advise me.

INOUYE: I believe this exchange has just convinced the Chair, as I feared, that about this time we all get testy. . . .

* * *

RUDMAN: I want to talk to you about Director Casey's legal opinions. And I want to start out by saying that I have concluded at the end of your testimony but actually before you came here, in reviewing literally hundreds and thousands of documents, that you indeed were authorized to do what you did in terms of the policies.

I'm not going to talk about the collateral issues—shredding, statements to the Congress, other personal matters—but the basic things that you did, not only is your testimony candid and believable, but it is true, it is supported, and it is corroborated by other witnesses. . . .

I guess the last thing I want to say to you, Colonel, is that the American people have the constitutional right to be wrong. And what Ronald Reagan thinks or what Oliver North thinks or what anybody thinks makes not a wit.

If the American people say enough, and that's why this Congress has been fickle and has vacillated, that's correct, but not because the people here necessarily believe differently than you do, but there comes a point that the views of the American people have to be heard.

* * *

On July 14, 1987, panel members wrapped up their questions for North and made their concluding statements.

[Sen. Sam] NUNN [D-Ga.]: Mr. McFarlane testified he had no knowledge of your activities with the private group raising funds for the contras. Specifically, quoting from his testimony, Mr. Liman asked him: "Were you involved at all in the activities of the Channell group to obtain moneys from the contras?"

Mr. McFarlane replied: "No, I wasn't."

Mr. Liman went on: "Did you know that Col. North was involved with them?"

Mr. McFarlane answered: "No, I didn't."

Now, could I ask you, Col. North, if Mr. McFarlane is correct on that point or was he in error?

NORTH: Sen. Nunn, I have over five and a half days, in some very difficult testimony, testified as to what I did and the authorities that I had to do it as I understood them.

One of the most difficult positions that a person can be in is to be in a situation where they are forced to contradict the testimony of anyone. I believe that within the volumes, as Mr. Liman has described them, of documents that were taken from my office is ample evidence that I sought approval from my superiors, that I kept them fully informed, and that I did nothing without permission. And I want that made very clear.

I did not come here to impugn the testimony of others. I did not come here to contradict others. But I have told you honestly and straightforwardly what I did. Some of it has been very, very unpleasant for me, as I am sure you know, and very difficult.

NUNN: Did you get authority from Mr. McFarlane for the activities in fund raising?

NORTH: There was never a speech that I made or a presentation I made that I didn't get approval to actually conduct that. . . .

NUNN: . . . Did you inform Mr. McFarlane that you were asking Ambassador [to Costa Rica Lewis A.] Tambs to open up the southern front?

NORTH: Yes, sir.

NUNN: So you had specific authority from Mr. McFarlane in respect to the airlift [of supplies to the contras] and Gen. Secord's participation therein?

NORTH: Everything that I have testified to, Sen. Nunn, is exactly the way it happened. Everything.

NUNN: One other point I want to ask along this line. Is it clear in your mind that you never received instructions from Mr.

McFarlane in regard to soliciting contributions?

I believe that he testified very clearly—I won't read all of it—that he did give instructions to his staff in the NSC not to in any way solicit contributions for the contras.

NORTH: And I never solicited contributions.

NUNN: I understand that.

The question really is—you made that very clear—did you get these instructions from him? Do you remember receiving those instructions?

NORTH: I may have been told to separate myself from dollar operations, or however one calls it, but I was very much of the understanding that I personally would not sit and solicit.

Every single activity that I conducted, as I described them to this committee, I conducted with the authority of my superiors; and to this day, Sen. Nunn, I do not believe any of them to be illegal. I don't now. . . .

* * *

The Boland Amendment

[Rep. Edward P.] BOLAND [D-Mass.]: Colonel, in my judgment, the law [the Boland amendment] was clear. It authorized the provision of certain types of intelligence information to the contras. It did not authorize CIA officials to coordinate the aerial supply or resupply of arms to the contra units in the field.

As you might agree, the supply of fighting units in the field is a military operation, and CIA participation in that type of operation was not authorized by law. That is correct, isn't it?

NORTH: I am not certain of that, Mr. Boland. In fact, it was my understanding that at the time these things were being done—

BOLAND: Wasn't the CIA barred from getting into any military operations, under the amendment?

NORTH: It certainly was barred from expending funds for those purposes. No doubt about it.

BOLAND: Was—and what was your understanding of the level of knowledge of CIA official Duane Clarridge in the Secord contra supply operation?

NORTH: My sense is that he had a general knowledge of the activities.

BOLAND: Did Clarridge assist the Secord operation in any way and, if so, in what way?

NORTH: I would say that his assistance was principally one of advising me on procedures. I don't believe he ever talked directly to any of those people involved and I don't believe he talked to any of the field officers involved.

I'm not certain of that, but I don't believe he did. But he certainly—he and I talked a good bit. I valued his expertise.

BOLAND: Are you aware of any efforts by Mr. Clarridge to provide the contras with weapons between June of 1984 and October of 1986?

NORTH: I'm talking off the top of my head now, Mr. Boland, but I do not know of any circumstances in which he was involved in those time periods with weapons.

BOLAND: Now, you've testified in great detail about Director Casey's knowledge of and interest in your activities on behalf of the contras.

What degree of control did he exert over these—did he exert over these activities?

You testified that on one occasion in connection with another activity Mr. Casey told you to get a ship, and you got a ship.

Was there ever a time when Director Casey told you to do something that you didn't do it?

NORTH: I didn't get a lawyer soon enough. . . .

BOLAND: . . . Now, you have testified that you had been advised that the National Security Council was not covered by the Boland Amendment. It won't surprise you to learn, I suppose, that I believe that that advice was wrong. I don't think we have to debate the coverage of NSC here with you.

I only want to know this. The CIA was covered by the Boland Amendment, so that the DoD [Department of Defense] and also the State Department, because everyone knows the State Department is an intelligence—has an intelligence capability. Why do you believe you had the ability to direct employees of those agencies to do things which the law said they couldn't do?

NORTH: Congressman Boland, I will take issue again with the word "direct." I certainly solicited from them help. If I didn't solicit money, I sought help, and I did seek a lot of that, and they provided it.

My understanding of the Boland proscription was that funds could not be expended for those purposes, and I don't know that any of those people engaged ever expended a nickel on behalf of the programs that I sought their help for.

BOLAND: Incidentally, the Boland Amendment in effect from October 1984 until October 1986 spoke about "funds available" to the CIA, DoD, or any other agency or entity of the United States involved in intelligence activities.

Would it surprise you to learn that Congress chose those particular words because it understood that the CIA, for example, operates proprietaries, and those proprietaries have funds available to them, and thus the CIA—which are not appropriated—but the funds would be available to the CIA even though not appropriated, but which Congress still wanted to include within the Boland proscriptions?

You've described the residuals in the Iran arms sales transactions as intended to support Director Casey's off-the-shelf covert operations entity. Weren't the residuals therefore funds available to the CIA?

NORTH: No, sir. The CIA never had—except for those monies transferred to the CIA from those entities to pay for weapons purchased under the Economy Act [a law controlling purchases between government agencies] from the DoD, the CIA never had available to it a nickel.

* * *

HAMILTON: . . . What strikes me is that despite your very good intentions, you were a participant in actions which catapulted a President into the most serious crisis of his Presidency, drove the Congress of the United States to launch an unprecedented investigation, and I think probably damaged the cause or the causes that you sought to promote.

It is not my task, and it is not the task of these committees, to judge you. As others have said, we are here to learn what went wrong, what caused the mistakes and what we can do to correct them. And the appropriate standard for these committees is whether we understand the facts better because of your testimony, and I think we do, and we are grateful to you.

In your opening statement you said that these hearings have caused serious damage to our national interest. But I wonder whether the damage has been caused by these hearings or by the acts which prompted these hearings. I wonder whether you would have the Congress do nothing after it has been lied to and misled and ignored.

Would we in the Congress then be true to our constitutional responsibilities? Is it better under our system to ignore misdeeds, or to investigate them behind closed doors as some have suggested, or is it better to bring them into the open and try to learn from them?

I submit that we are truer to our Constitution if we choose the latter course. . . .

I agree with you when you said in your opening statement that you were caught in a struggle between the Congress and the President over the direction of American foreign policy, and that most certainly is not your fault. And I agree with you that the Congress, whose record in all of this is certainly not unblemished, also must be accountable for its actions.

Now, let me tell you what bothers me. I want to talk about two things: first policy, and then process.

Chairman Inouye correctly said that the business of these select committees is not policy, and I agree with him. But you made such an eloquent and impassioned statement about policy that I wanted to comment.

I am very troubled by your defense of secret arms sales to Iran. There is no disagreement about the strategic importance of Iran or the desirability of an opening to Iran. My concern is with the means employed to achieve those objectives.

The President has acknowledged that his policy as implemented was an arms-for-hostage policy, and selling arms to Iran in secret was, to put it simply, bad policy. The policy contradicted and undermined long-held, often articulated, widely supported public policies in the United States. It repudiated U.S. policy to make no concessions to terrorists, to remain neutral in the Gulf war, and to stop arms sales to Iran.

We sold arms to a nation officially designated by our government as a terrorist state. This secret policy of selling arms to Iran damaged U.S. credibility. A great power cannot base its policy on an untruth without a loss of credibility. Friendly governments were deceived about what we were doing. You spoke about credibility of U.S. policy in Central America. You were right about that. But in the Middle East, mutual trust with some friends was damaged, even shattered. The policy of arms-for-hostages sent a clear message to the states of the Persian Gulf, and that message was that the United States is helping Iran in its war effort and making an accommodation with the Iranian Revolution and Iran's neighbors should do the same.

The policy provided the Soviets an opportunity they have now grasped and with which we are struggling to deal. The policy achieved none of the goals it sought. The Ayatollah [Ruhallah Khomeini, Iran's religious leader] got his arms, more Americans are held hostage today than when this policy began, subversion of U.S. interests throughout the region by Iran continues, moderates in Iran—if any there were—did not come forward, and today these moderates are showing fidelity to the Iran Revolution by leading the charge against the United States in the Persian Gulf.

In brief, the policy of selling arms to Iran, in my view at least, simply cannot be defended as in the interests of the United States. There were and there are other means to achieve that opening which should have been used.

Now, let me comment on process as well. First, with regard to the covert actions, you and I agree that covert actions pose very special problems for a democracy. It is, as you said, a dangerous world, and we must be able to conduct covert actions, as every member of this panel has said, but it is contrary to all that we know about democracy to have no checks and balances on them. We established a lawful procedure to handle covert actions. It is not perfect by any means, but it works reasonably well.

In this instance, those procedures were ignored. There was no Presidential finding in one case and a retroactive finding in another. The Intelligence committees of the Congress were not informed, and they were lied to. Foreign policies were created and carried out by a tiny circle of persons, apparently without the involvement of even some of the highest officials of our government. The administration tried to do so secretly what the Congress sought to prevent it from doing. The administration did secretly what it claimed to all the world it was not doing. Covert action should always be used to supplement, not to contradict, our foreign policy. It should be consistent with our public policies. It should not be used to impose a foreign policy on the American people which they do not support.

Mr. McFarlane was right. He told these committees it was clearly unwise to rely on covert action as the core of our policy; and, as you noted in your testimony, and I agree with you, it would have been a better course to continue to seek contra funding through open debate. You have spoken with compelling eloquence about the Reagan Doctrine. Laudable as that doctrine may be, it will not succeed unless it has the support of the Congress and the American people....

As you would expect, I am bothered by your comments about the Congress. You show very little appreciation for its role in the foreign policy process. You acknowledge that you were "erroneous, misleading, evasive, and wrong" in your testimony to the Congress. I appreciate, sir, that honesty can be hard in the conduct of government, but I am impressed that policy was driven by a series of lies: lies to the Iranians, lies to the Central Intelligence Agency, lies to the Attorney General, lies to our friends and allies, lies to the Congress, and lies to the American people.

So often during these hearings, not just during your testimony, but others as well, I have been reminded of President Thomas Jefferson's statement: "The whole art of government consists in the art of being honest."

Your experience has been in the Executive Branch, and mine has been in the Congress. Inevitably our perspectives will differ. Nonetheless, if I may say so, you have an extraordinarily expansive view of Presidential power. You would give the President free rein in foreign affairs. You said on the first day of your testimony, and I quote, "I didn't want to show Congress a single word on this whole thing."

I do not see how your attitude can be reconciled with the Constitution of the United States. I often find in the Executive Branch, in this administration, as well as others, a view that the Congress is not a partner but an adversary. The Constitution grants foreign policy-making powers to both the President and the Congress and our foreign policy cannot succeed unless they work together. You blame the Congress as if the restrictions it approved were the cause of mistakes by the administration; yet Congressional restrictions in the case of Nicaragua—if the polls are accurate—reflected the majority of the American people....

Your opening statement made the analogy to a baseball game. You said the playing field here was uneven and the Congress would declare itself the winner. I understand your sentiments, but may I suggest that we are not engaged in a game with winners and losers. That approach, if I may say so, is self-serving and ultimately self-defeating. We all lost.

The interests of the United States have been damaged by what happened. This country cannot be run effectively when major foreign policies are formulated by only a few, and are made and carried out in secret, and when public officials lie to other nations and to each other.

One purpose of these hearings is to change that. The self-cleansing process, the Tower Commission, and these joint hearings, and the report which will follow, are all part, we hope, of a process to reinvigorate and restore our system of government.

I don't have any doubt at all, Col. North, that you are a patriot. There are many patriots in this country, fortunately, and many forms of patriotism. For you, perhaps patriotism rested in the conduct of deeds, some requiring great personal courage, to free hostages and fight communism. And those of us who pursue public service with less risk to our physical well-being admire such courage.

But there's another form of patriotism which is unique to democracy. It resides in those who have a deep respect for the rule of law and faith in America's democratic traditions. To uphold our Constitution requires not the exceptional efforts of the few but the confidence and the trust and the work of the many.

Democracy has its frustrations. You've experienced some of them, but we—you and I—know of no better system of government; and when that democratic process is subverted, we risk all that we cherish....

* * *

Inouye's Advice

INOUYE: . . . I believe during the past week, we have participated in creating and developing very likely a new American hero. Like you, who has felt the burning sting of bullet and shrapnel and heard the unforgettable and frightening sounds of incoming shells, I salute you, sir, as a fellow combat man; and the rows of ribbons that you have on your chest forever remind us of the courageous service and your willingness, your patriotic willingness to risk your life and your limb.

I am certain the life and burdens of a hero will be difficult and heavy; and so, with all sincerity, I wish you well as you begin your journey into a new life.

However, as an interested observer, and as one who has participated in the making of this new American hero, I found certain aspects of your testimony to be most troubling. Chairman Hamilton has eloquently discussed them.

Because, as a result of your very gallant presence, and your articulate statements, your life, I am certain, will be emulated by many, many young Americans. I am certain we will, all of us, receive an abundance of requests from young citizens throughout the land for entrance into the privileged ranks of cadets of the Military Services.

These young citizens, having been imbued with the passion of patriotism, will do so; and to these young men and women, I wish to address a few words:

In 1964, when Col. North was a cadet, he took an oath of office like all hundreds throughout the service academies. And he also said that he will abide with the regulations which set forth the cadet honor concept.

The first honor concept, first because it is so important, over and above all others, is a very simple one: A member of the brigade does not lie, cheat, or steal. And in this regulation of 1964, the word "lie" was defined as follows:

"A deliberate oral or written untruth; it may be an oral or written statement which is known to be false or simple response to a question in which the answer is known to be false."

The words "mislead" or "deceive" were defined as follows: "A deliberate misrepresentation of a true situation by being untruthful or withholding or subtly wording information in such a way as to leave an erroneous or false impression of a known true situation."

And when the Colonel put on his uniform and the bars of a Second Lieutenant, he was well aware that he was subject to the Uniform Code of Military Justice. It is a special code of laws that apply to our men and women in uniform.

It is a code that has been applicable to the conduct and activities of Colonel North throughout his military career, and even at this moment. And that code makes it abundantly clear that orders of a superior officer must be obeyed by subordinate members. But it is lawful orders.

The uniform code makes it abundantly clear that it must be the lawful orders of a superior officer.

In fact, it says, "Members of the military have an obligation to disobey unlawful orders."

. . . Col. North, I am certain it must have been painful for you as you stated to testify that you lied to senior officials of our Government, that you lied and misled our Congress and believe me it was painful for all of us to sit here and listen to that testimony. It was painful.

It was equally painful to learn from your testimony that you lied and misled because of what you believed to be a just cause, supporters of Nicaraguan fighters, the contras.

You have eloquently articulated your opposition to Marxism and communism and I believe that all of us, I am certain all of us on this panel, are equally opposed to Marxism and communism.

But should we in the defense of democracy adopt and embrace one of the most important tenets of communism and Marxism, the ends justify the means?

This is not one of the commanders [*sic*] of democracy. Our Government is not a Government of men, it is still a Government of laws.

And finally, to those thousands upon thousands of citizens who have called, sent telegrams, and written letters, I wish to thank all of you most sincerely and commend you for your demonstrated interest in the well being of our Government, of our freedoms and our democracy.

Your support or opposition of what is happening in this room is important, important because it dramatically demonstrates the strength of this democracy. . . .

Throughout the past 10 days, many of my colleagues on this panel in opening their questions to the Colonel, prefaced their marks by saying, "Colonel, I am certain you know that I voted for the aid to the contras."

Ladies and gentlemen and Col. North, I voted against aid to the contras. I did so not as a communist. I did so not as an agent of the KGB. I did so upon information that I gathered as a member of the bipartisan Commission on Central America[,] based upon information that I gathered as Chairman of the Foreign Operations Committee, based upon information that I gathered as a senior member of the Defense Subcommittee, and based upon information that I gathered as Chairman and a Member of the Senate Intelligence Committee.

I voted against aid to the contras. It wasn't easy to vote

against your Commanding Chief. It is not easy to stand before my colleagues and find yourself in disagreement, but that is the nature of democracy.

I did so because I was firmly convinced that to follow the path or the course that was laid down by the Reagan proposal would certainly and inevitably lead to a point where young men and women of the United States would have to be sent into the conflict, and Colonel, I am certain, having experienced warfare, that is not what we want our young people to go through again.

John M. Poindexter

Following are excerpts from the July 15, 1987, testimony of Rear Adm. John M. Poindexter, one of the most important witnesses to appear before the special panel investigating the Iran-contra affair. Poindexter said President Reagan had not known about the diversion of funds from the Iranian arms sale to the contras. The admiral also said that Reagan had authorized the "arms-for-hostages" deal.

[Arthur L.] LIMAN [Senate committee chief counsel]: Now, Admiral, did there come a time in connection with this transaction [the November 1985 Hawk shipment to Iran] when the CIA sent over to you a proposed finding for the President to sign?

POINDEXTER: Yes, Mr. Liman. That is the [early December 1985] finding that I discussed with you earlier on the 2nd of May, which I destroyed.

LIMAN: Now, if we look at that finding, it is Exhibit 18 in the book, I will put it up there. Did you receive the letter of November 26, 1985, from [CIA director] William [J.] Casey addressed to you which says "Pursuant to our conversation, this should go to the President for his signature and should not be passed around in any hands below our level."

POINDEXTER: I did receive that.

LIMAN: Did you receive the finding with it? Is that correct?

POINDEXTER: Well, I must say, I don't actually remember getting it, but I am sure that I did. I am sure they came together.

LIMAN: Admiral, when you saw the finding, am I correct that the finding itself was essentially a straight arms-for-hostage finding?

POINDEXTER: That is correct. It had been prepared essentially by the CIA as a—what we call a CYA ["cover your ass"] effort.

LIMAN: Did the President of the United States sign that finding?

POINDEXTER: As I have testified before, he did, on or about the fifth of December. I am vague on the date. . . .

LIMAN: Do you recall who was present when the President signed the finding?

POINDEXTER: No, I don't. One of the things that I think my recollection is very important on the circumstances of the President actually signing this is recall that that was a day or so after Mr. [Robert C.] McFarlane had resigned [as national security adviser], and the President had just, I am not even—I guess we had announced it on the 4th.

Mr. McFarlane actually resigned on the 30th of November, we announced it on the 4th of December, and my recollection is that he signed this the following day, on the 5th.

My recollection now is that the CIA, especially the Deputy Director, John McMahon, was very anxious to get this signed. I frankly was never happy with it because it was not fully staffed, and I frankly can't recall when I showed it to the President whether—who was there or exactly what the discussion was or even what I recommended to him at this point.

I simply can't remember that.

LIMAN: But you do recall that whatever you recommended, the President read it and he signed it?

POINDEXTER: Yes, he did. He did sign it.

LIMAN: And there was, in fact, the recommendation from Bill Casey that he signed it and Bill Casey was a person whose advice the President valued?

POINDEXTER: He did.

LIMAN: What happened to that finding?

POINDEXTER: As I said earlier, I destroyed that by tearing it up on the 21st of November, because I thought it was a significant political embarrassment to the President, and I wanted to protect him from possible disclosure of this....

LIMAN: When you say the 21st of November, you are talking about the 21st of November, 1986?

POINDEXTER: 1986; that is correct.

LIMAN: Now, would you tell the panel the circumstances of your destroying this finding because you thought it would be a significant political embarrassment to the President?

POINDEXTER: I will. The finding, the existence of the finding I had completely forgotten in early November, 1986. As I said before, the finding initially was prepared by the CIA for the reason that I stated. I can recall in my time at the White House one or possibly two other findings that had a retroactive nature to them. I, frankly, was always uncomfortable with that, because I thought it didn't particularly make a lot of sense....

... [Attorney General Edwin] Ed Meese [III] and I had talked many times during the month of November, and when it became clear that there was a disagreement between Cabinet-level officials as to what had happened in November of 1985, he indicated that he wanted to come over and ask the President to have a fact-finding session, primarily with the Cabinet-level officials involved, to try to sort out what had happened, actually happened, in November of 1985.

And he called me early in the morning of the 21st of November and told me this, and he said he had an appointment to see the President at 11:30, and he wanted me and [White House chief of staff Donald T.] Don Regan to go with him, which we did, at 11:30. He told the President about the controversy—not really controversy—the different recollections as to what had happened in November and said he thought it would be useful if he would have a couple of his people that were close to him look into the matter to see if they could piece together what had happened. The President readily agreed, as I did, at that point. Because here we had Mr. McFarlane on one hand and Secretary [of State George P.] Shultz on the other hand recalling different recollections as to what had happened in the early days of November of '85.

So Ed called me after lunch, as I recall, and said he was going to send over a couple of his people either that afternoon or the next day, and I am not sure which, and he asked if I would have the appropriate documents pulled together so they could take a look at them. I said I would do that.

After he called, I called Cmdr. [Paul B.] Thompson, my military assistant, and asked him to take charge of pulling these documents together, and then I called [Lt. Col. [Oliver L.] North and told him of my conversation with Mr. Meese and asked him to cooperate with Cmdr. Thompson and Mr. Meese's people.

I called Col. North because he was very protective of the documents that he had, and I wanted to make sure that he understood the tasking that I had given Cmdr. Thompson.

Later in the afternoon or early evening, Cmdr. Thompson brought in to my office the envelopes that I had given him earlier containing the material we had on the Iranian project in the immediate office, which was essentially the various findings, and he pulled out this November finding, it was actually signed in December, and my recollection is that he said something to the effect that "They'll have a field day with this," or something to that effect.

And my recollection is that the import of his comment was that up until that time in November of 1986, the President was being beaten by the head and shoulders, that this was—the whole Iranian project was just an arms-for-hostage deal.

Well, this finding, unfortunately, gave that same impression. And I, frankly, didn't see the need for it at the time. I thought it was politically embarrassing. And so I decided to tear it up, and I tore it up, put it in the burn basket behind my desk. I can't recall, but I believe that Col. North was there in the office, but I am a little fuzzy on that point....

LIMAN: Admiral, you talked about the fact that the Presi-

dent was being beaten around the head and shoulders by the media for sanctioning an arms-for-hostage deal and that this finding seemed to corroborate it, and you, therefore, destroyed it in order to prevent significant political embarrassment.

Did you regard one of the responsibilities of the National Security Adviser to protect the President from political embarrassment?

POINDEXTER: I think that it's always the responsibility of a staff to protect their leader, and certainly in this case, where the leader is the Commander In Chief, I feel very strongly that that's one of the roles, and I don't mean that in any sense of cover-up. But one has to always put things in the President's perspective and to make sure that he is not put in a position that can be politically embarrassing.

LIMAN: Now, Admiral, a finding represents a decision of the President of the United States, correct?

POINDEXTER: It represents—a finding, I don't believe, is discussed in any statute. It is discussed in various Presidential directives. It is an artifact of what the statute calls a Presidential determination.

LIMAN: And the President, when he signed this finding, was making a determination?

POINDEXTER: That is correct. But it's important to point out that the finding, that early finding was designed for a very specific purpose, and was not fully staffed, and did not in any way ever represent the total thinking on the subject.

LIMAN: Well, the President didn't authorize you to destroy the finding, correct?

POINDEXTER: He certainly did not....

LIMAN: Admiral, I don't want to embarrass you by belaboring this any more than you want to embarrass the President. I just want to ask you this. The fact is that this finding remained in effect until January [1986], when there was a new finding. Am I correct?

POINDEXTER: That's correct. For a period of about six weeks, six or seven weeks.

LIMAN: And is it also a fact that findings get superseded or terminate all the time. Is that so?

POINDEXTER: That's correct.

LIMAN: And it is a fact that they are not destroyed just because they expire or because a new finding is adopted?

[Richard] BECKLER [Poindexter's lawyer]: Mr. Chairman, I'm going to object to that question. That is a conclusion. There is no basis for him asking that question, no foundation for it.

I would ask it be stricken.

[Rep. Lee H.] HAMILTON [D-Ind.]: Counsel, your objection is overruled.

I just want to say that I recognize, of course, Counsel is accustomed to rules of evidence in court, which, as you know, is much stricter than we have here, and for our purposes we will permit questions which go to a legislative purpose. That certainly includes the oversight responsibilities of the Congress, and it is the intention of the Chair to permit Counsel and members to have very broad leeway in asking questions.

The objection is overruled....

POINDEXTER: Mr. Liman, I honestly don't know whether other superseded findings are destroyed or not. We handled this series of three findings outside of our normal system. We did have a normal process through which most findings were managed, and I frankly don't know what the records people do with superseded findings.

LIMAN: In any event, you never destroyed a finding before that had been signed by the President?

POINDEXTER: I don't believe I did.

LIMAN: And the reason that you destroyed this was not because it was superseded but because it had the potential for political embarrassment.

BECKLER: Mr. Chairman, I have to object again. The testimony did not support that glittering generalization by Mr. Liman.

LIMAN: I withdraw the question.

HAMILTON: I think counsel has withdrawn his question.

LIMAN: Is the reason that you destroyed that finding because it would provide political embarrassment?

POINDEXTER: Yes, clearly.

* * *

Getting the Hostages Back

LIMAN: . . . It is also true that we did not want to authorize arms shipments to the Iranians unless we were assured of getting our hostages back; is that so?

POINDEXTER: As I was trying to lay out a moment ago, what our concerns were, what our major objective was, the President was clearly also concerned about the hostages. The President is a very sensitive person, and he is concerned about individuals when they are in difficulty. And so he, just as a human being, was concerned about the hostages.

I don't think that the President was overly concerned about them, but he recognized that we did have an opportunity here to try to get the hostages back, and there was no way that we could carry on discussions with Iranian officials about broader objectives until we got over the first obstacle and the first obstacle was to get the hostages back. And the President felt that—that it was worth taking some risk here.

LIMAN: Did the Secretary of State and the Secretary of Defense express objections?

POINDEXTER: They expressed, as opposed to some reports, very strong, vociferous objection, and clearly laid out for the President the other side of the issue. . . .

LIMAN: And there is no doubt in your mind that the President listened to and understood those objections?

POINDEXTER: I have a very vivid recollection of that meeting, and it was in the residence. The President pulled a footstool up to the coffee table and sat there very quietly, as is his nature, listening to all of the discussion up to that point, listening to Secretary Shultz, to Secretary [of Defense Caspar W.] Weinberger, Mr. McFarlane. I had very little comment. And I don't recall the Chief of Staff saying very much.

Mr. McMahon was there and commented a little bit about some of the technical aspects of the initiative. I had spoken to Director Casey about the meeting before it took place, and knew at that point that Director Casey was in favor of the idea.

And the President listened to all this very carefully, and at the end of the discussion, at least the first round, he sat back and he said something to the effect—and this is not a direct quote, but it was something to the effect that "I don't feel we can leave any stone unturned in trying to get the hostages back. We clearly have a situation here where there are larger strategic interests, but it is also an opportunity to get the hostages back, and I think that we ought to at least take the next step."

* * *

POINDEXTER: . . . One of the key reasons that Ed [Meese] decided or determined that the President could legally carry out such a project that involved arms—and you had testimony about this before, it goes back to the [former attorney general] William French Smith determination several years earlier on an arms issue. I understood that going into the 16 January meeting, but I didn't really understand up until that time that Ed felt that we should, rather than having the Israelis sell what was in their stock to the Iranians and then the U.S. replenish the Israeli stocks, he felt that we ought to go direct, that we ought to—

LIMAN: Why?

POINDEXTER: I will get to that, Mr. Liman.

He thought we ought to sell material out of U.S. stocks to Iran directly using the Israelis for logistics assistance. And the reason for that is that under the Arms Export Control Act, there was a congressional reporting requirement that we wanted to avoid. The President had decided, although he hadn't formally decided until he signed this [finding] on the 17th of January, but there had been discussions about whether to report this project to the Congress. I know that's a sensitive issue up here, and I think it deserves an answer on my part, but I would like to put that answer in perspective.

We had a significant problem with leaks in this administra-

tion, as with all administrations, but I frankly think that over the past five years they have gotten much worse than in earlier periods of time when I have been in Washington, and I have been here on and off for 15 or 16 years.

Now, I don't mean to imply by this that we felt, or I feel today, that all the leaks come from the Congress. That is pure nonsense. I think there are leaks that come from the Congress. There are leaks that come from the State Department. There are leaks that come from the Defense Department. There are leaks that come from the NSC [National Security Council] staff, and there are leaks that come from the White House staff. It has become an art form in this city to help influence policy.

So it wasn't simply a matter that we wanted just to postpone informing the Congress of this finding. We didn't want many people in the Executive Branch to know about it.

Our feeling was, the President's feeling was that the way that you carry out a secret covert activity is that you limit the knowledge to the absolute minimum number of people. And there were discussions about that.

I frankly don't recall anybody recommending that we do inform Congress. So some spoke against, some spoke in favor of postponing the notification as long as possible, and the President clearly agreed with that.

* * *

LIMAN: Now, Admiral, is it correct that in the discussions that you had leading up to the January 17 finding, there was no discussion with the President of the United States about the possibility of using proceeds of the sale to support the contras?

POINDEXTER: There was none.

LIMAN: And there was none with you?

POINDEXTER: There was none with me.

LIMAN: Would you tell us, and I am going to break this into different questions, when was the first time that you were told by Col. North about this possibility?

POINDEXTER: My best recollection is that this took place some time in February of 1986.

LIMAN: And would you tell us what Col. North said to you?

LIMAN: My recollection is that he had just come back from a meeting in London, and he was giving me a general update on the situation as he saw it, and he was reviewing the status of the work that was in progress at CIA and Defense, in addition to the results of his meeting in London.

And near the end of the conversation, my recollection is that he said something to the effect that, "Admiral, I think we can—I have found a way that we can legally provide some funds to the democratic resistance or as they have called been here," and I frankly agree with Congressman [Henry J.] Hyde [R-Ill.] that I have no problem with calling them contras—"through funds that will accrue from the arms sales to the Iranians."

LIMAN: Did he use the word "legally?"

POINDEXTER: My best recollection is that he did, but of course I know that Col. North is not a lawyer and so I was taking that in a layman's sense, that that was his conclusion.

LIMAN: Do you recall reciting this in your deposition you didn't use the word legally?

POINDEXTER: I don't recall that, that I didn't. I believe that he did. He may not have.

LIMAN: Did he tell you what the method would be for doing this?

POINDEXTER: This was a—this was a very general discussion, but this was clearly a new aspect that I had not thought about before. To make a long story short, in the end I thought it was a very good idea, the end of this conversation and I personally approved it.

LIMAN: Did he ask you for your approval?

POINDEXTER: I don't recall how he phrased his request, but he was clearly looking for a signal from me whether or not to proceed ahead along this line.

LIMAN: And you gave it?

POINDEXTER: And I gave it to him. . . .

After working with the President for 5½ years, the last 3 of which were very close, probably closer than any other officer in the

White House except the Chief of Staff, I was convinced that I understood the President's thinking on this and that if I had taken it to him that he would have approved it.

Now, I was not so naive as to believe that it was not a politically volatile issue, it clearly was, because of the divisions that existed within the Congress on the issue of support for the contras, and it was clear that there will be a lot of people that would disagree, that would make accusations that indeed have been made.

So although I was convinced that we could properly do it and that the President would approve if asked, I made a very deliberate decision not to ask the President so that I could insulate him from the decision and provide some future deniability for the President if it ever leaked out.

Of course, our hope was that it would not leak out.

LIMAN: When you say deniability, are you saying that your decision was not to tell the President so that he would be able to deny that he knew of it?

POINDEXTER: That is correct.

LIMAN: And did you at any time prior to the Attorney General's finding this on November 22 tell the President of the United States of the fact that [proceeds] from the Iranian arms sale were being used to support the contras?

POINDEXTER: I don't—I did not—I want to make this very clear, I understand it is an important issue—I did not talk to anybody else except Col. North about this decision until, to my knowledge, to my best recollection, and I don't want to quibble here over times in late November of 1986—but my recollection is the first mention that I made to anybody besides Col. North was on November 24th, 1986, to Ed Meese.

LIMAN: And so that the answer is you did not tell the President of the United States?

POINDEXTER: I did not.

LIMAN: And that for a period of whatever it is, nine months, you kept it from the President of the United States for the reasons you have given.

POINDEXTER: Mr. Liman, this clearly was an important decision, but it was also an implementation, a very clear policy if the President had asked me, I very likely would have told him about it. But he didn't.

And I think it is—you know, an important point here is that on this whole issue, you know, the buck stops here with me. I made the decision. I felt that I had the authority to do it. I thought it was a good idea. I was convinced that the President would in the end think it was a good idea. But I did not want him to be associated with the decision. . . .

LIMAN: Were there any other decisions that you withheld from the President that you had made because they were politically explosive?

POINDEXTER: I don't recall anything else that fell in that same category, although there were lots of—I want to make a distinction here between what I felt my authority was and why I didn't discuss it with the President.

Number one, I felt that it was within my authority because it was an implementation of a policy that was well understood, that the President felt very strongly about; it was not a secret foreign policy; that the President's policy with regard to the contras was clearly understood by every member of the Congress and the American people.

So it wasn't a matter of going out and making a secret foreign policy. The policy was clear. This was a—the way of going about, of carrying out that policy. So that was my thinking in terms that I felt that I had the authority to do it.

Now, the reason that—frankly, as Col. North has testified, I thought it was a neat idea, too, and I'm sure the President would have enjoyed knowing about it. But, on the other hand, because it would be controversial—and I must say that I don't believe that I estimated how controversial it would be accurately—but I knew very well that it would be controversial, and I wanted the President to have some deniability so that he would be protected, and at the same time we would be able to carry out this policy and provide the opposition to the Sandinista government.

* * *

LIMAN: Did you ever tell Col. North that you were not going to tell the President [about the diversion of funds to the contras]?

POINDEXTER: I did not. That was a private decision of mine. I did not tell Col. North one way or the other whether I would tell the President. I did give him broad general authority to carry out the plan in the same conversation in which he raised the issue.

LIMAN: Did you make any effort to lead him to believe that you were going to discuss this with the President?

POINDEXTER: I did not give him any reason to believe that because I didn't feel that was necessary. I was clearly his superior and Col. North, I think as you observed, is a very competent and capable staff officer, and he understood that and had no question, I don't think.

LIMAN: You have heard his testimony that up until mid-November he operated under the assumption that you had told the President.

Do you know what you said or did that gave him that assumption?

POINDEXTER: I think it was simply—again this is speculation on my part because I have not had a discussion with Col. North on this subject, but just based on experience and my relationship with Col. North over a period of several years, he would know that in general I briefed the President on most all aspects of all the projects that Col. North was involved with.

So it would not be surprising to—it would not be surprising to him if I had discussed it with the President.

LIMAN: And indeed not telling the President was an aberration here?

POINDEXTER: It was unusual. . . .

LIMAN: Was there ever a moment when you were tempted to tell him about the fact that the Ayatollah, instead of supporting the Sandinistas, was giving money for the contras?

POINDEXTER: Yes, Mr. Liman, there was. There was one point that I was very sorely tempted to tell him, but I didn't. And, as I recall, we were aboard Air Force One on the way back from the Economic Summit in Tokyo. . . . and he had a discussion with me on the airplane—this would have been in May, the middle of May 1986—and we had received via facsimile from the White House Office a paper that laid out the status of our legislative plans for getting the 100 million, and one of the options in the paper was that if were unable to get the 100 million, to pull out, drop our support of the contras.

And I had discussed that with the President, and he had been very adamant at the time. He says, look, I don't want to pull out our support for the contras for any reason. This would be an unacceptable option, isn't there something that I could do unilaterally?

And by that, I took it to mean he could do on his own that didn't require congressional approval. And I was sorely tempted at that point to tell him what we had working, but I thought better of it and did not.

LIMAN: And that was because you realized this would be so controversial?

POINDEXTER: That is correct.

LIMAN: So that, again, it is, the more controversial the issue, the less the President was to be told?

BECKLER: I am going to object.

LIMAN: I will proceed with the next question.

BECKLER: I would like to have that stricken. That is another bit of Arthur Liman bringing his conclusions to bear. His job is to give questions that elicit facts. We have never—my client has never testified that he does not bring things that are controversial forward to the President.

He has never said that. He has said over and over that the diversion or transfer was a detail implementing a policy. He did not—and he has also said, yes, it was politically controversial, but to imply that nothing controversial is brought to the President of the United States by Adm. Poindexter is just an unfair distortion of the record that Mr. Liman well knows was developed over four days and here today.

I would like to have at least one objection possibly sustained sometime. Brendan [V.] Sullivan [Jr., North's lawyer] didn't get one. I would like to get at least one.

* * *

LIMAN: What was the general charge that the President of the United States gave to you?

POINDEXTER: He wanted to be sure that the contras were supported. I don't recall the description body and soul, but that in essence in my view was what he wanted. He wanted to encourage private contributions, to get what support we could from third countries, and you know, the details—I think the President understood, from discussions I had with him, the limitations that were placed on the State Department, the Defense Department, and the CIA.

He knew that Col. North was the chief staff officer on Central America because of Col. North's attendance at various meetings in which these issues, the general issues of Central America were discussed.

But I did not get into the level of detail with him as to exactly how Col. North was carrying out his charter to keep the contras alive.

I generally know those details, but frankly, I didn't think those details were important to the President. The only thing that was important to him was that they were staying alive.

* * *

LIMAN: When he [North] was in negotiations with the second channel, did he tell you that he had, with his advisers and assistants, with Gen. Secord [retired major general Richard V. Secord] and [Albert] Hakim, negotiated the nine-point plan [negotiated in October 1986 to gain the release of two hostages in exchange for an arms shipment] with the Iranian second channel?

POINDEXTER: I believe he did. I don't have a strong recollection of this, but I believe he did.

LIMAN: Is your best recollection, and that is all we can talk about, that you approved it?

POINDEXTER: Yes, that is correct.

LIMAN: Is it your best recollection that you obtained the approval of the President of the United States?

POINDEXTER: Yes, it is.

LIMAN: You are aware of the plan because we have shown it to you as well as Col. North's testimony about the part of the plan that dealt with the Dawa [terrorists being held prisoner in Kuwait], correct?

POINDEXTER: That is correct.

LIMAN: And you were a subscriber to the policy of the United States, that the United States should not lean on the Kuwaitis to release these prisoners?

POINDEXTER: That is correct.

LIMAN: These were terrorists?

POINDEXTER: That is correct, and the President felt very strongly about the issue.

LIMAN: Did Col. North—

POINDEXTER: We had discussed that numerous times.

LIMAN: Did Col. North report to you that part of the plan was for Gen. Secord or Hakim to come up with a plan that the Iranians could use to attempt to convince the Kuwaitis to release the Dawa prisoners?

POINDEXTER: I believe he did. That was my understanding, that it was not something that Gen. Secord—I don't, I can't say that I really remember Albert Hakim's role in this, but my recollection would be that Gen. Secord was to come up with a plan which he could give the Iranians that the Iranians could execute, not that the U.S. Government would do it or not even that Gen. Secord would actually do anything.

LIMAN: Did you clear that with the President?

POINDEXTER: My best recollection is I did.

* * *

LIMAN: Did you tell the Secretary of State in May of 1986 that the [Iran] operation was over?

POINDEXTER: I do not recall making it that definitive.

LIMAN: Did you ever tell the Secretary of State that the United States had actually shipped arms to Iran?

POINDEXTER: Oh, I think that the Secretary of State knew that. I think that was covered in at least one family group lunch.

LIMAN: So your recollection is you did, in fact, tell him?

POINDEXTER: I think I did. In fact, I am almost certain of that.

LIMAN: Did the Secretary of State ever ask you not to keep him informed?

POINDEXTER: Not in those precise words. He, in at least one or more conversations, told me that—that I understood that he was opposed to the plan, that he also understood that the President wanted to go ahead with it, not that he liked that, he accepted it, and he indicated that he didn't particularly want to know the details.

He said just, in effect, tell me what I need to know.

* * *

LIMAN: . . . Admiral, the activities of Col. North began before you became National Security Adviser, correct?

POINDEXTER: They did.

LIMAN: And then you authorized him to continue them during your tenure.

POINDEXTER: That is correct. When I took over, I was, as I have testified, I was generally aware of what Col. North was doing, and when I took over, I recall a brief discussion with him that he should continue on track.

LIMAN: And Col. North testified that he wouldn't do things on his own and that his activities were authorized by his superiors. You recall that?

POINDEXTER: Yes, I do.

LIMAN: And to the best of your information and knowledge, were his activities in support of the contras authorized by either you or Mr. McFarlane?

POINDEXTER: During my tenure as National Security Adviser, I authorized, in general, the actions that I have heard described, and it was my understanding that Mr. McFarlane had authorized the activities that had taken place prior to December of 1985.

LIMAN: And just so that we can identify what it is that you understood that he was doing, am I correct that you understood that Col. North was looking for ways to support the contras through non-appropriated funds?

POINDEXTER: Yes.

LIMAN: Is it correct that you knew that Col. North had secured the services of—or encouraged, let me put it that way—Gen. Secord to set up the contra resupply operation?

POINDEXTER: I was aware that he did that, and I was certainly operating under the impression that Mr. McFarlane had approved that.

* * *

LIMAN: Did you have a conversation with Director Casey where he said that the contras would not be alive without Col. North?

POINDEXTER: Yes. I almost said that, but I figured you were going to ask that as the next question.

LIMAN: And you shared that view?

POINDEXTER: Yes, I did. I certainly did.

LIMAN: And I understand from your earlier testimony that you did not go into this degree of detail in briefing the President; is that so?

POINDEXTER: I certainly did not brief the President in detail of all of Col. North's activities. That would have been much too great a level of detail to cover [with] all of the other arms control and U.S.-Soviet issues that we were constantly struggling with. But I do think that the President understands that Col. North was instrumental in keeping the contras supported without maybe understanding the details of exactly what he was doing.

* * *

Poindexter resumed his testimony July 16, 1987:

LIMAN: Admiral, in saying that you are complying with the

letter and spirit of law, when you mean that the law doesn't apply and that you are supporting the contras, you do not consider that to be misleading Congress?

POINDEXTER: The only thing I meant, Mr. Liman, was withholding information from the Congress. We did not—I have not said that we weren't helping the contras. We were clearly helping the contras. But we were also trying very hard to stay within the letter and spirit of Boland by keeping the other departments that were covered by the Boland amendment out of the issue.

LIMAN: So that in saying that you are complying with the letter and spirit of Boland, what you mean is that the NSC was doing the support without the CIA?

POINDEXTER: That was my understanding.

LIMAN: And did the President understand that?

POINDEXTER: I think he did understand that.

LIMAN: What is that based on?

POINDEXTER: In a general way. He understood that the contras were being supported and that we were involved in—generally in coordinating the effort. He was aware of the contributions from country two [Saudi Arabia] and he himself felt personally, as related to me, that it was entirely appropriate for private individuals to support the contras and he was aware of the status of the contras in the field, the kinds of things that he was briefed on, I think, would have made that clear.

LIMAN: Did you—I am sorry.

POINDEXTER: I was just going to add that he was not briefed on every little issue involved in coordinating this effort. As I have testified before, the items that he was briefed on were primarily in the policy area and it was a judgment call every day as to exactly what level of detail I had to get into.

That doesn't mean that we were—or that I was trying to withhold information from him. It was just a matter of giving him the information that I felt it was most important depending upon the circumstances of the day....

LIMAN: Did you brief the President on the fact that the NSC staff was helping the contras?

POINDEXTER: Mr. Liman, as I have testified yesterday, I am not going to answer a question in a positive way unless I can remember a specific conversation. I have told you in general what I briefed the President on, and I don't recall a specific conversation that would allow me to answer your question in an affirmative way.

LIMAN: Now—or a negative way?

POINDEXTER: Or a negative way.

*   *   *

LIMAN: . . . Did the President designate the NSC to conduct the activities in support of the contras that you have described in your testimony yesterday?

POINDEXTER: In effect, he did, Mr. Liman, but not through a finding. A finding was not required.

LIMAN: I'm not talking about a finding. I said, in effect.

POINDEXTER: I want to make it clear, as I said yesterday and as Mr. McFarlane has testified, the President in effect wanted the National Security Council to make sure that the contras remained alive until we could turn the vote around in the Congress and return to a program that was supported with appropriated funds.

LIMAN: When we're talking about the President of the United States, I think we would both agree that we shouldn't talk about what he did in effect.

Did the President ever designate in words, in substance of words, the NSC to conduct the activities in support of the contras that you described yesterday?

POINDEXTER: I would not characterize it that way at all. As I said, if you take the totality of the President's actions, that was clearly his intent.

LIMAN: But you did not state that in words?

POINDEXTER: . . . There was no written finding on this activity because none was required.

LIMAN: . . . Did you brief the President about the fact that the NSC staff was, to use the words of the Tower Report, helping the contras?

POINDEXTER: Again, as I testified yesterday, I want to be very careful, and I want to recall a specific conversation with the President before I would answer that in an affirmative way. I do not recall a specific conversation in that regard, but I don't think that's unusual, because I would not get into the details with the President as to who was doing what. The President knew that there was a Boland Amendment, he knew there were restrictions on the government. As he has said, I think, since November of 1986, that he did not feel that the Boland Amendment applied to his personal staff and that that was his feeling all along. I knew that.

He knew the contras were being supported, and we simply didn't get into the details of exactly who was doing what. He understood that Col. North was the chief action officer on Central America. Col. North was always there when there were briefings in detail as to what was happening in Central America. Col. North was there with various foreign officials that were involved, and so the President, I think clearly associated with it.

Now, you know, the President doesn't recall apparently a specific briefing in which I laid out in great detail all of the ways that we were going about implementing the President's policy, and I frankly don't find that surprising. It would not, frankly, at that time have been a matter of great interest as to exactly how we were implementing the President's policy.

LIMAN: But yesterday, in explaining why you felt that the authorization of the diversion by you was consistent with the President's policies and with something—that had you told him, he would have approved, you were basing that on your discussions with the President.

POINDEXTER: That is correct.

LIMAN: Not discussions of the diversion which make it clear.

POINDEXTER: No.

LIMAN: But discussions of supporting the contras.

POINDEXTER: That is correct.

*   *   *

Residuals

LIMAN: Now, did you believe that all of what is—what Col. North called the residuals, called the profits, were going to be used for the contras?

POINDEXTER: That was my understanding.

LIMAN: And did you ever ask Col. North how much money these sales were generating for the contras?

POINDEXTER: No. I never did.

LIMAN: Did he ever tell you?

POINDEXTER: That I cannot remember.

LIMAN: Was there a reason why you didn't ask him how much money we are getting for the contras out of these sales?

POINDEXTER: Your question was, did I ask him?

LIMAN: My question was, why didn't you, given your interest in the financing of the contras, which you expressed and you have explained why you were interested in it, why didn't you ask Col. North, "How much are we getting out of these sales for the contras?"

POINDEXTER: I don't recall, frankly, ever thinking about that. I knew that the arms sales were going through. I had a rough idea of the amount of money involved from the early discussion in February. I knew that a portion of that would go, but with all of the other issues that I was involved with during the year, I simply didn't get into that detail of micromanagement of the project that Col. North was working on. I told you that was not my style.

*   *   *

Hawk Shipments

On November 20, 1986, Poindexter met with CIA director Casey, Attorney General Meese, and others to review the events surrounding the November 1985 shipment of Hawk antiaircraft missiles to Iran. The next day, during testimony before a closed House Intelligence Committee hearing, Casey left the impression that the shipment had contained only oil-drilling parts. (Casey testimony, p. C-1)

LIMAN: Is it a fact that whatever you may have remembered, you knew that it was a false story that the CIA and the NSC thought that these were oil drilling parts being shipped?

Did you know that that was false as far as that went, that it was oil drilling parts?

POINDEXTER: Mr. Liman, that isn't necessarily a false story.

LIMAN: I know, but you say not necessarily. I am asking you whether you knew that it was false to say that these were oil drilling parts so far as the United States knew.

POINDEXTER: I wasn't certain of that at all, because I did have a vague recollection, as the various conversations went forward, that there was something about oil drilling equipment. Since that time, I have thought back over it, and I believe what happened was that Col. North used that as a cover story with the CIA in arranging for the proprietaries [private airlines used by the CIA], so there were probably some people at CIA that thought that it was oil drilling equipment.

But, again, that is with a lot of additional information since that time. At the time, I remembered something about oil drilling equipment, but I was fairly certain in my mind that it was not as described in that version of the narrative of the chronology....

LIMAN: On the 21st [of November 1986], did Oliver North come into your office with his spiral notebook?

POINDEXTER: That is correct. This was the afternoon of the 21st.

LIMAN: And did he tell you that he had in that spiral notebook some notes that indicated that you knew that it was Hawk shipments, that the President had approved it?

POINDEXTER: That is correct. He came in some time middle to late afternoon with one of his old spiral notebooks and said he had just pulled these out of his files and gone back through to try to reconstruct what had happened in November of 1985, and he reported that conversation with me at the time.

I told him that I didn't recall it, but I didn't question that it happened. I am sure it did happen.

LIMAN: Did you reach a conclusion as to what Oliver North was going to do with his notebooks?

POINDEXTER: Yes. From something he said—and I don't recall exactly what it was—but I recall as he left the room that I had the impression that he was going to destroy that notebook.

LIMAN: Did you tell him not to?

POINDEXTER: I didn't tell him not to.

LIMAN: Now, if what you were interested in was telling the Congress, the public, the truth about what was known about the November shipment and the fact that the President had approved it, why didn't you say to Oliver North, "Don't destroy the note"?

POINDEXTER: My recollection of his reciting at that short meeting these events that had happened in November of 1985, my recollection was that there was nothing in the note that described whether or not the President had approved in Geneva [Switzerland] before the operation started the shipment of the Hawks, and the whole plan to get the hostages back the Israelis had come up with.

That in my mind was the crucial issue at the time, not related to what Col. North had just read to me.

LIMAN: Who did you think he was trying to protect by destroying those notes?

BECKLER: Objection, Mr. Chairman. I think—are you talking about Oliver North?

LIMAN: Col. North.

BECKLER: He was up here for six days. Isn't he the appropriate one to ask that question?

LIMAN: You came away with the conclusion he was going to destroy those notebooks; right?

POINDEXTER: That is right.

LIMAN: For what purpose did you think he was going to destroy those notebooks?

POINDEXTER: I don't think I really particularly focused on that at the time. The working notebooks and the working files I have never considered as official documents, and it was perfectly all right with me if Col. North destroyed his personal notebooks and working files that he had. I had no problem with that.

* * *

LIMAN: Did you tell the Attorney General that you had approved the diversion by Col. North?

POINDEXTER: I did not use those words. I told him that I was generally aware of the transfer—of the plan to transfer the funds. I was being very cautious at that point.

LIMAN: Can you tell us why you didn't tell him that Col. North was acting pursuant to your authority?

POINDEXTER: I wanted—in continuing the plan that I had always had of providing deniability to the President, I did not want to provide that detailed information at the time, because I wanted the President and his staff to be able to say they didn't know anything about it.

LIMAN: Is it a fact that the Attorney General didn't ask you whether you had told the President?

POINDEXTER: I do not recall his asking me whether I had told the President or his asking me whether I had approved it.

* * *

[John W.] NIELDS [Jr., House committee chief counsel]: I think you testified that you destroyed this [December 1985] finding [that retroactively ratified the November Hawk shipment] late on Friday, November 21st, 1986?

POINDEXTER: I did.

NIELDS: And I think you've testified that earlier that week a difference of opinion amongst Cabinet officers surfaced about the U.S. Government knowledge and involvement in that shipment?

POINDEXTER: Yes. The disagreement specifically related to conversations that had taken place in Geneva between Mr. McFarlane and George Shultz.

NIELDS: Mr. Shultz said that Mr. McFarlane—Secretary Shultz had said that Mr. McFarlane had told him in Geneva on November 18, 1985, that Hawks were being shipped to Iran for hostages, and Mr. McFarlane said that he had not known that the shipments were missiles at that time.

Is that about the size of the dispute?

POINDEXTER: As near as I could—can make out at this point. I don't think I ever saw or heard recited to me exactly what Secretary Shultz's recollection of that conversation was.

NIELDS: And again referring to Friday, November 21st, 1986, earlier that same day you had had a meeting with the Attorney General and the President of the United States at which the fact of this dispute was raised?

POINDEXTER: Yes. The question was one of the President's prior knowledge in Geneva of the Israeli plan and whether he had approved it or not, and we needed to get to the bottom of that.

NIELDS: And, indeed, you needed to get to the bottom of just what the facts were regarding this Government's knowledge and approval of the November Hawk shipment?

POINDEXTER: Yes, that's correct.

NIELDS: And, by the way, at that meeting did anybody ask the President whether he had approved?

POINDEXTER: That's an obvious question, but I don't recall if [*sic*] coming up. We were talking about events that had taken place over a year earlier, and I certainly didn't remember much about the year and I don't think I even thought about asking the President because I didn't think he would remember that level of detail either....

NIELDS: Do you have any document in your possession or in Col. North's that was more directly relevant to the Attorney General's inquiry into the question of Presidential approval of the Hawk shipment than the one up on the wall [the December 1985 finding]?

POINDEXTER: I don't know of any other document that—in fact—you know, at this point we wished that we had a lot more documents, but we didn't. I have explained why we didn't have many documents. We were very concerned about leaks.

NIELDS: I take it before—before the Attorney General had a chance to look at that document, you destroyed it?

POINDEXTER: I—when Cmdr. Thompson showed me this document, my concern was only that it would reinforce the story that the only objective we had in the whole project was arms for hostages. I did not think in terms of Hawk shipments or TOW [antitank missiles] shipments, or anything else, at that point.

NIELDS: Did you destroy it to give the President deniability?

POINDEXTER: I did not....

NIELDS: ... By destroying this document, did you not permit the President to deny that he had signed a finding on December 5th, 1985, relating to arms and hostages?

POINDEXTER: That was not the intent at all. I haven't—as I said, I haven't talked to the President since the morning of the 25th, and I don't know what he had in mind when he has made these statements.

NIELDS: Well, you did—I take it, it was your intent when you destroyed that document that no one would see the document?

POINDEXTER: Well, my concern was, as I have testified before, that any time a document left my office, I was concerned that it was susceptible to public exposure. I didn't—simply did not want this document to see the light of day.

* * *

Poindexter resumed his testimony July 17, 1987:

NIELDS: Now, Col. North, as you undoubtedly know, has testified about what he said during that face-to-face meeting [with members of the House Intelligence Committee August 1986]?

POINDEXTER: I understand that.

NIELDS: And he said this at page 225 of the transcript of last Wednesday, and I will read it to you.

He said—this is his testimony—"I will tell you right now, Counsel, and all the members here gathered, that I misled Congress. I misled—"—and then there is a question. "At that meeting?"

And the answer: "At that meeting."

Question: "Face-to-face?"

Answer: "Face-to-face."

Question: "You made false statements to them about your activities in support of the contras?"

Answer: "I did."

Now, my question to you is, did you authorize Col. North to do that?

POINDEXTER: I did not authorize him to make false statements. I did think that he would withhold information and be evasive, frankly, in answering questions. My objective all along was to withhold from the Congress exactly what the NSC staff was doing in carrying out the President's policy.

I felt that, as I have testified before, that the Boland Amendment did not apply to the NSC staff.

The Government, the U.S. Government, was complying with the letter and spirit of Boland, as I thought that was sufficient.

Don't misunderstand me. I thought that Col. North would withhold information. There was no doubt about that in my mind. There were a lot of stories in the press that had appeared that I had talked to Col. North about periodically.

Most of the stories were patently false and in error. I thought most of the questions would be about these rather outrageous stories in the press, and I felt that Col. North could knock those stories down by answering the questions truthfully.

NIELDS: My question to you is, did you put Col. North in an absolutely impossible position? How could he answer the questions raised by the resolution of inquiry truthfully and still withhold information?

POINDEXTER: First of all, Mr. Nields, as I testified a few moments ago, I don't believe I had actually read the resolution of inquiry as to the kinds of questions that were being raised there. I knew, in general, the issue was what was Col. North doing to help the contras. As I testified before, I felt that Col. North was a very capable officer. I did not micromanage him....

NIELDS: ... Was it the general understanding between you and Col. North that he was supposed to withhold information even if a member of the House Intelligence Committee asked him a direct question calling for it?

POINDEXTER: Col. North was a very competent individual, as I think you have observed. He had been in much tougher situations, I was sure. Col. North is very resourceful. I thought he could handle it some way.

The analysis as to exactly how he would do it did not enter my mind.

NIELDS: Well, he has testified here that he was unable to do that, that he was put in a position where he either had to give up the information that you didn't want him to or he had to lie.

Now, assume that he is faced and was faced with that choice. Which choice did you want him to make?

POINDEXTER: As I've said before, I did not expect him to lie to the committee. I expected him to be evasive, say that he didn't want to answer the question, be uncooperative, if necessary, but I rather think that with his resourcefulness, I thought he could handle it.

And furthermore, I—I understand that there isn't one, and it is unfortunate, but I would really like to know exactly what was asked and what his answers were. I'm sure they were very carefully crafted, nuanced. The total impact, I'm sure, was one of withholding information from the Congress, but I'm still not convinced—I know he testified that he lied and made false statements—but I'm not totally convinced of that myself.

* * *

INOUYE: Mr. Chairman [of the House select committee investigating the Iran-Contra affair, Rep. Lee H. Hamilton, D-Ind.], I have sat through the witness's testimony very quietly, and some would say rather meekly, listening to lectures from the counsel, and incidentally, he has spent nearly an hour telling us how we should question the witness, how we should pose and phrase our wording, how we are doing this wrong. He has lectured the members of the panel on improprieties of statements made and he has said that this has been done in the name of fairness. And in the name of fairness, I have not said anything.

But I would like to say a few words at this time, Mr. Chairman. In our rules it says, 54(a), "A witness's counsel shall be permitted to be present during the witness's testimony at any public or closed hearing or deposition or staff interview to advise the witness of his or her rights." That is all we say about counsel.

Secondly, Admiral, I think you are extremely fortunate in having your testimony under the able, courteous and gracious guidance of Chairman Hamilton. You can look far and wide, throughout the Congress of the United States, and you will not find any person much fairer, much more just than Chairman Hamilton. He has leaned over backwards to be fair.

But, at the same time, when we sit here and listen to your testimony, in which you tell us that you have either withheld information from or misled or misinformed the Congress of the United States, that you have withheld information from the President, that you have either withheld information from or misled or misinformed the highest-ranking Cabinet members of the United States, that you have withheld information from your most trusted deputy, Col. North, I don't think it is improper for any member of this panel to characterize that testimony as being incredible, mind-boggling, chilling. I think they are all proper....

POINDEXTER: Chairman Inouye, I don't think it is fair to say that I have misinformed Congress or other Cabinet officers. I haven't testified to that.

I testified that I have withheld information from Congress, and with regard to Cabinet officers, I didn't withhold anything from them that they didn't want withheld from them.

The only question I think that has come up is what Secretary Shultz said to me, and he was not aware of all the details but that was by his choice.

INOUYE: Admiral, I am not an expert on semantics. I will accept your correction, sir.

* * *

NIELDS: [What] was the reason to withhold information from Congress when they inquired about it?

POINDEXTER: Two reasons. One, we wanted to—we wanted to return to a covert implementation of the policy. If it had been—if it had become public as to exactly what we were doing, there would have been all sorts of press inquiries down in Central America. It would have been a very hot political issue. It would have caused problems for our friends and supporters in Central America, and if we had revealed all those details because the press understood it was a controversial, political issue in the Congress, there would have been a lot of attention to it, which would have essentially destroyed our ability to carry on the support for the contras under those very difficult situations.

The second point was that we didn't want more restrictive legislation introduced in some new form of the Boland Amendment. I knew that it would be controversial and that there were different interpretations of the Boland Amendment.

I felt that we were on strong legal ground with what we were doing and it was consistent with the President's policy, and I simply didn't want any outside interference. . . .

NIELDS: Now, the outside interference we are talking about was Congress, and I take it the reason they were inquiring about Col. North's activities, the Government's activities in support of the contras, was precisely so that they could fulfill with information their constitutional function to pass legislation, one way or the other. Isn't that true?

POINDEXTER: Yes, I suppose that is true.

NIELDS: And that you regarded as outside interference?

POINDEXTER: The point was, and still is, that the President has the constitutional right and, in fact, the constitutional mandate to conduct foreign policy. His policy was to support the contras.

Congress had put some restrictions on the use of proposed funds. Those restrictions didn't apply to private funds. They didn't apply to third-country funds.

And the restrictions in the Boland Amendment, as I have said, did not apply to the NSC staff.

* * *

The NSC's Role

[Richard] LEON [House counsel]: Now, I think you testified at one point in one of your depositions that you don't believe the NSC should be or is an ivory tower?

POINDEXTER: That is correct.

LEON: Do you still hold to that position?

POINDEXTER: I do.

LEON: Why don't you explain that?

POINDEXTER: The problem is that—as I have hinted at before, but this is an opportunity to expand on it—we live in a very imperfect world. You don't always have good decisions—good options to make, and decisions are necessary. The stakes are simply too high for us not to take actions. Invariably, because you don't always have good options, there are high risks involved.

The bureaucracy—and I don't mean to demean them in any way, because there are a lot of very fine, dedicated public servants out there in the bureaucracy—but the problem is that many of the options that a President has in managing foreign policy involve high risk, and because of the mechanics of our government, the bureaucracy doesn't handle risk very well, high-risk situations. They are always concerned about failure and the results of failure.

This episode that we are presently involved with, I think, is a good demonstration of the costs of failure, because clearly our Iranian project failed, we didn't achieve our objectives, it was exposed before we had a chance to achieve the success that we thought was possible.

Now, because the cost of failure is very high, the bureaucracy is not willing to recommend, often recommend, or certainly endorse high-risk operations, because of their fear of failure and the resulting harangue that comes about because of failing. Therefore, they don't make those kinds of hard options available to the President. And I think one of the roles of the NSC staff has got to be to bring these options to the President, and because the bureaucracy is often not willing to push them once a decision is made, push them vigorously, I feel that in the very real world that we live in, the NSC staff has got to be the catalyst that keeps the process moving forward, keeps the President's decisions moving along, and helps to make sure that they are implemented, and that often involves an operational role for the NSC staff. Their only loyalty is to the President. . . .

* * *

LEON: I would like to ask this, Admiral. Do you have any knowledge or information or any basis to believe that Col. North did tell the President about the diversion?

POINDEXTER: I have absolutely no reason to believe that he did.

LEON: Do you have any knowledge—

POINDEXTER: I would be almost willing to say absolutely he did not. There was never an opportunity, and furthermore, Col. North would not have done that without talking to me about it.

LEON: Do you have any knowledge or reason to think that the President learned about the diversion from some other source other than Col. North or yourself, as you have testified?

POINDEXTER: I don't have any reason to believe that.

* * *

[Sen. Sam] NUNN [D-Ga.]: . . . Admiral, after reading the denials by the White House issued since your testimony, do you still believe the President would have approved that decision if you had asked him?

POINDEXTER: I do.

NUNN: You have not changed your mind?

POINDEXTER: I have not changed my mind.

NUNN: Again, you said July 15, page 95, reading the words if you can find them, "I made the decision. I felt I had the authority to do it. I thought it was a good idea. I was convinced that the President would in the end think it was a good idea."

Do you see that?

POINDEXTER: Yes.

NUNN: Is that still your testimony?

POINDEXTER: It is.

NUNN: So that the denials from the White House have had no effect on your testimony?

POINDEXTER: No, they have not.

NUNN: That means, Admiral, you must believe the White House is now misleading the American people?

POINDEXTER: No, I don't think so.

NUNN: How can it not be?

POINDEXTER: Well, number one, what you have are reports of what [White House spokesman] Marlin Fitzwater said. I don't know exactly—

NUNN: You don't believe he is speaking for the President?

POINDEXTER: Well, I would—I would want to have a personal conversation with the President, which I have not had, and which would not be appropriate at this time.

NUNN: If Marlin Fitzwater really was speaking for the President, would you agree that those statements are in your opinion misleading the American people?

POINDEXTER: Senator, as I have testified before, and you have gone over some of the instances just now, I felt that the President would approve that if I had asked him.

I still feel that way. I am giving you my thought process at the time, my thought process now.

At this point, I can't speak for the White House. I don't know what they have got in mind over there, and I really can't comment on that.

NUNN: Well, I would just observe, Admiral, you can refute this if you like, a White House statement directly contradicts your testimony and you are standing by your testimony, so your testimony directly contradicts the White House statements.

POINDEXTER: That is correct. It appears to be obvious. People can draw their own conclusions I guess.

* * *

A Legal Opinion

[Sen. Warren B.] RUDMAN [R-N.H.]: . . . I have a question. I think the people of the country would like to know. Why didn't you, as the National Security Adviser, go to the Attorney General of the United States and say, General Meese, it is the view of the NSC that we are not covered by Boland, I want a secret legal opinion to the President, which he has a right to do as the President's client, telling us that we are right or we are wrong, so we can proceed?

Why didn't we avoid the situation we are in now where we had an opinion of the Attorney General essentially agreeing with your position. He is the highest legal officer in the land. It was the single, most important foreign policy initiative in this hemisphere that the President was concerned about, is one that you were immersed in enormously and put great stakes in, why not the Attorney General give an opinion?

POINDEXTER: The thought never crossed my mind. In carrying out my duties, I simply didn't think about them in terms of going to Ed and asking for a legal opinion from him. . . .

RUDMAN: I hesitate to ask this question, but I—I am going to ask this question. Was there any consideration of the fact that you didn't want to go outside for an opinion because you might get an answer you didn't like?

POINDEXTER: I don't think that crossed my mind.

RUDMAN: That was never discussed among your staff?

POINDEXTER: No, not that I initiated or participated in.

RUDMAN: Your answer, Admiral, you know I don't mean to make light of this, but it is like a book written a few years ago, like everything we always wanted to know about Boland but were afraid to ask. . . .

I will not get into the question of whether the President should have been notified or not, except with that last observation.

That, in my view, you acted in good faith. It is my view that presidents ought to be allowed to create their own political disasters. Nobody else ought to do it for them.

That was not your intention. Unfortunately, that is the way it has turned out.

*　*　*

Panel members questioned Poindexter on July 20, 1987:

[Rep. Thomas S.] FOLEY [D-Wash.]: Did you tell the President that it was Col. North who had requested Gen. Secord [retired major general Richard V. Secord] to construct the airfield [in Costa Rica]?

POINDEXTER: I don't believe that I covered that detail.

FOLEY: But you yourself knew that Gen. Secord was operating under the general instructions of Col. North with respect to the construction; is that fair?

POINDEXTER: I certainly knew that Gen. Secord was leading a private logistics organization and Col. North stayed in very close contact with him. I don't know that I was aware of the detail of Gen. Secord's involvement with that airstrip, but it would not have surprised me to learn that.

We simply—with all of the issues involved, simply didn't—I usually didn't get into that level of detail and I did not bring the President into that level of detail. He knew the contras were being supported. He knew they were being supported by third-country funds and by private support activity and that we were keeping close track of what was happening.

FOLEY: Under some interpretation, construction of the airfield might be considered a detail; isn't that true?

POINDEXTER: The point—the only reason for bringing that up with the President was that it was a dramatic display of cooperation and support for the President's policy by the country involved. That was the thing that was important to the President.

FOLEY: Col. North testified that he received approval to conduct the air resupply of weapons to the contras inside Nicaragua.

Did you authorize Col. North to direct the air resupply operation?

POINDEXTER: Again, Col. North was given a very broad charter to carry out a mission and I did not micromanage him. I don't think it is appropriate.

FOLEY: Did he tell you he was doing it?

POINDEXTER: I was aware that he had information on the times of delivery and I assume that he was indeed staying in close coordination with the private support effort.

FOLEY: In your method of managing subordinates, I think you've testified that you tend to give them responsibility and then not attempt to micromanage them?

POINDEXTER: I give them authority. I maintain the responsibility, Mr. Foley.

FOLEY: So you assumed the responsibility for the resupply effort because you knew it was being conducted by Col. North and you did not interrupt or countermand those efforts?

POINDEXTER: That's correct.

FOLEY: Did you authorize Col. North to use the air supply to drop lethal supplies in Nicaragua?

POINDEXTER: There was no distinction in my mind in the private logistics support organization between lethal and non-lethal weapons or material.

FOLEY: Even—

POINDEXTER: The whole question—excuse me—of lethal and non-lethal I think is a very difficult semantic question and it really only arose with regard to the $27 million appropriation [a fiscal 1986 appropriation for humanitarian aid for the contras].

FOLEY: And as far as you are concerned, that was not a very good distinction in law or in practice; is that correct?

POINDEXTER: I think, as you have all heard in the prior testimony here by [Assistant] Secretary [of State Elliott] Abrams, in practice, it was a very difficult issue to resolve as to what was lethal and what was non-lethal. . . .

FOLEY: With respect to the air resupply operation, did the President ever give specific authority for Col. North to conduct the air supply—resupply operations?

POINDEXTER: Mr. Foley, I have gone over this question numerous times now and I have told you what I feel was the President's understanding. It did not include something as specific as directing Col. North to conduct air supply operations.

FOLEY: I understand you have told us the President has general knowledge and I accept that answer. I am trying to find out whether the President had more specific knowledge. You told us that the President had specific knowledge about the construction of the airfield, which is a detail of the effort of air resupply.

I am just asking you if he knew about the general effort to resupply or authorized it and you have answered the question.

Col. North testified that in the summer of 1985, rather than route money directly to the contras, he participated in the establishment of a secret Swiss bank account under his control.

When you approved the diversion of funds from the sale of arms to Iran, did you also approve the use of the Swiss bank accounts, the secret Swiss bank account?

POINDEXTER: Mr. Foley, I don't think it is accurate to say that Col. North established a Swiss bank account under his control.

FOLEY: I said participated.

POINDEXTER: Well, I misunderstood you then. I was aware that Col. North was concerned about the logistics operation, the way it was going, and I was aware that he was going to Miami to talk to the contra leadership about this and I was aware that he was going to talk to Gen. Secord about setting up a more professional logistics support operation as a private operation.

With regard to details of bank accounts that Gen. Secord may or may not have had, I simply didn't get involved in that.

FOLEY: Did you know about it?

POINDEXTER: I suppose at some point I probably did, only from the standpoint of it being mentioned probably in passing, in talking about the amount of money that was available to the contra leadership.

But with regard to how many accounts and what their names were—

FOLEY: Were you told how much money was available to the contra leadership from these accounts?

POINDEXTER: The only figure that I can recall is the one that you have got in one of the exhibits where Col. North indicated to me that there was $6 million available.

Earlier on, when support was coming from what we have referred to as Country Two, I was generally aware of the amount of money that was available then.

FOLEY: Were you led to believe by Col. North that $6 million from the sale of arms to Iran was going to be available to the contras?

POINDEXTER: That is the reference I was just making.

FOLEY: Were you satisfied later that that $6 million was actually distributed to the contras?

POINDEXTER: I—again, that is a detail that I did not get into. I don't know that.

FOLEY: You don't have any knowledge at a later time that you can recall—you had no knowledge of how much actually went to the contras?

POINDEXTER: No, I do not know.

FOLEY: Do you know if the main force of the contras, the FDN, was ever provided with any of the funds from the diversion?

POINDEXTER: I have no basis on which to answer that question.

FOLEY: You don't actually know who got the money or—

POINDEXTER: I don't know that. . . .

FOLEY: You believe that the violation of our stated policy around the world through Operation Staunch [the administration's policy of trying to persuade foreign countries not to sell weapons to Iran and Iraq] and other activities was not seriously damaged by this undertaking?

POINDEXTER: Absolutely not, Mr. Foley. First of all, our policy was not an arms embargo against Iran. We don't just all of a sudden, out of the blue, decide to embargo arms to Iran.

The policy objective there was an end to the Iran-Iraq war. One of the methods to achieve that policy objective was to try to reduce the flow of arms into Iran. We weren't very successful.

As it turns out, Bill Casey and I—before he died—firmly believed that the actions that we had taken with the Iranians, the talks that we had had with them, were responsible for preventing or postponing a major Iranian attack across the border against Iraq.

That doesn't have anything to do with the fact that we provided arms; it had to do with our discussions with the Iranians, explaining to them that we didn't think the Soviets would ever allow them to defeat Iraq and they better rethink their situation.

Now, that is a step toward our objective of ending the Iran-Iraq war. The provision of the small amount of defensive arms was important to get them to listen to us, and listen to our reasoning.

FOLEY: So if you had it to do over again, you would not have stopped the process of this kind of exchange; is that fair?

POINDEXTER: If it had not been exposed, the next step was to bring in officials within the State Department in the actual discussions with the Iranians, and who knows where it would have led.

As I testified the other day, I think there is still a possibility.

FOLEY: The problem was in the exposure, not in the policy?

POINDEXTER: That's correct.

* * *

The President's Credibility

[Rep. Dick] CHENEY [R-Wyo.]: . . . The concern I have is that—I don't mean to moralize about not telling lies. A lot of people will do that. There has been—there has been plenty of expressions of moral indignation and outrage over some of these events and I think a lot is unjustified and excessive.

The reason for not misleading the Congress is a practical one. It is stupid. It is self-defeating.

Because while it may, in fact, allow you to prevail in the problem of the moment, eventually you destroy the President's credibility. The President's powers are for the most part the powers to persuade.

We can't compel anybody to do much of anything. He has to rely upon his capacity to persuade the Congress to support diffi-

cult policies, to persuade the public to make difficult decisions, and support difficult policies, and every time actions taken by the President or his subordinates raise questions about his credibility, it is just that much more difficult the next time around to argue that, in fact, the President is telling the truth, that he has solid information.

I look back at the events of the Reagan Administration. I can think of several incidents where the President's credibility was absolutely essential to having the American people understand and support what it was he wanted to do.

I think of the shoot-down of the Korean airliner, the charges the Soviets made that somehow this was an espionage mission. Or the Grenada operation, where there were charges this was just a willful use of power and there was no justification to take the action that was taken.

The Libyan raid, bombing raid, the Marine deployment in Lebanon, the need to aid the contras, the level of support that the Soviets provide to the contras—or to the Sandinistas in Nicaragua and thereby justify our involvement, the attractiveness of a potential arms deal with the Soviet Union, all of these things ultimately from the standpoint of the President and a successful policy depend upon his ability to be able to persuade the Congress and the American people that he understands the problems, that he has looked at it, and that the course of action he has recommended is based, in fact, on a sound policy.

If you go back and find instances where, whether it is the Iranian arms transaction, or the alleged diversion of funds to the contras, where there is a question about his credibility, then it seems to me you have destroyed his effectiveness for the future, or seriously weakened it, made his problems in governing more difficult than they otherwise might be.

Do you have concern about that?

Was that ever a subject of discussion?

POINDEXTER: Well, in my view I think that the President has remained very credible throughout this whole episode. That, of course, was part of my plan.

That is also why I recognized when I approved the diversion or the transfer of the residual funds to the contras that if, indeed, that ever did leak out, that I would have to resign, and I was prepared to do that.

You know, I approved it. I accept responsibility for it. And I don't think that the President has lost any credibility because of that. He has said all along that he was unaware.

Indeed, he was unaware. I think with regard to the Iranian project, in his speech that he made to the country, the statements were accurate, in my view. I still feel they were accurate. We weren't telling everything that we knew at that point, and that was very deliberate.

And I, frankly, think, Mr. Cheney, that the American people understand that. I don't think they want to know the secrets of all of the details of the actions that the U.S. Government takes in trying to implement foreign policy and to protect the national security of the United States.

The kinds of responses that I have been getting in telegrams since my appearance, my public appearance here, convinces me that that is the case.

I think the American people understand very well that they don't want to know all of the details.

* * *

Control of Contra Funds

[Rep. Dante B.] FASCELL [D-Fla.]: Now, you testified in answer to Mr. Foley that you'd never really received an accounting or a report on the amount of money that was raised, and also that you never really got an accounting or report on aid that actually went to the contras, and that you left all of that to North, as I understand your testimony.

And so you had no way of measuring or determining the attainment of your objectives, because that was all in North's hands; am I correct?

POINDEXTER: That's correct. The thing that I was interested in—that they were getting supplies and they were surviving as an effective fighting force in the country and in the surrounding countries.

FASCELL: So there was no review or accountability either with regard to funds or with regard to attainment of objective, except in the brain of Col. North, unless you knew that he was telling Bill Casey?

POINDEXTER: Mr. Fascell, as I said, I was unaware that Director Casey was in on this. But I think—you know, this business about accountability, it bothers me.

FASCELL: I didn't mean it in the sense of accounting for every dollar. But—

POINDEXTER: No. But even in general terms, I take exception to the claim that there is no accountability. Col. North is a very competent, trustworthy officer.

FASCELL: I am sure of that. I wasn't raising that question.

POINDEXTER: And Gen. Secord is, too.

FASCELL: Well, we are still trying to figure out his books. At least I am.

POINDEXTER: Well, my feeling is they are both trustworthy people who exercised good judgment and I frankly think that much of the accounting that goes on to provide accountability starts with the premise that people aren't trusted, and in this case I trusted both of these officers implicitly.

* * *

[Sen. Paul S.] TRIBLE [Jr., R-Va.]: . . . I would like to have your opinion of what is the role of truth for a public official. When should National Security Advisers and their top assistants be assumed to tell the truth, and when is it their right or prerogative not to do so, and I think that is a fair question and I think it is central to what we are about.

POINDEXTER: Ideally, Senator, good faith, and I think that is basically what you are talking about, is a two-way street. The problem is that in this struggle that we have ongoing now between our way of life, democracy and the totalitarianism represented by the Soviet Union, we are often faced with many, many issues that have lots of shades of gray.

The world is not black or white, the world is a very complex, dangerous place. Sometimes you have to make very tough decisions.

In the cases that I have been involved with, I have done my best to use my best judgment to help make those decisions and in some cases make those decisions.

The example that I would like to cite about good faith being a two-way street is the thing that I have referred to several times up to this point about the last $100 million that the Congress appropriated [in October 1986]. It took eight months for this Congress to appropriate those funds while men in Central America that were fighting for their freedom were dying. Now, I don't think that is good faith.

Now, the ex-Speaker of the House [Thomas P. "Tip" O'Neill, Jr., D-Mass.], in my view, this is my personal assessment, held up bringing that issue to a vote in the House for four months, for four of those eight months, even after both houses had voted, a majority of them, for the $100 million, he held up bringing the issue to a conference and putting it into an instrument that the President could sign for an additional two months.

So one man, who was not elected by all the people, was responsible, in my view, for holding up that funding for a period of six months.

Now, that is just one example of what I consider to be the lack of good faith on the part of some members of the Congress. Now, that is not an ideal situation.

I acknowledge that. But sometimes you have got to cope with things the way they are. That is what we were trying to do.

* * *

Deniability

[Sen. David L.] BOREN [D-Okla.]: Did you ever go the President after this story all started to come out and say, Mr. President, you didn't know about it at the time, but this thing looks like it is really going to be controversial, and I think you should know, you should hear it from me, you should know exactly what went on because you are going to be asked some questions?

Did you ever go to the President after the fact at any time?

POINDEXTER: With regard to the transfer—

BOREN: The diversion of funds?

POINDEXTER: Residuals?

BOREN: Yes.

POINDEXTER: No. I did not. Because, as I have testified earlier, up until the very last minute that month, I did not think that the transfer of residuals would come out. In fact, I specifically had directed Col. North to leave that out of the chronologies. I was treating that as a separate issue.

BOREN: So before you knew the President was going to make a speech to the American people on November 13th—

POINDEXTER: I didn't see that that—

BOREN: You still felt the President didn't need to know?

POINDEXTER: That is correct.

BOREN: I have to say that really troubles me. Going back to my experience as an executive on a very small scale, I used to say to my staff, if you did a mistake, you did something to inject me into controversy, I want to be the first person who knows about the mistake. Especially when trouble hits. I want to know all the facts.

POINDEXTER: Senator, I obviously didn't think it was a mistake. If I had discussed that in the White House before I left, I think it would have made it much more difficult for the President to distance himself from the decision. It would have raised a lot of questions as to when he knew it.

This way he didn't know.

BOREN: I suppose the President could have said, though, I didn't know it at the time and I found out about it later. He could have said exactly when he found out?

POINDEXTER: I know. But I think it would have been, in my opinion, more difficult to believe that and decided to do it the way I did it.

* * *

[Rep. Peter W.] RODINO [Jr., D-N.J.]: You knew, of course, that what the President was about to tell the American people [on November 13, 1986] was absolutely not only misleading, but deceptive; isn't that not the case?

POINDEXTER: No, I don't think it was, Mr. Rodino. What part are you referring to?

RODINO: Well, on November 13th, the charge has been made that the United States has shipped weapons to Iran as ransom payment for the release of American hostages.

POINDEXTER: We didn't think then, nor do I think now, that that is an accurate—I mean, saying that we were shipping arms as ransom for hostages is not an accurate description of what we were doing. I still believe that.

RODINO: And when you say that the United States has not swapped boatloads or planeloads [of] American weapons for the return of American hostages and we will not, and that again is a statement of the President, that again is not misleading?

POINDEXTER: As I have testified, Mr. Rodino, the President's view, and I agreed with it, was that it was not a swap of arms for hostages because the people that we were dealing with were the Iranians, they were not the captors of the hostages, they did not have control, total control, over those captors, and it is just as if you would go to another third country and ask them to intervene for you.

RODINO: You think that is the way the American public understood that statement?

POINDEXTER: Well, so far, Mr. Rodino, I have received probably a couple thousand telegrams since these hearings began, my appearance before you, and all but about 12 or 15 of those, the people say they understand, they support what we were trying to do, and I think it is very clear to them. I don't think that they felt misled.

RODINO: Notwithstanding the fact that the President stated time and again that it was American policy not to deal with terrorists and not to trade arms for hostages—you still insist on that position?

POINDEXTER: I don't think that he had, prior to November of 1986, had ever addressed the question of arms for hostages. But he has stated—

RODINO: You mean that was not the stated American policy?

POINDEXTER: No, the issue didn't come up before that. That is all I mean.

It is and has been our policy not to compromise with the terrorists that take the hostages, and we didn't think we were doing that. And that was—the President—that was very clear in his mind.

In my preparation with him for the speech and for the press backgrounder, there was no need to go over that point with him. That was firm in his mind from the very beginning.

Now, I am telling you the way he thinks about it. Now, some of the Cabinet officers that objected to it did not see it that way, and they argued with the President and he argued right back that he was comfortable in viewing it the way he did.

And so from his own heart and mind he did not see it as ransoming hostages by providing arms. . . .

RODINO: . . . You have testified here and stated that you were concerned about the disclosure of a lot of these facts concerning the diversion, concerning the sale of arms for hostages, and you wanted really to protect the President from political embarrassment. But isn't that political embarrassment that you talk of merely a consequence of a disclosure to the American people of misstatements and misleading information that the public might then be aware of?

Wouldn't that be the political embarrassment?

In other words, wouldn't it be, in effect, an attempt to keep the American people from knowing, from knowing what had taken place, and the political embarrassment as a consequence that would occur to the President, but weren't you keeping the American people from knowing what was happening?

POINDEXTER: No, I don't view it that way at all. The people knew that the President wanted to support the contras and was going to do everything he could to do that. He constantly talked about that, how important it was.

RODINO: He didn't tell them he wanted to divert funds or trade arms for hostages?

POINDEXTER: He told them, Mr. Rodino, that we were trying to get the hostages back and we were working very hard to do that, but he wasn't going to—he specifically told them that he was withholding information on how we were trying to get the hostages back.

I frankly don't think the American people want to know that, Mr. Rodino.

RODINO: I don't think the American people want to know what they shouldn't know, but I think, Admiral, that the political embarrassment that you speak about can't be other than a refusal on your part to get the American people to participate in the process of knowing what the President had been doing and what the Administration had done.

POINDEXTER: The main point, and maybe I wasn't clear on this, but I'll go over it again—I thought that the transfer, the use of residuals to support the contras, would be a politically volatile issue.

It wasn't withholding it from the American people; it was that there were a lot of opponents in the Congress that would have not agreed with our interpretation of the Boland Amendment. They wouldn't have agreed to the Iranian project, just as we have seen demonstrated, and if it came out it was going to be a very hot political issue that would be used to pound on the President.

And I wanted to be sure that the President could say that he didn't have anything to do with that part of it, and he has said that, and I think in the end I believe that the President is going to come out stronger for it.

* * *

Altering Documents

[Rep. Jack] BROOKS [D-Texas]: Col. North has testified that beginning in October of 1986, and right up until the day he was fired by the President from the staff on November 25th, that

he undertook to destroy and alter records from the NSC files related to both contra supply and the Iranian arms deal and you were his superior officer at the time, head of the NSC.

Did you authorize or instruct him to alter or destroy those records?

POINDEXTER: I don't believe I did, but I also don't think it is accurate to say that all—I don't know exactly what he destroyed, but based on his testimony, I would conclude that most of what he destroyed is not covered by this particular Act [the Presidential Records Act] that you are talking about here. They are working records of the NSC, which in this context are different than the presidential records.

The papers, for example, that I handled in my position as National Security Adviser fell in about three different categories. One, they were presidential records; two, they were official NSC records; and three, they were personal or working papers.

BROOKS: You were aware that he did destroy some records, though?

POINDEXTER: After the fact, I understand from his testimony that he did.

BROOKS: Section 2202 of the Presidential Records Act states that, "The United States shall reserve and retain complete ownership, possession and control of presidential records."

In 1978, Congress made a point of establishing the ownership of these presidential records because a few years previously a President and his staff had tried to alter history by destroying some papers.

I would just want to conclude this section by saying that the value of the paper that you destroyed, that you destroyed and the other documents that Col. North destroyed, what is at issue is not that value, but the effort of people like you and Col. North to make the historical record conform to what you wanted it to be by tampering with that record, by altering or destroying it and I think what you have done is to steal from the American people, this generation and future generations, their chance to learn what actually happened, what documents you were working with and what you have been doing since you are telling stories that are very interesting.

And I think that in addition to being a potential offense, which we are not [handling] here, the action most certainly is an enormous betrayal of the trust that I thought you held with the American people.

I have a couple other questions—

POINDEXTER: Could I respond to that?

BROOKS: Admiral, you are welcome to respond. You have been responding beautifully this time.

POINDEXTER: I obviously don't agree with your interpretation.

BROOKS: That is an understatement.

POINDEXTER: That particular version of the finding taken by itself, which would have been done if it leaked out as has been done since I have testified about it, taken out of context presents a misleading picture to the American public and that is what I was trying to avoid.

* * *

Upholding the Constitution

[Sen. George J.] MITCHELL [D-Maine]: . . . .One of the unusual features of the American system of government is that it combines in one person, the President, the duties of the chief of State and the executive head of government.

Most other countries separate those duties. One result of their being combined in our system is that for many Americans, the political interests of the President are seen as identical to the national interests. This is not a problem unique to the current Administration.

You are not the first, you will surely not be the last presidential aide to confuse those interests. But as a result of your making decisions based on your desire to protect the President's political interests, those very interests have been seriously damaged.

At the same time, at least in the opinion of some of us, the national interest has been damaged. If these hearings do nothing else, let's hope they remind all government officials that their first loyalty is not to any person and not to any office.

Their first and foremost obligation is to support and defend the Constitution and the laws of the United States. The Constitution and the laws. And if government officials remember that, they will best serve both the national interest and the President's political interests.

Thank you.

POINDEXTER: Senator, may I respond?

MITCHELL: You are free to do so. Certainly, Admiral.

POINDEXTER: The President also takes an oath of office where he will support and defend the Constitution of the United States against all enemies foreign and domestic, I believe.

What I meant by saying my loyalty and the loyalty of the NSC staff was to the President does not preclude or in any way supersede that oath of office that I took or the President took.

The job of the NSC staff is to assist the President and advise the President in carrying out his duties to support and defend the Constitution of the United States. That is exactly what we were doing. And I don't find that my expression of the loyalty of the NSC staff to the President in any way abrogates the responsibilities that I took and the other military officers on the staff and those civilians with commissions took to support and defend the Constitution of the United States.

That is what this is all about. That is what we were trying to do.

* * *

In closing statements on Poindexter's fifth day of testimony, July 21, 1987, panel members focused on the admiral's inability to recall pertinent facts and his decision to keep much of the information about the Iran-contra affair to himself and a few close colleagues.

INOUYE: ... Now, one would think that if you had a neat idea or a good idea, a legal idea, that others concur that would be a neat idea, I would like to brag about it. I would go to my boss and say, "Boss, I have got a neat idea. I have got a good idea. I can show you how we can pay for the contras, provide them with arms, and" as you said, "it won't cost the taxpayers any money."

But instead, you made a decision, according to your testimony, you and you alone, to set up a very elaborate scheme of keeping this secret.

Well, you decided not to tell the President because it would result in a political explosion. And this was done six weeks after you assumed the high position of National Security Adviser.

I am certain you were well aware that Mr. Casey was the campaign manager of the President. He was the political brains in the White House. He was an expert on covert activities, and yet here again you felt that you should not discuss this matter with him because, in the case of Mr. Casey, you didn't want to face that awful possibility of having to withhold information from the Congress.

Then you decided to withhold this information from members of the Cabinet, the Secretary of State, the Secretary of Defense [Caspar W. Weinberger], the Attorney General, and when asked earlier this morning about the Chairman of the Joint Chiefs of Staff [Gen. John W. Vessey, Jr.], well, he is subordinate to the Secretary of Defense, so if you are not going to give it to the Secretary of Defense, why give it to the Chairman of the Joint Chiefs?

Then, needless to say, if you are not going to give information to the above, you are not going to give it to the Congress, which you did not, but more specifically, you decided to withhold information not from the Congress of the United States, but from the leadership of the United States Congress; it was just a few people, and the members of the Intelligence Committees of both the House and the Senate.

I think with that type of testimony some of us are justified in asking ourselves, and in this case I will ask you this—you have had about a week to review your testimony, to sharpen your skills of recall.

Do you have any clarification you would like to make or can you tell us whether information is being withheld from us today or during the past week?

POINDEXTER: Mr. Chairman, absolutely not. I have not withheld any information in this hearing that I can accurately recall or have any recollection of, and what I have testified as I swore at the beginning of these hearings is the absolute truth and the whole truth.

* * *

A Secret Foreign Policy?

FOLEY: ... I think we have talked again and again about how to establish a basis of trust and a basis of better reaction, interaction between the Congress and the Executive Branch, and the only thing that I would observe, and I have tried not to make a lot of observations here, is that it is extremely difficult, it seems to me, if the view that you have, and I take it you sincerely express all your views here, is that the National Security Council is surrounded by a media that often deliberately distorts, deliberately mis-reports on the news and events, that the Congress is reflecting attitudes that are in bad faith in the attempt to confront the President's policies, that the normal agencies of government are lacking in enthusiasm and sort of affected by a cancer, a bureaucratic unwillingness to take risks—it leaves a very small group of people in the National Security Council to whom you would feel comfortable in sharing your plans and proposals for the Presidential action.

You didn't choose to share it with the Director of the Central Intelligence Agency, with whom you had high regard. You have given the impression, I think, that the less contact with the Congress, the better as an absolute rule, and I find it—that it would be a little distressing if I were in your position and felt that that was the case as to how in the future a democratic society can develop the kind of consensus and the President's program can be advanced with respect to the Congress and to the press, to the other agencies of the Executive Branch of Government if that pessimistic judgment is made about their intentions and attitudes.

POINDEXTER: Mr. Foley, I don't think it as accurate, as you are implying, that the NSC staff had some secret foreign policy. As I have stated before, the President's foreign policy was very open and understood by the people of this country. He campaigned on the issues in the 1984 campaign, and the people fully understand that. So that was not being withheld, and he was elected holding these positions.

What we have been talking about primarily in these hearings is how the NSC staff went about implementing these policies that were very public positions that the President took, and I think, under the conditions that have existed over the past few years that we were completely justified, and it was entirely proper that we keep the details of these implementations secret and highly compartmented, and I still contend that the majority of the people understand that and accept that and feel that that is a necessary way of doing business.

* * *

BROOKS: I have got just one question, really. You know, several times today you said that the American people when they vote for a President, they know what his foreign policy is, that they are voting for his foreign policy, he should be allowed to carry out that foreign policy without any interference.

Is that basically what you said?

POINDEXTER: What I said was that I think that the way our Constitution is written, the President is the chief architect of the foreign policy and the people when they vote for a President recognize the foreign policy position that he represents and that the President ought to be given an opportunity to carry out that foreign policy.

BROOKS: And are you suggesting that the millions of Americans that voted for the President were in favor of sending weapons to the Ayatollah [Ruhallah Khomeini, Iran's religious leader]? Iran?

POINDEXTER: I think that that is a tactical decision, using

[Rep. Jim] Courter's [R-N.J.] words, that most Americans would think that they didn't have enough information to make a decision one way or the other; and I think that most American people feel that that kind of tactical decision ought to be left up to the President who has the intelligence and who has the information on which to base that kind of decision.

* * *

Poindexter's Role

HAMILTON: ... Adm. Poindexter, I want to say that we have indeed appreciated your testimony. I've worked with you, I think, for about five years. I consider you to be honorable and able, certainly dedicated to this country and in all of my experience at all times, a gentleman....

Your home state of Indiana and your community are justifiably proud of your service to the country. You have experienced, as other witnesses have before these committees, something of the satisfaction, I think, and something of the frustration of public servants; and none of us, I think, can know all of the circumstances that you confronted as the National Security Adviser to the President.

But I know enough about those circumstances and about your responsibilities not to judge you personally. It is however—and I think you can appreciate this—our job to examine your role in the decision-making process so that we can understand what went on and try to correct the mistakes that occurred.

Your comments about secrecy in government or compartmentation, as you put it, concern me as it concerns my colleagues a great deal. You have testified that you intentionally withheld information from the President that denied him the opportunity to make probably the most fateful decision of his presidency on whether to divert the funds from the Iranian arms sales to aid the contras.

You said your objective was to withhold information from the Congress. Apparently, so far as I understood the testimony, without direction or authority to do so. As many have mentioned, you destroyed the December 5th, '85, finding.

You apparently intended to have original documents relating to the contras either altered or removed. You were unwilling to speak candidly with senior Justice and CIA officials about the Hawk missile shipments to Iran. And you kept the statements or the Secretaries of State and Defense uninformed about important initiatives in their areas of responsibility.

Now all of us recognize the need for secrecy in the conduct of government. This Member has been privileged to receive I believe the highest secrets of our government and I am quite sympathetic to your pleas that secrecy is often needed and too often violated. Even so, I believe that in this instance we have had testimony about excessive secrecy that has had serious consequences for the decision-making processes of government. All of us who work within our system of government sometimes feel impatient with its painstaking procedures. All of us disagree from time to time with the decisions reached. Yet, your comment about Congress—and I quote it directly—"I simply did not want any outside interference"—reflects an attitude which makes, in my judgment at least, our constitutional system of checks and balances unworkable.

Instead of bringing each agency dealing with foreign policy into the process, you cut those agencies out of the process. You told the committees, "I firmly believe in very tight compartmentation."

You compartmentalized not only the President's senior advisers, but, in effect, you locked the President himself out of the process. You began your testimony by saying that the function of a National Security Adviser is to present options and to advise the President.

Yet you told the committees the buck stops here with me. That is not where the buck is supposed to stop. You wanted to deflect blame from the President, but that is another way of saying you wanted to deflect responsibility from the President and that should not be done in our system of government.

You testified that diverting funds to the contras was a detail, a matter of implementation of the President's policies and you felt that you had the authority to approve it.

Yet this was a major foreign policy initiative as subsequent events have shown with very far-reaching ramifications, and this member, at least, wonders what else could be done in the President's name if this is mere implementation of policy.

As my colleague, Cheney, said yesterday, the secret methods you chose to determine and to implement policy were also self-defeating.

Both Mr. McFarlane and Lt. Col. North have acknowledged to these committees that it would have been better to continue the public debate, to seek contra funding. Both the contra resupply effort and the Iran initiative were highly controversial.

Decisions were made by only a few people. Many experts in the government were not consulted who should have been. Members of Congress were not informed.

Contacts with high officials did not take place. Information was compartmentalized. Decisions were made in secret. And discussion about them was limited.

May I suggest to you, sir, that this approach did not and will not work?

You cannot gain and sustain the support of the Congress of the United States and the American people for significant foreign policy decisions when they are uninformed. The secret means employed on behalf of the policy undermined its success, and when revealed, in my judgment, contributed to its failure.

Now, beyond that, excessive secrecy led to disarray in the process of government. That December 5th finding that has been so much talked about is a case study of excessive secrecy and how not to make policy in a covert operation....

Probably more important, secrecy contributed to disarray in the Oval Office. The President apparently did not know that you were making some of the most important foreign policy decisions of his presidency. You have testified, "I was convinced that the President would, in the end, think the diversion was a good idea."

Yet, the President has stated that he would not have approved the diversion. Excessive secrecy placed the President in an untenable position and caused him to make false and contradictory public statements. Let me cite some of them.

On November 6, 1986, the President said, "The speculation, the commenting and all on a story that came out of the Middle East has no foundation."

A week later the President said, "We did not, repeat, we did not trade weapons or anything else for hostages."

But on March 4, the President said, "A few months ago I told the American people I did not trade arms for hostages. My heart and my best intentions still tell me that is true, but the facts and the evidence tell me it is not."

Turning to the solicitation of private aid for the contras, the President said on May 5th, "I don't know how that money was to be used and I have no knowledge that there was ever any solicitation by our people with these people."

But on May 15, the President altered his view. He said, "As a matter of fact, I was definitely involved in the decisions about support to the freedom fighters. It was my idea to begin with."

May I suggest that the Preident was unaware of some important actions taken by his staff and, therefore, he misspoke? Because he lacked information, the President inflicted serious and repeated political wounds upon himself. Polls continue to indicate that a majority of the American people still feel that the President, despite his statements to the contrary, did know that the money from the Iran arms sales was channeled to the contras.

Let me finish, Admiral.

Two policies brought us here. The arms sales to Iran and the diversion of funds from those sales to the contras. The first began with a document the President forgot and you considered inoperative.

The second began without the President's knowledge. The President created the environment in the White House in which you and Lt. Col. North operated. He cared passionately about freeing the hostages and aiding the contras.

He gave you broad authority to carry out those purposes. Apparently he did not spell out how you were to achieve those goals. You believe that it was left to you and to Lt. Col. North to make key decisions, but the President cannot delegate such authority. No one can ask you or expect you to take responsibility for the President's decisions. Those are his and his alone. . . .

POINDEXTER: I just have one brief comment, Mr. Chairman.

With regard to your closing statement, I would just simply say that we will have to agree, you and I, to disagree on your interpretation of many of the events. And, finally, I leave this hearing with my head held high that I have done my very best to promote the long-term National Security interests of the United States.

Thank you.

George P. Shultz

Following are excerpts from the July 23, 1987, testimony of Secretary of State George P. Shultz. Shultz was asked about his knowledge of the 1985-86 U.S.-Iranian arms deals and the extent to which he participated in administration decison-making on the issue. Interest in his testimony had been heightened by Rear Adm. John M. Poindexter's statements that Shultz had not given President Reagan his full support and had said he did not want to know the details about the arms deals.

[Mark A.] BELNICK [Senate counsel]: There has been testimony here recently by Adm. Poindexter, that to the extent you were not informed [about the Iran arms sales], it was because you asked not to know or to be involved particularly with the Iran initiative after you lost the argument with the President regarding that initiative.

In particular, Adm. Poindexter testified that he did not withhold anything from you that you did not want withheld from you. With this in mind, Mr. Secretary, this testimony in mind, let me ask you, first, whether you ever told Adm. Poindexter or any other member of the administration that you did not want to be kept informed of the Iran initiative?

SHULTZ: I never made such a statement. What I did say to Adm. Poindexter was that I wanted to be informed of the things I needed to know to do my job as Secretary of State.

But he didn't need to keep me posted on the details, the operational details of what he was doing. That is what I told him. . . .

BELNICK: The main events you wanted to be kept informed of?

SHULTZ: Yes.

BELNICK: And that was true not only with respect to Iran, but with respect to all areas of foreign relations activity, including activities engaged in by the NSC [National Security Council] staff in Central America?

SHULTZ: Not only did I want to be informed, but when I found out things, sometimes by chance, I did my best to act on those things. . . .

BELNICK: Do you recall, Mr. Secretary, being briefed by Adm. Poindexter when he was about to assume the position of National Security Adviser on December 5, 1985, concerning the Iran initiative?

SHULTZ: Yes. He called me on the secure phone and gave me a lengthy briefing, and I felt very good about it, and I remarked to my executive assistant, who was there, that he told me more than I had known before of what went on in the latter half of 1985 and I felt this was a good thing and we were off to a good start.

BELNICK: Do you recall what you told Adm. Poindexter about your views concerning the Iran initiative as he described it to you in that briefing?

SHULTZ: Well, I told him that I thought it was a very bad idea, that I was opposed to it. That doesn't mean I was—I was in favor of doing things that had any potential for rearranging the behavior of Iran and our relationship with Iran, but I was very much opposed to arms sales in connection with that.

BELNICK: Did you tell him at that time that, in your view, the proposed policy amounted to paying for hostages and had to be stopped?

SHULTZ: Yes.

BELNICK: In that same conversation, sir, on December 5, the day that Adm. Poindexter briefed you on the initiative, did he tell you that on the very same day the President had signed a covert action finding authorizing an arms shipment to Iran?

SHULTZ: No.

BELNICK: Did Adm. Poindexter brief you about that finding two days later, on December 7, 1985, when you met at the White House with the President and other senior officials to discuss whether the proposed initiative ought to go forward?

SHULTZ: No. That was—I'm sure that was not mentioned in that session.

BELNICK: We will return to that December 7 meeting subsequently.

But let me ask you now about a subsequent meeting with the President and other senior U.S. officials on January 7, 1986, also concerning the Iran initiative and whether it ought to go forward.

Were you informed by Adm. Poindexter at that January 7 meeting that just one day earlier, on January 6, the President had signed another finding with respect to arms shipments to Iran from the United States?

SHULTZ: That was never mentioned in that meeting.

BELNICK: Then ten days later, on January 17, 1986, according to the chronology, you attended a family group luncheon with Adm. Poindexter and others, at which there was a discussion of the legality and wisdom of the proposed Iran initiative.

I understand you argued at that luncheon that the initiative, in your view, would be both unwise and unlawful?

SHULTZ: That is correct. I came back to my office and I told my assistant that we had had another discussion of this and I had once again said that I thought it was illegal and unwise.

BELNICK: Am I correct, sir, that at this January 17 luncheon the Admiral did not inform you that on that same day, January 17, the President had signed the third of the findings authorizing U.S. arms shipments to Iran?

SHULTZ: I would hardly have come back from the meeting saying that it was illegal if I had been informed that the Attorney General had provided a proper legal basis for proceeding. . . .

BELNICK: Now, sir, there came a time on July 26, 1986, that Adm. Poindexter according to the chronology advised you of the release from captivity of Father [Lawrence] Jenco. Did the Admiral inform you this release had been achieved in any way as a result of the U.S.-Iran initiative?

SHULTZ: No.

BELNICK: At that time, sir, in fact were you operating under the assumption that there was no initiative?

SHULTZ: I was operating under the assumption after the stand down discussion that we would continue to work at the problems presented by Iran, and we had normal ways of doing that. And I think by that time we had initiated one additional one that you never know what may have some promise, but, anyway, it was a different and official proper way of trying to have a sensible discourse with them.

So that I didn't assume that we had lost interest in the Iran problem, we didn't, we never lost interest in it but it is a question of how you do it.

BELNICK: By the way, the stand down discussion was in late May or early June 1986, am I right?

SHULTZ: That's my recollection. I don't have a note in my records about it, but that is my, what is in my head.

BELNICK: But you understood when Adm. Poindexter told you that the people involved had been told to stand down that it was over?

SHULTZ: Yes.

BELNICK: Now Adm. Poindexter has testified that in parlance, the term "stand down" means that there's only a temporary hiatus, it is an intermission. But that's not how you understood it.

SHULTZ: That's not how I understood it, but I'm not, I'm a Marine. I'm not a Navy man. So I may be wrong about that.

Somebody looked it up in the dictionary, though.

BELNICK: What did they find?

SHULTZ: Stand down means it's done. According to the dictionary. That's not necessarily a naval dictionary. I accede to Adm. Poindexter on that. What I understood that to mean was that this has been conducted and worked at and they went all the way to Tehran, and it fizzled.

BELNICK: Whether Army, Navy or Marines, the Admiral did not say to you we expect this to be rejuvenated within the next several weeks or any particular point in time?

SHULTZ: No. Although the initiative or effort that I mentioned a moment ago I think was something that he suggested, and I thought it was a good suggestion. I worked on it and a few of the key people who knew a lot about Iran in the State Department worked on it, and so it wasn't as though things were dead, as I said.

* * *

Shultz on North

BELNICK: Sir, did you ever express the view that [Lt.] Col. [Oliver L.] North was a loose cannon?

SHULTZ: No, I didn't. What I said—I think what you are referring to is an incident toward the end of a staff meeting in my office in which I told Elliott Abrams—the question was where are the freedom fighters getting their arms, as I remember; and I said to—Elliott said he didn't know. I said well, you're our point man here, you should find out. Or something like that.

BELNICK: As I understand, that conversation took place on September 4, 1985. Secretary Abrams has described that conversation here based on a note that he took in which he said you told him to "monitor Ollie."

Is that your recollection of the instruction you gave him?

SHULTZ: Well, my recollection is based on a note that was taken by somebody else who was in the meeting about what it was that I said and what I said is the way I put it. But no reason why Elliott shouldn't have taken it that way, because Col. North was commonly seen as a principal contact with the freedom fighters.

BELNICK: Did you have a view at that time that Col. North, because of any information that you had about him, was someone who had to be watched closely or that Elliott ought to monitor?

SHULTZ: There was talk about erratic behavior on his part, but I had no particular knowledge about it and didn't want to pass judgment. I'm not—and I can't get myself in the position of supervising people down the line working for others.

BELNICK: But you did expect, based on what you told Secretary Abrams, September 4, 1985, that he would keep himself informed about the activities; and as I have read the note specifically, about how the contras were getting supplied with arms and not simply shut his eyes to that?

SHULTZ: Yes.

BELNICK: All right, sir, in light of what you now know or have heard from the investigations regarding, for example, the role of Col. North and other NSC staff members in assisting the contras during the period of the Boland restrictions, the involvement in the [Eugene] Hasenfus flight [shot down over Nicaragua in October 1986 while transporting arms to the contras], the involvement of at least one of our ambassadors, [Ambassador to Costa Rica Lewis A.] Tambs, in negotiations for an airstrip to be used in Central America for contra resupply and in helping, as he testified to this panel on instructions from Col. North to open a southern military front against Nicaragua during the period of the Boland restrictions, in light of those facts and others that have come out during the investigations, is it your view that Secretary Abrams carried out your instructions to keep himself and you informed?

SHULTZ: What has been brought out in these hearings about all of the activities you mentioned has surprised a lot of people. It surprised me, it must have been a surprise to Chairman [Rep. Lee H.] Hamilton [D-Ind., chairman of the House panel investigating the Iran-contra affair], who looked into this a couple times and had assurances. So I imagine it has surprised the President. So things have come out that we didn't know about.

It wasn't too long, I think, after I had that conversation with Mr. Abrams that the results of inquiring into Col. North's activities—and at that time I think Mr. [Robert C.] McFarlane was the National Security Adviser—concluded with our feeling, and I think Chairman Hamilton's feeling, that we had looked into this matter and there was no problem. So this was part of the general understanding, and that is what Elliott thought, and that is what I thought.

* * *

Arms-for-Hostages

BELNICK: . . . Did Mr. McFarlane tell you that it was then proposed [in November 1985] that Israel would send an air shipment—through a European city—of some 100 Hawks to Iran?

SHULTZ: Yes. That was—he described the structure of a deal in which a plane would go from I think someplace in Portugal, as I remember, and it would be contingent on release of the hostages, a rather complex arrangement.

BELNICK: But the burden of it was if the hostages came out, the weapons would go to Iran; if they didn't, the weapons wouldn't?

SHULTZ: Exactly. It was a straight-out arms-for-hostages deal.

BELNICK: What did you tell Mr. McFarlane?

SHULTZ: I told him I hoped that the hostages would get out, but I was against it, and I was upset that he was telling me about it as it was just about to start so there was no way I could do anything about it.

But anyway, if it was happening, I hoped the hostages would get out.

BELNICK: After you objected, though, you learned within the next several days that no hostages had been released and your information was that the deal had, therefore, collapsed?

SHULTZ: Exactly.

* * *

BELNICK: On December 7, there was a meeting at the White House, and you have alluded to that meeting earlier, at which senior officials were present: you, Secretary [of Defense Caspar W.] Weinberger, [Chief of Staff] Donald [T.] Regan, Adm. Poindexter, and, of course, the President, in which the subject was the Iran initiative and the proposed dealings with Iran.

You spoke at that meeting, and, as I understand from your notes and prior testimony, expressed forceful opposition to the proposed policy?

SHULTZ: That is correct, and just as forceful was Secretary Weinberger.

BELNICK: If I could ask you, please, to turn to Tab 16? Tell us whether the document at that tab is a copy of the talking points which you prepared for the December 7 meeting and whether those points are a fair summary of the arguments you made against the Iran initiative to the President and others at that meeting?

SHULTZ: These were the talking points that I had and I worked from. In the flow of a meeting, you try to make your points as effectively as you can, and so I used these as a basis for my comments.

BELNICK: Who spoke in favor of the policy at that meeting?

SHULTZ: Well, I felt that Don Regan shared the view of Secretary Weinberger and I, and Mr. [John] McMahon, who was representing the CIA, seemed to be, as I recall, rather passive. He didn't seem to push one way or the other, but I may not be remembering that just right.

Mr. McFarlane and Adm. Poindexter seemed to be more pro doing this. The President, I felt, was somewhat on the fence but rather annoyed at me and Secretary Weinberger because I felt that he sort—he was very concerned about the hostages, as well as very much interested in the Iran initiative.

So it was a very vigorous discussion, and it took place in the family quarters in a rather informal kind of setting, and I think Secretary Weinberger started off by saying something like, "Are you really interested in my opinion?" And then the President said, "Yes." And so he gave it to him. So did I.

BELNICK: Was the President fully engaged in this conversation?

SHULTZ: Oh, yes. This idea that the President just sits around not paying attention, I don't know where anybody gets that idea. He is a very strong and decisive person.

BELNICK: Was he a strong proponent of the proposed policy at that meeting against your opposition and that of Secretary Weinberger?

SHULTZ: Well, I don't remember that he sort of argued with us. He listened, and you could feel his sense of frustration. He said at one time—because Cap [Weinberger] is a particularly good lawyer—he said, "There are legal problems here, Mr. President, in addition to all of the policy problems."

You know how people get sometimes when they are frustrated. He said, "Well, the American people will never forgive me if I fail to get these hostages out over this legal question or something like that."

And Secretary Weinberger—"but," he said, "visiting hours are Thursday," or some such statement.

So there was that kind of banter. I know people have looked at those notes and wondered if the Preident was advocating violating the law, and there was no such tone to that at all. It was the kind of statement that I'm sure we all make sometimes when we are frustrated.

* * *

BELNICK: When you left that meeting [January 7, 1986, at which Attorney General Edwin Meese III and CIA director William J. Casey were present as well as those who participated in the December 7, 1986, meeting], did you feel that a final decision had been made by the President to go forward?

SHULTZ: Well, it was very clear to me that he wanted to push in that direction. But, of course, I had been there before, in the sense of things starting and not really jelling, so I went away puzzled, distressed....

BELNICK: Mr. Secretary, feeling as you did at the time that the President may have reached a decision and was heading toward a final decision in favor of a policy that you thought would be disastrous, did you seek to speak to the President alone about that matter?

SHULTZ: No, I didn't. But there was no doubt in the President's mind about my opinion. It wasn't as though there was something that I had missed or that I felt he hadn't quite gotten. I felt I had made myself perfectly clear.

* * *

BELNICK: On Jan. 16, 1986, as your chronology reflects, you attended a Cabinet meeting at the White House from 2 to 3 p.m. in the afternoon. Adm. Poindexter and others have testified that subsequent to that Cabinet meeting, there was a post-Cabinet discussion among various senior officials about the Iran initiative, including the finding which the President would sign the very next day.

You were not at that meeting?

SHULTZ: I have no recollection of being at such a meeting, and my records show that I arrived back in the department at 3:20, I believe.

BELNICK: Yes, sir.

Just to take this one more step, Adm. Poindexter testified that while you were not at the meeting, the post-Cabinet meeting at which the finding was discussed, that you had been invited to it by Adm. Poindexter, that he had told you what the subject matter would be, but that you had said to him, in words or substance, that you had another engagement, that in any event the President and he—Adm. Poindexter—were aware of your view and you were opposed to it, period, and that you didn't attend the meeting.

SHULTZ: Well, I don't remember that, but if I was recorded as being opposed to it, that was certainly accurate.

BELNICK: Do you recall Adm. Poindexter telling you at the time, however, that they were going to discuss that day a proposed presidential finding that would authorize the very policy that you had been arguing against for six or seven months?

SHULTZ: I don't recall him using that term.

BELNICK: If Adm. Poindexter had said to you we are planning to discuss a finding, would you have considered that a watershed event, notwithstanding that you felt the President was in favor of the proposal as of Jan. 7?

SHULTZ: Yes.

BELNICK: Why, sir?

SHULTZ: In the sense that as it had been argued that without any new finding, an arms sale from the United States to Iran would be a violation of the Arms Export Control Act, and without that we are still basically in the area of talking in general about an Iran initiative and the kind of effort that Mr. McFarlane made in his London mission or other similar kinds of efforts, and you wouldn't have arms connected with it directly.

So a finding that specifically made it legal to do that would have been a change in the situation. It wouldn't necessarily mean that arms were going to be sold, but it would have clarified the legal point that was involved.

BELNICK: Was there—in addition to that, Mr. Secretary, did the finding itself have other significance in terms of the process that would have had to—it would have had to go through, the proposed covert action finding, before reaching the President's desk for signature?

SHULTZ: The normal way in which a finding is produced is that the—there is the policy part of it and there is a legal part of it. So in the case of the State Department, I rely on my legal adviser; and I happen to be blessed by having a very good one. So the legal adviser would look at it, and I would look at it, and presumably the same thing would be done in the Defense Department and the CIA and the Attorney General, of course, is the chief law officer of the United States. He would be involved. And then there would be a discussion of that and the President would then, in the light of the advice, both on the policy side and the legal side, make a decision on signing the finding or not. That's the general process that you presumably go through.

I don't think it's required by law that you do that, but certainly as a statutory member of the National Security Council, I would expect that we would go through a process of that sort. And I think it's very desirable to do it that way.

BELNICK: And it's been your experience that that was the process that was followed with other findings?

SHULTZ: Yes. That's generally the way it goes.

BELNICK: That process, though, was not followed so far as you know or the State Department was concerned with respect to the finding that you discovered had been signed in January 1986 that you learned about in November?

SHULTZ: I am sure it didn't go through that process.

BELNICK: That would be true with respect to what we now know were two other findings as well on the same matter, insofar as you know?

SHULTZ: The other two that you have mentioned didn't go through that process either. And I didn't know anything about either of those other two.

I want to be—the subject of legality was discussed periodically in all of these discussions. The precision of a finding is something different from that.

BELNICK: It would have mooted the discussion? That is, on Jan. 17, for example, the day after the 16th meeting, as you testified earlier, you were at a family group luncheon in which the subject of the legality of this initiative came up again?

SHULTZ: Yes. So there's no point in discussing it or I wouldn't have argued about it or reported back to my assistant when I debriefed on that meeting that I had said that I—I don't mean that I'm trying to act like a lawyer here, but that it was my sense that there were still legal problems and that it was unwise. That was the net of the meeting as far as I was concerned.

BELNICK: Nobody told the Secretary of State that those legal problems in the view of at least some in the Administration had been solved because the President had signed the finding the very same day?

SHULTZ: Not to my recollection.

* * *

What Did Shultz Know?

BELNICK: Sir, in the period Nov. 4 to roughly Nov. 10, when you attended the meeting at the White House that I will go into in a moment, there are indications in the records that we have seen of you expressing the view, in substance, that you weren't deceived or weren't cut out of events. This, again, as I say, is in the period between the 4th and the 10th of November.

In light of the facts, as you began to get them after Nov. 10 and have them now, is that still your view?

SHULTZ: We were discussing, I believe, what my role was, and people said, "Well, you didn't know anything about this." I said, "Yes, I did know something about it, I knew quite a bit about it." Because, after all, I had been—you have related quite a few things that took place in 1985, 1986, that I knew about and weighed in on, I didn't want to say I was uninformed, I was informed. I said my information at some point along here was fragmentary and sporadic or some such words, and, of course, I now know that was the understatement of the year.

But, at any rate, I didn't ever take the position and wouldn't have taken the position that I was totally uninformed, because that was not accurate.

BELNICK: Let's move then to the meeting on Nov. 10, 1986, at the White House, which you attended with the President; the Vice President [George Bush]; Adm. Poindexter; Don Regan; Mr. [Alton G.] Keel, who was Adm. Poindexter's Deputy; Director Casey; Secretary Weinberger and the Attorney General: And at Tab 39, Mr. Secretary, is a set of Mr. Casey's notes of that meeting which we have previously made available to you and, if I am correct, you think is a fair summary of what transpired at the meeting.

SHULTZ: Yes. And it is reasonably consistent with the notes that I gave to my Executive Assistant.

BELNICK: And if I may for the sake of time summarize what we understand from you in those notes: Adm. Poindexter gave a briefing concerning the operation with the President present, as I said, and he informed all of you at that time that a total of 1,000 TOWs [antitank missiles] and 240 Hawk spare parts were sold to Iran and also told you that this whole operation, as you said before, had started when an Israeli arms warehouse was located in Europe. That comports with your recollection?

SHULTZ: Yes.

Shortly thereafter at another briefing he said there were 2,000 TOWs, so I was very uneasy about these briefings.

BELNICK: And at this first briefing on Nov. 10, as you listened, notes indicate that you criticized the entire operation saying that it sounded like Hawks for hostages no matter what face was put on it, is that correct?

SHULTZ: That is correct.

BELNICK: But the President said that he disagreed with that view at that time.

SHULTZ: The President's view, as I have heard him express it, and I believe that he felt very clearly, was that this was basically about an initiative toward Iran and that as an aspect of it, we would get our hostages back and that a small sale of arms to Iran as a token of good intentions might or might not be part of that package, but he had no objection if it were. That is the way his mind was arranged on this, and I have heard him talk about it, and I am sure that is what he does believe....

BELNICK: And did you begin developing the view, particularly as of Nov. 10—we'll talk about the additional press guidance that you got on that day—that the President's advisers were misleading him and not giving him the facts concerning what actually transpired in the Iran initiative?

SHULTZ: I developed a very clear opinion that the President was not being given accurate information and I was very alarmed about it, and it became the preoccupying thing that I was working on through this period, and I felt that it was tremendously important for the President to get accurate information so he could see and make a judgment.

His judgment is excellent when he is given the right information, and he was not being given the right information, and I felt as this went on that the people who were giving him the information were, in a sense—had—I think I even used the word with some of my advisers, they had a conflict of interest with the President and they were trying to use his undoubted skills as a communicator to have him give a speech and give a press conference and say these things and, in doing so, he would bail them out.

At least that's the way it was—I don't want to try to attribute motives to other people too much, although I realize I have, but that's the way it shaped up to me.

So I was in a battle to try to get what I saw as the facts to the President and get—and see that he understood them.

Now, this was a very traumatic period for me because everybody was saying I'm disloyal to the President, I'm not speaking up for the policy, and I'm battling away here, and I could see people were calling for me to resign if I can't be loyal to the President, even including some of my friends and people who held high office and should know that maybe there's more involved than they're seeing.

And I frankly felt that I was the one who was loyal to the President, because I was the one who was trying to get him the facts so he could make a decision, and I must say as he absorbed this he did, he made the decision that we must get all these facts out.

But it was—it was a battle royal.

BELNICK: Mr. Secretary, in that battle royal to get out the facts which you waged and which the record reflects that you waged, who was the other side?

SHULTZ: Well, I can't say for sure. I feel that Adm. Poindexter was certainly on the other side of it, I felt that Director Casey was on the other side of it, and I don't know who all else. But they were the principals.

* * *

BELNICK: The [president's] press conference was that evening [November 19, 1986]. What was your reaction to what you heard?

SHULTZ: Well, I called him after the press conference.

BELNICK: Called the President?

SHULTZ: I always do, and I knew that he had been urged to have this press conference, and I told him that I thought it was personally a very courageous thing to do and to take on these subjects, but that I felt there were many statements that were wrong or misleading.

So I thought it was a very unfortunate press conference from that standpoint; and I said, "If you would like, I would welcome a chance to come around and go through it with you, and I will go through these points and tell you what I think is wrong with them and why."

BELNICK: And what did the President say?

SHULTZ: He said, "Well, I welcome seeing you." So I—the next day, I met with him in the family quarters. It is a little more—a good setting for that kind of discussion than in the office.

I asked Don Regan to be with me. I went through the things that I thought were wrong in the press conference with him. It was a long, tough discussion, not the kind of discussion I ever thought I would have with the President of the United States.

* * *

Comparisons to Watergate

[Sen. Daniel K.] Inouye [D-Hawaii]: ... Mr. Secretary, at the outset of these hearings which began about two months ago, I made a sad prediction that when the story began to unfold, the American people will have the right to ask, "How did this ever happen here or how could this ever happen in the United States?"

And I think at the same time Americans would have the right to demand that it never happen again.

The story we have heard over the past 10 weeks of testimony to some have been sad and depressing and distressing, and to many of us on this panel, and many of us are old-timers and a bit sophisticated, but we found it shocking and at times frightening. And I believe that may be the question the Americans will ask and the expectations they have a bit more compelling.

Mr. Secretary, you and I have lived through the agony and the nightmare of Watergate, and we saw it ruin a President, ruin senior advisers, demoralize the country, and cause the American people to lose faith in their political leaders.

Therefore, it is especially troubling to me, and I am sure it is to you, to see this nation once again faced with this breakdown of trust between the important branches of government....

How did this happen again and how did lifelong public servants, patriotic Americans like Adm. Poindexter, Bud McFarlane, Bill Casey, and Oliver North find themselves in a position where they misled you, kept information away from the Secretary of State, from the Secretary of Defense, lied to the Congress, withheld information from the President of the United States, destroyed, shredded, tore up, altered important documents....

And more importantly, Mr. Secretary, if you could also touch upon and advise us as to how we can prevent this from happening again and thus avoid the suffering of national self-doubt and international humiliation that follows such an ordeal?

SHULTZ: ... I would say with respect to the revelations that were brought out this morning and that I've been learning about of the deception and so on, and people coming and telling you that they lied to you and so on, as they did to others, that's not the way life is in government as I have experienced it. It is—government in the Congress and in the Executive Branch is basically full of people who are here because they want to help and they're honest, they work at it, we argue. But I would say, for example, right now in the State Department, the people I work with, I have never worked with more able and more dedicated people who just work their tails off when they see the substance in what we are doing and what we are trying to achieve.

So government is full of that, and I think, like you, I want to send a message out around our country that public service is a very rewarding and honorable thing, and nobody has to think they need to lie and cheat in order to be a public servant or to work in foreign policy. Quite the contrary: If you are really going to be effective over any period of time, you have to be straightforward and you have to conduct yourself in a basically honest way so people will have confidence and trust in you. So I think that's a second point I would like to make to people....

I think there are a lot of things to be learned myself reflecting on these events, if not from these events, that seem to me, as I have thought about it, worth mentioning. Some of them were brought out in the discussion this morning. One that I think was most vivid in response to Sen. [Sam] Nunn's [D-Ga.] question, and that is, I think that the importance of separating the functions of gathering and analyzing intelligence from the function of developing and carrying out policy, if the two things are mixed in together, it is too tempting to have your analysis on the selection of information that is presented favor the policy that you are advocating....

A second point has to do with accountability. I think the operations of the government of the Executive Branch of the government, I will confine my comments to that, but I want to get to the interactions between the branches. You stop me, Mr. Chairman, if I am carrying on here. You ought to interject.

But I think the Executive Branch ought to be so organized that to the maximum extent possible the people who are running things are accountable people. Accountable people are, number one, the President and the Vice President, they are accountable to the American people, they run for election, just like in the Congress the accountable people, in my opinion, are the Members of Congress, the Senate and House, you run for election, you are accountable to your constituents....

... We have a system that is described as checks and balances or division, separation of powers and it is a good system, I think.

Now, separation of powers to me means that there are different functions to be performed by the different branches. The two branches—I will just confine myself now to the Executive and Legislative—they shouldn't be trying to do each other's job, they should respect each other's job. It is for the legislature to pass the laws and appropriate the funds and raise the taxes.

A legislature can't manage government policy. It is wieldy, it doesn't work, it is not constitution [sic] that way. That is why there is an Executive Branch, to manage things and to develop policies and to push them.

But the Executive Branch can't do it unless it gets appropria-

tions and, of course, it has to live by the laws.

So I think—looking at it from the Executive Branch standpoint, we have to respect the fundamental duties of our colleagues on the Hill, but we have to expect them to respect ours and what that means is, as many have pointed out, that while we have a system of separation of powers in the way it is constituted, it inevitably means we also have a system of sharing powers, and there isn't any real way to say here is the answer by some kind of a formula.

* * *

[Sen. Warren B.] RUDMAN [R-N.H.]: Mr. Secretary, this morning in the course of one of our answers you made the point that if you present the President of the United States, this President, with facts, and all of the facts, that his instincts are good and he makes the decision based on those facts, he is not one to back away from decisions. Am I correct?

SHULTZ: That is right. He is comfortable with himself. He is decisive, he steps up to things, and when he decides, he stays with it. And sometimes you wish he wouldn't, but anyway, he does. He's very decisive, and he's very strong.

RUDMAN: You also testified that at the time following the disclosure of this entire matter, which in many ways, at least to me, is as disturbing as the issue itself, that you felt that the President did not have the facts in his possession that would enable him to be his usual forthright and direct self to the American people. Am I correct in that?

SHULTZ: He was forthright and direct, but he was not, I don't think he was given the correct information.

RUDMAN: Well, forthright, correct and accurate in what he said.

SHULTZ: I felt that the intelligence he was getting during that period was faulty about Iranian terrorism, I felt that he was not being—having described [to] him accurately, the operational aspects of arms for hostages—he had a perfectly good idea in his mind that was the basis for his decision to begin with. He had every right to make it, a perfectly good decision. I didn't agree with it because I felt underneath it was arms for hostages.

But nevertheless, that's what you got to do when you get elected President, you make those decisions, his decision to make, perfectly proper. People continued to try to sell him on that; when the time went by and he wasn't being given I felt the right kind of information—and I also feel that the intelligence that was the basis for the original recommendation was faulty and that it was tied in with policy....

RUDMAN: Mr. Secretary, again, you are not here to cast aspersions on other people. That is not why we want you here. But there is a basic question here troubling many people on this panel. I will put it to you generally.

Do you agree with me—and I think most members of this panel—that a Cabinet officer or someone of Cabinet rank who assumes responsibility for some sort of a major initiative—I'm referring to the diversion—without presidential authority has an obligation—law aside, courts aside—has an obligation to his President, who placed his trust in that individual, to tell the President, at the least, of what he did on his own authority?

SHULTZ: Well, I think the obligation goes earlier than that. I think a Cabinet officer must recognize that I—the Cabinet officer—I didn't get elected to anything, the President got elected, and it is one of my responsibilities to be sure that the things I'm doing are consistent with what the President wants; and when there's something of genuine significance, even if I am sure it's what he wants, I want to have him take part in it and be sure that he sees it and takes responsibility; and the more difficult it is, the more I should go out of my way to point it up to him so he doesn't miss the point of why it is that I am concerned about this....

RUDMAN: ... There is a term that is well-known around this town and the world about the arrogance of power. Ronald Reagan has never had the arrogance of power, in my view. But it seems to me that some people working for him surely did.

* * *

[Sen. Paul S.] SARBANES [D-Md.]: ... Adm. Poindexter,

in talking about the use of the proceeds of the Iranian arms sales for the contras, also addressed using it for a series of other covert projects, and he was asked was that the first time you ever heard about that, and he said, it is the first time that I've heard it discussed in that depth; I don't at all doubt that Col. North and Director Casey may have discussed that; frankly, it is an idea that has some attractive features in my mind.

Is it an idea that has any attractive features in your mind?

SHULTZ: None.

SARBANES: Would you explain why?

SHULTZ: Because it is totally outside of the system of government that we live by and must live by.

You cannot spend funds that the Congress doesn't either authorize you to obtain or appropriate. That is what the Constitution says, and we have to stick to it.

Now, I will join everybody in saying that sometimes it gets doggone frustrating with what the Congress does or doesn't do, and I can be critical. However, that's the system that—we have to accept it and then we have an argument about it and try to persuade you otherwise.

Just as I was saying about the funds for the Nicaraguan Freedom Fighters, when I was asked about third-country solicitations back in 1984, I think that in the end if this is going to work, we have to persuade the Congress to support it. And when we persuade the Congress to support it, which is the present situation, the results are much stronger.

That's where our long-term bet has to be. We have this very difficult task of having a separation of powers that means we have to learn how to share power. Sharing power is harder, and we need to work at it harder than we do.

But that's the only way. And this is not sharing power, this is not in line with what was agreed to in Philadelphia. This is a piece of junk and it ought to be treated that way.

* * *

[Rep. Dante B.] FASCELL [D-Fla.]: When you finally thought you had control over the foreign policy mechanism, after all this in-fighting and what-not, and your chief spokesman at that time was Elliott Abrams—still is, for Central—Latin American policy, etc.—and you instructed him, said you go find out what happened, how are these contras getting the arms. Curiosity. Did you ever get a report back.

SHULTZ: The report came back to me in the same way basically as it did to you. Questions were asked in the Congress about Col. North's activities, as I said this morning, just as I asked Elliott to find out what is—where is this coming from.

And while we didn't find out in an affirmative way, we did satisfy ourselves, as you did, basically relying upon the word of Mr. McFarlane in one instance and Adm. Poindexter in another.

There were records. You went through the same process. We both concluded everything was fine.

FASCELL: Mr. Secretary, so both the Department of State, the Secretary of State, and the Congress were out of the loop from the standpoint of getting information that was accurate.

SHULTZ: I believe the President was also out of the loop.

* * *

[Rep. William S.] BROOMFIELD [R-Mich.]: Mr. Secretary, no one can deny lying or deceiving Congress, but in the strategic sense of the word, as a nation have we benefited from Col. North and Adm. Poindexter's efforts to keep the contras alive in fighting against the Sandinista government in Nicaragua and bridging the gap, that theory? How important was that?

SHULTZ: Well, I think it is important to keep the freedom fighters alive. My feeling has always been they are a very legitimate group, and the amount of money they have to get along on, after all if you think of—I gather it is something like $1 million a month, and you are talking about 10,000 people, do that arithmetic, and you see it is not going to go very far. So their staying power is a measure of their legitimacy you might say.

But I think that the efforts made, I testified earlier about his incident where I complimented Col. North. As I understood it, he had extended himself personally to try to buck up the leaders and

keep them going, and I think that was a service. But I don't—I don't think that desirable ends justify means of lying, deceiving, of doing things that are outside of our constitutional processes. That is not in the picture as far as I am concerned.

* * *

Shultz resumed his testimony July 24, 1987:

BROOMFIELD: Do you feel the President continued to rely too much on Bill Casey as a result [of Shultz's opposition to the Iran initiative]?

SHULTZ: Well, he was the Director of Central Intelligence, so naturally he has access more than any other individual to this immense and impressive flow of information and to the analytical capabilities that go with it.

So you have to look to the Director of Central Intelligence as a principal person, without a doubt. That doesn't mean that the intelligence estimates can't be challenged, and they were.

For instance, I challenged the idea that Iran had dropped off in its use of terrorism.

BROOMFIELD: I am still troubled by your testimony yesterday that you have obviously been a very close friend of the President for some twenty years—at least you indicated yesterday—that you did not have the necessary influence with him, in other words, that you were not able to get to him. And I am just curious why you weren't able to see the President at any time, if you were so disturbed at what was developing on the Iran arms sales.

SHULTZ: I think I could see the President any time I wanted and I saw the President a great deal, and I'm sure if I, as I did one Sunday morning, called him up and said, Mr. President, I have something I need to see you about, and he said come on over—I had no problem with access to the President.

I used that access very sparingly because he is a very busy person.

BROOMFIELD: In retrospect, don't you feel you could have been more forceful? Why weren't you more forceful at an earlier date? Maybe you could have headed off some of this.

SHULTZ: I was present at the meetings in December and January with Secretary Weinberger and I expressed our views. I'm sure you will hear Secretary Weinberger. But I thought he was very forceful and I thought I was forceful, too. We didn't sit there and say, there's five arguments this way and four arguments that way. We were arguing.

So if your point is that the President was in some doubt about our views, your point is wrong.

* * *

Not a Watergate-Style Cover-Up

[Rep. Dick] CHENEY [R-Wyo.]: It is tentative for us to talk about a grave constitutional crisis. Some of my colleagues are fond of saying this is the worst thing that has happened in this case since Watergate, and I must say I have trouble with those arguments, the notion that this is a crisis strikes me as inappropriate. If it ever was a crisis it ended last December when the President put an end to those policies that are under investigation here and as to the extent we are focused on enforcing the Boland Amendment [which restricted U.S. aid to the Nicaraguan contras], we have to remind ourselves periodically that the Congress repealed that law over a year ago. I look at the arguments about Watergate which some of my colleagues on this committee are fond of pulling out as a relevant analogy, and I must say I don't see any relevant comparison at all. I think the analogy is grossly overdone, but you served in the Nixon Administration and went through those difficult years as well, and I just wonder if you would agree with my judgment that what we have here is a radically different set of circumstances and not a political crime, but rather fundamental disputes over policy and whatever the motives of the individuals involved might have been, and whether we agree or disagree with their policies it is clear that it was a policy struggle, not a struggle for domestic political advantage if you will, and it's also clear this President responded very aggressively when he found he had a problem, and contrary to running the so-called cover-up that was part of the Watergate incident, this President has done anything but that. He has made available even his own diary to the members of this committee, appointed the Tower Commission, cooperated in every single respect with our activities.

I wonder if you might comment based on your perspective of your service over the years, whether or not you think that analogy is appropriate.

SHULTZ: I believe that the Watergate problems were not so much about the burglary as they were about the cover-up. That was the essence of the Watergate problem. In this case we had a set of events involving an initiative toward Iran that were undertaken, broadly speaking, given the finding that we know about with attention to proper legality. And something happened in the course of that by way of fund diversion, which the President didn't know about. And as the events started to tumble out and then especially when the President and—the President set in motion a very quick investigation by the Attorney General as he began to sense that something was wrong very quickly, and then when he found something was definitely wrong he put it out immediately, and has gone in just the opposite direction of cover-up.

It was—you would have been inundated with materials, and to some extent I think some of the materials that have been put in the hands of the congressional committees, it is unwise to do it. But at any rate, the President has gone all out to see that all of the facts are available, and I think it's to his everlasting credit, that was his immediate instinct.

I think as a matter of fact with a great deal of—has been revealed by these investigations and I personally have been astonished at some of the things that have come out.

But the basic structure of what happened, the Iran initiative, the distortion and the fund diversion, that was brought out long ago, and I think that that is the essential set of facts, and that remains what you have before you, is to find out why did that happen and who knew about it and all that.

But the basic facts were set out at the President's direction in November.

* * *

Abrams's Mistake

[Rep. Jack] BROOKS [D-Texas]: Now, Mr. Secretary, when Elliott Abrams appeared before us in June, he told us that he misled the Congress about $10 million the Sultan of Brunei tried to send to the contras because he said he wasn't authorized to discuss that matter without going to you. That is his testimony of June 2nd, page 193. He explained that the reason he wasn't authorized to tell us the truth was because your Department had given assurances of confidentiality to the Sultan in the process of soliciting that money.

Now, did you or any other official of the Executive Branch instruct Mr. Abrams not to testify truthfully in regard to this matter?

SHULTZ: Everybody in the government, certainly anybody that works for me, should know that they must not lie and must not mislead. Nobody has to get my permission to tell the truth. They must tell the truth.

Now, in this case, Elliott had a piece of information that he could not reveal. To do so would have been a breach of faith with the country involved, and they had made—they had said that they would make this contribution on the understanding that it would be a confidential thing. They were going to contribute to the freedom fighters.

So there are all sorts of ways to handle it when you are in a session, as Elliott found himself in, he wasn't expecting to get questioned about this, but it came I think on the afternoon of the day when there were these revelations, and he was questioned by various Senators on the Senate Select Committee, particularly Sen. [Bill] Bradley [D-N.J.]—I say this because I had a very long and a good conversation with Sen. [David L.] Boren [D-Okla.] about all this, among other things he said, he asked me if I would get the transcript and read it.

And so I did that, both the first meeting with the Intelligence

Committee and the second one. And I think that a perfectly acceptable thing, I imagine, to the committee, would have been to say, "Senator, I don't want to testify on this. I would like to come back," or to say "The State Department is authorized by law to make solicitations, as you know, and we have made a solicitation that we believe is successful, but I cannot reveal the name of the country because we have given a pledge of confidentiality." That would have, I am sure, been quite satisfactory. There are all sorts of ways that you can respond with candor but without revealing the name.

Elliott made a mistake, and he knows it. He knew it more or less right away. He discussed it with various people in the department, what to do. And he was told what to do is to go back to Sen. Bradley and tell him. You don't have to tell him the name of the country, but tell him, so you correct the record.

In fairness, I didn't—he didn't lie, so to speak, directly. There wasn't any way for a Senate there to ask him if he had solicited Brunei. There was no way for them to know to ask that question. But it was clear enough that they were asking him about solicitation, as I read the transcript at your suggestion. So he knew he made a mistake. And then he corrected it in a later meeting, and again you asked me to read the transcript, which I did, and I think I told you that I agreed that he made a combative apology. Elliott is a combative person. That is one of his endearing qualities as far as I am concerned; he is a fighter.

But, anyway, he is full of remorse about this, and in my opinion, he is a first-class person, a person of high character, very able, a person with a real instinct for public service.

* * *

[Sen. George J.] MITCHELL [D-Maine]: . . . Now, your meeting with the President [in December 1986] occurred just two months after the plan was negotiated, and according to Adm. Poindexter, after it was approved by the President. You have said you told the President about it on a Sunday morning, and he reacted very negatively.

My next question is: Based upon your knowledge of the President and your personal observation of him during that meeting, are you convinced that the President could not have approved that plan in October, just two months before that?

SHULTZ: Absolutely.

MITCHELL: Now, you talked yesterday—

SHULTZ: And I would say, Senator, that any self-respecting person working for a President, if he were going to make such a proposal to the President has a responsibility to point it up to the President what is involved, because it clearly would be a gross violation of everything that we had said and stood for.

So, if—and I have no idea what Adm. Poindexter did or didn't do, but if he were to have undertaken that at all, that sense of responsibility, he had an obligation to make sure that the President understood fully what he was talking about, and I know that that couldn't possibly have happened. . . .

MITCHELL: Now, as you testified yesterday, you did not know about the findings that had been signed by the President authorizing the Iran initiative. The first of them was signed by the President on December 5, 1985.

You met with the President on December 7, 1985, with other officials, and you have described that meeting in some length about how you vigorously opposed the Iran initiative. Am I correct that the President did not then tell you that he had signed a finding authorizing the sale of arms to Iran two days before that meeting?

SHULTZ: I believe that the President said that he has no recollection of signing such a finding, and there is no company in existence, so—but he didn't inform me of signing it, but he has said that he has no recollection of doing so himself.

MITCHELL: Adm. Poindexter has testified that he was personally present when the President signed it.

SHULTZ: Yes, I understand that. All I can do is report the things that have been said.

MITCHELL: All right.

Then, we will go on to the next finding, which occurred on Jan. 6. The President signed a second finding on Jan. 6, 1986, and on the following day, met with you and the other principals of the National Security Council to discuss the Iran initiative.

And am I correct that the President did not tell you then that he had signed a finding on this matter on the day before?

SHULTZ: That is correct.

MITCHELL: And then, on Jan. 17, the President signed a third finding on Iran, and that same day, in the afternoon, met with you. Did the President—am I correct in my understanding that on that afternoon, the President did not tell you that he had signed a third finding on the Iran initiative on that very day?

SHULTZ: To the best of my recollection, the first I heard of the Jan. 17 finding was in the briefing on these matters on the 10th of November.

MITCHELL: Well, my point is with all due respect, Mr. Secretary, it wasn't just Adm. Poindexter who was keeping you in the dark, was it?

SHULTZ: Well, if the thrust of your question is that the President was part of an effort to see that I didn't know what was going on, I don't believe that.

MITCHELL: No, that is a conclusion.

SHULTZ: Yes, that is right.

MITCHELL: I think my point is that the President signed three findings related to Iran.

SHULTZ: He signed two that we know of for sure, and another that if he signed it in Adm. Poindexter's presence, it apparently didn't register with him very well, at least he doesn't remember it. And, quite possibly, the President assumed that somehow or other there was a process of discussion going on that wasn't in fact going on.

I am just speculating. But I don't know.

MITCHELL: In any event—

SHULTZ: I have a relationship with the President such that I don't think he is out to deceive me.

MITCHELL: No, and I certainly didn't mean to suggest that. My point was that the President, for whatever reason, did not inform you that he had signed these findings, even though you participated in discussions with him regarding the Iran initiative, we'll take just the last two, on one occasion, on the very same day and on the other day after.

SHULTZ: He didn't inform me and neither did any of the other people involved.

MITCHELL: Well—

SHULTZ: But I—

MITCHELL: I won't draw any conclusions.

SHULTZ: I'm not accepting the conclusion that somehow the President was deceiving me. I don't accept that.

MITCHELL: I want to make clear I'm not suggesting collusion. I guess all I'm suggesting is I think in fairness to Adm. Poindexter, I think the events as described and as they occurred could have led him to conclude that it was the President's wish that you not be informed since he knew that the President had signed the findings; he knew that you were Secretary of State and had participated in discussions on these matters almost contemporaneous with the findings, and chose not to tell you about them.

SHULTZ: I think it is equally arguable or maybe more so given my knowledge of the President that he assumed that what was happening I was aware of.

* * *

[Rep. Louis] STOKES [D-Ohio]: Mr. Secretary, wouldn't you also say, in line with your earlier comments about separating intelligence from policy functions, that one of the faults of the NSC staff was that it was both the staff element and the operational element for the Iranian initiative and for the contra-supply operation; that is, didn't the merging of those two functions create the conflicts and miscalculations, the short-sightedness and the mistakes that these hearings so amply detailed?

SHULTZ: Well, I've said I think there is a problem when intelligence is mixed in with operations. That is as distinct from operations having staff work done from them. They have to have staff work done for them. But the mixing of the task of gathering, sorting out, analyzing intelligence, I think, is something that we ought to separate from operations. Not that people in the opera-

tions don't look at intelligence and they may accept it or not, they have their own ideas, and should, but nevertheless I think to keep the functions separate is an important thing, and I believe there are instances in the set of events that you are examining that show the nature of the problem that comes when you mix the two things together, or can come.

* * *

[Rep. Michael] DEWINE [R-Ohio]: I think you have been a very good Secretary of State.

I have enjoyed having the opportunity on the Foreign Affairs Committee to work with you.

I think it is clear, the facts are very plain, that you were right about a lot of this, with regard to the arms sale, you were right about the whole thing.

In essence, you were a prophet, just about everything you said was going to go wrong did go wrong.

Having said that, I do feel that after listening to your testimony and after listening to the evidence for the last eight weeks, that I am in general agreement with the Tower Commission.

I think the basic problem, at least in this Congressman's mind, was that neither you nor the President really knew the essential facts.

You gave Adm. Poindexter complete authority to decide what you needed to know.

You took the risk, and it was a risk, that he would give you enough information about the Iran initiative for you to do your job.

In essence, you left the fox to guard the chicken coop.

SHULTZ: That is not correct. When I asked him—

DEWINE: Mr. Secretary.

SHULTZ: No, no. When I asked—

DEWINE: Mr. Secretary—

SHULTZ: —about the information I got in Tokyo, I was not leaving it up to him to decide whether to tell me about that or not. I was putting information to him and what I got in response was not accurate.

DEWINE: Mr. Secretary, I appreciate your comments, and I have my thoughts and I know you have yours, and if I could finish mine, then you can certainly say anything you want to.

You are a very articulate individual and you have impressed this committee very much.

If I could say what I think as a Congressman who has sat here for eight weeks listening to the testimony and I am in basic agreement with what the Tower Commission said.

I think it is very clear that you had and have and deserve to have good relations with the President of the United States. It is proper. It has been demonstrated very amply when you had what you describe as a barking session with the President after this whole thing started tumbling down, you went to the President, took the bull by the horns, and got the President and got him the essential facts and you got the facts as well.

So you have that relationship.

You have been a Secretary of State who has served along with and through the tenure of four National Security Advisers.

You have been a strong Secretary of State. You are well respected on Capitol Hill as the last two days have amply demonstrated, yet in my opinion, you let Adm. Poindexter cut you out.

You discussed your resignation on three separate occasions, on one of those occasions having to do with a polygraph, but you did not discuss it in regard to what has turned out to be the major foreign policy disaster of this Administration.

You stated you did not want to know the operational details. In my opinion, you purposefully cut yourself out from the facts.

In fairness to you, there is no doubt you were lied to, you were misled and you clearly were deceived. But in hindsight, Congress, those of us who sit up here, are always good with hindsight, no doubt about that.

In my opinion, you walked off the field when the score was against you. You took yourself out of the game.

It seems to me, Mr. Secretary, you permitted Adm. Poindexter to get between you and the President just as he got between the President and the American people.

As a result, our foreign policy suffered because the two key players, George Shultz and Ronald Reagan, were out of the game. Thank you very much.

SHULTZ: Well, I will just say that is one man's opinion and I don't share it.

* * *

[Rep. Lee H.] HAMILTON [D-Ind.]: Mr. Secretary, you have spent two full days with us. And I know that is a large hunk of time for a Secretary of State. And we deeply appreciate it. And I will not try to sum up. I simply want to say that I think the importance of your testimony for us is that you have really changed the focus of the committee's work.

Up until your appearance, we really have been focusing on the question of what went wrong, and in a sense, that is the easy part of our work, though it hasn't been easy. And I think from now on, as you have said several times in the course of your testimony, we have to begin to focus on what needs to be done, what kinds of constructive suggestions we can come up with to make this system of ours work better. . . .

Edwin Meese III

Following are excerpts from the July 28, 1987, opening statement and testimony of Attorney General Edwin Meese III:

MEESE: . . . I welcome this opportunity to come before these committees and assist in your review of this administration's Iranian policy initiatives, as well as other activities that were aimed at providing funding for the Freedom Fighters in Nicaragua. A number of witnesses have preceded me and provided an accounting of the policy decisions that were and were not made, and have described efforts undertaken for the ostensible purpose of furthering those policies.

Before continuing that description, let me discuss my role. As the Attorney General of the United States, it is, of course, one of my responsibilities to serve as the nation's chief law enforcement officer. In that capacity, I am privileged to assist the President in making sure that the laws of the United States are faithfully executed.

In addition, as prescribed in the Judiciary Act of 1789, which created the office of Attorney General, I am assigned the responsibility of providing legal advice and opinions to the President on such matters and at such times as he directs.

Further, the Attorney General is and has been since 1791 a member of the President's Cabinet, and thus has the distinctly separate role as one of the general advisers to the President and the Executive Branch.

My exposure to the Iran-contra matter was not confined to any one of those areas of responsibility, but from time to time has touched them all. I believe that one can better understand and appreciate my limited role in the events of the period by understanding in which of the several capacities I was approached for advice and assistance.

Some eight months ago the President asked me, as his principal legal adviser, to develop a factual overview of the events relating to the Iranian initiative. During that hectic weekend in November 1986, we were able to piece together a basic outline of what is now known as the Iran-contra story, which has been essentially validated during the extensive investigations which have occurred since.

I mention this because after many months of televised hearings and intensive press coverage, some might understandably have difficulty recalling that, as we embarked on our fact-finding inquiry on the 21st of November 1986, few people inside or outside the government understood the true nature and scope of the Iran matter, let alone knew of the many details of the related activities and events. I certainly had no such detailed knowledge. . . .

In early November of 1986, events occurred which were of great consequence to the Iranian initiative. On or about the 4th of November, following publication of a story in a Middle Eastern journal, American newspapers began to print widely varying accounts of this matter.

Therefore, on the 7th of November I advised Charles [J.] Cooper, the Assistant Attorney General for the Office of Legal Counsel—which is the office that assists me in my responsibility as legal adviser to the President and the Executive Branch, including on matters relating to national security—that his efforts would probably be needed on the legal issues that might arise in regard to the Iranian initiative.

The following Monday, which was the 10th of November, I attended a meeting with the President and other advisers, at which the Iranian initiative was generally discussed.

On the 13th of November, the President addressed the nation on the Iranian activities. Six days later, on the 19th of November, he held a press conference on the subject.

At [Rear] Adm. [John M.] Poindexter's invitation, I attended a meeting in his office the next afternoon, the 20th of November, with [CIA] Director [William J.] Casey, Assistant Attorney General Cooper, and for most of the time National Security Council counsel Paul [B.] Thompson and Lt. Col. [Oliver L.] North. There may have been others present from time to time.

I was invited to that meeting as the President's legal adviser, to review the legal aspects of the Iranian initiative prior to administration witnesses being called upon to give scheduled testimony and briefings before the Congress.

I recall seeing for the first time at that meeting a draft chronology of events that, from all appearances, had been prepared earlier in the day by the National Security Council [NSC] staff.

In addition, drafts of proposed testimony were distributed—again, which I was seeing for the first time. Those documents were reviewed and discussed, and corrections and revisions were made at the suggestions of those who had knowledge of specific events.

Mr. Chairman, questions have been raised during prior hearings of these committees here about my participation in this meeting and whether I so-called acquiesced in the statements included in the proposed testimony being prepared.

The truth is, I did not at the time have knowledge sufficient to allow me to make any sort of judgment regarding the accuracy of the proposed testimony, or the prepared chronology, or the revisions or corrections that were being suggested.

You will recall that the Iranian operation had been rigorously compartmentalized and only those, as I stated earlier, with a need to know were brought into the planning and the implementation.

Thus while I was generally aware on the 20th of November 1986 that there may have been arms transfers to Iran by Israel in 1985, I had no personal knowledge about such shipments, about our role (if any) in assisting with the transfers, or about the contemporaneous knowledge of other administration officials concerning the details of these shipments.

It was after that meeting, late in the evening, when I first learned in a secure telephone conversation with Mr. Cooper—I happened to be at West Point, New York, at the time—that there were apparent differences in the recollections of the Secretary of State, former National Security Assistant Robert [C.] McFarlane and perhaps others. I was concerned that great care be taken to resolve these differences so that accurate testimony would be given at the congressional hearings and briefings that were scheduled for the next day.

I believed that, because the Iranian initiative had been such a highly sensitive matter, and because it had been so rigidly compartmentalized, no one seemed to have all the facts and all seemed to me to be trying to piece together various parts of the story without full knowledge of the events.

As a consequence, there appeared to be considerable confusion as to what occurred when, and the many conflicting and inconsistent news stories only seemed to exacerbate the situation.

It was for this reason that I went to see the President the next day. I advised him of my concerns and recommended that he have someone undertake a fact-gathering review into the Iranian initiative to ascertain a fuller and more accurate picture of the events and the activities that had occurred.

The President agreed totally with my assessment and directed me to commence an immediate review. I had indicated that I would be willing to do that if he so decided.

He asked that I complete this task before the National Security Planning Group meeting which was to be on this subject and that had been scheduled for 2 p.m. on Monday, the 24th of November.

It might be helpful if I spend just a few minutes on the activity that took place during that weekend.

The essential point to keep in mind is that our purpose was not to conduct a criminal investigation. Indeed, on the 21st of November there was no hint that criminal activity was in any way implicated in the Iranian arms transactions. Indeed, I later learned that the Criminal Division of the Department of Justice had separately conducted its own independent review of criminal statutes that might possibly be involved and, as reflected in a memorandum dated the 22nd of November 1986, found no basis to suspect that crimes had been committed.

Early Friday afternoon—this is now the 21st of November, after my meeting with the President, I discussed the matter of the fact-gathering inquiry with FBI Director William [H.] Webster, who concurred that it would be inappropriate to utilize FBI investigators. Our purpose, plain and simple, was to find out what the facts really were and report to the President.

I therefore put together a small team of lawyers who were knowledgeable about national security matters and proceeded to systematically talk with each of the persons having information about the Iranian initiative and to review the applicable documents.

As Secretary [of State George P.] Shultz said in his testimony last week, our efforts in the space of just over three days turned up the essential facts that are still the essential facts today. Obviously much more information and many additional details have been uncovered by the various investigations, including those by these committees, and the months of effort that have taken place since that weekend.

But the basic outline of facts that the President and I related to Congress and to the public on the 25th of November 1986 remains intact today.

From the afternoon of Friday, Nov. 21, through the evening of Monday, Nov. 24th, a number of people were interviewed, documents were examined, and information was obtained from the relevant agencies that had participated in the strategic Iran initiative. Much of the information we obtained has previously been provided to these committees by the witnesses that have appeared before you and in the depositions and the documents which are part of your record.

Therefore, I will not chronicle in detail the events of that weekend, but will, of course, be happy to respond to any questions you may have about it.

During our review, we discovered facts indicating that funds obtained from the arms transfers in Iran had been diverted to the democratic resistance forces in Nicaragua. I brought this information to the President, who determined that it would be reported promptly to the Congress and to the American people and that immediate corrective action should be taken.

Therefore, on Tuesday, Nov. 25, 1986, a briefing for congressional leaders was held at 11 o'clock and a news conference was conducted at noon.

Although our information was by no means complete at that time, and we recognized that much investigative activity would follow, the President requested that I disclose all that we had learned to date so that there would be no claim of withholding of information or charge of cover-up.

Several actions were immediately commenced to pursue the necessary follow-up investigations and remedial actions.

The President announced that he was convening a special review board to investigate and make recommendations to ensure that the mistakes made in implementing national security policy in this case would not occur again.

We also took immediate action concerning the possible criminal law implications of the information which had been uncovered. I, therefore, met with Assistant Attorney General William Weld,

who heads the Department's Criminal Division, and did then, to discuss the initiation of an investigation by his attorneys and the FBI into the possible violation of criminal statutes. That process was well under way by the same evening.

I also directed Deputy Attorney General Arnold Burns to contact the White House Counsel to secure all files in the NSC offices.

As these steps were being taken, it was clear to me that the initiation of an independent counsel was probable. The activities of the Criminal Division included the initial inquiry to determine whether the legal and factual predicates required by the independent counsel statute were present.

By the 2nd of December, I had concluded that seeking an independent counsel was appropriate and advised the President of this fact.

On the 4th of December, the formal request for assignment of an independent counsel was presented to the Special Division of the Court of Appeals for the District of Columbia Circuit. That request was ultimately granted and Lawrence [E.] Walsh was appointed as independent counsel. Since then, I have continued, in accordance with the President's wishes and my own best judgment, to be fully supportive of and cooperative with all the official inquiries into this matter.

Today is my sixth session of testimony on this matter. Others in the department and elsewhere in the administration have also appeared multiple times; and there has been an unprecedented willing disclosure of perhaps millions of pages of sensitive government documents.

That in brief, Mr. Chairman, is my knowledge of events surrounding the matters under consideration by these committees, but I would be remiss if I did not acknowledge one of the often-stated goals of these hearings—the need for a constructive relationship between the Executive and the Legislative Branches in the conduct of foreign policy

*   *   *

Telling Congress

[John W.] NIELDS [Jr., House committee chief counsel]: At any of the meetings [on the Iranian initiative] in January of 1986 did anyone point out the advantage of consultation notice to Congress?

MEESE: I don't recall anyone pointing out the advantage of consultation with Congress or notification of Congress. It could possibly have been raised by someone on the 7th, but I certainly don't remember it. I think I said in my opening statement that there was no one who was arguing for notification. I don't remember anyone.

NIELDS: No one, for example, argued either that it would be helpful to get input from congressional leaders or that it would be helpful if the project failed to have some congressional support behind you?

MEESE: Not that I recall, Mr. Nields. Actually, the notification of Congress was a very brief part of the meeting on the 7th. The principal discussion at the meeting on the 7th was whether this should be done at all and there was a rather heated discussion of that in which I only had a very minor part.

It was primarily conducted on the one side by Secretary Shultz and Secretary [of Defense Caspar W.] Weinberger and on the other side by Adm. Poindexter and Director Casey.

*   *   *

NIELDS: Now, I take it then during the week of the third of November 1986 some newspaper reports appeared making reference to this [Iran] initiative.

MEESE: That is correct.

NIELDS: And I think that the record reflects that initially the President indicated publicly that these were without foundation, or words to that effect, but the articles continued, and there was a meeting of various members of the National Security Council on the 10th of November 1986. Do you have a recollection of that meeting?

MEESE: I don't recall statements by the President that you have characterized, but I do recall the meeting on the 10th of November, yes. . . .

I am looking now at my notes to refresh my recollection.

I see a note I took that says "Washington, D.C., too much talk," which may have to do with press accounts, and I see here my notes that say, "Lives of those with whom we deal, for example, in Iran could be jeopardized," which I am sure was at least possibly in reference to how they should be handled with the news media. I don't have any other notes, but I am sure that at least a part of that meeting was involved with how this should be handled with the press.

NIELDS: What was the President's position on that subject at that meeting?

MEESE: I think his position, as best I can recall, was that we should be very careful in statements to the press for a variety of reasons. He was concerned about the hostages who were still in Lebanon, he was concerned about the elements in Iran because at that time I believe there was some discussion that at least the communication with those elements could perhaps continue.

There was—I have a note here that says "debriefing of [newly-released hostage David P.] Jacobsen may lead to new opportunity," which would lead me to believe we felt there was still a possibility of getting hostages out, and I also have a note on my—a notation here on the second page of my note that says, "North, two more hostages by this weekend," which leads me to believe there was still hope we would get hostages out even in the course of this revelation.

So I believe the principal concern that the President had in regard to the way in which this was treated by the news media was to do nothing that would endanger either the hostages or the people in Iran.

NIELDS: There is another set of notes that relates to this meeting, which is Exhibit 19, they are Mr. Keel's [Alton G. Keel, Poindexter's deputy] notes. On page 7 of them, the President—it is attributed to the President. We don't talk TOWs [antitank missiles], don't talk specifics. Is that consistent with your recollection of the position that the President took at the meeting?

MEESE: I will assume it's here. I can't find it. As a matter of fact, I hardly read it. But in any event, I don't have any recollection one way or the other whether he said that specifically. I do know that the more details that were given, such as TOWs, the more danger there would have been to the people in Iran and presumably to the hostages as well, so that would not be inconsistent with what I recall as the general tenor of the meeting.

NIELDS: Do you recall any other contrary views being expressed?

MEESE: No, I do not. As a matter of fact, I think that was the general sentiment of most of the people there.

* * *

Interviewing North

NIELDS: Now, during this interview [of North by Meese and his aides, November 23], if I understand your testimony, Col. North told you in effect that Casey did not know of the diversion?

MEESE: That is correct. . . .

NIELDS: According to information the committee has, that was also false. He told you that Defense Minister [of Israel Yitzhak] Rabin had told him that oil drilling equipment was to be shipped in November of 1985. According to his testimony here before this committee that was also false.

Now, my question to you is: Following his interview, did you believe the representations that he had made? Did you accept them as true, or did you have question about them?

MEESE: I accepted them as true and had no reason to believe otherwise. He had been very forthcoming in response to what we had asked him and had laid out the whole scheme that was basically consistent with the memorandum that we have.

NIELDS: Will you describe his demeanor during the interview?

MEESE: Obviously he was a little more concerned and upset, I would say, because we had the memo, and that was a source of concern to him because, in effect, what had gone on there was

something he didn't realize anyone else knew, and it was a highly sensitive thing from his standpoint because it had to do with his efforts to get funds to the Nicaraguan democratic resistance, and so I think that my view was he was mostly concerned because if this got out this would impede his efforts to help the democratic resistance in Nicaragua.

NIELDS: In answering your questions, did he do so in a forthright manner?

MEESE: Yes. He was basically forthright, and I didn't think, he certainly did not appear to be concealing anything.

NIELDS: Now, at the end of your interview, you now confirmed the diversion. At that point in time did you believe that you were dealing with something other than confusion, something serious?

MEESE: Yes, very definitely, in that there was a whole new aspect of this situation.

NIELDS: Did you regard it at that point in time as now a matter proper for criminal experts?

MEESE: No. There was no—at that point we still hadn't figured out whether there was any criminality involved, whether this was an authorized activity, whether anyone else knew.

There was a possibility certainly down the line that there might be criminal aspects, but certainly what happened had happened per se there. There was no obvious criminality at that point.

NIELDS: Again, I must ask you this question because the committee has information that there may have been some more shredding between that time and the time when it was finally referred to the Criminal Division. Did you give any consideration at that time either referring it to your Criminal Division or independently taking some steps to secure files?

MEESE: No, I don't believe anybody did give any consideration to that at that time. I think there were various reasons. One is that there was no hint to us of any destruction of documents.

Secondly, we had all the documents, because we had been given access to all the documents to our knowledge at the National Security Staff offices. And Col. North had been very forthright and forthcoming in his answers.

So that there was nothing that at that point would have given us a hint. I must say it is always easy some eight months later to look back, and it certainly looks a lot different to us now than it did then but at that time there was nothing that did give us that hint.

* * *

NIELDS: . . . Whose decision was it to ask for John Poindexter's resignation?

MEESE: Well, ultimately it was the President's. And I think at that point it was [White House chief of staff Donald T.] Don Regan's strong recommendation that John Poindexter should resign.

NIELDS: What was done with respect to Col. North and whose decision was that?

MEESE: Well, that came later in the morning, when we were talking with the President, and the question was; should Col. North be allowed to resign? And I believe it was Mr. Regan, but I am not positive, but the resolution in any event was, well, he is just on detail from the Marine Corps, so he can just be transferred back to the Marine Corps.

NIELDS: Was it decided by anyone that he would be fired?

MEESE: Well, I think when you—I don't remember the words actually "fired," I remember the words "generally transferred back to the Marine Corps." That could be interpreted as being fired in the sense of a White House position, but there was a difference in the position that Col. North held related to that which Adm. Poindexter held.

Adm. Poindexter actually was appointed. He was a commissioned member of the White House staff as the Assistant to the President for National Security Affairs, whereas Col. North was one of many military personnel that were detailed to the White House, so there was a technical difference in terminology as to the two.

NIELDS: Whose decision was it that Col. North be transferred?

MEESE: Well, ultimately it was the President's decision, and I don't know who suggested it, I think it was Mr. Regan, but there was general agreement by all that were there that that should, in fact, happen.

NIELDS: What was your position on it?

MEESE: I certainly concurred.

NIELDS: And for what reason?

MEESE: On the basis of his involvement in the diversion of funds which was an unauthorized activity and something which had not been approved and would not be approved by the President had he known.

NIELDS: Now, were you under the impression that it had or had not been approved by Col. North's superior, Adm. Poindexter?

MEESE: I would say that my impression was exactly as I had been told by Adm. Poindexter, that he had condoned or allowed the activity to go forward.

* * *

Praising Meese

[Rep. Bill] McCOLLUM [R-Fla.]: . . . At the outset of talking with you today and having listened to what you have said up to this point, it seems to me from a public perspective, it is hard to determine who the players are in this or determine your role, if I am sitting out in the public somewhere listening to all this.

In my listening to all the weeks of testimony we have had, I have concluded, and I think just about anybody who thinks about this has, it wasn't the Justice Department that ran any of these operations regarding the Iranian or contra initiative, it was not the Justice Department that got involved with the Iranian arms transaction, it seems to me you made it very clear that from the standpoint of you, as the Attorney General, your only involvement with the Iran arms transaction until you got into your fact-finding inquiry in November 1986 was to make some determinations with regard to the legalities of the finding in 1986, in January, and to respond to a couple of inquiries of Adm. Poindexter on the phone to see if you could do some minor aiding in one or two very very minor aspects of it.

It also was not your office which destroyed or altered any documents involved in any of these matters. It was not you who misled Congress or misled the Secretary of State about any of the facts involved in these matters. And it seems to me that when we talk about all of this, it also is very clear that it was you and your office and your staff who unearthed the discrepancies with regard to the issue of the November 1985 arms shipment that led, in turn, to your fact-finding mission the weekend of Nov. 20 through 24, 1986, and that, in turn, it was you and your office who discovered the diversion memo, and it was you and your office who took the lead after questioning Col. North to point out that the diversion memo was indeed a diversion and a real potential problem. And you had recommended, you the Attorney General, to the President and to Mr. Regan that this matter be made public as quickly as possible, and it was over a period of approximately four days after you started into it all.

And so I guess the reason I went through that little litany was that I think we need to put all this in perspective today at the end of a day where we have been talking about so many details involved in this. . . .

* * *

Meese resumed his testimony July 29, 1987:

[Sen. George J.] MITCHELL [D-Maine]: . . . When the hearings end next week, the committee will begin to prepare a report. One of the problems we face is the conflict of evidence on several key points, how, if at all, can we determine credibility. You are in a unique position to help us. You knew most of the people involved and you personally interviewed them in the course of your fact-finding inquiry. So I would like to begin with a few questions about credibility.

You said yesterday that former CIA Director Casey told you he knew nothing about the diversion. Your words were, and I quote you, "It was Mr. Casey himself who told me on Tuesday morning that he had known nothing about it."

As you know, Col. North told this committee that he had told Mr. Casey of the diversion, that he showed Mr. Casey a written memorandum describing the diversion, and that Mr. Casey knew in advance of the diversion, and in Col. North's words, "was enthusiastic about it."

Now, those statements are in direct conflict as to Mr. Casey's knowledge. They cannot both be true.

My question to you is, which of those statements do you believe, Mr. Casey's statement to you that he knew nothing of the diversion, or Col. North's statement to this committee that Mr. Casey did know of the diversion?

MEESE: Well, Senator, it is always hard to judge credibility when you have not had the opportunity to observe the witnesses yourself, and in the case of Col. North, I was not here and did not see him testify. I saw an occasional glimpse of his testimony, but I could not really have the same vantage point that you had at that time. . . .

Rather than judging the credibility of the individuals, but rather as to which statement is true, it seems to me that we would have to look at the statement that was given to me at the time that this matter first came up when there was no jeopardy to the individuals involved and at a time when Mr. Casey was still available to refute any statement that might have been true or untrue.

And at that time Col. North said to me, without any question, that there were only three people in the government who knew anything about this: himself, Adm. Poindexter and Mr. McFarlane. And so it would seem to me, if I had to judge, that the statement given at that time probably has the most value as an accurate statement.

MITCHELL: You are saying then that you believe Mr. Casey's statement to you?

MEESE: I do believe Mr. Casey's statement to me, based upon that kind of rationale, yes.

MITCHELL: And you disbelieve the statement made later by Col. North?

MEESE: I'm not in a position to evaluate that, but it seems at odds with what he told me on the 23rd of November [when Meese interviewed North].

* * *

Saving the Documents

MITCHELL: On the securing of the documents, it is with hindsight, but a reasonable case can be made that the time at which preservation of documents should occur is the time when inspection of documents occurs, that is, if it is important enough to look at documents, it ought to be important enough to think about preserving them.

I gather from what you are saying is that you were acting in good faith, it simply didn't occur to you at that point on Friday that any steps should be taken to preserve documents from destruction?

MEESE: That is correct, it did not occur to me or anyone else, and we follow the same process as I mentioned that you do in your investigating committees here.

MITCHELL: When did you first think about the possibility of criminal investigation?

MEESE: The first real thought that I gave to the possibility of criminal investigation was probably on Monday afternoon—the investigation was probably Tuesday, the 25th.

MITCHELL: Well, before you go any further, recall what you just said in response to Sen. [William S.] Cohen [R-Maine].

MEESE: There I said the possibility that criminal laws might possibly have been violated.

MITCHELL: Criminal implications I think—

MEESE: Criminal implications, right.

MITCHELL: —was on Sunday when you talked to Col. North?

MEESE: That is correct.

MITCHELL: Would that have been the first time that entered your mind?

MEESE: Criminal implications, yes, I'm sure.

MITCHELL: But you still did not think about securing documents at that point?

MEESE: Well, Senator, we already had examined all the documents and we already, in fact, had the key document, the evidentiary document known as the diversion memo, which was the significant document—a copy of that in our possession.

MITCHELL: When you say we had examined all the documents, you had examined all the documents that you had seen until then, but in fact there were a great many documents that you never did see?

MEESE: Well, we don't know whether those were relevant documents, irrelevant documents, or what they were.

MITCHELL: Do you think Col. North spent from 11 in the evening until 4:15 the next morning destroying irrelevant documents?

MEESE: I think he probably did. I think there were a lot of documents that he destroyed that had no relationship to the Iranian initiative or had any relationship to the contra diversion of funds.

There were probably a lot of other things that he may well have destroyed, documents that he didn't want anyone to see.

MITCHELL: On what do you base that opinion?

MEESE: That is just a guess, as much speculation as yours that there were relevant documents.

* * *

'No Smoking Gun'

[Rep. Dick] CHENEY [R-Wyo.]: I think you covered a lot of territory.

I think it is important for us as a committee, though, to avoid trying to force the evidence to fit some preconceived notions or conclusions about what transpired. We have investigated for months the question of the charge that somehow the President had knowledge of the allegation that there had been a diversion of funds, and, of course, the fact of the matter is we found absolutely no evidence to support that.

I am somewhat suspicious now, in light of the fact that no smoking gun was found in connection with the diversion matter, that the focus has now shifted to a suggestion that somehow there was a cover-up of some kind; that at the direction of the President, with your active involvement, the administration undertook to obscure the facts of this particular case. Again, I find absolutely no evidence to support that allegation.

We had the story this weekend in *The Washington Post* on Sunday that implied that the President presided over a meeting on Nov. 10 where there was an initiation of an effort to cover up these events. Of course, when we analyze the basis for that story, that while that may have been the implication, the story simply doesn't support it. The President clearly was concerned on Nov. 10, as your notes and the notes of others clearly demonstrate, with trying to obtain the release of two additional hostages, that his basic message to his officials was not to discuss the subject at all.

I have a vivid recollection of that period of time when David Jacobsen, one of the hostages recently released from Lebanon, [was] standing on the steps of the Rose Garden at the White House pleading with the White House press corps not to dig too deeply in this matter because lives were at stake. I think it is clear that the allegation that somehow the Nov. 10 meeting involved a cover-up simply doesn't hold up.

* * *

Interviewing Poindexter

[Sen. Sam] NUNN [D-Ga.]: Did you ask Adm. Poindexter [during Meese's November 24, 1986, interview with Poindexter] who approved the diversion?

MEESE: I did not ask him in so many words. I did ask him whether he had ever told about this to anyone else in the White House and he said no.

NUNN: Did you ask him specifically whether he had told the President of the United States?

MEESE: I didn't ask him specifically whether he had told the President. I asked if he had told anyone in the White House or discussed it with anyone else in the White House, and he said no.

NUNN: So you didn't ask whether he had told the President directly?

MEESE: No, because that was included in the answer that I had received and the question I asked.

NUNN: Did you ask him if he had approved the diversion?

MEESE: Not in that many words, but I did ask him what he knew of it and he told me, in essence, that he had allowed it to go forward.

NUNN: So you took that as tacit approval?

MEESE: He told me that that was the extent of his involvement, and I took that as tacit approval, the fact that he allowed it to go forward.

NUNN: But I believe that you testified that you did not believe he had authority to approve that.

MEESE: That is correct.

NUNN: Did you ask him if he thought he had authority?

MEESE: No, sir, I did not.

NUNN: So you never discussed that with him.

Did you ask him when he learned of the diversion?

MEESE: I don't believe I asked him precisely when, nor did he tell me precisely when he had learned.

He indicated, as you quoted, that Col. North had given him hints over a period of time.

NUNN: Did you ask him why he did not tell the President of the United States about the diversion?

MEESE: No, sir, I did not.

NUNN: He just said he didn't tell anyone in the White House other than the named individuals.

Did you ask him if Col. North had discussed this or had approval from anyone other than him, that is, anyone other than Adm. Poindexter?

MEESE: No, I did not, because in our conversation with Col. North he had indicated that Adm. Poindexter was the only one in the White House who knew about it.

NUNN: What about outside the White House?

MEESE: The only one he had indicated outside the White House in the Government or had been in the Government was Mr. McFarlane.

NUNN: Did you ask him whether anyone outside the White House in the Government, other than Mr. McFarlane, knew about the diversion?

MEESE: He told me that. He said that there were only three persons in the United States Government who knew this, and those were himself, Mr. McFarlane and Mr. Poindexter.

NUNN: Did you ask him about who knew it outside of the United States Government?

MEESE: No, sir.

NUNN: That didn't occur to you?

MEESE: That did not occur to me.

NUNN: Did you ever have any conversation with Adm. Poindexter or ask him any question about whether Col. North and Director Casey had discussed this issue?

MEESE: No, sir, I did not ask Adm. Poindexter, because Col. North had told me that, again, just who in the Government knew about it, and I asked Adm. Poindexter only whether he had told anyone in the White House.

NUNN: So you never asked Adm. Poindexter if he had told or discussed this with Director Casey?

MEESE: No, sir, I did not.

NUNN: Did you ask Adm. Poindexter under what authority he had approved this diversion by Col. North?

MEESE: No, sir, I did not.

I don't know whether you were present earlier, Sen. Nunn, but at that time I testified why this was so brief and why I didn't go into more extensive questioning, and that was that I was literally on my way to talk with the President and my main purpose was to verify what I had been told by Col. North the previous day, and particularly as to whether anyone in the White House knew about it and what the knowledge was on the part of Adm. Poindexter.

NUNN: I heard that.

Did you ask Adm. Poindexter anything about the money, where it went?

MEESE: No, sir, I did not.

NUNN: And how much it was?

MEESE: No, sir.

NUNN: Did you ask him anything about whether the contras got the money?

MEESE: No, sir, I did not.

NUNN: I understand the rush of events that day, but it seems to me that there were almost no direct questions asked by you to Adm. Poindexter.

MEESE: That's correct. I mentioned already the time frame and also the fact that we had had a detailed account of this whole thing by Col. North the previous day.

Meese and the President

NUNN: But you were trying to determine—as you said, from the President your directive was to see how you would resolve various conflicts, and it seems to me you gave very short treatment to whether or not the two key players in this may themselves disagree.

MEESE: The purpose was to resolve the conflicts and to get a coherent story on the Iranian initiative.

We had a totally different situation with regard to discovery of the diversion of funds, and there the primary objective was to verify what in fact had happened, get an account of all of the essential facts and then determine what the next steps would be.

So the mission considerably changed from Friday noon when it started until roughly Sunday evening when we had a great deal more information.

NUNN: I believe yesterday you testified that when you told the President you had found the diversion memo, quoting you from yesterday's testimony, "The President was quite surprised and indicated he had not known anything of this, and I believe Don Regan said at that time, or at least indicated, that he was surprised."

Is that right?

MEESE: That is correct.

NUNN: When you said that the President said he had not known anything of this, what did the word "this" mean to you? Was that the diversion memo?

MEESE: He indicated that he did not know anything about the diversion scheme. I talked to him about the diversion scheme.

NUNN: Did you ask him that question?

MEESE: Not precisely, no.

NUNN: Did he volunteer that?

MEESE: He said this is a shock to me, or surprise to me. . . .

NUNN: Did the President ask you at that stage who had carried out this diversion?

MEESE: . . . Yes, sir. And I told him then what the scheme was, the sale of weapons, the profits, and then the profits being diverted.

I mentioned Col. North and I believe I told him about the bank accounts and that sort of thing.

NUNN: Did he ask you about the money? And how much there was?

MEESE: I don't remember whether he asked or whether I told him or gave him an estimate of what we thought it might be.

NUNN: Did he ask you whether the money went to the contras?

MEESE: I think I told him that we had been told the money did go to the contras.

NUNN: Did he ask you who authorized the decision?

MEESE: I believe I told him, particularly in the afternoon, what Adm. Poindexter had told me, namely that he knew about it, but had not stopped it and allowed it to go forward.

NUNN: Did the President ask you whether Adm. Poindexter thought he had authority to approve that diversion of funds?

MEESE: I don't believe that he did, no, sir.

NUNN: Did he ask you anything about whether Col. North

felt he had the authority to carry that out?

MEESE: I don't think the question of authority ever came up because it was clear to both the President and myself that nobody had that authority.

NUNN: It was clear in what way? Did you discuss it? Did you have a discussion with the President that no one had that authority?

MEESE: I don't know whether we said it in that many words, but there was certainly no question in either of our minds that no one had that authority.

NUNN: Did he say anything to the effect, golly gee, I wish they had consulted with me, or anything like that? Or why did they think they could possibly have the authority to do that? Did he express any sense of outrage?

MEESE: I think he expressed real concern that this had happened because—and a lot of this was obviously in both of our minds, that this was a major blow, that it cast a cloud upon both the Iranian initiative and on the assistance to the freedom in Nicaragua.

NUNN: It sounds as if it was more the terms of your reading each other's feelings rather than expressed words, is that a fair statement?

MEESE: I think on the part of all of us, Mr. Regan, the President, myself, we both had a generally similar reaction, yes.

* * *

Casey's Role

[Rep. Louis] STOKES [D-Ohio]: Mr. Attorney General, listening to our testimony over the last two days, it is obvious to me that Director Casey was a man for whom you had tremendous respect. He was a man whom you knew very well, you worked very closely with. And obviously in your testimony, he was a man of great integrity.

Knowing everything that you now know about this case, including conversations you had with Mr. North about it and your interviews with him, do you believe that Director Casey devised a so-called fall guy plan under which Col. North was to be the fall guy and the one, so to speak, to take the hit?

Do you believe that?

MEESE: Again, Mr. Stokes, I condition my answer only on the fact that I have not heard the testimony that you and the members of the committee have. But that to me would be uncharacteristic of Mr. Casey based upon my knowledge of him.

STOKES: Now, I want to ask you also with reference to Director Casey if you can conceive of him, knowing his relationship to the President of the United States, knowing the role he has played in the President's campaigns and his affection for the President, his high regard for him, if you can see him encouraging Col. North to divert these funds from Iran without the President's approval?

MEESE: It would be hard for me to imagine that occurring, based upon what I know of Mr. Casey, including what I believe would be his appreciation of the tremendous dangers of doing that to policies he thought were very important as well as to the legal and ethical aspects of it.

* * *

[Rep. Peter W.] RODINO [Jr., D-N.J.]: . . . Just let me say in closing that I recognize that a good many of us, of course, have been puzzled by the manner in which this whole matter has been handled.

Of course, you have come before us and you have explained and some of us, of course, will still have questions.

I wonder whether or not considering the fact that the President's credibility as the polls indicate has been damaged, why some of those key questions were really asked in order that maybe this matter might have been disposed of way back then right after November 25th, after you had conducted your inquiry, if those key questions had been asked.

I think that regrettably the issue that is going to remain in the minds of many is just that: Why weren't key questions asked?

MEESE: Mr. Rodino, the key questions were asked. As I

testified here innumerable times, the questions were asked who knew about this. The answers were given by Mr.—Col. North that the three people who knew about it were Mr. McFarlane, himself and Adm. Poindexter.

The question was asked of Mr.—of Adm. Poindexter, did he know about it. He said yes, which confirmed what Mr. North had told us. Col. North had told us. We asked the—Adm. Poindexter whether he told anyone else in the White House. He said no.

All of the things that were the key questions, as you call them, were all answered in the course of our weekend fact-finding inquiry, and all of those answers have stood right now to today.

* * *

Interpreting Boland

The following exchange came after Representative McCollum quizzed Meese on his interpretation of the Boland amendments, a series of laws that restricted U.S. aid to the Nicaraguan contras. At issue was whether the Boland amendments applied to the activities of the National Security Council.

[Sen. Daniel K.] INOUYE [D-Hawaii]: Mr. Attorney General, I must say that I was a bit surprised and quite distressed with your response to questions asked by Mr. McCollum.

As the chief law enforcement officer of the United States, are you suggesting, or is it your opinion that once the 1986 Boland Amendment was passed, setting forth certain activities that are forbidden to the CIA, the NSA [National Security Agency] and others, that the NSC could have assumed these forbidden functions without violating the law?

MEESE: Mr. Chairman, the question was directed to me as to whether the Boland Amendment applied to the NSC staff. I indicated that this was an issue on which we had not rendered an opinion in the Justice Department. I also indicated that if you look at the language, it is possible to make a strong case for the fact that the Boland Amendment does not apply to the NSC staff.

Whether it would be wise for the NSC staff to pursue things which were forbidden, as you call it, to the CIA and other entities of government is a question of policy rather than of law.

But if the Boland Amendment does not apply to the NSC staff, then they would not be included within the prohibitions.

INOUYE: Are you telling us that the staff of the NSC can carry out functions that are forbidden to the CIA without evading the laws of the United States?

MEESE: If the law doesn't apply to them, then they can without violating the law, obviously. That's a tautology. And when I say the law doesn't apply to them, the law by its language does not include them.

INOUYE: But if an agent of the CIA carried it out, that would have been a violation of the law?

MEESE: Because the law applies to the CIA by its very terms. But the law by its terms only applies to the CIA, I believe the Defense Department and entities, the government involved in intelligence activities. Normally, under the list that I read to you, that is not normally deemed to include the National Security Council staff.

INOUYE: Even if they carried out intelligence activities, covert activities?

MEESE: It would depend again on the circumstances. It is a hypothetical question. But by the language there I think a good case can be made that Congress in its enactment of that law did not include the National Security Council staff within the purview of the agencies that are listed in that section as involved in the prohibitions.

INOUYE: Did not Mr. McFarlane, when he was the director of the agency, communicate by letter with [Rep. Lee H.] Hamilton [D-Ind.], Chairman of the Intelligence Committee, to the effect that the Boland Amendment did apply to the National Security Council?

MEESE: Again, I don't know, because I don't know the letter, I don't know which Boland Amendment. Remember, we are talk-

ing about five different Boland Amendments.

INOUYE: In other words, from what you are telling me, employees of the Department of Agriculture could have done the same thing without evading the law.

MEESE: I think that is entirely possible—

INOUYE: To carry out covert activities?

MEESE: That, as the law is written here, where it says funds available to the Central Intelligence Agency, the Department of Defense or any other agency or entity of the United States involved in intelligence activities may be obligated and expended only as authorized in specific sections—now, as I read that, as I said earlier, a strong case can be made, I think, that that does not apply to the Agriculture Department, that it doesn't apply to Health and Human Services and a number of other entities which are not involved in intelligence activities.

INOUYE: But if some agent of the Department of Agriculture involved himself, with the approval of the President, in covert activity, would that law apply to him?

MEESE: By its language it does not appear to.

INOUYE: Then the Boland Amendment can be evaded very easily.

MEESE: I don't think it would be an evasion if the law itself doesn't apply to a particular entity. It certainly would not be an evasion.

Donald T. Regan

Following are excerpts from the July 30, 1987, testimony of Donald T. Regan, President Reagan's former chief of staff.

[Terry] SMILJANICH [Senate counsel]: . . . The contras and their success or failure were much on the President's mind during your tenure; is that a fair statement?

REGAN: Yes.

SMILJANICH: And much time was spent at the White House attempting to get Congress to repeal the Boland amendment [that restricted U.S. aid to the Nicaraguan contras]?

REGAN: Yes.

SMILJANICH: The Tower Board report quotes the President as saying he did not know the NSC [National Security Council] staff was engaged in helping the contras during the 1985-1986 time frame.

Did you know that the NSC staff was engaged in helping the contras?

REGAN: Well, I knew that Lt. Col. [Oliver L.] North would speak to various groups, I knew that through our public liaison person at the White House, meetings were set up, people brought into the White House for purposes of discussing the freedom fighters.

North was one of the ones that they had as a briefer.

SMILJANICH: Well, other than these types of jaw-boning activities, were you aware or familiar with any of Col. North's other activities in connection with helping or assisting the contras?

REGAN: No.

SMILJANICH: —paramilitary assistance, that type of thing?

REGAN: No.

SMILJANICH: All right.

Did you ever ask Mr. [Robert C.] McFarlane or [Rear] Adm. [John M.] Poindexter who was filling the void created by the fact the CIA could not engage in activities in Central America on behalf of the contras?

REGAN: No, I did not.

SMILJANICH: All right. Well, in any of the legislative strategy sessions, you did have strategy sessions in connection with attempting to get Congress to change its mind about assistance to the contras; is that correct?

REGAN: Yes, we did.

SMILJANICH: In any of those sessions, did anyone ever suggest that the NSC staff was already helping to coordinate assistance to the contras?

REGAN: No, not in that sense of the word. The NSC staff, and particularly when Bud McFarlane was there, and he enjoyed such a good relationship with the Congress, he was in charge of our legislative efforts, but as far as in the field or relationships with the contras outside of the legislative process, I never got into that.

SMILJANICH: Well, in any of these sessions, did anyone ever suggest that even if the Boland Amendment could not be repealed, the NSC staff could continue to engage in many activities which would assist the contras in Central America?

REGAN: I'm not conscious of any discussions of that in the legislative sessions or other sessions.

SMILJANICH: Mr. McFarlane told this committee that he believed that the Boland Amendment applied to the National Security Council staff; Adm. Poindexter testified that he believed that the Boland Amendment did not apply to the National Security Council staff, and that indeed the National Security Council had taken over the role of the CIA in Central America.

Now, you were Chief of Staff during the tenure of both of those gentlemen. What did you know or understand about that subject?

REGAN: Well, I never looked into the legality of the Boland Amendment. I've never had the privilege of being a lawyer, and I didn't think that I knew enough to be able to opine as to whether or not this was legal, who could do it, who couldn't do it. I left that up to the NSC.

* * *

SMILJANICH: In September of 1985, Mr. McFarlane specifically advised you and the President that the Israelis had in fact shipped 500 TOW [antitank] missiles to Iran; is that correct?

REGAN: That is right.

SMILJANICH: All right.

Is it your testimony that the—that you and the President did not know prior to that shipment of TOW missiles that Israel intended to do so?

REGAN: I certainly did not know it, and I have no recollection of anyone telling the President in my presence about the shipment prior to its being done.

SMILJANICH: What was said at that meeting in September of 1985 about the replenishment of the missiles that Israel had shipped to Iran?

REGAN: The President was quite upset that his hand was being forced this way. He still wasn't certain, because he had told McFarlane in the Aug. 6 meeting to go slow on this and let's make sure we know who we are dealing with before we get too far into this.

As a result, to have his hand forced that way was quite upsetting. And he said, "As far as any replenishment is concerned, we will cross that bridge later. I am not going to do anything about that now."

SMILJANICH: It would be fair to say he did not rule out the possibility at that time?

REGAN: He didn't, but he didn't volunteer to do it right away either.

* * *

SMILJANICH: All right, sir. Well, if you will turn to Exhibit 17 in your book.

REGAN: Yes.

SMILJANICH: Do you have that?

REGAN: Yes.

SMILJANICH: That is a Presidential covert action finding [that allowed the covert sale of arms to Iran], dated at the bottom, Jan. 17, 1986.

REGAN: Yes.

SMILJANICH: And the signature of Ronald Reagan appears on it?

REGAN: That is right.

SMILJANICH: Is it your testimony then—what you are saying is you don't specifically recall the President signing this document?

REGAN: That's right. I don't remember him signing it, but that certainly is his signature.

SMILJANICH: When did you first discover that the President had signed a finding on Jan. 17 allowing this matter to go forward?

REGAN: Sometime in October of 1986. [Director of Central Intelligence William J.] Bill Casey called me to ask if I had a copy of the finding of January. I asked my staff to see if we had a copy in our files. We had none.

I went back to him and said no, I don't have one, ask John Poindexter. I said how come you don't have one. He said we don't have one in our files, and he said that's why I'm trying to find one.

So I didn't realize that the thing had been signed or where it was until late October of '86.

SMILJANICH: So you are saying that in late October of 1986, after this operation had been going forward for eight, nine, 10 months, neither you nor Director Casey had specific knowledge that the President had signed a finding dated Jan. 17?

REGAN: I think both of us—although I shouldn't characterize what he was thinking, but I will say that I was thinking that all along I just assumed that he probably had signed it. I just didn't see it.

SMILJANICH: And you couldn't locate a copy and the Director of Central Intelligence couldn't locate a copy?

REGAN: That is correct.

SMILJANICH: You finally did determine who had the only copy of that finding; is that right?

REGAN: Yes.

SMILJANICH: Who did you call?

REGAN: I asked Poindexter about it the next day. I said did Casey call you about that finding. He said yes. I said where the hell has it been—excuse my language. That is normal for me. Excuse me.

And he said I have the only copy, it's in my safe, it's with me. . . .

SMILJANICH: Under the plan that had been discussed with the senior advisers in January, upon the shipment of this first 1,000 TOW missiles all of the American hostages held in Lebanon were supposed to be released; isn't that correct?

REGAN: Yes.

SMILJANICH: When no hostages were released after shipment of those TOW missiles, what did you recommend the President do about the fact that the Iranians had broken their word?

REGAN: I told him I thought we ought to break it off, that we had been snookered again, how many times do we put up with this rug merchant type of stuff—or words to that effect.

SMILJANICH: What did the—what was the President's attitude or decision?

REGAN: I think he shared my view that we had been had.

SMILJANICH: Did he instruct anyone to terminate their activities?

REGAN: No. There was a pause then and I sort of lost track of what was going on. At that point we were deep in the middle of the tax bill and the budget battle and I sort of lost track of what was going on. I wasn't paying that much attention to it.

* * *

SMILJANICH: Well, during the [president's November 13, 1986] speech and during the [November 19, 1986] press conference one of the matters that the President did volunteer was the statement that all of the weapons shipped to Iran could easily fit into a single cargo plane with plenty of space left over.

Now, obviously the President had to be told something like that in order for him to make a statement like that.

How did that particular information come to his attention?

REGAN: Somewhere in these notes I think you may find it. Somewhere in here are notes that have been furnished to this committee.

This was during a meeting where, discussing with Poindexter and [Poindexter's Deputy Alton G.] Keel, the President—I'm not sure whether the Vice President was there or not—we were discussing just how much had been done.

And the President said, well, we have only sent them a small amount. Poindexter volunteered the information, oh, hell yes, a very small amount. I said, well, you know, like that old "What's

My Line" type of questioning, you know, bigger than a breadbox.

I said, John, how big is it, can you tell me how big it is, I have no idea. I fought a different war—what a bigger TOW missile is, let alone how big spare parts for Hawks are.

He said, oh, hell, they'd fit on a small plane, a couple pallets.

So I said, well, can you find out the answer, and he came back and—a little red-faced—and said, well, make it a C-5. But it literally could fit on a C-5.

So that's where the statement came from, it all could fit on a plane. Most people think of it as a 727 or something—no. They are talking about a C-5, and I doubt even at that they would fit, but that's something else again.

SMILJANICH: I think the record will probably reflect eventually they would have a lot of difficulty getting into a C-5. Perhaps it could be done with a shoehorn. I'm not certain.

At any rate, when you first asked this question and Adm. Poindexter gave you his opinion about how big a TOW missile was, do you recall that you were in the Oval Office and he said every one they shipped could probably fit in that office?

REGAN: Yes, I think he did say something like that.

SMILJANICH: There wouldn't be much room in the Oval Office to get any work done if, as it turned out—when you find out how much it would take to ship these TOW missiles; is that right?

REGAN: The Secret Service would have quite a problem if they had that many TOWs in the Oval Office.

* * *

Poindexter's Resignation

SMILJANICH: The next morning, Nov. 25th, I think you have already briefly touched on it. When you came into the White House, you went and talked briefly with Adm. Poindexter?

REGAN: Well, that evening at home, the evening of the 24th, I drew up a rather lengthy plan of action as to what steps we would take in order to remind me of various things.

I got into the office early, at 6:30 in the morning, to work with the staff on the presidential statement, to check with [Attorney General Edwin] Meese [III] to see if he were ready, and—to answer all the media inquiry that would come about; and then I told my secretary that I wanted to see Adm. Poindexter, if she could find out was he in. He wasn't.

He didn't come in until much later than normal that morning, but then I did go see him.

SMILJANICH: And what did you tell Adm. Poindexter and what did he tell you?

REGAN: Well, again, this is a very vivid recollection in my mind. He was sitting at the end of his conference table having breakfast from a tray, and I went in and in my normal fashion said, you know, "What's going on, John?" You know, "What the heck happened here?"

And he was very careful, deliberate. John is a deliberate person. He adjusted his glasses, he dabbed at his mouth with his napkin, put it down. He said, "Well, I guess I should have looked into it more, but I didn't."

He said, "I knew that Ollie was up to something but," he said "I didn't know what." And he said, "I just didn't look into it."

I said to him, "Why not? What the hell? You are a vice admiral. What is going on?"

And he said, "Well, I suppose this will get me into trouble now with one of my old neighbors from my old neighborhood back in Cambridge, Mass., but," he said, "Well, that damned Tip O'Neill [D-Mass., former Speaker of the House]."

He said, "The way he is jerking the contras around, I was just so disgusted," he said, "I didn't want to know what he was doing."

SMILJANICH: You didn't have any discussion with Adm. Poindexter about any authorization he might have received in connection with this matter?

REGAN: No. I told him then—I said, "Well, John, when you go in to see the President at 9:30, I think you better make sure you have your resignation with you."

SMILJANICH: What did he say?

REGAN: He said, "I have been thinking of that." He said, "I will."

SMILJANICH: And at the 9:30 daily national security briefing, Adm. Poindexter submitted his resignation?

REGAN: He came in and immediately started the discussion by saying—he told the President he was sorry for what had happened and again repeated that he probably should have looked into it more, but didn't. And he was submitting his resignation.

SMILJANICH: What did the President say?

REGAN: Well, it was a very sorrowful moment, a very hushed moment. The Attorney General was there, as I recall. And the President nodded and said, "I understand." He said, "This is a shame that it has happened this way, that a man with your great naval record," so on, "has come to this end," but he said, "That is it," and there was sort of an awkward silence.

Poindexter left the room.

* * *

The Arms-for-Hostages Deal

[Sen. William S.] COHEN [R-Maine]: On July 26, 1986, [hostage] Father Lawrence Jenco was released. Again Counsel tried to bring this out. When Bud McFarlane went on this very dangerous mission to Tehran, he was told "Bring all the hostages or come back"; and he couldn't get all the hostages because the Iranians were—we will give them two now, we will give you two later. He pulled up and came back in a very controversial type of negotiation.

Then on July 26, Father Jenco was released, and according to the Tower Report, the Americans feared that if they didn't respond positively, they risked the death of the hostages, is that correct?

REGAN: That is what we were told.

COHEN: Did you play a part in the decision to then go forward and release the weapons to the Iranians?

REGAN: I offered no opposition. I won't say that I played a role in it, because it was more a passive role. I sat, I heard, I listened.

COHEN: Here we have a situation where Mr. McFarlane rejected an offer for two and came back to Washington and then a short time later, we ended up giving all of the weapons for one hostage.

I guess the question is, in your own language, we sort of got taken down a Persian alley and got mugged. No one said anything about it. It is hard to understand why we were capitulating in this fashion, and no one seemed to be raising objections and pounding on people's doors saying, "This has got to stop now."

REGAN: I think people were upset, very disgusted with what was going on. The bait was there, though, that we could save a life here, a life there. You weigh that sort of thing, and it is very hard to—with a degree of finality—say "to hell with it."

COHEN: You wanted to save the hostages?

REGAN: Definitely. That was the way to get arms.

COHEN: If it were not for the hostage issue, you agree it is unlikely the President would ever have agreed to sell weapons to the Iranians?

REGAN: I don't think he ever would have agreed, bona fides, or what have you.

COHEN: So from the very beginning, there is no question in anyone's mind, at least not yours, the hostages were in fact the driving force that kept holding this thing together?

REGAN: No. Not the driving force, but a force. Because the driving force was, and I believe still is, if this President doesn't make contact with Iran, the next one will certainly have to or his successor. We are going to have to make that contact.

COHEN: No one disputes that, but it is the fact that it was the hostages that kept the issue alive. The President could have walked away from the table at any time from dealing with [arms dealers Manucher] Ghorbanifar, [Adnan] Khashoggi, or anyone else?

REGAN: Oh, yes. To that extent, sure. But, again, you have to ask yourself what is the job of the President of the United States? Should he turn his back on people like this? If he has a chance to get them out, should he do it? This President tried, it didn't work.

* * *

COHEN: You indicated before there is a Wall Street term of NPH, "no profit here," but you added lightly that a 600 percent markup might be another way to balance the budget. I was wondering, because it raises the question about the whole diversion issue. What is wrong, from your point of view, having told Col. North to help get arms to the Iranians, having directed Col. North to get munitions and money to the contras, what is wrong in your mind with combining the two and killing two birds with one stone? Why did you react with horror to that?

REGAN: Well, this a major decision that having, as we thought, agreed to sell arms, and the normal practice when the United States sells arms to any nation is to sell them at our cost. As far as I know, we don't sell to make a profit. We might, but we don't.

And this, in my judgment, was an unauthorized action on the part of Col. North to make a markup without consulting his superiors.

COHEN: He did consult Adm. Poindexter? Adm. Poindexter testified clearly before this committee that he in fact—

REGAN: It was an unauthorized act on both of their parts.

COHEN: Yes.

REGAN: Because certainly I think the President of the United States should have been contacted on that one, or the Secretary of Defense, certainly. Had been alerted this type of thing was going on.

COHEN: Well, that is one of the other questions that I think all of us have, that John Poindexter has a reputation of—not of someone who takes bold leaps or engages in any sort of "Kissingerian"—if I can use that phrase—ingenuity, but straightforward, by the book. His whole history has been absolute chain of command.

How could he have been so wrong in this case to have presumed the President would have authorized such a major decision on his part?

REGAN: I notice that he testified that way before this committee or these committees. I would dispute that.

I don't think the President of the United States would have condoned this had he known about it. I don't think that he would have said, "Yes, let's go, mark this stuff up and divert the money to the contras." I don't think he would have participated in that. I know I wouldn't have.

That whole idea would have been, you know, very, very much contrary to the Ronald Reagan that I knew.

* * *

[Rep. Jack] BROOKS [D-Texas]: Do you think, Mr. Secretary, that it was primarily the aftermath of the Iran arms-contra scandal that precipitated your early retirement about three months later?

REGAN: Yes. I think it was a direct cause of that.

BROOKS: Col. North has been characterized by some as a national hero for having carried off this scheme to divert funds from the Iranian arms sales to the contras which he apparently did without the knowledge or approval of the President, according to the testimony of you and others.

Do you, as a former Marine with extensive overseas duty in World War II, consider Col. North to be a national hero for coming up with this neat idea?

REGAN: Well, let me put it this way: I admire the colonel's enthusiasm, his ingenuity, his—obviously I am very impressed by the courage he has shown previously on the battlefield and in his previous assignments.

My question, however, not recognizing him as a real hero, is insofar as I think he might have asked permission or shared with us his plan rather than to put it into effect in an unauthorized way and have this come out. Perhaps had more of us thought about it in a longer period of time, this wouldn't have happened and would have obviated the necessity for our being here today.

BROOKS: Are you concerned or disappointed or possibly angry about the damage that his and Adm. Poindexter's activities caused you and the Administration, the anguish that all of us have shared in the last—

REGAN: Oh, there were momentary frustrations on my part,

yes. At my age, and background, you learn to live with these things. So I bear them no ill will at this point.

* * *

[Sen. Warren B.] RUDMAN [R-N.H.]: . . . Do you think it is fair to say that the President's staff—and I am not talking about—I am talking about the National Security staff, not only ill-served the President by not advising him of the diversion scheme and allowing him to make that choice himself, but in fact did not adequately brief him on, during and after these events took place?

REGAN: Well, this may be an unkind characterization of them, but nevertheless, it's the way I feel. I do think they should have discussed this with the President, allowed him to make the decision to divert funds or not.

Secondly, knowing of that, that this money had been done but yet knowing that the cover had been blown and this would eventually come out, they should not have allowed this President to go to speak to this nation without revealing that fact, among others. That would have put a whole new light on the situation.

They also did him a very much grave disservice, hurt him badly by allowing him to go before the nation's media or its representatives, and not know that these deeds had been done. What if somebody that night had challenged the President, an enterprising reporter had found this information out one way or another? What would the President's embarrassment have been? As it so happened, it was the Attorney General that found it or one of his people, and the President himself was allowed to make this announcement. I say "allowed." There was no choice. I mean, the man wanted to do it. But it was certainly embarrassing to the President.

Now, that to me was a grave disservice that the National Security advisers did to the President in knowing that and nobody spoke up.

RUDMAN: Thank you. My time is up.

I'll simply wind up by just observing that a number of people on this panel, both Republicans and Democrats, have been criticized for being tough on certain witnesses and boring in on the facts, and I want to tell you, as a member, you and I are members of the same party, you served the President as Chief of Staff, I represent my constituents of New Hampshire here in this body, I happen to think that the greatest tragedy of this entire event is that this President, who has been good to the people, who has been reticent to fire people, who was known to be kindly and decent, was so ill-advised and deceived by key members of his own staff, I think it is an outrage, and frankly that has outraged me from the very beginning. And I would suspect it's probably outraged you.

REGAN: It has.

* * *

A Need to Lie?

[Sen. George J.] MITCHELL [D-Maine]: If you followed these hearings, you have heard a lot about lies to Congress and to the Attorney General, and you have dealt with Congress a great deal over the past several years.

And I want to ask you, have you ever felt you had to lie to Congress in order to do your job?

REGAN: No, never. There are times when I have regretted having to tell Congress some things. There are other times when I have bitten my tongue for not telling Congress some things, or maybe even where to go. But there is never an excuse for lying to the Congress, never, or dissembling from anyone in the Executive Branch. That simply shouldn't be tolerated, can't be tolerated.

MITCHELL: You have had a lot of experience. Indeed before you assumed your public positions, you were the Chief Executive Officer of what is the largest stock brokerage in the United States certainly, perhaps in the world. So you don't condone lying to Congress?

REGAN: Absolutely not.

MITCHELL: And you don't condone the destruction of important documents to prevent the information from ever becoming public?

REGAN: No.

MITCHELL: And you ran the White House and you would not have condoned that?

REGAN: As a matter of fact, I'll tell you this, I was questioned by—as my secretary has—by members of the staff of this committee and others, the Independent Counsel [Lawrence E. Walsh, appointed to conduct a criminal investigation into the Iran-contra affair], about shredding. I'll tell you this, we don't have a shredder or didn't have a shredder in my part of the West Wing. I don't know where that shredder is that supposedly is in the West Wing of the White House. I suspect it is downstairs in the Situation Room. But we did not have a shredder in my part of it, and the second point is, I wouldn't know how to operate one if I had one.

So we did not believe in shredding documents.

* * *

Regan resumed his testimony July 31, 1987:

[Rep. Louis] STOKES [D-Ohio]: Mr. Regan, during the period of time you were the Chief of Staff, after Poindexter and North had left the White House, did there come a time when there was a discussion with the President when you were present about congressional immunity for Col. North and Adm. Poindexter?

REGAN: Yes, there was such a time.

STOKES: And would that have been around approximately Dec. 15th, 16th?

REGAN: I think even earlier than that—probably around Dec. 8th, 9th, or 10th, in through there. I recall discussions of that.

STOKES: And who was present at that time?

REGAN: Well, I remember one discussion among the President, the Vice President and myself regarding this as to how to get the full story out. Both the Admiral and the Colonel were refusing to talk. We had said we didn't know the story, couldn't find out the story, granted, the Tower Commission was working but still in an effort to hasten this, I believe the President did suggest publicly some time in the period to which I referred that either the Senate or the House or both Intelligence committees should give limited immunity to both of these witnesses or to either one of them in order to get a story out.

But both of the committees, the House and the Senate Intelligence committees, said, no, they didn't want to do that, that there wasn't the proper time.

Presidential Pardons

STOKES: Now, either at that particular meeting or any other meeting, was the questions of presidential pardon for either Adm. Poindexter or Col. North ever discussed with the President?

REGAN: Yes, it was.

STOKES: Can you tell us when that was?

REGAN: Yes. Somebody brought it up to him. It was shot down right away. That was something the President wouldn't even listen to, the fact that he should grant a pardon. His reasoning went along this sort of line, to grant a pardon means you think somebody has committed a crime; you only pardon for a crime.

And he didn't know what the crime was. As yet, there had been no evidence brought to him, the Tower Commission report was not out, the Independent Counsel had been put in being, but he had no report, obviously neither the Senate nor the House Intelligence committees had finished, let alone the fact that this committee would be set up, so the President said not only is it premature, but I will be darned if I am going to accuse them of a crime in advance.

STOKES: Was that the extent of the conversation that day, as you recall?

REGAN: It never came up again. He put his foot down hard and it never came up again.

Caspar W. Weinberger

Following are excerpts from the July 31, 1987, testimony of Defense Secretary Caspar W. Weinberger:

[Neil] EGGLESTON [House deputy general counsel]: Let me ask you, sir, if you could discuss with us and tell us what occurred to the best that you recall on this meeting of Dec. 7 [1985], who was there, what it was, and what the issues were.

WEINBERGER: I think this meeting was in the White House in the Oval Office, I believe, and it could have been upstairs in the residence, I am just not quite sure at the moment, but the President was there, the Vice President, the Secretary of State [George P. Shultz], Mr. [Robert C.] McFarlane, I believe, was there. And the general discussion was now more specific than it had been in August, and it was about a specific plan to transfer some weapons to the Iranians and why this would produce a good result.

There was much more discussion of hostages at this time but there was also discussion of how important it was to have an opening to Iran. And I made very strong objection to the whole idea, as did the Secretary of State.

EGGLESTON: Now, do you recall any of the specific objections that you made to the plan?

WEINBERGER: Oh, yes. I ran through a whole group and raised every point that occurred to me, including the fact that we were at the same time asking other countries not to make sales of weapons to Iran, that there was no one of any reliability or, indeed, any sense with whom we could deal in Iran and the government, and that we would not have any bargain carried out, that if we were trying to help get hostages released, why there would be a real worry that the matter would not be held in any way confidential, that we would be subjected to blackmail, so to speak, by people who did know it in Iran and elsewhere, and that we had no interest whatsoever in helping Iran in any military way, even a minor way, and that in every way it was a policy that we should not engage in and most likely would not be successful.

EGGLESTON: Secretary Shultz has described your opposition at that meeting as quite forceful. Is that a fair characterization?

WEINBERGER: Well, I am afraid I argue that way about almost everything. I am told so, yes. But I think that is entirely a fair description, perhaps an understatement....

EGGLESTON: Let me ask you to direct your attention to Exhibit 20 in your exhibit book. Mr. Secretary, you would not have seen this document, I take it, contemporaneously?

WEINBERGER: No.

EGGLESTON: It is the cover memo to the Jan. 17th finding [authorizing the sale of arms to Iran in exchange for the release of hostages]. I want to ask you about a particular line in it—

WEINBERGER: This is a memorandum that you are directing my attention to from [Rear] Adm. [John M.] Poindexter to the President?

EGGLESTON: Yes, sir. It is dated Jan. 17th. The back page of this document contains the Jan. 17th finding with the President's signature on it and is also dated Jan. 17th.

WEINBERGER: Yes. There is, however, a page before that on which the President's initials are put on, but not in his handwriting.

EGGLESTON: That is correct. I think in the last sentence it indicates that the President was briefed verbally by Adm. Poindexter. If you could return to the very first page, there is just one line of this that I wanted to ask you about.

WEINBERGER: Right.

EGGLESTON: It is about halfway down the very first paragraph, and it reads as follows: "The Israelis are very concerned that Iran's deteriorating position in the war with Iraq,"—I want to ask you about that concept. Was it the view of the Department of Defense that Iran had a deteriorating position in the war with Iraq?

WEINBERGER: No, quite to the contrary, it wasn't my position or anybody's opinion that I talked to.

EGGLESTON: Were you consulted during this period about the relative positions of the Iranians and the Iraqis in the war?

WEINBERGER: No.

EGGLESTON: Do you know whether the President was advised that there was a contrary view to the one that is expressed in this memo?

WEINBERGER: I don't know that. I never saw this memo to the President, never had a chance to respond to it, but I certainly did not have the view that Iraq was winning or anything of that kind. Quite the contrary. As a matter of fact, it was basically Iraqi military strategy not to pursue any kind of decisive military end to that.

They have been trying to get a cease-fire and trying to get the war ended by negotiation. They have specifically eschewed the idea of a military victory as far as I can tell.

EGGLESTON: So if you had been consulted at that time, you would have advised the President that you disagreed with that Israeli view?

WEINBERGER: In the strongest possible terms.

EGGLESTON: To the extent the President relied upon that concept and decided to go forward, that in your view was simply as erroneous assumption on their part?

WEINBERGER: Yes.

* * *

[Rep. Les] ASPIN [D-Wis.]: . . . Let me ask a little bit about the policy that was undertaken and your attitude towards that policy. I take it that you, based upon your reaction to that NSDD [National Security Decision Directive] that was circulated, the draft that was circulated in 1985, that your opposition to this policy was opposition to the whole idea, not just to the opposition to the arms sales.

WEINBERGER: Oh, yes. I thought it, first of all, was not possible to get a better relationship with Iran, with the Iranian government and its present hands. I didn't think there was anybody we could deal with that was not virulently anti-American and I just didn't think it would work and I was, as you say, against the whole policy. . . .

I did add a word in my comment to the effect it would be good if we could get a relationship with Iran as we used to have it under the shah [of Iran, Mohammed Reza Pahlavi]. It would be desirable to try to do something like that, but we couldn't do it in this situation.

ASPIN: Let me ask you why you drew that conclusion. I take it that the opposition of other people, in principle, the Secretary of State, his view was if we could get some, he was not opposed to new initiatives with the Iranian government. He said he opposed the idea of selling arms in order to further that initiative. And that seems to be the general reaction of most people, was that the idea itself was not a bad idea, but that the particulars of it, namely selling arms as part of that, was wrong.

But you are saying you just flat-out did not think that the idea of pursuing any kind of relationship with a moderate element in Iran, that that was not a—

WEINBERGER: I didn't think it was a good idea. I didn't think it was possible to do it. I did not think and do not think there is any moderate element in Iran that's still alive, and I think it was not a good idea in any sense of the term.

I would like to have a relationship with a rational government in Iran of the kind we had when the shah was there, because I think geographically and strategically that's a very useful thing. I was, as you say, against the whole idea.

ASPIN: Does that—when the National Security Council, then Bud McFarlane, drafted the NSDD and circulated it, he had some intelligence from the CIA, particularly from Mr. Casey, that in fact there was some intelligence that would indicate that such an initiative was a good idea at that time.

Did you just not believe that intelligence or did you have some other intelligence? In other words, did DIA have a contrary—Defense Intelligence Agency—have a contrary view at that time?

WEINBERGER: My memory is that generally they did, but I didn't see anything in the estimate that accompanied the draft NSDD that supported such a conclusion.

There were no individuals named, and certainly everything that I had heard and known about Iran, particularly with respect to all of the statements, positions, their support of terrorism, all of that struck me as simply being contrary to that estimate. It was not an intelligence estimate with which I agreed.

ASPIN: So you just flat-out deny—I mean, there was a whole

series of options or intelligence estimates upon which this policy was based, either implicitly or explicitly. And let me just list them, and I guess you reject them all.

One, there was a moderate element in Iran—let me list them all, Mr. Secretary. One, that there was a moderate element that you could deal with.

Second, that somehow giving them weapons would strengthen them in some way, that this deal would somehow strengthen them.

Third, that Iran, and in particular this moderate element, held some influence over the people who are holding our hostages in Lebanon and that somehow, that they would have the ability to get the hostages loose and get these people to abate on their terrorist activities.

I take it you would just reject that whole litany. . . .

WEINBERGER: It was just contrary from everything I had heard, all the other intelligence that I've seen, my own personal views, and the knowledge that I had of the way the various battles in the war had gone and what they said about us, their support of international terrorism, just none of it rang true as far as I was concerned.

ASPIN: So it was essentially pretty much of a gut instinct reaction to it?

WEINBERGER: It was based on, as I say, a lot of other reports that I had that made that seem quite wrong.

* * *

The Hostage Situation

[Sen. Paul S.] SARBANES [D-Md.]: Now, as this thing [the Iran arms sales policy] was being driven, did you hear the argument made that the safety of the hostages was at stake if we did not continue the initiative and continue to send arms?

In other words, that the situation had reached the point not that the sending of arms would get the hostages out, the so-called arms-for-hostages exchange, but the failure to send arms would endanger the hostages so that just in order to sort of preserve them in the state in which they were, arms had to be sent, that we, in effect, had become hostages to the hostages.

WEINBERGER: Yes, I believe there were points made like that. There were a lot of arguments back and forth, and the point was continually made that we were on the verge of success, a point which I disputed all the time because it never, to my knowledge, had actually happened.

I never connected the release that took place with any of the activity that I disapproved of so strongly. But I think that the point was probably made that, I think it was more in the context, Senator, that we have had additional talks, if we could just give them a few more TOWs [antitank missiles], if we can just do a few more things, if we send over people they are convinced are bona fide representatives of the United States, then we will get the people out, and these will be people we can deal with later, and we have to keep doing this.

I think it was more in that context, but it is quite conceivable at some point someone may have mentioned the point, as you very eloquently phrase it, we become hostages to the hostages. . . .

SARBANES: What is your perception of what was occurring? You are the Secretary of Defense, a statutory member of the National Security Council. You are charged with major responsibility and, in fact, in the command and control function in the case of conflict, have a very unique and special responsibility that has been entrusted to you and yet here we are with you obtaining information about what your own Government is doing from foreign sources.

The National Security Adviser in effect is saying no, we don't want the Secretaries of State and Defense to consult with the President. What is your perception of what was taking place in our Government?

WEINBERGER: Senator, what was taking place, I believe, is what I described earlier and which I strongly disapprove of, that people with their own agenda who thought that this opening was a good thing, who knew that I opposed it and that George Shultz opposed it, did not want the President to hear these arguments after the decision had been made or perhaps indeed even to the extent that they were made before, I don't know.

But I think that that was basically the problem, and I think that people with their own agenda as I have said in the [National] Security Council were doing everything I can and maybe the motives were good, I don't know, but were doing everything they could to put this agenda into effect and one of the ways they were doing that was to keep away from the President views that they suspected, correctly most of the time, differ with theirs.

I think it was a bad procedure. I think it has been completely corrected now because we have totally different kinds of people who have a totally different approach.

I am not trying to lay blame, I am trying candidly to express to you how I think the situation came about.

* * *

Weinberger resumed his testimony August 3, 1987:

[Sen. Warren B.] RUDMAN [R-N.H.]: Mr. Secretary, I am very disturbed by one section of the Tower Report. I want to say at the outset that I think that the Tower Commission did an excellent job in very limited time. They, of course, did not have access to some of the key witnesses in this hearing; and it was looking at those witnesses in focus that have finally given us, I believe, a pretty complete picture of what happened. I particularly think that they were a bit premature in their judgment of certain Cabinet officials.

I want to just read a statement to you which I am sure you are familiar with. It says, "Given the importance of the issue and the sharp policy divergences involved, however, Secretary Shultz and Secretary Weinberger in particular distanced themselves from the march of events. Secretary Shultz specifically requested to be informed only as necessary to perform his job. Secretary Weinberger had access to intelligence, the details about the operation. Their obligation was to give the President their full support and continued advice with respect to the program; or if they could not in conscience do that, to so inform the President. Instead, they simply distanced themselves from the program. They protected the record as to their own positions on this issue. They were not energetic in attempting to protect the President from the consequences of his personal commitment to freeing the hostages."

. . . I wonder if you would like to respond a bit more than you have as to this particular part of that quote, "instead, they simply distanced themselves from the program and they protected the record and they were not energetic," etc.

Would you like to comment on that, Mr. Secretary?

WEINBERGER: I would like to comment on it, Senator. I think that is the kind of remark or the kind of conclusion that can only be drawn by people who don't have any knowledge of the facts.

There is no evidence to sustain that kind of conclusion at all that I am familiar with, nothing that the Commission talked with me about, nothing that as far as I know they heard, nothing that has come out in any of these hearings would sustain that conclusion.

I agree with you, I think it is a very unfair characterization. It's not based on any evidence that I know of at all. And indeed, it could not be if anybody had taken the trouble to explore the facts, and indeed, that is the view of the President, in his very generous and fair spirit, told the American public that that conclusion was exactly wrong.

RUDMAN: Indeed, Mr. Secretary, the record I think shows that on each and every occasion where you were part of a group discussing this with the President, you and Secretary Shultz—and I would use the word, from what I know of this—vehemently opposed the policy.

WEINBERGER: I think that's entirely a fair characterization. Some would even use stronger language. The President might.

But in any event, we did oppose it. We opposed it at every step of the way. And if the charge of distancing oneself were true, I would not have ever made any further inquiries when I first began

getting the intelligence reports that led me into what the facts actually were.

* * *

Operation Staunch

[Rep. Thomas S.] FOLEY [D-Wash.]: Did you have any knowledge of any transfers of weapons by any third country prior to 1985, from 1981 to 1985?

WEINBERGER: Not knowledge. There were some reports, but I do not have a specific personal knowledge, no, sir.

FOLEY: Those reports had to do with transfers of American weapons by a third country?

WEINBERGER: Well, they had to do with transfers and sales of weapons by other countries, some of which contained American technology, some of which were actually American weapons.

This was part of what we were trying to stop with this Operation Staunch [the administration's policy of convincing other countries not to sell arms to Iran or Iraq]. I did have information as I worked on that, as I talked with other countries' representatives, urging them not to make sales.

We had reports and I frequently would say we don't know if this is accurate or not, but here are the consequences and we hope you will stop, and so forth.

FOLEY: If these reports were true, would they be in violation of American law if they had not been reported to the United States?

WEINBERGER: Yes. We have a—two basic rules with respect to our weapons.

They cannot go to any country for any purpose except for its own self-defense and they cannot be re-exported by that country to any other country without specific permission from the United States.

FOLEY: And of course that permission requires notification?

WEINBERGER: Indeed.

FOLEY: To your knowledge, between 1981 and 1985, prior to the weapons that were transferred that we have discussed, were there any reports by any third country to the United States of sales or requests for permission to sell arms to Iran?

WEINBERGER: Not requests for permission that I ever recall. There were reports that various sales were being made, and it was this kind of thing that we were trying to stop with our Operation Staunch.

FOLEY: So if these sales had taken place, they would be taking place in violation of American law?

WEINBERGER: That is my understanding, yes, sir.

* * *

[Sen. George J.] MITCHELL [D-Maine]: . . . Did the transfers [of weapons] to Iran take place in such a way as to avoid established procedures?

WEINBERGER: Senator, the only way I can answer that question is, first of all, to say that this transaction was not one for which established procedures were set up or contemplated and; secondly, there was no bypassing, as you put it, of any of the procedures relating to price.

The pricing of the weapons was carried out in precisely the same way that it always is. But the procedures that I established much earlier, perhaps three years, four years ago, were designed for a situation in which an intelligence agency or an intelligence activity or individual assigned to intelligence would say that he had a requirement that could not be disclosed, but he needed—the reason for it couldn't be disclosed—but that he needed money or he needed the right to buy some equipment, ship, release a plane, something of that kind, and I found, and as a result of that, we have had a number of, well, fewer prosecutions, convictions growing out of some earlier activities because what was happening was that the intelligence aspects of his request were overriding any review at all, and, so we instituted a situation that when an intelligence activity was contemplated or when there was a request for some kind of support that then there would be a review of that by a number of people leading up to the Vice Chief of the Army

Staff, and that it would include members of the service as well as members of my office, and the Office of the Secretary General.

That system is still in effect and it is an important way of protecting against any abuses of the system.

This was a totally different transaction; this was a transaction in which the President of the United States directed that with as small a knowledge as possible because of the safety of the hostages and the desire to preserve any hope we had of getting them out that these weapons should be transferred to the CIA directly, and we did that, but there was a full review of the pricing because there was never any instruction of any kind about the price and the price was determined in the normal fashion.

Unfortunately, as we have talked about in the past, there were errors in that; in the computation of the price, but they were innocent errors.

* * *

[Rep. Louis] STOKES [D-Ohio]: . . . Do you see any conflict between the CIA Director sitting as a policy adviser within the National Security Council? In other words, say, between two models, the present one where the Director of Central Intelligence is not a member of the Cabinet, and the model we had under Mr. Casey where he is, which is preferable?

WEINBERGER: Well, Congressman, a member of the Cabinet is kind of a basically loose term. I don't see any way in which the intelligence advice that is requested by a President of anyone, whether he attends Cabinet meetings or doesn't attend Cabinet meetings, is not going to require some discussion of policy matters. You simply can't have the kind of relationship with the head of your—with your Director of Central Intelligence, I think as President or as a member of the Security Council, if you don't turn to them and ask for what their analysis shows and inevitably there is some subjective opinion type of comment that comes into that kind of discussion.

Bill Casey was a very close personal friend of the President, did sit as a member of the Cabinet meetings; but I don't recall his offering general opinions on matters that didn't derive from his intelligence analysis. He had a lot of conversation with the President when I wasn't there. I have no idea—was an old friend. I don't think that friendship should disqualify anybody from serving the government or the President; but basically, I think that [current CIA director William J.] Bill Webster, of course, is a person for whom I have very great admiration and has done a great job in all of the difficult assignments he has had over the years.

I think the main thing is that the analysis should be objective, as I think it is now, should be done by a professional. It should represent their best conclusions as a result of everything that they can secure from every source and evaluate the source; and then I think that ought to be presented to the President in distilled form and that the President then uses that in making up his own mind. In the course of that, he is very likely to ask for opinions of people, opinions of Bill Casey or of Bill Webster based on their general experience.

It's very hard to separate out and say that you must never, as a CIA or Director of Central Intelligence [DCI] man, you must never discuss policy. I don't think you can make quite that fine a line; but as long as the clear objective, impartial analysis given to the President, and that he makes up his own mind on the basis of that, I don't object to his supplementing that by discussions of a formal or informal nature with the DCI. I don't see how you can really avoid it. . . .

STOKES: Mr. Secretary, our committee heard testimony from Lt. Col. [Oliver L.] North about the desirability of what he called off-the-shelf, outside-the-system covert capability with rapid response capability, a central pool of ready funds, and the conduct of covert activities.

In his testimony before the committee on July 15, Adm. Poindexter, in response to a question from [Senate committee chief counsel Arthur L.] Liman, said: "I'm saying that a private organization, properly approved, using nonappropriated funds in an approved sort of way may be a solution to the problem."

My question to you, Mr. Secretary, is this: Is a private organization, using nonappropriated funds, a solution to any problem of which you are aware concerning covert activities; that is, do you agree with the Admiral and the Colonel on this type of thing?

WEINBERGER: No, I do not.

STOKES: Could you tell us why?

WEINBERGER: Well, I don't think—I think part of the problem is that—has been exemplified in the last three months here. I think that what you need is to have a proper degree of official oversight.

I am not in favor of unofficial, private people carrying out government activities. I think they are always subject to the worry that they will get engaged in things that are not subject to proper accountability.

I talked earlier this morning about how there are many things we do where the circle has to be kept narrow, and the circumference very limited of people who do know, because of the operational security and the objectives of a particular activity. And we have to do those kinds of activities. But I think it's all the more important for those to have proper accountability. And certainly where the use of funds are concerned, then I think that that becomes very much more critical because there are always additional temptations and so on.

* * *

The 'White House Mystique'

[Rep. Edward P.] BOLAND [D-Mass.]: Evidence has been presented to these committees indicating that in November of 1984, Lt. Col. North tasked Gen. Paul Gorman, who was the Commander of the Southern Command at the time, with furnishing information of the location and status of Sandinista Hind helicopters to Col. North for his passage to the contras.

To your knowledge, did Gen. Gorman make his superiors in DOD [Department of Defense] aware of this request?

WEINBERGER: I didn't know of it and Mr. North has no authority whatever to task anyone.

BOLAND: The evidence was presented to this committee—Exhibit 31 in the testimony of Mr. McFarlane when he was here.

Let me ask, given the disparity of their rank, between General and Lieutenant Colonel, would you attribute General Gorman's compliance with North's request to that "White House mystique" that you mentioned last Friday?

WEINBERGER: Well, if there was, indeed, compliance with it, yes. There are a number of people who feel that when the White House calls, that everything has to be done, but in accordance with that call. But I found this very shortly after I came to the Department and right after that time, I issued very strict instructions—which, to the best of my knowledge, have been followed—that any calls or requests for tasking of the military had to be referred to my office, to the Deputy Secretary, if I was away, and that they would be acted on only when we were—confirmed that this was indeed something that was desired by officials and not just by some building.

* * *

[Rep. Ed] JENKINS [D-Ga.]: With your forceful opposition to the proposal [to sell arms to Iran] as well as that of Secretary Shultz, who was the most persuasive person? I keep—during all of these hearings, we have not heard the person that was—that persuaded the President. Was it Casey? Was it McFarlane? Who?

WEINBERGER: Two things, sir. First of all, I heard Mr. McFarlane and Mr. Poindexter push the program for time to time at its beginning, and later. But the assumption seems to be that somebody has to persuade the President of something one way or the other.

This President is a man with very definite ideas. He is a superb leader, in my opinion, and he has his own judgments and his own ideas, and he's going to listen to advice and he's going to listen to recommendation, but he's not always going to follow them. I've had the great privilege of working with him for many, many years, and have made recommendations to him before that he has not agreed to and made recommendations that he has agreed to, and made recommendations that he partially agreed with. He has his own mind that he makes up after listening to a number of different views.

And so I don't—I think, as I say, there were two or three things that were very persuasive to him here, and one of them was certainly that it would be a good idea to get a better relationship with Iran, and I argued strenuously that we couldn't do that with the group that is there now. He also obviously was motivated by the hope of getting the hostages back, and I think all of these things were things that he was—that were significant. But I don't think he requires any one person to be for something or any one person to be against it, and then to follow that slavishly. He doesn't operate that way. He never has.

Closing Statements

Following are excerpts from the August 3, 1987, closing statements of the leaders of the select committees investigating the Iran-contra affair: Dick Cheney, R-Wyo., ranking minority member of the House panel; Warren B. Rudman, R-N.H., Senate panel vice chairman; Lee H. Hamilton, D-Ind., House panel chairman; and Daniel K. Inouye, D-Hawaii, Senate panel chairman:

CHENEY: . . . Questions have been raised about why we had these committees established. I think it was preordained that there would be such an investigation once it became clear the administration was trading arms to Iran. Congress clearly has a legitimate role of oversight in reviewing the conduct of foreign policy by the administration and the President himself supported these activities and encouraged us to form these select committees.

I also think it is important that credit be given to the President. He has given his complete cooperation and support to our investigation throughout. He has provided administration witnesses without ever claiming the executive privilege, provided thousands of pages of documents, classified and unclassified, provided access to his own personal diary, and given these committees and the nation an in-depth look at some of the most sensitive and excruciatingly painful event[s] of his Administration.

I think it is also important to point out that once President Reagan understood the serious nature of the problems associated with these events, he moved boldly and decisively to make corrections. He reassigned the responsible individuals, created the new NSC [National Security Council] staff under the able leadership of [national security adviser] Frank [C.] Carlucci and [Lt.] Gen. [Colin C.] Powell [deputy national security adviser], brought in a new White House Chief of Staff, a new Director of the CIA, appointed the Tower Commission, cooperated with the commission's investigation and took their criticisms to heart, supported the call for an independent counsel and, of course, gave his complete cooperation to these committees.

It takes a strong, confident leader to subject himself and his Administration to the very thorough nature of this investigation. We are here today concluding the public phase of our hearings on time in large part because of the cooperation of the President and his Administration.

President Reagan has enjoyed many successes during his more than six years in office. Clearly this was not one of them.

As the President himself has said, mistakes were made, mistakes in selling arms to Iran, allowing the transaction to become focused on releasing American hostages, diverting funds from the arms sale to support for the contras, misleading the Congress about the extent of NSC staff involvement with the contras, delaying notification of anyone in Congress of the transactions until after the story broke in Lebanese newspapers, and tolerating a decision-making process within the upper reaches of the administration that lacked integrity and accountability for key elements of the process.

But there are some mitigating factors, factors which—while they don't justify mistakes—go a long way to helping explain and make them understandable. The need is still evident today to find some way to alter our current relationships with Iran. The Presi-

dent's compassionate concern over the fate of Americans held hostage in Lebanon, especially the fate of [hostage] William Buckley, our CIA station chief in Beirut. The vital importance of keeping the Nicaraguan democratic resistance alive until Congress could reverse itself and repeal the Boland Amendment.

The fact that for the President and most of his key advisers these events did not loom as large at the time they occurred as they do now.

Congressional vacillations and uncertainty about our policies in Central America and finally a congressional track record of leaks of sensitive information sufficient to worry even the most apologetic advocate of an expansive role for the Congress in foreign policy making.

It is also, I think, important to point out what these hearings did not show. There is no evidence that the President had any knowledge of the diversion of profits from the arms sale to the Nicaraguan democratic resistance. In fact, all of the evidence indicates that he had no knowledge whatsoever of the diversion.

There is also no evidence of any effort by the President or his senior advisers to cover up these events.

On the contrary, the evidence clearly shows that the President and the Attorney General were the ones primarily responsible for bringing these events and matters to the attention of the nation.

In other words, these hearings have demonstrated conclusively in my opinion that the President has indeed been telling the truth.

What does it all mean? What does it signify? These events have been characterized by some pretty strong statements by my colleagues on the committees and by some in the press over the past eight months.

We have heard of a grave constitutional crisis, listened to expressions of moral indignation and outrage and even been treated to talk about a coup in the White House, a junta run by a Lieutenant Colonel and an Admiral.

My own personal view is that there has been far too much apocalyptic rhetoric about these events, most of it unjustified. If there ever was a crisis—which I doubt—it ended before these committees were established. And to the extent that corrective action was required, the President took it unilaterally before our committees had taken a single word of public testimony.

Saying that the investigators have sometimes gotten carried away in an effort to outdo one another's colorful phrase-making in no way justifies the mistakes that were made. But what is required here, it seems to me, is a little calm, dispassionate analysis if we are going to learn from our study of those events.

In some respects, what we have uncovered in the course of these hearings is just the latest chapter in an unfinished book about the conduct of U.S. foreign policy. The struggle between the President and the Congress for control over policy making and implementation continues unabated; nor should we be surprised that Secretaries of State and NSC Advisers find themselves at odds over the wisdom of various policies and engage in intense competition for the ear of the President.

Many of the substantive issues involved in the Iran-contra affair have challenged previous Presidents and are bound to arise again in future administrations.

Thomas Jefferson had to cope with the problem of Americans held hostage overseas and certainly Ronald Reagan's successor will confront the problem of Soviet efforts to expand their empire by military means through the use of surrogates and Third World conflict.

As these committees finish the fact-finding phase of our inquiry, the focus must now shift to the search for ways to improve our government's capability and performance in the conduct of foreign policy.

In the final analysis, an effective foreign policy needs cooperation and commitment from both ends of Pennsylvania Avenue. These hearings have concentrated on the Executive end of the avenue.

It is always easier to examine someone else's mistakes. But the Executive's problems are fairly easy to correct in principle. Indeed, the President has already taken a number of steps to guard against the kinds of actions that got him into trouble in the first place.

I would urge my colleagues to resist the temptation to enact new legislation designed to guarantee that no future President makes the mistakes that Ronald Reagan makes in this instance. In my opinion, this is no justification for further restrictions on the power and flexibility of future Presidents and I am pleased to note that Chairman Hamilton's statement this week indicates that he, too, does not believe additional legislation is required.

Congress' problems, on the other hand, will be harder to correct because they have to do with institutional proclivities rather than individual people. Let me touch on just two of them.

I am personally persuaded that the difficulties we have investigated here could have been avoided if the President had vetoed the Boland Amendment in 1984.

But that was an option only if the President was prepared to shut down the entire federal government since the Boland Amendment was part of that year's continuing resolution. Making significant change in foreign policy by adding amendments to continuing resolutions has become a fairly common practice in recent years.

We have seen it on everything from Central American policy to mandating compliance with unratified arms control agreements.

The effect of this practice is to, first of all, obscure the significance of certain foreign policy issues; secondly, to deny the President the opportunity to use his veto effectively; and third, to allow a simple majority of the Congress to reverse the President on important policy matters without having to muster the two-thirds vote that was envisioned in the Constitution.

This pernicious practice contributes significantly to the lack of stability and predictability in our foreign policy.

A second major institutional problem confronting the Congress is our inability to safeguard classified information. The fact that the Executive Branch also leaks is not justification for Congress ignoring its own problems in this area.

The fact is that nearly all sensitive information is generated in and controlled by the Executive Branch.

Those of us in the Legislative Branch pass statutes spelling out reporting requirements, but in the final analysis, the willingness of administration officials to share highly classified information is directly related to their confidence that we can keep a confidence.

Our track record in this area is not impressive. There are almost no recorded incidents of Congress disciplining its members for leaking classified information.

In my opinion, a Congressman or Senator who would divulge classified information to someone not authorized to receive it dishonors the Congress just as much as a member who would accept a bribe or sell his vote.

Discipline ought to be swift and appropriate. Unfortunately, as a body we are not yet very good at this disciplining our colleagues. I am personally persuaded that [Rep. Henry J.] Hyde's [R-Ill.] recommendation for the establishment of a small joint intelligence committee would significantly improve our ability to safeguard the nation's secrets.

I hope it will be considered by this committee as we prepare our final report.

Clearly, there is plenty of work to be done if Congress is going to equip itself to play a constructive role in the conduct of U.S. foreign policy in the years ahead. And I fervently hope that future Presidents will take away from these hearings one important lesson: That no foreign policy can be effective for long without the wholehearted support of the Congress and the American people.

It is often easier to develop a policy to be pursued overseas than it is to muster the political support here at home to sustain it.

Covert action has its place in the kind of world we live in, but it is no substitute for the kind of effective political leadership that brings around the recalcitrant Congress and persuades the American people of the importance of supporting those who share our faith in democracy.

* * *

RUDMAN: . . . When we embarked on these hearings on May 5th, we had a goal: to find out exactly what happened and to present that in an intelligible manner. We wanted to determine how a policy of selling arms to Iran was conceived, approved and implemented contrary to the stated, public, foreign policy of the United States.

We wanted to know about the diversion of proceeds from those sales to the contras—who initiated it, who approved it, and knew about it, the extent to which the diversion was proper, and what happened to the money. We wanted to know about other efforts by United States government officials to assist the Nicaraguan democratic forces when the Boland Amendments were in effect, and the extent to which those activities were properly authorized and in compliance with the law. To the extent things had gone wrong, we wanted to learn why—was it the people or the process?

The purpose of these hearings has not been to cast blame or point fingers. It has been to learn from our mistakes by examining them in the open daylight, to hold them under the magnifying eye of television so we can see where the Executive Branch and Congress went wrong, and to make such recommendations for change, if any, in federal law or the foreign policy process to ensure that we never face an episode like this again. And since it is impossible to write laws against all human frailty, a purpose of these hearings has been to educate the American people, especially the future leaders of our great country—to dispute the observation that the only thing we learn from history is that we learn nothing—so that they might learn from the mistakes of others and avoid some of the pitfalls that face [those] who are in power.

To accomplish this goal, the Senate and House Select Committees have taken on an unprecedented task. We have reviewed more than a quarter of a million pages of documents. We have interviewed nearly 500 people. When we conclude this week, we will have had 38 days of public testimony and three or four days of closed testimony, encompassing 32 witnesses.

To do this job properly, we needed and—I will emphasize this—received the total cooperation of the President. The President gave us access to the most sensitive documents in the possession of his administration, including minutes from National Security Council meetings, internal White House decision memoranda, and even drafts of documents that never had official status. The President allowed us to review his personal diaries. The President waived all claims of executive privilege, which could have been legitimately asserted at many times, and he instructed all Federal agencies to cooperate, which they did.

Neither I nor any of my colleagues are ready at this point to definitively state all our factual conclusions, much less our policy recommendations.

Speaking for myself, I am going to need the month of August to review, digest, and reflect on the mass of information we have collected.

However, there are some things that stand out after these weeks of testimony.

The policy of selling arms to Iran was duly authorized by President Reagan and, in the main, legally implemented. Whether it was in reality arms for hostages or whether that is just the common perception, will never be conclusively determined, but I suspect there is unanimous agreement on the Senate Committee that it was an act of folly as a means of re-establishing relations with Iran.

The testimony of both [Rear] Adm. [John M.] Poindexter and Attorney General [Edwin] Meese [III] establish that the legal route used for the transactions was agreed to by the President and the Attorney General exclusively to avoid having to notify the House and Senate Intelligence Committees or, in the alternative, the House and Senate leadership.

Although the presidential finding authorized the operation and gave control over it to the CIA, operational control was in fact at the NSC in the person of [Lt.] Col. [Oliver L.] North who reported fully to Adm. Poindexter.

While one can debate whether other agencies undertook sufficient effort to review the operation, it is clear that Adm. Poindexter attempted to deny the State Department, the Defense Department and White House staff the information necessary to enable them to engage in a review.

The diversion of funds to the contras would not have been

possible but for the mechanism chosen to conduct the Iranian arms sales.

According to the direct evidence, the diversion of funds was not authorized by or known to President Reagan. I am firmly convinced that statement is unequivocally correct having reviewed the entire documentary record, including the President's own personal diaries, to which we were given access in an extraordinary and unprecedented decision.

The only U.S. officials who knew of the diversion were Adm. Poindexter, Col. North, [NSC aide to North Lt.] Col. [Robert] Earl, and possibly [CIA] Director [William J.] Casey.

In addition, Mr. [Robert C.] McFarlane learned of the diversion in May 1986, but he was only informed of it in passing, and had no reason to assume it was not properly authorized, and was not involved in it.

The diversion of funds was not only improper, but it failed to provide any meaningful assistance to the contras. Although the amount paid to Gen. Secord's [retired major general Richard V. Secord] enterprise exceeded the cost of the weapons and related expense by $16.34 million, only $3.5 million ever found its way to the democratic resistance.

That this fact came as a total surprise to Col. North and Adm. Poindexter is interesting and perhaps reveals their naiveté in using private enterprise to conduct foreign policy initiatives.

With the exception of Adm. Poindexter, every high-level U.S. official who testified stated that Adm. Poindexter did not have the authority to approve the diversion; that the diversion was improper and possibly illegal, and that the President would not have approved of the diversion had he been consulted. These officials are Secretary [of State George P.] Shultz, Secretary [of Defense Caspar W.] Weinberger, former [White House] Chief of Staff [Donald T.] Regan, and Attorney General Meese.

Other covert operations run out of the National Security Council, specifically, certain other contra-support activities of Col. North and the hostage release effort involving the DEA [Drug Enforcement Administration], were not approved by the President.

This gives every appearance of violating President Reagan's order to his own Administration under Executive Order 12333 and National Security Decision Directive 159 and, in the case of the contra-support activities, may have been illegal on other grounds. The same four officials mentioned above testified that the National Security Council staff should not be conducting covert operations. That point is well taken inasmuch as the primary role of the National Security Council is to analyze and coordinate policy.

The CIA has recognized the dangers of mixing intelligence analysis and operational activities for years, and has gone to great lengths to separate the two.

This is further buttressed by the one-sided analyses prepared for the President by Col. North and Adm. Poindexter, when they bothered to consult him, in these matters in which they were exercising operational control.

Inadequate control was exercised over these covert operations run out of the NSC. This may be a result of the fact that neither Adm. Poindexter nor Col. North had any covert operations experience whatsoever prior to their time at NSC. Or, it may be the result of a single-minded pursuit of goals they thought justified virtually by any means.

One aberration found in this set of events is that private parties were involved in the making of foreign policy, as distinguished from being hired as agents to carry out a task which assists in the implementation of policy.

For example, there were instances where [Secord's business partner Albert] Hakim and Gen. Secord were apparently negotiating with foreign officials on behalf of the United States, where the outcome of the talks might make a tremendous difference to their own financial well being. The results speak for themselves.

NSC staff attempted to cover up all records of their questionable activities when the possibility of exposure arose. That cover-up accelerated when the Attorney General undertook his fact-finding inquiry at the behest of the President.

The cover-up included shredding of official documents, lying to the Attorney General and his representatives, and withholding information from the President.

The allegation that the Attorney General was himself involved in the cover-up is unfair and in my view false. Although some of us have strongly criticized some of the Attorney General's actions during the course of his inquiry, it was the Attorney General and his staff who initially uncovered some of the facts of wrongdoing and exposed them.

Certain NSC staff showed total disrespect for the laws of the United States and our system of government, in effect adopting a position that the end justifies the means.

Adm. Poindexter made major decisions without consulting the President, misled or lied to Cabinet officers and Congress, congratulated Col. North for lying to Congress, and shredded official government documents, including those reflecting presidential decisions.

Col. North lied to Congress and the Attorney General, shredded government documents thereby frustrating a fact-finding inquiry undertaken at the specific request of the President, and engaged in a number of questionable activities, admittedly with his superior's approval.

He may have accepted a gift from a private individual knowing that it was illegal, albeit for an understandable motive, and saw nothing wrong with commingling "official" and personal funds.

On this last point, while Col. North persuasively testified that he gained no personal benefit from the commingling, he destroyed the only records which would corroborate that.

Both of them flouted virtually every standard operating procedure that exists within the national security establishment for the development of government policy.

These actions and the attitudes they represent are antithetical to our democratic system of government. They cannot be justified by passion, patriotism, appropriate concern over the expansion of communism in Central America, or legitimate dismay over the policies enacted by Congress.

Good news also came out of this investigation. With the exception of those involved in the diversion, all government officials we heard from understand how our government is supposed to work and are dedicated to rebuilding the trust between the branches.

To the extent mistakes were made by them, they were errors in judgment. Errors in judgment, while regrettable, are not a threat to the core fabric of our political system. Infallibility is not yet a trait found among mankind, including, of course, those of us serving in Congress. . . .

Over the next month, we will be reviewing the record developed by these hearings and discussing recommendations for the future.

These recommendations should not only deal with changes in the process of the Executive Branch. It is also important for the committee to look at the way in which Congress is involved in the foreign policy process and to make recommendations to improve relations between Congress and the Executive Branch. I look forward to a bipartisan report which will reflect the views of all of us.

I would like to close these remarks with a few comments that are strictly my own.

The Tower Board essentially concluded that the problem in this so-called Iran-contra affair was that the normal processes had been ignored—and that is largely true. What the Tower Board missed, however—and this is through no fault of theirs since they lacked immunity power, subpoena authority, staff, and time—was the extent to which power was abused by a very small group of individuals.

Sen. [Sam] Nunn [D-Ga.] opened these hearings with the remark that "we cannot promote democracy abroad by undermining it at home." That is what these individuals did and, in my view, it is the most important revelation of these hearings.

This abuse of power is dangerous to and fundamentally unacceptable to our constitutional system of government. And the most important message that must come out of these hearings is that there is no room for such behavior in this country.

There are many different perspectives represented on this committee, and I have yet to hear anyone defend the diversion and the way it came about.

The Administration obviously shares that view—the Secretary of Defense, the Secretary of State, the Attorney General, and the former White House Chief of Staff all condemned the diversion.

No matter how well intentioned the actions were, the officials responsible did a great disservice to our President and the country they had sworn to serve.

* * *

HAMILTON: ... What we have heard, as many have suggested, has been depressing, but for me, at least, the process has been refreshing. It has been refreshing in two respects.

First, I view these hearings and other investigations of these events as an essential part of the self-cleansing process of our system of government. Because of them, we know better what happened and what mistakes were made. We can see more clearly what needs to be done to make our system work better. As a result of these inquiries, the process of restoring our institutions is already well advanced.

Second, I believe these hearings have contributed not only to the public's understanding of these events, but also the public's education on our Constitution and system of government. This, too, strengthens our system of government.

The committees have heard about 240 hours of testimony over the last 11 weeks from over 30 witnesses. They have examined well over 200,000 documents.

Several themes emerged.

There was too little accountability for decisions and actions taken in the name of elected officials.

There was too much secrecy and deception in government. Information was withheld from the Congress, other officials, friends and allies, and the American people. Information provided was misleading and evasive. Critical decisions were taken by a handful of people. The Congress and responsible officials, even the President, were cut out of the process.

There was too little regard for the rule of law. False statements to the Congress are violations of law, as the Attorney General reminded us. Key decisions were made and carried out without written legal analysis, and without written notice to Congress as the law requires.

There was too much reliance on private citizens, foreign nationals and foreign governments to execute American policy, which contributed to policy failure.

There was too much use of covert actions which contradicted public policies, and too little accountability for covert actions.

There was too much confusion at the highest levels of government. In the words of the Attorney General, "There appeared to be considerable confusion as to what occurred when." The President did not know what his own staff was doing; staff did not keep senior officials informed; policies were often contradictory.

These hearings have been about how the United States governs itself, and particularly how it runs its foreign policy. For this inquiry, the key question now is how we make our system of government work better.

The conduct of foreign policy in our democracy is difficult, because the Constitution gives important powers to the President and the Congress. The scholar Edward Corwin said the Constitution "is an invitation to struggle for the privilege of directing American foreign policy."

The Congress is a check on the Executive, but also a partner; the Congress is sometimes a critic, yet its support is essential if our policies are to succeed; the Congress sometimes has divisive foreign policy debates, but when debate ends, the country needs decisiveness and unity.

Some believe that a decision-making process that calls for shared powers and public debate just will not work in a dangerous world. They argue that sometimes bypassing normal checks and balances, through procedural shortcuts and secrecy, are necessary to protect our freedoms. They argue that the President, and those who work for him, must be given near-total power. Their views have been stated here with great force and eloquence.

But these hearings make another point: Shortcuts in the democratic process and excessive secrecy in the conduct of government are a sure road to policy failure. These hearings show us that policies formed under democratic scrutiny are better and wiser than policies formed without it.

Policies formed by shortcuts and excessive secrecy undermine a President's ability to make informed decisions; lead to confusion in his Administration; and deny him the opportunity to gain and sustain congressional and public support for his policies.

Shortcuts that bypass the checks and balances of the system, and excessive secrecy by those who serve the President, do not strenghten him. They weaken him and our constitutional system.

Properly conceived, the Constitution is not a burden in the making of policy, but a source of strength, because it specifies a process for making policy through informed consent.

In its joint report, the committees should focus on several areas.

First, accountability. Greater accountability to elected officials and ultimately to the American people will require rigorous oversight by the Congress, more openness and less secrecy, more consultation, a more thorough process of legal review, better record-keeping, use of appropriated funds rather than private or third-country donations to carry out policy, supervision and acceptance of responsibility up the chain of command, and decision-making by elected officials rather than by staff.

Second, intelligence analysis should be separated from policy formulation. Substantial testimony before these committees shows great confusion between intelligence and policy functions. Questionable intelligence was used to bolster poor decisions. Good intelligence is essential to good foreign policy, but intelligence should drive policy, not vice-versa. Too often intelligence is seen as a tool to make policy look good, rather than a tool for making good policy.

Covert actions, which are not really intelligence operations, can be an important instrument of foreign policy. These hearings show that we must reassess how we conduct them.

To be effective, covert actions must be based on statutory authority, including a written finding and notice to the Congress; they must meet a standard of accountability, including legal review by the Attorney General and policy review by the Secretaries of State and Defense; they must be determined by an intelligence assessment based on facts, not on preconceived notions of policy-making; they must be used to supplement policy, not become the policy itself; and they must meet a standard of acceptability. That standard includes consistency with public policies and a reasonable assurance that the American people would support a covert action if they knew about it.

Third, the President and the Congress need to exhibit a greater sensitivity to their respective roles. The President is the pre-eminent foreign policy-maker. Only he can make the hard decisions. The buck does not stop anywhere else. The President's decisions must be clean and crisp. Otherwise, as we have seen in these hearings, confusion follows and those who work for him cannot carry out his policies successfully. The President must understand that our system works better if he engages in consultation before, not after, policy has been formulated.

The Congress also needs to get its house in order. It must strengthen its ability to protect secrets. It must show a willingness to engage in consultation. It must avoid interference in day-to-day policy implementation. And it must take its share of responsibility for shared decisions on tough issues. The Congress must strike a balance between responsible criticism and necessary cooperation with the President.

Fourth, the Constitution and the rule of law work if we make them work. They are not self-executing. We must strengthen our allegiance to the concept that this is a nation of laws and of checks and balances.

The solution to the problem of decision-making revealed in these hearings lies less in new structures or new laws than in proper attitudes.

Secretary Shultz reminded us that "Trust is the coin of the realm." He insisted on honesty in public life.

Without trust in those who hold office, democratic government is not possible. Sometimes that trust is misplaced and the system falters. But to reject the system because it occasionally falters, and to rely instead on shortcuts and excessive secrecy—as was done in the events these committees have examined—is a prescription for disaster.

A deep respect for the shared powers of the Congress and the President is the predicate for making the Constitution work. President John Adams said, "A legislative, an executive and a judicial power comprehend the whole of what is meant and understood by government. It is by balancing each of these powers against the other two, that the efforts in human nature towards tyranny can alone be checked and restrained, and any degree of freedom preserved in the Constitution."

The separation of powers produces a healthy and creative tension. We believe—and these hearings teach us again—that through the process of open and democratic debate, better and stronger policies emerge. The democratic process is often time-consuming and frustrating. It is [never] tidy and precise. But we believe there is no better way; the alternatives are unacceptable.

The Constitution and the rule of law work if we understand them, and if those in public life practice prudence, discretion and honesty.

* * *

INOUYE: . . . When these hearings began three months ago, I stated that we would examine what happens when the "trust," which is the bond between the branches of our government, "is breached by high officials."

I promised that we would address the following questions: One, were the statutory restrictions on U.S. aid to the contras violated?

Two, was Congress misled?

Three, were the Executive Branch's own internal checks and balances bypassed in policy decisions on Nicaragua and Iran?

Four, was there a public foreign policy and, simultaneously, was there a very different, covert foreign policy?

Five, was American foreign policy privatized?

Six, were decisions on the most significant matters of national security driven or influenced by private profit motives?

We have kept our promise in examining these questions.

The story has now been told. Speaking for myself, I see it as a chilling story; a story of deceit and duplicity and the arrogant disregard of the rule of law. It is a story of withholding vital information from the American people, from the Congress, from the Secretary of State, from the Secretary of Defense, and, according to Adm. Poindexter's testimony, from the President himself.

It is also a story of a flawed policy kept alive by a secret White House junta despite repeated warnings and signs of failure; with concession piled upon concession, culminating even in a promise to help secure the release of the imprisoned Dawa terrorists who bombed the U.S. Embassy in Kuwait.

It is a story of the National Security Council staff becoming a dominant organ of foreign policy and shutting out those who disagreed with its views.

It is a story of how a great nation betrayed the principles which have made it great, and thereby became hostage to hostage-takers.

And, sadly, once the unsound policies began to unravel, it became a story of a cover-up, of shredding and altering the historical record, and of fall guy plans suitable for a grade-B movie, not a great power.

Whatever the motives of some of the participants, I can only echo the reaction of [vice] Chairman [Dante B.] Fascell [D-Fla.] upon hearing the story of self-proclaimed patriotism: "How come I don't feel good?"

I believe we have largely succeeded in piecing together the incredible chapters of this chilling story and presenting to our fellow citizens a chronology of events as they occurred.

However, we may never know, with precision and truth, why it ever happened.

Did this unseemly chapter in our history result from the disregard of our laws and Constitution by well-intentioned, patriotic zealots who believed in the doctrine espoused by the Marxists that the "ends justify the means"?

Or, are we here today because of the inadequacy of our laws and Constitution? Should they be clarified, amended or repealed?

Or, is this the result of an inadequacy in our national leadership?

Obviously, these hearings have been about issues much more profound than who did what or knew what in the Iran-contra affair. They have presented two visions of government, much as the Constitutional Convention was presented with different views of the relationship between government and its citizens 200 years ago.

One vision was described in the testimony of Adm. Poindexter, Lt. Col. North, Gen. Secord, and Mr. Hakim: that of a secret government, directed principally by NSC staffers, accountable to not a single elected official, including apparently the President himself—a shadowy government with its own air force, its own navy, its own fund-raising mechanism, and the ability to pursue its own ideas of the national interest, free from all checks and balances and free from the law itself.

It is an elitist vision of government that trusts no one, not the people, not the Congress, and not the Cabinet.

It is a vision of a government operated by persons convinced they have a monopoly on truth.

Albert Hakim, a businessman who admitted he was in it for the money, could boast to us that he was more competent to manage the Iran initiative than the Secretary of State.

Richard Secord could tell us he was more capable of running intelligence activities than the CIA.

Oliver North could describe, with enthusiasm, Director Casey's plan for a private, off-the-shelf organization that would conduct covert operations forbidden to the CIA with funds generated from the sale of U.S. arms.

John Poindexter could say that this all sounded like a good idea, maintain that Congress had no meaningful role in foreign policy, and act secure in the belief that the President would have approved the diversion of funds.

I believe these hearings will be remembered longest not for the facts they elicited, but for the extraordinary and extraordinarily frightening views of government they exposed.

Fortunately, our hearings were able to present another vision of government: one that is accountable to the people; a legitimate, not secret, government, in which "trust is the coin of the realm," as Secretary of State George Shultz said. This is the balanced government that our Founding Fathers contemplated in our Constitution.

In describing their motives for riding roughshod over the constitutional restraints built into our form of government, Adm. Poindexter and Lt. Col. North used almost the identical words: "This is a dangerous world," they said. That, my fellow citizens, is an excuse for autocracy, not for policy.

Because no times were more dangerous than when our country was born, when revolution was our midwife. Our system of government has withstood the tests and tensions of civil conflict, depression and two world wars, times hardly less challenging than our own present.

Indeed, as our greatest military leaders, such as [President George] Washington, [Secretary of State George C.] Marshall, and [President Dwight D.] Eisenhower have recognized, our form of government is what gives us strength. It must be safeguarded, particularly when times are dangerous and the temptation to arrogate power is the greatest.

Vigilance abroad does not require us to abandon our ideals or the rule of law at home. On the contrary, without our principles and without our ideals, we have little that is special or worthy to defend.

History records that almost 200 years ago, in September of 1787, as the Constitutional Convention was finishing its business, a bystander asked Benjamin Franklin: "Well, Doctor, what have we got, a republic or a monarchy?" Dr. Franklin replied: "A republic, if you can keep it."

By allowing the sunlight on this unseemly affair, and by showing what happens when foreign policy is conceived and executed by cabal and not by lawful consensus, we have tried to make our contribution to "keeping it."

My fellow Americans, out of this experience, may we all better understand and appreciate our Constitution, strive harder to preserve it, and make a fresh start at restoring the trust between the branches of government. For, in America, as 200 years ago, the people still rule.

Alan Fiers

Following are excerpts from the August 4-5, 1987, private testimony of Alan Fiers, chief of the CIA's Central American Task Force. The declassified testimony was released the week of August 24, 1987, by the House and Senate select Iran-contra committees.

FIERS: I learned [when becoming chief of the CIA Central American Task Force in October 1984] that I was in a charged political environment, that there were perils on all sides and I was going to have to learn to live in that environment and be very astute if I was to survive and I did that. Each step of the way I had the laws in mind, the political dynamics in mind, and I knew almost from the beginning that I was caught between the dynamics of a giant nutcracker of the Legislative on the one hand and the Executive on the other, and I was in the center in a very exposed position.

There were those who said I was not smart for taking the job but the Director [of Central Intelligence William J. Casey] had asked me to do it and I believed in what he had asked me to do, and so I did. During the three years that I have been in that job and particularly the two years that are the question of inquiry of the committee, I worked to serve the Administration, the Executive, within the bounds of the law as laid down by the Executive, by the Legislative and to do so to the fullest of my ability and to in every way possible work with the Congress to change that law [the Boland amendment, which restricted U.S. aid to the Nicaraguan contras] and to clear the contradiction that was at play to try to get myself out of the nutcracker I found myself in.

It was clear to me then, it is clear to me now that the words of Abraham Lincoln are as true as the sun rising in the east every morning—a house divided against itself cannot long endure, and in Nicaragua and in Central America we were clearly a house divided against ourselves and we had to change it. And I think that is what this hearing is all about.

I am here to answer your questions [on] how I handled myself during this period, why I did what I did, what my logic was. I don't claim that every decision I made was the right one. If I could turn the clock back I might do some things different, but not many. And in the end, I hope two things happen—one that the house is no longer divided and second, to persevere in Central America, because if we don't I don't want to think what the 21st century will be like for us as a great nation.

* * *

The Hasenfus Flight

[Patrick J.] CAROME [House committee associate counsel]: I would like you to turn to Exhibit 39. Exhibit 39 is excerpts of testimony which you and others gave to the House Intelligence Committee on Oct. 14, 1986, about a week after the Hasenfus flight went down. [Eugene Hasenfus's plane was shot down over Nicaragua in October 1986 while transporting arms to the contras.] I refer you first to page 17 in the excerpts about half way through. At that point, Mr. Clair George [CIA deputy director for covert operations] has just finished making his opening statement in which he has denied any CIA involvement in the flight, [Assistant Secretary of State Elliott] Abrams has also made a statement and he continues here on page 17, both of them, or Mr. George denies any CIA involvement, and then Mr. Abrams denies any U.S. Government involvement in the flight. Is that a fair summary of what the testimony was from those two gentlemen?

FIERS: I reviewed that testimony and both the text, the transcript and my recollection from that, that would be a fair presentation of it, yes.

CAROME: You were sitting there next to Mr. George and Mr. Abrams, weren't you?

FIERS: Yes. I don't think I was sitting next to Mr. Abrams. I was sitting next to George on the end, as I recall it.

CAROME: At the point where Mr. George and Mr. Abrams were making these denials of U.S. knowledge or involvement, you made an affirmative decision at that point to remain silent, didn't you?

FIERS: I think the decision was made before that point.

CAROME: By you?

FIERS: Yes. Well, let me now make a comment. I said there were three things I deeply regret in this undertaking. One was the involvement of [... classified ...] which bothers me the most, because it touches the most people and really was traumatic.

Second was the involvement of [... classified ...] because it was not part of the way that it was supposed to be.

Third is his testimony. I am troubled by it then, I am troubled by it now. I am not very happy about it. Probably it was the most difficult decision I have made in my life. I had a lot of facts racing around in my head. The decision that was taken, and I don't think it was taken actively, I don't think it was taken sort of like almost acquiescence, was to answer the questions narrowly defined. I think Elliott Abrams has testified to you a lot on this subject, and you will look at the construction of Clair George's discussions, I talk for the agency, I cannot talk for the U.S. Government.

Who was behind the flights? I didn't know where the money was coming from. I hadn't tied it altogether in a nice neat package. We took answers that I would best describe to you as cute, not the way I testify to Congress now or before or after. I was troubled by that. I am troubled by it now. There is not a lot I can do about it. You can go over this testimony word by word and beat me about the head and shoulders by it, and I will take it. It was what it is. You have got the facts. Judge for yourselves....

CAROME: I would like to go to page 21 where you say, at the bottom of page 20, "We knew in some cases much less frequently that they were flying [... classified ...] Nicaragua for the purpose of resupply, but as to who was flying the flights and who was behind them, we do not know."

The Chairman asks: "And you still don't?"

And you answer: "No."

Now, that was a false answer, wasn't it? You knew who was flying those flights?

FIERS: Let's go back again. I want to make one thing very, very clear. I don't lie and I don't provide false answers, and if I'm put in a situation that is untenable, I will find some way to avoid lying. Lying in my business is a kiss of death, a Judas kiss. I didn't know who was flying those flights.

CAROME: Or who was behind them, is what you said?

FIERS: You could have put me on a rack and I couldn't have told you who the pilots were, who was managing them. I at that time suspected, but didn't know that Gen. Secord [retired major general Richard V. Secord] was involved with them. I had no idea where the money was coming from. Had you made me guess, I would have said it was coming from some of the gentlemen that you had in front of this committee, the donors, some of the people—I would not have known that the money was being obtained in the manner that it was obtained. The pieces weren't together. It is not a lie. I could have been more forthcoming to the committee, but I frankly was not going to be the first person to step up and do that. You may call that a cowardly decision, some may call it a brave decision, it is a controversial decision, but so long as others who knew the details, as much as I, who knew more than I, were keeping their silence on this, I was going to keep my silence. That may be false loyalty, it may be folly, but I said before that I worked for the administration and I was to support the administration, and to stay within the bounds of the law. That answer was an attempt to do that and you can criticize me for it. I have no excuse for the answer and I have to stand by whatever accrues from it.

As I said, we can continue to pick this apart and I think you will find the same answer.

* * *

Partisan Politics

[Sen. George J.] MITCHELL [D-Maine]: You said this morning at one point that because of the circumstances you found yourself in, you were, I believe you said, bitter at the administration and at Congress.

FIERS: Yes, sir.

MITCHELL: Why were you bitter at Congress?

FIERS: Because I felt that it was frankly tough, rough, bipartisan politics that got us here. I think that the delaying—I am going to be very frank. I thought the delaying tactics of the Speaker of the House and the Rules Committee attendant to the $100 million program [to aid the contras] was tough, rough, first class, big-league political sort of legislative warfare, delaying it and tying up when that bill went to Conference, it got us into August, into September, it got us into October. That is one.

Frankly, I thought that the decision of the House of Representatives, once again, tough, tough partisan politics that ruled CIA out of the legislation and left us in an awkward and extended and difficult position, and I felt that the plea that we had made in October in large part in some measure, because I had pushed the issue very hard, to allow CIA to get back into support of the logistics game and was ruled down in the Senate-House Intelligence Committee Conference on the fiscal year '86 legislation, left us hanging out.

In short, I felt that I had made just Herculean efforts for a person in my position three times to get out from under the legislative vice I was in and three times, because of partisan politics, it was turned down, and I couldn't see any reason for it except for partisan politics, and I felt that left me in a continuing, exposed situation and that—to this day, it sticks in my craw.

The reason I am here is partly because of that.

MITCHELL: You are a career official in an intelligence agency and you regard disagreements over policy as partisan politics?

FIERS: I believe, and as a career intelligence official, it is my duty to serve the Administration. If that administration is right in its policies, I—in my—I serve them. If it is wrong I serve them and I try and change it. If the Congress is wrong in its policies and I am in a position as I was in, I serve the policy and try to work with the Congress to change it. That is how I see my job.

Now I have been in Democratic administrations as a career intelligence official and I have been in Republican administrations as an intelligence official, as a civil servant. I served in [. . .classified. . .] when it was the policy of the Carter Administration that the U.S. government had no strategic interest in [. . .classified. . .]. I thought it was dead wrong. I thought it was a silly policy. I stayed [. . .classified. . .]. I did what I was told. I served the Administration, I filed my reports and tried to change the policy.

I came back and in this job I was in a situation where I felt the Administration—I don't feel, I know, but it is still interpretive, so I will say my opinion is that the Administration is dead right about Central America, the Congress is wrong and I worked as hard as I could to change it. Maybe I am wrong, maybe I am naive, that there is every right to disagree, every right for the Congress to voice its disagreement, but when push comes to shove there's got to be a boss; someone has got to make a decision.

As I said in my opening statement a house divided against itself cannot long endure, and I think the final prerogative to make a decision and the man with his hand on the helm is the President. . . .

MITCHELL: I will just say that I think it is demeaning and insulting for you to suggest that those who happen to disagree with you on policy are engaged in partisan politics, obviously used in a pejorative manner as though there is something in our system that in which a person who disagrees is acting in a partisan manner but a person who agrees with you happens to be right, and I think it is simply preposterous to suggest that those who opposed contra aid did so because they didn't like Bill Casey. I would hope you would have a somewhat higher opinion of the motives of those who happen to disagree with you on an issue that people would vote on important policy issues on that basis. But—and every Executive Branch official has an obligation to obey and uphold the law, and not to select which laws will be obeyed or will not be.

* * *

Fiers on North

[Sen. Sam] NUNN [D-Ga.]: Do you know [Lt.] Col. [Oliver L.] North?

FIERS: Yes.

NUNN: Did you know him pretty well?

FIERS: I would say I knew him very well as a professional acquaintance. I didn't know him well as a social acquaintance.

NUNN: Did you hear his testimony where he said Director Casey knew and they talked about [the diversion of funds from the Iran arms deal to the Nicaraguan contras] many times?

FIERS: I didn't see it all, I saw snatches of it, and I read most of his deposition.

NUNN: I would like to ask you whether you believe that testimony.

FIERS: Sir, with your indulgence, I don't want to engage in opinions on it unless you really,—I don't know what to believe. I can tell you another vignette which I will, that will give you another side of Director Casey. At one point in time, I was in his office and he said, "You know, [. . . classified . . .]" he said, "so and so said that I had terminal cancer. Isn't that preposterous? Isn't that the most ludicrous thing you heard? Do I look like a man with cancer?" I said, "No, you don't." Well, he did. And I had no idea. So I mean the man—I just don't know what to make of it. It is possible he did, it is possible he didn't. I walked out of that office that day thinking he didn't have cancer and he was going up to New York, I guess, for treatment of prostate cancer sort of on a recurring basis and I didn't have a clue about it.

NUNN: So at the time he told you that he knew he had cancer?

FIERS: I would guess he did from what I understand. I don't know all the details but that is what I concluded.

NUNN: So you wouldn't know who to believe in that situation knowing both Casey and North?

FIERS: I wouldn't want to bet on it.

[Sen. William S.] COHEN [R-Maine]: If the Senator will yield. You talk about playing with words. He did say terminal cancer didn't he?

FIERS: Yes. I wouldn't want to bet on it one way or another. I wouldn't want to speculate on it. I will say this from where I stand, I think there was a lot of truth in Col. North's testimony, I never knew Col. North to be an absolute liar, but I never took anything he said at face value because I knew that he was bombastic and embellished the record, and threw curves, speed balls and spitballs to get what he wanted and I knew it and I knew it well.

NUNN: Have you every known anyone you would call an absolute liar?

FIERS: No, not absolute. I do know that I have seen, I have seen I guess the way to put it, I have seen Col. North play fast and loose with the facts. And I think the record will substantiate that. But, on the other hand, I believe that there is a, from where I sit, from the glimpses I saw of this thing as the train windows went by, there was a lot of fact in what he said too.

NUNN: A lot of what?

FIERS: Fact.

NUNN: Did Col. North every give you false information?

FIERS: I would assume he did.

NUNN: Can you tell us what that was? Do you recall? Do you know specific instances?

FIERS: No. Let—the specifics aren't in my mind where he did give me false information but I know there were lots of times I suspected he was putting the spin on something that wasn't exactly the way it was. An attempt to influence the way things come out. He dropped names a lot.

NUNN: Let me just ask you one closing question. In this business of covert activities you are involved in it, we are in a different world, we see part of your world, not all of it, and I sometimes have great sympathy for the position. I know you all find yourselves in dealing with covert activities, but how important is it in dealing with colleagues in covert areas—I am speaking of people in covert areas in the Executive Branch—how important is it to them?

FIERS: You can't lie. You have got to believe each other. Believe me, in the world in which I live and work, you have got to have a moral compass, a moral anchor. It keeps you clearly defined on where you are going, what you are, and what is truth and what is lie. If you don't, you will go virtually go and crash. We live in a schizophrenic world, a world where we deal with the lie as a tool of the trade. We deal with deceit, deception and manipulation in a positive and negative sense. You can't lose sight of your moral compass, or you will end up like [Frank] Terpil [a former CIA agent and arms dealer who was a fugitive from U.S. justice], [Edwin P.] Wilson [a CIA agent who was convicted in 1983 of illegally selling arms to Libya], [Thomas] Cline [a former CIA official who, in 1984, pleaded guilty to charges of defrauding the Pentagon on a contract for transporting military goods to Egypt], or those people who did lose sight of their moral compass.

NUNN: Col. North started his testimony before revealing he had misled people to the point, some would call it like that, covert activity is a lie in itself and the clear implication from that was once you undertake covert activity, being a lie in itself, everything that flows from that it seems by implication is excusable. Do you agree with that philosophy?

FIERS: I don't think covert activity is a lie, I think covert activity is a range; it is an operation undertaken to influence an event. You may deal in truth, in lie, coloration, wherever possible. As a standard operating procedure, we try to deal with truth. Truth is an easier thing to defend. We don't like to deal in lies even disinformation because you get caught up in it. That doesn't mean we won't. But by and large our preference is to deal with truth. It is a deception. It is something that is designed to deceive, and frequently the recipient of the action or the viewer of the action, but to call it a lie in itself is only true in some regard—with regard to its deniability.

NUNN: Well, is it fair to say, and I know my time has expired, this is the last question, Mr. Chairman: is it fair to say that those who deal with covert activities in the world of deception, in the world of secrets have to trust each other? Is that a fair assessment?

FIERS: Absolutely. If you can't trust each other, you are dead in this world.

Clair George

Following are excerpts from the August 5-6, 1987, private testimony of Clair George, CIA deputy director for covert operations. The declassified testimony ws released the week of August 24, 1987, by the House and Senate select Iran-contra committees.

[Charles] KERR [Senate committee associate counsel]: One of the purposes of that [the January 1986 polygraph test of Iranian middleman in the arms deal Manucher Ghorbanifar] was to try to establish by objective data, i.e., the test, some proof that this man could or could not be trusted?

GEORGE: Yes. We were totally prejudiced. I mean, we suffer every—all the faults of human nature. We convinced ourselves that Ghorbanifar was absolutely untrustworthy, but if you want us to put him back on the polygraph, we will do that. And the results—well, go ahead.

KERR: And the results were obtained when the polygraph was taken on the 11th of January.

GEORGE: He showed deception on 13 out of 15 questions. The only questions he passed were his name and his nationality.

KERR: We have at Exhibit 52 another entry from [Lt.] Col. [Oliver L.] North's diary. This one is at Q-1440. It shows that at 12:20 p.m. on the 13th of January, you called Col. North and said something to the effect Ghorbanifar is lying on 13 of 15 items?

GEORGE: I am sure I did. Because I was under pressure from Col. North—it is not fair to say "pressure." Col. North, as I said yesterday, and I were on the phone with some regularity. Col. North, if I can phrase it this way, wanted Mr. Ghorbanifar to pass his polygraph exam.

KERR: You wanted to make sure Col. North got the message.

GEORGE: I wanted him to get it from the horse's mouth that one more time Mr. Ghorbanifar in the exact phraseology shows

deception on 13 out of 15 issues.

KERR: At the time you talked to Col. North, were you aware Col. North was in the process of drafting a revision to a finding that had already been signed on about the 6th of January?

GEORGE: As I said to you yesterday, counsel, I am sort of the fool here. I am playing the fool. It wasn't whether Col. North was drafting a finding, using Ghorbanifar. The governments of Israel and the United States had been using Mr. Ghorbanifar since the summer of 1985 to involve themselves in a highly complicated international arms deal. So here is some guy running around talking about the polygraph when two major nations have already taken major foreign policy decisions based on his use.

KERR: So at least with the benefit of 20-20 hindsight, you perceive yourself having been participating in something of a charade at the time?

GEORGE: Well, you know, maybe I could have stopped it. I could have really raised hell and convinced everything in Jerusalem and Washington.

[Sen. William S.] COHEN [R-Maine]: Could you clarify, you were not aware at that time that Israel and the United States had been involved in a major, complicated arms deal?

GEORGE: At the time, no. But I am now—but in July of 1987, I realize how silly I may have looked at the time.

KERR: It is that concept, that feeling of silliness, did anyone, [CIA director William J.] Casey or otherwise, explain to you why you were put through that drill?

GEORGE: William Casey—who was always kind and courteous and a dear friend of mine and never—who never treated me otherwise, listened carefully to my pleas about Mr. Ghorbanifar. And if my memory serves me, I did something I rarely did with the Director. He is the Director, and I had great faith in him. I said, "Bill, I am not going to run this guy anymore," which means in our language "I will not handle him; he is a bum."

And Casey said, "Well, look, he does—"—see, there are levels of Ghorbanifar. Ghorbanifar knows endless things: hit teams in Europe, these Iranian terrorist centers [. . . classified . . .] plans to overthrow [. . . classified . . .] all these different things. Bill Casey said to me, "He has what appears to be valuable terrorist information."

This is another problem. Terrorist information you cannot dismiss no matter how foolish it looks. You have got to take terrorist information seriously even though you think who told you is crazy.

He said to me, "Would you mind if I had my National Intelligence Officer for Counterterrorism meet with Mr. Ghorbanifar to discuss terrorism?"

And I guess I said, "No, I don't mind."

KERR: . . . You have reached the conclusion Mr. Ghorbanifar continues to be someone you don't want to do business with?

GEORGE: That is correct.

KERR: And on Jan. 16 or 17, you all put out a notice, the Operations Directorate, put out a notice that says the CIA is going to do no further business with Mr. Ghorbanifar?

GEORGE: That is correct.

KERR: All right. We also know that that very day—

GEORGE: That is correct.

KERR: —the President of the United States signed a finding that required you to do business with Ghorbanifar.

GEORGE: On the 18th after having sent a cable, we will do no more business with Mr. Ghorbanifar, I was taken to the White House and given a finding which in its practical sense said you will be doing business with Mr. Ghorbanifar.

KERR: Now, as of the information you learned after the finding was signed, Jan. 18, that period of time, do you today have any knowledge as to whether the President of the United States had been given the benefit of the analysis that your people did have [on] Mr. Ghorbanifar as of that time?

GEORGE: I do not know.

* * *

North and Casey

KERR: One other aspect of North's relationships. Did you become familiar with or acquainted with North's relationship with Director Casey?

GEORGE: I knew they knew each other well. I remember sitting in the office and hearing Ollie North call Casey and talk to him and Casey would talk to him. They were, I think, among us, that Oliver North, and he's a friend of mine, had guts in approaching anybody anywhere any time in any conditions without any concern about their title, rank—you know, we all grew up that you don't just storm into the CEO's office the third day with the company, and Ollie did it. Bill Casey liked Ollie North. We all did.

* * *

[Rep. Edward P.] BOLAND [D-Mass.]: . . . Secretary [of State George P.] Shultz testified that information available to him caused him to conclude that the Government of Iran had absolute control over the hostage-takers. What degree of control did the CIA believe the Government of Iran exercised over the hostage-takers?

GEORGE: A great deal, but not all, and it was our judgment, which we passed regularly when asked, that under no conditions would the Government of Iran ever allow all the hostages to be released, nor will they ever all be released because the only leverage that those who hold the hostages have is the hostages, and so why would they give them up?

* * *

Views on Secord

[Sen. Paul S.] SARBANES [D-Md.]: Mr. George, did I understand your response to Sen. [David L.] Boren [D-Okla.] that you didn't know Gen. Secord [retired major general Richard V. Secord] before you met him in the Situation Room at the White House on the 19th of January?

GEORGE: That is absolutely correct. I knew of him, but I didn't know him.

SARBANES: What did you know of him?

GEORGE: Well, I knew a great deal about him. The good Gen. Secord's reputation inside the CIA was not of the highest. As I have testified previously, I had no evidence then, I have no evidence now—I have no knowledge of Gen. Secord engaged in illegal activities, but Gen. Secord worked the edges of the international arms market. Gen. Secord worked the edges of those guys out there in the world who were buying and selling in the arms business.

He had been associated in a I.G. [CIA inspector general] report of the CIA with Edwin [P.] Wilson, the famed renegade CIA agent who is now in Marion, Ill., [federal prison] and I know for a fact that he was in our minds, in my mind as a manager of the American Clandestine Service, an individual with whom I would not do business.

I will even go further and I maybe shouldn't, I went to Bill Casey soon after the famed Saturday, 18 January, meeting and urged Bill Casey not—if they are going to do this, if they are going to ship arms to Iran for hostages, and that is a complicated moral question, don't use Secord. I told him very strongly.

SARBANES: What reasons did you give Casey—

GEORGE: My knowledge of his involvement in what we considered to be not particularly wholesome—wholesome is a dumb word for a spy to use—particularly savory activities in the past, and he is mentioned in our Inspector General's report as being an associate. I had also read the book "Manhunt," which is the second book. He was just not a guy I wanted to do business with.

SARBANES: How did you understand that Secord got involved in all of this? Did you have an understanding—

GEORGE: You want to know what I thought now or what I thought then—

SARBANES: Both.

GEORGE: I didn't have a damn clue how he got involved when I saw him in January of that year. I was surprised, shocked. Stan Sporkin [former CIA general counsel], who was with me at this famous meeting and I understand it was testified to you, Stan and I agreed that this was a mistake and Stan and I went sepa-

rately to Bill Casey to try to talk him out of it. That is what I knew then, it was a dumb idea. Now, how did it happen—because starting in 1984 I assume—I have no personal evidence—when Oliver North was given the thankless task of supporting the contras or at least making sure they were supported, he turned to Secord. So by the time Secord was in the White House Situation Room in January 1986, Secord was probably—and I have no evidence of it—you may—I can't follow as closely as you do—already deeply engaged with Oliver North in the contra affair, and he would be a natural to move right on to the Iranian affair.

SARBANES: North testified that Secord in effect was sent to him by Casey?

GEORGE: I know that. I saw or heard that testimony.

SARBANES: What is your view of that?

GEORGE: I would doubt it.

SARBANES: Why?

GEORGE: Gut instinct, I know Bill Casey. If Casey sent Secord to North, someone else talked Casey into it. I don't know— why am I conjecturing—I can't believe that Bill Casey sent Secord to North because if he did he had to send him in the summer of 1984, I think as I put it back together historically. Bill Casey knew the problems with Secord. The problem—the problem is that when whomever it was told Ollie North that he had one little task, all Ollie had to do was get money or make sure money was obtained, obtain arms, make sure arms are sent to Central America, get somebody to give private support to the benefactors. Those who charged North with that activity were grossly unfair and who would walk into Ollie North's life first in the United States of America, you are not going to deal with foreigners, but Dick Secord who is in the international arms business and has experience in the United States Government in some version of clandestine activities.

* * *

Finding Hostages

[Rep. Peter W.] RODINO [Jr., D-N.J.]: . . . I referred to your deposition on page 60, Mr. George, where you were asked about the DEA [Drug Enforcement Administration] operations [a plan to use DEA agents to locate U.S. hostages in Lebanon], and you indicated that your Near East people would come to you and say, and I quote, on page 60: " 'The DEA case is running extreme. It is a bunch of hocus-pocus. It is phony. [. . . classified . . .] let's stop.' And I would say 'Let's stop.' "

Then you say again on page 62 of your deposition on lines 7 and 8: "Col. North's activities, as it related to the hostages and their plans that he came up with," you said it was "one of endless, harebrained schemes that took place at that time."

And you also went on to say in the same deposition on page 67, lines 18 through 20, you said: "I don't remember a single operation that involved bribery or purported bribery that I thought was worth anything, that anything would ever come out of it."

My question to you, Mr. George, in your position of responsibility there, having felt as you did and as strongly as you did, and we also note that the CIA people who were interviewed and deposed by the committee staff, have also said the same thing—my question is, how did you allow this to go on, feeling as strongly as you did? It went on for a period of time.

GEORGE: Well, I—the words are emotional here and I would have to sit down and look at this again. But the point I made was that—or I should have made, or the point I now make is that in the hostage business, which is what I'm speaking about, Mr. Chairman, unlike many other intelligence activities, you have to follow up on your leads, as silly or as impractical or as unprofessional as they sound.

So our communication system [. . . classified . . .] in the world because you can never not report it.

The point I tried to make here is that we were on several occasions and certainly in the DEA operation bypassed after we have voted in our directorate that the operation was, to use the words I used about DEA, a scam. How could that happen?

Mr. Rodino, sir, I'm the director of your foreign spy service, and have been involved for years in it. If someone decides in the White House that they do not like my opinion on an operation and we have seen the White House run operations outside of CIA over the last many administrations, they can do it. I just do not have the power other than to give you my honest, best advice based on my colleagues who I sit with, this is what your spies think about it. I certainly have no veto power on it.

I think in this case, and we are talking about hostages, and the emotionalism of the hostage issue throughout the entire affair, with Bill Casey, with the President, with me, people didn't want to stop. They wanted to get the hostages and it led them to do and run operations that are now after the fact foolish.

* * *

Covert Operations

[Sen. Sam] NUNN [D-Ga.]: . . . When Col. North testified, he started his testimony by saying that covert operation is a lie itself. The implication of that was that other lies that flow therefrom are neutral and recurring events in covert operations.

Would you give us your own view since you have been involved in this business for a long time about how you deal with your fellow officers and agents in carrying out a covert operation?

Whether lies are necessary within the operation itself?

GEORGE: I disagree with Col. North, as strongly as I can disagree with anyone. This is a business which you know, Sen. Nunn, from your experience on the Senate Committee and many of you who have dealt with me and more importantly with my agency, this is a business of trust. This is a business that works outside the law, outside the United States.

It is a business that is very difficult to define by legal terms because we are not working inside the American legal system. It is, and I have been asking you, and you heard me say many times, it is a business of being able to trust and have complete confidence in the people that work with you.

And to think that because we deal in lies, and overseas we may lie and we may do other such things, that therefore that gives you some permission, some right or some particular reason to operate that way with your fellow employees, I would not only disagree with, I would say it would be the destruction of a secret service in a democracy.

And I also believe, and I would like particularly to say this to you, and I said it to Sen. Cohen this morning. I want you to know, and I know we have recently had an agreement—disagreement over—that you may have thoughts otherwise, I deeply believe with the complexities of the oversight process and the relationship between a free legislative body and a secret spy service, that frankness is still the best and only way to make it work.

* * *

[Rep. Louis] STOKES [D-Ohio]: . . . When you look back at the Jan. 17, 1986, finding on Iran, it appears to be directed to the CIA. Yet you and others at the Agency have insisted that the CIA played only a support role in the Iranian operation.

There are some of us who, having some knowledge of intelligence operations, have commented upon the fact that the professionals in this business were not used particularly when it came to the DEA ransom operation, and in the case of the Iranian operation also. NSC [National Security Council] was chosen to conduct it.

I guess the logical question is, why didn't Director Casey fight this? If you know.

GEORGE: I'll let you in on a secret. The way to handle Bill Casey was outflank him to the right, charge him with being less than adventurous, suggest that maybe he really wasn't ready to take the high risk. What Bill Casey needed around him were cautious people to some degree, not frightened people, but cautious people.

I would suggest, and I guess I can suggest as well as anybody because God knows I dealt with him night and day, Bill Casey fell afoul to a charge in the White House that "come on, Bill, we have had enough of those"—as Dick Secord titles us—"shoe salesmen; let's get a real operation together and really do something."

STOKES: That is what I to a large extent sort of suspected, that there may have been a question—

GEORGE: Please, I'm not sure Bill Casey knew everything and I question a great deal, and it is not mine to question, of the charges made against Bill Casey before these committees and taking the fall after you're dead is the last great fall, but there is no doubt about it, Bill Casey was very vulnerable to the "oh, come on, Bill, those bureaucrats, let's get out and sock it to them." He may have allowed himself to be convinced.

Don't forget the significance of the fact of Mr. Ghorbanifar, contacts with Iran, plans for the release of hostages, plans for the development of contacts with moderates was brought to us by one of our very closest allies, in whom we have very great trust, in whom we place a Middle East role of unbelievable significance, the government of Israel—the Israelis will admit that this was a mistake, so there was a variety of things that happened. Casey's weakness was probably to say, "Oh, we'll take a chance."

[Rep. Henry J.] HYDE [R-Ill.]: Would you yield to me?

STOKES: Yes.

HYDE: Isn't it a fact that the CIA bureaucracy, as the State Department bureaucracy and possibly the Defense Department bureaucracy, were not hot for this thing at all and there was a fear of Director Casey's that had the CIA been into operations on this that there might have been leaks or there certainly would have been a lack of enthusiasm for it, and better to go with the gung-ho guys who felt this was a great, neat idea, is that too wild a speculation?

GEORGE: Mr. Hyde, I don't agree. I think we have—working within a government structure, we have as bold and as adventurous a government structure as there is, and we understand who the Director is and the President is.

I cannot buy the theory that you won't tell your CIA experts because you believe they are going to say no. Tell them and if they say no, and you think they are crazy, go ahead and do it, but see, they didn't tell us.

Donald P. Gregg

Following are excerpts from the May 18, 1987, private testimony of Donald P. Gregg, Vice President George Bush's national security adviser. The declassified testimony was released September 8, 1987, by the House and Senate select Iran-contra committees.

[Mark A.] BELNICK [Senate committee counsel]: From the time [former CIA agent] Felix [I. Rodriguez] went down to El Salvador until the summer of 1986—and let's start the summer as of June, so from the beginning of 1985 through June of 1986, did Felix tell you in any way about his role in assisting resupply or supply of the contras?

GREGG: No.

BELNICK: At any time during that same period, January '85 through June 1986, did he tell you about his involvement with [Lt.] Col. [Oliver L.] North?

GREGG: I don't recall Felix telling me about any structured involvement. I was aware that Ollie was traveling down there from time to time. I was aware from some things that Ollie said to me that he would run into Felix and from time to time Ollie would express irritation to me about some things Felix was doing. I now understand what Ollie was talking about.

I did not understand at that point. So I knew that they met, but I did not know that there was any continuing structure to that relationship.

BELNICK: What did you understand North's role to be vis-à-vis the contras and the Nicaraguan situation in that same period we've been discussing, roughly the beginning of January '85 through June 1986?

GREGG: I was aware that he was involved in what I took to be coordinating, aiding and abetting the informal private network of people who would contribute humanitarian assistance to the contras. There were groups that would come into the White House that one heard about and one knew that Ollie was involved in that. That's what I considered he was doing.

BELNICK: And what, Don, did you understand to be the nature of his involvement with these private fundraising groups?

GREGG: I didn't really have a clear sense as to what that was. I knew that he was very interested in Central America. I knew from his role in setting up the Vice President's trip in 1983, I knew he was interested in trying to keep the contras afloat during what was seen as a sort of hand-to-mouth period. But beyond that I did not have a clear sense of what he was doing on a day-to-day basis.

BELNICK: Now through June of '86 did you know whether he had any involvement with the contra resupply operation?

GREGG: "He" being North?

BELNICK: Col. North.

GREGG: No. I was out of the country for a fair part of June '86.

BELNICK: And you didn't know at any time prior to June '86?

GREGG: No.

* * *

What Did Bush Know?

BELNICK: Now did you report any of this [covert aid to the contras] to the Vice President?

GREGG: I did not.

BELNICK: None of what Felix told you?

GREGG: None.

BELNICK: What was the reason you decided not to make such a report?

GREGG: Well, I felt that it was a very murky business. I spend a great deal of my time trying to send things to the Vice President that I think are really Vice Presidential. I try to keep him focused, help him keep focused on arms control or Mideast peace or things of that nature. We had never discussed the contras. We had no responsibility for it. We had no expertise in it. I wasn't at all certain what this amounted to.

I had the names of four or five Americans on an obscure air base in Central America who apparently were ripping off donated funds and making unseemly profits. I felt I had passed along that material to the organizations who could do something about it, and I frankly did not think it was Vice Presidential level.

BELNICK: Did you confront North about his role?

GREGG: No. I didn't see Ollie for some time after that. This meeting was on the 12th of August. I went on leave on the 14th. I came back, I think, on the 19th. I had major surgery on the 21st, and was out of the office until the 3rd of September.

BELNICK: Before you left or after you returned on the 3rd of September did you try to see Ollie and talk to him about what Felix had told you of his role?

GREGG: No, I didn't because my feeling had always been with Ollie, as I saw him working as hard as he did and spread as thin as he was, was that he was stretched very thin and my assumption had been that he had gotten some people involved, thought they were doing a job, but was not in a position to really exercise quality control over what they were doing.

* * *

Contra Aid

BELNICK: What I'm trying to probe, then, is, with all respect here, you're told on Aug. 8, 1986, that there is this group, unsavory to boot, which is supplying lethal aid to the contras and North is using these people. North is involved with the group, right?

GREGG: Um-hum.

BELNICK: And North is a member of the staff of the National Security Council, correct?

GREGG: Um-hum.

BELNICK: The Vice President is a statutory member of the National Security Council, correct?

GREGG: Um-hum.

BELNICK: There is still a law in effect, at least until the next one kicks in, that bars this kind of activity, the Boland Amendment that has restrictions at that time. Didn't that strike you as a matter that was of some serious import?

GREGG: I had no sense at that point, nor do I now—and maybe that's from an insufficient reading of the Boland Amendment—I had no sense then nor do I now that anything I had heard was, ipso facto, against the law.

BELNICK: I'm not asking you for a legal opinion, but did you believe, leaving legal opinions out of it—well, let's not leave legal opinions out of it. As of that time, had you ever received a legal opinion that members of the National Security Council staff were exempt from the Boland Amendment?

GREGG: No.

BELNICK: Had you ever received any legal opinion on the Boland Amendment and what it applied to and what it didn't apply to?

GREGG: We were aware that the Boland Amendment was a moveable feast, that there had been various versions of it, that the CIA had been authorized, for example, [. . . classified . . .] that that had been briefed to the Boland Amendment. So I had no sense of illegality. I had a sense of corruption, which is what I thought I had taken care of by the meeting on the 12th.

BELNICK: But corruption is pretty important as well.

GREGG: Right.

BELNICK: Especially when the man involved with the corrupt, wittingly or not, and you had no reason to believe it was wittingly, is a member of the National Security Council staff.

GREGG: Okay, and his deputy attended that meeting, [Lt. Col. Robert L.] Earl, and I knew Bob Earl, Rhodes Scholar, very bright guy, and I think I said to him at the end of the meeting, Bob, I assume you will pass all of this along to Ollie. He said, I certainly will.

BELNICK: What about Ollie's superior? Earl was junior to Ollie, right?

GREGG: Yes.

BELNICK: What about getting the word to Ollie's superior?

GREGG: Until I had had—that's not the way I operate. If I see something that is questionable in the way somebody is going, I go to him and I say I think this is something you ought to know about, and I tried to do that with Ollie. It's just not my way to go running to his boss and say, hey, I think your guy's up to something.

BELNICK: So let me understand now, to go back to Boland and the restrictions. At the time, August of 1986, did you think, leaving legal analysis aside, did you think at that time that it would have been permissible for a member of the staff of the National Security Council to facilitate the provision of lethal aid to the contras?

GREGG: As long as the funds were private the flag of illegality did not arise in my mind at all.

BELNICK: So if a member of the National Security Council staff was directing lethal aid down to the contras but not paying for that lethal aid with government funds, in your mind that would have been okay?

GREGG: I had no question. The question of illegality did not arise in my mind.

BELNICK: And that was permissible, as far as you were concerned?

GREGG: Yes.

* * *

Bush and North

BELNICK: Don, there has been testimony at the hearing recently that the Vice President placed a telephone call to Oliver North on or about the day that he resigned. Have you heard that testimony?

GREGG: Yes.

BELNICK: Do you know anything about that phone call?

GREGG: I didn't know that it had been made. I remember that day the Vice President saying to me I wonder if I should call Ollie, because I knew we all had a lot of affection for him in terms of how hard he worked and how tireless he was, and we knew it was going to be a very difficult time. And I said something to the effect it would mean a lot to him if you did.

And he, I subsequently learned, did call him.

BELNICK: When did you learn that he had made the call?

GREGG: I think the Vice President told me a day or so later, yeah, I did call Ollie.

BELNICK: What did he tell you about the discussion?

GREGG: Just that he called. He just said I called Ollie very briefly.

BELNICK: Did the Vice President have any contact with Ollie that you were familiar with after the trip to Central America in December of '83?

GREGG: That's hard to answer with precision because there was some contact. Ollie's office, for example, was very much involved in terrorist matters. The Vice President was very much interested in the hostage situation. So yes, they would meet on those subjects but never to my knowledge did they meet to discuss contra supply.

Samuel J. Watson III

Following are excerpts from the June 16, 1987, private testimony of Col. Samuel J. Watson III, Vice President George Bush's deputy national security adviser. The declassified testimony was released September 8, 1987, by the House and Senate select Iran-contra committees.

[Mark A.] BELNICK [Senate committee counsel]: Do you remember—and we will get to it—that on Aug. 8th, 1986, [former CIA agent] Felix [I.] Rodriguez provided certain details of American citizens who were down purporting at least to help the contras, correct?

WATSON: That's true.

BELNICK: Prior to then, had you heard about any private network of U.S. citizens that was engaged in resupplying the contras or facilitating contra resupply?

WATSON: Not as a result of my questioning or asking anybody, but it was in the air, in the atmosphere.

BELNICK: Surely you had heard the stories.

WATSON: Surely.

BELNICK: You were aware of newspaper stories, for example, in 1986, the first half of 1986, that [Lt.] Col. [Oliver L.] North was somehow engaged in helping the contras in various ways? You were aware of stories to that effect?

WATSON: I was aware of the stories, aware of the Congressional interest.

BELNICK: Aware that Congressional inquiries had been made, correct?

WATSON: Correct.

BELNICK: Did you make any efforts to find out whether any of those stories were correct, were true or not?

WATSON: I can't recall any specific inquiries to that effect. I made the assumption that somebody was contributing money because the intelligence reports daily said that the contras were in combat and they seemed to be an effective fighting force and getting supplies from somewhere. And without inquiring, I made the assumption, because of the intelligence, that they were being supplied somehow, or monied, provided ammo.

But the answer to your question is no, I did not make specific inquiries.

BELNICK: Central America, the contras, you said was an area that was your responsibility?

WATSON: That's correct.

BELNICK: Why didn't you try to find out how the contras were getting all this money and military assistance?

WATSON: Two reasons. One is what I mentioned earlier, all the other things that I had to do.

BELNICK: But this was an important priority.

WATSON: It's an important priority.

BELNICK: You're not saying you didn't have enough time to ask, are you.

WATSON: Yes. I'm not sure I'm saying it quite that negatively, but I'm saying that when you have an awful lot of other things to do you don't spend all your time on one thing, and you have a lot of other responsibilities.

BELNICK: But this was one responsibility?

WATSON: This was one of many responsibilities.

BELNICK: So one reason you didn't ask was because—

WATSON: Because I had so much else to do and so many things to do that it didn't seem to be to be a high priority thing to ask about. And the second reason is, one never knows what is compartmented [restricted access by classification] or committed or authorized in a classified, compartmented government action, and I didn't see fit to ask.

BELNICK: Well, you would find out if it was compartmented if you asked and were told it is none of your business, right?

WATSON: I would have.

BELNICK: Did anyone tell you, don't ask these questions?

WATSON: No, nobody has ever told me not to ask questions.

BELNICK: Did you feel that if you asked you would get an answer you didn't want to hear?

WATSON: No.

BELNICK: Do you know—did you ever discuss with Mr. Gregg how the contras were being resupplied and assisted during this same period?

WATSON: I don't think so. You have to remember that we see intelligence every day and it shows the contras acting, and so you're assuming that they're getting something. And so it's not necessary to ask where they're getting it from.

You see the results of their actions in the combat reports.

BELNICK: These combat intelligence reports were coming to you from the CIA?

WATSON: That's correct, or the Defense Intelligence Agency.

BELNICK: Did those reports ever indicate the source or sources of the contras' materiel and money?

WATSON: I don't think so.

* * *

Contra Resupply Briefing

BELNICK: Do you recall telling [Donald P. Gregg's secretary] Phyllis Byrne that a purpose of the [May 1, 1986] meeting requested by Rodriguez was to discuss resupply of the contras?

WATSON: No, I do not.

BELNICK: Would it affect your recollection if I told you that Phyllis Byrne recalls that it was you who gave her the essence and substance of what appears as the purpose of the meeting on the schedule proposal, namely to brief the Vice President on the status of the war in El Salvador and resupply of the contras?

If I tell you again that Ms. Byrne recalls that it was you who told her that what I just read in effect was the purpose of the meeting, would that change your recollection in any way?

WATSON: That would not change my recollection.

BELNICK: Your view is that Phyllis is wrong.

WATSON: I can't say she's wrong. I can't say she's wrong. I can't say she's right.

BELNICK: She recalls that it was you who told her.

WATSON: Well, she can, but I do not recall giving those words.

BELNICK: Let me tell you where we are with this, Col. Watson. Mr. Gregg says he didn't write it. You say you didn't give it to Phyllis Byrne. She recalls that you did give it to Phyllis Byrne, that you did give it to her.

Do you have any explanation for where this language came from?

WATSON: The only explanation is that the Congress and the President and everybody was in the midst of a request for a vote, a request for an appropriation of funds, and the whole subject of continued or resumed military assistance for the United Nicaraguan Opposition was something that was being much discussed.

There were meetings going on constantly during that spring involving different members of the Administration to advocate the

President's policy of supplying, providing supplies to the Nicaraguans that were seeking freedom. And it was not an unusual issue.

The specific words "resupply of the contras" could have devolved or evolved from that general atmospheric. But as for the specific, no, I still do not know where that came from.

* * *

North's Role

BELNICK: What did Felix tell you about North's involvement with this group [in charge of the contra resupply effort and headed by Gen. Richard V. Secord and several renegade CIA agents]?

WATSON: As I recall, he mentioned that—I didn't take any notes. These were notes I wrote down afterwards. I think he mentioned that Ollie North was involved with these people and Ollie had some kind of directional role. I don't recall him discussing specific technical directive role that Ollie had; that Ollie was more the conceptualizer, the chairman of the board.

Those are my words, not his.

BELNICK: That's what you understood from Felix?

WATSON: That's what I understood, correct.

BELNICK: And did Felix associate North with the effort by Secord and the others to take away from the contras the planes which Felix [. . . classified . . .] said had been donated to the contras, right?

WATSON: Rather, Felix said that rather vehemently.

BELNICK: And that North was one of those who was trying to take those planes away from the contras, correct? That's what you testified a few moments ago?

WATSON: Yes, generally.

BELNICK: You testified that Felix said that North and Secord had no right to take those planes away from the contras, correct?

WATSON: Yes, I said that.

BELNICK: And that's what you recall Felix communicated to you?

WATSON: North, in the sense that he was chairman of the board; Secord, in that he was the chief operating officer.

BELNICK: Now, do you recall whether Felix told you at the Aug. 8th meeting anything about where the contras were getting money from or where the money was coming from to pay for contra weapons?

WATSON: No. What I recall was that he said that these people are buying the weapons or providing them to the contras. I don't recall him—he may have said that money was being donated by foreign governments. . . .

* * *

BELNICK: Did you have any understanding when the meeting ended as to whether Felix's allegations [about problems with the contra resupply effort, including that it was being run by corrupt former CIA agents and that a resupply aircraft may have been stolen] were going to be brought to the attention of the Vice President?

WATSON: I don't recall. I don't believe we had an understanding that it would go to the Vice President.

BELNICK: Did you have a view as of the end of the meeting on Aug. 8th, 1986, as to whether the information that Felix Rodriguez had just provided you should be brought to the Vice President's attention?

WATSON: No, I think the more proper thing was to take these allegations and talk to other people in the U.S. Government about them before you take something like this to the Vice President of the United States, a series of allegations, a case of many little pieces, of which nothing gels.

BELNICK: I don't want to put words in your mouth, but was it your view at that time when the meeting ended that the information you had just received should not then be reported to the Vice President?

WATSON: I don't think it was negative in that sense of the word.

BELNICK: Did you have a view one way or the other on that issue?

WATSON: No.

BELNICK: You didn't think about it?

WATSON: No. My thought was—and I think Don's thought was—that we ought to have a meeting of other government people and find out more about it; let's pass the word out to them, tell them what these warnings were.

BELNICK: You discussed that with Don after the Aug. 8th meeting?

WATSON: I don't know whether we discussed it immediately thereafter, but we had a meeting on Aug. 12th.

BELNICK: When the meeting ended, did you and Don talk about what you had just heard from Felix?

WATSON: I don't recall whether we did or whether the press of events carried us off to something else.

BELNICK: And this was fairly shocking news that Felix was giving you?

WATSON: Yes, we may well have. It's just that I don't recollect every single thing that we do in a day.

BELNICK: I understand. But Felix was now telling you that one of the most notorious, corrupt, and treacherous groups that had ever infected the United States Government was now involved in the contra resupply, correct?

WATSON: Yes.

BELNICK: These were people that were well known to Don because he was at the CIA, correct?

WATSON: Yes.

BELNICK: And they would have therefore also been well known to the Vice President, who had been DCI [Director of Central Intelligence], correct?

WATSON: Well, I guess they would have.

BELNICK: They were known to many Americans?

WATSON: They were known to many Americans.

BELNICK: He told you also that, lo and behold, involved with this group as in effect chairman of the board was a member of the staff of the National Security Council, correct?

WATSON: Yes.

BELNICK: Would you not consider this extremely significant information for the Vice President to have?

WATSON: At some point probably, but not immediately.

Michael Ledeen

Following are excerpts from the June 19, 1987, private testimony of Michael Ledeen, a former National Security Council consultant who played a pivotal role in early discussions between U.S. and Israeli officials about a plan to sell weapons to Iran. Ledeen testified on three occasions, in March, June, and September, in closed sessions. The declassified tesimony was released September 28, 1987, by the House and Senate select Iran-contra committees.

[Paul] BARBADORO [Senate panel deputy chief counsel]: What did [Lt.] Col. [Oliver L.] North tell you when you asked him about going public [in November 1986] with what your role was in the initiative?

LEDEEN: He said that I was not to do that, and that if and when it became possible for me to do that he would tell me, and that in the meantime, I should stay in touch with Mr. [Robert C.] McFarlane about the matter.

BARBADORO: What did Mr. McFarlane tell you when you asked him about going public to explain your role in the initiative?

LEDEEN: Well, he originally said the same thing as North, and then, a couple of days later, when I complained about it, he suggested that I talk to some journalists on background, but no public statements, and no on-the-record statements.

BARBADORO: The President gave his speech on the Iran initiative on Nov. 13. Prior to that, had you made attempts to contact [Rear] Adm. [John M.] Poindexter to discuss this matter with him?

LEDEEN: Yes. I had.

BARBADORO: Were you able to discuss it with Adm. Poindexter prior to the speech?

LEDEEN: No.

BARBADORO: Did you also try to contact [National Security Council aide Alton G.] Keel [Jr.]?

LEDEEN: Yes.

BARBADORO: Were you able to discuss this matter with Mr. Keel prior to the President's speech?

LEDEEN: Yes. I think it was prior to the President's speech.

BARBADORO: On Nov. 13, 1986, Wilma Hall [McFarlane's secretary] writes a note to Mr. Keel stating that you wanted to get in touch with Mr. Keel. When was it that you think you finally did get in touch with Mr. Keel?

LEDEEN: I think it was later that day, but I'm not certain, Mr. Barbadoro, but in any event, I did have a brief telephone conversation with Mr. Keel, in which I said essentially, how can you reconstruct what happens without listening to what I do?

BARBADORO: What was his response?

LEDEEN: He said that was a good point, and why didn't I type up a page or two, just giving a simple chronology of what I had done, and turn it in.

BARBADORO: Did you do that?

LEDEEN: Yes.

BARBADORO: When did you turn in that chronology of what you did?

LEDEEN: Probably a day or two after that, and I gave it to Col. North.

BARBADORO: Did you listen to the President's speech on Iran?

LEDEEN: Yes.

BARBADORO: Did you disagree with anything that the President said in his speech?

LEDEEN: Yes.

BARBADORO: What did you disagree with?

LEDEEN: I disagreed with the statement that all the weapons could fit into one small aircraft, and I disagreed with the statement—if I remember right, it's been a while since I've read it—but if I remember, he said that there had been at no time no arms for hostages. And I felt that the policy, although it had not begun as arms for hostages, that in fact it had become that, at least to a significant degree.

BARBADORO: When did you meet with Col. North to turn in your chronology?

LEDEEN: I don't remember, and I'm not even certain that I met with Col. North when I turned it in.

BARBADORO: Did you have a chance to raise your concerns about the President's speech with Col. North?

LEDEEN: Yes.

BARBADORO: What was his reaction?

LEDEEN: He said that I was not the only one to say that, and I said to him that I thought it was still not too late for the President simply to tell what had happened, and to say that we were looking for some kind of geopolitical démarche with regard to Iran, that we unfortunately became enmeshed in an arms-for-hostage affair in which the President, himself, had become emotionally involved with the hostage question, that he regretted it. He still felt quite passionately about the fate of the hostages, and would do anything reasonable to try to get them out, but felt that what had happened was probably wrong, and that he had put an end to it, and then would get on with it.

My understanding was that in fact Secretary [of Defense Caspar W.] Weinberger had recommended exactly that before the speech, and I thought it was a good idea, and I thought he should still do it.

*   *   *

Legal Tangles

BARBADORO: Do you recall a conversation with Col. North in which he suggested that you should get a lawyer?

LEDEEN: Yes.

BARBADORO: As best you can, what was the date of that conversation?

LEDEEN: I'm quite unsure about the date of this conversation.

BARBADORO: Would it have been before the President's speech, or after?

LEDEEN: My belief is that it was after the President's speech, but prior to the 21st of November.

BARBADORO: And would the conversation have been in person or over the telephone?

LEDEEN: I don't know. It could have been either.

BARBADORO: What do you recall Col. North saying to you about getting a lawyer?

LEDEEN: I remember Col. North saying to me that there were Justice Department people investigating the possibility of an illegal sale of Hawk [antiaircraft] missiles to Iran in November of 1985, and that they would undoubtedly be questioning me about it, and that I might consider getting an attorney.

BARBADORO: Did Col. North say anything about whether he—Col. North—had been advised to get a lawyer?

LEDEEN: I think that he said that he had been advised to get a lawyer.

BARBADORO: And did he say whether he would be getting a lawyer?

LEDEEN: I don't remember.

BARBADORO: How certain are you that this conversation occurred prior to Nov. 21?

LEDEEN: Look, I have a healthy amount of skepticism about the reliability of anybody's memory, and above all, about my own memory. However, I will explain to you why I think that it happened before the 21st of November.

On the 21st, when I went to see him in his office in the afternoon, he said, he asked me, what would you say if you were asked what do you know about shipment of Hawk missiles to Iran in November 1985? And when he said that to me I remember, or I think I remember remembering, a previous conversation in which he had spoken about Justice Department people looking into this, and telling me that I would undoubtedly be asked this question.

So I recall recalling that previous conversation on the 21st and remember it as having been precedent. Now it is conceivable—the only other possibility, because the only other time that I remember talking to him in that period, was the morning of the 21st at my house, but that was such a very brief encounter, that I don't think that that's when it happened, although that is possible, that it may have been the morning of the 21st. But I tend not to think so.

And I also lean towards believing that the conversation in which he said people were investigating it and I might consider getting a lawyer, was part of a telephone conversation rather than a face-to-face conversation. So that's what I think I recall, and how certain am I? I believe I have a fairly clear recollection of it, but I have been wrong about things in which I have had quite clear recollections in the past. So I'm doing my best to remember it.

BARBADORO: All right. Let's go back to the conversation where Col. North suggested that you should get a lawyer. Did Col. North explain to you what the problem with the legality of the November '85 Hawk shipment was?

LEDEEN: No.

BARBADORO: Did he say why it was being investigated by officials of the Justice Department?

LEDEEN: No, and indeed, I found it peculiar, and I found the suggestion that this sale of the Hawks had been illegal to be silly. I didn't believe it and I told him so. I told him I didn't think that there was the slightest possibility that that had been illegal, and I didn't think that anyone from the Justice Department was going to talk to me about it.

BARBADORO: Let me ask you as precisely, as you can remember, what did you tell Col. North when he suggested that you should get a lawyer?

LEDEEN: I said it's silly. I said all of that was perfectly proper. Everything that happened in that period was approved by the President.

BARBADORO: What was Col. North's reaction to that?

LEDEEN: He said he was just trying to advise me that this was going on, and to try to be helpful.

* * *

Going Public

BARBADORO: Did Mr. McFarlane come to your house at 11:00 o'clock on Nov. 21?

LEDEEN: Yes.

BARBADORO: What happened when he got there?

LEDEEN: We sat down and started talking, and we talked about all these various subjects.

BARBADORO: What did Mr. McFarlane say to you when you asked to go public?

LEDEEN: He said, first of all, that he did not think that this was—it was yet time to do it, that I could continue to talk to journalists on background, and try to help them understand what had taken place. But that in any event, when I spoke about my own role in this, that I must not—if I remember his words precisely, he said that I must not try to get too far out in front on this matter, and that I should not represent myself as having been on a mission for him when I went to talk to Prime Minister [of Israel Shimon] Peres in May of '85.

BARBADORO: Let me ask you about that. Do you feel that you were on a mission from Robert McFarlane when you went to talk to Mr. Peres in May of 1985?

LEDEEN: Yes.

BARBADORO: So you disagree with the assertion that Mr. McFarlane is making on Nov. 21, that you were not on a mission, is that right?

LEDEEN: That's right.

BARBADORO: What was your reaction when Mr. McFarlane told you this?

LEDEEN: I didn't say anything. Some time later in the conversation—I tried to figure out why he was saying this.

BARBADORO: What did you think about why he was saying that?

LEDEEN: Well, I thought there were several possibilities. One was that he simply did not remember what had happened, and had in his own mind made it a matter of, who knows, a happenstance conversation or chance encounter in which Peres and I had had a talk about Iran, and some interesting things had happened.

The second was that he was trying to protect me by attempting, publicly, at least, to minimize my role in it, and telling the story in such a way that I simply dropped out. Indeed, the way he was telling the story—and it looked that way to me for quite a while, I must tell you—because when he originally told the story, it tended to begin in July, always, with [former Israeli official David] Kimche's trip to Washington, and on that basis I simply dropped out of the story, as having any kind of important role.

And I said to him, whether towards the end of that conversation or at a later date I don't remember—but I said to him at a certain point, "Look, Bud, you cannot protect me in this, there is no way, because my name is already out and it's all over the place, and all the people who were in those meetings will eventually make that point, and people can add."

* * *

A Trip to Israel

BARBADORO: Let me start with a trip that your travel records show that you made to Israel on May 1, 1985. Do you recall that trip?

LEDEEN: Yes.

BARBADORO: Who did you meet with in Israel?

LEDEEN: I met with Prime Minister Peres, and I met subsequently with [former Israeli official] Shlomo Gazit.

BARBADORO: In general terms, would you just describe what you discussed in your meeting with Mr. Peres.

LEDEEN: I discussed the inadequate information that the Government of the United States had about Iran, and about Iran's

role in international terrorism. And I asked him if he felt that Israel had a satisfactory understanding of that situation. He said no, but that he agreed that it was an important matter and he proposed to create a study group, or whatever you care to call it, who would try to pull together what Israel knew about Iran, so that we could compare notes and try to achieve a better understanding together.

BARBADORO: Did he ask you to convey a message to Mr. McFarlane?

LEDEEN: Yes.

BARBADORO: What was that message?

LEDEEN: Said that they, Israel, had been asked by the Government of Iran to sell to Iran a certain quantity of—I think it was artillery shells, but it could have been artillery pieces—I don't recall—and that they would not do this without explicit American approval, and would I ask McFarlane if the United States approved.

BARBADORO: Did he mention a specific kind of artillery shell, or artillery?

LEDEEN: I don't recall.

BARBADORO: And you can't recall the quantity that he was talking about shipping to Iran?

LEDEEN: There was a quantity but I don't remember it.

BARBADORO: Was this shipment linked in any way to the potential release of hostages?

LEDEEN: No.

BARBADORO: Was there any discussion at your meeting with Mr. Peres about getting hostages released?

LEDEEN: No.

BARBADORO: Were TOW [antitank] missiles discussed at that meeting?

LEDEEN: No.

BARBADORO: Was [Iranian middleman in the arms deal Manucher] Ghorbanifar's name mentioned at that meeting?

LEDEEN: No.

BARBADORO: Was there any discussion at the meeting about improving U.S. relations with Iran by shipping weapons to Iran?

LEDEEN: No. There was no discussion of the relationship between the United States and Iran at all.

BARBADORO: Did Mr. Peres explain why he wanted to ship this artillery or artillery shells to Iran?

LEDEEN: He said that Israel had found it useful to have channels into Iran, that if we were interested in getting maximum information out of Iran, that this was one way. Those sort of channels helped them get information

[. . . classified . . .]

BARBADORO: And is it also fair to say that at this meeting, he expressed a willingness to try to cooperate with the United States in improving the quality of the intelligence that was available on Iran?

LEDEEN: Yes.

* * *

Meeting Kimche in London

BARBADORO: Your records show that you made a one-day trip to London on Aug. 20, 1986. Do you recall that trip?

LEDEEN: Yes.

BARBADORO: Did you obtain approval to make that trip from Mr. McFarlane before you made it?

LEDEEN: Yes.

BARBADORO: And what was your purpose in making that trip?

LEDEEN: To confirm with Kimche that the President had approved the test, and to give him a code in which we could communicate by telephone, should it be necessary for him to tell us when and where the possible pickup of American hostages in Lebanon would occur.

BARBADORO: Prior to going to that meeting, did Mr. McFarlane tell you that there were certain preferred locations where the hostages should be released?

LEDEEN: Yes.

BARBADORO: And did you tell that to Mr. Kimche when you met with him in London on the 20th?

LEDEEN: Yes.

BARBADORO: Other than telling him that the President had approved the initiative, that there were certain preferred locations for the hostages to be released, and that you gave him the one-time code to be used, what else did you talk about?

LEDEEN: I think that's it. Was there anything else?

BARBADORO: Was there any discussion of replenishment at this meeting on the 20th?

LEDEEN: Not that I recall.

BARBADORO: Was it your understanding at this time that the initiative involved 100 TOWs, or more than 100 TOWs?

LEDEEN: I don't really recall.

BARBADORO: Do you recall whether you understood the initiative to involve a one-time shipment of weapons or a sequence of shipments of weapons?

LEDEEN: I think I remember it as a staggered sequence. That is, a certain quantity of weapons would go in, and then something good would happen with regard to the hostages, and then a subsequent quantity of weapons, and however many hostages were finally going to come out.

BARBADORO: As we now know, 100 TOWs were shipped from Israel to Iran on Aug. 30, 1985, and no hostage was released. What happened after the TOWs were shipped and no hostage was released?

LEDEEN: They shipped more TOWs.

BARBADORO: Was there any discussion between you and Mr. McFarlane about the fact that the first shipment of TOWs had been made and no hostages had been released?

LEDEEN: Yes. And I think in fact that there was a meeting in Paris between the first shipment and the second shipment.

BARBADORO: Was that meeting scheduled because no hostages had been released, as you thought was going to happen after the first shipment?

LEDEEN: Yes.

BARBADORO: And did McFarlane approve you going to that meeting?

LEDEEN: Yes.

BARBADORO: And could you tell me what the purpose was of that meeting?

LEDEEN: The purpose of the meeting was to decide where—if anywhere—we were going to go from here.

BARBADORO: This meeting was attended by you, [Israeli arms dealers Al] Schwimmer, [Yaacov] Nimrodi, Mr. Kimche and Mr. Ghorbanifar, correct?

LEDEEN: Correct.

BARBADORO: Did Mr. Ghorbanifar have an explanation as to why no hostages have been released?

LEDEEN: Yes.

BARBADORO: What was it?

LEDEEN: The wrong people had gotten the missiles.

BARBADORO: What does he mean by that?

LEDEEN: Well, he meant that the missiles were supposed to go in such a way as to permit a moderate faction of the armed forces to get their—to obtain them, or at least to obtain the credit for having gotten them, and instead, some of the nasty revolutionary guards took possession of them.

BARBADORO: And did he promise that if more missiles were sent, that this time hostages would be released?

LEDEEN: Yes.

* * *

Shipping TOWs to Iran

BARBADORO: Did you understand prior to the TOW shipments that the Iranians were going to be asked to pay for TOWs?

LEDEEN: Oh, yes. They were going to pay for it. Indeed, some of the most entertaining discussions were the relationship between the timing of the arrival of the TOWs and the arrival of the money in some account.

BARBADORO: Okay. So you recall being present during some of these discussions?

LEDEEN: Yes. I remember, in particular, I shall remember it to my dying day being present at a discussion where we were searching for a method of achieving some kind of magical simultaneity whereby money could be electronically transferred at the precise [moment] that an aircraft entered Iranian airspace and all kinds of things of this nature.

BARBADORO: Did you understand that the price that was being charged would also include the Israeli expenses for shipping the TOWs to Iran?

LEDEEN: Sure. That was understood.

BARBADORO: Did you understand that there would be any other markup in the price of the TOWs?

LEDEEN: No.

BARBADORO: You don't recall any discussion about a profit being made so Ghorbanifar could make some profit?

LEDEEN: Look, there has been a lot of talk. Ghorbanifar also had expenses. I think that the Israelis believed that some of the money that Ghorbanifar was claiming for expenses actually represented something other than expenses—money for other persons. But it was—I never heard any discussion of organizing this thing in such a way that persons would be paid nor have I ever seen any evidence that that took place.

BARBADORO: Do I understand you to say that you assumed that Mr. Ghorbanifar would include the cost of his expenses in here and perhaps a markup as well but no one ever told you that?

LEDEEN: No. Mr. Ghorbanifar—I was present at discussions where people said that the expenses had to be covered. These expenses were not only Israeli expenses. Mr. Ghorbanifar also had expenses in connection with this and when they said that the expenses were going to be covered, it was going to be everybody's expenses and all those, including my expenses, were paid for by my Government. These people had quite extraordinary expenses in some cases. I mean, they were renting planes and flying them all over the world and so forth. It wasn't a minor matter. So the expenses were going to be covered in the pricing. That was understood. What I'm saying is that subsequently some of the Israelis suspected that Mr. Ghorbanifar's expenses were not just expenses, but that there was also some private money there for one person or another just as Mr. Ghorbanifar, on his side, suspected that the money that the Israelis took out of this also involved private money.

BARBADORO: So, everybody was suspicious of everyone else.

LEDEEN: Yes.

BARBADORO: But you had no knowledge of anybody making more than expenses out of the deal?

LEDEEN: I had no knowledge of it and I had their word that none would be made.

BARBADORO: Prior to the TOW shipments in August and September, was there any discussion about some of the money generated by the sale of these TOWs being used to pay expenses of other persons in Iran? Other than Ghorbanifar?

LEDEEN: Not that I can recall.

BARBADORO: No discussion of payments for expenses for any other purpose to other factions or leaders of factions in Iran to help improve Israeli or U.S. relationships with Iran?

LEDEEN: No.

* * *

Arms for Hostages

BARBADORO: Is it fair to say that Ghorbanifar [at an October 8, 1985, meeting] was discussing the possibility of Israel making additional arms shipments to Iran?

LEDEEN: Yes.

BARBADORO: And that he was making representations that additional arms shipments would result in additional hostages being released?

LEDEEN: Yes.

BARBADORO: Were there discussions of any particular type of weapons at this meeting?

LEDEEN: Oh, yes.

BARBADORO: Were Hawk missiles discussed?

LEDEEN: Hawks, Phoenixes, Harpoons, Sidewinders, every missile known to man or beast.

BARBADORO: And what was the reaction of the Israelis when Ghorbanifar would raise a possibility of additional arms shipments?

LEDEEN: Well, it didn't exactly happen that way. He gave us long lists of missiles that he'd like to have and I expressed an opinion that I thought that this was as good a time as any to get out of this whole business and that we ought to just stop talking about the hostages altogether.

BARBADORO: What caused you to be reluctant to continue with the initiative?

LEDEEN: Because I felt that what was important for us to establish was whether there were indeed these people in Iran that Mr. Ghorbanifar had told us about. People who wanted a better relationship between the two countries and were in a position to achieve it from the Iranian side. And I was convinced, first of all, that if we acted in such a way as to permit Iran to continue to obtain American weapons of whatever description, that it would make it impossible for us ever to gauge the real intention of our interlocutors because they would say anything, do anything in order to keep the weapons coming because they desperately needed these weapons. So since the important matter for the United States, in my opinion, was to establish who these people were, and what they were all about, and what they could deliver, I felt that so long as weapons were going there, we would never be able to answer that question. And that was the question that had to be answered.

Furthermore, I think that the business of bartering for hostages is a mistake and that in the end all you get for it, is more hostages taken, more hostages released, and I didn't want to encourage other people around the world to take Americans hostage.

* * *

Talking with Iranian Officials

BARBADORO: Mr. Ledeen, at some point that fall, did Mr. Ghorbanifar put you in touch with Iranian officials?

LEDEEN: Yes.

BARBADORO: I want to ask you about one senior Iranian official in particular. Did he put you in touch with a senior Iranian official?

LEDEEN: He did.

BARBADORO: And without referring to the time, place, or method of contact, could you describe in substance what was discussed between you and that senior Iranian official?

LEDEEN: The senior Iranian official told us that he believed it possible to, in essence, change the nature of the Iranian regime through peaceful, parliamentary methods—that this change in personnel would lead to a dramatic change in the policies of the country, including abandonments of terror and the abandonment of the policy of trying to violently export radical Shi'ism and to better relations with the western world in general, and with the United States in particular. And that he wanted to cooperate quite closely with the United States in this transformation, and asked us for various forms of modest support, more, again, along the lines of a gesture that would commit us to him rather than in terms of anything substantial.

BARBADORO: What did he want from the U.S. Government?

LEDEEN: Specifically, he wanted some small arms for the security of himself and his allies inside Iran, some training, and some secure communications.

BARBADORO: What would the secure communications equipment be used for?

LEDEEN: It would enable him to coordinate his moves with us and to advise us as to what the situation was and what he was thinking of doing.

BARBADORO: And what were the small arms to be used for?

LEDEEN: To protect him and his allies against the possibility of violence from people who he expected to be defeating in his political maneuvers.

BARBADORO: What kind of arms were discussed?

LEDEEN: I really don't remember.

The picture I have in my mind is of pistols and small caliber automatic weapons.

BARBADORO: Were silencers also discussed?

LEDEEN: They may have been, I don't recall.

BARBADORO: And how about quantities? How much was he looking for?

LEDEEN: I don't think we discussed the specific quantities, to tell you the truth. I think these were things that he listed as to things that he would like. It was clear to him that he was one step removed from a substantive discussion. So that we were talking about what would happen if we were able to work out such an arrangement.

BARBADORO: Did this official ask you for money?

LEDEEN: He did not.

BARBADORO: Did this official also provide you with information about the political situation inside Iran?

LEDEEN: The official did and the official also expressed considerable opposition to the sale of American weapons to Iran.

BARBADORO: What did he say about that?

LEDEEN: He said that he was quite angry about that because that had, in fact, strengthened his opponents. It had strengthened the very people that it was necessary to remove if one were going to transform the Iranian government into something more reasonable.

BARBADORO: Did his statement affect your view about the wisdom of continuing to ship arms to Iran?

LEDEEN: Well, I was encouraged to hear it since I had expressed similar views and so it surprised me.

In fact, many things about the exchange with this Iranian official surprised me but I was quite surprised and quite pleased to hear (a) that he was opposed to it and (b) that he thought it was counterproductive, because I thought it would strengthen my own arguments.

BARBADORO: Did this person provide you with any written information? A list of names of people who supported him?

LEDEEN: Yes. I don't see why it's important but I'll answer it.

BARBADORO: Did you provide the written information he gave you to Mr. McFarlane?

LEDEEN: I think so.

BARBADORO: After these discussions with this senior Iranian official, did you brief Mr. McFarlane?

LEDEEN: Yes.

BARBADORO: And did you raise with him the request from this senior Iranian official?

LEDEEN: Yes, I did and I told him that the general understanding at the meeting was that we would attempt to respond to him within a month.

BARBADORO: What was Mr. McFarlane's response?

LEDEEN: He said he would take it under consideration.

BARBADORO: Did he ever tell you whether the proposal was acceptable or not?

LEDEEN: No.

BARBADORO: Did you continue to try to get an answer from him?

LEDEEN: No.

BARBADORO: And it's fair to say that you were unsuccessful in getting an answer from him?

LEDEEN: That's correct.

BARBADORO: And it's also fair to say that to your knowledge, the U.S. Government never followed up on this proposal?

LEDEEN: The U.S. Government not only did not follow up on this proposal, but it did not follow up on other contacts with other Iranians which were arranged in the same period. . . .

* * *

Ledeen's Opposition

BARBADORO: Is it safe to say that as of that date [late November 1985], you had become a definite opponent of continued arms sales to Iran in order to effect the release of U.S. hostages?

LEDEEN: Since early October I had been. I don't think those events affected my feelings one way or another.

BARBADORO: But as of that date, you were opposed to continuing with the arms initiatives?

LEDEEN: That's right.

BARBADORO: And you had made Mr. McFarlane aware of your opposition to continuing with the initiative, correct?

LEDEEN: Yes.

BARBADORO: After that point, did you make attempts to contact a number of senior government officials to make them aware of your opposition to continuing with the arms part of this initiative and your desire to continue with the contacts with the senior Iranian official?

LEDEEN: Yes.

BARBADORO: Who did you first contact about that?

LEDEEN: I think the first person I contacted was [CIA director William J.] Casey.

BARBADORO: When was that?

LEDEEN: That was in December of 1985.

BARBADORO: What did you tell Casey?

LEDEEN: I told Casey the story. I briefed him on how I had met Ghorbanifar; how Ghorbanifar had arranged the various contacts, not simply the one with the senior Iranian official, but the range of contacts; and what these contacts could potentially do for us and urged Casey to tell the President that pursuing the hostage was backwards and it was permitting the tail to wag the dog, as it were, and that we should instead pursue the political manner.

BARBADORO: All right. Even before contacting Casey, had you prepared a memorandum for Col. North that had laid out your position on this issue?

LEDEEN: Well, I know the memorandum you're referring to. I don't remember exactly when that went to Col. North, whether it was December or January, so I can't place that.

BARBADORO: Somewhere around that time?

LEDEEN: Yes.

BARBADORO: Okay. What was Casey's reaction when you explained this to him?

LEDEEN: Well, Casey said he found it all very interesting and, indeed, I think it was that conversation with Casey, or at least in part that conversation with Casey, that led to the invitation to Ghorbanifar to be polygraphed.

BARBADORO: Did you meet with Casey again in the December-January period?

LEDEEN: I met with Casey several times in that period.

BARBADORO: We'll go into this in greater detail in a minute, but can you just summarize what was Casey's position as he expressed it to you?

LEDEEN: He expressed it to me—he agreed that the political matter was considerably more important than the hostage question, the geopolitical matter. However, he felt that there were internal Administration reasons or the politics of Washington, as he put it, that it was necessary to do the hostages first and get that out of the way and then pursue the other matter.

Shirley A. Napier

Following are excerpts from the April 10, 1987, deposition and May 11, 1987, affidavit of Shirley A. Napier, a secretary to retired Air Force major general Richard V. Secord. In her first deposition before the Senate Iran-contra committee April 10, Napier testified that she and others who worked for Secord's Vienna, Va., company shredded documents in early December 1986. Secord, during his May 6, 1987, public testimony, said the shredding took place in early November—before Attorney General Edwin Meese III's November 25, 1986, announcement that

profits from the sale of U.S. weapons to Iran had been diverted to the Nicaraguan contras. On May 11 Napier filed an affidavit with the committee lawyers that changed her earlier statements about the shredding.

In another conflict with public testimony, Napier said that retired Air Force colonel Robert C. Dutton, who worked directly under Secord at his company and supervised day-to-day logistics for the contra supply network, told her she would be picking up $16,000 in cash in Miami and bringing it back to Washington, D.C. During his May 27, 1987, public testimony, Dutton said he was unaware of the package's contents until Napier arrived in Miami and signed for the money.

Deposition

[Mark A.] BELNICK [Senate committee lawyer]: Could you describe for us the occasion in 1986 when you delivered money to the Old Executive Office Building?

NAPIER: Bob Dutton was trying to get in touch with Bill Cooper [William J. Cooper, a pilot in the contra supply network, shot down in October 1986 over Nicaragua], who was coming to D.C., and he wanted him to stop in Miami and pick up documents or papers, and he could not get a hold of Bill Cooper. And Mr. Secord was out of town and I didn't have much to do, so I volunteered to go down and pick up the papers.

Bob said he would have to make a phone call. He made his phone call, came back, said it was okay for me to pick it up, to make my reservations, and that he was going to make another phone call.

Well, I made my reservations and he came back, and at that time he told me that I would be picking up $16,000 in cash from a man who worked for Southern Air Transport.

BELNICK: All right.

NAPIER: And when I picked it up to bring it back to D.C. and to take it to [Lt.] Col. [Oliver L.] North at the Old Executive Office Building.

BELNICK: Before we go any further, who was Bob Dutton?

NAPIER: Bob Dutton, his title is staff director with Stanford Technology Trading Group International.

BELNICK: So he worked in the same group as you?

NAPIER: Yes.

BELNICK: Who is Bill Cooper?

NAPIER: Bill Cooper is a pilot that was down in Central America.

BELNICK: Do you know by whom he was employed?

NAPIER: I don't know who the employer was.

BELNICK: Did Mr. Dutton tell you the name of the man from Southern Air Transport that you were to see in southern Florida?

NAPIER: He did, and I can't remember the man's name. All I remember is I can describe him, and he said he was the controller for Southern Air.

BELNICK: Do you recall his name being Bill Langdon?

NAPIER: No, it was not Bill Langdon. He said I might meet Bill Langdon, but that another gentleman would meet me and it would not be Bill.

BELNICK: Did you fly to Miami?

NAPIER: Yes, I did.

BELNICK: Do you recall when this was?

NAPIER: It was August 26th.

BELNICK: 1986?

NAPIER: 1986.

BELNICK: Tell us what happened when you went to Miami?

NAPIER: I met the man at the gate that we had arranged and he had on an SAT ID badge, fit the description, and he recognized me by what I was wearing. We went to a lounge. He gave me a Federal Express overnight envelope, like an 8½-by-11 size. And he opened it up, showed me the money.

I did not count the money in the lounge because it was crowded. We went to the lounge. I went to the ladies room and counted the money, and there was $16,000.

BELNICK: In what denomination bills?

NAPIER: It was all twenties and under.

BELNICK: What did you do after you counted the money?

NAPIER: I boarded the plane back to D.C., to Dulles [International Airport].

BELNICK: Once you arrived at Dulles?

NAPIER: I left my car there. I got in my car and went down to the Old Executive Office Building. I went into the 17th Street entrance. There was a phone there, a house phone. I called Fawn's [Fawn Hall, North's former secretary] extension and told her I was downstairs with a package that I thought Ollie was waiting for.

BELNICK: What happened then?

NAPIER: I wait a few minutes and she came down and took the money.

BELNICK: Did she say anything to you? I'm talking about Fawn Hall. Did she say anything to you when she came down?

NAPIER: We exchanged a few words and she said something. It was either "Did you go to Miami and get this?" or "Did you go down there today?" I don't remember exactly what it was, but that was the extent of our conversation.

BELNICK: What did you do then?

NAPIER: I went to my home, because it was late in the afternoon.

BELNICK: Did you report to Mr. Dutton that evening?

NAPIER: No. I think I talked to him the next day. I think he might have called the office and asked me about it, and I told him I had delivered it. And he said, "Thank you for going down there."

* * *

BELNICK: Now, there was a day that we started to talk about some moments ago at the office, when you were asked to destroy certain documents; am I right?

NAPIER: Yes.

BELNICK: When was that?

NAPIER: That was in December, the first part of December.

BELNICK: Of?

NAPIER: '86.

BELNICK: Would you describe as best you recall it what happened on that day?

NAPIER: Mr. Secord came in and decided we needed to go through our files. I think he actually went through our subject files and took anything out that he wanted destroyed or put into the storage boxes.

I went through the telex files and my files and took all the summary sheets from telephone bills, telex bills, travel, and put those in the boxes. And the telexes, I took out anything that had company names, a person's name, anything that referenced money, or I think I took out things that referenced part numbers, lists of part numbers, gave those to Mr. Secord to go through.

BELNICK: And then what happened?

NAPIER: Anything he wanted destroyed, he gave back and we shredded them.

BELNICK: There was a shredder in the office?

NAPIER: Yes.

BELNICK: Where was that located?

NAPIER: It's in our little kitchen area.

BELNICK: Who participated in shredding the documents on that day?

NAPIER: I did, Joan Corbin [another secretary to Secord], and Bob Dutton. And I don't believe I ever saw Mr. Secord shred anything. I was not standing there. But again, that was in another room.

BELNICK: But Mr. Secord was telling you to shred the documents?

NAPIER: Yes.

BELNICK: Did Mr. Secord tell you, then or any other time after, why he wanted those documents shredded?

NAPIER: No.

* * *

Affidavit

During my April 10 testimony, I described an incident involving the transportation of documents at Richard Secord's direction from the offices of Stanford Technology Trading Group International to the Embassy Suites Hotel in Tysons Corner, Va., where Mr. Secord was meeting with his attorney. I also described some shredding activity which occurred at the Stanford offices. Using my best recollection at the time, I estimated that these events occurred in December.

On April 13, 1987, I testified before the grand jury.

On April 22, 1987, during an interview with members of the independent counsel's staff, I was shown, for the first time, a copy of an American Express Card receipt from the Embassy Suites Hotel in Tysons Corner. I recognized the receipt as the one I signed when I reserved and paid for the room later used by Mr. Secord for the meeting to which I brought the documents. The receipt was dated November 26, 1986, and it remains in the custody of the independent counsel.

Upon seeing the receipt, and in light of the investigators' focus upon pinpointing the dates involved, I invested considerable effort in an attempt to reconstruct these events and identify the dates more precisely.

It has been my belief that the shredding occurred prior to the trip to the Embassy Suites Hotel, and it is my present recollection that the shredding took place during the week of November 17, probably the 19th through the 21st. I informed the independent counsel of this information on April 27, and my counsel notified counsel for the Senate and House committees by letter dated April 29. There are several events which can be fixed in time, in addition to the Embassy Suites incident, which assist me in identifying these dates:

(a) I recall typing notes for Mr. Secord's use in a meeting with Oliver North on November 18 regarding the President's televised speech on November 19.

(b) The shredding could not have taken place on November 25 or 26, as Mr. Secord was out of the office on those days.

(c) On the date that I was directed to shred my old stenographer's notebooks, I decided that since the task of shredding individual pages was so time consuming, and since the notebooks contained so little information, I would take them home and burn them in the fireplace. I recall accomplishing this over a weekend.

(d) On or about November 28, I learned from a television news broadcast that Oliver North had been barred from the White House due to concerns that he had allegedly destroyed documents. I specifically recall that the shredding at Stanford had already occurred by the time I received that information.

The information above is drawn from my own recollection of these events. I was able to identify the dates involved after I learned the specific information about the date of the Embassy Suites Hotel incident during my interview with the independent counsel, and subsequently, I worked with a calendar. I did not consult with Richard Secord or his attorney in connection with these matters.

Documents

Following are texts of selected documents, speeches, press conferences, and statements that figured in the Iran-contra affair. Texts are presented in the order they were made public. The style of the original or official copy—the spelling, capitalization, and punctuation—has been retained. Use of *sic* in the original text has been set roman within brackets: [sic]. Where *sic* has been added, it appears in italics: [*sic*]. Excerpts from testimony of witnesses who appeared before congressional committees precede this documents section. *(Testimony, p. C-1)*

REAGAN ADDRESS ON IRAN ARMS SALES

Following is the text of President Reagan's November 13, 1986, address on U.S. shipments of arms to Iran:

Good evening. I know you have been reading, seeing, and hearing a lot of stories the past several days attributed to Danish sailors, unnamed observers at Italian ports and Spanish harbors, and especially unnamed government officials of my administration. Well, now you are going to hear the facts from a White House source, and you know my name.

Secret Discussions with Iran - 1

I wanted this time to talk with you about an extremely sensitive and profoundly important matter of foreign policy. For 18 months now we have had under way a secret diplomatic initiative to Iran. That initiative was undertaken for the simplest and best of reasons—to renew a relationship with the nation of Iran, to bring an honorable end to the bloody six-year war between Iran and Iraq, to eliminate state-sponsored terrorism and subversion, and to effect the safe return of all hostages.

Without Iran's cooperation, we cannot bring an end to the Persian Gulf war; without Iran's concurrence, there can be no enduring peace in the Middle East.

Getting to the Facts

For 10 days now, the American and world press have been full of reports and rumors about this initiative and these objectives.

Now, my fellow Americans, there is an old saying that nothing spreads so quickly as a rumor. So I thought it was time to speak with you directly—to tell you firsthand about our dealings with Iran. As Will Rogers once said, "Rumor travels faster, but it don't stay put as long as truth." So let's get to the facts.

No Arms-for-Hostages Swap

The charge has been made that the United States has shipped weapons to Iran as ransom payment for the release of American hostages in Lebanon—that the United States undercut its allies and secretly violated American policy against trafficking with terrorists.

Those charges are utterly false.

The United States has not made concessions to those who hold our people captive in Lebanon. And we will not. The United States has not swapped boatloads or planeloads of American weapons for the return of American hostages. And we will not.

Other reports have surfaced alleging U.S. involvement. Reports of a sealift to Iran using Danish ships to carry American arms. Of vessels in Spanish ports being employed in secret U.S. arms shipments. Of Italian ports being used. Of the U.S. sending spare parts and weapons for combat aircraft. All these reports are quite exciting, but as far as we are concerned, not one of them is true.

Arms Shipments to Iran

During the course of our secret discussions, I authorized the transfer of small amounts of defensive weapons and spare parts for defensive systems to Iran. My purpose was to convince Tehran that our negotiators were acting with my authority, to send a signal that the United States was prepared to replace the animosity between us with a new relationship. These modest deliveries, taken together, could easily fit into a single cargo plane. They could not, taken together, affect the outcome of the six-year war between Iran and Iraq—nor could they affect in any way the military balance between the two countries.

Those with whom we were in contact took considerable risks and needed a signal of our serious intent if they were to carry on and broaden the dialogue.

Iran's Influence in Hostages' Release

At the same time we undertook this initiative, we made clear that Iran must oppose all forms of international terrorism as a condition of progress in our relationship. The most significant step which Iran could take, we indicated, would be to use its influence in Lebanon to secure the release of all hostages held there.

Some progress has already been made. Since U.S. government contact began with Iran, there's been no evidence of Iranian government complicity in acts of terrorism against the United States. Hostages have come home—and we welcome the efforts that the government of Iran has taken in the past and is currently undertaking.

Strategic Importance of Iran

But why, you might ask, is any relationship with Iran important to the United States?

Iran encompasses some of the most critical geography in the world. It lies between the Soviet Union and access to the warm waters of the Indian Ocean. Geography explains why the Soviet Union has sent an army into Afghanistan to dominate that country and, if they could, Iran and Pakistan.

Iran's geography gives it a critical position from which adversaries could interfere with oil flows from the Arab states that border the Persian Gulf. Apart from geography, Iran's oil deposits are important to the long-term health of the world economy.

For these reasons, it is in our national interest to watch for changes within Iran that might offer hope for an improved relationship. Until last year, there was little to justify that hope.

No Need for Permanent Conflict

Indeed, we have bitter and enduring disagreements that persist today. At the heart of our quarrel has been Iran's past sponsorship of international terrorism. Iranian policy has been devoted to expelling all Western influence from the Middle East. We cannot abide that, because our interests in the Middle East are vital. At the same time, we seek no territory or special position in Iran. The Iranian revolution is a fact of history, but between American and Iranian basic national interests there need be no permanent conflict.

Since 1983, various countries have made overtures to stimulate direct contact between the United States and Iran. European, Near East, and Far East countries have attempted to serve as intermediaries. Despite a U.S. willingness to proceed, none of these overtures bore fruit.

With this history in mind, we were receptive last year when we were alerted to the possibility of establishing a direct dialogue with Iranian officials.

U.S. Interest in Dialogue - 1

Now, let me repeat. America's longstanding goals in the region have been to help preserve Iran's independence from Soviet domination; to bring an honorable end to the bloody Iran-Iraq war; to halt the export of subversion and terrorism in the region. A major impediment to those goals has been an absence of dialogue, a cutoff in communication between us.

It's because of Iran's strategic importance and its influence in the Islamic world that we chose to probe for a better relationship between our countries.

Secret Discussions with Iran - 2

Our discussions continued into the spring of this year. Based upon the progress we felt we had made, we sought to raise the diplomatic level of contacts. A meeting was arranged in Tehran. I then asked my former national security adviser, Robert [C.] McFarlane, to undertake a secret mission and gave him explicit instructions. I asked him to go to Iran to open a dialogue, making stark and clear our basic objectives and disagreements.

The four days of talks were conducted in a civil fashion, and American personnel were not mistreated. Since then, the dialogue has continued and step-by-step progress continues to be made.

U.S. Interest in Dialogue - 2

Let me repeat: Our interests are clearly served by opening a dialogue with Iran and thereby helping to end the Iran-Iraq war.

That war has dragged on for more than six years, with no prospect of a negotiated settlement. The slaughter on both sides has been enormous; and the adverse economic and political consequences for that vital region of the world have been growing. We sought to establish communication with both sides in that senseless struggle, so that we could assist in bringing about a ceasefire and, eventually, a settlement. We have sought to be evenhanded by working with both sides and with other interested nations to prevent a widening of the war.

This sensitive undertaking has entailed great risk for those involved. There is no question but that we could never have begun or continued this dialogue had the initiative been disclosed earlier. Due to the publicity of the past week, the entire initiative is very much at risk today.

Precedent for Secret Diplomacy

There is ample precedent in our history for this kind of secret diplomacy. In 1971, then-President Nixon sent his national security adviser on a secret mission to China. In that case, as today, there was a basic requirement for discretion and for a sensitivity to the situation in the nation we were attempting to engage.

Danger of False Rumors

Since the welcome return of former hostage David [P.] Jacobsen, there has been unprecedented speculation and countless reports that have not only been wrong, but have been potentially dangerous to the hostages and destructive of the opportunity before us. The efforts of courageous people like Terry Waite have been jeopardized. So extensive have been the false rumors and erroneous reports that the risks of remaining silent now exceed the risks of speaking out. And that's why I decided to address you tonight.

It's been widely reported, for example, that the Congress, as well as top Executive Branch officials, were circumvented. Although the efforts we undertook were highly sensitive and involvement of government officials was limited to those with a strict need to know, all appropriate Cabinet Officers were fully consulted. The actions I authorized were and continue to be in full compliance with Federal law. And the relevant committees of Congress are being and will be fully informed.

No Tilt toward Iran

Another charge is that we have tilted toward Iran in the Gulf war. This, too, is unfounded. We have consistently condemned the violence on both sides. We have consistently sought a negotiated settlement that preserves the territorial integrity of both nations. The overtures we've made to the government of Iran have not been a shift to supporting one side over the other. Rather, it has been a diplomatic initiative to gain some degree of access and influence within Iran—as well as Iraq—and to bring about an honorable end to that bloody conflict. It is in the interests of all parties in the Gulf region to end that war as soon as possible.

'No Concessions' Policy Intact

To summarize, our government has a firm policy not to capitulate to terrorist demands. That "no concessions" policy remains in force—in spite of the wildly speculative and false stories about arms for hostages and alleged ransom payments. We did not—repeat—did not trade weapons or anything else for hostages—nor will we. Those who think that we have "gone soft" on terrorism should take up the question with [Libyan leader] Colonel Gadhafi [Muammar el-Qaddafi].

We have not, nor will we, capitulate to terrorists. We will, however, get on with advancing the vital interests of our great nation—in spite of terrorists and radicals who seek to sabotage our efforts and immobilize the United States.

Our goals have been, and remain:
- to restore a relationship with Iran,
- to bring an honorable end to the war in the Gulf,
- to bring a halt to state-supported terror in the Middle East,

• and finally, to effect the safe return of all hostages from Lebanon.

As President, I've always operated on the belief that, given the facts, the American people will make the right decision. I believe that to be true now.

I cannot guarantee the outcome. But, as in the past, I ask for your support because I believe you share the hope for peace in the Middle East, for freedom for all hostages, and for a world free of terrorism. Certainly there are risks in this pursuit but there are greater risks if we do not persevere.

It will take patience and understanding; it will take continued resistance to those who commit terrorist acts; and it will take cooperation with all who seek to rid the world of this scourge.

Thank you and God bless you.

REAGAN'S NOVEMBER PRESS CONFERENCE

Following are excerpts from the text of President Reagan's November 19, 1986, press conference, followed by the text of a statement by the president issued shortly after the press conference:

PRESIDENT REAGAN: Good evening. I have a few words here before I take your questions—some brief remarks.

Secret Initiative to Iran

Eighteen months ago, as I said last Thursday, this administration began a secret initiative to the Islamic Republic of Iran. Our purposes were fourfold: to replace a relationship of total hostility with something better, to bring a negotiated end to the Iran-Iraq war, and to bring an end to terrorism and to effect the release of our hostages.

We knew this undertaking involved great risks, especially for our people and for the Iranian officials with whom we dealt. That is why the information was restricted to appropriate Cabinet officers and those officials with an absolute need to know. This undertaking was a matter of considerable debate within administration circles. Our policy objectives were never in dispute. There were differences on how best to proceed.

Waiver of Arms Embargo

The principal issue in contention was whether we should make isolated and limited exceptions to our arms embargo as a signal of our serious intent. Several top advisers opposed the sale of even a modest shipment of defensive weapons and spare parts to Iran. Others felt no progress could be made without this sale. I weighed their views. I considered the risks of failure and the rewards of success, and I decided to proceed, and the responsibility for the decision and the operation is mine and mine alone.

As Mr. Lincoln said of another presidential decision, "If it turns out right, the criticism will not matter. If it turns out wrong, 10 angels swearing I was right will make no difference."

Bringing Iran Back - 1

I understand this decision is deeply controversial and some profoundly disagree with what was done. Even some who support our secret initiative believe it was a mistake to send any weapons to Iran. I understand and I respect those views, but I deeply believe in the correctness of my decision. I was convinced then and I am convinced now that while the risks were great, so, too, was the potential reward. Bringing Iran back into the community of responsible nations, ending its participation in political terror, bringing an end to that terrible war, and bringing our hostages home— these are the causes that justify taking risks.

Risks Cannot Impede Action

In foreign policy the presence of risks alone cannot be reason enough not to act. There were risks when we liberated Grenada, when we went into Lebanon, when we aided the Philippines and when we acted against Libya, so we'll continue our efforts. However, to eliminate the widespread but mistaken perception that we have been exchanging arms for hostages, I have directed that no further sales of arms of any kind be sent to Iran. I have further directed that all information relating to our initiative be provided to the appropriate members of Congress. There may be some questions which for reasons of national security or to protect the safety of the hostages I will be unable to answer publicly. But again, all information will be provided to the appropriate members of Congress.

And now, I'll take your questions. Helen?

Damage to Credibility - 1

Q: Mr. President, in the recent past, there was an administration whose byword was: "Watch what we do, not what we say." How would you assess the credibility of your own administration in the light of the prolonged deception of Congress and the public in terms of your secret dealings with Iran, the disinformation, the trading of [convicted Soviet spy Gennadi F.] Zakharov for [American newsman Nicholas S.] Daniloff? And I'd like to follow up.

P: Well, Helen, let me take the last one first. I know you— some persist in saying that we traded Zakharov for Daniloff. We did not. We said that we would have no dealings with the Soviet Union, even on going to Iceland, until Daniloff was in our hands.

But to bring it up to date on this, there was no deception intended by us. There was the knowledge that we were embarking on something that could be of great risk to the people we were talking to, great risk to our hostages. And, therefore, we had to have it limited to only the barest number of people that had to know. I was not breaking any law in doing that. It is provided for me to do that. At the same time I have the right under the law to defer reporting to Congress, to the proper Congressional committees, on an action and defer it until such time as I believe it can safely be done with no risk to others.

And that's why I have ordered in this coming week the proper committees will be briefed on this. And we—there are still some parts of this that we cannot go public with because it will bring to risk and danger people that are held and people that we have been negotiating with. We were not negotiating government to government. We were negotiating with certain individuals within that country.

Observing Arms Embargo - 1

Q: You don't think your credibility has been damaged? And are you prepared now to disavow the finding which let you make end runs around the Iranian arms embargo? Are you going to tear it up?

P: No. As I say, I have—we are going to observe that embargo and it's part of the same reason, that as I've said, we were doing this in the first place. And that is to see, among the other issues involved, if we can help bring about peace between those two countries—a peace without victory to either one or defeat and that will recognize the territorial integrity of both. And this is something that all of our allies are seeking also.

But I think the people understand that sometimes you have to keep a secret in order to save human lives and to succeed in the mission, just as we went into Grenada without prior notice, because then we would have put to risk all of those men who were going to hit the beach.

Yes.

Shultz's Resignation

Q: Mr. President, has Secretary [of State George P.] Shultz discussed his resignation with you? Have you agreed to accept it or have you asked him to stay on?

P: Mike, he has never suggested to me in our meetings that—

resignation and, in fact, he has made it plain that he will stay as long as I want him, and I want him. So, there's never been any discussion there. He knows that I want him to stay and he has in advance said that he wants to. There's been no talk of resignation.

Q: If I may follow up, sir. Has he made his staying conditioned on your agreeing not to send further arms to Iran?

P: No. There have been no conditions. As I say, we didn't discuss that. And, as I've said now, there is no need to go further with this. We—the mission was served that made us waive temporarily that for that really minuscule amount of spare parts and defensive weapons.

Chris?

Arms-for-Hostages Swap - 1

Q: Mr. President, you have stated flatly and you stated flatly again tonight that you did not trade weapons for hostages. And yet the record shows that every time an American hostage was released—last September, this July and again just this very month—there had been a major shipment of arms just before that. Are we all to believe that was just a coincidence?

P: Chris, the only thing I know about major shipments of arms—as I've said, everything that we sold them could be put in one cargo plane and there would be plenty of room left over. Now, if there were major shipments—and we know this has been going on—there have been other countries that have been dealing in arms with Iran. There have been also private merchants of such things that have been doing the same thing. Now, I've seen the stories about a Danish tramp steamer and Danish sailors' union officials talking about their ships taking various supplies to Iran. I didn't know anything about that until I saw the press on it, because we certainly never had any contact with anything of the kind. And, so there's—it's just that we did something for a particular mission, that there was a risk entailed, and Iran held no hostages. Iran did not kidnap anyone, to our knowledge, and the fact that part of the operation was that we knew, however, that the kidnappers of our hostages did have some kind of relationship in which Iran could at times influence them—not always—but could influence them. And so three of our hostages came home.

U.S. Approval of Israeli Shipments - 1

Q: But on the—if I may follow up, sir—on that first point your own Chief of Staff, Mr. [Donald T.] Regan, has said that the U.S. condoned Israeli shipments of arms to Iran and aren't you, in effect, sending the very same message you always said you didn't want to send? Aren't you saying to terrorists either you or your state sponsor—which in this case was Iran—can gain from the holding of hostages?

P: Because I don't see where the kidnappers or the hostage holders gained anything. They didn't get anything. They let the hostages go. Now, whatever is the pressure that brought that about, I'm just grateful to it for the fact that we got them. As a matter of fact, if there had not been so much publicity, we would have had two more that we were expecting.

Sam.

Observing Arms Embargo - 2

Q: Mr. President, when you had the arms embargo on, you were asking other nations, our allies particularly, to observe it—publicly. But at the same time privately, you concede you were authorizing a breaking of that embargo by the United States. How can you justify this duplicity?

P: I don't think it was duplicity, and as I say, the so-called "violation" did not in any way alter the balance, military balance, between the two countries. But what we were aiming for, I think, made it worthwhile, and this was a waiver of our own embargo. The embargo still stays now and for the future. But the causes that I outlined here in my opening statement, first of all, to try and establish a relationship with a country that is of great strategic importance to peace and everything else in the Middle East. At the same time also, to strike a blow against terrorism and to get our

hostages back, as we did, and to—this particular thing was, we felt necessary in order to make the contacts that we made, and that could lead to better relations with us. And there was a fourth item, also, as I pointed out.

Damage to Credibility - 2

Q: Sir, if I may, the polls show that a lot of American people just simply don't believe you. But the one thing that you've had going for you more than anything else in your presidency, your credibility, has been severely damaged. Can you repair it? What does it mean for the rest of your presidency?

P: Well, I imagine I'm the only one around who wants to repair it, and I didn't do—have anything to do with damaging it. Bill.

Notification to Congress

Q: Mr. President, you say that the equipment which was shipped didn't alter the military balance. Yet, several things—we understand that there were 1,000 TOW anti-tank missiles shipped by the U.S. The U.S. apparently condoned shipments by Israel and other nations of other quantities of arms as an ancillary part of this deal—not directly connected, but had to condone it, or the shipments could not have gone forward, sir.

So how can you say that it cannot alter the military balance, and how can you say, sir, that it didn't break the law, when the National Security Act of 1977 plainly talks about timely notification of Congress and also, sir, stipulates that if the national security required secrecy, the President is still required to advise the leadership and the chairman of the Intelligence committees?

P: Bill, everything you've said here is based on a supposition that is false. We did not condone, and do not condone the shipment of arms from other countries. And what was the other point that you made here—

Q: They were the anti-tank missiles, sir.

P: Oh, no, about the—that it didn't—no, that it did violate the—or that did violate the law. No, as I said, the President, believe it or not, does have the power if, in his belief, national security can be served, to waive the provisions of that law as well as to defer the notification of the Congress on this.

Effect on Iran-Iraq War

Q: Is it possible that the Iraqis, sir, might think that 1,000 anti-tank missiles was enough to alter the balance of that war?

P: This is a purely defensive weapon—it is a shoulder-carried weapon and we don't think that in this defensive thing—we didn't add to any offensive power on the part of Iran. We know that Iraq has already announced that they would be willing to settle the conflict, as we've said, with no winners or losers. And that, and the other parts, happened to be spare parts for an anti-aircraft Hawk battery. And, as I say, all of those weapons could be very easily carried in one mission.

Now—I think—Charles.

U.S. Approval of Israeli Shipments - 2

Q: Mr. President, I don't think it's still clear just what Israel's role was in this—the questions that have been asked about a condoned shipment. We do understand that the Israelis sent a shipment in 1985 and there were also reports that it was the Israelis that contacted your administration and suggested that you make contact with Iran. Could you explain what the Israeli role was here?

P: No, because we, as I say, have had nothing to do with other countries or their shipment of arms or doing what they're doing. And, no—as a matter of fact, the first idea about the need to restore relations between Iran and the United States or the Western world, for that matter, actually began before our administration was here. But from the very first, if you look down the road at what could happen and perhaps a change of government there—that it was absolutely vital for the Western world and to the hope for peace in the Middle East and all, for us to be trying to establish this relationship. And we worked to—it started about 18 months ago, really, as we began to find out—some individuals that it might be possible for us to deal with, and who also were looking at the probability of a further accident.

Trude?

Presence of Iranian Moderates

Q: Can I follow up please, if I may, on that? The contacts that you're suggesting are with moderates in the Iranian government and in the Iranian system. Barry Goldwater tonight said in his judgment there are no moderates in Iran. I don't mean to suggest that there may not be, but how did you know that you were reaching the moderates and how do you define a moderate in that kind of a government?

P: Well, again, you're asking questions that I cannot get into with regard to the answers. But believe me, we had information that led us to believe that there is—there are factions within Iran and many of them with an eye toward the fact that they think sooner, rather than later, there is going to be a change in the government there and there is great dissatisfaction among the people in Iran. . . .

U.S. Approval of Israeli Shipments - 3

Q: Mr. President, going back over your answers tonight about the arms shipments and the numbers of them, are you telling us tonight that the only shipments with which we were involved were the one or two that followed your January 17th finding and that, whatever your aides have said on background or on the record, there are no other shipments with which the U.S. condoned?

P: That's right. I'm saying nothing but the missiles that we sold—and remember, there are too many people that are saying "gave." They bought them.

Andrea?

Q: Mr. President, to follow up on that, we've been told by the Chief of Staff, Donald Regan, that we condoned, this government condoned an Israeli shipment in September of 1985, shortly before the release of hostage Benjamin Weir. That was four months before your intelligence finding on January 17th that you say gave you the legal authority not to notify Congress. Can you clear that up why we were not—why this government was not in violation of its arms embargo and of the notification to Congress for having condoned American-made weapons shipped to Iran in September of 1985?

P: No, that—I've never heard Mr. Regan say that and I'll ask him about that, because we believe in the embargo and, as I say, we waived it for a specific purpose, in fact, with four goals in mind.

Yes.

Canceling Intelligence Finding

Q: Can I just follow up on that for a second, sir, because what is unclear to I think many people in the American public is why, if you are saying tonight that there will be no further arms shipments to Iran, why you won't cancel the January 17th intelligence finding so that you can put to rest any suggestion that you might again, without notification and in complete secrecy and perhaps with the objection of some of your Cabinet members, continue to ship weapons if you think that it is necessary?

P: No. This—I have no intention of doing that, but at the same time, we are hopeful that we're going to be able to continue our meetings with these people, these individuals.

Q: But you won't cancel the intelligence finding?

P: I don't know whether it's called for or whether I have to wait until we've reported to Congress and all. I don't know just what the technicality legally is on that.

Giving Weapons to Khomeini

Q: Yes, Mr. President. Why do you think, its strategic position notwithstanding, the American people would ever support weap-ons to the Ayatollah Khomeini?

P: We weren't giving them to the Ayatollah Khomeini. The—it's a strange situation. As I say, we were dealing with individuals and we believe that those—and some of those individuals are in government, in positions in government. But it was not a meeting officially of the United States' head of state and the Iranian head of state. But these people, we believed, and their closeness to the Iran military was such that this was necessary to let them know, number one, that we were serious and sincere in our effort about good relations and also that they were dealing with the head of government over here—that this wasn't something coming out of some agency or bureau—that I was behind it.

Arm Qaddafi and Bomb Khomeini?

Q: Well, sir, if that's the case, some have asked that if Libya occupied as strategic a position as Iran did, would you then arm [Libyan leader Muammar el-] Qaddafi and bomb Khomeini?

P: I know that's a—believe me, that's about as hypothetical a question as anyone could imagine. The situations are quite different.

Arms-for-Hostages Swap - 2

Q: Mr. President, you said that you were not swapping—or you did not think you were swapping arms for hostages. But did it ever occur to you or did it never occur to you that certainly the Iranians would see it that way and that they might take it as an inducement to take more hostages, especially in light of the fact that they've released three but taken three more?

P: No—to the best of our knowledge, Iran does not own or have authority over the Hezbollah. They cannot order them to do something. It is apparent that they evidently have either some persuasion and they don't always succeed, but they can somepersuade or pressure the Hezbollah into doing what they did in this instance. And, as I say, the Iranian government had no hostages and they bought a shipment from us and we, in turn—I might as well tell you—that we, in turn, had said when they wanted to kind of know our position and whether we were trustworthy and all of this, we told them that we were—we did not want to do business with any nation that openly backed terrorism. And they gave us information that they did not and they said also that they had some evidence that there had been a lessening of this on the part of—Khomeini and the government and that they'd made some progress. As a matter of fact, some individuals associated with terrorist acts had been put in prison there. And so that was when we said well, there's a very easy way for you to verify that if that's the way you feel, and they're being held hostage in Lebanon.

Q: Well, if I can follow up, if your arms shipments had no effect on the release of the hostages then how do you explain the release of the hostages at the same time that the shipments were coming in?

P: No. I said that at the time I said to them that there was something they could do to show their sincerity and if they really meant it that they were not in favor of backing terrorists, they could begin by releasing our hostages. And, as a matter of fact, I believe and have reason to believe, that we would have had all five of them by this last weekend, had it not been for the attendant confusion that arose here in the reporting room.

You don't have your red mittens on.

Leak of Secret Initiative

Q: On that point, you said earlier, and you said just now again that, but for the publicity, two other hostages would have been returned home by now. As you know, the publicity began in a Syrian-backed, pro-Syrian magazine—

P: Yes.

Q: —in Lebanon. My question is, therefore, are you suggesting that someone who was a party to this sabotaged it by deliberately leaking that original report?

P: To our best information, the leak came from a person in government in Iran and not one of the people that we were dealing with, someone that would be more hostile to us. And that individual gave the story to the magazine, and the magazine then printed the story there in Beirut.

U.S. Policy toward Nicaragua

Q: Mr. President, there has been an obvious change in policy towards Iran—from refusing to deal with a terrorist state, to even sending weapons as a gesture of good will. Would you consider, in the name of the same geopolitical interest that you invoked with Iran, changing your policy towards Nicaragua?

P: No, and I believe that I've answered that question, I think, more than once here—that no, we still hold to our position, and Iran officially is still on our list of nations that have been supporting terrorism. But I'm talking about the people that we were doing business with, and they gave us indication and evidence that that policy was changing. And so, as I said, to give them more prestige and muscle there, where they were, we made this sale.

Retaining Ties with Nicaragua

Q: Then, Mr. President, would you consider breaking diplomatic relations with Nicaragua to increase the pressure on the Sandinista government?

P: No, we have not thought of that, and we still believe very much in supporting the contras, because we believe in the contras' cause. The contras have made it plain that they—all they seek is to be able to put enough pressure on the Sandinista government for that government to negotiate with them and the people of Nicaragua for the kind of government that they altogether had promised when they were fighting the revolution against the Somoza dictatorship. And it was the Sandinistas who, as communist groups usually do, simply when the revolution was over, they did everything they could to get rid of their fellow revolutionaries, and they seized power and created a totalitarian communist state.

Now, the Sandinista, or the contras have never proposed overthrowing the government. They have repeatedly offered and said, we simply want to be able to negotiate and get—have a chance to have the government installed that we had promised the Organization of American States we were fighting for. So, I think we continue to help them, but we believe that there is a value in maintaining relations. It gives us a listening post in Nicaragua.

President on the Defensive

Q: Mr. President, there is a mood in Washington tonight of a President who is very much beleaguered, very much on the defensive. Why don't you seize the offensive by giving your Secretary of State a vote of confidence declaring that all future covert activities will have his support and by shaking up the National Security Council in such a way as to satisfy the concerns in Congress that [it] has been running a paramilitary operation out of the basement of the White House in defiance of the State Department and the Congress?

P: The State Department and the Secretary of State was involved, the Director of the CIA was involved in what we were doing and, as I said before, there are certain laws in which, for certain actions, I would not have been able to keep them a secret as they were. But these people you've mentioned have been involved—do know what was going on. And I don't see that the action that you've suggested has called for it, but what you've disappointed me the most in is suggesting that I sound defensive up here. I've just been trying to answer all of your questions as well as I can, and I don't feel that I have anything to defend about at all. With the circumstances the way they were, the decision I made I still believe was the correct decision and I believe that we achieved some portion of our goals.

Release of Remaining Hostages

Q: Mr. President do you believe that any of the additional hostages will be released?

P: I have to believe that.

Overthrow of Khomeini

Q: And, during any of these discussions with your administration, was there ever any hint or suggestion that these weapons might be used to topple the Ayatollah?

P: No, and I don't see in any way how that could be with the particular things that we were using. I don't see where the Ayatollah could be a logical target for an anti-aircraft missile or even for a TOW missile, for that matter.

Observing Arms Embargo - 3

Q: Mr. President, you made an exception for the arms embargo when you thought it was in the U.S. interest to do so. Why shouldn't other nations ship weapons to Iran when they think it's in their interests?

P: Well, I would like to see the indication as to how it could be in their interest. I know that there are other nations that feel as we do that the Western world should be trying to find an avenue to get Iran back where it once was, and that is in the family of democratic nations and the family of nations that want peace in the Middle East and so forth.

Bringing Iran Back - 2

Q: Mr. President, if I may follow up—how does shipping weapons to Iran help bring them back into the community of nations? You've acknowledged that you were dealing with only a small portion of the government.

P: I was talking of strengthening a particular group who needed the prestige that that could give them who needed that—well, that bargaining power, themselves, within their own ranks. Jerry?

Nature of TOW Weapon

Q: Mr. President, I believe you may have been slightly in error in describing a TOW as a shoulder-mounted weapon. It's a ground-to-ground weapon—Red-eye is the shoulder weapon, but that's beside the point. TOW—TOWs are used to destroy tanks.

P: Yes, I know, Jerry, I know it's a—

Q: I don't think it's fired from your shoulder.

P: Well, now—(laughter)—I have—if I have been misinformed, then I will yield on that, but it was my understanding that that is a man-carried weapon, and we have a number of other shoulder-borne weapons.

Q: I did have a question, though. (Laughter.)

P: You mean that wasn't a question? (Laughter.)

Q: No, sir, I thought I knew what a TOW was.

Admit Mistake Was Made

I just wanted to ask you, what would be wrong at this stage of the game, since everything seems to have gone wrong that could possibly go wrong, like the Murphy Law, the Reagan Law, the O'Leary Law, this week. What would be wrong in saying that a mistake was made on a very high-risk gamble and that—so that you can get on with the next two years?

P: Because I don't think a mistake was made. It was a high-risk gamble, and it was a gamble that, as I've said, I believe the circumstances warranted. And I don't see that it has been a fiasco or a great failure of any kind. We still have those contacts, we still have made some ground, we got our hostages back—three of them. And so I think that what we did was right, and we're going to continue on this path....

THE PRESS: Thank you.

Statement by the President

There may be some misunderstanding of one of my answers tonight. There was a third country involved in our secret project with Iran. But taking this into account, all of the shipments of the token amounts of defensive arms and parts that I have authorized or condoned taken in total could be placed aboard a single cargo aircraft. This includes all shipments by the United States or any third country. Any other shipments by third countries were not authorized by the U.S. government.

REAGAN, MEESE ON IRAN-CONTRA ARMS

Following is the text of the November 25, 1986, statements by President Reagan and Attorney General Edwin Meese III regarding the U.S. role in arms shipments to Iran and the transfer of funds to the contras. The statements were made before reporters, and a forty-minute question-and-answer session with Meese followed the attorney general's statement.

President Reagan's Statement

PRESIDENT REAGAN: Last Friday, after becoming concerned whether my national security apparatus had provided me with a security, or a complete factual record with respect to the implementation of my policy toward Iran, I directed the Attorney General to undertake a review of this matter over the weekend and report to me on Monday. And yesterday, Secretary Meese provided me and the White House Chief of Staff with a report on his preliminary findings. And this report led me to conclude that I was not fully informed on the nature of one of the activities undertaken in connection with this initiative. This action raises serious questions of propriety.

I've just met with my National Security advisers and Congressional leaders to inform them of the actions that I'm taking today. Determination of the full details of this action will require further review and investigation by the Department of Justice.

Looking to the future, I will appoint a special review board to conduct a comprehensive review of the role and procedures of the National Security Council [NSC] staff in the conduct of foreign and national security policy.

I anticipate receiving the reports from the Attorney General and the special review board at the earliest possible date. Upon the completion of these reports, I will share their findings and conclusions with the Congress and the American people.

Although not directly involved, Vice Admiral John [M.] Poindexter has asked to be relieved of his assignment as Assistant to the President for National Security Affairs and to return to another assignment in the Navy. Lieutenant Colonel Oliver [L.] North has been relieved of his duties on the National Security Council staff.

I am deeply troubled that the implementation of a policy aimed at resolving a truly tragic situation in the Middle East has resulted in such controversy. As I've stated previously, I believe our policy goals toward Iran were well-founded. However, the information brought to my attention yesterday convinced me that in one aspect, implementation of that policy was seriously flawed.

While I cannot reverse what has happened, I'm initiating steps, including those I've announced today, to assure that the implementation of all future, foreign, and national security policy initiatives will proceed only in accordance with my authorization.

Over the past six years, we've realized many foreign policy goals. I believe we can yet achieve, and I intend to pursue, the objectives on which we all agree—a safer, more secure and stable world.

And now, I'm going to ask Attorney General Meese to brief you.

Q: What was the flaw?

Q: Do you still maintain you didn't make a mistake, Mr. President?

P: Hold it.

No Mistake Was Made

Q: Did you make a mistake in sending arms to Tehran, sir?

P: No, and I'm not taking any more questions, and—just a second, I'm going to ask Attorney General Meese to brief you on what we presently know of what he has found out.

Q: Is anyone else going to be let go, sir?

Q: Can you tell us—did Secretary [of State George P.] Shultz—

Q: Is anyone else going to be let go? There have been calls for—

P: No one was let go; they chose to go.

Q: What about Secretary Shultz, Mr. President?

Q: Is Shultz going to stay, sir?

Q: How about Secretary Shultz and Mr. Regan [Chief of Staff Donald T. Regan], sir?

Q: What about Secretary Shultz, sir?

Q: Can you tell us if Secretary Shultz is going to stay?

Q: Can you give Secretary Shultz a vote of confidence if you feel that way?

P: May I give you Attorney General Meese?

Q: And who is going to run National Security?

Q: What about Shultz, sir?

Q: Why won't you say what the flaw is?

ATTORNEY GENERAL MEESE: That's what I'm going to say—what it's all about.

Q: Why can't he?

MEESE: Why don't I tell you what is the situation and then I'll take your questions.

Attorney General Meese's Statement

On Friday afternoon—or Friday at noon, the President asked me to look into and bring together the facts concerning the—particularly the implementation of the strategic initiative in Iran and more precisely, anything pertaining to the transfer of arms. Over the weekend this inquiry was conducted. Yesterday evening I reported to the President. We continued our inquiry and this morning the President directed that we make this information immediately available to the Congress and to the public through this medium this noon.

Let me say that all of the information is not yet in. We are still continuing our inquiry. But he did want me to make available immediately what we know at the present time.

What is involved is that in the course of the arms transfers, which involved the United States providing the arms to Israel and Israel in turn transferring the arms—in effect, selling the arms to representatives of Iran. Certain monies which were received in the transaction between representatives of Israel and representatives of Iran were taken and made available to the forces in Central America which are opposing the Sandinista government there.

In essence, the way in which the transactions occurred was that a certain amount of money was negotiated by representatives outside of the United States with Iran for arms. This amount of money was then transferred to representatives as best we know that can be described as representatives of Israel. They, in turn, transferred to the CIA [Central Intelligence Agency], which was the agent for the United States government under a finding prepared by the President—signed by the President in January of 1986. And, incidentally, all of these transactions that I am referring to took place between January of 1986 and the present time. They transferred to the CIA the exact amount of the money that was owed to the United States government for the weapons that were involved plus any costs of transportation that might be involved. This money was then repaid by the CIA to the Department of Defense under the normal procedures and all governmental funds and all governmental property was accounted for and statements of that have been verified by us up to the present time.

The money—the difference between the money owed to the United States government and the money received from representatives of Iran was then deposited in bank accounts which were under the control of representatives of the forces in Central America.

Meese Press Conference

Amount of Money Diverted

Q: How much money, Sir? How much involved?

MEESE: We don't know the exact amount, yet. Our estimate is that it is somewhere between $10 [million] and $30 million.

Discovery of Diversion - 1

Q: How did it come to your attention?

MEESE: In the course of a thorough review of a number of intercepts, and other materials, this—the hint of a possibility that there was some monies being made available for some other purpose came to our attention, and then we pursued that with the individuals involved.

Q: Why wasn't the President—why wasn't the President told?

MEESE: The President was told as soon as we found out about it.

Q: And he knew nothing about it?

MEESE: The President knew nothing about it until I reported it to him. I alerted him yesterday morning that we still had some more work to do, and then I gave him the detail that we had yesterday afternoon.

Q: Attorney General Meese—

MEESE: One at a time—right here.

Q: Is this what you were looking for when you began? Or is this just something that turned up in the course of your weekend investigation?

MEESE: This turned up in the course of the investigation. The first thing that triggered, if you will, an inquiry, was the fact that as people prepared their testimony—because this had been done in a rather compartmentalized way—as people prepared their testimony for the Hill on Friday, there were certain things where facts—there appeared to be more facts out there than we had already put together. And it was a matter, then, of the President requesting me to talk with everyone who had any participation at all, because one agency was doing one thing, another agency was doing another thing—there was very little paperwork—and to determine precisely what all of the facts were because he wanted to be sure that he had all of the information about anything that may have occurred in the course of this whole situation. That was—it was during the course of that inquiry that this information was found and then was followed out to the conclusions that I mentioned.

Okay?

Policy Management

Q: General Meese, can you tell us who is running national security policy? Can you clear up for the American people, is Secretary Shultz staying? Who is the new National Security Adviser? And what are you recommending in terms of possibly restructuring the White House Staff?

MEESE: In answer to your questions in order, at the present time, upon Admiral Poindexter actually leaving his post, Al [Alton G.] Keel [Jr.], his Deputy, will be the Acting Assistant to the President for National Security Affairs. The President has not yet selected a replacement, but he will do so as soon as possible. Secretary Shultz is remaining in his position as Secretary of State. That has not been a matter of conjecture, or discussion, or inquiry. And the third part of your question?

Q: Well, General Meese, will—

MEESE: Oh, what recommendations will we make?

We will make whatever recommendations for futher [sic] proceedings come out of it, but more particularly, the President will

be appointing a small commission which will look into the procedures and role of the NSC staff and will make specific recommendations to him as far as the process for the future.

Q: General Meese—

MEESE: Followup question, and then we'll get the rest.

Legal Opinion Given

Q: We've been told that the President was operating, from the beginning of this operation in June or July of 1985, on legal opinions, not written, but oral, from you. Now, one can ask, then, are you, at this point, sorry that you gave the advice that the NSC should do this operation overlooking the objections of State and Defense?

MEESE: The only—legal opinion that was involved had to do with the routine concurrence with the finding of January, 1986. That's the only legal opinion, or legal advice that was asked for, or that was given.

Q: General Meese?

Who Knew about Diversion? - 1

Q: General Meese, who in the NSC was aware that this extra amount of money was being transferred to the so-called "Contras" or under their control? Did Admiral Poindexter specifically know, who else knew, and did the CIA know? Was CIA Director [William J.] Casey aware of this?

MEESE: The only persons in the United States government that knew precisely about this, the only person, was Lieutenant Colonel North. Admiral Poindexter did know that something of this nature was occurring, but he did not look into it further.

Q: And what, if I could follow-up, sir, what about CIA Director Casey?

MEESE: CIA Director Casey, Secretary of State Shultz, Secretary of Defense [Caspar W.] Weinberger, myself, the other members in the NSC—none of us knew.

Poindexter Role - 1

Q: When you say that Poindexter knew, do you mean he approved of it?

MEESE: No. Admiral Poindexter knew generally that something of this nature was happening. He did not know the details.

Q: He did not try to stop it, however, though?

Q: When did he—

MEESE: He did not—

Q: He did not try to stop it, though?

MEESE: I don't know precisely when he learned it. He knew of it sometime during last year.

Q: But he didn't try to stop it, sir?

MEESE: He did not try to stop it.

Q: General Meese.

Iranian Arms Shipments - 1

Q: Let me ask you this. In the course of your investigation, did you satisfy yourself that you know exactly how many shipments of arms went from the United States or Israel to Iran, and exactly what they contained? There's quite a bit of controversy over that.

MEESE: We are fairly sure that we know of the shipments of arms, because we have some control. We know it was shipped out of DOD stocks. We will only know—we only know at this time what the United States participated in. We don't know of any other arms sales that may have been made, but we do know those that the United States participated in.

Israeli Shipments Approval - 1

Q: Well, let me just follow-up. Have you established in your investigation whether anyone in the United States government gave a wink, a nod, an accord, or any kind of approval for shipments which Israel or any other third country may have made?

MEESE: Well, all of the shipments that—in which the

United States' equipment was involved were made by—through Israel—were made by Israel.

Q: Was that legal? Was that legal?

MEESE: Yes.

Iranian Arms Shipments - 2

Q: Mr. Attorney General, do I understand, sir, that what you're reporting on this morning and what the President reported on this morning is a discovery of diversion of funds? The central questions that have been asked for the last three or four weeks about the propriety of shipment to—arms to Iran, about the U.S. arms embargo at the time, the questions that the Hill has been asking—you have, if I understand correctly, we have heard nothing new on those questions today. Is that correct?

MEESE: We have heard nothing new that hasn't been testified to essentially on the Hill. There may be—we may have more information than has been brought to light already. We've talked with Congress basically. I think Director Casey gave a pretty full exposition.

Legality of Diversion - 1

Q: But this today, the discovery and the announcement, rather, today, of the diversion of funds, we take it by Colonel North, that does not drive to any of those other questions. Did what Colonel North do, is that a crime? Will he be prosecuted?

MEESE: We are presently looking into the legal aspects of it as to whether there's any criminality involved. We're also looking precisely at his involvement and what he did, so that the conclusions as to whether there's any criminal acts involved is still under inquiry by us.

Q: General Meese—

Q: Isn't it at this time likely, even preferable from your point of view, that a special prosecutor be appointed to examine these questions? You're talking not only about the law about the Iranian transactions, but the Congressional strictures against the military aid to the Contras. Isn't it now time for a special prosecutor?

MEESE: No. If we find that there is any criminality, which as yet there have been no conclusions—and if we find that anyone who is a covered person under the Independent Counsel Act is involved, then that would be the time to request an independent counsel, as we would in any other matter.

Q: Mr. Meese, is the President angered by this?

Q: Is a grand jury to follow up—is a grand jury taking evidence on this?

MEESE: No. There is no grand jury at the present time.

Iran Policy Defended - 1

Q: —still saying it was not a mistake—the policy was not a mistake, General Meese?

MEESE: I think the policy, as the President said, to reestablish our relationship with Iran, to try to bring an end to the Iran-Iraqi war, to try to decrease the participation of Iran in terrorism in the Middle East, and to get our hostages back—all of these objectives—certainly were not mistake [sic].

Q: The way it was carried out led to this diversion of funds by not including the other agencies.

MEESE: It didn't lead to the diversion of funds. The funds were transferred and that's one of the things that has disturbed me and disturbed the President. That was not an inherent part of anything having to do with the policy itself. Instead, it was actually an aberration from the policy and from everything that had been described to the President and to the other members of the National Security Council.

Q: How did you discover this, sir?

Q: Perhaps he—

Q: How did you discover this? Did Colonel North—

MEESE: One question at a time.

Q: Did Colonel North give you testimony—

Q: —suggesting if Congress had been notified, don't you think it would have been unlikely for this to happen?

MEESE: No. I think exactly the same thing could well have happened, because this was something that was unknown to any of the officials that gave authorization for this in the first place.

Q: How did you discover it, sir?

MEESE: Yes?

Use of Diverted Funds

Q: Could you tell me what these funds were used for?

MEESE: I don't know. I don't know that anyone does. They were just provided to the Contras through this bank account and that was the end, so far as we know, of anyone in the United States government knowing anything about what happened to them.

Discovery of Diversion - 2

Q: How did you discover it, Mr. Attorney General?

MEESE: How did we discover it? In the course of a review of documents, we came across a reference to the possibility of differences in amount between the funds being paid by Iran and the amount of the actual weapons—that was one thing. And, secondly, there were some references to this in one particular document that we found. While it didn't reveal the whole situation, we then used that as the basis for proceeding further and discussing with one of the participants what this all meant and that's how this was discovered.

Q: When you talked to Colonel North over the weekend, did he admit that he had done this?

MEESE: I will talk about the facts. I think as far as anything that might possibly be involved in legal action as to who admitted what, I think it would not be appropriate for me to go into that.

How Money Was Diverted - 1

Q: One final follow up, then. How did Colonel North—let me put it this way—these transfers of monies, did they only go through one man—Colonel North? Were there no other people involved?

MEESE: No transfers of money went through anyone. Bank accounts were established, as best we know, by representatives of the forces in Central America. And this information was provided to representatives of the Israeli government and the funds—or representatives of Israel, I should say—and then these funds were put into the accounts. So far as we know at this stage, no American person actually handled any of the funds that went to the forces in Central America.

Q: —Israel deposited money to accounts that it had been asked to deposit the money to—Israel deposited money to accounts it had been asked—

MEESE: These are some of the details that we're still going into, because we haven't had a chance to interview everyone.

Q: You made the long march with the President—

NSC Role to be Examined

Q: General, have you made any finding regarding the use of the National Security Council staff as an operational wing of the government and that it would result in something like this?

MEESE: This is what the board or the commission that the President will set up will presumably be looking at. We will probably be making recommendations on this regard.

Q: Mr. Attorney General?

MEESE: Helen, you haven't talked yet.

Shultz Position - 1

Q: You made the long march with the President from California and there are many, many reports that his California friends and supporters do think there should be a real shake-up at the top. Yesterday, a number two man at the State Department really damaged the President's position in a way—publicly—by opposing it, differing and so forth. Do you think that Secretary Shultz has behaved in the proper style and should he stay on? And what do you think should happen? What's happening to the President?

MEESE: Well, Helen, I think you know that for the almost six years that I've been here I have never commented on any—on the conduct or tried to characterize the acts of any other member of the administration. I'm not going to change that now.

Q: Well, what is happening—

MEESE: I do think—I will say this. I think every member of the administration owes it to the President to stand shoulder-to-shoulder with him and support the policies that he has—the policy decisions he has made as well as to stand by him when something has happened which the President didn't know as in this case and where he has very courageously, I think, made it immediately available to the American public and to the Congress. And I intend to do that. Other people can speak for themselves.

Q: Mr. Meese, setting aside what the President didn't know until last night about the diversion of funds, you have the spectacle of the top members of this administration fighting one another like cats and dogs over policy and the President's credibility being damaged as a result. Have you done nothing to address that? Has anyone here addressed it?

MEESE: I think, again, this would involve commenting on other members of the administration, which I won't do. I've already said what my position is and my position is clearly that I think anyone who is a member of the President's staff or the President's Cabinet has an obligation either to support the policy decisions of the President or to get out.

Q: Where does that leave the Secretary of State?

MEESE: DeFrank—Tom?

Q: Would you clear up a discrepancy, sir, that you said—

MEESE: Let me get Tom DeFrank's question then we'll get the discrepancy.

Staff Shake-up - 1

Q: Thank you, Ed. Specifically, though, there have been published reports that you have recommended to the President or Mrs. Reagan or to someone that a change needed to be made at the White House staff. Is that so?

MEESE: No.

Q: Not true?

MEESE: I have not—the published reports I've seen are those which said that I was in league somehow with a—quote—"group of Californians" which had to do with major shake-ups in the government. I have not had any conversations with any Californians about such a group or making such recommendations.

Q: Have you had any conversations with Drew Lewis about replacing Donald Regan, sir?

MEESE: No.

Q: You have not called Drew Lewis?

MEESE: I have not called Drew Lewis and he has not called me about getting the job, no.

Now, the discrepancy back there.

Q: Is the job open?

Q: —said that—

MEESE: No.

Cost of Iranian Arms - 1

Q: Excuse me, sir. You said that between $10 million and $30 million surplus funds from the Iranian arms sale may have been diverted to sources in Central—

MEESE: I say may have been transferred.

Q: That's right. The public reports and what the White House has said suggested that only $12 million total was spent for these. What's the total cost of these arms?

MEESE: The difference is—it was $12 million worth—approximately—worth of arms that was transferred from DOD stocks. That's—

Q: Is that how the Israelis sold them for $10 [million] to $30 million more than that?

MEESE: That's my—that's the best of our understanding at the present time, yes.

Q: Did you know they were selling them at a premium?

MEESE: No one at a command level in the United States government did. No.

Q: Attorney General Meese—

MEESE: Wait a minute—let's—

Q: Attorney General, just to follow-up—

MEESE: Yes.

Reason for Diversion - 1

Q: What was the purpose, as you determined it, for setting up this special—given the funding that's been approved, why was it that someone in the White House felt it necessary to funnel this extra money to the Contras?

MEESE: Well, I don't know precisely—except that this was all done during a period when the funding was not being provided by the Congress. This was all done prior to the first of this fiscal year when funding was resumed. So, it was at a time when no funds were being provided by the United States government.

Q: Therefore, it was in violation of the—wasn't it?

MEESE: What?

Legality of Diversion - 2

Q: Is this definitely in violation in the law, then?

MEESE: That's something we're looking at at the present time because it depends on two things: precisely what was done and precisely who did it, in terms of what people who are United States officials, or United States citizens—actually participated, and what their conduct was. That's what we're still looking at.

Q: General Meese—

Q: General Meese—

MEESE: One at a time.

Eleanor?

Poindexter Role - 2

Q: In your conversations with Admiral Poindexter, how does he explain not having alerted anyone that this was going on? As you said, he was aware of those happenings and—

MEESE: Again, I'm not going in to [sic] any precise conversations with anyone while the inquiry is still proceeding. Let me just say that he did not notify anyone of this, particularly the President, or any of the other members of the National Security Council.

Poindexter Resignation - 1

Q: General?

MEESE: Yes.

Q: Did he quit, or was he fired?

MEESE: Admiral Poindexter resigned—or actually requested reassignment to the Navy of his own accord before anyone ever raised any question about this. He did this of his own volition because he felt—

Q: When?

MEESE: —because he felt that it was his responsibility to take that action to avoid any possible confusion over this matter and to allow the President to have a new start in terms of his national security operations.

Q: When did he do that, Sir?

Q: When did he do it?

MEESE: He discussed it with me, yesterday, and he actually—and he—

Q: That was after the information had come out about this diversion of funds to the Contras, yes?

MEESE: It was during the same conversation that I discussed with him that he mentioned what his feeling had been as to what he ought to do in regard to the whole matter.

Q: But, it was only after he was aware that this had become public, and you knew about it.

MEESE: No, it had not become public at that time.

Q: But, that you knew about it, correct?

MEESE: This is correct. However, I was led to believe that he had already planned to resign prior to his conversation with me, and he actually told the President this morning.

Shultz Position - 2

Q: You say the members of the administration should support the President or get out. Where does that leave the Secretary of State?

MEESE: I'm not talking about any particular person. Conclusions are your business, not mine.

Yes?

Israeli Shipments Approval - 2

Q: Would you, please, clarify the whole question of the President condoning a third country shipment prior to signing this order—this intelligence finding in January. Exactly what did the President know, and when did he know it? Who told him the details were, in terms of Israel shipping arms to Iran, apart from this additional question of shipping arms to the Contras?

MEESE: This is still being looked into.

The President did not have full details of all of the aspects of transactions that took place prior to the finding. There were—there was at least one transaction that we know about in which Israel shipped weapons without any authorization from the United States. There was another transaction of a similar nature, although there was probably knowledge on the part of people in the United States about it, and this—

Q: When was that?

MEESE: —is one of—there was a transaction, one transaction in late August or September, and there was another transaction in—

Q: Of '85?

MEESE: —of '85—in November. And in the November transaction, actually, those weapons were returned to Israel, it's our understanding. That was—that whole—both of those transactions took place between Israel and Iran, did not involve, at that time, the United States.

Q: Mr. Attorney General, on that transaction in September—

Q: Did the President know about it afterwards, or at what point—

MEESE: Wait a minute.

Q: —at what point did the President know? You said he didn't have the full details.

MEESE: Yes.

Q: What details did he have about those transactions, and when did he have them?

MEESE: The President—this is one of the things that we're recollecting now. The President was informed generally that there had been an Israeli shipment of weapons to Iran sometime during the late summer, early fall of 1985, and then he later learned in February of 1986 details about another shipment that had taken place in November of '85, which had actually been returned to Israel in February of '86.

Q: Mr. Attorney General, Admiral Poindexter—

Q: If he didn't really know, why did he call Shimon Peres to thank him right after Benjamin Weir's release? Why did he call the then Israeli Prime Minister to thank him for Israel's help in sending that shipment of arms?

MEESE: Well, he thanked—he called—I don't know, because that's something I have not discussed with the President specifically the call to [Yitzhak] Shamir, but I think there was no question that the Israelis had been helpful in terms of their contacts with other people in regard to Weir.

Q: Attorney General, Admiral Poindexter has told reporters that the President verbally authorized that shipment in September of 1985 from Israel to Iran. Does your information dispute that?

MEESE: Our information is that the President knew about it probably after the fact and agreed with the general concept of continuing our discussions with the Israelis concerning these matters. That's the information I have.

Q: But who had the authorization ability, if not the President?

Who can authorize—

Q: —why did he condone—

MEESE: Well, nobody—to my knowledge—

Q: Let me just ask the question.

MEESE: To my knowledge, nobody authorized that particular shipment specifically.

Q: The Israelis did it on their own?

MEESE: That's my understanding, yes.

Q: Do you know the Israelis claim that they never did anything without the full knowledge, understanding and consent of the United States government?

Q: That's what [Israeli defense minister Yitzhak] Rabin says.

MEESE: My understanding is that in terms of that particular shipment—and this is one of the—

Q: Which one? The September '85?

MEESE: The September—the August or September—it's either August or September—that on that particular occasion, it was done at their—on their own motion by the Israelis. It was known to us, and it's uncertain as to whether it was known before or after and—

Q: Didn't [Robert C.] Bud McFarlane meet with an Israeli official just at that time?

MEESE: Wait a minute. Let me finish my answer—and that it was, however, after the fact, at least, was condoned by the United States government.

Q: Mr. Meese—

MEESE: Wait. One at a time.

Q: You made a careful distinction, Mr. Meese, between the—

LARRY SPEAKES (White House spokesman): Let's let—hey, hold it. Let's let the Attorney General call on one person—he's called on you—and conclude, because he has a lunch.

Q: Okay, great. You corrected yourself to make a distinction between the Israeli government and Israelis that were involved in the diversion of funds. Are you implying that there was somebody outside the government and that they are in fact the kingpins behind the—this operation to divert the funds?

MEESE: Well, one of the things that's very difficult is to be talking about this in the middle of an inquiry which is not yet complete. We don't know all the facts. And so, as far as things that are happening other than involving United States persons or United States government officials that we have talked to, we don't know all the facts. That's why I'm being very careful to say that as best we know, they were representatives of Israel. Whether they were specifically authorized by the government or not is one of the things I would assume we will find out.

Q: You have—

Q: What about notifying Congress in a timely fashion?

Q: Will there be more resignations?

Disclosure of Diversion

Q: Andrea's had a few questions already. (Laughter.) What's to prevent an increasingly cynical public from thinking that you went looking for a scapegoat and you came up with this whopper, but it doesn't have a lot to do with the original controversy?

MEESE: Well, the only thing that I can say is that we have been very careful to lay out the facts for you and for the American public just as rapidly as we've gotten them, much—much different that we would do in a normal inquiry or investigation when we usually wait until the inquiry is complete. But the President felt that in the interests of getting the full story out that he should make the statement that he did today and that I should appear before you and answer questions, which I think you will agree is doing everything we can to be sure that there is no hint that anything is trying to be concealed.

All right, now, in the back. Yes.

Who Knew about Diversion? - 2

Q: Mr. Meese, how high did this go? In other words, do you believe, and are we being asked to believe, that a Lieutenant Colonel took this initiative and had these funds transferred, and that only Admiral Poindexter knew about it? How high did it go?

MEESE: Well, what you have just said is an accurate picture of what we know at this time, and to the best of our knowledge, and we have checked this rather extensively, it did not go any higher than that.

Private Aid Network

Q: Mr. Meese, was General Singlaub [retired major general John K. Singlaub] or General Secord [retired major general Richard V. Secord] or anybody in that network—providing aid to the Contras, were they involved in this?

MEESE: Well, I can't tell you because we have not completed our inquiry, and the only names that I have used are people with whom we have already talked and have pretty good information as to who's who.

Q: Well, did you uncover—sir, did you uncover any other evidence?

Legality of Diversion - 3

Q: You've talked about giving us this information about the funds to Nicaragua. Congress specifically forbade you in the Boland Amendment from directing or providing support to the Contras. Haven't you, based strictly on the information you've given us today, violated the Boland Amendment, and hasn't one of the President's staff members overseen that?

MEESE: This is something that we are looking into at the present time. As to the specific applicability of variety of laws and whether the acts that particular persons committed were in violation of those laws, I'm not prepared at this time to make a legal conclusion, because that's still under consideration.

Q: Would you tell the President that the Boland Amendment might have been violated, and that's why you were taking this action?

MEESE: My answer remains the same. Yes.

Poindexter Resignation - 2

Q: Mr. Meese, you say Admiral Poindexter is being reassigned. Should he be reassigned without any determination being made as to whether or not there has been any criminality involved here?

MEESE: Well, he is a Naval officer, a very distinguished Naval officer. He has asked to be returned to the Navy, and the President has agreed to allow him to do that. So it's a matter of him deciding to relinquish his position as the Assistant to the President for National Security Affairs, so he automatically goes back to the Navy, as he's requested.

Q: Do you—staff changes?
Q: You've spoken of several instances—
Q: Where is Colonel North going?

Management Style

Q: —where the President did not have information. Do you believe, or has the President expressed to you some concern that perhaps he needs to change some of his staff operations in order for him to receive more information and have more of a hands-on presidency?

MEESE: It's not a matter of having a hands-on president, it's making sure that those people who are working for him are following the procedures. That's the reason why he has this commission which will be reviewing specifically what those procedures and what those standards of conduct are. As far as what the President didn't know, I only mentioned two times where he knew nothing, which was the transfer of funds to the forces in Nicaragua. The other thing was where he didn't have complete information at the time regarding the November transaction. And in the summer, the August situation in which he was informed of that, but after the fact. And it's my understanding that the United States individuals involved were also informed after the fact.

Q: But does he believe that he has been badly served? Is he angered by this?

MEESE: I think what—that that calls for a conclusion. I'm just talking about facts.
Q: Do you—
Q: Mr. Meese—
MEESE: All right. Back there.

Relations with Congress - 1

Q: What does this do to your credibility with Congress. I mean, how can your people now go down to Congress and look them in the eye when they passed a law opposing funds for the contras and your administration, however it happened, wound up sending that money?

MEESE: I think the same way you do when anybody in the administration does something that is not correct. And that is you go down to Congress and you tell them exactly what happened, which is what the President and what I did today. I don't think anyone can be responsible if someone on the lower echelons of government, does something that we don't feel—or that—objectively viewed as not correct. But when that happens and you find out about it, you investigate it and you take the necessary action, which is exactly what we did and what the President has done.

Q: Will you cooperate with Congress, Mr. Attorney General? Clearly there—
Q: —lower echelon did this.
SPEAKES: Please. Quiet.
Q: Well, will you cooperate with Congress?
SPEAKES: One second. Let's let the Colonel have the privilege of asking the concluding question.
Q: Well, let me just follow up on the previous one. Mr. Attorney General, will you cooperate with Congress?
MEESE: It's my—I don't like to—I want to get Larry's permission, but I'm not really a sado-masochist.
SPEAKES: The more questions you answer the less I have—
Q: —Congress, sir, on an investigation. Congress will undoubtedly require its own investigation.
MEESE: I think—did I hear question here?
Q: Congress will undoubtedly require its own investigation on the theory that the administration cannot properly investigate itself in this matter. Will you cooperate with a Congressional investigation?
MEESE: I don't accept your premise that Congress will feel that we can't investigate ourselves. We're not investigating ourselves. We're investigating certain people within the administration. There's no question whatsoever or no implication that anything that was done was administration policy or directed by—top administration officials. However, the President has already directed, as he told you, I think almost two weeks ago, that he wanted all members of the government to cooperate fully with the Congress so that all the facts would be presented to them and that's why such an immediate presentation to the Congress was made, as it was this morning.

Reason for Diversion - 2

Q: Sir, was there—can I ask you, what did Colonel North actually tell you? Why did he do it and where was the money deposited? Was it in one bank or several banks?

MEESE: I'm not going to go into specific conversations for the reasons that I mentioned earlier. My—the information we have at the present time is that it was done because this was during a period when Congress had not provided money to the Contras; it was done during a time in which, it is my understanding, that provisions had been made by Congress to permit the United States to seek funding of the forces in Nicaragua from third countries and—what was the other part of your question?

How Money Was Diverted - 2

Q: —bank accounts?
MEESE: And the bank accounts—my understanding is that the bank accounts were in Switzerland and that they were—where normal deposits are made into accounts—into numbered accounts

and then this was withdrawn by the representatives of the forces in Nicaragua.

Q: Was Adolfo Calero involved? Was he the man that North contacted?

MEESE: I'm not going to be able to talk about people where I don't know specific facts, Frank.

Q: General?

Q: Do you expect further resignations?

Q: —It was a UNO operation—

MEESE: It's very hard—until we get silence, I'll answer one question—

Q: I've already been called on.

SPEAKES: Yes.

Q: Nobody will let me ask—

MEESE: All right, Jerry. It's your turn.

North Returns to Marines

Q: I would like to know what's going to become of Lieutenant Colonel North and if he's going back to the Marine Corps.

MEESE: Lieutenant Colonel North has requested to return to the Marine Corps and that has been accomplished.

Q: Mr. Meese, do you expect—

MEESE: As a matter of fact, I think—my understanding is—I believe—that he has already indicated that he is retiring from the Marine Corps, but that I'd have to check.

Q: Mr. Meese—

Q: General—

Q: You said—

MEESE: All right. Right in front of Jerry there.

Cabinet Instructions

Q: You said that it is time for the President's men to stand shoulder-to-shoulder—that that is your belief. But specifically, what has the President instructed of his Cabinet members in that meeting yesterday that lasted for two hours—that he wants to have happen now?

MEESE: You know that I never comment on meetings with the President and who said what.

Q: General?

MEESE: Yes?

Whose Money Diverted? - 1

Q: General, could you say—since that money was owed to the U.S. government, the $30 million or $40 million, are you going to—

MEESE: No. It was not owed to the U.S. government. All the money that was owed to the United States government was paid to the United States government.

Q: Are you going to require that that additional money that went to the Contras go back to the U.S. government?

MEESE: We have no control over that money. It was never United States funds, it was never the property of United States officials, so we have no control over that whatsoever.

Q: General, what about the role of Bud McFarlane, sir, the former National Security Adviser?

MEESE: Quiet. Pardon?

Relations with Congress - 2

Q: —Congressional criticism of the arms sale itself. Your showing this additional factor as a possible violation of—Can the President legitimately expect to get anything accomplished on Capitol Hill unless he makes some changes?

MEESE: I think the President has already indicated that he will make some changes. One of the things he's going to do is to have a commission to review the procedures and the role of the National Security Council staff. Already, Admiral Poindexter has requested return to the Navy so the President can make some changes in that particular spot.

Q: General, what about the—

Q: other changes?

MEESE: So, I think the changes are already underway.

Q: General—

McFarlane Role - 1

Q: —Robert McFarlane, the former National Security Adviser who was deeply involved in this whole project, did he know about this diversion of funds to the Contras?

MEESE: Bud McFarlane knew about it. He was told about it in the middle of the year—April or May of 1986 at a time when he was no longer in the government.

Q: So he was aware of this while it was going on?

MEESE: That's my understanding, yes.

Q: And possibly an illegal act—an illegal diversion of funds?

MEESE: You're coming to conclusions that we haven't made yet.

Q: —have you suggested—

Foreign Policy Question

Q: Why did the administration decide not to send medicine and humanitarian aid and isn't it true that if you had decided to go that route, you wouldn't be in the mess you're in?

MEESE: That's a matter for foreign policy expertise. Justice is my routine.

Q: General—

Staff Shake-up - 2

Q: Do you expect further resignations or some other way for this administration to establish its credibility and to show that its Cabinet is functioning?

MEESE: I think that the administration has already demonstrated its credibility by the full disclosure of the facts. I think there's no question the Cabinet is functioning right now—as witness the meetings we've had yesterday and today, and I know of no other resignations that are either contemplated or requested.

Legality of Diversion - 4

Q: Do you mean to suggest, sir, that the Congress may have authorized what Colonel North did in seeking funds for the Contras and third countries? Did you mean to suggest that?

MEESE: I—certainly, Congess never specifically authorized what Colonel North did. The question that has to be looked at as a legal matter, [sic] is whether he committed any violation of law at the time he did that.

Q: But, were you suggesting that the Intelligence Committee may have given the go-ahead to the CIA, for instance, to raise money from third countries?

MEESE: No, I did not. I did not comment on that aspect of it at all. All I said—the only point that I'm making is, that before determining whether there is any criminal offense, you have to find out what—how the law applies to specific acts—and that's going on at the present time.

Regan Not Informed

Q: To follow-up sir, could you explain how it is that the President's National Security Adviser, who has the President's ear, could not, at least, inform the Chief of Staff, Mr. Regan, of this?

MEESE: I cannot explain it other than the fact that it happen [sic].

Q: Mr. Meese?

MEESE: Yes?

Discovery of Diversion - 3

Q: General Meese, since—since no one other than those two men knew about this, and since the President insists that he did not make a mistake in the Iran deal to begin with, why was the investigation begun? Why did he come to you last week and say, "Look into this?"

D-14   The Iran-Contra Puzzle

MEESE: He didn't. I came to him.
Q: Why?
MEESE: Because as the various—I had been in meetings—in looking at the various aspects of the testimony, and there appeared to be things that we didn't know because one person had done this, and one person had done that, and because of the very necessary secrecy involved in this, and the highly compartmentalized nature of the operation, a lot of people did not know certain things that were going on, that were being done by others. My suggestion to the President was that we get all of the facts together to be sure that anyone testifying before Congress was being absolutely accurate, not only as to what they knew, but as to other facts, since they were representing the administration. The President suggested that that be done—that the facts all be pulled together. It was in the course of that, that this information came to light.
Q: Mr. Meese?
MEESE: Yes.

Shultz Position - 3

Q: In your inquiry, did you determine how much information the State Department has gotten—not in reference to Contra money, but in the whole respect of this Iran connection, did—were they informed, or weren't they?
MEESE: Well, I think Mr. Shultz has said that he participated in certain meetings, and did get certain information, that he had opposed the concept of any transfer of arms, and that he was not involved, nor was he informed about any of the implementing steps. And everything that I have found, including my discussions with Mr. Shultz himself, verify that that is essentially correct.
Okay, we're drawing to a close here. If we—
Yes?

Whose Money Diverted? - 2

Q: Whose money was misappropriated? If it wasn't the United States government funds—
MEESE: I don't know that anybody's money was misappropriated.
Q: Attorney General?
MEESE: Yes?

Cost of Iranian Arms - 2

Q: Can you explain a little more about how the pricing of these weapons took place? I mean, who it was who set the price for the Iranians, and how that occurred? Was it North? Was it the Israelis?
MEESE: My understanding is that all of that took place in negotiations between people which we might call "loosely" representing Israel and people representing Iran. And, so—that this was not done in the presence of, or with the participation of any American persons, to the best of our knowledge at this time. That's one of the things that we'll be looking into.

Israeli Role

Q: Did Israeli officials know that this money then was being transferred to the Contras—that that was the goal or the target of it?
MEESE: I don't know whether Israeli officials, as opposed to representatives, depending on who the people were, knew—that's one of the things again that we will be looking at.
Q: Who were the Israelis and who were the Iranians?
MEESE: Again, I can't mention any names until we actually have those things pinned down, which is one of the things we'll be looking at.
Q: Well, did the Iranian government—

Bush Allegations

Q: Was this Colonel North's idea? Was it Colonel North's idea—if we can bid up the amount of money the Iranians are

paying, we can take that extra money and divert it to the Contras? Did he come up with the original idea? Was it an Israeli idea? And a second question, sir—there have been allegations that Vice President [George] Bush was involved in supplying money or aiding the supply of money to the Contras. Do you know whether or not he was aware of this project at all?
MEESE: First, I don't know precisely what the conversations were—who said what to who—when this thing first got started. Again, it's a matter that is still under investigation. I do know that the President—that the Vice President did not know about any of this until yesterday when I informed him of essentially the same information I had given the President.
Q: Mr. Meese, did the Iranian government—

Why Didn't Reagan Know?

Q: How is it that so much of this can go on and the President not know it? He is the President of the United States. Why doesn't he know?
MEESE: Because somebody didn't tell him, that's why. And remember, we're talking about three situations over a period of some six or eight months, and the people who were involved in the situation didn't tell anybody, including the President. So, it's common understanding why the President wouldn't know, because no one in the chain of command was informed.
Yes?

Whose Money Diverted? - 3

Q: Mr. Meese, if they weren't U.S. funds, whose money was this?
MEESE: Well, I think that's—I would assume that it either belonged to the party that—who had sold the weapons to the Iranians, or it belonged to the party who had bought the weapons and given the money. That's—but I think it would probably be the party that had sold the weapons to the Iranians.

Justice Department Investigations

Q: Sir, were any of the principals on the Iranian or the Israeli side—were they involved in cases that the Justice Department was prosecuting or investigating separately—first? And second, was that—
MEESE: Not to our knowledge, in answer to your question.

CIA Involvement

Q: Were those bank accounts—is there any evidence or indication those bank accounts were set up by the CIA?
MEESE: No. There's no indication at all.
Q: Or that the Contras did it with the help of the CIA?
MEESE: No. There's no indication whatsoever, to the best of our knowledge—that no one in the CIA knew anything about it.

Iran Policy Defended - 2

Q: Can you explain, sir, why if it was the people who are leaving today—they were the ones who proposed to the President the idea of arms shipments to Iran—if, perhaps, they had other information from the President on that policy, as well, why doesn't the President ask for a re-examination of that policy? Perhaps the four goals that you mentioned, which they proposed—that there's a question about them, as well? Perhaps the President has been misled about this larger policy, as well, since we know that Secretary Shultz opposes it and Secretary Weinberger opposes it, but the main advice came from NSC, from the people who are now leaving. Don't you think the President should re-examine that policy as well?
MEESE: No, because the people who are leaving today were not the people that proposed the policy to the President. The policy was proposed initially as a result of conversations with Israel. It was then presented to the President by the then Assistant to the President for National Security Affairs. It was discussed

with all of the members, in January, with all of the members of the National—or almost all of the members of the National Security Council and that on the National Security Council there was a split of opinion. But after hearing all of the arguments, pro and con, the President decided that the potential for achieving the goals of effecting peace in the Middle East, helping secure that area, stopping a war, and obtaining our hostages was worth the risks involved.

McFarlane Role - 2

Q: Can you say that when the President made that decision who was his National Security Adviser?

MEESE: Admiral Poindexter was actually—it really was at the time when Bud McFarlane was leaving. The discussions with the President about this specific series of events had gone on under Mr. McFarlane during 1985 and the specific discussions of some of these things that led to the finding in January had actually started in December, while Mr. McFarlane was here.

He was transferring out during the latter part of December and the early part of January. At that time, Admiral Poindexter came in.

Q: So he knew about details of this operation but didn't tell anyone in the administration for—

MEESE: Mr. McFarlane?

Q: Yes,

MEESE: He didn't learn of this, of the transactions involving the forces in Central America until probably April or May of 1986.

Q: Why didn't he say anything?

Q: Why didn't he tell you?

Q: Why did he not say anything to the President?

MEESE: I don't know. He didn't.

Q: He did go on a mission for the President—

MEESE: He didn't—

Q: —in May of that year, right? He was a representative of the President—

MEESE: That's correct. Whether he talked with the President during that period of time, I don't know.

Cabinet Split

Q: Well, why should the President take these people's advice, sir?

MEESE: Well, because—the President didn't just take these people's advice as to the overall policy. He had the advice of the entire range of his national security advisers.

Q: Most of them advised against it.

MEESE: All of his advisers. What?

Q: Do you know what—

MEESE: Two of—some of whom advised against it, some of whom advised in favor of it.

Q: Who else advised in favor of it besides members of the NSC?

MEESE: As you know, I don't talk about who gives advice to the President.

McFarlane Role - 3

Q: How did McFarlane learn of it?

Q: The people who you say profited from this diversion of funds, these then are the people that we were working with, people perhaps that were even aboard the plane with Mr. McFarlane into Iran.

MEESE: No, no. The people who profited? I don't know that anyone profited. The fund—

Q: In Israel who you say—

MEESE: I don't know that anyone in Israel—

Q: —owed the money that got diverted into—

MEESE: The money that was transferred to the forces in Nicaragua—I don't know that anyone who was involved in that transaction was necessarily on the plane with Mr. McFarlane. That's something we haven't gone into yet.

Q: How did he learn of it?

Number of Diversions

Q: We now know of three specific shipments, unless I'm mistaken—the one in late August, early September, as you've described it; one in November, which was returned to Israel; and then another one in May.

MEESE: And there were—

Q: The diversion of funds took place from which of those or all three of those?

Q: Or none of those?

MEESE: There were several shipments—there were, I believe, three or four shipments during 1986. I can't give you the precise date. The transfer of funds were [sic] involved with at least one and possibly three of those shipments during the period from roughly January of 1986 or February through probably September of 1986.

Hasenfus Mission

Q: Mr. Meese, Mr. [Eugene] Hasenfus is in jail in Nicaragua, as you know, for running supplies into Nicaragua to help the Contras. Did his mission, can you now say, was it in any way funded by any of these diverted funds?

MEESE: I have no knowledge and I doubt if we'll ever find out since we have no information about how those funds were used once they were ultimately received.

THE PRESS: Thank you.

EXECUTIVE ORDER ON REVIEW BOARD

Following is the text of President Reagan's December 1, 1986, executive order (No. 12575) establishing a special review board to investigate activities of the National Security Council concerning secret arms sales to Iran, and the transfer of funds to the contras.

Executive Order 12575

President's Special Board

By the authority vested in me as President by the Constitution and laws of the United States of America, and in order to establish, in accordance with the Federal Advisory Committee Act, as amended (5 U.S.C. App. I), a Special Review Board to review activities of the National Security Council, it is hereby ordered as follows:

Section 1. Establishment. (a) There is established the President's Special Review Board on the future role of the National Security Council staff. The Board shall consist of three members appointed by the President from among persons with extensive experience in foreign policy and national security affairs.

(b) The President shall designate a Chairman from among the members of the Board.

Sec. 2. Functions. (a) The Board shall conduct a comprehensive study of the future role and procedures of the National Security Council (NSC) staff in the development, coordination, oversight, and conduct of foreign and national security policy; review the NSC staff's proper role in operational activities, especially extremely sensitive diplomatic, military, and intelligence missions; and provide recommendations to the President based upon its analysis of the manner in which foreign and national security policies established by the President have been implemented by the NSC staff.

(b) The Board shall submit its findings and recommendations

to the President within 60 days of the date of this Order.

Sec. 3. Administration. (a) The heads of Executive departments, agencies, and independent instrumentalities, to the extent permitted by law, shall provide the Board, upon request, with such information as it may require for purposes of carrying out its functions.

(b) Members of the Board shall receive compensation for their work on the Board at the daily rate specified for GS-18 of the General Schedule. While engaged in the work of the Board, members appointed from among private citizens of the United States may be allowed travel expenses, including per diem in lieu of subsistence, as authorized by law for persons serving intermittently in the government service (5 U.S.C. 5701-5707).

(c) To the extent permitted by law and subject to the availability of appropriations, the Office of Administration, Executive Office of the President, shall provide the Board with such administrative services, funds, facilities, staff, and other support services as may be necessary for the performance of its functions.

Sec. 4. General Provision. The Board shall terminate 30 days after submitting its report to the President.

RONALD REAGAN

THE WHITE HOUSE,
December 1, 1986.

REAGAN CALLS FOR INDEPENDENT COUNSEL

Following is the text of President Reagan's December 2, 1986, address in which he supported appointment of an independent counsel to investigate the Iran-contra affair and announced the appointment of Frank C. Carlucci as his new national security adviser:

Good afternoon. Since the outset of the controversy over our policy relating to Iran, I've done everything in my power to make all the facts concerning this matter known to the American people. I can appreciate why some of these things are difficult to comprehend, and you're entitled to have your questions answered. And that's why I've pledged to get to the bottom of this matter.

Independent Counsel

And I have said earlier that I would welcome the appointment of an independent counsel to look into allegations of illegality in the sale of arms to Iran and the use of funds from these sales to assist the forces opposing the Sandinista government in Nicaragua.

This morning, Attorney General [Edwin] Meese [III] advised me of his decision that his investigation has turned up reasonable grounds to believe that further investigation by an independent counsel would be appropriate. Accordingly, consistent with his responsibilities under the Independent Counsel Act, I immediately urged him to apply to the court here in Washington for the appointment of an independent counsel.

Tower Commission

Yesterday, I had my first meeting with the Special Review Board. That Review Board is made up of three men of unquestioned integrity and broad experience in foreign and national security policy. In the meeting with the Board, they promised me a tough, no-nonsense investigation, and I promised them the full cooperation of the White House staff and all agencies of the Executive Branch.

No area of the NSC staff's activities will be immune from review. And when the Board reports to me, I intend to make their conclusions and recommendations available to Congress and to the American people. With the appointment of an independent counsel, we will have in place a dual system for assuring a thorough review of all aspects of this matter.

If illegal acts were undertaken, those who did so will be brought to justice. If actions in implementing my policy were taken without my authorization, knowledge or concurrence, this would be exposed and appropriate corrective steps will be implemented.

Cooperation with Congress

I recognize fully the interest of Congress in this matter and the fact that in performing its important oversight and legislative role, Congress will want to inquire into what occurred. We will cooperate fully with these inquiries. I have already taken the unprecedented step of permitting two of my former National Security Advisers to testify before a committee of Congress.

These Congressional inquiries should continue. But I do believe Congress can carry out its duties in getting the facts without disrupting the orderly conduct of a vital part of this nation's government. Accordingly, I am urging the Congress to consider some mechanism that will consolidate its inquiries—such a step has already been requested by several members of Congress. I support the idea.

In closing, I want to state again that it is my policy to oppose terrorism throughout the world—to punish those who support it and to make common cause with those who seek to suppress it. This has been my policy and will continue to be my policy.

If the investigative processes now set in motion are given an opportunity to work, all the facts concerning Iran and the transfer of funds to assist the anti-Sandinista forces will shortly be made public. Then the American people—you—will be the final arbiters of this controversy. You will have all the facts and will be able to judge for themselves—yourselves.

Carlucci Appointment

I am pleased to announce today that I am appointing Frank Carlucci as Assistant to the President for National Security Affairs. A former Deputy Secretary of Defense, Deputy Director of the CIA, and Ambassador to Portugal, Mr. Carlucci has the depth of experience in foreign affairs, defense, and intelligence matters that uniquely qualify him to serve as my National Security Adviser. The American people will be well-served by his tenure.

Thank you and God bless you.

BUSH SPEECH ON IRAN ARMS SALES

Following is the text of a speech by Vice President George Bush, delivered December 3, 1986, to a public policy forum of the American Enterprise Institute (AEI). The text was taken from the New York Times *and Federal News Service.*

Well, Mr. President, at the outset of these remarks, let me just pay my respects to you and thank you for all you do for this wonderful institution, AEI, an institution for which I have so much respect, and I'm delighted to see you. Bob Millot, too. And, of course, I was invited some time ago by Paul McCracken to come here. And I hope that you'll all be interested in the topic that Paul asked me to address: special drawing rights, the snake and its effect on disintermediation. (Laughter.)

No, I am delighted to be here at this AEI forum, and you couldn't have scheduled a better time to discuss public policy. A great many citizens currently are troubled about recent revelations. And I'm grateful for this chance to address some of those concerns of the American people.

Damaged Credibility

There has been much criticism and confusion in recent weeks, over the administration's—our policies regarding Iran. And I understand the skepticism of the American people. The result, as you all know, according to these opinion surveys, is that the administration's credibility has been hurt. And this is especially painful to the President, and to me, as well. And after all, we're in the White House because of the trust that the American people placed in us. And we must restore that trust.

And so today I'd like to discuss some of the basic concerns that the American people rightfully have about our policy toward Iran, questions of why we tried to open channels, open channels with a regime that all of us Americans despise, questions of how we can have a policy of not sending arms to Iran and then seemingly do just the opposite, and questions about the operation of the National Security Council [NSC] staff.

Let me start with a basic concern.

Why a Dialogue with Iran?

Why did we open a dialogue with Iran? Here was a country that deeply humiliated the United States by kidnapping our diplomats, burning our flag, and we still have vivid memories of blindfolded Americans being paraded around our embassy there in Tehran. And there is, in the hearts of the American people, an understandable animosity, a hatred really, to [Ayatollah Ruhollah] Khomeini's Iran.

I feel that way myself, to be very honest with you.

And so does the President, who has been vilified time and time again by Iran's radical leaders. We're told that most Iranians feel the same way about us, the country that they call the Great Satan.

And so why have anything to do with them?

I'm sorry I didn't bring a map, but if you look at a map, Iran is all that stands between the Soviets and the Gulf oil states. It's all that stands between the Soviets and a warm water port. Either a disintegrating Iran or an overly powerful Iran could threaten the stability of the entire Middle East and especially those moderate Arab states, our friends, whose stability and independence are absolutely vital to the national security of the United States.

We may not like the current Iranian regime, and I've said we don't. But it would be irresponsible to ignore its geopolitical and strategic importance. And that doesn't mean we should simply appease any Iranian regime. It does mean, however, that we can't ignore this looming transition that will soon take place in Iran.

Khomeini will pass from the scene.

A successor regime will take power.

And we must be positioned to serve America's interests and indeed the interests of the entire free world. Apart from the strategic reasons, humanitarian concern about American hostages in Lebanon provided another reason to open a channel to Iran.

The Iranians themselves are not holding our hostages.

But we believe they have influence over those who do hold some of our hostages.

But let me add something very important.

In spite of our bitter feelings toward Iran's leadership, we would've tried to begin a dialogue with Iran whether we had hostages in Lebanon or not.

In fact for three years prior to the first hostage kidnapping, this Administration attempted to find reliable, hopefully moderate, Iranian channels through which to conduct a responsible dialogue.

And more recently, we've been receiving intelligence that pragmatic elements within Iran were beginning to appreciate certain sobering realities. To the east, in Afghanistan, we estimate 115,000 Soviet troops are committing atrocities on Iran's Islamic brothers. To the north, 26 Soviet divisions right there on Iran's border for whatever opportunities might arise. To the west, Iran is engaged in a war of unbelievably horrible human dimensions—war with Iraq. Twelve-year-old kids, 14-year-old kids pressed into service and then ground up in combat.

And at home, Iran is teetering on the economic brink right there in its own front yard, a 40 percent unemployment rate. Many Iranian leaders understand that their own survival and certainly the rebuilding of their economy may depend on normalizing ties with their neighbors and with the Western world.

Violation of Arms Embargo

And so we, for our reasons, and certain elements in Iran for their reasons, in spite of this mutual hatred, began a tentative, probing dialogue, which brings us to another question:

How can the United States Government have a policy against countries sending arms to Iran and then turn around and itself send arms?

I understand, I know the American people simply don't understand this. And when we started talking to the Iranians, both sides were deeply suspicious of each other, and remain so, I might say.

Those Iranians who were taking enormous personal risks by just talking to us felt that they needed a signal that their risks were worth it. And we were told the signal that they required and we gave them that signal by selling a limited amount of arms, about one-tenth of 1 percent of the arms that have been supplied by other countries.

And likewise, we needed proof of Iranian seriousness. We required signs of a cessation of Iranian use of terrorism, and help in gaining the release of our hostages in Lebanon. And we did see certain positive signs, we have seen them.

They opposed, for example, the Pan American hijacking in Karachi; and immediately after, they denied landing rights. They interceded with the TWA hijackers in Beirut.

And of course, three hostages, once [held] in Lebanon by the Islamic Jihad, are today with their families here in the United States of America.

'Simple Human Hope'

And I—perhaps President Ford would agree with this—but when you are President, any American held captive against his will anywhere in the world is like your own son or daughter. I know that's the way our President feels about it. But you must remain true to your principles and I can tell you that the President is absolutely convinced that he did not swap arms for hostages. And still the question remains of how the Administration could violate its own policy of not selling arms to Iran.

Simple human hope explains it perhaps better than anything else.

'Mistakes Were Made'

The President hoped that we could open a channel that would serve the interests of the United States and of our allies in a variety of ways. Call it leadership. Given 20-20 hindsight, call it a mistaken tactic if you want to. It was risky but potentially of long-term value.

The shaping of the Iranian policy involved difficult choices. As complex as the public debate on the issue would be, the matter was further clouded by the way in which the President's goals were executed. Specifically allegations about certain activities of the National Security Council staff. Clearly mistakes were made. Our policy of conducting a dialogue with Iran, which was legitimate and arguable, has become entangled with the separate matter of this NSC investigation.

Reagan's Moves for Disclosure

A week ago Monday afternoon, the President learned of proper, of possible improprieties. A week ago Monday. On Tuesday, he disclosed the problem to the public and instructed the Attorney General to go forward with a full investigation. On Wednesday, he created a bipartisan commission, outstanding three individuals, outstanding individuals, to review the role of the NSC staff and make recommendations for the future. And just yesterday, he moved to appoint, have the court appoint an independent counsel to ensure a full accounting for any possible wrongdoing.

The President pledged full cooperation with the United States Congress, urging it to consolidate and expedite its inquiry. Yesterday, he also named Frank [C.] Carlucci, a seasoned professional with broad experience so well-known to many people here, to serve as his national security adviser.

Now this is fast action in anybody's book. And these are actions I fully support and which I believe the American people will judge commendable. And the President has moved swiftly, strongly. But let me add this: I am convinced that he will take whatever additional steps may be necessary to get things back on track and get our foreign policy moving forward.

As the elected representatives of, of all the people, the President and the Vice President, he and I have a duty to preserve the public trust and uphold the laws of this country and we take, take that duty very, very seriously.

Bush's Role

I'd like to say something about my own role in all of this. I was aware of our Iran initiative and I support the President's decision. And I was not aware of and I oppose any diversion of funds, any ransom payments or any circumvention of the will of the Congress or the law of the United States of America.

And as the various investigations proceed, I have this to say: Let the chips fall where they may. We want the truth. The President wants it. I want it. And the American people have a fundamental right to it. And if the truth hurts, so be it. We've got to take our lumps and move ahead.

Politics do not matter. Personalities do not matter. Those who've served the President haven't served the President well don't matter. What matters is the United States of America. And we mustn't allow our foreign policy to become paralyzed by distraction. There can be no denying that our credibility has been damaged by this, this entire episode and its aftermath.

Moving Foreign Policy Forward

We have a critical role to play internationally and I intend to help the President tackle the challenges that lie before us in the last two years of this Administration. Putting U.S.-Soviet relations on a new footing, pursuing a breakthrough in arms reduction, building on the potential that I saw so clearly just this past summer for making new strides for peace between Israel and its Arab neighbors, working to end apartheid and creating a more hopeful future for all Africans, solidifying the remarkable changes taking place in Asia, combating international terrorism in close conjunction with our allies, and, of course, fostering the development of democracy in Central America.

And let me add, the freedom of the people of Central America should not, must not, be held hostage to actions unrelated to them.

This nation's support of those who are fighting for democracy in Nicaragua should stand on its own merits, not hang upon events related to Iran. The Marxist-Leninist regime in Managua must not benefit from the errors of some people in Washington.

Our Administration has a duty to follow a foreign policy that reflects the values of its citizens. This sounds simple and yet it is often, as so many of you here know, a very complex matter. It's not easy translating general values into specific foreign policy programs and this is why there's always so much internal debate over our nation's role in world affairs from Iran to arms reduction.

The Reagan Administration has two years left in which to pursue our particular vision of how America's foreign policy should fit America's values. There's one thing, however, on which critics and supporters would agree. U.S. foreign policy must move forward.

The U.S. has obligations as leaders of the free world. It has opportunities and responsibilities unmatched by any other country to bring stability to the world. And we must move forward with the trust of the American people; to the extent that that trust has been damaged, it must be repaired. And only the truth can repair that. Our government rules not by force or intimidation, but by earning the confidence and respect of the American people. Our duty must be to uphold that confidence and restore that respect.

Sometimes, true bipartisanship is really, is called for. And in my view, now is just such a time, and I have been very pleased that Republicans and Democrats alike have pledged to help get the facts out and move on.

A storm is now raging, but when the full truth is known—and it will be—and when the people of American—American people, come to understand that this strong and honest President moved swiftly to correct what might have been wrong, then a forgiving American people, in spite of their misgivings about Iran and weapons and diverted funds will say: "Our president told the truth. He took action. Let's go forward together."

Thank you very much.

REAGAN RADIO ADDRESS ON IRAN ARMS, CONTRA AID

Following is the text of a December 6, 1986, radio address by President Reagan on the Iran arms and contra aid controversy:

I'm speaking to you today from Camp David, and because the atmosphere here is a bit more informal than everyday Washington, I thought it would be a good opportunity to think and reflect with you about those crucial foreign policy matters so much in the news lately. It's also a chance to do something I've wanted to do throughout the course of these events: and that's share some personal thoughts with you, to speak to you, the American people, from the heart.

I realize you must be disappointed and probably confused with all the furor of the last couple of weeks. You must be asking: What were we doing in the Middle East? What was our policy? Where was it wrong? Were we engaged in some kind of shenanigans that blew up in our face? I can understand if these are the questions you're asking, and I'd like to provide some answers.

First of all, the Middle East is critically important to our nation's security. Right now it's a major troublespot that could easily set off the sparks of a wider conflict. Much of our effort has been aimed at stopping terrorism—putting an end to the bombing of innocent civilians and the kidnapping of hostages, especially our own citizens—and bringing about an end to the bloody war between Iran and Iraq.

When word came to me that individuals in Iran, including some members of the government there, had asked through an intermediary in a third country for a meeting with a representative of our government, I said yes. And even though these were responsible elements in Iran that might be able to assist us in stopping the violence and possibly helping us get back the hostages being held in Lebanon, there was a risk involved. But I believed then and believe now there was a greater risk in doing nothing, of not trying.

So, I gave the order to proceed. We had some notable success: There was some reduction in terrorism, and three of our hostages were released—one at a time—and others were about to follow. Then someone in the Government of Iran leaked information about our contacts with Iran to a newspaper in Lebanon. You know the rest. This effort to establish a relationship with responsible moderates in Iran came to light and was broken off. But I think you can see the purposes behind our policy: to end the war in the Middle East, to prevent Soviet expansionism, to halt terrorism, and to help gain release of American hostages.

But now I want to speak to you about something else, not the policies themselves but how they were carried out. And while we are still seeking all the facts, it's obvious that the execution of these policies was flawed and mistakes were made. Let me just say it was not my intent to do business with [Ayatollah Ruhollah] Khomeini, to trade weapons for hostages, nor to undercut our policy of antiterrorism.

And let me say again, I know the stories of the past few weeks have been distressing. I'm deeply disappointed this initiative has resulted in such a controversy, and I regret it's caused such concern and consternation. But I pledge to you I will set things right.

That's what I am doing now. When our Iranian initiative came to light, I spoke to you from the Oval Office and explained it. When revelations regarding a transfer of money from Iran to those attempting to fight the Sandinista government were reported to me, they were immediately shared with you and the Congress. I then appointed a distinguished, independent board chaired by former Senator and Ambassador John Tower to review our National Security Council staff apparatus. And to ensure a complete legal inquiry, I urged the appointment of an independent counsel. They used to be called special prosecutors, and that's what they are. They just changed the title. And finally, I have stated we will cooperate fully with the Congress as they undertake their proper review.

If illegal acts were undertaken in the implementation of our policy, those who did so will be brought to justice. If actions in implementing my policy were taken without my authorization, knowledge, or concurrence, this will be exposed and appropriate corrective steps will be implemented. I will continue to make all the facts known surrounding this matter. We live in a country that requires we operate within the rules and laws—all of us. Just cause and deep concern and noble ends can never be reason enough to justify improper actions or excessive means.

In these past 6 years we have done much together to restore the faith and confidence and respect of our people and our country. We've done so not by avoiding challenges or denying problems but when confronted with these problems dealing with them directly and honestly. We will continue to do so.

Until next week, thanks for listening, and God bless you.

VICE PRESIDENT'S STAFF DENIES CONTRA AID ROLE

Following is the text of a December 15, 1986, press statement and chronology of contacts between the office of Vice President George Bush and Felix Rodriguez, a former Central Intelligence Agency (CIA) agent who was involved in counterinsurgency work in El Salvador and assisted in the contra supply operation. A subsequent addition to the chronology was issued by the vice president's office May 14, 1987. The text follows the chronology.

Press Secretary's Statement

The Vice President has reviewed the attached chronology of meetings with Felix Rodriguez, prepared by his National Security Advisor Donald Gregg. The meetings and telephone calls show that Donald Gregg and his staff maintained periodic communication with Felix Rodriguez, but were never involved in directing, coordinating, or approving military aid to the contras in Nicaragua. Nor was there any awareness of the diversion of funds to the contras. Felix Rodriguez indicated on August 8, 1986, in a meeting with Don Gregg that he had knowledge of the contra aid network which he wanted to discuss with U.S. officials. Mr. Gregg passed Mr. Rodriguez's concerns along to the appropriate officials on August 12, 1986. The Vice President was not informed of these meetings.

The communications with Felix Rodriguez concerning his work as a counterinsurgency expert in El Salvador were entirely appropriate. On the three occasions when the Vice President met with Mr. Rodriguez, the discussions dealt entirely with the insurgency in El Salvador and there was no discussion, direct or indirect, of the contra aid network.

Donald Gregg has been invited to meet with staff from the House Intelligence Committee, which he anticipates scheduling this week. The Vice President has full confidence in his National Security Advisor. This chronology will be made available to the independent counsel and appropriate Congressional committees. Our purpose from the beginning has been to end speculation about the relationship between Felix Rodriguez and the Office of the Vice President. Our intent continues to be full disclosure and cooperation with the Congress to make all of the facts known.

Summary of Contacts with Felix Rodriguez

Donald Gregg, Assistant to the Vice President for National Security Affairs, first met Felix Rodriguez in Vietnam in 1970. Working together with other CIA officials, they developed an effective operational concept for use against guerrilla units operating in the provinces near Saigon. Mr. Rodriguez, a Cuban born intelligence officer of great courage and experience, was instrumental in implementing this concept. It involved the use of small helicopters to launch pinpoint operations against small guerrilla units. The concept was extremely successful. Mr. Gregg and Mr. Rodriguez maintained sporadic contact during the intervening years. Mr. Rodriguez had retired from CIA on a disability, having injured his back in a helicopter crash in Vietnam. Mr. Rodriguez became interested in the insurgency in El Salvador and traveled frequently to the area in 1983 and 1984. Mr. Rodriguez is extremely knowledgeable of low intensity warfare operations and it was for these reasons that Mr. Gregg aided Mr. Rodriguez when he expressed a desire to go to El Salvador to help the counterinsurgency effort in that country.

On November 3, 1983, Mr. Rodriguez met with Mr. Gregg to discuss the general situation in Central America. Mr. Rodriguez had just returned from a trip to the area.

On December 21, 1984, Mr. Rodriguez expressed an interest in going to El Salvador and working with the El Salvador Air Force to help them in their counterinsurgency effort which Mr. Rodriguez felt was very similar to that which he had assisted in Vietnam. Subsequent to this meeting, Mr. Gregg called Ambassador [Thomas R.] Pickering, Assistant Secretary of State [Langhorne A.] Motley, and Deputy Assistant Secretary of Defense [Nestor D.] Sanchez to recommend that they meet and talk with Mr. Rodriguez to assist him in going to El Salvador. Mr. Rodriguez met with these officials and also subsequently met with General Paul Gorman, Commander of the Southern Command.

On January 22, 1985, Mr. Rodriguez met with the Vice President and Mr. Gregg to inform the Vice President that Mr. Rodriguez wanted to work in El Salvador against the insurgency.

On February 19, 1985, Mr. Rodriguez met with Mr. Gregg to report growing support for his work in El Salvador. In March, having been accepted by the El Salvador Air Force, Mr. Rodriguez moved to El Salvador.

On June 5, 1985, Mr. Gregg met with Mr. Rodriguez and Colonel [James] Steele [former commander of U.S. military forces in El Salvador] to discuss the situation in El Salvador.

On December 20, 1985, Mr. Rodriguez joined in a Christmas party with members of Mr. Gregg's office, where he met all members of Mr. Gregg's staff.

During the period January 19-21, 1986, Colonel Samuel Watson, Mr. Gregg's Deputy, met with Mr. Rodriguez, Colonel Steele and others in El Salvador to discuss counterinsurgency operations. This was part of an orientation trip to the area for Colonel Watson.

On April 30, 1986, Colonel Watson and Mr. Rodriguez met to discuss progress of the insurgency and the need for helicopter parts.

On May 1, 1986, Mr. Rodriguez met with the Vice President for approximately ten minutes. Mr. Gregg and Colonel Watson attended. Mr. Rodriguez showed pictures taken during the counterinsurgency operations in El Salvador. Former Senator Nicholas Brady [R-N.J., 1982] also sat in on the meeting. At the end of the brief session Ambassador [Edwin G.] Ed Corr, accompanied by Lieutenant Colonel Oliver [L.] North, joined the group in the Vice President's office. At that time, Ambassador Corr strongly praised Mr. Rodriguez' performance in El Salvador.

On May 20, 1986, the Vice President spoke briefly with Mr. Rodriguez and El Salvador Air Force Commander Bustillo at a large reception in Miami, Florida on Cuban Independence Day.

On August 8, 1986, Mr. Rodriguez met with Mr. Gregg and Colonel Watson to express his concerns that the informal Contra supply organization which then existed might not survive until a United States Government organization directed by CIA to implement delivery of funds and equipment recently authorized by Congress could be established. This was the first time that such a subject had been discussed by Mr. Rodriguez in any of his meetings with the Vice President's office. Mr. Rodriguez was also concerned about the poor quality of the aircraft being used in the Contra supply operation.

On August 12, 1986, Mr. Gregg and Colonel Watson met with Ambassador Edwin Corr, Deputy Assistant Secretary of State William Walker, [Raymond F.] Ray Burghardt and [Robert L.] Bob Earl of the NSC [National Security Council], and a CIA officer, to pass along the concerns mentioned by Mr. Rodriguez. This meeting was convened since the Vice President's office had no jurisdiction or responsibility with regard to Contra supply operations. It was believed, however, that Mr. Rodriguez' observations were sufficiently important to pass along. In talking to the *New York Times* and the *Washington Post,* Mr. Gregg incorrectly placed Mr. Rodriguez in the August 12 meeting. This was not the case as Mr. Rodriguez had already departed from Washington.

On October 5 and 6, 1986, Mr. Rodriguez called Colonel Watson twice to say that he had received information that one of the Contra resupply aircraft was missing, possibly in Nicaragua. Following established practice, Colonel Watson advised the Situation Room and the NSC staff of this information. It was subsequently learned that the aircraft had crashed in Nicaragua.

On November 6, 1986, Mr. Rodriguez delivered a speech at the National War College on low intensity conflict in El Salvador.

On November 6, 1986, Colonel Watson and Mr. Rodriguez had dinner in McLean, Virginia.

On November 7, 1986, Mr. Rodriguez met with Mr. Gregg and Colonel Watson in Gregg's office. Mr. Rodriguez described his role in El Salvador as having been primarily directed toward the insurgency in that country. Mr. Rodriguez also indicated that he, himself, had been able to assist the Contra resupply effort.

On November 11-12, 1986, Mr. Rodriguez was again in Washington, this time accompanying General Bustillo. They had dinner on November 11 with Colonel Watson and on November 12 met with Mr. Gregg. At that time, General Bustillo made it clear that he would welcome Mr. Rodriguez' return to El Salvador to continue his assistance in the counterinsurgency operation.

Additional Comments:

On the three occasions when the Vice President met with Mr. Rodriguez, discussions dealt entirely with the insurgency in El Salvador. There was no mention of supply or support operations for the Contras whatsoever.

At no point in his discussions with anyone in the Vice President's office did Mr. Rodriguez mention diversion of funds to the Contra operation from Iran. There is no indication that Mr. Rodriguez knew of such a diversion, and he has stated categorically to Mr. Gregg that he was unaware of the diversion.

During the period covered by this chronology, Mr. Rodriguez called Mr. Gregg and Colonel Watson from El Salvador and from his home in Miami, Florida. These calls concerned his counterinsurgency activities in El Salvador, and until the calls of October 5 and 6, contained no references to Contra operations.

Chronology Revision

On December 15, 1986, Bush spokesman Marlin Fitzwater disclosed that Col. Sam Watson, Bush's deputy national security adviser, had visited two contra military camps in Honduras during his orientation trip January 19-21, 1986. Fitzwater said the information was not included in the chronology because it did not pertain to Felix Rodriguez.

The following press statement, acknowledging an additional meeting between Watson and Rodriguez, was issued May 14, 1987:

The Office of the Counsel to the Vice President has provided the following information concerning the document search requested on behalf of the Independent Counsel and the Congressional Committees.

The Office of the Vice President has completed a comprehensive review of its files and records and has transmitted or made available all documents related to the Iran-Contra investigations to the Independent Counsel and the Congressional Committees investigating the Iran-Contra matter. In the course of the search, the Office verified the meetings and contacts with Feliz Rodriguez made public as a chronology on December 15, 1986. In particular, the review confirms that the Vice President's contacts with Felix Rodriguez dealt "entirely with the insurgency in El Salvador and there was no discussion, direct or indirect, on the Contra aid network."

The review also confirmed all meetings and telephone calls listed in the chronology between Rodriguez and Donald Gregg and his staff, confirmed that those contacts never involved "directing, coordinating or approving military aid to the Contras in Nicaragua" and confirmed that there was no "awareness of the diversion of funds to the Contras."

The review indentified [*sic*] an additional meeting between Samuel J. Watson and Rodriguez on June 25, 1986 that was not indicated in the original chronology. This meeting was not scheduled ahead of time and did not appear on Colonel Watson's schedule which had been consulted in preparing the original chronology. It was discovered when Watson's personal notes were reviewed. The meeting was short and involved the counter insurgency operations in El Salvador and needed helicopter parts to support it. The Vice President was neither in the meeting nor aware it had taken place. Donald Gregg was overseas at the time and not aware of the meeting. Finally, the review also confirmed that the first discussion of the private resupply network was in connection with the August 8, 1986 meeting described in some detail in the chronology.

The Office of the Vice President will continue to cooperate fully in the pursuit of the facts.

INTELLIGENCE FINDING AUTHORIZES IRAN SALES

Following is the text of President Reagan's January 17, 1986, secret intelligence "finding" that allowed the sale of weapons to Iran. The text was released by the White House January 9, 1987.

Finding Pursuant to Section 662 of The Foreign Assistance Act of 1961 As Amended, Concerning Operations Undertaken by the Central Intelligence Agency in Foreign Countries, Other Than Those Intended Solely for the Purpose of Intelligence Collection

I hereby find that the following operation in a foreign country (including all support necessary to such operation) is important to the national security of the United States, and due to its extreme sensitivity and security risks, I determine it is essential to limit prior notice, and direct the Director of Central Intelligence to refrain from reporting this Finding to the Congress as provided in Section 501 of the National Security Act of 1947, as amended, until I otherwise direct.

SCOPE: Iran

DESCRIPTION: Assist selected friendly foreign liaison services, third countries and third parties which have established relationships with Iranian elements, groups, and individuals sympathetic to U.S. Government interests and which do not conduct or support terrorist actions directed against U.S. persons, property or interests, for the purpose of: (1) establishing a more moderate government in Iran, (2) obtaining from them significant intelligence not otherwise obtainable, to determine the current Iranian Government's intentions with respect to its neighbors and with respect to terrorist acts, and (3) furthering the release of the American hostages held in Beirut and preventing additional terrorist acts by these groups. Provide funds, intelligence, counterintelligence, training, guidance and communications and other necessary assistance to these elements, groups, individuals, liaison services and third countries in support of these activities.

The USG will act to facilitate efforts by third parties and third countries to establish contact with moderate elements within and outside the Government of Iran by providing these elements with arms, equipment and related materiel in order to enhance the credibility of these elements in their effort to achieve a more pro-U.S. government in Iran by demonstrating their ability to obtain requisite resources to defend their country against Iraq and intervention by the Soviet Union. This support will be discontinued if the U.S. Government learns that these elements have abandoned their goals of moderating their government and appropriated the materiel for purposes other than that provided by this Finding.

Ronald Reagan

The White House,
Washington, D.C.
Date January 17, 1986

POINDEXTER MEMO ACCOMPANIES FINDING

Following is the text of the background paper from Vice Adm. John M. Poindexter that accompanied the January 17, 1986, intelligence "finding" authorizing weapons sales to Iran. The document was prepared by National Security Council aide Lt. Col. Oliver L. North. A notation at the bottom of the memorandum said that the "president was briefed verbally from this paper" with Vice President George Bush, Chief of Staff Donald T. Regan, and Donald R. Fortier, the deputy national security adviser, present.

ACTION

MEMORANDUM FOR THE PRESIDENT
FROM: JOHN M. POINDEXTER
SUBJECT: Covert Action Finding Regarding Iran

Prime Minister Peres of Israel secretly dispatched his special advisor on terrorism with instructions to propose a plan by which Israel, with limited assistance from the U.S., can create conditions to help bring about a more moderate government in Iran. The Israelis are very concerned that Iran's deteriorating position in the war with Iraq, the potential for further radicalization in Iran, and the possibility of enhanced Soviet influence in the Gulf all pose significant threats to the security of Israel. They believe it is essential that they act to at least preserve a balance of power in the region.

The Israeli plan is premised on the assumption that moderate elements in Iran can come to power if these factions demonstrate their credibility in defending Iran against Iraq and in deterring Soviet intervention. To achieve the strategic goal of a more moderate Iranian government, the Israelis are prepared to unilaterally commence selling military materiel to Western-oriented Iranian factions. It is their belief that by so doing they can achieve a heretofore unobtainable penetration of the Iranian governing hierarchy. The Israelis are convinced that the Iranians are so desperate for military materiel, expertise and intelligence that the provision of these resources will result in favorable long-term changes in personnel and attitudes within the Iranian government. Further, once the exchange relationship has commenced, a dependency would be established on those who are providing the requisite resources, thus allowing the provider(s) to coercively influence near-term events. Such an outcome is consistent with our policy objectives and would present significant advantages for U.S. national interests. As described by the Prime Minister's emissary, the only requirement the Israelis have is an assurance that they will be allowed to purchase U.S. replenishments for the stocks that they sell to Iran. We have researched the legal problems of Israel's selling U.S. manufactured arms to Iran. Because of the requirement in U.S. law for recipients of U.S. arms to notify the U.S. government of transfers to third countries, I do not recommend that you agree with the specific details of the Israeli plan. However, there is another possibility. Some time ago Attorney General William French Smith determined that under an appropriate finding you could authorize the CIA [Central Intelligence Agency] to sell arms to countries outside of the provisions of the laws and reporting requirements for foreign military sales. The objectives of the Israeli plan could be met if the CIA, using an authorized agent as necessary, purchased arms from the Department of Defense under the Economy Act and then transferred them to Iran directly after receiving appropriate payment from Iran.

The Covert Action Finding attached at Tab A provides the latitude for the transactions indicated above to proceed. The Iranians have indicated an immediate requirement for 4,000 basic TOW weapons for use in the launchers they already hold.

The Israeli's [sic] are also sensitive to a strong U.S. desire to free our Beirut hostages and have insisted that the Iranians demonstrate both influence and good intent by an early release of the five Americans. Both sides have agreed that the hostages will be immediately released upon commencement of this action. Prime Minister Peres had his emissary pointedly note that they well understand our position on not making concessions to terrorists. They also point out, however, that terrorist groups, movements, and organizations are significantly easier to influence through governments than they are by direct approach. In that we have been unable to exercise any suasion over Hizballah during the course of nearly two years of kidnappings, this approach through the government of Iran may well be our *only* way to achieve the release of the Americans held in Beirut. It must again be noted that since this dialogue with the Iranians began in September, Reverend [Benjamin] Weir has been released and there have been no Shia terrorist attacks against American or Israeli persons, property, or interests.

Therefore it is proposed that Israel make the necessary arrangements for the sale of 4000 TOW weapons to Iran. Sufficient funds to cover the sale would be transferred to an agent of the CIA. The CIA would then purchase the weapons from the Department of Defense and deliver the weapons to Iran through the agent. If all of the hostages are not released after the first shipment of 1000 weapons, further transfers would cease.

On the other hand, since hostage release is in some respects a byproduct of a larger effort to develop ties to potentially moderate forces in Iran, you may wish to redirect such transfers to other groups within the government at a later time.

The Israelis have asked for our urgent response to this proposal so that they can plan accordingly. They note that conditions inside both Iran and Lebanon are highly volatile. The Israelis are cognizant that this entire operation will be terminated if the Iranians abandon their goal of moderating their government or allow further acts of terrorism. You have discussed the general outlines of the Israeli plan with Secretaries [George P.] Shultz and [Caspar W.] Weinberger, Attorney General [Edwin] Meese [III] and Director [William J.] Casey. The Secretaries do not recommend you proceed with this plan. Attorney General Meese and Director Casey believe the short-term and long-term objectives of the plan warrant the policy risks involved and recommend you approve the attached Finding. Because of the extreme sensitivity of this project, it is recommended that you exercise your statutory prerogative to withhold notification of the Finding to the Congressional oversight committees until such time that you deem it to be appropriate.

STATE OF UNION ADDRESS, MAJORITY LEADER'S REPLY

Following are comments on the Iran-contra affair included in President Reagan's January 27, 1987, State of the Union address and in a response delivered by Senate majority leader Robert C. Byrd, D-W.Va.

Reagan Comments

But though we've made much progress, I have one major regret. I took a risk with regard to our action in Iran. It did not work, and for that I assume full responsibility.

The goals were worthy. I do not believe it was wrong to try to establish contacts with a country of strategic importance or to try to save lives. And certainly it was not wrong to try to secure freedom for our citizens held in barbaric captivity. (Applause.) But we did not achieve what we wished, and serious mistakes were made in trying to do so. We will get to the bottom of this, and I will take whatever action is called for.

But in debating the past—(applause)—in debating the past, we must not deny ourselves the successes of the future. Let it never be said of this generation of Americans that we became so obsessed with failure that we refused to take risks that could further the cause of peace and freedom in the world. (Applause.)

Much is at stake here, and the nation and the world are watching—to see if we go forward together in the national interest, or if we let partisanship weaken us.

U.S. Policy on Terrorism

And let there be no mistake about American policy: we will not sit idly by if our interests or our friends in the Middle East are threatened, nor will we yield to terrorist blackmail....

Commitment to Contras

In Central America, too, the cause of freedom is being tested. And our resolve is being tested there as well. Here, especially, the world is watching to see how this nation responds.

Today, over 90 percent of the people of Latin America live in democracy. Democracy is on the march in Central and South America. Communist Nicaragua is the odd man out—suppressing the Church, the press, and democratic dissent and promoting subversion in the region. We support diplomatic efforts, but these efforts can never succeed if the Sandinistas win their war against the Nicaraguan people.

Our commitment to a Western Hemisphere safe from aggression did not occur by spontaneous generation on the day that we took office. It began with the Monroe Doctrine in 1823 and continues our historic bipartisan American policy. Franklin Roosevelt said we "are determined to do everything possible to maintain peace on this hemisphere." President Truman was very blunt: "International communism seeks to crush and undermine and destroy the independence of the Americans. We cannot let that happen here."

And John F. Kennedy made clear that "communist domina-

tion in this hemisphere can never be negotiated." (Applause.)

Some in this Congress may choose to depart from this historic commitment, but I will not. (Applause.)

This year we celebrate the second century of our Constitution. The Sandinistas just signed theirs two weeks ago—and then suspended it. We won't know how my words tonight will be reported there, for one simple reason: there is no free press in Nicaragua.

Nicaraguan freedom fighters have never asked us to wage their battle, but I will fight any effort to shut off their lifeblood and consign them to death, defeat, or a life without freedom. There must be no Soviet beachhead in Central America. (Applause.) . . .

Byrd Comments

The Administration's recent dealings with Iran have cast a long shadow over this country. There's a gathering sense of mistrust.

The sale of arms to Iran—in direct contradiction to our stated foreign policy—raises real questions about trust. But it also raises real doubts about competence. Without competence—and a good measure of common sense—government will have a tough time earning the nation's trust.

And government without trust is government without power.

'A Breach of Faith'

That's why so many find the Iranian affair so troubling. It was a breach of faith—both here and abroad.

Like people, a nation is only as good as its word. If our word is good—our nation is strong. If our word is in doubt—our nation is weak. We do not hold the free world together at gunpoint. It is a mutual trust that binds us—a respect for one another and a common commitment to human dignity and to peace.

This Democratic Congress wants to work with the President and the administration in advancing our national interests abroad. We need a coherent foreign policy that aggressively seeks to get the peace movement back on track in the Middle East; a policy that does not just offer the contras as a solution to our problems in Central America; a foreign policy that utilizes all the resources available to us—diplomatic, political, economic, and military—to achieve America's goals in the world.

For the moment, our allies and our friends are bewildered and question our motives. They wonder how we can rail against terrorism—and then sell arms to terrorists. Many of you are wondering, too.

Open Debate on Foreign Policy

Foreign policy is too crucial in today's world to be decided in the dark. Tonight, Americans are once again held hostage by terrorists. We must stand together and have the courage of our convictions. Americans love liberty and human freedom. All of us want to see our hostages brought home. But if risks must be taken, then all Americans must understand those risks—and take them together.

Bold actions can succeed, but they must be based on carefully considered and sound judgment. The President owes us all a more open debate on foreign policy in return for our trust. And, we owe our allies and friends a firmer handshake in return for theirs.

The Administration has the obligation to tell the American people exactly what led to the arms-for-hostage deal—and what happened to accountability in the White House....

SENATE INTELLIGENCE IRAN-CONTRA INQUIRY

Following is the text of the Senate Intelligence Committee's report (S Rept 100-7) on its investigation into the

Iran-contra affair. The report, Preliminary Inquiry into the Sale of Arms to Iran and Possible Diversion of Funds to the Nicaraguan Resistance, *was released January 29, 1987.*

Letter of Transmittal

U.S. Senate,
Select Committee on Intelligence,
Washington, DC, January 29, 1987.

Hon. Daniel K. Inouye,
Chairman, Select Committee on Secret Military Assistance to Iran and the Nicaraguan Opposition, U.S. Senate, Washington, DC.

Dear Dan: Pursuant to Senate Resolution 23, transmitted herewith is the report prepared by the Select Committee on Intelligence summarizing the results of our preliminary inquiry into the sale of arms to Iran and the possible diversion of funds to the Contras. In accordance with the terms of Senate Resolution 23, the report describes in narrative form information which the Committee was able to learn during the course of its study and identifies areas of inquiry that the Committee believes should be among these [*sic*] pursued by the Special Committee.

In transmitting this report to your Committee, we would like to share briefly with you the limited objectives of the Committee, a sense of how the Intelligence Committee conducted the inquiry upon which the report is based, and where we stand in terms of gathering relevant information.

At the outset, it should be emphasized that the study by the Intelligence Committee was necessarily limited, both in scope and in time. It was never the goal or the mandate of the Intelligence Committee during this initial phase to conduct a definitive investigation into this complex matter. Rather, the Intelligence Committee undertook its inquiry pursuant to its responsibility for oversight of the nation's intelligence activities. Furthermore, we sought to gather as much information as possible while recollections were fresh and to collect in one place as many documents as possible that would be pertinent to any future comprehensive investigation. In addition, it was our hope that this preliminary work would help the new Committee to accomplish its task more quickly insofar as some of the groundwork would have been done. The Intelligence Committee, we believe, succeeded in accomplishing this goal.

For all intents and purposes, the Committee commenced its inquiry on December 1 by issuing subpoenas to 15 individuals and entities, as well as a series of invitations to appear, and concluded the information gathering process on December 18. During this period, the Committee received testimony from 36 witnesses and received thousands of pages of documents. While it was impossible to include all details of documents and all information received because of constraints of time and resources, nonetheless, the complete record of information received, including any additional data which was received after December 18, is herewith transmitted to the Special Committee in addition to our report.

While documents and testimony received by the Committee during the course of its study of this matter were voluminous, the work of our Committee was only preliminary in nature for a number of reasons related primarily to the time constraints described above. First, a number of potentially useful witnesses could not be called by the Committee or were out of the country and therefore unable to testify. Secondly, while a total of 36 witnesses appeared before the Committee, such key witnesses as Admiral John [M.] Poindexter, Lieutenant Colonel Oliver [L.] North, Retired Major General Richard [V.] Secord, Retired Colonel Robert [C.] Dutton, and Colonel Robert [L.] Earl asserted their constitutional rights and declined to testify. Director of Central Intelligence William [J.] Casey appeared before the Committee just before this inquiry was commenced and before the full scope of the situation was known by the public or by the Committee, and prior to his unfortunate illness. Accordingly, his testimony was general in nature and was not under oath. Third, because of the pressure of time, the witnesses that appeared before the Committee did so

without the benefit of prior interviews. Obviously, from an investigative standpoint, this precluded a comprehensive examination. And, when the witnesses did testify, consistent with the Committee's objectives, the questioning was geared toward information gathering purposes rather than toward prosecution and confrontation. Fourth, except in two instances, witnesses were not recalled to be questioned regarding information acquired by the Committee subsequent to their initial appearance. Any such information or documents, of course, are included in this transmittal to the new Special Committee. Fifth, again consistent with the Committee's information gathering purposes, subpoenas were narrowly drawn. Consequently, there may still be documents that we have not obtained that would be helpful to you. And, while the staff has reviewed the vast majority of documents that were received by the Committee, including all documents received from public sources, time constraints have prevented a detailed analysis of all documents from private sources. Finally, as noted above, new information has come to light since the close of the fact finding period with respect to which the Committee could not follow up if it was to complete this report to the new Special Committee. This includes information both reported in the media and contained in documents that are still being delivered to the Intelligence Committee in response to our subpoenas. It was felt that since the new Special Committee has now been charged with overall responsibility for the investigation, this information should simply be transmitted to the new Committee rather than subjecting it to analysis by the Intelligence Committee.

As noted above, the Committee heard testimony from 36 witnesses and gathered thousands of pages of documents from both public and private sources. When witnesses testified before us, they did so behind closed doors and before only Senators and limited Committee staff. The Committee was careful to sequester witnesses as a precaution against coordinated or otherwise compromised testimony. Again, our goal was to preserve the record for any future investigation.

With respect to the report itself, we have attempted to set forth information received by the Committee in an objective manner, without evaluation. We believe that this is necessary because any conclusions based upon such inherently limited fact finding would be necessarily premature. Therefore, the report seeks solely to be an accurate and fair representation of the information which has been presented to us. We have tried to indicate where there are discrepancies in testimony about specific events or decisions and where there are gaps in the information that we have learned. Indeed, it is evident that this preliminary inquiry cannot provide a final resolution to the fundamental questions facing the new Special Committee.

Because so much attention has been given to earlier staff drafts of reports which were not approved by the Intelligence Committee, we would like to touch briefly on why this report has been adopted by the Committee. First, the Committee believes that its report should be primarily a summary of the information that we have gathered and that it could not appropriately reach conclusions or findings because of its preliminary nature, other than to note discrepancies and gaps and to identify areas of inquiry which might merit future consideration by your Committee. We believe that this report accomplishes that goal.

Secondly, since January 6, the testimony of a dozen witnesses has been transcribed and made available for preparation of this report and thousands of pages of documents which had not been previously indexed and reviewed, have now been analyzed. While much of this information does not dramatically change the thrust of the report, some of the information is clearly useful. If some of the documents which were in our possession had not been reviewed and analyzed before the issuance of a report, such an omission could have adversely affected the credibility of the Committee's work.

What we are presenting to you is, as we indicated, still necessarily incomplete. We believe, however, that it is as complete and consistent as it can be based upon the information made available to us. This report describes the essence of much of the documents and testimony that we have gathered, and it is our hope and belief that the report, along with the documents and testimony transmitted herewith, will provide a useful tool to your Committee staff as you begin your work.

We look forward to working with you in this vital endeavor to determine all the facts regarding this matter and the implications for our national security and our foreign policy decision making process. If the Members or the staff of the Senate Select Committee on Intelligence can be of any assistance to you in the upcoming weeks and months, please do not hesitate to call upon us.

Sincerely,

David L. Boren, *Chairman*
William S. Cohen, *Vice Chairman*

Introduction

In response to public and private reports and in accordance with its responsibility for oversight of the nation's intelligence activities, the Senate Select Committee on Intelligence on December 1, 1986, undertook a preliminary inquiry into the sale of arms to Iran and possible diversion of funds to the Contras. It was not the goal of the Committee to conduct a definitive investigation into this complex matter. Rather, the Committee sought only to gather as much information as possible while recollections were fresh and to collect in one place as many relevant documents as possible.

Accordingly, two objectives were served: first, the Committee learned a great deal of information that will be extremely useful in the future as the Committee continues to perform its intelligence oversight function; and, secondly, testimony and documents have been preserved that the Committee hopes will contribute to the Select Committee on Secret Military Assistance to Iran and the Nicaraguan Opposition as it performs its investigative function. As a result, the Select Committee should be able to save time by moving more rapidly through the preliminary stages of its investigation and thereby get the facts to the American public that much sooner.

Consistent with these twin objectives, and pursuant to Senate Resolution 23 (100th Congress), this report is in two parts: first, Section I summarizes in narrative form the information given to the Committee during the course of its inquiry which the Committee believes is materially relevant to the mandate of Senate Resolution 23. Since the fact finding of the Committee encompassed only 18 days, this narrative is necessarily incomplete and thus endeavors only to provide a general chronological framework of events derived from the documents and testimony received by the Committee. Secondly, again consistent with Senate Resolution 23, Section II sets forth certain unresolved questions and issues that the Committee recommends be pursued by the Select Committee.

The Iran Initiative

Origins

The Committee's inquiry suggests that the Iran initiative originated as a result of the confluence of several factors including:
—A reappraisal of U.S. policy toward Iran by the National Security Council [NSC], beginning in late 1984, with special emphasis on building a constructive relationship with moderate elements in Iran;
—Deep concern at the highest level of the U.S. Government over the plight of American citizens held hostage in Lebanon;
—Israel's strong and continuing interest in furthering contacts with Iran;
—Efforts on the part of private parties, including international arms dealers and others.

Reappraisal of U.S. Policies

The formal reappraisal of U.S. policy toward Iran began in late 1984 when the National Security Council issued a National Security Study Directive (NSSD). An NSC official involved in the

policy review testified that he was disappointed with the bureaucracy's lack of imagination in responding to this study directive and with the absence of any recommendation for change in policy.

In May 1985, the CIA [Central Intelligence Agency] National Intelligence Officer for the Middle East prepared a five-page memo which went to the NSC and the State Department, arguing for a change in U.S. policy that would seek a more constructive relationship with Iranian leaders interested in improved ties with the West. The memo argued in part that the U.S. could permit allies to sell arms to Iran as one of the alternative means of establishing Western influence so as to offset growing Soviet inroads in Iran. Apparently using the arguments in this memo two members of the NSC staff then prepared a draft National Security Decision Directive (NSDD) which proposed a departure in U.S. policy toward Iran. Describing the Iranian political environment as increasingly unstable and threatened by Soviet regional aims, the draft NSDD stated that the U.S. is compelled to undertake a range of short and long term initiatives to include the provision of selected military equipment to increase Western leverage with Iran and minimize Soviet influence.

National Security Adviser Robert [C.] McFarlane transmitted the draft NSDD on June 17, 1985 to Secretaries [George P.] Shultz and [Caspar W.] Weinberger for their comment. State Department logs and Secretary Shultz's testimony indicate that he responded in writing on 29 June that the proposed policy was "perverse" and "contrary to our own interests." Weinberger made the following comment in the margin of the draft, "This is almost too absurd to comment on." According to Weinberger's testimony and that of Assistant Secretary of Defense [Richard L.] Armitage, Weinberger responded in writing opposing such sales.

The Hostage Factor

Testimony by several senior Administration witnesses indicate that during 1985, the Administration was preoccupied on a regular basis with matters relating to terrorism and the state of U.S. hostages. In particular, documents and testimony reflect a deep personal concern on the part of the President for the welfare of U.S. hostages both in the early stages of the initiative and throughout the program. The hostages included William Buckley, a U.S. official in Lebanon. Information was received that in late 1985 the Syrians informed Ambassador Vernon Walters that Buckley's captors had tortured and killed him. The reports indicate that this information was conveyed to Vice President [George] Bush who found it very distressing. The possibility of the release of U.S. hostages was brought up repeatedly in conjunction with discussion of the program.

Israeli Interests

According to documents and testimony received by the Committee, Israel had a strong interest in promoting contacts with Iran and reportedly had permitted arms transfers to Iran as a means of furthering their interests. A series of intelligence studies written in 1984 and 1985 described Israeli interests in Iran. These studies also reported Israeli shipments of non-U.S. arms to Iran as well as the use of Israeli middlemen as early as 1982 to arrange private deals involving U.S. arms. In an interview with the Chairman and Vice Chairman of the Committee on November 21, 1986, National Security Adviser John Poindexter described Israel's interest in much the same terms.

McFarlane testified that he was never informed by the CIA that Israel has been engaged in such activities during 1981-85. In fact, McFarlane, prompted by news accounts of such activity on the part of Israel, asked the CIA—and the DCI specifically—several times whether the news reports were true. He was told they were not. McFarlane testified that if he had known that the Israelis had previously shipped arms to Iran it would have made him less responsive to later Israeli proposals to resume shipments. However, in his first cable to Shultz in the matter, he stated that it was obvious to him the Israeli channel into Iran had existed for some time. One of the NSC staffers who drafted the NSDD testified that he was aware of allegations that Israel was selling arms to

Iran but discounted such reports because he believed they failed to offer conclusive evidence and because Prime Minister [Shimon] Peres had assured the U.S. that there was no such trade.

Private Parties

Documents and testimony indicate that Adnan Khashoggi and other international arms dealers, including Manucher Ghorbanifar, were interested in bringing the U.S. into an arms relationship with Iran, and had discussed this at a series of meetings beginning in the summer of 1984 and continuing into early 1985. These discussions reportedly included the idea of an "arms for hostages" deal in part as a means of establishing each country's bona fides. Khashoggi reportedly met with various leaders in the Middle East to discuss policy toward Iran during this same period.

In July 1985 Khashoggi sent McFarlane a lengthy paper he had written dealing with the political situation in Iran. McFarlane testified that he did not recall seeing these papers, but indicated the existence of prior "think pieces" Khashoggi had sent him on the Middle East. A staff member of the NSC testified that McFarlane gave the Khashoggi paper to another NSC staffer. Michael Ledeen, a professor at Georgetown University, and a part-time NSC consultant beginning in February 1985, appears to have played a key role in the initial contacts between the U.S. and Israel vis-a-vis Iran. According to Ledeen, while on a trip to Europe in April 1985, he spoke with a European intelligence official who had just returned from Iran. The official characterized the internal situation in Iran as more fluid than previously thought, and suggested it was time for the U.S. to take a new look at Iran. He said that the U.S. should discuss this with the Israelis, who the official believed were unusually well-informed about Iran.

According to testimony by McFarlane, Ledeen apprised McFarlane of a forthcoming trip Ledeen planned to Israel and asked whether he was interested in knowing whether Israel had any Iranian contacts. McFarlane testified that he responded affirmatively. McFarlane stated that he was aware that Ledeen was a friend of Israeli Prime Minister Peres. Ledeen testified that he talked to McFarlane in April 1985 about the possibility of raising contacts with Iran with the government of Israel and that McFarlane agreed, and requested specifically that Ledeen get Israel's perspective on fighting Iranian terrorism.

According to Ledeen, he traveled to Israel on 4-5 May 1985, and discussed the situation in Iran with Prime Minister Peres. Peres referred Ledeen to a retired Israeli intelligence official who agreed with Ledeen that both countries needed to work together to improve their knowledge of Iran. Ledeen testified that he reported his talks in Israel to McFarlane in mid-May, and that McFarlane subsequently arranged to task the Intelligence Community to produce a Special National Intelligence Estimate (SNIE) on Iran.

Secretary of State Shultz learned of Ledeen's activities and, in a message dated 5 June, complained to McFarlane that Ledeen's contact with Israel had bypassed the Department of State. Shultz noted that Israel's agenda regarding Iran "is not the same as ours" and that an intelligence relationship with Israel concerning Iran "could seriously skew our own perception and analysis of the Iranian scene." He added that we "are interested to know what Israel thinks about Iran, but we should treat it as having a bias built in," and concluded that this initiative "contains the seeds of . . . serious error unless straightened out quickly." McFarlane responded in a cable of June 7 that Ledeen had been acting "on his own hook." With regard to the Iran initiative, McFarlane stated "I am turning it off entirely," but added "I am not convinced that that is wise."

On June 14, 1985, TWA Flight 847 was hijacked. According to testimony by White House Chief of Staff Donald [T.] Regan, McFarlane mentioned the possibility of requesting use of the Israeli channel to Iran in briefings to the President during the crisis. Regan said that this was his first awareness of any such contacts.

According to testimony by McFarlane, on July 3, 1985, David Kimche, Director General of Israel's Foreign Ministry and a former intelligence officer, contacted McFarlane and reported to him that Israel had succeeded in establishing a dialogue with Iran. Kimche stated that as a result of growing concerns with Soviet pressures, Iranian officials had asked Israel to determine whether the U.S. would be interested in opening up political talks with Iran. According to McFarlane, Kimche stated that the Iranians understood U.S. concerns regarding their legitimacy and therefore had proposed to use their influence with radical elements holding U.S. hostages in Lebanon. Although there was no specific Iranian request for arms, Kimche admitted to the possibility that Iranians might raise the arms issue in the future.

In a cable from McFarlane to Shultz on July 14, 1985, McFarlane stated that the proposal had also been raised several weeks earlier by Peres to Ledeen. In the cable, McFarlane said that he had instructed Ledeen to say we did not favor such a process. McFarlane also reported that Kimche, on instructions from Peres, had come to inquire about the U.S. disinclination to pursue the initiative and ask McFarlane to take up the proposal with appropriate authorities. Then on July 14, "a private emissary" from Prime Minister Peres came to press the point.

McFarlane further noted to Shultz the advantages and disadvantages of the Kimche proposal, and gave a positive assessment of the Iranian channel based upon his confidence in his Israeli contacts. Finally, he stated that in the short term seven hostages might be released and therefore that he tended to favor going ahead.

Shultz responded to McFarlane by cable the same day, noting that the U.S. should make a tentative show of interest without making any commitment and should listen and seriously consider the idea of private U.S.-Iran relations. Shultz stated that McFarlane should manage the initiative, while making it known to the Israelis that McFarlane and Shultz would be in close contact and full agreement at every step.

McFarlane testified that he visited the President in the hospital on either July 13 or 14, 1985. According to testimony by Regan, he also attended the meeting and believes that it occurred three days after the President's operation (i.e., July 16 or 17). Regan further testified that at the meeting McFarlane requested the President's authority to use an Israeli contact with an Iranian as a channel to higher-ups in Iran. According to Regan, McFarlane was vague about the specifics of the plan, and the President then questioned McFarlane on his confidence in the Iranian contact, Ghorbanifar. Regan testified that McFarlane defended Ghorbanifar on the basis of Israeli assurances and the President authorized McFarlane to explore the channel. Regan testified that it was his own opinion that the release of hostages would have been a collateral benefit of such an opening.

McFarlane testified that the plan he conveyed to the President was essentially what Kimche had suggested. McFarlane stated that he told the President that he would not be surprised if arms entered into the relationship later. According to McFarlane, the President was enthusiastic about the opening, hoped it would lead to the release of hostages, and authorized McFarlane to explore the plan.

In his testimony, McFarlane categorically denied any discussion of Ghorbanifar with the President, recalling that it was only in December that McFarlane became aware of Ghorhanifar's [Ghorbanifar] identity. It should be noted, however, that McFarlane made reference to Ghorbanifar in his July 14 cable to Shultz describing the proposal. In describing his contacts with the emissary from Peres and Kimche, McFarlane stated that the Iranian officials named in the context of the proposal are an ayatollah and "an advisor to the Prime Minister named Ghorbanifar."

Meanwhile, according to testimony by Ledeen, in early July he was called by Kimche who said a friend, Al Schwimmer, was coming to Washington and wanted to talk to Ledeen. Ledeen testified that he met with Schwimmer in early July. Schwimmer recounted a meeting he had attended a week or two before in Europe with Kimche, Khashoggi and Ghorbanifar. Schwimmer said Ghorbanifar had a lot of useful information about the situation in Iran and that Ledeen should meet him as soon as possible.

According to Ledeen he reported his meeting with Schwimmer to McFarlane. Ledeen told McFarlane he was going to Israel on vacation from mid-July to mid-August, and would, if McFarlane thought it appropriate, meet Ghorbanifar. Ledeen testified that McFarlane agreed.

Ledeen met Ghorbanifar in Israel in late July. Kimche, Schwimmer and Yaacov Nimrodi, an arms dealer and former Israeli military attache in Tehran, also attended. At the meeting Ghorbanifar gave what Ledeen described as "a great quantity" of information on Iran. Ledeen testified that Ghorbanifar said that if relations between Iran and the U.S. were to improve, each side would have to send the other clear signals about its seriousness, and that the Iranian signal could be a release of the hostages in Lebanon (referring specifically to U.S. Government official William Buckley) and cessation or moderation of Iran-sponsored terrorism. According to Ledeen, Ghorbanifar said that for the U.S. the only convincing gesture would be to help Iran buy weapons it otherwise could not obtain.

According to documents received by the Committee, Kimche phoned McFarlane on July 30 to request an August meeting. According to testimony by Shultz, Kimche and McFarlane met at the beginning of August 1985, at which Kimche indicated that the Iranian not only wanted "a dialogue with America" but also wanted arms from the U.S. and TOW anti-tank missiles from Israel. In return the Iranians could produce hostages.

The August-September Shipment of TOWs

On August 8, 1985 at a meeting of the National Security Planning Group in the White House residence, McFarlane, with Poindexter, briefed the President, the Vice President, Shultz, Weinberger, Regan, and Casey on the Kimche proposal to permit the sale of TOWs to Iran through Israel. There is a divergence of views as to whether approval was granted for the Israelis to ship arms to Iran either at that meeting or subsequent to it. There is also conflicting testimony on which of the participants supported the proposal, although opposition to the plan by Shultz and Weinberger is clear.

According to testimony by Regan, the President declined to authorize the sale of TOWs because of misgivings about Ghorbanifar's credentials and influence in Iran. Regan testified that the other participants agreed it was premature to get involved in arms sales to Iran. McFarlane, on the other hand, testified that Ghorbanifar's name never came up at the August meeting.

In a November 1986 interview in conjunction with the Attorney General's inquiry, Shultz "dimly recalled" a meeting at the White House residence in August on the subject of an Israeli shipment of TOWs to Iran. In his testimony before the Committee in December, however, Secretary Shultz said there was a meeting on August 6, 1985 where McFarlane briefed the President on an Israeli request for U.S. replenishment of Israeli TOW missiles proposed for shipment to Iran. In return, according to Shultz, the U.S. was to get four hostages and the entire transaction would be deniable. Shultz said he opposed the proposal, but the President did not make a decision.

According to testimony by McFarlane, the transfer was supported by Casey, Regan, and Bush while Shultz and Weinberger opposed it. McFarlane testified that subsequent to the meeting President Reagan approved the Israeli request to ship arms to Iran and to purchase replacements from the U.S. Presidental [sic] approval was on the condition that the transfers would not contribute to terrorism or alter the balance of the Iran-Iraq war. Although there is no written record of a decision at this time, McFarlane testified that the President informed Shultz, Weinberger and Casey of his decision.

According to his testimony, McFarlane believed at the time that the President's decision constituted an "oral Finding," which was formally codified on January 17 in a written Finding. McFarlane testified that when he and Attorney General Meese discussed the legality of an oral Finding November 21, 1986, Meese told him that he believed an oral, informal Presidential decision or determination to be no less valid then [sic] a written Finding. According to documents received by the Committee, McFarlane, when interviewed by Meese, made no mention of Presidential approval of the TOW shipment of August-September 1985 or of an "oral Finding." McFarlane did tell Meese that he told Kimche at a December 1985 meeting in London that the U.S. was disturbed about the shipment of TOWs, and could not approve it.

One White House Chronology prepared in November 1986 simply notes that McFarlane conveyed to Kimche a Presidential decision that a dialogue with Iran would be worthwhile. However, a second White House chronology presents conflicting accounts about whether the U.S. acquiesced in the Israeli delivery of 508 TOWs to Iran on August 30.

According to testimony by McFarlane, Israel did not feel bound to clear each specific transaction with the U.S. Israel proceeded on the basis of a general authority from the President based on a U.S. commitment to replace their stocks. Also Israel's negotiations on hostages would not necessarily require U.S. approval.

According to testimony by Ledeen, when he returned to the U.S. in Mid-August, 1985, McFarlane informed him that the program of contact with Iran would go forward and that a test of the kind Ghorbanifar had proposed would occur. Accordingly, McFarlane told Ledeen to work out arrangements with Kimche for receipt of the hostages. McFarlane said he believed at this time that the sale of TOWs would secure the release of all U.S. hostages.

Ledeen testified that he attended a meeting in Paris on September 4 with Kimche, Ghorbanifar, Schwimmer and Nimrodi. The discussions were in two parts: (1) technical questions about transfers of weapons from Israel to Iran and getting the hostages out of Lebanon; and (2) conversation with Ghorbanifar about events in Iran. Ghorbanifar told them they would soon see public statements by leading Iranian officials making clear their intention to improve U.S.-Iranian relations. Subsequently, according to testimony by Ledeen, in the second week of September on the anniversary of the Iranian revolution, the President and Prime Minister gave speeches in which the Soviets were attacked, but not the U.S. Ledeen saw this as "in accordance with" Ghorbanifar's prediction.

According to testimony from a senior CIA analyst, in early September 1985 Ledeen provided him with information on Iranian-sponsored terrorism and on Ghorbanifar. According to this analyst, this was the first time Ledeen had identified Ghorbanifar by name to the CIA. According to testimony by Ledeen, the subject of Ghorbanifar's bona fides first came up in September 1985. However, Shultz testified that he saw an intelligence report on July 16, 1985, two days after he cabled McFarlane from Geneva, which indicated that Ghorbanifar was a "talented fabricator." Ledeen testified that he knew that the CIA was suspicious of Ghorbanifar, and that Ghorbanifar had raised the subject himself, in one of their meetings. According to testimony by Ledeen, it appeared to him that Ghorbanifar's credentials were well-documented.

The Committee received testimony and documents, however, indicating that the CIA had long been aware of Ghorbanifar's suspect character. In August 1984 CIA had issued a notice to other government agencies warning that Ghorbanifar was a fabricator. Documents indicate CIA was aware, [sic] of one instance in which Ghorbanifar had reportedly offered to provide intelligence on Iran to a third country in return for permission from the third country to continue the drug smuggling activities of Ghorbanifar's associates with the country concerned.

According to the CIA analyst, North called him on September 9, 1985, and requested increased intelligence collection on Lebanon and Iran. North told him there was a possibility of release of American hostages. In mid-September North asked him for intelligence collection on specific individuals in Iran who were in contact with American officials. North later gave him a very restricted distribution list for the intelligence collected, which specifically left out the Department of State. North said Shultz would be briefed orally by McFarlane. As the intelligence began to come in, this senior CIA analyst did not understand all the parties involved. However, he felt the intelligence clearly showed that hostages and some forms of arms sales were involved.

According to documents received by the Committee, the shipment of 508 TOWs left Israel on August 30, 1985, transited a third country and arrived in Iran on September 13. North later asserted to Meese that he was totally unaware of the TOW shipment at the time it occurred. He believed he first learned of it in a November 25 or 26 conversation with Secord while in Tel Aviv. North also claimed that he did not know who had otherwise been aware of the shipment. McFarlane told Meese that he thought he learned of the shipment from Ledeen. He then informed the President, Shultz, Weinberger, and Casey, but noted that the shipment had not achieved the objective of release of all the hostages. According to McFarlane, there was no official contact between the U.S. and Israeli governments regarding the shipment.

On September 15, 1985, the Reverend Benjamin Weir was released from his captivity in Lebanon. According to testimony received by the Committee, there was reason to believe at the time that Ghorbanifar played a direct role in the event. In addition, Ledeen testified that it was clear to the Israelis that there was a causal relationship between the September arms shipment and Ghorbanifar's role in it and the release of Weir. The view that the Iranians helped to secure Weir's release appears to have been shared by McFarlane.

It should be noted that the Committee also received testimony inconsistent with this description of events. Secretary of Defense Weinberger testified in response to a specific question that he knew nothing about any connection between the release of Weir and Israeli arms sales to Iran. Regan testified that McFarlane told the President—in his presence—that the Israelis, "damn them," had sold 500 TOWs to the Iranians without U.S. knowledge. Regan further testified that he, the President, McFarlane and Poindexter decided to "ignore" the incident except to "let the Israelis know of our displeasure" and "keep the channel open." According to Regan's testimony this shipment of arms to Iran was not sanctioned by the U.S. Government.

One White House chronology states that after discussing the matter with the President, it was decided not to expose the action, thus retaining the option of "exploiting the Israeli channel to establish a strategic dialogue."

The testimony of McFarlane is inconsistent with that of Regan. McFarlane in testimony, disputed Regan's characterization of his reaction to the TOW shipment and denied that the President had ever expressed disapproval of the Israeli action. McFarlane testified that the President was "elated" at Weir's release and denied that the President had ever instructed him to reproach the Israelis.

According to evidence received by the Committee, concurrently with the arms shipment and hostage release—and perhaps connected with both—was an airplane flight out of Tabriz, Iran which made an emergency landing in Tel Aviv. Ghorbanifar was very interested in this event, and a CIA analyst studying the situation was convinced that there was a correlation between Ghorbanifar, the aircraft flight to Tel Aviv, and the release of Weir. The Committee has not established that there was a correlation between these events.

The November 1985 Shipment of Hawks

After the first shipment of TOWs, Ledeen continued to be active. He held meetings in the Fall of 1985 with Kimche, Schwimmer, Ghorbanifar, and Nimrodi. These meetings reportedly dealt with intelligence on the situation in Iran and who might want to cooperate with the U.S. Ghorbanifar also discussed the offer to get hostages released and the weapons that Iran needed, including Hawk missiles. Iran demanded an arms shipment before each release while the United States and Israel pushed for release in advance of any further arms shipments.

It is clear from testimony that the Iranians believed the new channel with the U.S. would be productive. For example, they appeared to expect to receive sophisticated weaponry such as Phoenix and Harpoon missiles at some point in the future.

Ledeen testified that he briefed McFarlane on these meetings. He stated that this was a promising channel to pursue but that if it continued on an arms for hostages basis, it would be difficult to determine Iran's motives. Ledeen also suggested that if the program were to continue there was a need to bring in an intelligence service. Ledeen said McFarlane had a "bad feeling" about the program and was going to stop it.

McFarlane testified that on November 17, while in Geneva for the Summit, he received a call from Israeli Defense Minister [Yitzhak] Rabin. Rabin requested assistance in resolving difficulties Israel was having in a shipment of military equipment through a European country onward to Iran. McFarlane told the Committee that he called Colonel North, briefed him on the President's August 1985 decision, and requested that he contact Rabin and offer assistance.

According to notes from the Attorney General's Inquiry, North said he suspected that the Israeli shipment McFarlane mentioned consisted of U.S. arms. Reportedly, North told Meese that he called Rabin and was told Israel was having difficulty in getting clearance for a flight to a European country. Rabin told him the flight involved moving "things" to support a U.S. rapprochement with Iran. North said he then contacted retired Air Force Major General Richard Secord, whom he described as a close personal friend, for assistance. Secord was to try to arrange a large cargo aircraft of neither U.S. nor Israeli origin for the flight.

McFarlane testified that North called him in Geneva to explain the problem. The Israelis had failed to make proper customs arrangements for a flight to the European country. Further, the only aircraft they had available was an El Al plane, which was believed unsuitable because of national markings and documentation. McFarlane testified that North told him McFarlane might have to call the Prime Minister of the European country to get the necessary approval. McFarlane stated that he did so, explaining to the Prime Minister that a transfer from Israel to Iran was in progress and that the U.S. Government would appreciate assistance. North also contacted a CIA official and obtained CIA's support in trying to arrange the necessary flight clearances.

A White House electronic message from North to Admiral Poindexter on November 20 indicates that North had a detailed understanding of the Hawk plan by that time. This message indicates that Israel would deliver 80 Hawks through the European country on November 22 for shipment to Tabriz; five U.S. hostages would then be released to the U.S. Embassy in Beirut; $18 million in payment had already been deposited in appropriate accounts; retired USAF Major General Richard Secord would make all arrangements; and replacements would be sold to Israel. According to documents received by the Committee, North continued to keep Poindexter informed on a daily basis about plans for an impending shipment of Hawk missiles to Iran and the release of American hostages.

The Committee received evidence that McFarlane contacted Secretary of State Shultz and Donald Regan and advised them that hostages were to be released and some type of arms were to be transported to Iran by Israel. This evidence indicates that McFarlane told Regan and Shultz that Israel would buy replacements for these arms from the United States. While Shultz was advised that Hawk missiles were involved, Regan said that he was informed of this fact sometime later.

Regan testified that McFarlane informed the President in Geneva that some type of arms shipment was being considered, and that if the operation were successful, hostages might be freed. Shultz expressed reservations to McFarlane, but according to Shultz, was told by McFarlane that he had cleared it with the President.

After many communications between Washington and this European country, efforts to obtain flight clearances failed. Secord was central to the effort to obtain flight clearances. U.S. officials in the European country were instructed to expect to be contacted by a Mr. "Copp" and to cooperate with him. The messages between CIA Headquarters and the European capital indicate Secord was essentially directing the effort to make arrangements for the flight.

Several witnesses testified that North then asked the CIA to identify a charter aircraft that might be used. In response, CIA proposed using its proprietary aircraft and advised the company to accept this NSC related mission.

The CIA proprietary flew from Israel in the latter part of November, carrying 18 Hawk missiles identified as oil drilling spare parts. According to testimony received by the Committee, there was speculation at the CIA that the cargo was actually arms. When queried by nations responding to requests for overflight clearances as to the nature of the cargo, the CIA office again asked North, who reaffirmed that the flight was carrying oil drilling equipment and was on a humanitarian mission. According to copies of cables received by the Committee, in order to overcome reservations of some countries to granting flight clearance, U.S. officials in certain cases were authorized to inform high host government officials that the humanitarian purpose of the flight was related to hostages and that highest levels of the U.S. Government would appreciate assistance.

According to his testimony to the Committee and memoranda for the record he prepared, it was on Saturday, November 23, that John McMahon, Deputy Director of Central Intelligence, was first informed of CIA's support role. In John McMahon's view, the Agency was merely providing a secure channel of communications to assist NSC personnel seeking flight clearances for the Israeli flight. According to the evidence available to the Committee, McMahon approved provision of this support, and asked for a full briefing on the next business day.

On November 25, McMahon learned that a CIA proprietary had flown the arms to Iran in support of an "NSC mission" without his knowledge or approval. According to McMahon, he instructed that no further CIA activity in support of the NSC operation was to be conducted without a Presidential Finding authorizing covert action. McMahon also directed that involved CIA officials brief the CIA General Counsel, Stanley Sporkin, on what had transpired.

Sporkin testified that he recalled meeting with CIA personnel in late November or early December at the DDCI's request, and learned from them that the CIA was involved in a shipment of arms to Iran. Later in the day, November 25, Sporkin informed McMahon that a Finding would indeed be necessary for such activity to be authorized. McMahon directed that a draft finding be prepared for the President's signature which would provide the necessary authority for the CIA's activity in support of the NSC Iran initiative.

This draft finding was prepared by Sporkin, approved by DCI Casey and delivered to Poindexter on November 26. The draft Finding authorized CIA to provide assistance to "private parties" seeking to free American hostages. It also contained language retroactively ratifying all previous activities undertaken by U.S. officials in pursuit of this effort and directed that the Congress not be informed until directed by the President.

Subsequent to the flight, no U.S. hostages were released. The Iranians were dissatisfied with the type of Hawk missile they received and believed they had been cheated. The Secretary of State later stated that at that point he believed the operation had collapsed and expressed relief that it was over. However, in the CIA, planning and support for future missions in support of the NSC operation continued. The CIA officials who had responded to North's first request testified that he was responsible for this contingency planning and believed the direction from DDCI McMahon to cease support did not prohibit such efforts. Until mid-December, a series of messages relating to possible future missions was exchanged between CIA headquarters and U.S. posts in various European and Middle Eastern countries. Documents received by the Committee indicate that a variety of government officials, liaisons, and other sources were involved during this time.

The Committee received testimony that senior CIA officials made repeated calls to NSC staff in late November and early December urging that the draft November 26 Presidential Finding be signed. According to a memorandum for the record prepared by McMahon on December 7, CIA was informed on December 5 that the President had signed the finding and had directed the CIA not to inform Congress for reasons of safety of the hostages. Sporkin testified that one of his assistants had been informed by North that the finding had been signed and was in Poindexter's safe. CIA believed the December 5 finding contained the provision retroactively ratifying previous actions. However, the Committee has received no documentary evidence that any finding of November 26 or December 5 was ever signed.

At the end of November, according to McFarlane's testimony, he obtained the President's approval to go to London on December 8 to meet with Iranian intermediaries. A meeting of principals in the White House was scheduled for December 7 to discuss Iran.

The Presidential Finding

In an electronic message of December 4, North provided Poindexter with a status report on the situation. North's message stated that it was based on discussions held in Geneva between Kimche, Secord, Ghorbanifar and the Iranian contact. The message recounted Iranian unhappiness with the Hawk shipment in late November. It indicated that release of the hostages is tied to a series of arms shipments beginning later in December, and that North, Secord, Kimche and Schwimmer were to meet in London on December 7 to go over arrangements for the next shipments. It stated that North had gone over all the plans with the CIA official who had assisted in the November 25 flight. He indicated that the only officials fully informed about the longer term goals are McFarlane, Poindexter and North.

On December 7, the President met with Shultz, Weinberger, McMahon representing Casey, McFarlane and Poindexter to discuss the Iran initiative. Most participants who testified before the Committee believed there was a consensus at this discussion that McFarlane would inform the Iranians in London that the U.S. would not trade arms for hostages. Shultz and Weinberger both testified that they left the meeting believing that the arms component of the contacts with elements in Iran was over.

However, at least one participant, DDCI McMahon, testified that there was no decision or consensus. He testified that the meeting was divided over whether to proceed with the Iran initiative, with White House staff supporting continuation and all others disagreeing. There also is disagreement in the Committee's record about whether McFarlane's meeting with the Iranians in London was discussed at the December 7 meeting, or what specific guidance was approved. Two participants did not recall any discussion of instructions McFarlane claimed to have received—to make clear that the U.S. remained open to a political dialogue, but would not exchange arms for hostages.

McFarlane testified that prior to meeting the Iranians in London, he and North met Kimche. Kimche urged the U.S. to be more patient and permit the Iranians to demonstrate their bona fides. According to McFarlane, he told Kimche his mission was "to close down" the operation. He and North then met with Kimche, Nimrodi and Ghorbanifar, to whom McFarlane made it "emphatically" clear that the U.S. would engage in no more arms transfers. According to McFarlane, Ghorbanifar argued strongly for continued U.S. arms transfers, and McFarlane came away convinced the U.S. should not "do business" with Ghorbanifar.

On McFarlane's return, he reported to the President and others on his London meeting. According to Casey's written account of that meeting, McFarlane recommended that the U.S. not pursue a relationship with the Iranians through Ghorbanifar, of whom he did not have a good impression, but that we should work through others. Casey's memo said that "everyone" supported this idea, though it stated that the President "argued mildly" for letting the Israelis go ahead without any U.S. commitment except to replace arms they might ship. The memo indicated the President was concerned for the fate of the hostages if we stopped the discussions, and stated that Casey told the President that the contacts could be justified later as trying to influence events in Iran.

At this time, CIA sent a message through its channels to posts in countries involved in preparations for future missions, advising them that "the deal" was apparently off and everyone should stand down.

McFarlane resigned from the Government on December 11. He testified that he had no further involvement with the Iran matter during the period of January to April 1986.

In a memorandum of December 9, 1985 the day before McFarlane reported on his trip, North summarized the options on the Iran program to Poindexter. North wrote that Ghorbanifar was a reliable interlocutor. He noted that the U.S. should gain operational control to avoid past problems experienced with Schwimmer, [sic] He then posed five options: (1) allow the Israeli shipment of TOWs to go forward, with U.S. replenishment; (2) attempt to rescue the hostages; (3) allow Israel to make only a token shipment of TOWs as a sign of good faith; (4) do nothing; (5) issue a covert action finding and make arms deliveries ourselves through Secord. North indicated that there was little to lose by allowing Israel to go ahead with the delivery of TOWs.

Meanwhile, as a result of Ledeen's activities, the question of Ghorbanifar's bona fides as an intermediary arose again. Ledeen testified that, at Ghorbanifar's request, they met during a private trip made by Ledeen to Europe. At this time, Ghorbanifar again provided information on developments in Iran and complained about his treatment by the CIA.

According to Ledeen, when he returned to the United States in late December 1985, he briefed DCI Casey and other CIA officials about his conversations with Ghorbanifar. He said he stressed to them that Ghorbanifar was a useful channel in gaining a political opening to elements in Iran, and that with proper precautions we should keep working with him. Subsequent to this discussion, Casey asked him to arrange for Ghorbanifar to submit to a CIA polygraph. Ledeen contacted Ghorbanifar abroad and obtained his agreement to the polygraph which was administered in mid January.

Ledeen also had Ghorbanifar visit Washington in late December. There Ghorbanifar met for the first time with CIA officials who were aware of the arms sale efforts. Ghorbanifar discussed many matters of interest to U.S. officials, but the CIA's past experience with him prompted caution. On December 23, Director Casey wrote to the President that Ghorbanifar's information "could be a deception to impress up [sic]. It is necessary to be careful in talking with Ghorbanifar." Casey told the President that the polygraph in January would help.

According to evidence received by the Committee, the polygraph indicated deception by Ghorbanifar on virtually all questions, including whether he was under control of the Iranian government, whether he knew in advance that no American hostages would be released as part of the November Hawk transactions, whether he cooperated with Iranian officials to deceive the U.S., and whether he independently acted to deceive the U.S.

According to testimony received by the Committee, the results of this polygraph, as well as the fact that CIA had instructed all its components in August 1984 to have no dealings with Ghorbanifar were made known to the White House in January, 1986. Nevertheless, the White House chose to continue to work with him and, according to one CIA witness, it was North who was responsible for keeping Ghorbanifar on the project after he failed the polygraph. A senior Directorate of Operations official testified that while CIA had suspicions about the cargo on the November 1985 flight, it was not until these discussions with Ghorbanifar in early January that they knew that the aircraft carried arms. Other documentation submitted to the Committee, however, indicates that at least some CIA officials overseas were aware of the nature of the cargo much earlier, and at least one reported this back to headquarters.

In early January, 1986, Prime Minister Peres sent Amiram Nir, Terrorism Advisor to the Israeli Prime Minister, as an emissary to meet the President about the Iran initiative. According to evidence received by the Committee, Nir urged the President and Poindexter to reconsider the transfer of arms to Iran for the release of hostages.

The Committee received copies of various draft findings prepared during early January. One finding, dated January 6, was signed by the President apparently after review and discussion with the Vice President, Regan and Poindexter. This finding instructed that the DCI not notify Congress until otherwise directed by the President. The cover memorandum attached to this finding, written by North, stated that he had spoken to Casey about this and Casey concurred. According to testimony and documents received by the Committee, prior to the signing of the January 6 finding, Casey, North and Sporkin had met to discuss it. Sporkin testified that he recommended that the revised finding specifically refer to release of the hostages, but North objected. The purpose of the program was described as helping to establish a more moderate government in Iran. It was agreed not to refer to hostages because of the anticipated objections from Shultz.

On January 7, the President met in the Oval office with the Vice President, Shultz, Weinberger, Casey, Meese, and Poindexter to discuss the Iran program. According to participants who testified, two officials—Shultz and Weinberger—argued strongly against providing arms to Iran. According to these participants, the President wished to keep the channel open, and left unresolved the issue of providing arms to Iran. However, this Committee received conflicting testimony as to whether a finding was discussed and, if so, what the content of that discussion was.

Some participants clearly recall discussion of a finding, approval by the President of a finding to authorize the program. They also recall a discussion that withholding of notification of Congress would be legal. Others do not recall specific discussion of a finding, but agree the thrust of the meeting was to go ahead with the Iran initiative. There was little discussion of the issue of notification of Congress, but the Attorney General testified that his impression was that the operation was to be completed within a short time, 60-90 days.

Subsequent to the January 7 meeting, legal analysis of the finding and various means to implement the program continued. The Department of Defense insisted that the sale of arms by the Defense Department to a foreign country, be it Iran or Israel, could not be hidden from Congress under the law. This argument applied not only to future direct or indirect sales to Iran, but also to the replenishment of Israel's TOW stocks, which had to be done under this program because Israel could not afford the replacement cost for the TOWs. The solution was to have DoD sell the arms to the CIA under the Economy Act, an approach that CIA General Counsel Sporkin had urged on legal grounds despite the Agency's desire not to be involved. The CIA could then resell the arms, as part of a covert action operation, to a private company that in turn would sell them to Iran and (for the 508 TOWs) Israel. A small change in the January 6 Finding, adding the words "and third parties," sufficed to authorize this new approach.

A final meeting was held in Poindexter's office on January 16 to review a final draft of the finding. Attending were Poindexter, Casey, Meese, Sporkin and Weinberger. Weinberger again voiced opposition to the program. There was also discussion of the question of notification of Congress.

The Attorney General testified that he gave his opinion that withholding notification was legal, on the basis of the President's constitutional powers and justifiable because of jeopardy to the hostages. Meese testified that it was his recollection that Congress was to be notified as soon as the hostages were freed. Sporkin testified that his recollection was that the participants agreed to defer notification of Congress until release of the hostages, even though they understood this might mean a lengthy delay.

According to a memorandum from North to Poindexter, the final finding was presented to the President on January 17 for signature. Poindexter orally briefed the President on the contents of the finding, in the presence of the Vice President and Regan. According to the North memorandum, Poindexter indicated that in the opinion of the Attorney General, the Finding would provide CIA with the necessary authority to transfer arms legally. The memorandum noted that both sides had agreed that the hostages would be released upon commencement of the arms shipments. It stated that if the hostages were not released after the first shipment, the remaining shipments could be suspended, or redirected to other Iranian groups later. It recommended against notifying Congress. The memorandum contained a notation that the President approved. The Committee has received a copy of the signed finding.

Weinberger testified before the Committee that later that day he received a call from Poindexter informing him of the President's action. Weinberger testified that he instructed his military aide, Major General Colin Powell, to arrange for transfer of the weapons under the Economy Act to the CIA, and that the matter was to be closely held at the direction of the President.

General Powell had had previous discussions with North about the program and about Israel's problems in getting replacement TOWs. Assistant Secretary Armitage testified that Weinberger gave his aide authority to inform Armitage, which was done at a later date. Armitage testified that Deputy Secretary [William H.] Taft [IV] later told him that in April, Taft had seen the finding in Poindexter's office, where it was kept. According to Armitage and a CIA official, Powell worked with Major General Vincent Russo of the Defense Logistics Agency to provide the materiel securely and without any loss of funds for the Army.

CIA's Deputy Director for Operations testified that he was informed by the DDCI or the DCI that CIA was going to provide support to a White House initiative which had two aims: (1) strategic dialogue with Iran; and (2) the release of the hostages. On January 18, 1986, he and two other CIA officials, accompanied by the CIA General Counsel, met with North and Poindexter at the White House where they were told that the President had signed a Finding the day before and that CIA would provide support for the activity, which was to be run out of NSC. They were also told, according to testimony, that the Finding stipulated that Congress was not to be informed because of the sensitivity of the hostage situation. Documents received by the Committee indicate that on January 21, the CIA was asked to assist LTC North in preparing for a meeting in Europe with Ghorbanifar. They did so later that day.

The February Shipment of TOWs

According to documents received by the Committee, full-scale implementation of the January 17 Finding began immediately. LTC North flew to London to brief and negotiate with Ghorbanifar, who was told what the United States was prepared to do as a sign of good faith and interest in a long-term relationship. He was told particularly that the United States would provide intelligence on Iraqi positions in the war zone. Ghorbanifar also was told that more TOW missiles would be sold to Iran and that the unwanted Hawk missiles would be picked up and removed from Iran in connection with the first delivery of 1,000 TOWs. (Then-General Counsel Sporkin later told Attorney General Meese that a planned European meeting that was discussed on January 18 never came off.)

According to documents received by the Committee, by January 24, LTC North had prepared a detailed plan of the program. The plan provided for: provision of intelligence samples to Iran; the financing and delivery of 1,000 TOW missiles to Iran, to be followed by the release of all U.S. hostages and 50 Hizballah prisoners held by Land in southern Lebanon, and the return of Hawk missiles to Israel; and the financing and delivery of 3,000 more TOWs for Iran and 508 TOWs for repayment to Israel. Secord was to be in charge of aircraft requirements. The plan included a prediction that Khomeini would step down on February 11, the anniversary of the Iranian Islamic Revolution; Ghorbanifar was telling U.S. officials that other senior Iranians were urging Khomeini to do this so as to ensure a smooth transition. A memorandum from North to Poindexter contains a "notional timeline" and lists the persons who were fully briefed on the plan: in the NSC, Poindexter, North and Donald Fortier; in CIA, Deputy Director McMahon (as Director Casey was out of the country), the Deputy Director for Operations, one division chief, and one other official, on the outside, Richard Secord; and in Israel, Amiram Nir and Prime Minister Peres. The NSC's Executive Secretary later testified that he was kept out of the program throughout.

North's plan called for intelligence samples to be given to Ghorbanifar in Europe on January 26, 1986. According to testimony and a cable from Deputy Director McMahon to Director Casey, McMahon argued strongly with Poindexter that this should not be done, both because Ghorbanifar could not be trusted and because intelligence could give Iran an advantage in the war; but, McMahon testified, Poindexter insisted, and he obeyed.

According to testimony of Robert Gates, who was Deputy Director for Intelligence at the time, a meeting was held on January 25 at CIA to discuss preparation of intelligence material which was to be passed to the Iranians. Participants testified that the meeting was attended by officials from CIA and LTC North from the NSC. Gates testified that he objected to the release of some specific intelligence relating to Iraq but that he was overruled by the NSC, and CIA was directed to prepare the intelligence material. A CIA official was directed to take the intelligence sample to Ghorbanifar.

The intelligence material was given to Ghorbanifar in a meeting held in Europe in late January, according to testimony and documents received by the Committee. Ghorbanifar complained

bitterly about his polygraph and argued as he had done in Washington on January 13, that his Iranian contacts could be of great use to the United States. (The CIA official testified that in early February, the whole arms sale plan was discussed at a White House meeting that included North, Secord, Deputy Assistant Secretary of Defense Noel Koch, and two CIA officials. The Committee found no other indication of a meeting at this time.)

According to documents received by the Committee, North's "notional timeline" for the Iran arms sale program provided for a funding mechanism in which Iranian funds would be put into an "Israeli account" in Switzerland and then transferred to an account in the same bank that was controlled by Secord. Secord's account manager, in turn, would transfer enough funds to the CIA to cover the actual cost of the arms and transportation. Those funds would be transferred by the CIA to a Defense Department account, at which point DoD could begin to move the materiel to a staging area. According to testimony received by the Committee, on January 21, North tasked the CIA to open a Swiss bank account for their part of the funding chain. According to testimony by CIA officials, CIA personnel decided that the fastest and most secure mechanism would be to use an existing account that also contained funds for an unrelated operation. A CIA official gave the number of that account to North; it was used for several months, until a separate account was created in a routine manner. CIA testimony indicates that there was on commingling of funds between the two projects that used the same bank account for these months. Testimony and documents also indicate that, in practice, DoD needed only an assurance that CIA had the requisite funds in its possession. Actual payment occurred months later, after DoD had formally billed the CIA for the arms.

On January 18, MG Russo was tasked to provide 3,504 TOW missiles to CIA upon certification that CIA had the funds set aside. On February 7, the Army began to consider whether a provision of the Intelligence Authorization Act for FY 1986 required congressional notification of this transfer of arms to CIA. On the 13th of February, the Army's Office of the General Counsel determined that congressional notification was the responsibility of the CIA, rather than the Army. A note of March 5 from MG Russo to MG Powell conveyed Russo's belief that CIA had this responsibility and said that CIA was fully aware of this. In the meantime, the Army had given CIA a price of $3,515,000 for 1,000 TOWs.

On February 12 the CIA notified the Army that funds were available, and on February 13 the TOWs were turned over to the CIA. The 1,000 TOWs were shipped to Israel on February 15-16, and half of them were flown to Iran on February 17. The plane that delivered the remaining TOWs, and picked up the 18 Hawks returned them to Israel on February 18. Testimony indicates that Khashoggi received four checks for $3 million each from Ghorbanifar, and that $1 million went to the investors as interest, while another $1 million covered expenses and profit.

According to documents and testimony received by the Committee, the next step was for a second set of intelligence materials to be given to Ghorbanifar in Europe in mid-February. (This meeting was originally scheduled for early February, and this date was used in one White House chronology prepared in November 1986; it also appeared in Director Casey's testimony on November 21. The Committee has no other indication that a meeting took place at that time.) CIA prepared, with some reluctance, according to CIA witnesses, the intelligence material that was provided to Iran. At one point, according to testimony and documents, North asked Poindexter to urge Director Casey to provide the needed material.

The meeting with Ghorbanifar took place a short time after the first half of the 1,000 TOWs had been delivered to Iran. The U.S. side included North and Secord, with Albert Hakim, and [sic] Iranian-American and business associate of Secord, as interpreter. The intelligence was given to Ghorbanifar, and there was discussion of the common Soviet threat that both Iran and the United States saw in the region.

Later in February, the same Americans met with Ghorbanifar and an Iranian official. Before this meeting, certain Hizballah prisoners were expected to be released; the capture of two Israeli soldiers by Hizballah in mid-February derailed any such expectations. The meeting with the Iranian official was not very successful. North reported by memo to McFarlane that Iran shared the American concern about the Soviet threat, but that their distrust of the United States was also very great. In an electronic memorandum to McFarlane, North stated that Ghorbanifar's translation of his remarks had distorted much of what North had said and that this was a particular problem. A later North memo stated, moreover, that "it became apparent that our conditions/demands had not been adequately transmitted to the Iranian Government by the intermediary.["] According to testimony received by the Committee, the Iranian official indicated that Iran especially needed spare parts for its Hawk anti-aircraft missile systems, rather than just more TOWs. The U.S. side took his request and ordered the second half of the 1,000 TOWs to be delivered; the Iranian agreed to consult with his superiors on the prospects for a higher-level meeting and to return for further meetings. The 500 TOWs were delivered later in February; no U.S. hostages were released. North later wrote that it was agreed at the February meeting that the hostages would be released during a high-level meeting in Iran, after which the U.S. would sell Iran 3,000 more TOWs. Regan testified that the President was informed of the sale of the 1,000 TOWs to Iran.

According to documents received by the Committee, in the wake of the February meeting with the Iranian official, North remained confident that the hostages would be released shortly. He proposed that McFarlane be sent to a meeting in Europe the next week, but found both Poindexter and Casey unenthusiastic, so he appealed to McFarlane for help with Poindexter. By the next day, Poindexter had agreed that McFarlane should go to Europe for the meeting. Shultz testified that Poindexter showed him the terms or [sic] reference that McFarlane would be given, which Shultz approved. Shultz testified that he was told the hostages would be released at the time of the meeting.

Evidence received by the Committee indicates Director Casey may have agreed to another meeting with the Iranian official. The talking points prepared for him the day Poindexter showed the terms of reference to Shultz indicate great concern over who would attend that meeting. Ghorbanifar had been the original interpreter, but the CIA retained severe doubts of his reliability. Although one CIA official had been in close contact with him and had advised working more closely with him, others indicated that Ghorbanifar continued to be untrustworthy. The use of Hakim as interpreter was preferable, but CIA was concerned over Hakim's possible private interests in arms deals with Iran. Casey proposed that a retired CIA officer who still consulted for the Agency be brought on as an interpreter and as a knowledgeable advisor to the program. This was done in early March.

At the end of February, Israeli Prime Minister Peres wrote to President Reagan encouraging him to continue his efforts to gain a strategic opening in Iran and pledging to assist in this effort. Director Casey proposed that the President call Peres to reassure him that the program would continue and to thank him for Israel's assistance. His talking points also argued, however, that the next meeting should be U.S.-Iranian, without a direct Israeli role.

The McFarlane Mission to Tehran

In the period of March through May, 1986, all efforts in the Iran arms sale program were directed at arranging a high-level meeting between U.S. and Iranian officials. These efforts led to the McFarlane mission to Tehran in late May and the associated transfer of Hawk missile parts to Iran. Throughout this period, no hostages were released.

In early March, Ghorbanifar asked for another meeting with U.S. and Israeli officials in Europe. Ghorbanifar was demanding that the U.S. sell Harpoons and 200 Phoenix missiles to Iran, which the U.S. Government was not prepared to do. One CIA official noted that North was planning to take a hard line with Ghorbanifar, while Israel was possibly providing additional non-U.S. arms on the side to move the process along.

The CIA officer brought on as an interpreter was briefed on the program just before leaving for Europe. His testimony indi-

cated that he was told this was an NSC operation, with CIA providing required support. The CIA officer had known of Ghorbanifar in past years, and testimony indicates that he was horrified when he learned that this was the channel being used by the U.S. Government.

At the meeting in early March, Ghorbanifar conveyed the information that senior Iranian officials agreed to a U.S. delegation visiting Tehran for negotiations. He indicated that 240 types of spare parts for the Hawk missile system would have to be provided by the United States, but said that the arrival of the U.S. delegation in Tehran with half of the parts would result in the release of all the hostages. Testimony indicates that prices for the Hawk parts were not discussed. North later wrote that the U.S. team emphasized the February understanding that deliveries would not precede the hostage releases. They deflected the demand for Phoenix and Harpoon missiles by arguing that Iran's launchers for the missiles were inoperable. On March 11, according to Secretary Shultz's testimony, Poindexter told him that a McFarlane trip to Europe was off; this was ascribed to reservations on McFarlane's part.

During the first or second week of March, Gates asked analysts to prepare briefing materials on the Soviet military threat to Iran for use by McFarlane in briefing the Iranians. A week later, other CIA analysts met with Gates and some of the participants in the early March meeting with Ghorbanifar. They were provided a list of Iranian intelligence requirements regarding Iraq and they discussed how to respond to it. The tasking and discussions in early March eventually led to the materials that CIA would hand over in mid-May and that would be used in Tehran in late May.

In mid-March, Ghorbanifar visited Tehran. He told U.S. officials that he had met with several high officials and that the meetings had been difficult. According to a CIA official, [Amiram] Nir, with whom Ghorbanifar also spoke, said Iran's proposals were still unacceptable; Nir worried that Ghorbanifar might be losing credibility with the Iranians and urged U.S. officials to work more closely with Ghorbanifar. Ghorbanifar had been ill and was also having money problems, which he pressed the U.S. Government to help solve. Nir indicated that he and his associates were helping out Ghorbanifar financially.

In late March, U.S. officials were told that Ghorbanifar was especially upset. An "NSC consultant," probably Ledeen, told one official that Ghorbanifar suspected the CIA of entering the office of one of his associates, Roy Furmark, as well as the home of a friend in California. Ghorbanifar told both Nir and a CIA official that Albert Hakim had tried to convince Ghorbanifar's Iranian channel to leave Ghorbanifar out of the negotiations. To demonstrate their support for Ghorbanifar, U.S. officials asked him to return to Washington for another meeting.

U.S. officials met with Ghorbanifar in Washington on April 3 and, less formally, the morning of April 4. Discussions of the proposed visit to Iran covered a wide range of detailed issues: where the meetings would be held; how the U.S. delegation would fly in, and with what passports; what communications they would have; what arms or material they would bring to sell to Iran; and how the delivery of the arms and the release of hostages would be orchestrated. In addition to the 240 types of Hawk parts, Iran wanted Hawk radars and mobile I-Hawk missile batteries, as well as more TOW missiles. The Soviet threat to Iran and Afghanistan was an area of agreement and Ghorbanifar said that Ayatollah Khomeini was going to issue a "fatwa" against hostage-taking. The United States insisted that all the hostages be released before the 240 Hawk parts were delivered, and only then would it discuss further arms deals.

It is unclear whether the subject of devoting some profits to the contras arose at this meeting. One memorandum indicated that support for the mujahedin in Afghanistan was mentioned. Another memo indicated that Ghorbanifar discussed using the profits to support "Afghan rebels, etc." A third, undated memorandum apparently referring to this April meeting indicated that Ghorbanifar said the United States could do the same with Nicaragua.

A memorandum of April 4 set forth the results of the Washington meeting. The U.S. delegation visit was scheduled for April

20. Before then, Iran would pay $17 million into an Israeli account; $15 million of that would be moved into "a private U.S. corporation account." Of that amount, $3.65 million would go to the CIA to cover Hawk missile parts. This price, which testimony indicates the Defense Department had been developing since March, was for those parts that DoD could find in its stocks. Several hours after the arrival of the U.S. delegation, which was to be met by Majlis Speaker Rafsanjani, the hostages would be released; eight hours later, the Hawk parts would be delivered. The memo states that broader U.S. interests in the Soviet threat and in ending the Iran-Iraq war were made clear. Ghorbanifar had proposed that if further agreements were reached to sell TOWs to Iran, a portion of those would be devoted to the Afghan rebels. This memorandum also states that $2 million of the proceeds would finance Israel's purchase of 508 TOWs to replace those sold to Iran in September 1985, and that "$12 million will be used to purchase critically needed supplies for the Nicaraguan Democratic Resistance Forces." The memo is discussed further in the section on the diversion of funds.

Attached to the April 4 memorandum were draft "terms of reference" for use by McFarlane in a high-level meeting with Iranian officials. Testimony and a retrospective memorandum for the record indicate that North and Howard Teischer [Teicher] of the NSC staff prepared the draft in late March, and that it was then revised by Donald Fortier and reviewed by Admiral Poindexter for submission to the President. The "terms of reference" attached to the April 4 memorandum are the same as those in documents of six weeks later, when the mission to Tehran finally took place.

After his return to Europe, Ghorbanifar worked on the details of the planned talks and on raising the "bridge" loan funds needed to start the arms transfer process in light of Iran's refusal to pay until it had received and inspected the materiel. Ghorbanifar told a CIA official that LTC North had promised to sell Iran two Hawk radars, as well as the 240 types of parts Iran had requested. He also described his progress in gaining support for the visit among high-level Iranian officials whom he intended the American delegation to meet.

In mid-April, further difficulties arose. Although Ghorbanifar assured the United States that Iranian officials were prepared to meet with McFarlane, he also reported that Iran was insisting upon not releasing all the hostages before the Hawk parts were delivered; Iranian intransigence was increased, he said, by the realization that McFarlane could not possibly carry all the parts on the plane that would take him to Iran. Iran also continued to insist upon Hawk radars, as well as the other parts.

On April 14, the United States attacked Libyan targets in response to Libyan involvement in terrorism directed at U.S. interests. In the aftermath of that action, hostage Peter Kilbourn was killed by his captors, reportedly at the behest of Libyan leader Muammar Qadhafi [el-Qaddafi]. Some press stories have suggested that the U.S. attack resulted in delays in the mission to Iran. A White House chronology indicates that instead Iran wanted to accelerate planning for the mission, so that it would not be accused of involvement in the Kilbourn death. The Committee has found no other documentation or testimony indicating that these events had an impact on the arms sale program. The Defense Department, meanwhile, continued to track down the Hawk spare parts. CIA formally requested 234 types of Hawk parts in mid-April, and two Hawk radars later in the month. By the end of April, the cost of the Hawk spare parts that the Army had located was fixed at $4.4 million, including transportation.

On April 22, the U.S. Customs Service announced several arrests in a major "sting" operation involving the sale of arms to Iran; an Iranian arms dealer, Cyrus Hashemi, had agreed to co-operate with Customs authorities. Ghorbanifar, who was in Switzerland, was jailed for a day. According to testimony of the CIA consultant, officials surmised that he had been held because he was an investor in the failed scheme. This development seemed likely to make Ghorbanifar (and Iran) more eager to do business through the one reliable channel to the United States, but it also made Iran ever more insistent upon not giving Ghorbanifar the money in advance.

By late April, the lack of progress in arranging the high-level visit to Iran had led the U.S. officials to decide that the operation would be shut down unless there was movement within 2-3 weeks. A CIA official wrote that the differences between the United States and Iran appeared intractable. He suggested the sale of two Hawk radars to Iran and renewed emphasis upon a long-term military supply relationship with Iran. The CIA official noted that Israel was eager for such a relationship and might be quietly supplementing U.S. sales. Then Ghorbanifar and/or Nir apparently proposed that the mission to Iran be only a preliminary meeting. U.S. officials rejected this idea, noting that if Iran understood and abided by what had been agreed to in February, there would be no need for any preliminary meeting. On May 5, a CIA official warned Director Casey and the Deputy Director that "the White House initiative to secure release of American hostages in Lebanon remains dead in the water."

At the end of April, documents indicate that the U.S. Embassy in London became aware of the fact that Ghorbanifar and Khashoggi had approached a British businessman in hopes of getting a $50 million line of credit for arms sales to Iran with U.S. approval. The businessman had been assured by Israeli officials that this was a White House operation and did indeed have U.S. approval. U.S. Ambassador [Charles H.] Price [II] reported this to the Department of State on May 1. The next day, Under Secretary [Michael H.] Armacost sent Secretary of State Shultz a cable at the Tokyo economic summit; Armacost summarized Ambassador Price's report which noted that "the State Department has been cut out." On May 3, Admiral Poindexter spoke with the ambassador and recommended that he discourage the British businessman from getting involved. The ambassador's memo on the call indicates that Poindexter assured the ambassador that there was only a "small shred of truth" in the claim that the White House approved of this operation. Meanwhile, in Tokyo, Secretary Shultz, according to his testimony, tried to find Poindexter to get an explanation; being unable to find him, Shultz went to Chief of Staff Regan instead. Shultz testified that he recommended that Regan speak to the President and end the matter once and for all. According to Secretary Shultz, he was later told by both Admiral Poindexter and Director Casey that the operation had ended.

In early May, just a few days after the incident just recounted, U.S. officials again met with Ghorbanifar in Europe. Ghorbanifar assured them that financing for the arms sale would be no problem. Testimony and documents indicate Ghorbanifar frequently left the talks to call Tehran. On one occasion, according to later testimony, the CIA officer who was serving as interpreter joined in the talks with Tehran to explain that the United States could not or would not bring all the Hawk spare parts at the same time that the McFarlane delegation arrived. The Iranian at first was unwilling to agree to the release of all the hostages before all of the parts arrived, but it was agreed that McFarlane's plane would bring as many of the parts as possible, with the rest to arrive after release of the hostages. A White House chronology indicates that at this meeting, Israel privately indicated to the United States that it wanted the replacement TOWs that the April 4 memo indicated would be funded by this sale. The price for the Hawk spares that was discussed at this meeting was roughly $22.5 million, plus over $20 million for the Hawk radars, but the CIA officer who attended the talks later testified that he was not present when such matters were discussed. However, testimony indicates that LTC North discussed the overpricing problem with another CIA official. And the CIA officer who attended the talks wrote that the dispute over how many Hawk parts to deliver before the release of hostages remained a problem. A CIA official has testified that reporting on these matters was available to the McFarlane delegation.

Immediately after the Europe meeting in early May, U.S. officials moved to get ready for a trip to Tehran. The Defense Department was told to be ready to transfer the Hawk spare parts. Prices were quoted as $4.4 million for the Hawk parts and transportation; $1.8 million for the 508 TOWs; and $6.2 million for the two radars.

On May 15, according to testimony, Adnan Khashoggi paid $15 million into the account of Lake Resources. CIA officials were later told that Khashoggi had obtained this money from an Arab investor and two Canadians. Testimony indicates that Khashoggi was given post-dated checks totalling $18 million, which included 20 percent interest for the one-month loan. Testimony and documents indicate that CIA officials were told in October 1986, that at the May meeting of Khashoggi and Ghorbanifar, Ghorbanifar stated that the high price was because the money was being used to support the Contras.

Director Casey has testified that on May 15, the President approved the McFarlane mission to Tehran. On the same day, according to a later CIA letter to the Committee, the Hyde Park Square Corporation deposited $6.5 million in the CIA's account in Switzerland, to cover both the Hawk parts and the 508 TOWs. (A White House chronology lists the date as May 16, and a different CIA memo cites May 20 as the date. Director Casey's testimony follows the White House chronology. The May 20 date may reflect a second deposit that was expected for the Hawk radars.) On May 16, the CIA notified the Army of the availability of funds for both the Hawk parts and the TOWs. The TOWs were transferred to the CIA on May 19 and shipped to Israel on May 23. According to testimony, the Hawk parts were also supposed to be shipped to Israel during this period. On May 20, the CIA certified the availability of funds to test, inspect and service the old Hawk radars; the next day, it received more detailed cost information on the radars.

A CIA official spoke with Ghorbanifar on May 18 and was assured that the hostages would be available when the Americans arrived in Tehran. He was also assured that McFarlane would meet the top three political officials in Iran (i.e., President Khamenei, Prime Minister Musavi and Majlis Speaker Rafsanjani). Three days later, Ghorbanifar thanked the official for information relayed to him by Richard Secord and described the greeting and accommodations that the U.S. team could expect.

McFarlane has testified that he received pre-trip briefings during the week of May 19. He indicated that he was assured by Admiral Poindexter that Secretary Shultz was involved in the planning for the trip and that Secretary Weinberger had been apprised. His terms of reference emphasized long-term U.S. and Iranian common interests in opposing the Soviet threat. They accept the Iranian revolution as a fact, but note the need for Iran to end its support of terrorism and hostage-taking and its efforts to undermine American interests. They indicate that the United States wants neither an Iraqi victory or [sic] an overwhelming Iranian victory in the Iran-Iraq war. McFarlane's terms of reference show him to offer the prospect of a limited military supply relationship, but say that this depended upon whether Iran and America's convergent or divergent interests come to loom larger in the overall picture.

The McFarlane delegation traveled from the United States to Iran via Europe and Israel on May 23-25. In Israel they took on a single pallet of the Hawk missile parts that Iran had requested. McFarlane later testified that Secord met the plane in Israel, but that McFarlane identified his role primarily in connection with the aircraft. McFarlane's delegation included LTC North, Howard Teischer [Teicher] (North's formal superior on the NSC staff), the CIA officer who served as an interpreter, and others, including U.S. communicators. McFarlane told Attorney General Meese that he brought no inscribed Bible and that LTC North brought the cake that was mentioned in Iranian reports. McFarlane later testified that he carried his own passport, and did not carry a cake or a Bible. Teischer [Teicher] and the CIA officer testified that North brought the cake, and the CIA officer remembered a Bible as well. Documents indicate that, whether or not McFarlane actually carried a false passport, one was prepared for him and has returned after the trip with a one-week Iranian tourist visa and an entry cachet. Teischer [Teicher] later testified that he took detailed notes on the meetings, and the interpeter later wrote a memorandum on the meetings. This report's treatment of the Tehran discussions is based upon the latter source, plus McFarlane's cable to Poindexter.

The Tehran discussions got off to a slow start on May 25, with the arriving delegation having to wait some time before any Iranian officials greeted them. They were taken to a Tehran hotel where, late that afternoon, the first session was held. The Iranians listed past sins of the United States and demanded that the U.S. Government do more than had been agreed in February. The U.S. delegation insisted that the February schedule be adhered to.

On the 26th, there were, [sic] again no discussions until late in the afternoon. The interpreter later noted that the Moslem holy period of Ramadan, during which one fasts during daylight hours, may have interferred [sic] with normal schedules. McFarlane began the discussions by presenting the U.S. position, emphasizing the long-term interests as stated in the terms of reference. This was reasonably well received, but the Iranians then presented a list of demands from the captor of the U.S. hostages. They also accused the United States of going back on its commitments, because McFarlane had not brought half of the Hawk missile parts. Members of the U.S. delegation were surprised at this allegation, but they subsequently learned that Ghorbanifar had given the Iranians the impression that they would bring half of the Hawks with them. The U.S. delegation continued to insist that the hostages must first be freed before any further delivery of arms.

When no progress could be made, McFarlane threatened to end the discussion and leave. The Iranians protested that this was not proper behavior; McFarlane then retired from the negotiations, indicating that he would return if there were an agreement. The Iranians then emphasized how risky it was for them to have this set of discussions, and the American team came to the conclusion that top-ranking officials—particularly Khomeini himself—had not been informed of the meeting.

In a message to Admiral Poindexter after the May 26 session, McFarlane indicated that the Iranians were saying the right generalities and continually assured the U.S. team that they were making progress on the hostages. But McFarlane, while suggesting the sorts of future steps that the U.S. and Iran could take insisted upon concrete acts from Iran before such steps could be taken. He wired Poindexter that the Iranians had produced a competent negotiator to lead their team on the second day, but that McFarlane had remained outside the negotiations to demonstrate the need for more than rhetorical progress.

On May 27, it appeared to the U.S. team that the Iranians were stalling, although they did drop nearly all of the Lebanese demands that had been raised the previous day. The American team drafted an agreement that became the topic for discussion that evening. At midnight the Iranians broke to caucus among themselves. At about 2 a.m. on the 28th, the chief Iranian official asked to see McFarlane. They asked for more time to gain control of the hostage situation and obtained assurances that the remainder of the Hawk parts would arrive within a few hours of the release of the hostages. McFarlane gave them until early the next morning, claiming that he had instructions to leave on the evening of the 27th. In a second message to Admiral Poindexter, McFarlane indicated that his discussions had been low-key and that the common interests between the two countries had been understood. The Iranian official had clearly been told, however, that the balance of the Hawk parts would be forwarded only after the hostages were released. McFarlane recommended that, despite the vastly improved tone in the discussions, the President authorized him to leave on the 28th unless there was clear evidence on an impending hostage release. McFarlane added that he had told the Iranian that further discussions could be arranged after the visit.

On the morning of May 28, one of the Iranians asked whether the United States would settle for two of the hostages to be released before the delivery. McFarlane replied that although the U.S. team was departing, the delivery would not be called off until 9:30. There was [sic] no signs of an impending release, however, and the President gave McFarlane authority to decide when to leave. The U.S. team left at 9. A later White House chronology, drawing upon McFarlane's messages, stated that despite Iran's unwillingness or inability to obtain the release of the hostages, the visit "established the basis for a continuing relationship" and the CIA officer later noted that the U.S. team did meet senior Iranians. One NSC staff member later testified, however, that McFarlane was not pleased with the results.

The CIA officer who served as interpreter later testified that Ghorbanifar had told him at one of the sessions that other Iranians might protest the price of $24 million for the Hawk spare parts.

Ghorbanifar, according to this testimony, asked the CIA officer to uphold that price. The CIA officer says that he then spoke to LTC North who could not explain it, and both approached another delegation member about the matter, again without obtaining a satisfactory explanation.

June-September, 1986

According to testimony by McFarlane, on May 29 he returned from his mission to Tehran reinforced in his belief that the sale of arms was a mistake and that it ought to be terminated. One NSC staffer testified that the word quickly came down that the President had decided there would be no move by the United States to further the sales; the next step was up to Iran.

An intelligence officer on the trip to Tehran with McFarlane, while similarly discouraged by Iran's unwillingness or inability to hold high-level meetings with McFarlane and to secure the release of more hostages, felt that the United States had made its point to Iranian officials regarding its seriousness and that, by the time the trip ended, the Iranians truly wanted further talks. While not quarreling with the idea that Iran would have to move first, an intelligence officer on the trip to Tehran with McFarlane recommended that if they continued talks with Iran, LTC North and he should meet them in Europe to continue the negotiations.

Iranian officials soon heard of the American reaction to the Tehran talks. A November 1986 chronology of the program prepared by the NSC stafff [sic] indicates that on June 10, 1986 Majlis speaker Rafsanjani made a speech that guardedly mentioned Iranians [sic] interest in improved relations with the United States. The Committee does not know whether that speech was seen as a signal at the time, but CIA personnel were soon told that there might be another meeting, and Iranian officials were made aware that a meeting in Europe was possible.

In late June, all the parties were apparently trying to patch together a new schedule of arms deliveries and hostage releases. According to one report, Iran was considering whether to release a hostage before any further deliveries of arms. Another report suggests that Israel offered to "sweeten the pot" by adding some free equipment to the proposed arms sale package.

According to testimony received by the Committee, the Iranians were upset by the high prices being charged, especially for spare parts for Hawk missile systems and by the fact that the U.S. had not upheld its part of the deal in shipping one half of the Hawk missile spare parts to Tehran with the U.S. delegation in May of 1986. A CIA official who participated on the trip contends that no such promise had been made. At the same time, according to the testimony of a CIA official it became clear that Iran was unable to control the captors of U.S. hostages. By early July, two CIA officers were comparing notes on whether the program was in danger; one has testified that he also made LTC North aware of Iranian anger over the high prices. Through early July, various schedules were floated without success. Iran had a price list for Hawk parts, and the gross discrepancies between that list and the prices being charged to Iran were too large to explain away or to ignore.

During this same period, Iranian officials privately told officials of two other countries that they desired better relations with the United States; in one case they noted the possibility of hostage releases. LTC North noticed both these approaches and by July 17 had secured approval for positive responses to Iran through those countries.

In mid-July, there was some progress. It was made clear to Iran through multiple channels that there would be no further movement by the United States unless a hostage was released. According to documents received by the Committee, the Iranians accepted this and took steps to arrange for the release of a hostage. Iran also agreed to pay $4 million for the Hawk parts that had been delivered on McFarlane's plane.

A Casey memo to Poindexter indicates that in late July, when no hostage had yet been released, the United States told Ghorbanifar that the deal was off. A day later, however, it was learned that a hostage would indeed be released, and Father [Lawrence] Jenco was released on July 29.

In this memorandum, to Poindexter, dated July 29, Director Casey detailed the role of participants in the arms sales program and made the case for meeting Iranian expectations about what would happen next. Casey argued that Ghorbanifar, while uncontrollable, "appears to respond generally to Nir's direction." Nir and Israeli officials would continue to work for the release of American hostages, Casey said, because their reputations were on the line and because the program was consonant with Israeli interests. Were the United States not to respond to this Iranian move, on the other hand, "matters could turn ugly" and "it is entirely possible that Iran and/or Hizballah could resort to the murder of one or more of the remaining hostages." Casey admitted that piecemeal releases were unpleasant, but he saw this as perhaps "the only way to proceed." He also felt that resolution of this issue could lead to longer term "contacts with moderate factions in Iran."

LTC North sent a memorandum to Admiral Poindexter, also dated July 29, proposing that Poindexter get the President's approval to ship the remaining Hawk parts to Iran. North also sent an electronic message to McFarlane emphasizing that Father Jenco's release had been on [sic] outgrowth of McFarlane's mission to Iran, rather than the result of any Syrian role. The document includes a notation by Admiral Poindexter, dated July 30, that the President had approved the shipment of the remaining Hawk parts to Iran. On the same day, Vice President Bush was given a briefing in Jerusalem by Mr. Nir. The Vice President attended the meeting at the suggestion of LTC North. According to a memorandum dated a week later by an official who was present at the briefing, Nir indicated he was briefing the Vice President at the request of Prime Minister Peres. He conceded the problems encountered in the program, but argued that the Iranians with whom they were dealing were ones who could "deliver." He also discussed the problem of the sequence of release of additional hostages. According to the memo, the Vice President made no commitments and gave no direction to Nir.

Apparently in response to the approval of President Reagan, the Hawk parts reached Iran on August 3.

During the same period, according to documents received by the Committee, the United States was developing an alternative channel of communications with Iranian officials. In mid-July, Albert Hakim and a U.S. Government employee met with an acquaintance of Hakim's who was interested in putting together arms deals. The acquaintance knew of an Iranian official who wanted to contact the U.S. Government and talk about arms sales. Hakim had things arranged so that the Iranian would be steered toward him, rather than toward participants in the existing channel. By late July, LTC North reported to Admiral Poindexter that there had been meetings with some people to see whether they could become intermediaries; it is not clear whether he was referring to the mid-July meeting or to a later one. Hakim was pleased because his acquaintance was willing also to consider deals for non-lethal items; Hakim reportedly stated that he wanted to pursue that avenue irrespective of whether the U.S. Government used the channel. One proposal that later bore fruit was for some medical supplies to be sold at cost.

According to testimony received by the Committee, in August, Secord and Hakim met with the Iranian official who had sought to contact the U.S. Government to arrange arms sales. Secord reported to North that he was impressed with the Iranian, who knew about the existing channel but reportedly viewed Ghorbanifar and other intermediaries as untrustworthy. The Iranian promised not to disrupt the existing channel, but said that he would consult with his government about opening a second channel to the U.S. Government.

For the first channel, August 1986 was a time of continuing efforts and growing concern. Two CIA officials testified that they became more upset over Ghorbanifar's situation as they tried to understand the financing of this program and could not make sense of it. Ghorbanifar admitted to trying for a profit of 60 percent on top of the base price, but it would have taken a margin at least five times that to explain the figures that the CIA officials now understood to be involved. At some point during the summer of 1986, CIA's Near East Division asked another office to help it prepare a fake list to justify the inflated Hawk part prices. The latter office later recalled that it had recommended that the division go to the Defense Department for help instead, and the Committee does not know whether a fake price list was ever actually prepared.

According to documents and testimony received by the Committee, in early August, efforts were resumed in the old channel to arrange for possible shipment of the two Hawk radars that Iran wanted. In mid-August, Amiram Nir told CIA personnel that he had authorized most of what Ghorbanifar had offered in the way of price cuts and alternative schedules, although Ghorbanifar had offered at least one item that was not authorized. Nir also conceded that Ghorbanifar was probably no longer trusted by the Iranians. The latest proposal involved the Hawk radars, some electron tubes for the Hawk systems, 1,000 TOWs, another trip to Tehran, and an Israeli sale, along with the staggered release of the three remaining hostages.

Later in August, at a meeting of Ghorbanifar, Nir and North, a new schedule was proposed that added still another 1,000 TOWs, instead of the Israeli sale, and added the requirement that William Buckley's body be returned for proper burial. By late August, preparations for a shipment of 500 TOWs had begun.

According to documents received by the Committee, on September 2, North sent Admiral Poindexter a memorandum on "Next Steps with Iran." Among other things, he recounted the messages being sent through two friendly countries, the latest Ghorbanifar proposal, and the emergence of a possible new channel. His proposal, reached in conjunction with the CIA, was that the Ghorbanifar channel be pursued as the primary effort.

North's proposal appears to have been rejected by either Poindexter or the President, for a September 8 memorandum from North to Poindexter mentions "guidance" to seek the simultaneous release of all three hostages, rather than sequential releases. This memorandum was a supplement to the September 2 memo, and again states that it was prepared in conjunction with the CIA. The memo noted that it had proved impossible to convince the first channel to consider simultaneous release of all the hostages; that DOD had located enough material [sic] to make a sequential release approach attractive to the Iranians; that the first channel may now have been acting pursuant to direction by the new channel; and that Director Casey, having conducted a review of the Iranian project that day, considered Ghorbanifar's channel "the only proven means" to get hostage releses [sic], and so supported expeditious efforts to meet the plan proposed by Ghorbanifar, while holding out hopes that the new channel might make modifications later in September. The memo argued that "our window of opportunity may be better than it will ever be again".

After meeting with Poindexter, LTC North told a CIA official that the old channel was to be shut down and put on hold, and the new channel was to be developed instead. According to a memorandum received by the Committee, LTC North had been warned that the Ghorbanifar channel would have to be closed in a secure manner, which meant finding enough money to get Ghorbanifar out of trouble. The memo noted a figure of $4 million. Further, according to testimony received by the Committee, others were warned of the risks associated with closing down the Ghorbanifar channel at that time.

A CIA official testified that he began at this time to consider the possibility that one reason for Ghorbanifar's problems was a diversion of funds, in light of Secord and Hakim's roles in providing aid to anti-Sandinista forces. These concerns, especially the concern that Ghorbanifar's problems could lead somebody to go public, led the CIA official to raise the issue with Director Casey and Deputy Director Gates in early October, just as another source began to warn of a possible lawsuit. These events are discussed later in this report.

In mid-September, the visit of Israeli Prime Minister Peres and other officials to Washington prompted lower-level meetings with Nir, followed by briefings of the President and Poindexter for their meetings with Peres and Nir respectively. North's paper for Poindexter's use in briefing the President noted that the Israelis were nervous about U.S. intentions regarding the Iran program. The memorandum recommended that the President note his

appreciation of the Israeli role and indicate our intentions to continue to coordinate closely with Israel vis-a-vis Iran. Ledeen attempted to see Secretary Shultz around this time to discuss the program, as he would again in October, but Shultz testified that he declined to meet with Ledeen.

According to testimony and documents received by the Committee, during September there was a shift to the new channel. In early September, the shipment of medical supplies that Hakim had proposed in July began to move forward as the CIA took steps to purchase and pack the materials.

In the early fall, there was a meeting between the new channel and U.S. officals, arranged by Secord. According to documents and testimony received by the Committee, the Iranian official said that he was meeting the U.S. team in order to upgrade the channel between the United States and Iran. The Iranian said that Iran would handle the old channel, and that he should be considered the new one.

According to documents received by the Committee, the hostage issue was treated at the meeting "as an obstacle, not a key issue in arriving at a strategic relationship". The Iranian said that Iran opposed hostage taking and terrorism, and that the Ayatollah Khomeini had prepared a "fatwa" condemning the taking of hostages (which had been promised by Ghorbanifar in April). Another Iranian told a U.S. participant that the hostage matter "would soon be settled." Iran's intelligence needs were also presented in detail, and there was a discussion of a joint U.S.-Iranian committee that could handle the improving relations—first in secret, then in the open.

According to documents and testimony received by the Committee, the U.S. team told the Iranian official that to show U.S. seriousness, the Voice of America would mention Iran as one of the countries the United States wished to thank for refusing to grant landing rights to the hijackers of a TWA aircraft in Karachi. A few days later, NSC and CIA officials met to discuss a draft of the editorial. Working through State Department officials, the NSC staff convinced USIA [United States Information Agency] that this unusual request came from "the highest levels" of the government, and the editorial was broadcast over a three-day period.

By the end of September, the stage was set for a complete switch to the new channel, and, in effect, the first channel was left to fend for itself.

Compromise of the Program

According to Roy [M.] Furmark, at the end of September 1986, Khashoggi asked Furmark to visit Casey and ask for his assistance. Khashoggi was deeply involved in financing arms deals between the U.S. and Iran, and he was owed $10 million. The funds belonged to some investors and had been deposited in an account belonging to Lake Resources, a firm connected to North, Secord, and Hakim. According to Furmark, Khashoggi assumed that Lake was a U.S. Government account. The solution, he said, was for the U.S. Government either to refund the $10 million or to complete the weapons shipment.

According to the testimony of Gates and a CIA officer, in early October 1986 a CIA officer expressed concern to DDCI Gates that abandoning the old channel altogether for the new channel might be a risk to operational security because the old channel had not been taken care of financially.

At the same time, Gates was reportedly informed of speculation by this CIA officer that there was the possibility of funds from Iranian arms sales having been diverted to other U.S. projects, including the "Contras". Gates directed that Casey be briefed and the CIA officer testified that he met with Casey on October 7 and repeated what he had told Gates. At this meeting, Casey told the CIA officer that he had received a call that day from Roy Furmark, a former legal client and long-time acquaintance. Casey said that Furmark had told him that Khashoggi had put up the money to finance the purchase of arms by Iran, but that the money was not actually Khashoggi's; that Khashoggi had borrowed the money from two Canadians for a 20 percent return on the investment after 30 days; and that the Canadians had not been repaid and were threatening to go public with the details of the operation.

According to the CIA officer, Casey called Poindexter that same day and told him of Furmark's call. (It should be noted that Furmark testified that he had met with, not called, Casey that day.)

According to documents received by the Committee, during this same timeframe a meeting was scheduled in Europe with the new Iranian channel. In preparation for this meeting, North drafted a memorandum for Poindexter to send to Casey, stating that the President had authorized the delivery of intelligence information to the Iranians. The January 6, 1986, Presidential Finding was cited as the authority.

The CIA assembled an intelligence package in preparation for a meeting in Europe with the new Iranian channel. The CIA author of the memorandum transmitting the package cautioned, however, that "such information, if it were to come into Iranian possession, would likely help Iran plan and execute military operations against Iraq".

According to testimony received by the Committee, the European meeting took place between the U.S. team, which consisted of North, Secord, and a CIA officer, and the new Iranian channel, and, subsequently, on October 9, North visited CIA headquarters and briefed Casey and Gates on the meeting. According to testimony by Gates, during the course of this briefing, he asked North if there was any CIA involvement in North's efforts on behalf of private funding for the Contras. Gates testified that North responded that there was no CIA involvement. Gates further testified that at this same meeting, he urged Casey to insist on getting a copy of the Iran Finding, a document which the CIA did not have. North said that he would assist in this effort, and a few days later the CIA received the Finding.

According to documents received by the Committee, shortly thereafter, a CIA officer drafted a memorandum analyzing the NSC arms to Iran initiative which, in part, proposed certain damage control procedures in the event the initiative became public and speculated that creditors might assert that money from the arms sales was being "distributed to other projects of the U.S. and Israel". Upon seeing the memo, Casey called Poindexter and set up an appointment for the next day.

Casey and Gates saw Poindexter on October 15 and gave him a copy of the memorandum. Gates testified that he and Casey recommended to Poindexter that the President ought to reveal the initiative to the public, to avoid having it "leak out in dribs and drabs." Meanwhile, according to Gates, he directed the CIA's General Counsel to review all aspects of the Iran project to insure that the CIA was not doing anything illegal. The General Counsel subsequently reported to Gates that he had looked into the situation and that there was "nothing amiss from the CIA standpoint".

On October 16, at Casey's direction, a CIA officer met with Furmark to discuss the Iran initiative and Khashoggi's involvement in financing the arms sales. Subsequent to the meeting, a memo to Casey was drafted recounting the conversation with Furmark, which provided in part that Furmark had recommended an Iranian arms shipment "to maintain some credibility with the Iranians . . . and to provide Ghorbanifar with some capital so that the investors can be repaid partially and so that Ghorbanifar can borrow money to finance additional shipments." This, according to Furmark, would keep the process rolling and could result in release of additional hostages.

A follow-up meeting with Furmark in New York with two CIA officers occurred on October 22. According to documents and testimony received by the Committee, in addition to discussing the sources of financing for the various shipments of arms to Iran, Furmark said that Ghorbanifar firmly believed that "the bulk of the $15 million [for the Hawk spare parts] had been diverted to the Contras." The CIA officer testified that it was his impression that Furmark shared Ghorbanifar's belief. Upon their return, the two CIA officers briefed Casey, including the subject of possible diversion of funds to the Contras. A summary memorandum was drafted for Casey to send to Poindexter, but it was never signed by the DCI and was apparently never sent to Poindexter.

The next arms shipments to Iran continued during this period. At a meeting in late October, the Iranians produced a check for $4 million to pay for 500 TOWs. Of this amount the CIA

received $2.037 million on October 28, and on October 29, 500 TOW missiles were shipped from Israel to Iran. On that same day, North sent a message to Poindexter providing a status report on the meeting with the Iranians. According to that document, the United States was assured of getting two hostages back "in the next few days". On November 2, hostage [David] Peter Jacobsen was released.

According to testimony received by the Committee, the October 29 shipment of arms from Israel to Iran—for which the Israelis received 500 TOWs in reimbursement on November 6—marked the end of U.S.-Iranian arms deals. On November 3, the Lebanese newspaper Al Shiraa [sic] reported that the United States had been supplying arms to Iran and stated that McFarlane had visited Tehran earlier in the year to meet with Iranian officials.

According to documents and testimony received by the Committee, Secretary of State Shultz, upon learning of the revelations, sent a cable to Poindexter in which he expressed his concern over possible press attempts to portray the arms deal as a violation of U.S. counterterrorism policy. Shultz suggested that the best course of action would be to go public on the NSC initiative in an attempt to make it "clear that this was a special one time operation based on humanitarian grounds and decided by the President within his Constitutional responsibility to act in the service of the national interest." Shultz testified that he did not know at this time about the January 17 Presidential Finding authorizing the arms transfers to Iran and that neither he nor Secretary Weinberger learned of the Finding until it was revealed at a White House meeting on November 10.

According to documents received by the Committee, Poindexter, by cable, rejected the Secretary's advice, citing a need to get the hostages out and a desire to brief the Congressional Intelligence Committees. According to the cable, Poindexter had spoken with Vice President Bush, Weinberger, and Casey and they had all agreed with the necessity for remaining "absolutely close-mouthed while stressing that basic policy toward Iran, the Gulf War and dealing with terrorists had not changed".

On November 7, Furmark told the CIA officer with whom he had been meeting that the Canadian investors who had not received their funds from Khashoggi were planning to sue the Saudi arms dealer and a private firm into which they paid the $11 million to cover the cost of the Hawk missile parts" [sic]. According to documents received by the Committee, Furmark said that he had persuaded the Canadians to delay their lawsuit. Furmark indicated he was unimpressed with the new Iranian channel and expressed support for the ability of Ghorbanifar, who "coordinated his initiatives . . . with all significant factions in Iran".

In November, the U.S. team, including North, met again with the new Iranian channel. During three days of meetings with the Iranians, the topics included hostages release, Dawa Prisoners being held by Kuwait, the Israeli role in the arms transfers, and Iranian intelligence requirements. The new channel admitted that Iran owed Ghorbanifar $10 million, but stated that Ghorbanifar owed Iran 1,000 TOW missiles.

According to testimony received by the Committee, by this point the Executive branch had come to believe that the Senate and House Intelligence Committees would have to be briefed on the Iranian initiative. The CIA thereupon began to prepare the materials needed for Casey's presentation. The CIA officer who had dealt directly with the Iranians was asked to prepare an outline of the meetings he had attended, and the CIA Comptroller attempted to reconstruct the financial aspects of the Iran program.

Casey testified before the Senate Intelligence Committee on November 21, 1986. He did not mention any possibility that there had been a diversion of funds from the arms sales to Iran. When asked about this omission, Gates later testified that the reason for the omission was that "the information was based on analytical judgments of bits and pieces of information by one intelligence officer, and that they [Casey and Gates] didn't consider that very much to go on, although it was enough to raise our concerns to the point where we expressed them to the White House."

According to the Attorney General's inquiry, prior to appearing before the Senate Intelligence Committee, Shultz went to the White House and informed the President that some of the statements being made about the Iran arms affairs would not stand up to scrutiny. Shultz also informed Meese of his feelings on this matter. A Justice Department staff member then obtained information from the State Department about the November 1985 Hawk missile shipments that did not fit with other information gathered by the Attorney General. At that point, Meese decided to go see the President.

The same day that Casey testified before the Senate Intelligence Committee, the Attorney General met with the President and Chief of Staff Regan to discuss the need for an accurate account of the arms deals, particularly in light of the upcoming testimony before Congressional Committees. According to Meese, the President asked him to "review the facts" to get an accurate portrayal of the various agencies and their involvement. Meese later testified that he "didn't smell something was wrong," but was bothered by "things we didn't know." This was not an investigation said Meese, but simply an attempt "to pull the facts together so that we would have a coherent account." Regan suggested that the review be completed prior to the 2 p.m. NSC meeting on Monday. According to testimony by Meese, he then discussed his mission with FBI Director [William H.] Webster, and the two of them agreed that it was not a criminal matter and it would not be appropriate to involve the FBI.

Meese testified that on the afternoon of November 21, he assembled a team of three lawyers "who had experience with this type of matter." Meese then made a list of people to talk with, including North, Shultz, Weinberger, Poindexter, McFarlane, and the CIA's General Counsel.

According to the Attorney General's inquiry, one of the first persons interviewed by Meese was McFarlane, who said he had told Kimche at a December meeting in London that the United States was "disturbed about TOWs—can't approve it." By contrast, McFarlane testified that he had told Meese during this interview that the President had favored the Iran initiative from the beginning. McFarlane stated that Meese seemed glad to hear this, as an early Presidential approval would legitimize subsequent acts. According to McFarlane, Meese then opined that an oral, informal Presidential decision or determination was no less valid than a written Finding.

At 8:00 a.m. Saturday, Meese spoke with Shultz to discuss the Secretary of State's recollection of certain events. Meese testified that he was not shocked to learn that Shultz had not known of the January 17 Presidential Finding and stated that he himself had heard nothing of it after it had been signed.

According to testimony by Meese, on the morning of November 22, the Meese team discovered the early April NSC memo which referred explicitly to the diversion of arms profits to the Contras. Assistant Attorney General William Bradford Reynolds told Meese about the document at lunch Saturday. Meese testified that this was the first time that he felt as if something was "not in accord with the President's plan."

According to the Attorney General's inquiry, the next day, the Meese team—including the Attorney General—met with North. Meese reportedly told North that there would be some people who were concerned with protecting the President, but that facts were what was needed. In response to Meese's question about whether McFarlane's problem was the perception or the fact of arms to Iran for hostages, North stated that he believed the President himself authorized the deal. North said that when he spoke with the President it was in terms of a strategic linkage. With the President, said North, it always came back to hostages. According to Meese, North said it was a terrible mistake to say that the President wanted a strategic relationship, because the President wanted the hostages.

According to testimony by Meese, on November 24, 1986, at 11 a.m. he met with the President and the Chief of Staff and told them of indications that money from the Iran arms sales might have gone to the Contras. The Attorney General's announcement of this on November 25, led the Committee to begin the inquiry herewith reported.

As recently as mid-December, State Department and CIA officials met with an Iranian representative to discuss U.S. policy toward Iran. The State Department official relayed the message

that there would be no more arms to Iran unless Iran stopped supporting terrorism and agreed to negotiate an end to the war with Iraq. U.S. hostages, said the official, must be released unconditionally. The Iranians, in turn, cited a previously-agreed upon nine-point agenda which included the repair of Phoenix missiles, an approach toward Kuwait about releasing Dawa prisoners, and shipment of 1,000 TOWs to Iran. Following this unsuccessful session, the CIA officer met privately with the Iranian, without the State Department's knowledge or approval.

According to testimony received by the Committee, on December 19 Senator Dave Durenberger, Chairman of the Intelligence Committee, and Bernard McMahon, the Committee's staff director, met with the President, Peter Wallison, Don Regan, and Alton Keel, at the request of the White House to discuss matters relating to the sale of arms to Iran and possible diversion of funds to the Contras. The Committee was not informed of this meeting until January 20, 1987.

According to testimony received by the Committee, on December 20 Senator Dave Durenberger and Bernard McMahon met with the Vice President, Craig Fuller and a second member of his staff to discuss matters relating to the sale of arms to Iran and possible diversion of funds to the Contras. The Committee was not informed of this meeting until January 20, 1987.

Support to the Nicaraguan Resistance

The Committee initiated its preliminary inquiry on December 1, 1986 after the Attorney General disclosed evidence of the possible diversion of funds from the Iran arms sales to the Nicaraguan resistance. According to documents and testimony received by the Committee, several individuals played key roles in both the arms sales to Iran and the possible diversion of funds to the Nicaraguan resistance, including Lt. Colonel North, Retired Major General Richard Secord, and Secord's business associate, Albert Hakim. North was assigned NSC responsibility for the Nicaragua-Central America account.

McFarlane testified that in preparing his response to press reports and Congressional inquiries in the summer of 1985, he went to considerable length in interviews with North and looking at files to determine the nature of North's activities in connection with the Nicaraguan resistance. He further testified that North assured him categorically at that time that his role was nothing more than encouraging the Contras and advising people who volunteered support that they should contact the Contras. McFarlane further testified that he had learned nothing since that time to contradict this view of North's activities.

The initial CIA action officer on the Iran project met with North on several occasions in 1986. The CIA officer described Secord and Hakim as "almost co-equal lieutenants" of North. The CIA action officer testified that on a trip in February he learned from North that Secord and Hakim were the principal aides to North in his Contra activities. North did not describe those activities to the CIA officer other than saying that Hakim was responsible for the effort in Europe to help the Contras. In March 1986, the CIA officer knew that North was very active in the Contra program. It seemed to the CIA officer as if North was splitting his time between the Contras and the Iran project and that he was having trouble keeping up with both. North was visiting Honduras and going to meetings and otherwise working hard on support for the fighters. The CIA officer testified that North's activities were widely known in the CIA and the NSC.

A White House document indicates that Lt. Colonel North described Albert Hakim to Admiral Poindexter on February 18, 1986 as Vice President of one of the European companies set up to "handle aid to resistance movements."

Another White House document reflects that in a secure message from North to McFarlane on February 27, 1986, summarizing a meeting in Europe, North described Hakim as an American citizen who "runs the European operation for our Nicaraguan resistance support activity."

According to documents reviewed by the Committee, in late November 1985, North received assistance from Secord in resolving problems with an arms transfer to Iran. A White House document dated November 22, 1985, indicates that North and Secord were already involved in an enterprise North referred to as, "our Swiss Company," Lake Resources, and that an aircraft belonging to Lake Resources was in a European country in November to pick up arms for the Nicaraguan resistance. It was to be the first direct flight to the resistance at Bocay and the arms packages had parachutes attached. This flight was to be delayed so that the plane could be used for the transfer to Iran (ultimately another plane was used for the arms transfer).

This document also reflects that North described these circumstances to Poindexter. The document also shows North saying that he (North) would meet with Adolfo Calero, a Contra leader, to advise him of the delay in arrival of the arms.

A separate White House document reflects that North advised Poindexter on December 4, 1985 that North was using an operations code for Iranian matters similar to the one used to oversee deliveries to the Nicaraguan resistance. North reported that the latter code had never been compromised.

According to evidence received by the Committee, a direct connection between the arms sales to Iran and aid to the Nicaraguan resistance was made in January, 1986 in discussions between North and Amiram Nir, terrorism advisor to Israeli Prime Minister Peres. Notes taken at the interview of North by Meese on November 23, 1986 quote North as saying that he had discussed support for the Nicaraguan resistance with Nir in January, 1986 and that Nir proposed using funds from arms sales to Iran for that support. [According to some notes, North believed Nir made the suggestion on his own.] The Attorney General testified that he was uncertain as to whether North or Nir brought up the subject of Nicaraguan resistance. North also recalled turning down other Nir suggestions that U.S. funds to Israel or Israel's own funds could be used to support the Nicaraguan resistance.

Other notes of that interview reflect only that Nir told North in January that the Israelis would take funds from a residual account and transfer them to a Nicaraguan account.

Notes of the Meese-North interview further reflect that North commented that he had discussed Israeli help in general with Defense Minister Rabin, but could not recall asking specifically for help from the Israelis.

According to documents received by the Committee, by the time of the North-Nir discussion in January, the Israelis may have been holding funds from the November 1985 Hawk transfer available to use for the Nicaraguan resistance. A CIA document reflects that during one of the breaks in a CIA polygraph examination of Ghorbanifar in January 1986, he commented that the Israelis received $24 million as soon as the Hawk shipment was delivered and that they were holding all of the funds. The Iranians were requesting the funds be returned. Ghorbanifar reportedly stated that the Israelis told him they had "doubled" the cost of the shipment apparently because the Americans were involved. Ghorbanifar reportedly stressed how upset the Iranians were at not getting the $24 million back.

On November 24, 1986, the day after Meese met with North, an attorney, Tom Green, met with Assistant Attorney General Charles [J.] Cooper. According to Cooper's notes, Green said he represented North and Secord and described the role played by Secord and Hakim in the Iran project. Green reportedly said that at a meeting on the arms sales in Europe in early 1986, where Hakim served as interpreter for the Americans, Hakim told the Iranians that in order to foster the relationship and show their bona fides, the Iranians should make a contribution over the purchase price for use of the Contras or "of us." Green added that Hakim probably said the U.S. Government was desirous of this. Green said that was the basis upon which the February shipment of TOWs was priced.

According to Cooper's notes, Green said the money from that sale was routed through Israelis into Hakim's financial network. Hakim, in his private capacity, routed money into other accounts belonging to foreigners. The same thing happened again in May. Green reportedly said none of this violated the law because no U.S.

money was involved—only Iranians making a contribution.

On of [sic] after April 4, 1986, an undated White House document (the "Undated Memorandum") was prepared that outlines past developments and future plans for the Iran program. Evidence received by the Committee, including the text of the Undated Memorandum and an attachment styled "Terms of Reference" and dated April 4, suggests the Undated Memorandum was written in this time period. The Undated Memorandum provided that $12 million of the residual funds from an arms transaction would be used to purchase critically needed supplies for the Nicaraguan Democratic Resistance Forces. The Undated Memorandum described this material as essential to cover shortages in resistance inventories resulting from their current offensive and Sandinista counter-attacks and to "bridge" the period until Congressionally-approved lethal assistance beyond "defensive" arms could be delivered. At the bottom of the page on which this discussion appears was a recommendation that Presidential approval be obtained for certain parts of the plan for the Iran program that did not include the diversion of funds to the Nicaraguan resistance. The Undated Memorandum was unsigned and specified no addressee, and it is not clear to the Committee who, if anyone, saw it.

The Undated Memorandum was discovered in the files of the NSC on November 22, 1986 by members of the Attorney General's staff. Meese made an appointment to meet with North the next day, at which time North was questioned at some length about the Iran program and then confronted with the Undated Memorandum.

Notes taken at the November 23 meeting indicate that North confirmed the accuracy of the Undated Memorandum as reflecting the plan for use of residual funds from the Iran arms sale for the Nicaraguan resistance. Notes of the meeting recount North saying the $12 million figure in the memo was based on what he was told by the Israelis and that he did not know how much was moved to the Nicaraguans—the Israeli (Nir) decided what amount given to the resistance, with no involvement by the CIA or NSC.

According to the notes of the Attorney General inquiry, North stated that he had not discussed the matter with the President. According to documents received by the Committee, North was in 17 meetings with the President over the two year period, 1985-1986, and none alone, and had one phone conversation with the President on December 4, 1986.

According to testimony by Meese, North said that he did not know the amount of money involved. North said the CIA did not know about the handling of the money, although some might suspect.

Notes taken at the meeting further reflect that North said Presidential approval of something would be reflected in the working files. Asked whether he would have a record if the President approved in this case, the notes reflect that North replied affirmatively, and said he didn't think it was approved.

Notes taken at the meeting further reflect that North described the money that the Israelis were to get to the Nicaraguans as Iranian money from profits of the arms deals and saying he understood this part of the deal. The notes further reflect that North said he had told McFarlane in April or May 1986 about the deals and that the only three people who could know in the U.S. were McFarlane, Poindexter and North.

According to testimony by McFarlane, during their return trip from Tehran, North told McFarlane that part of the profit from the arms transaction was going to the Nicaraguan resistance. McFarlane testified that he took it from the summary reference that this was a matter of policy sanctioned by higher authority.

McFarlane testified that he did not ask North whether there was a Finding specifically sanctioning the transfer of funds to the Contras. He testified that North's portrayal of the Contra connection was "part and parcel of a series of activities that had been going on." McFarlane testified that he did not report what he had been told by North about the use of Iran arms profits for the Nicaraguan resistance.

Moreover, McFarlane testified that when he asked North on November 23, 1986 who had approved such action, North responded that he would never do anything without it being approved by higher authority and that he could not account for who was involved beyond Poindexter.

The notes of the Attorney General's inquiry further reflect that North said after the meeting with Nir in January 1986, he had contacted Adolfo Calero and as a result of the contact three accounts were opened in Switzerland. The notes quote North as saying he gave the account numbers to the Israelis, and money was deposited in those accounts. North guessed the money got to the Contras; they knew money came and were appreciative.

Notes taken at the meeting further reflect that North identified two transaction [sic] from which money may have been diverted to the Contras; 1) the transfer of 1,000 TOWs in February [1986], from which $3-4 million may have gone to the Contras; and 2) the transaction [in May 1986] involving payment for Hawk parts and payment for replenishment of the 508 TOWs.

Notes taken at the meeting indicated North said there was no money for the Contras in the October shipment of 500 TOWs to avoid a perception of private profit and because the resumption of U.S. funding made it unnecessary. According to North, Nir was upset because the October price was not the same as charged earlier.

When Attorney General Meese testified before the Committee, he said that North was surprised and visibly shaken when shown the Undated Memorandum. According to testimony by Meese, North said that he did not recall the account numbers which were given to the Israelis and that Israelis arranged for the money to be deposited. Meese testified that North was very definite that the money got to the Nicaragua resistance forces, but could not remember or did not know the amount apart from an estimate of $3-4 million on one occasion.

Meese testified that he got the impression that the three bank accounts were set up by somebody representing the Nicaraguan resistance forces, that the numbers were given to North, and that North gave them to the Israelis.

Meese further testified that he was not positive that North told him the Undated Memorandum was not used or sent for approval. Meese testified that North did not mention any problem in his mind that, by some interpretations, U.S. money was being used for the Nicaraguan resistance. Meese testified that he did not go into that with North and that there was no discussion of the Congressional restriction on soliciting funds.

Meese testified that he did not advise North of his right to counsel because he did not consider his inquiry to be a criminal investigation.

Meese testified that North did not explain how he reported the arms sale matter to Poindexter. Meese testified that he got the impression that there was very little real communication about it between North and Poindexter and that North was not acting on orders from anyone.

Regan testified that he never saw the Undated Memorandum until shown it by White House counsel several days before his testimony and that his reaction on seeing it was he could not believe it. Mr. Regan further testified that the President was never in his presence briefed on anything of that nature and that he is confident the President would not have approved it if he had been told by Poindexter or North. Regan testified that he had not shown the document to the President.

During the same general time period, the President had two meetings which appeared to relate to Central American policy at which North was present. The exact topic of discussion cannot be determined from records available to the Committee. Both meetings occurred on April 23. White House documents list as the general topic of one meeting a discussion of a recent trip by Elliott Abrams to El Salvador, Honduras, and Costa Rica. The meeting was attended by the President, the Vice-President, Deputy Secretary of State John [C.] Whitehead, Abrams, Regan, Poindexter, and Fortier in addition to North. The other meeting for which no topic is listed was attended by the President, North, Regan, Poindexter, a Central American security official and his wife, and the senior CIA officer in that country. The CIA officer was later the subject of an internal CIA investigation initiated in the Fall of 1986 concerning unauthorized contacts with private supporters of the Nicaraguan resistance.

According to documents and testimony received by the Committee, it is possible that the following two events occurred on the same day, May 15, 1986. First, according to a chronology of the Iran program prepared at the White House in November 1986, the Terms of Reference for Mr. McFarlane's trip to Tehran were approved on May 15, 1986. These Terms of Reference appear to be identical to the Terms of Reference dated April 4 which were found in NCS files attached to the Undated Memorandum discussing diversion of funds to the Contras. Second, Poindexter gave the President a status report on the Nicaraguan resistance in preparation for an NSPG meeting on Central America scheduled for the next day. According to Poindexter's memorandum, Poindexter included in his status report a note that outside support for the Nicaraguan resistance would be consumed by mid-June and no further significant support appeared readily available. The memorandum stated that the $100 million aid request was stalled in Congress. Poindexter identified as options: reprogramming; Presidential appeal for private donations; and direct and very private Presidential overture to certain heads of state.

Regan testified that the President met with McFarlane prior to his trip to Tehran and discussed the objectives for McFarlane's talks with the Iranians. Regan testified that he did not recall seeing a document entitled "Terms of Reference" similar to the Undated Memorandum, nor did he recall approval ever being given for such a document. Regan testified, however, that the President's approval should have been required if those instructions were given to McFarlane for his visit to Tehran. A copy of Terms of Reference identical to those attached to the Undated Memorandum and bearing the date May 21, 1986 has been located in White House files.

According to documents received by the Committee, on May 16, 1986, the President held an NSPG meeting where solicitation of third-country humanitarian support for the Nicaraguan resistance was discussed. Those present included the President, Vice President, Craig Fuller, Secretary Shultz, Ambassador Habib, Assistant Secretary Abrams, Secretary Baker, Secretary Weinberger, Under Secretary Ikle, Director Casey, the CIA task force chief, General Wickham, Lt. Gen. Moellering, Don Regan, Admiral Poindexter, William Ball, Djerejian, McDaniel, Burghart, and North. White House documents reflect that the issues discussed at this meeting included the negotiation process and the status of Contadora, and the $100 million aid package before Congress for the Nicaraguan resistance. The document states that the situation with the resistance was good but could reverse abruptly as they were running out of money. Two options to get the money were considered—seek to get reprogramming through Congress or go to other countries. The final decision was to look at both approaches. According to the documents, Secretary Shultz was to provide a list of countries which could be approached.

Abrams testified that the State Department had legal authority from Congress to solicit humanitarian assistance from third countries. According to Abrams, Secretary Shultz agreed it was a good idea to do so. According to testimony by Shultz, in June 1986 Abrams came to Shultz with a proposal to seek such aid and said there was a Swiss account that could receive the money and Shultz approved. Shultz testified that apart from a request for communications equipment, which was not honored, only one country was asked for a contribution pursuant to this policy.

Regan recalled such an NSPG discussion, although not the precise date of May 16, and testified that there was absolutely no mention of the possible use of funds from the Iran arms sale, including sales by third parties or countries, to provide humanitarian or military assistance to the Nicaraguan resistance.

Shultz testified that in June, McFarlane telephoned him to report that a third country had previously contributed $31 million to the Nicaraguan resistance. McFarlane, in his testimony, recalled a similar phone call to Shultz informing him of a $30 million third country contribution to the FDN.

August-September, 1986

According to testimony received by the Committee, in August, pursuant to the policy approved by the President in May, Abrams approached a third country and asked it to contribute $10 million for humanitarian assistance to UNO. Abrams reportedly met with a representative of that country on August 8; he pointed out that Congress had approved $100 million but it had not been appropriated yet and money was needed to bridge this gap between the previous $27 million [in humanitarian aid] and passage of the appropriation by Congress, which the Contras had not yet received. When the third country agreed, Abrams asked the CIA task force chief and North for advice on handling the contribution.

According to testimony received by the Committee, the task force chief recommended having UNO open a bank account in its name and then having NHAO or the State Department monitor the expenses and authorize them from that account. Abrams agreed, and the task force contacted UNO Secretary General Naio Sommariba and asked him to open an offshore bank account for use to deposit the funds. According to testimony received by the Committee, this was done at a bank in the Bahamas, with signatures of Sommariba and his accountant on the bank account. According to testimony received by the Committee, Abrams needed the account number urgently and the number was obtained and passed on to Abrams at a meeting in the NSC situation room. The task force chief said he provided this assistance on his own authority after consulting with the task force lawyer to make sure it was legal. He testified that he informed CIA Deputy Director for Operations and the Latin America Division Chief after the fact, and they raised no questions as to legality. The task force chief went on to testify that this was the way he handled 95 percent of his activities. CIA officials considered that the State Department was legally within its bounds to solicit the money and did not consider CIA's assistance to be in any way circumventing the law.

Abrams testified that he asked both the CIA task force chief and North to provide accounts for the donation from the third country. He testified that the account opened by North was with Credit Suisse. Abrams testified that he discussed the situation with Charles Hill, Executive Assistant to Secretary Shultz, and they decided to use the account opened by North without procedures for monitoriing expenditures from the account.

Abrams testified that in September and October the State Department sought assurances from the donating country that they were going to give the $10 million and would deposit it in the account provided by North. Documents received by the Committee confirm this statement.

Abrams testified that on several occasions after that he checked with North to see if the money had been deposited. According to Abrams, North reported to him on several occasions that the money had not reached the account. According to documents and testimony received by the Committee, in late November, Abrams turned over the information on the account to the State Department legal advisor, and the FBI began looking into the matter.

According to a document submitted by the Justice Department to the Swiss government in December 1986, the Credit Suisse account number that North gave Abrams is the same as the number of the account suspected of being used by North, Hakim, and Secord for proceeds from Iran arms sales.

In preparation for a meeting on September 15, 1986 between the President and Israeli Prime Minister Peres, North prepared a memorandum for National Security Advisor Poindexter on matters the Prime Minister might raise with the President. The memorandum reported that on the previous Friday, September 12, Israeli Defense Minister Rabin had offered a significant quantity of captured Soviet bloc arms for use by the Nicaraguan resistance. These arms were to be picked up by a foreign flag vessel the week of September 15 and delivered to the resistance. The memorandum advised that if Peres raised this issue, the President should thank him because the Israelis held considerable stores of bloc ordnance compatible with arms used by the Nicaraguan resistance. Poindexter noted on the memorandum received by the Committee, that he discussed it with the President.

Regan testified that he attended a briefing of the President one hour before the Peres meeting and that the Rabin offer was discussed. Regan testified that the subject was not expected to come up at the President's meeting, but that if Peres raised it, the President should "just say thanks." Regan recalled no discussion as to legality under American law.

Regan testified that the President never told him what came up in a 15 minute private meeting between the President and the Prime Minister, and the subject did not come up in the open meeting.

According to a document received by the Committee, two days before the President's meeting with Peres, Poindexter had replied by note to a message from North advising him to "go ahead and make it happen" as a "private deal between Dick and Rabin that we bless." Poindexter's note also referred to another note providing that Poindexter had talked to Casey that morning about Secord. Poindexter instructed North to keep the pressure on "Bill" to "make things right for Secord."

CIA

In testimony to the Committee, the senior CIA analyst on the Iran project stated that he began a thorough analysis of the intelligence on the program in mid-September 1986 and became concerned that Iran was being overcharged and that the funding might have been diverted for other projects including support for the Nicaraguan resistance.

He testified that he had conversations with Ghorbanifar and with Nir in August and September about funding problems with the Iran arms transfers. He knew, he said, that North was active in political support of the Contras and that Hakim and Secord were involved in flights to supply the Contras as well as the Iran program. Because the money issue was unresolved, he suspected money was already spent or allocated.

The CIA analyst testified that on October 1, 1986, he brought his concerns to the Deputy Director of Central Intelligence, Robert Gates. He explained that given the individuals involved, he was concerned that funds were being diverted to Central America.

According to testimony, Gates was surprised and disturbed and told the analyst to see Director Casey. The analyst testified that he and Gates did not discuss the legality or illegality of diversion. They talked about it being an inappropriate commingling of separate activities and the risk to operational security.

Gates testified to the Committee that the analyst viewed the problems as a serious threat to the operational security of the Iran project. Gates recalled that the analyst's conclusion [sic] that some of the money involved was being diverted to other U.S. projects, including the Contras.

Furmark

According to testimony by Roy Furmark, a New York businessman and a lawyer for Adnan Khashoggi, Ghorbanifar told him in a meeting in August in Paris, that proceeds from the inflated Iran arms sale prices may have gone to Afghanistan or Nicaragua. Furmark testified that at the end of September, Khashoggi asked him to visit Casey to get the U.S. to resolve the financial problems. Furmark testified that all those involved considered the Lake Resources account at Credit Suisse to be an American account. Furmark testified that he had known Casey for twenty years in business matters, OSS dinners, et cetera.

In a letter to Attorney General Edwin Meese dated late November 25, 1986, Casey described Furmark as a friend and former client—someone he had not seen in six or seven years.

Furmark and Casey met on October 7, 1986 and, according to Furmark's testimony, he told Casey about the financial problems with the Iran project and that Casey seemed unaware of details. Furmark testified that Casey tried to call Poindexter who was not in and that Casey said he would look into it.

In a letter to Attorney General Meese dated November 25, 1986, Casey said Furmark had provided him with more information than Casey had ever heard about the Ghorbanifar-Israeli channel to the Iranians. The letter quotes Furmark as saying that he had been involved in a Ghorbanifar-Israeli channel to the Iranians from its inception. Casey advised the Attorney General that he and Gates had passed Furmark's information on to Poindexter a day or so after the October 7 meeting.

Also on October 7, a meeting was held between a senior CIA analyst, the Deputy Director of CIA, Bob Gates, and Casey. This senior CIA analyst testified he believed Furmark did not mention to Casey on October 7 the possibility that Iran arms proceeds had gone to the Nicaraguan resistance.

Casey later told the analyst that he, Casey, called Poindexter on October 7 and that Poindexter knew of the problem raised by Furmark.

Gates testified that it was possible that during the October 7 meeting Furmark may have raised with Casey the possible diversion of money to the Contras.

At the meeting with Casey on October 7, Gates told Casey of the senior analyst's concerns about the possible diversion of funds to Central America. Casey directed the analyst to put all his concerns in writing. Gates testified that Casey was startled by the information.

Gates further testified that on October 9, 1986, Casey, Gates, and North met for lunch to give North an opportunity to debrief Casey and Gates on a meeting on the Iran project that had recently taken place in Europe. Gates testified that problems with the Iran program were discussed and that, during lunch North made a very cryptic reference to a Swiss account and money for the Contras. Gates recalled that he and Casey did not pursue it but instead asked North whether there was any direct or indirect CIA involvement in any funding efforts for the Contras. North's response reportedly was that CIA was "completely clean" and that he had worked to keep them separate. Gates testified that he and Casey discussed after lunch the fact that they did not understand North's comments. After the lunch, Gates noted for the record that North had "confirmed" that the CIA "is completely clean on the question of any contact with those organizing the funding and operation," and that a clear separation between all CIA assets and the private funding effort had been maintained. A senior CIA analyst testified that Gates later told him that there had been a discussion with North of integration of the private effort to support the Contras and CIA activities, and that North had told Gates there was no commingling and CIA was clear.

On October 14, 1986, Gates and the senior CIA analyst met with Casey and gave him the memorandum prepared by the analyst pursuant to the October 7 meeting. A cover memorandum from the analyst to Casey and Gates said the analyst had not consulted with North or other individuals involved on the U.S. side in drafting the memorandum. The attached 7-page memorandum discussed the risk that Ghorbanifar might disclose to the press an account, charging that the U.S. Government had failed to keep several promises to him and that both the U.S. and Israeli governments had acquired substantial profit from the Iran arms transactions, some of which was redistributed to "other projects of the U.S. and Israel." The analyst testified that the reference in his memo to "other projects" related only to speculation about possible allegations of improper diversions of money to Central America, misappropriation of funds by arms dealers, and indications of funds needed for some unknown purpose by an Israeli official.

Casey advised the Attorney General in his November 25, 1986 letter that he had this memorandum prepared and believed it was delivered to the NSC to review the state of play on the channel to the Iranian government. Gates testified that the next day, October 15, 1986, he and Casey met with Poindexter and delivered a copy of the analyst's memorandum. Gates testified that they advised Poindexter, in view of the people who knew about it, to think seriously about having the President lay the project before the American public to avoid having it leak in dribs and drabs.

According to his November letter to Meese, Casey said that he and Gates urged Poindexter to get all the facts together and have a comprehensive statement prepared because it seemed likely that the litigation which Furmark said his clients were contemplating would require it.

In the same letter, Casey stated that Gates had said he would apprise the CIA General Counsel of the matters and get his advice. Gates testified that he did ask CIA General Counsel Dave Doherty to review all aspects of the project and to ensure that the Agency was not involved in any illegalities. According to Gates, Doherty later told him that he had looked into things and not found

anything wrong. Doherty testified that Gates mentioned that Southern Air Transport was involved, linking the whole thing to Central America, because Southern Air transport [sic] was also shipping material to the Nicaraguan resistance. According to Doherty, the FBI was looking at the issue of humanitarian funds to see if any were being spent unlawfully.

According to testimony by Doherty, Gates also mentioned to the General Counsel speculation and rumors that Iran funds could have been sent to Central America as part of private funding efforts. Doherty testified that Gates told him he was concerned that CIA did not know how funding transfers were being handled by the NSC and middlemen.

Doherty further testified that he undertook no review other than to evaluate the activities as described to him by Gates. He testified that he did not interview other CIA employees, nor did he suspect NSC involvement in diversion to the Contras. According to other testimony received by the Committee, Doherty did, however, direct in late October or early November that nothing relating to the Iran program be destroyed. Two CIA employees, concerned, subsequently put all notes, documents, et cetera in a box.

Furmark testified that he next talked to Casey on October 16, 1986, and again asked for Casey's help in getting the U.S. Government to resolve his clients' financial claims. According to his letter to the Attorney General of November 25, Casey had a senior CIA analyst and a CIA contract employee go up to New York to discuss the whole thing at length with Furmark. Memoranda dated October 17 and November 7 discussed their meetings with Furmark.

The memorandum dated October 17 recounted a brief conversation between the senior CIA analyst and Furmark on October 16. It did not mention use of arms sale profits for "other projects," but did relate Furmark's allegation that $3 million of the $8 million paid by the Iranians for the May 1985 [1986] transaction had been used "to cover expenses and for other matters" and that $10 million was still owed to the Canadian investors who financed the May transaction.

The senior CIA analyst's memorandum dated November 7 described a meeting between Furmark and the senior CIA analyst on the afternoon of November 6 in Washington in which Furmark warned that the Canadian investors intended to expose fully the U.S. Government's role in the Iran arms transactions. Furmark, according to the memorandum, said they knew that Secord was heavily involved in managing the Iran arms transactions for North, and that Secord was also involved in assisting North in support of the Contras in Nicaragua. Furmark also said the Canadians believed they had been swindled and the money paid by Iran for the arms may have been siphoned off to support the Contras in Nicaragua.

According to testimony by Gates, on November 6, Casey and Gates met with Poindexter at the White House. According to testimony by Gates, Casey recommended that Poindexter bring in the White House counsel, but Poindexter replied that he did not trust the White House counsel and would talk instead to Paul Thompson (a lawyer and military assistant to Poindexter). Gates also said he learned at that meeting that Casey had a prior discussion with Poindexter in which he may have recommended that North obtain legal counsel. A similar rendition of this conversation was later contained in Casey's November letter to the Attorney General.

The senior CIA analyst and the CIA contract employee returned to New York on October 22 to meet with Furmark and afterward drafted a memorandum for Casey to send to Poindexter. The memorandum reported that Ghorbanifar had told Furmark and Khashoggi that he believed the bulk of the original $15 million price for the May shipment was earmarked for Central America. The memorandum continued that in this regard, Ghorbanifar told Furmark that he was relieved when the $100 million aid to the Contras was passed by Congress.

According to the memorandum, Furmark also presumed that $2 million of the $8 million paid by the Iranians to Ghorbanifar went to Nir, as agreed to at a meeting among the financiers, Ghorbanifar, and Nir in May.

A signed copy of this memorandum has not been received by the Committee. In his November 25, 1986 letter to the Attorney

General, Casey said he had not read it "until this morning" and did not recall ever having read it before. In this letter Casey further said that he had been told the memorandum was prepared but apparently never went forward.

The senior CIA analyst testified that he was not looking at the question of improprieties but rather as an intelligence officer was focusing on damage control.

The analyst testified that Furmark felt Ghorbanifar firmly believed money was diverted to the Contras, and the analyst had the impression Furmark also believed the money was diverted.

According to testimony by the analyst, the October 22 meeting with Furmark was the first time he had heard a direct allegation that Ghorbanifar suspected the bulk of funds raised for Hawk spare parts had gone to the Contras. He testified that the quick briefing he and the CIA contract employee gave Casey after their October 22 meeting with Furmark included mention of diversion. The contract employee who drafted the memo to Poindexter, testified that Casey may have conveyed its substance to Poindexter by phone and that Casey remembered seeing the memo.

According to notes of the Attorney General's inquiry, North told Meese on November 23, 1986 that Poindexter had asked North in mid-November to compile a history of the Iran program. North reportedly told Meese that he went to the files and also talked to McFarlane, Poindexter, and others in compiling the chronology. None of the materials prepared in the White House during this period and received by the Committee referred to the use of Iran arms sales proceeds for the Nicaraguan resistance, although one chronology dated November 17 and labeled "maximum version" has in handwriting at the end of a list of Iran program accomplishments the notation "Nicargua" [sic].

NSC Executive Secretary Rod McDaniel testified that sometime during October or November, North commented to the effect that "one of the great ironies was how the Iranians were helping the contras." McDaniel testified that he did not give much thought to the comment at the time because North was given to hyperbole.

According to testimony received by the Committee, on Wednesday, November 19, Casey was briefed in preparation for his appearance before the Senate Intelligence Committee set for November 21. Testimony received by the Committee indicated that in this briefing Casey may have been made aware that there might be a problem in the area of diversion of Iran project funds to the Contras. The CIA task force chief recalled being totally flabbergasted upon learning of the possible interconnection between Nicaragua and the Iran program from Casey's aide.

The CIA Comptroller testified that he learned of the possible diversion of funds to the Contras on November 18-19. The Comptroller recalled that a CIA operations officer speculated that money may have been diverted as they were preparing Casey's testimony for November 21.

The Comptroller's testimony [sic] that he shared this information with the CIA Executive Director and learned that Casey and Gates had made their concerns known to Poindexter after learning of the subject in October.

The CIA Inspector General testified before the Committee and described as "fairly significant" the evidence that had begun to develop in the CIA by early November that some diversion might be taking place. The IG testified that he asked for the senior CIA analyst memos about suspected diversion of money to Central America prepared on October 14 and confirmed, [sic] that Casey and Gates saw Poindexter the next day to discuss the issue.

In other testimony, the executive assistant to Deputy Director for Operations at CIA testified that although there is a record in the DO registry of a memo from the senior CIA analyst on the analyst's third meeting with Furmark, he had only a vague recollection of the DDO having viewed the memo. The executive assistant said he had helped draft Casey's testimony for November 21, but in none of the drafts was there ever any mention of diversion of funds.

According to testimony by Meese, he spoke with Poindexter after the President's news conference on November 19. Meese testified that he was concerned about the absence of a "factual chronology" and Casey's forthcoming testimony. Meese said he had also talked to Poindexter earlier in the day in Poindexter's

office after a meeting where Casey was present. Poindexter reportedly asked Meese to come back the next day to help prepare Casey's testimony.

The NSC staff had prepared a 17-page historical summary of the Iran program dated November 20 which appears to contain numerous important omissions and misstatements of fact about the program (the White House chronology). According to testimony by Meese, on November 20 he and Assistant Attorney General Charles Cooper went to a meeting at the White House where Casey, Poindexter, and others from the NSC staff reviewed Casey's testimony and a chronology to see if they squared with Meese's recollection of the legal discussions and the facts. Meese testified that he left before the meeting was over, but that Cooper stayed. In the evening, Meese received a secure call advising him that other Justice Department officials working on the Iran matter were concerned about gaps in information and inconsistent recollections.

On the same night of November 20, according to notes of the Attorney General's inquiry, Secretary Shultz went to the White House residence to see the President and told him that some of the statements would not stand up to scrutiny.

Meese testified that on the morning of Friday, November 21, when Casey was testifying on the Hill, after learning from his staff of more discrepancies with State Department information, he met with the President and Regan. Meese testified that he reported his concerns about the need for an accurate accounting, particularly in view of upcoming testimony to Congressional committees. The President reportedly asked Meese to review the facts to get an accurate portrayal by the different agencies involved. Meese testified that he "didn't smell something was wrong," but was bothered "that there were things we didn't know." According to Meese, the President did not request an investigation but asked Meese to pull the facts together so they could have a coherent account. Regan reportedly suggested that Meese's review be completed by 2:00 p.m. on Monday, November 24, when an NSC meeting on Iran was scheduled.

Meese testified that he later discussed the Iran matter with FBI Director Webster and told him what the President has [sic] asked Meese to do. According to Meese, he and Webster agreed that, as there was no criminal matter involved, it would not be appropriate to bring in the FBI.

On the afternoon of November 21, Meese assembled a small team of Justice Department officials and aides, including Assistant Attorneys General Charles Cooper and Bradford Reynolds. This team did not include any senior Department officials responsible for criminal investigations.

According to testimony received by the Committee, in this same time period, on November 21 Poindexter briefed the leadership of SSCI in the White House in the morning. In the afternoon Casey appeared before the Committee on the Hill, accompanied by other CIA officials. The possibility of use of Iran arms sale proceeds for the Nicaraguan resistance was not mentioned.

Gates later testified that the reason Casey said nothing about the possible diversion of funds was that they knew nothing more on November 21 than they did on October 14, i.e., bits and pieces of information and analytical judgments by one intelligence officer, and that this was not considered very much to go on. The senior CIA analyst testified that he helped prepare the DCI's testimony which focused on what CIA knew and what support they gave the NSC. He said there was no discussion in his presence of the possibility of diversion of funds.

The next morning, Saturday, November 22, while Meese was meeting with Shultz, members of the Attorney General's staff including Reynolds, examined documents in NSC files at the White House. Meese later testified that Poindexter had given permission for this file review and that NSC staff including North and Paul Thompson were present in the NSC offices when it was conducted. Meese testified that he received no information that North shredded documents in his office.

Meese's staff went through the documents presented to them and had copies made of those they thought important. The Attorney General's staff discovered in NSC files the Undated Memorandum which included a discussion of use of Iran arms sale proceeds for the Nicaraguan resistance. Reynolds advised Meese of this discovery at lunch. Meese testified that following a meeting with former CIA General Counsel Sporkin in the afternoon, Meese made an appointment with North to meet the following day. Meese testified that he had planned to interview North in the morning, but agreed to a delay until 2:00 p.m. because North wanted to have time to go to church and be with his family.

According to testimony received by the Committee, North arranged to consult with an attorney after meeting with lawyers from the Justice Department on Saturday, November 22, to obtain legal counsel.

According to testimony by Meese, that Saturday evening Meese met with Casey at Casey's home. They had talked on the phone earlier in the day. At their meeting Casey discussed Furmark and the Canadian investors. Meese recalled no mention of the Contras, Nicaragua, anti-Sandinistas, Democratic Resistance, Freedom Fighters or Central America. At one point he said it was possible that Casey may have mentioned something similar, but he subsequently said he was sure Casey did not mention the possible diversion of funds.

McFarlane testified that on Sunday morning, November 23, North called him and asked to meet him in McFarlane's office. According to McFarlane, North arrived at 12:30 p.m. and the two had a private discussion for about fifteen minutes. North said he would have to lay the facts out for the Justice Department later that day on the diversion of Iran money to the Contras. McFarlane testified that North also stated it was a matter of record in a memorandum North had done for Poindexter. McFarlane asked if it was an approved matter, and was told that it was.

According to McFarlane, North stated that McFarlane knew North wouldn't do anything that was not approved.

McFarlane testified that after their private meeting, an attorney named Tom Green arrived; as the meeting ended, Secord arrived. McFarlane testified that he learned later that Green was Secord's lawyer.

At 2:00 that afternoon North met with Meese, Reynolds and Cooper, and another Justice Department official named Richardson, who took extensive notes. According to the notes, Meese began by explaining that he wanted to get all the facts from everyone involved and flesh out different recollections. Meese said he had talked to the President and Poindexter. He stated that the worst thing that could happen was if someone tried to conceal something to protect themselves or the President or put a good "spin" in it.

Meese testified that he did not know North well on a personal basis, but did have considerable contact with him in and out of the White House on a casual basis. Based on his discussion with North and what he read subsequently, Meese was convinced North was "zealous about the mission he felt he had." Meese concluded that North had let Poindexter know what he was doing and had not been forbidden from doing it. Meese testified that it never occurred to him that there would be any collusion of an untoward nature and that it was at the time still not a criminal matter. North was questioned at some length about the Iran program before being confronted with the Undated Memorandum with the passage on use of residual arms sale funds for the Nicaraguan resistance.

Meese testified that he recalled being disturbed and troubled, but not apprehensive. Steps were taken, however, to get McFarlane in right away, the next morning—North had said he told McFarlane during the Tehran trip about use of Iran arms proceeds for the Nicaraguan resistance.

Meese was asked by the Committee if he sought out Poindexter immediately so as to prevent any communications between Poindexter and North on what North had just told Meese and the other Justice Department officials. Meese testified that he did not.

Meese testified the next morning, Monday, November 24. Meese met with his staff and went over what they had found. Meese recalled asking his attorneys to look over what criminal laws or others [sic] laws might be applicable. Meese was not sure whether he talked to the FBI Director on Monday.

Later that morning Meese also talked to McFarlane to find out what he knew about money being available to the Nicaraguan resistance. According to Meese, McFarlane said he knew nothing until his trip to Tehran, and that was the only thing he knew about it. Meese's conversation with McFarlane was brief; he said he was only trying to verify certain facts. Meese also talked briefly to Weinberger by phone; Weinberger did not have much to add.

Meese testified that at 11 a.m. that morning he met with the President and Regan telling them that during his review, Meese had come across indications that money from Iranian arms transactions may have gone to the Nicaraguan resistance. Meese testified he told them he had talked to North who had acknowledged that in fact that had happened.

Meese told the President he had not completed his review and would get back to him later that afternoon after talking to other people, including Poindexter. Meese said the President looked shocked and very surprised, as did Regan, who uttered an expletive.

Meese recalled that at this meeting or at one later in the day, the President said it was important "to get this out as soon as possible." Regan recalled a discussion with Meese in the morning at which Meese told him he needed to arrange a meeting with the President about what he had found out on Monday afternoon.

Meese testified that he talked to Poindexter in the latter's office very briefly on Monday afternoon. No notes were taken and Meese was alone. Meese recalled telling Poindexter what had been learned from North and asking if he knew about the matter. According to Meese, Poindexter said yes, he knew about it generally. According to Meese, Poindexter said North had given him "enough hints" that he knew there was money going to the Contras, but he "didn't inquire further." Meese further testified that Poindexter said he had already decided he would probably have to resign because of it.

Meese testified that he asked Poindexter if he had told anyone about the money going to the Contras, and Poindexter said he had not. Their conversation lasted about ten minutes, because Meese needed to get back to see the President. Meese testified that he did not consider his talk with Poindexter an "investigation" or a "criminal investigation," and Meese said he did not consider the matter a law violation "on its face." He was trying, he said, to find out what happened from a respected member of the Administration.

Meese testified that he met with the President and Regan at 4:30 p.m. that afternoon and related what he had learned, including Poindexter's acknowledgement that he had knowledge of the Contra funds. Meese said he discussed looking at what applicable criminal laws there might be. They arranged to meet again the next morning at 9:00 after sorting things out because it was "a tremendous surprise and shock to everybody." Meese testified that he knew that "neither Don Regan nor Ronald Reagan knew anything about this." Regan recalled the President's dismay and surprise at the discovery, and his decision to go public with it. Regan testified that the President had made clear to his staff that while he strongly supported the Nicaraguan resistance, such support should be provided by lawful means.

Meese testified that he talked with the Vice President that Monday and told him what had been learned. Meese "asked him if he had known anything about it, and the Vice President said no, he had not." Meese also recalled that the possibility of Poindexter's resignation was discussed Monday evening, possibly between Regan and the President. Meese learned that Regan talked to Casey on Monday night.

Two other meetings occurred on Monday, November 24. According to his notes, Assistant Attorney General Cooper met with Tom Green who said he represented North and Secord. After discussing Hakim's role in proposing use of Iran arms proceeds to the Nicaraguan resistance, Green said Hakim and Secord felt like they were doing the Lord's work. They believed they were not violating any laws. Cooper's notes say Green warned that if the matter blew up, Iran would kill one or more of the hostages and two other individuals would also probably be killed.

According to testimony by Furmark, also on Monday, he met again with Casey at CIA headquarters. According to Furmark, Casey told him there was $30,000 in the account. Furmark assumed he meant the Lake Resources account. Furmark testified that Casey called North. Then Casey stated repeatedly that he did not know where the money was. Casey also called Assistant Attorney General Cooper. Furmark testified that Casey's staff told him the only way they knew about the Lake Resources account was because Furmark had told them about it. According to Furmark, North apparently told Casey that the Iranians or the Israelis owed Ghorbanifar and Khashoggi the money. Furmark said Casey tried and failed to reach Regan and Meese.

Meese testified that he met with Casey at Casey's home the next morning at 7 a.m., Tuesday, November 25. Casey had called Meese at 6:30 to ask him to stop by. Meese could not recall the conversation, except that it was generally about the situation and what Meese had learned. Casey told Meese that Regan had talked to him the night before about the money-to-the-Contras situation. While with Casey, Meese received a call from Regan who said he was going to talk with Poindexter. Regan verified that Meese would be at the White House at 9:00. Casey also apparently told Meese he would send him the Furmark memoranda, which he did by letter. At 8:00, according to his testimony, Regan talked with Poindexter and indicated he felt Poindexter should be ready to resign when he saw the President at 9:30. Regan testified that when he questioned Poindexter about his negligence, Poindexter responded that he had felt sorry for the Contras and wanted them to get help. He had, therefore, not questioned where the money came from.

Meese testified that at 9:00 he met with the President and Regan. He testified that he told them more of what he had found out and that a criminal investigation would probably be convened. According to Meese, they realized this was "a very momentous occasion" and that the worst thing for the President would be the appearance of covering up. The emphasis was on getting it out to the Congressional leadership and the public and, in parallel with that, commencing a criminal investigation.

Meese disclosed his findings at a noon press conference. Meese testified that he arrived at the $10-30 million figure he used at the press conference by taking North's statement that $3-4 million went to the Nicaraguan resistance on one occasion and the April 4 document which referred to $12 million. North had said two or three shipments were involved. Multiplying the sums for one transaction by three gave $10-30 million as an approximation.

Meese told the Committee that after his press conference and a luncheon with the Supreme Court, Meese walked back to the Oval Office with the President. He told the President that he was going back to the Justice Department because they were pursuing a criminal investigation.

Meese recalled that, at the press conference, he did not know if any criminal violations were possibly involved. According to his testimony, Meese commenced a criminal investigation that afternoon.

He directed the Deputy Attorney General notify the White House Counsel to be sure that security precautions were taken on all documents, and directed the Assistant Attorney General for the Criminal Division to meet with the Assistant Attorney General for the Office of Legal Counsel (Mr. Cooper) to discuss possible laws that might apply, including criminal laws. Meese testified he also met with FBI Director Webster and told him he was turning the matter over to the Criminal Division and would "probably" need FBI resources. According to Meese, FBI resources were requested the next day, November 26.

Meese testified that Israeli Foreign Minister Peres called him on the afternoon of November 25. According to Meese, Peres said they had heard what had happened and that all they had done was tell the Iranians where to put the money. They had not handled the money. They had told the Iranians what bank accounts to put the money into, and how much.

According to an NSC staff member who shared North's office suite, a security officer came to the office on the evening of November 25 for the purpose of sealing the office. The staff member said he had no knowledge that any papers were destroyed.

On November 25, 1986, Assistant Secretary Abrams and the CIA task force chief appeared before the Committee at a regular hearing to review implementation of U.S. Nicaragua programs. In response to questions about third-country support for anti-Sandi-

nista forces, neither witness revealed the solicitation of $10 million in August. In testimony on December 8, 1986, under oath, Mr. Abrams apologized to the Committee for withholding this information. He said he did not feel he had been asked a direct question and did not realize until shown the transcript that his statements clearly left a misleading impression.

After the initiation of the Committee's initial investigation on November 28, the Committee received information indicating that profits from Iranian arms sales were deposited in account(s) in a Swiss bank called Credit Fiduciere Services (CFS) and that such accounts were opened and/or controlled by Richard Secord, Thomas Clines, and Theodore Shackley. CFS then transferred money to its subsidiaries in Grand Cayman which disbursed it to the Nicaraguan resistance.

This report was based on sources of unknown reliability and the committee has not been able to verify its contents.

According to testimony received by the Committee, private funding for the Nicaraguan resistance generally was funnelled through offshore bank accounts in the Cayman Islands and Panama controlled by Adolfo Calero. However, the Committee received no direct testimony regarding the actual receipt of specific amounts of money by the Nicaraguan resistance. According to testimony by the CIA task force chief who was responsible for monitoring the financial status of the Nicaraguan resistance, there was no unusual infusion of funds to the Nicaraguan resistance in 1986.

Unresolved Issues

The Intelligence Committee has, as reflected in this report, gathered a considerable amount of information, both through testimony and documentation, regarding the sale of arms to Iran and possible diversion of funds to the Nicaraguan resistance. This information, we believe, will be helpful to the Select Committee as it undertakes its investigation into these matters.

In accordance with Senate Resolution 23, the Committee recommends that the Select Committee pursue a number of questions and issues on which this information bears. These items are not meant to be limiting in any way to the work of the Select Committee, but, consistent with provisions of Senate Resolution 23, they are areas of inquiry that the Intelligence Committee believes the Select Committee might consider as part of its investigation.

1. What role did members of the White House staff play in planning and implementing the sale of arms to Iran and the possible diversion of funds to the Nicaraguan resistance?

2. What role did the CIA and other U.S. Government agencies or their officials play in planning and implementing the sale of arms to Iran and the possible diversion of funds to the Nicaraguan resistance?

3. What role did private individuals, both citizens of the U.S. and citizens of foreign countries, including private arms dealers and financiers, play in planning and implementing the sale of arms to Iran and the possible diversion of funds to the Nicaraguan resistance? Why did U.S. officials rely upon such private individuals in lieu of established U.S. Government agencies?

4. What role did officials, agents, representatives and emissaries of foreign countries, including, without limitation, Israel and other Mideast nations, play in planning and implementing the sale of arms to Iran and the possible diversion of funds to the Nicaraguan resistance?

5. When, by whom and to what extent were the activities of individuals acting independently or on behalf of the U.S. in planning and implementing the sale of arms to Iran and the possible diversion of funds to the Nicaraguan resistance authorized by the officials of the U.S. Government?

6. When, by whom and to what extent were the activities of individuals acting independently or on behalf of the U.S. in planning the sale of arms to Iran and the possible diversion of funds to the Nicaraguan resistance made known to officials of the U.S. Government?

7. How were funds raised by or with the participation of U.S. officials for the benefit of the Nicaraguan resistance from any and

all sources, including, without limitation, private individuals, third countries, and the sale of arms to Iran? How and by whom were such funds administered? In what way, to whom and for what purposes were such funds expended?

8. Except as authorized by Congress, what forms of assistance, other than funds, were provided by or with the participation of U.S. officials to the Nicaraguan resistance and by whom? When, by whom and to what extent were such other forms of assistance authorized by or known to officials of the U.S. Government?

9. To what extent was assistance, both financial and otherwise, that was provided to the Nicaraguan resistance by private citizens and officials of the U.S. Government consistent with applicable law?

10. To what extent was assistance to Iran, including, without limitation, the sale of arms and the provisions of intelligence, consistent with applicable law?

11. To what extent were the objectives of U.S. officials in selling arms to Iran frustrated by the participation and possible enrichment of private individuals?

12. To what extent were the objectives of U.S. officials in raising funds for the Nicaraguan resistance, whether or not such objectives were authorized by applicable law, frustrated by the participation and possible enrichment of private individuals?

13. Whether upon being made aware of information with regard to the unauthorized and possibly unlawful provision of financial and other assistance to the Nicaraguan resistance, U.S. officials acted properly in investigating and reporting such information.

14. How, when, and by whom were financial decisions made and implemented with respect to the sale of arms to Iran, including, without limitation, the basis upon which prices for arms were determined, the way in which funds were raised, administered and expended to effect the sales, and by whom, when, how and to whom the proceeds from such sales were distributed?

BUSH AIDE'S MEMO ON IRAN SALES BRIEFING

Following is the text of a memo written by Craig Fuller, Vice President George Bush's chief of staff, on a meeting Bush and Fuller had with Amiram Nir on July 29, 1986. Nir, antiterrorism adviser to Israeli prime minister Shimon Peres, briefed the vice president on U.S. arms sales to Iran. The top secret memo was published in the Washington Post *February 8, 1987, and was included in the Tower Commission report.*

THE VICE PRESIDENT'S MEETING WITH MR. NIR— 7/29/86 0735-0805

PARTICIPANTS: The Vice President, Mr. Nir, Craig Fuller

DATE/TIME: 7/29/86 0735-0805

LOCATION: Vice President's suite/King David Hotel, Jerusalem

1. SUMMARY. Mr. Nir indicated that he had briefed Prime Minister Peres and had been asked to brief the VP by his White House contacts. He described the details of the efforts from last year through the current period to gain the release of the U.S. hostages. He reviewed what had been learned which was essentially that the radical group was the group that could deliver. He reviewed the issues to be considered—namely that there needed to be ad [sic] decision as to whether the items requested would be delivered in separate shipments or whether we would continue to press for the release of the hostages prior to delivering the items in an amount agreed to previously.

2. The VP's 25 minute meeting was arranged after Mr. Nir called Craig Fuller and requested the meeting and after it was discussed with the VP by Fuller and [Lt. Col. Oliver L.] North. Only Fuller was aware of the meeting and no other member of the VP's staff or traveling party has been advised about the meeting. No cables were generated nor was there other reporting except a brief phone call between Fuller and North to advise that "no requests were made."

3. Nir began by indicating that Peres had asked him to brief the VP. In addition, Nir's White House contacts with whom he had recent discussions asked him to brief the VP.

4. Nir began by providing an historical perspective from his vantage point. He stated that the effort began last summer. This early phase he said "didn't work well." There were more discussions in November and in January "we thought we had a better approach with the Iranian side," said Nir. He said, "[national security adviser John M.] Poindexter accepted the decision."

5. He characterized the decision as "having two layers—tactical and strategic." The tactical layer was described as an effort "to get the hostages out." The strategic layer was designed "to build better contact with Iran and to insure we are better prepared when a change (in leadership) occurs." "Working through our Iranian contact, we used the hostage problem and efforts there as a test," suggested Nir. He seemed to suggest the test was to determine how best to establish relationships that worked with various Iranian factions.

6. Nir described Israel's role in the effort by saying, "we activated the channel; we gave a front to the operation; provided a physical base; provided aircraft." All this to "make sure the U.S. will not be involved in logistical aspects." Nir indicated that in the early phase they "began moving things over there."

7. Before a second phase a meeting was desired. Nir indicated a February meeting took place with "the Prime Minister on the other side." Nir did not make it clear who else attended the meeting. He said the meeting was "dramatic and interesting." He said "an agreement was made on 4,000 units—1,000 first and then 3,000." The agreement was made on the basis that we would get the group," Nir said. "The whole package for a fixed price," he said.

8. Although there was agreement the other side changed their minds and "then they asked for the other items," according to Nir. "We were pleased because these were defensive items and we got to work with the military," said Nir. He continued, "there were 240 items on the list we were provided and we agreed to it."

9. A meeting was organized for mid May in Tehran to finalize the operation. The VP asked Nir if he attended the meeting and Nir indicated he did attend. Nir said "two mistakes were made during this phase." "Two people were to be sent to prepare for the meeting but the U.S. had concerns about [Robert C.] McFarlane," according to Nir. He described the meetings as "more difficult—total frustration because we didn't prepare." And he said, "their top level was not prepared adequately." During the meeting in Tehran the other side kept reminding the group that "in 1982 there was a meeting which leaked and the Prime Minister was thrown out of office." Nir said that at the end of the May meeting, "they began to see the light." "McFarlane was making it clear that we wanted all hostages released," Nir reported and, "at the last moment the other side suggested two would be released if those at the meeting stayed six more hours." According to Nir, "the Deputy Prime Minister delivered the request (to delay departure) and when the group said 'no,' they all departed without anything."

10. According to Nir, "the reason for delay is to squeeze as much as possible as long as they have assets. They don't believe that we want overall strategic cooperation to be better in the future. If they believed us they would have not bothered so much with the price right now." Further, according to Nir, "there are serious struggles now within the Iran power groups. Three leaders share the view that we should go ahead but each wants to prove his own toughness."

11. Turning to what Nir said was the final or most recent phase, he reported, "we felt things would just die if we didn't push forward to see what could be delivered. They asked for four sequences, but we said no to talks until they showed something."

12. According to Nir, he told them about 10 days ago he would cancel the deal. Then nine days ago their Prime Minister called saying that they were taking steps to release one—the Priest. The second one to be released would be [David P.] Jacobson. The Prime Minister also said that one would be released and then "we should give some equipment." Nir indicated to the VP that the bottom line on the items to be delivered was understood to be the same or even less but it was not the way the deal was originally made. The items involved spares for Hawks and TOWs. No denial or approval was given according to Nir. Nir said he made it clear that no deal would be discussed unless evidence is seen of a release.

13. On Tuesday or Wednesday a message was intercepted between Tehran and the guards according to Nir. On Friday, three hostages were taken out and on Saturday [Rev. Lawrence Jenco] Janco [sic] was taken out, put into a trunk and driven to a village in the Bakka [sic] Valley. Nir then described what Janco reported with regard to the conditions under which he was held and what he knew of the other hostages including [William] Buckley. (I assume we have detailed briefing already.) The VP asked Nir if he had briefed Peres on all of this and he indicated that he had.

14. Nir described some of the lessons learned: "we are dealing with the most radical elements. The Deputy Prime Minister is an emissary. They can deliver . . . that's for sure. They were called yesterday and thanked and today more phone calls. This is good because we've learned they can deliver and the moderates can't. We should think about diversity and establish other contacts with other factions. We have started to establish contact with some success and now more success is expected since if these groups feel if the extremes are in contact with us then it is less risky for the other groups—nothing operational is being done . . . this is contact only."

15. Nir described some of the problems and choices: "Should we accept sequencing? What are alternatives to sequencing? They fear if they give all hostages they won't get anything from us. If we do want to move along these lines we'd have to move quickly. It would be a matter still of several weeks not several days, in part because they have to move the hostages every time one is released."

16. Nir concluded with the following points: "The bottom line is that we won't give them more than previously agreed to. It is important that we have assets there 2 to 3 years out when change occurs. We have no real choice than to proceed."

17. The VP made no commitments nor did he give any direction to Nir. The VP expressed his appreciation for the briefing and thanked Nir for having pursued this effort despite doubts and reservations throughout the process.

BY: CRAIG L. FULLER [initialed:] "CF 8/6/86"

PRESIDENT'S STATEMENT ON TOWER REPORT RELEASE

Following is the text of President Reagan's remarks opening the Tower Commission's February 26, 1987, press conference on its final report:

PRESIDENT REAGAN: On behalf of myself and the American people, I want to extend my thanks to [former] Senator [John] Tower, [former] Secretary [of State Edmund S.] Muskie, and [retired Air Force Lt.] General [Brent] Scowcroft. Whatever this report may say, I have appointed—or I'm proud to have appointed this distinguished Board, because it fulfills my commitment to get the facts and share them with the American people. This is why I asked Attorney General [Edwin] Meese [III] to conduct his review and why, when that review uncovered unauthorized actions, I ordered full disclosure of what we then knew. It

was why I urged the appointment of an Independent Counsel and why I appointed David Abshire as my Special Counselor on this matter. And it is also why I ordered full cooperation with congressional inquiries. And it's why I appointed this Board—the Tower board.

The significance of this Board's work is reflected in the size of this volume, which I am going to carefully study over the next several days. But Senator Tower, Secretary Muskie, and General Scowcroft, in completing the task so well, you've again demonstrated a willingness—one you've shown all your lives—to help your country, to devote yourself to public service. In a highly charged atmosphere, I know it wasn't easy to interrupt your lives. But this was an important contribution to your nation and the American people are grateful to you for it.

And now, in addition to thanking these distinguished gentlemen, I want to make it clear that I consider their work far too important for instant analysis. I intend to read and digest it first, think carefully about its findings, and promptly act on its recommendations.

Next week I will address the nation and give the American people my response to this report. But I pledge to the American people today that I will do whatever is necessary to enact the proper reforms and to meet the challenges ahead.

I want to thank the members of the Board again. And now, John [Senator Tower], I'm sure there'll be a few questions for you.

Q: Mr. President—

Q: —Donald [T.] Regan be leaving as Chief of Staff?

Q: —Iranian.

Q: Mr. President—

Q: Is Donald Regan—

P: The Board will take your questions.

Q: Sir, will Donald Regan be leaving as your Chief of Staff?

TOWER COMMISSION PRESS CONFERENCE

Following is the text of the February 26, 1987, press conference held by the members of the President's Special Review Board: former senator John Tower, R-Texas, board chairman; former senator and secretary of state Edmund S. Muskie, D-Maine; and retired Air Force lieutenant general Brent Scowcroft, a former national security adviser to President Gerald R. Ford:

Tower Statement

SENATOR TOWER: The Special Review Board has completed its work. Senator Muskie and General Scowcroft will have their own statements in a moment. But it might be helpful to give you the highlights of this rather lengthy report to the President.

Before we begin, I want to note that I have never been privileged to work with two more public-spirited, perceptive and intellectually honest men than Ed Muskie and Brent Scowcroft. Our working relationship was congenial and collegial. The report represents the collective understandings, evaluations and judgments of all three of us. There were never any significant disagreements among us.

It was incumbent upon us to put aside all partisan or personal loyalties and prejudices in fulfilling this demanding and challenging assignment. I emphasize that it was not our function to make judgments on criminal culpability. I want to express my gratitude to my colleagues for the considerable time they devoted, their dedication, and their sense of purpose.

We would be remiss if we did not pay tribute to the small but dedicated, diligent, and highly professional staff that supported us. Under the circumstances of deadlines and our expectations, they put together a product I consider to be remarkable. Now, let me discuss this report for a few minutes. Ed and Brent will each expand on this in their own statements at the completion of my remarks.

We began our work December 1st of last year [1986], the same day President [Ronald] Reagan appointed us and signed the Executive Order. The President, in the Executive Order, asked all departments and agencies to cooperate with us. When President Reagan appointed us, he urged that all the facts come out on the Iran-Contra matter. The President wanted us to examine this matter, to find lessons for the future so that it can be put right.

We considered the development of the NSC [National Security Council] system over time. As part of that review, we interviewed former Presidents [Richard] Nixon, [Gerald R.] Ford, and [Jimmy] Carter, as well as most of the living Secretaries of State, Secretaries of Defense, Directors of Central Intelligence, National Security Advisers, as well as two former Chairmen of the Joint Chiefs of Staff.

In addition, we looked at specific case studies of the NSC system from the administration of President [Dwight D.] Eisenhower to date in an effort to understand how the system works under stress. The Iran initiative and Contra diversion served as the primary case study in our review. The summary of the facts on Iran-Contra is located in Part III of our report. Here and elsewhere, we have presented these facts as we understand them. Some information, we have concluded, must remain in the classified domain. No material—I emphasize no material—was deleted on the grounds that it might prove politically embarrassing to this administration. What was left out did not alter the substance of the report.

Our conclusion is that there are indeed many powerful lessons to be learned. Part IV of our report, called, "What Was Wrong," is intended to instruct on those lessons. It is important to emphasize, however, that putting into practice those lessons is not susceptible of quick fixes or easy answers. Our principal recommendation illustrates that point. Let me quote from the report here: "Using the process will not always produce brilliant ideas, but history suggests it can at least help prevent bad ideas from becoming Presidential policy."

Now, the report you have is a lengthy one. Here are a few points you might keep in mind while reading through it. Mistakes were made. But those mistakes that attract headlines may give a distorted picture of how the NSC really works. We looked at case studies from crises of this and previous administrations. The Iran-Contra affair was clearly an aberration. The NSC system is alive, and has served us well for the 40 years of its existence. We should profit from those mistakes. The President obviously desires to do so. It is a tribute to President Reagan that he had the courage to invite three outsiders in, give them complete access to sensitive national security files and administration personnel, and deal with the consequences. This act clearly demonstrates the strength and resilience of American democracy with its inherent capacity for a constructive self-analysis and self-criticism.

To make the NSC system work, it must be used. One of the mistakes made in the Iran initiative was to ignore the system. Process is no substitute for substance. However, steady and consistent governance has a better opportunity of success if there is an orderly process for decision-making.

The President is the ultimate decision maker in national security. No one can, or should, pretend otherwise. We could not long endure or exercise executive power by committee. A strong executive with a flexibility to conduct foreign and diplomatic affairs is an essential feature of our form of government.

Those who serve as presidential advisers on national security issues have a special responsibility. This is true for this or any administration. The advisers must assure that the President gets the best counsel possible. A President may not follow their advice, but the advisers have a clear responsibility to continue to bring to his attention matters that are pertinent even after the decision is made. Our report follows these principles. Taken as a whole, they constitute a guide to sound management.

The Board went to considerable lengths to obtain the facts about Iran-Contra. To the extent that we've obtained them, they are in Appendix B. There the story is told as best we know how.

We also looked into the issue of NSC involvement in support of the Nicaraguan rebels—the so-called Contras. We did not have the time to do so thoroughly. However, what we learned is at Appendix C. The handling of the matter after it became known was of interest to us also. The Board was able to take a broad look at this but not in the detail which we devoted to the Iran initiative. That is included in Appendix D and summarized at the end of Part IV.

The Congressional investigating committees and the Independent Counsel will carry on. We leave it to them to analyze new evidence. The value of this effort we leave to the judgment of the American people and to history.

Senator Muskie will now give his statement and discuss Part IV of the report. General Scowcroft will follow him and discuss our recommendations.

Senator Muskie.

Muskie Statement

SENATOR MUSKIE: Thank you very much, John. I share John's evaluation of the work that we've done together. I have total respect for both of my colleagues and I emphasize that this is a unanimous report and I think it was clear from the beginning that it would be.

I would also like to emphasize the President, after all, appointed us to conduct the study. We wouldn't be here discussing the report except for that fact. We were given two extensions of time to conclude our work. We were given the kind of access to departments and agencies of the government which he promised us.

I will address my remarks, as John has said, to Part IV of the report which is entitled "What Was Wrong". I commended [sic] to those who would like a summary of our findings. It goes to our mandate to draw conclusion [sic] about the NSC system and it forms the basis our of [sic] recommendations. So Part IV and Part III taken together are the meat of what it is that we present.

Now the following are the [sic] among the conclusions you will find in this section.

Item: The Iran initiative was handled almost casually and through informal channels. Always, apparently, with an expectation that the process would end with the next arms-for-hostages exchange. And, of course, it did not. It was subjected neither to the general procedures for interagency consideration and review of policy nor the procedures for covert operations.

Item: The opportunity for a full hearing before the President was inadequate.

Item: Interagency consideration of the initiative was limited to the Cabinet level and inadequate at that. It was never examined at the staff level where expertise on the situation in Iran, the difficulties of dealing with terrorists and the mechanisms of conducting diplomatic openings may have made a difference.

Item: Intelligence analysis may—could also have provided an independent evaluation of the Israeli proposals, a systematic vetting of those engaged as intermediaries and a thorough examination of the effect of the initiative on the balance in the Iran-Iraq war.

Item: Insufficient attention was given to the implications of the NSC staff having operational control of the initiative rather than the CIA.

Item: Concern for preserving the secrecy of the initiative provided an excuse for abandoning sound process.

Item: The informality of the initiative meant that it lacked a formal institutional record and informed analysis. The result was that we were too often dependent on mere recollection instead of a clear and complete record.

Item: The implementation of the initiative was never subjected to a rigorous review at appropriate times in this long 18-month history.

The Board also received—reached several conclusions regarding responsibility. This is not an exhaustive list, but some of the highlights. I would be surprised if the list answered all the questions that you would like to put, but I hope that these will get you started.

Item: The NSC system will not work unless the President makes it work. After all, this system was created to serve the President of the United States in ways of his choosing—by his actions, by his leadership. The President, therefore, determines the quality of its performance.

Item: The President did not force his policy to undergo the most criticial review of which the NSC participants and the process were capable.

Item: The Board found a strong consensus among NSC participants that the President's priority in the Iran initiative was the release of U.S. hostages. But setting priorities is not enough when it comes to sensitive and risky initiatives that directly effect [sic] U.S. national security, for it is the President who must take responsibility for the NSC system and deal with the consequences.

Item: President Reagan's personal management style places an especially heavy responsibility on his key advisers. Knowing his style, they should have been particularly mindful of the need for special attention to the measures in which this arms sales initiative developed and proceeded. On this score, neither the National Security Adviser nor the other NSC principals deserve high marks.

Item: The National Security Adviser failed in his responsability [sic] to see that an orderly process was observed.

Item: The Chief of Staff also shares in this responsibility. More than almost any Chief of Staff of recent memory, he asserted personal control over the White House staff and sought to extend his control to the National Security Adviser. He as much as anyone should have insisted that an orderly process be observed. In addition, he especially should have insured that plans were made for handling any public disclosure of the initiative.

Item: Given the importance of the initiative, Secretary [of State George P.] Shultz and Secretary [of Defense Caspar W.] Weinberger, while indicating their opposition, distanced themselves from the march of events.

Item and period: There is no evidence that [CIA] Director [William J.] Casey made clear to the President that Lieutenant Colonel [Oliver L.] North, rather than the CIA, was running the operation. The President does not recall ever being informed of this fact. Indeed, Director Casey should have gone further and pressed for operational responsibility to be transferred to the CIA.

I now yield to my colleague, General Scowcroft.

Scowcroft Statement

GENERAL SCOWCROFT: By way of echoing John's and Ed's introductory remarks, let me just say that I consider we operated not in a bipartisan, but a nonpartisan fashion. We had a great many arguments about semantics, but I recall not a single one about substance.

As for our staff who worked days, nights, weekends and holidays, they bring honor to the term staff, or bureaucrat, as the case may be. The country owes them a major debt of gratitude.

As Senator Tower said, we studied with care the operation of the NSC system over the 40 years of its existence. As far as we know, we're the first such official study to have focused exclusively on this institution.

People tend to forget what the National Security Council system is all about. The NSC system, the Council itself, the NSC staff and the National Security Adviser is the President's creature. The President is accountable to the American people for its successes and its failures. It is not just another agency of the Executive Branch. It is not intended to be subject to the reach of Congress. It is the President's own instrument. It is through this system that he brings his creative impulses in national security to bear on the permanent government, the departments and agencies. It is one of the few structures in government that is unequivocally his. The National Security Act recognized this by giving the President wide latitude to fashion it to his liking. Each President has done so with the result that over the years there have been many different operational styles, many different operational organizational modes for the NSC staff and the National Security Adviser.

Given its role, there is no ideal structure for the system. It should be sufficiently flexible to be adaptable to the management style and operating philosophy of any President. But there are certain functions which in some manner must be performed to provide every President with the tools he requires to do his job.

The National Security Council exists for only one purpose—to advise the President in his awesome task of directing a national security policy of the country. It does not make decisions. The agency heads who participate in its deliberations are there, not simply to represent their department views. They are there as individual advisers to offer their best judgment to the President.

As the manager of this system, the National Security Adviser must insure, at a minimum, that matters which come before the NSC cover the full range of issues on which a review is required, that a full range of options is considered together with their opportunities and their risks, that all relevant intelligence and other information is available to all the participants, especially the President, and that Presidential decisions are fully understood and are implemented in the manner in which the President intended.

But the National Security Adviser is not simply the manager of the process. We believe that he, himself, should be an important source of advice to the President. His is advice unburdened by agency burdens and perspectives. But he must, to play his role properly, also represent the views of the other principals fully and fairly. This is an essential, a difficult, but not an impossible task.

The NSC staff which serves the National Security Adviser and the President should be small, highly competent and experienced in policy making. It should be able neither to substitute for, nor to duplicate the work of the agencies. It should not undertake operational functions except in the rarest of circumstances. Even then, that should be done only at the express direction of the President, following a judgment there are no feasible alternative ways to accomplish the task.

We have described in the report a very general model of an NSC system to serve any President. We do not believe any amendment in the provisions of the National Security Act, dealing with the structure and operation of the NSC system, is required or is desirable.

The Iranian affair, of course, has led to concerns for which legislative remedies have been suggested. One is Senate confirmation of the National Security Adviser. Our report cites several troubling aspects of the performance of the National Security Adviser. However, this is the President's problem, not that of the Congress. And confirmation would introduce a number of new difficulties, which we believe would be damaging.

Another is a ban on an operational role for the NSC staff. We are opposed to the staff having such a role, rather than a legislative prscription [sic], however, we believe that if an operational assignment to the NSC staff appears essential, it should be undertaken only after explicit approval by the President.

Our analysis of the Iranian affair, as Senator Muskie has stated, indicates to us that the problem at the heart was one of people, not of process. It was not that the structure was faulty, it is that the structure was not used. The President is a powerful figure under the Constitution. The objective should be to give him tools which will help and not inhibit the performance of his tasks. Unless the system is flexible enough to serve any President's needs, it will either become an obstacle and a source of frustration to the President, or an institutional irrelevance as he fashions an informal structure more to his liking.

We believe the recommendations we've outlined provide for a system which can be operated so as to minimize the likelihood of major error in national security policy, without destroying the creative impulses of the President.

Presidential Responsibility - 1

Q: Did the President take responsibility or deal with the consequences, as you say, in this case?

SENATOR TOWER: I think the President has said that he would take the responsibility for what happened. In this particular instance, I believe that the President was poorly advised and poorly served. I think that he should have followed-up more and monitored this operation more closely. I think he was not aware of a lot of the things that were going on and the way the operation was structured and who was involved in it. He very clearly didn't understand all that.

Q: Senator Tower, you list a number of things you say the President should have done but did not do. To put it in plain English, are you saying the President made mistakes?

SENATOR TOWER: Yes, the President made mistakes. I think that's very plain English. The President did make mistakes. A lot of his subordinates made mistakes. I might note that every President has made mistakes from time to time—some of far greater consequence than the ones that President Reagan has made. I think that the whole initiative could be justified on the grounds of a geostrategic opening, but that the arms-for-hostage exchange cannot be justified, and was actually counterproductive of the long-term objective of a geostrategic opening.

Reagan Management Style - 1

Q: Senator Tower—and I'd like all three of you to answer this if you will, because you've all had long experience dealing with Presidents. If you could put this in comparison to other Presidents you've all worked with, how disengaged was this President from the process, how troubling is that to you, and how dangerous was it to have a foreign policy that the President wasn't running?

SENATOR TOWER: Let me make my comment on that, and other—my colleagues will have their own observations. President Reagan has a particular type of management style of delegating authority, and that style, to work, means that the President must be surrounded by experts who will act responsibly. At the same time, the president must from time to time monitor the actions of those to whom he delegates authority. Now, there are other Presidents that have had different styles. Some have gotten heavily involved in the details of operations to the point where they fail to see the big picture. They lose vision and concept.

I think that President Reagan is a man of great vision and concept. And I think for the most part, the operation of the foreign policy of this administration has been good. And I think the policy has been fundamentally sound. In this particular instance, it wasn't the public policy of the United States that was in question. But the fact is that there was a covert activity that was going absolutely contrary to the public policy of the United States that was set by the President himself.

I think the others should be permitted to—

GENERAL SCOWCROFT: Yes. I think the key to the system is that it ought to be able to adapt to management style of different Presidents, and we've had some, as John said, going from the—if you will, the laid-back style, I think that was the term used, to a highly intrusive kind of a President.

Now, what happened in this case is that the system did not compensate for the management style of the President. He did not, perhaps, ask enough questions. But it was incumbent upon the other participants in the system to ensure that the President was absolutely clear about what was going on. There should have been bells ringing, lights flashing, and so on, so that there was no question. Not to try to steer him or anything, but no question with [*sic*] the consequences of his pursuing this policy was.

SENATOR TOWER: Let Senator Muskie comment.

SENATOR MUSKIE: A follow-up question to each of us?

SENATOR TOWER: He asked that our whole panel comment.

SENATOR MUSKIE: Yes, I know. Well, let me put it this way. The policy was a wrong policy, and it was the President's policy. And there's no question but what he felt deeply about that policy and about its purposes and objectives. He did truly believe that we ought to be thinking about developing an opening to Iran at the right time under the right circumstances. And that was not a casual position on his part, it was a deeply-felt one.

At the same time, he was emotionally and heavily involved in the fate of the hostages. And if you'll recall the last 18 months, there were many opportunities in which the President was exposed to the tragedy of these various hostage situations. And in July, for example, of 1985, the TWA hostages came back, and there was the funeral at Arlington Cemetery, and that day and those circum-

stances happened to coincide with the first initiative taken by the Israelis to present a proposal to him. And he reacted strongly. And it's clear that he was driven by that compassion for the hostages from beginning to end. So there was this coincidence of Presidential interest which it is appropriate for the President to take. But given his heavy personal and emotional commitment to both objectives, it was then incumbent upon his staff to make sure that all of the implications of the policy were investigated, and I think I've made some comments on that in my opening statement.

SENATOR TOWER: The lady in red in the back there. The lady in red back there.

Resupplying the Contras

Q: Senator, I'm interested in the corporate involvement in the financing of the situation—particular on Page C-6, it states that Colonel North had some connecting—some political action committees. In particular, I'd like to know about the Fortune—any of the Fortune 500—whether they themselves or subsidiaries financed this through charitable contributions from nations or political action committees?

SENATOR TOWER: Let me say that we did not deal with individual or private contributors to the Contras. That's not dealt with here. We did deal with the fact that NSC staff were obviously engaged in activities that—in helping to manage and coordinate activities that were clearly not sanctioned by the Boland Amendment.

Q: Senator—

SENATOR TOWER: The lady here in red.

Q: In your conclusions on that, you have a lengthy appendix which says that Colonel North reported to both [former national security advisers] Mr. [Robert C.] McFarlane and later to Admiral [John M.] Poindexter about his involvement in resupplying the Contras. Now, do you conclude from that that that was the policy of this government in contradiction to the Boland Amendment and that others in the NSC, including Shultz, Weinberger, the President, the Vice President, were aware of it?

SENATOR TOWER: I don't believe that we—and my colleagues can comment on this if they choose—but I don't believe that we found anything that would lead us to believe that the President was directly involved in this effort—that it was, indeed, an operation that was going on in the NSC staff, but that they were not personally involved or knowledgeable.

Q: Well, how—

SENATOR TOWER: Let me call on General Scowcroft on that.

Q: Let me just ask how both McFarlane and Poindexter could have been running this operation through Colonel North without the President's knowledge or Director Casey's knowledge or anyone else higher up knowing?

GENERAL SCOWCROFT: First of all, I think it's important to underscore that the legislative provisions dealing with Nicaragua and the Contras are extraordinarily complex, ambiguous. And it's not at all clear what—whether they were or were not operating in violation. Secondly, it was not our job to review criminal culpability. We looked at what happened and tried to figure out why it happened, not whether or not it was specifically in contravention of laws other than was it, in fact, considered. It's a very murky question.

Q: Senator Tower?

Reagan Truthfulness

Q: You indicated that the President has not been involved in a cover-up. Does that mean that the President has, in fact, been honest with the American people at all stages of this investigation?

SENATOR TOWER: I think the President did not direct—and we don't use the term cover-up—the President did not direct the preparation of the materials that were employed in his public presentations of November 13th and November 19th, I believe. There was a deliberate effort to mislead by those who prepared these materials. I don't believe that the President wittingly mislead [*sic*] the American people. I think the President was convinced himself of the voracity [sic] of what he was saying. I think at the same time, that he was very—that he felt that there was still an opportunity, perhaps, for additional hostages to be released. I think he felt very strongly that any public comment that he might make could conceivably have some impact on the safety—the personal safety of people—of both hostages and people in Iran.

Q: Senator Tower—

Q: Senator, you heard from the President—

SENATOR TOWER: Right here.

Q: —on three occasions—twice in testimony and once by letter—and there are variances in that testimony about the authorization from the Israeli shipment. Could you address what you find and what you believe the President's position on that is and whether the Board finds it—and what its finding is in terms of an authorization for the Israelis to make that shipment?

SENATOR TOWER: Absent any evidence to the contrary, we have to conclude that the President's recollection of when the first shipment was approved is faulty. Now, he does acknowledge having approved it. The question is whether it was approved prospectively or retrospectively. The Board has made a plausible [sic] judgment, in my view, that the shipment was approved prior to the first August 30th transfer of arms. Now, again, that is a judgment on our part.

Q: Senator Tower—

Q: Yes, Senator Tower—

SENATOR TOWER: Miss White. Miss White.

Q: You're considered a Reagan loyalist, you headed up the Reagan-Bush campaign in Texas, viewed as sympathetic to the President. What steps do you think he needs to take to, I guess, restore public confidence in his ability to govern?

SENATOR TOWER: Well, I think the President must respond with great candor. I think that there is a great deal that he will learn from reading our report that has not been brought to his attention by his subordinates. As you know, we criticized his subordinates a great deal here. Even though I have been a supporter of this President and still regard myself as a supporter of this President, I'm not going to give public advice on how he should handle—

Advisers Failed Reagan

Q: Senator Tower, you painted a rather damning picture of the top aides that surround the President—Mr. Casey, Poindexter, North—that many of them misled the President, did not do their jobs basically. The nation's been through a nightmare before in terms of White House staff. How can this not happen again?

SENATOR TOWER: Well, I don't think that you can guarantee that mistakes will not be made in the future. What happened here was a failure to use the process that was available to the President—the failure to follow guidelines that had already been set down by this administration in a classified document in January of 1985. Had the prescribed system been followed, probably all of this would not have happened. But one thing is very, very clear—that members of the system who were privy to what was going on failed the President. They failed to advise him, they failed to insist on a periodic review, they failed to expose him to expert judgments and briefings on matters that he should have been made privy to—

Q: Senator Tower—

SENATOR TOWER: —because the President, clearly, didn't understand the nature of this operation, who was involved, and what was happening.

Q: Senator Tower, were there any heroes at all in this? We've read parts of this, and you're pretty critical of almost everybody, including the President. Did anybody do his or her job? Did anybody blow the whistle or attempt to? Is there anything good in here?

SENATOR TOWER: Well, we're not in the business of either determining criminal culpability or finding heroes. We tried to present an objective report, and all of our comments on individual personalities, I think, are very objectively done.

Q: Did anybody do the—

SENATOR TOWER: I wouldn't—I wouldn't try to single

out heroes because this is really a story of people whose performance was perhaps somewhat short of heroic.

Q: Senator Tower, there are two things here that seem to stand out. One, that the staff did not inform the President, that they excluded him from knowing about things. And two, that the President did not insist on knowing when he had started this operation and must have known it was proceeding. Why do you think the people were afraid to tell the President what was going on? And why do you think the President didn't insist on knowing?

SENATOR TOWER: Well, that would be speculative for me to answer that question, Sarah. But—

Q: Well, I want you to be. You've got a right to be speculative.

SENATOR TOWER: —it's not my position here to be speculative, I'm here as a member of the Board. Maybe later on I'll do a little speculation, but I don't propose to do it now because I want to try [sic] give you objective answers to the questions.

Q: From your experience, can't you answer that?

Secrecy Obsession - 1

Q: Question for Senator Muskie. The report would seem to suggest at every—almost every step along the way, a disregard for what was legal or what might not have been legal—an almost deliberate attempt to avoid pursing [sic] that question at each step. Does anything need to be done to prevent that?

SENATOR MUSKIE: Well, I think the single most important factor here is the over-obsession with secrecy. In a system of this kind when you—and there are occasions when it's necessary to hold closely information about—especially covert operations, but even possibly other operations of the government—well, every time that you are over-concerned with secrecy, you tend to abandon process. I mentioned some of those points in my opening statement. And the result is that, in this case, control of the operation slipped into the hands of Lt. Colonel North and the people that he assemble [sic] to pursue it. And the details, I think, are spelled out here and I won't try to summarize them here in the answer to your question. But once that happened, you see, then it was operating outside established government circles and was in the hands of intermediaries from outside the government and others, so that it was very difficult, then, for the President, or those who have direct responsibility to him, to get the information.

Arms-for-Hostages Exchange

Q: The one question we're [sic] been wondering about is, has the President's policy been an arms-for-hostages exchange? Was it or wasn't it?

SENATOR TOWER: That's what it became. Regardless of what it started out as—and I have no reason to believe that it didn't start out as anything but a geostrategic opening to Iran, which fundamentally is desirable because Iran occupies a very strategic position, and we have certain long-term objectives in which a formal relationship with Iran would serve. However, I think it very quickly became an arms-for-hostage deal. And the whole chronology of the affair, I think, very clearly demonstrates that that's what it became. In which event, of course, the idea of a geostrategic opening provided the rationale.

Reagan Management Style - 2

Q: Senator Tower, you say the NSC staff does not deserve high marks for this, but what kind of marks does the President deserve? And do you think he's had a weak style of management?

SENATOR TOWER: Well, this goes back to a question that was asked earlier. Now, after all, the system has performed pretty well during the course of this administration, up to this instance. As we noted in our report, this was an aberration—the Iran-Contra affair—and the system broke down. It's already—my colleagues already commented on the fact that every President has his own style. Now you can say that perhaps this President holds himself a little bit too aloof from the implementation of policy. I think a lot of people made the criticism of his predecessor President Carter, that he got too much involved in details. Perhaps there's a happy medium somewhere in between. But up to this point, I know a lot of members of the press complained that they could never get a handle on this President and a lot of his detractors did. Well, the reason is, because the performance to date has been pretty satisfactory—this is an aberration.

Secrecy Obsession - 2

Q: Senator Tower, the—in your conclusions in your recommendations you suggested Congress fold its intelligence agencies and merge them into one. And in your—the findings you suggest that the covert—the secrecy was one the problems. Is there any justification in the minds of the NSC staff for withholding the information from Congress? In light of your recommendations, is there justification that they felt Congress might leak it?

SENATOR TOWER: I think our report also says that Congress very often gets disproportionate blame for leakage, and one could certainly believe that if one scrutinizes the history of the past two months. But there is the natural tension between the President and Congress that always exists. The President has the unique responsibility in the field of foreign affairs—only the President really can formulate and implement foreign policies that are subject to certain constitutional checks by the Congress. And Presidents do get obsessed with secrecy. They all do. And they don't want to expose an operation or see the security of it violated. So, there's a natural inclination not to want to share.

However, I think, on the other hand, that consultation with Congress can be a protection for the President, and can be a useful tool for him. In fact, there are times when deferring notification of the Congress may be really essential. Let's take the Iran hostage rescue operation in 1980, for example. I think that President Carter was perfectly justified in not notifying the Congress until the mission was aborted. In this instance, I think a case can be made for deferring notification of the Congress because of the danger that hostages or certain Iranian contacts might be in as a result of information leaking. But I think that Presidents must not get too obsessed with this, and I think that one thing that might tend to cure this obsession will be for Congress to abandon the system of Select Intelligence committees with large staffs in both Houses, and have a joint committee, patterned after the old Joint Committee on Atomic Energy, with a relatively small, tight staff. We've simply recommended that Congress consider that.

Presidential Responsibility - 2

Q: Senator Muskie, we have seen a process that involves many nations, foreign and covert operations. In describing the management style of the President, it appears to have been without the oversight of the President, and Congress also seems to have been deprived of oversight. My question is, then, to whom devolves responsibility, constitutionally speaking, for this wide range of operations?

SENATOR MUSKIE: Well, to the extent that other countries were involved in one way or another, there are limits to how much of that we can disclose. But with respect to the principle [sic] operation here, we're talking about an initiative that began either in Iran or in Israel or in the United States. Now, we cannot—and I think the report clearly presents the facts that might lead to any of those three conclusions, but those—

Q: But—

SENATOR MUSKIE: Wait—the responsibility, obviously. Since the President conducts foreign policy, the responsibility lies in the Executive Branch. And this is why our report concentrates very heavily on the failure of the NSC system to perform as it should have.

Q: I have another one here.

Were Laws Broken?

Q: Yes. Senator Tower, in just talking about how you feel about all of this, I wonder, as a former Senator—and Mr. Muskie, the same thing, and Mr. Scowcroft—do you actually think after all that you know that some laws were broken? What do you personally think about this?

SENATOR TOWER: I think you've asked for the whole panel to comment, so I'll refer first to General Scowcroft and then to Senator Muskie.

GENERAL SCOWCROFT: I am, A, not a lawyer; B, that is not what we focused on. What we did identify is that there were a number of laws that did apply in one way or another to the kinds of operations that were conducted. And what we did determine is that there was apparently no clear searching, legal analysis as to what was or was not permitted by them.

SENATOR TOWER: Senator Muskie, would you—

SENATOR MUSKIE: Well, with respect to the laws which one could bear on—on individual or criminal culpability—that was outside our area. I would not speculate on an—

SENATOR TOWER: Well, we really—

SENATOR MUSKIE: —criminal culpability. There were obviously people whose performance was wrong, but that is something different than reaching a conclusion that it was criminal.

SENATOR TOWER: And we were not charged to doing that. That's the job of the special prosecutor. We can't make any judgment on that.

Reagan Management Style - 3

Q: General Scowcroft, you talked about that [sic] the process was basically—a good part of the problem was that the President's management style didn't challenge it. Is there any reason to believe anything is going to change? He's had this management style for a long time? [sic]

GENERAL SCOWCROFT: Well, I don't think that you can expect the President to change his management style or basically any President to adapt to the NSC structure. The NSC structure ought to adapt to the President. Now, I think Senator Tower said maybe the President is a little too casual in challenging the system. But the people in the system have the fundamental responsibility to keep the President aware and to keep under his sight the pitfalls of every policy that he wants to pursue.

Q: But is it not your finding that they were doing—that they thought they were doing what he wanted done?

GENERAL SCOWCROFT: Oh, I don't think there's any question they thought they were doing what he wanted done. And they probably were. That is not the point. It is not the point of the system to tell a President he can't do this or he can't do that. But to make crystal clear to him what the possible consequences of pursuing that—and I think we see the consequences in this case that were not laid out.

SENATOR TOWER: Yes, ma'am?

Bush Role

Q: Thank you, Senator. Senator Muskie, in your litany of people who—subordinates to the President who failed in advising him properly—you listed the Secretary of State and Defense, and people at the NSC, notably absent was Vice President [George] Bush. What is his responsibility in either having been aware of some of this, or having failed to properly advise the President?

SENATOR MUSKIE: Of course, Vice President Bush doesn't have a management responsibilty [sic], but he has a responsibilty [sic] as one of the four statutory members of the National Security Council. And he was present at several of the—there were not too many—as a matter of fact, all too few full meetings of the National Security Council. And I ought to take this question as an opportunity to point out that people refer to the National Security Council, which is four statutory people: the Secretary of Defense, Secretary of State, Vice President and the President. And then the President usually nominates a couple of others: the Director of the CIA, and of course, the National Security Adviser, and occasionally others.

But that's the Council. But they confuse that often with the National Security Staff, which is in place to serve the Council. Well, the Council itself is an advisery [sic] body. The Council doesn't perform staff operations, it's the staff that does that. Now, Vice President Bush, of course, is a member of the Council. Now, in this case, I think there were not more than two or three—at most three—meetings of the National Security Council to consider this policy, its consequences, its progress, its results, and its problems. So there were too few meetings at which Vice President Bush and the other members of that Council were given an opportunity or had an opportunity to influence the results.

Q: Did your review indicate, though, whether there were circumstances outside of the formal meetings of the NSC where Vice President Bush might have been made aware or learned what was going on?

SENATOR MUSKIE: Well, it's a little difficult to get that kind of a record.

Q: Senator Tower—

Diversion of Funds

Q: You were not able to interview Colonel North or Vice Admiral Poindexter, you weren't able to get access to Swiss bank accounts. How much of the story is still out there, still untold?

SENATOR TOWER: We feel that there is some out there that is untold, of course. For example, we—although we had strong—we had evidence of a Contra diversion, there was no way we could conclude that there had actually been a diversion to the Contras, because we didn't have access to these accounts, we didn't have access to Colonel North or Admiral Poindexter. And we can't establish what happened to the money. So quite frankly, that's something that we couldn't uncover, and that remains to others to try to solve that riddle.

Q: Are you satisfied the evidence won't show in the future that the President may have known that?

SENATOR TOWER: I won't speculate about what will happen in the future. We are statisfied [sic] that the President had no knowledge of any diversionary effort.

Q: Senator Tower—

Missing Documents

Q: There are references in your report to missing documents, specifically some of Admiral Poindexter's documents. Do you believe that any relevant documents were destroyed or altered, and if that's the case, who did that?

SENATOR TOWER: There's no way for us to know whether or not documents that have been destroyed were relevant, because we weren't—they didn't have access to them before they were destroyed. So, that would be a question that we could only speculate on.

Q: Senator Muskie.

Q: Senator Tower.

Presidential Responsibility - 3

Q: Senator Tower, General Scowcroft said that you had no differences in substance, but in semantics. My question is did you argue over language about the President's involvement—the President's responsibility? Was there a watering down of language?

SENATOR TOWER: No, there was not and I will ask my colleagues to comment on that. Nothing about watering down. We got in a lengthy debate about split infinitives one time I remember. (Laughter.) But let me ask Senator Muskie to comment on that.

SENATOR MUSKIE: There was no cover-up within our operation.

Q: Senator Muskie—

Scope of Inquiry

Q: Senator Tower, the commission could have taken a much narrower focus on the National Security Council staff operations and still fulfilled its mandate. Can you enlighten us a little bit on how you—how and why you decided to broaden the scope of your inquiry and enlighten us a bit on what the White House's response to this was.

SENATOR TOWER: We actually did not broaden the scope of our inquiries. The White House—we were brought into being by

the Iran-Contra affair; that's what prompted the White House to appoint this Board. And the President specifically directed us to study the Iran-Contra case and other cases. Well, there's already available a number of studies on other cases that we accessed and that we cited from time to time. This one we had to do our own study because it wasn't all out. And that's why this occupied a great deal of our time.

Our conclusions and our—our recommendations, I should say, really are based not just on the Iran-Contra affair, but on the performance and operation of the National Security Council and the National Security Council staff, the National Security Adviser historically.

Israeli Role

Q: Could the members of the Board give their understanding of the role of Israel in the whole affair, both in policy formulation, in the provision of intelligence, and in the facilitation of the—

SENATOR TOWER: You want us all to comment?

Q: Please.

SENATOR TOWER: General Scowcroft.

GENERAL SCOWCROFT: Well, we don't have a full picture of the role of Israel in this, partly because we have testimony only from one side; the Israelis did not make themselves available to us. There's no question that the Israelis encouraged, if not—did not initiate this policy, and that they did whatever they could when it appeared to be flagging from time to time, to renew its vigor.

I think the problem is that our goals and the Israeli goals were not synonymous, indeed, in some respects, they may have been in conflict. But the Israelis certainly supported if they did not take a lead in the policy.

SENATOR MUSKIE: That is essentially it. We tried—we met with the Ambassador here in Washington to request their participation or to request that they make available to us servants of the Israeli government and Israeli citizens who could contribute to our understandings of this sytem. They found it—they rejected that idea and so we are not in a position to evaluate from their point of view. But I think that General Scowcroft has summarized our impression of the situation.

SENATOR TOWER: Yes. And I would emphasize that there was heavy Israeli involvement. Of course, the final decision on our participation was our own. But, clearly, there were people—members of the Israeli government that perceived the service of their own national interest in involving themselves in this matter.

Thank you very much ladies and gentlemen.

Q: Sir, could you clear up one point? There have been reports that [Donald T.] Don Regan had been involved in—

Q: A cover-up.

Q: —cover-up. Could you address that, please?

Q: Israeli people—the NSC—the Israeli—

Q: What about Regan?

Q: Could you answer—just clarify that report, sir, whether Mr. Regan was involved in bringing together a false chronology?

SENATOR TOWER: I think we'll just have to stand on what's in the report.

TOWER PANEL REPORT ON IRAN-CONTRA AFFAIR

Following is the main body of the Report of the President's Special Review Board. *The board, chaired by former senator John Tower, submitted its report to President Reagan on February 26, 1987. The report's appendices have been omitted. Footnotes appear at the end of the text.*

The Honorable Ronald W. Reagan
The President of the United States
Washington, D.C. 20500

Dear Mr. President:

We respectfully submit to you the Report of the Special Review Board. This Report is the product of our study of the National Security Council, its operation and its staff.

For the last three months, we have reviewed the evolution of the NSC system since its creation forty years ago. We had extensive discussions with almost every current and former senior official involved in national security affairs. Case studies from several Administrations were also conducted to inform our judgments.

At your direction, we also focused on the Iran/Contra matter and sought to follow your injunction that "all the facts come out." We attempted to do this as fairly as we knew how so that lessons for the future could be learned.

The Report is based in large part on information and documentation provided to us by U.S. departments and agencies and interviews of current and former officials. We relied upon others in the Executive Branch to conduct the search for materials or information we requested. In general, we received a positive response to our inquiries from every agency, including the White House, although the Independent Counsel and the Federal Bureau of Investigation responded negatively to our request for material. We found that the individuals from agencies that appeared before us generally did so in a forthcoming manner.

The portions of this Report that recite facts were reviewed by appropriate agency representatives in order to identify classified material. This was done to enable you to make the Report public. These representatives performed this security review without regard for domestic political consequences. No material was deleted on the grounds that it might prove embarrassing to your Administration. There was, however, some information that we concluded had to remain in the classified domain. The appropriate Congressional committees may find this information of use.

While the publication of the material in this Report may be troublesome to some in the short term, we believe that, over time, the nation will clearly benefit by your decision to commission this review. We commend this Report to you and to future Presidents in the hope that it will enhance the effectiveness of the National Security Council.

We are honored to have had the opportunity to serve on this Board.

Sincerely,

Edmund S. Muskie
John Tower
Brent Scowcroft

Part I. Introduction

In November, 1986, it was disclosed that the United States had, in August, 1985, and subsequently, participated in secret dealings with Iran involving the sale of military equipment. There appeared to be a linkage between these dealings and efforts to obtain the release of U.S. citizens held hostage in Lebanon by terrorists believed to be closely associated with the Iranian regime. After the initial story broke, the Attorney General announced that proceeds from the arms transfers may have been diverted to assist U.S.-backed rebel forces in Nicaragua, known as Contras. This possibility enlarged the controversy and added questions not only of policy and propriety but also violations of law.

These disclosures became the focus of substantial public attention. The secret arms transfers appeared to run directly counter to declared U.S. policies. The United States had announced a policy of neutrality in the six-year old Iran/Iraq war and had proclaimed an embargo on arms sales to Iran. It had worked actively to isolate Iran and other regimes known to give aid and comfort to terrorists. It had declared that it would not pay ransom to hostage-takers.

Public concern was not limited to the issues of policy, however. Questions arose as to the propriety of certain actions taken by the National Security Council [NSC] staff and the manner in which the decision to transfer arms to Iran had been made. Congress was never informed. A variety of intermediaries, both private and governmental, some with motives open to question, had central roles. The NSC staff rather than the CIA seemed to be running the operation. The President appeared to be unaware of key elements of the operation. The controversy threatened a crisis of confidence in the manner in which national security decisions are made and the role played by the NSC staff.

It was this latter set of concerns that prompted the President to establish this Special Review Board on December 1, 1986. The President directed the Board to examine the proper role of the National Security Council staff in national security operations, including the arms transfers to Iran. The President made clear that he wanted "all the facts to come out."

The Board was not, however, called upon to assess individual culpability or be the final arbiter of the facts. These tasks have been properly left to others. Indeed, the short deadline set by the President for completion of the Board's work and its limited resources precluded a separate and thorough field investigation. Instead, the Board has examined the events surrounding the transfer of arms to Iran as a principal case study in evaluating the operation of the National Security Council in general and the role of the NSC staff in particular.

The President gave the Board a broad charter. It was directed to conduct "a comprehensive study of the future role and procedures of the National Security Council (NSC) staff in the development, coordination, oversight, and conduct of foreign and national security policy." [1]

It has been forty years since the enactment of the National Security Act of 1947 and the creation of the National Security Council. Since that time the NSC staff has grown in importance and the Assistant to the President for National Security Affairs has emerged as a key player in national security decision-making. This is the first Presidential Commission to have as its sole responsibility a comprehensive review of how these institutions have performed. We believe that, quite aside from the circumstances which brought about the Board's creation, such a review was overdue.

The Board divided its work into three major inquiries: the circumstances surrounding the Iran/Contra matter, other case studies that might reveal strengths and weaknesses in the operation of the National Security Council system under stress, and the manner in which that system has served eight different Presidents since its inception in 1947.

At Appendix B [Appendix omitted.] is a narrative of the information obtained from documents and interviews regarding the arms sales to Iran. The narrative is necessarily incomplete. As of the date of this report, some key witnesses had refused to testify before any forum. Important documents located in other countries had yet to be released, and important witnesses in other countries were not available. But the appended narrative tells much of the story. Although more information will undoubtedly come to light, the record thus far developed provides a sufficient basis for evaluating the process by which these events came about.

During the Board's work, it received evidence concerning the role of the NSC staff in support of the Contras during the period that such support was either barred or restricted by Congress. The Board had neither the time nor the resources to make a systematic inquiry into this area. Notwithstanding, substantial evidence came before the Board. A narrative of that evidence is contained at Appendix C [Appendix omitted.].

The Board found that the issues raised by the Iran/Contra matter are in most instances not new. Every Administration has faced similar issues, although arising in different factual contexts. The Board examined in some detail the performance of the National Security Council system in 12 different crises dating back to the Truman Administration.[2] Former government officials participating in many of these crises were interviewed. This learning provided a broad historical perspective to the issues before the Board.

Those who expect from us a radical prescription for wholesale change may be disappointed. Not all major problems—and Iran/Contra has been a major one—can be solved simply by rearranging organizational blocks or passing new laws.

In addition, it is important to emphasize that the President is responsible for the national security policy of the United States. In the development and execution of that policy, the President is the decision-maker. He is not obliged to consult with or seek approval from anyone in the Executive Branch. The structure and procedures of the National Security Council system should be designed to give the President every assistance in discharging these heavy responsibilities. It is not possible to make a system immune from error without paralyzing its capacity to act.

At its senior levels, the National Security Council is primarily the interaction of people. We have examined with care its operation in the Iran/Contra matter and have set out in considerable detail mistakes of omission, commission, judgment, and perspective. We believe that this record and analysis can warn future Presidents, members of the National Security Council, and National Security Advisors of the potential pitfalls they face even when they are operating with what they consider the best of motives. We would hope that this record would be carefully read and its lessons fully absorbed by all aspirants to senior positions in the National Security Council system.

This report will serve another purpose. In preparing it, we contacted every living past President, three former Vice Presidents, and every living Secretary of State, Secretary of Defense, National Security Advisor, most Directors of Central Intelligence, and several Chairmen of the Joint Chiefs of Staff to solicit their views. We sought to learn how well, in their experience, the system had operated or, in the case of past Presidents, how well it served them. We asked all former participants how they would change the system to make it more useful to the President.[3]

Our review validates the current National Security Council system. That system has been utilized by different Presidents in very different ways, in accordance with their individual work habits and philosophical predilections. On occasion over the years it has functioned with real brilliance; at other times serious mistakes have been made. The problems we examined in the case of Iran/Contra caused us deep concern. But their solution does not lie in revamping the National Security Council system.

That system is properly the President's creature. It must be left flexible to be molded by the President into the form most useful to him. Otherwise it will become either an obstacle to the President, and a source of frustration; or an institutional irrelevance, as the President fashions informal structures more to his liking.

Having said that, there are certain functions which need to be performed in some way for any President. What we have tried to do is to distill from the wisdom of those who have participated in the National Security Council system over the past forty years the essence of these functions and the manner in which that system can be operated so as to minimize the likelihood of major error without destroying the creative impulses of the President.

Part II. Organizing for National Security

Ours is a government of checks and balances, of shared power and responsibility. The Constitution places the President and the Congress in dynamic tension. They both cooperate and compete in the making of national policy.

National security is no exception. The Constitution gives both the President and the Congress an important role. The Congress is critical in formulating national policies and in marshalling the resources to carry them out. But those resources—the nation's military personnel, its diplomats, its intelligence capability—are lodged in the Executive Branch. As Chief Executive and Commander-in-Chief, and with broad authority in the area of foreign affairs, it is the President who is empowered to act for the nation and protect its interests.

A. The National Security Council

The present organization of the Executive Branch for national security matters was established by the National Security Act of 1947. That Act created the National Security Council. As now constituted, its statutory members are the President, Vice President, Secretary of State, and Secretary of Defense. The President is the head of the National Security Council.

Presidents have from time to time invited the heads of other departments or agencies to attend National Security Council meetings or to participate as de facto members. These have included the Director of Central Intelligence (the "DCI") and the Chairman of the Joint Chiefs of Staff (the "CJCS"). The President (or, in his absence, his designee) presides.

The National Security Council deals with the most vital issues in the nation's national security policy. It is this body that discusses recent developments in arms control and the Strategic Defense Initiative; that discussed whether or not to bomb the Cambodia mainland after the *Mayaguez* was captured; that debated the timetable for the U.S. withdrawal from Vietnam; and that considered the risky and daring attempt to rescue U.S. hostages in Iran in 1980. The National Security Council deals with issues that are difficult, complex, and often secret. Decisions are often required in hours rather than weeks. Advice must be given under great stress and with imperfect information.

The National Security Council is not a decision-making body. Although its other members hold official positions in the Government, when meeting as the National Security Council they sit as advisors to the President. This is clear from the language of the 1947 Act:

> *"The function of the Council shall be to advise the President with respect to the integration of domestic, foreign, and military policies relating to the national security so as to enable the military services and the other departments and agencies of the Government to cooperate more effectively in matters involving the national security."*

The National Security Council has from its inception been a highly personal instrument. Every President has turned for advice to those individuals and institutions whose judgment he has valued and trusted. For some Presidents, such as President Eisenhower, the National Security Council served as a primary forum for obtaining advice on national security matters. Other Presidents, such as President Kennedy, relied on more informal groupings of advisors, often including some but not all of the Council members.

One official summarized the way the system has been adjusted by different Presidents:

> *"The NSC is going to be pretty well what a President wants it to be and what he determines it should be. Kennedy—and these are some exaggerations and generalities of course—with an anti-organizational bias, disestablished all [the Eisenhower created] committees and put a tight group in the White House totally attuned to his philosophic approach * * *. Johnson didn't change that very much, except certain difficulties began to develop in the informality which was [otherwise] characterized by speed, unity of purpose, precision * * *. So it had great efficiency and responsiveness. The difficulties began to develop in * * * the informality of the thing."*

The Nixon Administration saw a return to the use of the National Security Council as a principal forum for national security advice. This pattern was continued by President Ford and President Carter, and in large measure by President Reagan.

Regardless of the frequency of its use, the NSC has remained a strictly advisory body. Each President has kept the burden of decision for himself, in accordance with his Constitutional responsibilities.

B. The Assistant to the President for National Security Affairs

Although closely associated with the National Security Council in the public mind, the Assistant to the President for National Security Affairs is not one of its members. Indeed, no mention of this position is made in the National Security Act of 1947.

The position was created by President Eisenhower in 1953. Although its precise title has varied, the position has come to be known (somewhat misleadingly) as the National Security Advisor.

Under President Eisenhower, the holder of this position served as the principal executive officer of the Council, setting the agenda, briefing the President on Council matters, and supervising the staff. He was not a policy advocate.

It was not until President Kennedy, with McGeorge Bundy in the role, that the position took on its current form. Bundy emerged as an important personal advisor to the President on national security affairs. This introduced an element of direct competition into Bundy's relationship with the members of the National Security Council. Although President Johnson changed the title of the position to simply "Special Assistant," in the hands of Walt Rostow it continued to play an important role.

President Nixon relied heavily on his National Security Advisor, maintaining and even enhancing its prominence. In that position, Henry Kissinger became a key spokesman for the President's national security policies both to the U.S. press and to foreign governments. President Nixon used him to negotiate on behalf of the United States with Vietnam, China, the Soviet Union, and other countries. The roles of spokesman and negotiator had traditionally been the province of the Secretary of State, not of the National Security Advisor. The emerging tension between the two positions was only resolved when Kissinger assumed them both.

Under President Ford, Lt Gen Brent Scowcroft became National Security Advisor, with Henry Kissinger remaining as Secretary of State. The National Security Advisor exercised major responsibility for coordinating for the President the advice of his NSC principals and overseeing the process of policy development and implementation within the Executive Branch.

President Carter returned in large part to the early Kissinger model, with a resulting increase in tensions with the Secretary of State. President Carter wanted to take the lead in matters of foreign policy, and used his National Security Advisor as a source of information, ideas, and new initiatives.

The role of the National Security Advisor, like the role of the NSC itself, has in large measure been a function of the operating style of the President. Notwithstanding, the National Security Advisor has come to perform, to a greater or lesser extent, certain functions which appear essential to the effective discharge of the President's responsibilities in national security affairs.

● He is an "honest broker" for the NSC process. He assures that issues are clearly presented to the President; that all reasonable options, together with an analysis of their disadvantages and risks, are brought to his attention; and that the views of the President's other principal advisors are accurately conveyed.

● He provides advice from the President's vantage point, unalloyed by institutional responsibilities and biases. Unlike the Secretaries of State or Defense, who have substantial organizations for which they are responsible, the President is the National Security Advisor's only constituency.

● He monitors the actions taken by the executive departments in implementing the President's national security policies. He asks the question whether these actions are consistent with Presidential decisions and whether, over time, the underlying policies continue to serve U.S. interests.

● He has a special role in crisis management. This has resulted from the need for prompt and coordinated action under Presidential control, often with secrecy being esssential.

● He reaches out for new ideas and initiatives that will give substance to broad Presidential objectives for national security.

● He keeps the President informed about international developments and developments in the Congress and the Executive Branch that affect the President's policies and priorities.

But the National Security Advisor remains the creature of the President. The position will be largely what he wants it to be. This presents any President with a series of dilemmas.

● The President must surround himself with people he trusts and to whom he can speak in confidence. To this end, the National Security Advisor, unlike the Secretaries of State and Defense, is not subject to confirmation by the Senate and does not testify before Congress. But the more the President relies on the National Security Advisor for advice, especially to the exclusion of his Cabinet officials, the greater will be the unease with this arrangement.

● As the "honest broker" of the NSC process, the National Security Advisor must ensure that the different and often conflicting views of the NSC principals are presented fairly to the President. But as an independent advisor to the President, he must provide his own judgment. To the extent that the National Security Advisor becomes a strong advocate for a particular point of view, his role as "honest broker" may be compromised and the President's access to the unedited views of the NSC principals may be impaired.

● The Secretaries of State and Defense, and the Director of Central Intelligence, head agencies of government that have specific statutory responsibilities and are subject to Congressional oversight for the implementation of U.S. national security policy. To the extent that the National Security Advisor assumes operational responsibilities, whether in negotiating with foreign governments or becoming heavily involved in military or intelligence operations, the legitimacy of that role and his authority to perform it may be challenged.

● The more the National Security Advisor becomes an "operator" in implementing policy, the less will he be able objectively to review that implementation—and whether the underlying policy continues to serve the interests of the President and the nation.

● The Secretary of State has traditionally been the President's spokesman on matters of national security and foreign affairs. To the extent that the National Security Advisor speaks publicly on these matters or meets with representatives of foreign governments, the result may be confusion as to what is the President's policy.

C. The NSC Staff

At the time it established the National Security Council, Congress authorized a staff headed by an Executive Secretary appointed by the President. Initially quite small, the NSC staff expanded substantially under President Eisenhower.

During the Eisenhower Administration, the NSC staff assumed two important functions: coordinating the executive departments in the development of national policy (through the NSC Planning Board) and overseeing the implementation of that policy (through the Operations Coordination Board). A systematic effort was made to coordinate policy development and its implementation by the various agencies through an elaborate set of committees. The system worked fairly well in bringing together for the President the views of the other NSC principals. But it has been criticized as biased toward reaching consensus among these principals rather than developing options for Presidential decision. By the end of his second term, President Eisenhower himself had reached the conclusion that a highly competent individual and a small staff could perform the needed functions in a better way. Such a change was made by President Kennedy.

Under President Kennedy, a number of the functions of the NSC staff were eliminated and its size was sharply reduced. The Planning and Operations Coordinating Boards were abolished. Policy development and policy implementation were assigned to individual Cabinet officers, responsible directly to the President. By late 1962 the staff was only 12 professionals, serving largely as an independent source of ideas and information to the President. The system was lean and responsive, but frequently suffered from a lack of coordination. The Johnson Administration followed much the same pattern.

The Nixon Administration returned to a model more like Eisenhower's but with something of the informality of the Kennedy/Johnson staffs. The Eisenhower system had emphasized coordination; the Kennedy-Johnson system tilted to innovation and the generation of new ideas. The Nixon system emphasized both. The objective was not inter-departmental consensus but the generation of policy options for Presidential decision, and then ensuring that those decisions were carried out. The staff grew to 50 professionals in 1970 and became a major factor in the national security decision-making process. This approach was largely continued under President Ford.

The NSC staff retained an important role under President Carter. While continuing to have responsibility for coordinating policy among the various executive agencies, President Carter particularly looked to the NSC staff as a personal source of independent advice. President Carter felt the need to have a group loyal only to him from which to launch his own initiatives and to move a vast and lethargic government. During his time in office, President Carter reduced the size of the professional staff to 35, feeling that a smaller group could do the job and would have a closer relationship to him.

What emerges from this history is an NSC staff used by each President in a way that reflected his individual preferences and working style. Over time, it has developed an important role within the Executive Branch of coordinating policy review, preparing issues for Presidential decision, and monitoring implementation. But it has remained the President's creature, molded as he sees fit, to serve as his personal staff for national security affairs. For this reason, it has generally operated out of the public view and has not been subject to direct oversight by the Congress.

D. The Interagency Committee System

The National Security Council has frequently been supported by committees made up of representatives of the relevant national security departments and agencies. These committees analyze issues prior to consideration by the Council. There are generally several levels of committees. At the top level, officials from each agency (at the Deputy Secretary or Under Secretary level) meet to provide a senior level policy review. These senior-level committees are in turn supported by more junior interagency groups (usually at the Assistant Secretary level). These in turn may oversee staff level working groups that prepare detailed analysis of important issues.

Administrations have differed in the extent to which they have used these interagency committees. President Kennedy placed little stock in them. The Nixon and Carter Administrations, by contrast, made much use of them.

E. The Reagan Model

President Reagan entered office with a strong commitment to cabinet government. His principal advisors on national security affairs were to be the Secretaries of State and Defense, and to a lesser extent the Director of Central Intelligence. The position of the National Security Advisor was initially downgraded in both status and access to the President. Over the next six years, five different people held that position.

The Administration's first National Security Advisor, Richard [V.] Allen, reported to the President through the senior White House staff. Consequently, the NSC staff assumed a reduced role. Mr. Allen believed that the Secretary of State had primacy in the field of foreign policy. He viewed the job of the National Security Advisor as that of a policy coordinator.

President Reagan initially declared that the National Security Council would be the principal forum for consideration of national security issues. To support the work of the Council, President Reagan established an interagency committee system headed by three Senior Interagency Groups (or "SIGs"), one each for foreign policy, defense policy, and intelligence. They were chaired by the Secretary of State, the Secretary of Defense, and the Director of Central Intelligence, respectively.

Over time, the Administration's original conception of the role of the National Security Advisor changed. William [P.] Clark, who succeeded Richard Allen in 1982, was a long-time associate of the President and dealt directly with him. Robert [C.] McFarlane, who replaced Judge Clark in 1983, although personally less close to the President, continued to have direct access to him. The same was true for VADM [Vice Admiral] John [M.] Poindexter, who was appointed to the position in December, 1985.

President Reagan appointed several additional members to his National Security Council and allowed staff attendance at meetings. The resultant size of the meetings led the President to turn increasingly to a smaller group (called the National Security Planning Group or "NSPG"). Attendance at its meetings was more restricted but included the statutory principals of the NSC. The NSPG was supported by the SIGs, and new SIGs were occasionally created to deal with particular issues. These were frequently chaired by the National Security Advisor. But generally the SIGs and many of their subsidiary groups (called Interagency Groups or "IGs") fell into disuse.

As a supplement to the normal NSC process, the Reagan Administration adopted comprehensive procedures for covert actions. These are contained in a classified document, NSDD-159, establishing the process for deciding, implementing, monitoring, and reviewing covert activities.

F. The Problem of Covert Operations

Covert activities place a great strain on the process of decision in a free society. Disclosure of even the existence of the operation could threaten its effectiveness and risk embarrassment to the Government. As a result, there is strong pressure to withhold information, to limit knowledge of the operation to a minimum number of people.

These pressures come into play with great force when covert activities are undertaken in an effort to obtain the release of U.S. citizens held hostage abroad. Because of the legitimate human concern all Presidents have felt over the fate of such hostages, our national pride as a powerful country with a tradition of protecting its citizens abroad, and the great attention paid by the news media to hostage situations, the pressures on any President to take action to free hostages are enormous. Frequently to be effective, this action must necessarily be covert. Disclosure would directly threaten the lives of the hostages as well as those willing to contemplate their release.

Since covert arms sales to Iran played such a central role in the creation of this Board, it has focused its attention in large measure on the role of the NSC staff where covert activity is involved. This is not to denigrate, however, the importance of other decisions taken by the government. In those areas as well the National Security Council and its staff play a critical role. But in many respects the best test of a system is its performance under stress. The conditions of greatest stress are often found in the crucible of covert activities.

Part III. Arms Transfers to Iran, Diversion, and Support for the Contras

The Iran/Contra matter has been and, in some respects, still is an enigma. For three months the Board sought to learn the facts, and still the whole matter cannot be fully explained. The general outlines of the story are clear. The story is set out here as we now know it.

Given the President's injunction that he wanted "all the facts to come out," the Board sought to include all relevant materials. The Board tried to be faithful to the testimony and documents that came before it. This Board was not established, however, as an investigative body nor was it to determine matters of criminal culpability. Rather, the Board was established to gather the facts, to place them in their proper historical context, and to make recommendations about what corrective steps might be taken.

The limits of time, resources, and legal authority were handicaps but not unreasonable ones.

The Board had no authority to subpoena documents, compel testimony, swear witnesses, or grant immunity.

But these limitations did not prevent the Board from assembling sufficient information to form a basis for its fundamental judgments. The Board received a vast quantity of documents and interviewed over 80 witnesses. The Board requested all affected departments and agencies to provide all documents relevant to the Board's inquiry. The Board relied upon these agencies to conduct thorough searches for all relevant materials in their possession. In addition, the Board reviewed the results and relevant portions of working files from both the CIA and Department of the Army Inspectors General reports.

Several individuals declined our request to appear before the Board: VADM John Poindexter; General Richard [V.] Secord, USAF Ret.; LtCol Oliver [L.] North; LtCol Robert [L.] Earl; Mr. Albert Hakim; and Miss Fawn Hall. The Board requested that the President exercise his powers as Commander-in-Chief and order VADM Poindexter and LtCol North to appear. The President declined.[1]

Despite the refusal of VADM Poindexter and LtCol North to appear, the Board's access to other sources of information filled much of this gap. The FBI provided documents taken from the files of the National Security Advisor and relevant NSC staff members, including messages from the PROF system[2] between VADM Poindexter and LtCol North. The PROF messages were conversations by computer, written at the time events occurred and presumed by the writers to be protected from disclosure. In this sense, they provide a first-hand, contemporaneous account of events.

In the closing days of the Board's inquiry, we gained access to a considerable number of additional exchanges on PROFs between VADM Poindexter, LtCol North, and Mr. McFarlane.

The Board had access to another contemporaneous record of events. The President keeps a diary in which he chronicles, in long hand, key events that occurred during the day. President Reagan reviewed his notes and, at the Board's request, culled from them the relevant notes he had made on particular dates requested by the Board. The Board was permitted to review but not to retain a typewritten copy of these diary entries.

No one interviewed by the Board seemed able to provide a unified account of the events in August independent of calendars or meeting notes. In the lives of these particularly busy individuals this should not be surprising. This lack of a total and accurate recall may suggest an equally important point: when these events occurred, they were not treated by many of the participants as sufficiently important.

Those that are present at meetings or privy to conversations will retain different impressions of what occurred. That certainly happened here. Many of these events occurred almost two years ago, and memories fade. There is also the chance that, for whatever reason, individuals concealed evidence or deliberately misled the Board. In any event, the Board's mandate was not to resolve conflicts among various recollections but to attempt to ascertain the essential facts as they affect conclusions about the national security process.

The Independent Counsel at various points denied the Board access to some materials in which he had established an interest. The Government of Israel was asked to make certain individuals available in any way that would be convenient to them. They declined to do so. They agreed to answer written interrogatories. We dispatched those to the Government of Israel but no response has, as yet, been received.

The first section of this Part III summarizes the evidence before the Board concerning the arms transfers to Iran. A more detailed narrative of this evidence is set out in Appendix B [Appendix omitted.].

The second section summarizes the evidence before the Board concerning a diversion of funds from the arms sales to the support of the Contras fighting in Nicaragua.

The third section summarizes the evidence accumulated by the Board concerning the role of the NSC staff in the support of the Contras during the period that support from the U.S. govern-ment was either barred or restricted by Congress. A more detailed narrative of this evidence is set out in Appendix C [Appendix omitted.].

Section A: The Arms Transfers to Iran

Two persistent concerns lay behind U.S. participation in arms transfers to Iran.

First, the U.S. government anxiously sought the release of seven U.S. citizens abducted in Beirut, Lebanon, in seven separate incidents between March 7, 1984, and June 9, 1985. One of those abducted was William Buckley, CIA station chief in Beirut, seized on March 16, 1984. Available intelligence suggested that most, if not all, of the Americans were held hostage by members of Hizballah, a fundamentalist Shiite terrorist group with links to the regime of the Ayatollah Khomeini.

Second, the U.S. government had a latent and unresolved interest in establishing ties to Iran. Few in the U.S. government doubted Iran's strategic importance or the risk of Soviet meddling in the succession crisis that might follow the death of Khomeini. For this reason, some in the U.S. government were convinced that efforts should be made to open potential channels to Iran.

Arms transfers ultimately appeared to offer a means to achieve both the release of the hostages and a strategic opening to Iran.

The formulation, development, and implementation of the Iran initiative passed through seven distinct stages. Each is analyzed in this section of the report. For the purposes of the Board's mandate, the critical questions for each stage are: What was U.S. policy? How were decisions made? What action was authorized and by whom? How was this action carried out? What happened as a result?

Stage 1: The NSC Staff Seeks a New Look at U.S. Policy on Iran

The Shah of Iran was overthrown on January 16, 1979, ending an intimate, twenty-five year relationship between the United States and Iran. Mutual hostility and tension characterized U.S. relations with the regime of the Ayatollah Khomeini, which, after some months, succeeded the Shah's rule. On November 4, 1979, radical Iranian elements seized the U.S. embassy in Tehran and held its staff hostage. The United States responded by blocking the transfer of all property of the Iranian government, imposing a trade embargo, freezing all other Iranian assets, and breaking diplomatic relations. In addition, the United States imposed an embargo on all arms shipments to Iran, including arms that had been purchased under the Shah but not yet delivered.

On January 19, 1981, many of these restrictions were lifted, as part of the agreement that led to the release of the embassy staff. However, this did not extend to the embargo on arms transfers. Iraq had attacked Iran on September 22, 1980. The United States had adopted a policy of neutrality and refused to ship arms to either side. The result was a continuation of the arms embargo against Iran.

The Reagan Administration had adopted a tough line against terrorism. In particular, the United States adamantly opposed making any concessions to terrorists in exchange for the release of hostages—whether by paying ransom, releasing prisoners, changing policies, or otherwise. Some time in July of 1982, the United States became aware of evidence suggesting that Iran was supporting terrorist groups, including groups engaged in hostage-taking. On January 20, 1984, the Secretary of State designated Iran a sponsor of international terrorism.[3] Thereafter, the United States actively pressured its allies not to ship arms to Iran, both because of its sponsorship of international terrorism and its continuation of the war with Iraq.

The NSC Staff Initiates a Reevaluation. By early 1984, Robert McFarlane, the National Security Advisor, and members of the NSC staff, had become concerned about future U.S. policy toward Iran. They feared that the death of Khomeini would touch off a succession struggle which would hold important consequences for U.S. interests. They believed that the United States lacked a strategy and capability for dealing with this prospect.

Initially, Mr. McFarlane tried to use the formal interagency policy process to address this issue. On August 31, 1984, he requested an interagency study of U.S. relations with Iran after Khomeini. On October 19, 1984, the State Department sent Mr. McFarlane the interagency response to his request. It concluded that the United States had "no influential contacts" within the Iranian government or Iranian political groups. The study suggested little that the United States could do to establish such contacts. Separately, in a letter dated December 11, 1984, to Mr. McFarlane's deputy, VADM John Poindexter, the CIA professed only a limited capability to influence events in Iran over the near term.

The Reevaluation Yields No New Ideas. Howard Teicher, one of the NSC staff members involved, told the Board that the interagency effort failed to identify any new ideas for significantly expanding U.S. influence in Iran. It resulted in no change in U.S. policy. The U.S. government continued aggressively to discourage arms transfers by other nations to Iran under a program called "Operation Staunch."

Stage 2: The NSC Staff Tries a Second Time

Mr. Teicher, Donald Fortier, and perhaps other NSC staff members were unhappy with the result of the interagency effort. They placed a high priority on fashioning a strategy for acquiring influence and checking the Soviets in Iran. Graham Fuller, then the National Intelligence Officer for the Near East and South Asia, told the Board that in early 1985 the U.S. intelligence community began to believe that serious factional fighting could break out in Iran even before Khomeini died. This change in the community's assessment provided a second opportunity for a policy review.

The NSC Staff Suggests Limited Arms Sales. Mr. Teicher, and to a lesser extent Mr. Fortier, worked closely with CIA officials to prepare an update of a previous "Special National Intelligence Estimate" (or "SNIE") on Iran. Dated May 20, 1985, the update portrayed the Soviets as well positioned to take advantage of chaos inside Iran. The United States, by contrast, was unlikely to be able directly to influence events. Our European and other allies could, however, provide a valuable presence to help protect Western interests. The update concluded that the degree to which these allies "can fill a military gap for Iran will be a critical measure of the West's ability to blunt Soviet influence."

On June 11, 1985, Mr. Fortier and Mr. Teicher submitted to Mr. McFarlane a draft Presidential decision document (a National Security Decision Directive or "NSDD") drawing on the intelligence update. The draft set out immediate and long-term U.S. goals and listed specific steps to achieve them. First on the list was to "[e]ncourage Western allies and friends to help Iran meet its import requirements * * * includ[ing] provision of selected military equipment * * *."

The memorandum from Mr. Fortier and Mr. Teicher transmitting the draft NSDD to Mr. McFarlane suggested that "[b]ecause of the political and bureaucratic sensitivities," Mr. McFarlane should provide copies of the NSDD only to Secretary of State [George P.] Shultz and Secretary of Defense [Caspar W.] Weinberger. "Whether to proceed with a restricted SIG [Senior Interagency Group], NSPG [National Security Planning Group], or other forum [for consideration of the draft] would depend on their reactions." Mr. McFarlane circulated the draft on June 17, 1985, to Secretary Shultz, Secretary Weinberger, and Director of Central Intelligence Casey. His transmittal memorandum requested that further distribution remain limited to lessen the risk of leaks. In letters to Mr. McFarlane dated June 29, 1985, and July 16, 1985, respectively, both Secretary Shultz and Secretary Weinberger objected sharply to the suggestion that the United States should permit or encourage transfers of Western arms to Iran. By contrast, in his reply of July 18, 1985, Director Casey "strongly endorse[d]" the thrust of the draft NSDD and particularly its emphasis on the need to take "concrete and timely steps to enhance U.S. leverage." He did not specifically address the issue of arms sales.

The Suggestion Dies. Mr. Teicher told the Board that the strong objections from Secretary Shultz and Secretary Weinberger apparently killed the draft NSDD. In mid-August he was told to "stand down" on the effort. The draft was never submitted to the President for his consideration or signature.

The abandonment of the draft NSDD marked the end of efforts by Mr. McFarlane and the NSC staff to use the formal interagency policy process to obtain an explicit change in U.S. policy toward Iran. From this point on, the matter moved along a different track.

Stage 3: The Israelis Provide a Vehicle

While the NSC staff was seeking a reexamination of U.S. policy toward Iran, several staff members were growing ever more concerned about the hostage issue. On June 14, 1985, TWA flight 847 was hijacked enroute from Athens to Rome, with 135 U.S. citizens aboard. It was not until June 29 that all the hostages were released. One U.S. citizen was executed. The event dominated the news in the United States and dramatized the hostage issue. Frustration at the lack of progress in freeing the hostages in Beirut grew perceptibly within the U.S. government, especially in the face of pleas to the President for action by the families of the hostages. In the summer of 1985, a vehicle appeared that offered the prospect of progress both on the release of the hostages and a strategic opening to Iran.

Israel had long-standing interests in a relationship with Iran and in promoting its arms export industry. Arms sales to Iran could further both objectives. It also offered a means of strengthening Iran against Israel's old adversary, Iraq. Much of Israel's military equipment came originally from the United States, however. For both legal and political reasons, Israel felt a need for U.S. approval of, or at least acquiescence in, any arms sales to Iran. In addition, elements in Israel undoubtedly wanted the United States involved for its own sake so as to distance the United States from the Arab world and ultimately to establish Israel as the only real strategic partner of the United States in the region.

Iran badly wanted what Israel could provide. The United States had been the primary source of arms for the Shah, but U.S. shipments to Iran were now barred by the embargo. Iran desperately wanted U.S.-origin TOW and HAWK missiles,[4] in order to counter Iraq's chief areas of superiority—armor and air forces. Since Israel had these weapons in its inventory, it was an alternative source of supply. Israel was more than willing to provide these weapons to Iran, but only if the United States approved the transfer and would agree to replace the weapons.

Iranian interest in these weapons was widely known among those connected with the arms trade. These included Manucher Ghorbanifar, an Iranian businessman living in France, and Adolph Schwimmer and Yaacov [Jacob] Nimrodi, private Israeli arms dealers with contacts throughout the Middle East including Israel [sic]. Since September, 1984, Mr. Schwimmer had also been a consultant to then-Prime Minister of Israel Shimon Peres. In a series of meetings beginning in January, 1985, these men had discussed using arms sales to obtain the release of the U.S. citizens held hostage in Beirut and to open a strategic dialogue with Iran. Some of those meetings included Amiram Nir, since September, 1984, an advisor to Prime Minister Peres on counterterrorism. Also involved was Saudi businessman Adnan Khashoggi, a man well-connected in the Middle East and enjoying a special relationship with key Israeli officials. All these men subsequently played a role in the brokering of the arms deals that later did occur.

These men believed that the United States, Israel, and Iran, though with different interests, were susceptible to a relationship of convenience involving arms, hostages, and the opening of a channel to Iran. The catalyst that brought this relationship into being was the proffering by Israel of a channel for the United States in establishing contacts with Iran.

An Opening to Iran. On the 4th or 5th of May, 1985, Michael Ledeen, an NSC staff consultant, with the knowledge of Mr. McFarlane, went to Israel and met with Prime Minister Peres. Mr. Ledeen told the Board that he asked about the state of Israeli intelligence on Iran and whether Israel would be willing to share its intelligence with the United States. Two months later, the United States received the first of three separate requests regarding Iran from the Israeli government. The first two occurred in July, 1985.

(i) *The July Requests.* On July 3, 1985, David Kimche, the Director General of the Israeli Foreign Ministry, met at the White House with Mr. McFarlane. Mr. McFarlane told the Board that Mr. Kimche asked the position of the U.S. government toward engaging in a political discourse with Iranian officials. He recalled Mr. Kimche as saying that these Iranian officials had conveyed to Israel their interest in a discourse with the United States. Contact was to be handled through an intermediary (later disclosed to be Mr. Ghorbanifar) who was represented as having good connections to Iranian officials.

This was not the first time that Mr. Ghorbanifar had come to the attention of the U.S. government. The CIA knew of Mr. Ghorbanifar and had a history of contacts with him. CIA's first contact with Ghorbanifar was through a European intelligence service in January 1980. From the beginning, CIA found it "difficult to filter out the bravado and exaggeration from what actually happened." Other intelligence services had similar experiences with Mr. Ghorbanifar. By September of 1980, CIA decided to drop efforts at recruiting Ghorbanifar. It considered him neither reliable nor trustworthy. In addition, Theodore Shackley, a former CIA official, had met Mr. Ghorbanifar in Hamburg, West Germany, between November 19-21, 1984. Mr. Ghorbanifar at that time suggested payment of a cash ransom for the hostages in Beirut, with himself as middleman. This proposal, contained in a memorandum prepared by Mr. Shackley dated November 22, 1984, apparently reached the State Department where it elicited no interest. A memorandum from Mr. Shackley dated June 7, 1985, containing a later suggestion by Mr. Ghorbanifar that the ransom involve items "other than money," also drew no response. At the time of his meeting with Mr. Kimche, Mr. McFarlane apparently did not know this background or even that Mr. Ghorbanifar was the intermediary Mr. Kimche had in mind. He learned this later in the month from Mr. Ledeen.

Mr. McFarlane told the Board that Mr. Kimche told him the Iranians understood that they would have to demonstrate their "bona fides" and that the Iranians believed they could influence Hizballah to release the hostages in Beirut. But Mr. McFarlane also recalled Mr. Kimche expressing the view that ultimately the Iranians would need something to show for the dialogue, and that this would "probably" be weapons.

Mr. McFarlane testified that he informed the President of his conversation with Mr. Kimche within three or four days after the meeting, shortly before the President entered the hospital for his cancer operation. Mr. McFarlane also stated that on July 13, 1985, he briefed Secretary Shultz, Secretary Weinberger, and Director Casey in separate conversations. Mr. McFarlane told the Board that the President was interested in the proposal and said that he believed we should explore it. Mr. McFarlane said this may have occurred in the first week of July, before the President entered the hospital.

On July 13, 1985, Mr. McFarlane apparently received a second request, this time brought by an emissary directly from Israeli Prime Minister Peres. The "emissary" was Mr. Schwimmer, who delivered the request to Mr. McFarlane through Mr. Ledeen. The emissary carried word of a recent meeting with Mr. Ghorbanifar and another Iranian in which the Iranians had said that others inside Iran were interested in more extensive relations with the West, and particularly, the United States. The Iranians reportedly said that their contacts in Iran could achieve the release of the seven Americans held in Lebanon but in exchange sought 100 TOW missiles from Israel. This was to be part of a "larger purpose" of opening a "private dialogue" on U.S./Iranian relations. The emissary asked for a prompt response. Mr. McFarlane stated that he passed the President's decision to David Kimche by telephone.

On July 14, 1985, Mr. McFarlane cabled this proposal to Secretary Shultz, who was traveling in Asia. Mr. McFarlane recommended a tentative show of interest in a dialogue but with no commitment to the arms exchange. He asked for Secretary Shultz's guidance and indicated he would "abide fully" by the Secretary's decision. By return cable on the same day, Secretary

Shultz agreed to "a tentative show of interest without commitment." He said this was consistent with U.S. policy of "maintaining contact with people who might eventually provide information or help in freeing hostages." Secretary Shultz advised Mr. McFarlane to "handle this probe personally" but asked that he stay in close contact.

White House Chief of Staff [Donald T.] Regan told the Board that he and Mr. McFarlane met with the President on this issue in the hospital a few days after the President's cancer operation on July 13. Mr. Regan told the Board that the matter was discussed for 20 to 25 minutes, with the President asking quite a few questions. He recalled the President then saying "yes, go ahead. Open it up."

In his meeting with the Board on February 11, 1987, the President said he had no recollection of a meeting in the hospital in July with Mr. McFarlane and that he had no notes that would show such a meeting.

(ii) *The August Request.* On August 2, 1985, Mr. McFarlane again met at the White House with Mr. Kimche. According to Mr. McFarlane, Mr. Kimche said that the Iranians had asked whether the United States would supply arms to Iran. Mr. McFarlane recalled responding that he thought not. He told the Board that Mr. Kimche then asked what the U.S. reaction would be if Israel shipped weapons to Iran, and whether the United States would sell replacements "whether it's HAWKs or TOWs or whatever else." Mr. McFarlane recalled telling Mr. Kimche he would "get you our position."

What followed is quite murky.

Most NSC principals apparently had an opportunity to discuss this request with the President in and around the first two weeks of August. There clearly was a series of meetings with one or more of the principals in attendance. In addition, a number of the participants seem to recall a single meeting at which all the principals were present. White House records, however, show no meetings of the NSC principals in August scheduled for the purpose of discussing this issue. Other evidence suggests that there were meetings of the NSC principals in August at which this issue could have been discussed.

It is also unclear what exactly was under consideration at this time. No analytical paper was prepared for the August discussions and no formal minutes of any of the discussions were made.

Mr. McFarlane said that Mr. Kinche [*sic*] made a special proposal that 100 TOWs to Iran would establish good faith and result in the release of all the hostages. Mr. McFarlane told the Board that he discussed this proposal with the President several times and, on at least one occasion, with all the "full" members of the NSC. Within days after the meeting, the President communicated his decision to Mr. McFarlane by telephone. He said the President decided that, if Israel chose to transfer arms to Iran, in modest amounts not enough to change the military balance and not including major weapon systems, then it could buy replacements from the United States. Mr. McFarlane said that the President also indicated that the United States was interested in a political meeting with the Iranians. Mr. McFarlane said he reminded the President of the opposition expressed by Secretary Shultz and Secretary Weinburger [*sic*], but that the President said he wanted to go ahead—that he, the President, would take "all the heat for that."

Mr. McFarlane told the Board that he subsequently conveyed the President's decison to Mr. Kimche. He said that he emphasized to Mr. Kimche that the U.S. purpose was a political agenda with Iran, not an exchange of arms for hostages. Mr. McFarlane told the Board that he also conveyed this decision to the NSC principals.

Secretary Shultz told the Board on August 6, 1985, during one of his regularly scheduled meetings with the President, he discussed with the President a proposal for the transfer of 100 TOW missiles from Israel. The Iranians were for their part to produce the release of four or more hostages. Secretary Shultz told the Board that he opposed the arms sales at the meeting with the President. He said that Mr. McFarlane was present at this meeting. Secretary Shultz did not recall a telephone call from Mr. McFarlane regarding a decision by the President.

Secretary Weinberger recalled a meeting with the President at his residence after the President's return from the hospital. He told the Board that he argued forcefully against arms transfers to Iran, as did George Shultz. He said he thought that the President agreed that the idea should not be pursued.

Mr. Regan also recalled an August meeting with the President. He told the Board that the President expressed concern with any one-for-one swap of arms for hostages and indicated "we should go slow on this but develop the contact." Mr. Regan also told the Board that in early September, Mr. McFarlane informed the President that Israel had sold arms to the Iranians and hoped to get some hostages out. Mr. Regan stated that the President was "upset" at the news and that Mr. McFarlane explained that the Israelis had "simply taken it upon themselves to do this." Mr. Regan said that after some discussion, the President decided to "leave it alone."

In his meeting with the Board on January 26, 1987, the President said that sometime in August he approved the shipment of arms by Israel to Iran. He was uncertain as to the precise date. The President also said that he approved replenishment of any arms transferred by Israel to Iran. Mr. McFarlane's testimony of January 16, 1986, before the Senate Foreign Relations Committee, which the President embraced, takes the same position. This portion of Mr. McFarlane's testimony was specifically highlighted on the copy of testimony given by the President to the Board.

In his meeting with the Board on February 11, the President said that he and Mr. Regan had gone over the matter a number of times and that Mr. Regan had a firm recollection that the President had not authorized the August shipment in advance. The President said he did not recall authorizing the August shipment in advance. He noted that very possibly, the transfer was brought to him as already completed. He said that subsequently there were arms shipments he authorized that may have had to do with replenishment, and that this approval for replenishment could have taken place in September. The President stated that he had been "surprised" that the Israelis had shipped arms to Iran, and that this fact caused the President to conclude that he had not approved the transfer in advance.

In a subsequent letter to the Board received on February 20, 1987, the President wrote: "In trying to recall events that happened eighteen months ago I'm afraid that I let myself be influenced by others' recollections, not my own ...

> "... I have no personal notes or records to help my recollection on this matter. The only honest answer is to state that try as I might, I cannot recall anything whatsoever about whether I approved an Israeli sale in advance or whether I approved replenishment of Israeli stocks around August of 1985. My answer therefore and the simple truth is, 'I don't remember—period.'"

The Board tried to resolve the question of whether the President gave prior approval to Israel's transfer of arms to Iran. We could not do so conclusively.

We believe that an Israeli request for approval of such a transfer was discussed before the President in early August. We believe that Secretary Shultz and Secretary Weinberger expressed at times vigorous opposition to the proposal. The President agreed to replenish Israeli stocks. We are persuaded that he most likely provided this approval prior to the first shipment by Israel.

In coming to this conclusion, it is of paramount importance that the President never opposed the idea of Israel transferring arms to Iran. Indeed, four months after the August shipment, the President authorized the United States government to undertake directly the very same operation that Israel had proposed. Even if Mr. McFarlane did not have the President's explicit prior approval, he clearly had his full support.

A Hostage Comes Out. On August 30, 1985, Israel delivered 100 TOWs to Iran. A subsequent delivery of 408 more TOWs occurred on September 14, 1985. [5] On September 15, 1985, Reverend Benjamin Weir was released by his captors.

Mr. Ghorbanifar told the Board that the 100 TOWs were not linked to a hostage release. They were to evidence U.S. seriousness in reestablishing relations with Iran. The next step was to be the delivery of 400 more TOWs, for which Iran was to free a hostage. The goal was to establish a new relationship between the two countries, which would include a pledge by Iran of no further terrorist acts against the United States or its citizens by those under Iran's control.

Mr. McFarlane said that he received a telephone call from Mr. Kimche informing him of Rev. Weir's impending release about a week before it occurred. LtCol North, the NSC staff officer with responsibility for terrorism policy, made arrangements for receiving and debriefing Rev. Weir.

Although it appears that Israel and the United States expected the release of the remaining hostages to accompany or follow the release of Rev. Weir, this did not occur.

Stage 4: The Initiative Appears to Founder

The United States had only a supporting role in the August and September deliveries to Iran. Israel managed the operation. The next three months saw an increasing U.S. role.

A number of important developments regarding the Iran initiative occurred between September and December, 1985. However, it proved difficult for the Board to establish precisely what happened during this period. This is in part because the period was one of great activity for the President, the NSC principals, and Mr. McFarlane. Issues that seemed to be both more important and more urgent than the Iran initiative clearly preoccupied them.

Mr. McFarlane described the foreign policy agenda for the period. The Soviet foreign minister visited Washington. Preparations for the Geneva Summit with General Secretary Gorbachev were under way; this included four Presidential speeches on arms control, human rights, regional issues, and U.S./Soviet bilateral [sic] relations. The President delivered an address to the United Nations on the occasion of its 40th Anniversary. The President met with twelve to fifteen heads of State in New York and Washington. In the middle of this hectic schedule, on October 7, 1985, the Achille Lauro was seized by four Palestinian hijackers.

An Arms for Hostages Deal. On October 8, 1985, LtCol North's calendar indicated that he met with Mr. Ledeen, Mr. Schwimmer, Mr. Nimrodi, and Mr. Ghorbanifar (using the alias of Nicholas Kralis). Other meetings may have occurred. There is little evidence of what exactly went on in these meetings. All that is known for sure is that shortly after those meetings, David Kimche advanced a third proposal.

Mr. Kimche met with Mr. McFarlane and LtCol North on November 9, 1985. John McMahon, the Deputy Director of Central Intelligence, told the Board that Mr. McFarlane spoke with him on November 14. Mr. McFarlane told Mr. McMahon that Mr. Kimche had indicated that the Israelis planned to provide some arms to moderates in Iran who would oppose Khomeini. Mr. McFarlane suggested that the Israelis interpreted the Presidential authorization as an open charter for further arms shipments as long as the shipments were modest and did not alter the military balance between Iran and Iraq. Indeed, he did not recall any specific request by Israel in the late fall. He did, however, remember that early in November, Yitzhak Rabin, Israel's Defense Minister, asked whether U.S. policy would still permit Israel to buy replacements from the U.S. for arms it transferred to Iran. Mr. McFarlane confirmed that it would, although he indicated U.S. reservations about any trade of arms for hostages. They asked nothing further.

In a message to VADM Poindexter on November 20, 1985, LtCol North described the following plan. The Israelis were to deliver 80 HAWK missiles to a staging area in a third country, at noon on Friday, November 22. These were to be loaded aboard three chartered aircraft, which would take off at two hour intervals for Tabriz, Iran. Once launch of the first aircraft had been confirmed by Mr. Ghorbanifar, directions would be given to release the five U.S. citizens held hostage in Beirut. No aircraft was to land in Tabriz until all the hostages had been delivered to the U.S. embassy in Beirut. Israel would deliver forty additional HAWKs at a later time. The Iranians would commit to seeing that there were no further hostages seized.

Secretary Shultz told the Board that Mr. McFarlane told him on November 18, 1985, about a plan that would produce the release of the hostages on Thursday, November 21. Secretary Shultz told the Board he told Mr. McFarlane that had he known of it earlier, he would have stopped it. He nonetheless expressed the hope to Mr. McFarlane that the hostages would be released. It is not clear what other NSC principals, if any, were told in advance about the plan.

Secretary Shultz said he told an associate on November 22 that "Bud says he's cleared with the President" on the plan. Chief of Staff Regan told the Board that the President was informed in advance of the Israeli HAWK shipment but was not asked to approve it. He said that Mr. McFarlane told the President early in the month on the margins of his briefings for the Geneva Summit to expect that a shipment of missiles would come from Israel through a third country to Iran, and that the hostages would come out.

In his first meeting with the Board on January 16, 1987, the President said he did not remember how the November shipment came about. The President said he objected to the shipment, and that, as a result of that objection, the shipment was returned to Israel.

In his second meeting with the Board on February 11, 1987, the President stated that both he and Mr. Regan agreed that they cannot remember any meeting or conversation in general about a HAWK shipment. The President said he did not remember anything about a call-back of the HAWKs.

Nonetheless, that the United States would sell replacement HAWKs to Israel seems to have been assumed at least by VADM Poindexter from the start. LtCol North informed VADM Poindexter on November 20, 1985, that "IAW [in accordance with] your instructions I have told their [Israel's] agent that we will sell them 120 items [HAWKs] at a price that they can meet."

Failure. In contrast to the August TOW shipment, the United States became directly involved in the November transfer of the HAWK missiles. Sometime on November 17 or 18, 1985, while Mr. McFarlane was in Geneva for the November summit, Mr. Rabin called Mr. McFarlane to say that a problem had arisen. Mr. McFarlane referred the matter to LtCol North.

North signed a letter for Mr. McFarlane dated November 19, 1985, requesting Richard Secord, a retired U.S. Air Force general officer, to proceed to a foreign country, to arrange for the transfer of "sensitive material" being shipped from Israel. That day Mr. Secord made arrangements for transshipment of the Israeli HAWKs.

But late in the day on November 21, these arrangements began to fall apart. The foreign government denied landing clearance to the aircraft bringing the HAWKs from Israel. LtCol North contacted Duane Clarridge of the CIA for assistance in obtaining the required landing clearance. When the CIA's efforts failed, LtCol North asked Mr. Clarridge to find a reliable commercial carrier to substitute for the Israeli flight. Mr. Clarridge put Mr. Secord in contact with a carrier that was a CIA proprietary.

The plan went awry again on November 22, when Mr. Schwimmer allowed the lease to expire on the three aircraft they had chartered to take the HAWKs to Tabriz. Mr. Secord was able to provide an aircraft for this leg of the journey, however. The CIA arranged for overflight rights over a third country. On November 25 the aircraft left a European country. Delivery was three days late, however, and the aircraft carried only 18 HAWKs. Contrary to LtCol North's description of this plan, the aircraft delivered the HAWKs before the release of any hostages. In fact, no hostages were ever released as a result of this delivery.

Not only were just 18 of the initial shipment of HAWKs delivered, the HAWKs did not meet Iranian military requirements. In addition, they bore Israeli markings. Mr. Ghorbanifar told the Board that this caused great unhappiness in Iran and had disastrous consequences for the emerging relationship. Ultimately the Iranians returned 17 of the HAWKs to Israel. The eighteenth had been test-fired at an Iraqi aircraft flying over Kharg Island to determine the missile's effectiveness.

When Deputy Director McMahon learned of the CIA role in the shipment some three or four days after the fact, he directed the

CIA General Counsel to prepare a Covert Action Finding[6] providing Presidential authorization for the CIA's past support and any future support to the Iran initiative. A Findipg [sic] was drafted and delivered to VADM Poindexter, but the evidence strongly suggests it was never signed by the President.

Stage 5: The United States Sells Directly to Iran

On November 30, 1985, Mr. McFarlane resigned as National Security Advisor. VADM Poindexter was named National Security Advisor on December 4. That same day, LtCol North raised with VADM Poindexter a new proposal for an arms-for-hostages deal. It involved the transfer of 3,300 Israeli TOWs and 50 Israeli HAWKs in exchange for release of all the hostages. The arms were to be delivered in five installments, spread over a 24-hour period. Each installment was to result in the release of a one or two hostages, so that in the end all five U.S. citizens held in Beirut and a French hostage would be freed.[7] If any installment did not result in a hostage release, all deliveries would stop.

An Attempt to Break the Arms/Hostages Link. This proposal was considered at a meeting with the President on December 7 in the White House residence. The President, Secretary Shultz, Secretary Weinberger, Mr. Regan, Mr. McMahon, Mr. McFarlane, and VADM Poindexter attended. Secretary Shultz described the meeting as the first "formal meeting" on the Iran initiative where the participants were informed in advance of the subject and had time to prepare. Mr. McFarlane said that the participants reviewed the history of the program. However, no analytical paper was circulated for discussion at the meeting; the Board was not able to acquire any minutes of this meeting. State Department notes of Secretary Shultz's contemporaneous report of a conversation he had with VADM Poindexter on December 5 indicate that VADM Poindexter asked that Secretary Shultz's calendar not show the meeting.

Recollections of the meeting are quite diverse. In his meeting with the Board on January 26, 1987, the President said he recalled discussing a complex Iranian proposal for weapons delivered by the Israelis in installments prior to the release of the hostages. The President said that Secretary Shultz and Secretary Weinberger objected to the plan, and that this was the first time he "noted down" their disapproval. The President said that the discussion at the meeting produced a stalemate.

Secretary Weinberger told the Board he argued strongly against the complicated arms and hostages plan, and that he was joined in his opposition by Secretary Shultz. Mr. Regan told the Board that he supported the plan. But notes written that day by the President and State Department notes of Secretary Shultz's contemporaneous report of the meeting indicate that Mr. Regan joined Secretary Shultz and Secretary Weinberger in opposing the plan. Whatever disagreements were expressed at the meeting, a consensus emerged that Mr. McFarlane should go to London and deliver a message to the Iranians.

No written Presidential decision resulted from the meeting. Immediately after the meeting, Mr. McFarlane left for London to meet with Mr. Ghorbanifar and others to discuss the plan. There is no evidence that Mr. McFarlane was given any written instructions for the trip.

Mr. McFarlane's message at the London meeting was that, while the United States wanted the U.S. hostages released, and would be interested in better relations with Iran, it was making no offer of arms. According to a memorandum written by LtCol North, Mr. Ghorbanifar refused to transmit this message to his Iranian contacts, reportedly stating that to do so would endanger the lives of the hostages. There appears to be no formal record of the London meeting.

Mr. McFarlane reported the results of his trip directly to the President at a meeting held in the Oval Office on December 10. Once again, no analytical paper was distributed in advance, no minutes were kept, and no formal Presidential decision resulted. The President, Secretary Weinberger, Director Casey, Chief of Staff Regan, and VADM Poindexter were present. Secretary Weinberger has no recollection of the meeting though Mr. McFarlane recalled that the Secretary asserted his opposition to the operation. Secretary Shultz was in Europe, but his staff reported to him on the meeting apparently after talking to VADM Poindexter.

Mr. McFarlane reported that an impasse in the talks developed when he refused to discuss the transfer of arms to Iran. Mr. McFarlane also told the Board he recommended against any further dealings with Mr. Ghorbanifar or these arms transfers and left government thinking the initiative had been discontinued.

The President also noted on December 9 that Mr. McFarlane had returned from London. He had met with an Iranian agent described as "a devious character." The President noted that the Iranian agent had said that Mr. McFarlane's message would kill the hostages. The President told the Board at the meeting on December 10, Mr. McFarlane expressed no confidence in the Iranian intermediary he met in London [Mr. Ghorbanifar]. The President noted that Mr. McFarlane recommended rejection of the latest plan.[8] The President said he agreed. "I had to."

Mr. Regan told the Board that at the meeting the President said the United States should try something else or abandon the whole project. Mr. Regan also said that the President noted that it would be another Christmas with hostages still in Beirut, and that he [the President] was looking powerless and inept because he was unable to do anything to get the hostages out.

Director Casey prepared a memorandum of the meeting dated the same day (December 10). It states that the President "argued mildly" for letting the Israelis sell the equipment but without any commitment from the United States other than replenishment. It reports that the President was concerned that terminating the ongoing discussions could lead to early action against the hostages. Director Casey ended the memorandum saying that as the meeting broke up: "I had the idea that the President had not entirely given up on encouraging the Israelis to carry on with the Iranians. I suspect he would be willing to run the risk and take the heat in the future if this will lead to springing the hostages."

The Arms/Hostages Link Reestablished. The President was clearly quite concerned about the hostages. Mr. McFarlane told the Board that the President inquired almost daily about the welfare of the hostages. Chief of Staff Regan is reported to have told reporters on November 14, 1986, that "the President brings up the hostages at about 90 percent of his briefings." Mr. Regan is reported to have said that each morning at the daily intelligence briefing, the President asked VADM Poindexter: "John, anything new on the hostages?"

The premise of the McFarlane December 7 trip had been to try to break the arms/hostage link. However, on December 9, LtCol North submitted to VADM Poindexter a memorandum proposing direct U.S. deliveries of arms to Iran in exchange for release of the hostages, using Mr. Secord to control Mr. Ghorbanifar and the delivery operation. The December 9 memorandum raises at least a question as to whether LtCol North, who accompanied Mr. McFarlane to the London meeting, fully supported the thrust of McFarlane's instructions in his own conversations in London with Mr. Ghorbanifar and others.

During the rest of December, LtCol North, Mr. Ghorbanifar, Mr. Ledeen, Mr. Secord, and Mr. Nir met variously among themselves. Again we know little of the proceedings. It is not clear who took the lead in developing the arms-for-hostages proposal that was soon presented by the Israelis. It is clear, however, that on January 2, 1986, Mr. Nir advanced a proposal just when the initiative seemed to be dying.

Mr. Nir met with VADM Poindexter in his office on January 2. Secretary Shultz recalls being told by VADM Poindexter that Mr. Nir proposed an exchange of certain Hizballah prisoners held by Israeli-supported Lebanese Christian forces, together with 3000 Israeli TOWs, for the release of the U.S. citizens held hostage in Beirut. On January 7, 1986, this proposal was discussed with the President at a meeting, probably held in the Oval Office, attended by the Vice President, Secretary Shultz, Secretary Weinberger, Attorney General Meese, Director Casey, Mr. Regan, and VADM Poindexter. Although the President apparently did not make a decision at this meeting, several of the participants recall leaving the meeting persuaded that he supported the proposal. Secretary Shultz told the Board that the President, the Vice-President, Mr.

Casey, Mr. Meese, Mr. Regan, and VADM Poindexter "all had one opinion and I had a different one and Cap shared it."

At his meeting with the Board on January 26, 1987, the President said he approved a convoluted plan whereby Israel would free 20 Hizballah prisoners, Israel would sell TOW missiles to Iran, the five U.S. citizens in Beirut would be freed, and the kidnappings would stop. A draft Covert Action Finding had already been signed by the President the day before the meeting on January 6, 1986. Mr. Regan told the Board that the draft Finding may have been signed in error. The President did not recall signing the January 6 draft.

The President told the Board that he had several times asked for assurances that shipments to Iran would not alter the military balance with Iraq. He did not indicate when this occurred but stated that he received such assurances. The President also said he was warned by Secretary Shultz that the arms sales would undercut U.S. efforts to discourage arms sales by its allies to Iran.

The President did not amplify those remarks in his meeting with the Board on February 11. He did add, however, that no one ever discussed with him the provision of intelligence to Iran.

On January 17, a second draft Finding was submitted to the President. It was identical to the January 6 Finding but with the addition of the words "and third parties" to the first sentence.

The President told the Board that he signed the Finding on January 17. It was presented to him under cover of a memorandum from VADM Poindexter of the same date. The President said he was briefed on the contents of the memorandum but stated that he did not read it. This is reflected in VADM Poindexter's handwritten note on the memorandum. That note also indicates that the Vice President, Mr. Regan, and Donald Fortier were present for the briefing.

Although the draft Finding was virtually identical to that signed by the President on January 6, the cover memorandum signaled a major change in the Iran initiative. Rather than accepting the arrangement suggested by Mr. Nir, the memorandum proposed that the CIA purchase 4000 TOWs from DoD and, after receiving payment, transfer them directly to Iran. Israel would still "make the necessary arrangements" for the transaction.

This was an important change. The United States became a direct supplier of arms to Iran. The President told the Board that he understood the plan in this way. That day, President Reagan wrote in his diary: "I agreed to sell TOWs to Iran."

It is important to note, however, that this decision was made at a meeting at which neither Secretary Shultz, Secretary Weinberger, nor Director Casey were present. Although Secretary Weinberger and Director Casey had been present at a meeting with Attorney General Meese, General Counsel Sporkin, and VADM Poindexter the preceding day to review the draft Finding, the new U.S. role does not appear in the text of the Finding. Attorney General Meese told the Board he did not recall any discussion of the implications of this change. Secretary Weinberger told the Board he had no recollection of attending the meeting.

The President made the point to the Board that arms were not given to Iran but sold, and that the purpose was to improve the stature within Iran of particular elements seeking ties to the Iranian military. The President distinguished between selling to someone believed to be able to exert influence with respect to the hostages and dealing directly with kidnappers. The President told the Board that only the latter would "make it pay" to take hostages.

The President told the Board that he had not been advised at any time during this period how the plan would be implemented. He said he thought that Israeli government officials would be involved. He assumed that the U.S. side would be on its guard against people such as Mr. McFarlane had met in London in early December. He indicated that Director Casey had not suggested to him at any time that the CIA assume operational responsibility for the initiative, nor was he advised of the downside risks if the NSC staff ran the operation. He recalls understanding at the time that he had a right to defer notice to Congress, and being concerned that any leaks would result in the death of those with whom the United States sought to deal in Iran.

The January 17 Finding was apparently not given or shown to

key NSC principals. In particular, Secretary Shultz, Secretary Weinberger, and Mr. Regan stated that they did not see the signed Finding until after the Iran initiative became public. The Finding marked, however, a major step toward increasingly direct U.S. participation in, and control over, the Iran initiative.

Stage 6: The NSC Staff Manages the Operation

In the months that followed the signing of the January 17th Finding, LtCol North forwarded to VADM Poindexter a number of operational plans for achieving the release of all the hostages. Each plan involved a direct link between the release of hostages and the sale of arms. LtCol North, with the knowledge of VADM Poindexter and the support of selected individuals at CIA, directly managed a network of private individuals in carrying out these plans. None of the plans, however, achieved their common objective—the release of all the hostages.

Plans for "Operation Recovery." The plan described in the cover memorandum to the January 17 Finding called for Israel to arrange for the sale of 4000 U.S. TOW missiles to Iran. The memorandum stated that both sides had agreed that the hostages would be released "immediately" upon commencement of the operation. It provided, however, that if all the hostages were not released after the first shipment of 1000 TOWS, further transfers would cease.

At this point elements of the CIA assumed a much more direct role in the operation. On January 18, 1986, VADM Poindexter and LtCol North met with Clair George, Deputy Director of Operations at CIA, Stanley Sporkin, CIA General Counsel[,] and one of the primary authors of the January 17 Finding, the Chief of the Near East Division with the Operations Directorate at CIA. They began planning the execution of the plan. Because of an NSC request for clearance of Mr. Ghorbanifar, on January 11, 1986, the CIA had administered a polygraph test to Mr. Ghorbanifar during a visit to Washington. Although he failed the test, and despite the unsatisfactory results of the program to date, Mr. Ghorbanifar continued to serve as intermediary. A CIA official recalls Director Casey concurring in this decision.

On January 24, LtCol North sent to VADM Poindexter a lengthy memorandum containing a notional timeline for "Operation Recovery." The complex plan was to commence January 24 and conclude February 25. It called for the United States to provide intelligence data to Iran. Thereafter, Mr. Ghorbanifar was to transfer funds for the purchase of 1000 TOWs to an Israeli account at Credit Suisse Bank in Geneva, Switzerland. It provided that these funds would be transfered [sic] to an account in the same bank controlled by Mr. Secord; that $6 million of that amount would be transferred to a CIA account in that bank; and that the CIA would then wire the $6 million to a U.S. Department of Defense account in the United States.[9] The 1000 TOWs would then be transferred from the DoD to the CIA.

Mr. Secord and his associates, rather than the CIA, had the more substantial operational role. He would arrange for the shipment of the TOWs to Eilat, Israel. From there, an Israeli 707, flown by a crew provided by Mr. Secord, would deliver the TOWs to Bandar Abbas, Iran. On the return flight, the aircraft would stop in Tehran to pick up the HAWK missiles delivered in November of 1985 but later rejected by Iran. The plan anticipated that the next day (February 9) all U.S. citizens held hostage in Beirut would be released to the U.S. embassy there. Thereafter, 3000 more TOWS would be delivered. The plan anticipated that Khomeini would step down on February 11, 1985, the fifth anniversary of the founding of the Islamic Republic.[10]

Mr. Ghorbanifar's recollection of the terms of the arrangements are [sic] radically different. Mr. Ghorbanifar stated adamantly that the 1000 TOWs were to reestablish U.S. good faith after the disasterous [sic] November shipment of HAWK missiles. Mr. Ghorbanifar said there was no agreement that the U.S. hostages were to be released as a result of the sale.

On February 18, the first 500 TOWs were delivered to Bandar Abbas, and the HAWK missiles were brought out. On February 24-27, LtCol North, a CIA official, Mr. Secord, Mr. Nir, and Mr.

Albert Hakim (a business associate of Mr. Secord) held a series of meetings in Frankfurt, Germany with Mr. Ghorbanifar and other Iranians to review the details of the operation. On February 27, the second 500 TOWs were delivered to Bandar Abbas. Although a hostage release and a later meeting between senior U.S. and Iranian officials had been agreed upon at the Frankfurt meeting, the plan fell through. No hostages were released and the meeting failed to materialize until much later.

Although the cover memorandum to the January 17 Finding stated that further arms transfers would cease if all the hostages were not released after delivery of the first 1000 TOWs, the United States continued to pursue the initiative and arranged for another delivery of arms two months later.

Authorization for "Operation Recovery." LtCol North appears to have kept VADM Poindexter fully advised of the progress of Operation Recovery. Director Casey also appears to have been kept informed both by LtCol North and by a CIA official. Both LtCol North and VADM Poindexter were in touch with Mr. McFarlane. In a message to LtCol North on February 27, 1986, Mr. McFarlane noted that he had just received a note from VADM Poindexter asking whether Mr. McFarlane could undertake the senior level meeting with the Iranians and indicating that "the President is on board." Mr. Regan told the Board that the President authorized the shipment of 1000 TOWs during one of VADM Poindexter's morning briefings to the President.

Secretary Shultz told the Board that on February 28, 1986, VADM Poindexter informed him the hostages would be released the following week. Secretary Shultz said VADM Poindexter reported nothing about arms. VADM Poindexter said the Iranians wanted a high-level dialogue covering issues other than hostages, and that the White House had chosen Mr. McFarlane for the mission.

Preparation for the May Trip. Preparation for a meeting between Mr. McFarlane and senior Iranian officials began shortly after LtCol North's return from Frankfurt on February 27. That same day, VADM Poindexter met with Director Casey, Mr. George, and another CIA official to discuss plans for the meeting. On March 5, 1986, George Cave joined the group. He was a retired CIA officer who since retirement had served as a full-time paid consultant to the agency. He was a Farsi speaker and an expert on Iran.

LtCol North, Mr. Cave, and a CIA official met with Mr. Ghorbanifar in Paris on March 8, 1986. LtCol North reported on this conversation to Mr. McFarlane on March 10. He said he told Mr. Ghorbanifar that the United States remained interested in a meeting with senior Iranian officials as long as the hostages were released during or before the meeting. He said he briefed Mr. Ghorbanifar on the Soviet threat to Iran using intelligence supplied by Mr. Robert Gates, then the CIA Deputy Director for Intelligence. Mr. Ghorbanifar responded by presenting a list of 240 different types of spare parts, in various quantities, needed by Iran for its HAWK missile units. He also emphasized the importance of an advance meeting in Tehran to prepare for the meeting with Mr. McFarlane. This advance meeting would establish the agenda and who should participate from the Iranian side.

While further discussion occurred over the next month, it resulted in little progress. On April 3, 1986, Mr. Ghorbanifar arrived in Washington, D.C. He met with LtCol North, Mr. Allen, Mr. Cave, and another CIA official between April 3-4. In a message to Mr. McFarlane on April 7, 1986, LtCol North indicated that, at the request of VADM Poindexter, he had prepared a paper for "our boss" laying out the arrangements agreed upon at the meeting.

An unsigned, undated memorandum was found in LtCol North's files entitled "Release of American Hostages in Beirut."[11] It appears to have been prepared in early April.

In an interview with Attorney General Meese on November 23, 1986, LtCol North said he prepared this memorandum between April 4-7. Although in a form for transmittal by VADM Poindexter to the President, LtCol North indicated that he did not believe the President had approved the memorandum.

The memorandum provided for the following sequence of events:

—On April 9, the CIA would commence procuring $3.641 million worth of parts for HAWK missile units.

—On April 18, a private U.S. aircraft would load the parts and fly them to an Israeli airfield. The parts would then be transferred to an Israeli military aircraft with false markings.

—On April 19, Mr. McFarlane, LtCol North, Mr. Teicher, Mr. Cave, and a CIA official would board a CIA aircraft in Frankfurt en route to Tehran.

—On April 20, they would meet with a delegation of senior Iranian officials. Seven hours later, the U.S. hostages would be released in Beirut. Fifteen hours later, the Israeli military aircraft with the HAWK missile parts would land in Bandar Abbas, Iran.

That schedule was not met. On April 16, 1986, LtCol North wrote VADM Poindexter seeking approval for a meeting with Mr. Ghorbanifar in Frankfurt on April 18. In his reply of the same date, VADM Poindexter approved the trip but insisted that there be no delivery of parts until all the hostages had been freed. He expressly ruled out half shipments before release. "It is either all or nothing." He authorized LtCol North to tell Mr. Ghorbanifar: "The President is getting very annoyed at their continual stalling." On April 21, VADM Poindexter sent a message to Mr. McFarlane informing him of this position.

The Frankfurt meeting was not held. On May 6, 1986, LtCol North and Mr. Cave met with Mr. Ghorbanifar in London. Mr. Ghorbanifar promised a meeting with senior Iranian officials but asked that the U.S. delegation bring all the HAWK spare parts with them. Mr. Cave recalls the Americans agreeing that one-quarter of the spare parts would accompany the delegation. Notwithstanding, LtCol North informed VADM Poindexter on May 8: "I believe we have succeeded. * * * Release of hostages set for week of 19 May in sequence you have specified."

On May 22, 1986, LtCol North submitted the final operating plan for the trip to VADM Poindexter. It provided that the McFarlane delegation would arrive in Tehran on May 25, 1986. The next day (but no later than May 28), the hostages would be released. One hour later, an Israeli 707 carrying the balance of the spare parts would leave Tel Aviv for Tehran.

Authorization for the May Trip. On May 3, 1986, while at the Tokyo economic summit, Secretary Shultz received word from the U.S. Ambassador to London that Mr. Khashoggi, Mr. Ghorbanifar, and Mr. Nir had sought to interest a British businessman in the shipment of spare parts and weapons to Iran. That same day, Secretary Shultz expressed his concern about any such transaction to Mr. Regan. Secretary Shultz told the Board that Mr. Regan said he was alarmed and would talk to the President. Secretary Shultz said he talked later to VADM Poindexter and was told that "that was not our deal." He recalls being told soon thereafter by both VADM Poindexter and Director Casey that the operation had ended and the people involved had been told to "stand down." The Tokyo Summit closed with a statement from all the heads of state strongly reaffirming their condemnation of international terrorism in all its forms.

Rodney McDaniel noted that during the national security briefing on May 12, 1986, VADM Poindexter discussed with the President the hostages and Mr. McFarlane's forthcoming trip.[12] The notes indicate that the President directed that the press not be told about the trip. On May 15, 1986, Mr. McDaniel's notes indicate that the President authorized Mr. McFarlane's secret mission to Iran and the Terms of Reference for that trip. Those notes indicate that the trip was discussed again with the President on May 21.

On May 17, LtCol North "strongly urged" that VADM Poindexter include Secretary Shultz and Secretary Weinberger along with Director Casey in a "quiet" meeting with the President and Mr. McFarlane to review the proposed trip. VADM Poindexter responded, "I don't want a meeting with RR, Shultz and Weinberger."

The May Trip to Tehran. LtCol North noted in a message to VADM Poindexter on May 19 that CIA was providing "comms, beacons, and documentation for the party." All the other logistics had been arranged through Mr. Secord "or affiliates." Mr. McFarlane, along with LtCol North, Mr. Cave, and a CIA official, left the United States on May 23. Mr. Nir had pressed to be included in the delegation. The Chief of the Near East Division in the CIA operations directorate told the Board that this request was initially rejected, and that position was transmitted by the White House to Israeli Prime Minister Peres who appealed it. He said that ultimately, the decision was left to Mr. McFarlane, who decided to let Mr. Nir join the group. Mr. Ghorbanifar recalls that in meetings with Iranian officials, Mr. Nir was always presented as an American.

On May 25 the delegation arrived in Tehran. Without the prior knowledge to [*sic*] Mr. McFarlane, the aircraft carried one pallet of HAWK spare parts. The delegation was not met by any senior Iranian officials. No hostages were released. Because of this, a second plane carrying the rest of the HAWK spare parts was ordered not to come to Tehran. Two days of talks proved fruitless. The Iranians initially raised demands for additional concessions, but later appeared to abandon them. Mr. McFarlane demanded the prior release of all hostages and the Iranians insisted on the immediate delivery of all HAWK spare parts. On May 27, Mr. McFarlane demanded the release of the hostages by 6:30 a.m. the next day. When no hostages were released, Mr. McFarlane and his party departed, but not before the pallet of HAWK spare parts had been removed from their aircraft by the Iranians.

In a report to VADM Poindexter on May 26, Mr. McFarlane stated: "The incompetence of the Iranian government to do business requires a rethinking on our part of why there have been so many frustrating failures to deliver on their part."

Mr. Ghorbanifar placed blame for the failure of the May trip squarely on the United States. Mr. Ghorbanifar said that he had proposed that he and LtCol North go to Tehran first to prepare the way. But after Mr. Ghorbanifar had made all the arrangements, LtCol North advised that VADM Poindexter had disapproved the trip. The failure to hold this preparatory meeting may have resulted in substantial misunderstanding between the two sides as to just what would occur and be discussed at the meeting with Mr. McFarlane. Mr. Ghorbanifar stated that the Iranians failed to meet Mr. McFarlane's plane because it arrived three hours ahead of schedule. Mr. Ghorbanifar also claimed that the delegation did meet with a senior-level foreign policy advisor.

The Board found evidence that LtCol North, Mr. Cave, Mr. Allen, and another CIA official knew as early as mid-April that if all the HAWK spare parts were not delivered with the delegation, then only one U.S. hostage would be released. Mr. McFarlane may not have been advised of this. While in Tehran, he insisted upon the release of all U.S. hostages prior to more than the token delivery of HAWK spare parts. This was apparently his and VADM Poindexter's understanding of the agreed arrangements. This led Mr. McFarlane to refuse an even better Iranian offer than the one LtCol North and his associates had reason to expect: two hostages immediately and the remaining two after delivery of the rest of the spare parts.

Notes made by Mr. McDaniel indicate that on May 27 the President received a report on the McFarlane trip. Those notes also indicate that Mr. McFarlane reported on his trip in person to the President on May 29. The notes indicate that the Vice President, Mr. Regan, VADM Poindexter, Mr. Teicher, and LtCol North also attended. Mr. McFarlane told the Board, and the notes confirm, that he told the President that the program ought to be discontinued. It was his view that while political meetings might be considered, there should be no weapons transfers.

A Hostage Comes Out. Mr. McDaniel's notes indicate that on June 20, 1986, the President decided that no further meeting with the Iranians would be held until the release of the hostages. Early in July, LtCol North called Charles Allen, a CIA official, and asked him to take over the day-to-day contact with Mr. Nir. LtCol North wrote in a memorandum to VADM Poindexter about this same time that he believed he had "lost face" because of his failure to obtain the release of an American hostage. Mr. Allen recalled that Mr. Nir was alarmed at losing direct contact with LtCol North. Mr. Allen told the Board that as a result, Mr. Nir worked closely with Mr. Ghorbanifar to obtain the release of an American hostage.

Notes made by the NSC Executive Secretary indicate that on July 18, VADM Poindexter informed the President of the latest communications with the Iranian interlocutors. On July 21, LtCol North, Mr. Cave, and Mr. Nir met with Mr. Ghorbanifar in London. They discussed the release of the hostages in exchange for the HAWK spare parts that remained undelivered from the May mission to Tehran. On July 26, Father Lawrence Jenco was released.

VADM Poindexter briefed the President on the Jenco release that same day over a secure telephone. He used a memorandum prepared by LtCol North that claimed the release was "undoubtedly" a result of Mr. McFarlane's trip in May and the continuing contacts thereafter. A July 26, 1986 memorandum to VADM Poindexter from Director Casey reached the same conclusion.

In a memorandum to VADM Poindexter dated July 29, 1986, LtCol North recommended that the President approve the immediate shipment of the rest of the HAWK spare parts and a follow-up meeting with the Iranians in Europe. Notes of the NSC Executive Secretary indicate that the President approved this proposal on July 30. Additional spare parts were delivered to Tehran on August 3.

Stage 7: The Second Channel Is Opened But the Initiative Leaks

From the start, U.S. officials had stressed to Mr. Ghorbanifar that Iran must use its influence to discourage further acts of terrorism directed against the United States and its citizens. Whether as a result of those efforts or for some other reason, from June 9, 1985, until September 9, 1986, no U.S. citizen was seized in Lebanon.[13] But on September 9, 1986, terrorists seized Frank Reed, a U.S. educator at the Lebanese International School. Two more U.S. citizens, Joseph Cicippio and Edward Tracey [sic], were taken hostage on September 12 and October 21.

The McFarlane mission to Tehran marked the high-water mark of U.S. efforts to deal with Iran through Mr. Ghorbanifar. For a year he had been at the center of the relationship. That year had been marked by great confusion, broken promises, and increasing frustration on the U.S. side. LtCol North and other U.S. officials apparently blamed these problems more on Mr. Ghorbanifar than on Iran. The release of Rev. Jenco did little to mitigate their unhappiness.

Sometime in July, 1986, an Iranian living in London proposed to Mr. Hakim a second Iranian channel—the relative of a powerful Iranian official. On July 25, Mr. Cave went to London to discuss this possibility. On August 26, 1986, Mr. Secord and Mr. Hakim met with the second channel and other Iranians in London. The Iranians said they were aware of the McFarlane visit, the Israeli connection, and Mr. Ghorbanifar's role. They referred to Mr. Ghorbanifar as a "crook." Notes taken by Mr. McDaniel indicate that the President was briefed about the second channel on September 9, 1986.

LtCol North, Mr. Cave, and a CIA official met with the second channel and two other Iranians in Washington between September 19 and 21, 1986. The two sides discussed the Soviet threat, cooperation in support of the Afghan resistance, and improved relations between the United States and Iran. The bulk of the time, however, was spent discussing the "obstacle" of the hostages and Iran's urgent need (within two months) for both intelligence and weapons to be used in offensive operations against Iraq. LtCol North reviewed a list of military equipment and agreed "in principle" to provide that equipment, subject to the constraints of what was available within the United States or obtainable from abroad. The parties discussed the establishment of a secret eight-man U.S.-Iranian commission to work on future relations. Finally, LtCol North told the Iranians that unless contact came from North, Richard Secord, or George Cave, "there is no official message from the United States." Notes by Mr. McDaniel indicate that on

September 23, the President was briefed on recent discussions with the second channel.

On October 5-7, 1986, LtCol North, Mr. Cave, and Mr. Secord met with the second channel in Frankfurt, Germany. They carried a Bible for the Iranians inscribed by the President on October 3. During the meeting, LtCol North misrepresented his access to the President and attributed to the President things the President never said.

In presenting the Bible, LtCol North related the following story to the Iranians:

> *"We inside our Government had an enormous debate, a very angry debate inside our government over whether or not my president should authorize me to say "We accept the Islamic Revolution of Iran as a fact * * *." He [the President] went off one whole weekend and prayed about what the answer should be and he came back almost a year ago with that passage I gave you that he wrote in front of the Bible I gave you. And he said to me, "This is a promise that God gave to Abraham. Who am I to say that we should not do this?"*

In reality, the idea of the Bible and the choice of the inscription were contained in an October 2, 1986, memorandum from LtCol North to VADM Poindexter. The Bible was to be exchanged for a Koran at the October 5-7 meeting. VADM Poindexter approved the idea and the President inscribed the Bible the next morning. The President told the Board that he did inscribe the Bible because VADM Poindexter told him this was a favorite passage with one of the people with whom the U.S. was dealing in Iran. The President said he made the inscription to show the recipient that he was "getting through."

At two points during the October 5-7 Frankfurt meetings, LtCol North told two stories of private discussions with the President at Camp David. The first had the President saying that he wanted an end to the Iran/Iraq war on terms acceptable to Iran. The second had the President saying that the Gulf states had to be convinced that it was Saddam Husain [Saddam Hussein] of Iraq that was "causing the problem."

When pressed by the Iranians for an explicit statement of what the United States means by "an honorable victory" for Iran, LtCol North replied: "We also recognize that Saddam Husain must go."

The President emphasized to the Board that these statements are an "absolute fiction" and that there were no meetings as LtCol North describes. In addition, Mr. McDaniel noted that on October 3, 1986, the President reaffirmed that the United States wanted neither Iran or Iraq to win the war.

At the October 5-7 meeting, LtCol North laid out a seven-step proposal for the provision of weapons and other items in exchange for Iranian influence to secure the release of all remaining U.S. hostages, the body of William Buckley, a debrief by his captors, and the release of John Pattis, a United States citizen whom the Iranians had arrested on spying charges several months earlier. The Iranians presented a six-point counter-proposal that, in part, promised the release of one hostage following receipt of additional HAWK parts and a timetable for future delivery of intelligence information. The Iranians made clear that they could not secure the release of all the hostages. Mr. Cave recalls that the Iranians proposed exchanging 500 TOWs for the release of two hostages. He stated that the U.S. side agreed.

A second meeting was held in Frankfurt on October 26-28 at which the parties finalized the payment and delivery schedule for the TOWs. At that meeting, the parties apparently discussed a nine-point U.S. agenda with Iran. That agenda included delivery by the U.S. of the 500 TOWs, an unspecified number of HAWKs, discussion of the 17 Da'Wa prisoners held by Kuwait, additional arms including 1000 more TOWs, and military intelligence. In exchange the Iranians promised release of one and perhaps two U.S. citizens held hostage in Beirut and "further efforts to create the condition for release of other hostages."

At a meeting between representatives of the State Department and the second channel on December 13, 1986, the Iranian said that both sides had agreed to this nine-point agenda. The Board found no evidence that LtCol North had authority to agree to such an agenda. Secretary Shultz told the Board that he informed the President the next day. He said that the President was "stricken" and could not believe anything like this had been discussed. Of particular concern was the point that the United States had consistently given strong support to Kuwait in resisting terrorist demands for the release of the Da'Wa prisoners.

At the October 26-28 meeting, the Iranian participants said the story of the McFarlane mission to Tehran had been published in a small Hezbollah newspaper in Baalbek, Lebanon. The article was based on a series of leaflets distributed in Tehran on 15 or 16 October.

Mr. Regan recalls the President authorizing the shipment of 500 TOWs on October 29, 1986.

Because of a delay in the transfer of funds the TOWs actually delivered to Iran on October 29, 1986, were Israeli TOWs. The 500 U.S. TOWs were provided to Israel as replacements on November 7.

On November 2, hostage David Jacobsen was released. The next day, a pro-Syrian Beirut magazine published the story of the McFarlane mission. On November 4, Majlis Speaker Rafsanjani publicly announced the mission.

The President, VADM Poindexter, and LtCol North hoped that more hostages would be released. Notes taken by the NSC Executive Secretary indicate that on November 7, 1986, the President decided not to respond to questions on this subject for fear of jeopardizing the remaining hostages. No further hostages were released.

Mr. Ghorbanifar told the Board that the switch to the second channel was a major error. He claimed that he had involved all three major lines or factions within the government of Iran in the initiative, and that the second channel involved only the Rafsanjani faction thus stimulating friction among the factions and leading to the leak of the story to embarrass Rafsanjani. In addition, the price offered to this faction was lower ($8000 per TOW) than the price charged for the earlier TOW deliveries ($10000 per TOW).

Section B: Contra Diversion

Sizable sums of money generated by the arms sales to Iran remain unaccounted for. Determining whether these funds from the sale of arms to Iran were diverted to support the Contras proved to be extremely difficult. VADM Poindexter, LtCol North, Israeli participants, and other key witnesses refused to appear before the Board, and records for relevant bank accounts maintained in Switzerland and elsewhere could not be obtained by the Board. Notwithstanding, there was considerable evidence before the Board of a diversion to support the Contras. But the Board had no hard proof.

Early in 1986, the need to find funds for the support of the Contras was desperate. At the same time, the idea of diverting funds from the arms sales to Iran surfaced. Attorney General Meese told the Board that VADM Poindexter and LtCol North both told him that a diversion had occurred.

Money Was Available. Israel made three arms deliveries to Iran in 1985. One of these was the November shipment of HAWK missiles. After the November deal collapsed, 17 of the 18 HAWK missiles were returned to Israel and available evidence suggests that all of the money for that shipment was returned or credited to Iran. In the case of the TOW shipments in August and September 1985, the price charged to Iran by Israel was far in excess of what Israel paid the U.S. Department of Defense to replenish the arms it delivered. This excess amount was roughly $3 million for the August/September TOW shipments. Nothing is known by the Board about the disposition of those funds.

The United States directly managed four arms deliveries in 1986. In each case, the purchase money was deposited in Swiss bank accounts held in the name of Lake Resources and under the control of Richard Secord. Again, the price charged to Iran was far in excess of what was paid to the Department of Defense for the arms. The excess amounts totaled almost $20 million for the four deliveries: $6.3 million for the February shipment of TOWs, $8.5 million for the May and August shipments of HAWK parts, and $5 million for the October shipment of TOWs.[14]

Most of these monies remain unaccounted for. Mr. Khashoggi and other investors claim they are still owed $10 million from these transactions.

The Contras Desperately Needed Funds. In January, 1986, the President requested $100 million in military aid to the Contras. The request revived the often bitter Congressional debate over whether the United States should support the Contras. The obligational authority for the $27 million in humanitarian aid to the Contras approved by the Congress in 1985 would expire on March 31, 1986. LtCol North, who had primary NSC staff responsibility for matters relating to the Contras, became increasingly concerned. While anticipating Congressional approval of the President's January 1 request, LtCol North feared the Contras would run out of funds before then. On April 22, 1986, he wrote Mr. Fortier: "[T]he picture is dismal unless a new source of 'bridge' funding can be identified * * *. We need to explore this problem urgently or there won't be a force to help when the Congress finally acts."

A Diversion Was Suggested. It is unclear who first suggested the idea of diverting funds from the arms sales to Iran to support the Contras. The evidence suggests that the idea surfaced early in 1986.

Attorney General Meese told the Board that during his interview with LtCol North on November 23, 1986, North indicated that the idea surfaced during a discussion with Mr. Nir in January, 1986, about ways Israel could help the Contras. LtCol North recalled the Israeli official suggesting that the "residuals" from the Iran arms sales be transferred to the Contras. Contemporaneous Justice Department notes of the November interview indicate that LtCol North said the diversion was an Israeli idea; that the Israelis wanted to be helpful.

Mr. Ghorbanifar told the Board that he had a conversation with LtCol North and Mr. Secord sometime in February of 1986 concerning arrangements for the upcoming delivery of 1000 TOW missiles to Iran. He said that LtCol North and Mr. Secord were extremely worried about a shortfall in funding for the Contras. Mr. Ghorbanifar said that LtCol North asked him if the Iranians would pay $10,000 per TOW missile, instead of $6,500. When told that Iran would pay that price, Mr. Ghorbanifar said LtCol North was greatly relieved—"he was a changed man."

In a memorandum of a meeting with Mr. Ghorbanifar in Paris on March 7-8, George Cave reported that Mr. Ghorbanifar, in an aside, "proposed that we use profits from these deals and others to fund support to the rebels in Afghanistan. We could do the same with Nicaragua."

Before the Board, Mr. Cave said that neither he nor Mr. Ghorbanifar made any mention of diversion.

North and Poindexter Said Diversion Occurred. Attorney General Meese told the Board that during his interview with LtCol North on November 23, 1986, North said that $3 to $4 million was diverted to the support of the Contras after the February shipment of TOW missiles and that more (though how much LtCol North was not sure) was diverted after the May shipment of HAWK parts. Contemporaneous Justice Department staff notes of that interview indicate that LtCol North said that the Israelis handled the money and that he gave them the numbers of three accounts opened in Switzerland by Adolpho [Adolfo] Calero, a Contra leader. The notes also indicate that LtCol North said there was no money for the Contras as a result of the shipment in October, 1986. By then Congressional funding had resumed.

Mr. McFarlane testified that while standing on the tarmac at a Tel Aviv airport after the trip to Tehran in May of 1986, LtCol North told him not to be too downhearted because "this government is availing itself of part of the money [from the Iran initiative] for application to Central America." Assistant Secretary of Defense Richard Armitage told the Board that North told him sometime in November of 1986 that: "it's going to be just fine * * * as soon as everyone knows that * * * the Ayatollah is helping us with the Contras."

Authorization. It is unclear whether LtCol North ever sought or received prior approval of any diversion of funds to the support of the Contras. LtCol North prepared in early April an unsigned memorandum entitled "Release of American Hostages in Beirut," which sought Presidential approval for what became Mr. McFarlane's May trip to Tehran. In that memo, LtCol North stated that $12 million in "residual" funds from the transaction would "be used to purchase critically needed supplies for the Nicaraguan Democratic Resistance Forces." No evidence has emerged to suggest that this memorandum was ever placed before VADM Poindexter, the President, or any other U.S. official.

As a general matter, LtCol North kept VADM Poindexter exhaustively informed about his activities with respect to the Iran initiative. Although the Board did not find a specific communication from Lt. Col North to VADM Poindexter on the diversion question, VADM Poindexter said that he knew that a diversion had occurred. Mr. Regan told the Board that he asked VADM Poindexter on November 24, 1986, if he knew of LtCol North's role in a diversion of funds to support the Contras. VADM Poindexter replied that, "I had a feeling that something bad was going on, but I didn't investigate it and I didn't do a thing about it. * * * I really didn't want to know. I was so damned mad at Tip O'Neill for the way he was dragging the Contras around I didn't want to know what, if anything, was going on. I should have, but I didn't." Attorney General Meese told the Board that after talking to LtCol North, he asked VADM Poindexter what he knew about the diversion. "He said that he did know about it * * * Ollie North had given him enough hints that he knew what was going on, but he didn't want to look further into it. But that he in fact did generally know that money had gone to the Contras as a result of the Iran shipment."

The President said he had no knowledge of the diversion prior to his conversation with Attorney General Meese on November 25, 1986. No evidence has come to light to suggest otherwise. Contemporaneous Justice Department staff notes of LtCol North's interview with Attorney General Meese on November 23, 1986, show North telling the Attorney General that only he, Mr. McFarlane, and VADM Poindexter were aware of the diversion.

Section C: The NSC Staff and Support for the Contras

Inquiry into the arms sale to Iran and the possible diversion of funds to the Contras disclosed evidence of substantial NSC staff involvement in a related area; private support for the Contras during the period that support from the U.S. Government was either banned or restricted by Congress.

There are similarities in the two cases. Indeed, the NSC staff's role in support for the Contras set the stage for its subsequent role in the Iran initiative. In both, LtCol North, with the acquiescence of the National Security Advisor, was deeply involved in the operational details of a covert program. He relied heavily on private U.S. citizens and foreigners to carry out key operational tasks. Some of the same individuals were involved in both. When Israeli plans for the November HAWK shipment began to unravel, LtCol North turned to the private network that was already in place to run the Contra support operation. This network, under the direction of Mr. Secord, undertook increasing responsibility for the Iran initiative. Neither program was subjected to rigorous and periodic inter-agency overview. In neither case was Congress informed. In the case of Contra support, Congress may have been actively misled.

These two operations also differ in several key aspects. While Iran policy was the subject of strong disagreement within the Executive Branch, the President's emphatic support for the Contras provoked an often bitter debate with the Congress. The result was an intense political struggle between the President and the Congress over how to define U.S. policy toward Nicaragua. Congress sought to restrict the President's ability to implement his policy. What emerged was a highly ambiguous legal environment.

On December 21, 1982, Congress passed the first "Boland amendment" prohibiting the Department of Defense and the Central Intelligence Agency from spending funds to overthrow Nicaragua or provoke conflict between Nicaragua and Honduras. The following year, $24 million was authorized for the Contras. On October 3, 1984, Congress cut off all funding for the Contras and prohibited DoD, CIA, and any other agency or entity "involved in intelligence activities" from directly or indirectly supporting military operations in Nicaragua.

The 1984 prohibition was subject to conflicting interpretation. On the one hand, several of its Congressional supporters believed that the legislation covered the activities of the NSC staff. On the other hand, it appears that LtCol North and VADM Poindexter received legal advice from the President's Intelligence Oversight Board that the restrictions on lethal assistance to the Contras did not cover the NSC staff.

Confusion only increased. In December 1985 Congress approved classified amounts of funds to the Contras for "communications" and "advice." The authorization was subject, however, to a classified annex negotiated by the Senate and House intelligence committees. An exchange of letters, initiated the day the law passed, evidences the extreme difficulty even the Chairmen of the two committees had in deciding what the annex permitted or proscribed.

The support for the Contras differs from the Iranian initiative in some other important respects. First, the activities undertaken by LtCol North with respect to the Contras, unlike in the Iranian case, were in support of the declared policy of at least the Executive. Second, the President may never have authorized or, indeed, even been apprised of what the NSC staff was doing. The President never issued a Covert Action Finding or any other formal decision authorizing NSC staff activities in support of the Contras. Third, the NSC staff's role in support of the Contras was not in derogation of the CIA's role because, CIA involvement was expressly barred by statute.

The Board had neither the time nor the resources to conduct a full inquiry into the role of the NSC staff in the support of the Contras that was commensurate with its work on the Iran arms sales. As a consequence, the evidence assembled by the Board was somewhat anecdotal and disconnected. The most significant evidence is summarized in this Section C. A fuller treatment is contained in Appendix C [Appendix omitted.].

The Bid for Private Funding. Because of Congressional restrictions, the Executive Branch turned to private sources to sustain the Contras militarily. In 1985 and 1986, Mr. McFarlane and the NSC staff repeatedly denied any direct involvement in efforts to obtain funds from these sources. Yet evidence before the Board suggests that LtCol North was well aware of these efforts and played a role in coordinating them. The extent of that role remains unclear.

In a memorandum to Mr. McFarlane dated April 11, 1985, LtCol North expressed concern that remaining Contra funds would soon be insufficient. He advised that efforts be made to seek $15 to $20 million in additional funds from the current donors which will "allow the force to grow to 30-35,000." The exact purpose to which these private funds were to be put was unambiguous. A number of memoranda from LtCol North make clear that the funds were for munitions and lethal aid.

Asked by the Board about the source of such funds, Mr. McFarlane provided a written response that indicated that "without solicitation" a foreign official offered $1 million a month from what he described as "personal funds." At Mr. McFarlane's request, LtCol North provided the numbers of a Contra bank account in Miami. Mr. McFarlane wrote that in 1985, the foreign official doubled his contribution to $2 million a month, a fact confirmed by two other U.S. officials.

Contributions appear to have been channeled through a series of non-profit organizations that LtCol North apparently had a hand in organizing. A diagram found in LtCol North's safe links some of these organizations to bank accounts controlled by Richard Secord and others known to be involved in purchasing and shipping arms to the Contras.

Other documents and evidence suggest that private contributions for the Contras were eventually funnelled into "Project Democracy," [15] a term apparently used by LtCol North to describe a network of secret bank accounts and individuals involved in Contra resupply and other activities. In a message to VADM Poindexter dated July 15, 1986, LtCol North described "Project Democracy" assets as worth over $4.5 million. They included six aircraft, warehouses, supplies, maintenance facilities, ships, boats, leased houses, vehicles, ordnance, munitions, communications equipment, and a 6520-foot runway. The runway was in fact a secret airfield in Costa Rica. LtCol North indicated in a memorandum dated September 30, 1986, that the airfield was used for direct resupply of the Contras from July 1985 to February 1986, and thereafter as the primary abort base for damaged aircraft.

On September 9, 1986, following Costa Rica's decision to close the airfield, LtCol North received word that the Costa Rican government was planning to call a press conference to announce the existence of the airfield. The same day, LtCol North informed VADM Poindexter that he had held a conference call with then U.S. Ambassador to Costa Rica, Louis Tambs, and Assistant Secretary Elliott Abrams to discuss the potential public revelation of the airfield. All three participants confirm the conference. North said that they had decided North would call Costa Rican President [Oscar] Arias and tell him if the press conference went forward the U.S. would cancel $80 million in promised A.I.D. assistance and Arias' upcoming visit with President Reagan. North added that both Ambassador Tambs and Assistant Secretary Abrams reinforced this message with Arias. VADM Poindexter replied: "You did the right thing, but let's try to keep it quiet."

Assistant Secretary Abrams and Ambassador Tambs told the Board that the conference call took place, but only Tambs was instructed to call Arias and that no threat to withhold U.S. assistance was made. They each doubted that North ever called the President of Costa Rica on this matter. The Costa Rican Government later announced the discovery and closure of the airfield.

Coordinating the Resupply Operation. The CIA Headquarters instructed its field stations to "cease and desist" with action which can be construed to be providing any type of support either direct or indirect to the various entities with whom we dealt under the program. The Chief of the CIA Central American Task Force added that in other respects the interagency process on Central America was in disarray in October 1984 and that "it was Ollie North who then moved into that void and was the focal point for the Administration on Central American policy until fall 1985."

As early as April 1985, LtCol North maintained detailed records of expenditures for Contra military equipment, supplies, and operations. On April 11, 1985, LtCol North sent a memorandum to Mr. McFarlane describing two sealifts and two airlifts "[a]s of April 9, 1985." The memorandum set out the kind of munition purchased, the quantity, and in some instances the cost. LtCol North also noted that from July 1984 to April 9, 1985: "$17,145,594 has been expended for arms, munitions, combat operations, and support activities."

Evidence suggests that at least by November 1985, LtCol North had assumed a direct operational role, coordinating logistical arrangements to ship privately purchased arms to the Contras. In a note to Poindexter on November 22, 1985, he described a prospective delivery as "our first direct flight (of ammo) to the resistance field [in] Nicaragua." This shipment was delayed when Mr. Secord was asked to use the aircraft instead to deliver the 18 HAWK missiles to Iran in November, 1985.

In 1986, North established a private secure communications network. North received 15 encryption devices from the National Security Agency from January to March 1986, provided in support of his counter-terrorist activities. One was provided to Mr. Secord and another, through a private citizen, to a CIA field officer posted in Central America. Through this mechanism, North coordinated the resupply of the Contras with military equipment apparently purchased with funds provided by the network of private benefactors. The messages to LtCol North from Mr. Secord and the CIA officer: (a) asked him to direct where and when to make Contra munitions drops; (b) informed him of arms requirements; and (c) apprised him of payments, balances, and deficits.

At least nine arms shipments were coordinated through this channel from March through June, 1986. The CIA field officer in Costa Rica outlined his involvement in the resupply network and described the shipments: "This was all lethal. Benefactors only sent lethal stuff." The CIA officer added that the private benefactor operation was, according to his understanding, controlled by LtCol North.

Mr. Secord was in charge of arranging the actual deliveries, using at least in part Southern Air Transport ("SAT"). Assistant Commissioner William Rosenblatt told the Board that LtCol North contacted him after a SAT C-123 aircraft crashed in Nicaragua, prompting a Customs investigation. North told him that the Customs investigation was focused on "good guys" who committed "no crimes." The Customs Service then narrowed the investigation to the specific aircraft involved in the crash rather than on the activities of the whole company. U.S. Customs Commissioner William von Rabb [Raab] said that LtCol North had previously contacted him to complain that Custom's agents were conducting an investigation involving a Maule aircraft. A former CIA officer in Central America said that at least one Maule aircraft was used in support of the Contra forces. Mr. Rosenblatt and Mr. von Raab told the Board that LtCol North never asked them to close out their investigations. The Board obtained evidence that at least one Maule aircraft was used in Contra military operations. This evidence was referred to the Independent Counsel.

Authorization. The evidence before the Board contained no record that LtCol North's role to support the Contras was formally authorized. It appears, however, that LtCol North did keep the National Security Advisor informed, first Mr. McFarlane and then VADM Poindexter. It is not clear to what extent other NSC principals or their departments were informed. On May 15, 1986, VADM Poindexter cautioned North: "From now on, I don't want you to talk to anybody else, including Casey, except me about any of your operational roles."

The President told the Board on January 26, 1987, that he did not know that the NSC staff was engaged in helping the Contras. The Board is aware of no evidence to suggest that the President was aware of LtCol North's activities.

Part IV. What Was Wrong

The arms transfers to Iran and the activities of the NSC staff in support of the Contras are case studies in the perils of policy pursued outside the constraints of orderly process.

The Iran initiative ran directly counter to the Administration's own policies on terrorism, the Iran/Iraq war, and military support to Iran. This inconsistency was never resolved, nor were the consequences of this inconsistency fully considered and provided for. The result taken as a whole was a U.S. policy that worked against itself.

The Board believes that failure to deal adequately with these contradictions resulted in large part from the flaws in the manner in which decisions were made. Established procedures for making national security decisions were ignored. Reviews of the initiative by all the NSC principals were too infrequent. The initiatives were not adequately vetted below the cabinet level. Intelligence resources were underutilized. Applicable legal constraints were not adequately addressed. The whole matter was handled too informally, without adequate written records of what had been considered, discussed, and decided.

This pattern persisted in the implementation of the Iran initiative. The NSC staff assumed direct operational control. The initiative fell within the traditional jurisdictions of the Departments of State, Defense, and CIA. Yet these agencies were largely ignored. Great reliance was placed on a network of private operators and intermediaries. How the initiative was to be carried out never received adequate attention from the NSC principals or a tough working-level review. No periodic evaluation of the progress of the initiative was ever conducted. The result was an unprofessional and, in substantial part, unsatisfactory operation.

In all of this process, Congress was never notified.

As noted in Part III, the record of the role of the NSC staff in support of the Contras is much less complete. Nonetheless, what is known suggests that many of the same problems plagued that effort as well.

The first section of this Part IV discusses the flaws in the process by which conflicting policies were considered, decisions were made, and the initiatives were implemented.

The second section discusses the responsibility of the NSC principals and other key national security officials for the manner in which these initiatives were handled.

The third section discusses the special problem posed by the role of the Israelis.

The fourth section of this Part IV outlines the Board's conclusions about the management of the initial public presentation of the facts of the Iran initiative.

A. A Flawed Process

1. Contradictory Policies Were Pursued.—The arms sales to Iran and the NSC support for the Contras demonstrate the risks involved when highly controversial initiatives are pursued covertly.

Arms Transfers to Iran.—The initiative to Iran was a covert operation directly at odds with important and well-publicized policies of the Executive Branch. But the initiative itself embodied a fundamental contradiction. Two objectives were apparent from the outset: a strategic opening to Iran, and release of the U.S. citizens held hostage in Lebanon. The sale of arms to Iran appeared to provide a means to achieve both these objectives. It also played into the hands of those who had other interests—some of them personal financial gain—in engaging the United States in an arms deal with Iran.

In fact, the sale of arms was not equally appropriate for achieving both these objectives. Arms were what Iran wanted. If all the United States sought was to free the hostages, then an arms-for-hostages deal could achieve the immediate objectives of both sides. But if the U.S. objective was a broader strategic relationship, then the sale of arms should have been contingent upon first putting into place the elements of that relationship. An arms-for-hostages deal in this context could become counter-productive to achieving this broader strategic objective. In addition, release of the hostages would require exerting influence with Hizballah, which could involve the most radical elements of the Iranian regime. The kind of strategic opening sought by the United States, however, involved what were regarded as more moderate elements.

The U.S. officials involved in the initiative appeared to have held three distinct views. For some, the principal motivation seemed consistently a strategic opening to Iran. For others, the strategic opening became a rationale for using arms sales to obtain the release of the hostages. For still others, the initiative appeared clearly as an arms-for-hostages deal from first to last.

Whatever the intent, almost from the beginning the initiative became in fact a series of arms-for-hostages deals. The shipment of arms in November, 1985, was directly tied to a hostage release. Indeed, the August/September transfer may have been nothing more than an arms-for-hostages trade. By July 14, 1985, a specific proposal for the sale of 100 TOWs to Iran in exchange for Iranian efforts to secure the release of all the hostages had been transmitted to the White House and discussed with the President. What actually occurred, at least so far as the September shipment was concerned, involved a direct link of arms and a hostage.

The initiative continued to be described in terms of its broader strategic relationship. But those elements never really materialized. While a high-level meeting among senior U.S. and Iranian officials continued to be a subject of discussion, it never occurred. Although Mr. McFarlane went to Tehran in May of 1986, the promised high-level Iranians never appeared. In discussions among U.S. officials, the focus seemed to be on the prospects for obtaining release of the hostages, not on a strategic relationship. Even if one accepts the explanation that arms and hostages represented only "bona fides" of seriousness of purpose for each side, that had clearly been established, one way or another, by the September exchange.

It is true that, strictly speaking, arms were not exchanged for the hostages. The arms were sold for cash; and to Iran, rather than the terrorists holding the hostages. Iran clearly wanted to buy the arms, however, and time and time again U.S. willingness to sell was directly conditioned upon the release of hostages. Although Iran might claim that it did not itself hold the hostages, the whole arrangement was premised on Iran's ability to secure their release.

While the United States was seeking the release of the hostages in this way, it was vigorously pursuing policies that were dramatically opposed to such efforts. The Reagan Administration in particular had come into office declaring a firm stand against terrorism, which it continued to maintain. In December of 1985, the Administration completed a major study under the chairmanship of the Vice President. It resulted in a vigorous reaffirmation of U.S. opposition to terrorism in all its forms and a vow of total war on terrorism whatever its source. The Administration continued to pressure U.S. allies not to sell arms to Iran and not to make concessions to terrorists.

No serious effort was made to reconcile the inconsistency between these policies and the Iran initiative. No effort was made systematically to address the consequences of this inconsistency—the effect on U.S. policy when, as it inevitably would, the Iran initiative became known.

The Board believes that a strategic opening to Iran may have been in the national interest but that the United States never should have been a party to the arms transfers. As arms-for-hostages trades, they could not help but create an incentive for further hostage-taking. As a violation of the U.S. arms embargo, they could only remove inhibitions on other nations from selling arms to Iran. This threatened to upset the military balance between Iran and Iraq, with consequent jeopardy to the Gulf States and the interests of the West in that region. The arms-for-hostages trades rewarded a regime that clearly supported terrorism and hostage-taking. They increased the risk that the United States would be perceived, especially in the Arab world, as a creature of Israel. They suggested to other U.S. allies and friends in the region that the United States had shifted its policy in favor of Iran. They raised questions as to whether U.S. policy statements could be relied upon.

As the arms-for-hostages proposal first came to the United States, it clearly was tempting. The sale of just 100 TOWs was to produce the release of all seven Americans held in Lebanon. Even had the offer been genuine, it would have been unsound. But it was not genuine. The 100 TOWs did not produce seven hostages. Very quickly the price went up, and the arrangements became protracted. A pattern of successive bargained exchanges of arms and hostages was quickly established. While release of all the hostages continued to be promised, in fact the hostages came out singly if at all. This sad history is powerful evidence of why the United States should never have become involved in the arms transfers.

NSC Staff Support for the Contras.—The activities of the NSC staff in support of the Contras sought to achieve an important objective of the Administration's foreign policy. The President had publicly and emphatically declared his support for the Nicaragua resistance. That brought his policy in direct conflict with that of the Congress, at least during the period that direct or indirect support of military operations in Nicaragua was barred.

Although the evidence before the Board is limited, no serious effort appears to have been made to come to grips with the risks to the President of direct NSC support for the Contras in the face of these Congressional restrictions. Even if it could be argued that these restrictions did not technically apply to the NSC staff, these activities presented great political risk to the President. The appearance of the President's personal staff doing what Congress had forbade other agencies to do could, once disclosed, only touch off a firestorm in the Congress and threaten the Administration's whole policy on the Contras.

2. The Decision-making Process Was Flawed.—Because the arms sales to Iran and the NSC support for the Contras occurred in settings of such controversy, one would expect that the decisions to undertake these activities would have been made only after intense and thorough consideration. In fact, a far different picture emerges.

Arms Transfers to Iran.—The Iran initiative was handled almost casually and through informal channels, always apparently with an expectation that the process would end with the next arms-for-hostages exchange. It was subjected neither to the general procedures for interagency consideration and review of policy issues nor the more restrictive procedures set out in NSDD 159 for handling covert operations. This had a number of consequences.

(i) The Opportunity for a Full Hearing before the President Was Inadequate.—In the last half of 1985, the Israelis made three separate proposals to the United States with respect to the Iran initiative (two in July and one in August). In addition, Israel made three separate deliveries of arms to Iran, one each in August, September, and November. Yet prior to December 7, 1985, there was at most one meeting of the NSC principals, a meeting which several participants recall taking place on August 6. There is no dispute that full meetings of the principals did occur on December 7, 1985, and on January 7, 1986. But the proposal to shift to direct U.S. arms sales to Iran appears not to have been discussed until later. It was considered by the President at a meeting on January 17 which only the Vice President, Mr. Regan, Mr. Fortier, and VADM Poindexter attended. Thereafter, the only senior-level review the Iran initiative received was during one or another of the President's daily national security briefings. These were routinely attended only by the President, the Vice President, Mr. Regan, and VADM Poindexter. There was no subsequent collective consideration of the Iran initiative by the NSC principals before it became public 11 months later.

This was not sufficient for a matter as important and consequential as the Iran initiative. Two or three cabinet-level reviews in a period of 17 months was not enough. The meeting on December 7 came late in the day, after the pattern of arms-for-hostages exchanges had become well established. The January 7 meeting had earmarks of a meeting held after a decision had already been made. Indeed, a draft Covert Action Finding authorizing the initiative had been signed by the President, though perhaps inadvertently, the previous day.

At each significant step in the Iran initiative, deliberations among the NSC principals in the presence of the President should have been virtually automatic. This was not and should not have been a formal requirement, something prescribed by statute. Rather, it should have been something the NSC principals desired as a means of ensuring an optimal environment for Presidential judgment. The meetings should have been preceded by consideration by the NSC principals of staff papers prepared according to the procedures applicable to covert actions. These should have reviewed the history of the initiative, analyzed the issues then presented, developed a range of realistic options, presented the odds of success and the costs of failure, and addressed questions of implementation and execution. Had this been done, the objectives of the Iran initiative might have been clarified and alternatives to the sale of arms might have been identified.

(ii) The Initiative Was Never Subjected to a Rigorous Review below the Cabinet Level.—Because of the obsession with secrecy, interagency consideration of the initiative was limited to the cabinet level. With the exception of the NSC staff and, after January 17, 1986, a handful of CIA officials, the rest of the executive departments and agencies were largely excluded.

As a consequence, the initiative was never vetted at the staff level. This deprived those responsible for the initiative of considerable expertise—on the situation in Iran; on the difficulties of dealing with terrorists; on the mechanics of conducting a diplomatic opening. It also kept the plan from receiving a tough, critical review.

Moreover, the initiative did not receive a policy review below cabinet level. Careful consideration at the Deputy/Under Secretary level might have exposed the confusion in U.S. objectives and clarified the risks of using arms as an instrument of policy in this instance.

The vetting process would also have ensured better use of U.S. intelligence. As it was, the intelligence input into the decision process was clearly inadequate. First, no independent evaluation of the Israeli proposals offered in July and August appears to have been sought or offered by U.S. intelligence agencies. The Israelis represented that they for some time had had contacts with elements in Iran. The prospects for an opening to Iran depended

heavily on these contacts, yet no systematic assessment appears to have been made by U.S. intelligence agencies of the reliability and motivations of these contacts, and the identity and objectives of the elements in Iran that the opening was supposed to reach. Neither was any systematic assessment made of the motivation of the Israelis.

Second, neither Mr. Ghorbanifar nor the second channel seem to have been subjected to a systematic intelligence vetting before they were engaged as intermediaries. Mr. Ghorbanifar had been known to the CIA for some time and the agency had substantial doubts as to his reliability and truthfulness. Yet the agency did not volunteer that information or inquire about the identity of the intermediary if his name was unknown. Conversely, no early request for a name check was made of the CIA, and it was not until January 11, 1986, that the agency gave Mr. Ghorbanifar a new polygraph, which he failed. Notwithstanding this situation, with the signing of the January 17 Finding, the United States took control of the initiative and became even more directly involved with Mr. Ghorbanifar. The issues raised by the polygraph results do not appear to have been systematically addressed. In similar fashion, no prior intelligence check appears to have been made on the second channel.

Third, although the President recalled being assured that the arms sales to Iran would not alter the military balance with Iran, the Board could find no evidence that the President was ever briefed on this subject. The question of the impact of any intelligence shared with the Iranians does not appear to have been brought to the President's attention.

A thorough vetting would have included consideration of the legal implications of the initiative. There appeared little effort to face squarely the legal restrictions and notification requirements applicable to the operation. At several points, other agencies raised questions about violations of law or regulations. These concerns were dismissed without, it appears, investigating them with the benefit of legal counsel.

Finally, insufficient attention was given to the implications of implementation. The implementation of the initiative raised a number of issues: should the NSC staff rather than the CIA have had operational control; what were the implications of Israeli involvement; how reliable were the Iranian and various other private intermediaries; what were the implications of the use of Mr. Secord's private network of operatives; what were the implications for the military balance in the region; was operational security adequate. Nowhere do these issues appear to have been sufficiently addressed.

The concern for preserving the secrecy of the initiative provided an excuse for abandoning sound process. Yet the initiative was known to a variety of persons with diverse interests and ambitions—Israelis, Iranians, various arms dealers and business intermediaries, and LtCol North's network of private operatives. While concern for secrecy would have justified limiting the circle of persons knowledgeable about the initiative, in this case it was drawn too tightly. As a consequence, important advice and counsel were lost.

In January of 1985, the President had adopted procedures for striking the proper balance between secrecy and the need for consultation on sensitive programs. These covered the institution, implementation, and review of covert operations. In the case of the Iran initiative, these procedures were almost totally ignored.

The only staff work the President apparently reviewed in connection with the Iran initiative was prepared by NSC staff members, under the direction of the National Security Advisor. These were, of course, the principal proponents of the initiative. A portion of this staff work was reviewed by the Board. It was frequently striking in its failure to present the record of past efforts—particularly past failures. Alternative ways of achieving U.S. objectives—other than yet another arms-for-hostages deal—were not discussed. Frequently it neither adequately presented the risks involved in pursuing the initiative nor the full force of the dissenting views of other NSC principals. On balance, it did not serve the President well.

(iii) The Process Was Too Informal.—The whole decision process was too informal. Even when meetings among NSC princi-

pals did occur, often there was no prior notice of the agenda. No formal written minutes seem to have been kept. Decisions subsequently taken by the President were not formally recorded. An exception was the January 17 Finding, but even this was apparently not circulated or shown to key U.S. officials.

The effect of this informality was that the initiative lacked a formal institutional record. This precluded the participants from undertaking the more informed analysis and reflection that is afforded by a written record, as opposed to mere recollection. It made it difficult to determine where the initiative stood, and to learn lessons from the record that could guide future action. This lack of an institutional record permitted specific proposals for arms-for-hostages exchanges to be presented in a vacuum, without reference to the results of past proposals. Had a searching and thorough review of the Iran initiative been undertaken at any stage in the process, it would have been extremely difficult to conduct. The Board can attest first hand to the problem of conducting a review in the absence of such records. Indeed, the exposition in the wake of public revelation suffered the most.

NSC Staff Support for the Contras.—It is not clear how LtCol North first became involved in activities in direct support of the Contras during the period of the Congressional ban. The Board did not have before it much evidence on this point. In the evidence that the Board did have, there is no suggestion at any point of any discussion of LtCol North's activities with the President in any forum. There also does not appear to have been any interagency review of LtCol North's activities at any level.

This latter point is not surprising given the Congressional restrictions under which the other relevant agencies were operating. But the NSC staff apparently did not compensate for the lack of any interagency review with its own internal vetting of these activities. LtCol North apparently worked largely in isolation, keeping first Mr. McFarlane and then VADM Poindexter informed.

The lack of adequate vetting is particularly evident on the question of the legality of LtCol North's activities. The Board did not make a judgment on the legal issues raised by his activities in support of the Contras. Nevertheless, some things can be said.

If these activities were illegal, obviously they should not have been conducted. If there was any doubt on the matter, systematic legal advice should have been obtained. The political cost to the President of illegal action by the NSC staff was particularly high, both because the NSC staff is the personal staff of the President and because of the history of serious conflict with the Congress over the issue of Contra support. For these reasons, the President should have been kept apprised of any review of the legality of LtCol North's activities.

Legal advice was apparently obtained from the President's Intelligence Oversight Board. Without passing on the quality of that advice, it is an odd source. It would be one thing for the Intelligence Oversight Board to review the legal advice provided by some other agency. It is another for the Intelligence Oversight Board to be originating legal advice of its own. That is a function more appropriate for the NSC staff's own legal counsel.[1]

3. Implementation Was Unprofessional.—The manner in which the Iran initiative was implemented and LtCol North undertook to support the Contras are very similar. This is in large part because the same cast of characters was involved. In both cases the operations were unprofessional, although the Board has much less evidence with respect to LtCol North's Contra activities.

Arms Transfers to Iran.—With the signing of the January 17 Finding, the Iran initiative became a U.S. operation run by the NSC staff. LtCol North made most of the significant operational decisions. He conducted the operation through Mr. Secord and his associates, a network of private individuals already involved in the Contra resupply operation. To this was added a handful of selected individuals from the CIA.

But the CIA support was limited. Two CIA officials, though often at meetings, had a relatively limited role. One served as the point man for LtCol North in providing logistics and financial arrangements. The other (Mr. Allen) served as a contact between LtCol North and the intelligence community. By contrast, George Cave actually played a significant and expanding role. However,

Clair George, Deputy Director for Operations at CIA, told the Board: "George was paid by me and on the paper was working for me. But I think in the heat of the battle, * * * George was working for Oliver North."

Because so few people from the departments and agencies were told of the initiative, LtCol North cut himself off from resources and expertise from within the government. He relied instead on a number of private intermediaries, businessmen and other financial brokers, private operators, and Iranians hostile to the United States. Some of these were individuals with questionable credentials and potentially large personal financial interests in the transactions. This made the transactions unnecessarily complicated and invited kick-backs and payoffs. This arrangement also dramatically increased the risks that the initiative would leak. Yet no provision was made for such an eventuality. Further, the use of Mr. Secord's private network in the Iran initiative linked those operators with the resupply of the Contras, threatening exposure of both operations if either became public.

The result was a very unprofessional operation.

Mr. Secord undertook in November, 1985, to arrange landing clearance for the Israeli flight bringing the HAWK missiles into a third-country staging area. The arrangements fell apart. A CIA field officer attributed this failure to the amateurish way in which Mr. Secord and his associates approached officials in the government from which landing clearance was needed. If Mr. Ghorbanifar is to be believed, the mission of Mr. McFarlane to Tehran was undertaken without any advance work, and with distinctly different expectations on the part of the two sides. This could have contributed to its failure.

But there were much more serious errors. Without adequate study and consideration, intelligence was passed to the Iranians of potentially major significance to the Iran/Iraq war. At the meeting with the second channel on October 5-7, 1986, LtCol North misrepresented his access to the President. He told Mr. Ghorbanifar stories of conversations with the President which were wholly fanciful. He suggested without authority a shift in U.S. policy adverse to Iraq in general and Saddam Husain in particular. Finally, in the nine-point agenda discussed on October 26-28, he committed the United States, without authorization, to a position contrary to well established U.S. policy on the prisoners held by Kuwait.

The conduct of the negotiators with Mr. Ghorbanifar and the second channel were handled in a way that revealed obvious inexperience. The discussions were too casual for dealings with intermediaries to a regime so hostile to U.S. interests. The U.S. hand was repeatedly tipped and unskillfully played. The arrangements failed to guarantee that the U.S. obtained its hostages in exchange for the arms. Repeatedly, LtCol North permitted arms to be delivered without the release of a single captive.

The implementation of the initiative was never subjected to a rigorous review. LtCol North appears to have kept VADM Poindexter fully informed of his activities. In addition, VADM Poindexter, LtCol North, and the CIA officials involved apparently apprised Director Casey of many of the operational details. But LtCol North and his operation functioned largely outside the orbit of the U.S. Government. Their activities were not subject to critical reviews of any kind.

After the initial hostage release in September, 1985, it was over 10 months before another hostage was released. This despite recurring promises of the release of all the hostages and four intervening arms shipments. Beginning with the November shipment, the United States increasingly took over the operation of the initiative. In January, 1986, it decided to transfer arms directly to Iran.

Any of these developments could have served as a useful occasion for a systematic reconsideration of the initiative. Indeed, at least one of the schemes contained a provision for reconsideration if the initial assumptions proved to be invalid. They did, but the reconsideration never took place. It was the responsibility of the National Security Advisor and the responsible officers on the NSC staff to call for a review. But they were too involved in the initiative both as advocates and as implementors. This made it less likely that they would initiate the kind of review and reconsideration that should have been undertaken.

NSC Staff Support for the Contras.—As already noted, the NSC activities in support of the Contras and its role in the Iran initiative were of a piece. In the former, there was an added element of LtCol North's intervention in the customs investigation of the crash of the SAT aircraft. Here, too, selected CIA officials reported directly to LtCol North. The limited evidence before the Board suggested that the activities in support of the Contras involved unprofessionalism much like that in the Iran operation.

iv. Congress Was Never Notified.—Congress was not apprised either of the Iran initiative or of the NSC staff's activities in support of the Contras.

In the case of Iran, because release of the hostages was expected within a short time after the delivery of equipment, and because public disclosure could have destroyed the operation and perhaps endangered the hostages, it could be argued that it was justifiable to defer notification of Congress prior to the first shipment of arms to Iran. The plan apparently was to inform Congress immediately after the hostages were safely in U.S. hands. But after the first delivery failed to release all the hostages, and as one hostage release plan was replaced by another, Congress certainly should have been informed. This could have been done during a period when no specific hostage release plan was in execution. Consultation with Congress could have been useful to the President, for it might have given him some sense of how the public would react to the initiative. It also might have influenced his decision to continue to pursue it.

v. Legal Issues.—In addition to conflicting with several fundamental U.S. policies, selling arms to Iran raised far-reaching legal questions. How it dealt with these is important to an evaluation of the Iran initiative.

Arms Transfers to Iran.—It was not part of the Board's mandate to consider issues of law as they may pertain to individuals or detailed aspects of the Iran initiative. Instead, the Board focused on the legal basis for the arms transfers to Iran and how issues of law were addressed in the NSC process.

The Arms Export Control Act, the principal U.S. statute governing arms sales abroad, makes it unlawful to export arms without a license. Exports of arms by U.S. government agencies, however, do not require a license if they are otherwise authorized by law. Criminal penalties—fines and imprisonment—are provided for willful violations.

The initial arms transfers in the Iran initiative involved the sale and shipment by Israel of U.S.-origin missiles. The usual way for such international retransfer of arms to be authorized under U.S. law is pursuant to the Arms Export Control Act. This Act requires that the President consent to any transfers by another country of arms exported under the Act and imposes three conditions before such Presidential consent may be given:

(a) the United States would itself transfer the arms in question to the recipient country;
(b) a commitment in writing has been obtained from the recipient country against unauthorized retransfer of significant arms, such as missiles; and
(c) a prior written certification regarding the retransfer is submitted to the Congress if the defense equipment, such as missiles, has an acquisition cost of 14 million dollars or more. 22 U.S.C. 2753 (a), (d).

In addition, the Act generally imposes restrictions on which countries are eligible to receive U.S. arms and on the purposes for which arms may be sold.[2]

The other possible avenue whereby government arms transfers to Iran may be authorized by law would be in connection with intelligence operations conducted under the National Security Act. This Act requires that the Director of Central Intelligence and the heads of other intelligence agencies keep the two Congressional intelligence committees "fully and currently informed" of all intelligence activities under their responsibility. 50 U.S.C. 413. Where prior notice of significant intelligence activities is not given, the intelligence committees are to be informed "in a timely fashion." In addition, the so called Hughes-Ryan Amendment to the Foreign Assistance Act requires that "significant anticipated intelligence activities" may not be conducted by the CIA unless and until the President finds that "each such operation is important to the national security of the United States." 22 U.S.C. 2422.

When the Israelis began transferring arms to Iran in August, 1985, they were not acting on their own. U.S. officials had knowledge about the essential elements of the proposed shipments. The United States shared some common purpose in the transfers and received a benefit from them—the release of a hostage. More importantly, Mr. McFarlane communicated prior U.S. approval to the Israelis for the shipments, including an undertaking for replenishment. But for this U.S. approval, the transactions may not have gone forward. In short, the United States was an essential participant in the arms transfers to Iran that occurred in 1985.

Whether this U.S. involvement in the arms transfers by the Israelis was lawful depends fundamentally upon whether the President approved the transactions before they occurred. In the absence of Presidential approval, there does not appear to be any authority in this case for the United States to engage in the transfer of arms or consent to the transfer by another country. The arms transfers to Iran in 1985 and hence the Iran initiative itself would have proceeded contrary to U.S. law.

The Attorney General reached a similar judgment with respect to the activities of the CIA in facilitating the November, 1985 shipment by the Israelis of HAWK missiles. In a letter to the Board,[3] the Attorney General concluded that with respect to the CIA assistance, "a finding under the Hughes-Ryan Amendment would be required."[4]

The Board was unable to reach a conclusive judgment about whether the 1985 shipments of arms to Iran were approved in advance by the President. On balance the Board believes that it is plausible to conclude that he did approve them in advance.

Yet even if the President in some sense consented to or approved the transactions, a serious question of law remains. It is not clear that the form of the approval was sufficient for purposes of either the Arms Export Control Act or the Hughes-Ryan Amendment. The consent did not meet the conditions of the Arms Export Control Act, especially in the absence of a prior written commitment from the Iranians regarding unauthorized retransfer.

Under the National Security Act, it is not clear that mere oral approval by the President would qualify as a Presidential finding that the initiative was vital to the national security interests of the United States. The approval was never reduced to writing. It appears to have been conveyed to only one person. The President himself has no memory of it. And there is contradictory evidence from the President's advisors about how the President responded when he learned of the arms shipments which the approval was to support. In addition, the requirement for Congressional notification was ignored. In these circumstances, even if the President approved of the transactions, it is difficult to conclude that his actions constituted adequate legal authority.

The legal requirements pertaining to the sale of arms to Iran are complex; the availability of legal authority, including that which may flow from the President's constitutional powers, is difficult to delineate. Definitive legal conclusions will also depend upon a variety of specific factual determinations that the Board has not attempted to resolve—for example, the specific content of any consent provided by the President, the authority under which the missiles were originally transferred to Israel, the knowledge and intentions of individuals, and the like. Nevertheless, it was sufficient for the Board's purposes to conclude that the legal underpinning of the Iran initiative during 1985 was at best highly questionable.

The Presidential Finding of January 17, 1986, formally approved the Iran initiative as a covert intelligence operation under the National Security Act. This ended the uncertainty about the legal status of the initiative and provided legal authority for the United States to transfer arms directly to Iran.

The National Security Act also requires notification of Congress of covert intelligence activities. If not done in advance, notification must be "in a timely fashion." The Presidential finding of January 17 directed that Congressional notification be withheld, and this decision appears to have never been reconsidered.

While there was surely justification to suspend Congressional notification in advance of a particular transaction relating to a hostage release, the law would seem to require disclosure where, as in the Iran case, a pattern of relative inactivity occurs over an extended period. To do otherwise prevents the Congress from fulfilling its proper oversight responsibilities.

Throughout the Iran initiative, significant questions of law do not appear to have been adequately addressed. In the face of a sweeping statutory prohibition and explicit requirements relating to Presidential consent to arms transfers by third countries, there appears to have been at the outset in 1985 little attention, let alone systematic analysis, devoted to how Presidential actions would comply with U.S. law. The Board has found no evidence that an evaluation was ever done during the life of the operation to determine whether it continued to comply with the terms of the January 17 Presidential Finding. Similarly, when a new prohibition was added to the Arms Export Control Act in August of 1986 to prohibit exports to countries on the terrorism list (a list which contained Iran), no evaluation was made to determine whether this law affected authority to transfer arms to Iran in connection with intelligence operations under the National Security Act. This lack of legal vigilance markedly increased the chances that the initiative would proceed contrary to law.

NSC Staff Support for the Contras. The NSC staff activities in support of the Contras were marked by the same uncertainty as to legal authority and insensitivity to legal issues as were present in the Iran initiative. The ambiguity of the law governing activities in support of the Contras presented a greater challenge than even the considerable complexity of laws governing arms transfers. Intense Congressional scrutiny with respect to the NSC staff activities relating to the Contras added to the potential costs of actions that pushed the limits of the law.

In this context, the NSC staff should have been particularly cautious, avoiding operational activity in this area and seeking legal counsel. The Board saw no signs of such restraint.

B. Failure of Responsibility

The NSC system will not work unless the President makes it work. After all, this system was created to serve the President of the United States in ways of his choosing. By his actions, by his leadership, the President therefore determines the quality of its performance.

By his own account, as evidenced in his diary notes, and as conveyed to the Board by his principal advisors, President Reagan was deeply committed to securing the release of the hostages. It was this intense compassion for the hostages that appeared to motivate his steadfast support of the Iran initiative, even in the face of opposition from his Secretaries of State and Defense.

In his obvious commitment, the President appears to have proceeded with a concept of the initiative that was not accurately reflected in the reality of the operation. The President did not seem to be aware of the way in which the operation was implemented and the full consequences of U.S. participation.

The President's expressed concern for the safety of both the hostages and the Iranians who could have been at risk may have been conveyed in a manner so as to inhibit the full functioning of the system.

The President's management style is to put the principal responsibility for policy review and implementation on the shoulders of his advisors. Nevertheless, with such a complex, high-risk operation and so much at stake, the President should have ensured that the NSC system did not fail him. He did not force his policy to undergo the most critical review of which the NSC participants and the process were capable. At no time did he insist upon accountability and performance review. Had the President chosen to drive the NSC system, the outcome could well have been different. As it was, the most powerful features of the NSC system—providing comprehensive analysis, alternatives and follow-up—were not utilized.

The Board found a strong consensus among NSC participants that the President's priority in the Iran initiative was the release of U.S. hostages. But setting priorities is not enough when it comes to

sensitive and risky initiatives that directly affect U.S. national security. He must ensure that the content and tactics of an initiative match his priorities and objectives. He must insist upon accountability. For it is the President who must take responsibility for the NSC system and deal with the consequences.

Beyond the President, the other NSC principals and the National Security Advisor must share in the responsibility for the NSC system.

President Reagan's personal management style places an especially heavy responsibility on his key advisors. Knowing his style, they should have been particularly mindful of the need for special attention to the manner in which this arms sale initiative developed and proceeded. On this score, neither the National Security Advisor nor the other NSC principals deserve high marks.

It is their obligation as members and advisors to the Council to ensure that the President is adequately served. The principal subordinates to the President must not be deterred from urging the President not to proceed on a highly questionable course of action even in the face of his strong conviction to the contrary.

In the case of the Iran initiative, the NSC process did not fail, it simply was largely ignored. The National Security Advisor and the NSC principals all had a duty to raise this issue and insist that orderly process he imposed. None of them did so.

All had the opportunity. While the National Security Advisor had the responsibility to see that an orderly process was observed, his failure to do so does not excuse the other NSC principals. It does not appear that any of the NSC principals called for more frequent consideration of the Iran initiative by the NSC principals in the presence of the President. None of the principals called for a serious vetting of the initiative by even a restricted group of disinterested individuals. The intelligence questions do not appear to have been raised, and legal considerations, while raised, were not pressed. No one seemed to have complained about the informality of the process. No one called for a thorough reexamination once the initiative did not meet expectations or the manner of execution changed. While one or another of the NSC principals suspected that something was amiss, none vigorously pursued the issue.

Mr. Regan also shares in this responsibility. More than almost any Chief of Staff of recent memory, he asserted personal control over the White House staff and sought to extend this control to the National Security Advisor. He was personally active in national security affairs and attended almost all of the relevant meetings regarding the Iran initiative. He, as much as anyone, should have insisted that an orderly process be observed. In addition, he especially should have ensured that plans were made for handling any public disclosure of the initiative. He must bear primary responsibility for the chaos that descended upon the White House when such disclosure did occur.

Mr. McFarlane appeared caught between a President who supported the initiative and the cabinet officers who strongly opposed it. While he made efforts to keep these cabinet officers informed, the Board heard complaints from some that he was not always successful. VADM Poindexter on several occasions apparently sought to exclude NSC principals other than the President from knowledge of the initiative. Indeed, on one or more occasions Secretary Shultz may have been actively misled by VADM Poindexter.

VADM Poindexter also failed grievously on the matter of Contra diversion. Evidence indicates that VADM Poindexter knew that a diversion occurred, yet he did not take the steps that were required given the gravity of that prospect. He apparently failed to appreciate or ignored the serious legal and political risks presented. His clear obligation was either to investigate the matter or take it to the President—or both. He did neither. Director Casey shared a similar responsibility. Evidence suggests that he received information about the possible diversion of funds to the Contras almost a month before the story broke. He, too, did not move promptly to raise the matter with the President. Yet his responsibility to do so was clear.

The NSC principals other than the President may be somewhat excused by the insufficient attention on the part of the National Security Advisor to the need to keep all the principals fully informed. Given the importance of the issue and the sharp policy divergences involved, however, Secretary Shultz and Secretary Weinberger in particular distanced themselves from the march of events. Secretary Shultz specifically requested to be informed only as necessary to perform his job. Secretary Weinberger had access through intelligence to details about the operation. Their obligation was to give the President their full support and continued advice with respect to the program or, if they could not in conscience do that, to so inform the President. Instead, they simply distanced themselves from the program. They protected the record as to their own positions on this issue. They were not energetic in attempting to protect the President from the consequences of his personal commitment to freeing the hostages.

Director Casey appears to have been informed in considerable detail about the specifics of the Iranian operation. He appears to have acquiesced in and to have encouraged North's exercise of direct operational control over the operation. Because of the NSC staff's proximity to and close identification with the President, this increased the risks to the President if the initiative became public or the operation failed.

There is no evidence, however, that Director Casey explained this risk to the President or made clear to the President that LtCol North, rather than the CIA, was running the operation. The President does not recall ever being informed of this fact. Indeed, Director Casey should have gone further and pressed for operational responsibility to be transferred to the CIA.

Director Casey should have taken the lead in vetting the assumptions presented by the Israelis on which the program was based and in pressing for an early examination of the reliance upon Mr. Ghorbanifar and the second channel as intermediaries. He should also have assumed responsibility for checking out the other intermediaries involved in the operation. Finally, because Congressional restrictions on covert actions are both largely directed at and familiar to the CIA, Director Casey should have taken the lead in keeping the question of Congressional notification active.

Finally, Director Casey, and, to a lesser extent, Secretary Weinberger, should have taken it upon themselves to assess the effect of the transfer of arms and intelligence to Iran on the Iran/Iraq military balance, and to transmit that information to the President.

C. The Role of the Israelis

Conversations with emissaries from the Government of Israel took place prior to the commencement of the initiative. It remains unclear whether the initial proposal to open the Ghorbanifar channel was an Israeli initiative, was brought on by the avarice of arms dealers, or came as a result of an American request for assistance. There is no doubt, however, that it was Israel that pressed Mr. Ghorbanifar on the United States. U.S. officials accepted Israeli assurances that they had had for some time an extensive dialogue that involved high-level Iranians, as well as their assurances of Mr. Ghorbanifar's bona fides. Thereafter, at critical points in the initiative, when doubts were expressed by critical U.S. participants, an Israeli emissary would arrive with encouragement, often a specific proposal, and pressure to stay with the Ghorbanifar channel.

From the record available to the Board, it is not possible to determine the role of key U.S. participants in prompting these Israeli interventions. There were active and ongoing consultations between LtCol North and officials of the Israeli government, specifically David Kimche and Amiram Nir. In addition, Mr. Schwimmer, Mr. Nimrodi, and Mr. Ledeen, also in frequent contact with LtCol North, had close ties with the government of Israel. It may be that the Israeli interventions were actively solicited by particular U.S. officials. Without the benefit of the views of the Israeli officials involved, it is hard to know the facts.

It is clear, however, that Israel had its own interests, some in direct conflict with those of the United States, in having the United States pursue the initiative. For this reason, it had an incentive to keep the initiative alive. It sought to do this by interventions with the NSC staff, the National Security Advisor, and the President. Although it may have received suggestions from LtCol North, Mr. Ledeen, and others, it responded affirmatively to these suggestions by reason of its own interests.

Even if the Government of Israel actively worked to begin the initiative and to keep it going, the U.S. Government is responsible for its own decisions. Key participants in U.S. deliberations made the point that Israel's objectives and interests in this initiative were different from, and in some respects in conflict with, those of the United States. Although Israel dealt with those portions of the U.S. Government that it deemed were sympathetic to the initiative, there is nothing improper *per se* about this fact. U.S. decision-makers made their own decisions and must bear responsibility for the consequences.

D. Aftermath—The Efforts To Tell the Story

From the first hint in late-October, 1986 that the McFarlane trip would soon become public, information on the Iran initiative and Contra activity cascaded into the press. The veiled hints of secret activities, random and indiscriminate disclosures of information from a variety of sources, both knowledgeable and otherwise, and conflicting statements by high-level officials presented a confusing picture to the American public. The Board recognized that conflicts among contemporaneous documents and statements raised concern about the management of the public presentation of facts on the Iran initiative. Though the board reviewed some evidence[5] on events after the exposure, our ability to comment on these events remains limited.

The Board found evidence that immediately following the public disclosure, the President wanted to avoid providing too much specificity or detail out of concern for the hostages still held in Lebanon and those Iranians who had supported the initiative. In doing so, he did not, we believe, intend to mislead the American public or cover-up unlawful conduct. By at least November 20, the President took steps to ensure that all the facts would come out. From the President's request to Mr. Meese to look into the history of the initiative, to his appointment of this Board, to his request for an Independent Counsel, to his willingness to discuss this matter fully and to review his personal notes with us, the Board is convinced that the President does indeed want the full story to be told.

Those who prepared the President's supporting documentation did not appear, at least initially, to share in the President's ultimate wishes. Mr. McFarlane described for the Board the process used by the NSC staff to create a chronology that obscured essential facts. Mr. McFarlane contributed to the creation of this chronology which did not, he said, present "a full and completely accurate account" of the events and left ambiguous the President's role. This was, according to Mr. McFarlane, done to distance the President from the timing and nature of the President's authorization. He told the Board that he wrote a memorandum on November 18, which tried to, in his own words, "gild the President's motives." This version was incorporated into the chronology. Mr. McFarlane told the Board that he knew the account was "misleading, at least, and wrong, at worst." Mr. McFarlane told the Board that he did provide the Attorney General an accurate account of the President's role.

The Board found considerable reason to question the actions of LtCol North in the aftermath of the disclosure. The Board has no evidence to either confirm or refute that LtCol North destroyed documents on the initiative in an effort to conceal facts from threatened investigations. The Board found indications that LtCol North was involved in an effort, over time, to conceal or withhold important information. The files of LtCol North contained much of the historical documentation that the Board used to construct its narrative. Moreover, LtCol North was the primary U.S. government official involved in the details of the operation. The chronology he produced has many inaccuracies. These "histories" were to be the basis of the "full" story of the Iran initiative. These inaccuracies lend some evidence to the proposition that LtCol North, either on his own or at the behest of others, actively sought to conceal important information.

Out of concern for the protection of classified material, Director Casey and VADM Poindexter were to brief only the Congressional intelligence committees on the "full" story; the DCI before the Committees and VADM Poindexter in private sessions with the chairmen and vice-chairmen. The DCI and VADM Poindexter undertook to do this on November 21, 1986. It appears from the copy of the DCI's testimony and notes of VADM Poindexter's meetings, that they did not fully relate the nature of events as they had occurred. The result is an understandable perception that they were not forthcoming.

The Board is also concerned about various notes that appear to be missing. VADM Poindexter was the official note taker in some key meetings, yet no notes for the meetings can be found. The reason for the lack of such notes remains unknown to the Board. If they were written, they may contain very important information. We have no way of knowing if they exist.

Part V. Recommendations

*"Not only * * * is the Federal power over external affairs in origin and essential character different from that over internal affairs, but participation in the exercise of the power is significantly limited. In this vast external realm, with its important, complicated, delicate and manifold problems, the President alone has the power to speak or listen as a representative of the nation."* United States v. Curtiss-Wright Export Corp., 299 U.S. 304, 319 (1936).

Whereas the ultimate power to formulate domestic policy resides in the Congress, the primary responsibility for the formulation and implementation of national security policy falls on the President.

It is the President who is the usual source of innovation and responsiveness in this field. The departments and agencies—the Defense Department, State Department, and CIA bureaucracies—tend to resist policy change. Each has its own perspective based on long experience. The challenge for the President is to bring his perspective to bear on these bureaucracies for they are his instruments for executing national security policy, and he must work through them. His task is to provide them leadership and direction.

The National Security Act of 1947 and the system that has grown up under it affords the President special tools for carrying out this important role. These tools are the National Security Council, the National Security Advisor, and the NSC Staff. These are the means through which the creative impulses of the President are brought to bear on the permanent government. The National Security Act, and custom and practice, rightly give the President wide latitude in fashioning exactly how these means are used.

There is no magic formula which can be applied to the NSC structure and process to produce an optimal system. Because the system is the vehicle through which the President formulates and implements his national security policy, it must adapt to each individual President's style and management philosophy. This means that NSC structures and processes must be flexible, not rigid. Overprescription would, as discussed in Part II, either destroy the system or render it ineffective.

Nevertheless, this does not mean there can be no guidelines or recommendations that might improve the operation of the system, whatever the particular style of the incumbent President. We have reviewed the operation of the system over the past 40 years, through good times and bad. We have listened carefully to the views of all the living former Presidents as well as those of most of the participants in their own national security systems. With the strong caveat that flexibility and adaptability must be at the core, it is our judgment that the national security system seems to have worked best when it has in general operated along the lines set forth below.

Organizing for National Security. Because of the wide latitude in the National Security Act, the President bears a special responsibility for the effective performance of the NSC system. A President must at the outset provide guidelines to the members of the National Security Council, his National Security Advisor, and the National Security Council staff. These guidelines, to be effective, must include how they will relate to one another, what procedures will be followed, what the President expects of them. If his advisors are not performing as he likes, only the President can intervene.

The National Security Council principals other than the President participate on the Council in a unique capacity.[1] Although holding a seat by virtue of their official positions in the Administration, when they sit as members of the Council they sit not as cabinet secretaries or department heads but as advisors to the President. They are there not simply to advance or defend the particular positions of the departments or agencies they head but to give their best advice to the President. Their job—and their challenge—is to see the issue from this perspective, not from the narrower interests of their respective bureaucracies.

The National Security Council is only advisory. It is the President alone who decides. When the NSC principals receive those decisions, they do so as heads of the appropriate departments or agencies. They are then responsible to see that the President's decisions are carried out by those organizations accurately and effectively.

This is an important point. The policy innovation and creativity of the President encounters a natural resistance from the executing departments. While this resistance is a source of frustration to every President, it is inherent in the design of the government. It is up to the politically appointed agency heads to ensure that the President's goals, designs, and policies are brought to bear on this permanent structure. Circumventing the departments, perhaps by using the National Security Advisor or the NSC Staff to execute policy, robs the President of the experience and capacity resident in the departments. The President must act largely through them, but the agency heads must ensure that they execute the President's policies in an expeditious and effective manner. It is not just the obligation of the National Security Advisor to see that the national security process is used. All of the NSC principals—and particularly the President—have that obligation.

This tension between the President and the Executive Departments is worked out through the national security process described in the opening sections of this report. It is through this process that the nation obtains both the best of the creativity of the President and the learning and expertise of the national security departments and agencies.

This process is extremely important to the President. His decisions will benefit from the advice and perspective of all the concerned departments and agencies. History offers numerous examples of this truth. President Kennedy, for example, did not have adequate consultation before entering upon the Bay of Pigs invasion, one of his greatest failures. He remedied this in time for the Cuban missile crisis, one of his greatest successes. Process will not always produce brilliant ideas, but history suggests it can at least help prevent bad ideas from becoming Presidential policy.

The National Security Advisor. It is the National Security Advisor who is primarily responsible for managing this process on a daily basis. The job requires skill, sensitivity, and integrity. It is his responsibility to ensure that matters submitted for consideration by the Council cover the full range of issues on which review is required; that those issues are fully analyzed; that a full range of options is considered; that the prospects and risks of each are examined; that all relevant intelligence and other information is available to the principals; that legal considerations are addressed; that difficulties in implementation are confronted. Usually, this can best be accomplished through interagency participation in the analysis of the issue and a preparatory policy review at the Deputy or Under Secretary level.

The National Security Advisor assumes these responsibilities not only with respect to the President but with respect to all the NSC principals. He must keep them informed of the President's thinking and decisions. They should have adequate notice and an agenda for all meetings. Decision papers should, if at all possible, be provided in advance.

The National Security Advisor must also ensure that adequate records are kept of NSC consultations and Presidential decisions. This is essential to avoid confusion among Presidential advisors and departmental staffs about what was actually decided and what is wanted. Those records are also essential for conducting a periodic review of a policy or initiative, and to learn from the past.

It is the responsibility of the National Security Advisor to monitor policy implementation and to ensure that policies are executed in conformity with the intent of the President's decision. Monitoring includes initiating periodic reassessments of a policy or operation, especially when changed circumstances suggest that the policy or operation no longer serves U.S. interests.

But the National Security Advisor does not simply manage the national security process. He is himself an important source of advice on national security matters to the President. He is not the President's only source of advice, but he is perhaps the one most able to see things from the President's perspective. He is unburdened by departmental responsibilities. The President is his only master. His advice is confidential. He is not subject to Senate confirmation and traditionally does not formally appear before Congressional committees.

To serve the President well, the National Security Advisor should present his own views, but he must at the same time represent the views of others fully and faithfully to the President. The system will not work well if the National Security Advisor does not have the trust of the NSC principals. He, therefore, must not use his proximity to the President to manipulate the process so as to produce his own position. He should not interpose himself between the President and the NSC principals. He should not seek to exclude the NSC principals from the decision process. Performing both these roles well is an essential, if not easy, task.

In order for the National Security Advisor to serve the President adequately, he must have direct access to the President. Unless he knows first hand the views of the President and is known to reflect them in his management of the NSC system, he will be ineffective. He should not report to the President through some other official. While the Chief of Staff or others can usefully interject domestic political considerations into national security deliberations, they should do so as additional advisors to the President.

Ideally, the National Security Advisor should not have a high public profile. He should not try to compete with the Secretary of State or the Secretary of Defense as the articulator of public policy. They, along with the President, should be the spokesmen for the policies of the Administration. While a "passion for anonymity" is perhaps too strong a term, the National Security Advisor should generally operate offstage.

The NSC principals of course must have direct access to the President, with whatever frequency the President feels is appropriate. But these individual meetings should not be used by the principal to seek decisions or otherwise circumvent the system in the absence of the other principals. In the same way, the National Security Advisor should not use his scheduled intelligence or other daily briefings of the President as an opportunity to seek Presidential decision on significant issues.

If the system is to operate well, the National Security Advisor must promote cooperation rather than competition among himself and the other NSC principals. But the President is ultimately responsible for the operation of this system. If rancorous infighting develops among his principal national security functionaries, only he can deal with them. Public dispute over external policy by senior officials undermines the process of decision-making and narrows his options. It is the President's responsibility to ensure that it does not take place.

Finally, the National Security Advisor should focus on advice and management, not implementation and execution. Implementation is the responsibility and the strength of the departments and agencies. The National Security Advisor and the NSC Staff generally do not have the depth of resources for the conduct of operations. In addition, when they take on implementation

responsibilities, they risk compromising their objectivity. They can no longer act as impartial overseers of the implementation, ensuring that Presidential guidance is followed, that policies are kept under review, and that the results are serving the President's policy and the national interest.

The NSC Staff. The NSC staff should be small, highly competent, and experienced in the making of public policy. Staff members should be drawn both from within and from outside government. Those from within government should come from the several departments and agencies concerned with national security matters. No particular department or agency should have a predominate role. A proper balance must be maintained between people from within and outside the government. Staff members should generally rotate with a stay of more than four years viewed as the exception.

A large number of staff action officers organized along essentially horizontal lines enhances the possibilities for poorly supervised and monitored activities by individual staff members. Such a system is made to order for energetic self-starters to take unauthorized initiatives. Clear vertical lines of control and authority, responsibility and accountability, are essential to good management.

One problem affecting the NSC staff is lack of institutional memory. This results from the understandable desire of a President to replace the staff in order to be sure it is responsive to him. Departments provide continuity that can help the Council, but the Council as an institution also needs some means to assure adequate records and memory. This was identified to the Board as a problem by many witnesses.

We recognize the problem and have identified a range of possibilities that a President might consider on this subject. One would be to create a small permanent executive secretariat. Another would be to have one person, the Executive Secretary, as a permanent position. Finally, a pattern of limited tenure and overlapping rotation could be used. Any of these would help reduce the problem of loss of institutional memory; none would be practical unless each succeeding President subscribed to it.

The guidelines for the role of the National Security Advisor also apply generally to the NSC staff. They should protect the process and thereby the President. Departments and agencies should not be excluded from participation in that process. The staff should not be implementors or operators and staff should keep a low profile with the press.

Principal Recommendation

The model we have outlined above for the National Security Council system constitutes our first and most important recommendation. It includes guidelines that address virtually all of the deficiencies in procedure and practice that the Board encountered in the Iran/Contra affair as well as in other case studies of this and previous administrations.

We believe this model can enhance the performance of a President and his administration in the area of national security. It responds directly to President Reagan's mandate to describe the NSC system as it ought to be.

The Board recommends that the proposed model be used by Presidents in their management of the national security system.

Specific Recommendations

In addition to its principal recommendation regarding the organization and functioning of the NSC system and roles to be played by the participants, the Board has a number of specific recommendations.

1. *The National Security Act of 1947.* The flaws of procedure and failures of responsibility revealed by our study do not suggest any inadequacies in the provisions of the National Security Act of 1947 that deal with the structure and operation of the NSC system. Forty years of experience under that Act demonstrate to the Board that it remains a fundamentally sound framework for national security decision-making. It strikes a balance between for-

mal structure and flexibility adequate to permit each President to tailor the system to fit his needs.

As a general matter, the NSC Staff should not engage in the implementation of policy or the conduct of operations. This compromises their oversight role and usurps the responsibilities of the departments and agencies. But the inflexibility of a legislative restriction should be avoided. Terms such as "operation" and "implementation" are difficult to define, and a legislative proscription might preclude some future President from making a very constructive use of the NSC Staff.

Predisposition on sizing of the staff should be toward fewer rather than more. But a legislative restriction cannot forsee [sic] the requirements of future Presidents. Size is best left to the discretion of the President, with the admonition that the role of the NSC staff is to review, not to duplicate or replace, the work of the departments and agencies.

We recommend that no substantive change be made in the provisions of the National Security Act dealing with the structure and operation of the NSC system.

2. *Senate Confirmation of the National Security Advisor.* It has been suggested that the job of the National Security Advisor has become so important that its holder should be screened by the process of confirmation, and that once confirmed he should return frequently for questioning by the Congress. It is argued that this would improve the accountability of the National Security Advisor.

We hold a different view. The National Security Advisor does, and should continue, to serve only one master, and that is the President. Further, confirmation is inconsistent with the role the National Security Advisor should play. He should not decide, only advise. He should not engage in policy implementation or operations. He should serve the President, with no collateral and potentially diverting loyalties.

Confirmation would tend to institutionalize the natural tension that exists between the Secretary of State and the National Security Advisor. Questions would increasingly arise about who really speaks for the President in national security matters. Foreign governments could be confused or would be encouraged to engage in "forum shopping."

Only one of the former government officials interviewed favored Senate confirmation of the National Security Advisor. While consultation with Congress received wide support, confirmation and formal questioning were opposed. Several suggested that if the National Security Advisor were to become a position subject to confirmation, it could induce the President to turn to other internal staff or to people outside government to play that role.

We urge the Congress not to require Senate confirmation of the National Security Advisor.

3. *The Interagency Process.* It is the National Security Advisor who has the greatest interest in making the national security process work, for it is this process by which the President obtains the information, background, and analysis he requires to make decisions and build support for his program. Most Presidents have set up interagency committees at both a staff and policy level to surface issues, develop options, and clarify choices. There has typically been a struggle for the chairmanships of these groups between the National Security Advisor and the NSC staff on the one hand, and the cabinet secretaries and department officials on the other.

Our review of the operation of the present system and that of other administrations where committee chairmen came from the departments has led us to the conclusion that the system generally operates better when the committees are chaired by the individual with the greatest stake in making the NSC system work.

We recommend that the National Security Advisor chair the senior-level committees of the NSC system.

4. *Covert Actions.* Policy formulation and implementation are usually managed by a team of experts led by policymaking generalists. Covert action requirements are no different, but there is a need to limit, sometimes severely, the number of individuals involved. The lives of many people may be at stake, as was the case in the attempt to rescue the hostages in Tehran. Premature disclosure might kill the idea in embryo, as could have been the case in

the opening of relations with China. In such cases, there is a tendency to limit those involved to a small number of top officials. This practice tends to limit severely the expertise brought to bear on the problem and should be used very sparingly indeed.

The obsession with secrecy and preoccupation with leaks threaten to paralyze the government in its handling of covert operations. Unfortunately, the concern is not misplaced. The selective leak has become a principal means of waging bureaucratic warfare. Opponents of an operation kill it with a leak; supporters seek to build support through the same means.

We have witnessed over the past years a significant deterioration in the integrity of process. Rather than a means to obtain results more satisfactory than the position of any of the individual departments, it has frequently become something to be manipulated to reach a specific outcome. The leak becomes a primary instrument in that process.

This practice is destructive of orderly governance. It can only be reversed if the most senior officials take the lead. If senior decision-makers set a clear example and demand compliance, subordinates are more likely to conform.

Most recent administrations have had carefully drawn procedures for the consideration of covert activities. The Reagan Administration established such procedures in January, 1985, then promptly ignored them in their consideration of the Iran initiative.

We recommend that each administration formulate precise procedures for restricted consideration of covert action and that, once formulated, those procedures be strictly adhered to.

5. *The Role of the CIA.* Some aspects of the Iran arms sales raised broader questions in the minds of members of the Board regarding the role of CIA. The first deals with intelligence.

The NSC staff was actively involved in the preparation of the May 20, 1985, update to the Special National Intelligence Estimate on Iran. It is a matter for concern if this involvement and the strong views of NSC staff members were allowed to influence the intelligence judgments contained in the update. It is also of concern that the update contained the hint that the United States should change its existing policy and encourage its allies to provide arms to Iran. It is critical that the line between intelligence and advocacy of a particular policy be preserved if intelligence is to retain its integrity and perform its proper function. In this instance, the CIA came close enough to the line to warrant concern.

We emphasize to both the intelligence community and policymakers the importance of maintaining the integrity and objectivity of the intelligence process.

6. *Legal Counsel.* From time to time issues with important legal ramifications will come before the National Security Council. The Attorney General is currently a member of the Council by invitation and should be in a position to provide legal advice to the Council and the President. It is important that the Attorney General and his department be available to interagency deliberations.

The Justice Department, however, should not replace the role of counsel in the other departments. As the principal counsel on foreign affairs, the Legal Adviser to the Secretary of State should also be available to all the NSC participants.

Of all the NSC participants, it is the Assistant for National Security Affairs who seems to have had the least access to expert counsel familiar with his activities.

The Board recommends that the position of Legal Adviser to the NSC be enhanced in stature and in its role within the NSC staff.

7. *Secrecy and Congress.* There is a natural tension between the desire for secrecy and the need to consult Congress on covert operations. Presidents seem to become increasingly concerned about leaks of classified information as their administrations progress. They blame Congress disproportionately. Various cabinet officials from prior administrations indicated to the Board that they believe Congress bears no more blame than the Executive Branch. However, the number of Members and staff involved in reviewing covert activities is large; it provides cause for concern and a convenient excuse for Presidents to avoid Congressional consultation.

We recommend that Congress consider replacing the existing Intelligence Committees of the respective Houses with a new joint committee with a restricted staff to oversee the intelligence community, patterned after the Joint Committee on Atomic Energy that existed until the mid-1970s.

8. *Privatizing National Security Policy.* Careful and limited use of people outside the U.S. Government may be very helpful in some unique cases. But this practice raises substantial questions. It can create conflict of interest problems. Private or foreign sources may have different policy interests or personal motives and may exploit their association with a U.S. government effort. Such involvement gives private and foreign sources potentially powerful leverage in the form of demands for return favors or even blackmail.

The U.S. has enormous resources invested in agencies and departments in order to conduct the government's business. In all but a very few cases, these can perform the functions needed. If not, then inquiry is required to find out why.

We recommend against having implementation and policy oversight dominated by intermediaries. We do not recommend barring limited use of private individuals to assist in United States diplomatic initiatives or in covert activities. We caution against use of such people except in very limited ways and under close observation and supervision.

Epilogue

If but one of the major policy mistakes we examined had been avoided, the nation's history would bear one less scar, one less embarrassment, one less opportunity for opponents to reverse the principles this nation seeks to preserve and advance in the world.

As a collection, these recommendations are offered to those who will find themselves in situations similar to the ones we reviewed: under stress, with high stakes, given little time, using incomplete information, and troubled by premature disclosure. In such a state, modest improvements may yield surprising gains. This is our hope.

Footnotes

Part I

1. See Appendix A, Executive Order No. 12575. [Appendix omitted. For text, see p. D-15.]
2. A list of those case studies is contained in Appendix E. [Appendix omitted.]
3. A list of the witnesses interviewed by the Board is contained in Appendix F. [Appendix omitted.]

Part III

1. The correspondence to the President from the Board's Chairman and the reply, on his behalf, of White House Counsel Peter Wallison, are at Appendix G. [Appendix omitted.]
2. The "PROF" system, The Professional Office System, is an interoffice mail system run through an IBM main frame computer and managed by the White House Communications Agency for the NSC. All NSC officers have personal passwords which enable them to send and receive messages to each other from terminals at their desks.
3. On August 27, 1986, a new section was added to the Arms Export Control Act which prohibited the export of arms to countries which the Secretary of State has determined support acts of international terrorism. Such a determination was in effect at that time for Iran.
4. The acronym "TOW" stands for tube-launched, optically-tracked, wire-guided missile. It is a man-portable anti-tank missile. A "HAWK" is a type of ground-launched, anti-aircrafrt missile.
5. The financing of these and other arms transactions discussed in this Part III is described in detail in the charts annexed to the end of Appendix B. [Appendix omitted.]
6. Section 662 of the Foreign Assistance Act, the so-called Hughes-Ryan Amendment, prohibits covert operations by the CIA unless and until the President "finds such operation is important to the national security of the United States."
7. In October, 1985, the United States obtained reliable evidence that William Buckley had died the preceding June.
8. This appears to be the plan discussed at the meeting on December 7, 1985.
9. The financing of this and the other transactions involved in the arms sale initiative is covered in the charts annexed to the end of Appendix B. [Appendix omitted.]
10. The Board has found no evidence that would give any credence to this assumption.
11. This memorandum also contained a reference to the diversion of funds to the Contras, discussed in Section B of this Part III.
12. Mr. McDaniel became Executive Secretary of the NSC in February, 1986. Though uninvolved in both the policy and implementation of the Iran initiative, Mr. McDaniel accompanied VADM Poindexter to his morning briefings of the President as a note taker.
13. This excludes two and possibly three dual-national U.S. citizens seized during this period.
14. Charts describing the various arms sales transactions involved in the initiative are annexed to Appendix B. [Appendix omitted.]
15. We have no information linking the activities described herein as "Project Democracy" with the National Endowment for Democracy (NED). The latter was created in 1983 by Congressional act and is funded by legislation. Its purpose is to strengthen democratic institutions around the world through private, non-governmental efforts. NED grew out of an earlier Administration public initiative to promote democracy around the world, which came to be known as "Project Democracy". It appears that North later adopted the term to refer to his own covert operations network. We believe this is the only link between the NED and North's activities.

Part IV

1. The issue of legal advice to the NSC staff is treated in more detail in Part V of this report.
2. It may be possible to authorize transfers by another country under the Arms Export Control Act without obtaining the President's consent. As a practical matter, however, the legal requirements may not differ significantly. For example, section 614(2) permits the President to waive the requirements of the Act. But this waiver authority may not be exercised unless it is determined that the international arms sales are "vital to the national security interests of the United States." Moreover, before granting a waiver, the President must consult with and provide written justification to the foreign affairs and appropriations committees of the Congress. 22 U.S.C. 2374(3).
3. A copy of the letter is set forth in Appendix H. [Appendix omitted.]
4. Apparently no determination was made at the time as to the legality of these activities even though serious concerns about legality were expressed by the Deputy Director of CIA, a Presidential finding was sought by CIA officials before any further CIA activities in support of the Iran initiative were undertaken, and the CIA counsel, Mr. Stanley Sporkin, advised that as a matter of prudence any new finding should seek to ratify the prior CIA activities.
5. See Appendix D. [Appendix omitted.]

Part V

1. As discussed in more detail in Part II, the statutory members of the National Security Council are the President, Vice President, Secretary of State, and Secretary of Defense. By the phrase "National Security Council principals" or "NSC principals," the Board generally means those four statutory members plus the Director of Central Intelligence and the Chairman of the Joint Chiefs of Staff.

NORTH'S APRIL 1986 MEMO ON DIVERSION TO CONTRAS

Following is the text of a memorandum written by Lt. Col. Oliver L. North between April 4-7, 1986, on the Iran arms sales and diversion of funds from those sales to the Nicaraguan contras. The undated and unsigned memo, reprinted in the Tower Commission report, was written for Vice Adm. John M. Poindexter to forward to President Reagan. However, the Tower Commission stated: "No evidence has emerged to suggest that this memorandum was ever placed before VADM Poindexter, the President, or any other U.S. official." Following the North memo is the text of "Terms of Reference U.S.-Iran Dialogue," a document dated April 4, 1986, and attached to the memo.

Release of American Hostages in Beirut

Background.—In June 1985, private American and Israeli citizens commenced an operation to effect the release of the American hostages in Beirut in exchange for providing certain factions in Iran with U.S.-origin Israeli military materiel. By September, U.S. and Israeli Government officials became involved in this endeavor in order to ensure that the USG would:

—not object to the Israeli transfer of embargoed material to Iran;
—sell replacement items to Israel as replenishment for like items sold to Iran by Israel.

On September 13, the Israeli Government, with the endorsement of the USG, transferred 508 TOW missile [*sic*] to Iran. Forty-eight hours later, Reverend Benjamin Weir was released in Beirut.

Subsequent efforts by both governments to continue this process have met with frustration due to the need to communicate our intentions through an Iranian expatriate arms dealer in Europe. In January 1986, under the provisions of a new Covert Action Finding, the USG demanded a meeting with responsible Iranian government officials.

On February 20, a U.S. Government official met with an official in the Iranian Prime Minister's office—the first direct U.S.-Iranian contact in over five years. At this meeting, the U.S. side made an effort to refocus Iranian attention on the threat posed by the Soviet Union and the need to establish a longer term relationship between our two countries based on more than arms transactions. It was emphasized that the hostage issue was a "hurdle" which must be crossed before this improved relationship could prosper. During the meeting, it also became apparent that our conditions/demand had not been accurately transmitted to the Iranian government by the intermediary and it was agreed that:

—The USG would establish its good faith and bona fides by immediately providing 1,000 TOW missiles for sale to Iran. This transaction was covertly completed on February 21, using a private U.S. firm and the Israelis as intermediaries.
—A subsequent meeting would be held in Iran with senior U.S. and Iranian officials during which the U.S. hostages would be released.
—Immediately after the hostages were safely in our hands, the U.S. would sell an additional 3,000 TOW missiles to Iran using the same procedures employed during the September 1985 transfer.

In early March, the Iranian expatriate intermediary demanded that Iranian conditions for release of the hostages now included the prior sale of 200 PHOENIX missiles and an unspeci-

fied number of HARPOON missiles, in addition to the 3,000 TOWs which would be delivered after the hostages were released. A subsequent meeting was held with the intermediary in Paris on March 8, wherein it was explained that the requirement for prior deliveries violated the understanding reached in Frankfurt on February 20, and were [*sic*] therefore unacceptable. It was further noted that the Iranian aircraft and ship launchers for these missiles were in such disrepair that the missiles could not be launched even if provided.

From March 9 until March 30, there was no further effort undertaken on our behalf to contact the Iranian Government or the intermediary. On March 26, [the official in the Prime Minister's office] made an unsolicited call to the phone-drop in Maryland which we had established for this purpose. [He] asked why we had not been in contact and urged that we proceed expeditiously since the situation in Beirut was deteriorating rapidly. He was informed by our Farsi-speaking interpreter that the conditions requiring additional materiel beyond the 3,000 TOWs were unacceptable and that we could in no case provide anything else prior to the release of our hostages. [The Iranian official] observed that we were correct in our assessment of their inability to use PHOENIX and HARPOON missiles and that the most urgent requirement that Iran had was to place their current HAWK missile inventory in working condition. In a subsequent phone call, we agreed to discuss this matter with him and he indicated that he would prepare an inventory of parts required to make their HAWK systems operational. This parts list was received ~~on March~~ 28, and verified by CIA.

Current Situation.—On April 3, Ari Gorbanifahr [*sic*] [Manucher Ghorbanifar], the Iranian intermediary, arrived in Washington, D.C. with instructions from [his Tehran contact] to consummate final arrangements for the return of the hostages. Gorbanifahr [Ghorbanifar] was reportedly enfranchised to negotiate the types, quantities, and deliver procedure for materiel the U.S. would sell to Iran through Israel. The meeting lasted nearly all night on April 3-4, and involved numerous calls to Tehran. A Farsi-speaking CIA officer in attendance was able to verify the substance of his calls to Tehran during the meeting. Subject to Presidential approval, it was agreed to proceed as follows:

—By Monday, April 7, the Iranian Government will transfer $17 million to an Israeli account in Switzerland. The Israelis will, in turn, transfer to a private U.S. corporation account in Switzerland the sum of $15 million.
—On Tuesday, April 8 (or as soon as the transactions are verified), the private U.S. corporation will transfer $3.651 million to a CIA account in Switzerland. CIA will then transfer this sum to a covert Department of the Army account in the U.S.
—On Wednesday, April 9, the CIA will commence procuring $3.651 million worth of HAWK missile parts (240 separate line items) and transferring these parts to . . . This process is estimated to take seven working days.
—On Friday, April 18, a private U.S. aircraft (707B) will pickup the HAWK missile parts at . . . and fly them to a covert Israeli airfield for prepositioning (this field was used for the earlier delivery of the 1000 TOWs). At this field, the parts will be transferred to an Israeli Defense Forces' (IDF) aircraft with false markings. A SATCOM capability will be positioned at this location.
—On Saturday, April 19, [Robert C.] McFarlane, North, [Howard J.] Teicher, [George] Cave, [C/NE], and a SATCOM communicator will board an aircraft in Frankfurt, Germany, enroute [*sic*] to Tehran.
—On Saturday, April 20, the following series of events will occur:

—U.S. party arrives [*sic*] Tehran (A-hour)—met by [Ali Akbar Hashemi] Rafsanjani, as head of the Iranian delegation.
—At A+7 hours, the U.S. hostages will be released in Beirut.
—At A+15 hours, the IDF aircraft with the HAWK missile parts aboard will land at Bandar Abbas, Iran.

Discussion.—The following points are relevant to this transaction, the discussions in Iran, and the establishment of a broader relationship between the United States and Iran:

—The Iranians have been told that our presence in Iran is a "holy commitment" on the part of the USG that we are sincere and can be trusted. There is great distrust of the U.S. among the various Iranian parties involved. Without our presence on the ground in Iran, they will not believe that we will fulfill our end of the bargain after the hostages are released.

—The Iranians know, probably better than we, that both [Yasir] Arafat and Qhadhaffi [Muammar el-Qaddafi] are trying hard to have the hostages turned over to them. Gorbanifahr [Ghorbanifar] specifically mentioned that Qhadhaffi's [Qaddafi's] efforts to "buy" the hostages could succeed in the near future. Further, the Iranians are well aware that the situation in Beirut is deteriorating rapidly and that the ability of the IRGC [Iranian Revolutionary Guard Corps] to effect the release of the hostages will become increasingly more difficult over time.

—We have convinced the Iranians of a significant near term and long range threat from the Soviet Union. We have real and deceptive intelligence to demonstrate this threat during the visit. They have expressed considerable interest in this matter as part of the longer term relationship.

—We have told the Iranians that we are interested in assistance they may be willing to provide to the Afghan resistance and that we wish to discuss this mattter [*sic*] in Tehran.

—The Iranians have been told that their provision of assistance to Nicaragua is unacceptable to us and they have agreed to discuss this matter in Tehran.

—We have further indicated to the Iranians that we wish to discuss steps leading to a cessation of hostilities between Iran and Iraq. . . .

—The Iranians are well aware that their most immediate needs are for technical assistance in maintaining their air force and navy. We should expect that they will raise this issue during the discussion in Tehran. Further conversation with Gorbanifahr [Ghorbanifar] on April 4, [*sic*] indicates that they will want to raise the matter of the original 3,000 TOWs as a significant deterrent to a potential Soviet move against Iran. They have also suggested that, if agreement is reached to provided the TOWs, they will make 200 out of each 1,000 available to the Afghan resistance and train the resistance forces in how to use them against the Soviets. We have agreed to discuss this matter.

—The Iranians have been told and agreed that they will receive neither blame nor credit for the seizure/release of the hostages.

—The residual funds from this transaction are allocated as follows:

—$2 million will be used to purchase replacement TOWs for the original 508 sold by Israel to Iran for the release of Benjamin Weir. This is the only way that we have found to meet our commitment to replenish these stocks.

—$12 million will be used to purchase critically needed supplies for the Nicaraguan Democratic Resistance Forces. This materiel is essential to cover shortages in resistance inventories resulting from their current offensives and Sandinista counter-attacks and to "bridge" the period between now and when Congressionally-approved lethal assistance (beyond the $25 million in "defensive" arms) can be delivered.

The ultimate objective in the trip to Tehran is to commence the process of improving U.S.-Iranian relations. Both sides are aware that the Iran-Iraq War is a major factor that must be discussed. We should not, however, view this meeting as a session which will result in immediate Iranian agreement to proceed with a settlement with Iraq. Rather, this meeting, the first high-level U.S.-Iranian contact in five years, should be seen as a chance to move in this direction. These discussions, as well as follow-on talks, should be governed by the Terms of Reference (TOR) (Tab A) with the recognition that this is, hopefully, the first of many meetings and that the hostage issue, once behind us, improves the opportunities for this relationship.

Finally, we should recognize that the Iranians will undoubtedly want to discuss additional arms and commercial transactions as "quids" for accommodating our points on Afghanistan, Nicaragua, and Iraq. Our emphasis on the Soviet military and subversive threat, a useful mechanism in bringing them to agreement on the hostage issue, has also served to increase their desire for means to protect themselves against/deter the Soviets.

Recommendation

That the President approve the structure depicted above under "Current Situation" and the Terms of Reference at Tab A.

Approve_____   Disapprove_____

Terms of Reference
U.S.-Iran Dialogue

I. Basic Pillars of U.S. Foreign Policy

—President Reagan came into office at a time when Iran had had a certain impact on the American political process—perhaps not what you intended.

—The President represented and embodied America's recovery from a period of weakness. He has rebuilt American military and economic strength.

—Most important, he has restored American will and self-confidence. The U.S. is not afraid to use its power in defense of its interests. We are not intimidated by Soviet pressures, whether on arms control or Angola or Central America or Afghanistan.

—At the same time, we are prepared to resolve political problems on the basis of reciprocity.

—We see many international trends—economic, technological, and political—working in our favor.

II. U.S. Policy toward Iran: Basic Principles

A. U.S. Assessment of Iranian Policy

—We view the Iranian revolution as a fact. The U.S. is not trying to turn the clock back.

—Our present attitude to Iran is not a product of prejudice or emotion, but a clear-eyed assessment of Iran's present policies.

—Iran has had "revolutionary Islam" as a weapon to undermine pro-Western governments and American interests throughout the Middle East. As long as this is Iran's policy, we are bound to be strategic adversaries.

—Support for terrorism and hostage-taking is part of this strategic pattern. We see it used not only against us, but against our friends. We cannot accept either. Your influence in achieving the release of *all* hostages/return or those killed (over time) is essential.

—We see your activity in many parts of the world, including even Central America.

—The U.S. knows how Iran views the Soviet Union. But subversion of Western interests and friends objectively serves Soviet interests on a global scale.

—Thus, our assessment is that a decisive Iranian victory in the war with Iraq would only unleash greater regional instability, a further erosion of the Wester position, and enhanced opportunities for Soviet trouble-making.

—The U.S. will therefore do what it can to prevent such a development. We regard the war as dangerous in many respects and would like to see an end to it.

B. Possible Intersection of U.S.-Iranian Interests

—Despite fundamental conflicts, we preceive several possible intersections of U.S. and Iranian interests. I propose to explore those areas.
—First, the U.S. has had a traditional interest in seeing Iran preserve its territorial integrity and independence. This has not changed. The U.S. opposes Soviet designs on Iran.
—Second, we have no interest in an Iraqi victory over Iran. [Discussion of US-Iran Relationship] We are seeking an end to this conflict and want to use an improved relationship with Iran to further that end.
—Third, we have parallel views on Afghanistan. Soviet policy there is naked aggression, a threat to all in the region. Our mutual friends—China and Pakistan—are threatened. We have ties with different elements of the Mujahideen. But our objective is the same: the Soviets must get out and let the Afghan people choose their own course.

C. U.S. Objective Today

—We have no illusions about what is possible in our bilateral relations. Perhaps this meeting will reveal only a limited, momentary, tactical coincidence of interests. Perhaps more. We are prepared either way.
—In essense, we are preparing to have whatever kind of relationship with Iran that Iran is prepared to have with us.

III. Soviet Military Posture

—[Discussion of Soviet interests in Iran]
—Afghanistan illustrates the price the Soviets are ready to pay to expand areas under their direct control.
—Summarize Soviet capabilities along border and inside Afghanistan which could threaten Tehran.
—U.S. is aware of Soviet activity in Baluchistan, air strikes.
—Iranian support to Sandinista regime in Nicaragua aids and abets Soviet designs—makes U.S.-Iranian relationship more difficult ($100 million in oil last year, plus arms).
—U.S. can help Iran cope with Soviet threat.

IV. Afghanistan

—[Discussion of situation in Afghanistan]

V. Hardware

—We may be prepared to resume a limited supply relationship.
—However, its evolution and ultimate scope will depend on whether our convergent or our divergent interests come to loom larger in the overall picture.
—What does Iran want?

REAGAN RESPONSE TO TOWER REPORT

Following is the text of President Reagan's March 4, 1987, address, responding to the Tower Commission report on the Iran-contra affair:

My fellow Americans, I've spoken to you from this historic office on many occasions and about many things. The power of the Presidency is often thought to reside within this Oval Office. Yet it doesn't rest here; it rests in you, the American people, and in your trust.

Your trust is what gives a President his powers of leadership and his personal strength and it's what I want to talk to you about this evening.

For the past three months, I've been silent on the revelations about Iran. And you must have been thinking, "Well, why doesn't he tell us what's happening? Why doesn't he just speak to us as he has in the past when we've faced troubles or tragedies?" Others of you, I guess, were thinking, "What's he doing hiding out in the White House?"

Well, the reason I haven't spoken to you before now is this: You deserved the truth. And, as frustrating as the waiting has been, I felt it was improper to come to you with sketchy reports, or possibly even erroneous statements, which would then have to be corrected, creating even more doubt and confusion. There's been enough of that.

The Price of Silence

I've paid a price for my silence in terms of your trust and confidence. But I've had to wait, as you have, for the complete story. That's why I appointed Ambassador David Abshire as my special counselor to help get out the thousands of documents to the various investigations. And I appointed a special review board, the Tower Board, which took on the chore of pulling the truth together for me and getting to the bottom of things. It has now issued its findings.

I'm often accused of being an optimist, and it's true I had to hunt pretty hard to find any good news in the Board's report. As you know, it's well-stocked with criticisms, which I'll discuss in a moment, but I was very relieved to read this sentence, ". . . the Board is convinced that the President does indeed want the full story to be told." And that will continue to be my pledge to you as the other investigations go forward.

I want to thank the members of the panel—former Senator John Tower, former Secretary of State Edmund Muskie, and former National Security Adviser Brent Scowcroft. They have done the nation, as well as me personally, a great service by submitting a report of such integrity and depth. They have my genuine and enduring gratitude.

I've studied the Board's report. Its findings are honest, convincing and highly critical, and I accept them. And tonight I want to share with you my thoughts on these findings and report to you on the actions I'm taking to implement the Board's recommendations.

First, let me say I take full responsibility for my own actions and for those of my administration. As angry as I may be about activities undertaken without my knowledge, I am still accountable for those activities. As disappointed as I may be in some who served me, I am still the one who must answer to the American people for this behavior. And as personally distasteful as I find secret bank accounts and diverted funds—well, as the Navy would say, this happened on my watch.

Arms for Hostages

Let's start with the part that is the most controversial. A few months ago I told the American people I did not trade arms for hostages. My heart and my best intentions still tell me that is true, but the facts and the evidence tell me it is not. As the Tower Board reported, what began as a strategic opening to Iran deteriorated in its implementation into trading arms for hostages. This runs counter to my own beliefs, to administration policy, and to the original strategy we had in mind. There are reasons why it happened, but no excuses. It was a mistake.

I undertook the original Iran initiative in order to develop relations with those who might assume leadership in a post-Khomeini government. It's clear from the Board's report, however, that I let my personal concern for the hostages spill over into the geopolitical strategy of reaching out to Iran. I asked so many questions about the hostages' welfare that I didn't ask enough about the specifics of the total Iran plan.

Let me say to the hostage families, we have not given up. We never will. And I promise you we'll use every legitimate means to free your loved ones from captivity. But I must also caution that those Americans who freely remain in such dangerous areas must know that they're responsible for their own safety.

Transfer of Funds

Now, another major aspect of the Board's findings regards the transfer of funds to the Nicaraguan Contras. The Tower Board wasn't able to find out what happened to this money, so the facts here will be left to the continuing investigations of the court-appointed Independent Counsel and the two Congressional investigating committees. I'm confident the truth will come out about this matter as well. As I told the Tower Board, I didn't know about any diversion of funds to the Contras. But as President, I cannot escape responsibility.

Management Style

Much has been said about my management style, a style that's worked successfully for me during eight years as Governor of California and for most of my Presidency. The way I work is to identify the problem, find the right individuals to do the job, and then let them go to it. I have found this invariably brings out the best in people. They seem to rise to their full capability, and in the long run you get more done.

When it came to managing the NSC staff, let's face it, my style didn't match its previous track record. I have already begun correcting this. As a start, yesterday I met with the entire professional staff of the National Security Council. I defined for them the values I want to guide the national security policies of this country. I told them that I wanted a policy that was as justifiable and understandable in public as it was in secret. I wanted a policy that reflected the will of the Congress as well as of the White House. And I told them that there'll be no more freelancing by individuals when it comes to our national security.

You have heard a lot about the staff of the National Security Council in recent months. I can tell you, they are good and dedicated government employees, who put in long hours for the nation's benefit. They are eager and anxious to serve their country.

One thing still upsetting me, however, is that no one kept proper records of meetings or decisions. This led to my failure to recollect whether I approved an arms shipment before or after the fact. I did approve it; I just can't say specifically when. Well, rest assured, there's plenty of record-keeping now going on at 1600 Pennsylvania Avenue.

For nearly a week now, I've been studying the Board's report. I want the American people to know that this wrenching ordeal of recent months has not been in vain. I endorse every one of the Tower Board's recommendations. In fact, I'm going beyond its recommendations, so as to put the house in even better order.

I'm taking action in three basic areas—personnel, national security policy, and the process for making sure that the system works.

Personnel

First, personnel. I've brought in an accomplished and highly respected new team here at the White House. They bring new blood, new energy, and new credibility and experience.

Former Senator Howard [H.] Baker, [Jr.,] my new Chief of Staff, possesses a breadth of legislative and foreign affairs skills that's impossible to match. I'm hopeful that his experience as Minority and Majority Leader of the Senate can help us forge a new partnership with the Congress, especially on foreign and national security policies. I'm genuinely honored that he's given up his own presidential aspirations to serve the country as my Chief of Staff.

Frank [C.] Carlucci, my new National Security Adviser, is respected for his experience in government and trusted for his judgment and counsel. Under him, the NSC staff is being rebuilt with proper management discipline. Already, almost half the NSC professional staff is comprised of new people.

Yesterday I nominated William [H.] Webster, a man of sterling reputation, to be Director of the Central Intelligence Agency. Mr. Webster has served as Director of the FBI and a U.S. District Court Judge. He understands the meaning of "rule of law."

So that his knowledge of national security matters can be available to me on a continuing basis, I will also appoint John Tower to serve as a member of my Foreign Intelligence Advisory Board.

I am considering other changes in personnel, and I'll move more furniture as I see fit in the weeks and months ahead.

National Security Policy

Second, in the area of national security policy, I have ordered the NSC to begin a comprehensive review of all covert operations. I have also directed that any covert activity be in support of clear policy objectives and in compliance with American values. I expect a covert policy that if Americans saw it on the front page of their newspaper, they'd say, "That makes sense."

I have had issued a directive prohibiting the NSC staff itself from undertaking covert operations—no ifs, ands or buts.

I have asked Vice President [George] Bush to reconvene his task force on terrorism to review our terrorist policy in light of the events that have occurred.

Making the System Work

Third, in terms of the process of reaching national security decisions I am adopting in total the Tower Report's model of how the NSC process and staff should work. I am directing Mr. Carlucci to take the necessary steps to make that happen. He will report back to me on further reforms that might be needed. I've created the post of NSC Legal Adviser to assure a greater sensitivity to matters of law.

I am also determined to make the Congressional oversight process work. Proper procedures for consultation with the Congress will be followed, not only in letter but in spirit. Before the end of March I will report to the Congress on all the steps I've taken in line with the Tower Board's conclusions.

Going Forward

Now, what should happen when you make a mistake is this: You take your knocks, you learn your lessons, and then you move on. That's the healthiest way to deal with a problem. This in no way diminishes the importance of the other continuing investigations, but the business of our country and our people must proceed. I've gotten this message from Republicans and Democrats in Congress, from allies around the world—and if we're reading the signals right, even from the Soviets. And, of course, I've heard the message from you, the American people.

You know, by the time you reach my age, you've made plenty of mistakes. And if you've lived your life properly—so you learn. You put things in perspective. You pull your energies together. You change. You go forward.

My fellow Americans, I have a great deal that I want to accomplish with you and for you over the next two years. And, the Lord willing, that's exactly what I intend to do.

Good night and God bless you.

REAGAN'S MARCH PRESS CONFERENCE

Following are excerpts from the text of President Reagan's March 19, 1987, press conference:

THE PRESIDENT: . . . Now before we get started, let me also add that, after our last press conference, I felt it was important for the Tower commission to complete its work and report its findings. And that has now happened. I have accepted their recommendations and many are in the process of being implemented. . . .

Release of Hostages - 1

Q: Sir, Terry Anderson was taken captive in Lebanon two years and four days ago, and today there are eight Americans held hostage there. How has the Iran-Contra affair complicated your efforts to win the release of the hostages?

P: Well, that's rather hard to tell right now. Indeed the affair did get some hostages released, and if it hadn't leaked I don't know whether the word of what we were doing there—I don't know whether we would have gotten more out. As the day that the information leaked and everything went public, it was my understanding that there were—the other two were due out in the next few days. But, we're going to continue to explore, as we always have, every opportunity to try and get them out.

I happen to believe that when an American citizen anyplace in the world, is unjustly denied their constitutional rights to life, liberty, and the pursuit of happiness, it is the responsibility of this government to restore those rights.

Q: Sir, if I may, former President Carter will be in Syria this weekend. Is he carrying a message from you about the hostages?

P: No.

Q: Is he making any effort in that regard as far as you know?

P: I don't know. I wouldn't be surprised if he—if he was, but—and I'd be grateful if he did.

Helen?

Diversion of Funds - 1

Q: Mr. President, there have been reports that you were told, directly or indirectly, at least twice that the Contras were benefiting from the Iran arms sale. Is that true or were you deceived and lied to by Admiral [John M.] Poindexter and Colonel [Oliver L.] North? And I'd like to follow up.

P: Helen, let me just say, no, that is not true at all. When I went on the air right after the news broke and told what we had been doing and how we—what our policy was in getting into this affair, I did not know at that time that there was any money involved. I only knew that we had received our $12 million for the weapons which we had agreed to sell. Then, a little later, when the Attorney General told me that he had come upon something that indicated that there was something to do with money in Swiss bank accounts—and I couldn't imagine what it could be, because as I say, we got our money—but I said that I thought we ought to go public with that again so that you had all the information that we had and not wait and have someone uncover this and think we were trying to cover up or something.

So that was late on Monday afternoon. Tuesday morning, the first thing, we went before the joint leadership of the Congress and told them what we'd learned, that all we'd learned was that there was evidently some money having to do with this whole arrangement over there and involving some Swiss bank accounts. And then I came into the press room to all of you and told you.

Q: Mr. President, is it possible that two military officers who are trained to obey orders grabbed power, made major foreign policy moves, didn't tell you when you were briefed every day on intelligence? Or did they think they were doing your bidding?

P: Helen, I don't know. I only know that that's why I've said repeatedly that I want to find out, I want to get to the bottom of this and find out all that has happened. And so far I've told you all that I know and, you know, the truth of the matter is, for quite some long time, all that you knew what was I'd told you.

Sam.

Remembering the Facts

Q: Sir, Robert [C.] McFarlane, who was then your National Security Adviser, says that in August of 1985, he called you on the telephone and asked if you wanted to give the green light to Israel to send arms to Iran and have them replenished from U.S. stocks, and you said you did. And he said that he reminded you in that conversation that your Secretaries of State and Defense were against it and you said you understood that, but you explained to him the reasons why you wanted to authorize it. Do you have no memory of that, whatsoever?

P: Sam, all I know is that I was never—my memory didn't fail me on the fact that I had agreed to this thing. The only thing I could not recall was at what point was I asked. And as a result of that and not being able to recall when I gave this permission, we now have quite a system installed of people taking notes in all our meetings and all our doings.

Q: If you don't recall, when Benjamin Weir—Reverend Weir, was released in mid-September of that year, why did you think they had released him if you couldn't recall that you had authorized Israel to do that?

P: No. As I say, I'm aware—I can't remember just when, in all the calls and meetings and so forth, this was presented and when I gave the go-ahead. But this was a thing in which the Israelis were willing to sell weaponry—mainly TOW missiles—and wanted to know if they did, if we would agree to sell them replacements when and if they needed it.

Q: A shipment only went the day before he was released, sir.

P: I know that I agreed to that and I've heard—and there are other people that don't remember either who were present at meetings. One of them was Bud [McFarlane] and what his memory was—I don't think it was a phone call. He has described it as a visit to the hospital where I was after surgery. But others who were there present, they didn't remember that conversation. But I know that it must have come up and I must have verbally given the okay.

Bill?

A Flawed Policy?

Q: Mr. President, you said that in your heart you still believe that it wasn't an arms-for-hostages deal, but that the weight of the evidence presented by the Tower commission convinced you that it was. In your heart do you now believe that it was an arms-for-hostages deal from the beginning, as the Tower commission said, and that the policy was flawed?

P: But it could be that the policy was flawed in that it did deteriorate into what I myself and when I went on the air recently said—was arms for hostages. But let me just as briefly as I can take you through the steps which I did from the very beginning.

We had, by way of Israel, a report that there were responsible people, some from the government of Iran but not necessarily in the inner circle of—with [Ayatollah Ruhollah] Khomeini, who wanted to see if they could not open a dialogue with representatives from the United States that would lead to a better understanding—and I'm sure that they had in mind a future government of Iran—that we could have the kind of relationship that we'd had once earlier. I thought, because our policy had always been based on trying to restore a relationship with a country that is very important strategically, and also behind the scenes to try and get an end to that war—and end with no victor, no vanquished, both countries retiring to their own boundaries, and so forth. So I wasn't going to miss that opportunity. And I approved our going ahead.

One of the first things brought up in the meeting with those who were representing us was that these people said that they, for two reasons, needed something like—and they mentioned the arms sales. It came from them, not us. They said, one, for their own prestige it would give them a standing with the people that they would have to be dealing with in the future, including the military leaders. And, at the same time, it would assure them that the people they were dealing with did have access to our government at the highest levels and they could trust them to deal. And, so, our answer to that was we had a policy of not doing business with a country that supported terrorism, and Iran was on that list. Well, they made quite a pitch that they, too, were opposed to terrorism and that they had even done some things counter to terrorism—terrorist activities and so forth. Well, our reply to them was, there is a very practical way in which you can prove that, and that is, help the—use your influence to get the hostages out. Now, I have never believed, and I don't believe now, that Iran can give orders to the Hezbollah, but there is a philosophical relationship there that we thought they might be able to be persuasive and they've indicated that that was true. Now, with no further information than that, until I read the Tower commission report, after appointing the Tower commission to get to the bottom of this thing and see what was going on, then I found that the strategy talks had disappeared completely, and led by the Iranians, the conversation was totally arms-for-hostages. So I don't see where I could say now that isn't what it degenerated into.

Release of Hostages - 2

Q: Mr. President, they faulted you in the Tower commission report for caring too much about the hostages. If you had it to do all over again, sir, would you do it again?

P: No, I would not go down that same road again. I will keep my eyes open for any opportunity again for improving relations. And we will continue to explore every legitimate means of getting our hostages back for the reason that I explained earlier....

A Question of Misstatements

Q: Mr. President—thank you. At your last news conference four months ago, you said that Israel has nothing to—U.S. had nothing to do with Israeli arms shipments to Iran when you knew that that was not true. Why did you say that?

P: Chris, I'm glad you asked that, because I've read at great length references to that, and heard them on the air. I'm glad to explain. When I left here, after that press conference and went back there, and our people were waiting back there and they had been watching on the monitor what was going on, they told me what I had said. And it was evidently just a misstatement on my part. I did not know that I had said it in such a way as to seemingly deny Israel's participation. And when they told me this, and when I finished bumping my head, I said to them, "Quick, write down a correction of this." I didn't realize that in there maybe I'd talked too long. I said, "I didn't realize that I had said that or given that impression. We've got to get this message to all of you before you went to work on your stories."

So it was just a misstatement that I didn't realize that I made.

Q: But the fact is that you were asked it four times in that news conference, and you made this inadvertent statement four times you were specifically asked about Israel's role. And during that early period, it now turns out that there were a series of statements you made that were misleading. One of the first statements was, you said that the whole story that came out of the Mideast was without foundation.

P: No. That wasn't at the press conference. That was on Nov. 6, when you were shouting questions at me.

Q: Well—

P: And at that—well, right. But then, what I was trying to do, and I think some of you will recall this, I was trying to plead with all of you, hoping that this leak that came from that weekly paper in Beirut could be corraled, because I wanted to explain that we didn't know but what the lives of the people we'd be dealing with would be endangered, and certainly our hostages could be in danger. And so this was all I was trying to say, and I remember saying, "Please—stop speculating and stop asking questions." I didn't know how far we could go before we could get someone killed. And when David [P.] Jacobsen came here and met with you in the Rose Garden, he repeated that without knowing that I had said it. He said the same thing, and quite passionately, that you could get some people killed if we kept on with that story.

Telling the Truth

Q: If I may ask my question, sir, do you feel an obligation always to tell the truth to the American people? Or sometimes do you feel you may have to mislead, as in that case, saying it's without foundation for a higher diplomatic purpose?

P: No, there are things in which I—there are times in which I think you can't answer because of national security or other people's security. But no, I'm not—I'm not going to tell falsehoods to the American people. I'll leave that to others.

"A Sacred Trust"

Q: Mr. President, speaking to young people in your re-election campaign in '84, you referred to government as a sacred trust and you said we're going to keep this trust. The Tower report says that some of your officials in your administration made untruthful statements, and you've acknowledged here that it became a trade of arms for hostages. Do you feel that you kept your promise that you made in that campaign to the young people and that your government has?

P: Yes, I do. And from the very first, I told you all everything I know about this situation. I am still waiting to find out the source of extra money, the bank accounts, and where that extra money went. And that's why I appointed the Tower commission to get to the bottom of this and a special prosecutor. You see, I'm old-fashioned—I call these independent counsels—I still call them special prosecutors.

Q: If I could follow, sir—are you distressed that even your own polls show that a majority of American people, including many who voted for you, believe that you're not telling the full truth on the Iran-Contra affair?

P: Well, in view of what they've been reading and hearing for all these several months—I can understand why they might think that.

Diversion of Funds - 2

Q: Mr. President, in view of what you told the Tower board, and what they concluded—that you had difficulty recalling the decision and the timing of the decision to send the arms to Iran—is it at all conceivable that you may also have forgotten being told about diversion of funds to the Contras?

P: Oh, no. You would have heard me from—without opening the door to the office if I had been told that at any time. No. And I still do not have the answer to that money. The only thing that I can see is that somebody in the interplay of transporting the weapons, must have put an additional price on them. We asked for $12 million, which was the cost—no profit on those weapons—and we got our $12 million back. And it was a complete surprise to me to discover that there was any additional money—and this, I think is the thing—we're still waiting for that to be explained.

Private Funds for the Contras - 1

Q: If I could follow in a related element, then—Mr. North is quoted in the Tower report in a memo he wrote as saying the President obviously knows why—he has been meeting with select people to thank them for their support for democracy in Central America. Were you aware that such meetings that you attended were being used to solicit funds from private citizens in the U.S. for Central America for the Contras?

P: I knew that there were many people privately giving money to things of that kind—in the country here—but the people I met with—and I subsequently found out that some of them were doing this. But when I met with them, I met with them to thank them because they had raised money to put spot ads on television in favor of the Contras in an effort to try and influence Congress to continue giving aid. And I thought that was worth a thanks. I've gone to the public many times since I've been here to get the public to help put the pressure on the Congress for us to get some worthwhile cause....

Right or Wrong?

Q: Mr. President, to follow up Bill's question, the Tower report said that the arms deal with Iran should never have been made in the first place. You have said that you accept the Tower commission report.

P: Yes.

Q: And yet your friends say that in private you still have a deep feeling that you do not feel it was wrong to sell arms in the beginning. I want to know, Mr. President, in your heart, do you feel that you were right or were you wrong in selling arms to Iran?

P: We had quite a debate, and it was true that two of our Cabinet members were very much on the other side. And it turned out they were right because, as I say, it did deteriorate into that.

But what my position was, and still is, you are faced with some kidnappers—they have kidnapped some of our citizens. Now, you cannot do business with them. There's no way that you can discuss ransom or do them any favor which makes taking hostages profitable. But suddenly, an opportunity to get into a conversation with a third party—and you find that that third party maybe can do something you can't do, that they can have an influence on these people over there, these kidnappers, and get your people free—I did not see that as trading anything with the kidnappers. They didn't get any advantage out of this; they didn't show any profit on what was going on. And the place where I was wrong was in not realizing that once that pressure was put on from the other side—and it did stem from the Iranian representatives—they saw an opportunity, they thought, to start bargaining for more weapons than that, more or less, token amount that we had agreed to sell, and to put the price at varying numbers of hostages.

So I still believe that if someone in my family was kidnapped and I went out and hired someone that I thought could get that person safely home, that would not be engaging in ransom of the victim.

Q: If I could follow, Mr. President, you're still arguing that somehow this event deteriorated, it went awry as it went along. I want to know whether you think it was wrong or right in the beginning.

P: Well, if I hadn't thought it was right in the beginning, we never would have started that. It was an opportunity presented by people evidently of some substance in the Iranian government to open up a channel to probably better relations between our two countries, maybe even leading to more influence in getting this terrible war ended there in the Middle East. And they themselves—there was never—when we entered into this, there wasn't any thought of hostages in this particular thing, they'd never been mentioned. It was only when they put in this request, as I've explained, for arms and we had to explain that we didn't do business with people that supported terrorism, that they offered to prove that they weren't supportive of terrorism, either. And this is how we weren't going to overlook an opportunity if we could get those hostages back. And we're not going to overlook an opportunity in the future. But we're not going to try the same thing again, because we see how it worked.

U.S.-Arab Relations

Q: Mr. President, setting aside what the Iran initiative turned into, as you were setting the policy in motion, did you give consideration to how our Arab friends in the region would think about the United States sending arms to their mortal enemy?

P: I think we have a very good relationship—better than we've had in many, many decades—with the countries in the Middle East. And I think that we have proven our friendship for them to the place that they could understand what we were doing. But I also think it ought to be noted that countries in the Middle East, countries in Europe, countries in Asia, and the communist bloc have been selling arms to both sides in this war for the last few years and they've been selling about almost four times as much to Iraq as they have to Iran. And the biggest amount of sales is coming from the communist bloc to both countries. So, what I was sure of was that we were not affecting the balance—military balance between the two countries with the small amount that we were going to sell.

Q: If I could follow up, sir, you've said that Defense Secretary [Caspar W.] Weinberger and Secretary [George P.] Shultz opposed the policy, that you weighed their views and decided to go ahead anyway. Given all the other concerns that you have to deal with as President, how much thought did you give to this policy? Was it a casual thing or did you give it quite an extensive going over before you embraced the policy?

P: The only thing I've done casually since I've been here in these six years is hold a press conference....

Private Funds to the Contras - 2

P: I remembered I promised you I'd call on you.

Q: Thank you, Mr. President, I'm afraid I've caught your laryngitis.

P: Well, imitation is the sincerest form of flattery.

Q: Long before the diversion of funds to the Contras, the Tower board has documented two years of an extensive U.S. military support for the Contras at a time when Congress ruled that to be illegal—air strips, phony corporations, tax-exempt foundations—all directed by Oliver North, and John Poindexter, and before them Robert McFarlane, out of the White House. And, the question is, how could all of this be taking place—millions and millions of dollars—without your having known about it, especially at a time when you were calling the Contras the moral equivalent of our Founding Fathers?

P: Andrea, I don't believe—I was aware that there are private groups and private individuals in this country—I don't believe it was counter to our law, but these people were voluntarily offering help, just as we have in the past. We had a thing called the Abraham Lincoln Brigade in Spain in the Civil War there. And I don't know how much that would amount to. I don't know whether it's enough to keep them in business or not. But I do know that it is absolutely vital that we not back away from this. We've had some experiences in our country where the Congress has turned on a President. Angola was the most recent example, perhaps—when in Angola, when it ceased being a colony, and the civil war broke out there, and there was a communist faction, and there was a group that wanted democracy. And an American President asked Congress just for money. No blood, just money to help the democratic people of Angola have a democratic government. They don't have a democratic government, they have a communist government now, and there are 37,000 Cuban soldiers fighting their battle.

Management Style

Q: But sir, if you were truly unaware of the millions of dollars in government money and government operations that North and Poindexter were directing to the Contras, what does this—respectfully, what does this say about your management style? You have said in your speech that your management style in the Contra-Iran affair did not match your previous track record. The Tower board criticized your management style. If you were unaware of these things and forgot when you actually approved the Iranian arms sales, what does it say about the way you've been managing the Presidency?

P: Andrea, I've been reading a great deal about my management style. I think most people in business will agree that it is a proper management style. You get the best people you can to do a job, then you don't hang over their shoulder criticizing everything they do or picking at them on how they're doing it. You set the policy and I set the policy in this administration, and they are then to implement it. And the only time you move is if the evidence is incontrovertible that they are not following policy or they have gone down a road in which they're not achieving what we want. And I think that that is a good management policy.

Q: Would you—

P: I'm not going to comment now because all that you've mentioned are involved in investigations and I, more than anyone, want these investigations to proceed so that I know, and will know, what has been going on that had been kept from me in various covert operations.

Q: Thank you.

Q: Mr. President, you didn't answer the question on North or Poindexter. Did they deceive you? You didn't answer whether Poindexter or North deceived you.

P: They just didn't tell me what was going on—

Q: Did [Donald T.] Don Regan deceive you?

Q: Did they lie to you?

Q: Did Don Regan pressure you, sir, to change your testimony?

Q: When are you going to come back and see us again, sir? When are you going to come back—

Q: How soon?

Q: Let's have another press conference.

Q: Let's do it again.

Q: How about another half hour?

Q: Did the Vice President—did the Vice President object to this plan in Iran, Mr. President? You said that—

Q: Would you come back and talk to us?

Q: You said that Shultz and Weinberger didn't. Did the Vice President?

P: No.

Q: He didn't object to it? Thank you, sir.

Q: When will you be back, sir?

Q: Come back soon, Mr. President.

Q: We missed you.

Q: Bring Maureen with you.

Q: —Baker here—

Q: Go on back to your reading.

Q: Thank you.

REPORTERS' INTERVIEW WITH PRESIDENT REAGAN

Following are excerpts from the text of President Reagan's April 28, 1987, session with six reporters chosen by the White House:

Iran-Contra and Poindexter

Q: Mr. President, as you know, next week Congress opens hearings on the Iran-Contra matter. Are you worried that when your former National Security Adviser, John [M.] Poindexter, testifies that he won't some way implicate you in the knowledge of diversion of funds to the Contras?

P: No, John Poindexter's an honorable man. And since I was not informed—as a matter of fact, since I did not know that there were any excess funds until we, ourselves, in that check-up after the whole thing blew up, and that was, if you'll remember, that was the incident in which the Attorney General came to me and told me that he had seen a memo that indicated that there were more funds. We had gotten our $12 million dollars back for the weapons that we have provided. I have no way of knowing why or how. I can speculate as to how there was additional money. But we had no indication of it until that time. And that was at 4:30 p.m. on a Monday afternoon. And first thing Tuesday morning he and I met with the joint leadership of the House and Senate, told them what we had learned, that there evidently was something of this kind, and then went before you in the press room and told all of you. And that, as far as I know, factually, that is all I know. I am still waiting to find out exactly how did there turn out to be more money and where did that money go?

Confusion over North

Q: Have you thought about how it was possible that a close adviser who you saw daily, a career military man, failed to notify you of something so important in advance?

P: Well, this is what we're waiting to find out in both instances. Apparently, he told more to Admiral Poindexter, who was my National Security Adviser.

Q: Do you mean Colonel [Oliver L.] North?

P: Yes. And I was—assumed that's—because those were the only two military.

Q: Well, I mean, how is it possible that Poindexter, who you describe as an honorable man—

P: Well, that I don't know.

Q: —and who saw you daily and is a military man—

P: Maybe he thought he was being, in some way, protective of me. I don't know. But that's what we're continuing to investigate to find out.

Q: Protective of what?

P: What?

Q: Protective of what?

P: Well—

Q: Possible wrong-doing?

P: Well, I don't know. The—apparently—and on such things as the Tower commission has come up with and others so far, apparently, there were some go-betweens on the Iranian side who, meeting the problem of did we deliver weapons before we got the money or did we get the money and then deliver the weapons and so forth, arranged some bridge loans so that a post-dated check and so forth could be given and that money could be handled in that way, the transfer. Now, as I said before, my only—the only thing I knew was that weapons were delivered and we received $12 million by way of what's called a sterile bank account, which I understand is the way of transferring money across the ocean. And the only thing that, apparently, from what has been learned so far in these investigations, that, evidently, those with this bridge loan, evidently, put a retail price instead of our wholesale price for the weapons. And, thus, there was more money paid than we had asked for.

Now, that's where my knowledge ends. Who got that, who handled it, what did they do with it and who was involved in that extra money?

Who's in Charge?

Q: Mr. President, in your early years as President, you were credited with restoring faith in government and in the power of the Presidency. But since the Iran affair, polls have reported that people are deeply concerned about who is in charge of the country and where the nation is headed. Now, this lack of trust in government is widespread according to the polls, and I'm wondering what you can do now to reverse that and restore confidence.

P: Well, I don't think the mistrust is justified.

I do think that the manner in which the whole thing when it—it was a covert operation to begin with.

And when the information was leaked through that rag in Beirut and then picked up worldwide—if you will remember, my first reaction was, please, don't. You can get some people killed—meaning the people that we were dealing with on the Iranian side and possibly our hostages. But—and the—Mr. [David P.] Jacobsen when he came home, if you'll recall, made the same plea publicly—and for the same reason.

But, I know that this has been created on the basis that the people have been led to believe I'm covering up—that I do know all about the money and I'm somehow covering. I was interested in one poll that went a step further. It asked another question of the people. And that was, did they think it was all right for me to be covering up. And that poll was taken just of the people that believed I was covering up. And about two-thirds or more of those people said, yes, there are times when a President has to keep his mouth shut and not tell people certain things.

So—but, no, it—as I say, I didn't have any more knowledge than that and I do hope that we can restore to them their faith in government because we have not betrayed the people of this country in any way nor would I—nor would I permit it.

Dealing with Iran

Q: But, is it possible that Admiral Poindexter and Colonel North got the idea that you approved of their actions and that they were acting with your authority? Is that possible?

P: I wouldn't see how, no. No. The things that—now, there again, we don't know their involvement with that money thing, as I said that it was done—that some of the go-betweens put up a bridge loan to enable the transaction to go through with. We don't know the extent of their knowledge of that and why there was extra money or whether they even participated in that in any way or agreed to it. The other thing that the Tower commission report revealed to me was that contrary to what our purpose had been—

in other words, to establish that contact and see if we could not get a basis for a better relationship between our two countries—that we, in return for their asking, as a measure of good faith on our part for this—really it wasn't much more than a token sale of weapons—that we turned around and said, because of the support by Iran of terrorism we're not—we can't do business. They protested that they were opposed to terrorism themselves and would never have—remember, we were talking not to [Ayatollah Ruhollah] Khomeini, as so many of your colleagues have indicated. We were talking to people that had sought a meeting with us on the basis that they were thinking of the government that was going to succeed the Khomeini. And this is why it had to be covert—because of—they were kind of sticking their necks out. And we went along with this and then we put as a condition that said, well, you can prove this anti-terrorism procedure or provision on your part if you can seek to impress on the Hezbollah, who is—sort of have a relationship with Iran—to start turning—give us our hostages back. And the other thing that did develop, then, was that somehow the whole thing just began to deteriorate into a hostage sale thing. And they—suddenly, they were demanding more arms and more deals as to what would be necessary for the hostages and so forth. Well, I wasn't aware of that. We had made an arrangement based on the two things—yes, all right, we'd break our practice and provide those arms. They in turn would do their best—and they did—deliver some hostages to us. And so, the whole distortion of the picture that this was—that we were dealing with the Khomeini, and that in spite of all that he had done to us, and we weren't.

We thought we were going around behind his back with some of his people. And therefore, I don't think there was anything wrong to have accepted the proposal by people from Iran who wanted, apparently, to talk a better relationship with us in the government yet to come. And as I have often said, I didn't think it was trading arms for hostages when the hostages, or the kidnappers weren't getting anything. We were doing business with these people in Iran.

And as I say, there is more yet to come out now as to who was doing what and how much of it was being known. I do know that from the Tower commission report that at one point, [Robert C.] Bud McFarlane was demanding—now, we know this afterward in their report—demanded that they get away from this just straight bargaining about hostages and arms trading and get back to the process of the better relationship. And when they refused to do that, he walked away and wouldn't negotiate any further.

INDEPENDENT COUNSEL ISSUES INTERIM REPORT

Following is the text of independent counsel Lawrence E. Walsh's first interim report to Congress on his investigation, issued April 28, 1987:

Immunity and Prosecution: A First Interim Report

The Independent Counsel statute provides that an "independent counsel appointed under this chapter may make public from time to time, and shall send to the Congress statements or reports on the activities of such independent counsel. These statements and reports shall contain such information as such independent counsel deems appropriate." 28 U.S.C. Section 595(a). On December 19, 1986, the Division for the Purpose of Appointing Independent Counsels of the United States Court of Appeals for the District of Columbia Circuit appointed Lawrence E. Walsh as

Independent Counsel in the Iran/Contra matter. This submission represents his first interim report.

Under the governing statute, Independent Counsel's responsibilities are threefold. First, he has an investigative role. 28 U.S.C. Section 594. Second, he has a prosecutorial role. 28 U.S.C. Section 594. Third, he has a reporting role. 28 U.S.C. Section 595.

As the Select Committees of the House and Senate prepare to begin their joint hearings on the Iran/Contra matter, it is an appropriate time for a first interim report.

The purpose of this report is: (1) to review the scope of Independent Counsel's investigation; (2) to explain the correlation between his investigation and that of the Congressional Committees; and (3) to analyze the problem of immunity.

Events Leading to the Appointment of Independent Counsel

On Tuesday, November 25, 1986, President Reagan announced that the preceding Friday he had directed Attorney General Edwin Meese III to conduct a review of certain activities of the National Security Council with respect to Iran. Attorney General Meese then reported that it had been learned that some of the moneys paid by representatives of Iran for United States arms transferred to Iran had been deposited in bank accounts which were under the control of representatives of the Contras.

On Tuesday, December 2, 1986, the Attorney General announced that he had concluded that he should apply for the appointment of an Independent Counsel; that a possible conflict of interest might result if the Department of Justice continued the investigation; and that the national interest would be served by the appointment of an outside counsel. Two days later, he filed an application for this purpose with the Division for the Purpose of Appointing Independent Counsels of the United States Court of Appeals for the District of Columbia Circuit.

The Appointment of Independent Counsel

On December 19, 1986, the Division of the United States Court of Appeals filed an order appointing the present Independent Counsel. It directed the investigation of:

> *"(1) the direct or indirect sale, shipment, or transfer since in or about 1984 down to the present, of military arms, materiel, or funds to the Government of Iran, officials of that government, persons, organizations or entities connected with or purporting to represent that government, or persons located in Iran;*
> *(2) the direct or indirect sale, shipment, or transfer of military arms, materiel or funds to any government, entity, or person acting, or purporting to act as an intermediary in any transaction above referred to in section (1);*
> *(3) the financing or funding of any direct or indirect sale, shipment or transfer referred to in section (1) or (2);*
> *(4) the diversion of the proceeds from any transaction described in section (1) or (2) to or for any person, organization, foreign government, or any faction or body of insurgents in any foreign country, including, but not limited to Nicaragua;*
> *(5) the provision or coordination of support for persons or entities engaged as military insurgents in armed conflict with the Government of Nicaragua since 1984[.]"*

Organization of the Investigation

On December 19, 1986, William H. Webster, Director of the Federal Bureau of Investigation, assigned to Independent Counsel the group of FBI Special Agents already working on the Iran/Contra matter. By December 31, 1986, the first several Associate Counsel had been appointed and Chief Judge Aubrey E. Robinson, Jr. had assigned temporary space in the United States Courthouse. By early January, additional Associate Counsel were appointed and as security clearances were completed, teams were created—based upon groupings of witnesses and records as well as subject matter. Later, several Special Agents were assigned by the Commissioner of Internal Revenue and Customs Agents were added. At present, there are 23 Associate Counsel, 35 Agents of the FBI, 11 Agents of the IRS, and 4 Customs Agents working on the investigation. The Office has finally obtained permanent quarters.

A grand jury was empaneled on January 28, 1987. It has been hearing testimony regularly two or three full days a week. In addition, 800 interviews have been conducted. Hundreds of boxes of documents from the White House and National Security Council have been examined, as well as approximately 200,000 pages of documents from the Central Intelligence Agency.

Ongoing investigations are presently being conducted at the White House, the Office of the Vice President, the National Security Council, the President's Intelligence Oversight Board, Department of Defense, Department of Justice, Department of State, Department of Transportation, Department of the Treasury, and the Central Intelligence Agency. Requests for documents and information have been addressed to thirteen foreign countries. Others are about to be added. The Swiss Government has supported Independent Counsel's application for certain records of Swiss financial institutions.

An action to block the investigation by constitutional objections to the appointment of Independent Counsel was dismissed by Honorable Barrington D. Parker. *North v. Walsh*, No. 87-0547 (D.D.C. Mar. 12, 1987). The Attorney General supported the investigation by giving Independent Counsel a back-up appointment.

I. The Scope of Independent Counsel's Investigation

The policy of grand jury secrecy underlying Rule 6(e) of the Federal Rules of Criminal Procedure counsels that the fruits of these extensive investigative efforts—the facts uncovered, the crimes, if any, revealed, the leads to be investigated—remain secret at this time. It can be said, however, that the grand jury has been heavily occupied and that the investigation has produced extensive and specific evidence relating to Independent Counsel's mandate from the Court.

The Senate Intelligence Committee report and the Tower Commission report portray an effort by a combination of certain Government officers, former Government officers, and other individuals to supply military assistance to the Contras notwithstanding the legal restrictions of government support of such activities. These activities included government sponsored fund raising to purchase military equipment, the purchase of such equipment, and its transportation to Nicaragua, as well as efforts to conceal these activities from Congress. Subsequently, these reports relate, members of this combination became active in the sale of United States weapons to Iran and the diversion of part of the proceeds thereof.

Independent Counsel must determine whether crimes were committed and whether evidence is available to prove these crimes. It is not sufficient to merely determine what happened. The process requires the identification of individuals and proof beyond a reasonable doubt of the participation of each. In some cases it is not sufficient merely to prove an act, it is also necessary to prove intent. The investigation of this complex series of transactions must be extensive.

The progress of the investigation must also be uneven—much more rapid in some areas than in others. For example, an investigation into financial dealings in the United States may be well advanced, whereas that part of the investigation which depends upon Swiss financial records may be retarded by the delay in obtaining those records. For the purpose of this report, it is sufficient to say that the investigation is being pursued with earnest-

ness and ample basis has been developed for its continuation.

The Vice Chairman of the Senate Select Committee [Warren B. Rudman, R-N.H.], in a recent public statement, suggested that Independent Counsel's investigation should not be unduly prolonged; that any conspiracy to defraud the United States would be difficult to prove; that the inquiry should be narrowed to obstruction of justice; and that grand jury action should not be further delayed. The Senator may well express the point of view of others and his comment demonstrates the timeliness of this report.

There are many reasons why these suggestions may not be adopted:

First, there is no appropriate basis for narrowing Independent Counsel's investigation at this time. Most lines of inquiry are proving fruitful. None has yet been abandoned.

Second, factors affecting the timing of indictments preponderate against haste. Although in other investigations, segments of a broad activity have been singled out for early grand jury action, there are several contrary considerations under present circumstances. The likelihood of conflict between court proceedings and the oncoming Congressional public hearings cannot be ignored. Further, a partial indictment often precipitates the distraction of defense motion practice, which would divert the efforts of Independent Counsel from the ongoing investigation.

Third, an indictment in advance of immunized testimony does not eliminate problems of the testimony's impact on the trial.

Fourth, prudence and justice to individuals may, even in the absence of other factors, justify awaiting the completion of some or all of the Congressional hearings.

Accordingly, this is not the time to narrow or conclude the grand jury process. The Office of Independent Counsel and the grand jury have been proceeding at an accelerating rate and the acceleration promises to continue.

II. The Correlation between the Congressional Inquiry and the Investigation of Independent Counsel

Except for possible problems regarding the grant of immunity which are discussed hereafter, the Congressional Select Committees and Independent Counsel have pursued mutually supportive courses. Honorable Lee H. Hamilton, Chairman of the House Select Committee, foresaw the possible problems of exchange of information and immunity. As a result, a satisfactory mechanism has evolved for the exchange of information through weekly meetings of counsel. Also, as the result of Chairman Hamilton's early warning, Independent Counsel quickly doubled the number of Associate Counsel and was assigned additional FBI Agents by Director Webster. Both committees have been generous in hearing Independent Counsel in an effort to minimize problems.

Independent Counsel has recognized from the outset the extraordinarily important role of the Congressional Select Committees. It is they who are responsible for the accurate public disclosure of the facts concerning transactions of immense national importance. Ultimately, it is they who are empowered to formulate recommendations, not only for the avoidance of similar transactions in the narrow sense, but also for consideration of possible mechanisms for less abrasive formulation of views and policy for the country's external affairs.

The law is clear in the event of conflict as to immunity between the Congressional Committees and Independent Counsel; it is the Congressional Committees which must prevail. This is no more than a recognition of the high political importance of their responsibility. It is further a recognition that the decision as to these priorities calls for the judgment of seasoned political figures who have over the years become experts in the choice between conflicting national options.

Although Independent Counsel has a reporting responsibility, his first responsibility is the prosecution of such crimes as may be exposed. This applies not only to disclosures in his own investigation, but also to crimes exposed by the investigation of the Congressional Committees. In addition, he must monitor the committee hearings for possible perjury. Accordingly, it is not his primary responsibility to develop for the public a knowledge of what occurred. This is the primary responsibility of Congress. In the absence of some factor compelling a different course, it is the plan of Independent Counsel during the period of the public hearings to continue his investigation of possible crimes.

III. Congressional Immunity May Jeopardize Criminal Prosecutions

The immunity statute provides that either House of Congress, or a Committee of either House, may confer immunity on a witness. 18 U.S.C. Section 6005. If either House or a Committee thereof decides to do so, it must notify the Independent Counsel ten days before requesting the court order; the Independent Counsel may then defer the issuance of an immunity order for up to twenty days. 18 U.S.C. Section 6005; 28 U.S.C. Section 594(a) (7).

According to public court documents, Congress has already conferred immunity on at least eleven witnesses.[1] The Independent Counsel neither objected to immunity nor requested a deferral for seven witnesses.[2] He requested a deferral for at least four witnesses.[3] With respect to Lieutenant Colonel Oliver [L.] North and Vice Admiral John [M.] Poindexter, the Committees and the Independent Counsel reached an agreement in which the Committees agreed to defer voting on immunity for the two individuals, and the Independent Counsel agreed not to invoke the twenty-day deferral option if and when such immunity was voted by the Select Committees. Additionally, it has been suggested that the Committees may grant immunity to other individuals, including other central figures in the Iran/Contra investigation.

A. Congressional Grants of Use Immunity Erect Serious Barriers to Prosecution

The Supreme Court held in *Kastigar v. United States,* 406 U.S. 441, 458, 459-60 (1972), that any grant of use immunity results in "a sweeping proscription of any use, direct or indirect, of the compelled testimony and any information derived therefrom", and casts upon the prosecution "the heavy burden of proving that all of the evidence it proposes to use was derived from legitimate independent sources." It is sometimes suggested that *Kastigar* requires only that the prosecution demonstrate that each item of evidence it proposes to use against the immunized witness was obtained from some source independent of the immunized testimony. However, this burden—while in itself an onerous one—may not be the only burden imposed upon the prosecution by *Kastigar.*

Although the Supreme Court has not yet determined the issue, some lower courts have held that use immunity bars a prosecutor not only from making any evidentiary use of immunized testimony, but also from making any significant nonevidentiary use, including "assistance in focusing the investigation, deciding to initiate prosecution, planning cross-examination, and otherwise generally planning trial strategy." *United States v. McDaniel,* 482 F.2d 305, 311 (8th Cir. 1973); accord, e.g., *United States v. Semkiw,* 712 F.2d 891, 894-95 (3d Cir. 1983). But see *United States v. Byrd,* 765 F.2d 1524, 1531 (11th Cir. 1985). In practice, the burden of proving that the prosecution has made no significant nonevidentiary use of the immunized testimony could be difficult to satisfy, particularly in a highly publicized matter. See, e.g., *United States v. Romano,* 583 F.2d 1, 7-9 (1st Cir. 1978).

As stated in the United States Attorneys' Manual of the United States Department of Justice: "Although the person may still be prosecuted on the basis of independent evidence for any offense about which he/she testifies, in practice, the government's burden of proving the independent nature of its evidence is so great that successful prosecution would usually be extremely difficult. Consequently, under the circumstances of many cases, use of the statute will effectively preclude a future prosecution of the matters to which his/her testimony related." United States Attorneys' Manual at 1-11.212.

It is sometimes suggested that the experience of the Watergate prosecutions demonstrates that Congressional grants of use immunity do not significantly impede successful prosecutions.

This is very misleading. If anything, the Watergate experience demonstrates the contrary. Although two immunized witnesses in the Watergate matter—John Dean and Charles Colson—subsequently pleaded guilty, *no immunized Watergate witness who refused to plead guilty was successfully tried and convicted.* Gordon Strachan, the only immunized witness who was included in the Watergate coverup indictment, never went to trial because the Watergate Special Prosecutor conceded that there was "a significant possibility that Strachan eventually might prevail on his [taint] claim." Strachan, *Self-Incrimination, Immunity and Watergate,* 56 Tex. L. Rev. 791, 814-20 (1978). The same happened in the case of Felipe De Diego, who was granted immunity by State authorities in connection with the break-in of the offices of Daniel Ellsberg's psychiatrist. See *United States v. De Diego,* 511 F.2d 818, 822-25 (D.C. Cir. 1975).

Thus, use immunity cannot be granted without a full recognition that it will have a serious and possibly destructive impact upon a subsequent prosecution.

B. The Independent Counsel Has Undertaken Extensive Efforts to Protect the Possibility of Prosecution

Recognizing the imminence of Congressional immunity, the Independent Counsel has made extensive efforts to protect the possibility of prosecution.

First, as described above, the Independent Counsel has expedited some parts of the investigation most likely to be the subject of Congressional immunity.

Second, the Independent Counsel has developed and instituted a filing procedure to preserve evidence in a demonstrably "untainted" form. Before Congressional immunity becomes effective for an individual who is under investigation, the Independent Counsel gathers pertinent evidence and possible leads which are sealed and then lodged with the court. This procedure helps establish the independent origin of this investigative evidence and leads.

Third, the Independent Counsel has taken steps to insulate the attorneys and investigators concerned with the possible prosecution of an immunized individual from his immunized testimony. Some attorneys will be designated as an "exposed" team, and they will be familiar with the immunized testimony. This team is necessary, among other reasons, for liaison work with other government agencies and the Select Committees, and to monitor the hearings for possible perjury.

Through these steps Independent Counsel is making a determined effort to preserve the possibility of prosecutions.

C. Additional Grants of Immunity to Central Figures in the Investigation Could Have a Devastating Effect on Possible Prosecutions

Despite the rigorous efforts of the Independent Counsel to protect possible prosecutions, grants of immunity to central figures in the investigation might preclude future prosecution of those individuals.

The unique nature of the Iran/Contra matter poses special problems. Few cases even remotely approach the exposure of immunized testimony created by nationally televised—and nationally scrutinized—Congressional hearings. The underlying issues involve matters of great public import and interest. High government officials are involved, and the investigations have received intense national attention. Except, perhaps, for Watergate, the situation is virtually unprecedented.

The Watergate experience suggests the extreme difficulty of prosecution after the grant of immunity: again, not one immunized Watergate witness who refused to plead guilty was successfully tried and convicted after the grant of immunity.

Given the special nature of this investigation, it would be particularly unfortunate if otherwise appropriate prosecutions were precluded by Congressional grants of immunity. The allegations in the investigation concern possible violations of public trust and possible misuse of position by high government officials and their manipulation by former government officials. Large sums of public money are unaccounted for and those most knowledgeable resist public disclosure. In such matters, the public is entitled to a fair and deliberate prosecutive judgment. Additional grants of Congressional immunity to central figures may frustrate the even-handed application of justice which would be expected as a matter of course for principal figures in less spectacular activities.

D. A Central Figure in the Investigation Should Be Immunized Only on the Basis of an Overriding and Compelling Need

Since any grant of use immunity endangers a subsequent prosecution of the immunized witness, such immunity should not be granted to a central participant in a suspected scheme to defraud the United States unless an overriding need compels such amnesty.

The question whether immunity should be granted to aid the Congressional inquiry is, of course, itself a policy question of great magnitude. The Select Committees and the Houses they represent have the ultimate decision as to the extent to which prosecution for crime shall be subordinated to legislative interests. At the same time, Independent Counsel finds it imperative to report that further grants of immunity to central figures in the investigation will jeopardize their prosecutions and may prevent a fair and judicious assessment of individual culpability.

For this reason Independent Counsel respectfully urges the following standards for consideration in granting immunity:

1. What assurance is there that the prospective witness will in return for immunity tell the truth? Has there been a proffer of his testimony which can be checked for honesty against the evidence already assembled?
2. Would the prospective witness ordinarily be a logical subject for prosecutive consideration? Is there substantial evidence of an enterprise designed to frustrate the enacted legislative policy of the United States? Was the prospective witness a sophisticated and deliberate leader of that enterprise? Did he personally profit from it? Did he corrupt government officers of the United States or of foreign governments? Did he, if an officer of the United States, accept, or agree to accept, proceeds of transactions ostensibly for the benefit of the United States?
3. Is there no less culpable person to supply the evidence sought by grant of immunity?

Conclusion

Reasonable restraints in the grant of immunity by the Congressional Committees will enable both investigations to achieve the important results properly expected of them. The investigation of Independent Counsel is progressing and accelerating. It promises a result which will satisfy the public interest in even-handed application of the rule of law.

LAWRENCE E. WALSH
Independent Counsel

April 28, 1987

---

[1] These witnesses are Joan Corbin, John Cupp, Edward de Garay, Cynthia Dondlinger, Robert [C.] Dutton, Robert [L.] Earl, Richard Gadd, Fawn Hall, Albert Hakim, Shirley Napier, and Robert [W.] Owen.
[2] Corbin, Cupp, de Garay, Dondlinger, Dutton, Hall, and Napier.
[3] Earl, Gadd, Hakim, and Owen.

REAGAN ADDRESS, DEMOCRATS' RESPONSE

Following are excerpts from the text of President Reagan's August 12, 1987, address on the Iran-contra affair and his plans for his last seventeen months in office, and excerpts from the Democrats' response given by Sen. George J. Mitchell, D-Maine:

President Reagan's Address

My fellow Americans, I've said on several occasions that I wouldn't comment about the recent Congressional hearings on the Iran-Contra matter until the hearings were over. Well, that time has come, so tonight I want to talk about some of the lessons we've learned.

But rest assured, that's not my sole subject this evening. I also want to talk about the future and getting on with things, because the people's business is waiting.

These past nine months have been confusing and painful ones for the country. I know you have doubts in your own minds about what happened in this whole episode. What I hope is not in doubt, however, is my commitment to the investigations themselves.

So far, we've had four investigations—by the Justice Department, the Tower Board [a special review board, appointed by the president and headed by former senator John Tower, R-Texas], the Independent Counsel, and the Congress. I requested three of those investigations, and I endorsed and cooperated fully with the fourth—the Congressional hearings—supplying over 250,000 pages of White House documents, including parts of my own private diaries. Once I realized I hadn't been fully informed, I sought to find the answers.

Some of the answers I don't like. As the Tower Board reported, and as I said last March, our original initiative rapidly got all tangled up in the sale of arms, and the sale of arms got tangled up with hostages. Secretary [of State George P.] Shultz and Secretary [of Defense Caspar W.] Weinberger both predicted that the American people would immediately assume this whole plan was an arms for hostages deal and nothing more. Well, unfortunately, their predictions were right.

As I said to you in March, I let my preoccupation with the hostages intrude into areas where it didn't belong. The image—the reality of Americans in chains, deprived of their freedom and families so far from home, burdened my thoughts. And this was a mistake.

My fellow Americans, I've thought long and often about how to explain to you what I intended to accomplish, but I respect you too much to make excuses. The fact of the matter is that there's nothing I can say that will make the situation right. I was stubborn in my pursuit of a policy that went astray.

Diversion of Funds

The other major issue of the hearings, of course, was the diversion of funds to the Nicaraguan Contras.

[Lt.] Col. [Oliver L.] North and [Rear] Adm. [John M.] Poindexter believed they were doing what I would've wanted done—keeping the democratic resistance alive in Nicaragua. I believed then and I believe now in preventing the Soviets from establishing a beachhead in Central America.

Since I have been so closely associated with the cause of the Contras, the big question during the hearings was whether I knew of the diversion. I was aware the resistance was receiving funds directly from third countries and from private efforts, and I endorsed those endeavors wholeheartedly. But, let me put this in capital letters, I did not know about the diversion of funds. Indeed, I didn't know there were excess funds.

Yet the buck does not stop with Adm. Poindexter, as he stated in his testimony; it stops with me. I am the one who is ultimately accountable to the American people. The Admiral testified he wanted to protect me; yet no President should ever be protected from the truth. No operation is so secret that it must be kept from the Commander-in-Chief. I had the right, the obligation, to make my own decision.

I heard someone the other day ask why I wasn't outraged. Well, at times, I've been mad as a hornet. Anyone would be—just look at the damage that's been done and the time that's been lost. But I've always found that the best therapy for outrage and anger is action.

Making Changes

I've tried to take steps so that what we've been through can't happen again, either in this administration or future ones. But I remember very well what the Tower Board said last February when it issued this report. It said the failure was more in people than in process.

We can build in every precaution known to the world. We can design the best system ever devised by man. But in the end people are going to have to run it. And we will never be free of human hopes, weaknesses and enthusiasms.

Let me tell you what I've done to change both the system and the people who operate it.

First of all, I've brought in a new and knowledgeable team. I have a new National Security Adviser, a new Director of the CIA [Central Intelligence Agency], a new Chief of Staff here at the White House. And I've told them that I must be informed and informed fully.

In addition, I adopted the Tower Board's model of how the NSC [National Security Council] process and staff should work and I prohibited any operational role by the NSC staff in covert activities.

The report I ordered reviewing our nation's covert operations has been completed. There were no surprises. Some operations were continued and some were eliminated because they'd outlived their usefulness.

I am also adopting new, tighter procedures on consulting with and notifying the Congress on future covert action findings.

We will still pursue covert operations when appropriate, but each operation must be legal and it must meet a specific policy objective.

The problem goes deeper, however, than policies and personnel. Probably the biggest lesson we can draw from the hearings is that the executive and legislative branches of government need to regain trust in each other. We've seen the results of that mistrust in the form of lies, leaks, divisions and mistakes. We need to find a way to cooperate while realizing foreign policy can't be run by committee. And I believe there's now the growing sense that we can accomplish more by cooperating.

And in the end, this may be the eventual blessing in disguise to come out of the Iran-Contra mess.

Looking Ahead

But now let me turn to the other subject I promised to discuss this evening—the future. There are now 17 months left in this administration and I want them to be prosperous, productive ones for the American people.

When you first elected me to this office, you elected me to pursue a new, different direction for America. When you elected me the second time, you reaffirmed your desire to continue that course. My hopes for this country are as fervent today as they were in 1981. Up until the morning I leave this house, I intend to do what you sent me here to do—lead the nation toward the goals we agreed on when you elected me.

Let me tell you where I'm going to put my heart and my energies for the remainder of my term....

Democratic Resistance in Nicaragua

And there's another area that will occupy my time and my heart—the cause of democracy. There are Americans still burning for freedom—Central Americans, the people of Nicaragua. Over the last 10 years, democrats have been emerging all over the world. In Central and South America alone, 10 countries have been added to the ranks. The question is, will Nicaragua ever be added to this honor roll?

As you know, I am totally committed to the democratic resistance—the freedom fighters and their pursuit of democracy in Nicaragua. Recently there's been important progress on the diplomatic front, both here in Washington and in the region itself.

Central American Peace Plan

My administration and the leadership of Congress have put forth a bipartisan initiative proposing concrete steps that can bring an end to the conflict there. Our key point was that the communist regime in Nicaragua should do what it formally pledged to do in 1979—respect the Nicaraguan people's basic rights of free speech, free press, free elections, and religious liberty. Instead, those who govern in Nicaragua chose to turn their country over to the Soviet Union to be a base for communist expansion on the American mainland.

The need for democracy in Nicaragua was also emphasized in the agreement signed by the five Central American presidents in Guatemala last Friday. We welcome this development and pledge our support to democracy and those fighting for freedom. We have always been willing to talk—we have never been willing to abandon those who are fighting for democracy and freedom.

I'm especially pleased that in the United States' diplomatic initiative we once again have the beginnings, however uncertain, of a bipartisan foreign policy. The recent hearings emphasized the need for such bipartisanship, and I hope this cautious start will grow and blossom.

These are among the goals for the remainder of my term as President. I believe they're the kinds of goals that will advance the security and prosperity and future of our people. I urge the Congress to be as thorough and energetic in pursuing these ends as it was in pursuing the recent investigation.

My fellow Americans, I have a year-and-a-half before I have to clean out this desk. I'm not about to let the dust and cobwebs settle on the furniture in this office, or on me. I have things I intend to do, and with your help, we can do them.

Good night and God bless you.

Democrats' Response

A great theologian once said, "There's just enough bad in human beings to make democracy necessary, and there's just enough good in them to make it possible."

The men who wrote the American Constitution shared that view.

They recognized the immense strength of freedom.

But they also understood the corrupting capacity of political power.

This year we observe the 200th anniversary of our Constitution.

It's been a success because it protects individual liberty, and at the same time it shares and limits the power of government, preventing any individual or institution from achieving total control.

It's a delicate, even a fragile balance.

But it works.

We're blessed to be citizens of the most free, the most open, the most prosperous, the most just nation in human history.

We enjoy those blessings because Americans understand that the balance can be maintained only if we adhere to certain basic beliefs and govern ourselves by certain rules.

None is more important than the rule of law.

In America, every person is equal before the law, no person is so high as to be above the law, and no end, however noble, justifies illegal means.

The Iran-Contra scandal is about the rule of law.

It reminds us of how much democracy asks of us, how quickly

its demands can become frustrating to those who, even though acting with patriotic motives, are convinced that they alone know what's best.

It reminds us of the continuing need to affirm our commitment to the rule of law, the need for our leaders to say, clearly and unequivocally, that we condemn any violation of law, we condemn lying to the American people or to Congress, we condemn the destruction of important documents.

America will remain a free and democratic society only if the people demand of the Government what the Government demands of the people: Obey the law.

Another basic principle of our democratic system is accountability, which means simply that public officials, like private citizens, are responsible for the consequences of their acts.

If accountability in our democracy means anything, it means, as the President said tonight, that the buck stops with him.

Let there be no misunderstanding.

The mistakes were not only in the execution of policies.

The major mistakes were in the policies themselves.

And the policies were the President's.

The President personally approved, in writing, the sale of weapons to Iran.

That was a mistake, a mistake that contradicted our publicly stated policy, that worked against our interests in the Persian Gulf, a mistake so grave that Americans now risking their lives in that region face the terrible possibility of attack by a nation we've helped to arm.

The President personally approved, in writing, the exchange of arms for hostages.

That was a mistake, a mistake that also contradicted our publicly stated policy, that left American policy against terrorism in ruins, a mistake so grave that there are just as many Americans now held hostage in Lebanon as there were when this effort began.

Those were serious mistakes.

But once recognized and corrected they should be put behind us.

For there's much to be done together. . . .

We're encouraged by recent progress toward peace in Central America.

The leadership of the President and the Speaker of the House of Representatives, Jim Wright [D-Texas], and the courage of the leaders of the Central American democracies—especially President [Oscar] Arias of Costa Rica—combine to offer hope for a peaceful resolution of the problems in that troubled region. . . .

Bibliography

Books

Arms for Hostages: The Official Report of the President's Special Review Board (Tower Commission Report). Torrance, Calif.: Diane Books Publishing, 1987. (Report also published by New York: Bantam Books/Time Books, 1987.)

Bahbah, Bishara. *Israel and Latin America: The Military Connection.* New York: St. Martin's Press, 1986.

Berman, Karl. *Under the Big Stick: Nicaragua and the U.S. since 1848.* Boston: South End Press, 1987.

Burns, E. Bradford. *At War in Nicaragua: The Reagan Doctrine and the Politics of Nostalgia.* New York: Harper and Row, 1987.

Ferrari, Paul L., Jeffrey W. Knopf, and Raul L. Madrid. *U.S. Arms Exports: Policies and Contractors.* Washington, D.C.: Investor Responsibility Research Center, 1987.

Hammond, Paul Y., David J. Louscher, Michael D. Salomone, and Norman A. Graham. *The Reluctant Supplier: U.S. Decision-Making for Arms Sales.* Boston: Oelgeschlager, Gunn and Hain, 1983.

Hunter, Jane, Jonathan Marshall, and Peter D. Scott. *The Iran-Contra Connection: Secret Teams and Covert Operation in the Reagan Era.* Boston: South End Press, 1987.

Klieman, Aaron S. *Israel's Global Reach: Arms Sales as Diplomacy.* Elmsford, N.Y.: Pergamon Press, 1985.

Labrie, Roger. *U.S. Arms Sales Policy: Background and Issues.* Washington, D.C.: American Enterprise Institute for Public Policy Research, 1982.

LaFeber, Walter. *Inevitable Revolutions: The United States in Central America.* New York: W. W. Norton, 1983.

Lieverman, Theodore, and Peter Schneider. *Memorandum of Law on the United States Policy toward Nicaragua.* New York: National Lawyers Guild, n.d.

Louscher, David J., and Michael D. Salomone, eds. *Marketing Security Assistance: New Perspectives on Arms Sales.* Lexington, Mass.: Lexington Books, 1987.

McKinlay, R. D., and A. Mughan. *Aid and Arms to the Third World: The Distribution and Impact of U.S. Official Transfers.* New York: St. Martin's Press, 1984.

Meyer, Peter. *Defiant Patriot: The Life and Exploits of Lt. Colonel Oliver L. North.* New York: St. Martin's Press, 1987.

National Security Archive. *The Chronology: The Documented Day-by-Day Account of the Secret Military Assistance to Iran and the Contras.* New York: Warner Books, 1987.

Norsworthy, Kent, and William Robinson. *David and Goliath: The U.S. War against Nicaragua.* New York: Monthly Review Press, 1987.

Pastor, Robert A. *Condemned to Repetition: The United States and Nicaragua.* Princeton, N.J.: Princeton University Press, 1988.

Pierre, Andrew J. *The Global Politics of Arms Sales.* Princeton, N.J.: Princeton University Press, 1981.

Prados, John. *President's Secret Wars: CIA and Pentagon Covert Operations since World War II.* New York: Morrow, 1986.

Ra'Anan, Uri, Robert L. Pfaltzgraff, and Geoffery Kemp. *Arms Transfer to the Third World: Problems and Policies.* Boulder, Colo.: Westview Press, 1978.

Ranelagh, John. *The Agency: The Rise and Decline of the CIA.* New York: Simon and Schuster, 1987.

Sanchez, James J. *Index to the Tower Commission Report.* Jefferson, N.C.: McFarland and Company, 1987. (Index is to *Tower Commission Report,* New York: Bantam Books/Time Books, 1987.)

Siegel, Mark A., Nancy Jacobs, and Carol Foster, eds. *Arms Sales: A Reflection of Foreign Policy.* Plano, Texas: Information Aids, 1986.

Taking the Stand: The Testimony of Lieutenant Colonel Oliver L. North. New York: Pocket Books, 1987.

Tessendorf, K. C. *Uncle Sam in Nicaragua: A History.* New York: Macmillan, 1987.

The Middle East, 6th ed. Washington, D.C.: Congressional Quarterly, 1986.

Turner, R. F. *Nicaragua vs. United States: A Look at the Facts.* Elmsford, N.Y.: Pergamon Press, 1987.

Varas, Augusto. *Militarization and the International Arms Race in Latin America.* Boulder, Colo.: Westview Press, 1985.

Woodward, Bob. *VEIL: The Secret Wars of the CIA, 1981-1987.* New York: Simon and Schuster, 1987.

Bibliography

Articles

Alterman, Eric. "Elliott Abrams: The Teflon Assistant Secretary." *Washington Monthly,* May 1987, 19-26.

———. "Inside Ollie's Mind: A Catalog of Lies." *New Republic,* February 16, 1987, 12-15.

"America's Shadow Network: Behind the Secret Deals with Iran and the Contras." *U.S. News & World Report,* December 15, 1986, 22-32.

"Arms to Iran: Reverberations." *American-Arab Affairs,* Spring 1987, 1-29.

Arnold, Terrell E. "The King Is Hostage: Hostage Negotiations in Iran-Contra Arms Sale." *National Review,* April 10, 1987, 34-37.

Aronson, James. "Times Change: The Fifth Remembered." *Nation,* December 27, 1986, 731-734.

"Assistance for Nicaraguan Democratic Resistance: February 25th Message to the Congress." *Department of State Bulletin,* May 1986, 81-85.

Barnes, Fred. "By a Thread: Elliott Abrams." *New Republic,* July 13, 1987, 11-13.

"Bent Arrow: An Arms-for-Iran Plot That Failed." *Time,* August 12, 1985, 16.

Ben-Yishai, Ron. "The Murky World of Weapons Dealers: How Arms Traders Bartered with U.S. Policy." *Time,* January 19, 1987, 26-29.

Brookhiser, Richard. "The Public Brawl, the Secret War." *National Review,* January 30, 1987, 34-37.

Brownstein, Ronald. "Coping with Iran: Preoccupation with the Iran Arms Scandal Has Forced All the Candidates for the Presidency, Democrats as Well as Republicans, to Rethink Their Political Strategies." *National Journal,* January 3, 1987, 13-16.

Brzezinski, Zbigniew. "Deciding Who Makes Foreign Policy." *New York Times Magazine,* September 18, 1983, 56-61.

Brzoska, Michael. "Profiteering on the Iran-Iraq War." *Bulletin of the Atomic Scientists,* June 1987, 42-45.

"Central America: Ronald Reagan's Letter to the Congress." *Department of State Bulletin,* September 1986, 91.

"Change of Plea and Iran-Contra Affair." *Economist,* May 23, 1987, 26-27.

"Charging up Capitol Hill: How Oliver North Captured the Imagination of America." *Time,* July 20, 1987, 12-27.

Church, George J. "Arguing about Means and Ends: Legality of United States Military Aid to Nicaragua." *Time,* April 18, 1983, 30-31.

———. "But What Laws Were Broken?" *Time,* June 1, 1987, 24-26.

———. "What He Needs to Know." *Time,* December 22, 1986, 14-20.

"CIA Support for Nicaraguan Rebels." *U.S. News & World Report,* November 7, 1983, 93.

Codevilla, Angelo. "The Reagan Doctrine: (As Yet) a Declaratory Policy." *Strategic Review,* Summer 1986, 17-26.

Coll, Alberto R. "Soviet Arms and Central American Turmoil." *World Affairs,* Summer 1985, 7-17.

Colson, Charles. "Must Governments Deal in Deceit?" *Christianity Today,* February 6, 1987, 66.

"Contra Aid and the Reagan Doctrine: A Major Issue Forum." *Congressional Research Service Review,* March, 1987, 1-25.

"Contretemps: Snags in Push for Aid." *Time,* June 23, 1986, 36.

Cooper, Ann. "Third World Insurgent Groups Learning to Play the Washington Lobbying Game." *National Journal,* February 8, 1986, 329-333.

Cordesman, Anthony H. "Realities and Unrealities of the Middle Eastern Arms Market." *RUSI, Journal of the Royal United Services Institute for Defence Studies,* March 1987, 47-56.

"Council of Mutual Economic Assistance-Nicaragua: Agreement on Cooperation." *International Legal Materials,* September 1985, 1408-1410.

Cox, Archibald. "Iranian Arms and Contra Aid: Some Underlying Questions." *Vital Speeches,* June 15, 1987, 531-533.

Crovitz, L. Gordon. "Congress Is Hoist by Its Boland Petard." *Wall Street Journal,* July 7, 1987, 28 (Eastern edition); 24 (Western edition).

Cuau, Yves. " 'Reasonable Goals,' 'Sadness and Concern' for the President." *World Press Review,* January 1987, 13-14.

Cutler, Lloyd. "Self-Incrimination Privilege: From Star Chamber to Irangate." *Legal Times,* May 11, 1987, 16.

Depalo, William A., Jr. "The Military Situation in Nicaragua." *Military Review,* August 1986, 28-41.

Destler, I. M. "A Job That Doesn't Work." *Foreign Policy,* Spring 1980, 80-88.

———. "National Security Advice to U.S. Presidents: Some Lessons from Thirty Years." *World Politics,* January 1977, 143-176

———. "National Security Management: What Presidents Have Wrought." *Political Science Quarterly,* Winter 1980-81, 573-588.

Doerner, William R. "Retreating on Rebel Aid: Congress Forces the President to Compromise on His Contra Request." *Time,* April 29, 1985, 40-42.

Donnelly, Harrison. "National Security Council." *Editorial Research Reports,* January 16, 1987, 17-27.

Draper, Theodore. "Reagan's Junta." *New York Review of Books,* January 29, 1987, 5-10.

Duffy, Brian. "What Did They Know, and When? The Iran-Contra Scandal Promises to Spread, Touching Other Administration Officials, Damaging Ronald Reagan and Threatening His Presidency." *U.S. News & World Report,* December 8, 1986, 16-21+.

———. "Who's in Charge Here? Secret Iran Contacts Spell Trouble for Reagan with Congress, Allies." *U.S. News & World Report,* November 24, 1986, 18-22.

Eisler, Kim I. "Elliott Abrams, Esq.: Defiant and Elusive." *Legal Times,* June 8, 1987, 2.

———. "Mark Belnick: Liman's Deft Deputy." *Legal Times,* May 25, 1987, 4.

Elmer-DeWitt, Phillip. "Can a System Keep a Secret? The Iranscam Revelations Raise Thorny Issues about Privacy." *Time,* April 6, 1987, 68-69.

Fialka, John J. "War Center: How Iranian Dealers Buy Arms of All Sorts through British Office: They Spend $3 Billion or More a Year on Iraq Campaign, Much Favor U.S. Weaponry: An Alleged Israeli Connection." *Wall Street Journal,* January 30, 1987, 1.

FitzGerald, Frances. "Reagan's Band of True Believers." *New York Times Magazine,* May 10, 1987, 36.

Frank, Allan Dodds. "Shopping the Great Satan: Smuggling of U.S. Weapons to Iran." *Forbes,* January 27, 1986, 32-33.

Friend, David. "A Man of Many Faces: Oliver North May Go to Jail, But Iranscam's Central Player Shows Another Side—as a Suburban Father." *Life,* August 1987, 12-17.

Garment, Leonard. "Garment I, II." *New Republic,* April 13, 1987, 6.

Gerassi, John. "Pluralism vs. Centralism in Nicaragua: The Sandinistas under Attack." *Scandinavian Journal of Development Alternatives,* March 1986, 77-94.

Geyelin, Philip. "The Reagan Crisis: Dreaming Impossible Dreams." *Foreign Affairs,* 1986, 447-457.

Ginsberg, Marc. "Sciaroni Findings Were Faulty: Legal Memo on Contra Aid." *Legal Times,* June 29, 1987, 20.

"Gipperdammerung? Cui bono?" *National Review,* January 30, 1987, 19-21.

Gomez, Linda. "Tracking Oliver North." *Life,* May 1987, 30-36.

Goodman, Allan E. "Reforming U.S. Intelligence." *Foreign Policy,* Summer 1987, 121-136.

Greenberger, Robert S., and Monica Langley. "Intrepid Marine: Col. North's Ideology and Zealousness Led Him to Contra's Cause; Big Desire to Please Superiors Also Seems a Motivation." *Wall Street Journal,* December 31, 1986, 1+.

Gutman, Roy. "Nicaragua: America's Diplomatic Charade." *Foreign Policy,* Fall 1984, 3-23.

Hackett, George. "The Canonization of Ollie." *Newsweek,* December 22, 1986, 26.

Halperin, Morton. "The Case against Covert Action." *Nation,* March 21, 1987, 345-347.

"Have Guns, Will Travel." *Newsweek,* November 3, 1986, 32-39.

Hitchens, Christopher. " 'Stab-in-the-Back' Culture." *New Statesman,* January 9, 1987, 19-20.

Hodgson, Godfrey. "Not for the First Time: Antecedents of the 'Irangate' Scandal." *Political Quarterly,* April/June 1987, 125-138.

Hoffman, David. "Reagan Gives Abrams a Mild Nod: President Says He Isn't Covered by Boland Amendment." *Washington Post,* June 12, 1987, A1.

Horowitz, Irving Louis. "The Unraveling of the Reagan Presidency: Government by Satrapies." *New Leader,* December 29, 1986, 5-7.

Hosenball, Mark. "The Culture of Lying: A Catalog of Whoppers." *New Republic,* July 13, 1987, 16-18.

———. "The Khashoggi Memo: Tips from Iranamok's Middleman." *New Republic,* February 2, 1987, 14-15.

Hunter, Shireen T. "After the Ayatollah." *Foreign Policy,* Spring 1987, 77-97.

Ignatius, David. "Volatile Spy Chief: Casey Raises Morale and Budget at CIA, But Not Public Image." *Wall Street Journal,* January 11, 1985, 1+.

"Issues of Law and Ethics." *Time,* March 2, 1987, 16.

Jameson, Donald F. B. "The Iran Affair, Presidential Authority and Covert Operations." *Strategic Review,* Winter 1987, 24-30.

Jenkins, Tony. "Administration Strategy: One Last Chance for the Contras." *Nation,* May 16, 1987, 638-640.

Johns, Michael. "The Lessons of Afghanistan: Bipartisan Support for Freedom Fighters Pays Off." *Policy Review,* Spring 1987, 32-35.

"Joint Chiefs Chairman Denies Significance of Iran Arms Deals." *Aviation Week and Space Technology,* December 1, 1986, 41.

Kaplan, David A. "Prosecutor of Few Words, A Low-Key Approach in Iran-Contra Affair." *National Law Journal,* March 16, 1987, 25.

Kapstein, Jonathan, and John Rossant. "How the World Keeps the Iran-Iraq War Going." *Business Week,* December 29, 1986, 46-48.

"Khashoggi in the Middle." *Fortune,* January 5, 1987, 12.

Kirkpatrick, Jeane J., Daniel P. Moynihan, Trent Lott, and Zbigniew Brzezinski. "Lessons of the Iran-Contra Affair." *Reader's Digest,* June 1987, 72-77.

Kirschten, Dick. "Competent Manager: If He Lacks the Aura of a Kissinger or Brzezinski, National Security Adviser Frank C. Carlucci III May Still Be the Right Man to Clean Up after the Iran-Contra Mess." *National Journal,* February 28, 1987, 468-469+.

Knowlton, Christopher. "The Man Asking Iranscam's Tough Questions: Champion Litigator Arthur Liman Is Also the Fellow Whose Testimony Helped Send Texaco into Bankruptcy." *Fortune,* June 8, 1987, 76-81.

Kohn, Alan. "U.S. Cracks Scheme to Ship American-Made Arms to Iran." *New York Law Journal,* April 23, 1986, 1.

Kornbluh. "Ollie's Follies: What North Might Have Wrought." *Nation,* June 27, 1987, 871-874.

———. "The Selling of FDN: Contraprop." *Nation,* January 17, 1987, 40-44.

Krauss, Clifford. "Revolution in Central America?" *Foreign Affairs,* Winter 1987, 564-582.

Krauss, Clifford, and Robert S. Greenberger. "Latin Focus: Despite Fears of U.S., Soviet Aid to Nicaragua Appears to be Limited; White House Still Will Push to Aid Contras to Lessen Risk of Region Revolution." *Wall Street Journal,* April 3, 1985, 1+.

Krauthammer, Charles. "Divided Superpower: The Real Cause of the North Affair." *New Republic,* December 22, 1986, 14-16.

Krepon, Michael. "The Iran-Arms Control Connection." *Bulletin of the Atomic Scientists,* March 1987, 9-10.

Lacovara, Philip. "A Watergate Counsel Reflects: What Laws Apply to Iran Deal?" *Legal Times,* February 23, 1987, 14.

Lamar, Jacob V., Jr. "A Big Bonus for 'Belly Button': Iran-Arms Money Turns Up in an Account Reserved for Oliver North." *Time,* June 15, 1987, 18-19.

———. "From Many Strands, a Tangled Web." *Time,* December 8, 1986, 28-31.

———. "The Right Man at the Right Time: Howard Baker Is a Popular Choice as the New Chief of Staff." *Time,* March 9, 1987, 27.

"Left in Limbo: Congress and Contra Aid." *Time,* April 28, 1986, 34.

"Legal Limits on Aid to the Contras." *Washington Post,* May 28, 1987, A14.

Maas, Peter. "Oliver North's Strange Recruits." *New York Times Magazine,* January 18, 1987, 20.

Madison, Christopher. "Iran: Act Two: With the Opening of Congressional Hearings on the Iran-Contra Arms Affair, Expectations of a Dramatic Watergate-Like Summer Will Be High—Perhaps Too High." *National Journal,* May 2, 1987, 1050-1055.

———. "The Arms Sale Say-So: The Iran Affair Has Lent Steam to Congress's Efforts to Gain Control over Arms Sales." *National Journal,* March 21, 1987, 667-671.

———. "The Widening Gap: The Crisis over Arms Sales to Iran Is Only the Latest Episode in a Long-Running War Between Congress and the White House on the Conduct of Foreign Policy." *National Journal,* December 20, 1986, 3060-3064.

Magnuson, Ed. "Once More into the Breach: Reagan Renews His Bid for Military Aid To 'Freedom Fighters.' " *Time,* February 3, 1986, 21.

Bibliography

____. "Plumbing the CIA's Shadowy Role: What Bill Casey Didn't Know—and When He Didn't Know It." *Time,* December 22, 1986, 26-32.

Mallison, Sally V., and W. Thomas Mallison. "The Changing U.S. Position on Palestinian Self-Determination and the Impact of the Iran-Contra Scandal." *Journal of Palestine Studies,* Spring 1987, 101-114.

Mangan, David. "The Kingdom and the Iran-Contra Affair." *Middle East Executive Reports,* March 1987, 8-9.

Martz, Larry. "The Contra Crusade: Reagan's Strident Plea for Aid Polarizes Congress." *Newsweek,* March 17, 1986, 20-22.

Martz, Larry, et al. "Ollie Takes the Hill." *Newsweek,* July 20, 1987, 12-18.

Mashek, John W., and Melissa Healy. "Can They Live Up to the Laws?" *U.S. News & World Report,* December 8, 1986, 25.

McManus, Doyle. "Dateline Washington: Gipperdammerung." *Foreign Policy,* Spring 1987, 156-172.

Menashri, David. "The American-Israeli-Iranian Triangle." *New Outlook,* January/February 1987, 11-15.

Millman, Joel. "Dead Men Tell No Tales: Some Contragate Players Will Never Get to Testify." *Mother Jones,* April 1987, 46-51.

"Missile Smuggling Charge: Hawk Missile Parts to Iran." *Aviation Week and Space Technology,* February 18, 1985, 21.

Morganthau, Tom. "Ollie North's Secret Network." *Newsweek,* March 9, 1987, 32-37.

____. "Rekindling the Magic: Reagan Wins a Congressional Victory to Aid the Contras." *Newsweek,* July 7, 1986, 20-21.

Morley, Jefferson. "Oliver's Army: Ends and Means, 'Contra'-Style." *New Republic,* December 22, 1986, 12-13.

____. "Ollie's Blueprint: The Strategic Planning of the Iran-Contra Operation." *New Republic,* May 25, 1987, 16-18.

Morrison, David C. "Tilting with Intelligence: The Tower Commission's Criticism of the CIA on the Iran-Contra Affair Is Echoed in Other Questions Raised about the Integrity of the Intelligence Process." *National Journal,* May 9, 1987, 1110-1115.

Mudge, Arthur W. "A Case Study in Human Rights and Development Assistance: Nicaragua." *Universal Human Rights,* October/December 1979, 93-102.

Mulcahy, Kevin V. "The Secretary of State and the National Security Adviser: Foreign Policymaking in the Carter and Reagan Administrations." *Presidential Studies Quarterly,* Spring 1986, 280-299.

Nairn, Allan. "The Bush Connection." *Progressive,* May 1987, 19-24.

Norland, Ron. "The Secret World of General Secord." *Newsweek,* May 11, 1987, 20-22.

Parker, Alan A. "A Nation of Laws?" *Trial,* July 1987, 13-14.

____. "The Integrity of Institutions." *Trial,* January 1987, 13.

Parry, Robert, and Brian Barger. "Reagan's Shadow CIA: How the White House Ran the Secret 'Contra' War." *New Republic,* November 24, 1986, 23-28.

Pasley, Jeffrey L. "Inside Dopes: Washington Journalists and Col. Oliver L. North." *New Republic,* February 23, 1987, 14-16.

Perry, Mark. "The ISA behind the NSC: Underground Cowboys." *Nation,* January 17, 1987, 33-36.

Plattner, Andy. "Anti-Nicaragua Aid—a Capitol Resurrection." *U.S. News & World Report,* July 7, 1986, 6-7.

Powell, Stewart. "Whose War Is It? Nobody Owns Up: Nicaragua and Hasenfus Affair." *U.S. News & World Report,* November 3, 1986, 35.

Rabbaniha, Sally. "Shock among Arabs: The Regional Balance Tilts." *World Press Review,* January 1987, 18-19.

Rielly, John. "American Opinion: Continuity, Not Reaganism." *Foreign Policy,* Spring 1983, 86-104.

Riley, Fred, and John Strasser. "Hearings Throw Spotlight on Meese." *National Law Journal,* May 11, 1987, 31.

Riley, John. "A Legal Thicket That's Thicker Than Watergate." *National Law Journal,* May 11, 1987, 29.

____. "North: A Good, But Not Flawless, TV Performance." *National Law Journal,* July 20, 1987, 7.

Riley, John, and Fred Strasser. "In Search of Justice and the Story That Wouldn't Go Away." *National Law Journal,* March 16, 1987, 26.

____. "Looking for Loopholes: The Administration's Legal Hall of Mirrors." *National Law Journal,* June 29, 1987, 13.

Roberts, Charley. "Few Experts Back Reagan's View of Contra-Aid Laws: Is Congress Limited to Power of Purse in Foreign Affairs? Area Called Murky." *Los Angeles Daily Journal,* May 22, 1987, 1.

____. "Shultz Says Deal Attempts Went on Despite Exposure and Wanted Legal Analysis." *Los Angeles Daily Journal,* July 24, 1987, 1.

Robinson, Timothy S., John Riley, and Marcia Coyle. "Focus of Iran-Contra Investigation Shifts to Bush." *National Law Journal,* May 25, 1987, 5.

Rogers, David, and David Ignatius. "The Contra Fight: How CIA-Aided Raids in Nicaragua in '84 Led Congress to End Funds; But Officials Help Insurgents Raise Private Funds Here." *Wall Street Journal,* March 6, 1985, 1+.

Rogers, William. "Summary Procedure in Hasenfus Trial Offends Basic Rights." *Legal Times,* November 24, 1986, 13.

Rosenfeld, Mordecai. "Colonel North and Doctor Freud." *New York Law Journal,* February 17, 1987, 2.

Russell, George. "Everybody's Doing It: Selling Arms to Iran, That Is, Notably the Europeans." *Time,* March 16, 1987, 31.

Salpeter, Eliahu. "Triple Trouble In Israel: Israeli Role in the Iran Arms Sale Affair." *New Leader,* March 23, 1987, 5-7.

Schlesinger, James. "Reykjavik and Revelations: A Turn of the Tide?" *Foreign Affairs,* 1986, 426-446.

Schorr, Daniel. "McFarlane's Folly." *New Leader,* February 9, 1987, 3-4.

Schroeder, Richard C. "Decision on Nicaragua." *Editorial Research Reports,* February 28, 1986, 147-164.

Scott, Peter Dale. "The Secret Team behind Contragate." *Nation,* January 31, 1987, 97-100.

Seib, Gerald F. "White House Case against Boland Amendment Attempts End Run around Charges of Violation." *Wall Street Journal,* May 18, 1987, 56 (Eastern edition); 50 (Western edition).

Sharkey, Jacqueline. "Back in Control: The CIA's Secret Propaganda Campaign Puts the Agency Exactly Where It Wants to Be." *Common Cause Magazine,* September/October 1986, 28-40.

____. "Disturbing the Peace." *Common Cause Magazine,* September/October 1985, 20-32.

Shaw, Gaylord. "Iranian Connection: Iran's Quest for U.S. Military Equipment." *Military Logistics Forum,* November/December 1986, 20-24.

Shipp, E. R. "Use of Fifth Amendment: It's Re-emerging as a Legal Issue." *New York Times,* December 14, 1986, Section 1, 8+.

Shultz, George P. "Iran and U.S. Policy." *Department of State Bulletin,* February 1987, 22-33.

——. "Secretary's Interview on 'Meet the Press.'" *Department of State Bulletin,* March 1987, 20-23.

Sick, Gary. "Iran's Quest for Superpower Status." *Foreign Affairs,* Spring 1987, 697-716.

Smolowe, Jill. "Pouncing on a Transgressor: Nicaragua Steps over the Line, Helping the Contras Get Aid." *Time,* April 7, 1986, 24-25.

Spiro, Peter J. "The Iran-Contra Affair, the Neutrality Act, and the Statutory Definition of 'At Peace.'" *Virginia Journal of International Law,* Winter 1987, 343-368.

Stengel, Richard. "Khashoggi's High-Flying Realm." *Time,* January 19, 1987, 30-34.

——. "True Belief Unhampered by Doubt: From Small Town Boy to Shadow Secretary of State, Oliver North Did Not Know When to Stop." *Time,* July 13, 1987, 28-31.

Strasser, Fred. "The Right Lawyers for the Job? The Iran Probe's Legal Lineup." *National Law Journal,* January 26, 1987, 3.

Strasser, Fred, and John Riley. "A 'Guerrilla' Lawyer for Lt. Col. North's Legal Battles." *National Law Journal,* July 13, 1987, 8.

Taylor, Stuart, Jr. "Limited Use Immunity Would Hinder Iran-Contra Probe." *Chicago Daily Law Bulletin,* December 17, 1986, 1.

Telang, G. M. "Compromising Moves: A Complex Diplomatic Maneuver Misfires." *World Press Review,* January 1987, 16-17.

"The Ayatollah's Big Sting: The Iranians Planted a Phony Story of a Dying Leader and a Bitter Power Struggle and Used It to Spring a Stunning Superpower Trap." *U.S. News & World Report,* March 30, 1987, 18-28.

"The Boland Deviation." *National Review,* June 19, 1987, 17-18.

"The Egyptian Angle." *Economist,* June 13, 1987, 37.

"The Fifth Freedom: Invoking the Fifth Amendment in Iran Scandal." *Progressive,* February 1987, 10-11.

"The 'Iranagua' Blunder: President Reagan Is Weakened at a Critical Moment." *World Press Review,* January 1987, 11-12.

"The Iranian Connection." *New Outlook,* November/December 1986, 11-13.

"The Pro-American Activities Committee." *National Review,* July 3, 1987, 16-17.

"The Route to Sales in Iran Starts in Istanbul and Izmir." *Middle East Executive Reports,* December 1985, 11-12.

"The Untelevised Iranian Show." *Economist,* May 9, 1987, 37-38.

"The Vagaries of Boland." *Economist,* June 6, 1987, 22-23.

"The White House Crisis." *Newsweek,* December 8, 1986, 32-50.

Thomas, Evan, and Amy Wilentz. "Tough Tug of War: In His Crusade against Managua, Reagan Loses a Battle in Washington." *Time,* March 31, 1986, 14-20.

Treverton, Gregory F. "Covert Action and Open Society." *Foreign Affairs,* Summer 1987, 995-1114.

Uhlfelder, Mark N. "Iran-Contra Aid Scandal Develops

Tax Twist, Pickle Meets with Gibbs to Discuss Activities of Tax-Exempt Organizations." *Tax Notes,* December 22, 1986, 1093.

Ullman, Richard H. "At War with Nicaragua." *Foreign Affairs,* Fall 1983, 39-58.

"Vietnam and Nicaragua: U.S. Foreign Policy." *Monthly Review,* March 1987, 1-6.

Walcott, John. "Under Siege: Revitalized for a Time, the CIA Is Now Jolted by Variety of Setbacks; Its Iran-Contra Role Damages Relations with Congress." *Wall Street Journal,* January 21, 1987, 1+.

Walczak, Lee, Richard Fly, and Douglas Harbrecht. "How Much Damage? Reagan May Never Regain His Credibility." *Business Week,* July 27, 1987, 24-25.

Walsh, Kenneth T. "Can Reagan Bounce Back? Congress Flexes Its Muscles with House Rejection of Aid to Contras." *U.S. News & World Report,* March 31, 1986, 16-18.

Watson, Russell, and Colleen O'Connor. "'Project Recovery': A Handful of 'Cowboys' Leads Reagan into the Biggest Blunder of His Presidency." *Newsweek,* December 1, 1986, 26-32.

Watson, Russell, and John Barry. "A Stunning Indictment: The Tower Report Exposes a System Betrayed by the People Who Ran It." *Newsweek,* March 9, 1987, 25-31.

"When Privatisation Goes Wrong." *Economist,* June 13, 1987, 34-36.

Whitaker, Mark, and John Walcott. "Sending Managua a Message: Reagan's Nicaragua Policy Gains Support as the Senate Approves Aid to the Contras." *Newsweek,* June 17, 1985, 46-48.

Whitaker, Mark, and Joseph Contreras. "Nicaragua: A War of Words: The Sandinistas and the Reagan Administration Are Battling for the Hearts and Minds of Congress." *Newsweek,* March 11, 1985, 20-22.

Wieseltier, Leon. "Democracy and Colonel North: Oliver's Apologists and the American Idea." *New Republic,* January 26, 1987, 22-27.

Willey, Fay, Carroll Bogert, and Robert B. Cullen. "Peking Guns for Hard Cash: Arms Sale to Iran, Iraq and Others Profit China." *Newsweek,* March 23, 1987, 36.

Woodward, Bob. "CIA Aiding Iraq in Gulf War: Target Data from U.S. Satellites Supplied for Nearly Two Years." *Washington Post,* December 15, 1986, A1.

Wright, Connie. "'No Watergate,' Baker Says of Iran Arms-Sale Issue." *Nation's Cities Weekly,* December 8, 1986, 2.

Government Documents

Executive Office of the President. President's Special Review Board 1987. *Report of the President's Special Review Board (Tower Commission Report).* Washington, D.C.: Government Printing Office, 1987.

Fauriol, Georges. *Latin American Insurgencies.* U.S. Defense Department. National Defense University, 1985.

Preece, Richard M. *Arms Shipments to Iran.* (Issue Brief #87022) Washington, D.C.: Congressional Research Service, 1987.

Preece, Richard M., and Robert D. Shuey. *Iran Arms and Contra Funds: A Chronology of Events.* Washington, D.C.: Congressional Research Service, 1987. Updated monthly.

Serafino, Nina M. *Contra Aid: 1981-1986: Summary and Chronology of Major Congressional Action on Key Legislation Concerning U.S. Aid to the Anti-Sandi-*

Bibliography

nista Guerrillas. Washington, D.C.: Congressional Research Service, 1987.

U.S. Congress. House. Committee on Foreign Affairs. *Concerning U.S. Military and Paramilitary Operations in Nicaragua. Markup, May 18; June 6, 7, 1983*. 98th Cong., 1st sess., 1983.

——. *The Foreign Policy Implications of Arms Sales to Iran and the Contra Connection. Hearings, November 24; December 8, 9, 1986*. 99th Cong., 2d sess., 1986.

U.S. Congress. House. Committee on Foreign Affairs. Subcommittee on Europe and the Middle East. *Islamic Fundamentalism and Islamic Radicalism. Hearings, June 24; July 15; September 30, 1985*. 99th Cong., 1st sess., 1985.

——. *The Media, Diplomacy, and Terrorism in the Middle East. Hearing, July 30, 1985*. 99th Cong., 1st sess., 1985.

U.S. Congress. House. Committee on Foreign Affairs. Subcommittee on Western Hemisphere Affairs. *Investigation of United States Assistance to the Nicaraguan Contras. Hearings and Markup, March 5, 6; April 9; May 1, 8; June 11, 1986*. 99th Cong., 2d sess., 1986.

——. *U.S. Support for the Contras. Hearing, April 16, 17, 18, 1985*. 99th Cong., 1st sess., 1985.

U.S. Congress. House. "Legislative Histories of Statutory Restrictions on Funding for Covert Assistance for Military or Paramilitary Operations in Nicaragua, FY 1983-FY 1986." *Congressional Record*. 100th Cong., 1st sess., 1987, Vol. 133, pt. 97, H4585-H4987.

U.S. Congress. Senate. Committee on Appropriations. Subcommittee on Defense Appropriations. *Covert Assistance to Nicaragua, FY86. Special Hearing, April 18, 1985*. 99th Cong., 1st sess., 1985.

U.S. Congress. Senate. Committee on Foreign Relations. *The National Security Advisor: Role and Accountability. Hearings, April 17, 1980*. 96th Cong., 2d sess., 1980.

——. *U.S. Policy toward Nicaragua: Aid to Nicaraguan Resistance Proposal. Hearings, February 27; March 4, 1986*. 99th Cong., 2d sess., 1986.

U.S. Congress. Senate. Select Committee on Intelligence. *Preliminary Inquiry into the Sale of Arms to Iran and Possible Diversion of Funds to the Nicaraguan Resistance*. 100th Cong., 1st sess., 1987.

U.S. Government Accounting Office. *Problems in Controlling Funds for the Nicaraguan Democratic Resistance*. Washington, D.C.: Government Printing Office, 1986.

U.S. State Department and Defense Department. *Challenge to Democracy in Central America*. Washington, D.C.: Government Printing Office, 1986.

——. *Sandinista Military Build-up*. Washington, D.C.: Government Printing Office, 1985.

Index

Index

Index

Index

Index

Index